Business Essentials Fachwörterbuch

Deutsch - Englisch
Englisch - Deutsch

von

Prof. Dr. Axel Noack

FH Stralsund

Rebekka Stettnisch

R. Oldenbourg Verlag München Wien

Bibliografische Information der Deutschen Nationalbibliothek

Die Deutsche Nationalbibliothek verzeichnet diese Publikation in der Deutschen Nationalbibliografie; detaillierte bibliografische Daten sind im Internet über <http://dnb.d-nb.de> abrufbar.

Rosenheimer Straße 145, D-81671 München
Telefon: (089) 45051-0
oldenbourg.de

Lektorat: Wirtschafts- und Sozialwissenschaften, wiso@oldenbourg.de
Herstellung: Anna Grosser
Satz: DTP-Vorlagen des Autors
Coverentwurf: Kochan & Partner, München
Gedruckt auf säure- und chlorfreiem Papier
Druck: Memminger MedienCentrum, Memmingen

ISBN 978-3-486-58261-1

Vorwort

dieses Wörterbuch möchte dem Nutzer das Fachvokabular des modernen internationalen Geschäftslebens in einer besonders anwenderfreundlichen Weise an die Hand geben.

So enthält der englisch-deutsche Teil die 11.000 wichtigsten Wörter und Begriffe des anglo-amerikanischen Sprachgebrauchs und ist damit zugleich:

- umfassend - alle grundlegenden Bereiche werden abgedeckt,
- aktuell - alle neuen Entwicklungen sind berücksichtigt, und
- fundiert - die wichtigsten Begriffe werden detailliert definiert und erklärt.

Der deutsch-englische Teil enthält entsprechend 14.000 aktuelle Fachbegriffe mit ihren Übersetzungen.

Im dritten Teil werden 3.000 Abkürzungen aus dem internationalen Wirtschaftsgeschehen mit ihren verschiedenen Bedeutungen aufgeführt.

Abgedeckt werden nicht nur alle zentralen Bereiche (Handel, Banken, Versicherungen, Finanzen, Börse, Rechnungswesen, Controlling, Produktion, Marketing, Organisation, Recht, Computer, Internet); auch Managementdenker und ihre Ideen, internationale Institutionen, sowie grundlegende Konzepte der Wirtschaftswissenschaften werden behandelt.

Ein Novum ist die konsequente Umsetzung einer umfassenden Internetstrategie. So ist der Inhalt des Buches nicht nur komplett in die Datenbank von www.leo.org, des bekanntesten deutschen Übersetzungsportals, aufgenommen worden. Bei www.talx.net sind darüber hinaus aktuelle Versionen für PDA und PPC verfügbar.

Das Lexikon richtet sich somit an Studierende der Wirtschaftswissenschaften sowie alle Fach- und Führungskräfte, die Wirtschaftsenglisch für Ihren Beruf benötigen. Für ausländische Studenten bietet es einen Einstieg in das hiesige Wirtschaftsleben.

Abschließend möchte ich mich bei allen bedanken, die zur Fertigstellung beigetragen haben: Herr Stefan Kansy, Frau Andrea Kasten, Frau Nicole Richter, Frau Astrid Nehls, Herr Sebastian Ille, Herr Siddharth Mudgal und Frau Margarita Kolesheva. Des weiteren bei Herrn Martin Weigert und insbesondere bei Herrn Dr. Schechler vom Oldenbourg Verlag.

Axel Noack

Inhalt

A

AAA/Aaa erstklassige Bonität; erstklassiges Wertpapier

"Triple A", the highest credit rating awarded by the two leading US rating agencies Standard & Poor's and Moody's. It indicates a very high level of reliability for a corporate, country or municipal bond.

abandon aufgeben; preisgeben; *(to desert)* im Stich lassen; *(insurance)* abtreten; *(a claim)* fallenlassen; *(controls)* aufheben; nicht ausüben; außer Betrieb nehmen

abandonment Aufgabe; Stilllegung; Außerbetriebnahme; Nichtannahme; *(property)* Verzicht; *(insurance)* Abtretung; *(shipping)* Abandon

In general: act of giving up the ownership of something, normally covered by an insurance policy, and treating it as if it has been completely lost or destroyed.

Property: voluntary, intentional surrender of property, or of a right to it, without naming a successor as owner or tenant.

Shipping: act of giving up a ship and its cargo to the underwriters against payment for the total loss.

abandonment option Aufgabeoption

Option of terminating an investment earlier than originally planned.

abatement Kürzung; Minderung; *(law)* Prozesseinstellung; Abnahme; Linderung; Beseitigung; Verringerung

In general: a reduction in some amount of money owed, usually given by the creditor.

Law: either a termination or a temporary suspension of a lawsuit.

Taxes: an abatement of taxes is a tax rebate or decrease.

abbreviated accounts vereinfachter Jahresabschluß

In most countries, there are provisions for small or medium-sized companies to file abbreviated accounts instead of the full report and accounts.

ABC agreement ABC Abkommen

Stock exchange: contract between an employee and a brokerage firm outlining the rights of the firm purchasing an NYSE membership for that employee.

ABC method ABC Analyse

Inventory management method that classifies products or services in three classe, A, B, and C, based on the revenues that they generate. More importance should be placed on higher value items ("A"s) than on lesser value items ("B"s), while the least important items ("C"s) receive the least time and attention.

ability Fähigkeit; Befähigung; Können; Begabung; Talent; Qualifikation

Individual's capacity to perform the various tasks in a job. An individual's overall abilities essentially are made up of two sets of factors: intellectual and physical abilities.

ability to pay Zahlungsfähigkeit; Solvenz

Finance: refers to the borrower's ability to make interest and principal payments on debts.

Industrial relations: ability of an employer to meet a union's financial demands from operating income.

Bonds: describes the issuer's present and future ability to create sufficient revenues to fulfill his contractual obligations.

ability-to-pay taxation Besteuerung nach Zahlungsfähigkeit

Taxation on the basis of the taxpayer´s ability to pay, determined according to income or wealth.

The approach is based on the view that as income or wealth increases, its marginal utility decreases so that progressive rates of tax can be levied on higher income.

able fähig; *(efficient)* tüchtig; *(law)* berechtigt; *(to be able to do)* können; im Stande sein

abnormal anormal; nicht normal; ; ungewöhnlich; regelwidrig

abnormal returns anormale Einkünfte aus Kapitalvermögen

Component of the return that is not due to systematic (market-wide) influences. In other words, abnormal returns are returns above those predicted by the market movement alone.

abolish (*to do away with)* beseitigen; abschaffen; (*to void)* aufheben; abbauen

abolition Abschaffung; Aufhebung

above par über dem Nennwert

Security whose market value is above its nominal (or face, or par) value.

Fall in long-term interest rates after a bond has been issued will raise the bond's price above par.

above-the-fold oben auf der ersten Seite

General: an advertisement displayed above the fold in printed media.

Internet: a banner advertisement or other content on a web page that is displayed without the need to scroll. This is likely to give higher click through.

above the line über dem Strich; (*government*) Posten des ordentlichen Haushalts; (*advertising*) normale Werbemaßnahmen

Taxation: amounts on a tax return that are deductible from gross income before arriving at adjusted gross income. In case of companies, it is the income and expenditure before tax.

Government: revenue items in a government budget dealing with taxes and government expenditure.

Advertising: advertising for which a payment is made (such as an ad in a magazine or a stand at a trade fair) and for which a commission is paid to the advertising agency.

abridgment *(shortening)* Ab-; Ver-; Kürzung; Abriss; *(abridged work)* gekürzte Ausgabe; Zusammenziehung

abroad im (ins) Ausland; auswärts; überall; aus dem Haus; draußen

abrogate aufheben; außer Kraft setzen; auflösen; abschaffen; kündigen

Any action that makes a former rule, order, law, or treaty void or inoperative.

absence Abwesenheit; *(from work)* Fehlen; Nichtvorhandensein; Fehlen; Mangel

Not being at work or at a meeting.

absence rate Fehlzeitenquote

Measure of the frequency of employees failing to report to work.

absent abwesend; fehlend

absentee Fehlender; Abwesender

Worker or employee who stays away from work for no valid reason.

absenteeism Abwesenheit; Krankfeiern; Absentismus; unentschuldigtes Fernbleiben

Staying away from work for no valid reason, but can also be involuntary due to a cause outside the control of the employee (e.g. breakdown of public transport).

In large organizations it can be a major problem. Some countermeasures are: flexible working hours, increased annual leave, introduced personal days leave in addition to normal holiday entitlement, and devised incentive schemes for full attendance

absolute unumschränkt; absolut

absolute advantage absoluter Kostenvorteil

Theory first presented by Adam Smith, which holds that because certain countries can produce some goods more efficiently than all other countries can, i.e. they have an absolute advantage in their production, they should specialize in and export those goods and trade for other things they need.

The costs of producing similar products vary between countries because certain resources, such as labor, raw materials, and energy, can be cheaper in some countries than in others.

In a globalized world, multinational enterprises are able to take advantage of these cost differences by buying components or products from countries that have these advantages. For example, a motor vehicle manufacturer in an economy with high labor costs may purchase certain components from another country with significantly lower labor costs.

absolute liability volle Haftung; Gefährdungshaftung

Products: manufacturers and retailers are strictly liable for products that can cause injuries and have been shown to be defective, even though the manufacturer or retailer was not proven to be at fault or negligent.

absolute monopoly uneingeschränktes oder vollkommenes Monopol; reines Monopol

Persistent market situation where there is only one producer or supplier of a product or service, and many buyers. Monopolies are characterized by a lack of economic competition for the good or service that they provide and a lack of viable substitute goods.

absolute priority absolute Priorität; absoluter Vorrang; Gläubigervorrecht; strikte Priorität

Rule in bankruptcy proceedings requiring senior creditors to be paid in full before junior creditors receive any payment.

absorb abschöpfen; aufnehmen; *(liquids)* aufsaugen; *(costs)* auffangen; *(expenses)* übernehmen; *(shock)* dämpfen; tragen; übernehmen; absorbieren

absorbed absorbiert; aufgefangen

Business: cost, such as a tax increas, that is carried by the firm and not passed on to a customer.

Cost accounting: indirect manufacturing costs, such as property taxes and insurance.

Securities: an issue that has been completely sold to the public.

absorption costing Vollkostenrechnung

Method of cost accounting where all costs incurred by the business are charged to the individual products and services.

Full costs include either all costs which have arisen during the manufacturing of a product or delivery of a service (full manufacturing costs) or all costs which have arisen for the products sold within a period (full cost price).The calculation of full costs is only possible if structure costs can be allocated through their proportionalization, since not all costs arising in a business stand in a direct causal relationship with the goods manufactured or sold.

absorption limit Sättigungsgrenze

absorption point Sättigungspunkt

abstain sich enthalten; sich zurückhalten

abstention Enthaltung; Stimmenthaltung

Decision to deliberately refrain from an action or practice. An abstention normally is recorded and occurs when someone has a conflict of interest.

abstract *(summary)* Zusammenfassung; Übersicht; Abriss; (*to summarize*) einen Auszug machen

abstract of title Grundbuchauszug; Eigentumsnachweis

Record summarizing all details of the ownership of a property. These can include conveyances, transfers, grants, wills and judicial proceedings as well as encumbrances and liens. It also lists evidence of satisfaction and any other facts affecting title.

abundance Überfluss; Fülle; Reichtum

abundant reichlich

abuse Missbrauch; *(mistreatment)* Misshandlung; Missstand; (*to use wrongly)* missbrauchen; (*to mistreat)* misshandeln; übermäßig beanspruchen; schmähen

accelerate beschleunigen; *(car)* Gas geben

accelerated depreciation Sonderabschreibung; beschleunigte Abschreibung

Legal method of calculating depreciation which permits greater amounts of deductions in earlier years than possible under the straight line method, which assumes equal depreciation during each year of the asset's life.

Example: a computer may be expected to have a useful life of four years when it is purchased, but it is replaced after two years. By accelerating the depreciation the full charge could be made earlier, reflecting the short life cycle of high- technology products.

acceleration Beschleunigung

acceleration clause Verfallsklausel; Fälligkeitsklausel

Clause in a loan contract giving the lender the right to declare the entire amount immediately due and payable if a specific provision of the loan is violated, such as the failure to make payments on time.

acceleration principle Akzeleratorprinzip

Hypothesis that investment responds to growth in output. If the rate of growth of output changes, the level of investment will change.

accelerator coefficient Akzelerator; Akzelerator-Koeffizient

Factor which determines how much investment is induced by a change in output: Its value is influenced by the availability of spare capacity, the productivity of capital; the rate of interest and the price of labor.

accept annehmen; hinnehmen; abnehmen; *(invitation)* zusagen; gelten lassen; *(bill of exchange)* akzeptieren

acceptability Annehmbarkeit

acceptable annehmbar; angenehm; akzeptabel

acceptable quality level annehmbares Qualitätsniveau

Concept of quality control whereby managers are willing to accept a certain level of production defects, which are dealt with through repair facilities and service centers.

acceptance Zuschlag; Abnahme; Annahme; Billigung; *(invitation)* Zusage; *(bill of exchange)* Akzept; Wechsel

Contract: act of consenting to the terms of an offer, thereby creating a valid contract with binding terms.

Banking: procedure by which a bank on which a check is drawn promises to honor the draft by paying the stated amount to the payee named on the check.

Bill of exchange: Short-term bill of exchange which has been accepted by the financial institution on which it is drawn.

acceptance bank Akzeptbank; Akzepthaus; Wechselbank

Merchant bank which accepts bills of exchange; i.e. it promises to pay them, at a discount, in return for immediate payment to the issuer.

acceptance credit Akzeptkredit; Rembourskredit; Wechselkredit; Trassierungskredit

acceptance financing Akzeptfinanzierung

Method of financing exports and imports through a short-term line of credit. A borrower draws a bill of exchange on a bank for the required amount. The bill is accepted by the bank, which it returns to the drawer, who can then discount it.

The lending bank may include specific documentation to show evidence of title to the merchandise. The required documentation normally consists of a warehouse receipt or a bill of lading.

acceptance of liability Haftungszusage

acceptance sampling Stichprobenabnahmekontrolle

Statistical procedure used in quality control that involves testing a batch of data to determine if the proportion of units having a particular attribute exceeds a defined limit.

This technique leads to the acceptance or rejection of a batch of products.

accepting house Akzeptbank

An institution specializing in accepting or guaranteeing bills of exchange. A service fee is charged for guaranteeing payment. enabling the bill to be discounted at preferential rates on the money marker.

There has been a decline in the use of bills of exchange, which has forced the accepting houses to widen their financial activities. many of whom have returned to their original role as merchant banks.

acceptor Akzeptant; Bezogener; Trassat

Person or company which accepts a bill of exchange, normally by signing it, and so undertakes to pay it.

access *(Internet)* Zugang; Zugriff; Zutritt

access control Zugangskontrolle

E-Marketing: places its emphasis on laws and standards that enable persons to reasonably regulate the information that they are giving up.

access lag verzögerter Zugriff

A delay caused by the limited data-transmission speed between the user and the Internet.

access provider Dienstanbieter

A company providing services to enable an organization or individual to access the Internet.

Access providers can be divided into Internet service providers and on-line service providers.

access time Zugriffszeit

The time taken to obtain information from a computer memory or to write information to the memory.

Access times can vary from a thousand millionth of a second (a nanosecond) in a fast electronic memory to a second or longer with magnetic-tape memories.

accessibility Zugänglichkeit, Erreichbarkeit

Marketing: the degree to which a market segment can be reached and served.

accessible zugänglich; erreichbar

accessories Zubehör; hinzukommend

accessory equipment Zubehörausstattung

Portable factory equipment and tools and office equipment that are not part of the finished product.

accessory after the fact Helfer nach der Tat

Someone who knowingly aids a criminal after a criminal act.

accessory before the fact Helfer vor der Tat; Anstifter

Someone who instigates or aids in a crime but takes no part in its commission.

accident Unfall; *(chance)* Zufall; Zwischenfall

accident and health insurance Unfall- und Krankenversicherung

Insurance against accidental injury, accidental death, or sickness, including payment of medical, surgical, and hospital expenses and income payments.

An employer can offer this insurance to his employees and is entitled to a tax deduction for such payments.

accident insurance Unfallversicherung

Insurance cover against bodily injury and/or death resulting from accidental means.

The insurance pays a specified amount of money to the policyholder in a certain event, like the loss of an eye or limb. It also pays a sum to the dependants of the policyholder.

accommodate *(housing)* unterbringen; (to *oblige)* entgegenkommen; aushelfen; sich anpassen; schlichten

accommodating Nachgeben; entgegenkommend; gefällig

Willingness of one party in a conflict to place the opponent's interests above his or her own.

accommodation Unterbringung; Unterkunft; Räumlichkeit; *(settlement)* Verständigung; Anpassung; *(concession)* Entgegenkommen; Kulanz

accommodation paper Gefälligkeitspapier

Negotiable instrument (e.g. bill of exchange) signed by one party (the maker, drawer, acceptor, or endorser), without receiving value. It has the purpose of enabling another party to obtain money or credit.

accompany begleiten; zugehören

accomplish schaffen; zu Stande bringen; erreichen; (*task*) bewältigen; (*to complete*) vollenden; Zweck erreichen

accomplishment Leistung; (*achievement*) Errungenschaft; (*completion*) Bewältigung

accord Übereinkunft; Vereinbarung; (*to ~*) gewähren; bewilligen; einander entsprechen; zugestehen; übereinstimmen

accordance Übereinstimmung; Einverständnis

accord and satisfaction vergleichsweise Erfüllung; Abfindung

A legal device enabling one party to a contract to avoid an obligation that arises under the contract. provided that the other party agrees.

Example: under a contract of sale the seller of goods may discharge the contractual obligation by delivering goods of different quality to that specified in the contract, provided there is agreement with the buyer (the accord) and the seller after a reduction in the contract price (the satisfaction). The seller has therefore purchased the release from the obligation.

according to gemäß; nach; entsprechend

according to schedule termingerecht

according to value wertmäßig

account Konto; (*advertising*) Kundenetat; (*report*) Bericht; (*bill*) Rechnung; (*business*) Kundenkonto; Erzählung; Rechenschaft; Wert; Bedeutung; Grund; Ursache

Banking: formal arrangement to transact business in a bank by depositing money and making payments.

Business: customer who regularly does business under a particular name, usually evidenced by a deposit against which withdrawals can be made.

Accounting: assets, liabilities, income, and expenses as represented by individual ledger pages to which debit and credit entries are chronologically posted to record changes in value.

accountability Verantwortlichkeit, Haftung; Rechenschaftspflicht

Management: concept for justifying management organizational actions.

It means to identify persons making management decisions and to develop a measurement standard to determine if decisions were correct.

Example: junior manager is accountable to a senior manager for the completion of a project by a particular date and within given budget guidelines.

accountable verantwortlich; haftbar; rechenschaftspflichtig

accountancy Rechnungswesen; Buchhaltung; Buchführung

Term used in UK English for the theory and practice of accounting.

accountant Buchhalter; Bilanzbuchhalter; Rechnungsprüfer; (*certified public accountant*) Wirtschaftsprüfer

Someone who works in the area of accounting. This can be as an independent auditor, or as an employee of a business, providing internal accounting services.

Qualifications awarded include Certified Public Accountant (U.S.) and Chartered Accountant (U.K.).

accountant's opinion Bestätigungsvermerk des Abschlussprüfers; Gutachten

Documet signed by an independent certified public accountant describing the examination of a company´s annual report.

The accountant's opinion represents an important measure to an investor. Major types of opinions are clean, qualified, adverse, and disclaimer.

account balance Saldo; Kontensaldo; Kontostand

Difference between the debit and the credit side of an account, necessary to balance the two sides of an account.

If total debits exceed total credits, the account is in a debit balance. If total credits exceed total debits, the account is in a credit balance.

account executive Kundenbetreuer; Großkundenbetreuer; (*Advertising*) Werbeetatbetreuer

Business: executive/employee of a business who is personally responsible for a particular client and who is the principal coordinator and contact person for the client within the agency.

Finance: employee of a brokerage firm who advises clients and handles orders on their behalf. He has the legal powers of an agent. Account executives have to pass certain tests set by securities regulatory boards.

account for Rechenschaft ablegen; abrechnen; erklären; nachweisen

account holder Kontoinhaber

accounting Buchhaltung; Rechnungswesen; Abrechnung; Rechnungslegung

Process of identifying, recording, and interpreting quantifiable economic transactions and events. The two basic types of accounting are financial and management accounting.

Financial accounting, also called bookkeeping, records, analyzes and interprets all the assets and liabilities of a business and the monetary transactions with the outside world.

Management accounting, also called cost accounting, provides information to the management of a business required for decision-making about the costs of production etc.

accounting change Änderung in der Rechnungslegung

Occurs when a company changes its accounting principles (e.g. a new depreciation method), its accounting estimates (e.g. revised projections of doubtful accounts receivable), or the reporting entity (such as a merger of companies).

Such accounting changes have to be justified and explained in the footnotes, so that readers can make appropriate investment and credit judgments.

accounting concepts Buchhaltungsgrundsätze; Buchhaltungsvorschriften

Basic theoretical concepts devised to support the activity of accounting. There is no universal agreement, but four concepts are normally accepted as important:

The going concern concept assumes that the business is a going concern until there is evidence to the contrary. This is done so that assets are not stated at their break-up value

The accruals concept involves recording income and expenses as they accrue, as distinct from when they are received or paid.

The consistency concept demands that accounts be prepared on a consistent basis from one period to another

The prudence concept calls for accounts to be prepared on a conservative basis, i.e. not taking credit for profits or income before they are realized but making provision for losses when they are foreseen.

accounting cycle Buchungszyklus; Buchungsdurchlauf

All steps in the accounting process, beginning with an initial entry, such as recording the first sale of the year, and ending with the closing entries, at the year-end, and the preparation of the financial statements.

accounting differences Unterschiede im Rechnungswesen

Difference in national accounting and reporting standards which can be based upon social, cultural, legal, political and economic factors.

Several efforts have been made to harmonize standards internationally, such as the International Accounting Standards Committee (ISAAC) and the International Coordination Committee for the Accounting Profession (ICCAP).

accounting equation Bilanzgleichung

Fundamental accounting formula and the basis of double-entry book-keeping.

assets = liabilities + owners' equity

It shows how assets were financed: either by borrowing money from someone else (liability) or by paying one´s own money (shareholder's equity).

Example: If a student buys a computer for 600 Euros by borrowing 200 Euros from his friend and taking another 400 Euros from his savings, his assets are worth 600 Euros, liabilities 200 Euros, and equity 400 Euros.

accounting entity Buchhaltungseinheit

A unit for which accounting records are maintained and for which financial statements are prepared.

By law limited companies constitute the accounting entity. For sole traders and partnerships accounts are also prepared to reflect the transactions of the business as an accounting entity, not those of the owner.

accounting error Buchungsfehler; Fehlbuchung

Incident where accounting information is represented inaccurately, but not intentionally so.

accounting exposure Gefährdung durch Rechnungslegung

Risk of foreign exchange movements that may alter the monetary values of accounting entries. Accounting exposure includes translation risk and transaction risk.

accounting insolvency bilanzielle Überschuldung

When total liabilities exceed total assets, the firm has a negative net worth and is insolvent in the books.

accounting liquidity Liquidierbarkeit

Ease and quickness with which assets can be converted to cash.

accounting method Bilanzierungsweise; Buchführungsmethode; Rechnungslegungsmethode; Gewinnermittlungsmethode

Method a company uses to keep its books and records with the purpose of computing income and all related information.

This includes not only the overall method of accounting, but also such details as the accounting treatment of inventory or long-term contracts.

accounting period Rechnungsperiode; Abrechnungszeitraum

Time covered by an income statement, which is normally a year, such as January 1st through December 31st, but can also be a quarter or six months.

accounting principles Bilanzierungsrichtlinien; Buchführungsgrundsätze; Bilanzierungsgrundsätze

Principles that govern a company´s accounting practices. They serve as a reference to prove the application of the appropriate treatment of complex transactions.

In most countries, the accounting principles are determined by the state or professional associations.

accounting rate of return Gewinnvergleichsrechnung; rechnerische Rendite

Way of calculating the rate of return from an investment with a straight-line approach, that is not discounted or compounded. It is not as sophisticated as the discounted approach.

Profit is calculated by totaling investment inflows and substracting investment costs, and then divided by the number of years invested to estimate an annual rate of return.

accounting records Buchführungsbelege; Buchhaltungsunterlagen; Buchungsbeleg

All the documents and records used in the preparation of financial statements, including the general ledger, subsidiary ledgers, sales slips, invoices or digital records.

account number Kundennummer; Kontonummer

Customers: Unique code assigned to any customer, supplier, lender, or other business partner.

Banking: the number under which a bank maintains a customer´s account.

account sales Zwischen- oder Schlussabrechnung eines Kommissionärs

Record delivered by a broker or commission agrent to the owner of a consignment of goods, which shows the amount and sale prices of goods sold and deductions for commissions, freight and other expenses.

accounts Jahresabschluß

The financial statements produced at the end of an accounting period, especially the balance sheet and profit and loss account.

accounts payable Verbindlichkeiten; Kreditoren; Gläubiger; Lieferkonto

Money the firm owes to suppliers. It represents a list of debts currently owed by a person or business, which have been incurred for the purchase of services, inventory, and supplies.

Accounts payable normally do not include accrued salaries payable, accrued interest payable, or rent payable.

accounts payable ledger Lieferantenbuch

Detailed listing of accounts that shows how much is owed to each supplier. The balance in the accounts payable ledger should agree with the balance in the general ledger.

accounts receivable Außenstände; Forderungen; Debitoren

Money owed to the firm by its customers. It represents a list of money owed by a creditor which is kept in the normal course of the creditor's business and represents unsettled claims and transactions.

Accounts receivable normally arise from the sale on credit of a company's products or services to its customers.

accounts receivable financing Debitoren-finanzierung

Method of short-term financing whereby accounts receivable serve as collateral for working-capital advances. A secured short-term loan that involves either the assigning or factoring of receivables.

Under assignment, the lender has a lien on the receivables and recourse to the borrower. Factoring involves the sale of accounts receivable. Then the purchaser, called the factor, collects the receivables.

accounts receivable ledger Debitorenkartei; Kontokorrentbuch

Detailed listing of a firm´s accounts, originally in the form of a book, showing how much each customer owes.

Each transaction that generated a receivable is listed under that customer's account and a balance by the customer is determined. The balance in this ledger must corrsepond to that in the general ledger.

accounts receivable ratio Debitoren-Umschlag; Umschlagskennzahl der Debitoren

Ratio obtained by dividing total credit sales by accounts receivable. It shows how many times the receivables portfolio has been collected during the accounting period.

A high ratio indicates that management is efficient in granting credits and collecting debts. Also called accounts receivable turnover.

accounts receivable turnover Forderungsumschlag

Credit sales divided by average accounts receivable.

accredited akkreditiert; autorisiert; bevollmächtigt; bestätigt; beglaubigt

Someone who is appointed by a company to act on its behalf.

accretion Wertsteigerung; Wertzuwachs; Zunahme; Wachstum; Verschmelzung

Growth in the value of an asset through internal expansion, acquisition or other causes.

Example: the aging of whisky or the growth of timber.

accrual Zugang; Zuwachs; Zufluss; Ansammlung; Auflaufen

Gradual increase by addition.

accrual accounting Prinzip der Periodenabgrenzung; periodengerechte Aufwands- und Ertragsrechnung

Accounting method that books income and expense items as they are earned or incurred, even if they may not yet have been received or paid in cash. Also called accrual basis or accrual method.

Most companies have to use this method for their inventories: a sale has to be booked as soon as an article has been shipped, even if payment is not received for days or months. Exceptions to the accrual method for tax purposes include the recognition of bad debts and payments received in advance for services or merchandise.

accruals and deferrals Abgrenzungen; Rückstellungen; Abgrenzungsposten; antizipative Posten

Distinguishing *expense* and *revenue* in financial accounting on one hand, from costs and income in cost accounting on the other hand.

Any sums like *neutral and extraordinary expenses,* expenses on real estate, donations and gifts and expenses arising from speculative transactions, i.e. expenses which are not direct-lee necessary for the running of the business, should not appear in cost accounting. The same principle applies to the accrual and deferral of revenue.

Accruals and deferrals are also undertaken to even out profits; this is done above all by deferring costs from one period to the next to avoid showing results that are either too good or too poor.

There is a tendency in *management accounting* nowadays, to show only those costs which relate to actual expenses. In this way imputed *cost elements* disappear and depreciation e.g. on debtors and inventory can be regarded as costs. Thus the publicly presented result can be more easily reconciled with the internal result, but here we are overlooking the fact that *external reporting* and management accounting serve different purposes.

accrue auflaufen; anwachsen; erwachsen; anfallen; zufallen; sich ansammeln; auflaufen; entstehen; *(Bilanz)* abgrenzen

Accounting: to include an event on the accounting records regardless of whether cash changed hands.

accrued expense passive Anrechnungsabgrenzung; antizipative Passiva

accrued interest aufgelaufene Zinsen; Zinszuwachs; Stückzinsen

Interest that has been earned but not paid.

accrued liabilities Verbindlichkeiten

Liabilities which are recorded amounts owed but not yet paid; does not necessarily indicate a default or delinquency; also called accruals.

accrued taxes aufgelaufene Steuern

Taxes owed to tax authorities but not yet paid.

acculturation kulturelle Anpassung

Process someone goes through to become as comfortable as possible in another culture. Normally, acculturation does not mean giving up one's own culture, but adding those features of the new culture which allow one to operate more effectively.

accumulate anhäufen; ansammeln; auflaufen; akkumulieren; anwachsen

To grow larger by adding.

accumulated depletion aufgelaufene Wertberichtigung auf Bodenschätze

Way of accounting for a depletable asset, such as a mine. The balance is accumulated in a contra account, which is then subtracted from the asset account when shown on the balance sheet.

accumulated depreciation aufgelaufene Abschreibung; akkumulierte Abschreibung

Total amount of depreciation expense that has been claimed to a specific date. Same as accrued depreciation.

Example: a computer bought for € 2,000 and with an estimated life of five years, will have after two years an accumulated depreciation of € 800.

accumulated dividend aufgelaufene Dividende

Total dividend that is due, usually to holders of cumulative preferred stock, but not yet paid. It is carried on the books as a liability until it has been paid.

accumulated earnings tax Körperschaftssteuer auf einbehaltene Gewinne

Surcharge on earnings retained in a corporation which exceed a level deemed reasonable by the Internal Revenue Service.

This is done to counter the attempts by shareholders to avoid the higher personal income taxes to which they would be subject if paid out as dividends to the owners.

accumulated profit Gewinnvortrag; thesaurierter Gewinn

Profit which is not paid out as a dividend to the shareholders, but is taken over into the accounts of the following year.

accumulation Auflaufen; Anhäufung; Ansammlung; *(assets)* Vermögensbildung; Aufzinsung

accuracy Genauigkeit; Richtigkeit; Präzision

accurate genau; richtig; exakt; pünktlich

achieve erreichen; erzielen; leisten

achievement Erreichen; Erzielen; *(performance)* Leistung; *(thing achieved)* Errungenschaft; Ausführung

achievement motivation Leistungsmotivation

Theory that establishes a relationship between personal characteristics, social background, and achievement.

For a person with a strong need for achievement the task can become more important than any relationship.

The need for achievement is based on a combination of an intrinsic motivation and extrinsic motivation.

acid test ratio Liquidität ersten Grades, Verhältnis der liquiden Aktiva zu den laufenden Verbindlichkeiten

Accounting term for a measure of a company's ability to pay immediate liabilities. It is calculated by dividing liquid assets by current liabilities.

Liquid assets are cash plus money owed by debtors, normally excluding long-term debtors. The ratio is an indicator of a company's ability to pay its debts as they become due. It should be at least 1 or higher.

acknowledge *(to confirm)* bestätigen; *(to recognize)* anerkennen; quittieren

acknowledgment *(confirmation)* Bestätigung; *(recognition)* Anerkennung; *(legal)* notarielle Beglaubigung; Empfangsbestätigung; Quittierung

Legal: declaration by a person who has signed a document that his or her signature is a voluntary act.

acquire erwerben; anschaffen; erlangen; aneignen; ankaufen

acquirer Erwerber

acquisition Erwerb; Beschaffung; Akquisition; Gewinn; Ankauf; Kauf; Errungenschaft; Betriebsübernahme

Event when one company takes over the controlling interest in another company.

A means of obtaining new products or services by buying a whole company, a patent or a license to produce someone else's product or market someone else's service.

acquisition accounting Übertragungsbilanz; Anschaffungswertprinzip

The accounting procedures followed when one company is taken over by another.

The fair value of the target company has to be allocated between the underlying net tangible and intangible assets, other than goodwill, on the basis of the fair value to the acquiring company.

Any difference between the fair value of the target company and the aggregate of the fair values of the separable net assets (including identifiable intangibles, such as patents, licenses, and trademarks) will represent goodwill.

acquisition costs Anschaffungs-; Beschaffungs-; Akquisitionskosten

All the expenses required to obtain a property or business, including the price and all fees.

Marketing: The average cost of acquiring a prospect or a customer. This is often calculated for setting marketing budgets in direct marketing.

acronym Akronym

An abbreviation that is formed out of the first letters of a series of other words. An acronym is pronounceable, whereas normal abbreviations do not have to be.

across-the-board pauschal; allgemein; linear; übergreifend

Applying to everything or everyone.

Example: if a movement in the stock market affects almost all stocks in the same direction.

across-the-board tariff reductions allgemeine Zollsenkung

With an across-the-board tariff reduction all tariffs are reduced by a specified amount, and each country which is signatory to the agreement must abide by the arrangement.

Across the board tariff reductions are reached when a reduction is desired but a detailed examination of each product is too time-consuming.

act Tat; Handlung; *(law)* Gesetz; *(legal)* Rechtsgeschäft; *(to ~)* handeln; *(to behave)* sich verhalten; tätig sein; *(to ~ as)* fungieren als; *(to ~for)* vertreten

act of bankruptcy Konkursvergehen; Konkursgrund

Any behavior indicating that a person or business might be judged as bankrupt. This could be the suspension of debt payments, but also the transfer of property abroad.

act of God höhere Gewalt

Any violent or catastrophic event caused by nature which could not have been prevented.

Act of God makes the performance of a contractual duty, such as delivery of a product, impossible and may excuse performance of that duty.

acting partner geschäftsführender Gesellschafter; tätiger Teilhaber

Any member of a partnership who is actively involved in running day-to-day business.

A partner who has contributed to the business capital of a partnership and who participates in its management. All partners are deemed to be active partners unless otherwise.

action Tat; *(activity)* Tätigkeit; Handlung; *(lawsuit)* Klage; Prozess; Rechtsstreit; Aktion; Maßnahme

Law: case in a law court where a person or a company sues another person or company.

actionability Handlungsfähigkeit; *(lawsuit)* Prozessfähigkeit

Degree to which effective programs can be designed for attracting and serving a given market segment.

actionable klagbar; belangbar

action for damages Schadensersatzklage

Case in a law court where a person or a company seeks compensation for a loss that results from a broken contract.

action learning Tätigkeitslernen

action plan Aktionsplan

One of the phases of the marketing plan, in which the marketer identifies specific tactics to implement selected strategies.

action planning Maßnahmeplanung

action research anwendungsbezogene Forschung; Aktionsforschung

Refers to a change process based on the systematic collection of data and then selection of a change action based on what the analyzed data indicate.

Process of action research consists of five steps: diagnosis, analysis, feedback, action, and evaluation. These steps closely parallel the scientific planned change. Their importance lies in providing a scientific methodology for managing planned change.

activation Aktivierung

active aktiv; lebhaft; *(market)* lebhaft; tätig; wirksam; produktiv; zinsbringend

active income aktives Einkommen

Tax category of income that includes salaries, wages, and commissions. It does not include interest, dividends or passive income, i.e. real estate and businesses in which the taxpayer does not materially participate.

active listening aktives Zuhören

active market lebhafter Markt

Market with a high volume of trading in a particular stock, bond, or commodity. The spread between bid and asked prices is usually narrower in an active market than in a quiet market.

Active Server Page (ASP)

Internet: type of HTML page (denoted by an .asp file name) that includes scripts (small programs) that are processed on a web server before the web page is served to the user's web browser.

ASP is a Microsoft technology that usually runs on a Microsoft Internet Information Server (usually on Windows NT). The main use of such programs is to process information supplied by the user in an online form. A query may then be run to provide specific information to the customer such as delivery status on an order, or a personalised web page.

ActiveX

Programming language standard developed by Microsoft, which permits complex and graphical customer applications to be written and then accessed from a web browser.

ActiveX components are standard controls that can be incorporated into web sites and are then automatically downloaded for users. Examples are graphics and animation or a calculator form for calculating interest on a loan or a control for graphing stock prices. A competitor to Java.

activity Aktivität; Tätigkeit; *(function)* Aufgabenbereich; Betätigung; Maßnahme; Wirksamkeit; Organisation; Arbeitseinheit; Dienststelle

activity level Beschäftigungsgrad; *(cost accounting)* Beschäftigung

Cost accounting: the output of a cost center expressed in units of the cost center concerned. Actual performance is measured either manually or automatically.

activity-based costing (ABC) Prozesskostenrechnung

Cost accounting procedure focussed on the indirect process along the value chain, mainly used in German speaking countries. It assigns costs to main and sub-processes, plans and ascertains from cost drivers, cost rates for the process output. Its results can be applied to cost management and to differentiated costing. Activity-based management is a part of a broader process management that aspires to an optimization of all processes.

Activity-based costing (ABC) first assigns resource costs to the activities performed by the organization. Then activity costs are assigned to the products, customers, and services that benefit from them or are creating the demand for these activities.

activity-on-arrow (AOA) Aktivität auf Pfeil

One of two alternative conventions for the visual representation of network diagrams. In AOA the activities, which make up the network, are depicted as arrows, with durations attached. The direction of the arrow indicates the direction of time.

activity-on-node (AON) Aktivität auf Knoten

One of two alternative conventions for the visual representation of network diagrams. In AON the activities, which make up the network. are located on nodes, with the lines in between simply indicating the logical sequence.

activity ratio Auslastungsgrad

A ratio used in management accounting consisting of the production achieved for an accounting period divided by the production level regarded as achievable for that period.

actual Ist-; tatsächlich; real; *(costs)* effektiv; wirklich; gegenwärtig

actual activities Istleistungen

Accounting: the performance that a cost center has effectively achieved over the month reported, in terms of work tickets. If the activity is measured in allowed standard time then the term used is *'actual-target-activity'*. If, on the other hand, the actual time worked is measured, then the term is *'actual-actual-activity'*. With this measurement, the variance in the degree of utilisation (intensity variance) can be calculated.

Actual activity, derived from *plant data collection,* is a tool for registering consumption and performance in the manufacturing process. The collection of operational data, in terms of cost center activities (measured in output units of the cost center), shows which center has performed to what degree and during what period. Since these particulars are in any case required for the correct control of the production process, no additional demands are made for cost accounting purposes.

actual costs Istkosten

Accounting: costs that have effectively occurred over a period, recorded on the basis of vouchers in the accounts payable department, payroll and materials accounts as well as in the general ledger and then transferred to cost accounting. The actual costs of can never be exactly ascertained since the real costs of a fixed asset can only be determined only once it has been liquidated

actual damages tatsächlicher Schadenersatz; tatsächliche Beschädigungen

Any losses that are directly related to a breach of contract. They can readily be proven, and the injured party is normally compensated.

actual data Istdaten

Accounting: all the data of the past period, as recorded in the costing process.

actual product Regelprodukt; eigentliches Produkt

Product's parts, quality level, features, design, brand name, packaging and other attributes that combine to deliver product benefits.

actual situation tatsächliche Situation, Sachverhalt

actual wage Reallohn; Effektivlohn

actual wage level reales Lohnniveau

actuary Versicherungsmathematiker; Versicherungsstatistiker

Person who calculates insurance and property costs, such as the cost of life insurance risks and insurance premiums. To become an actuary requires passing a set of difficult mathematical examinations.

ad Anzeige; Inserat; Werbespot; Annonce

See: advertisement.

Adair, John (* 1934)

Thinker in the theory and practice of leadership, most famous for his teaching concept Action-Centered Leadership (ACL).

Adair was the first to demonstrate that people can be trained for leadership as a transferable skill rather than a matter of inborn aptitude. He has helped to alter the concept of management to include the wider element of leadership, with which he associated the neighbouring skills of decision-making, communication, and the ability to manage time. In his teaching concept of ACL, he defined leadership in terms of three overlapping circles – task, team and individual.

Biography: Educated at Cambridge University, service in the Bedouin regiment, lecturer at the Royal Military Academy, Sandhurst, visiting fellow to the Oxford Center for Management Studies, assistant director of the Industrial Society, first chair in leadership studies in the UK, University of Surrey, 1979-1983, since 1991 visiting professor in leadership studies at the University of Exeter.

Major publications: (1983) Effective Leadership, (1986) Effective Teambuilding, (1988a) Not Bosses but Leaders, (1988b) Developing Leaders, (1989) Great Leaders, (1990) Understanding Motivation, (1996) Effective Communication

adapt anpassen; *(to rework)* umarbeiten; *(machine)* umstellen; *(text)* bearbeiten

adaptability Anpassungsfähigkeit

adaptability screening Prüfung der Anpassungsfähigkeit

Process of determining a potential expatriate's ability to deal with overseas assignments.

Example: screening takes the form of testing the ability to deal with change, handle stress, make decisions without full knowledge.

adaptation Angleichung, Anpassung; Bearbeitung

In international marketing, a policy whereby the marketing mix is adapted to local market requirements.

Example: advertisements showing nude skin would offend the values of viewers in Arab countries and have to be altered.

adaptive exponential smoothing adaptive exponentielle Glättung

A quantitative forecasting method in which averages derived from historical data are smoothed by a coefficient, which is allowed to fluctuate with time in relation to changes in the demand pattern. The larger the coefficient, the greater the smoothing effect.

adapted marketing mix angepasster Marketing Mix

An international marketing strategy for adjusting the marketing-mix elements to each international target market, leading to higher costs but hoping for a larger market share and return.

Adaptation can concern all aspects of the marketing mix, e.g. the product's labeling, the pricing strategy, the distribution and the promotion.

ad clicks Anzahl des Anklickens von digitalen Werbebannern

Internet: The number of times a user "clicks" on an online ad, often measured as a function of time ("ad clicks per day").

ad click rate Rate des Anklickens von digitalen Werbebannern

Internet: number of ad clicks as a percentage of ad views, or the number of times an ad is clicked on by users as a percentage of the number of times an ad was downloaded and viewed by users.

ad concept testing Überprüfung des Werbekonzeptes

Technique aimed at obtaining the reactions of target customers to preliminary versions of a number of alternative approaches to an advertisement.

add addieren; zusammenrechnen; *(to append)* hinzufügen; hinzutun; hinzurechnen; aufsummieren; sagen

added value Mehrwert; Wertzuwachs; Wertschöpfung

addendum Zusatz; Nachtrag

Attachment or addition to a written document, such as a contract.

Example: commonly added addenda in real estate purchase agreements describe financing terms and property inspection requirements.

addition Addition; Zusammenrechnung; *(supplement)* Zusatz

additional Zusatz-; zusätzlich

additional mark-on Handelsaufschlag; Vertriebskosten- und Gewinnaufschlag; *(price)* Bruttoaufschlag; zusätzlicher Aufschlag

Further increase in a retail merchandise price; often done to take advantage of holiday periods or periods of peak demand.

additional paid in capital zusätzlich eingezahlte Kapital

Amount paid for stock above its stated par value, as shown in the owner's equity section of a balance sheet.

additions to net working capital zusätzliches Nettoumlaufvermögen

Component of cash flow of firm, along with operating cash flow and capital spending.

add-on Zugabe

A supplementary accessory or a premium version of a product sold to a customer.

add-on interest Teilzahlungszinsen

Interest that is added to the principal of a loan. The amount of interest for the entire life of a loan is computed on the original amount, so the stated rate is much lower than the annual percentage rate (APR).

address Adresse; Anschrift; *(form of address)* Anrede; *(speech)* Ansprache; *(to ~)* adressieren; richten an; ansprechen

adequacy Angemessenheit; Eignung; ausreichende Menge

adequate angemessen; ausreichend

adhesion contract *(law)* diktierter Vertrag; Knebelvertrag; Standardvertrag mit einseitig auferlegten Bedingungen

Contract in which the consumer must accept the standard provisions and does not have the ability to change them.

The consumer is normally unable to negotiate with the seller which can lead to inequality of bargaining power. An example is a standard warranty clause.

ad impression Werbeeindruck

Concept similar to a page impression; describes one viewing of an advertisement by a single member of its audience. Same as ad view, a term that is less commonly used.

ad inventory Anzeigebestand

Total number of ad impressions that a web site can sell over time (usually specified per month).

adjacent benachbart; angrenzend; anliegend

Nearby, but not necessarily touching.

adjoining angrenzend; benachbart

In actual contact with another object, such as properties with a common border. Same as contiguous.

adjourning stage Adjourning, letzte Phase des Gruppenprozesses; Vertagung

Final stage in group development for temporary groups, characterized by concern with wrapping up activities rather than task performance.

In this stage, the group prepares for its disbandment. High task performance is no longer the group's top priority. Instead, attention is directed toward wrapping up activities. Responses of group members vary in this stage. Some are upbeat, enjoying the group's accomplishments, others may be depressed over the loss of camaraderie and friendships gained during the work group's life.

adjudicate entscheiden; Urteil fällen; urteilen

Decide a legal problem; to give a judgment between two parties in law.

adjudication Entscheidung; Beschluss; Gerichtsentscheidung; richterliches Urteil

Act of giving a judgment; of deciding a legal problem determination of a controversy and pronouncement of judgment.

adjust anpassen; *(to balance)* ausgleichen; *(accounts)* bereinigen; *(entry)* berichtigen; ver-; ein-; richtig stellen; schlichten

adjustable einstellbar; regulierbar

adjustable-rate *(loan)* mit flexibler Verzinsung

Mortgage loan: interest rate that changes at specific intervals over the maturity of the loan.

adjusted gross income (AGI) Roheinnahmen; steuerrelevante Einnahmen

The share of income that is taxable. AGI consists of gross income minus certain items, such as payments to a pension plan. AGI minus deductions and personal exemptions equals taxable income

adjusted selling price berichtigter Verkaufspreis; *(accountancy)* angepasster Verkaufspreis

The selling price of an item less all expenses related to the sale, such as commissions.

adjusted tax basis angepasste Besteuerungsgrundlage

Original cost or other basis of property, reduced by depreciation deductions and increased by capital expenditures; base amount from which to measure gains and losses for tax purposes.

adjusting entry Ausgleichsbuchung; Berichtigungsbuchung

A bookkeeping entry made at the end of an accounting period to correct the data and adjust them to a prior period.

adjustment Anpassung; *(balance sheet)* Wertberichtigung; *(correction)* Richtigstellung; Schlichtung; Bereinigung

The process of arriving at an amount of settlement for a claim. It may involve calculations and discussions of liability.

adjustment program Anpassungsprogramm

adjustor Schiedsmann; Vermittler

Person who makes the settlement in claims arising out of losses or complaints with the purpose of avoiding possible litigation.

administer verwalten; bewirtschaften; *(price)* regulieren; handhaben; regeln; verabreichen

General term describing the management actions of planning, directing, budgeting, and implementing.

administered price kontrollierter Preis; vertikale Preisbindung; regulierter Preis

A price of a good or service that is fixed by government or some other non-market agency.

administered VMS kontrolliertes vertikales Marketingsystem

Vertical marketing system that coordinates successive stages of production and distribution, not through common ownership or contractual ties, but through the size and power of one of the parties.

administration Verwaltung; *(US)* Regierung; Behörde; Leitung; Unternehmensführung; Nachlassverwaltung

administrative Verwaltungs-; verwaltungsmäßig

administrative expense Verwaltungsausgaben; Verwaltungskosten; Verwaltungsgemeinkosten

Expenses that are not as easily associated with a specific function as are direct costs of manufacturing and selling and are often grouped with general expenses. They typically include expenses of the headquarters office and accounting expenses.

administrative law Verwaltungsrecht

The body of law that arises from the activities of government agencies of, which includes rulemaking, adjudication, or the enforcement of a specific regulatory agenda. Administrative law is a considered a branch of public law.

administrative management Bürokratisches Management

A traditional view of management that centers on how a business should be organized and the practices an effective manager should follow.

Prominent contributors to this school of thought were Henri Fayol (1930) and Max Weber (1922).

administrative skills Verwaltungsfähigkeiten; Verwaltungsfertigkeiten

Organizational and technical skills, including planning, organizing, staffing, scheduling, and computer skills.

administrative trade policies verwaltungsmäßige Handelspolitiken

administrator Verwalter; Verwaltungsfachmann; Verwaltungsleiter; Verwaltungsbeamter; *(legal)* Nachlassverwalter; Geschäftsführer; Behördenleiter

Law: Administrators are appointed by court when a person dies without having made a will or without having named an executor, or when the named executor cannot or will not serve.

admissible zulässig; erlaubt; annehmbar

admission Zulassung; *(entrance)* Einlass; Zutritt; Eintritt; Aufnahme; *(price)* Eintrittspreis; *(acknowledgement)* Zugeständnis

admit einlassen; zulassen; *(membership)* aufnehmen; *(to concede)* zugeben

adopt feststellen; *(procedure)* beschließen; *(budget)* verabschieden; annehmen; übernehmen

adoption Feststellung; Annahme; *(budget)* Verabschiedung; Einführung; Übernahme

Decision by an individual to become a regular user of the product.

adoption barriers Annahmebarrieren

Internet: sociological, cultural, technological, legal, and political issues that pose barriers to consumer use of particular products (in this case the internet).

adoption of innovations Annahme von Innovationen

Consumers can be divided into five different groups with respect to their willingness to adopt an innovation. A good understanding of these groups can help a company in devising effective marketing strategies.

Innovators are the first to buy and use new products. They demonstrate the innovation and persuade others to try the product. Normally this group is rather small, around 2% of consumers.

Early adapters tend to be opinion leaders, adopting new ideas early but more carefully, the next 13% of consumers.

Early majority are deliberate in their decisions, but not leaders. They constitute the next 34% of the adopting consumers.

Late majority are skeptics who only adopt an innovation after most other people have done so. They form the next 34% of consumers.

Laggards are the most conservative, suspicious of changes and innovations. They tend only to adopt the innovation when it has become widely accepted (16 %).

adoption curve Adoptionskurve

E-Marketing: Representation of the adoption process, consisting of five decision-making steps consumers go through before buying goods or services: (1) unawareness, (2) awareness, (3) interest, (4) evaluation, and (5) trial.

adoption process Annahmeprozess

Mental process through which an individual passes from first hearing about an innovation to the final adoption.

The stages are: awareness, interest, evaluation, trial, and finally adoption.

adrate Anzeigenpreis

adrate card Anzeigenpreisliste

A summary issued by a publication giving the space rates, mechanical requirements, closing dates for advertisements.

ad rotation Anzeigenrotation

Internet: Term for change of advertisements on a web site for different user sessions. This may be in response to ad targeting or simply displaying different advertisements from those on a list.

ADSL (Asymmetric Digital Subscriber Line)

Internet: variation of DSL, in which the information coming to the user's home is delivered faster than the information that the user sends upstream.

ad space Werbefläche

Area of a web page that is set aside for banner advertising.

ad valorem dem Wert entsprechend; nach Wert

Latin for "according to value". A method of taxation using the value of the thing taxed to determine the amount of tax. Can be applied to any goods or property.

ad valorem duty Wertzoll

Tariff levied as a proportion of the value of an imported good or service.

ad valorem tax Wertsteuer

Indirect tax that is levied as a percentage of the price of a good or service.

Examples: Value added tax and most sales taxes.

advance (*progress*) Fortschritt, (*credit*) Vorschuss; Kredit; Vorsprung; *(to ~)* vorwärts kommen; vorwärts rücken;

vorwärts bringen; fortschreiten; vordringen; aufsteigen; *(to prepay)* vorauszahlen; anheben; erhöhen

General: Amount paid before it is earned or incurred, such as a cash advance for travel expenses.

Credit: bankers' word for a loan. Normally short term, two or three years, the form of an overdraft to a company or individual.

advance against documents Dokumentenvorschuss

Loan extended by a bank or the buyer of goods to the seller of goods, usually on the basis of a sales contract or bill of lading. The loan is paid back upon delivery of the goods and presentation of documents that allow the release of funds from the letter of credit or other payment instruments.

advancement Fortschritt; Förderung; *(promotion)* Beförderung

advance on current account Kontokorrentkredit, offener Kredit

advance payment Vorauszahlung

advantage Vorteil; Nutzen; Überlegenheit

advantageous vorteilhaft; günstig

adversary Gegner; Teufel

Opponent or litigant, as, for example, in a legal controversy or litigation.

adverse ungünstig; nachteilig; widrig

adverse opinion nachteilige Meinung; (*Accounting*) negativer Prüfvermerk

Accounting: accountant's opinion that the financial statements are not in conformity with generally accepted accounting principles and/or that they do not present results fairly.

This situation can arise when there is a disagreement between the auditor and the directors, and the auditor considers the effect of the disagreement to be so substantial that the financial statements are seriously misleading.

adverse possession ungerechtfertigter Besitz

The possession of land belonging to another person in a manner deemed adverse to the interest of the owner.

advertise werben; Reklame machen; *(in newspapers)* annoncieren; inserieren; öffentlich bekannt machen; Anzeige aufgeben

advertisement Werbung; Reklame; *(in newspaper)* (Werbe-)Anzeige; Annonce; Inserat; *(for position)* Ausschreibung

The paid promotion of goods, services, companies and ideas by an identified sponsor.

advertisement heading Anzeigenüberschrift

advertisement photograph Werbebild

advertisement viewer Anzeigenbetrachter

advertiser Werber; Inserent; *(sponsor)* Werbekunde; Anzeigenkunde; Werbeagentur

advertising Werbung; Reklame

Commercial promotion of goods, services, or companies by an identified sponsor, and performed through differnet of media. Advertising is part of an overall promotional strategy, which can also include publicity, public relations, personal selling, and sales promotion.

Advertising is persuasive and informational and is designed to influence the purchasing behavior and/or thought patterns of the audience.

The media that carry advertising range from the press, television, cinema, radio, and posters to company logos on apparel.

advertising account executive Werbeetatbetreuer

advertising agency Werbeagentur

A business organization specializing in planning and handling advertising on behalf of its clients.

A full-service agency provides comprehensive services, including booking of advertising space, designing and producing advertisements, devising media schedules, commissioning research, providing sales promotion advice, and acting as a marketing consultant. Specialized agencies would only concentrate on part of that spectrum.

The departments within an agency include research, planning, creative design, media bookings. production. and accounts. Most advertising agents work on the basis of a commission on the total sums spent by the client.

advertising appeal Werbeappell; Werbewirkung

The central theme or idea behind an advertising message.

The purpose is to tell potential buyers what the product offers and why the product should appeal to them.

advertising briefing Werbebriefing

An agreement between an advertising agency and a client on the objectives of an advertising campaign.

A briefing outlines exactly what the objectives are, and helps to plan the overall strategy, and to set the budgets.

Once the brief has been agreed the agency can prepare and evaluate the advertisements themselves and develop the media plan.

advertising brochure Werbeprospekt

advertising budget Werbeetat; Werbebudget

advertising campaign Werbekampagne; Werbefeldzug

advertising circle Werbekreis

advertising consultant (freiberuflicher) Werbeberater

advertising copy Werbetext; Reklametext; Anzeigentext

advertising design Werbegestaltung

advertising director Werbechef

advertising evaluation Messung der Werbewirkung

An attempt to measure the effectiveness of an advertising campaign. This involves an assessment of the communications and sales effects of the advertisement as well as copy testing.

Testing can be done before or after an advertisement is broadcast or published. Testing before would include direct rating, portfolio tests, and laboratory tests. Testing after would include recall tests (aided and unaided) as well as recognition tests.

advertising expenditure Werbeaufwendung

advertising expense Werbekosten; Werbeaufwand

advertising gimmick Werbemasche

advertising idea Werbeeinfall; Werbeidee

advertising impact Werbeeffekt; Werbewirkung

advertising material Werbemittel; Werbematerial

advertising message Werbebotschaft

advertising networks werbende Netzwerke

Internet: Collection of independent web sites of different companies and media networks, each of which has an arrangement with a single advertising broker to place banner advertisements.

advertising objective Werbeauftrag; Werbeziel

Specific communication *task* to be accomplished with a specific *target* audience during a specific period of *time*.

advertising rates Anzeigenpreis, Anzeigentarif, Werbepreis, Werbetarif

The basic charges made by the advertising media for use of their services or facilities.

advertising section Anzeigenteil

advertising schedule Anzeigenschaltplan

A list of the planned or already booked advertisements, giving details of the specific media involved, sizes, timing, and costs.

advertising slogan Werbebotschaft; Werbemotto; Werbeslogan

advertising specialties Werbegeschenke

Useful articles imprinted with an advertiser's name, given as gifts to consumers.

advertising strategy Werbestrategie

advertising tactic Werbemaßnahme

advertising theme Werbetenor; Hauptthema der Werbung

An advertising appeal used in several different advertisements to give continuity to an advertising campaign.

For example, Visa credit cards are advertised as the "most widely accepted card", while the theme of American Express card advertising is "the card has no spending limits".

advertising war Werbekrieg; Werbeschlacht

advertorial (advertisement + editorial) redaktionell aufgemachte Anzeige

Print advertisement styled to resemble the editorial format and typeface of the publication in which it runs.

advice Rat; Ratschlag; *(notification)*

advice note Benachrichtigung;

A note sent to a customer by a supplier of goods to advise rum that an order has been fulfilled.

The advice note may either accompany the goods or be sent separately, preceding the invoice and any delivery note.

ad view Werbebannerbetrachtung

Internet: concept similar to a page impression; describing one viewing of an advertisement by a single member of its audience. The same as ad impression, the term that is more commonly used.

advise raten; be-; anraten; *(to notify)* benachrichtigen; avisieren; mitteilen; hinweisen

adviser Berater; Ratgeber

advisory Beratungs-; beratend

advisory board Beirat; Beratungsgremium; beratendes Gremium

advisory group Beratergruppe

advocacy advertising defensive Werbung

Advertisements by companies presenting their own opinion on public issues, such as laws or government polics.

advocate Fürsprecher; Befürworter befürworten; empfehlen; plädieren; eintreten für

affair *(business)* Geschäft; *(concern)* Angelegenheit; Sache

affect Affekt; *(to~)* beeinflussen; sich auswirken auf; angreifen; in Mitleidenschaft ziehen

affective behavior affektives Verhalten

Behavior aimed at producing a desired result, such as trying to satisfy the needs of another party in a negotiation.

affective component of an attitude affektive Komponente einer Einstellung

Covers a broad range of feelings that people experience, encompassing both emotions and moods.

Marketing: The affective component is concerned with the customer's emotional reactions to a product or a brand.

affiant Abgeber; *(law)* Vereidigte; Vereidigter

Signer of an affidavit.

affidavit eidesstattliche Erklärung; beeidete schriftliche Erklärung

Written attestation of the truth of a statement made under oath before a legally authorized person to certify that statement.

affiliate Partner; Zweiggesellschaft; *(to ~)* anschließen; verbinden; vereinigen; Konzerngesellschaft angliedern

Company or individual in legal and financial association with another.

affiliated angeschlossen; angegliedert; verbunden mit

affiliate network Partnerprogramm, verbundenes Netzwerk

Internet: reciprocal arrangement between a company and third-party sites where traffic is directed to the company from third-party sites through banner advertisements and links and incentives.

In return for linking to the destination site the third-party site will typically receive a proportion of any resulting sale.

affiliated chain angeschlossene Ladenkette

Group of small retail stores who form an association in order to gain economic advantage such as large-scale purchasing.

In so doing, they can achieve larger discounts. The group can also purchase advertising time and space as if it were a large advertiser.

affiliated company Tochter-; Schwester-; Konzern-; Zweig-; Beteiligungsgesellschaft

In general: two companies that are connected by ownership but have less than a majority of the voting stock of the other.

Banking: organization that a bank owns or controls by stock holdings, or which the bank's shareholders own, or whose officers are also directors of the bank.

affiliated group Konzernverbund; Konzern; Firmenzusammenschluß

Group of companies whose common parent owns at least 80% of the voting power and value of the stock of the includable corporations.

affiliated retailer Einzellhändler im Verbund

Independent retailer who affiliates with other independent retailers under a common trade name for merchandising purposes. A group of such independent retailers will advertise under this common trade name.

affiliated wholesaler Großhändler im Verbund

Wholesaler who supports or owns a affiliated retailers or who affiliates with other wholesalers under a common trade name.

affiliate program Partnerprogramm

Internet: firms put a link to an e-tailer' s web site and make a commission on all purchases by referred customers.

affinity card Kreditkarte für bestimmte Zielgruppen

A credit card issued to an affinity group, such as the members of a club, college etc.

affinity group Affinitätsgruppe

Internet: people with a common interest. On the internet, typically a subject-oriented mailing list, a newsgroup, or a conference on a website.

affirm versichern; bekräftigen; bestätigen

affirmative action aktive Förderungsmaßnahmen; positive Diskriminierung

Measures taken to correct conditions resulting from past discrimination or violations of a law, particularly with respect to employment.

affirmative relief positive Abhilfe

Relief or compensation that may be granted to the defendant in a trial.

affluence Wohlstand; Reichtum

affluent reich; wohlhabend

afford *(can afford)* sich leisten; erschwingen; *(to offer)* bieten; *(to grant)* gewähren; liefern; bereiten

affordable erschwinglich

affordable method finanzmittelbezogene Budgetmethode; Residualmethode

Setting the promotion budget at the level management thinks the company can afford.

affreightment Beförderungsvertrag; Befrachtung; Befrachtungsvertrag; Seekonnossement

Contract between a customer and a carrier for the transportation of goods, in which cargo space is reserved on a vessel for a specified time and at a specified price..

afloat verschifft

Trade: denoting goods, especially commodities, that are on a ship from their port of origin to a specified port of destination. For example, "afloat Rotterdam" means the goods are on their war to Rotterdam.

after date ab Ausstellungsdatum; ab dato

The words used in a bill of exchange to indicate that the period of the bill should commence from the date inserted on the bill e.g. "... 30 days after date, we promise to pay".

after-sales service Kundendienst

Maintenance of products by the manufacturer or his agent after purchase, often in the form of a guarantee which is effective for a stated period during which the service is free in respect of both parts and labor.

Credible after-sales service is an essential component of any good marketing policy, especially for such consumer durables as cars and computers.

after sight nach Sicht

The words used in a bill of exchange to indicate that the period of the bill should commence from the date on which the drawee is presented with it for acceptance. i.e. has sight of it.

after-tax basis nach Steuern

Investment: Method of comparing the returns on different types of bonds (taxable and non-taxable).

against all risk gegen alle Gefahren

age Alter; *(length of life)* Lebensdauer; *(of age)* Mündigkeit; *(period)* Zeitalter; bisherige Nutzungsdauer; lange Zeit; *(to ~)* altern; *(to mature)* reifen; ausreifen

age and life-cycle segmentation Alters- und Lebenszyklussegmentation

Dividing the market into different age and life-cycle groups, e.g. 30-35 years old, married, three children under 10 years old.

age discrimination Altersdiskriminierung

Discrimination of employees on the basis of age. In most countries explicitly prohibited by law.

age of consent Geschäftsfähigkeit

An age defined by law when a person can enter into contracts, in most cases 18 years. A contract entered into by a minor (i.e. someone below the age of consent) is not always capable of being enforced

aging schedule Fälligkeitstabelle

Compilation of accounts receivable by the age of account.

agency Agentur; Vertretung; *(public authority)* Amt; Behörde; Geschäftsstelle; *(administration)* Verwaltungsstelle; Vertretung

General: relationship between a principal and an agent who represents the principal in transactions with a third party.

Finance: certain types of account where a trust officer acts on behalf of the customer.

Investment: act of buying or selling for the account and risk of a client.

Personnel: company that refers potential employees to employers for a fee.

Government: an administrative unit of government.

agency costs Agency-Kosten

Costs of resolving the conflicts of interest among shareholders, bondholders and managers. They include the costs of providing managers with an incentive to maximize shareholder wealth and then monitoring their behavior and the cost of protecting bondholders from shareholders. Agency costs are borne by shareholders.

Agency for International Development (AID) Agentur für internationale Entwicklung

agency theory Agency-Theorie

Theory of the relationship between principals and agents. It involves the nature of the costs of resolving conflicts of interest between princ-ipals and agents.

agenda Tagesordnung; Agenda

agenda item Tagesordnungspunkt

agent *(representative)* Vertreter; Agent; *(authorized person)* Bevollmächtigter; Vermittler; Stellvertreter

In general: person or company acting for another person or company. Wholesaler who represents buyers or sellers on a relatively permanent basis, performs only a few functions, and does not take title to the goods.

Internet: intermediary representing either the buyer or the seller, not taking title to the goods, and making a commission for work completed.

Insurance: individual who sells and services insurance policies in either of two classifications:

An *independent agent* represents at least two insurance companies and (at least in theory) serves clients by searching the market for the most advantageous price for the most coverage. The agent's commission is a percentage of each premium paid and includes a fee for servicing the insured's policy.

A *direct writer* represents only one company and sells only that company's policies. This agent is paid on a commission basis in much the same manner as the independent agent.

agents (*Internet*) Agenten

Software programs that can assist people to perform tasks such as finding particular information such as the best price for a product.

agglomeration Anhäufung; Ballung; Zusammenballung

Urbanization: an extended urbanized area comprising the built-up area and related suburbs and satellite towns.

Business: Accumulation of several unrelated activities into a single entity, such as a holding company.

agglomeration diseconomies Agglomerationsnachteile

Loss resulting from agglomeration, often caused by unfamiliarity of the holding company management with the activities and the management of subsidiaries.

aggravate verschlimmern; erschweren; verschärfen

aggregate *(insurance)* Aggregat; aggregierte Größe; gesamt ansammeln; vereinigen; aggregieren

Sum total of the whole. Aggregate output is the total of all output during a given period.

aggregate demand Gesamtnachfrage; gesamtwirtschaftliche Nachfrage

Economics: The sum of demands for all the goods and services in an economy at any particular time.

A central concept in the macroeconomic thinking of J M Keynes, it is usually defined as the sum of consumers′ expenditure, investment, government expenditure, and imports less exports.

Keynes proposed that the free market will not always maintain a sufficient level of aggregate demand to ensure full employment and that at such times governments should seek to stimulate aggregate demand.

The feasibility of such policies has been questioned and it remains a critical issue in macroeconomics.

aggregate income Volkseinkommen

Economics: Sum of all payments made for the services of all the factors of production in an economy during a specified time. There is no adjustment for inflation, taxes, or double-counting. The gross domestic product is one of many measures of aggregate income.

aggregate supply Gesamtangebot; gesamtwirtschaftliches Angebot

Economics: total amount of goods and services supplied in the economy in a certain period available to meet aggregate demand.

The agregate supply curve describes the relationship between price levels and the quantity of output that firms are willing to provide.

aggregation Ansammlung; Gesamtsumme; Aggregation

Finance: Process in corporate financial planning whereby the smaller investment proposals of each of the firm's operational units are added up and in effect treated as a big picture.

E-Marketing: gathering of products from multiple suppliers so that the consumer can have more choices in one location.

aging of accounts receivable Fälligkeitsanalyse der Debitoren

Classification of trade accounts showing how long accounts receivable have been outstanding. It is an important tool in analyzing the quality of a company's receivables and where collection efforts should be concentrated.

aging schedule Fälligkeitsliste

agree *(to consent)* zustimmen; *(to settle)* abmachen; *(to reach an agreement)* vereinbaren; übereinkommen; *(to concur)* übereinstimmen

agreeableness Verträglichkeit; Annehmlichkeit; Freundlichkeit; Einverständnis

Factor of the Big Five Model describing a personality that is good-natured, cooperative, and trusting. People who score low on this dimension are easily distracted, disorganized, and unreliable.

agreement *(understanding)* Abmachung; Übereinkommen; Vereinbarung; Verständigung; *(opinion)* Einigung; *(treaty)* Abkommen; *(consent)* Zustimmung; Einverständnis

An expression of mutual assent between two or more legally competent parties, which normally leads to a contract.

agreement of sale Kaufvereinbarung

A legal contract between a seller and a purchaser stating the terms and conditions of the sale.

agricultural landwirtschaftlich; Agrar-

agricultural act Agrarbeschluss

agricultural budget Agrarhaushalt

agricultural market Agrarmarkt

agricultural price policy Agrarpreispolitik

agricultural price support Agrarpreisstützung

agricultural product Agrarerzeugnis; Agrargut; Agrarprodukt

agricultural surplus Agrarüberschuss

agricultural technology Agrartechnik

agricultural trade Agrarhandel

agriculture Landwirtschaft; Agrarwirtschaft

aid Hilfe; Beistand; Unterstützung; *(promotion)* Förderung; Hilfsmittel; *(to ~)* helfen; unterstützen; *(to promote)* fördern

AIDA Attention, Interest, Desire, Action

Acronym used in communications analysis, describing a model for the hierarchy of communication effects.

It is a very basic approach, but can still be useful as a rough guideline in creating advertisements.

aided brand awareness

One of the variables observed in ad tracking research.

Usually a researcher will ask respondents to indicate whether they are aware of various brands not mentioned in an unaided brand awareness question.

aim *(goal)* Ziel; *(purpose)* Zweck; *(intention)* Absicht; zielen auf; abzielen auf; *(to strive for)* erstreben; richten; werfen; sich bemühen

aimless ziellos; planlos

AIO

Internet: Activities, Interests, and Opinions of consumers.

air bill Luftfrachtbrief

A bill of lading used for the air transport of goods, normally not negotiable. It is a contract for carriage that includes conditions, shipping instructions, a description of the commodity and transportation charges.

The sender completes a form with multiple copies which provide a receipt for the sender, another for the carrier's billing records, and at least one copy with the address to accompany the package to its destination.

air consignment note Luftfrachtbrief

aircraft Flugzeug

air freight Luftfracht

The transport of goods by aircraft, either in a scheduled airliner or chartered airliner carrying passengers (an all-traffic service) or in a freight plane (an all-freight service).

Air cargo usually consists of goods that have a high value compared to their weight.

airline Fluggesellschaft

air mail Luftpost

airplane Flugzeug

airport Flughafen

airspace Luftraum

airtime Sendezeit; Werbezeit

The amount of time allocated to an advertisement on radio or television.

air transport Luftverkehr

air waybill Luftfrachtbrief

See: air-bill.

algorithm Algorithmus

A mathematical rule or procedure for solving a problem, including a sequence of detailed, precisely specified instructions.

A computer program is an *algorithm* written in a language that a computer can understand.

alien *(foreigner)* Ausländer; Gebietsfremder; *(foreign)* ausländisch; *(different)* fremd

Person who is not a citizen of the country in which he lives.

alien corporation ausländische Aktiengesellschaft; ausländische Kapitalgesellschaft

Company incorporated under the laws of a foreign country.

In US state law, corporations formed in another federal US state other than that in which it does business, are called foreign corporations, whilst corporations from outside the US are called alien corporations.

Example: Microsoft, incorporated in the state of Washington, is foreign in the state of California. DaimlerChrysler AG, incorporated in Germany, is alien in the US.

alienation Entfremdung

A feeling of detachment that causes employees to believe that their work is neither relevant nor important.

Some of the principal causes of alienation are: powerlessness: the inability to influence work conditions; meaninglessness: the absence of recognition of the contribution made by the individual; isolation: the absence of human interaction during working hours; low self-esteem: a lack of value placed on individuals by an organization and its managers; loss of identity with the organization: the absence of pride in working for the organization; lack of prospects: the feeling of frustration at being trapped in a situation that offers little prospect of advancement; lack of equality: the result of strict differentiation between the grades and levels in a hierarchical organization.

Managers need to be aware of its existence and its causes if they are to improve relationships within a work force.

alimony Alimente; Unterhalt

Regular payments for the support of one's divorced or separated spouse.

alleviate erleichtern; mildern; lindern

alliance Bündnis; Bund; Gemeinschaft; Verbindung; Verwandtschaft

alliance partner Bündnispartner

all-inclusive price Pauschalpreis

allocate *(to allot)* zuteilen; zuwenden; zuweisen; *(to set apart for a specific purpose)* bereitstellen

Accounting: to spread a single cost over a number of products, customers, people, or time. For example, depreciation accounting attempts to allocate the cost of a wasting asset over its estimated useful life.

allocation *(allotment)* Zuweisung; Zuteilung; *(setting apart for a specific purpose)* Bereitstellung; Zuweisung; Vergabe; Allokation

General: Apportionment of goods in short supply so that all companies or customers may secure a share according to their comparative immediate needs.

Broadcast: range of wavelengths assigned to a TV or radio station by state regulators.

Marketing: the quantity of products designated for a particular market.

Investment: The amount of securities assigned to an investor, broker, or underwriter in an offering. An allocation can be equal to or less than the amount demanded by the investor during the subscription process.

allocation of profit Gewinnzuschreibung

allocation of resources Mittelverwendung; Ressourcen-Allokation

Manner in which scarce factors of production are apportioned among producers, and in which scarce goods are apportioned among customers. It is the central topic of economics.

allocative function Verteilungsfunktion

allot zuteilen; zuweisen; verteilen

allotment Zuteilung; Zuweisung; *(Aktien)* Kontingentszuteilung

allow erlauben; *(to grant)* gewähren; *(to admit)* zulassen; voll vergüten; anerkennen; zubilligen; einräumen; bewilligen

allowable *(admissible)* zulässig; *(deductible)* abziehbar

allowance Preisnachlass; Pauschale; *(compensation)* Vergütung; Zulage; *(discount)* Abzug; *(allotment)* Zuteilung; Zuschuss; *(planning)* zulässige Abweichung

General: A price reduction or rebate given to a customer or intermediary on a large order or for any other specific reason.

Marketing: price reduction offered to a retailer by a manufacturer or wholesaler. It is designed to compensate the retailer for expenses incurred in marketing the product.

Promotion: money paid by manufacturers to retailers in return for an agreement to feature the manufacturer's product in some way.

Taxation: an amount that may be deducted before a particular tax is calculated. Typical allowances in assessing a person's liability to income tax are personal allowances, age allowances. It also includes tax-free annual amounts, such as the annual allowances available in respect of capital gains tax or inheritance tax.

Banking: gradual liquidation of a mortgage or other debt by periodic payments in addition to interest.

allowed time Vorgabezeit

Sheduled time in which a job should be completed at standard performance, including all contingencies; also called standard time.

all risk all peril Globalversicherung; Versicherung gegen alle Gefahren

Insurance covering each and every loss, except specifically excluded. If the insurance company does not specifically exclude a particular loss, it is automatically covered. This is the broadest type of policy that can be purchased.

ally Verbündeter; Helfer; Alliierter; (*to ~*) sich verbünden; sich zusammenschließen

alpha Alpha

Investment: Measurement of returns from an investment apart from market returns. Represents the amount of return expected from fundamental causes such as the growth rate in earnings per share; *contrast with beta*, which is a measure of volatility.

A positive alpha is the extra return awarded to the investor for taking a risk, instead of accepting the market return. In case of *mutual funds*, it is a measure of selection risk (also known as residual risk) of a mutual fund in relation to the market.

alpha equation Alpha-Gleichung

The alpha of a fund is determined as follows:

[(sum of y) - ((b)(sum of x))] / n

where: n = number of observations (36 mos)

b = beta of the fund

x = rate of return for the S&P 500

y = rate of return for the fund

alpha-release stage Alpha Version

The first stage of testing a product or service in which lead users, often company employees and loyal customers, test a new version.

alter ändern; verändern; umändern

alteration Änderung; Veränderung; Umänderung

alternate *(substitute)* Ersatz; Ersatzmann; abwechselnd; wechselnd; *(on alternate days)* jeden zweiten Tag wechseln; abwechseln

alternative Alternative; Ausweichsmöglichkeit; Ersatz; Ersatzwerk; Ersatzlösung; abwechseln; alternativ

alternative dispute resolution alternative Beilegung von Rechtsstreitigkeiten

alternative evaluation alternative Auswertung

Stage of the buyer decision process in which the consumer uses information to evaluate alternative brands in the choice set.

alternative hypothesis Alternativhypothese

In statistical testing, a hypothesis is accepted if a sample contains sufficient evidence to reject the null hypothesis. It is usually denoted by H_1.

In most cases, the alternative hypothesis is the expected conclusion (why the test was completed in the first place).

altitude Höhe

amalgamation Verschmelzung

The combination of two or more companies, either by one company acquiring others, by the merging of two or more companies, or by existing companies being dissolved and a new company formed to take over the combined business.

ambassador Botschafter

ambiguity Ungewissheit; Doppeldeutigkeit; Zweideutigkeit; mangelnde Eindeutigkeit

ambiguous ungewiss; zweideutig; nicht eindeutig; unklar

ambition Ehrgeiz; Strebsamkeit

ambitious ehrgeizig; strebsam; anspruchsvoll

amend berichtigen; ergänzen; novellieren

amendment Zusatz; Neufassung; *(law)* (Gesetzes-)Novelle; Gesetzesänderung; Nachtrag

American Accounting Association Amerikanischer Buchhaltungsverband

American Customer Satisfaction Index Amerikanischer Kundenzufriedenheits-Index

American Depository Receipt (ADR)

Security certificates issued by a U.S. Depositary Bank, representing shares of a foreign company held by the bank, usually by a branch or correspondent in the country of issue, enabling those shares to be traded in the United States.

One ADR may represent a portion of a foreign share, one share or a bundle of shares of a foreign corporation. ADR's carry the same currency, political and economic risks as the underlying foreign share; the prices of the two, adjusted for the SDR/ordinary ratio, are kept essentially identical by arbitrage. American Depositary Shares (ADS) are a similar form of certification.

If the ADR's are "sponsored", the corporation provides financial information and other assistance to the bank and may subsidize the administration of the ADR's. "Unsponsored" ADR's do not receive such assistance.

American option Amerikanische Option; terminoffene Anleihe

Option contract that can be exercised at any time between the date of purchase and the expiration date. Most exchange-traded options are American style. A European option, however, may be exercised only on the expiration date.

America Online (AOL)

Internet Service Provider (ISP) offering internet access, web-services, e-mail, etc.

amortization Schuldentilgung; Amortisation; Kredittilgung; *(depreciation)* Abschreibung; Tilgung; periodische Rückzahlung

The process of gradually reducing a debt through regular installment payments of principal and interest.

Accounting: the systematic write-off of costs incurred to acquire an intangible asset, such as patents, copyrights, or goodwill.

amortization amount Tilgungsbetrag

amortization mortgage Tilgungshypothek

amortization rate Tilgungsrate

amortization term Tilgungszeit

The amount of time required to amortize a debt.

amortize tilgen; amortisieren; *(to depreciate)* abschreiben

amount Betrag; Summe; *(quantity)* Menge; Höhe; Geldbetrag; Quantität; *(to ~)* betragen; ausmachen; sich belaufen auf; hinauslaufen

amount at risk Risikosumme

The difference between the face value of a life insurance policy and its accrued cash value.

amount invested Investitionssumme

amount of capital Kapitalbetrag; Kapitalhöhe

amount saved Sparbetrag

amounts differ abweichende Beträge

The words written on a cheque or bill of exchange by a banker who returns it unpaid because the amount in words differs from that in figures.

ample ausreichend; reichlich; genügend

amplitude Umfang; Fülle

AMTRAK

National Railway Passenger Corporation; federal agency that runs passenger trains throughout the United States.

analysis Analyse; Aufgliederung; Darlegung; Zerlegung

A systematic approach to problem solving. Complex problems are separated into more understandable elements. This involves the identification of purposes and facts, the statement of assumptions, and the formulation of conclusions

In a business-related situation the problem is divided into major elements in order to understand the item in question and make appropriate recommendations.

Example: evaluation of a product line in terms of pricing, quality, service, demand, and market share done by the marketing staff.

analysis of needs Bedarfsanalyse

analysis of variance (ANOVA) Abweichungsanalyse

A commonly used method for examining the statistically significant differences between the means of two or more populations.

In its simplest form it involves only one dependent variable and one or more independent variables.

Example: establish if there is a statistically significant difference in the average amount spent on alcohol per week between two samples of population (say, male and female). Here, the dependent variable is the amount spent and the independent variable is the gender of the participants.

analysis phase Analysephase

Internet: phase of a website design, related to identification of the requirements of a website. Techniques to achieve this may include focus groups, questionnaires sent with existing customers or interviews with key accounts.

analyst *(finance)* Berater; Analytiker; Analyst

Investment: Employee of a brokerage or fund management house who studies companies and makes buy and sell recommendations on their stocks. Most specialize in a specific industry.

analytic process Analyseverfahren; Analyseprozess

Procedures employed to analyse a situation or event. For example, an investor would engage in financial statement analysis by looking at trends in the accounts and financial ratios.

analytical analytisch

analytical estimating analytische Schätzung

A work measurement technique providing an estimate of the time required to carry out the elements of a job to be produced at a defined level of performance.

analytical review analytische Untersuchung

Auditing: analysis of significant ratios and trends for unusual change and questionable items.

Practically, this includes reading important documents and analyzing their accounting and financial effects; reviewing the activity in an account between interim and year-end; comparing current period account balances to prior periods as well as to budgeted amounts.

analyze analysieren; genau untersuchen

ancillary Neben-; Zusatz-; Hilfs-; ergänzend; zusätzlich; untergeordnet

ancillary income Nebeneinkünfte

Income generated by non-core business activiteis, for a hotel this may come from vending machines dispensing drinks.

anchor store Schlüsselgeschäft

Key retailers which form the nucleus of a shopping cluster. Their presence makes it all the more attractive for other retailers to set up shop in that shopping zone.

ANDEAN

Agreement reached in 1969 between Bolivia, Chile, Ecuador, Colombia, and Peru to establish a customs union.

animated banner advertisements animierte Bannerwerbung

Internet: Banner advertisements, on the internet, typic-ally involving several different images, disp-layed in sequence to help attract attention to the banner and build up a theme, often ending with a call to action and the injunction to click on the banner.

These advertisements are achieved through supplying the ad creative as an animated GIF file with different layers or frames, usually a rectangle of 468 by 60 pixels. Animated banner advertisements are an example of rich media advertisements.

annexation Anschluss; Eingemeindung; Annexion

Real estate: proces by which municipalities incorporate a certain amount of land or territory into the existing town or city limits.

The rules of annexation normally require a public ballot within the city and the area to be annexed.

annotation Erläuterung; Anmerkung; Kommentar

announce ankündigen; bekannt machen; *(to report)* melden

announcement Bekanntmachung; Ankündigung

announcer Ansager; Sprecher

Person hired by a radio station to introduce radio programs and performers.

annual *(book)* Jahrbuch; jährlich; einjährig; Jahrbuch; einjährige Pflanze

annual accounts Jahresabschluss

The financial statements of an organization. published annually.

Annual accounts consist of a profit and loss account, balance sheet and cash-flow statement, together with supporting notes, the directors´ report and auditor´s report.

Non-incorporated bodies, such as partnerships, are not legally obliged to produce accounts but may do so for their own information. or for their banks.

annual amount Jahresbetrag

annual average Jahresdurchschnitt

annual balance sheet Jahresabschluss; Jahresbilanz

annual basis Jahresbasis

Statistical technique extending figures covering a period of less than a year to cover a 12-month period. The procedure must take seasonal variations into account to be accurate.

annual budget Jahresetat; Jahresbudget

annual comparison Jahresvergleich

annual conference Jahrestagung

annual convention Jahrestagung

annual debt service jährlicher Schuldendienst

Finance: the cash required in a year for payments of interest and current maturities of principal on outstanding debt.

annual earnings Jahresgewinn; Jahresverdienst

A company's net profit, after expenses, investing and taxes.

Taxable income and the annual income indicated by financial statements may be significantly different.

annual financial statement Jahresabschluss

annual general meeting (AGM) Jahreshauptversammlung

A meeting of the owners (shareholders) of a corporation, which must be held every year.

The usual business conducted at an AGM is the presentation of the audited accounts, the appointment of directors and auditors, the fixing of their remuneration, and recommendations for the payment of dividends.

The chief executive officer usually comments on the outlook for the coming year and, with other senior officers, answers questions from shareholders.

annualized rate auf Jahresbasis; auf das Jahr umgerechnet

The translation of periods of less than a year into an annual rate for comparative purposes. *Example*: To annualize quarterly figures, they have to be multiplied by four.

annual output Jahresproduktion

annual percentage rate (APR) effektiver Jahreszins

The cost of credit shown as a yearly figure. It will be higher than the interest rate stated due to the fact that it includes the interest rate, discounts, fees and insurance.

annual plan Jahresplan

Short-term plan that describes the company′s current situation, its objectives, strategy, controls and budgets for the year ahead.

annual report Jahresbericht; Geschäftsbericht; Lagebericht; Jahresgutachten

Accounting: Financial statement issued at the end of every accounting year showing the company's financial condition. It includes a description of the firm's operations, its balance sheet and income statement.

In case of publicly owned corporations, the annual report must comply with reporting requirements defined by law or such organizations as the SEC in the U.S. Balance sheet, income statement, and cash-flow reports must be audited by an independent certified public accountant.

annual returns Jahresergebnis

annual sales Jahresumsatz

annual statement of accounts Jahresabschluss

annual working hours Jahresarbeitszeit

annualized holding-period return durchschnittliche Jahresrendite

Annual rate of return that, when compounded T times, would have given the same T-period holding return as actually occurred from period 1 to period T.

annuity Jahresrente; Jahreszahlung; Annuität; Rente

A contract sold by a life insurance company that provides fixed or variable payments to an annuitant in the future, either monthly, quarterly, semiannual, or annual.

annuity factor Rentenfaktor; Annuitätenfaktor

Mathematical calculation showing the present value of an income.

annuity in advance vorschüssige Rente

Annuity with an immediate initial payment.

annuity in arrears nachschüssige Rente

Annuity with a first payment at the end of one full period, rather than immediately. The first pay-ment occurs on date 1 rather than on date 0.

annuity index Rentenindex

annuity insurance Rentenversicherung

annuity value Rentenwert

Ansoff, H. Igor (1918-2002)

Pioneer of strategic management and corporate planning.

His seminal work *Corporate Strategy* has been ranked as one of the best business books of all time. After analyzing the three main types of decision-making – strategic, administrative and operating – he explains the specific questions addressed by strategy: what are the firm's objectives and goals? Should the firms seek to diversify, in what areas and how vigorously? How should the firm develop and exploit its present product-market position?

Biography: Born in Vladivostok, Russia; father American diplomat; studied mechanical engineering and physics in New York; 1948 joined Rand Foundation; worked for Lockheed and became vice-president and general manag-er of Lockheed Electronics Company; became professor at Carnegie School of Industrial Administration, later founding dean of the Graduate School of Management at Vanderbilt University.

Major publications: (1965) Corporate Strategy, (1969) Business Strategy, (1971) Behavior of US Manufacturing Firms 1946-65, (1976) From Strategic Planning to Strategic Manage-ment, (1979) Strategic Management, (1984) Implanting Strategic Management.

Ansoff matrix Ansoff'sche Matrix

A strategic marketing planning model, based on the assumption that companies can either sell existing or new products, and that they can sell them either in markets familiar to them (existing markets) or in new markets.

The resulting two by two matrix gives four alternative strategies for increasing sales:

- Market penetration, i.e. concentrate on selling more existing products into existing markets. This can be achieve by such means as price reductions and increased advertising. It is regarded as a low-risk strategy.
- Product development, to modify or improve its existing products and sell these to current customers.
- Market development, to sell existing products to a new market, for example to export the current range of products to America. The second and the third strategies are medium risk.
- Diversification, is to develop new products for new markets, for example, for a lawn-mower manufacturer to develop printing machinery. This is the highest the risk strategy.

Also referred to as product-market matrix.

answer Antwort; Bescheid; *(solution)* Lösung; antworten; *(a question)* beantworten; *(to be responsible)* verantwortlich sein; entsprechen

answer in the affirmative zusagen

anthropology Menschenkunde; Anthropologie

Study of societies to learn about human beings and their activities.

Anthropologists' work on cultures and env-ironments has helped understand differences in fundamental values, attitudes, and behavior among people in different countries and within different organizations.

Much of current understanding of organizational culture and organizational environments, is the result of the work of anthropologists or those using their methodologies.

anticipate *(to await)* erwarten; *(to forestall)* vorwegnehmen; vorweg verwenden; zuvorkommen; vorausahnen; voraussehen

anticipation *(expectation)* Erwartung; *(forestalling)* Vorwegnahme; Vorgefühl; -freunde; Zuvorkommen; Hoffnung; zusätzlicher Nachlass

anticipatory breach antizipierter Vertragsbruch

Breaking a contract before the actual time of required performance.

anti-diversion clause Anti-Ablenkungs-klausel

anti-dumping duty Anti-Dumping-Abgabe; Antidumpingzoll

anti-dumping law Anti-Dumping-Gesetz

Law designed to restrict the sale of goods for less than their fair market price.

anti-dumping policies Anti-Dumping-Politik

Policies designed to punish foreign firms that engage in dumping and thus protect domestic producers from unfair foreign competition.

antitrust agency Kartellamt

antitrust laws Kartellrecht

Laws enacted to protect individuals and businesses from monopolies and unfair restrictions.

application service provider (ASP)

Allows businesses to outsource value chain functions to separate providers. These providers act as third party service providers.

apology Entschuldigung; Verteidigung(srede; -sschrift)

apparatus Vorrichtung; Gerät; Apparat;

apparent authority Scheinvollmacht; *(contracts)* Anscheinsvollmacht

Concept in agency theory describing authority that an agent has on the basis of actions or inactions of the principal. This is so despite the fact that the agent may not have actual authority.

appeal Bitte; *(against sentence)* Berufung; *(against decision)* Einspruch; *(to customers)* Anklang; *(request)* Aufruf; Appell; *(to appeal a sentence)* Berufung einlegen; *(to appeal a decision)* Einspruch erheben; *(to customers)* Anklang finden bei; appellieren; dringend bitten; Eindruck machen auf

Legal: Resort to a higher court for a review of a lower court's decision in hope of hearing it reversed; or the case retried.

appear erscheinen; in Sicht kommen; auftreten

appearance Erscheinung; *(in public)* Auftreten; Aussehen

appellant Revisionskläger

A person or organization that appeals against the decision of a court. The party resisting the appeal is called the respondent.

applet (*Software*) kleine Anwendung; kleines Programm

Small program that performs a limited set of tasks. Internet-based programs that use the Java programming language are often referred to as applets.

appliance Vorrichtung; (Haushalts-)Gerät

applicable anwendbar; zutreffend; *(usable)* verwendbar

applicant Bewerber; Antragsteller; *(for a job)* Stellenbewerber

application *(use)* Anwendung; *(request)* Antrag; *(for a position)* Bewerbung; *(handling)* Handhabung; Bitten; Gesuch; Bewerbung; Fleiß; Hingabe

application for listing Antrag auf Börsenzulassung

The process by which a company applies to a stock exchange for its securities to be traded on that exchange.

A company will be required to abide by the rules of the exchange. The advantage for a company in obtaining a listing is that it will be able to raise funds by issuing shares on the stock exchange and the marketability of the shares it issues will attract investors.

application form Bewerbungsforumular; Anmeldeformular

application of funds Mittelverwendung

Section in the statement of changes in financial position outlining the uses of the funds.

In the working capital concept of funds, the applications are: net loss; increase in non current assets; decrease in non current liabilities; and decrease in stockholders' equity.

In the cash concept of funds flow, two additional applications are: increase in current assets other than cash; and decrease in current liabilities.

application service provider (ASP)

Internet: acompany that allows businesses to outsource value chain functions to separate providers. The software is developed at the ASP's site.

applications software Anwendungssoftware

Computer programs that are designed for a particular purpose or application. Examples would be accounting programs, games programs, or educational programs.

applied research angewandte Forschung

Original investigations undertaken to gain new knowledge with respect to a specific practical objective.

Example: any testing in the search for a product alternative would normally be considered as applied research because it is aimed at a specific practical objective.

Pure research, on the other hand, is primarily undertaken to acquire new scientific knowledge for its own sake.

apply anwenden; *(funds)* verwenden; *(for a position)* sich bewerben; *(to make a request)* beantragen; *(results, findings)* verwerten für; *(efforts)* zuwenden; *(pressure)* ausüben; betätigen; *(paint)* auftragen

apply oneself sich anstrengen.

appoint to a post ernennen; berufen; *(to designate)* bestimmen

appointment Verabredung; Termin; *(nomination)* Ernennung; *(office)* Anstellung; Berufung; Einsetzung; Stellung; Posten; *pl* Einrichtung

appointment calendar Terminkalender

appointment schedule Terminkalender; Terminplan

apportion zuweisen; (gerecht) verteilen; aufteilen

apportionment Verteilung; Zuteilung; Einteilung; Erteilung; Aufschlüsselung; *(public finance)* Aufteilung

Distribution of expenses, such as taxes and insurance, between buyer and seller.

Property: Partitioning of land into individual parcels by tenants in common.

appraisable bewertbar

appraisal Schätzung; Bewertung; Auswertung; Taxierung, *(value)* Taxwert

In general: act of appraising or the stated result after appraising.

Property: estimate of the value of a property.

Insurance: to determine the amount of hazard insurance to carry.

appraisal report Gutachten eines Schätzers

Report describing the findings of an appraisal engagement.

appraisal rights Bewertungsrechte

Rights of minority stockholders who object to an extraordinary action taken by the management of a corporation such as a merger.

appraise ab-; ein-; schätzen; bewerten; beurteilen; *(to assess)* taxieren

Estimate the value of property. To set a value on goods, land, the estate of a deceased person; to estimate loss as by fire, etc.

appraiser Schätzer; *(insurance)* Schadensabschätzer

Person qualified to estimate the value of real property. One designated by court or appointed by agreement to set a value on property.

appreciate *(to value)* schätzen; *(to rise in value)* im Wert steigen; würdigen anerkennen; dankbar sein

appreciation Wertschätzung; *(rise in value)* Wertsteigerung; Aufwertung; Werterhöhung; Würdigung

appreciation of principal Kapitalzuwachs

apprentice Lehrling; Auszubildender; in die Lehre gehen

A young employee who signs a contract agreeing to be trained in a particular skill for a set amount of time by a specific employer.

During this time, the apprenticeship, the wages will be relatively low, but upon its completion they increase to reflect the increased status of the employee and to recognize the skills acquired.

apprenticeship Lehrstelle; Lehre; Berufsausbildung; Lehrzeit

apprenticeship offer Lehrstellenangebot

approach Vorgehen; *(access)* Annäherung; Nahen; (*to* ~) sich nähern; näher kommen; sich wenden an; herangehen an

Marketing: step in the selling process in which the salesperson meets and greets the buyer to get the relationship off to a good start.

approachable erreichbar; ansprechbar

appropriate *(adequate)* angemessen; passend; gemäß *(to allocate)* bewilligen; *(to take possession)* aneignen

appropriation *(allocation)* Bewilligung; *(taking possession)* Aneignung; Verwendung

approval Zustimmung; Genehmigung; Billigung; Bewilligung

approve zustimmen; genehmigen; billigen; anerkennen

approximate annähernd; nahe bringen; nahe kommen; ungefähr; annähernd

approximately zirka; schätzungsweise; ungefähr

approximation annähernde Berechnung; Näherungswert; Annäherung

a priori statement Annahme; Vermutung

Statement that is accepted as true without being verified or tested.

aptitude Eignung; Fähigkeit; Geschick; Befähigung; Begabung; Talent

Natural ability of an individual to learn material sufficiently so that he can properly perform the business task required on the job.

aptitude test Eignungsprüfung; Eignungstest

A selection test intended to assess a candidate's promise, trainability, and potential rather than his previously acquired competence.

Arab League Arabische Liga

arbiter Schiedsrichter

Person appointed by a court to decide a controversy according to the law.

An arbiter needs the court's confirmation of his decision for it to be final, whilst an arbitrator has the power himself.

arbitrage Arbitrage; Ausnutzung von Preisunterschieden

In general: A technique employed to take advantage of differences in price. Practically, it involves the simultaneous purchase of an asset in one market at a lower cost and sale in a different market with a higher price.

Stocks: purchase of securities in one market for immediate resale in another to profit from a price discrepancy.

True *arbitrage* positions are completely hedged, i.e., the performance of both sides of the transaction is guaranteed at any time. This involves no risk.

arbitrage bond Arbitrageschuld-verschreibung

A lower-rate debt security issued by a municipality prior to the call date of the municipality's existing higher-rate security. The aim is to gain an interest rate advantage.

arbitrageur Arbitragehändler; Arbitrageur

A person who engages in arbitrage.

arbitrage pricing theory (APT) Arbitrage-Pricing-Theorie

Equilibrium asset pricing theory that is derived from a factor model by using diversification and arbitrage. It shows that the expected return on any risky asset is a linear combination of various factors.

arbitrary willkürlich; eigenmächtig

arbitrate schlichten; schiedsrichterlich entscheiden

arbitration Schlichtung; Schlichtungsverfahren; Schiedsgerichtsverfahren; Schiedsspruch

Act of submitting a dispute for judgment to an impartial third party, the arbitrator. Where the parties agree to be bound by the determination of the arbitrator, the process is called *binding arbitration.*

arbitration agreement Schlichtungsabkommen; Schiedsvertrag

arbitration decision Schlichtungsspruch

arbitration pricing theory Schlichtungspreistheorie

arbitration result Schlichtungsergebnis

arbitrator Schlichter; Schiedsrichter; Vermittler

A person who decides disputes between two or more parties. He has to be impartial and agreed upon by all parties of a conflict to solve a dispute. An arbitrator is empowered to make a final decision concerning the controversy and is bound only by his own discretion.

archie

Database containing information on what documents and programs are located on FTP servers

archive Archiv

A store for documents and other storage media containing records that are seldom used.

A computer file, usually in a compressed format, holding data that is no longer current.

area Fläche; *(region)* Gebiet; Bereich; Gegend; Zone

argue diskutieren; *(to dispute)* sich auseinandersetzen; argumentieren; streiten

argument Argument; *(dispute)* Wortstreit; Streit; Auseinandersetzung; Behauptung; mathematischer Beweis; Diskussion; Wortwechsel

Argyris, Chris (* 1923)

Organizational psychologist specializing in the personal development of individuals within organizations, and the resistance of managers to change.

Biography: Professor of Educational and Organizational Behavior at Yale University, since 1971 Professor of Educational and Organizational Behavior at Harvard University.

Major publications: (1957) Personality and Organization, (1965) Organization and Innovation, (1978) Organizational Learning: A theory of Action Perspective, (1985) Strategy, Change and Defensive Routines, (1991) 'Teaching Smart People how to Learn', Harvard Business Review (May/June), (1994) 'Good communication that blocks learning' Harvard Business Review (July/August)

arithmetic average arithmetischer Durchschnitt

arithmetic mean arithmetisches Mittel; Mittelwert

An average obtained by adding together the individual numbers concerned and dividing the total by their number.

For example, the arithmetic mean of 7, 20, 107, and 350 is 484/4 = 121. This value, however, gives no idea of the spread of numbers.

arms index Arms Index

An advance/decline market indicator. Less than 1.0 indicates bullish demand, while above 1.0 is bearish. The index often is smoothed with a simple moving average.

arm's length auf geschäftlicher Grundlage; unabhängig

Denoting a transaction in which the parties to the transaction are financially unconnected.

For example, a transaction between two subsidiaries of the same parent organization could only be said to be at arm's length if it could be shown that the deal had been carried out at current market prices With no preference of any kind being shown in the trading terms.

arm´s-length transaction Abschluss auf rein geschäftlicher Grundlage; Abschluss auf Basis von Marktpreisen; Transaktion zwischen unabhängigen Partnern

Transaction among parties, each of whom acts in his or her own best interest.

Example: transactions between the following parties would, in most cases, not be considered arm's length: a husband and wife; a father and son; a corporation and one of its subsidiaries.

arrange arrangieren; ordnen; *(to agree upon)* vereinbaren; *(to plan)* Vorkehrungen treffen; *(to organize)* veranstalten; einrichten; beilegen; Vorkehrungen treffen

arrangement Anordnung; *(agreement)* Abmachung; Vereinbarung; *(plan)* Vorkehrung; *(compromise)* Vergleich; Arrangement

Formal summoning of an accused into court where indictment is read by him and he is called up on to plead "guilty" or "not guilty".

array Datenreihe; Reihe; Ordnung; große Anzahl; Aufgebot; *(to ~)* (an)ordnen; aufstellen

Statistics: A series of variables or objects that are of the same type and size. Each element can be identified by a set of numbers known as subscripts, which indicate the row and column in which the element is located.

arrearage Rückstand; rückständige Zahlung

General: The past due amounts to be repaid in accordance with the terms of a repayment plan.

Investment: amount by which interest on bonds or dividends on cumulative preferred stock is due and unpaid.

arrears Schulden; Rückstand

A liability that has not been settled by the due date.

arrears, in im Rückstand; rückständig

Debt: debts not paid by the due date.

Payments: at the end of a term. Interest on a mortgage is normally paid *in arrears;* i.e. at the end of a month. Rent and insurance premiums are normally paid in advance, i.e. at the beginning of the month.

arrival Ankunft; Ankommen; Eintreffen; *(of shipment)* Eingang; Ankömmling

arrival notice Eingangsbestätigung

Announcement by transportation company to consignee when shipment reaches destination.

arrive ankommen; eintreffen; *(shipment)* eingehen; eintreten

arson Brandlegung; Brandstiftung

Crime of deliberately setting fire to a property; a statutory crime.

article (Waren-; Zeitungs-)Artikel; *(item)* Posten; *(goods)* Ware; *(object)* Gegenstand; *(clause)* Klausel; *(section)* Abschnitt; Stück

articles of incorporation Gründungsurkunde; Gesellschaftsvertrag; Satzung

An official document that creates a private corporation according to the general corporation laws of the state.

In the U.K., this document is called memorandum of association

artificial intelligence künstliche Intelligenz

The ability of a computer to perform tasks normally associated with human intelligence, such as reasoning and learning from experience.

An expert system uses the computer's ability to store, organize and retrieve large volumes of information. Also called intelligent knowledge-based systems, these store the knowledge and experience of an expert in a particular field. The system can be questioned by a non-expert and will give the answer that the expert would give.

artificial person künstliche Person

A person whose identity is recognized by the law but who is not an individual.

For example, a company is a person in the sense that it can sue and be sued, hold property, etc. in its own name. It is not, however, an individual or real person.

ascertain feststellen; festsetzen; *(costs)* ermitteln

ascertainment Feststellung; Ermittlung; Erhebung

ASCII Acronym for American Standard Code for Information Interchange.

Acronym for American Standard Code for Information Interchange. A Standard 8 bit code used in data communications representing numbers, letters, and symbols.

ASEAN (Association of South East Asian Nations)

Association formed in 1967, as an attempt to establish a free trade area between Brunei, Indonesia, Malaysia, the Philippines, Singapore, and Thailand.

as is wie besichtigt; wie gesehen

Commercial term indicating that a product is sold in its present conditions with no warranties. The buyer has to accept delivery of the goods in the condition in which they are found on inspection prior to purchase, even if they are damaged or defective.

ask Preisangebot; *(a question)* (er)fragen; *(for a favor)* bitten; *(to demand)* (auf)fordern; ersuchen; einladen

asking price ursprüngliche Preisforderung; offizieller Verkaufspreis

Price at which an investment is offered for sale; also called *ask price, asked price, ask,* or offering price. Per-share price at which mutual fund shares are offered to the public, usually the net asset value per share plus a sales charge, if any.

aspect Gesichtspunkt; Aspekt; Blickpunkt; Erscheinung; Seite

aspirational group angestrebte Gruppe

A type of reference group to which people would like to belong. Quite often. the aspiring person assumes the values, attitudes, and even the dress of the group.

assemble *(people)* versammeln; *(objects)* ansammeln; *(industry)* montieren; zusammensetzen; -bauen

assembly *(industry)* Montage; *(people)* Versammlung

assembly chamber Kongresshalle

assembly line Fließband; Taktstraße; Fertigungsstraße; Montageband

Mechanical system in a factory whereby a product is conveyed through different production sites at which successive operations are performed on it. Processes are highly standardized and rationalized.

assembly plant Montagewerk

A factory where manufactured parts are assembled into a finished product

assembly operation Montagevorgang

assert behaupten; *(rights)* geltend machen; zur Geltung bringen; behaupten

assertion Behauptung; *(rights)* Geltendmachung; Durchsetzung; Erklärung

assertive bestimmend

assertiveness Selbstbehauptung; Durchsetzungsvermögen

assertiveness training Selbstbehauptungstraining

Training courses designed to help employees to maximize their potential by developing their abilities, exercising initiative, presenting themselves convincingly, and translating ideas into action.

assess *(to appraise)* einschätzen; abschätzen; beurteilen; bewerten; *(to charge with a tax)* besteuern; *(a fine)* festsetzen; festlegen; bemessen; veranlagen

To determine the value of something, e.g. the value of property on the basis of which property taxes will be calculated.

assessed value Einheitswert

Value assigned to property by a municipality for the purpose of assessing taxes.

assessment *(appraisal)* Einschätzung; Beurteilung; Bewertung; *(taxes)* Veranlagung; *(duty)* Abgabe; Umlage

assessment center Assessment-Center

Set of performance simulation tests, specifically designed to evaluate a candidate's managerial potential. Line executives, supervisors, and/or trained psychologists evaluate candidates as they go through several days of exercises that simulate real problems that they would confront on the job.

Based on a list of descriptive dimensions that the actual job incumbent has to meet, activities might include interviews, in-basket problem-solving exercises, leaderless group discussion, and business decision games. The results of this test predict later job performance in managerial positions.

assessment ratio Bemessungsverhältnis

The ratio of assessed value to full market value as set by a taxing authority.

assessment roll *(property)* Grundsteuerliste

Public record of the assessed value of property in a municipality, listing each individual tract of land with its assessed value.

assessor Schadensgutachter; Schadensregulierer; Schätzer; Taxator; Beisitzer; Steuereinschätzer

Appointed or elected official who determines property values, generally for real estate taxation purposes.

asset *(balance sheet)* Aktivposten; *(possession)* Vermögensgegenstand; Aktivposten; Wirtschaftsgut; Vorzug; Plus; Vorteil

Any object, tangible or intangible, that is of value to its possessor.

Tangible assets include land and buildings, plant and machinery, fixtures and fittings, trading stock. investments, debtors, and cash. Intangible assets include goodwill, patents, copyrights, and trademarks.

asset allocation Portfolio-Strukturierung

The process of dividing investments among different kinds of assets, such as stocks, bonds, real estate and cash, to optimize risk and reward to the investor.

asset account Bestandskonto

asset-creating vermögenswirksam

asset currency Vermögenswährung

Banking: currency secured exclusively by the general assets of the issuing bank as distinguished from that secured by special deposit issuing bank as distinguished from that secured by special deposit of government, bonds, commercial paper, etc.

asset depreciation range (ADR) *(property)* betriebsgewöhnliche Nutzungsdauer

Limitation on the period over which assets may be depreciated.

asset management Anlagenverwaltung; Vermögensverwaltung

The management of the financial assets of a company in order to maximize the return on the investments.

asset stripping Zerschlagung eines Unternehmens

The acquisition of a firm for a price that is well below its total asset value, and the subsequent sale of these assets.

This may be done either because a particular asset, such as property, is valued in the firm's balance sheet at well below its potential market price, or because the firm has been poorly managed.

No consideration is given to the interests of other stakeholders, such as employees, suppliers, or customers.

assets *(balance sheet)* Aktiva; Aktivseite; *(property)* Vermögens-; Konkursmasse; Guthaben; Besitz

Balance sheet: assets can be categorized in different ways. For example: fixed or permanent assets - land, building, machinery, capital stock of another company which can be used repeatedly; current, liquid or floating Assets - cash or materials which can be used only at one time; quick assets - cash or goods which can be immediately disposed of without loss.

asset value Vermögenswert; Wert eines Wirtschaftgutes

asset valuation Anlagenbewertung; Vermögensbewertung

An assessment of the value at which the assets of an organization, usually the capital assets, should be entered into its balance sheet.

assign *(to allot)* zuweisen; zuteilen; zuordnen; *(to transfer)* übertragen; übereignen; *(debt)* abtreten; anweisen; auftragen; bestimmen

assignee Beauftragter; *(law)* Abtretungsempfänger; Zessionar; Begünstigter; Rechtsnachfolger; Assignat

Person to whom an agreement or contract is sold or transferred.

assignment *(allotment)* Zuweisung; Anweisung; *(transfer)* Übertragung; *(debt)* Abtretung; *(task)* Aufgabe

Property: A document transferring ownership from one party to another. The party who assigns is the assignor and the party who receives the transfer of title, i.e., the assignment - is the assignee.

Insurance: Transfer of the rights of an insurance policy to someone else. Life insurance policies are normally freely assignable, whilst property and casualty insurance policies are not.

assignment of income Einkommensabtretung

Taxpayer's direction that income earned by him be paid to another person so that it will be considered the other person's income for tax purposes.

assignment of lease Pachtabtretung

A transfer by the lessee of his or her interest in the lease to a third person. The assignee acquires the same rights and privileges as the assignor. The assignor remains liable unless released by the property owner.

assignment status Zuweisungsstatus

assignor Abtretender; *(law)* Zedent; Rechtsvorgänger; Altgläubiger

Party who assigns or transfers an agreement or contract to another.

assimilate angleichen; anpassen

assimilation Angleichung; Anpassung; Einverleibung

assist helfen; unterstützen

assistance Hilfe; Unterstützung

assistant Gehilfe; Gehilfin; Assistent; Hilfskraft; Mitarbeiter; *(deputizing)* stellvertretend

assistive technologies Unterstützungstechnologie

Internet: help people with disabilities use their computers to communicate over the net. These include voice-activated computers, large type screen displays, type-to-speech or Braille: speech-to-text telephony, and eye gaze-to-type.

associate *(business)* Geschäftspartner; Teilhaber; Partner; *(to~)* sich verbinden; sich assoziieren

associated establishment Partnerinstitut

association *(organization)* Verband; Verein; Vereinigung; Gemeinschaft; Genossenschaft; Gesellschaft; *(with other people)* Umgang; Verkehr

Group of persons united without a formal charter in order to follow a common aim.

association representative Verbandsvertreter

assortment *(selection)* Auswahl; *(set of goods)* Kollektion; Sortiment; Mischung

assume *(to suppose)* annehmen; unterstellen; voraussetzen; vermuten; *(an office)* übernehmen

assumed shelter cost angenommene Schutzkosten

assumption Annahme; Vermutung; *(prerequisite)* Voraussetzung; *(duty)* Übernahme

assumption of office Amtsübernahme

assumption of risk Risikoübernahme; *(contracts)* Gefahrübernahme

Technique of risk management under which business assumes expected losses that are not catastrophic, but protects against catastrophic losses through the purchase of insurance.

assurance Zusicherung; Versicherung; Sicherheit; Assekuranz

assure sichern; versichern; zusichern; sicherstellen; überzeugen

assured zusichern; versichern

atmosphere Atmosphäre

Marketing: designed environment that creates or reinforces the buyer's propensity to consume a product.

attach beifügen; anheften; *(to fasten)* befestigen; *(to seize)* beschlagnahmen; pfänden

attaché Gesandschaftsbeamter; Attaché

attachment *(to a document)* Beilage; *(seizure)* Beschlagnahme; *(implement)* Zusatzgerät; Zubehörteil; Zusatzteil

attain erreichen; erlangen

attainable erreichbar

attainment Erlangung; Errungenschaft; Kenntnisse; Leistungen

attempt Versuch; versuchen

attend besuchen; *(to take care of)* besorgen; bedienen; Beachtung schenken; behandeln; begleiten

attendance Anwesenheit; Besuch; (Auf-) Wartung; Behandlung; *(number of visitors)* Teilnehmerzahl; Besucherzahl

attendant Begleiter; *(guard)* Wärter; *(care taker)* Pfleger; Wärter; Platzanweiser; begleitend; dazugehörig; Dienst tuend

attention Aufmerksamkeit; Beachtung; *(to the attention of)* zu Händen von

attentive aufmerksam; sorgfältig

attest beglaubigen; bezeugen; bestätigen; bescheinigen; beweisen; Zeugnis ablegen; vereidigen

To bear witness to an act or event. The law requires that some documents are only valid and binding if the signatures on them have been attested to by a third party.

at the money am Geld

Option when the value of its underlying security is equal to the option strike price. An option is at-the-money if the strike price of the option is equal to the market price of the underlying security.

Example: if xyz stock is trading at 54, then the xyz 54 option is at-the-money.

attitude Haltung; Einstellung

The way in which a person views and evaluates something or someone. Attitudes are made up of cognitive, affective, and behavioral components.

In modern marketing, the emphasis is mainly on defining attitude in terms of affect, i.e. a person's feelings towards a product or a brand.

attitude surveys Mitarbeiterbefragung

Eliciting responses from employees through questionnaires about how they feel about their jobs, work groups, supervisors, and the organization.

Regular attitude surveys provide managers with valuable feedback on how employees perceive their working conditions.

attorney Bevollmächtigter; *(attorney-at-law)* Rechtsanwalt; Anwalt

attract anziehen; auf sich lenken; (an)lenken

attraction Attraktion; *(power to attract)* Anziehungskraft; *(focus of attraction)* Anziehungspunkt; Reiz

attractive anziehend; reizend; attraktiv; zugkräftig; reizvoll; *(price)* günstig

attribute Eigenschaft; Merkmal; Kennzeichen; *(to ~)* zurechnen; zurückführen auf; zuschreiben

attribution Zurechnung; Zurückführung

attribution theory Attributionstheorie

Theory explaining the ways in which we judge people differently, depending on what meaning we attribute to a given behavior.

It suggests that when individuals observe an individual behavior, they attempt to determine whether it is internally or externally caused.

Internally caused behaviors are those that are believed to be under the personal control of the individual. *Externally* caused behavior is seen as resulting from outside causes; that is, the person is seen as having been forced into the behavior by the situation.

attrition Zermürbung; Verschleiß; Arbeitskräfteabgang

Employment: Normal and uncontrollable reduction of a work force because of retirement, death, sickness or relocation.

auction Versteigerung; Auktion, *(to~)* versteigern

Public sale by competitive bidding of prospective buyers.

Bids are taken orally on the spot, by phone, by mail, by telegram, etc., and the item is sold to the highest bidder.

auction exchange Auktionsbörse

Securities: Centralized market where securities including equities, bonds, options, etc. are bought and sold through bid and offer prices by security brokers.

auctioneer Auktionator; Versteigerer

Person whose job is to conduct auction sales.

The auctioneer normally acts as agent for the seller and receives a commission on the price. He must have the authority of the seller to sell, and must know of no defect in the seller's title to the goods.

auction market Auktionsmarkt

Market where all traders in a certain good meet at one place to buy or sell an asset. A stock exchange is an example.

audience *(reception)* Empfang; *(public)* Publikum; Zuhörerschaft; Zielgruppe

General: group of people assembled in a studio, theater, or auditorium to witness a presentation or performance.

Advertising: total number of people who may receive an advertising message delivered by a medium or a combination of media.

Communications: total number of readers, viewers, or listeners reached by the appropriate medium.

audience accumulation Publikumskumulierung

Process of adding new audiences to a media vehicle's total reach.

Accumulation takes place because audiences constantly expand from a base as new audiences are reached, while old ones are lost.

From the advertiser's point of view, the new audiences are accumulated, providing him with an expanding number of people who have seen his or her ad message.

audience composition Zielgruppenzusammensetzung

audience research Publikumsforschung

Research to establish readership, audience and circulation data of an advertisement.

audience turnover Publikumsfluktuation

The ratio of a cumulative audience over several periods of time (e.g., four weeks) to the average audience per period of time (e.g., per week).

The ratio serves as an indication of the relative frequency with which the audience of a program changes.

audit Revision; Bilanzprüfung; Wirtschaftsprüfung; Rechnungsprüfung; *(to ~)* Revision durchführen; prüfen; auditieren

Accounting: An independent inspection, correction and verification of the accounting records and procedures of a business by a qualified auditor, for the purpose of verifying the accuracy and completeness of the records.

It may be conducted by a member of the organization (internal audit) or by an outsider (independent audit).

audit, external Prüfung des Unternehmensumfeldes

Marketing: Examination of the business and economic environment in which a company operates. This includes the political, economic, social, fiscal, legal, cultural and technological factors (PESTL).

auditor Wirtschaftsprüfer; Rechnungsprüfer; Bilanzprüfer; Revisor

Person authorized and trained to examine, correct and verify accounts.

Public officer charged by law with the duty of examining and verifying the expenditure of public funds. Accountant who performs a similar function for private parties.

auditor's certificate Bestätigungsvermerk; Prüfungsbericht; Revisionsbericht

See: accountant's opinon.

auditor's opinion Bestätigungsvermerk; Prüfungsbericht

See: accountant's opinion.

audit program Prüfungsprogramm

Detailed description of the steps to be taken by an auditor when analyzing transactions to determine the acceptability of financial statements.

Accounting firms may prepare an audit program for each client and require the person who does the work to sign or initial each step performed.

audit report Revisionsbericht; Prüfbericht

A report by the auditors appointed to audit the accounts of a company or other organization.

Auditors' reports may take many forms depending on who has appointed the auditors and for what purposes.

The auditors of a limited company are required to form an opinion as to whether the annual accounts of the company give a true and fair view of its profit or loss for the period under review and of its state of affairs at the end of the period; they are also required to certify that the accounts are prepared in accordance with the legal requirements.

audit trail Prüfungskette; Prüfungsweg

Step-by-step record by which accounting data can be traced to their source.

Any questions concerning the validity or accuracy of an accounting figure can then be resolved by reviewing the sequence of events from which the figure resulted.

augment vergrößern; vermehren; zunehmen

augmentation Vergrößerung; Vermehrung; Zunahme

augmented product erweitertertes Produkt; Zusatznutzen des Produktes

Additional consumer services and benefits built around the core and actual products.

These include warranty, repair service, phone number for problems, and possibly lessons on how to use the device.

The augmented product can be critical to the success of the core product.

austerity *(severity)* Strenge; *(simplicity)* Einfachheit; *(hardship)* Entbehrung; Knappheit

austerity program Sparprogramm; Sanierungsprogramm

autarchy Autarkie; Alleinherrschaft

Term describing a closed economy that is self-sufficient and does not trade with the rest of the world.

authentic echt; verlässlich; authentisch

authentication Anerkennung; Beglaubigung

Legal verification of the genuineness of a document, as by the certification and seal of an authorized public official.

Stocks: Identification of a bond certificate as having been issued under a specific indenture, thus validating the bond.

authenticity Echtheit; *(legal validity)* Rechtsgültigkeit

author Urheber; Autor; Verfasser

authoritarian autoritär

Dictatorial and domineering. Authoritarian managers value employees' unquestioned obedience.

authoritarian society autoritäre Gesellschaft, autoritäres System

Existence of governmental authority over numerous phases of human conduct while approval by the people for governmental action does not exist.

An *authoritarian society* is distinguished from a totalitarian society in that the latter covers all phases of human conduct.

authoritative maßgeblich

authority *(government)* Behörde; *(expert)* Autorität; *(right to act)* Befugnis; *(attorney)* Vollmacht; *(expert)* Sachverständiger; Fachmann

The power or right to give orders or make decisions. With authority comes responsibility for one's actions.

Example: managers have the *authority* to hire and fire personnel in an organization.

authorization Ermächtigung; Bevollmächtigung; *(approval)* Genehmigung; Befugnis; Billigung

authorize (to *grant power)* er-; bevollmächtigen; *(to approve)* genehmigen; gutheißen

autocorrelation Autokorellation

Correlation of a variable with itself over successive time intervals.

autodraft Eigenwechsel

automate automatisieren

automated guided vehicle (AGV) fahrerloses Transportfahrzeug

A self-propelled vehicle used to transport materials or components without human intervention.

They are most often used in manufacturing plants, especially if these involve hazardous chemicals or structures, where AGVs can form an integrated part of the process design.

automated screen trading (AST) elektronischer Handel

Electronic dealing in securities using computers to display prices and to enter, match, and execute deals.

automated teller machine (ATM) Geldausgabeautomat; Geldautomat

Computer-controlled terminal through which customers of a bank may make deposits, withdrawals or other transactions as they would through a bank teller.

automatic automatisch

automatic customization automatische Kundenausrichtung

Internet: tailoring of the content presented to the user based on information known about the user and the user's historical surfing behavior.

automatic identification automatische Indentifizierung

A way of identifying a product mechanically and entering the data obtained automatically into a computer.

The most widely used methods are bar codes, optical character recognition (OCR), magnetic ink character recognition (MICR), magnetic stripes, and voice systems.

automatic vending automatisierter Verkauf

The use of coin operated self-service machines to sell small, standardised, routinely purchased products such as chewing gum, sweets, newspapers, cigarettes, soft drinks and coffee.

automation Automatisierung

Controlling industrial processes automatically by using electronically-controlled systems.

autonomous unabhängig; autonom

autonomy Autonomie; Selbstregierung; Selbstverwaltung; Selbstständigkeit

Employment: Depth to which a job provides substantial freedom, independence, and discretion to the individual in scheduling the work and in determining the procedures to be used in carrying it out.

autoregressive moving average autoregressiver gleitender Durchschnitt

Statistical model applied to time series date in order to understand and, predict future values in this series.

auto responder Autoresponder

Software tools or agents running on web servers, which automatically send a standard reply to the sender of an e-mail message. This may provide information to a standard request; also known as *mail bots*.

auxiliary materials *(balance sheet)* Hilfsstoffe

availability Verfügbarkeit

availability float Pufferzeit der Gültigkeit

Refers to the time required to clear a check through the banking system.

availability heuristic Heuristik nach Verfügbarkeit

Tendency of people to base their judgments on information that is readily available to them. Events that evoke emotions, that are particularly vivid, or that have occurred more recentlee tend to be more available in memory.

Example: managers, when doing annual performance appraisals, tend to give more weight to recent behaviors of an employee than those behaviors of six or nine months ago.

available verfügbar; vorhanden; benutzbar; erhältlich; gültig

available market vorhandener Markt

Set of consumers who have interest, income and access to a particular product or service.

average Durchschnitt; *(mean value)* Mittelwert; durchschnittlich; *(to~)* durchschnittlich betragen; den Durchschnitt berechnen

Finance: weighted and adjusted arithmetic mean of selected securities designed to be representative of an entire market. *Example:* Dow Jones Industrial & Transportation Average.

average accounting return (AAR) durchschnittliche Buchrendite

Average project earnings before taxes but after depreciation divided by the average book value of the investment during its life.

average audience durchschnittliche Anzahl der Nutzer/Zuhörer

Internet: in broadcast, the average number of homes (or individuals) tuned to a given time segment of a program. In print media, the number of individuals who looked into an average issue of a publication and are considered "readers."

average collection period durchschnittliche Forderungslaufzeit

Average amount of time required to collect an account receivable. Also referred to as day's sales outstanding.

average costs Durchschnittskosten

Total of all costs for all units bought (or produced), divided by the number of units acquired (or produced).

average cost of capital durchschnittliche Kapitalkosten

Firm's required return to the bondholders and the shareholders expressed as a percentage of capital contributed to the firm. Average cost of capital is computed by dividing the total required cost of capital by the total amount of contributed capital.

average figure Durchschnittszahl

average daily sales durchschnittlicher Tagesumsatz

Annual sales divided by 365 days.

average maturity durchschnittliche Laufzeit

Average time to maturity of securities held by a mutual fund. Changes in interest rates have greater impact on funds with longer average life.

average number Durchschnittszahl

average order value durchschnittlicher Auftragswert

Calculation that reflects dollar sales divided by the number of orders.

average price Durchschnittspreis

average rent Durchschnittsmiete

aviation Luftfahrt; Luftwesen

aviation industry Luftfahrtindustrie

avoid vermeiden; umgehen; ausweichen; anfechten

avoidable vermeidlich; vermeidbar

avoidance Vermeidung

avoidance strategy Vermeidungsstrategie

avoiding Ausweichen

Psychology: Technique employed by a person who may recognize that a conflict exists and wants to withdraw from it or suppress it.

award *(reward)* Belohnung; Zuerkennung; *(price)* Preis; *(of contract)* Vergabe; *(to ~)* belohnen; zuerkennen; *(a prize)* verleihen; vergeben

Legal: Decision rendered by a court or arbitrator that one party in a dispute is owed money and that the other party or parties are liable.

Competition: Prize or gift given to the winner of a competition as an incentive for good performance.

B

baby boom Baby Boom

An increase in the annual birthrate after World War II, which lasted until the early 1960s.

baby bond Kleinobligation; Kleinschuldverschreibung; Baby-Bonds

Bond with a par value of less than $1,000, usually $500 to $25.

bachelor Junggesselle; (*akad*) niedrigster akademischer Grad in GB und USA

bachelor of arts Hochschulabschluss in Geisteswissenschaften

bachelor of business administration (BBA) Betriebswirt

Degree from a three- or four-year college with concentration in business studies.

back Rücken; *(back page)* Rückseite; *(overdue)* rückständig; zurück; rückwärts; *(to support)* unterstützen

backdating (zu)rückdatieren

Dating any statement, check, or other document earlier than the date it was actually drawn.

back freight Rückfracht

The cost of shipping goods back to the port of destination after they have been overcarried.

background Hintergrund; Untergrund; Grundlage; *(preceding events)* Vorgeschichte; *(professional experience)* Berufserfahrung; *(training)* Ausbildung; Wissen u. Können

background check Hintergrundüberprüfung

Complete investigation by the management of an employee's job history and personal references.

Though very time consuming & expensive at times, it is used to ensure that qualified personnel are placed in an organization.

backing *(help)* Hilfe; *(support)* Stütze; Unterstützung; *(bank notes)* Deckung; *(currency exchange)* Stützungskäufe

backing money Stützungsgelder

backlog of orders unerledigte Aufträge; Rückstand an Aufträgen

Unfilled orders placed with a manufacturing company or any other customer.

back office Abwicklungsabteilung; Abrechnungsstelle; Abteilung ohne Kundenkontakt; Backoffice

Department in a bank or brokerage house that supports, but does not practice direct selling or trading.

Includes all written confirmation and settlement of trades, accounting record keeping, communication between branches and government regulatory compliance.

The terms can also be used to describe similar departments in other industries, e.g. travel agents.

back translation Rückübersetzung

back-to-back letter of credit Gegenakkreditiv

A method to conceal the identity of the seller from the buyer in a credit arrangement.

When a finance house arranges the credit, the foreign seller provides the relevant documentation. The finance house then issues its own documents to the buyer, omitting the seller's name.

back-to-back loan wechselseitiger Kredit; Prallelkredit

A loan from one company to another, often a subsidiary in a different country.

A financial institution acts as an intermediary to provide the loan but not the funding, which comes from a third party.

backward vertical integration vertikale Rückwärtsintegration

Attempts by a firm to take ownership or control of its supply chain.

bad abgelehntes Gut; schlecht; ungünstig; *(check)* ungedeckt

bad buy Fehlkauf; schlechtes Geschäft

bad debt uneinbringbliche Forderung; zweifelhafte Forderung

Debt that is not collectible because the debtor is insolvent, and is therefore worthless to the creditor. A business bad debt may be written off under a specific method.

bad debt insurance Kreditversicherung

bail Kaution; Bürge; Bürgschaft

Monetary guarantee that an individual released from jail will be present in court at the appointed time. If the individual is not present in court at that time *(has jumped bail),* the monetary value of the bond is forfeited to the court.

balance Gleichgewicht; *(balance sheet)* Bilanz; *(debit or credit account surplus)* Saldo; Differenz; Restsumme ausgleichen; *(to balance an account)* bilanzieren; saldieren; Konto ausgleichen

Accounting: Amount shown in an account; difference between debits and credits in an account. If credits exceed debits' it is called a credit balance.

balance of current accounts Leistungsbilanz

balance of payments Zahlungsbilanz

Economics: A systematic record of all of a country's economic transactions with the rest of the world during a particular period.

The balance of payments is typically divided into three accounts – current account, capital account, and official reserves. These accounts can show a surplus or a deficit, but there can be no surplus or deficit on the overall balance of payments, as it has to be by definition always in balance.

balance of prices Preisgleichgewicht

balance of trade Handelsbilanz

Economics: The difference between the value of a country's imports and its exports during a period, normally a year.

The balance of trade is a component of the balance of payments, forming part of the current account.

When a country exports more than it imports, it is said to have a surplus, *or favorable* balance of trade; when imports predominate, the balance is in deficit, and is called *unfavorable.*

balanced scorecard Balanced Scorecard

Balanced Scorecard is a way to measure performance that allows equilibrated control and thus integration in reporting with the help of ratios.

Special attention is given to the weighing of different ratios and it concentrates not only on the ratio figures but mainly on the realisation of the objectives according to formulated strategies.

Ordinary reporting systems concentrate on mere financial and profit ratios but in a balanced scorecard non-financial elements are taken into account when evaluating results.

In its classical form the balanced scorecard is built with four perspectives of control in mind.

1. Financial and value perspective
2. Market and customer perspective
3. Process perspective
4. Knowledge and innovation perspective.

The ratios for the four perspectives should be linked through cause-effect-chains and can guide managers to use personnel and physical resources to realize the future potentials for success.

balance sheet Bilanz; Bilanzaufstellung; Handelsbilanz; Kassenbericht; Rechnungsabschluss

Accounting: Financial statement that gives a picture of a company's property, including assets and liabilities and of claims against the property on a particular date.

It reflects the equation: Assets = Liabilities + Shareholders' equity. The left (debit) side of a balance sheet states assets; the right (credit) side shows liabilities and owners' equity. The two sides must be equal (balance). To calculate a company's net worth, liabilities have to be substracted from its assets.

The balance sheet is like a snapshot of the financial position of a business at one point in time.

balance sheet approach Bilanzansatz

balance sheet guidelines Bilanzrichtlinien

balance sheet item Bilanzposten

balance sheet structure Bilanzstruktur

balance sheet total Bilanzsumme; Bilanzvolumen

Baldridge Award (Malcolm Baldridge National Quality Award; MBNQA)

Annual award, named after a US Secretary of State for Commerce, given to companies in the USA that have "excelled in quality management and quality achievement".

There are three categories of winners: manufacturing, services, and small business, with up to two awards in each category.

The first-level categories are: leadership, information and analysis, strategic planning, human resource development and management, process management, business results, and customer focus and satisfaction.

balloon Ballon; *(to ~)* (künstlich) hinauftreiben; rasch steigen

Finance: Principal amount repaid on maturity of a loan that is significantly larger than the annual repayments. For example an issue could have six payments of 10 per cent, followed by a balloon of 40 per cent at maturity.

balloon payment Ballonzahlung

ballot *(ticket)* Wahlzettel; Stimmzettel; *(act)* Abstimmung; Wahl; *(to ~)* abstimmen

ballot vote Urabstimmung; geheime Abstimmung

Baltic Exchange

A freight-chartering exchange in the City of London, which started in the 18th century trading in grain with Baltic ports.

band Band; Bandbreite; Bereich; Streifen; Gruppe

Finance: trading range, set by upper and lower limits, of a commodity or currency.

For example, the European Monetary System used to set a band against a central rate of conversion to the euro of +/- 15%.

bandwagon effect Mitläufereffekt

Descriptive term for the phenomenon that successful business strategies gain a lot of momentum and are copied, sometimes without the necessary reflection.

For example, after the fall of the Berlin Wall, many businesses invested in Eastern Europe, because it was generally believed that those would be punished that did not position themselves early.

bandwidth Bandbreite

Amount of data that a transmission line can carry, usually measured in bits per second (bps).

High-bandwidth internet connections such as a T-1 line, DSL or cable modem can transfer millions of bits per second (megabits per second, or Mbps), while standard PC modems transfer thousands of bits per second (kilobits per second, or Kbps).

bank Bank; *(to ~)* Bankgeschäfte machen; auf eine Bank einzahlen; Bankkonto haben

A financial institution that can perform a variety of tasks: maintain savings and checking accounts, issue loans and credit, and deal in negotiable securities issued by government agencies and by corporations.

Banks are strictly regulated and in the US fall into the following three: commercial banks; savings and loan associations; savings banks.

bankable bankfähig; diskontfähig

bank account Bankkonto

bank affiliate Bankentochter

bank assets Bankvermögen

bank automation Bankautomation

bank bill Bankakzept; Bankwechsel

A bill of exchange issued or guaranteed (accepted) by a bank.

A bank bill is normally considered more acceptable than a trade bill as there is less risk of non-payment. It therefore can be discounted at a more favorable rate.

bank charges Bankgebühren; Bearbeitungsgebühren einer Bank

The money charged to customers by a bank, for specific services, such as transactions, paying by cheque, or withdrawing money from an automated teller machine.

bank clientele Bankenkundschaft

bank code number Bankleitzahl

bank counselor Bankberater

bank credit Bankkredit

bank customer Bankkunde; Bankkundin

bank customers Bankenkundschaft

bank deposit Bankguthaben; Einlage

A certain sum of money placed by a customer in a bank account, usually either a deposit account or a current account.

The depostit may or may not attract interest, and it may be instantly accessible or accessible at a later time agreed by the two parties.

bank depositor Einleger

bank draft Bankwechsel

A cheque drawn by a bank on itself or its agent.

A person who owes money to someone else can buy the draft from a bank for cash and then give it to the creditor. A bank draft can be used if the creditor is unwilling to accept ordinary checks.

bank employee Bankmitarbeiter; Bankangestellter

banker Bankier

banker's acceptance Bankakzept

Agreement by a bank to pay a given sum of money at a future date. A short-term credit investment created by a non-financial firm and guaranteed by a bank as to payment.

Time draft drawn on and accepted by a bank; the customary means of effecting payment for merchandise sold in import-export transactions and a source of financing used extensively in international trade. Acceptances are traded at discounts from face value in the secondary market. These instruments have been a popular investment for money market funds.

Bank for International Settlements Bank für internationalen Zahlungsausgleich

International banking facility located in Switzerland that promotes cooperation among central banks and serves as the lender of last resort to some less developed countries.

bank group Bankenkonsortium

bank guarantee Banksicherheit

An guarantee given by a bank to settle a debt should the debtor fail to do so.

The banks themselves will normally require good cover in cash or counter-value before they issue a guarantee. A bank guarantee has to be in writing to be legally binding, and it can be used as a security for a loan.

Bank Holiday öffentlicher Feiertag (in UK)

Public holiday in the UK, when the banks are closed.

They are New Year's Day, Easter Monday, May Day (the first Monday in May), Spring Bank Holiday (the last Monday in May), August Bank Holiday (last Monday in August), and Boxing Day.

In banking, Bank Holidays have a similar status to Sundays, as bills of exchange falling due on a Bank Holiday are postponed until the following day.

banking Bankwesen

The activities undertaken by banks. The main areas are: personal banking (non-business customers), commercial banking (small and medium-sized business customers), and corporate banking (large international and multinational corporations).

banking activity Bankaktivität; Banktätigkeit

banking business Bankgewerbe; Bankgeschäft

banking center Bankplatz

banking expertise Bankfachwissen

banking house Bank(haus)

banking institution Bankinstitut

banking rule Bankregel

banking service Bankdienstleistung; Bankleistung

banking syndicate Bankenkonsortium

bank line Kreditlinie

Line of credit granted by a bank to a customer. It represnts a moral commitment to make loans up to a specified maximum during a certain period.

A bank line is not a legal commitment, it is not customary to charge a fee.

bank management Bankleitung; Bankvorstand

bank manager Bankleiter; Filialleiter

bank note Banknote

bank officer Bankangestellte/r

bankroll finanzieren; Geldmittel bereitstellen

bankrupt bankrott; pleite; ruiniert; zahlungsunfähig; *(debtor)* Konkursschuldner; Gemeinschuldner

bankrupt company Pleitefirma

bankruptcy Bankrott; Konkurs

Legally declared inability of an individual or an organization to pay debts as they become due.

Under U.S. law, there are two kinds of bankruptcies: Chapter 7, or involuntary, when one or more creditors petition to have a debtor judged insolvent by a court; and Chapter 11, or voluntary, when the debtor brings the petition. In both cases the objective is an orderly and equitable settlement of obligations.

In case of a firm's bankruptcy, the ownership of the firm's assets is transferred from the shareholders to the bondholders.

bankruptcy case Konkursfall

bankruptcy costs Konkurskosten

bankruptcy judge Konkursrichter

bankruptcy law Insolvenzrecht

bankruptcy petition Konkursantrag

Formal document filed with a court to initiate a bankruptcy proceeding.

bank service charges Bankspesen

bank statement Kontoauszug

A regular record, issued by a bank or other financial institution. It normally shows the credit and debit entries in a customer's account, together with the current balance.

bank stocks Bankkapital

bank subsidiary Bankentochter

bank supervision Bankenaufsicht

bank top management Bankvorstand

banner Banner; Fahne; Spruchband; Transparent

banner ad Banneranzeige; Bannerinserat

Internet: most common form of online advertising,.

Banner ads appear on a web page as a box containing text, images, animation or other effects for the purposes of brand building or driving traffic to another site.

Users who click on a banner follow a hyperlink to the advertiser's website.

bar Schranke; Hindernis; Sperre; Barren; Streifen; *(law)* Anwaltsstand

Legal: Association of people related to the legal profession.

bar ausschließen; verriegeln; zusperren; erschweren

bar chart Balkendiagramm

A chart showing statistical data by means of rectangles (i.e. bars) of differing heights.

Important presentation technique, as the different sizes of the bars enable viewers to grasp the information much more quickly.

bar code Strichcode; Barcode; Balkencode

A small white label with closely spaced black stripes that can be read by a computer by scanning it with a laser beam.

Bar codes can bee utilized to encode many different kinds of data, such as the Universal Product Code for cash registers in supermarkets.

bar code scanner Strichcodeleser

Electronic device used to read bar codes into the computer.

bargain Geschäft; Handel; Schnäppchen; *(favorable purchase)* Gelegenheitskauf; *(to ~)* feilschen; (aus)handeln; verhandeln

A mutual and voluntary agreement between two parties, regarding the price of a good or service and the conditions of sale.

bargain and sale deed Abtretungsvertrag

Form of a contract, which conveys property and transfers title to the buyer but lacks any guarantee from the seller as to the validity of the title. It is commonly used to convey title to real estate and in effect transfers to the new owner whatever interest the grantor had.

bargain basement Abteilung für Sonderangebote; Restposten-Abteilung

Department of a main store, often in the basement, where discounted merchandise is sold.

bargain hunter Schnäppchenjäger

Buyers who are very sensitive to price, and will buy the product or service from the cheapest seller.

bargaining verhandeln

A type of negotiation in which the buyer and seller of a good or service dispute the price which will be paid and the exact nature of the transaction that will take place.

bargaining agent Tarifpartner

Union or individual certified through a secret ballot process to be the exclusive representative of all the employees in a bargaining unit or group; also called *bargaining representative.*

In order for a bargaining agent to be certified, it must receive a majority of the ballots cast in the bargaining unit.

bargaining agreement Betriebsvereinbarung; Tarifvereinbarung

bargaining power starke Verhandlungsposition; Verhandlungsstärke; Verhandlungsmacht

bargaining round Verhandlungsrunde; Tarifrunde

bargaining strength Verhandlungsstärke

bargain-purchase-price option Erwerbsoption

Gives lessee the option to purchase the asset at a price below fair market value when the lease expires.

barrel Faß

A unit of capacity used in the oil industry equal to 42 gallons (159 litres).

barrier Schranke; Barriere; Sperre; Hemmnis; Hindernis

barriers to entry Marktzutrittsbarrieren; Zugangsbeschränkungen; Markteintrittsschranke; Markteintrittshemmnisse

Legal, natural or other impediments preventing a firm from entering certain industries.

These include funding requirements, technological or trade learning curves, unknown or little-known business practices, tightly controlled markets, licensing procedures, the need for highly skilled or trained employees, long lead times, and specially designed facilities.

barriers to exit Marktaustrittsbarrieren; Marktaustrittsschranken

Conditions that make it harder for a company to get out of a particular industry than it would otherwise have been.

They include the costs of laying off staff and contractual obligations, such as the payment of rent.

barriers to mobility Mobilitätsbarrieren

Factors that prevent a company to move from one industry or market into another.

For example, supermarkets cannot easily start a banking business. Insteasd, they have to form an alliance with an existing registered bank.

barrister Rechtsanwalt; Barrister

Legal practitioner in England, whose function is similar to that of a U.S. trial lawyer, although the barrister does not prepare the case from the start.

His *solicitor* assembles the materials necessary for presentation to the court and settles cases out of court.

barter Tausch(geschäft); Tauschhandel; Naturaltausch; *(to~)* Tauschhandel treiben

Direct exchange of commodities and services without use of money. Income from a *barter* transaction is taxable income.

Internet: exchange of goods and services without the use of cash. Usually, the acquisition of media time or space by a media company in exchange for similar time/space in return.

barter economy Tauschwirtschaft

barter trade Kompensationshandel; Tauschgeschäft

barter transaction Tauschhandel; Tausch-; Kompensations-; Gegengeschäft; gebundenes Geschäft

base Basis; Grundlage; Boden; Bezugsgröße; Bezugswert; *(to ~)* basieren; begründen; beruhen auf

base currency Basiswährung; Bezugswährung

The currency used as the basis for an exchange rate.

An exchange rate is quoted per single unit of the base currency, for example 1.25 Euros per 1US dollar (base currency).

base pay Grundgehalt

Employee's hourly wage; regular rate of pay upon which overtime and other wage supplements are computed.

base period Basisperiode; Basiszeitraum; Zeitbasis

A selected period of time, frequently one year, against which changes to other points in time are calculated.

base price *(cost price)* Einkaufspreis; Grundpreis; Basispreis

base rate Basiszinssatz

The rate of interest used as a basis by banks for the rates they charge their customers.

Normally, most customers have to pay a premium over base rate, reflecting the bank's risk involved in lending.

base salary Grundgehalt

base-year analysis Basisjahranalyse

An analysis using a particular year as the base period. It is used to express trends in economic data, such as the gross national product, without the effect of inflation.

basic Grund-; grundlegend; grundsätzlich; fundamental

BASIC

Computing: acronym for Beginner's All-purpose Symbolic Instruction Code.

BASIC is a popular language used especially to program small computers. It is an easy-to-learn and easy-to-use, using a small number of ordinary English words (called keywords) to give instructions to the computer.

basic cable Grundverkabelung

Television: basic service agreement in which a subscriber pays a cable TV operator or system a monthly fee. Does not include "pay" services that might be offered by the cable operator.

basic IRR rule IZF-Grundregel

Investment analysis using the internal rate of return method. The basic rule suggest that a project should be accepted if IRR is greater than the hurdle rate and rejected IRR is less than the hurdle rate.

basic need Grundbedürfnis

basic prerequisite Grundvoraussetzung

basic regulation Rahmenregelung

basic research Grundlagenforschung

Research aimed at expanding the boundaries of knowledge, rather than solving a specific problem.

basic research center Basisforschungszentrum; Grundlagenforschungszentrum

Centers for fundamental research located in regions where valuable scientific knowledge is being created; they develop the basic technologies that become new products.

basic strategy Grundstrategie

basing-point pricing Preisgestaltung im Frachtbasissystem

Geographic pricing strategy in which the seller designates some city as a basing point and charges all customers the freight cost from that city to the customer location, regardless of the city from which the goods are actually shipped.

basis Basis; (Bemessungs-)Grundlage; Fundament

Taxation: The original cost of an asset, plus additional expenses, that is used to determine gain or loss when the asset is sold.

basis of calculation (Be)Rechnungsgrundlage

basis of information Informationsbasis

basis point 1/100 Prozentpunkt; Vergleichspunkt

Smallest measure used in quoting yields on mortgages, bonds, and notes. One basis point is 0.01% of yield in bonds. One percentage point of yield equals 100 basis points.

Example: if a bond yield changes from 7.25 % to 7.39 %, that's a rise of 14 *basis points*.

basket Korb

basket of commodities Warenkorb

Artificial measurement that includes a variety of products and services an average household would normally consume.

The money to be spent on that basket is continuously monitored by statistical offices to determine consumer spending and inflation.

basket of currencies Währungskorb

Artificial currency, based on a mixture of actual currencies. For example, the ECU was an artificial currency based upon a basket of EU currencies.

batch Stapel; Charge; Ladung; Menge; Liefermenge

batch costing Produktbündelrechnung; Serienkalkulation

A form of casting in which the unit costs are expressed on the basis of a batch produced.

Batch costing is particularly appropriate where the cost per unit of production would result in a very small number.

batch processing Stapelverarbeitung; schubweise Verarbeitung; Verarbeitung von Aufgabensätzen

Computing: a mode of data processing in which data is gathered over a period of time and aggregated for subsequent sequential processing.

Batch processing contrasts with *interactive* processing, in which the user communicates with the computer by means of a terminal while the program is running.

batch production Serienfertigung; Serienproduktion

A manufacturing technique in which medium to high volumes of similar items are made in batches, rather than continuously. The product moves from process to process in batches.

Important in batch production is the careful scheduling of work to ensure good utilization of capacity and to minimize the capital locked up in work in progress.

Examples of batch production would be a run of a certain book at a book printer.

Baye´s theorem Theorem von Bayes; Bayes Regel der Entscheidungsfindung

A method that is used to compute posterior probabilities by revising prior probabilities.

It is used in decision making when insufficient empirical estimates are available. As more information becomes available, the original assumptions are refined and/or corrected.

bear *(stock exchange)* Baissespekulant; Baissier; *(market)* flau; *(to carry)* tragen; *(costs)* bestreiten; *(interest)* sich verzinsen

Stock market: investor who thinks a stock or overall market will fall/decline. Bears may sell a stock short or buy a put option to take advantage of the anticipated drop.

bearer (Vollmachts-)Inhaber; Überbringer

A person who presents for payment a cheque or bill of exchange marked "pay bearer".

As a bearer cheque or bill does not require endorsement it is considered a high-risk form of transfer.

bearer bond Inhaberpapier; Inhaberschuldverschreibung; Inhaberobligation

Bond issued without record of the owner's name. Security not registered on the books of the issuing corporation and thus payable to the person possessing it, i.e., the owner or bearer of the bond.

A *bearer bond* has coupons attached, which the bondholder sends in or presents on the interest date for payment, hence the alternative name *coupon bonds.*

bearer savings bond Inhabersparbrief

bearer share Inhaberaktie

bearer stock Inhaberaktie

bear market Baisse; Baissemarkt

Stock market: Prolonged period of falling prices. A bear market in stocks is usually brought about by the anticipation of declining economic activity, and a bear market in bonds is caused by rising interest rates.

bear raid Leerverkauf

Situation in which large traders sell positions with the intention of driving prices down.

begin anfangen; beginnen

beginning Beginn; Anfang; Start

behavior Verhalten; *(attitude)* Einstellung; *(manners)* Benehmen

behavioral component of an attitude Handlungskomponente einer Einstellung

Intention to behave in a certain way toward someone or something.

behavioral control Verhaltenssteuerung

behaviorally anchored rating scales (BARS) verhaltensverankerte Beurteilungsskalen

Evaluation method in which actual job-related behaviors are rated along a continuum. BARS specify definite, observable and measurable job behavior.

behavioral norm Verhaltensnorm

behavioral segmentation Marktsegmentierung nach Verhaltenskriterien

Process of dividing a market into groups based on consumer knowledge, attitude, use or response to a product.

behavioral theories of leadership Verhaltenstheorien der Führung

Theories proposing specific behaviors differentiating leaders from non-leaders. Normally, four different behavioral theories of leadership are distinguished:

Ohio State leadership studies: resulting from research that began at Ohio State University in the late 1940s, where attemps were made to identify independent dimensions of leader behavior. Beginning with over a thousand dimensions, the list was reduced into two categories: initiating structure and consideration.

University of Michigan leadership studies: similar to the Ohio State studies, the objective was to locate behavioral characteristics of leaders that appeared to be related to measures of performance effectiveness. They also came up with two dimensions: employee-oriented leaders, and production-oriented leaders.

Managerial Grid: a graphic portrayal of a two-dimensional view of leadership style, developed by Blake and Mouton.

Scandinavian leadership studies: researchers in Finland and Sweden believed that the three reviewed studies failed to capture the more dynamic realities of modern leadership. Their basic premise is that in a changing world, effective leaders would exhibit development-oriented behavior.

behavior modification Verhaltensänderung

Change in personality or attitude based on new information and experiences. Employment of positive or negative reinforcement to alter the actions of an individual or group.

Example: a salesperson may change the approach of dealing with a customer once the customer's likes and dislikes are known. Such a change in behavior often occurs with maturity and greater understanding about oneself and others.

behavior of markets Marktverhalten

behavior pattern Verhaltensweise; Verhaltensmuster

Belbin, Meredith (* 1926)

Psychologist who developed the system of building teams out of complementing and balancing the strengths and 'allowable weaknesses' of individuals.

His team selection system grew out of research program with Henley Management College in 1967 into the effectiveness of management teams. He found that the more complementary the contributions or roles, the better the team performed. Belbin developed psychometric tests to assess the contributions which each individual could make.

Belbin defined the eight main roles which contribute to the ideal and their basic characteristics as: company worker (conservative, predictable, hardworking), chairman (calm, controlled), shaper (outgoing, dynamic), plant (individualistic, ingenious), resource investigator (extroverted, curious), monitor-evaluator (sober, prudent), team worker (socially orientated, sensitive) and computer-finisher (orderly, conscientious).

Biography: educated at Cambridge University, specializing in experimental psychology, gerontology. His main interest were in training and in the development and employment of older workers, worked as a consultant for the OECD in Paris, devloping the 'guided discovery' method of enabling older workers to learn new skills.

Major publications: (1981) Management Teams: Why they Succeed or Fail, (1993) Team Roles at Work, (1996) The Coming Shape of Organizations, (1997) Changing the way we work.

belief Glaube; *(opinion)* Meinung; *(conviction)* Überzeugung; Zutrauen; Vertrauen

Descriptive thought that a person holds about something.

believe glauben; meinen; Vertrauen haben

bell curve glockenförmige Kurve

bells and whistles Schnickschnack

Additional features of a product or service intended to attract buyers.

belong gehören; *(to be a member of)* angehören

below par unter Nennwert; unter pari

At a price below the face, or nominal, value of a security, especially a bond..

below the line unter dem Strich; (*advertising*) nicht vergütungsfähige Werbung

Accounting: entries below the horizontal line on a company's profit and loss account that separates the entries that establish the profit (or loss) from the entries that show how the profit is distributed or where the funds to finance the loss have come from.

Advertising: advertising expenditure in which no commission is payable to an advertising agency. For example, direct mail, exhibitions, point-of-sale material, and free samples.

belt *(geography)* Streifen; Zone; *(clothing)* Gürtel; *(machinery)* Riemen

benchmark Bezugswert; -punkt; -marke; Maßstab; Vergleichspunkt

Standard used for the basis of comparison; it must be identified with sufficient detail so that other similar classifications can be compared as being above, below, or comparable to the benchmark.

benchmarking Benchmarking; Leistungsvergleich

Analysis and planning tool, which allows companies to compare themselves with the their competitors in order to improve quality and performance.

Unlike traditional methods of comparing businesses, where figures from profit and loss accounts and balance sheets are analyzed, benchmarking makes comparisons with the best practice demonstrated by companies in a different industry. It is, therefore, a process which compares the methods, operations and results of business functions with one or more other enterprises in order to discover opportunities for rationalisation.

Generally, ther are considered to be four groups of benchmarking:

Internal benchmarking: similar to the process of quality management, it is an internal checking of the organization's standards.

Competitive benchmarking: the comparison of one company's standards with those of another (rival) company.

Industry benchmarking: comparison between a company's standard and those of the industry to which it belongs.

Best-in-class benchmarking: comparison of a company's level of achievement with the best anywhere in the world, regardless of industry or national market.

beneficial vorteilhaft; nutzlich; nutzbringend; wohltätig; von Vorteil

beneficial interest Nießbrauch

Equitable interest in a trust held by the beneficiary of the trust, as distinguished from the interest of the trustee who holds legal title.

Any person who under the terms of a trust instrument has the right to the income or principal of the trust fund has a *beneficial interest* in the trust.

beneficial owner Nießbrauchsberechtigter; wirtschaftlicher Besitzer; wirtschaftlicher Eigentümer

The person entitled to the benefits of ownership of an asset, such as a security, even though the title is in another name.

When securities are held by a bank, the real owner is the *beneficial owner,* even though the bank holds title.

beneficial use Genuss

beneficiary Begünstigter; Bezugsberechtigter; Genussberechtigter; *(law)* Nutznießer

Person who receives or is to receive the benefits resulting from certain acts. In a tax context, a person entitled to the benefits from trust property or from an insurance policy.

benefit Vorteil; Nutzen; Vergünstigung; *(insurance)* Leistung; *(compensation)* Nebenleistung; *(aid)* Beihilfe; Zuschuss; Rente; *(to favor)* begünstigen; *(to profit from)* Nutzen ziehen aus

Organization: Something that contributes to an organization, such as better efficiency, enhanced profitability, or reduced risk.

Insurance: Payment made by an insurance company to an individual due to the occurrence of an event, such as death or sickness.

Marketing: The advantage that a feature of a product or service provides to the customer, such as ease of use, low costs etc.

benefit analysis Nutzwertanalyse

benefit in kind Sachleistung; Lohnnebenleistung

Benefits other than cash arising from employment.

Examples of benefits in kind are: company cars and associated fuel provided by the employer, beneficial loans, mobile telephones, medical insurance provided by the employer, subscriptions paid, and any costs paid on the employee's behalf.

These benefits will be assessed to tax. This often takes the form of a restriction to the income tax code.

benefit segmentation Nutzensegmentierung; Marktsegmentierung nach Nutzwert

The process of dividing a market according to the different benefits that consumers seek from a product.

For example, some car buyers want comfort and reliability from their car, whilst others look for style and speed. A manufacturer has to decide which benefits to offer.

Benelux Benelux

A customs union formed in 1947 between Belgium, the Netherlands, and Luxembourg.

Bennis, Warren (* 1925)

Leading thinker of leadership theory, famous for his aphorism 'Managers do things right. Leaders do the right thing'.

In his 1985 standard work, *Leaders: The Strategies for Taking Charge*, Bennis identified four factors or 'competencies' common to all leadership personalities which he had studied: the ability to manage attention, meaning, trust and self.

Biograpy: born in New York, educated at MIT's Sloan School of Management, where he was influenced by Douglas McGregor and his 'Theory X and Theory Y', from 1971 to 1977 president of the University of Cincinnati, worked internationally in France, Switzerland, and India. Distinguised Proessor of Business Adminstration and founder of the Leadership Institute at the University of Southern California in San Diego.

Major publications: (1968) The Temporary Society, (1976) The Unconscious Conspiracy, (1985, with B. Nanus) Leaders: The Strategies for Taking Charge, (1989) On Becoming a Leader, (1993) An Invented Life: Reflections on Leadership and Change, (1997 with P. Biedermann) Organizing Genius.

bequeath hinterlassen; vermachen

To make a bequest; i.e. to transfer personal property through a will.

bequest Nachlass; Erbe; Vermächtnis

The transfer of personal property by will. Real property is usually transferred by a devise.

Berne Union Berner Union

Informal name for the International Union of Credit and Investment Insurers, an association of credit insurers from the main industrial countries.

Its main function is to facilitate an exchange of information. especially over credit terms.

best alternative to a negotiated settlement (BATNA) beste Alternative zu einer Verhandlungslösung

Determines the lowest acceptable value to an individual for a negotiated agreement.

best-efforts underwriting Platzierung ohne Risikoübernahme durch Konsortium

Offering in which an underwriter agrees to distribute as much of the offering as possible and to return any unsold shares to the issuer.

bet Wette; *(to ~)* wetten

beta coefficient Beta-Faktor; Betakoeffizient

A measure of a stock´s or a fund´s volatility relative to the rest of the market.

The Standard & Poor's index has a *beta coefficient* of 1. Any stock with a higher beta is more volatile than the market, and any with a lower beta can be expected to rise and fall more slowly than the market. A beta of 0.7 means a stock price is likely to move up or down 70% of the market change; 1.3 means the stock is likely to move up or down 30% more than the market.

beta software Beta-Software

Software companies often release test, or beta, versions of their software before the final commercial release. Beta software may include serious flaws.

Some vendors release beta software only to select users, others make it available to the general public. Most vendors, however, don't provide technical support for beta releases.

betterment Verbesserung; Wertzuwachs

bid Angebot; Offerte; *(estimate)* Kostenvoranschlag; *(auction)* Gebot; Geldkurs; Submissionsangebot; *(to auction)* bieten; *(to make an offer)* Angebot machen

A prospective buyer's indication or offer of a price he is willing to pay..

bid and asked Gebots- und Nachfragepreis

Bid is the highest price a prospective buyer is prepared to pay at a particular time; *asked* is the lowest price acceptable to a prospective seller.

Together, the two prices constitute a quotation; the difference between them is called the *spread.*

bidder Bieter; Anbieter

bid invitation Ausschreibung

bid price Angebotspreis; gebotener Preis; Geldkurs

bilateral zweiseitig; bilateral

bilateral monopoly bilaterales Monopol

A situation in which a monopoly seller bargains with a monopoly buyer (also called monopsony).

The classic application of bilateral monopoly is to the negotiation of wages between a union and a firm.

bilateral netting bilaterales Netting

Settlement in which the amount one subsidiary owes another can be canceled by the debt the second subsidiary owes the first.

bilateral tax agreement bilaterales Steuerabkommen

bilateral trade bilateraler Handel

bilateral trade agreement bilaterales Handelsabkommen

An agreement between two countries on trade policy, usually concerning a reduction in tariffs or other protective barriers.

bilateral treaty bilateraler Vertrag

bill Rechnung; Faktura; *(banknote)* Banknote; *(bill of exchange)* Wechsel; Konnossement; *(government)* Gesetzentwurf; *(to ~)* berechnen; in Rechnung stellen

General: A bill is a document requesting payment for goods and services previously supplied.

Legislation: draft of a proposed statute submitted to the legislature for enactment.

Commercial law: an account for goods sold, services rendered and work done.

Currency: any form of paper money.

bill holdings Wechselportefeuille

billing cycle Abrechnungszeitraum; Abrechnungsperiode

The interval between periodic billings for goods sold or services rendered, normally 28-32 days.

bill of entry Zollanmeldung; Zolleinfuhrschein; Einfuhrdeklaration

A detailed description of the nature and value of a consignment of goods prepared by the shipper of the consignment for customs entry.

bill of exchange Wechsel; Akzept; Tratte

Negotiable instrument which requires one person, the drawee, to pay a certain sum of money to another named person, the drawer, on demand or at a certain future time

International Trade: order written by an exporter instructing an importer, or an importer's agent, to pay a specified amount of money at a specified time.

If the drawee, or acceptor, of the bill is a bank, the bill is a known as a banker's acceptance; if it is a trader, the bill is a trade bill; if it is the UK or US government, it is a Treasury bill.

Such bills are normally issued with 90-day lives, and their marketability depends on the standing of the drawee or acceptor, the nature of the underlying transaction and whether the bill is eligible for rediscounting with the central bank. Such bills of exchange are called eligible bills.

bill of health Gesundheitsbescheinigung

bill of lading Konnossement; Frachtbrief; Seefrachtbrief; Ladebrief

Certificate signed and issued by a merchandise transportation company to an exporter, listing articles being shipped. It serves as a receipt, a contract, and a document of title(creating in the person possessing the bill ownership of the goods shipped).

bill of materials Materialliste; Stückliste

Manufacturing: a detailed list that contains information about the composition of a product and lists the parts required for manufacturing, including planned or standard prices of the material to be used for the product in question, cost rates of the manufacturing cost centers, possible planned wage rates per hour in as far as single wages can be charged to orders and products.

The bill of materials is one of the tender documents that goes out to contractors who wish to quote for carrying out the work.

bill of sale Übereignungsurkunde; Kaufurkunde; Kaufbrief; Verkaufsnota; Übereignungsvertrag; Lieferschein

A document by which a person or a company transfer the ownership of goods to another.

The goods are normally transferred conditionally, as security for a debt. A conditional bill of sale is therefore a mortgage of goods.

bill of sight provisorische Zolldeklaration; Zollerlaubnisschein

A temporary customs document that an importer, who is unable to fully describe an imported cargo, gives to authorities to authorize them to inspect the goods on landing.

After the goods have been landed and the importer supplies the missing information the entry is completed and the importer is said to have perfected the sight.

bills in hand Wechselportefeuille

bills payable offene Rechnungen

The amounts owed by a business to its creditors, such as trade suppliers.

bills receivable offene Forderungen; Aussenstände

The amounts owed to a business by its debtors, i.e. its customers.

binary numbers Binärzahlen

Numbers written in a positional number system that uses only two digits: 0 and 1. Each digit of a binary number represents a power of 2. The rightmost digit is the 1s digit, the next digit to the left is the 2s digit, and so on.

binder Vorvertrag; vorläufige Zusage

A preliminary agreement, outlining the important terms of a contract that gives temporary protection to the contract while further details are clarified.

Often used for insurances, e.g. when buying a car, the owner is insured whilst the policy is prepared.

binominal distribution Binominalverteilung

biographical characteristics biographische Merkmale

Factors that are easily definable and readily available; data that can be obtained, for the most part, simply from information available in an employee's personnel file. Obvious characteristics would be an employee's age, gender, marital status, and length of service with an organization

bit vendor Bitverkäufer

E-Marketing: type of e-tailer that sells digital products such as media, software, and music and delivers them via the internet.

black box Blackbox; Fahrdatenschreiber; Unfallschreiber

Air-transport: data and voice recorder, used to save important information in case of emergency like air crash, forced landing, etc.

Computers: slang for central processing unit; also any device that provides answers to complex problems without explaining the solution.

black economy Schattenwirtschaft

Economic activity that is undisclosed, largely in order to avoid taxation.

The black economy is thought to be significant in many countries, and earnings do not appear in national statistics.

Black Monday scharzer Montag

Either of the two Mondays on which the two largest stock market crashes in the 20th century occurred.

The original Wall Street crash occurred on Monday. 28 October 1929, when the Dow Jones Industrial Average fell by 13%. On Monday, 19 October 1987, the Dow Jones Average lost 23%.

Black Wednesday schwarzer Mittwoch

Wednesday, 16 September 1992, when the Pound sterling and the peseta left the Exchange Rate Mechanism, which led to a 15% fall in sterling´s value against the Deutsche Mark.

Black Friday schwarzer Freitag

Day signifying a sharp drop in a financial market. The original Black Friday was September 24, 1869, when a group of financiers tried to corner the gold market and precipitated a business panic followed by a depression.

The panic of 1873 also began on Friday, and *Black Friday* has come to apply to any debacle affecting the financial markets.

blacklist schwarze Liste

A list or register of people who, for one reason or another, are being denied a particular privilege.

It normally refers to people who are unacceptable for employment in an organization. But also used for Internet sites that are connected with spamming.

black market Schwarzmarkt; Schwarzhandel

Illegal markets in which market exchange occurs in commodities and goods whose prices and/or supply are regulated or rationed by government.

Black markets normally exist in wartime, when rationed goods are in short supply. Another example is the market for drugs that cannot legally be sold, or sold without a prescription.

Black-Scholes Call Pricing Equation Black-Scholes-Formel zur Call-Bewertung

Exact formula for the price of a call option. The formula requires live variables: the risk free interest rate, the variance of the underlying share the exercise price, the price of the underlying share, and the time to expiration.

Black-Scholes Option Pricing Model Black-Scholes Operationspreismodell

Statistical formula developed by Fischer Black and Myron Scholes to estimate whether options contracts are fairly valued.

The model incorporates such factors as the volatility of a security's return, the level of interest rates, the relationship of the underlying stock's price to the exercise price of the option, and the time remaining until the option expires.

blame Tadel; Schuld; *(to ~)* tadeln; Schuld geben

blank Vordruck; Formular; *(space)* leere Stelle; Leere; *(lottery)* Niete; *(Scheck)*; blanko; leer; ausdruckslos

blank credit Blankokredit

blanket insurance Pauschalversicherung; Kollektivversicherung

A type of property insurance that covers through a single contract more than one type of property in one location or one or more types of property at more than one location.

Blanket insurances are very useful for such businesses as chain stores.

blanket inventory lien Pauschalpfandrecht

Secured loan that gives the lender a lien against all the borrower' s inventories.

blanket medical expense insurance Pauschalarztkostenversicherung; Pauschalkrankheitskostenversicherung

Health insurance policy providing coverage for all medical expenses except specifically excluded.

blanket mortgage Gesamthypothek

Single mortgage covering more than one property owned by the same owner

A developer can subdivide a tract of land into lots and obtain a blanket mortgage on the whole tract.

blind testing anonymer Test; Blindversuch

Generally, any procedure designed to ensure that subjects and/or experimenters are not aware of the true nature of the treatment being administered or assessed.

In marketing research, a technique in which the test persons are unaware of the product's brand that is tested.

block Block; Sperre; *(to ~)* blockieren; sperren; durchkreuzen; hemmen

blocked account gesperrtes Konto

A bank account from which money cannot be withdrawn. This can be for individual reasons, such as bankruptcy, or political reasons, when a government is so short of foreign currency that it has to block all accounts that require the use of a foreign currency

blocked currency blockierte Währung; nicht frei konvertierbare Devisen; nichtkonvertible Währung

A currency that is not freely convertible to other currencies due to exchange controls.

Governments that are trying to keep the value of their currency up sometimes block its supply to the foreign exchange market.

block sampling Blockauswahl

Accounting: non-statistical method in which accounts or items are chosen in a sequential order. After the initial item in the block is chosen, the balance of the block is automatically selected.

blue chip stock Spitzenaktie; erstklassiges Wertpapier

Shares of normally large companies that have a history of strong earnings growth and dividend payments, and a reputation for quality management, products, and services.

Named after the color of the most valuable gambling tokens.

blue-collar worker Arbeiter; gewerblicher Arbeitnehmer

An employee who performs manual or technical labor, such as in a factory or in technical maintenance.

The work often requires a work uniform, which may be blue in color, hence *blue-collar*. Blue-collar workers range from unskilled to skilled employees.

board Ausschuss; Rat; *(executive)* Vorstand; *(directors)* Aufsichtsrat;

Direktorium; *(billboard)* Anschlagtafel; *(to enter)* einsteigen; *(ship)* sich einschiffen

board meeting *(directors)* Aufsichtsrats-sitzung; *(management)* Vorstands-sitzung

board of directors Aufsichtsrat; Verwaltungsrat

A group of individuals that are elected by the shareholders of a corporation and empowered to carry out certain tasks, such as appointing executive management, issuing additional shares and declaring dividends.

Directors, who are paid for their services, are considered insiders and meet several times a year.

board of directors' seat Aufsichtsrats-mandat

Board of Governors of the Federal Reserve System Direktorium des US Zentralbankensystems

Managing body of the federal reserve system; commonly called *Federal Reserve Board.* The board has seven members and sets policy on issues relating to banking regulations as well as to the money supply.

board of management Vorstand

board representative Arbeitnehmervertreter im Aufsichtsrat

Employees who sit on an company's board of directors and represent the interests of the firm's employees.

In some countries such as Germany, large companies are legally required to make sure that employee representatives have the same number of board seats as stockholder representatives.

body language Körpersprache

A broad term for several forms of communication using body movements or gestures. Body language is therefore non-verbal and often unintended on the part of one individual to another.

Body language includes facial expressions, head movements, eye contact, hand gestures, body positions and acts, tones of voice, and others. In general, body language expresses an individual's emotions, feelings, and attitudes.

boilerplate Materplatte; Vorlage

A master copy intended to make other copies.

Sometimes used to describe a detailed standard form of words used in a contract, guarantee, etc.

bona fide gutgläubig; auf Treu und Glauben; angemessen

Latin for "in good faith" , used as a legal term which refers to any actions, situations, or persons that are honest, in good faith.

bona fide purchaser (BFP) gutgläubiger Erwerber

Someone who buys in good faith, pays a valuable consideration, and has no notice of outstanding rights of others.

bond Schuldverschreibung; Anleihepapier; Obligation; festverzinsliches Wertpapier; *(mortgage)* Pfandbrief; *(customs)* Zollverschluss

An obligation to pay, issued by a borrower to a lender. Bonds often take the form of a fixed-interest security, and can be issued by governments, local authorities, or companies.

Bonds can take on many forms: with fixed or variable rates of interest, redeemable or irredeemable, short- or long-term, secured or unsecured, and marketable or unmarketable.

Interest payments are usually made twice a year but may alternatively be credited at the end of the agreement (typically 5 to 10 years). The borrower then repays a specific sum of money plus the face (par) value of the bond.

In the U.S., interest on municipal bonds is generally non-taxable for federal income tax purposes and in the municipality of issue. Corporate bond interest is generally fully tax-able.

bond broker Makler; Fondsmakler; Obligationenmakler

Broker who executes bond trades on the floor of an exchange; also, one who trades corporate U.S. government, or municipal debt issues over the counter, mostly for large institutional accounts.

bond discount Obligationsdisagio

The difference between the face value and the sales price when bonds are sold below their face value.

bonded goods Waren unter Zollverschluss; zollpflichtige Waren; Zollverschlussware

Goods brought into a country that are placed in a bonded warehouse until all duties are paid, or the goods re-exported.

bonded storage Zolllager

bonded warehouse Zolllager; -speicher; Freilager

A warehouse, usually close to a sea port or airport, where goods on which customs duties are due, are stored after being imported.

bond index Anleihenindex

bond market Anleihenmarkt

bond ownership Anleihenenbesitz

bond premium Anleiheemissionsagio

Amount the purchaser of a bond pays that exceeds the face value of the bond.

bond price Anleihekurs

bond rating Bewertung einer Schuldverschreibung; Anleihebewertung

A method of evaluating the expected performance, quality and safety of a bond issue.

Standard & Poor's, Moody's Investors Service, Fitch Investors Service, and Duff and Phelps analyze the financial strength of each bond's issuer, whether a corporation or a government body.

Ratings range from AAA (highly unlikely to default) to D (in default).

bond valuation Wertberechnung einer Obligation; Anleihebewertung; Kursrechnung

Bono, Edward de (* 1933)

De Bono became famous for his concept of 'lateral thinking' and the generation of new ideas and the escape from old, conventional ones. Describing himself as a thinker about thinking, he tried to break out of established patterns in order to look at things differently.

De Bono argues that creativity comes into every aspect of managing a business – not only innovation, but information systems, planning, design, R&D, communications, finance, marketing, advertising, labor and public relations and problem solving. Unlike vertical or traditional, logical thinking which proceeds step by step, directly from one state of information to another state, lateral thinking is based on discontinuity.

The two systems do not cancel each other out, but are complementary. Where vertical thinking operates on a 'Yes/No' regression of alternatives, seeking always the solution that is right, lateral thinking proceeds by provocative leaps in unlikely directions, seeking what can be used in an idea rather than accepting or rejecting the whole idea outright.

Biography: born in Malta, studied psychology and medicine at Oxford University, acted as consultant to various leading companies such as Shell, IBM, Exxon, 3M, Apple, General Foods, Proctor and Gamble, Unilever, has taught at Oxford, Cambridge, London and Harvard universities, is the founder-director of the Cognitive Research Trust in Cambridge and the Center for the Study of Thinking.

Major publications: (1967) The use of lateral thinking, (1968) The five-day course in thinking, (1969) The mechanism of the mind, (1971) Lateral thinking for management, (1985) Tactics- the art and science of success, (1990) I am right, you are wrong, (1994) Parallel thinking, (1995) Teach yourself to think.

bonus Prämie; Sondervergütung; Zugabe; Dividende; Gehaltszuschlag; *(Christmas)* Gratifikation

An extra payment made by management to employees, usually as a reward or a compensation, e.g. for dangerous work.

A bonus is normally above and beyond either a commission or a salary. It is therefore an unexpected benefit occurring as the result of making a particular action.

Example: a salesperson who achieves the million-dollar mark in sales may be entitled to a one-time bonus. A corporation achieving a

10% increase in profits may distribute part of the earnings as a bonus to its employees.

bonus system Bonussystem

book Buch; *(ledger)* Geschäftsbuch; Heft; Block; *(to make a reservation)* buchen

The books of a company is a descriptive term for all its journals, ledgers, and other accounting records.

Securities: preliminary indications of interest on the part of prospective buyers of the issue.

As a verb, to book means to give accounting recognition to something. For example, to book a profit on the transaction.

book cash buchmäßige liquide Mittel

Firm's cash balance as reported in its financial statements.

book credit Buchkredit

book depreciation Buchwertabschreibung

book-entry securities buchmäßig verwaltete Wertpapiere

Securities that are not represented by a certificate. Purchases and sales of some municipal bonds, for instance, are merely recorded on customers, accounts; no certificates change hands.

booking center Buchungszentrum

Offshore financial center whose main function is to act as an accounting center in order to minimize the payment of taxes.

booking system Buchungssystem; Auftragssystem

book inventory Buchinventar

Stock in hand according to recorded figures.

bookkeeper Buchhalter; Rechnungsführer

A person who records the basic transactions of a business: receipts, payments, sales invoices. He also prepares the books of account to trial balance, makes the deposits and pays the wages. Normally, a *bookkeeper* does not have the advanced education of an accountant.

bookkeeping Buchführung; Buchhaltung

The keeping of the books of account of a business. The records enable the compilation of a profit and loss account and the balance sheet.

bookkeeping entry Buchungsposten

bookmark Lesezeichen

Internet: on the web, it is an address book entry for a web address. Most browsers contain a list where the reader can store the addresses of their favorite places.

book of commissions Auftragsbuch; Orderbuch

book profit Buchgewinn; buchmäßiger Gewinn

book loss Buchverlust; buchmäßiger Verlust

book value (Netto-)Buchwert; fortgeführter Anschaffungswert Bilanzwert

The value of an asset as recorded in the books of an organization. This is normally the purchase price of the asset reduced by amounts written off for depreciation.

Except at the time of purchase of the asset, the book value will rarely be the same as the market value of the asset.

book value per share Buchwert pro Aktie

Per-share accounting equity value of a firm. Total accounting equity divided by the number of outstanding shares.

boom Hausse; *(demand)* starke Nachfrage; Konjunkturaufschwung; Hochkonjunktur; (to *rise in value)* im Wert steigen; hochschnellen; blühen

The phase of a business cycle that follows a recovery, when the economy is working at full capacity. Demand, prices, and wages rise, while unemployment falls.

If fiscal controls are insufficient, a boom can lead to a recession and ultimately to a slump.

boost Auftrieb; Ankurbelung; Förderung; Auftrieb; *(to~)* ankurbeln; fördern; erhöhen; steigern; verstärken

border Rand; *(state)* Grenze; *(to ~)* angrenzen; begrenzen

borderline case Grenzfall

borrow borgen; entleihen; verschulden; *(loan)* ein Darlehen aufnehmen

Obtain or receive money on loan with the promise or understanding of returning it or its equivalent.

borrowed money Fremdgeld; aufgenommenes Kapital

borrower Kreditnehmer; Kreditkunde; Entleiher; Schuldner

borrower's bank Hausbank

borrowing Kreditaufnahme

boss Chef; Meister; Boss; Parteimanager; *(to ~)* leiten; kommandieren

Boston matrix (BCG matrix) Boston Consutling Group Matrix

See: growth-share matrix.

bottleneck Engpass

bottom Tiefstand; Boden; unterer Rand; *(business cycle)* Tiefpunkt

Economics: lowest level of prices for a market as a whole, often measured by an index, such as the lowest point in an economic cycle..

Securities: lowest market price of a security or commodity during a day, a season, a year, a cycle; also,.

Economic policy: support level for market prices of any type.

bottom line Saldo; Endgewinn oder Endverlust

The last line of a company's profit and loss calculation, usually stating the net profit.

The expression is used colloquially when seeking the result without asking for the reasons: "What is the *bottom line?"*

bottom-up planning Planung von unten nach oben

An approach to planning starting from the operational, shop-floor level

boundary Grenze; Grenzlinie

boundary-less organization grenzenlose Organisation

Organization that seeks to eliminate the chain of command, have limitless spans of control, and replace departments with empowered teams.

bounded rationality begrenzte / eingeschränkte Rationalität

Individuals make decisions by constructing simplified models that extract the essential features from problems without capturing all their complexity. Individuals can then behave rationally within the limits of the simply model.

box Kasten; Kiste; *(cardboard)* Karton; Schachtel; *(post office)* Schließfach; *(to ~)* verpacken

box office Hauptkasse; *(movie)* Kinokasse; *(theater)* Theaterkasse

boycott Boykott; *(to ~)* boykottieren

An organized refusal with the objective of winning concessions. It can be used by employees of a firm and their unions, by businesses who refrain from commercial dealing with others, or be ordered by a government that prohibits dealings with another country.

brainstorming Brainstorming; Ideenfindungsprozess

Technique for generating creative ideas in a group environment with normally not more than 10 participants. The purpose is to come up with originality in thinking without inhibitions.

To be most effective, brainstorming sessions require a trained facilitator and some basic rules. The three basic rules are:

1. Participants should be encouraged to come up with as many ideas as possible, however wild they are.

2. No judgment should be passed on any idea until the end of the session.

3. Participants should be encouraged to build on each other's ideas, putting together unlikely combinations and taking each one in unlikely directions.

Additionally, it is important to identify a precise topic to be discussed; make each group choose a secretary to record the ideas that are generated; explain clearly the three basic rules; invite all ideas, with the secretary listing all that come up; establish criteria for selecting the best ideas; then evaluate each idea against these criteria.

branch Ast; *(of company)* Zweigstelle; Filiale; Geschäftsstelle

branch bank Tochterbank; Filialbank; Bankzweigstelle

branch network Filialnetz; Geschäftsstellennetz

branch office Zweigniederlassung; Niederlassung; *(of a bank)* Depositenkasse

branch office manager Direktor einer Niederlassung; Filialleiter; Zweigstellenleiter;

brand *(make)* Marke; Schutzmarke; Sorte; *(brand product)* Markenerzeugnis; Markenartikel; *(to ~)* mit seinem Warenzeichen versehen

One useful definition (of many) : "A name, term, sign, symbol or design, or a combination of these, intended to identify the product of one seller and to differentiate it from those of its competitors" (Bennet).

Brands play a central role in advanced consumer markets, as without a brand a company can only market its product as a commodity, which means that it can only compete on price.

Any attempt to charge a premium are dependent on identifying the product and equipping it with certain real or perceived qualities. All these efforts depend on the existence of a brand.

Neither can a company effectively communicate about its products with its customers and stakeholders.

From the consumer´s point of view, brands not only offer orientation in a vast sea of products, but increasingly become vehicles to communicate messages to their environment and give meaning to their lives.

brand advertising Markenwerbung; Markenartikelwerbung

Advertising that creates a distinctly favorable image that customers associate with a product at the moment they make buying decisions.

brand association Markenassoziation

The degree to which a particular brand is associated with the general product category, such as Kleenex or Sello Tape.

brand awareness Markenbekanntheit; Bekanntheitsgrad einer Marke

The degree to which consumers are aware of a particular brand.

It can be measured as the percentage of all brand for a given category of product that is enjoyed by a particular brand in that category.

brand development Marententwicklung; Markenkonsumanteil

Policies and practices used to establish and maintain a successful brand.

Also: Measure of the strength of a product's sales, usually per thousand population. If 100 people in 1,000 buy a product, the product has a *brand development* of 10%.

brand development index (BDI) Markenkonsumindex; Index des Markenwarenkonsums

A measure of the relative strength of a brand's sales in a geographic area. Calculated as the percentage of total national brand sales which occur in an area divided by the percent of households which reside in that area

The BDI allows the media planner to see the concentration of current customers of a brand and concentrate advertising expenditure accordingly.

brand equity Markenwert

The value of a brand beyond its purely functional purpose.

Brand equity is a function of a number of factors: the extent to which a brand commands brand loyalty, in particular its potential for repeat buying, brand name awareness, perceived quality, strong brand associations, as well as other assets, such as patents, trademarks, and channel relationships.

brand extension Markenerweiterung

Using a successful brand name to launch a new or modified product in a new category. Addition of a new product to an already established line of products under the same brand name.

Brand extension allows the new product the benefit of the older product's established reputation.

For example, a food manufacturer with an established brand for its chocolate, can extend the brand to a new line of ice cream.

brand image Markenimage; Markenprofil

Set of beliefs that consumers hold about a particular brand.

Qualities that consumers associate with a specific brand, expressed in terms of human behavior and desires, but that also relate to price, quality, and situational use of the brand.

Example: a brand such as Mercedes Benz will conjure up a strong public image because of its sensory and physical characteristics as well as its price. This image is not inherent in the brand name but is created through advertising.

branding Markenpolitik; Warenzeichnpolitik

Alle efforts aimed at imposing a distinctive identity on goods and services. A brand's image is conveyed in a variety of ways, including advertising, packaging and the attitudes of employees.

Branding has a number of benefits, most important: it reassures consumers about the quality of the product; and for the company it provides an enduring platform on which to communicate with its consumers.

brand loyalty Markentreue

Degree to which a consumer will repeatedly purchase a brand. For advertisers brand loyalty is very important, as consumer must believe that the brand offers the right combination of quality and price.

There are many factors that influence brand loyalty, such as consumer attitudes, family or peer pressure, and friendship with the salesperson. The advertiser must try to consider all such factors.

brand manager Produktmanager; Produktmanagerin; Markenbetreuer; Markenbetreuerin

Marketing manager for a brand, who takes most of the decisions for that brand; also called *product manager.*

Responsibilities can range from setting strategic objectives, analysing consumers and competition; to managing and coordinating its distribution and all communication decisions.

Often in a company with many different brands, each brand will have its own *brand manager.* Each may use a different advertising agency, and each will have his or her own budget.

brand mark Markenzeichen; Markensymbol

A unique symbol that is part of a brand. Most successful brands use a unique symbol that helps to conjure up the image of the product or service.

brand name Markenname; *(trademark)* Warenzeichen

Part of a brand, trademark, or service mark that can be spoken, as distinguished from an identifying symbol. A brand name may consist of a word, letter, or group of words or letters.

brand new fabrikneu

brand potential index (BPI) Markenpotentialindex

Relationship between a brand's market development index and brand development index (BDI) in a particular market area.

The brand potential index is used to predict future sales and to aid in planning future advertising budget allocations.

brand share Markenanteil einer Marke

Measure similar to market share: the total amount spent by consumers on a particular brand as compared to the amount spent on all competing brands in the same category. Companies often set marketing goals to achieve a specific *brand share,* and plan their strategies to meet those goals.

brand value Markenwert

Attempt to measure the monetary value of a brand, based on a variety of factors: for example the extent to which it has high brand loyalty, name awareness, perceived quality, strong brand associations, and other assets such as patents, trademarks, and channel relationships.

The value of a company's brands may be of importance in a takeover bid; they may be shown in a company's balance sheets as intangible assets.

The most valueable brands, such as Coca Cola and Marlboro can be valued at US$70bn.

breach Bruch; *(violation)* Verstoß; Verletzung; Übertreten; *(to ~)* brechen; verletzen

Failure to perform some agreed-upon act or to comply with a legal duty owed to another or to society.

breach of contract Vertragsbruch; Vertragsverletzung

A failure by a party to a contract to perform the obligations in that contract. The injured party can sue for damages for the loss sustained.

breach of warranty Garantieverletzung; Verletzung einer Gewährleistungs-pflicht; Gewährleistungsbruch

Infraction of an express or implied agreement as to the title, quality, content, or condition of a thing sold.

break Bruch; *(pause)* Arbeitspause; Einschnitt; *(to ~)* brechen; *(rules)* nicht einhalten

breakdown Zusammenbruch; Unfall; Störung; Panne; Aufgliederung; Analyse; Liste

break even ohne Gewinn und Verlust abschneiden; kostendeckend arbeiten

break even analysis Break-Even-Analyse; Gewinnschwellenanalyse

An analysis that identifies the sales volume a business needs to generate before it can begin making profit. At that point expenses equal gross revenue for a zero net difference, and fixed and variable costs will be covered.

The technique is used in decision making to assist management to determine the profit or loss likely to arise from any given level of production or sales, the impact on profitability of changes in the in fixed or variable costs, and the levels of activity required to generate a desired profit.

Breakeven analysis may either be carried out by drawing a breakeven chart or by calculation.

The formula is: (total fixed costs + desired level of profit) / contribution per unit of production.

break-even point Kostendeckungspunkt; Gewinn-/Rentabilitätsschwelle; Break-Even-Punkt

In general: volume of sales at which a business begins to make profit. On the way to reaching the break-even point all contribution margins are consumed by the structure costs incurred by the business. Only when passing the break-even point a surplus of sales revenue over all the cumulated costs is to be stated. The break-even point may be analyzed in terms of units or currency.

Example: if a fixed costs are $100 and each item generates $5 in net revenue, the break-even point is at 20 items sold. A profit will be made on items sold in excess of 20. A loss will result on sales under 20.

Finance: point at which revenues equal costs. All sales over the break-even point produce profits; any drop in sales below that point will produce losses.

Real estate: occupancy level needed to pay for Operating expenses and debt service, but leaving no cash flow.

breakout Überschreitung des Widerstandsniveaus bei Aktienkursen

Rise in a security's price above a resistance level (commonly its previous high price) or drop below a level of support (commonly the former lowest price.) A breakout is taken to signify a continuing move in the same direction. Can be used by technical analysts as a buy or sell indication.

breakthrough Durchbruch

breakup Auflösung; Abbruch; Aufhebung; Aufteilung

Dissolution of any unit, organization, or group of organizations.

break up *(conglomerate)* entflechten; auseinander brechen; abbrechen; *(to dissolve)* auflösen

break-up value Liquidationswert

The value of an asset once a organization goes out of business. Assets are then normally sold in a rush and piecemeal, and their value is going to be rather low.

Bretton Woods

Name of a small town in New Hampshire, where in July 1944 representatives of 40 countries led by the United States and the United Kingdom held a conference to design the post-war international economic and monetary system.

The name has become synonimous with efforts at international cooperation to build a structured and predictable world order in the areas of international finance and international trade.

The main institutions that resulted from the decsions taken at Bretton Woods were the International Monetary Fund (IMF), the International Bank for Reconstruction and Development (World Bank), and, after four decades of negotiating rounds under the GATT, the World Trade Organization (WTO).

bribe Bestechung; Bestechungsgeschenk; Lockmittel; *(to ~)* bestechen; locken

Voluntary payment offered, usually surreptitiously, in expectation of a special favor. While offering a bribe is not always illegal, accepting one is unethical or frequently illegal.

bribery Bestechung

bridge a gap überbrücken

bridge loan Überbrückungskredit; Zwischenkredit

Short-term loan, also called *swing loan,* made in anticipation of intermediate-term or long-term financing.

bridges Brücken

Individuals in a social network who serve as linking pins by belonging to two or more clusters.

bridging of a gap Überbrückung

brief *(law)* Schriftsatz; kurz; *(to ~)* informieren; Anweisung geben; instruieren

briefcase Aktentasche

briefing Einweisung; Unterrichtung

broad breit; weit; ausgedehnt; voll; umfassend; großzügig

broadband Breitband

High-speed transmission medium. T-1, ISDN, DSL and cable modems are broadband media. Besides downloading web pages more quickly, broadband can also transmit high-quality streaming video.

broadband technology Breitband-technologie

Term referring to methods of delivering information across the internet at a higher rate by increasing bandwidth.

broadcast advertising Werbefunk; Werbefunk

broad product line breit gestreutes Warensortiment

brochure Broschüre; Druckschrift; Werbeschrift; Prospekt

Flyer or small book used to advertise or describe a product for sale or service available.

brochure price Prospektpreis

brochure ware rein darstellende Internetseite

Web-site that provides information about a company's products and services. In this approach, the company has simply transferred its existing paper-based promotional literature on to the internet without recognizing the differences required by this medium.

broke pleite; bankrott

broken lot unvollständiges Warenset

Incomplete set of merchandise. Broken lots often are the result of breakage or improper packaging.

broker Makler; Broker

Agent whose functions is to bring buyers and sellers together and assist in negotiation, but who does not take title to goods.

Brokers are used because they have specialized knowledge of certain markets or to conceal the identity of a principal.

brokerage Maklergeschäft; Maklergebühr; Courtage; Provision

Profession: Business of being a broker. One may open a brokerage office, upon receiving a broker's license, for the purpose of engaging in *brokerage.*

Payment: Commission received by a broker for his services, usually a percentage of the total sale. For example, the *brokerage* on the sale of a $100,000 house was $6,000.

brokerage allowance Maklergebühr

Commission paid by the seller in a transaction to the broker who arranged the sale, normally a percentage of the selling price. A brokerage allowance usually refers only to transactions in which the broker does not take possession of the goods sold.

brokerage house Brokerhaus; Maklerunternehmen; Maklerfirma

brownfield development

A housing or industrial development within an existing urban area. Distinct from greenfield development, where a new area is dedicated.

brown goods braune Ware

Televisions, hi-fi equipment, etc., which are usually housed in wood or imitation wood cabinets.

browser Browser

Software tool, often bundled with operating systems, used to access web-pages on the internet.

The most widely used browsers are Microsoft Internet Explorer, Netscape, and Mozilla Firefox.

browser and server Browser und Server

Internet: Every webpage requires two machines: the sender's host or server, and the reader's browser. The server is a sender, a transmitter, that sends the webpage to the reader. The browser is the receiver, which displays it on the reader's computer.

bubble theory (of speculative markets) Theorie der Spekulationsblase

Theory suggesting that security prices sometimes move wildly above their true values, and that this speculative bubble will have to burst sooner or later.

budget Budget; Haushalt; Staatshaushalt; Etat; Plan; Finanzplan; *(to ~)* Haushaltsplan aufstellen; einplanen; einkalkulieren

A detailed plan of revenue and expenditure for a specified period in the future.

In the broader sense the word *budget* is used to characterise the accounting side of planning (budgetary accounting), e.g. sales volumes, turnover, costs, head counts, output.

Of the many kinds of budgets, a cash budget shows future cash flow, an *expense budget* shows projected expenditures, and a capital budget shows anticipated capital outlays. In a *balanced* budget, revenues equal expenditures.

Government: A government's annual budget, which is presented to parliament for ratification.

budgetary control Budget-Finanzkonktrolle

The process by which financial control is exercised within an organization using budgets.

Income and expenditure for each function of the organization are set in advance of an accounting period, and budgets are then compared with actual performance to establish any variances.

Managers are made responsible for the controllable activities within their budgets, and are expected to take action if the adverse variances are regarded as excessive.

budgetary policy Haushaltspolitik

budget committee Haushaltsausschuss

budget deficit Haushaltsdefizit; Etatdefizit; Budgetdefizit

The excess of government expenditure over government income.

A budget deficit must be financed either by borrowing or by printing money.

budgeting Finanzplanung; Planungsrechnung; Budgetierung

Process of the annual planning of the result expressed in financial terms resulting in a budget.

The tools used in budgeting are the planned balance sheet, the planned profit & loss account, the financial budget and the liquidity budget.

budget limitation Budgetbeschränkung

budget mortgage Budgethypothek; Etathypothek

Mortgage that requires monthly payments for taxes and insurance in addition to interest and principal.

budget proposal Haushaltsvoranschlag; Haushaltsentwurf; Haushaltsgericht

budget reduction Budgetbeschränkung

budget reorganization Haushalts-sanierung

budget specialist Haushaltsexperte

buffer Reserve; Stoßpolster; Puffer; Prellbock; Zwischenspeicher

Computing: device for the temporary storage of electronic data that is located between two other devices of differing speeds.

A computer is much faster than a printer output device, so the output from the computer will be sent to the buffer before it is sent to the printer. This allows a computer to continue working instead of waiting for the printer to catch up.

buffer stock Vorratslager; Reservelager; Ausgleichslager

A partially managed system that utilizes stocks of commodities to regulate their prices.

Stock used in agriculture to stabilize the price of commodities. The government purchases excess production for storage and sells that storage stock in years of low production. In general the use of buffer stocks stabilizes commodity market price swings.

bug Programmfehler; Defekt

Computing: Error in a computer program. Bugs can be either *syntax errors,* meaning that the rules of the programming language were not followed, or *logic errors,* meaning that the program does not do what it is supposed to do.

The term originated when a wayward insect caused a short circuit in the ENIAC, the world's first electronic digital computer.

build Gestalt; Bauart; *(to ~)* bauen; aufbauen; errichten

builder Bauherr; Baumeister; (Er-)Bauer; Bauträger

building funds Baugelder

building design Bauzeichnung; Bauplanung

building permit Baugenehmigung

Permission granted by a local government to build a specific structure at a particular site.

building society Bausparkasse

A financial institution in the UK that accepts deposits, upon which it pays interest, and makes loans for house purchase or house improvement secured by mortgages.

Loans made to persons wishing to purchase property are usually repaid by regular monthly installments of capital and interest over a number of years.

build to order Konstruktion zeitnah zur Bestellung

Complex product created as it is ordered. This helps to eliminate inventory and reduce cost.

bulk Masse; Menge; lose; unverpackt

bulk buyer Gossabnehmer

bulk buying Masseneinkauf; Großeinkauf

The buying of products or commodities in sufficiently large quantities to take advantage of discounts.

bulk carrier Massengutfrachter; Frachtschiff

A vessel in which the cargo is carried in bulk, rather than in bags, containers, etc.

Bulk cargoes are usually homogeneous such as ores, coal, wheat. etc.

bulk commodity Massengut

bulk transaction Massengeschäft

bull Haussespekulant; Haussier; Preistreiber

Investor with an optimistic attitude who expects the price of shares, and/or stock markets, to rise. Opposite of Bear.

A *bullish* can refer to the prospects for an individual stock, bond, or commodity, an industry segment, or the market as a whole. In a more general sense, *bullish* means *optimistic.* The symbol of a bull and bear locked in combat represents the stock market.

bull market Haussemarkt; optimistischer Markt

Any market in which prices are in an upward trend.

bullet endfällige Anleihe

Straight debt issue with repayment in one go at maturity.

bulletin amtliche Bekanntmachung; Mitteilungsblatt; Nachrichtenblatt; Bericht

1. Written announcement that arrives with urgency.

2. Description or title of a business or trade periodical that displays merchandise and price information.

bulletin board Bulletin Board

A software tool on the Internet enabling users of a network to communicate asynchronously by sending and replying to messages.

bullion (Edelmetall-)Barren

Bars of gold and silver intended for coinage.

bullish phase Haussephase

bull market Hausse

Prolonged period in a market associated with a consistent upward trend of rising prices.

bundling Bündelung

Marketing technique of giving away a relatively cheap product together with a relatively expensive one.

For example, giving free audio cassettes with each purchase of a tape recorder, or incorporating one or more CDs with the software package supplied with a computer.

burden Last; Belastung; Bürde *(to ~)* belasten; aufbürden

burden of proof *(law)* Beweislast

The obligation to prove what is alleged. A plaintiff in a trial normally has to substantiate an allegation or issue and convince the court of the truth of his claim in order to prevail in a civil or criminal suit.

bureau Dienststelle; Amt; Büro

bureaucracy Bürokratie

A hierarchical administrative organization designed to deal with large quantities of work in a routine manner, largely by adhering to a set of strict and impersonal rules and procedures.

Tasks are grouped into functional departments, centralized authority, narrow spans of control, and decision making that follows the chain of command.

bureaucrat Bürokrat

Government employee who follows a rigid procedure in administering the responsibilities of a position. A classical bureaucrat follows a set of rules and procedures in an impersonal manner.

bureaucratic bürokratisch

bureaucratic controls bürokratische Kontrollen

Achieving control though establishment of a system of rules and procedures.

burglary *(law)* Einbruch; Diebstahl

Crime of breaking into and entering another person's building with intent to steal or commit another crime.

burnout Zustand totaler Erschöpfung

Psychology: a condition of emotional and often physical exhaustion. Often interest in work, personal achievement, and efficiency decline sharply and the sufferer is no longer capable of making decisions.

The condition is brought about by stress and pressures at work and is frequently experienced by individuals who derive a major part of their self-esteem from their work, because they have few other interests.

burnout syndrom Burnout Syndrom

business *(company)* Geschäft; *(firm)* Firma; *(plant)* Betrieb; *(trade)* Gewerbe; Handel; Beruf; Sache; Pflicht; Angelegenheit

Activity: commercial, professional, and industrial activity undertaken to earn a profit.

Organization: A commercial enterprise, profession, or trade operated for the purpose of earning a profit by providing a product or service; also called *business enterprise.*

Businesses are created by entrepreneurs who invest money in a particular venture in order to earn a profit. They vary in size from a one-person sole proprietorship to an international corporation having billions of dollars in assets and thousands of employees.

Industry: business can also be used to refer to a particular area of economic activity, such as the or the computer business.

business activity code Geschäftstätigkeitscode

Four-digit code numbers used in the US for principal business activities, designed to classify enterprises by type of activity for the administrative purposes of the IRS. They are similar in format to Standard Industry Classification codes.

business analysis Unternehmensanalyse; betriebswirtschaftliche Analyse

An attempt to evaluate the current performance of a firm as part of the strategic planning process.

It normally includes an analysis of its current market performance, measured by market share, a competition analysis, such as SWOT, and an environmental analyisis, such as PESTL.

business buying process Kaufprozess bei Unternehmen

Decision-making process by which business buyers define their needs and identify, evaluate and choose among alternative brands and suppliers.

The amount of time and effort devoted to the process will depend on a number of factors, including the importance of the decision, the costs involved, the number of alternatives available, and the experience of the participant.

business buying situation Kaufsituation bei Unternehmen

When businesses make complex buying decisions, three typical situations can be destinguished:

Straight rebuy: a familiar product (e.g. stationery, electricity) is bought from a regular supplier.

Modified rebuy: searching a product with improved performance, perhaps reflecting dissatisfaction with current suppliers.

New-task: the buyer is attempting to fulfill a need or solve a problem that has not been previously encountered.

Each situation requires a different approach by marketers.

business call Kundenbesuch; Dienstgespräch

business center Geschäftszentrum

business client Firmenkunde; Geschäftskunde

business community Geschäftswelt; Wirtschaftskreise

business condition Geschäftsbedingungen; wirtschaftliche Rahmenbedingungen

General climate of the economy and/or the political situation as they relate to the profitability and prosperity of business.

business culture Unternehmenskultur; Geschäftskultur

business cycle Konjunkturzyklus; Konjunkturverlauf

The periodic but irregular up-and-down movement in economic activity, measured by fluctuations in real GDP and other macroeconomic variables.

From historical research, economists have identified short-term (2 to 3 years) to long-term (50- to 60-year Kondratieff cycle) business cycles; however, while economic activity in recent years has experienced both booms and lulls, there is little evidence that these periods occur on a regular, predictable basis.

Economists identify four separate phases in a classic business cycle:

1. Prosperity phase, when production and sales rise, and so too do prices.

2. Liquidation phase, when customers decide to remain liquid.

3. Recession phase, when there is widespread unemployment and business closures.

4. Recovery phase, when consumers regain their confidence.

business day Geschäftstag

In general: time of a day when most businesses are in operation, normally from 9 am to 5 pm.

Finance: day when financial marketplaces are open for trading. Saturday, Sunday, and/or a legal holidays do not count as business days.

business development Geschäftsentwicklung

business ethics Geschäftsethik; Wirtschaftsethik

A branch of ethics that examines ethical rules and principles within a commercial context, i.e. what is acceptable and unacceptable behavior by business people.

An example of a lack of *business ethics* is when an advertising firm develops a deceptive and grossly misleading ad campaign.

business etiquette Geschäftsetikette

Generally accepted behavior in normal business situations, based on social guidelines.

business expenses Geschäftskosten

business financing Geschäftsfinanzierung; Unternehmensfinanzierung; Finanzwirtschaft

business gift Werbegeschenk

Small presents given by a business for goodwill, without obligation to its customers and employees.

business hours Verkaufszeiten; Öffnungszeiten; Geschäftszeiten

business intelligence Informationsdienst eines Unternehmens

Gathering of secondary and primary information about competitors, markets, customers, and more.

business interruption insurance Betriebsunterbrechungsversicherung

Insurance against the loss of profits and continuing fixed expenses when some disaster, such as a fire, prevents business from being carried on.

business investment Anlagegeschäft; Anlagengeschäft

business journal Wirtschaftszeitung

business liability insurance Betriebshaftpflichtversicherung

Coverage for liability exposures of a business to include policies covering individual specific areas of a given business or industry, any of which may be subject to liability.

business life and health insurance Teilhaberlebens- und Krankenversicherung; Partnerlebens- und Krankenversicherung

Insurance against the loss of a key person, owner, or partner, that assures the maintenance of a business as closely to normal.

business loan Betriebskredit; Geschäftskredit; Gewerbedarlehen; gewerblicher Kredit

businessman Geschäftsmann; Kaufmann; Unternehmer

business management Geschäftsführung; Unternehmensführung; Betriebsführung; Verwaltung

business market Geschäftsmarkt; Absatzmarkt

All the organizations that buy goods and services to use in the production of other products and services, or for the purpose of reselling or renting them to others at a profit.

business meal Geschäftsessen

business modeling Geschäftsprozess-modellierung

Modelling based on widely available software that allows non-technical general managers to try out different options on (electronic) paper before deciding which one to use.

It also can help to democratize decision-making by diffusing it throughout the organization. Other common uses of business modeling include financial planning, with the help of spreadsheets, forecasting, mapping processes, and data mining.

business name Handelsname; *(business on joint account)* Konsortialgeschäft

business office Geschäftslokal

Place of business where professional or clerical duties are performed.

business organization Betriebsstruktur; Firmenorganisation; Unternehmens-organisation

A commercial or industrial enterprise and the people who constitute it. Also: th structure of a particular business in terms of how it functions.

business outlook Konjunkturaussichten; Geschäftslage

business page *(newspaper)* Wirtschaftsteil

businesspeople Geschäftsleute

business plan Geschäftsplan

Comprehensive document drawn up by management or entreprenuers that provides information to managers and employees on the one hand and on the other inform the board and external business partners like investors and banks about plans for the development of the company and its business units.

Core elements of a business plan are the descriptions of the actual situation of the company and its finances, the plans for the future development of the business units, the formulated objectives and programs, plans for personnel, finance and know how requirements, together with plans for individual option and benefit plans. Business planning requires the know how and the commitment of all involved persons.

An important part of business plans are strategies. They should be formulated in the form of measurable and traceable objectives. This has to demonstrate how the company is going to adapt to changing situations (in the environment) and which actions have to be performed to succeed.

business portfolio Geschäftsfelder-Portfolio; Unternehmensportefeuille

Collection of businesses and products that make up the company.

business premises Betriebsstätte

business process re-engineering (BPR) Umgestaltung von Geschäftsprozessen

A fundamental and often radical re-assessment of the organizational processes that results in a comprehensive restructuring of an organization

BPR asks fundamental questions: what does the organization want to achieve, what are its core processes, and what are its predominant competencies. Based on the answers, it attempts to plan the most efficient, effective, and direct ways of achieving the desired ends.

business property Geschäftsgrundstück; Betriebsvermögen

Any property used in a trade or business that is not a capital asset, generally for tax purposes.

This would include assets specifically excepted from capital asset status, such as: inventory, property held for sale to customers in the ordinary course of business, trade receivables from the sale of property or services in the normal course of business, depreciable personal property used in a trade or business, real property used in a trade or business, intangible assets such as a copyright or trademark.

business publication Wirtschaftsmagazin

business purpose Geschäftszweck

business reply card (BRC) Antwortkarte

business reply envelope (BRE) Freiumschlag

business reply mail (BRM) Rückantwort

Preaddressed cards, envelopes, labels, or cartons that can be mailed without prepayment of postage.

After delivery of the mailing piece, the postal service collects the postage due, based upon a printed permit number on the envelope that identifies the addressee.

business report Geschäftsbericht

business revival Konjunkturbelebung

business risk Geschäftsrisiko; unternehmerisches Risiko

Risk that the firm's shareholders bear if the firm is financed only with equity.

business school Wirtschaftshochschule; Handelsschule

business segment Unternehmenssegment

business strategy Geschäftsstrategie; Unternehmensstrategie

business summary Unternehmensüberblick

Field of information that will give the investor a brief description of what the company's line of business is. It also gives information regarding the current period's revenues and earnings vs. the prior periods results.

business tax Gewerbesteuer

business-to-business marketing (B2B) Unternehmensmarketing

Marketing of products to businesses, governments, and institutions for use in the business operation, as components in the business products, or for resale.

business-to-consumer marketing (B2C) Konsumentenmarkting

Marketing of products to the end consumer.

business volume Geschäftsvolumen; Geschäftsumfang

businesswoman Geschäftsfrau

busy beschäftigt; tätig; *(street)* belebt; *(telephone)* besetzt

button Knopf

E-Marketing: like banners ads, buttons are paid for by an advertiser but are square or round instead of rectangular.

buy Kauf; Erwerb; *(to ~)* kaufen; ein-; aufkaufen; erwerben

buy-and-sell agreement Rückkaufklausel

Approach used for sole proprietorships and partnerships in which the business interests of a deceased or disabled partner are sold according to a predetermined formula to the remaining member(s) of the business.

buy back (Aktien)rückkauf

The buying back by a corporation of its shares to reduce the number on the market.

The purpose of a buy back can be either to increase the return on those shares still available, or to remove threatening shareholders

buy-back agreement Ruckkaufvereinbarung

A contract between a purchaser and vendor in which the vendor agrees to buy the property back from the purchaser if a certain event occurs within a specified period of time

Example: the buyer is transferred by his company to another position.

buyer Käufer; Einkäufer; Abnehmer

A person who purchases goods or services; also called *customer.*

A consumer makes purchases for his or her own use or purpose. A professional buyer makes bulk purchases on behalf of a retailer or wholesaler. A media buyer purchases media space or time for an advertiser.

buyer behavior Käuferverhalten; Einkaufsverhalten

An important part of the marketing process is to gain an understanding of how buyers behave. Without that knowledge, businesses would find it difficult to respond to customer needs.

The qustions to be answered are: who buys; why does he buy; where does he buy; when does he buy; how does he buy; who influences hime, etc?

Buyer behavior is influenced by such factors as personality, socio-demographic characteristics, and lifestyle.

buyer aggregator Abnehmergemeinschaft

Type of online purchasing agent that brings buyers together for the purpose of buying in larger quantities and, thus, reducing prices.

buyer cooperative Abnehmergenossenschaft

buyer's market Käufermarkt

Market situation in which supply exceeds demand, and where buyers have a wide choice and may negotiate lower prices.

buyer-readiness stages Stufen der Kaufbereitschaft

Stages that consumers normally pass through on their way to purchase, including awareness, knowledge, liking, preference, conviction and purchase.

buyers Einkäufer; Aufkäufer

People in an organization's buying center with formal authority to select the supplier and arrange terms of purchase.

buy-in Stützungskäufe der Notenbanken; *(stock market)* Deckungskauf

Trading: procedure whereby the responsibility to deliver or accept stock can be terminated.

Securities: transaction between brokers wherein securities are not delivered on time by the broker on the sell side, forcing the buy-side broker to obtain shares from other sources.

buying agent Einkaufsagent; Einkäufer; Einkaufskommissionär

buying center Beschaffungsteam; Einkaufsgremium

The informal group of individuals within an organization that decides which items the organization should buy.

The group's composition varies according to the cost and complexity of the purchase, but normally includes: the purchasing manager, the proposed user, influencers, i.e. people indirectly associated with the use of the product, and the decider one or more people. such as a director who authorize the purchase.

It is important for the seller to discover the composition of this group and to recognize that membership changes periodically.

buying country Abnehmerland

buying forward Terminkauf

The act of buying commodities, securities, foreign exchange, etc., for delivery at a date in the future.

The aim of buying forward is to establish a strong market position or to cover a forward sale. In the case of foreign exchange, a forward purchase may be made to cover a payment that has to be made at a later date in a foreign currency.

buying incentive Kaufanreiz

buying process Kaufprozess

The decision process that leads to the purchase of a product. Consumers go through a five-stage process when they buy something:

Problem recognition: The individual recognizes a need, a desire, or problem.

Information search: the consumer begins to collect information about available product and purchase alternatives.

Evaluation of altervatives: the consumer evaluates the various purchase alternatives by applying certain decision criteria.

Purchase decision: the consumer makes a selection one option from the varous purchase alternatives.

Postpurchase behavior: the consumer experiences some degree of satisfaction or dissatisfaction with his or her purchase decision, and takes certain actions, e.g. rebuy.

buying resistance Kaufzurückhaltung; Kaufwiderstand

buying the index Indexkauf

Purchasing the shares in an index, for example the Financial Times Stock Exchange 100, in the same proportion as the index to achieve the same return.

buy local legislation Rechtssetzung, die den Kauf inländischer Produkte fördert

Laws that are intended to favor the purchase of domestically sourced goods or services over imported ones, even though the imports may be a better buy.

buyout Aufkauf; Übernahme

Purchase of at least a controlling percentage-/interest of a company's stock in order to take over its assets and operations.

A buyout can be accomplished through negotiation or through a tender offer. A leveraged buyout is done with borrowed money.

buy up aufkaufen

buzz word Modewort; Fachsprache

An idiom used in technical, administrative, and sometimes political environments by in-groups, often not understandable to outsiders.

bylaws Statuten; Satzung

Rules adopted for the regulation of an association's or a corporation's own actions.

In corporation law, bylaws are self-imposed rules that constitute an agreement or contract between a corporation and its members to conduct the corporate business in a particular way.

by-product pricing Nebenproduktpreis

Setting a price for by-products in order to make the main product's price more competitive.

by-products Nebenprodukte; Nebenerzeugnis

Items produced as a result of the main factory process, such as waste and rejected items. Residue arising at various stages in the production of a principal commodity.

Example: by-products of the meat-packing industry are glue and hair. Certain industries produce toxic by-products that can become environmental hazards.

byte

Amount of computer memory space needed to store one character, which is normally 8 bits. A computer with 8-bit bytes can distinguish 2^8 = 256 different characters. The size of a computer's memory is measured in *kilobytes,* where 1 kilobyte (K) = 1024 bytes.

by the book streng nach Vorschrift

Method of working in a very rigid manner, according to pre-established written guidelines and regulations.

Saying an business is run *by the book* often represents a criticism, implying lack of flexibility and unresponsiveness to changing needs.

C

cable Kabel; Telegramm

An international telegram. Cables have now been replaced almost entirely by fax. e-mail, and the Internet.

cable modem Kabelmodem

Device that allows transmission of internet traffic over the cable TV wire connected to the home. The speed of transmission over a cable modem ranges between 500 Kbps and 2.5 Mbps.

cable rate Kabelkurs

cable TV Kabelfernsehen

Reception of TV signals via cable (wires) rather than over the air (i.e., via a TV antenna).

cache

Internet: cache (pronounced cash), is a file on the internet user's computer where their system stores a copy of sites they have visited recently.

If the user asks for the same thing again, instead of issuing another internet request, the computer can simply use the copy from the cache, sometimes saving as much as 10 or 20 seconds.

caching

Internet: phenomenon that occurs when access providers or browsers store or buffer web page data in a temporary location on their networks or in their disk space to speed access and reduce traffic. Reduces the number of measured page views at the original content site.

calculable berechenbar

calculate (be)rechnen; kalkulieren; errechnen; *(to estimate)* schätzen

calculation Berechnung; Kalkulation; *(estimate)* Voranschlag; Rechnung

calculation of earning power Ertragsschätzung

calculator Rechenmaschine; (Taschen-)Rechner

calendar Kalender

calendar year Kalenderjahr

Continuous period beginning January 1 and ending December 31. Not necessarily identical with fiscal year.

call Ruf; Berufung; Ernennung; Kaufoption; *(telephone)* Anruf; Gespräch; *(visit)* Besuch; *(demand)* Nachfrage; *(to ~)* rufen; anrufen; nennen; *(a loan)* abrufen

Banking: demand by a bank to repay a secured loan. When a banker *calls* a loan, the entire principal amount is due immediately.

Bonds: the right to redeem outstanding bonds before their scheduled maturity. The first dates when an issuer may *call* bonds are specified in the call provisions.

Bonds are usually called when interest rates fall so significantly that the issuer can save money by floating new bonds at lower rates.

Options: the right to buy a specific number of shares at a specified price by a fixed date.

callable abrufbar; fällig; rückkaufbar; rückforderbar

Security that can be redeemed by the issuer before the scheduled maturity. The issuer normally has to pay the holders a premium price if such a security is retired early.

callable bond kündbare Schuldverschreibung

Bond that may be repurchased at a stated call price before maturity.

callback service Rückrufservice

Internet: direct response facility available on a web site to enable a company to contact a customer by phone at a later time as specified by the customer.

call center Call-Center

An organization whose sole purpose is to handle large amounts of telephone calls. It is used for inbound and outbound telemarketing, customer-service, or market research.

call for additional cover Nachschusspflicht

call for funds Einforderung

calling in Einforderung

calling on customers Kundenbesuch

call money Tagesgeld

call option Bezugsoption; Kaufoption

Option contract that gives the holder the right but not the obligation to purchase, and obligates the writer to sell, a specified number of shares of the underlying stock at a predetermined (strike) price, on or before the expiration date of the contract.

call premium Bezugsprämie; Kündigungsaufgeld; Vorprämie; Optionspreis

Amount the buyer of a call option has to pay to the seller for the right to purchase a stock or stock index at a specified price by a specified date.

In bonds and preferred stock, the amount over par an issuer has to pay to an investor for redeeming the security early.

call price Rückkaufpreis; Rücknahmepreis

Price at which a bond or preferred stock with a call feature can be redeemed by the issuer; also known as *redemption* price.

call protected Schutz vor vorzeitiger Kündigung; Kündigungsschutz

Describes a bond that is not allowed to be called, usually for a certain early period in the life of the bond.

call provision Rückkaufklausel

call report Kontaktbericht

Advertising: Report kept by an advertising agency of its meetings with current or prospective clients; also called *conference report, contact report.* The *call report* records when the meeting took place, who was present, and what was discussed.

call up abrufen; wecken; wachrufen; *(military)* einziehen

campaign Kampagne; Feldzug; Aktion; *(to ~)* eine Kampagne führen; Propaganda machen

cancel rückgängig machen; annullieren; streichen; aufheben; *(order)* stornieren; *(meeting)* absagen; *(subscription)* kündigen

cancellation Streichung; Aufhebung; Annullierung; *(order)* Stornierung; *(entry)* Löschung; *(subscription)* Kündigung; *(meeting)* Absage

cancellation clause Rücktrittsklausel

Provision in a contract that gives the right to terminate obligations upon the occurrence of specified conditions or events.

candidate Kandidat; Anwärter; Bewerber

canned sales approach vorgefertigte Verkaufspräsentation

Sales presentation prepared by the company, which the sales representatives has to memorize and then repeat verbatim when making a sales presentation.

This approach can be effective for inexperienced sales personnel, but is normally inadequate for complex selling transactions.

cannibalization Kannibalisierung

Introduction of a new product or service into a market where there is little scope for further growth. That product or service will either eat into the share of the market's existing products, or fail.

Example: two drinks marketed by the same manufacturer and positioned to the same target audience could cause increased sales of one to be achieved at the expense of decreased sales of the other.

But firms may also choose to cannibalize their own products by introducing marginally improved products and to persuade existing customers to purchase an upgraded version (e.g. the PC market).

canvass Kundenwerbung; Stimmenwerbung; *(to ~)* Kunden werben; Stimmen werben

canvassing Dirketvertrieb; Akquisition; *(politics)* Direktansprache von Wählern

cap Deckel; festgeschriebenes Maximum

A ceiling on a charge or payment. An interest-rate cap, for example, would set a maximum interest rate to be charged on a loan, regardless of prevailing general interest-rate levels. A lender will normally charge a fee for including a cap.

capability Fähigkeit; Leistungsfähigkeit; Tüchtigkeit

capable fähig; tüchtig; imstande

capacity Kapazität; Leistungsfähigkeit; *(content)* Fassungsvermögen; *(official role)* Eigenschaft; *(power)* Kraft; Leistungsstärke

Production: the amount that can be produced by a factory or production unit. Can be expressed in units, weights, size, man hours, labor cost, etc. Typically, there are five different dimensions of capacity.

Ideal capacity: volume that could be attained under ideal operating conditions, with minimum allowance for inefficiency.

Practical capacity: highest level at which a factory can operate, taking into consideration unavoidable losses of productive time, such as vacations, holidays, and repairs.

Normal capacity: average level of operating activity that is sufficient to fill the demand for the company's products or services for a prolonged period of time.

Planned capacity: similar to *normal capacity* except it is projected against a particular single year.

Operating capacity: similar to *planned capacity* except the time period is within a smaller part of a year.

capital Kapital; Stammvermögen; Geldmittel; *(city)* Hauptstadt; *(letter)* Großbuchstabe

Economics: in economic theory, a factor of production, usually either machinery and plant (physical capital) or money (financial capital).

Capital is generally used to enhance the productivity of other factors of production, (e.g. harvesters enhance the productivity of land; tools enhance the value of labor). Its return is the reward following from this enhancement, the rate of return on capital is therefore called profit.

Finance: money and other property of a corporation or other enterprise used in transacting its business.

capital account Kapitalkonto; Kapitalbilanz; Vermögensrechnung

Finance: group of accounting records that involve transactions in the equity or ownership of a business.

Economics: part of the balance of payments that records a nation's inflow and outflow of financial securities.

capital accumulation Kapitalakkumulation

capital allocation Kapitalallokation

capital allowance Abschreibungsbetrag; steuerliche Abschreibung

Allowances against income tax or corporation tax available to a business. Capital allowances can be given on capital spent on plant and machinery used in the business, or on commercia l buildings in enterprise zones, agricultural buildings, industrial buildings, and hotels.

capital appreciation Anlagewertsteigerung; Vermögenszuwachs

capital assets Anlagegüter; Anlagevermögen; Kapitalgut; Wirtschaftsgut

An asset is that is expected to be used for a considerable time in a trade or business

Examples of capital assets in most businesses are land and buildings, plant and machinery, investments in subsidiary companies, goodwill, and motor vehicles.

The costs of these assets are normally written off against profits over their expected useful life spans by deducting an item for depreciation from their book value each year..

capital asset pricing model (CAPM) Bewertungsmodell für risikobehaftete Wertpapiere

Mathematical model of the relationship between *expected risk* and *expected return.* The model is grounded in the theory that investors demand higher returns for higher risks.

capital base Kapitalbasis

capital budget Investitionsplan; Investitionshaushalt; Finanzbudget

The sums allocated by an organization for future capital expenditure. The capital budget normally encompasses a longer period than the next accounting period.

capital budgeting Investitionsrechnung; Investitionsplanung

The process of evaluating proposed investments, such as plant expansion, research and development, and advertising.

Among the sophisticated methods used in arriving at a capital budget are net present value and internal rate of return.

capital consumption Kapitalverbrauch; Kapitalverschleiß

Amount of depreciation included in the gross domestic product (GDP), normally around 10% of GDP. This amount is subtracted from GDP, on the theory that it is "used up" during the year, to arrive at net domestic product.

capital contributed excess of par value Zahlbetrag über den Nennwert

Amount paid for stock above its stated par value, as shown in the owner's equity section of a balance sheet.

capital contribution Einlage; Kapitaleinzahlung; Eigenkapital

Cash or property acquired by a corporation from a shareholder without the receipt of additional stock. Such amount is added to the basis of the shareholder's existing stock, and the corporation's basis is carried over from the shareholder.

capital controls Kapitalverkehrskontrolle

Restrictions on cross-border capital flows that segment different stock markets; limit amount of a firm's stock a foreigner can own; and limit a citizen's ability to invest outside the country.

capital employed Nettogesamtvermögen; betriebsnotewendiges Kapital

Either the sum of the shareholders' equity in a company and its long-term debts, or the capital assets of a company plus its net current assets. This concept is an important element of ratio analysis.

capital expenditure Investitionsausgaben; Investitionen

The amount spent by an organization during a particular period of time (normally one year) to acquire or improve long term assets such as property, plant, or equipment.

Capital expenditures are not charged against the profits of the organization when they take place, but are regarded as an investment to be capitalized in the balance sheet as a fixed asset and subsequently charged against profits by depreciating the asset over its estimated useful life.

capital expenditure program Investitionsprogramm

capital export Kapitalexport; Kapitalausfuhr

capital flight Kapitalflucht

capital flow Kapitalwanderung; Kapitalbewegung; Kapitalstrom; Kapitalfluss

capital formation Kapitalbildung; Vermögensbildung

Creation or expansion, through savings, of capital buildings, machinery, equipment which produces other goods and services.

capital gain Kapitalgewinn; Veräußerungsgewinn; Vermögenszuwachs aus Veräußerungen

The gain achieved on the disposal of an asset. It is calculated by deducting the cost of the asset from the proceeds received on its disposal.

A negative capital gain is a capital loss. If a stock is sold below cost, the difference is a capital loss.

capital gains tax Steuer auf Veräusserungsgewinne

Most countries have a form of income tax under which they tax substantial disposals of assets either by traders or by individuals (e.g. sales of shares by an investor).

If an asset has only been held for a limited time, tax rates tend to be higher than for the normal capital gains tax.

capital goods Investitionsgüter; Produktionsmittel; Anlagegüter

Industrial goods that are used in the production of other goods, such as industrial buildings, machinery, and equipment, as well as highways, office buildings, and government installations. In the aggregate, such goods are key determiners of a country's productive capacity.

capital growth Kapitalzuwachs

An increase in the value of invested capital. Investment in fixed-interest securities or bonds provides limited capital growth, whilst the value of equities should increase with inflation.

capital improvement Teilanschaffungswert

An expenditure for a physical improvement to an existing capital asset such as additions and major alterations that are intended to improve performance or increase useful life.

capital income Kapitaleinkommen

capital intensive anlageintensiv; kapitalintensiv

Project or purchase requiring large investments in capital assets. The term *capital intensive* is sometimes also used to mean having a high proportion of fixed assets to labor.

Motor-vehicle and steel production are capital-intensive industries. To provide an acceptable return on investment, such industries must have a high margin of profit or a low cost of borrowing.

capital investment Kapitalanlage; Investitionskapital; Anlageinvestition

capitalism Kapitalismus

An economic and political system in which individual ownership and profit plays a central role, as opposed to socialist and communist systems, where the collective has a higher value.

Cenral to a capitalst system are the following features (1) private ownership of property exists; (2) the income from property or capital belongs to the individuals or firms that accumulated and own it; (3) individuals and firms are relatively free to compete with others for their own economic gain; and (4) the profit motive is basic to economic life.

Most of the developed economies are capitalistic, even though governments do interfere to some extent with the movements of capital.

capitalist Kapitalist; kapitalistisch

capitalistic kapitalistisch

capitalization Kapitalisierung; Kapitalausstattung; *(capital stock)* Gesellschaftskapital

The structure of the capital of a company, in particular the extent to which its capital is divided into share or loan capital and the extent to which share capital is divided into ordinary and preference shares.

capitalize kapitalisieren; Kapitalwert berechnen; Nutzen ziehen; (*Grammatik*) groß schreiben

capitalized value Kapitalwert; Ertragswert

The value at which an asset has been recorded in the balance sheet of a company or other organization. usually before the deduction of depreciation.

capital lease Finanzierungs-Leasing; aktivierungspflichtiger Leasingvertrag

Type of lease arrangement classified and accounted for by a lessee as a purchase and by the lessor as a sale or financing.

capital loss Kapitalverlust; Kapitalwertminderung; Kapitalveräußerungsverlust

Loss from the sale of a capital asset. Corporations may offset capital losses against capital gains but not against ordinary income.

capital market Kapitalmarkt

A market in which long-term capital is raised by industry, commerce, and governments. The money comes from private investors, insurance companies, pension funds, and banks.

Stock exchanges are also part of the capital market because they provide a market for the shares and loan stocks that represent the capital once it has been raised.

capital market line Kapitalmarkt-Linie

The efficient set of all assets, both risky and risk less, which provides the investor with the best possible opportunities.

capital movement Kapitalverkehr; Kapitalbewegungen

capital-output ratio Kapitalkoeffizient

capital rationing Kapitalzuteilung; Kapitalrationierung

Situation when a company has a limit on the budget for capital spending and has to select the right mix of acceptable projects that provides the highest overall net present value (NPV).

capital reduction Kapitalminderung

capital requirement Kapitalbedarf

Expenses and financing needed for the normal operation of a business; this includes the long-term and working capital.

capital reserves Kapitalreserven

Undistributed profits of a company, including certain profits on the revaluation of capital assets and any sums received from share issues in excess of the nominal value of the shares.

capital resources Eigenmittel; *(bank)* Eigenkapital; Kapitalausstattung

capital spending Kapitalaufwand; Investitionen

capital stock Grundkapital; Anfangskapital; Aktienkapital; Kapitalbestand

All ownership shares of a company, both common and preferred, representing money or property contributed by stockholders to be used as the financial foundation for the corporation.

capital structure Kapitalstruktur; Kapitalzusammensetzung

Corporation's financial framework, including long-term debt, preferred stock, and net worth. It is distinguished from financial structure, which includes additional sources of capital, such as short-term debt, accounts payable, and other liabilities.

capital surplus Kapitalreserven; Kapitalrücklage

The difference between the par value of a share and its issue price.

capital turnover Kapitalumschlag; Kapitalumsatz

A measure of the productivity of capital, calculated by dividing annual sales by average stockholder equity (net worth). When compared over a period, it reveals the extent to which a company is able to grow without additional capital investment.

caption Schlagzeile; Titelzeile; Überschrift

Text accompanying an illustration or photograph.

captive audience unfreiwilliges Publikum

An audience that is unlikely to be able to escape and has to view an entire advertisement, such as in a cinema.

captive market Markt eines monopolistischen Anbieters

Purchasers who are obliged to buy a particular product because they have no choice, e.g. the absence of an alternative supplier or product.

captive-product pricing Preissetzung von Komponenten

Setting a price for products that must be used along with a main product, such as blades for a razor and film for a camera.

capture Eroberung; *(to ~)* Markt erobern

card Karte; *(ticket)* Billett; *(business card)* Visitenkarte

care Sorge; Fürsorge; Sorgfalt; Betreuung; Pflege; *(responsibility)* Obhut; *(to ~)* sorgen für; sich kümmern um

care of *(mail)* bei

career Laufbahn; Karriere; Werdegang; Beruf

career opportunity Berufschance

cargo Fracht; Ladung; Frachtgut

Goods or products transported on a ship, plane, train or lorry, generally for commercial gain.

cargo insurance Ladungsversicherung; Gütertransportversicherung; Güterversicherung

An insurance policy protecting cargo being transported by a carrier, normally covering exposures on all risk/all peril basis. Exclusions include war, nuclear disaster, and other eventualities.

cargo ship Frachtschiff; Linienfrachter

carnet Zollbegleitscheinheft; Carnet; Zollpassagierscheinheft; Zollcarnet

carriage and insurance paid to frachtfrei versichert; Fracht und Versicherung bezahlt

carriage paid to frachtfrei; Fracht bezahlt

carrier Fuhrunternehmen; Transporteur; Spediteur; Frachtführer; *(airline)* Lufttransportgesellschaft;

carrier's lien Pfandrecht des Frachtführers

The right of a carrier to retain cargo as collateral for payment of the transportation services provided.

carrot and stick Zuckerbrot und Peitsche

Strategy often used in negotiations where one side offers the other something desirable while threatening negative sanctions if it does not accept the offer.

carry tragen; *(to transport)* befördern; mitführen; transportieren

carry back zurücktragen; verrechnen

Practice by which the deductions or credits of one taxable year that cannot be used to reduce tax liability in that year are applied against tax liability in an earlier year or years.

carry forward übertragen; vortragen

carrying costs Nebenkosten; Bestandskosten; Speditionskosten; Transportkosten

Real estate: The expenses of living in and maintaining a home and property, including mortgage payments, property taxes, heating, repairs, maintenance fees, etc

Retailing: charge for carrying the actual commodity, including interest, storage, and insurance costs.

Securities: fee that a broker charges for carrying securities on credit (margin).

carry on weitermachen; *(business)* betreiben

carry out durchführen; ausführen; vollziehen

carryover Saldovertrag; Übertrag; (Lager) alte Bestände

cartel Kartell

A group of producers who enter a collusive agreement to restrict or regulate output in order to raise prices and profits.

An example of a cartel would be the Organization of Petroleum Exporting Countries (OPEC).

cartelize kartellisieren

case Fall; *(container)* Kasten; *(law)* Rechtssache; Rechtsfall; *(to ~)* in Kisten verpacken

case of need Notfall

case presentation Fallpräsentation

case study Fallstudie

case study method Fallstudienmethode; Fallmethode

Approach to learning that works with information from a hypothetical or actual business situation. The aim is to formulate a recommended policy based on the facts provided. Data have to be gathered, organized, evaluated and generalized.

It involves looking at how a company's management handled an actual situation and determining if this was the best course of action.

cash Bargeld; Barmittel; Geldmittel; *(balance sheet)* Kassenbestand; bar; *(to ~)* einkassieren; *(check)* einlösen

Legal tender in the form of banknotes and coins.

Asset account on a balance sheet representing paper currency and coins, negotiable money orders and checks, and bank balances

cash account Kassenkonto

cash accounting Kassenbuchführung

cash against documents Barzahlung gegen Dokumente; Kasse gegen Dokumente

Payment terms for exported goods in which the seller sends the shipping documents to a bank in the destination country, and the buyer then obtains the documents by paying the invoice amount in cash to the bank.

cash and carry Selbstbedienungsgroßhändler

Wholesalers that stock a limited line of fast-moving goods such as groceries, toys, household goods, clothes, electrical supplies and building materials and that sell to small retailers and industrial firms for cash and normally do not provide a delivery service.

cash and equivalents Bargeld und Gegenwerte

Value of assets that can be converted into cash immediately, as reported by a company. Cash equivalents on balance sheets include securities that mature within ninety days.

cash assets reserve Bestandsreserve; Barreserve

cash bonus Barprämie; Bardividende

cash book Kassenbuch

Accounting book that combines cash receipts and disbursements. Its balance ties to the cash account in the general ledger on which the balance sheet is based.

cash budget Einnahmen-Ausgaben-Planung; Liquiditätsplan; Liquiditätsbudget

A projection of cash spendings and receipts during the next planning period. A detailed cash budget covers daily, weekly, or monthly expenditures together with the anticipated cash flow from collections and other operating sources.

cash contribution Bargeldbeitrag; Bareinlage

cash cow Unternehmen mit hohen Liquiditätsreserven

Business or product that generates a continuing flow of cash, which can be reinvested. Often in low-growth markets, but with a high market share.

cash cycle Liquiditätszyklus

In general, the time between cash disbursement and cash collection. In net working capital management, it can be thought of as the operating cycle less the accounts payable payment period.

cash discount Skonto; Barzahlungsrabatt; Kassaskonto

Reduction in a selling price for prompt cash payment for purchase. One reason a cash discount may be offered is to speed up the collection of receivables.

cash distribution Barausschüttung

cash dividend ausgeschüttete Dividende; Bardividende; Barausschüttung

Cash payment to a corporation's stockholders, distributed from current earnings or accumulated profits.Taxable as income.

cash earnings Bareinnahmen; Barverdienst

Cash revenues less cash expenses, specifically excluding non cash expenses such as depreciation.

cash equivalent Bargegenwert

Form of payment that is just like cash, such as a *traveler's check* or cashier's check.

cash flow Cashflow; Kapitalflussrechnung; geschäftsnotwendige Barmittel; liquiditätswirksamer Ertrag

Accounting: Measure of the actual cash generated by a business rather than the accounting profit. Calculated as turnover surplus over the liquidity-related expenses incurred by a company's business activity. It is regarded as an indicator for a company's profit situation and its *self-financing strength.*

Finance: calculation of all the changes that affect the cash account during an accounting period. Cash flow from operations is one factor in a breakdown, usually shown as *sources of cash* and *uses of cash.*

Investment: net income plus depreciation and other non cash charges, synonymous with cash earnings. Important to investors because of their concern with a firm's ability to pay dividends.

cash flow after interest and taxes Cashflow nach Zinsen und Steuern

cash flow analysis Cashflow-Analyse

cash flow statement Cashflow-Bericht; Kapitalflussrechnung; Bruttoertragsanalyse

Summary of a company's cash receipts and cash disbursements over a period of time; listing cash to and cash from operating, investing, and financing activities, along with the net increase or decrease in cash for the period.

cash flow time line Cashflow-Verlauf

Line depicting the operating activities and cash flows for a firm over a particular period.

cashier Kassierer; Kassenführer

A person in a business responisble for accepting payments, providing change, and recording all transactions.

cashier's check Barscheck; Kassenscheck

Check issued by a bank on its own account for the amount paid to the bank by the purchaser with a named payee, and stating the name of the party purchasing the check (the remitter).

cash in advance Vorkasse; Vorauszahlung

cash ledger Kassenbuch

cash management Kassenhaltung; Kassenmanagement

cash market *(stock exchange)* Kassamarkt

Market in which transactions are promptly completed. Ownership of the commodity is transferred from seller to buyer and payment is given on delivery of the commodity.

cash method Barwertmethode

An accounting method under which income is subject to tax when actually received and deductions are allowed when actually paid. Used by most individual taxpayers.

cash on delivery (COD) zahlbar bei Lieferung; Lieferung gegen Nachnahme

Method of payment requiring that goods be paid for in full by cash or certified check or the equivalent at the point of delivery. The term *collect on delivery* has the same abbreviation and same meaning.

cash position Liquiditätslage; Geldmittelbestand

cash price Barpreis; Barzahlungspreis

cash ratio Barliquidität; Liquidität ersten Grades

Ratio of cash and marketable securities to current liabilities: Refinement of the quick ratio. The *cash ratio* tells the extent to which liabilities could be liquidated immediately. Sometimes also called liquidity ratio.

cash refund offer Rückvergütungsangebot

Offer to refund part of the purchase price of a product to consumers who send a "proof of purchase" to the manufacturer.

cash squeeze Liquiditätsdruck

cash transaction Bargeschäft

Transaction where exchange is immediate, as contrasted to a forward contract, which calls for future delivery of an asset at an agreed-upon price.

cashout Liquiditätsengpass

Refers to situation where a firm runs out of cash and cannot readily sell marketable securities.

cash value Barwert; Kapitalwert *(insurance)* Versicherungswert

cash with order Kassa bei Auftragserteilung; Zahlung bei Auftragserteilung; Zahlung mit Anweisung

caste system Kastensystem

System of hereditary social stratification in which social position is determined by the family into which a person is born. Change in that position is usually not possible.

casualty Opfer; Verletzter

casualty insurance Unfallversicherung

catalog Katalog; Verzeichnis; Liste; *(to ~)* katalogisieren

Internet: Catalogs are similar to directories and provide a structured listing of registered web sites in different categories. Yahoo! and Excite are the best known examples of catalogs.

catalog aggregator Sammelbesteller

Brings together many catalog companies, creating a new searchable database of products for buyers.

catalog firm Versandhaus

catalog marketing Katalogmarketing

Direct marketing through catalogues that are mailed to a selected list of customers or made available in stores.

catalog showroom Versandhaus

Retail operation that sells a wide selection of high mark-up, fast moving, brand-name goods at discount prices.

catch-up effect Nachholeffekt

category Klasse; Gruppe; Kategorie

category killer Branchenkiller

Large and mostly very aggressive retailers that offer branded merchandise in clearly defined product categories at heavily discounted prices. In so doing they threaten the existence of an entire category of shops who can no longer compete on price, as for example, toys′ shops and Toys′r us.

category of goods Gütergruppe

causal ursächlich; kausal

causal chain ursächliche Verkettung; Kausalkette

causal quantitative models kausale quantitative Modelle

Research techniques used to forecast future demand for a product, by finding a causal relationship between two or more variables.

For example, average temperature, season and demographic data can be used to predict ice-cream sales.

causal loop ursächlicher Kreislauf

causal research Ursachenforschung

Marketing research to test hypotheses about cause-and-effect relationships. For example, it might determine whether a rise in temperature was the cause of an increase in sales of ice-cream

cause Ursache; Anlass; Grund; *(public interest)* Anliegen; *(law)* Rechtsstreit; Streitsache; *(to ~)* verursachen; veranlassen; bewirken

cause-effect diagram Grund-Folge Diagramm

A diagram that attempts to identify the main categories of possible causes of a problem in order to generate detailed lists of specific possible causes.

The method involves four steps; (1) identifying the problem or effect to be analyzed; (2) identifying the main classes of possible causes; (3) identifying possible detailed causes; (4) recording these possible causes on a diagram.

cause of loss Schadensursache; *(caution)* Vorsicht; *(prudence)* Umsicht; *(warning)* Warnung; *(to ~)* warnen

cautiou vorsichtig; behutsam

caveat emptor Ausschluss der Gewährleistung; Gewährleistungsausschluss

Latin term for "Let the buyer beware." A legal maxim stating that the buyer takes the risk regarding quality or condition of the property purchased, unless protected by warranty.

C curve C-Kurve

"C" like looking curve showing a relationship between corporate growth and reconstruction. The company's capital employed is plotted against the return on that capital. Developed in the 1990s by the Boston Consulting Group (BCG).

At first the capital employed shrinks without any improvement in the return. If the structuring is being successful, the returns start to improve.

CD-ROM

(Abbrev. Compact Disc - Read Only Memory) Optical storage technology that encodes data on a laminated metallic disc. One CD-ROM holds about 600 megabytes. Unlike a floppy disk, the data on a CD-ROM cannot be erased or edited.

cease aufhören; *(firm)* erlöschen; *(payment)* einstellen

ceiling Höchstbetrag; Obergrenze; Plafond

censure Tadel; *(to ~)* tadeln

Censure is a formal act by which a reprimand is issued to an individual by an authoritative body, such as a governmental agency or professional organization, indicating significant disapproval.

census Volkszählung; (Total-)Erhebung; *(year)* Erhebungsjahr;

center Zentrum; Zentralstelle; Mittelpunkt; *(to ~)* sich konzentrieren; in den Mittelpunkt stellen

center of learning Bildungszentrum

central Haupt-; Zentral-; zentral

central bank Notenbank; Zentralbank

A bank that provides financial and banking services for the government of a country and its commercial banks.

The task of a central bank normally include: to issue currency; to administer monetary policy; to hold deposits representing the reserves of other banks; and to engage in transactions designed to facilitate the conduct of business and protect the public interest.

central bank money Zentralbankgeld

central bank system Notenbanksystem

central buying zentraler Einkauf

Practice whereby all purchasing is done through a central or main office. Used by large organizations or chain stores.

central department Hauptabteilung

centralization Zentralisierung; Zusammenlegung

Organizational structure in which decision making is concentrated at the top. Strictly hierarchical model where no delegation of authority is permitted. The benefits are clear direction and facilitated planning, the disadvantages its inflexibility as well as poor accountability.

centralize zentralisieren

centralized depository zentralisierte Hinterlegungsstelle

Practice of centralizing corporate cash balances in a single depository.

centralized management zentralisiertes Management

central market Großmarkt

central pay office Hauptkasse

central planning staatliche Planung; zentrale Planung

century Jahrhundert;

certain sicher; gewiss; bestimmt

certainty Gewissheit; Tatsache; Bestimmtheit; Sicherheit

certificate Bescheinigung; Attest; Schein; Bestätigung; Beglaubigung; *(customs)* Geleitzettel; *(stock)* Anteilschein; Zertifikat; *(diploma)* Zeugnis; Urkunde

Formal document attesting to the truth of certain stated facts, such as a *birth certificate.*

Certificate of Deposit (CD) Depositenzertifikat, Geldmarktzertifikat; Einlagenzertifikat

A document issued by a bank or other financial institution that is evidence of a deposit, with the issuer's promise to return the deposit plus earnings at a specified interest rate within a specified time.

Maturities range from a few weeks to several years, interest rates are set by competitive forces in the marketplace.

certificate of health Gesundheitszeugnis

certificate of incorporation amtliche Registrierungsbescheinigung; Gründungsurkunde

A legal document, filed with the local government, which describes the legal organizational structure of a corporation, and any amendments and restatements of the certificate of incorporation. Once the certificate is issued; the corporation begins to exist.

certificate of inspection Beschaffenheitszeugnis

certificate of manufacturing Ursprungszeugnis; Ursprungszertifikat

certificate of origin Ursprungszeugnis; Ursprungszertifikat

certificate of quality Qualitätszeugnis

certificate of title Eigentumsnachweis

Official document issued by a registrar, which is considered conclusive evidence of the present ownership and state of the title to the property described.

certificate of use Nutzungsbescheinigung; Gebrauchsbescheinigung

certificate of weight Gewichtsbescheinigung

certificates of deposit Geldmarktzertifikat; Einlagenzertifikat

certification Bestätigung; Beglaubigung; Bescheinigung; Beurkundung

certification authority (CA) Zertifizierungbehörde

Organization issuing and managing certificates or public keys and private keys to individuals or organizations together with identification information.

certification mark Prüfzeichen; Gütezeichen

Type of trademark used in connection with goods or services to indicate geographic origin, material, mode of manufacture, quality, accuracy or other characteristics.

certified accountant zugelassener Wirtschaftsprüfer (UK)

A member of the Chartered Association of Certified Accountants in the UK. Its members are trained in industry, in the public service, and in the offices of practicing accountants.

certified check bestätigter Scheck

A personal check drawn by an individual which is guaranteed to be good, i.e. that the drawer of the check has sufficient funds in the bank to cover payment.

certified financial statement Abschluss mit Bestätigungsvermerk; testierter Abschluss

Financial statment, including balance sheet and income statement, that are attested to by a certified public accountant who audited the company.

certified mail Einschreiben

Service offered by postal service at extra cost, which provides proof of mailing and delivery.

certified public accountant (CPA) konzessionierter Wirtschaftsprüfer; zugelassener Wirtschaftsprüfer (US)

A title given to an accountant in the US who has passed the required examinations and has met other certifying requirements, such as practical experience and a certain age. CPA certificates are issued and monitored by state boards of accountancy. In addition to accounting and auditing, CPAs prepare tax returns for corporations and individuals.

cessation Beendigung; Einstellung; Aufhören

cession Überlassung, Zession; Abtretung

chain Kette; Reihe; Einzelhandelskette

chain of command Weisungskette; Dienstweg; Leitungsorganisation

The reporting relationships which result from delegating authority and responsibility to successively lower levels within an organization. It reflects the structure of decision-making from the highest to the lowest levels of authority.

chain of stores Handelskette

chain store Kettenladen; Filialgeschäft; -betrieb; Filiale

Two or more outlets that are commonly owned and managed, have central buying and merchandising, and sell similar lines of merchandise.

chairman, -person, -woman Vorsitzender; Präsident

chairman of the board Aufsichtsratsvorsitzender; Präsident

The most senior officer in a company, who chairs the annual general meeting and the meetings of the board of directors.

He may also have the role managing director, especially in a small company of which he is the majority shareholder, or he may be a figurehead, without executive powers. Sometimes this person is also called the president.

challenge Herausforderung; Aufgabe; Anregung; *(to ~)* herausfordern; auffordern; *(to contest)* anfechten

chamber Kammer; Raum

chamber of commerce Handelskammer

champion Verfechter; Vorkämpfer

championing Verfechten

To champion something is to support or defend it. The word became a management concept in the late 20th century when many companies came to believe that each new project, in order to succeed, needed a champion.

Championing is often applied to people as well: bright, talented people within an organization are deemed to need a champion, someone higher up the corporate leader.

Chandler, Alfred (* 1918)

American economic historian whose main contribution to management theory has been to explain the relationship in organizations between strategy and structure, arguing that structure follows strategy in organizations.

Chandler´s work has largely been based on studies of major US companies between 1850 and 1920, the period when modern capitalism was shaped and new economic units came into being – the business with a range of distinct operating units, each managed autonomously, and completely different from its historical predecessor, the traditional single-unit firm, personally owned and managed.

Chandler believes that his work contributed to a nationwide restructuring of corporations, with the multidivisional form of organization becoming the standard for large industrial firms producing multiple products in multiple markets. He was one of the first management thinkers to perceive the importance of creating a strategic plan for a business before framing its organizational structure.

Major publications: (1962) Strategy and structure, (1977) The visible hand: the managerial revolution in American business, (1980 and H. Deams, eds.) Managerial hierarchies: comparative perspectives on the rise of modern industrial enterprises, (1985 with R.S. Tedlow) The coming of managerial capitalism

change Änderung; Veränderung; *(transition)* Übergang; Wandel; *(money)* Wechselgeld; *(small coin)* Kleingeld; *(to ~)* ändern; umwandeln; wandeln; *(money)* wechseln; tauschen

change agent Berater in der Organisationsentwicklung

Person who acts as catalyst and assumes the responsibility for managing change in organizations. The options essentially fall into four groups:

Structure: involves making an alteration in authority relations, coordination mechanism, job redesign, or similar structural variables.

Technology: encompasses modifications in the way work is processed and in the methods and equipment used.

Physical setting: covers altering the space and layout arrangements in the workplace.

People: refers to changes in employee attitudes, skills, expectations, perception, and/or behavior.

change in financial position Änderung in der Kapitalflussrechnung

Sources of funds internally provided from operations which alter a company's cash flow position: depreciation, deferred taxes, other sources, and capital expenditures.

change management Change Management; Management von Veränderungsprozessen

Management concept that recocgizes the need of organizations to overcome their desire to stay static, and instead adapt to a changing environment.

This change can take many forms: a decline in market share, because of cost-cutting by new rivals; a new technology (such as the mobile phone) that transforms entire markets.

As a consequence, business projects had to be broken up into a series of small steps, and managers were supposed to learn to live with uncertainty, not knowing precisely where they might end up.

The concept was discussed by academics such as Rosabeth Moss Kanter, Tom Peters and Robert Waterman, and Charles Handy.

change purse Portemonnaie

channel Kanal; Weg; Vertriebsweg; Dienstweg; *(television)* Programm; *(to ~)* lenken; einschleusen; kanalisieren

Advertising: Medium through which a communication message travels. It is selected by the source, who must determine which channel is best suited to reach the desired target audience.

Distribution: the chain of intermediaries involved in getting a product from the producer to the consumer. Each unit passes the product or service down the chain to the next organization, before it finally reaches the end-user. Each participant will have their own specific needs, which the producer must take into account.

Organization: Formal channels established by an organization that transmit messages that pertain to the job-related activities of members. They follow the authority network within the organization. Other forms of messages, such as personal or social, follow the informal channels in the organization.

channel conflict Konflikte in den Vertriebskanälen

Disagreement between members of a distribution channel.

Horizontal channel conflict can occur among retailers, e.g. if one feels threatened by another. Vertical conflict can occur between retailers and their suppliers when either side feels dominated by the other.

Conflicts can also arise when a manufacturer creates a new channel. such as direct e-commerce.

channel of distribution Absatzkanal; Distributionsweg

All intermediaries involved in getting a product from the manufacturer to the end user.

Intermediaries who actually take title to the merchandise and resell the goods are called merchants, e.g wholesalers and retailers. Those who act as broker but do not take title are called agents, e.g. manufacturer's representatives, brokers, and sales agents.

chapter Kapitel; Abschnitt

chapter 11

The statute of the Bankruptcy Reform Act (1978) in the USA that refers to the reorganization of partnerships, corporations, and sole traders, who are in financial difficulties. Unde chaper 11, the debtor remains in control of the business and can enter into arrangements trying to save the situation.

chapter 7

The statute of the Bankruptcy Reform Act (1978) in the USA that refers to liquidation proceedings. It provides for a trustee to be appointed by the court to make operational decisions.

character Zeichen; Charakter; Persönlichkeit; Leumund

characteristic Merkmal; Kennzeichen; charakteristisch; bezeichnend

characteristic line charakteristische Wertpapierlinie

Line relating the expected return on a security to different returns on the market.

characterization Charakterisierung

charge Gebühr; Aufwendung; Kosten; *(bookkeeping)* Belastung; Abbuchung; *(responsibility)* Verantwortung; Aufsicht; *(to ~)* belasten; abbuchen; berechnen; in Rechnung stellen; *(to entrust)* beauftragen; *(law)* zur Last legen

charging of costs Kostenbelastung

charisma Ausstrahlung; Charisma

charismatic leadership charismatische Führung

Followers make attributions of heroic or extraordinary leadership abilities when they observe certain behaviors. The five key characteristics of charismatic leaders are: 1.) vision and articulation 2.) personal risk 3.) environmental sensitivity 4.) sensitivity for follower needs 5.) unconventional behavior

chart Karte; Tabelle; *(graph)* Schaubild; Graphik; Diagramm

charter Mieten; *(by-laws)* Satzung; *(flight)* Charterflug; *(bank)* Konzession; Statut; *(to ~)* chartern; mieten

Law: document issued by a government establishing a corporate entity. Many kinds of organizations including cities are chartered.

Transportation: to hire a vehicle, usually for exclusive use.

chartered accountant zugelassener Wirtschaftsprüfer

Professional designation for British accountant. To be one, a candidate must pass rigorous examinations, as CPAs must do in the United States.

chartist Wertpapieranalytiker; Börsenkurs-; Chart-Analytiker

chartism Chartanalyse

chat room

Internet: Virtual space where internet users can communicate in real time using special software.

cheap billig; preiswert; *(inferior)* minderwertig

check Scheck; *(bill)* Rechnung; *(control)* Aufsicht; Überprüfung; *(voucher)* Gutschein; *(baggage)* Aufbewahrungsschein; *(to ~)* nachprüfen; *(to mark)* ankreuzen

Banking: a written order instructing a financial institution to pay on demand a specified amount of money from the check writer's account to the person named on the check or, to whoever bears the check to the institution for payment.

check guarantee Scheckbürgschaft

check guarantee card Scheckkarte

checking account Scheckkonto; Girokonto; Bankkonto

check list Prüfliste; Kontrollliste

check presentation Scheckeinreichung

cheque (*UK*) Scheck

cherry-picking sich die Rosinen rauspicken; wählerisches Verhalten

Metaphorical expression for the act of selecting only the best quality or products. It can be applied in many different contexts, whenever an individual or a firm are very concerned with making the best choices.

chief Leiter; Chef; Haupt-; hauptsächlich

chief executive Vorstandsvorsitzender; Vorstandschef; Firmenchef; Vorstandssprecher

chief executive officer (CEO) Vorstandsvorsitzender; Vorstandschef; Firmenchef; Vorstandssprecher

Officer who has ultimate management responsibility for an organization. The CEO reports directly to a board of directors, which is accountable to the company's owners. The CEO appoints other managers, including a president, to assist in carrying out the responsibilities of the organization. The CEO can also have the title CEO-President if the responsibilities of both positions are combined.

chief financial officer (CFO) Finanzchef; Finanzleiter

Corporate officer having full financial authority to make appropriations and authorize expenditures for an organization.

chief operating officer (COO) Betriebsleiter

Person who has full operational responsibilities for the day-to-day activities of an organization.

Children's Online Protection Act (COOPA)

Internet: act that requires websites and other online media that knowingly collect information from children under 12 years of age, amongst others, to provide notice to parents and obtain verifiable parental consent.

child support Kinderbeihilfe; Unterhalt

The legal obligation of a parent to pay money toward the care and maintenance of his/her children.

choice Wahl; Auswahl; *(best quality)* Auslese; auserlesene Qualität; Sortiment; ausgesucht; erstklassig

choose wählen; auswählen

churning Provisionsschneiderei; Spesenreiterei; Gaunerei

Excessive trading by a broker of a client's account in order to increase the broker's commissions.

CIF (cost, insurance, and freight) Kosten, Versicherung und Fracht

A term in a sales contract meaning that the cost of the goods, the insurance, and the freight to the destination are included in the contract price.

The seller normally completes the contract when the merchandise is delivered to the shipper, the freight to the point of destination is paid, and the buyer has been forwarded the bill of lading, invoice, insurance policy, and receipt showing payment of freight.

circa zirka

circle Kreis; Ring; Zyklus

circular Rundschreiben; Rundbrief; kreisförmig

circular letter of credit Kreditbrief; Reisekreditbrief

circulation Umlauf; Kreislauf; *(newspaper)* Auflage; Auflagenhöhe

In print media, the number of copies sold or distributed by a publication. In broadcast, the number of homes owning a TV/radio set within a station' s coverage area. Or, in cable TV, the number of households that subscribe to cable services for a given network. In out-of-home media, the number of people passing an advertisement who have an opportunity to see it.

circulation of money Geldumlauf; Geldverkehr

circumstance Umstand; Fall

circumstances Sachlage; Sachverhalt; Umstand; *(financial)* Vermögensverhältnisse

city-center shopping zone Einkaufszone in der Innenstadt

Store cluster situated in a city center. Major retail chain stores, department stores, speciality shops and superstores form the anchor stores in the shopping center. The stores attract shoppers from a wide region, even outside the city.

civil zivil; zivil-

Applying to ordinary citizens.

Law: Relating to private rights and remedies sought by civil actions as contrasted with criminal proceedings

civial action Zivilklage

A lawsuit that is not criminal in nature; relating to private rights and remedies sought by civil actions.

civil law Zivilrecht

The law applied by civil courts, as opposed to ecclesiastical, criminal, or military law. It is the law that regulates dealings between private citizens that are not subject to interference by the state.

civil law system Zivilrechtssystem

System of law based on a very detailed set of written laws and codes.

civil liability zivilrechtliche Haftung

Negligent acts and/or omissions for which a remedy can be provided in a court of law. For example, a person injured in someone's home can bring suit under *civil liability* law.

civil penalty Bußgeld

Monetary relief against an individual as restitution for wrongdoing by the individual. Civil penalties are imposed as a criminal sanction, while civil remedies redress wrongs between private parties.

civil remedy zivilrechtliche Einigung

civil rights Bürgerrechte

Personal rights guaranteed and protected by the Constitution, ie, freedom of speech, press, freedom from discrimination. These rights can be enforced by court action.

claim Anspruch; Forderung; *(statement)* Behauptung; *(to ~)* beanspruchen; fordern; *(to state)* behaupten

Insurance: request by an insured person for indemnification by an insurance company for loss incurred from an insured peril.

class Klasse; Gattung; *(rank)* Stand; Rangstufe; *(lecture)* Vorlesung; *(to ~)* klassifizieren; einstufen; einordnen

class action suit Gruppenklage

class barrier Klassenschranke

class consciousness Klassenbewusstsein

Tendency for individuals to perceive themselves in terms of their class background

classical conditioning klassische Konditionierung

Type of conditioning in which an individual responds to some stimulus that would not ordinarily produce such a response.

The classical conditioning grew out of experiments to teach dogs to salivate in response to the ringing of a bell, conducted at the turn of the twentieth century by the Russian physiologist, Ivan Pavlov.

classification Klassifizierung; Einteilung; Aufgliederung; Anordnung

Any method of delineating and categorizing business activities and products.

classified advertisement Kleinanzeige

Small advertisements, listed alphabetically, in a print or electronic media.

classified stock kategorisierte Aktie

Separation of ownership interest into more than one class of common stock, frequently called Class A and Class B. Class A shares usually possess an advantage in terms of voting power and additional dividend privileges.

classify einstufen; einordnen; einteilen; unterteilen; gruppieren; klassifizieren

class of stocks Aktiengattung

class society Klassengesellschaft

class struggle Klassenkampf

Antagonism between social classes resulting from different economic and social interests; first identified by Karl Marx.

One of Marx's examples is the conflict between the owners of capital (bourgeoisie) and the non-owning employees (proletariat). According to the Communist Manifesto, written during the Industrial Revolution, the workers will rise up and take over the state by force.

class system Klassensystem

System of social stratification in which social status is determined by the family into which a person is born and by subsequent socio-economic achievements. Mobility between classes is possible.

clause Klausel; Bestimmung

Insurance: sentences and paragraphs describing various coverages, exclusions, duties of the insured, locations covered, and conditions which suspend or terminate coverage.

clean sauber; unbeschränkt; geschickt; glatt; *(finance)* schuldenfrei

Accounting: unqualified audit report.

Finance: free of debt.

International trade: without documents.

clean bill of lading reines Konnossement

A receipt for goods issued by a carrier indicating that the goods were received without damages or other irregularities.

clean collection einfaches Inkasso

clean payment reine Zahlung; nichtdokumentäre Zahlung

clear klar; *(pure)* rein; *(claim)* unanfechtbar; unbelastet; *(to ~)* freigeben; *(check)* verrechnen; *(debt)* bezahlen; *(customs)* zollamtlich abfertigen

Banking: the collection of the funds on which a check is drawn, and the subsequent payment of those funds to the holder of the check.

Customs: to pass a shipment through all the examinations and requirements set by customs authorities.

clearance Freigabe; *(check)* Verrechnung; *(customs)* Zollabfertigung; *(debts)* Zahlung; *(of stock)* Lagerräumung; Leerung; Abrechnung; Genehmigung

clearing *(banking)* Verrechnung; Giroverkehr; Abwicklung

Exchange of checks and balancing of accounts between banks.

clearing balance Verrechnungssaldo

clearing bank Girobank; Verrechnungsbank; Geschäftsbank

clearinghouse Girozentrale; Abrechnungsstelle; Clearingzentrum

clearinghouse association Giroverband

clearinghouse balance Verrechnungssaldo

clearing system Verrechnungsverkehr

clearing unit Verrechnungseinheit

clerical Büro-; Schreib-; geistlich

clerical worker Büroangestellter

clerk kaufmännischer Angestellter; Büroangestellter; Schreibkraft; Sekretär

An employee who performs clerical work on behalf of his boss.

click *(to ~)* klicken, anklicken; knacken; schnappen

Term referring to pressing a mouse button to initiate an action on the computer screen.

click and mortar virtueller und nicht-virtueller Verkauf

Shopping stores with both offline and online selling.

click-stream Klickstrom; Folge von Seitenaufrufen

Record of the path a user takes through a web site. Clickstreams enable website designers to assess how their site is being used.

clickstream data Daten über Klickstrom

Data that are recorded by software either on the user PC or a web-server. Includes every page that the user visits and the frequency with which the user returns to a page.

click-through Klicken

Click-through (ad click) occurs each time a user clicks on a banner advertisement with the mouse to direct them to a web page that contains further information.

click-through rate Klickrate

Expressed as a percentage of total ad impressions, and refers to the proportion of users viewing an advertisement who click on it. It is calculated as the number of click-throughs divided by the number of ad impressions.

click-tracking Klickverfolgung

Java technology that can be used to track movements of individual users to a website.

client Klient; *(customer)* Kunde; Kundin; *(law)* Mandant

In general: a person, company, or organization that buys products or services from another.

Advertising: a manufacturer that uses the services of an advertising agency to advertise his product or service; also called account.

clientele Kundschaft; Klientel

clientele effect Klientel-Effekt

Argument that shares attract clienteles based on dividend yield or taxes. For example, a tax clientele effect is induced by the difference in tax treatment of dividend income and capital gains income; high tax-bracket individuals tend to prefer low-dividend yields.

client-side auf Seite des Clients

Refers to activities that occur on the user's computer, such as writing and sending e-mail.

client-side data collection Datensammlung über die Clienten

Information about consumer surfing is gathered at the user' s PC. One example of this is the cookie file.

climax Höhepunkt; Gipfel; Steigerung

climb steigen; klettern

clique Clique

Relatively permanent informal group that involve friendships.

clone Klon; *(to ~)* klonen

In general: An exact copy made of biological material.

Business: exact or almost exact duplicate of a product.

close Schluss; Ende; *(accounting)* Abschluss; *(business)* Geschäftsschluss; *(to ~)* schließen; *(accounting)* abschließen; zumachen

closed account abgeschlossenes Konto; ausgeglichenes Konto

Banking: account that has been terminated.

Accounting: ledger account that has been closed.

closed economy geschlossene Volkswirtschaft

An economy that does not permit economic transactions with the outside world, and in which all production and consumption is contained within itself.

closed-end question geschlossene Frage

Question in marketing research that include all the possible answers and allow subjects to make choices among them.

closed loop marketing

Internet: tracks user with cookie files as long as the user remains in one of the web sites on that loop or network.

closed shop gewerkschaftspflichtiger Betrieb

Organization where workers are required to be in a union before they can be hired.

closed stock Sammelware

Products sold only in sets, individual parts of which cannot be purchased separately. Example: set of glasses.

closely held corporation Gesellschaft mit beschränkter Mitgliederzahl

Corporation in which five or fewer individuals owned more than 50% of the value of all outstanding stock during the last half of the year.

close of the year Jahresschluss

closing Auflösung; Auflassung; Abschluss

Step in the selling process in which the salesperson asks the customer for an order.

closing date Anmeldeschluss; Einsendeschluss; Abgabefrist; Schlusstermin; Anzeigenschluss

Real estate: The date specified in the contract on which a sale becomes final and the new owner takes possession.

Advertising: The date by which all material for an advertisement to appear in a forthcoming publication has to be submitted.

closing inventory Endbestand; Schlussbestand

The value and quantitiy of stock on hand at the end of an accounting period, measured either at cost or retail value.

closing of account Kontoauflösung

closing purchase Abschlusskauf; Kauf zum Börsenschluss

Transaction in which the purchaser's intention is to reduce or eliminate a short position in a stock, or in a given series of options.

closing sale Ausverkauf; Schlussverkauf

Transaction in which the seller's intention is to reduce or eliminate his long position in a stock, or a given series of options

closing session Abschlusssitzung

closure Schließung; Schluss

clout Einfluss; Macht; Durchschlagkraft

club Verein; Treff; Klub; Schläger

cluster Cluster, Anhäufung; Traube; Gruppe; *(to ~)* anhäufen

cluster analysis Clusteranalyse; Gruppenanalyse

A statistical technique for grouping similarities or differences between a set of objects or persons.

One common application is to characterize the interests of customer clusters such as yuppies, so that promotion can be specifically targeted to them.

clustering Clustering

Description of the phenomenon that firms from the same industry gather together in close proximity.

Clustering is particularly evident in industries like banking. Banking centres in cities such as London and New York have thrived for centuries.

The proximity enables firms to benefit from a pool of expertise, skilled workers, and information channels.

cluster sampling Clusterstichprobenverfahren; Clusterauswahl

coalition Koalition; Vereinigung; Bund

Informal group bound together by the active pursuit of a single issue. Successful coalitions have been found to contain fluid membership and are able to form swiftly, achieve their target issue, and quickly disappear.

co-branding gemeinsame Markenpraxis

Practice of using the established brand names of two different companies on one product, e.g. Bacardi Coke.

The aim is that the brands are strengthened if they are seen as complementary. This is a reciprocal arrangement, which can occur without payment.

code Code; Chiffrierschlüssel; *(law)* Gesetzbuch; Kodex; *(to ~)* kodieren

co-decide mitentscheiden

code law Gesetzbuch

code of commerce Handelsgesetzbuch

codetermination Mitbestimmung

Process by which both labor and management participate in the management of a company.

codetermine mitbestimmen

coercive power Macht durch Bestrafung; Macht durch Zwangsausübung

Power based on fear. People react to this power out of fear of the negative results that might occur if they failed to comply.

cofounder Mitbegründer

cognitive behavior kognitives Verhalten

cognitive component of an attitude kognitive Komponente einer Einstellung

cognitive dissonance kognitive Dissonanz

Marketing: state of mental conflict a consumer might find himself in if perception and reality don´t seem to fit.

For example, a consumer may believe the advertising for a product, which claims that the product is the most effective one. A competitor's advertisement, however, might seem to prove conclusively that this competitive product is better.

cognitive evaluation theory Theorie der kognitiven Evaluation

Allocating extrinsic rewards for behavior that had been previously intrinsically rewarding trends to decrease the overall level of motivation. The individual experiences a loss of control over the own behavior so that the previous intrinsic motivation diminishes.

cognitive resource theory kognitive-Ressourcen-Theorie

Theory of leadership that states that stress notably effects the situations, and intelligence and experience can lessen the influence of stress on the leader. The essence of the new theory by Fiedler and Joe Garcia, is that stress is the enemy of rationality. Intelligence and experience interfere with each other.

cognitive skill kognitive Fähigkeiten

cohesiveness Kohäsion; Gruppenzusammenhalt

Degree to which group members are attracted to each other and are motivated to stay in the group.

Cohesiveness is important, because it has been found to be related to the group's productivity. The relationship of cohesiveness and productivity depends on the performance-related norms established by the group.

cohort Kohorte

Individuals who, as a part of a group, hold a common attribute. Groups and organizations are composed of cohorts.

coin Münze; Geldstück; *(to ~)* münzen; prägen

coin changing machine Geldwechselautomat

coin collection Münzensammlung

co-insurance effect Mitversicherungseffekt

Refers to the fact that the merger of two firms decreases the probability of default on either's debt.

cold calling unangemeldete Kundenansprache

Approach to selling in which a sales representative makes calls, door-to-door, by post, or by telephone, to people who have not previously shown any interest in the product.

The primary objective in cold calling is to establish a favorable relationship quickly, enabling the representative to explain the benefits of their product or service before being dismissed.

collaborate zusammenarbeiten; mitarbeiten

collaborating Zusammenarbeit

Conflict resolution: Situation in which the conflicting parties each desire to satisfy fully the concerns of all parties. They try to find a win-win solution that allows both parties' goals to be completely achieved and seeking a conclusion that incorporates the valid insights of both parties.

collaboration Zusammenarbeit; Mitarbeit

collaborator Mitarbeiter

collaborative filtering Filtern von gleich gesinnten Meinungen

Internet: Software that gathers opinions of like-minded users online and returns those opinions to the individual in real time.

collapse Zusammenbruch; Scheitern *(to ~)* zusammenbrechen; -fallen; stürzen;

collateral Pfand; Sicherheit; *(cover)* Deckung;

In commercial transactions, collateral is an assets that is offered to secure a loan.

colleague Kollege; Mitarbeiter

Fellow member of a profession, association, occupation, or organization.

collect sammeln; *(to cash)* kassieren; einziehen; *(to demand)* einfordern; abholen

collect call R-Gespräch

collection Sammlung; *(cashing)* Inkasso; Einziehung; *(demand)* Einforderung

In general: the conversion of accounts receivable into cash.

Banking: the presentation of a negotiable instrument such as a draft or a check to the place at which it is payable.

collective bargaining Tarifverhandlung

Process of negotiation between employers or their representatives and workers, normally organized in unions, on wages and other employment conditions.

collection float Inkassofloat

Increase in book cash with no immediate change in bank cash, generated by checks deposited by the firm that have not cleared.

collection item Inkassopapier

collection paper Inkassopapier

collection policy Inkassopolitik

Procedures followed by a firm in attempting to collect accounts receivable.

collection ratio Forderungsumschlag

Ratio of a company's accounts receivable to its average daily sales. The *collection ratio* is the average number of days it takes the company to convert receivables into cash. It is also called *average collection period.*

collective Gemeinschaft; gemeinsam

collective agreement Tarifabkommen

collective bargainer Tarifpartner

collective bargaining Tarifverhandlung; Tarifautonomie

collective consignment Sammelsendung; Beipacksendung

collective shipment Sammelsendung

collective transfer Sammelüberweisung

collectivism Kollektivismus; zentrale Wirtschaftsplanung

Emphasis on collective goals as opposed to individual goals. A national culture attribute describing the degree to which people prefer to act as individuals rather than a member of a group.

collector Sammler; *(debts)* Inkassobeamter; *(taxes)* Steuereinnehmer; Kollektor

collector's item Sammlerobjekt

collector's value Sammlerwert

collusion geheime Absprache; geheimes Einverständnis; Kollusion

The illegal practice of two or more companies making secret agreements for their mutual benefit. Example: price fixing or other market interference.

column Säule; *(newspaper)* Rubrik; Spalte; *(figures)* Zahlenreihe

combination Verbindung; Zusammenschluss; Kombination

combine Trust; Pool; Kombinat; *(to ~)* zusammenschließen; *(to merge)* fusionieren; vereinen; verbinden

combined shipment gebrochener Güterverkehr; Sammelladung

Transport of goods using different modes of transport

combined transport bill of lading kombiniertes Transportkonnossement; Sammel(ladungs)konnossement

combined transport operator Kombinationstransportunternehmer

comeback Wiederaufstieg

come to terms sich einigen

Council for Mutual Economic Aid (COMECON)

Former economic association of Eastern European communist states headed by the former Soviet Union.

command Befehl; *(leadership)* Führung; Herrschaft; *(mastery)* Beherrschung; *(to ~)* befehlen; kommandieren; anordnen; *(to have available)* verfügen über

An instruction by a superior to carry out an action.

command economy Planwirtschaft

Economic system where the allocation of resources, including determination of what goods and services should be produced, and in what quantity and what price, is planned by the government or a central non-market authority.

command group Weisungsgruppe

Is determined by the organization chart. It is composed of the individuals who report directly to a given manager.

commence beginnen; anfangen

commensurate im rechten Verhältnis; angemessen; entsprechend

comment Kommentar; Bemerkung; Erläuterung; *(to ~)* kommentieren; Bemerkung machen

commentary Kommentar

commerce *(trade)* Handel; *(flow of merchandise)* Warenverkehr

commercial geschäftlich; kaufmännisch; kommerziell; *(advertising)* Werbesendung

Advertising: an advertising message that is broadcast on television or radio.

A commercial is normally produced by an advertising agency as it must be creatively designed to deliver a message with words, sound, music, sight and motion.

commercial attaché Handelsattaché

commercial bank Geschäftsbank; Handelsbank

A bank that offers a broad range of services to individuals and businesses, most commonly deposit accounts, including checking, savings, and time deposits, and the extension of loans.

commercial center Geschäftszentrum

commercial code Handelsgesetzbuch

commercial debt Warenschuld

commercial draft Handelswechsel

commercial establishment Handelshaus; Handelsunternehmen

commercial invoice Handelsrechnung; Faktura

commercial interest reference rates kommerzielle Referenzzinssätze

commercialization Kommerzialisierung; Vermarktung

commercial law Handelsrecht

Body of law that which governs business and commerce. It is concerned with the rights and obligations of persons in their commercial dealings with one another.

commercial lender Geschäftskreditgeber

commercial loan Geschäftskredit; Warenkredit; gewerblicher Kredit

commercial paper Handelspapier; Warenwechsel; Wertpapier

commercial relationship Handelsbeziehung

commercial risk wirtschaftliches Risiko

commercial sector gewerblicher Bereich

Economy: the sector which includes non-manufacturing businesses, such as hotels, motels, restaurants, wholesale businesses, retail stores, and health, social, and educational institutions.

commercial shipment Warenversand

commercial treaty Handelsabkommen

commercial visa Handelsvisum

commission Provision; Courtage; *(committee)* Ausschuss; Kommission; *(to ~)* beauftragen; bevollmächtigen; bestellen

Organization: a type of organizational body that is formed to solve a particular problem. Commissions normally have a limited life, but they can also be permanent, such as governmental trade commission.

Commerce: a fee paid to an employee or agent for services performed, normally as a percentage of a total amount received in a transaction. A salary, on the other hand, is a fixed amount payable periodically.

commission agent Kommissionär

commission earnings Provisionseinnahme; Provisionsertrag

commissioner Beauftragter; Bevollmächtigter; Kommissar

commission on sales Umsatzprovision

commission rate Provisionsgebühr

commission receipts Provisionsertrag

commit *(to entrust)* anvertrauen; *(to commit oneself)* sich verpflichten; *(to perpetrate)* übergeben; festlegen

commitment *(obligation)* Verpflichtung; Obligo; Engagement; *(consignment)* Überweisung

The act of binding oneself to a course of action.

Commerce: A binding financial obligation typically in the form of a purchase order, such a purchaser entering into *commitment* to buy goods from a supplier at a specified price by a specified date.

committee Komitee; Ausschuss

A formal working group within a larger organisation, with a defined authority or legitimacy. Often made up of members from across departmental lines.

commodities Güter; Waren; Rohstoffe; Massenartikel

commodities futures Warentermingeschäfte

Contracts, up to one year, in which sellers promise to deliver a given commodity by a certain date at a predetermined price. The contract specifies the item, the price, the expiration date, and a standardized unit to be traded. Price is agreed to by open outcry on the floor of the commodities exchange.

commodity Ware; Erzeugnis; Massenartikel

A product that is traded primarily on the basis of price, and not on differences in quality or features. *Examples:* agricultural products, fuels, and minerals. Manufactured goods are considered as commodities if purchasing decisions are made almost solely on the price of the product.

commodity futures Warenterminhandel

commodity futures market Warenterminmarkt

commodity price Warenpreis; Rohstoffpreis

commodity sale Warenverkauf

common üblich; gewöhnlich; *(shared)* gemeinsam; *(public)* öffentlich; allgemein; häufig

Common Agriculture Policy (CAP) gemeinsame Agrarpolitik (GAP)

EU policy to support free trade within the Common Market and to protect farmers in the member states.

The Commission fixes a threshold price, below which cereals may not be imported into the EU. It also buys surplus cereals at an agreed intervention price in order to help farmers achieve a reasonable average price, called the target price.

Prices are also agreed for meats, poultry, eggs, fruit, and vegetables with similar arrangements.

Common Budget Gemeinsamer EU Haushalt

The fund, administered by the European Commission. into which all levies and customs duties on goods entering the European Union are paid and from which all subsidies due under the Common Agricultural Policy are taken.

Common External Tariff (CET) gemeinsamer Außenzoll

The tariff of import duties payable on certain goods entering any country in the European Union from non-member countries. Income from these duties is paid into the Common Budget.

Common Gateway Interface (CGI)

CGI provides a standard way to run gateway programs or scripts, on a web server.

CGI programs can process data from web page forms, generate web pages dynamically from database and perform many other useful functions

common law Gewohnheitsrecht

Law based on judicial precedent (court decisions) rather than on legislative enactment (statutes). It is therefore derived from principles rather than rules.

common law system Rechtssystem basierend auf dem Gewohnheitsrecht

System of jurisprudence found in the United Kingdom and former British colonies, ranging from Australia to the United States. System of law based on tradition, precedent, custom and usage. When law courts interpret common law, they do so with regard to these characteristics.

common market gemeinsamer Markt

Form of regional economic integration in which a group of countries is committed to (1) removing all barriers to the free flow of goods, services, and factors of production between each other and (2) the pursuit of a common external trade policy.

Example: the *European Economic Community (EEC).*

common stock Stammaktie

Financial security representing an ownership interest in a corporation. Ownership may also be shared with preferred stock, which has prior claim on any dividends to be paid and, in the event of liquidation, to the distribution of the corporation's assets.

Balance sheet: Value of outstanding common shares at par, plus accumulated retained earnings. Also called shareholders' equity

common stock equivalent stammaktiengleiches Papier; stammaktienäquivalent

Preferred stock or bond convertible into common stock, or warrant to purchase common stock at a specified price or discount from market price. Common stock equivalents represent potential dilution of existing common shareholder equity.

common stockholders Aktionäre

The common stockholders are the owners of a corporation, assuming the primary risk and entitled to a share of the profit in the form of dividends.

common stock ratio Stammaktienanteil

Percentage of total capitalization represented by common stock. From a creditor's standpoint, a high ratio represents a margin of safety in the event of liquidation. From an Investor's standpoint, a high ratio can mean a lack of leverage.

Commonwealth of Independent States (CIS) Gemeinschaft Unabhängiger Staaten (GUS)

communicate mitteilen; in Verbindung stehen; übertragen; verkehren

communication Kommunikation; *(message)* Mitteilung; Benachrichtigung; *(relationship)* Verbindung; *(telecommunication)* Fernmeldewesen; *(flow)* Informationsfluss

communications and collaboration Kommunikation und Zusammenarbeit

Part of internet commercialization, which includes gathering and processing information, communicating, collaborating, and publishing. All media that place their content online for subscription or as advertising fall into this category.

communication apprehension Kommunikationsangst

Undue tension and anxiety about oral communication, written communication, or both. As a result, people may rely on memos or faxes to convey messages when a phone call would not only be faster but also appropriate.

communication network Informationsnetz; Kommunikationsnetzwerk

Channels by which information flows. These channels are either formal or informal.

communication policy Informationspolitik

communication process Kommunikationsprozess

Steps between a source and a receiver that result in the transference and understanding of meaning.

The communication process is made up of seven parts: (1) communication source, (2) encoding, (3) message, (4) channel, (5) decoding, (6) receiver, and (7) feedback.

communication skills Kommunikationsfähigkeiten

communication system Informationssystem

communication technology Informationstechnik; Kommunikationstechnik

communism Kommunismus

Collectivistic ideology advocating that socialism can be achieved only through a revolution and a totalitarian dictatorship of the proletariat.

Amongst the many communist writers, Karl Marx has been the most influential. Common to most is the call for collective ownership of the means of production as the basis for a better society.

Communism was first achiveved in practice in the Soviet Union after the revolution of 1917, and until the revolutions of 1989 proposed an existing alternative economic system in which production facilities were state-owned and production decisions made by official policy and not directed by market action.

community Gemeinde; Gemeinschaft ; Kommunion

commute pendeln

commuter Pendler

A person who travels regularly between two places, normally working in one and living in the other.

commuting Pendeln

The process of traveling between one´s place of residence and place of work.

company (Handels-)Gesellschaft; *(firm)* Firma; *(enterprise)* Unternehmen; *(plant)* Betrieb; Gesellschaft; Gruppe

A group of people united to pursue a common interest, synonymous with association, but used specifically to identify associations formed for profit, such as a partnership, a joint-stock company, or a corporation. A company is not necessarily a corporation and does not have a separate existence from its members.

company brand Firmenmarke

company car Firmenwagen

Car owned by the firm, but available for use to certain employees.

company earnings Betriebsergebnis

company management Unternehmensleitung

company pension Betriebsrente

company union Betriebsgewerkschaft

A labor union sympathetic to the management of the company where it operates which may not necessarily represent the true interests of the workers it represents.

comparability Vergleichbarkeit

comparable vergleichbar

comparative vergleichend; relativ; komparativ

comparative advantage komparativer Vorteil

International trade theory holding that countries should specialize in the production of goods and services they can produce most efficiently.

Countries increase their economic prosperity by exporting the goods that they are relatively more efficient at producing and importing the goods that other countries are relatively more efficient at producing.

comparative advertising vergleichende Werbung

Advertising that compares one product or brand, either directly or indirectly, with one or more other products or brands.

The practice is legally restricted in many markets, and even if it not, consumers often react with a feeling of uncertainty. This reflects to a degree their cultural disposition.

Examples of comparative advertising is in the car industry, comparing the availability of a range of features on competitors' models in the same price bracket

comparatively vergleichsweise

compare vergleichen

comparison Vergleich

compartment *(department)* Abteilung; Fach; *(railroad)* Abteil

compatible verträglich; vereinbar; zusammenpassend; *(computer)* kompatibel

Term describing a device capable of being used with or connected to other devices or components without modification. For example, two computers that can run the same programs.

compensate *(to make up for)* entschädigen; ausgleichen; *(to pay)* entlohnen; erstatten; kompensieren

compensating balance Mindestguthaben; Sicherheitsguthaben

A minimum account balance that a borrower is required to maintain as a condition for obtaining a loan.

A standard requirement for a bank line of credit is 10% of the line plus an additional 10% of the borrowings.

compensation *(for damage)* Schadensersatz; Abfindung; Ausgleich; *(salary)* Vergütung; Entlohnung

General: something given or received as payment or reparation for a service performed or a loss or injury.

Employment: any kind of reward given to an employee for their performance, can be direct or indirect, moneatar or non-monetary.

compensation charge Ausgleichsabgabe

compensation package Gesamtvergütung

compensation trade Kompensationshandel

compensatory entschädigend; ausgleichend; kompensierend

compensatory duty Ausgleichsabgabe

compensatory trade Ausgleichshandel

compete konkurrieren; im Wettbewerb stehen

compete for sich bewerben

competence *(ability)* Befähigung; *(authority)* Zuständigkeit; Kompetenz; Befugnis

competent fähig; kompetent; fachkundig

competing Selbstbehauptung

Desire to satisfy one's interests, regardless of the impact on the other party to the conflict.

competing country Konkurrenzland

competition Konkurrenz; Wettbewerb; *(competing)* Konkurrenzkampf; Wettkampf; *(lottery)* Wettspiel

Rivalry between suppliers providing goods or services for a market.

Lottery: promotional event that gives consumers the chance to win something – such as cash, trips or goods – by luck or through extra effort.

competition policy Wettbewerbspolitik

Regulations by states and organizations designed to promote competition and restrict monopoly practices.

competitive konkurrenzfähig; wettbewerbsfähig; auf Wettbewerb beruhend; *(individual)* ehrgeizig

competitive advantage Wettbewerbsvorteil

Concept which was given new significance by Michael Porter with his influential book *Competitive Advantage*. It provided managers with a framework for strategic thinking about how to beat their competitors.

Porter argued that competitive advantage is "...a function of either providing comparable buyer value more efficiently than competitors (low cost), or performing activities at comparable cost but in unique ways that create more buyer value than competitors and, hence, command a premium price (differentiation)."

Behind the conept lay an innovative way of looking at the firm as a series of activities which link together into what Porter called "a value chain".

Each of the links in the chain adds value, that is, something that customers are prepared to pay for. Even a company's support activities, such as training and compensation systems, can be links in the chain and sources of competitive advantage in their own right.

competitive analysis Wettbewerbsanalyse

competitive bid geheime Gebotsabgabe

Sealed bid, containing price and terms, submitted by a prospective contractor to a purchaser, who awards the contract to the bidder with the best price and terms.

Example: municipalities, railroads and public utilities use this bid system.

competitive dynamics Wettbewerbsdynamik

competitive disadvantage Wettbewerbsnachteil

competitive intelligence Wettbewerbsforschung; Wettbewerbsanalyse

Analysis of the industries in which a firm operates as input to the firm's strategic positioning and to understand competitor vulnerabilities.

competitiveness Wettbewerbsfähigkeit; Konkurrenzfähigkeit

competitive offer Konkurrenzangebot

Method of selecting an investment banker for a new issue by offering the securities to the underwriter bidding highest.

competitive parity method Methode der Wettbewerbsparität

Setting the promotion budget to match competitors' outlays.

competitive position Wettbewerbsposition

competitive pricing konkurrenzfähige Preisfestsetzung

competitive strategy Wettbewerbsstrategie

In general: strategy that seeks to establish a profitable and sustainable position against the forces that determine industry competition.

Advertising: promotional strategy used in an advertising campaign that is designed to compete with rival brands, such as trying to discredit another brand or undercut it in terms of price.

competitor Konkurrent; Wettbewerber; Mitbewerber

Company whose product or service can be used to satisfy consumer needs in a market where other companies try to satisfy the same needs.

competitor analysis Konkurrenzanalyse

Process of identifying key competitors; assessing their objectives, strategies, strengths and weaknesses, and reaction patterns; and selecting which competitors to attack or avoid.

competitor-centered company konkurrenzorientiertes Unternehmen

Company whose moves are mainly based on competitors' actions and reactions; it spends most of its time tracking competitors' moves and market shares and trying to find strategies to counter them.

compilation Zusammenstellung; Aufstellung; Erstellung; Erfassung

Accounting: Process of transferring the data from a general ledger or trial balance to a financial statement, normally prior to the accountant's assurance as to conformity with generally accepted accounting principles.

complain sich beschweren; sich beklagen; *(faulty merchandise)* reklamieren; beanstanden

complaint Beschwerde; Klage; Leiden; *(faulty merchandise)* Reklamation; Beanstandung

A written statement that begins a civil lawsuit, in which the plaintiff details the claims against the defendant.

In criminal law, the preliminary charge or accusation made by one person against another to the appropriate court. Court proceedings, such as a trial, are only instituted after an indictment or information has been handed down against the defendant.

complement Ergänzung; volle Anzahl *(to ~)* ergänzen

complementary komplementär; ergänzend

complementary asset komplementäres Wirtschaftsgut

complementary goods komplementäre Güter; Komplementärgüter

Products that usually are consumed together, such as cars and gasoline. Demand for one falls when the other's price rises; demand for one increases when the price of the other decreases.

complete vollständig; vollendet; komplett; *(to ~)* beenden; vollenden; vervollständigen; *(a form)* ausfüllen

complete financials date Termin der letzte vollständigen Finanzaufstellung

Date that indicates the last quarter or annual update with a complete set of financial records.

completion Vollendung; Fertigstellung; Beendigung; Abschluss; *(of a form)* Ausfüllen

completion allowance Abschlußbonus

complex kompliziert; komplex; verzweigt; verflochten; verwickelt

complex buying behavior komplexes Einkaufsverhalten

Consumer buying behavior in situations characterized by high consumer involvement in a purchase and significant perceived differences among brands.

complexity Kompliziertheit; Verflechtung; Verzweigtheit; Schwierigkeit

compliance Befolgung; Einhaltung; Willfährigkeit

comply befolgen; einhalten; sich richten; sich fügen

component Bestandteil; Komponente

component part Einzelteil; Bestandteil

composite zusammengesetzt

compound Zusammensetzung; *adj* zusammengesetzt; *(to ~)* zusammensetzen

compound duty gemischter Wertzoll

compound growth rate Gesamtwachstumsrate

The rate of growth of a figure, compounded over some period, generally years. The rate accounts for growth from the base period to the ending period in the same manner as compound interest.

compounding Aufzinsung

Process of reinvesting each interest payment to earn more interest. Compounding is based on the idea that interest itself becomes principal and therefore also earns interest in subsequent periods.

compound interest Zinseszinsen

Interest that is earned not only on the initial principal but also the accumulated interest of prior periods. The interest earned in one period becomes part of the principal in a following period. Interest can be compounded on daily, quarterly, annually or other basis.

Example: if €100 are invested at 10% interest, the depositor will be credited with €110 at the end of the first year and €121 at the end of the second year. That extra €1, which was earned on the €10 interest from the first year, is the *compound interest.*

comprehend verstehen; erfassen; begreifen

comprehensive umfassend; umfangreich

comprehensive coverage *(car insurance)* Vollkasko

compressed workweek komprimierte Arbeitswoche

Four-day week, with employees working 10 hours a day. The program was conceived to allow workers more leisure time and shopping time.

Such a program can increase employee enthusiasm, morale, and commitment to the organization, increase productivity and reduce costs.

comprise enthalten; einschließen; erfassen; umfassen; einbeziehen

compromise Kompromiss; Vergleich; Gefährdung; *(to ~)* einen Kompromiss schließen; *(to endanger)* gefährden; *(to expose)* bloßstellen

The process or result of concessions from both sides of a dispute with the aim of finding a solution acceptable to both. In a true compromise each party concedes something the other side finds acceptable.

compromising Kompromisse suchen; kompromittierend

Situation in which each party to a conflict is willing to give up something. There is no clear winner or loser. Rather, there is a willingness to ration the object of the conflict and accept a solution that provides incomplete satisfaction of both parties' concerns. Intentions provide general guidelines for parties in a conflict situation. They define each party's purpose.

Examples: willingness to accept a raise of $1 an hour rather than $2, to acknowledge partial agreement with a specific viewpoint, and to take partial blame for an infraction.

comptroller (amtlicher) Rechnungsprüfer; Kostenprüfer; *(auditor)* Revisor; Controller

Term for a corporate or public official; its meaning and pronunciation are identical to *controller*.

compulsory obligatorisch; zwingend; pflichtmäßig; zwangsweise

compulsory insurance Pflichtversicherung

compulsory loan Zwangsanleihe

compulsory registration Meldepflicht

compulsory retirement Zwangspensionierung

Practice of being forced to resign from one's employment at an age specified by contract or company policy.

CompuServe

Pioneering internet company and oldest internet service provider, bought in 1997 by America Online (AOL) and maintained as a separate brand.

computation Berechnung; Rechnung

computation of interest Zinsrechnung

compute be-; errechnen; kalkulieren

computer Computer; Elektronenrechner

computer-aided manufacturing (CAM) computerunterstützte Fertigung

All approaches to use computers to control industrial processes, from brewing, to chemical manufacture, oil refining, and steel making.

computer aided personal interview (CAPI) computerunsterstützes Interview

A method of interviewing using laptop computers to conduct personal interviews and transmit the resulting data immediately. This approach dramatically reduces the time of the research process.

computer-assisted design (CAD) computergestützte Entwicklung

The use of computers to aid in product design and development. It consists of developing three-dimensional designs where the computer performs all mathematical calculations and dynamically develops the resulting images.

CAD enables experimentation without large costs or extensive time delays, resulting in faster product development.

computer-assisted telephone interview (CATI) computerunterstütztes Telefoninterview

An approach to telephone interviewing where the interviewer uses a computer and a computerized questionnaire. The interviewer keys in the answers directly which reduces errors and enables the required statistics to be extracted automatically.

computer-assisted trading (CAT) computergestützter Handel

The use of computers by brokers and traders on a market, such as a stock exchange or foreign-exchange market, to facilitate trading by displaying prices, recording deals, etc

computer center Rechenzentrum

computer company Computerfirma

computer-controlled computergesteuert

computer data Computerdaten

Computer Decency Act (CDA)

Amendment in 1996 in the 1934 federal Telecommunications Act, to include the legislation which made it a criminal act to send an obscene or indecent communication to a recipient who was known to the sender to be under 18 years of age.

computer game Computerspiel

computer integrated manufacturing (CIM) computerintegrierte Fertigung; computerintegrierte Herstellung

Fully integrated computerized manufacturing system combining all the processes from design, engineering, manufacturing, and marketing.

computerize computerisieren; auf Datenverarbeitung umstellen

computerized cash register Computerkasse

computer keyboard Computertastatur

computer operation Computerverfahren

computer program Computerprogramm

computer programming Computerprogrammierung

The process of writing the instructions that a computer must follow to solve a problem. The list of all instructions is called the program.

The steps involved in writing a program are: problem definition, planning, program prepartion, testing, removing errors, and documenting.

computer room Rechenzentrale

computer screen Computerbildschirm

computer technology Computertechnologie

conceal verheimlichen; verbergen; verhehlen; *(balance sheet)* verschleiern

concealment Geheimhaltung; Verbergen; Verhehlen; Versteck

In general: an attempt to hide or to prevent for recognition or disclosure.

Insurance: if an insured withholds information about which the insurance company has no knowledge, the company can void the contract.

Example: the insured in a life insurance does not teell the company that he is suffering from a heart disease.

concede zugestehen; einräumen; gewähren

concentrate sich konzentrieren; konzentrieren

concentrated marketing Konzentriertes Marketing

Technique when a firm selects one segment and develops one or more marketing mixes to meet the needs of that segment; also called *niche marketing.*

concentration Konzentration; Anhäufung; Aufmerksamkeit; Dichte; Gehalt

concept Begriff; Auffassung; Erfindung; Konzept

concept testing Akzeptanztest eines Werbekonzeptes

The process of evaluating consumer response to a product idea prior to the introduction of a product to the market.

Adverstising: Research testing an advertsing idea or concept that has been developed, in order to assess the effectiveness of an advertising campaign in reaching its objectives.

conceptual skills konzeptionelle Fähigkeiten

Mental ability to analyze and diagnose complex situations. Decision making, for instance, requires managers to spot problems, identify alternatives that can correct them, evaluate those alternatives, and select the best one.

concern *(business)* Betrieb; Unternehmen; Konzern; *(interest)* Interesse; Angelegenheit; *(worry)* Besorgnis; *(to ~)* betreffen; angehen; *(to occupy with)* sich beschäftigen mit

concern director Konzernchef

concerning hinsichtlich; betreffend

concern leadership Konzernführung

concern management Konzernführung

concerted gemeinschaftlich; aufeinander abgestimmt; wohlausgewogen

concession Konzession; *(conceding)* Zugeständnis; *(granting)* Gewährung; *(trade license)* Gewerbeerlaubnis

The right to operate a business, either granted by a government or by a some other business holding the relevant rights. *Examples*: a service station on a highway, a small shop in a hotel, or a catering business in a theme park.

conciliation *(arbitration)* Schlichtung; Versöhnung; *(settlement)* Ausgleich

A form of dispute resolution in which the parties search the help of a neutral third party, who helps lower tensions, improve communications, and explore possible solutions. Conciliation is similar to mediation, but normally less formal.

conciliator Friedensstifter; Schiedsrichter; Schlichter

Trusted third person who provides an informal communication link between the negotiator and the opponent.

His approach includes fact-finding, interpreting messages, and persuading disputants to develop agreements.

conclude abschließen; schließen; *(to finish)* erledigen; enden; beenden; *(to deduce)* folgern; beschließen

conclusion Abschluss; Ende; *(deduction)* Schlussfolgerung

conclusion of an agreement Vertragsabschluss

conclusion of a sale Auftragsabschluss; Verkaufsabschluss

conclusive beweiskräftig; endgültig; überzeugend; schlüssig

concur zusammentreffen; zusammenwirken; *(to agree)* übereinstimmen

concurrence Zusammenwirken; *(agreement)* Übereinstimmung

concurrent gleichzeitig; übereinstimmend

condition Lage; Zustand; Beschaffenheit; Verfassung; *(prerequisite)* Bedingung; Kondition; *(to ~)* bedingen; konditionieren

conditional Bedingungs-; bedingt

conditionality Bedingtheit

conditional sales contract Kaufvertrag unter Eigentumsvorbehalt

Arrangement whereby the firm retains legal ownership of the goods until the customer has completed payment.

condominium Eigentumswohnung

A form of property ownership in which the homeowner holds title to an individual unit, such as an appartment, and pays a maintenance fee for the upkeep of common property such as gardens, lobbies, and elevators.

conduct Führung; Leitung; *(behavior)* Verhalten; Betragen; *(to ~)* führen; leiten; betreiben; *(to behave)* sich verhalten; sich betragen

confer *(to grant)* gewähren; *(a degree)* verleihen; *(to discuss)* sich beraten; konferieren

conference Konferenz; Besprechung; Sitzung

confidence Vertrauen; Zutrauen; Zuversicht;

confidence indicator Vertrauensanzeiger

Measure of investors' faith in the economy and the securities market. A low or deteriorating level of confidence is considered by many technical analysts as a bearish sign.

confidence interval Konfidenzintervall; Vertrauensintervall

confidence level Aussagewahrscheinlichkeit

The level of certainty to which an estimate can be trusted.

confident zuversichtlich

confidential vertraulich; geheim

A type of information that may be disclosed only to authorized individuals, such as conversations and records between an attorney and his client.

confidentiality Vertraulichkeit

confine beschränken; einschränken; einsperren

confirm bestätigen; bekräftigen; rechtsgültig vollziehen

confirmation Bestätigung; Konfirmation, Firmung

confirmed letter of credit bestätigtes Akkreditiv

confiscation Beschlagnahme; Einziehung; Konfiszierung

conflict Konflikt; Widerspruch; *(to ~)* in Widerspruch stehen; sich entgegenstehen; widerstreiten

conflict between bondholders and shareholders Interessenkonflikt zwischen Gläubigern und Aktionären

These two groups may have interests in the company that conflict. Sources of conflict include dividends, dilution, distortion of investment and underinvestment. Protective covenants work to resolve these conflicts.

conflicting widersprüchlich; widersprechend; widerstreitend; sich entgegenstehend

conflict management Konflikt-management; Konflikthandhabung

Use of resolution and simulation techniques to achieve the desired level of conflict.

Conflict resolution techniques include: problem solving, superordinate goal, expansion of resources, avoidance, smoothing, compromise, authoritative command, altering the human variable, and altering the structural variables.

conflict of interest Interessenkonflikt

A conflict between an individual's personal interest and his public duty.

conflict process Konfliktverlauf

Process of removing or solving conflict situations between two or more parties. Five stages can be distinguished:

Potential opposition or incompatibility: presence of conditions that create opportunities for conflict to arise.

Cognition and personalization: the perception of the conflict is required. Conflict issues have to be defined and the parties have to spell out what the conflict is about.

Intentions: decisions to act in a given way. Each party infers the other's intent in order to know how to respond to that behavior.

Behavior: conflict becomes visible. The behavior stage includes the statements, actions, and reactions made by the conflicting parties.

Outcomes: the action-reaction interplay between the conflicting parties results in consequences, which may be functional, i.e. the conflict results in an improvement, or dysfunctional, i.e. further performance is hindered.

conflict resolution Konfliktlösung

conflict settlement Konfliktregelung

conflict situation Konfliktfall

conform übereinstimmend; konform; *(to ~)* anpassen; sich anpassen; sich fügen; *(to agree)* übereinstimmen

conformed copy bestätigte Kopie

An exact copy of a document in which essential legal features, such as signature and seal, have been replaced by a notation.

conformity Übereinstimmung; Angepaßtsein; Konformität

Groups: adjusting one's behavior with the norms of the group. Conformity to social norms is higher in collectivist cultures than in individualistic cultures.

confused positioning unklare Positionierung

Positioning error that leaves consumers with a confused image of the company, its product or brand.

conglomerate Konzern; Großkonzern; Ansammlung; *(to ~)* zusammenballen

A corporation that has diversified its operations, usually by acquiring enterprises in widely varied industries. The perceived advantages of conglomerates are better management and sounder financial backing, and therefore the potential to generate more profit than small independent companies.

conglomerate acquisition unverbundene Akquisition

Acquisition in which the acquired firm and the acquiring firm are not in a related industry, unlike a horizontal or a vertical acquisition.

congress Tagung; Kongress

connect verbinden; in Verbindung stehen; *(train)* Anschluss haben

connection Anschluss; Anschließung; Verbindung;

connoisseur Kenner

conscientious gewissenhaft

conscientiousness Gewissenhaftigkeit; Pflichtbewusstsein

Personality dimension that describes someone who is responsible, dependable, persistent, and organized.

consecutive aufeinander folgend; hintereinander; konsekutiv

consensus Übereinstimmung; übereinstimmende Meinung (aller)

consent Zustimmung; Einwilligung; Einverständnis; *(to ~)* zustimmen; einwilligen

consequence Folge; Auswirkung

consequent konsequent; folgerichtig; folgend

conservation Erhaltung; Bewahrung; *(protection)* Schutz

conservative konservativ; *(cautious)* vorsichtig; zurückhaltend; Konservativer

conservatism Konservatismus; *(accounting)* Grundsatz der Vorsicht

Accounting: a conservative view assumes that in financial reporting it is preferable to be pessimistic rather than optimistic. Practically, this means that financial statements understate assets and revenues and overstate liabilities and expenses, and expenses are recognized sooner, revenues later, and reported earnings are lower.

conserve erhalten; bewahren; schonen; konservieren

consider in Erwägung ziehen; erwägen; überlegen; berücksichtigen; Rücksicht nehmen auf

considerable beträchtlich; erheblich; bedeutend

consideration Überlegung; Erwägung; Berücksichtigung; Rücksicht; *(for services)* Entgelt; Gegenleistung

Management: extent to which a leader is likely to have relationships characterized by mutual trust, respect for subordinates' ideas, and regard for their feeling. He shows concern for his followers' comfort, well-being, status, and satisfaction.

consign übergeben; übertragen; *(on commission)* in Kommission geben; *(goods)* versenden

consignee Empfänger; Warenempfänger

A person or company to whom a consignment is shipped. Only to a consignee may a carrier lawfully make delivery.

consignment *(assigning)* Übertragung; *(of goods)* Versand; (Waren-)Sendung; *(commission)* Kommissionsauftrag

Commission: transaction in which purchase is not final; unsold goods may be returned to consignor.

consignment note Frachtbrief

consignor Absender

The person or business from whom a consignment has been received for shipment, either the seller, shipper, or exporter.

consistency Festigkeit; Konsistenz; Kontinuität; Beständigkeit; Konsequenz

Accounting: use of the same accounting concepts and procedures for related items within the company's financial statements from period to period. Otherwise, it would be difficult for financial statement users to make reliable projections.

consistent vereinbar; beständig; konsequent

consolidate festigen; vereinigen; konsolidieren; zusammenlegen

consolidated konsolidiert; zusammengelegt, vereinigt

consolidated accounts Konzernabschluss

Final accounts prepared for a group of companies as if they were single company.

consolidated balance sheet Konzernbilanz; konsolidierte Bilanz

The balance sheet of a consolidated group of companies. It has to provide the financial information contained in the individual financial statements of the parent company of the group and its subsidiaries.

consolidated company Konzernfirma

consolidated profit and loss account Gewinn- und Verlustrechnung eines Konzerns; konsolidierte GuV

A combination of the individual profit and loss accounts of the members of a group of consolidated companies.

consolidated sales Konzernumsatz

consolidation *(loan)* Konsolidierung; *(merger)* Fusion; Zusammenlegung

Consolidation is the process of merging many things into one. In business, it refers to the merger or acquisitions of companies that together form a larger unit.

consolidator Sammelladungsagent; Verfrachter

Entity that combines *less-than-carload* shipments into full carloads to take advantage of lower shipping rates for full carloads.

consortium Konsortium; Arbeitsgemeinschaft; Zusammenschluss

Temporary combination of two or more companies to promote a common objective or engage in a project of benefit to all members.

The relationship normally entails cooperation and a sharing of resources, sometimes even common ownership.

constant beständig; treu; ständig; konstant; gleich bleibend

constant dollars Basisdollar; Dollar im Bezugsjahr

Dollars of a base year, used as a gauge in adjusting the dollars of other years in order to ascertain actual purchasing power.

constant growth model konstantes Wachstumsmodell

constant returns to specialization konstante Erträge der Spezialisierung

Units of resources required to produce a good are assumed to remain constant no matter where one is on a country's production possibility frontier.

constituency Wählerschaft; Wahlkreis; Kundenkreis;

constitution Verfassung;

constituent company verbundenes Unternehmen

Company that is one of a group of affiliated, merged, or consolidated corporations.

constitution Verfassung; Wesen; Art; Gestaltung; Errichtung *(bylaws)* Satzung; Statuten

A constitution lays down the fundamental principles of law by which a country is administered and a government is created.

In western democratic understanding, a constitution must be based on a mandate from the people in their sovereign capacity.

constitutional Verfassungs-; verfassungsmäßig

constitutional state Rechtsstaat

constrain beschränken, hemmen

constraint Beschränkung; Hemmung; Gehemmtsein

constraints Hemmnisse; Grenzen

construct bauen; errichten; konstruieren

construction Bau; Errichtung; Konstruktion

construction business Baugewerbe

construction company Baufirma; Baugesellschaft

construction financing Baufinanzierung

construction industry Bauindustrie; Bauwirtschaft

construction loan Baudarlehen; Baugelder

construction trade Baugewerbe; Bauindustrie

consul Konsul

consular declaration konsularische Erklärung; Konsulatserklärung

consular invoice Konsulatsfaktura

consulate Konsulat

consul general Generalkonsul

consult sich beraten lassen; nachsehen in; konsultieren

consultant Berater; Gutachter; Facharzt

An independent individual or business, providing professional advice to a business for a fee. The areas covered range from organization, management, accounting, finance, to legal and technical matters.

consultant as negotiator Berater in Verhandlungen

Impartial third party who attempts to facilitate problem solving through communication and analysis.

In this role, the consultant's task is not to settle the issues but to improve relations between the conflicting parties so that they can reach an amicable settlement.

consultation Beratung; Rücksprache

consulting firm Beratungsfirma

consume verbrauchen; aufbrauchen; konsumieren

consumer Verbraucher; Konsument; *(customer)* Kunde

Ultimate user of the *final* product or service. The consumer is not always the purchaser of a product (customer).

Example: in the case of pet food, the pet is technically the consumer because it is the ultimate user, although the advertising is aimed at the pet owner, the customer.

consumer advertising Endverbraucher-Werbung

The advertising of goods or services aimed at the potential end-user, rather than at an intermediary in the selling chain.

consumer analysis Verbraucheranalyse

Phase of marketing research that attempts to answer basic questions about the consumer, e.g. who is buying, who is using the product, what is the decision-making process, is there a basis for segmentation, etc.

For marketing to be effective, a good understanding of the consumer should be essential and come first.

consumer bank Kundenkreditbank

consumer behavior Verbraucherverhalten; Konsumentenverhalten

Attempts to analyse and predict the buying behavior of final consumers – individuals and households who buy goods and services for personal consumption.

Normally, a number of different people, playing different roles, are involved in the purchase decision:

Initiator, the person who first suggests or thinks of the idea of buying a particular product or service.

Influencer, a person whose views or advice influences the buying decision.

Decider, the person who ultimately makes the decision to buy; including whether to buy, what to buy, how to buy, and where to buy.

Buyer, the person who makes the actual purchase.

User, the person who uses the product or service.

consumer buying process Kaufprozess

Theoretical model analysing the different activities consumers perform in making a purchase. This decision process is considered to be sequential and combining several mental and physical activities.

Usually, five stages are distinguished: (1) problem recognition, (2) information search, (3) evaluation of alternatives, (4) choice, (5) post purchase experience

consumer choice Verbraucherwahl

consumer credit Konsumentenkredit

Short-term loans to the end user for the purchase of goods. The most common forms are credit accounts, personal loans from banks and finance houses, hire purchase, and credit cards.

consumer demand Verbrauchernachfrage; Konsumentenwunsch; Endnachfrage

consumer finance company Ratenkreditbank

consumer goods Konsumgüter

Goods bought for personal or household use, as distinguished from capital goods, which are used to produce other goods.

A broad distinction is between consumer durables, such as cars, refrigerators, and television sets, whose useful life extends over a relatively long period, and consumer non-durables or disposables, which are used up within a short time after purchase, such as food, drink, newspapers, etc.

consumer groups Konsumentengruppen

Groups to which consumers belong and which influence their behavior. Small primary groups are the family or a work group, larg secondary groups are professional associations or trade unions.

Further, reference groups serve as direct or indirect points of reference, providing comparisons that help to form a person's attitudes or behavior, and aspirational groups offer values, attitudes, which an individual wants to copy.

consumer income Verbrauchereinkommen

consumerism Verbraucherschutzbewegung

Organized social movement seeking to protect and augment the rights and powers of buyers in relation to sellers.

consumer lending Kundenkreditgewährung

consumer loan Kleinkredit; Kundenkredit; Anschaffungsdarlehen; *(installment loan)* Abzahlungskredit

consumer market Verbrauchermarkt

Individuals and households who buy or acquire goods and services for personal consumption.

consumer-oriented marketing verbraucherorientiertes Marketing

Principle of enlightened marketing which holds that a company should view and organize its marketing activities from the consumers' point of view.

consumer price Verbraucherpreis

consumer price index Verbraucherpreisindex

A measure of the average change in prices over time in a fixed basket of goods and services typically purchased by consumers.

The index is composed of the costs of housing, food, transportation, and utilities.

consumer products Konsumgüter; Verbrauchsgüter

Products bought by final consumers for their personal consumption; any tangible personal property normally used for personal, family, or household purposes.

consumer promotion Verkaufsförderung

Sales promotion designed to stimulate consumer purchasing, including samples, coupons, rebates, prices-off, premiums, patronage rewards, displays, and contests and sweepstakes.

consumer protection Verbraucherschutz

Government regulation to protect the interests of consumers, for example against unfair contract terms by requiring businesses to disclose detailed information about products, and to aid them if goods and services have been improperly manufactured, delivered, handled, or described.

consumers' association Verbraucherverband

consumer research Konsumforschung; Verbraucherforschung

Research conducted to obtain information about consumers and determine what influences their buying behavior. Techniques include focus groups, in-depth interviews, inquiry tests, aided recall interviews, consumer surveys, and attitude testing,.

This type of research aids the advertiser in planning an advertising strategy and in defining the target market.

consumer survey Verbraucherumfrage; Verbraucherbefragung

consumer-to-consumer (C2C) von Verbraucher zu Verbraucher

Business transaction from one consumer to another. Once limited to classified advertising and garage sales, C2C has grown enormously with the spread of the Internet and the advent of such new forms as online auctions and aggregate buying.

consumption Verbrauch; Konsum; *(food)* Verzehr

consumption expenditure Konsumausgabe

consumption function Konsumfunktion

The consumption function calculates the amount of total consumption in an economy and relates personal consumption expenditures to disposable income.

consumption of goods Güterkonsum

consumption reduction Verbrauchsminderung

consumption sector Konsumsektor

contact Verbindung; Beziehung; Kontakt; Berührung; Kontaktperson; *(to ~)* Beziehungen aufnehmen; in Verbindung treten

contain enthalten; *(to comprise)* (um)fassen; *(to set limits)* eingrenzen.

container Behälter; Container

Metal box structure of standard design, used to carry cargo in units. Containers are either 20 or 40 foot in length. The standardized design means that containers can be loaded on container ships, railroad cars, and trucks, and the goods can be shipped directly from the producer to the buyer. Invented in the 1950s, containers have revolutionized transportation and were a crucial precondition for the expansion of international trade.

container freight station Containerladestelle; Container-Packstation

containerization Verladung in Container; Verpackung in Container; Umstellung auf Containerverkehr

The use of large rectangular containers for the shipment of goods. The goods are packed into containers at the factory and transported by road to the port of shipment, where they are loaded direct onto a ship without unpacking. At the port of destination they can again be transported by road to the final user.

container yard Container-Depot

contemporary Zeitgenosse; zeitgenössisch

contend sich bewerben; *(to assert)* behaupten; *(to fight)* kämpfen; im Wettbewerb stehen

contender (Mit)Bewerber; *(rival)* Rivale

content Inhalt; Gehalt; *adv* zufrieden; willens

In general: the material or information contained in a source like a book, magazine or brochure.

Internet: any text, graphics, audio, or video online that informs or persuades the user of an internet site.

content filtering Herausfiltern bestimmter Inhalte

Process by which web users may block unwanted material.

contention Behauptung; Streit

contest Wettkampf; Preisausschreiben; *(to ~)* anfechten; bestreiten; kämpfen um

contingencies *(balance sheet)* Rückstellungen

Balance sheet: Potential gains and losses that cannot be clearly defined at the balance-sheet date, but that have to be recorded somehow.

contingency Eventualfall; Zufall; Möglichkeit; eventueller Umstand

contingency approach Kontingenzansatz; situativer Ansatz

contingency fund außerordentlicher Rücklagenfonds

Amount reserved for a possible loss, such as caused by a business setback. Contingency funds and other reserves set aside are not deductible for tax purposes.

contingency plan Alternativplan; Eventualplan

An alternative for action if things don't go as planned or if expected results fail to materialize. For example, if the contingency was an unexpected increase in demand for a product, the plan would have to include means of increasing production quickly.

contingency variables Kontingenzvariablen

Situational factors; variables that moderate the relationship between two or more other variables and improve the correlation.

contingent Anteil; Kontingent; eventuell; unvorhergesehen

contingent claim bedingter Anspruch; Eventualforderung

Claim whose value is directly dependent on the value of its underlying assets. For example, the debt and equity securities issued by a firm derive their value from the total value of the firm.

continuance Fortbestand; *(adjournment)* Vertagung; Dauer; Bleiben

continuation Fortsetzung; Fortdauer; Weiterführung

continue fortsetzen; fortführen; *(to go on)* fortfahren; fortdauern; *(to adjourn)* vertagen

continuing education weiterführende Bildung

Courses offered by colleges or other organizations that are not for degree credit. Many professions require those licensed in the profession to take a certain number of *continuing education* hours each year.

continuity Kontinuität; Stetigkeit; ununterbrochener Zusammenhang

continuous Dauer-; laufend; fortlaufend; kontinuierlich; ununterbrochen; zusammenhängend

continuous compounding stetige Verzinsung

Interest compounded continuously, every instant, rather than at fixed intervals.

continuous improvement fortwährende Verbesserung

continuous reinforcement laufende Verstärkung

In motivational theory, reassuring an individual with positive feedback on a continuous basis. It can apply to having an employee receive immediate feedback on the outcome of performance.

continuous replenishment andauerndes Auffüllen

contraband Schmuggel; Schmuggelware; Kontrabande

contract Vertrag; Kontrakt; Abkommen; Vorhaben; *(to ~)* Vertrag abschließen; sich vertraglich verpflichten; verkürzen

A legally binding agreement, arising from an offer and an acceptance. Tto be legally binding, the parties (1) must have an intention to create legal relations, (2) must have capacity to contact, and (3) the agreement must not be rendered void by some law or by some inherent defect.

No particular formality is required for the creation of a valid contract: tt may be oral, written, partly oral and partly written, or implied from conduct.

contract amount Vertragssumme

contract frustration Vertragsvereitelung

contracting out aus der staatlichen / firmeneigenen Rentenversicherung austreten; Freizeichnung

contraction Zusammenziehung; Schrumpfung; Abschwung; *(debts)* Aufnahme

Economics: a downturn in the business cycle, also called *recession,* that results in a reduction in the level of national aggregate income or gross domestic product.

contract manufacturing vertragliche Fertigung

Joint venture in which a company contracts with manufacturers, often in a foreign market, to produce a product.

contract of employment Dienstvertrag

contract of affreightment Verfrachtungsvertrag; Schiffsfrachtvertrag; Chartervertrag

contractor Vertragsschließender; Auftragnehmer; *(building)* Bauunternehmer; *(supplier)* Lieferant

Someone who contracts to do work for another or is engaged in a profession in which they offer their services to the public.

An independent contractor makes an agreement to do a specific piece of work, retaining control of the means and method of doing the job. *Example:* architects, lawyers, authors, etc.

contract repudiation Vertragsablehnung

contract repudiation coverage Versicherung gegen Vertragsnichtanerkennung

contractual vertraglich

contractual obligation Schuldverhältnis; Vertragsverpflichtung

contractual VMS vertragliches vertikales Marketing System

Vertical marketing system in which independent firms at different levels of production and distribution join together through contracts to obtain more economies or sales impact than they could achieve alone.

contrast Gegensatz; Vergleich; Kontrast; *(to ~)* gegenüberstellen; vergleichen; kontrastieren

contrast effect Vergleichseffekt

Evaluations of a person's characteristics that are affected by comparisons with other people recently encountered who rank higher or lower on the same characteristics.

contribute beitragen; *(capital)* einbringen; beisteuern; *(charity)* spenden.

contribution Beitrag; *(capital)* Einlagekapital; *(donation)* Spende; *(coinsurance)* Schadensbeteiligung;

contribution accounting Deckungsbeitragsrechnung

Analytical tool for planning and controlling the profitability of a business's activities. By calculating the contribution margin, management can determine how much each individual article contributes towards covering the structural costs of a business as well as towards the generating a profit.

contribution margin Deckungsbeitrag

The amount that each transaction contributes towards covering fixed costs and to generating profit.

The formula to calculate the contribution margin is: sales price of a given product, less the variable costs of producing it. In trade, it correponds to the difference between the net sales price and the acquisition costs of an item and is called the *trade margin.*

Once the total contributions exceed the fixed overheads, all further contributions represent pure profit. The total contribution is the product of the unit contribution and the number of units produced. This is based on the assumptions that the marginal cost and the sales value will be constant.

contribution receipt Spendenquittung

contributor Spender; Beitragsleistender; *(capital)* Kapitaleinleger; Beitragender; Mitarbeiter

control Beherrschung; Kontrolle; Überwachung; *(supervision)* Aufsicht; *(guidance)* Steuerung; Lenkung; *(to ~)* beherrschen; kontrollieren; überwachen; regeln, *(to supervise)* beaufsichtigen; *(to guide)* lenken

Managerial control: a non-delegatable task of management including ascertaining the difference between budgeted and actual figures as well as deciding on *corrective actions* like checking whether the new measures are effective and/or need of sanctions. Controllers interpret the results actually obtained for the managers without depriving the managers of their controlling task.

controllable costs beeinflussbare Kosten

Costs for which the head of an organizational unit (cost center, service center, profit center) is directly responsible, because he can influence them independently. The most important are: personnel costs, maintenance and repair costs, materials and supplies for the cost center and other primary costs.

controlled corporation kontrolliertes Unternehmen

A corporation in which another firm owns more than *50%* of the voting shares. Decisions are therefore effectively by the owners.

controller Aufseher; Kontrolleur; Leiter; *(auditor)* Rechnungsprüfer; Controller

Controllers provide services for managers by designing and maintaining the tools for planning and budgeting, and for comparison of budgeted and actual figures and forecasts.

Controllers therefore help to ensure transparency of costs and results at every level of management: from corporate policy to strategy, over operative planning down to day-to-day operations.

Controllers must make sure that the systems they develop and which they keep up-to-date, are fit for management. In particular this means, that they build up their systems with an eye to objectives, decision-making and allocation of responsibilities.

In small companies the controller may also serve as treasurer. In large companies there may be a chief accountant who reports to the controller.

controller organization Controller-organisation

controlling Kontrollieren; Controlling

The whole process that helps an organization to determine whether or not its objectives are being achieved and whether or not adjustments need to be made.

A good control system helps managers to determine why goals and objectives are not being met; so they can decide on the corrective actions.

The entire controlling process normally consist of the following steps: (1) long-term strategic goals and plans are set, (2) managers determine short-term tactical and operational objectives and plans, (3) control standards are established in line with objectives, (4) performance is measured, (5) comparisons are made between performance and standards, (6) corrective action is taken, if necessary, the standard is changed or performance is continued.

controlling function Kontrollfunktion

controlling interest Mehrheitsbeteiligung; Kapitalmehrheit; Mehrheit

Ownership of more than 50% of a corporation's voting shares. Firm has a controlling interest in another business entity when it owns more than 50 percent of that entity's voting stock.

A much smaller interest, owned individually or by a group in combination, can be controlling if the other shares are widely dispersed and not actively voted.

controlling stockholder Großaktionär

controlling year planner Controlling-Kalender

Organized dates, deadlines and schedules in which the controller's work of controlling must be carried out.

convene sich versammeln; einberufen; vorladen

convenience Komfort; Bequemlichkeit; Zweckmäßigkeit; Angemessenheit; Annehmlichkeit

convenience food Fertiggerichte

Any packaged dish or food that can be prepared quickly and easily in an oven or a microwave.

Convenience foods appeal to those who have neither the desire nor the time to prepare and cook a meal because they are quick and easy.

convenience goods Güter des täglichen Bedarfs; Waren des täglichen Bedarfs

Goods bought for consumption on a regular basis and with a minimum of comparison and buying effort.

convenience store Nachbarschaftsladen; Bedarfsartikelgeschäft; kleiner Lebensmittelladen

A small retailer that is centrally located, is open long hours, and carries a moderate number of items. Convenience stores charge above average prices compared to large supermarkets that generate large-volume sales.

convenient zweckdienlich; geeignet; angenehm; günstig gelegen

convention Zusammenkunft; Versammlung; Konvention; Übereinkommen; Vertrag; Abmachung; *(custom)* Gewohnheit; Sitte

conventional herkömmlich; höflich; herkömmlich; konventionell

conventional distribution channel herkömmlicher Vertiebsweg

Channel consisting of one or more independent producers, wholesalers, and retailers, each a separate business seeking to maximize its own profits even at the expense of profits for the system as a whole.

convergence Zusammenlaufen; Konvergenz; Konzentration

In general: movement towards a common point.

Example: banking and insurance in the 1990s - bank getting into the insurance business.

Technology: trend in which different hardware devices such as televisions, computers and telephones merge and have similar functions.

conversion Umwechslung; Umstellung; Umwandlung; *(foreign currency)* Umtausch; Umrechnung

Stock exchange: exchange of a convertible security such as a bond into a fixed number of shares of the issuing corporation's common stock.

Insurance: switch from short-term to permanent life insurance.

conversion costs Umstellungskosten; Konvertierungskosten

All the costs that have to be incurred when changing from one kind of equipment or process to another. They include the cost of new equipment plus training, but also hidden costs, such a compatibility.

conversion of debts Umschuldung

conversion premium Wandlungsprämie

Difference between the conversion price and the current share price divided by the current share price.

conversion price Wandlungspreis

Term referring to the share price and meaning the cash amount of the bond's face value that is exchangeable.

conversion ratio Wandelverhältnis

Number of shares that a bondholder would receive if the bond were converted into shares.

conversion value Umwandlungswert

Value a convertible bond would be worth if it were immediately converted into ordinary shares at the current price.

convert verändern; umstellen; *(currency)* umrechnen; umtauschen; umwandeln

convertibility Umwandelbarkeit; Umtauschbarkeit; Konvertierbarkeit; Konvertibilität

convertible umwandelbar; konvertierbar; *(cash)* realisierbar; *(car)* Cabriolet

convertible bond Wandelschuldverschreibung; Wandelanleihe

Bond that may be converted into another form of security, typically ordinary shares, at the option of the holder at a specified price for a specified period of time.

convertible currency konvertierbare Währung; konvertierbare Devisen

Currency for which there are not barriers or restrictions in the foreign exchange market.

convertible loan Wandelanleihe

convey übertragen; übermitteln; ausdrücken; *(to transport)* transportieren; befördern

conveyance Übermittlung; Beförderung; Versendung; *(real estate)* Umschreibung

Real estate: the transfer of the title of real estate from one person to another.

cookie

String of text sent by a web server that a browser stores in a small text file on the user's hard drive. Cookies store information supplied by the user and read it back later to keep track of user behavior.

cooperate zusammenarbeiten; zusammen-; mitwirken; mitarbeiten

cooperation Zusammenarbeit; Mitarbeit; Mitwirkung; Kooperation

cooperation agreement Koorperationsabkommen

cooperative Genossenschaft; genossenschaftlich; hilfsbereit; kooperativ

Organization for the production or marketing of goods owned collectively by members who share the benefits, for example, an agricultural *cooperative.*

cooperative advertising Gemeinschaftswerbung; Verbundwerbung

In general: an advertisement that is sponsored by two or more manufacturers or retailers. The sponsors cooperate in deciding on the copy as well as in sharing the costs. Example:

cooperative bank Genossenschaftsbank

cooperative exchange agreements kooperatives Wechselabkommen

cooperative store Konsumladen

coordinate koordiniert; gleichgestellt; *(to ~)* einheitlich leiten; koordinieren

coordinating committee Koordinierungsausschuss

coordination Koordinierung; Koordination

Inter and/or intra-level linking of sub-systems, especially sub-plans. It can be the result of directives, personal and departmental initiatives or the regular planning process.

cope with bewältigen; fertig werden mit

copy Abschrift; Kopie; Ausfertigung; *(advertisement)* Reklametext; *(book)* Exemplar; *(to ~)* kopieren; Abschrift anfertigen

copy of invoice Fakturakopie

copyright Urheberrecht; *(to ~)* urheberrechtlich schützen

Legal protection giving authors, composers, playwrights, publishers and other artists the exclusive right to publish and dispose their works or to determine who may do.

With the advent of the Internet, copyright questions have become a matter of serious concern, as it has become very easy to download music, movies and other digitalized works of art.

copy testing *(advertising)* Testprüfung; Werbetextwirkungsuntersuchung

The process of measuring the communication effect of an advertising copy on a potential buyer, either before or after it is printed or broadcast.

copywriter Werbetexter

A person whose job is to write the text for advertisements or other promotional material.

Copywriters usually work for an advertising agency, but if the subject is highly technical, they are often employed by the company manufacturing or distributing the product

core capabilities Kernfähigkeiten

core competence Kernkompetenz

A set of skills that have been integrated in a unique way by a firm in order to add value.

The idea was first introduced into management literature in 1990 by CK Prahalad and Gary Hamel. They argued that core competencies are "...the collective learning in the organisation, especially how to co-ordinate diverse production skills and integrate multiple streams of technologies ...core competence is communication, involvement and a deep commitment to working across organizational boundaries ...core competence does not diminish with use Unlike physical assets, which do deteriorate over time, competencies are enhanced as they are applied and shared."

There are three fields of core competences that are separated: (1) market-access competences facilitate focussed market penetration and make the contact to the buyers, (2) "integrity-related competences" are important for fast and reliable cooperation between different organizational units and functions within the company, whereas (3) "functionality-related competences" serve to include outstanding functions in the sold products.

core job characteristics die wichtigsten Motivationsfaktoren einer Tätigkeit

Five characteristics that have been identified as creating motivation at work because they are important to the psychological well-being of an individual:

skill variety: the degree to which the job draws on several skills and abilities;

task identity: the extent to which a person is able to complete a task from start to finish;

task significance: the degree to which a person perceives his task to be important to the organization and its clients;

autonomy: the degree to which a person can decide how and when to do his task;

feedback: the extent to which the person receives feedback on the quality of performance.

core product Kernprodukt

Problem-solving services or benefits that consumers are really looking for when buying a product. For example, a person buying a power drill really wants a hole in the wall.

core strategy Kernstrategie

Central part of a marketing strategy which has two parts: the identification of a group of customers for whom the firm has a differential advantage; and then positioning itself in that market.

core values Grundwerte

Primary or dominant values that are accepted throughout the organization. The core values are essentially retained but modified to reflect each separate unit's distinct situation.

corner a market Waren zu Spekulationszwecken aufkaufen; zu spekulativen Zwecken den Markt aufkaufen

Attempt to purchase enough of the available supply of a commodity or stock in order to manipulate its price.

corner shop Nachbarschaftsladen; Laden an der Ecke; Tante-Emma-Laden

Small store, serving the immediate neighborhood, usually owned and managed by a person who lives in the local neighbourhood. It is typically a grocery store, a convenience store or confectioner-tobacconist-newsagent (CTN).

corporate Gesellschafts-; gesellschaftlich; körperschaftlich

corporate bond Industrieanleihe; Industrieobligation; Industrieschuldverschreibung; Obligation einer Aktiengesellschaft

A debt instrument issued by a corporation, as distinct from one issued by a government agency or a municipality.

Corporate bonds typically have four distinguishing features: (1) they are taxable; (2) they have a par value of $1000; (3) they have a fixed maturity; (4) they are traded on major exchanges, with prices published in newspapers.

corporate brand strategy unternehmenseigene Markenstrategie

Brand strategy whereby the firm makes its company name the dominant brand identity across all its products.

corporate characteristics Unternehmensmerkmale, die eine Aktiengesellschaft definieren

Characteristics considered unique to corporations, namely perpetual life, limited liability, free transferability of interests, centralized management.

In the U.S., if a business entity has more *corporate characteristics* than non-corporate, it will be taxed as a corporation.

corporate concept Unternehmenskonzept

corporate culture Unternehmenskultur

The values, beliefs, and traditions within an organization that influence the behavior of its members and generate a general organizational operating environment.

Corporate culture is considered to be comprehensive, affecting employees, management, and customer relations, extending to the types of products and services the organization creates, and including production methods, marketing practices, advertising, and service quality.

corporate customer Firmenkunde

corporate equity Firmenvermögen

corporate governance Grundsätze der Unternehmensführung

The manner in which organizations, especially large corporations, are managed and the nature of accountability of the managers to the owners.

corporate licensing Lizenzerteilung

Form of licensing whereby a firm rents a corporate trademark or logo made famous in one product or service category and uses it in a related category.

corporate management Firmenleitung; Unternehmensleitung; Vorstand

corporate merger Gesellschaftsfusion

corporate objective Gesellschaftsziel; Geschäftszweck

corporate officer Vorstandsmitglied

corporate planning Unternehmensplanung

corporate policy Unternehmungspolitik; Geschäftspolitik

Corporate policy essentially seeks to create a match between the compamy´s environment and its business objectives.

To achieve this, management must establish the basic values and standards of conduct, at the same time determining the principles of behavior for dealing with customers, suppliers and employees.

Corporate policy is laid down for the company as a whole and is valid for everybody concerned. Generally it is seen to consist of three main elements: vision, mission statement and business concept.

corporate portal Unternehmensportal

Internet: intranet site attempting to merge all of the employee's information and communication needs into a single interface, accessing internal documents, data warehouses, groupware, e-mail, and calendars, in addition to the web.

corporate relations service Firmenbetreuung

corporate reorganization Unternehmensumstrukturierung; Unternehmensneugestaltung

Merger, acquisition, divisive acquisition, or other restructuring of a corporation.

corporate strategy Unternehmensstrategie

corporate structure Unternehmensstruktur

Basic setup of an organization in terms of departments and agencies, as well as distribution of power and delegation of functional responsibilities throughout an organization. Henry Mintzberg identified five basic structures:

(1) the simple structure, (2) the machine bureaucracy, (3) the professional bureaucracy, (4) the divisionalized form, and (5) the adhocracy. His classification embraces the fundamental distinction between vertical organizations (types 1, 2 and 4), and horizontal ones (types 3 and 5).

corporate takeover Gesellschaftsübernahme

corporate VMS unternehmensbezogenes vertikales Marketingsystem

Vertical marketing system that combines successive stages of production and distribution under single ownership – channel leadership is established through common ownership.

corporation *(jomt stock company)* Kapitalgesellschaft; Aktiengesellschaft

A legal business entity created under federal or provincial statutes in the U.S. It is regarded by the courts as an artificial person that is separate and distinct from the persons who own it may. In particular, it can own property, incur debts, sue, or be sued.

A corporation has four chief distinguishing features:

(1) Limited liability (owners can lose only what they invest); (2) easy transfer of ownership through the sale of shares of stock; (3) continuity of existence; and (4) centralized management.

It can obtain capital through expanding ownership, and the shareholders profit from the growth of the business.

correct korrekt; richtig; einwandfrei; *(to ~)* berichtigen; richtig stellen

correction Berichtigung; Korrektur; Richtigstellung

Stock exchange: reverse movement, usually downward, in the price of an individual security or the entire index. For example, if the DAX has been rising steadily and then falls dramatically, it is considered a correction of the upward trend.

correlation Korrelation

Standardized statistical measure of the dependence of two random variables. It is defined as the covariance divided by the standard deviations of two variables. Its value is always between -l and 1.

correspond *(letter)* im Briefwechsel stehen; *(to relate to)* entsprechen; korrespondieren

correspondence Briefverkehr; Schriftwechsel; Korrespondenz; Briefwechsel; Übereinstimmung

correspondent Korrespondent; Briefpartner; *(newspaper)* Berichterstatter

correspondent bank Korrespondenzbank; Partnerbank; Bankverbindung

corrupt bestechlich; korrupt; verdorben

corruption Bestechlichkeit; Korruption; Verderben; Verdorbensein; Verfall

co-sign Mitunterzeichnung

Act of affixing one's signature on a contract, such as a loan, in addition to the principal signature of another. Both signers are liable for the loan or other contract.

cost Kosten; *(expenses)* Aufwand; *(price)* Preis; Anschaffungs-preis; *(to ~)* kosten; erfordern; veranschlagen; kalkulieren

An expression in terms of money units of the effect of activating or consuming resources, or simply the amount of money that must be paid to acquire something.

For accounting purposes, product and structural costs can be differentiated. Product costs (proportional costs) are the direct and causal consequence of producing an product-item or a service. Structural costs are defined by a business's capacity and organizational structure; costs that are not directly dependent on output but are determined by decisions over the business's capability to produce goods and services.

cost accounting Selbstkostenrechnung; Kostenrechnung; Betriebsabrechnung

Branch of accounting concerned with collecting, processing, and presenting financial and quantitative data within an organization. The main purpose is to ascertain the cost of cost centers, cost units, and various operations.

In detail, *cost accounting* embraces various accounting subsystems, analysing different areas of an organization. These include (1) cost, (2) output, (3) revenue, (4) result, (5) account.

Taken together, these subsystems enable management to answer questions concerning different objects in plan, actual, variance and forecast.

cost advantage Kostenvorteil

cost containment Kostenbeschränkung; Kostendämmung

cost allocation Umlagen; Kostenverrechnung

Charging of cost centers or cost objects with structure costs from cost centers upstream without establishing a causal connection between them. Structure costs are thus distributed in a proportional way.

By allocating structure costs (e.g. building, material administration, factory administration, sales and general administration costs) it becomes possible to calculate the *manufacturing cost.*

cost and freight Kosten und Fracht

cost application Kostenzurechnung

The process of allocating costs between different entities, such as products, processes, or departments. For example, rent expense can be allocated to a department based on square footage.

cost-benefit analysis Kosten-Nutzen-Analyse; Nutzwertanalyse

Method of measuring the benefits expected from a decision by calculating the costs of the decision, then determining whether the benefits outweigh the costs.

Usually, the analysis comprises seven steps: (1) definition of the objectives, (2) establish requirements, (3) determine selection criteria, (4) weight selection criteria, (5) elaborate options, (6) evaluate options, (7) choose the best option.

cost center Kostenstelle

Non-revenue-producing element of an organization, where costs are separately figured and allocated, and for which someone has formal responsibility. The personnel function is a cost center in that it does not directly produce revenue.

cost center accounting Kostenstellenrechnung

One of the three elements of cost accounting. Cost center accounting serves as the cost center's planning and controlling tool and as a basis for the calculation of *cost rates* and *allocation rates* for product costing. It answers the question, *where* costs have occurred or may be expected to occur.

cost containment Kosten(ein)dämmung, Kostensenkung

Process of maintaining organizational costs within a specified budget; restraining expenditures to meet organizational or project financial targets.

cost control Kostenkontrolle; Kostenüberwachung

cost cutting Kosteneinsparung; Kostenreduzierung

cost differential Kostenunterschied

cost drivers Kostentreiber

Any activity within an organisation that causes costs to be incurred. Cost drivers are used to charge costs to products or services and are applied to cost pools, which relate to common activities.

cost-effectiveness Kostenwirksamkeit; Kostenrentabilität; Wirtschaftlichkeit; Nutzwert von Kosten

Ability to generate sufficient value to offset an activity's costs. The value can be interpreted as revenue in the case of a business.

cost-efficient kostengünstig

cost increase Kostenerhöhung; Kostensteigerung

cost inflation Kosteninflation

cost, insurance and freight (CIF) Kosten, Versicherung und Fracht

costly kostspielig; teuer

cost method Kostenmethode; Kostenverfahren

Method of accounting for investments by a parent company in its subsidiary companies.

The parent maintains the investment in a subsidiary account as its cost without recognizing periodically its share of subsidiary income or loss.

The method is usually practiced when the parent only holds a small share of the stock (below 20%), because there is a lack of effective control.

cost-minimization-strategy Kostenminimierungsssstrategie

Strategy that emphasizes tight cost controls, avoidance of unnecessary innovation or marketing expenses, and cuts prices in selling a basic product. *Example:* the strategy pursued by companies like Wal-Mart or Aldi.

cost models Kostenmodelle

Internet: Approaches to charge costs for internet advertising, the most important ones being per-exposure, per-response and per-action.

cost objective Kostenvorgabe; Kostenziel

A limit on the cost of an activity. A project cannot exceed the *cost objective* that has been set for it in the budget.

cost of capital Kapitalaufwand; Kapitalkosten

The amount, expressed in terms of an interest rate, that an organisation is required to pay for the capital used in financing its activities.

The mix of sources of capital, e.g. equity share capital, loan capital, and debt, leads to some uncertainty if the cost of capital actually increases if the gearing increases.

cost of equity capital Eigenkapitalkosten

Required return on the company's ordinary shares in capital markets. It is also called the equity holders' required rate of return because it is what equity holders can expect to obtain in the capital market. It is a cost from the firm's perspective.

cost of fringe benefits Lohnnebenkosten

cost of goods Herstellungskosten

cost of goods manufactured Kosten der hergestellten Waren; Herstellungskosten

An accounting measure of the total costs during an accounting period of all goods produced, which includes costs of material, labor, and overhead, whether fixed or variable.

cost of goods sold Verkaufskosten; Umsatzkosten; Umsatzaufwendungen

All direct costs allocated to goods sold. Included are clear-cut and variable factors used in making a product, such as direct factory labor and raw material, as well as others that are less clear-cut, such as overhead.

An attempt to measure what a product or service costs when all the functions that are involved in the production of the finished product are considered.

The costs included are: direct material costs and the proportional manufacturing costs which together give the product costs, material overheads, such as purchasing and warehousing, and manufacturing structure costs.

cost of labor Lohnkosten

cost of living Lebenshaltungskosten

cost of living allowance Lebenshaltungszuschuss; Lebenskostenzuschlag; Teuerungszulage

cost of money Geldbeschaffungskosten

cost of production Produktionskosten

cost of sales method Umsatzkostenverfahren

The cost of sales method is one way of setting out the income statement. The costs incurred in the manufacturing of a specific product are set against the revenue achieved in the sale of that product.

The calculation: revenues less deductions from revenue equal cost of goods sold less research and dvelopment cost less administration and sales overheads equal operating result.

cost overrun Kostenüberschuss; Kostenüberschreitung; Mehrkosten

Excess of a project's cost over budget. A cost overrun necessitates an additional allocation of funds in the budget equaling the size of the overrun.

cost per click Kosten pro Klick

Internet: Total advertisement cost divided by number of clicks on an ad or hyperlink.

cost per mille (CPM) Kosten pro Tausend

Advertising: The cost of an advertisement per thousand people who will see or hear it.

cost per order Kosten pro Auftrag

Direct marketing: The total cost of a mailing divided by the total number of orders received

cost per targeted mille (CPTM) Kosten pro zielgerichtete Tausend

Advertising: The cost of an advertisement per targeted thousand people who will see or hear it.

cost-plus pricing kostenorientierte Preisbildung; Verkaufspreisermittlung durch Gewinnzuschlag

An approach to pricing, in which the total cost of producing the product or service is estimated, and a certain percentage mark-up is added.

cost price Selbstkostenpreis; Anschaffungs- oder Herstellungspreis

cost-push inflation Kostendruckinflation; kosteninduzierte Inflation

A theory to explain the increase in the prices of goods as caused by an increase in the cost of inputs, especially wages and raw materials.

The simple causal chain looks like this: the demand for raw materials exceeds the supply, prices go up, manufacturers pay more for raw materials, they raise the prices they charge merchants for their finished products, merchants in turn raise the prices they charge consumers.

cost savings Kostenersparnis

cost schedule Kostensatz

cost structure Kostengliederung; Kostenstruktur

cost trend Kostenentwicklung

cost types Kostenart

The different types of costs that arise in a cost center or in a cost object, the most important: personnel costs, material costs, outside services, repair and maintenance costs, other costs, cost allocations, depreciation and interest.

Cost type accounting serves to collect and break down all the different cost elements within a given period and register them systematically.

cost unit Kosteneinheit

A unit of production for which the costs incurred are calculated. The cost unit may be the final item produced, e.g. a chair or a light bulb, or it may be a sub-assembly, e.g. an aircraft wing or a gear box.

council Rat

council of economic advisors Wirtschaftsrat

Council for Mutual Economic Assistance (COMECON) Rat für gegenseitige Wirtschaftshilfe

An organization in the former Communist Block, formed in 1949 to promote the development of the national economies and the science and technology of its member states.

The members were Bulgaria, Cuba. Czechoslovakia, German Democratic Republic, Hungary, Mongolia, Poland, Romania, USSR, and Vietnam.

It was replaced in 1991 by an organisation designed to help those economies integrate with the rest of Europe

counsel Rat, Ratschlag; *(adviser)* Berater; *(to ~)* raten; beraten

counselor Berater; Ratgeber; Rechtsberater

count Zählung; *(total)* Gesamtsumme; *(to ~)* zählen; rechnen; berechnen

counter Ladentisch; Schalter; Theke; *(counting device)* Zähler; *(to ~)* entgegnen; parieren; kontern

counterbalance Gegengewicht; *(bookkeeping)* Gegensaldo; *(to ~)* kompensieren

counterbid Gegengebot

A bid made in an auction that exceeds a bid already made, which then becomes the underbid.

countercyclical policy antizyklische Politik

Economic policies pursued by a government to smooth out the negative effects of the business cycle.

During an inflation, the central bank can for example raise interest rates in order to reduce demand and thus end inflationary expansion.

counterentry Gegenbuchung

counterfeit Fälschung; gefälscht; falsch; *(to ~)* fälschen; nachahmen

A counterfeit is an illegal copy of a product that is made with the intent of deceiveing consumers.

counteroffer Gegenangebot

A reply made to a bid. If a seller makes an offer, the buyer may accept it or make a bid against the offer. Sellers who find the bid unacceptable may make a counteroffer. If the buyer still finds the counter offer unacceptable he may make a counterbid.

counterorder Abbestellung; *(to ~)* abbestellen

counterpart Gegenstück; *(counter value)* Gegenwert

counterproposal Gegenvorschlag

counterpurchase Kompensationskauf

Form of international trade based on a reciprocal buying agreement and involving the direct or indirect exchange of goods for other goods instead of cash.

counter-trade Kompensationshandel

Practice in international trade involving the direct or indirect exchange of goods for other goods instead of cash. Forms include barter compensation (buyback) and counterpurchase.

counter-trade economy Tauschwirtschaft

countervail ausgleichen; entgegenwirken

countervailing duty Ausgleichszoll; Kompensationszoll

An extra import duty imposed by a country on specific goods. It is used to prevent dumping or to counteract export subsidies given by foreign countries

country Land; Staat

country analysis Länderanalyse

country of origin Herkunftsland

country risk Länderrisiko

The risk that a foreign government will either prevent the fulfilment of a contract or take over control of the management of overseas subsidiaries

country risk assessment Risikoeinschätzung eines Landes

county Kreis; Grafschatz

coupon *(bond interest)* Kupon; *(gift certificate)* Gutschein

Banking: stated interest on a debt instrument.

Marketing: certificates that give buyers a saving when they purchase a product. They normally must be presented with the purchase to claim the discount..

coupon bond Inhaberobligation

coupon rate Anleihezins; Zins für festverzinsliche Anleihen

In bonds, notes or other fixed income securities, the stated percentage rate of interest, usually paid twice a year.

course Ablauf; Verlauf; *(studies)* Kurs; *(lecture)* Vorlesung

course of business Geschäftsverlauf

course of one year Jahresverlauf

course of the economy Wirtschaftsverlauf

court Hof; Hinterhof; *(law)* Gericht; Gerichtshof; Kammer

court of arbitration Schiedsgericht

courtesy Höflichkeit; Entgegenkommen; Gefälligkeit

covariance Kovarianz

A statistical measure used in computing the correlation coefficient between two variables.

A positive covariance indicates that the two variables tend to move up and down together; a negative covariance indicates that when one moves higher, the other tends to go lower.

covenant Zusage, Verpflichtung; Vertrag

A promise made in a deed, which can be enforced as a contract, even if the promise is gratuitous: for example, if A covenants to pay B €100 per month, B can enforce this promise even without having done anything in return.

cover Deckung; Schutz; *(book)* Deckel; Hülle; Umhüllung; *(under separate cover)* mit getrennter Post; *(to ~)* decken; *(to comprise)* umfassen; erfassen; *(to report)* berichten

coverage *(insurance)* Versicherungsschutz; *(backing)* Deckung; *(spread)* Verbreitung; Geltungsbereich

Advertising: Percentage of a population covered by a medium. Commonly used with print media to describe an average issue's audience within defined demographic or purchasing groups

cover letter Begleitbrief

covered call gedeckte Kaufoption

A short call option position in which the writer owns the shares of the underlying stock.

This limits the risk the writer takes because the stock does not have to be bought at the market price if the holder of the option decides to exercise it.

covered put gedeckte Verkaufsoption

A put option position in which the option writer is short the corresponding stock. This limits the risk the writer takes because stock is already set aside.

cracker Hacker

Person who breaks into computer systems in order to steal or destroy data, deliberately performing criminal acts.

craft Handwerk; Gewerbe; Zunft; *(boat)* Boot; *(aircraft)* Flugzeug

craftsman, -person, -woman, Handwerker; Gewerbetreibender

crash Absturz; *(stocks)* Sturz; *(to ~)* abstürzen; zertrümmern

Finance: rapid and serious drop in stock prices and economic activity, as in the *crash* of 1929, which initiated the Great Depression. Crashes are usually brought on by a loss in investor confidence.

Computers: hardware failure or program error causing an application to quit working or a computer to become inoperable. In such a case, the computer usually needs to be restarted.

crate Lattenkiste; -verschlag

create schaffen; gründen

creation Schöpfung; Gründung; Erzeugung; Werk

creation of money Geldschöpfung

creative schöpferisch

creative accounting aktive Bilanzgestaltung; kreative Buchführung

creative strategy kreative Strategie; Kreativstrategie

creativity Kreativität; Schöpferkraft

Ability to produce novel and useful ideas which are different from what has been done before.

creator Schöpfer; Urheber

credentials Zeugnis; *(reference)* Empfehlungsschreiben; *(diplomacy)* Beglaubigungsschreiben

credibility Glaubwürdigkeit; Glaubhaftigkeit

credible glaubwürdig; glaubhaft

credit Kredit; *(account)* Haben; *(tax)* Freibetrag; *(reputation)* Kreditwürdigkeit; *(recognition)* Anerkennung; *(to ~ an account)* gutschreiben; zuschreiben; kreditieren

General: the reputation and financial standing of a person or an organisation.

Commerce: the sum of money that a trader allows his customer before requiring payment.

Consumers: the ability of a consumer to purchase goods with money borrowed from banks or other financial institutions.

*Accounting: a*n entry on the rig hand side of an account in double-en book-keeping. showing a positive asset.

credit agreement Kreditvertrag

credit amount Kreditsumme

credit analysis Kreditanalyse

Process of determining whether a credit applicant meets the firm's standards and what amount of credit the applicant should receive.

credit association Kreditanstalt

credit balance Guthaben; Aktivsaldo

credit business Kreditgewerbe

credit card Kreditkarte

A plastic card issued by a bank or finance organisation, enabling its holders to obtain credit with retailers.

The retailer receives the amount less a service charge through monthly payments from the credit card company.

Customers receive monthly statements from the credit card company, which have to be paid within a certain number of days, with interest charged on the outstanding balance.

credit contraction Kreditschrumpfung

credit cooperative Kreditgenossenschaft

credit entry Gutschrift; Habenbuchung

credit expansion Kreditexpansion; Kreditzuwachs

credit flow Finanzierungsstrom

credit institution Kreditinstitut

credit instrument Finanzierungsmittel

Device by which a firm offers credit, such as an invoice, a promissory note, or a conditional sales contract.

credit insurance Kreditversicherung

An insurance policy that continues the repayments of a debt if the policyholder is unable to do so.

credit item Gutschrift; Habenposten

credit line eingeräumter Kredit; Kreditlinie; Kreditrahmen; Dispositionskredit

The amount of credit extended to a borrower.

credit multiplier Kreditmultiplikator

creditor Gläubiger; Kreditor

Someone to whom money is owed by the debtor

The total amount owed to creditors is shown in the balance sheet of a company, with a distinction being made between creditors who will be paid during the coming accounting period and those who will be paid later.

creditor bank Gläubigerbank

creditor country Gläubigerland

creditor of a bankrupt's estate Konkursgläubiger

creditor protection Gläubigerschutz

credit period Zahlungsziel

Time allowed a credit purchaser to remit the full payment for credit purchases.

credit rating Kreditbeurteilung; Kreditwürdigkeit; Bonitätseinstufung

An assessment of the creditworthiness of an individual or a firm, giving a formal evaluation of credit history and capability to repay obligations.

Traditionally performed by banks, a number of companies now investigate, analyze, and maintain records on the credit responsibility of individuals and businesses. In the U.S., e.g. TRW and Dun & Bradstreet. The bond ratings by Standard & Poor's and Moody's are also a form of credit rating.

credit rationing Drosselung der Kreditgewährung; Kreditbeschränkung; Kreditkontigentierung

Allocation of loans to borrowers not according to market criteria. Credit rationing occurs when interest rates are below the regular market level or the amount lenders are willing to lend to borrowers is limited.

credit risk Kreditrisiko

credit risk insurance Kreditrisikoversicherung

credit scoring Beurteilung der Kreditwürdigkeit

credit standing Bonität; Kreditwürdigkeit

The ability to conclude legally-binding credit agreements. Individuals who are in full-time employment, corporations and business partnerships normally have credit standing. Credit rating tends to be more quantitative than credit standing.

credit system Kreditwesen

credit terms Kreditkonditionen

credit transaction Kreditgeschäft

credit union Volksbank; Kreditgenossenschaft

credit volume Kreditvolumen

credit voucher Gutschrift

creeping inflation schleichende Inflation

A moderate but continuous increase in the general price level that may appear tolerable in the short run but leads to significant long-run price increases. For example, a sustained inflation of 2% per year will cause prices to increase over fivefold in a century.

crisis Krise

crisis management Krisenmanagement

A crisis is a serious disruption for a business, which can have various causes: acts of God (storms, earthquakes), mechanical problems (metal fatigue), human errors (miscommunication), management decisions (underestimating a problem).

Because crises often accompanied by a high level of public attention, crisis management requires special skills. It is especially important to be well prepared in advance, move fast, consider getting outside help and advice, be honest, and to look to the long term.

criterion Kennzeichen; Kriterium; Maßstab; Prüfstein

critical incident kritischer Zwischenfall, kritischer Vorfall

critical path method (CPM) kritischer Pfad Methode; CPM-Methode

The Critical Path Method (CPM) is an algorithm for finding a critical path of an order-requirement network, i.e. a technique for planning the most efficient way to achieve a given objective by determining the activities and events required and showing how they relate to each other.

CPM is used in manufacturing to plan and control the entire process of material deliveries, organization, inspections, and production.

critical success factors kritische Erfolgsfaktoren

Strengths and weaknesses that most critically affect an organization's success. These are measured relative to competition.

crop Ernte; Pflanze; Haufen; *(to ~)* beschneiden; besäen; bepflanzen

cross Kreuz; Querstrich; *(opposite)* entgegengesetzt; *(to ~)* überqueren; kreuzen; sich kreuzen

cross-cultural communication interkulturelle Kommunikation

cross-cultural competence interkulturelle Kompetenz

cross-cultural training interkulturelles Training

cross-elasticity Kreuzelastizität

cross-functional teams funktionsübergreifende Teams

Employees from about the same hierarchical level, but from different work areas, who come together to accomplish a task.

Example: at an airline, cross-functional teams include flight crew, ramp personnel, mechanics, dispatchers, and reservation agents.

cross licensing gegenseitiger Austausch von Lizenzen; Lizenzaustausch

Arrangement in which a company licenses valuable intangible property to a foreign partner and receives a license for the partner's valuable knowledge.

cross merchandising kombinierte Absatzförderung; Cross Merchandising

Technique of arranging displays of related products close to each other in a supermarket in order to induce customers to cross over from one product to another.

Example: a display of shaving cream and skin care products.

crossing Überfahrt; Überquerung; *(intersection)* Kreuzung; Bahnübergang; *(crosswalk)* Fußgängerübergang

cross rate Kreuzrate; Kreuzparität

The exchange rate between two foreign currencies, neither of which is the US dollar.

cross-selling Verbundverkauf; Gegenseitigkeitsgeschäft

The practice of selling related products and services to existing customers. For example, a car dealer may offer servicing of the vehicle, an insurance broker may offer car insurance additionally to an existing life insurance.

crown jewels Kronjuwelen

Anti-takeover tactic in which an option is written to sell major assets - the crown jewels – to a friendly firm if control should be lost to a predator.

crucial entscheidend; kritisch; wichtig

crude oil Rohöl

culmination Erreichen des Höhepunkt; Kulmination

cultivate bebauen; kultivieren; pflegen; *(soil)* bearbeiten; ausbilden; üben; pflegen

cultivation Anbau; Bebauung; Kultivierung; *(soil)* Ackerbestellung

cultural Kultur-; kulturell

cultural adaptation kulturelle Anpassung

cultural adoption kulturelle Annahme

cultural assimilation kulturelle Angleichung; kulturelle Anpassung; kulturelle Assimilation

cultural diversity kulturelle Verschiedenheit

cultural emphathy kulturelles Einfühlungsvermögen

cultural environment kulturelles Umfeld

Institutions and other forces that affect society's basic values, perceptions, preferences and behaviors.

cultural norms kulturelle Normen

cultural relativism kultureller Relativismus

cultural universals allgemeingültige Eigenschaften; kulturübergreifende Eigenschaften

Cultural characteristics and attributes that are found in a wide range of cultures: that is, features that transcend national cultures.

cultural variables kulturelle Variablen

culture Kultur; Bildung

The concept of culture tries to explain the fact that groups of people have something in common, which expresses itself in collective ways of thinking and acting. These groups can be nations, regions, business groups, youth groups.

There exist some 200 definitions of culture and various models that try to explain and analyse this phenomenon.

In German usage, culture refers often more to the level of education and artistic disposition of individuals.

culture model Kulturmodell

Attempt at providing a scientific framework for analysing and understanding cultural differences.

One of the best-known culture models is by Geert Hofstede, a Dutch academic who spent long periods at IBM, where he studied the employees of one multinational company in 40 different countries. Many later studies followed that approach.

Hofstede devised a model that classifies cultures along five dimensions:

(1) Individual versus collective: refers to the extent to which individuals expect only to look after themselves and their immediate families, compared with the extent to which there is a tight social framework in which people expect the groups to which they belong to look after them. In exchange for the care of the group, they give their absolute loyalty.

(2) Power distance: refers to the extent to which a society accepts and expects the fact that power in institutions and organisations is distributed unequally.

(3) Uncertainty avoidance, describes the extent to which people feel threatened by ambiguity, and the relative importance that they attach to rules, security and steady progression up a well-defined career ladder.

(4) Masculinity versus femininity: refers to the nature of the dominant values in a society. Masculine values are considered to be assertiveness and monetary focus, feminine values concern for others and the quality of relationships.

(5) Short term versus long term, refers to the different time frames used by different people. Those with a short-term view are more inclined towards consumption, whilst with a long- term attitude the focus is on preserving status-based relationships.

culture matrix Kulturmatrix

culture shock Kulturshock

cum div abbr. cum dividend

With dividend declared or pending.

cume (cumulative) kumulierte Publikumszahlen

Rating the reach of a radio or TV program or station as opposed to the "average."

cumulative steigernd; verstärken; kumulativ; anhäufend

cumulative abnormal return (CAR) kumulative abnormale Rendite

Sum of differences between the expected return on a share and the actual return that comes from the release of news to the market.

cumulative preference dividend kumulative Vorzugsdividende

Dividend on preferred shares that takes priority over dividend payments on ordinary shares. Dividends may not be paid on the ordinary shares until all past dividends on the preferred shares have been paid.

cumulative probability kumulierte Wahrscheinlichkeit

Probability that a drawing from the standardized normal distribution will be below a particular value.

cumulative voting kumulative Stimmabgabe

A method of voting for corporate directors, that allows shareholders to multiply the number of shares owned by the number of directorships being voted. The system is designed to give minority stockholders representation on the board.

curb Bordsteinkante; *(restraint)* Drosselung; *(to ~)* dämpfen; drosseln

currency Währung; Zahlungsmittel; Valuta; *(foreign)* Devisen; Fremdwährung

A unit of exchange that facilitates the transfer of goods and services. It is a form of money, i.e. coins and bills that are authorized by a government as legal tender for the payment of obligations.

currency account Fremdwährungskonto; Valutakonto; Devisenkonto

currency adjustment Währungsausgleich

currency crisis Währungskrise

Occurs when an exceptional event, such as a speculative attack, results in a sharp depreciation in the value of the currency or forces authorities to expend large volumes of international currency reserves and sharply increase interest rates to defend the prevailing exchange rate.

currency depreciation Währungsabwertung

currency exposure unsichere Währungspositionen

The effect which changes in exchange rates have on the net worth of a business.

currency fund Währungsfonds

currency future Devisentermingeschäft

A futures contract in which a currency for forward delivery is bought or sold at a certain exchange rate.

currency hedging Wechselkurssicherung

currency inconvertibility Nichtkonvertierbarkeit einer Währung

currency market Devisenmarkt; Devisenbörse

currency needs Währungsbedarf

currency option Währungsoption

A contract giving the right to buy or to sell a currency at a fixed exchange rate within a given period. The price agreed is called the strike price or exercise price.

currency profit Währungsgewinn

currency rate Währungskurs; Wechselkurs

currency speculation Währungsspekulation; Devisenspekulation

Involves short-term movement of funds from one currency to another in hopes of profiting from shifts in exchange rates.

currency stability Währungsstabilität; Geldwertstabilität

currency swap Swapgeschäft

Simultaneous purchase and sale of a given amount of foreign exchange for two different values.

currency translation Währungsumrechnung

Converting the financial statements of foreign subsidiaries into the currency of the home country.

current Strom; umlaufend; laufend; *(present)* gegenwärtig; aktuell

current account Girokonto; laufendes Konto; Kontokorrentkonto; *(balance of payments)* Leistungsbilanz

Banking: An active account at a bank or other financial institution into which deposits can be paid and from which withdrawals can be made

Balance of payments: The part of the balance of payments account of a country that records non-capital transactions, including international trade in goods and services along with transfer payments and short-term credit.

current account advance Kontokorrent-kredit

current account deficit Leistungsbilanzdefizit; Kontokorrent-defizit

The current account of the balance of payments is in deficit when a country imports more goods and services than it exports.

current account ledger Kontokorrentbuch

current account surplus Leistungsbilanzüberschuss; Kontokorrent-guthaben

Current account of the balance of payments is in surplus when a country exports more goods and services than it imports.

current assets Umlaufvermögen

Balance sheet: Assets of a company that are expected to be converted to cash within 12 months, such as cash, inventory, accounts receivable, marketable securities.

current costs Kosten zum Gegenwartswert

Present market value of a product or asset, as contrasted with its acquisition cost.

current cost accounting Buchführung zum Tageswert; Bilanzierung auf der Basis des Wiederbeschaffungswertes; Rechnungslegung zum Tages- oder Marktwert; inflationsbereinigte Bilanzierung

Method of accounting where assets are valued at their value to the business, also known as their deprival value.

The deprival value of an asset is the loss that a business would suffer if it were to be deprived of the use of the asset. This may be the replacement costof the asset, its net realisable value. or its economic value of the business.

current liabilities kurzfristige Verbindlichkeiten

Debts or obligations incurred by a company that are expected to be repaid during the following year or the operating period.

Example: accounts payable, short-term loans, and that portion of long-term loans due in one year.

current market situation gegenwärtige Marktsituation

current rate method Umrechnungsmethode zum geltenden Satz; Fremdwährungsumrechnung zu Stichtagskursen

Using the exchange rate at the balance sheet date to translate the financial statements of a foreign subsidiary into the home currency.

current ratio Verhältnis von Umlaufvermögen zu kurzfristigen Verbindlichkeiten; Liquidität dritten Grades

A ratio to test a corporation's liquidity, calculated by dividing current assets by current liabilities, i.e., the ratio shows a company's ability to pay its current obligations from current assets. The higher the ratio, the more liquid the company.

current transfer laufende Transfer-zahlungen

current yield laufender Ertrag; laufende Rendite

The annual rate of return that an investor purchasing a security at its market price would realize. This is calculated by dividing the annual income from a security by the current price of the security; also known as the return on investment.

*Example:*a security paying 10% with a par value of $1000 is bought at a market price of $800. The annual income is $100, but the current yield is $100 divided by $800, or 12½%.

curriculum vitae Lebenslauf

Biographical resume of one's career, including educational credentials and professional experience. Its purpose is to give the prospective employer an understanding of the professional abilities of the applicant. In the U.S. it is often called a resume.

cursor Mauszeiger

The blinking symbol on a computer screen that shows where the next charter will appear.

curtail einschränken; verkürzen; beschneiden

curtailment Verkürzung

curve Kurve; Biegung; Krümmung; *(to ~)* biegen; kurven

cushion Kissen; Polster; Sicherheitsfaktor; *(to ~)* abdämpfen; polstern; unterdrücken

custodial account Depotkonto; Treuhandkonto

Account that parents create for a minor, usually at a bank or brokerage firm. Minors cannot make securities transactions without the approval of the account trustee.

custodian Treuhänder; Verwahrer; Wärter; Verwalter

Real estate: A person having care of a facility or a building, cleaning and maintaining it. Also called caretaker or janitor.

custodian bank Depotbank; verwahrende Bank

A bank or other financial institution that holds in custody and for safekeeping the securities and other assets of an investment company.

custodianship account Kundendepot

custody Verwahrung; Depot; *(supervision)* Aufsicht; Obhut; Haft

Property: Legal responsibilities for the assets of another person that are within one's personal care and control.

Persons: The right to or responsibility for a child's care and control, which includes the obligation of providing food, shelter, medical care, education and discipline.

custody bill of lading Lagerhallenkonnossement

custom Gewohnheit; Gebrauch

customary Gewohnheits-; gewohnheitsmässig; üblich

customary within an industry branchenüblich

customer Kunde; *(purchaser)* Abnehmer

buyer of a product or service.

customer base Kundschaft; Kundenbestand

customer-centered company Kundenorientiertes Unternehmen

Company that focuses on customer developments in designing its marketing strategies and on delivering superior value to its target customers.

customer contract Kundenvertrag

custumer contribution accounting Kundendeckungsbeitragsrechnung

Amount of contribution a particular customer makes to profits, once all costs which can be attributed to this customer have been deducted from the revenues.

Customers can then be classified according to the revenues they generate, possibly using an ABC approach. This can be a useful basis for the development of marketing policy and for strategic management.

customer database Kundendatenbank

Organized collection of comprehensive data about individual customers or prospects, including geographic, demographic, psychographic and buying behavior data.

customer demands Kundenwünsche

customer loyalty Kundentreue

customer needs Kundenbedürfnisse

customer orientation Kundenorientierung

customer profiling Kundenprofil

The use of data warehouse information to help marketers understand the characteristics and behavior of specific target groups.

customer proximity Kundennähe

customer relationship management (CRM) Kundenbeziehungsmanagement

Holistic process of identifying, attracting, and retaining the most valuable customers of a business to sustain profitable growth.

Consisten CRM requires structures and systems to be put in place that cut across the vertical lines of the traditional firm and focus on individual customers.

customer sales force structure Struktur der kundenspezifischen Verkaufspersonals

Sales force organization under which sales people specialize in selling only to certain customers or industries.

customer satisfaction Kunden-zufriedenheit

Extent to which a product's perceived performance matches a buyer's expectations. If the product's performance falls short of expectations, the buyer is dissatisfied.

customer service Kundendienst; Kundenberatung; Kundenservice

The services a business offers to its customers. Customer service used to be offered especially for industrial goods, but with increasing competition, more and more consumer goods, such as computers or cars, require good customer service as well.

Customer services can take many forms, including after-sales servicing, such as a repair and replacement service, extended guarantees, regular mailings of information, and freephone telephone calls in case of complaints.

customer service representative Kundenberater

customer value Kundenwert; Kundennutzen

Attempt to measure the value of a customer to a company by quantifying the revenues to be gained from a long-term relationship with a customer.

Practically, the expected revenues, contribution margins and direct marketing costs have to be investigated. The cash streams are projected into the future, discounted and shown as a net present value.

customer value analysis Analyse des Kundennutzens

Analysis conducted to determine what benefits target customers value and how they rate the relative value of various competitors' offers.

customer value delivery system System für Erbringung von Kundennutzen

System made up of the value chains of the company and its suppliers, distributors, and ultimately customers who work together to deliver value to customers.

customization Anpassung an kundenspezifische Anforderungen

Design and development of a product to meet the specific requirements of a single customer.

Because of the high costs involved in producing a unique product, most firms offer a standard product with certain features that can be modified.

Many cars, for example, can be bought with various additional features, such as stronger engines or trims. Additionally, optional extras, such as exhausts, enable buyers to customise their cars even further.

customs Zoll; *(administration)* Zollbehörde

Government agency responsible for checking all imported goods, assessing their value, and collecting duties.

customs agency Zollagentur

customs authority Zollverwaltung

customs bill of entry Zolleinfuhr-erklärung; Zolleinfuhrschein; Import-erklärung

customs broker Zollagent; Zollspediteur

customs classification Tarifierung; Zollklassifizierung

customs declaration Zollerklärung; Zollanmeldung; Zollab-fertigungsschein

customs forwarding firm Zollspedition

customs guarantee Zollgarantie

customs house Zollstelle

customs invoice Zollfaktura

An invoice for goods imported or exported, which is prepared especially for the customs authorities.

customs officials Zollverwaltung

customs territory Zollgebiet

customs union Zollunion

Form of regional economic integration in which a group of countries is committed to (1) removing all barriers to the free flow of goods and services between each other and (2) the pursuit of a common external trade policy.

customs valuation Zollbewertung; zollamtliche Bewertung; Zollwertfest-setzung

cut Schnitt; *(reduction)* Kürzung; Verkürzung; *(price)* Ermäßigung; Senkung; *(to ~)* schneiden; abschnei-den; beschneiden; kürzen; *(price)* ermäßigen

cutback Einschränkung; Abbau; Rückgang; Kürzung

cut back einschränken; abbauen; zurückblenden

cutthroat Halsabschneider; Mörder; ruinös; halsabschneiderisch

cybermediaries Cyber-Intermediäre

Intermediaries on the internet who bring together buyers and sellers or those with particular information or service needs.

cyberspace virtueller Raum

Terms used colloquially to indicate the futuristic nature of the internet.

cyber-squatting Domain-Piraterie

Type of trademark violation that involves the registration of domains that resemble or duplicate the names of existing corporations or other entities.

cycle Zyklus; Kreislauf; Periode; *(business cycle)* Konjunkturzyklus; zyklische Konjunkturschwankungen;

Wave-like movement of sales resulting from changes in general economic and competitive activity.

cyclical Konjunktur-; zyklisch; konjunkturell; konjunkturbedingt

cyclical demand zyklische Nachfrage; konjunkturbedingte Nachfrage

Demand for products and services that changes cyclically over time. This can happen in response to some seasonal changes or to the business cycle.

Example: demand for ice cream is seasonally cyclical; demand for housing is affected by the effects of the business cycle on interest rates.

cyclical downturn Konjunkturabschwung

cyclical industry konjunkturempfindliche Branche

An industry whose performance is closely tied to the condition of the general economy and in which variations in output occur frequently.

Example: the construction industry depends on the business cycle, especially changes in interest rates and demand.

cyclical pattern Konjunkturschema

cyclical trend Konjunkturverlauf

cyclical unemployment konjunkturelle Arbeitslosigkeit

Unemployment caused by fluctuations in the economy.

D

daily quotations *(stock market)* Kursblatt; Tageskurs; Einheitskurs

daily statement of account Tagesauszug

daisy wheel printer Typenraddrucker

damage Schaden; *(loss)* Verlust; Einbuße; *(to ~)* schaden; beschädigen

damages Schadensersatz

Monetary compensation for a damage suffered, such as loss, injury, breach of contract, tort, or infringement of a right.

Damages describes only the compensation awarded, not the damage itself, and represents an attempt to restore injured parties to the position they were in before the event occurred. The aim is therefore to provied a restitution not an opportunity for profit.

data Daten; Werte; Angaben; Datenmaterial; Tatsachen; Sachverhalt

data bank Datenbank; Datenbestand; Datensammlung

database Datenbasis; Datenbank

An organized collection of data stored on a computer storage medium for access by a number of users and for a number of different applications.

Example: the name and address of the same customer may be in a marketing file, a billing file, and an addressing file. In database systems, this information is retrievable for each application from a shared file that is not dependent upon the application programs.

database management Datenbank-verwaltung

A systematic approach to creating, maintaining, accessing, reporting, and analyzing large amounts of data.

database marketing Datenbankmarketing

Marketing based on the extensive use of computerized databases of customers. The databases can be owned by the company itself, or they can be purchased from specialized companies supplying consolidated lists.

Database marketing is becoming increasinly accurate, and even if is still expensive, it is becoming rapidly more widespread with technical progress.

data collection Datenerfassung; Datenerhebung

data exchange Datenaustausch

data fusion Datenzusammenführung; Datenverschmelzung

Combining data from different complementary sources (e.g. geo-demographic and lifestyle or market research and lifestyle) to build a wholesome picture on a particular topic.

data mining Datenbankauswertung; Auswertung grösserer Datenmengen

Extraction of previously hidden predictive information from the warehouse via statistical analysis in order to find patterns and other information in databases.

data processing Datenverarbeitung

data protection Datenschutz

Legal safeguards protecting the personal information about individuals.

Some of the principles of data protection should be: information should be processed, fairly and lawfully, Personal data should be held only for specified and lawful purposes and should be relevant to those purposes, data should not be kept longer than necessary, and security measures have to be taken against unauthorized access.

data storage Datenspeicherung

data transmission Datenübertragung

data warehouse universelle Datenbanken

Data repository for an entire organization's historical data, designed specifically to support analyzes necessary for decision making.

Through data mining, the data contained in a data warehouse can be used for targeted marketing activities, but also executive information systems and other decision support systems.

date Datum; *(appointment)* Verabredung; *(business)* Termin

date draft Datowechsel

date of bookkeeping entry Buchungstag

date of issue Ausgabezeitpunkt

date of maturity Fälligkeitstermin

date of record Eintragungszeitpunkt

Securities: The date on which a shareholder must officially own shares in order to be entitled to a dividend.

dates convention exakte Datumskonvention

Treating cash flows as being received on exact dates-date 0, date 1, and so forth-as opposed to the end-of-year convention.

daughter window Nebenfenster

Internet: Separate window that overlays the current browser window and contains content or advertisements. Sometimes called pop-up window.

day order Tagesauftrag

Order to buy or sell stock that automatically expires if it can't be executed on the day it is entered

days in receivables Forderungslaufzeit

dead freight Fehlfracht

deadline letzter Termin; Stichtag; Schlusstermin; Einsendeschluss; Annahmeschluss

A date by which specific requirements must be satisfied or actions taken, such as the latest time for the completion of a negotiation, project, service, or product. The failure to meet a deadline normally results in negative consequences.

deal Geschäft; Handel; Transaktion; *(agreement)* Abmachung; *(to ~)* handeln; Handel treiben; Geschäfte machen

dead stock totes Inventar; unverkäufliche Ware; unverkaufte Ware

dealer Händler; Kaufmann; Kauffrau; *(sales agent)* Vertreter

General: someone who buys and sells from his own account. The merchandise is inventory, any gain on sales is ordinary income.

Stock exchange: a merchant who regularly engages in the purchase and resale of securities, such as stocks, bonds, and other financial instruments, to customers.

dealer network Händlernetz

dealership Verkaufsagentur; Verkaufsvertretung

dealings geschäftlicher Umgang; Verkehr

debenture Schuldschein; Schuldverschreibung; Obligation; ungesicherte langfristige Verbindlichkeiten

An unsecured debt instrument backed only by the general credit standing and earning capacity of the issuer..

Debentures are issued by large, well-established corporations. Holders of debentures are creditors and entitled to payment before shareholders if the corporation should be dissolved.

debit Soll; Kontobelastung; Lastschrift; *(accoun)* Abbuchung; Schuldenposten; *(to ~ an account)* belasten; abbuchen

Accounting: an entry on the left-hand side of an account record in which amounts are recorded in a double-entry system of bookkeeping. Debits include the acquisition cost of assets and amounts of deductible expenses.

Banking: a charge to a customer's bank account.

debit advice Lastschriftanzeige; *(debit balance)* Verlustvortrag; Schuldsaldo

debit card Kundenkreditkarte; Lastschriftkarte

Card used for making electronic transfers of cash from a customer's bank account to a store's account.

debit carryover Passivüberhang

debit column Sollseite

debit entry Lastschrift; Sollbuchung

debt Verschuldung; Schulden; Verbindlichkeit

Loan agreement that is a liability of the firm. An obligation to repay a specified amount at a particular time.

debt burden Schuldenlast

debt buy-backs Schuldenrückkäufe

debt capacity Verschuldungsfähigkeit

Ability to borrow; amount a firm can borrow up to the point where the firm value no longer increases.

debt ceiling Verschuldungsgrenze

debt crisis Schuldenkrise; Verschuldungskrise

debt displacement Verschuldunglimit durch Leasing

Amount of borrowing that leasing displaces. Firms that do a lot of leasing will be forced to cut back on borrowing.

debt/equity ratio Verschuldungsgrad; Verhältnis von Schulden zu Aktienkapital

A ratio used to examine the financial structure of a business. Long term debt is divided by common stockholders' equity, comparing assets provided by creditors to assets provided by shareholders.

In a highly geared company the debt is higher than the equity. It offers higher returns to shareholders when it is performing well, but must be regarded as a speculative investment.

debt equity swap Umwandlung von Bankkrediten in Beteiligungskapital; Schuldenhandel

debt financing Fremdfinanzierung; Fremdmittelaufnahme; Außenfinanzierung

Raising capital through borrowing, as with the sale of bonds; as contrasted with equity financing, which is raising capital through the sale of an ownership portion (stock).

debt instrument Schuldpapier

Written promise to repay a debt; such as a bill, bond, banker's acceptance, note, certificate of deposit, or commercial paper.

debt level Schuldenstand

debt management Schuldenmanagement

debt market Schuldenmarkt

debt obligation Schuldschein

debtor Schuldner; Debitor

One who owes another something or is under obligation to pay money or to fulfill some other obligation; in bankruptcy or similar proceedings, the person who is the subject of the proceeding.

debtor nation Schuldnerland

debt rating Schuldenrating

debt reduction Schuldensenkung; Schuldenrückführung; Schuldenabbau

debt rescheduling Umschuldung

A negotiation between a debtor and his creditor concerning outstanding loans in which the debtor has repayment difficulties.

The rescheduling can take various forms, such as an entirely new loan, an extension of the existing loan repayment period, deferring interest or principal repayments.

debt retirement Schuldenabbau; Schuldenrückzahlung

Repayment of debt, usually on a term-wise or regular payment basis.

debt risk Schuldenrisiko

debt security Schuldensicherheit

Security representing money borrowed that must be repaid and having a fixed amount, a specific maturity or maturities, and usually a specific rate of interest or an original purchase discount.

debt service Schuldendienst

The payments of principal and interest by a borrower to a lender.

Debt service in mortgage loans includes interest and principal; in corporate bond issues, the annual interest plus annual sinking fund payments; in government bonds, the annual payments into the debt service fund.

debt service ratio Schuldendienstquote

A ratio showing the degree of a country's indebtedness, shown as the proportion of annual export earnings of a country needed to service its external debts, including interest payments and repayment of principal.

debt service reduction Schuldendienstreduktion

decelerate verlangsamen

deceleration Verlangsamung

decentralization Dezentralisierung; Auflockerung

Business situation where essential decision making and policy formulation done at several locations throughout an organization.

The objective is to give decision-making authority to those most directly responsible for the outcome of those decisions, with first-hand experience and knowledge about the issues involved.

decentralize dezentralisieren; auflockern

decentralized management dezentrale Leitung; dezentralisiertes Management

deception Täuschung; Irreführung; Betrug; Trick

deceptive advertising irreführende Werbung

Advertising that is intended to mislead consumers by creating a false impression.

Deceptive practices include false promises, incomplete descriptions, false testimonials unsubstantiated claims, or comparisons, small-print qualifications of advertisements, partial disclosure, or visual distortion of products.

deceptive packaging irreführende Verpackung; Mogelpackung

Packaging that is intended to mislead consumers by creating a false impression, either about the quantity or the quality of the product.

decide entscheiden; beschließen; bestimmen; (to *make up one's mind)* sich entscheiden;

decider Entscheidungsträger; Entscheider

Buying: person who ultimately makes a buying decision or any part of it – whether to buy, what to buy how to buy, or where to buy.

decimal dezimal

decimal currency Dezimale Währung

A currency system in which the standard unit is subdivided into 100 parts.

decision Entscheidung; Entschluss; Entschlusskraft; Beschluss; *(law)* Urteil

decision accounting Entscheidungsrechnung

Accounting information prepare specifically for managers to take decisions. Only those figures of costs, revenues and volumes are included that can really and directly be changed by the decision to be taken.

decision and reward system Entscheidungs- und Vergütungssystem

Formal and informal operating procedures that guide planning, targeting, compensation and other activities.

decision maker Entscheider; Entscheidungsträger

decision making Entscheidungsfindung

The act of deciding between two or more alternative courses of action. In business, various techniques are used to facilitate decision making, such as discounted cash flow, critical-path analysis, marginal costing, and breakeven analysis.

decision-making unit entscheidungsfindende Einheit; Entscheidungsträger

All the individuals who participate in the process of reaching a decision.

decision model Entscheidungsmodell

Formal or informal conceptualization of the relationship of the various factors that are relevant in decision making and planning.

decision process Entscheidungsprozess

decision support system (DSS) Entscheidungsfindungssystem; Entscheidungsunterstützungssystem

Information system that provides answers to problems and that integrates the decision maker into the system as a component. Branch of the broadly defined management information system (MIS).

decision tree Entscheidungsbaum

Diagram that illustrates all possible consequences of different decisions at different stages of a decision making process.

declaration Erklärung; *(customs)* Zolldeklaration; Zollerklärung; *(property)* Vermögensangabe; *(bankruptcy)* Konkurserklärung

declaration date Dividendenstichtag

Corporate finance: date on which the board of directors passes a resolution to pay a dividend of a specified amount to all qualified holders of record on a specified date.

declaration of intention Grundsatzerklärung; Willenserklärung

declare erklären; aussagen; feststellen; bekannt machen; *(customs)* deklarieren; *(bankruptcy)* anmelden

decline Rückgang; Abnahme; Verschlechterung; *(to ~)* abnehmen; geringer werden; sinken; *(invitation)* absagen; ablehnen

decline in earnings Ertragsrückgang

decline in prices Preisrückgang; Preisverfall; *(stock)* Kursabschlag

decline in sales Umsatzrückgang; Absatzrückgang

decline stage Degenerationsphase

Product life-cycle stage at which a product's sales decline.

declining-balance method degressive Abschreibung

An accelerated depreciation method that charges more depreciation in the early life of an asset, based on the view that the asset is used to generate profits less and less as it gets older.

decoding Dekodierung; Entschlüsselung; Dechiffrierung

As part of the communication process, retranslating in a sender's communication message. Before the message can be received, the symbols in it must be translated into a form that can be understood by the receiver.

decontrol Freigabe; Aufhebung; Abbau; Liberalisierung; *(to ~)* freigeben; aufheben; abbauen; liberalisieren

Removal of government restrictions on prices, rents, etc.

decrease Abnahme; Verminderung; Rückgang; *(cutback)* Kürzung; *(to ~)* abnehmen; vermindern; zurückgehen; fallen

decryption Dechiffrierung; Entzifferung; Entschlüsselung

Process of decoding (unscrambling) a message that has been encrypted using defined mathematical rules.

deduct abziehen; *(taxes)* absetzen

deductible abziehbar; *(taxes)*absetzbar

deduction Abzug; *(taxes)* Absetzung; *(rebate)* Abschlag; Folgerung

Taxation: a reduction in the gross amount on which a tax is calculated.

deductive reasoning schlussfolgerndes Denken

A mental conclusion drawing from a given set of facts (premises), to reach certain consequences (conclusions).

deed Tat; Handlung; *(law)* gesiegelter Vertrag, förmliche Urkunde; *(to ~)* urkundlich übertragen

Written legal document, that has been signed, sealed, and deliverd. Usually about ownership or rights, it conveys an interest in land from the grantor to the grantee. Its main function is to pass title to land.

deed of assignment Abtretungsurkunde

deed of partnership Gesellschaftsvertrag

deep-discount bond stark diskontierte Anleihe

Bond issued with a very low coupon or no coupon, and selling at a price far below par value. When the bond has no coupon, it is also called a zero coupon bond or pure-discount or original-issue-discount bond.

de facto faktisch; tatsächlich

Existing in actual fact, although not by official legal recognition.

defalcation Unterschlagung von Geldern; unterschlagene Summe; Veruntreuung; Betrug

Misappropriation of money placed in trust, or the sum misappropriated.

default Nichterfüllung; Nichteinhaltung; *(contract)* Vertragsverletzung; Säumnis; *(payment)* Verzug; Nichtzahlung *(to ~)* seinen Verpflichtungen nicht nachkommen; *(payments)* in Verzug geraten

Payment: Failure of a debtor to make timely payments of interest and principal as they come due, or to meet some other provision of a bond, mortgage, lease, or other contract

default clause Default-Klausel

defaulted interest Verzugszinsen

Interest that has not been paid on time.

default judgment Säumnisurteil

Law: A judgment passed by a court against a defendant who did not respond to a plaintiff's action or who did not appear at the trial.

default risk Ausfallrisiko

Chance that interest or principal will not be paid on the due date and in the promised amount.

defect Fehler; Mangel; Defekt; Manko

defective fehlerhaft; mangelhaft

Incomplete, faulty, not reasonably safe for a use that can be reasonably anticipated.

defective title mit Rechtsmängeln behafteter Rechtstitel; Rechtsmangel

Property: a title that might be subject to partial or complete ownership by someone else.

Bonds: title obtained through fraud or other illegal means.

defense Verteidigung; Schutz

defend verteidigen; eintreten für

defendant Beklagter; Angeklagter

A person or institution against whom an action is brought in a court; in civil proceedings, the party responding to the complaint; in criminal proceedings, the accused.

defensive behaviors defensives Verhalten

Reactive and protective behaviors to avoid action, blame, or change.

defer veschieben; aufschieben; verzögern; *(meeting)* vertagen

deferral Aufschub; Verschiebung; Verzögerung

deferral of taxes transitorische Steuerabgrenzung

The deferment of making tax payments from the current year to a later year. The aim is to earn interest on money not yet paid in taxes.

deferral principle Prinzip der transitorischen Abgrenzung

Taxation practice under which parent companies are not taxed on the income of a foreign subsidiary until they actually receive a dividend from that subsidiary.

deferred billing Rechnungsaufschub

A way of offering customers to make purchases and not pay for them for some weeks or months, normally without interest.

deferred charge aufgeschobene Ausgaben; aktive Rechnungsabgrenzung

An expenditure that is considered an asset until it becomes relevant to the business and amortized over the life it represents.

deferred compensation nachträgliche Vergütung

Plan under whose terms an employee defers payment of a portion of salary in return for the employer's promise to pay the employee the salary at some time in the future.

deferred item *(balance sheet)* Ausgleichsposten; transitorischer Posten

deferred payment credit Ratenkredit

deferred payment letter of credit Nachsicht-Akkreditiv; Zielzahlungs-Akkreditiv

deferred payments aufgeschobene Zahlungen

Money payments to be delayed for a future date or extended period of time.

deferred tax aufgeschobene Steuer; latente Steuer

Non-cash expense that provides a source of free cash flow. Amount allocated during the period to cover tax liabilities that have not yet been paid.

deficiency Mangel; Manko; *(deficit)* Fehlbetrag; Ausfall

deficient unzureichend; unzulänglich; fehlerhaft; ungenügend

deficient product fehlerhaftes Produkt; Ausschuss

deficit Fehlbetrag; Defizit; *(loss)* Verlust; Ausfall; *(balance sheet)* Passivsaldo

General: insufficiency in an account or number, possibly the result of defaults misappropriations or mistakes.

Government: excess of government spending over its revenues. Many economists believe that deficits lead to inflation.

deficit decrease Defizitkürzung

deficit financing Defizitfinanzierung; Staatsverschuldung

Borrowing by a government to compensate revenue shortfalls. Deficit financing stimulates the economy for a time but eventually can become a drag on the economy by pushing up interest rates.

deficit spending Defizitfinanzierung; öffentliche

define definieren; bestimmen; abgrenzen; erläutern; umreißen

definite bestimmt; deutlich; genau; klar

definition of a project Aufgabenstellung

deflation Deflation; Entwertung

Deflation is the reverse of inflation, accompanied by a decline in prices, or volume of production of goods and services, usually accompanied by unemployment. Not to be confused with disinflation, which is a slowing down in the rate of price increases.

deflationary deflationistisch

deflator Deflationsfaktor; Deflationierungsfaktor; Deflator

Statistical factor or device designed to remove the effect inflation has on variables. Inflation-adjusted variables are said to be in real, or constant-value terms.

Example: inflation-adjusted gross national product figures are said to show *real GNP.*

defraud betrügen

defunct company erloschene Gesellschaft

Company that no longer exists; company that has suspended all operations and is out of business.

degression Degression; degressive Abnahme

Tendency to descend or decrease; progressive decline in an item, such as value, over time.

Example: deterioration in a company's market share for a specific product line.

de jure von Rechts wegen; rechtlich gesehen

By right; lawful; legitimate. Generally used in contrast to de facto; *de jure* connotes "as a matter of law" whereas *de facto* connotes "as a matter of practice not founded upon law".

delay Aufschub; Verzögerung; Verzug; *(loss of time)* Zeitverlust; *(to ~)* verzögern; hinausschieben; aufhalten

delayering Hierarchieabbau

Reducing the number of levels in an organization's hierarchy, making the pyramid mor flat or horizontal. As a consequence, the average span of control of managers is increased.

delegate Abgeordneter; Delegierter; Bevollmächtigter; *(to ~)* delegieren; bevollmächtigen

To appoint, authorize, or commission, transferring authority from one person to another. Efficient management requires delegating authority but not necessarily responsibility.

delegation Bevollmächtigung; *(group of delegates)* Abordnung; Delegation

delete streichen; ausstreichen; löschen; *(debt)* tilgen

deletion Streichung; Löschung

deliberate absichtlich; wohlüberlegt; bedachtsam; *(to ~)* überlegen; nachdenken; *(to discuss)* sich beraten; beratschlagen

deliberation Beratung; *(consideration)* Überlegung; Bedächtigkeit

delinquency Pflichtvergessenheit; Schuld; Vergehen; Säumnis; Nichtzahlung bei Fälligkeit

deliver liefern; ausliefern; zustellen; übergeben; *(a speech)* halten

deliverable lieferfähig; zustellbar

deliverable instrument lieferbarer Wert

Asset in a forward contract, that will be delivered in the future at an agreed-upon price.

delivered at frontier an der Grenze abgeliefert; geliefert Grenze benannter Bestimmungsort im Einfuhrland

delivered duty paid geliefert verzollt; zollfrei geliefert

delivered duty unpaid geliefert unverzollt

delivered ex quay duty paid geliefert verzollt ab Kai

delivered ex quay duty unpaid geliefert unverzollt ab Kai

delivery Lieferung; Auslieferung; Ablieferung; Zustellung; Überbringung

delivery clause Lieferklausel; Auslieferungsklausel; Übergabeklausel

delivery ex ship Lieferung ab Schiff

delivery date Empfangsdatum; Fälligkeits-termin; Liefertermin; Lieferdatum

Stock exchange: first day on which delivery is to be made under a futures contract.

delivery guarantee Lieferungsgarantie

delivery note Lieferschein; Versandanzeige

delivery order Teilschein; Lieferauftrag; Lieferschein

delivery risk Lieferrisiko

delivery stop Liefersperre

delivery terms Lieferbestimmungen; Lieferklausel

delivery verification certificate Verbleibsnachweis bei der Einfuhr

delphi technique Delphi-Methode

A group technique that seeks to eliminate the effects of personal relationships.

Each member writes down his thoughts on a problem and submits them to a coordinator. The coordinator then compiles all comments received and sends them to every member for review. Each member then provides feedback on the other comments and submits recommendations to the coordinator. The coordinator then attempts to reach a consensus based on all comments received.

demand Nachfrage; Bedarf; *(claim)* Forderung; Einforderung; *(aggregate)* Endnachfrage; Verlangen; *(to ~)* fordern; verlangen

Buyer behavior: The combined desire, ability and willingness on the part of consumers to exchange value (goods, labor, money) for goods or services, depending upon the price asked.

demand analysis Bedarfsanalyse; Nachfrageanalyse

demand creditor Sichtkreditor

demand curve Nachfragekurve

A graph showing the relationship between the quantity demanded of a product and its price.

Price is normally shown on the vertical axis, and quantity on the horizontal. The demand curve normally slopes downward from left to right, reflecting higher quantity demanded at lower prices.

demand deposit Sichteinlage

demand for credit Kreditnachfrage

demand forecast Nachfragevorhersage; Nachfrageprognose; Bedarfsprognose

demand growth Nachfragezuwachs; Bedarfszunahme

demand-pull inflation Nachfragedruckinflation; Nachfrageinflation; nachfrageinduzierte Inflation

Price increases occurring when supply is not adequate to meet demand.

Deming, W. Edwards (1900-1993)

American statistician and founder of the quality movement. Deming's approach was based on the assumption that if the levels of variation are managed, they can be decreased and quality raised.

Together with Joseph Juran, Deming introduced quality management into post-war Japanese industry, which is considered the basis for its later success. The core element in his approach was the 'management circle' of planning, implementation, check and action. Deming's basic management philosophy regarded the consumer as the most important part of the production line.

Biography: studied electrical engineering at the University of Wyoming and mathematical physics at Yale, worked at the Western Electric Hawthorne plant in Chicago as a government statistician, in 1950 invited to Japan, where his teachings led to resounding success. His achievements were only widely recognized in the United States from 1980 onwards.

Major publications: (1982) Quality, productivity and competitive position, (1986) Out of the crisis, (Walton, Mary, 1986) The Deming management method, (Neave, H.R., 1990) The Deming dimension.

demographic demographisch; bevölkerungsstatistisch; bevölkerungswissenschaftlich

Related to statistics about human population characteristics such as size, growth rates, density, distribution, migration, birth rates and mortality rates.

demographic segmentation demographische Segmentierung

Dividing the market into groups based on demographic variables such as age, sex, family size, family life cycle, income, occupation, education, religion, race and nationality.

Demographic segmentation is used mostly in combination with other techniques, such as benefit, life-stage, and life-cycle segmentation in order to produce more predictable market information.

demography Demographie; Bevölkerungswissenschaft

The statistical study of human populations, analyzing such factors as size, density, distribution, age, sex, family size, family life cycle, income, occupation, education, religion, race and nationality.

demolition Abbruch; Abriss; Niederreißen; Zerstörung

Destruction and removal of an existing structure from a site; necessary to prepare a site for new construction.

demonstrate beweisen; vorführen; demonstrieren

demonstration Darstellung; Ausführung; Äußerung; Demonstration

demoralize demoralisieren; Sitten/Moral untergraben

In general: to lower someone's spirits.

Personnel: to decrease employee morale, e.g. by lack of appreciation, layoffs, wage cuts. As a result, productivity and accuracy will fall, whilst employee turnover will rise.

demote degradieren; in den nächst niederen Rang versetzen

demurrage Überliegegebühr; Liegegeld

Charge applied to shipping vehicles when they are held by the consignor or the consignee for an excessive amount of time.

denationlization Reprivatisierung; Entstaatlichung

denomination Benennung; *(class)* Klasse; Kategorie; *(bank note)* Nennwert; *(church)* Konfession

density Dichte

deny verweigern; abschlagen; *(to declare untrue)* leugnen; dementieren

department Abteilung; Arbeitsgebiet; Fachgebiet; Branche *(government)* Ministerium; Ressort

A specialized division of a large organization, set up to accomplish particular functions. It contains a number of positions and normally a head or manager who has the responsibility of coordinating the group.

departmentalization Abteilungsbildung

Process of setting up groups of employees in specialized divisions to accomplish specific organizational goals.

Departments can be organized according to a number of criteria: (1) functions workers perform, as in accounting and human resource departments; (2) products, as in a department store organized by retail product categories; (3) type of customer, as in men's wear or women's wear; or (4) geographic divisions.

department store Kaufhaus; Warenhaus

Large retail store organized into departments that carry a wide variety of product lines, normally clothing, home furnishings, appliances and household goods.

depend abhängig sein von; angewiesen sein auf; abhängen von

dependence Abhängigkeit; Vertrauen; Stütze

dependent Abhängiger; *(tax)* Unterhaltsberechtigter; unselbständig; abhängig

Tax: any person for whom a taxpayer can claim a *dependency exemption,* defined as any individual supported by the taxpayer who is related to the taxpayer in specified ways or who makes his principal abode in the taxpayer's household.

dependent coverage Mitversicherung für Familienmitglieder

Health insurance coverage extended to the spouse and unmarried children of the primary insured member.

dependent on price preisabhängig

dependent on the exchange rate Wechselkurs bedingt

dependent on time zeitabhängig

dependent upon sales umsatzabhängig

dependent variable abhängige Variable

Statistics: A mathematical variable - usually expressed as "Y" - whose value is determined by that of one or more other variables in the function, the *independent variables* - usually expressed as "X". The amount of variation of the dependent variable caused by the independent variables can be measured by regression analysis.

deplete *(to empty)* entleeren; *(to exhaust)* erschöpfen; *(to use up)* aufbrauchen; *(to reduce)* verringern

depletion *(exhaustion)* Erschöpfung; Entleerung; *(of assets)* Substanzverringerung; Abnutzung

Process of using up a natural resource, such as coal.

deploy *(to use)* einsetzen; entfalten

deployment Einsatz; Aufmarsch; Entfaltung; Verwendung

deployment of machines Maschineneinsatz

deport ausweisen; deportieren; abschieben

deposit Geldeinlage; Einzahlung; Einlage; *(down payment)* Anzahlung; *(safety)*

Hinterlegungssumme; *(minerals)* Vorkommen; *(to ~)* einzahlen; *(safety)* hinterlegen; anzahlen

Banking: money paid to a bank or other financial institution, in the form of cash, checks, or drafts, that will be credited to a customer's account.

Security: money paid as a security in a transaction intended to protect the other party in the event that the contract is not completed.

deposit account Sparkonto; Einlagenkonto

deposit account balance Guthaben

deposit insurance Depotversicherung; Einlagenversicherung

depositor Einzahler; Hinterleger; *(down payment)* Anzahler; *(account holder)* Depositeninhaber; Deponent; Kontoinhaber

depository Lagerhaus; Verwahrungsort; Hinterlegungsstelle; Depot

deposit transaction Einlagengeschäft

depth and breadth of a product line Tiefe und Breite einer Produktlinie

depreciate abschreiben; im Wert sinken

To decrease in value over a period in time

Accounting: To systematically write off the cost of an asset over a period of time.

depreciated cost abgeschriebene Kosten

Accounting: The original cost of an asset less accumulated depreciation.

depreciation Abwertung; Entwertung; Wertminderung; Geringschätzung

Economics: decline in the value of an asset, whether due to physical changes, obsolescence, or factors outside the asset

Accounting: The reduction in the balance sheet value of a company asset to reflect its loss of value, through age and usage.

depreciation allowance Abschreibungsbetrag; zulässiger Abschreibungssatz; Abschreibungsmöglichkeit

An allowance for a loss in valued due to depreciation defined by tax law.

depreciation methods Abschreibungsmethode; Abschreibungsverfahren

Generally accepted accounting techniques for allocating the cost of an asset over its useful life.

The most important depreciation methods include: (1) the straight-line method, (2) the diminishing-balance method, (3) the sum- of-the-digits method, (4) the production-unit method, and the (5) revaluation method.

depreciation of a currency Geldentwertung

depreciation tax shield Steuerbegünstigung durch Abschreibung

Portion of an investment that can be deducted from taxable income.

depress drücken; niederdrücken; herabsetzen

depression Vertiefung; Senkung; *(economy)* Depression; Wirtschaftskrise; Konjunkturtief; *(stock market)* Baisse

Economics: a sustained downturn in the economy, normally characterized by a decrease in business activity, falling prices, reduced purchasing power, an excess of supply over demand, rising unemployment, accumulating inventories, deflation, an plant contraction, often accompanied by public apprehension, and caution.

depth interview Tiefeninterview; offenes Interview; Intensivinterview

Interview technique conducted in person in the field by a trained interviewer. The aim is to get detailed information about the attitudes and motivation of consumers.

deregulate freigeben; deregulieren

deregulation Freigabe; Deregulierung; Entregulierung; Liberalisierung

The reduction or removal of government restrictions and regulations on the operation of markets, in order to to create a more efficient marketplace.

Industries such as transportation, communications, banking, and securities have been deregulated recently, which usually leads to increased competition and heightened innovation. Some government oversight normally remains after deregulation.

derivative Derivat; abgeleitet; sekundär; derivat

derivative security derivate Sicherheit

Financial security, such as an option, or future, whose value is derived in part from the value and characteristics of another security, the underlying security.

derive ableiten; herleiten; *(to receive from)* erzielen

derived demand abgeleitete Nachfrage

Business demand for capital goods and/or labor that ultimately comes from (is derived from) the demand for consumer goods.

Since production depends upon demand for the finished output, demand for goods and services used in production is derived from demand for finished goods. *Example*: the demand for excarvators is ultimately derived from the housing market.

describe beschreiben; bezeichnen; schildern

description Beschreibung; Schilderung; Bezeichnung

descriptive research beschreibende Forschung

Marketing research to better describe marketing problems, situations or markets, such as the market potential for a product or the demographics and attitudes of consumers.

design Gestaltung; Design; *(form)* Form; Gestalt; Entwurf; *(construction)* Konstruktionszeichnung; Ausführung; *(pattern)* Muster; *(to ~)* entwerfen; planen

designate bezeichnen; bestimmen

design phase Designphase

First stage in the development of a product, when basic qualities and functionalities are determined.

desirable wünschenswert; erwünscht

desirable products wünschenswerte Produkte

Products that give both high immediate satisfaction and high long-run benefits.

desire Wunsch; *(to ~)* wünschen; ersehnen

desk Schreibtisch; *(school)* Pult; Schalter

desk research Sekundärforschung

Research technique using mainly external published data and material, but also existing internal reports and company records.

desktop computer Schreibtischcomputer

desktop publishing (DTP) Desktop Publishing

Computer application that enables small companies and individuals to produce professional publications.

destabilize destabilisieren; unsicher machen; ins Schwanken bringen

destination Bestimmungsort; Ziel

destined bestimmt; vorgesehen

destroy zerstören; vernichten; kaputtmachen

destruction Zerstörung; Ruin

destructive zerstörerisch

detach ablösen; abmachen; losmachen; abtrennen

detail Einzelheit; Detail

detail person Handelsvertreter

Representative of a manufacturer's who visits the manufacturer's customers with the pupose of increasing business.

detailed ausführlich; eingehend

detain zurückhalten; aufhalten; vorenthalten

detection Ermittlung; Entdecken; Feststellung

deteriorate verfallen; sich verschlechtern; verschlimmern; *(trade)* zurückgehen; *(to spoil)* verderben

deterioration Verschlechterung; Verfall; Wertminderung; *(wear and tear)* Verschleiß; *(spoilage)* Verderb

determinable bestimmbar; festsetzbar

determination Entschlossenheit; Entscheidung; *(decision)* Entschluss; *(will)* Wille; Festlegung

determine bestimmen; festsetzen; festlegen; *(to decide)* entscheiden; *(to find out)* feststellen; veranlassen

determining factor Einflussgröße

deterministic deterministisch

Events that have no random or probabilistic aspects but proceed in a fixed predictable fashion. The opposite of stochastic, ie known and certain.

deterrence Abschreckung

detrend Trend bereinigen

Remove the general drift, tendency or bent of a set of statistical data as related to time.

detriment Schaden; Nachteil; Beeinträchtigung

detrimental abträglich; schädlich

devaluation Abwertung; Entwertung

A decline in the value of a currency relative to gold or to other currencies. Governments can devalue their currency to make exports cheaper and imports dearer, which also causes a certain loss of confidence in the economy.

devalue entwerten; abwerten

develop (sich) entwickeln; *(to expand)* ausbauen; *(to promote)* fördern; *(land)* erschließen; schaffen

developer Grundstückserschließer; *(construction)* Bauunternehmer

Real estate: a person or a company who increases the value of land through the use of labor, capital, and entrepreneurial efforts.

developing countries Entwicklungsländer

Countries with a low average income per head and a standard of living far below that of industrial nations. The main reasons are often a lack the capital and skills required to develop.. Close to 80% of the world's population lives in developing countries, often characterized by poverty, over-population, and poor educational facilities.

development Entwicklung; Entfaltung; Ausbau; *(promotion)* Förderung; *(land)* Erschließung; *(housing)* Wohnsiedlung

Real estate: process of making improvements to a parcel of land, such as drainage, utilities, subdividing, access, buildings, and any combination of these elements.

development bank Entwicklungsbank

development costs Entwicklungskosten

development impetus Entwicklungsimpuls

development of sales Umsatzentwicklung

development-oriented leader entwicklungsorientierter Leiter

A leader who values experimentation, seeking new ideas, and generating and implementing change.

development phase Entwicklungsphase

development policy Entwicklungspolitik

development process Entwicklungsprozess

development stage Entwicklungsstadium

Stage in the development process of a new product when the concept is transformed into a prototype and a basic marketing strategy is developed.

deviate abweichen

deviation Abweichung

deviation clause Abweichungsklausel

deviation policy Abweichungspolitik

Policy for dealing with occurrences that differ from what is expected. This can relate to employee behavior, production norms, or sales figures. When deviations are detected, management actions have to be taken.

device Vorrichtung; Gerät; Apparat; *(trick)* Kunstgriff

devise erfinden; entwerfen; sich ausdenken

diagnose erkennen; feststellen; bestimmen; diagnostizieren

diagnosis Diagnose; Feststellung

diagram graphische Darstellung; Schaubild; Übersicht; Diagramm

dictate Gebot; *(to ~)* diktieren; bestimmen

differ sich unterscheiden; *(disagreement)* anderer Meinung sein

difference Unterschied; Differenz; Gefälle; *(money)* Unterschiedsbetrag; Streitigkeit

difference from S&P Unterschied von S&P

Mutual fund's return minus the change in the Standard & Poor's 500 Index for the same time: -5.00 means the fund return was 5 percentage points less than the gain in the S&P, while 0.00 means that the fund and the S&P had the same return.

difference in exchange rate Kursdifferenz

difference in interest Zinsunterschied; Zinsgefälle

differential Differenz; Unterschiedsmerkmal; *(difference in prices)* Gefälle

differential advantage Wettbewerbsvorteil

International trade: advantage a country has in the production of a good which arises from unique economic characteristics, such as raw materials or labor costs.

differential duty Differenzialzoll

differentiate unterscheiden; verschieden(artig) werden

differentiated marketing differenziertes Marketing

Market-coverage strategy in which a firm carefully selects two or more segments and designs separate offers and marketing mix strategies for each. Most firms today use a multi-segment strategy. Also called *multi-segment marketing.*

differentiation Unterscheidung; Differenzierung

differentiation strategy Differenzierungsstrategie

Marketing: strategy of distinguishing similar products by real or imaginary means, thus enabling them to be sold at higher prices and profit.

Differentiation can take place on the basis of a variety of factors, such as quality, design, customer service, or any other means that is important to the consumer.

Differentiation is normally based on a *segmentation strategy,* establishing coherent groups of consumers and offering them a tailored marketing mix.

differing unterschiedlich

difficult schwierig; schwer

difficulty Schwierigkeit

diffusion process (of innovations) Diffusion; Verbreitung von Innovationen; Innovationsausbreitung; Innovationsdiffusion

Process by which the sale of new products and services spreads to new customer groups.

Initially, the innovators accepted the product, followed by the larger group of early adapters. These groups can be considere as opinion leaders, who bring about a wider acceptance by consumers.

The diffusion process can be speeded up by making new products more attractive, for example by giving away free samples or by special introductory prices

digital digital

digital audio, digitales Audiomaterial

Audio materials stored in a digital format for inclusion on web pages and other electronic transmission over the Internet.

digital brand digitale Marke

Brand identity used for a product or company online that differs from the traditional brand; also called *online brand.*

digital cash digitales Bargeld

Electronic version of cash in which the buyer of an item is typically anonymous to the seller.

Also referred to as virtual cash, electronic cash or e-cash.

digital certificate digitales Zertifikat

Special e-mail attachment that confirms the identity of the person sending the message

Digital Millennium Copyright Act (DMCA)

Complex piece of legislation in the U.S. that contains several provisions, among them it grants Internet Service Providers (ISP' s) protection from acts of user infringement as long as certain procedures are followed, including the prompt reporting and disabling of infringing material, and criminalizes the circumvention of software protections and the development or distribution of circumvention products.

digital signature digitale Signatur

Electronic equivalent of written signature that is used as an online method of identifying individuals or companies using public key encryption.

digital subscriber line (DSL)

Telecommunications protocols designed to allow data communications over standard telephone lines at speeds up to 1.5 Mbps. DSL service lets users receive voice and data transmissions simultaneously over the same phone line, allowing permanent internet access

digital television digitales Fernsehen

Form of television in which information is received and displayed on using binary information, which allows better picture and sound quality as well as interactivity.

digital video digitales Videomaterial

Video materials stored in a digital format for inclusion on web pages and other electronic transmission over the Internet

dilemma Dilemma; Verlegenheit

diligence Sorgsamkeit; Gewissenhaftigkeit; Fleiß; Sorgfalt

diligent sorgsam; gewissenhaft; fleissig

dilute verwässern; verdünnen; abstumpfen

dilution Verwässerung; Verdünnung

Shares: effect on earnings per share and book value if all convertible securities were converted and stock options were exercised.

dime Zehncentstück (US)

dimension Dimension; Ausmaß; Maß; Abmessung; Größenordnung

diminish abnehmen; geringer werden; reduzieren; schrumpfen

diminishing-balance method degressive Abschreibung

A method of computing the depreciation of a capital asset, in which the percentage to be charged is based on the depreciated value at the beginning of the period. As a result, the annual depreciation charged against profits is reduced year by year.

diminishing marginal utility abnehmender Grenznutzen

Economic theory stating that successive units of a good or service provide less and less satisfaction to a consumer, given that the previous units already have been consumed.

Example: the first helping of food is very satisfying, whilst subsequent helpings are less and less so.

diminishing returns abnehmende Erträge; Ertragsrückgang

A law first described by David Ricardo, that states that as extra units of one factor of production are employed, the output generated by each additional unit will eventually fall.

For example, a farmer can pick 100 apples a day. By hiring an additional worker, the two of can pick 200 apples a day. However, after hiring a second worker, the three can only pick 250 a day.

Beyond a certain point, adding additional units of resources to a production process will provide successively smaller increments of additional product.

diminishing returns to specialization abnehmende Erträge der Spezialisierung

Applied to international trade theory, the more of a good that a country produces, the greater the units of resources required to produce each additional item.

diminution Verminderung; Abnahme; Reduzierung; Verjüngung

dinks (double income no kids)

Affluent couple without children who will spend substantial amounts on the purchase of consumer goods.

diplomacy Diplomatie

General:. the art and practice of carrying out relations between nations by their representatives.

Business: attempts to deal carefully with clients, suppliers, and employees in order to avoid conflict and bad relations.

direct direkt; unmittelbar; unverblümt; unmittelbar; *(to ~)* führen; leiten; lenken; anweisen *(film)* Regie führen

direct costing Teilkostenrechnung, einstufige Deckungsbeitragsrechnung

Cost accounting method that includes only variable manufacturing costs in the cost of a unit of product - direct materials, direct labour, and variable manufacturing overhead.

direct costs direkte Kosten; Einzelkosten

Those costs that can be identified specifically with a particular activity or product, for examples labor and materials that can be identified directly in the product produced.

direct exchange rate direkter Wechselkurs; direkter Umrechnungskurs

direct exporting direkter Export

A form of the export in which a domestic producer sells products directly to foreign buyers. Other than transportation, there are no other intermediaries.

directed information search gezielte Informationssuche

direct foreign investment Direktinvestition im Ausland

Investment of capital by an investor in the equity of an organization that is located in a foreign country. It is a quick yet expensive way of entering a foreign market by developing foreign-based assembly or manufacturing facilities.

direct investment Direktinvestition; Direktanlage

Investment of capital by an investor in the equity of an organization that is located in the investor´s home country.

direct importing Direktimport

direction Anweisung; Richtung; *(managing)* Führung; Leitung; *(traffic)* Fahrtrichtung

directive Direktive; (An-)Weisung; Verfügung; Richtlinie

direct labor Fertigungslohn; Lohneinzelkosten; unmittelbarer Arbeitsaufwand

Labor costs directly attributed to the production of specific units or products, such as the salary of the person who works at the production machine.

direct lease direktes Leasing

Lease under which a lessor buys equipment from a manufacturer and leases it to a lessee.

direct liability unmittelbare Haftung

Legal obligation resulting from negligent acts or omissions that cause bodily injury and/or property damage or destruction to another party.

direct mail Direktversandwerbung; Postwurfsendung

Mail sent to large numbers of potential customers with the purpose of advertising a product or service and soliciting orders. Even if the response rate tends to be very low, it is widely used because it can be directed at specific target audiences.

direct marketing Direktmarketing

Marketing through various advertising media that interact directly with consumers, generally calling for the consumer to make a direct response. The result of a promotion are normally measurable in terms of response.

Traditional direct marekting methods include mail order, direct-mail selling, cold calling, telephone selling, and door-to-door calling. More modern methods include telemarketing, direct radio selling. magazine and TV advertising. and on-line computer shopping.

direct marketing channel direkter Absatzweg

Marketing channel that has no intermediary levels, such as mail order, telemarketing or internet.

director Direktor; *(manager)* Geschäftsführer; Leiter; *(board member)* Aufsichtsratsmitglied; *(film)* Regisseur; *(television)* Sendeleiter

General: any person who leads or supervises a project or entity.

Corporations: a person elected by corporate shareholders to serve on the corporation's board of directors, sharing with other directors the legal responsibility of control over the officers and affairs of the corporation.

directorate Direktion; Geschäftsleitung; Vorstand; Aufsichtsrat; Direktorium; Direktorat

Office or group of organizational directors, also called *directorship.* It is a group of people elected by shareholders to establish company policies.

director of a company Direktor; Geschäftsführer; Leiter; Firmenchef

directorship Aufsichtsratsposten; Direktorat

direct overhead direkte Gemeinkosten

Share of overhead costs in the manufacturing sector of a firm devoted to cover expenses such as rent, lights, insurance, by the application of a standard factor termed a *burden rate.*

direct producer Haupthersteller

A firm that has the primary responsibility to produce a certain product.

direct response Direktantwort

direct response advertising auf spezielle Kaufreaktion abgestellte Werbung

Form of advertising when a consumer can react directly to the advertisement by phone or mail.

Direct response advertising is geared to eliminate an intermediary in the purchase process, utilizing a wide range of media, from print to radio and television.

direct response marketing auf spezielle Kaufreaktion abgestelltes Marketing

direct response television marketing (DRTV) speziell auf Kaufreaktion abgestelltes Fernsehmarketing

Marketing of products or services via television commercials and programs which involve a responsive element, typically the use of a free-phone.

direct sales Direktverkauf; Direktabsatz

Publishing: magazine or periodical subscriptions sold by the publisher without the use of a subscription agent; also called *direct-to-publisher sales.*

dirty bill of lading unreines Konnossement

A bill of lading carrying a not by the mate of the ship that the goods arrived for loading in a damaged condition.

dirty float system System des „schmutzigen Floaten“

System under which a country’s currency is nominally allowed to float freely against other currencies, but in which the government will intervene, buying and selling currency, if it believes that the currency has deviated too far from its fair value.

disability Unvermögen; Unfähigkeit; *(of employee)* Behinderung; Invalidität; Arbeitsunfähigkeit; Erwerbsunfähigkeit

Personnel: any restriction or lack of ability to perform an activity in a manner that is considered normal.

disadvantage Nachteil; ungünstiger Umstand; *(situation)* ungünstige Lage

disadvantageous nachteilig; schädlich; abträglich

disagio Disagio; Abgeld

disagree nicht übereinstimmen; in Widerspruch stehen; uneinig sein; verschiedener Meinung sein

disagreement Meinungsverschiedenheit; Widerspruch; Nichtübereinstimmung

disallow nicht gestatten; nicht zulassen; nicht zugeben; *(to reject)* abweisen

disappear verschwinden; verloren gehen

disappointment Enttäuschung; *(failure)* Fehlschlag; Misserfolg

disappoint enttäuschen; nicht befriedigen

disappointing enttäuschend; unbefriedigend; nicht den Erwartungen entsprechend

disapproval Missbilligung; Missfallen

disaster Unglück; Unglücksfall; Katastrophe

disastrous verheerend; katastrophal

disburse auszahlen; ausgeben

disbursement Auszahlung; Ausgabe; Auslage

A payment made by a professional person, such as a solicitor or banker on behalf of a client.

disbursement float Auszahlungsfloat

Decrease in book cash, but no immediate change in bank cash, generated by checks written by the firm.

discharge Entlassung; Entlastung; *(debt)* Tilgung; *(cargo)* Entladen; *(to ~)* entlassen; *(to release)* entlasten; *(to unload)* entladen; ausstoßen

disclaim ablehnen; abstreiten; nicht anerkennen; verleugnen; dementieren

disclaimer Verzicht; Verzichtserklärung; Aufgabe einer Anspruchs; Dementi; Widerruf; Gegenerklärung

General: a statement denying responsibility for a particular fact, action, or content.

Accounting: statement whereby a certified public accountant refuses to express an opinion.

disclose offenbaren; aufzeigen; bekannt geben; offen legen

disclosure Enthüllung; Aufdeckung; Bekanntgabe; Eröffnung

General: providing information which might otherwise be kept secret, usually voluntarily or in compliance with regulations.

Stock exchange: publication of all relevant company information, positive or negative, that might influence an investment decision. For listed companies, required by the stock exchange.

disclosure obligation Offenlegungspflicht

disclosure statement Offenlegungsvermerk

Banking: A document issued by a lender to a borrower in which he states all the terms and conditions of the loan.

discontinue einstellen; aufhören; unterbrechen

discount Rabatt; Abschlag; *(payment)* Skonto; *(bond)* Disagio; *(bill of exchange)* Diskont; *(to ~)* abziehen; Rabatt gewähren; *(bill of exchange)* diskontieren; *(to depreciate)* im Wert herabsetzen

General: a deduction made from the normal selling price.

Bonds: difference between a bond's current market price and its face value.

Securities: manner of selling securities such as treasury bills, which are issued at less than face value and are redeemed at face value.

Foreign exchange: relationship between two currencies, for example the Euro may sell at a *discount* to the U.S. dollar.

discount broker Diskontmakler; Wechselmakler; Wechselhändler

A brokerage firm that executes buy and sell orders at lower commission rates than those charged by a full service broker.

discounted cash flow abgezinster Cashflow; diskontierter Bargeldfluss; diskontierter Einnahmeüberschuss

A method of analysing investment opportunities in which annual cash flows are discounted and accumulated to arrive at their present value (PV)., using net present value (NPV) or internal rate of return (IRR).

The NPV method applies a discount rate to future cash flows to express them in terms of current money. The IRR method determines the average return on investment earned through the life of the investment.

discounted payback period rule dynamische Amortisationsdauer

Investment decision rule in which the cash flows are discounted at an interest rate and the payback role is applied on these discounted cash flows.

discounted present value diskontierter Barwert; diskontierter Zeitwert

discounted value Diskontwert

discounter Billiganbieter

discount factor Abzinsungsfaktor

A factor that, when multiplied by a year's predicted cash flow, brings the cash flow to a present value.

discounting Abzinsung

Process of converting a stream of income or costs incurred in the future to a single present value. The result reflects the time value of money. Discounting is the opposite of compounding.

discount merchant Billighändler

discount quotation Kursabschlag

discount rate Diskontsatz; Rabattdiskont; Abzinsungssatz

Banking: interest rate that a central bank, such as the Federal Reserve, charges banks for loans, using government securities as collateral.

Accounting: interest rate used in determining the present value of future cash flows.

discount rate increase Diskontsatz-erhöhung

discount store Verbrauchermarkt; Discountgeschäft; -laden

Retail store having a broad merchandise assortment, similar to a department store, yet selling at lower prices by accepting lower margins and higher volumes.

discount yield Diskontertrag

Yield on a security sold at a discount; for example, U.S. Treasury bills sold at $9,750 and maturing at $10,000 in 90 days.

discover entdecken; feststellen

discovery Entdeckung; Auffindung; Feststellung

discreet überlegt; umsichtig; verschwiegen; diskret

discrepancy Gegensatz; Widerspruch; Abweichung; Diskrepanz

Deviation between what is expected and what actually occurs.

Example: variation in a marketing performance report between budgeted sales and actual sales.

discrete abgesondert; getrennt; abstrakt; getrennt; diskontinuierlich

discretion Besonnenheit; Klugheit; Umsicht; Diskretion; *(decisions)* Gutdünken; Ermessen

Freedom of a person to make choices, within the limits of his authority, among possible courses of action.

discretionary beliebig; willkürlich; uneingeschränkt

discretionary costs Ermessenskosten

Costs that arise form periodic appropriation decisions and which therefore can be changed easily by management decisions, such as advertising or research and development.

discretionary income verfügbares Einkommen

The amount of a person´s income available for spending after all fixed and necessary expenses (such as food, clothing and shelter) have been paid.

Producers of goods and services other than necessities compete for the consumer's discretionary income of consumers by trying to appeal to psychological needs, rather than physical needs.

discriminate unterscheiden; *(to treat unequally)* unterschiedlich behandeln; diskriminieren

discrimination Diskriminierung; ungleiche Behandlung; *(judgement)* Feingefühl; Scharfsinn; Unterscheidungsvermögen; Urteilsfähigkeit

The illegal practice of treating someone in a special way solely on the basis of the person's ethnicity, age, religion, or sex.

discriminating tariff diskriminierende Einfuhrsteuer

A tariff that is not imposed equally on all trading partners.

discuss besprechen; erörtern; diskutieren

discussion Besprechung; Diskussion; Erörterung

diseconomies of scale negative Skaleneffekte; Kostenprogression

Like economies of scale. but with the implication that they are negative, so larger volumes of productions would increase cost per unit.

disequilibrium Unausgeglichenheit; Ungleichgewicht; gestörtes Gleichgewicht

dishonor Annahmeverweigerung; Akzeptierverweigerung; Nichteinlösung; *(to ~)* nicht akzeptieren

Refuse, rightly or wrongly, to make payment on a negotiable instrument when such an instrument is duly presented for payment.

disinflation Verringerung des Inflationsanstiegs; Disnflation

Disinflation is a decrease in the rate of inflation, which usually occurs during a recession. Volumes of sales drop and retailers can´t pass on higher prices to consumers. Different from deflation, when prices actually drop.

disintermediation Abschaffung von Vermittlerstellen; Disintermediation

Removal of intermediaries such as distributors or brokers that formerly linked a company to its customers.

In particular disintermediation enables a company to sell direct to the customer by cutting-out the middleman.

disinvestment Deinvestition; Investitionsabbau

diskette Diskette

dismantle *(factory)* auseinander nehmen; zerlegen; demontieren; abbauen; *(committee)* auflösen

dismiss entlassen; fortschicken; freistellen; *(complaint)* zurückweisen; *(lawsuit)* Verfahren einstellen

dismissal Entlassung; Kündigung; *(law)* Abweisung

Employment: the termination of someone's employment.

Law: the termination of a lawsuit. A dismissal without prejudice allows a lawsuit to be brought before the court again; a dismissal with prejudice prevents the lawsuit from being brought before a court again.

disorder Unordnung; Verwirrung; Durcheinander

disorganization Auflösung; Zerrüttung; Störung

disparate ungleichartig; unvereinbar; disparat; ganz verschieden

disparity Ungleichheit; Verschiedenheit; Unterschied

dispatch Absendung; Versand; *(message)* Nachricht; Nachrichtensendung; *(to ~)* abschicken; befördern; senden

disperse *(funds)* verteilen; *(news)* verbreiten; *(gathering)* auflösen; zerstreuen

displace verlagern; verdrängen; ersetzen

display Zurschaustellung; *(marketing)* Auslage; *(store)* Schaufensterauslage; *(to ~)* auslegen; ausstellen; zeigen

displayed emotions gezeigte Emotionen

Emotions that are organizationally required and considered appropriate in a given job. They're not innate but learned. Example: flight attendants have to be friendly.

disposable verfügbar; disponibel; *(throwaway)* wegwerfbar

disposable goods Einweggüter; Wegwerfgüter

disposable income verfügbares Einkommen

Personal income remaining after personal taxes and government fees have been paid. This money cen be spent on essentials like food and shelter, nonessentials like going to the movies, or it can be saved.

disposal Verfügung; Veräußerung; *(waste)* Beseitigung; *(sale)* Absatz

dispose *(to arrange)* anordnen; disponieren; *(to sell)* absetzen; veräußern; *(to remove)* beseitigen

disposition of funds Mittelverwendung

dispossess Besitz entziehen; enteignen; berauben

To to remove a person from his real property by lawful means, including, the use of force.

disproportion Missverhältnis

disproportionate unverhältnismäßig

disregard Missachtung; Geringschätzung; *(to ~)* missachten; nicht achten; gering schätzen

disrupt unterbrechen; *(market)* spalten; zerbrechen; zerstören

dissatisfaction Unzufriedenheit; Missfallen

dissatisfy nicht befriedigen; unzufrieden machen

disseminate ausstreuen; verbreiten

dissemination Verbreitung; Ausstreuung

dissent Meinungsverschiedenheit; *(to ~)* nicht zustimmen; abweichen

dissociate trennen; loslösen; scheiden; lossagen von

dissolution *(firm)* Auflösung; *(cartel)* Entflechtung; Liquidation; Tod; Zerfall

Corporation law: the termination of the legal existence of a corporation. This can happen by expiration of charter, decree of court, act of legislature, vote of shareholders, or other means.

dissolve *(firm)* auflösen; liquidieren; *(cartel)* entflechten

dissonance-reducing buying behavior konfliktminimierndes Kaufverhalten

Consumer buying behavior in situations characterized by high involvement but few perceived differences among brands. *Example*: buying carpets for a new flat.

distance Entfernung; Strecke; Zeitraum; *(distant)* fern; weit entfernt

distinctive competencies unterscheidende Kompetenzen

Defines what the organization is more superior at delivering than its competition. Identifying distinctive competencies can influence decisions regarding what activities are crucial to the organization's success.

distinguish unterscheiden; *(to characterize)* kennzeichnen; charakterisieren; *(merit)* auszeichnen; klar erkennen

distinguishable unterscheidbar; klar erkennbar

distinguished ausgezeichnet; berühmt; hervorragend

distribute verteilen; austeilen; einteilen; streuen; *(to allocate)* zuteilen; *(to sell)* vertreiben; absetzen; *(dividend)* ausschütten

distributed e-mail verteilte E-Mail

E-mail sent to distribution lists and redistributed to the entire subscription list.

distribution Verteilung; Verbreitung; Streuung; Aufteilung; *(allocation)*

Zuteilung; *(marketing)* Vertrieb; Absatz; *(dividend)* Ausschüttung

Marketing: one of the elements of the marketing mix dealing with the transporting and selling goods from a producer to the end user, either directly, or through intermediaries such as wholesalers and retailers. This involves a multitude of decisions, ranging from transporation and storage to areas and segments to be covered.

Corporate finance: the allocation of income and expenses to the appropriate subsidiary accounts.

Economics: the way in which wealth and income is distributed amongst the members of an economy.

distribution allowance Vertriebsprovision

A reduction in price reduction offered by a manufacturer to an intermediary, such as a distributor, retail chain, or wholesaler as a reward for distributing the product.

distribution center Absatzzentrum; Verteilerzentrum; Vertriebszentrum

Large, highly automated warehouse designed to receive goods from various plants and suppliers, take orders, fill them efficiently, and deliver goods to customers as quickly as possible.

distribution channel Vertriebsweg

Group of interdependent firms necessary to distribute goods or services from the manufacturers to the consumers. The channel can consist of manufacturers, distributors, wholesalers, and retailers.

distribution cost analysis Vertriebskostenanalyse; Distributionskostenanalyse

Detailed analysis of all costs incurred in getting a product from the manufacturer to the end user.

distribution network Vertriebsnetz

distribution of profit Gewinnausschüttung

distribution strategy Absatzstrategie; Vertriebsstrategie

distribution system Verteilungssystem; Vertriebssystem

distributive bargaining Verteilungsverhandlung

Bargaining situation where a fixed amount of resources have to be distributed. Because it operates under zero-sum conditions, it will always result in a win-lose situation.

distributive justice Verteilungsgerechtigkeit

In a bargaining situation, the perceived fairness with which shares and rewards are distributed amongst the participants. It has a great influence on satisfaction and motivation.

distributor Verteiler; Großhändler; Zwischenhändler; Wiederverkäufer; *(agent)* Vertreter; *(film)* Verleiher; *(engine)* Zündverteiler

Logistics: an agent or a business that sells or delivers merchandise to customers, such as retail stores.

Distributors are intermediaries between manufacturers and retailers, often with their own warehouse. They often purchase products from many different manufacturers and sell them to various retailers.

distributorship Vertriebsagentur Verteilernetz

district Bezirk; Distrikt; *(city)* Viertel; Kreis; Gebiet

district court Amtsgericht

disturb stören; beunruhigen; durcheinander bringen

disturbance Störung; Unruhe

diverge abweichen; auseinander gehen

divergence Abweichung; Divergenz

divergent abweichend; auseinander laufend

diverse verschieden; anders; ungleich; *(varied)* vielfältig; mannigfaltig

diversifiable risk diversifizierbares Risiko

Risk that specifically affects a single asset or a small group of assets. Also called unique or unsystematic risk.

diversification Diversifizierung; Diversifikation; *(investment)* Streuung; Risikostreuung; *(products)* Auffächerung

Corporate: strategy for company growth by starting up or acquiring businesses outside the company's current products and markets.

Investment: reduction of risk by putting assets in several categories of investments: stocks, bonds, money market instruments, precious metals, and real estate.

diversification strategy Diversifikationsstrategie

diversified abwechslungsreich; mannigfaltig; *(capital)* gestreut angelegt

diversified company diversifiziertes Unternhemen; breit gefächertes Unternehmen

A company that sells a variety of products and services in several markets.

The main advantages of diversification is the ability to better weather business cycles, since some of the products or services may always be countercyclical.

diversify diversifizieren; abwechslungsreich gestalten; variieren; *(investment)* gestreut anlegen

diversity Verschiedenheit; Ungleichheit; *(variety)* Vielfalt; Mannigfaltigkeit; Nuance

divert umleiten; umlenken; *(attention)* ablenken; *(funds)* abzweigen; *(to amuse)* zerstreuen; unterhalten

divide teilen; verteilen; aufteilen; trennen

dividend Dividende; Gewinnanteilung; *(math)* Dividend

Distribution of a portion of a company's earnings, cash flow or capital to shareholders, in cash or additional stock.

It is usually taxed as ordinary income, for which most corporations receive no deduction. Such amount may be taxed to the shareholder as ordinary income (to the extent of current and accumulated earnings and profits) or capital gain (to the extent of stock basis), or the amount may be treated as a return of capital.

dividend coupon Dividendenschein; Gewinnanteilsschein

dividend declared angekündigte Dividende

dividend declaration Dividendenerklärung

dividend ex-date Dividendenstichtag

First date on which a person purchasing the stock is no longer eligible to receive the last announced dividend.

dividend growth model Dividenden-Wachstums-Modell

Model wherein dividends are assumed to be at a constant rate in perpetuity.

dividend income Dividendeneinnahme

dividend-paying stock Dividendenpapier

dividend payout Dividendenausschüttung

Amount of cash paid to shareholders expressed as a percentage of earnings per share.

dividend payout ratio Ausschüttungssatz

A measure of the percentage of earnings paid out to shareholders in the form of dividends. Computed by dividing cash dividends by the net income available to each class of stock.

Mature companies, such as utilities, tend to have a higher payout ratios than fast-growing companies, who usually reinvest all earnings and pay no dividends.

dividend policy Ausschüttungspolitik

dividends payable auszuschüttende Dividenden

Balance sheet: a current liability item disclosing dividends which have been declared or recommended by management but have not been paid out to the shareholders at the balance sheet date.

dividend payment date Ausschüttungstag

Date on which payment for the last dividend declared will be made to the shareholders.

dividend rate Dividendensatz

Value of the total of the expected dividend payments over the next twelve months. It is generally the most recent cash dividend paid or declared multiplied by the dividend payment frequency, plus any recurring extra dividends.

dividend reinvestment plans (DRP) Reinvestmentpläne für Dividenden

Plans offered by many corporations for the reinvestment of dividends, sometimes at a discount from market price, on the dividend payment date.

Many DRPs also allow the investment of additional cash from the shareholder. The DRP is usually administered by the company without charges to the holder. Some plans provide for the purchase of additional shares at a discount to market price.

dividends per share Dividende pro Aktie

Dividends paid for the past 12 months divided by the number of common shares outstanding, as reported by a company.

The number of shares often is determined by a weighted average of shares outstanding over the reporting term.

dividend yield Dividendenertrag; Dividendenrendite; Effektivrendite; Kursrendite

Stocks: the annual percentage of return that the dividend provides to the investor on either common or preferred stock.

Funds: return on a share of a mutual fund held over the past 12 months, reflecting sales charges, but not redemption charges.

dividend yield, five year average Dividendenrendite, 5-Jahres-Durchschnitt

Value of the average of the dividend yield over the last 60 months.

divisibility Teilbarkeit

divisible teilbar

division Teilung; Auf-; Verteilung; Trennung; Division *(department)* Geschäftsbereich; Unternehmensbereich

Organization: self-sufficient unit within a company, that contains all the departments necessary to operate independently from the parent company.

Example: Opel is a division of the General Motors Corporation.

division manager Abteilungsleiter

division of labor Arbeitsteiligkeit; Arbeitsteilung

Organization: Splitting a production process into different tasks, each beaing performed by different workers who do the same task repeatedly rather than having a single worker perform all tasks.

The advantage of division of labor is that each worker can practice and perfect a particular set of skills which results in increased productivity, individually and overall.

dock receipt Kaiempfangsschein; Übernahmeschein

doctrine Lehre; Doktrin

document Dokument; Urkunde; Akte; Unterlage; *(to ~)* beurkunden; schriftlich belegen; dokumentieren; mit Urkunden belegen

documentary collection Dokumenteninkasso

documentary credit Dokumentenakkreditiv

documentary draft Rembourstratte

documentary letter of credit Dokumentenakkreditiv; Dokumententratte; Dokumentenkredit

documentation Dokumentation

Computing: written description of a computer program, usually in several categories: (1) internal documentation, consisting of comments within the program; (2) on-line documentation, displayed as the program runs or called up with a command such as help; (3) reference cards, containing easily forgotten details for quick reference; (4) reference manuals, setting auto complete instructions for the program in a systematic way; and (5) tutorials, serving as introduction for new users.

documented dokumentiert; urkundlich festgelegt; durch Unterlagen belegt

documents against acceptance Dokumente gegen Akzept

documents against payment Dokumente gegen Zahlung

dodge Umgehungsmanöver; Täuschung; Methode; Vorgehen; *(to ~)* umgehen; vermeiden; sich drücken; ausweichen; springen

dog wenig erfolgreiches Produkt; perspektivloses Produkt mit geringem Marktanteil und schwachen Marktwachstum

Portfolio analysis: low-growth, low-share businesses and products that may generate enough cash to maintain themselves, but do not promise to be large sources of cash.

dogma Dogma; Lehrsatz; Glaubenssatz

domain Bezirk; Gebiet; Bereich; Feld; *(area of responsibility)* Aufgabengebiet

domain name Domain-Name

Text-based URL or address of a web site, usually consisting of several different parts, separated by periods. A given server may have more than one domain name, but a given domain name points to only one machine.

Example: the name www.google.com includes the generic "www" and ".com" identifiers, along with the unique name "google".

domain name registration Domain-Name Registrierung

Process of reserving a unique web address that can be used to refer to the company web site.

domain name system (DNS)

Internet database that translates between numeric IP addresses and text-based domain names. When users type www.microsoft.com into their web browser, for example, the request goes to a DNS server that translates the name into the appropriate numeric IP address. Domain names are divided into the following categories:

1. Top level domain names such as *.com* or *.de* (also known as global or generic) top level domain names.

2. Second-level domain names. This refers to the company name and is sometimes referred to as the enterprise name, e.g. *novel.com.*

3. Third-level or sub-enterprise domain names. This may be used to refer to an individual server within an organization such as *support-.novel.com.*

domestic inländisch; einheimisch; innerstaatlich; *(home)* häuslich; heimisch

domestic bank Inlandsbank

domestic business Inlandsgeschäft

domestic capital Inlandskapital

domestic client Inlandskunde

domestic commerce Binnenhandel

domestic consumption Inlandsverbrauch

domestic content nationaler Anteil an der Wertschöpfung

domestic content requirement nationaler Mindestanteil an der Wertschöpfung

domestic corporation inländisch Kapitalgesellschaft

domestic demand Binnenbedarf; Binnennachfrage

domestic division Inlandsabteilung

domestic economy Binnenwirtschaft

domestic investment inländische Anlagen; Inlandsanlage; Inlandsinvestition

domestic loan Inlandsanleihe

domestic market Binnenmarkt

domestic order Inlandsbestellung

domestic production Inlandsproduktion; Eigenerzeugung

domicile fester Wohnsitz; *(firm)* Sitz, Gesellschaftssitz

In general: the place where a person has his permanent legal home.

Business: address where the business is maintained or where the governing power is exercised.

Domicile is not the same as residence, since a person can have many residences but only one legal domicile.

dominance Vorherrschen; Herrschaft

dominant culture dominante Unternehmenskultur

Expresses the core values that are shared by a majority of the organization's members.

dominion Besitzrecht; Herrschaft(-sgebiet); Dominion

donate spenden; schenken; *(to endow)* stiften

donation Spende; Schenkung; *(endowment)* Stiftung

donee Zuwendungsempfänger

The person who receives a gift, bequest, or a grant, or any other power, right, or interest.

donor Spender; Geber

A person, group or organization that gives or donates something, can be funding, e.g. to a charity, or confers a power, right, or interest.

door-to-door retailing Haustürverkauf

dormant partner stiller Teilhaber

dot-com Internetunternehmen

Start-up companies selling products or services somehow related to the Internet. The name derived from the ".com" built into their company name.

double declining balance degressive Abschreibung

Method of accelerated depreciation, in which double the straight-line depreciation amount is taken the first year, and then that same percentage is applied to the remaining amount in subsequent years.

double-entry accounting doppelte Buchführung

System of recording every transaction of a business in at least two accounts. This double aspect enables the business to be controlled because all the books of accounts must balance.

For example, when a person (debtor) pays cash to a business for goods purchased, the cash held by the business is increased and the amount due from the debtor is decreased by the same amount. When a purchase is made on credit, the stock is decreased and the amount owing to creditors is increased by the same amount.

double entry bookkeeping doppelte Buchführung

double-loop learning kontinuierliches Lernen

Process where errors are corrected by modifying the organization's objectives, policies, and standard routines. Executives continually question the policies and objectives within which the decision-making power is constrained.

double taxation doppelte Besteuerung

International: Taxation of the same source of income in more than one country. A large number of treaties have been concluded between countries to ensure that their own residents are not doubly taxed.

Corporations: in the U.S., the term is often used to describe *dividend taxation*, i.e. the fact that shareholders are taxed on the dividends they receive.

Dow Jones & Co.

Publishing and financial information company based in the United States; issuer of The Wall Street Journal, Barron's National Business and Financial Weekly, and other influential publications, as well as computer data bases and additional financial information.

Dow Jones Industrial Average Dow Jones Index

An index of security prices issued by Dow Jones & Co. used on the New York Stock Exchange. It is a narrowly based index, having 30 constituent companies. The index was founded in 1884, but was reorganized in 1928 when it was given the value of 100.

downgrade niedriger einstufen; verschlechtern

download heruntergeladene Daten; herunterladen

Internet: process of retrieving electronic information such as a web page or e-mail from another remote location such as a web server.

down payment Anzahlung

The amount or percentage of the purchase price paid by the buyer in advance.

downscale auf eine niedrigere Ebene verlagern

The intended movement of business activity from a higher to a lower level, such as selling lower grade merchandise.

downside risk Risiko des Kursrückgangs

The risk of a loss, which an investor may weight more heavily than the possibility of a profit, taking into account the total range of factors affecting market price.

downsizing Verkleinerung; Verringerung; Personalkürzung; Abbau

Process whereby a corporation reduces the layers of management and the work force in order to increase organizational productivity and profits, often in response to changed market circumstances

downstream nachgelagert; stromabwärts

In general: flow of corporate activity from parent to subsidiary.

Management: usually refers to instructions from headquarters.

Finance: refers to loans, since dividends and interest generally flow upstream.

downturn Abwärtsbewegung; *(economic cycle)* Konjunkturabschwung

The movement of business cycle from rising to falling. An economy is in a *downturn* when it moves from expansion to recession, a stock market is in a downturn when it changes from a bull market to a bear market.

dowry Aussteuer, Mitgift

A gift of money, property, or valuables given by the bride's family to that of the groom to permit their marriage.

draft Entwurf; Zeichnung; (*bank*) Zahlungsanweisung; (*bill of exchange*) Tratte; Wechsel; (*account*) Geldabhebung

Commerce: an order issued by a seller against a purchaser directing payment, usually through an intermediary bank. Typical bank drafts are negotiable instruments and are similar to checks on checking accounts in a bank. Synonymous with bill of exchange.

Law: preliminary form of a legal document; for example, the draft of a contract, often called *rough draft.*

draft at sight Sichttratte

draft budget Budgetentwurf

draft credit Wechselkredit

draft guarantee Wechselbürgschaft

draft treaty Vertragsentwurf

draw *(lottery)* Verlosung; *(tie)* Unentschieden; *(to ~)* anziehen; *(to issue)* ausstellen; *(salary)* beziehen; ziehen

drawback Nachteil; *(customs)* Zollrückschein; Zollrückvergütung

drawee Akzeptant; Bezogener, Angewiesener; Trassat

Commerce: The individual or firm on whom a draft is drawn and who owes the stated amount.

In a typical checking account situation, the bank is the *drawee,* the person writing the check is the maker or drawer, and the person to whom the check is written is the payee.

drawer Aussteller; Trassant; Zeichner

The individual or firm that issues or signs a draft and therefore is entitled to receive payment of the stated amount from the drawee.

drawing *(bill of exchange)* Ausstellen; Ziehung; *(account)* Abhebung; Trassierung

drawing right Ziehungsrecht

drift *(inactivity)* Treibenlassen; *(tendency)* Tendenz; *(customers)* Abwanderung; Strömung; Trift; Verwehung; *(to ~)* treiben

drive Fahrt; Anfahrt; *(advertising)* Werbefeldzug; *(energy)* Schwung; Geldsammlung; *(to ~)* treiben; *(car)* fahren; lenken; kutschieren

drive to succeed Erfolgszwang

driving forces treibende Kräfte; fördernde Kräfte

Forces that direct behavior away from the status quo.

drop Tropfen; *(prices)* Rückgang; *(stock exchange)* Baisse; Sturz; Sinken; *(to ~)* fallenlassen; *(prices)* fallen

Drucker, Peter (1909-2005)

Highly admired management thinker who invented or shaped many of the main management trends and theories of the second half of the 20th century; amongst others: 'Management by objective', privatization, 'putting the customer first', 'structure follows strategy', decentralization and the implications of the information age.

Drucker´s five basic principles of management remain valid: setting objectives, organizing, motivating and communicating, establishing measurements of performance, and developing people. Apart from his works on management theory and technique, Drucker wrote just as prolifically and successfully on political and social analysis.

Biography: born in Vienna, went to Britain in the late 1920s and worked as an economist, emigrated to the US in 1937, worked as a consultant with General Motors and then with most other leading companies, taught at New York University Business School, since 1971 at Claremont Graduate School, California.

Major publications: (1946) Concept of the corporation, (1951) The new society, (1954) The practice of management, (1964) Managing for results, (1969) The age of discontinuity, (1974) Management: tasks, responsibilities, practices, (1985) Innovation and entrepreneurship, (1989) The new realities, (1994) Frontiers of management, (1997) Drucker on Asia, (1998) On the profession of management

dry goods Textilwaren

Fabrics, textiles, and clothing made from cotton, wool, silk, and other materials, including ready-to-wear clothing and bedding.

dual currency bond Doppelwährungsanleihe

dual use goods zivil und militärisch nutzbare Güter

due *(charge)* Gebühr; gebührend; *(maturing)* fällig; *(owing)* zustehend

due bill Schuldanerkenntnis; fälliger Wechsel

A written acknowledgment of the existence of a debt owed to another party.

due diligence angemessene Sorgfalt; Due Diligence

An investigation and evaluation of a company that is preparing to go public, conducted with a reasonable amount of care.

dues Gebühren; *(membership)* Beitrag

dummy Strohmann; Attrappe

Individual or entity that stands in the place of the principal to a transaction; sometimes used to avoid personal liability.

dummy variables Scheinvariable

dump Abladeplatz; Halde; *(to ~)* abladen; *(sell cheaply)* billig abstoßen; *(export trade)* zu Schleuderpreisen verkaufen

dumping Ausfuhr zu Schleuderpreisen; Dumping; Preisunterbietung

The sale of goods or services in a foreign market for a lower price than in the domestic market or for a lower price than their cost of production. The aim can be to eliminate a surplus or to gain an edge in foreign competition.

dumping duty Ausgleichszoll gegen Schleuderausfuhr

Dun & Bradstreet (D&B)

Company providing business and credit information. The information is obtained directly from firms and solicited from their creditors. This information is available to subscribers in reports and a ratings directory.

Dun's number

Short for Dun's Market Identifier. It is published as part of a list of firms giving information such as an identification number, address code, number of employees, corporate affiliations, and trade styles.

duopoly Duopol

A market situation in which there are only two producers or sellers of a particular product or service and many buyers.

duplicate Duplikat; zweite Ausfertigung; *(to ~)* kopieren; vervielfältigen; verdoppeln; Kopien herstellen

Du Pont analysis Werbewirksamkeitsanalyse nach Du Pont

Experiment conducted by Du Pont measuring the effectiveness of advertising by comparing different budgets in different market situations.

DuPont ROI Model Du Pont Kennzahlsystem

System of financial analysis developed by Du Pont to show the different dimensions of the company´s financial performance.

durable langlebig; dauerhaft; haltbar

durable products langlebige Konsumgüter

Consumer products that are usually used over an extended period of time and that normally survive many uses. *Example*: consumer electronics, furniture, cars etc.

duration Dauer

dutiable gebührenpflichtig; zollpflichtig

duty Pflicht; Aufgabe; *(customs)* Zollgebühr; Abgabe

duty charge Zollforderung

duty claim Zollforderung

duty-free gebührenfrei; zollfrei

duty remission Zollerlass

dwelling Wohnhaus; Wohnung; Wohnsitz; Behausung; Obdach

A building or a portion thereof used exclusively for residential purposes.

dwindle zusammenschrumpfen; *(prices)* sinken; sich vermindern; schwinden

Dynamic Hypertext Mark-up Language (DHTML)

Umbrella term used to include HTML and related technologies such as Cascading Style Sheets (CSS) and JavaScript that bring animation and other interactivity to web pages.

dynamic pricing dynamische Preiskalkulation

Personalized and up-to-date price information received by internet users, on demand from product databases.

dysfunctional conflict dysfunktionaler Konflikt

Conflict that does not support the goals of the group and diminishes its performance.

E

early Früh; Anfangs-; früh; frühzeitig

early adopters frühe Imitatoren; Person, die ein Produkt früh annimmt

Buyer bahavior: Second group of consumers, comprising around 13.5%, to purchase the product, after the innovators, who comprise the first 2.5%. Early adopters are eager to buy new products, but they are more community minded than innovators and tend to communicate with others about new products.

early majority frühe Mehrheit

Buyer bahavio: Consumers comprising the next 34% after innovators and early adopters. These consumers do not rush to try new products but collect information first, perhaps talking to opinion leaders, and purchasing only after thoughtful consideration.

early retirement Vorruhestand

Leaving a job before normal retirement age, subject to minimum requirements of age and years of service.

This makes it possible for the company to promote younger employees without layoffs.

early-retirement benefits Frührente; Vorruhestandsrente; vorzeitige Rente

Benefits a person is entitled to when retiring before the formal retirement age.

early warning Frühwarnsystem

earmark Kennzeichen; Eigenschaft *(to ~)* kennzeichnen; bestimmen; vorsehen

earmarked gezeichnet; vorgemerkt; zurückgestellt; *(tax)* zweckgebunden; *(account)* gesperrt

earn erwerben; *(wages)* verdienen; *(interest)* Zinsen erbringen

earner Erwerbstätiger; Verdiener

earning Verdienen; Erwerb; Ertrag

earning capacity *(company)* Ertragsfähigkeit; *(person)* Erwerbsfähigkeit

earnings Einkommen; Einkünfte; *(profit)* Gewinn; Ertrag; *(salary)* Gehalt; *(wages)* Verdienst; Lohn; Einkünfte

The amount of money that a company earns after paying for all its costs. Often used synonymously with profit.

Earnings are calculated starting with revenues, and deducting all costs, such as employees' salaries and depreciation.

earnings announcements Gewinnankündigung; vorläufige Gewinnangabe

A company's preliminary operating results which includes the most recent date announced as well as revenue, earnings, and EPS information.

earnings and profits Einkommen und Profite

Tax term that refers to the economic capacity of a corporation to make a distribution to shareholders that is not a return of capital. Similar to retained earnings, although its calculation starts with taxable income.

earnings before interest and taxes (EBIT) Gewinne vor Zinsen und Steuern

The profit of a company as shown on the profit and lass account, before deducting interest and tax. This figure is used for the calculation of many ratios because it enables better comparisons to be made with other companies.

earnings before taxes Gewinn vor Steuern

Sales revenues less cost of sales, operating expenses, and interest, before taxes have been paid.

earnings per share (EPS) Gewinn pro Aktie

A measure of profitability derived by dividing the net income of the company by the average number of shares outstanding.

Example: a corporation that earned $10 million a year and has 10 million shares outstanding would report earnings of $1 per share.

earnings report Gewinn- und Verlustrechnung

A financial statement that provides the operating results of a corporation for a specific period. Same as income statement.

earnings statement Erfolgsrechnung; Ertragsrechnung; Gewinn- und Verlustrechnung

earnings yield Gewinnrendite; *(stock)* Gewinn je Stammaktie nach Steuern zum Kurs der Stammaktie

Ratio of earnings per share after allowing for tax and interest payments on fixed interest debt, to the current share price. The inverse of the Price/Earnings ratio.

It is calculated by taking the total twelve months earnings divided by number of outstanding shares, divided by the recent price, multiplied by 100.

ease Leichtigkeit; Ruhe; Behagen; *(to ~)* entspannen; *(stock prices)* nachgeben; *(monetary policy)* lockern; erleichtern

easement Grunddienstbarkeit; Nutzungsrecht; Erleichterung

The right of use by one party over the property owned by another. There are many forms of easements that define specific cases.

easing Erleichterung; Lockerung

easy leicht; bequem; ungezwungen; *(terms)* zu günstigen Bedingungen

easy money leichtes Geld; Politik des billigen Geldes

Fiscal policy: a policy of keeping interest rates at a low level in order to encourage an expansion in the level of economic activity by reducing the cost of borrowing and investment. The policy eventually leads to inflation.

e-business

See: electronic business.

e-cash

See: digital cash.

e-check

Method of automatically paying for goods or services.

eclectic eklektisch; zusammengestellt

eclectic paradigm eklektisches Paradigma

Argument that combining location specific assets and the firm's own unique assets often requires FDI; it requires the firm to establish production facilities where those foreign assets or resource endowments are located.

ecological Umwelt-; ökologisch

ecology Umwelt; Ökologie; Umweltschutz

ecology-minded umweltbewusst

e-commerce elektronischer Handel

See: electronic commerce.

econometric ökonometrisch

A combination of mathematical economics, statistics, economic statistics and economic theory. It is an approach to describe in mathematical terms the numerical relationship between key economic forces such as labor, capital, interest rates, and government policies.

economic wirtschaftlich; volkswirtschaftlich; ökonomisch; *(productive)* rentabel

Relating to the science of economics or to an economy.

economic advisor Wirtschaftsberater

economic agreement Wirtschaftsabkommen; Handelsabkommen

economic analysis Wirtschaftsanalyse

A systematic approach to the study and understanding of trends, phenomena and information which are economic in nature.

economical wirtschaftlich; *(thrifty)* sparsam

Economic and Monetary Union (EMU) Europäische Wirtschafts- und Währungsunion (EWWU)

economic appraisal Wirtschaftlichkeitsrechnnung

A method of capital budgeting that makes use of discounted cash flow techniques to determine a preferred investment.

Instead of using annual projected cash flows, the technique discounts the expected annual economic costs and economic benefits.

economic base wirtschaftliche Basis

Major industries within an economy that provide productivity, tax revenues and employment.

economic boom Wirtschaftsaufschwung

economic condition Wirtschaftslage

economic cycle Konjunkturzyklus

economic depreciation ökonomische Abschreibung; ökonomische Abwertung

Real estate: the decline in the value of a property caused by reasons outside of the property itself, such as a decline in the neighborhood.

economic development Wirtschafts-entwicklung

economic domain Wirtschaftsbereich

economic efficiency ökonomische Effizienz; Wirtschaftlichkeit

A concept refering to the optimal production and consumption of goods and services. It assumes the a llocation of resources to their highest valued use and the production and distribution of goods and services at the lowest possible cost.

economic entity Wirtschaftseinheit

economic environment wirtschaftliches Umfeld

economic expert Wirtschaftsexperte

economic exposure wirtschaftliche Gefährdung

Extent to which a firm's future international earning power is affected by changes in exchange rates.

economic freedom wirtschaftliche Freiheit; Gewerbefreiheit

Freedom to engage in economic transactions, without government interference. In a capitalist system, economic freedom is supposed to lead to efficient allocation of resources.

The role of government is to provide support and the institutions necessary for that freedom, such as the rule of law, sound money, and open markets.

economic growth Wirtschaftswachstum; wirtschaftliches Wachstum

The increase in the capacity of an economy to produce goods and services and to improve the well-being of its citizens. Commonly expressed as increase in gross national product.

economic growth rate Wachstumsrate der Volkwirtschaft

Rate of change in the gross national product (GNP), expressed as an annual percentage. If the rate rises in two consecutive quarters, it is considered to indicate an expanding economy, it drops in two consecutive quarters, it is considered to mean a recession. The 'real' economic growth rate is obtained when the rate is adjusted for inflation.

economic indicators Konjunkturindikatoren; Konjunkturanzeichen;

Key statistics indicating the state of an economy, including GNP, unemployment figures, new orders, vendor performance, stock prices, and changes in the money supply.

economic inefficiency Unwirtschaftlichkeit

economic integration wirtschaftliche Integration

economic journal Wirtschaftszeitung

economic life wirtschaftliche Lebensdauer; wirtschaftliche Nutzungsdauer

The period of time during which an asset can be used to create economic value, i.e. when it generates more income than operating expenses costs.

economic loss Vermögenseinbuße; Vermögensschaden

The amount by which total costs, including all opportunity costs, exceeds total revenue.

economic miracle Wirtschaftswunder

economic model Wirtschaftsmodell

economic performance Wirtschaftsleistung

economic plan Wirtschaftsplan

economic policy Wirtschaftspolitik

economic process Wirtschaftsablauf; Wirtschaftsgeschehen

economic recession Wirtschaftsflaute; Rezession

economic recovery Konjunkturbelebung

economic rent Grundrente

Economics: The income received by the owner of a factor of production in excess of the minimum income they would require in order to be willing to make the resource available for use.

economic report Konjunkturbericht

economic research Wirtschaftsforschung; Konjunkturforschung

economic researcher Wirtschaftsforscher; Konjunkturforscher

economic risk wirtschaftliches Risiko

Likelihood that events, including economic mismanagement, will cause drastic changes in a country's business environment that adversely affect the profit and other goals of a particular business enterprise.

economics Volkswirtschaftslehre; Nationalökonomie; Ökonomie; wirtschaftliche Gegebenheiten

The branch of social sciences dealing with the production, distribution and consumption of goods and services, as well as their management.

The two main branches of economics are microeconomics, where the unit of analysis is the individual agent, such as a household or firm, and macroeconomics, where the unit of analysis is a whole economy.

economic sanctions Wirtschaftssanktionen

Restrictions upon trade and financial dealings that a country imposes upon another for political reasons.

economic sector Wirtschaftszweig; Wirtschaftssektor

economic specialist Wirtschaftsfachmann

economic spokesman Wirtschaftssprecher

economic stabilization policy Konjunkturpolitik

economic statistics Wirtschaftsstatistik

economic structure Wirtschaftsstruktur

economic system Wirtschaftsordnung; Wirtschaftssystem

The set of institutions and mechanisms by which a society organizes the production, distribution and consumption of goods and services. The major economic systems are capitalism, socialism and communism.

economic theory Wirtschaftstheorie

economic trend Wirtschaftskurs; Konjunkturverlauf

economic union Wirtschaftsunion

Group of countries committed to (1) removing all barriers to the free flow of goods, services, and factors of production between each other, (2) the pursuit of a common external trade policy, (3) the adoption of a common currency, (4) the harmonization of tax rates.

economic value wirtschaftliches Wohl; wirtschaftlicher Wert

An alternative term for net present value in the context of asset valuation. It is the value of an asset expressed in terms of its exchangeability for other goods, taking into account all relevant costs and benefits provided by it.

economic value added (EVA) Residualgewinn; Geschäftswertbeitrag

EVA is a measure of the economic value of an investment or project, calculated as the surplus profit over the weighted average cost of capital.

economies of scale Skalenertrag; Skaleneffekt; Größenkostenersparnis

Reductions in the cost of producing a unit of a product that occurs as the output increases. This enables a producer to offer his product at more competitive prices and thus to capture a larger market share. Two types of economies of scale can be distinguished:

Internal: costs savings that accrue to a firm regardless of the industry, market or environment in which it operates.

External: economies that benefit a firm as a result of the way in which its industry is organized.

economies of scope Verbundvorteile; Verbundeffekt

Factors that make it cheaper to produce a range of products together, rather than to produce each one of them on its.

Efficiencies to be achieved arise from demand-side changes, such as increasing or decreasing the scope of marketing and distribution, of *different types of products*. Resultant strategies are product bundling, product lining, and family branding.

economist Wirtschaftswissenschaftler; Volkswirt; Ökonom

An expert in the science of economics .

economize sparsam wirtschaften; sparsam; haushalten

economy Wirtschaft; *(national economy)* Volkswirtschaft; *(thrift)* Sparsamkeit; Ersparnis

A cohesive system producing, distributing, and consuming wealth. It includes the activities of producers, labor and consumers and their interaction.

e-coupons

Like traditional coupons, but available on the internet.

edge-of-town retail cluster Gewerbezentrum in Stadtrandlage

Cluster of stores, usually supermarkets, superstores or hypermarkets, that are located at the edge of town, yet that are not organized as a unit.

edict Verordnung; Edikt

A legally binding command or decision arrived at by a court.

editor-in-chief Chefredakteur

educate ausbilden; erziehen; aufziehen

education Ausbildung; Erziehung; Pädagogik

educational Ausbildungs-; bildend; erzieherisch; *(informative)* belehrend

education allowance Ausbildungsbeihilfe

education field Bildungswesen

effect Auswirkung; *(in force)* Gültigkeit; *(to ~)* bewirken

effective effektiv; wirksam; wirkungsvoll; *(in force)* gültig

effective annual interest rate jährlicher Effektivzinssatz

Interest rate as if it were compounded once per time period rather than several times per period.

effective frequency effektive Häufigkeit

Marketing: Number of exposures or ad impressions required for an advertisement to become effective.

effectiveness Wirksamkeit; Erfolgswirksamkeit; Effektivität

Effectiveness measures how successfully a system achieves its desired outputs. This involves the subjective reaction of customer, and is therefore difficult to measure.

effective reach effektive Reichweite

Marketing: Percentage of a population group reached by a media schedule at a given level of frequency.

effective tax rate Effektiver Steuersatz

The average tax rate that is applicable in a given circumstance, which may not be the published rate of the tax.

efficiency Effizienz; Wirtschaftlichkeit; *(capacity)* Leistungsfähigkeit; *(person)* Tüchtigkeit

The ratio of the output to the input of any system, measuring how successfully inputs have been transformed into outputs.

Originally a measure of the effectiveness of a machine in terms of the ratio of work output to energy input. Applied to economics, it describes the conditions that create the biggest possible profit with the smallest possible costs

efficiency frontier Effektivitätsgrenze

efficiency ratio Effizienzkennzahl

efficient wirtschaftlich; effizient; tüchtig; ergiebig; *(productive)* leistungsfähig

efficient market hypothesis Hypothese effizienter Märkte

The hypothesis that the stock market is a efficient pricing mechanism, meaning that at any time all available information is fully reflected by shares prices.

Investors buying shares in an efficient market can expect to obtain an equilibrium rate of return, whilst business can expect to receive a fair value for the securities they sell.

efficient set Kurve effizienter Portfolios

Graph representing a set of portfolios that maximize expected return at each level of portfolio risk.

effort Bemühung; Anstrengung; Mühe; Leistung; Fleiß; *(time)* Arbeitsaufwand

elasticity Elastizität; Spannkraft

A ratio to measure a cause-effect relationship by calculting the incremental percentage change in one variable with respect to an incremental percentage change in another variable.

elasticity of demand Nachfrageelastizität; Elastizität der Nachfrage

Measure for the responsiveness of buyers to changes in price. Calculated as the percentage change in the quantity demanded divided by the percentage change in price. Deamand is said to be elastic if the elasticity exceeds -1, and inelasitc, when it is between 0 and -1.

elasticity of supply Angebotselastizität

Measure for the responsiveness of output to changes in price; calculated as the percentage change in the quantity supplied divided by the percentage change in the price. Supply is said to be elastic if the elasticity exceeds -1, and inelastic it is between 0 and -1.

elect wählen

election Wahl

electronic cash elektronisches Bargeld

electronic business (e-business)

Term, used often interchangeably with e-commerce, describing all electronic activities conducted by organizations such as business intelligence, e-commerce, supply chain management, customer relationship management and enterprise resource planning.

electronic commerce (e-commerce) elektronischer Handel

General term for a buying and selling process that is supported by electronic means, i.e., trading of goods and services using digital media.

Includes buying/selling online, digital value creation, virtual marketplaces and storefronts, and new distribution channel intermediaries.

Electronic Communication Privacy Act (ECPA)

As with the Fair Credit Reporting Act, this provides sanctions for misuse of consumer data.

electronic data interchange (EDI) Elektronischer Datenaustausch

Exchange of standardized document forms between computers for business use.

EDI has traditionally been a very complex and expensive undertaking. As more companies build inexpensive, standards-based networks around the internet, however, EDI systems are becoming cheaper and easier to use

electronic mall elektronisches Einkaufszentrum

electronic marketing (e-marketing) elektronisches Marketing; e-Marketing

Marketing activities that seek to achieve its objectives through the use of electronic communications technology such as Internet, e-mail, database, and mobile phone.

Sometimes used instead of online marketing, which is, however, limited to the use of internet technology to attain marketing objectives.

electronic marketspace elektronischer Marktplatz

Virtual marketplace such as the internet in which no direct contact occurs between buyers and sellers.

electronic meeting elektronisches Treffen

Meeting in which members interact on computers, allowing for anonymity of comments and aggregation of votes.

electronic shopping cart Elektronischer Einkaufswagen

Software that allows customers of an online-shop to place items in a virtual cart. Upon checkout the software calculates a total for the order, including shipping and handling.

electronic tokens elektronische Münzen

Units of digital currency that are in a standard electronic format.

eligibility Eignung; Qualifikation; *(for benefits)* Berechtigung

eligible geeignet; annehmbar; *(qualified)* qualifiziert; *(authorized)* berechtigt; passend; wünschenswert

eliminate eliminieren; beseitigen; aussondern; ausschließen; *(competition)* ausschalten

elimination Eliminierung; Beseitigung; Aussonderung *(competition)* Ausschaltung

e-mail elektronische Post; E-Mail

Electronic form of communication over the internet where the user types in the message and posts it to the electronic address of the recipient.

With the emergence of cheap internet service, it has become an inexpensive form of communication, providing fast, real-time communication.

e-mail advertising E-Mail Werbung

Advertisements such as newsletters, contained within an e-mail.

The least expensive type of online advertising, e-mail ads are generally just a few sentences of text embedded in another firm's e-mail content.

embargo Ausfuhrsperre; Handelssperre; Embargo; Verbot

Government prohibition against the shipment or import of certain goods to another country, most common during wartime but sometimes applied for economic reasons as well.

embassy Botschaft

embezzle unterschlagen; veruntreuen

embezzlement Unterschlagung; Veruntreuung

Fraudulent appropriation for one's own use, of property lawfully in one's possession but actually owned by others.

emerge hervortreten; zutage treten; herauskommen; bekannt werden

emergence Hervortreten; Auftauchen

emergent clusters gewachsene Cluster

emergency Notlage; Notfall; Ernstfall

emergency measure Notmaßnahme; Hilfsmaßnahme

emerging markets Schwellenländer

emotional emotional

emotional appeal emotionaler Anreiz

Advertising message that attempts to appeal to negative or positive emotions which will motivate a purchase. *Example:* fear, guilt, shame, love, humour, pride and joy.

emotional intelligence emotionale Intelligenz

Non-cognitive skills, capabilities, and competencies that influence a person's ability to cope with environmental demands and pressures. It is composed of five dimensions:

Self-awareness: the ability to be aware of what one is feeling.

Self-management: the ability to manage one's own emotions and impulses.

Self-motivation: the ability to persist in the face of setbacks and failures.

Empathy: the ability to sense how others are feeling.

Social skills: the ability to handle the emotions of others.

emotional labor Emotionsarbeit

Expression of organizationally desired emotions during interpersonal transactions by an employee.

Example: airline flight attendants are expected to be cheerful, funeral counselors sad, and doctors emotionally neutral.

emotional selling proposition emotionales Alleinstellungsmerkmal

Non-functional attribute that has unique association for consumers, even if the product may be similar to that of competitors. *Example*: Ferrari cars and Rolex watches.

emotional stability emotionale Stabilität

Personality dimension that characterized someone as calm, self-confident, secure (positive) versus nervous, anxious, depressed, and insecure (negative).

emotions Emotionen

Intense feelings that are directed at someone or something. Object specific reactions to an object, not a trait.

emphasis Betonung; Schwerpunkt; Nachdruck

emphasize betonen; hervorheben; herausstellen

employ anstellen; beschäftigen; *(to use)* verwenden

employed angestellt; berufstätig

employed person Erwerbsperson

employee Angestellter; Arbeitnehmer

A person who performs work for an employer under a verbal or written understanding where the employer gives direction as to what tasks are to be performed. Compensation may be paid on an hourly, daily, or annual wage basis.

employee association Berufsverband

Organization of employees, which are not labor unions.

employee categories Arbeitnehmergruppen

employee deviance Fehlverhalten von Mitarbeitern

Counter-productive behavior by employees that violate established norms and that threaten the organization, its members, or both.

Examples include: leaving early, intentionally working slowly, stealing, sabotage, gossiping, blaming co-workers, sexual harassment, verbal abuse.

employee evaluation Mitarbeiterbewertung

employee involvement Mitarbeiterbeteiligung

Participative process that uses the entire capacity of employees and is designed to encourage increased commitment to the organi zation's success.

By involving workers in those decisions that affect them and by increasing their autonomy and control, employees become more satisfied with their jobs.

employee layoff Belegschaftsabbau

employee-oriented leader mitarbeiterorientierter Führer

Leader who emphasizes interpersonal relations and takes a personal interest in the needs of the employees and accepts individual differences among members. They are associated with higher group productivity and higher job satisfaction.

employee profiling Mitarbeiterprofil erstellen

employee profit sharing Gewinnbeteiligung der Arbeitnehmer

A trust that enables an employer to share business profits with some or all of its employees.

employee representation Personalvertretung; Arbeitnehmervertretung

employee selection test Personalauswahltest

employee stock option Aktienbezugsrecht für Mitarbeiter; Vorzugsaktien

Stock options for the company's own stock that are offered to top managers as part of the executive compensation package.

Employee stock options carry the right, but not the obligation, to buy a certain amount of shares in the company at a predetermined price.

employee stock ownership plan (ESOP) Plan für den Belegschaftsaktienbesitz

A trust established by a company for the allocation of shares to its employees.

employee turnover Mitarbeiterfluktuation

employer Arbeitgeber

A person or a firm that employs workers and pays wages, thereby providing a livelihood to individuals who perform work.

The authority of an employer normally includes the right to control and direct the work to be performed.

employer association Arbeitgeberverband

employer interference Einsatz unlauterer Arbeitskampfmethoden seitens des Arbeitgebers

Range of unfair labor practices by employers against employees, like putting pressure on them in one-to-one interviews or threatening to fire them.

employer representative Arbeitgebervertretung

employment Anstellung; Arbeitsverhältnis; Beschäftigung;; *(use)* Verwendung

General: a contract between an employer and an employee resulting in a paid occupation.

employment agency Arbeitsvermittlung

A public or private organization charged with finding employment or jobs for individuals who are seeking employment.

employment contract Arbeitsvertrag

An agreement between an employer and an employee describing the exact nature of their relationship, specifically what compensation the employee will receive in exchange for which specific work to be performed

employment office Arbeitsamt

An employment agency run by the state that finds people to fill particular jobs or finds jobs for unemployed people.

empower bevollmächtigen; ermächtigen; befähigen

empowerment Bevollmächtigung; Übertragung von Verantwortung auf Untergebene

Form of participative management attempting to encouragie and authorize workers in order to improve operations, reduce costs, and improve product quality and customer service.

empty nesters Paar, dessen Kinder einen eigenen Haushalt haben

Stage in the family life cycle describing couples whose children have established separate households.

As all other households in the family life cycle, empty nesters have specific requirements, e.g. in the housing market, since they often seek to smaller housing units.

enable befähigen; ermöglichen; möglich machen

enabling technology technologische Voraussetzung

Internet: electronic products unique to the internet that operate behind the scenes and assist in the creation of customer value.

enact verordnen; beschließen; verfügen

enactment Verordnung; Erlass; Verfügung

enclose einschließen; *(with letter)* beilegen

encoding Verschlüsselung; Kodierung

The process of converting a message into a certain code. Often as a control to assure confidentiality, especially when messages or documents are to be transmitted via the internet.

encounter stage Eintrittsphase

Second stage in the socialization process in which a new employee sees what the organization is really like and confronts the possibility that expectations and reality may diverge.

encourage ermutigen; aufmuntern; *(to support)* fördern

encouragement Ermutigung; Aufmunterung; *(support)* Förderung

encroach beeinträchtigen; übergreifen

To gradually infringe upon the rights or property of another.

encroachment Beeinträchtigung; Rechtsverletzung; Ein-; Übergriff

encryption Chiffrierung; Kodierung, Verschlüsselung

Translation of plain-text data, such as an e-mail message, into an unreadable code in order to ensure its safe transmission over the internet.

To read encrypted data, one needs software that allows to decrypt it. There are several different types of encryption, the most popular form is called public-key encryption.

encumber belasten; behindern; versperren

encumbrance Belastung; *(land)* Hypothekenschulden; *(assessment)* Umlage

ending rate Schlussrate

Spot exchange rate when budget and performance are being compared.

end of the year Jahresende; Jahresultimo

end-of-year convention nachschüssige Zahlungen

Treating cash flows as if they occur at the end of a year (or, alternatively, at the end of a period), as opposed to the date convention. Under the end- of-year convention, the end of year 0 is the present, the end of year 1 occurs one period hence, and so on.

endorse billigen; zulassen; bestätigen; *(a check)* indossieren; *(to support)* unterstützen; *(to approve)* zustimmen

Banking: sign one's name as a payee or to indicate co-responsibility for payment on a check, bill, note or other document

endorsement Zustimmung; *(support)* Unterstützung *(of a check)* Indossament; Giro; Vermerk

Banking: the signature of a payee or drawee on the back of a check to assign or transfer the paper to another.

Insurance: a written amendment attached to a policy that modifies the terms of the insurance contract.

endow ausstatten; stiften; ausstatten

endowment Stiftung; Ausstattung

A bequest, gift, or other funds intended to be kept permanently and invested to generate regular income, which is used to serve the specific purpose for which the gift was intended.

endowment contract Zuwendungsvertrag; Risikolebensversicherung

Insurance: an endowment contract is an annuity that also provides life insurance protection.

energy Energie; Kraft; Arbeitsvermögen

enforce durchsetzen; durchführen; geltend machen; *(law)* vollstrecken; erzwingen

enforcement Durchsetzung; Durchführung; *(law)* Vollstreckung; Zwang

Implementation or putting into practice a rule, law or activity.

engage *(contract)* verpflichten; *(to employ)* ein-; anstellen; angreifen

engagement *(appointment)* Verabredung; *(employment)* Anstellung; Beschäftigung; *(obligation)* Verpflichtung

Engel's Law Engelsches Gesetz

Observation by 19th-century economist Ernst Engel that when a family's income increases, the proportion of money they spend on food decreases.

engineer Ingenieur; Mechaniker

engineering Ingenieurswesen

engineering works Maschinenfabrik; Konstruktionswerk

enhance steigern; verbessern; erhöhen

enhancement Steigerung; Verbesserung; Vergrößerung

enjoyment Vergnügen; Genuss

enlarge ausweiten; vergrößern

enlargement Vergrößerung; Erweiterung

enlightened marketing aufgeklärtes Marketing

Marketing philosophy holding that a company's marketing should support the best long-run performance of the marketing system; based on principles like consumer-oriented marketing, innovative marketing, value marketing, sense-of-mission marketing, and societal marketing.

enlist anstellen; in Anspruch nehmen; anwerben lassen; eintreten

enough genug; hinreichend

enrichment Bereicherung

enrollment period Einschreibungszeitraum; Eintragungszeitraum

Insurance: The amount of time an employee has to sign up for a health insurance plan.

ensurance Versicherung; Zusicherung

ensure sicherstellen; sichern

enter eintreten; *(contract)* eingehen; *(record)* eintragen; verbuchen; *(country)* einreisen

enterprise Unternehmen; Unternehmung; *(business)* Geschäft; *(plant)* Betrieb

An organization created to pursue business ventures. It consists of a group of departments, divisions, or companies which together make up an entire business.

enterprise knowledge management Wissensmanagement des Unternehmens

Combination of the database contents and the technology used to create the system: the marketing information system (MIS) at a company-wide level. Marketing knowledge contributes to the EKM system through the MIS.

enterprise resource planning Resourcenplanung eines Unternehmens

Combination of electronic information systems throughout an organization that enables to plan coherently, even if for disparate parts.

enterprise zone Industriefördergebiet; Industriegebiet; Gewerbegebiet; Wirtschaftsentwicklungsgebiet

An area set up by a government where businesses enjoy favorable tax credits and other advantages, such as planning exceptions in order to stimulate development and to generate inward investment.

entire ganz; voll; komplett

entire income Gesamteinkommen

entire territory Gesamtgebiet

entirety Gesamtheit

entitle berechtigen; betiteln

entitlement Berechtigung

entity Gebilde; Wesen; *(agency)* Dienststelle; *(legal)* juristische Person

Organization: Options for business entities include, amongst others, a corporation or sole proprietorship, a joint venture, a limited partnership, or a partnership.

entrance Eingang; *(admission)* Eintritt; Zugang

entrepreneur Unternehmer

A person who undertakes and operates a new enterprise or venture, and assumes some accountability for the inherent risks.

entrepreneurial unternehmerisch

entrepreneurial behavior Unternehmerverhalten

entrepreneurship Unternehmertum

Special collection of skills possessed by an entrepreneur, including a propensity to take risks over and above the normal, and a desire to create wealth.

entrust anvertrauen; betrauen

entry Eingang; Eintritt; *(record)* Eintragung; Buchung; Posten; *(into country)* Einreise; Vermerk

entry barrier Markteintrittsbarriere; Marktzugangsbeschränkung

entry documents Einreisedokumente

entry page Eingangsseite

Internet: page at which visitors enter a web site. It is identified by a log file analyzer.

enumerate aufzählen

environment Umwelt; Umgebung; Milieu

Business: those institutions and forces outside the organization that potentially affect the organization's aims and performance.

Business environments can have three key dimensions: c*apacity,* the degree to which it can support growth, *volatility,* the degree of instability, an *complexity,* the degree of heterogeneity and concentration among environmental elements. Simple environments are homogeneous and concentrated.

environmental Umwelt-; umweltbedingt

environmental burden Umweltbelastung

environmental factors Umweltfaktoren

environmental impact analysis Umweltverträglichkeitsuntersuchung

Analysis of the expected effects of a course of action on the surrounding natural and fabricated environment.

environmental group Umweltgruppe

environmental management Umweltmanagement

The management of a business´s interaction with and impact upon the environment.

environmental scanning Umfeldbeobachtung; Milieuabfrage

The continual process of collecting information to carry out a systematic analysis of the forces affecting a business and identifying potential threats and opportunities.

environmentalism Umweltschutzbewegung

Organized movement of concerned citizens and government agencies to protect the environment and improve people's living conditions.

environmentally aware umweltbewusst

environmentally compatible umweltverträglich

environmental orientation Umweltorientierung

environmental problem Umweltproblem

environmental protection Umweltschutz

environmental protectionist Umweltschützer

environmental quality Umweltqualität

equal Gleichgestellter; gleich; gleichmäßig; *(equal rights)* gleichberechtigt; *(to ~)* gleich sein; gleichen; gewachsen

equal opportunity Chancengleichheit

equal opportunity employer Arbeitgeber der Chancengleichheit fördert

Employer who has made a commitment to practice affirmative action and create a workplace free of discrimination and harassment.

equality Gleichheit; Gleichwertigkeit; *(rights)* Gleichberechtigung; Parität

equalization Ausgleich; Gleichstellung

equalize ausgleichen

equal treatment Gleichstellung; Gleichbehandlung

equate gleichsetzen; als gleich ansehen

equation Gleichung; Ausgleich

equilibrium Gleichgewicht

Economics: status of stability of a market in which there are no forces operating that would bring about changes in the quantity demanded or the prevailing price.

equilibrium price Gleichgewichtspreis

Price at which the quantity of goods producers wish to supply matches the quantity demanders want to purchase.

equilibrium quantity Gleichgewichtsmenge

Quantity at which the price of goods producers wish to supply matches the price demanders are prepared to pay.

equilibrium rate of interest Gleichgewichtszinssatz

Interest rate that clears the market. Also called market-clearing interest rate.

equip ausrüsten; einrichten

equipment Einrichtung; Ausrüstung; Ausrüstungsgegenstand; *(tool)* Gerät; *(machine)* Anlage

equitable gerecht; angemessen; vernünftig

equity Billigkeit; Gerechtigkeit; *(business)* Nettoanteil; *(capital)* Eigenkapital; *(capital stock)* Grundkapital

Investment: a financial term for the difference between a company's assets and liabilities, representing the ownership interest possessed by ordinary shareholders in a company.

Real estate: the interest of the owner in a property over and above all claims against the property, usually calculate as the difference between the market value of the property and any outstanding encumbrances.

equity capital Grundkapital; Aktienkapital; Eigenkapital

equity financing Aktienfinanzierung; Beteiligungsfinanzierung; Eigenfinanzierung

Method of raising money by selling part of the ownership of a company, such as stock in a corporation, in contrast with debt financing.

equity holder Kapitaleigner

equity kicker Option auf Wandlung in Eigenkapital

equity markets Aktienmärkte

A market where investors buy and sell securities providing ownership of a company's shares. Same as stock market.

equity method Equitymethode; Eigenkapitalanteilsmethode

Valuation method for holdings in companies when an investor owns between 20% and 50% of the voting common stock of a company.

equity options Aktienoptionen

Securities that give the holder the right to buy or sell a specified number of shares of stock, at a specified price for a certain (limited) time period. Typically one option equals 100 shares of stock.

equity participation Kapitalbeteiligung

equity share Dividendenpapier

Ownership interest which bears most risk in a company and participates in any residual return.

equity-theory Equity-Theorie; Trachten nach fairen Gegenleistungen

A process theory in social psychology seeking to explain the origins of motivation. Basically, individuals compare their job inputs and outcomes with those of others and then respond so as to eliminate any inequities.

There are four reference comparisons that an employee can use:

Self-inside: an employee's experiences in a different position inside the current organization.

Self-outside: an employee's experiences in a situation or position outside the current organization.

Other inside: another individual or group of individuals inside the employee's organization.

Other outside: another individual or group of individuals outside the employee's organization.

equity yield rate Eigenkapitalverzinsung

The return on the portion of an investment financed by equity capital. It takes into account periodic cash flow and the proceeds from resale and considers the timing and amounts of cash flow after annual debt service, but not income taxes.

equivalent Gegenwert; Gegenleistung; gleichwertig; entsprechend; äquivalent

equivalent annual cost äquivalente jährliche Kosten

equivalent treatment gleichwertige Betrachtung

era Ära; Zeitalter

ergonomic ergonomisch

Machines and equipment, such as computers, chairs and lighting, designed to work with the human body. Ergonomic equipment is intended to reduce injuries and increase productivity.

ergonomics Ergonomie, Arbeitswissenschaft

The applied science that studies the relationship of humans to their working environment and seeks to improve working conditions and increase efficiency by designing machines and equipment for the dynamics and needs of human physiology.

erosion Erosion; Abnutzung; Verschleiß; Beeinträchtigung

The gradual wearing away of land or soil by the action of wind, water, or ice. In a business context the term indicates a gradual decline in business figures such as *sales* and *market - share.*

err sich irren; auf Abwege geraten

erroneous irrig; irrtümlich

error Irrtum; Fehler; Versehen; Verfehlung

error rate Fehlerquote

errors and omissions liability insurance Haftpflichtversicherung

Policies available to professionals that require protection for negligent acts and/or omissions resulting in bodily injury, personal injury, and/or property damage liability to a client.

escalate eskalieren; steigern; steigen; sich ausweiten

escalation Eskalation; Steigerung

escalation of commitment Steigerung des Engagements

Increased commitment by management to a previous decision in spite of negative information. Can easily lead to large losses only because a manager wants to prove that the original decision was right.

escape Entkommen; *(to ~)* entkommen

escape clause Rücktrittsklausel

escrow Treuhandvertrag; Treuhänder

A deed that has been signed and sealed, but is delivered on the condition that it will not become effective until some condition is fulfilled. As soon as that has happened, it will become effective and cannot be revoked. *Example*: escrow account, in which funds accumulate to pay taxes, insurance on mortgaged property, etc.

e-shock

Speculation by M. de Kare-Silver in 1998, that by 2005-2007 consumers will use the internet as their preferred method of making purchases. Those will account for 15-20 per cent of total purchases, which will lead to decreasing margins for retailers, who will be forced to close substantial parts of their retail networks.

espionage Spionage

essential industry Schlüsselindustrie

Industry which, for political or economic reasons, is considered by society to be necessarily located within its own economy, regardless of its comparative advantage or disadvantage with other economics. *Example:* the defense industry, coal mining.

establish gründen; errichten; *(to ascertain)* einwandfrei feststellen

established gegründet; *(well-established)* alteingeführt; bestehend

establishment Niederlassung; Betrieb; Institution; *(society)* Führungsschicht

establishment of contact Kontaktnahme

establish oneself sich etablieren

estate Eigentum; *(land)* Grundbesitz; Grundstück; Landbesitz; *(bankruptcy)* Konkursmasse *(after death)* Erbschaftsmasse; Vermögensmasse

In general: all that a person owns, including personal property (car, household items, and other tangible items), real property, and intangible property, such as stock certificates and bank accounts.

estate tax Erbschaftssteuer

Amount due to the government, generally based on the fair market value of one's property at death, less liabilities.

estimate *(of costs)* Voranschlag; *(estimation)* Schätzung; *(to ~)* schätzen; abschätzen; *(to calculate)* berechnen

estimated value Schätzwert

estimate of profits Gewinnschätzung

estimation Veranschlagung; *(cost)* Kostenkalkulation; *(esteem)* Wertschätzung; Schätzung

e-tailer Internet-Händler

Intermediary firm that buys products and resells them online, just as traditional retailers do offline.

et al. und andere

Abbreviation of *et alii,* Latin for "and others." Used in scientific publications.

Ethernet

Most common method of transferring data over a LAN. Fast Ethernet runs at up to 100Mbps, and Gigabit Ethernet runs at up to 1Gbps.

ethical ethisch; moralisch vertretbar; standesgemäß; sittlich; dem Berufsethos entsprechend

Conforming to accepted standards of social or professional behavior, i.e. that work is performed in an honest and diligent way.

ethical business Unternehmensethik

ethical code Ehrenkodex

Code developed by trade associations, commercial standards groups, and the professions, outlining proper behaviors.

ethical dilemma ethisches Dilemma

Situation in which an individual is required to define right or wrong conduct.

Example: successful executives use insider information for personal financial gain.

ethics Ethik; Moral; Standesethik; Sittenlehre

Branch of classical philosophy attempting to distinguish what is right from what is wrong. Ethics tends to be more global than morality, which allows more leeway for individual interpretation.

ethnic ethnisch

Referring to people grouped according to a common racial, national, tribal, religious, linguistic, or cultural origin.

ethnocentrism Ethnozentrismus

Behavior that is based on the belief in the superiority of one's own ethnic group or culture; often shows disregard or contempt for the culture of other countries.

ethnocentric staffing ethnozentrische Stellenbesetzung

Staffing approach within multinational enterprises in which all key management positions are filled by parent country nationals.

Euro Euro

eurobanks Eurobanken

Banks that make loans and accept deposits in foreign currencies.

eurocurrency Eurowährung

Money deposited by businesses and governments in banks away from their home countries. The currencies held are, however, not European, such as the Eurodollar.

eurobonds Euroanleihen

Bond placed in countries other than the one in whose currency the bond is denominated.

eurocheque Euroscheck

A cheque drawn on a European bank, which can be cashed at any bank in the world that displays the ec sign. It can also be used to pay for goods and services in shops, hotels, restaurants. In most cases, a commission of 1.25% is added to the foreign currency value of the cheque.

Eurodollar Eurodollar

US currency held in banks outside the US, primarily in Europe. Eurodollars were created after World War II by U.S. defense and foreign aid expenditures. Since the dollar was backed by gold, it became a popular reserve currency in Europe and widely used for settling international transactions.

European Atomic Energy Community (Euratom) Europäische Atomgemeinschaft

Organization set up by the six members of the European Coal and Steel Community in 1957 to create the technical and industrial conditions necessary to produce nuclear energy on an industrial scale.

European Bank for Reconstruction and Development (EBRD) Europäische Bank für Wiederaufbau und Entwicklung

European Central Bank (ECB) Europäische Zentralbank

The central bank of the European Union, established on 1 July 1998 in Frankfurt to direct the monetary policy needed for European Monetary Union.

The bank became fully functional on 1 January 1999 when the single European currency was launched. The president, vice-president and board members are appointed by the participating governments but the bank is otherwise entirely independent. Its main objective is achieving and maintaining price stability.

European Coal and Steel Cornmunity (ECSC) Montanunion

The first of the European Communities, founded in 1953 to create a common market in coal, steel, iron ore, and scrap between the original six members of the EC, Belgium, France, West Germany, Italy, Luxembourg. and the Netherlands. These six countries signed the Treaty of Rome in 1957, setting up the European Economic Community

European Commission Europäische Kommission

The executive body formed in 1967 from the three separate executive bodies. In 2004 it consisted of 20 Commissioners: two each from the UK, France, Germany, Spain, and Italy; and One each from Belgium, the Netherlands, Luxembourg, Ireland, Denmark. Greece, Portugal, Austria, Finland, and Sweden. The Commissioners accept joint responsibility for their decisions, which are taken on the basis of a majority vote.

The Commission initiates and implements EU legislation and mediates between member governments. The Commissioners are backed by a staff of same 15000 civil servants located mainly in the Berlaymont Building in Brussels.

European Communities Europäische Gemeinschaften

European Communities is the name given collectively to the European Coal and Steel Community (ECSC), the European Economic Community (EEC), and the European Atomic Energy Community (Euratom), when in 1967, they were first merged under a single institutional framework.

European Community (EC) Europäische Gemeinschaft

The European Community was originally founded on March 25, 1957 by the signing of the Treaty of Rome under the name of European Economic Community. The 'Economic' was removed from its name by the Maastricht treaty in 1992, which at the same time effectively made the European Community the first of three pillars of the European Union.

European company Europagesellschaft

A form of business corporation proposed by the European Union and defined by statute in 2001, not subject to the national laws of the member states but to European law.

European Council Europäischer Rat

The European Council is a meeting of the heads of state and/or government of the

European Union, and the President of the European Commission. Held two to four times a year, it is the venue for discussion on the key policy issues and direction of the EU.

European Council of Ministers Europäischer Ministerrat

The Council of the European Union (also referred to as Council, Council of Ministers, or European Council of Ministers) is the EU's main decision making institution.

It consists of the Ministers of the Member States responsible for the area of activity on the agenda. Its main responsibilities are:

Legislation: the Council passes EU law on the recommendations of the European Commission and the European Parliament.

Budget: the Council and the Parliament must agree on the budget.

Foreign and defence policy: the Council seeks to achieve a common European foreign and defence policy.

Economic policy: the Council seeks to achieve a common economic policy.

Justice: the Council seeks to co-ordinate the justice system of the member states.

European Currency Unit (ECU) Europäische Währungseinheit

Former currency unit of the European Union, created in 1979 as the reserve asset and accounting unit of the European Monetary System (EMS); it was superseded by the euro in January 1999.

The value of the ECU was calculated as a weighted average of a basket of European Union currencies, its value was reviewed periodically.

European Economic Area Europäischer Wirtschaftsraum

Organization formed in 1992 between the members of the European Union and the members of the European Free Trade Association (EFTA) except Switzerland.

European Economic Community (EEC; Common Market) Europäische Wirtschaftgemeinschaft

The common market set up by the six member states of the European Cool and Steel Community in 1957. At the same time the European Atomic Energy Community was set up, and the European Parliament and the European Court of Justice were formed in accordance with the Treaty of Rome in 1957.

The treaty aimed to build a closer union between the countries of Europe by removing the economic effects of their frontiers, including the elimination of customs duties and quotas between members, a common trade policy to outside countries, the abolition of restrictions on the movement of people and capital between member states, and a Common Agricultural Policy.

The UK, Ireland, and Denmark joined the EC in 1973, Greece joined in *1979,* and Portugal and Spain became members in 1986, making a total of 12 nations. In 1993 the European Community became the European Union, which was joined by Austria, Finland, and Sweden in 1995.

European Free Trade Association (EFTA) Europäische Freihandelszone

A trade association formed in 1960 between Austria, Denmark, Norway, Portugal, Sweden, Switzerland. The UK; Finland, Iceland, and Liechtenstein joined later. The UK, Denmark, Portugal, Austria, Finland, and Sweden left again on joining the European Union.

EFTA is a looser association than the EU, dealing only with trade barriers rather than generally coordinating economic policy.

European Interbank Offered Rate (EURIBOR)

A daily reference rate based on the interest rates at which banks offer to lend *unsecured* funds to other banks in the euro wholesale money market.

European Investment Bank (EIB) Europäische Investitionsbank

A bank set up under the Treaty of Rome in 1958 to finance capital-investment projects in the European Economic Community. The EIB grants long-term loans to private companies and public institutions for projects that further the aims of the Community.

The members of the EIB are the member states of the European Union, all of whom have subscribed to the Bank's capital, but most of the funds lent by the bank are borrowed on the EU and inter- national capital markets.

European Monetary System (EMS) Europäisches Währungssystem (EWS)

A system of exchange-rate stabilization for the European Union, established in 1979, with two main elements: the Exchange Rate Mechanism (ERM), under which participating countries committed themselves to maintaining the values of their currencies within agreed limits, and a balance of payments support mechanism, organized through the European Monetary Cooperation Fund.

European Monetary Union (EMU) Eurpäische Währungsunion

The decision to create a single currency was part of the Maastricht Treaty of 1991. In June 1998 11 EU countries, all member states except Denmark. Greece, Sweden, and the UK, committed themselves to monetary union. Their currencies were then locked together irrevocably and the European Central Bank was established to direct the single monetary policy essential for EMU.

The euro was launched for all purposes except cash transactions in January 1999, Euro bank notes and coins were brought into circulation in January 2002, replacing all national currencies of the participating states.

European option Europäische Option

Finance: Option contract that may be exercised only on the expiration date. An American option may be exercised any time up to the expiration date.

European Parliament Europäisches Parlament; Europaparlament

The parliamentary body of the European Union (EU), directly elected by the citizen of the EU once every five years. It meets in Strasbourg and Brussels, and together with the Council of Ministers it composes the legislative branch of the Union.

The European Parliament cannot initiate legislation, which is done by the Commission, but it can amend or veto it in many areas. In certain other areas, it can only be consulted. The Parliament also supervises the Commission, approving all appointments to it, and dismissing it with a vote of censure. It also has the right to control the EU budget.

European Quality Award (EQA) Europäische Qualitätsauszeichung

A prize set up in 1992 by the European Foundation for Quality Management. It is awarded to companies that can demonstrate excellence in their management of quality and that their approach to total quality management has contributed to the satisfaction of customers, employees, and other stakeholders.

The first-level categories of the EQA model are: leadership, policy and strategy, people, management, resources, processes, customer satisfaction, people satisfaction, impact on society, and business results.

European Union (EU) Europäische Union

Economic and political union between 25 European nations (2005): Austria, Belgium, Cyprus, Czech Republic, Denmark, Estonia, Finland, France, Germany, Greece, Hungary, Ireland, Italy, Latvia, Lithuania, Luxembourg, Malta, Poland, Portugal, Slovakia, Slovenia, Spain, Sweden, the Netherlands, the United Kingdom.

The EU was created in 1993 from the European Community. Its executive body is the European Commission which initiates and implements European policy. The legislative process is a dialog between the Commission, the Council, which takes the major policy decisions, the European Parliament, which exercises democratic control over policy, and the European Court of Justice, which imposes the rule of law on the EU.

evaluate bewerten; *(data)* auswerten; zahlenmäßig bestimmen

evaluation Bewertung; *(data)* Auswertung

evaluation of international managers Bewertung internationaler Manager

evaluation plan Bewertungsplan; Auswertungsplan

Internet: System whereby the site is continually evaluated after it is created and published. This requires tracking systems that must be in place before the site is launched.

even gleich; ruhig; ausgeglichen; *(number)* gerade; *(surface)* ebenmäßig; glatt

event Ereignis, Veranstaltung

Advertising: occurrences staged to communicate message to target audiences; examples news conferences, grand openings.

event risk Risikowahrscheinlichkeit

The risk that an unforeseen event will affect a a given business or investment; *contrast with market* or *systematic risk,* which affects all in the same class.

event study Event-Studie

Statistical study that examines how the release of information affects prices at a particular time.

eviction Zwangsräumung; Vertreibung; Ausweisung

Physical expulsion of someone from real estate by the assertion of superior title or through legal proceedings.

evidence Beweismittel; Nachweis; Anzeichen; Anhaltspunkt; *(testimony)* Zeugenaussage; *(to ~)* beweisen

evidence of title Eigentumsnachweis

Document, such as a deed, which demonstrates ownership, usually kept in safe places, such as a bank vault.

evolution Evolution; Entwicklung; Heranwachsen; natürliches Werden

ex *(sbipping point)* ab; *(former)* ehemalig

exact genau; sorgfältig; *(to ~) (to collect)* eintreiben; fordern; erzwingen

examination Prüfung; *(accounts)* Revision; Kontrolle; *(investigation)* Untersuchung

examine prüfen; untersuchen; *(accounts)* durchsehen

examiner Prüfer; *(accountant)* Revisor; *(investigator)* Untersuchender

example Beispiel; Muster; Vorbild

exceed übersteigen; überschreiten; größer sein als

excellence Spitzenleistung; Vortrefflichkeit; hervorragende Eigenschaft

In business and management, excellence is considered to have eight attributes: bias for action, close to the customer, autonomy and entrepreneurship, productivity through people, hands-on, value driven, stick to the knitting, simple form, lean staff, and simultaneous loose-tight properties.

exception Ausnahme; Vorbehalt; *(objection)* Einwand

exceptional case Ausnahmefall

excess Übermaß; Überschuss; Mehr-; Über-

excess capacity Überkapazität

excess reserves außerordentliche Reserven; Überschussreserven; Sonderrücklagen

Banking: amount of reserves held by a banking institution in excess of its reserve requirement. The money may be on deposit with the central bank or in the bank's possession.

excessive übermäßig

excessive indebtedness Überschuldung

exchange Umtausch; Austausch; *(currency)* Währungsumtausch; *(rate)* Wechselkurs; *(foreign exchange)* Devisen; *(stock market)* Börse; *(to ~)* umtauschen; austauschen; auswechseln

General: act of obtaining a desired object from someone by offering something in return.

Market: marketplace in which shares, options and futures on stocks, bonds, commodities and indices are traded.

exchangeable austauschbar; auswechelbar

exchange bank Wechselbank

exchange controls Devisenkontrolle; Währungskontrollen

Restrictions imposed by a country on the convertibility of a currency or on the movement of funds in that currency.

exchange equilibrium Zahlungsausgleich

exchange of views Meinungsaustausch

exchange process Austauschprozess

Market mechanism where one thing of value is given for another of equal value. Although barter can be used as the exchange method, in the modern economy the normal unit of exchange is money.

exchange profit Kursgewinn

exchange rate Wechselkurs; Devisenkurs; Umrechnungskurs; Währungskurs; Tauschrate

Rate at which one currency is converted into another, or simply the price of one currency expressed in another.

Most exchange rates float freely and follow the laws of supply and demand, others are fixed and do not change as a result of market forces.

exchange rate change Wechselkursänderung

exchange rate fluctuations Wechselkursschwankungen

exchange rate increase Wechselkursanstieg

exchange rate mechanism (ERM) Wechselkursmechanismus

A system of intervention in the foreign exchange markets designed to keep participating European countries within a narrow range versus the ECU.

exchange rate profit Wechselkursgewinn

exchange rate risk Wechselkursrisiko

exchange relation Tauschrelation

excise tax Verbrauchssteuer

A tax imposed on on the manufacture, sale, or consumption of certain non-essential goods or services, such as gasoline, alcohol, tobacco, etc

The term covers every tax except the income tax and the property tax.

exclude ausschließen

exclusion Ausschließung; Ausschluss

Insurance: something that is not covered by an insurance policy and specifically stated so in the policy contract.

exclusive ausschließlich; nicht eingerechnet; exklusiv

exclusive agent Alleinvertreter

exclusive channel exklusiver Vertriebskanal

Distribution channel that outsiders find difficult to access.

exclusive distribution exklusive Distribution

Giving a limited number of dealers the exclusive right to distribute the company's products in their territories.

ex dividend ohne Dividende

ex-dividend rate Kurs ex Dividende

execute ausführen; erledigen; *(a contract)* Bedingungen erfüllen; *(a judgment)* vollstrecken; vollziehen; hinrichten

ex dock frei Dock

execution Ausführung; Durchführung; Erledigung; *(judgment)* Vollstreckung

Law: the process of signing, sealing, and delivering of a contract, thus making it valid.

Securities: process of completing an order to buy or sell. A broker who buys or sells shares has *executed* an order.

executive Vollzugs-; Exekutiv-; *(government)* Exekutive; *(company)* leitender Angestellter; Führungskraft; geschäftsführender Vorstand; *(managing)* leitend; verwaltend

Politics: the branch of the government responsible for the enforcement of laws and administrative decision making.

Management: a company employee in a top-level management position who has major decision-making authority.

executive committee Leitungsausschuss, Leitungsgremium; geschäftsführender Vorstand; *(law)* Exekutivausschuss

Elected management committee empowered to make and implement major organizational decisions.

In a supervisory function it has the authority to request justification of certain matters as well as to plan activities.

executive position Führungsposition

executive secretary Vorstandssekretär

A secretary having administrative duties and responsibilities, acting as an assistant to top-level management personnel. Executive secretaries have substantial clerical as well as administrative responsibilities.

executive staff Führungsstab; leitende Angestellte

executive suite Chefetage

executor Testamentsvollstrecker; Nachlaßverwalter

A person appointed by a testator to carry out the terms of the will, especially the distribution of the assets in it.

exempt befreien; befreit; frei von

exemption Befreiung; Freistellung; Ausnahmeregelung; *(income tax)* (Steuer-)Freibetrag

Taxation: deduction allowed to a taxpayer reducing the amount of income upon which he is taxed. Can be on the due to the taxpayer's status or circumstances, for example, a married couple having three children are allowed substantial exemptions.

exercise Anwendung; (Aus)Übung; Bewegung; *(to~)* üben; trainieren

exercise of functions Aufgabenwahrnehmung

exercise of influence Einflussnahme

exercise price Basispreis einer Option; Optionspreis; Abschlusskurs

Price at which the holder of an option can buy (in the case of a call option) or sell (in the case of a put option) the underlying share. Also called the strike price.

exercising the option Optionsausübung

The act of buying or selling the underlying asset via an option contract.

exert oneself sich bemühen

ex factory ab Fabrik; ab Werk

exhibit Ausstellungsstück; *(proof)* Beweisstück; *(voucber)* Beleg; *(to ~) (to display)* ausstellen; zeigen; an den Tag legen

exhibition Ausstellung; *(fair)* Messe; Schau; Bekundung

exhibitor Aussteller

exim bank Ausfuhr-Einfuhr-Bank

exist existieren; *(to be in existence)* bestehen; (to *live)* leben

existence Dasein; Existenz; Vorhandensein; *(life)* Leben

existence, relatedness and growth (ERG) theory Existenz-, Beziehungs- und Wachstums-Theorie

Theory by Clayton Alderfer, developing Maslow's need hierarchy further. He defines three groups of core needs: existence, relatedness, and growth.

Existence: is concerned with providing basic material existence requirements. They include the items that Maslow considered to be physiological and safety needs.

Relatedness: the desire for maintaining important interpersonal relationships. These social status desires require interaction with others if they are to be satisfied, and they align with Maslow's social need and the external component of Maslow's esteem classification.

Growth: an intrinsic desire for personal development. These include the intrinsic component from Maslow's esteem category and the characteristics included under self-actualization.

existing commitment Altengagement

existing installation Altanlage

exit Ausgang; Abwanderung

Motivation: Dissatisfaction expressed through behavior directed toward leaving the organization, including looking for a new position as well as resigning.

exit interview Abgangsgespräch

HRM: Interview conducted when an employee's leaves an organization in order to obtain feedback.

exit page Ausgangsseite

Internet: Page from which a visitor exits a web site. It is identified by a log file analyzer.

exit visa Ausgangsbescheinigung; Ausreisevisum

ex officio von Amts wegen

By virtue of an office or position, and therefore not requiring further appointment.

expand erweitern; ausdehnen; sich entwickeln; expandieren; weiten

expansion Erweiterung; Ausdehnung; Expansion; Ausweitung

Any increase of the commercial activities of a company, as a result of modernization, replacement, upgrade, or increased workload.

Expansion may be necessary to meet new competitive demands as well as to open new markets for a company.

expatriate Führungskraft im Ausland; Ausgebürgerter; Auswanderer; *(to ~)* ausbürgern; verbannen; *adj* ständig im Ausland lebend; nicht einheimisch

expatriate failure Scheitern eines Managers im Ausland

expatriate manager Manager im Auslandseinsatz

National of one country appointed to a management position in another country.

expect erwarten; annehmen

expectancy theory Erwartungstheorie

Theory suggesting that the strength of a tendency to act in a certain way depends on the strength of an expectation that the act will be followed by a given outcome and on the attractiveness of that outcome to the individual. The theory identifies three relationships:

Effort-performance relationship: the probability perceived by the individual that exerting a given amount of effort will lead to performance.

Performance-reward relationship: the degree to which the individual believes that performing at a particular level will lead to the attainment of a desired outcome

Rewards-personal goals relationship: the degree to which organizational rewards satisfy an individual's personal goals or needs and the attractiveness of those potential rewards for the individual.

expectation Aussicht; Erwartung

expectation for the future Zukunftserwartung

expectation of profits Gewinnerwartung

expectations hypothesis Erwartungshypothese

Theory that forward interest rates are unbiased estimates of expected future interest rates.

expectations theory (of foreign exchange rates) Erwartungstheorie (der Wechselkurse)

Theory that forward exchange rates are unbiased estimates of expected future exchange rates.

expected voraussichtlich; erwartet

expected monetary value erwarteter Geldwert

expected return erwartete Rendite

Average of possible returns weighted by their probability.

expected value Erwartungswert

Average value that would appear if a ransom variable were observed many times; also called the *expectation.*

expedient Hilfsmittel; zweckdienlich; vorteilhaft; nützlich

expeditious prompt; rasch; schnell

expend aufwenden; ausgeben; verbrauchen

expenditure Ausgabe; Aufwand; Aufwendung; *(expenses)* Spesen

expense Ausgabe; Aufwand; *(costs)* Kosten; *(expenses)* Spesen

General: a term for an outgoing payment made by a business or individual.

Accounting: costs that are deductible, as opposed to capital expenditures, which may not be deducted but must be depreciated or amortized over the useful life of the property.

expense account Aufwandskonto; Spesenkonto; Kostenkonto

Accounting: account used to accumulate expenses such as interest, advertising, and administrative.

Personnel: allowance or account for travel and business entertainment purposes.

expense item Ausgabenposten

expense ratio Verhältnis Aufwand zu Umsatzerlös; Kostensatz

Ratio of operating expenses to gross income, especially for a real estate property.

expense report Spesenabrechnung

List of expenses incurred by an employee, submitted to the employer for reimbursement.. It contains expenses such as transportation, lodging, meals away from home, and client entertainment.

expensive teuer; aufwendig; kostspielig

experience Erlebnis; *(knowledge)* Erfahrung; Kenntnissee *(to ~)* erfahren; erleben; durchmachen

experience curve Erfahrungskurve

Phenomenon in production that unit costs decline as volume increases, resulting from the accumulated production experience over the life of a product. It has been observed that when the cumulated volume of goods produced is doubled, the total costs per unit may be reduced by between 20 and 30 percent.

The causes of the experience effect are: (1) learning in the narrower sense, (2) rationalisation; (3) standardisation, (4) technical progress, (5) more favorable procurement, (6) changes in the materials used, (7) distribution of the structure costs over a greater production volume.

experience curve pricing Preispolitik nach der Erfahrungskurve

Aggressive pricing designed to increase volume and help the firm realize experience curve economies.

experienced erfahren; sachkundig

experiment Versuch; Experiment; Erprobung; *(to ~)* experimentieren

experimental research experimentelle Forschung

Gathering of primary data by selecting matched groups of subjects, giving them different treatments, controlling related factors and checking for differences in group responses.

experimental series Versuchsreihe

expert Experte; Fachmann; Sachverständiger; Sachkenner; *adj.* fachmännisch; erfahren; geübt

expert advisory board Sachverständigenrat

expertise Sachwissen; Expertise

expert opinion Gutachten; Expertenmeinung; Begutachtung

expert power Expertenmacht

The power derived from advanced knowledge or experience in a particular subject, resulting in the ability to influence someone else. A person may be given the power to make decisions for others because he is an expert on the particular subject.

expert report Expertenbericht

expert system Expertensystem

A system designed for solving problems in a particular application area. It consists of a computer software designed to implement the thought processes of experts in a given subject area. The knowledge is integrated into a database the program references when solving a problem. Medical diagnosis was one of the earliest applications of expert systems.

expiration Erlöschen; *(becoming due)* Fälligwerden; *(termination)* Ablauf

In general: date on which a contract, agreement, license, magazine subscription, etc., ceases to be effective.

Options: last day on which an option can be exercised.

expiration cycle Auslaufrhythmus; Verfallsrhythmus

Expiration cycle relates to the dates on which options on a particular security expire.

expiration date Verfallsdatum

Finance: Last day (in the case of American-style) or the only day (in the case of European-style) on which an option may be exercised.

expire erlöschen; außer Kraft treten; *(to run out)* ablaufen

explain erklären; erläutern

explanation Erklärung; Erläuterung

explanatory erklärend

explicit ausdrücklich; klar; eindeutig

exploit ausbeuten; ausnutzen

exploitation Ausbeutung; Ausnutzung

Taking advantage of someone for one's own benefit.

exploration Erforschung

exploratory research Vorabaforschung; erste Nachforschungen

Marketing research to gather preliminary information that will help to better define problems and suggest solutions.

explore untersuchen; sondieren; erkunden

exponential smoothing exponentielle Glättung

Technique for short-run forecasting, usind a weighted average of past data as the basis for the forecast. More recent information is given heaviest weight.

export Export; Ausfuhr; *(article)* Exportgut; *(to ~)* ausführen; exportieren

exportation Ausfuhr

export agent Ausfuhragent; Exportvertreter; Exportkommissionär

export barriers Ausfuhrbeschränkungen

export commission house Ausfuhrkommissionär; Exportkommissionär

export contract list Exportvertragsliste

export credit Exportkredit; Ausfuhrkredit

export department Exportabteilung

Form of international marketing organization that comprises a sales manager and a few assistants whose job is to organize the shipping out of the company's goods to foreign markets.

export documents Ausfuhrdokumente; Exportdokumente; Exportpapier

export duty Ausfuhrzoll; Ausfuhrabgabe; Ausgangszoll; Exportabgabe; Exportsteuer; Exportzoll

export earnings Exportertrag; Ausfuhrertrag

export economy Exportwirtschaft

exporter Exporteur

export financing Exportfinanzierung; Ausfuhrfinanzierung

export growth Exportwachstum; Exportzuwachs; Ausfuhrzuwachs

export guarantee Ausfuhrgarantie

export house Exportgeschäft

export industry Exportindustrie

exporting Ausfuhr; Exporttätigkeit; *adj* ausfuhrorientiert; exportorientiert

Entering a foreign market by sending products and selling them through international marketing intermediaries (indirect exporting) or through the company's own department, branch, or sales representatives or agents (direct exporting).

exporting country Exportland; Ausfuhrland

export license Ausfuhrgenehmigung; Exportlizenz

export management company Außenhandelsunternehmen

Export specialists who acts as an export marketing department for client firms.

export market Auslandsmarkt

export order Exportauftrag; Ausfuhrauftrag

export oriented exportorientiert

export product Exportprodukt

export promotion Exportförderung; Ausfuhrförderung

export prospects Exportaussichten

export quota Ausfuhrkontingent; Exportkontingent; Ausfuhrquote; Exportquote

export receipts Exporteinnahmen; Ausfuhreinnahmen

export restriction Exportbeschränkung; Ausfuhrbeschränkung

export sales subsidiary Exportgeschäfte

export strength Exportkraft

export subsidy Exportsubvention; Ausfuhrsubvention

export surplus Exportüberschuss; Ausfuhrüberschuss

export trading company Außenhandelsgesellschaft; Exporthandelsgesellschaft

export value Ausfuhrwert

exposure offene Position; Kontakt; Werbemittelkontakt

Finance: the total amount of money loaned to a borrower or a country which is potentially at risk.

Marketing: advertising, whether free or paid, provided through such media as radio and television, newspapers, and billboards.

express Eilbeförderung; *(letter)* Eilbrief; *(train)* Eilzug; Eil-; ausdrücklich; express; als Eilsendung *(to ~)* ausdrücken

expression Ausdruck

expropriate enteignen

expropriation Enteignung

The act of taking private property into public ownership without compensation, such as the property of a foreign investors or foreign industry.

ex quay ab Pier; ab Kai

ex rights ohne Bezugsrecht

Phrase used to indicate that a share is selling without a recently declared right.

ex ship ab Schiff

extend verlängern; *(to expand)* ausdehnen; *(bill of exchange)* prolongieren

Extended Fund Facility (EFF) Erweiterte Fondsfazilität

Extensible Markup Language (XML)

Internet: latest generation of HTML that allows web browsers to pull information from databases on-the-fly and display in web pages.

extension Verlängerung; *(expansion)* Ausdehnung; Erweiterung; Ausweitung; *(bill of exchange)* Prolongierung

A mutual agreement between two parties to extend the time specified in a contract for payment or delivery.

extension of demand Nachfrageausweitung

extent Umfang; Höhe; Ausdehnung

external äußerlich; *(foreign)* ausländisch; *(trade)* außenwirtschaftlich

external audit externe Revision

Marketing: detailed examination of the company´s external environment, including markets, competition, business and economic environment, and other relevant information.

Accounting: the examination of financial records and reports of a company conducted by an outside firm, generally a CPA firm.

external debts Auslandsschulden

external funds Fremdfinanzierung

Outside funds brought in from outside the corporation, in the form of a bank loan, proceeds from a bond offering, or an infusion of cash from venture capitalists.

external growth externes Wachstum

The means by which a business can grow other than by growing organically through its own internal development. External growth is attractive to companies as it can offer greater speed than internal development.

Typically, firms can increase their market share by merging with or taking over a competitor in the same field (horizontal diversification). Alternatively, a company can seek greater control of its supply chain by merging or taking over a supplier or distributor (vertical integration).

External growth also carries risks, since the expected gains may often be slow to appear due to the restructuring and organizational changes involved as well as the high costs of financing.

externals fremdbestimmte Menschen

People who believe that what happens to them is controlled by outside forces such as luck or chance.

Externals are usually less satisfied with their jobs, have higher absenteeism rates, are more alienated from the work setting, and are less involved on their jobs.

external value Außenwert

externally convertible currency nicht frei konvertierbare Währung

Government policy that permits non-residents to convert their holdings of domestic currency into foreign currency, but the ability of residents to convert the currency is limited in some way.

extinguish löschen; auslöschen; *(debt)* tilgen

extortion Erpressung

A criminal offense, which occurs when a person obtains money or property from another through coercion or intimidation.

Extortion has to be distinguished from blackmail, as the blackmailer threatens to do something which would be legal or normally allowed.

extra Zugabe; *(charge)* Zuschlag; zusätzlich; extra

extra charge Extragebühr

extra cost Mehraufwand

extraction *(mining)* Gewinnung

extra earnings Mehrerlös

extraneous *(costs)* betriebsfremd

extranet Extranet

Network formed by extending the intranet beyond a company to customers, suppliers, collaborators or even competitors, for the purpose of sharing information.

Extranets are usually password protected to prevent access by general internet users.

extraofficial nebenamtlich

extraordinary item Sonderposten

Accounting: nonrecurring occurrence that must be explained to shareholders in an annual or quarterly report.

Examples include write-offs, acquisitions, sale of a large amount of real estate, or uncovering of employee fraud that negatively affects the company's financial condition.

extrapolation Hochrechnung; Weiterführung; vermuteter Schluss

Prediction of values by a statistical model outside of or beyond the range of the data used.

extras Zugaben; *(costs)* Nebenkosten

extroversion Extrovertiertheit

Quality of an individual to be gregarious, assertive, and sociable. Ability to capture one's comfort level with relationships.

extrovert extrovertierter Mensch; *adj* extrovertiert; *(to ~)* extrovertieren

ex works ab Werk

Delivery term for goods in which the buyer pays for transporting them.

F

fabricate anfertigen; erzeugen; fabrizieren; *(story)* erfinden

face Gesicht; das Äußere; *(coin)* Vorderseite; *(to ~)* gegenüberstehen; *(facts)* ins Gesicht sehen

face amount Nennbetrag

face value Nennwert; Nominalwert

The value displayed on a financial instrument, such as a bank check or a bond; also called its par value or *nominal value.* The interest rate normally refers to the face value, not the market value.

face value of policy Versicherungswert

facilitate erleichtern; fördern

facilitation Erleichterung

facilities Einrichtungen; *(plant)* Betriebsanlagen

facility Einrichtung; Anlage; *(ease)* Leichtigkeit; *(aptitude)* Gewandtheit

A building or a location that provides a particular service or is used for a specific function. *Example:* a factory is *a facility* uniquely designed for the purpose of production.

fact Tatsache; Umstand

faction Fraktion; Splittergruppe; Parteigruppe; Uneinigkeit

Formal or informal group of people within a larger organization, that have similar beliefs but different goals then the whole of the organization. Similar to a *clique,* a faction is formed through voluntary membership.

factor Faktor; Umstand; Grund; *(factoring)* Absatzfinanzierungsinstitut

Factoring: financial institution that buys a firm's accounts receivables at a discount and collects the debt.

factor analysis Faktoranalyse

A statistical technique used to reduce a large amount of data into a structure that can be studied more easily. The information is summarized and condensed into a smaller number of factors containing variables that are interrelated.

Example: characteristics of a group of people such as hobbies, activities, and interests might be condensed into one factor, lifestyle.

factor mobility Faktorbeweglichkeit; Substituierbarkeit der Produktionsfaktoren;

factor price Faktorpreis

factorial Fakultät

Mathematics: product of all whole numbers up to the number considered. For example, eight factorial, abbreviated 8!, is 8 x 7 x 6 x 5 x 4 x 3 x 2 x l, or 40,320.

Statistics: design of experiment to investigate a number of variables or factors. *Factorial* design minimizes the number of observations required to test numerous variables.

factoring Factoring; Forderungsverkauf

Type of financial service that involves the purchase of commercial accounts receivable (invoices) from a business at a discount. The *factoring* company then acts as the principal, not as agent.

Factors normall pay 70% to 90% of the invoice amount up front, followed by an additional payment when they collect the invoice. Ultimately, factors discount the invoice from 2% to 5% or more.

factors Faktoren

Economic resources that go into the production of a good. Economic factors include (a) capital, (b) human resources or labor, and (c) property resources including land. Entrepreneurial ability is considered by some a fourth factor since it organizes the other three factors plus innovation while bearing a capital risk; also *called factors of production.*

factory Fabrik; Fertigungsanlage; Industriewerk

factory closing Werkschließung

factory outlets Fabrikverkäufe; Direktverkäufe

Off-price retailing operations that are owned and operated by manufacturers and that normally carry the manufacturer's surplus, discontinued, or irregular goods.

factory overheads Fertigungsgemeinkosten

Insurance, electricity, janitorial services, and other expenses of a factory that are allocated to goods manufactured; all manufacturing expenses except direct materials and direct labor.

factory workshop Werkhalle

facts of the case Sachverhalt

fads Modewellen; Marotten; Launen

Short lived fashions that enter quickly, are adopted with great zeal, peak early and decline very fast. They seldom have any lasting impact.

fail misslingen; keinen Erfolg haben; scheitern; *(to go bankrupt)* Bankrott machen; in Konkurs geraten; *(examination)* durchfallen

failure Misserfolg; Fehlschlag; *(bankruptcy)* Konkurs; Bankrott; *(insolvency)* Zahlungseinstellung; *(nonperformance)* Unterlassung; Nichterfüllung; *(machine)* Ausfall

failure rate Ausfallquote

fair Messe; Ausstellung; *(just)* gerecht; *(equitable)* angemessen; *(business)* reell; fair; *(impartial)* unparteiisch

fairground Messeplatz

fair market value fairer Marktwert

The estimated price at which an asset or a service would pass from a willing seller to a willing buyer under the following assumptions: both buyer and seller are acting rationally, at arms length, in an open and unrestricted market, neither is under compulsion to buy or sell and both have reasonable knowledge of all the relevant facts.

fair rate of return angemessener Gewinn

The amount of profit that a public utility is allowed to earn, normally determined by the utility's needs to provide the expected service and maintain and expand plant and equipment.

fair trade lauterer Wettbewerb

International trade: a movement with the aim of improving the position of disadvantaged producers in developing countries in order to ensure that they work in safe conditions, are paid fair wages, don´t exploit the environment.

fair value üblicher Marktpreis

faq (frequently asked questions) häufig gestellte Fragen

fall Fallen; Rückgang; Niedergang; *(season)* Herbst; *(stock exchange)* Kurseinbruch; *(to ~)* fallen; sinken; zurückgehen

false falsch

false entry Falschbuchung

false prognosis Fehlprognose

falsify verfälschen; fälschen

Legal: change something that is true. It may be statements, representations, or acts made to deceive others through distortion, such as an unauthorized altering of the contents of a contract.

family background Herkunft

family brand Dachmarke

A marketing strategy that involves selling several related products under one brand name. The aim is to encourage recognition, ease the introduction of new products, increase market acceptance, and lowers marketing costs.

family firm Familienunternehmen

Enterprise that has been in the control of a single family since its foundation. It can be either private or public, as long as family members have an input in the operation and future of the business.

family focus Familienorientierung

family-friendly workplaces familienfreundliche Betriebe

Companies that offer a variety of programs such as paid paternity and adoption leave, on-site child care, flexible working hours, compressed work-weeks, job sharing, temporary part-time employment, and relocation assistance.

Creating a family-friendly work climate is motivated by management's concern with improving employee moral and productivity and reducing absenteeism.

family life cycle Familienlebenszyklus

Analytical model that examines the different demographic stages through which families usually pass as they mature over time, which result in different buying patterns.

Usually, six stages are distinguished: (1) young single people; (2) young couples with no children; (3) young couples with youngest child under six years; (4) couples with dependent children; (5) older couples with no children at home; (6) older single people.

As each group has its own specific and distinguishable needs and interests, marketers can devise specific products and advertising for them.

family status Familienstand

fare Fahrpreis; Fahrgeld; *(airfare)* Flugpreis; *(food)* Kost

farm Bauernhof; *(to ~)* einen Bauernhof bewirtschaften; Feld bestellen

farmer Landwirt; Bauer

farming area Agrargebiet

farm policy Agrarmarktpolitik

farm policy regulation Agrarmarkt-ordnung

farm product Agrargut; Agrarprodukt

fascism Faschismus

A collection of aggressive concepts involving hostile nationalistic attitudes, racism, together with private economic ownership under rigid government control.

fashion Mode

Currently accepted or popular taste or style in a given field, followed by substantial groups of consumers. Marketing has to keep fashion trends in mind and develops products that meet the current tastes and inclinations of consumers.

fast food Fastfood; Schnellessen

Food served in restaurants with limited and standardized menus. They are often self-service establishments offering the same quality of product throughout the country or, in same cases, the world.

fast tracking rascher Aufstieg; geförderte Karriere

HRM: strategy of selecting certain workers, such as future mangers, for rapid advancement and putting them in training programs allowing them to bypass remaining workers.

fault Mangel; Fehler; *(mechanics)* Defekt

faultfinding Krittelei; krittelig

faulty mangelhaft; fehlerhaft

favor Gefallen; Gefälligkeit; *(preference)* Vorzug; *(in favor of)* zu Gunsten von; *(to ~)* bevorzugen; begünstigen

favoritism Begünstigung; Günstlingswirtschaft

FAX-on-demand Faxabruf

Process where customers can request that a FAX on a certain topic of interest be sent to them.

Fayol, Henri (1841-1925)

French engineer and one of the first managers to formulate a comprehensive theory of management.

His keys elements of managerial activity – to plan, to organize, to command, to coordinate and to control – remain foundation-stones on which all later management thinkers have built. Fayol believed that a manager obtained the best performance from his workforce by leadership qualities and by his knowledge of the business and his workers. Furthermore by the ability to instil a sense of mission. He distilled the 14 General Principles of Management.

Major publications: (1949) General and Industrial Management, (1990) Organization Theory

feasibility Durchführbarkeit; Machbarkeit; Ausführbarkeit

feasibility study Durchführbarkeitsstudie; Machbarkeitsstudie

A detailed investigation and analysis of a proposed project to determine whether it is technically and economically viable.

Practically, a feasibility should normally produces the following results: estimate the demand in the planned area; estimate the absorption rate for the project; discuss legal and other considerations; forecast cash flows; and approximate investment returns likely to be produced.

feasible durchführbar; ausführbar; machbar; brauchbar

feature Kennzeichen; Eigenschaft; *(advertising)* Aufhänger; *(newspaper)* Sonderartikel; *(to ~)* besonders herausstellen

federal Bundes-; bundesstaatlich; föderalistisch

federal deficit Staatsdefizit

The difference between what the US federal government spent and what it received in tax receipts in a given year.

To cover the shortfall, the government has to borrow from the public by floating long and short-term debt.

Federal Deposit Insurance Corporation

A US government corporation that operates throughout the Federal Reserve System and provides deposit insurance for US banks through the Bank Insurance Fund.

federal funds rate Leitzins der US Zentralbank

A highly volatile and sensitive interest rate that is charged between member banks of the Federal Reserve System.

Federal Home Loan Bank Refinanzierungsbanken von Hypothekarkrediten

Twelve regional organizations in the USA that supply credit for savings and loans associations and other organizations providing domestic mortgages.

Federal Home Loan Mortgage Corporation börsennotierte US-Hypothekenbank

A corporation established in the USA in 1970 to buy mortgages from savings and loans associations in order to resell them in the secondary market. It is usually referred to inofficially as 'Freddie Mac'.

Federal National Mortgage Association staatliche amerikanische Hypothekenbank

A government sponsored company in the USA trading in mortgages, guaranteed by the Federal Housing Finance Board. It is the largest source of housing finance in the USA, and often referred to inofficially as 'Fannie Mae'.

Federal Open Market Committee Offenmarktausschuss des Federal Reserve System

Key committee in the Federal Reserve System, which sets short-term monetary policy for the Fed. The committee comprises the seven governors of the Federal Reserve System, the president of the New York Federal Reserve Bank, and the presidents of four other Federal Reserve Banks.

Federal Reserve Bank Mitgliedsbank im amerikanischen Zentralbanksystem

One of the 12 banks in the US constituing the federal reserve system. Its task is to monitor the commercial and savings banks in its region to ensure that they follow federal reserve board regulations and to provide those banks with access to emergency funds from the discount window.

The federal reserve banks are located in Boston, New York, Philadelphia, Cleveland, Richmond, Atlanta, Chicago, St. Louis, Minneapolis, Kansas City, Dallas, and San Francisco.

Federal Reserve Board Zentralbankvorstand

The governing board of the Federal Reserve System. It is comprised of seven members who are appointed by the President of the United States, subject to Senate confirmation, and serve 14-year terms.

The tasks of the Board Federal Reserve System include: to establish policies on reserve requirements and other bank regulations; set the discount rate; to tighten or loosen the availability of credit in the economy, and to regulate the purchase of securities on margin.

Federal Reserve System (FED) Zentralbanksystem der Vereinigten Staaten

The central banking system of the US comprising 12 Federal Reserve Banks controlling 12 districts under the Federal Reserve Board. Established by the Federal Reserve Act of 1913, its task is to regulate the monetary and banking system in the USA.

The FED´s main functions are: to regulate money supply, set reserve requirements for member banks, supervise the printing of currency at the mint, act as clearinghouse for the transfer of funds throughout the banking system, and to examine member banks to make sure they meet regulations.

Federal Savings and Loan Accociation

A federally chartered savings and loan association in the US. It acts as a savings and loan association, but in contrast to one with a state charter, has the ability to branch across state lines.

Federal Trade Commission (FTC) Ausschuß zur Bekämpfung des unlauteren Wettbewerbs; Bundeskartellbehörde

US government agency responsible for protecting the public against unfair business practices.

The commission consists of five members serving seven-year terms. It is empowered to investigate interstate and foreign commerce as well as to take legal action to enforce the laws that fall under its jurisdiction.

Fédération Internationale des Associations de Transitaieres et Assimilés (FIATA) Internationale Dachorganisation des Speditionsgewerbes

fee Gebühr; Honorar; *(remuneration)* Bezahlung; *(government fee)* Abgabe

A charge for services.

feedback Rückmeldung; Resonanz; Rückkopplung

Management: Degree to which carrying out the work activities required by the job results in the individual obtaining direct and clear information about the effectiveness of his or her performance.

feedback control Resonanzkontrolle

Controlling: refers to the reporting of actual figures as compared to budgeted figures. The feedback creates the possibility of a variance analysis on the basis of which regulating mechanisms can be set in motion (introduction of measures).

feeder plant Zulieferbetrieb

feedforward control Feedforward Kontrolle

Controlling: method of analysing the performance of a system by comparing the budgeted figures with the expected actuals (forecasting). So measures can be taken before the advent of any disruption.

It is an important strategic management tool since the decisions concerning the appropriateness of the budgets have to be taken before any actuals can be consulted.

fee increase Gebührenerhöhung

fee waiver Gebührenverzicht

fellow manager Vorstandskollege; Vorstandskollegin

fellow partner Mitgesellschafter

felt conflict empfundener Konflikt

Emotional involvement in a conflict creating anxiety, tenseness, frustration, or hostility.

felt emotions empfundene Emotionen

FIATA Combined Transport Bill of Lading (FBL) FIATA-Konnossement des kombinierten Transports

FIATA-Forwarding Agent's Certificate of Receipt (FCR) Spediteursübernahmebescheinigung

FIATA Warehouse Receipt (FWR) FIATA Lagerschein

fiber optics Glasfaserkabel; Lichtleitfaserkabel

Technology that transmits data as beams of light along tiny strands of glass. Fiber-optic networks can transmit a greater amount of data than other kinds of networks, and are much less likely to cause data errors.

fiduciary Treuhänder; Apotropos; treuhänderisch; auf Vertrauen beruhen

Person, company, or association holding assets in trust for a beneficiary, charged with the responsibility of investing the money wisely for the beneficiary's benefit. A fiduciary is responsible for the filing of tax returns and estimated tax for estates, trusts, and bankruptcy estates.

Example: executors of wills and estates, receivers in bankruptcy, trustees, and those who administer the assets of underage or incompetent beneficiaries.

Fiedler contingency model Fiedlers Kontingenzmodell

First comprehensive contingency model for leadership developed by Fred Fiedler, arguing that effective groups depend upon a proper match between a leader's style of interacting with subordinates and the degree to which the situation gives control and influence to the leader.

field Feld; Gebiet; *(market)* Absatzgebiet; *(service)* Außendienst; *(business)* Sparte; *(subject)* Fach; Fachgebiet; *(to ~ questions)* Fragen beantworten

field experience Außendiensterfahrung

field office Außenstelle

field of industry Industriebranche

field operation Außendiensttätigkeit

field sales force Verkaufsorganisation

FIFO method FIFO-Methode

See: First In First Out.

fight Kampf; *(to ~)* bekämpfen; sich zur Wehr setzen

figure Zahl; Ziffer; *(amount)* Betrag; *(diagram)* Diagramm; Zeichnung; Abbildung; *(person)* Figur; *(to ~)* berechnen; ausrechnen; kapieren

figures Zahlenmaterial

file Akte; *(folder)* Aktenordner; *(record)* Vorgang; *(to ~)* ablegen; einordnen; *(to submit)* einreichen

file transfer protocol (FTP)

Internet: most common way to download and upload files over the internet, requiring special software.

filing Aktenablage; *(registration)* Anmeldung; *(submission)* Einreichen

fill einfüllen; *(form)* ausfüllen; *(order)* ausführen; *(position)* besetzen

filling a contract Auftragsabwicklung

filtering Filterung

Communication: the sender's manipulation of information so that it will be seen more favorably by the receiver.

Filtering is most likely to occur in organizations in which there is emphasis on status differences and among employees with strong career mobility aspirations.

final Schluss-; End-; endgültig

final account Endabrechnung

final assembly Endmontage

Stage of the production process when all components are assembled into a finished product.

final goods Endprodukte

Goods that are ultimately consumed rather than used in the production of another good.

final inventory Endbestand

final product Endprodukt

final report Schlussbericht

final result Endergebnis

finance Finanzwesen; Finanzwirtschaft; Finanzen; *(science)* Finanzwissenschaft; *(to ~)* finanzieren

finance business Finanzgeschäft

finance company Finanzierungsgesellschaft; Finanzgesellschaft; Geldinstitut; *(consumer loan)* Kundenkreditgesellschaft

A financial institution that provides financial services, first and foremost in the form of loans. Unlike a bank, it does not receive deposits from the public.

finance department Finanzabteilung

finance function Finanzierungsfunktion

financial Finanz-; finanziell; fiskalisch

financial accounting Bilanzierung; Rechnungslegung

Branch of accounting concerned with classifying, measuring, and recording the transactions of a business. At the end of a year, a profit and loss account and a balance sheet are prepared to show the performance and position of the business.

Financial accounting is primarily concerned with providing a true and fair view of the activities of a business and can be separated into a number of specific activities, such as conducting audits, taxation, book- keeping, and insolvency.

Financial Accounting Standards Board (FASB) Gremium, dass die US-Bilanzierungsrichtlinien festlegt

Independent board responsible for establishing & interpreting Generally Accepted Accounting Principles. It was formed in 1973 to succeed and continue the activities of the Accounting Principles Board (APB).

financial affairs Finanzgeschäfte; finanzielle Angelegenheiten

financial aid Kredithilfe; Finanzhilfe

financial analysis Finanzanalyse

The analysis of financial statements and the calculation of ratios, in order to monitor and evaluate the financial performance and position of a business.

financial assets Geldvermögen

financial budget Finanzplan

Finance: plan detailing the income and expenses incurred by an organization.

financial business Kreditgewerbe

financial center Finanzplatz; Finanzzentrum

financial control Finanzkontrolle

All actions of the management of an organization taken to ensure that the costs incurred and revenue generated are sufficient.

financial crisis Finanzkrise

financial distress Insolvenzgefahr

Events preceding and including bankruptcy, such as violation of loan contracts.

financial distress costs Insolvenzkosten

Legal and administrative costs of liquidation or reorganization (direct costs). Also included are indirect costs, such as an impaired ability to do business.

financial futures Finanztermingeschäft; Terminhandel mit Finanztiteln

A futures contract in currencies or interest rates, that can be bought and sold on specialized markets. The main purpose is to manage risks effectively, but can also be sought as a source of additional profit.

financial infrastructure finanzielle Infrastruktur

financial institution Kreditinstitut; Geldinstitut

financial instrument Kreditinstrument

financial intermediaries Finanzvermittler; Finanzintermediäre

Banks, credit companies, insurance companies and other businesses that help finance transactions or insure against the risk associated with the buying and selling of goods.

financial interest Kapitalbeteiligung

financial investment Geldanlage

financial leasing Finanzierungs-Leasing

Form of leasing in which the service provided by the lessor to the lessee is limited to financing a project. All other responsibilities, such as maintenance, insurance, and taxes, are borne by the lessee.

financial leverage Verschuldungsgrad

Extent to which a firm relies on debt. Also called *gearing*. It is calculated by dividing net total borrowings by shareholders' equity.

financial management Finanzmanagement; Finanzverwaltung; Finanzwesen; Finanzwirtschaft

Area of finance that deals with the financial decisions made by corporations and the tools as well as analyses used to make these decisions.

financial market Finanzmarkt; Geldmarkt

A market for the exchange of capital and credit in an economy. Financial markets include: the stock market, bond market, commodities market, and the foreign exchange market.

A further distinction is between money markets that deal in short term debt instruments, and capital markets that trade in long term debt and equity instruments.

financial planning Finanzplanung

All efforts aimed at maintaining the liquidity and financial stability of a business. These include a planned *cash flow statement*, the balance sheet and the transactions in the profit & loss account, and planning the in and out payments in accordance with strict deadlines.

financial report Jahresabschlußbericht; Lagebericht; Bericht über die Vermögenslage; Jahresbericht

financial requirements Finanzbedarf

Financing arrangements detailed in the financial plan, that are necessary to meet the overall corporate objective.

financial restructuring Umschuldung; Sanierung

financial risk finanzielles Risiko

Additional risk that the firm's shareholders bear when the firm is financed with debt as well as equity.

financial section *(newspaper)* Finanzteil

financial service Finanzdienstleistung

financial statements Jahresabschluß; Geschäftsbericht; Bilanzabschluss

Written statements summarizing a company's activities over the last year. They consist of the profit and loss account, balance sheet, statement of total recognized gains and losses, and, if required, the cash-flow statement, together with supporting notes.

financial statement date Bilanzstichtag

financial statement information Bilanzdaten

financial straits Geldnot ; finanzielle Zwangslage

financial structure Finanzierungsstruktur; Kapitalstruktur

Structure of the right-hand side of a company's balance sheet, which describes the way in which a company´s assets are financed, including short-term borrowings, long-term debt, and ownership equity.

Financial structure differs from capital structure, which accounts for long-term debt and equity only.

Financial Times-Stock Exchange 100 (FTSE) Financial-Times-Börsenindex

Composite index of 100 British ordinary shares.

financial transaction Finanzgeschäft; Transaktion

financial worth Vermögenswert

financial year Geschäftsjahr; Bilanzjahr; Wirtschaftsjahr

financier Geldgeber; Kapitalgeber; Financier

financing Finanzierung; Kapitalbeschaffung; Kreditwesen

financing deficit Finanzierungsdefizit

financing flow Finanzierungsstrom

financing rule Finanzierungsregel

find Fund; Entdeckung; *(to ~)* finden; *(to procure)* beschaffen; besorgen

find fault with bemängeln

find out feststellen; herausfinden

finder's fee Vermittlungsprovision; Maklerprovision

Fee paid to an individual or company whose function is to bring together the parties involved in a business deal. The fee is usually a percentage of either the profit created by the deal or its value.

fine Geldstrafe; Ordnungsstrafe; Geldbuße; *(to ~)* mit einer Geldstrafe belegen

fine tuning Feinabstimmung

finish Schluss; Ende; Fertigstellung; *(coating)* Überzug; *(to ~)* fertig stellen; beenden; *(manufacturing)* veredeln; fertig bearbeiten

finished goods Fertigwaren

finished product Fertigprodukt

finishing Veredelung; Fertigstellung; Weiterverarbeitung

fire Feuer; *(to ~) (worker)* hinauswerfen; *(gun)* schießen

firewall Zugangsschutzsystem; Firewall

Software that acts as a security barrier between a company's internal systems and outside systems and thus protects a private network, such as a LAN or an intranet, from intruders or unauthorized traffic.

Firewall software usually screens traffic by IP address or other traits, admitting certain types of traffic while blocking others

firm Firma; *(enterprise)* Unternehmen; *(plant)* Betrieb; *(business)* Geschäft

Organization: Legal term, referring only to non incorporated businesses. The term is, however, often used generally for any business, corporation, partnership, or proprietorship.

firmness Festigkeit

firm commitment underwriting Festübernahme

Securities: a form of underwriting in which the underwriter agrees to purchase the entire issue from the issuer.

firm offer Festangebot; festes Angebot; verbindliche Offerte; verbindliches Angebot

An offer to sell goods that remains in force for a stated period, thus binding the seller to sell if the buyer accepts the offer within this time. An offer that is not firm is usually called a quotation.

firm order Festbestellung

Commerce: written or oral order that has been confirmed and is not subject to cancellation.

Securities: (1) order to buy or sell for the proprietary account of the broker-dealer firm; (2) buy or sell order not conditional upon the customer's confirmation.

first in, first out (FIFO) FIFO-Methode; zuerst eingekauft, zuerst verbraucht

Method of valuing inventories which assumes that inventories acquired first were used first in production, and inventories acquired later are being used later.

In times of rapid price rises, FIFO inflates profits, since the least expensive inventory is charged against cost of current sales, which results in *inventory profits.*

first-line management unterste Leitungsebene; unterste Führungsschicht

Supervisors on an organizational level immediately above non-managerial workers who primarily oversee performance on line tasks.

Example: some typical titles are foreman, shift boss, sergeant, section head, and ward nurse.

first-order change Wandel erster Ordnung

Linear and continuous change which implies no fundamental shifts in the assumptions that organizational members hold about the world and how the organization can improve its functioning.

first purchaser Ersterwerber

first-rate securities Spitzenpapiere

fiscal Finanz-; Steuer-; finanziell; fiskalisch; steuerrechtlich

Anything pertaining to public finance and financial transactions; belonging to the public treasury.

fiscal authority Finanzverwaltung

fiscal policy Fiskalpolitik

The economic term which describes the actions of a government in setting the level of public expenditure and how that expenditure is funded. Three basic types of fical policy can be distinguished:

Expansionary fiscal policy - an increase in government spending, a decrease in net taxes, or a combination of the two for the purpose of increasing aggregate demand and expanding real output.

Contractionary fiscal policy - a decrease in government spending, an increase in net taxes, or some combination of the two for the purpose of decreasing aggregate demand and controlling inflation.

Neutral fiscal policy - modest policy with no intention of effecting economic activity (rare).

fiscal system Fiskalsystem

fiscal year Haushaltsjahr; Wirtschaftsjahr; Geschäftsjahr; Rechnungsjahr

Any continuous 12-month period used by a business or government as its accounting period.

Fisher effect Fisher-Effect; Preiserwartungseffekt

Proposition by Irving Fisher that the real interest rate is independent of monetary measures, especially the nominal interest rate. The Fisher equation is $r_r = r_n - \pi^e$.

This means, the real interest rate equals the nominal rate minus expected inflation (π^e). Therefore, if π^e rises, so must r_n, if you assume r_r to be constant.

According to the principle of monetary neutrality, an increase in the rate of money growth raises the rate of inflation but does not affect any real variable.

fit Zusammenpassen; Sitz;Passung; Passen; *(qualified)* befähigt; tauglich; qualifiziert; geeignet; passend; *(physically)* in Form; fit; *(to ~) (in size)* passen; *(to adjust)* anpassen; *(to equip)* ausrüsten

Situation where the features of a particular product, such as an investment, match the requirements of a buyer.

fit for work erwerbsfähig

five factor model of personality Fünf-Faktoren-Modell der Persönlichkeit

A descriptive model of personality comprised of five dimensions (acronym OCEAN): Openness to Experience, Conscientiousness, Extraversion, Agreeableness, and Neuroticism.

five forces theory Branchenstruktur-analyse nach dem Fünf-Kräfte-Modell

A theoretical framework for industry analysis developed by Michael Porter that describes comptetition in an industry to be influenced by five forces: (1) rivalry amongst existing competitors, (2) the power of suppliers, (3) the power of buyers, (4) the threat of subsitutes, and (5) barriers to access.

five stage group development model Fünf-Phasen-Modell der Gruppenentwicklung

Model that characterizes groups as proceeding through five distinct stages: forming, storming, norming, performing, and adjourning.

Groups do not always proceed clearly from one stage to the next. Sometimes, in fact, several stages go on simultaneously, as when groups are storming and performing at the same time.

fix *(dilemma)* Klemme; *(to ~)* festsetzen; festlegen; *(to repair)* reparieren; befestigen; fixieren

fixed festgesetzt; fixiert

fixed assets Sachanlagen; materielle Vermögensgegenstände; Anlagevermögen

Term used in accounting for assets and property which a business owns and uses in the production of its income.

Fixed assets cannot be converted into cash easily, as compared with current assets such as cash or bank accounts, which are also described as liquid assets.

fixed capital revenue Sachkapitalrendite

fixed costs Fixkosten; feste Kosten; fixe Kosten

All items of expenditure that remain constant regardless of sales volumes because they are incurred in order to ensure that the company can produce and sell. Fixed costs include salaries of executives, interest expenses, rent, depreciation, and insurance expenses. They contrast with *variable costs* and *semi-variable costs,* which vary, but not necessarily in direct relation to sales.

fixed exchange rate fester Wechselkurs

A rate of exchange between one currency and another that is fixed by a government and maintained by that government through buying or selling its currency.

At the Bretton Woods International Monetary Conference in 1944, a system of fixed exchange rates was set up, which existed until the early 1970s, when a floating exchange rate system was adopted.

fixed expenses Fixkosten

fixed fee feste Gebühr

Set price for the completion of a project.

fixed income feste Einkünfte; feststehende Einkünfte

A guaranteed rate of interest on an investment that is not adjusted to reflect changes in prices. Examples: interest on most bonds and income from most annuities and some pensions.

fixed interest Festzinsen; festverzinslich

fixed-interest bearing festverzinslich

fixed-interest security festverzinsliches Wertpapier

A type of security that gives a fixed stated interest payment once or twice per annum. They include gilt-edged securities, bonds, preference shares, and debentures. They entail less risk than innquiries but offer less scope for capital appreciation.

fixed-interval schedule fixierter Intervallplan

System in which events take place on a regular interval. The critical variable is time, and it is held constant.

Example: employees get their salary on a weekly, monthly, or other predetermined time basis.

fixed rate loan Festzinsanleihe

fixed rate of interest Festzins; Festzinssatz

fixed-ratio schedule fixierter Quotenplan

Rewards that are initiated after a fixed or constant number of responses.

Example: a piece-rate incentive plan is a fixed ratio schedule; the employee receives a reward based on the number of work pieces generated.

fixed term license Lizenz mit einer Festlaufzeit

flag Flagge; Fahne; Kennzeichen; Markierung; *(to ~)* kennzeichnen, markieren

flag of convenience Billigflagge

The national flag of a small country, such as Panama, Liberia, Honduras, or Costa Rica, flown by ships that are registered in one of these countries, although they are owned by a national of another country. The aim of the ship owners is to avoid taxation and the more stringent safety and humanitarian conditions imposed on ships and their crews by larger states.

flame Drohbrief

Internet: hostile letter or nasty note, either written to a public forum or sent privately. Flamers usually think they are justified, and are particularly fierce in attacking what they see as misuses of the internet.

flat rate Pauschalpreis; Einheitstarif

A fixed price for goods or services that does not vary with changes in the amount used, volume consumed, or units purchased.

flexibility Flexibilität; Elastizität; Beweglichkeit; Biegsamkeit; Anpassungsfähigkeit

flexible elastisch; flexibel; wendig; anpassungsfähig

flexible benefits flexible Zusatzleistungen

Tailored benefit program to meet the personal needs of employees by picking and choosing from a menu of benefit options.

Examples: medical plans with different coverage, a variety of savings and pension plans, life insurance, college tuition reimbursement plans, and extended vacation time.

flexible budget flexibles Budget

A budget that takes into account circumstances resulting in the actual levels of activity achieved being different from those on which the original budget was based. As a result, in a flexible budget the budget cost allowances for each cost item are changed for the variable items to allow for the actual levels of activity achieved.

The flexible budget shows what the *actual activity* should have cost, had it gone strictly according to plan.

flexible manufacturing flexible Fertigung

Manufacturing process that is largely computer controlled which provides flexibility in adapting machinery to different products. This allows customization to customer needs at competitive costs.

flexible manufacturing systems flexible Fertigungssysteme

Integration of computer-aided design, engineering, and manufacturing to produce low volume products at mass-production costs.

flexitime gleitende Arbeitszeit

A time management system in which employees are given a degree of flexibility in the hours they work. Provided they work an agreed number of hours per day, they may start or finish work at different times.

flier Handzettel

flight Flug; *(escape)* Flucht

flight of capital Kapitalflucht

float freigegebener Wechselkurs; *(banking)* schwebende Überweisung; *(to ~ a currency)* Währung freigeben; *(bond issue)* auflegen

Banking: delay in the clearing of payments between banks, especially the period between the presentation of a check and the actual payment to the payee.

floatation *(issue)* Auflegung; Emission

floater zinsvariable Anleihe; erstklassiges Inhaberpapier

floating currency exchange rate flexibler Wechselkurs

The exchange rate of a currency that is determined by the market forces of supply and demand; also known *as flexible exchange rate.*

The forces affecting the exchange rate of a currency include: a nation's reserves of hard currency and gold, its international trade balance, its rate of inflation and interest rates, and the general strength of its economy.

floating rate freier Wechselkurs; variabler Zins

floating-rate bond Anleihe mit variabler Verzinsung

Debt obligation with an adjustable coupon payment.

floor Grund; Boden; *(story)* Stockwerk; Stock; Geschoß; Etage; *(minimum of prices)* Mindestpreishöhe; *(stock exchange)* Börsensaal; Parkett

floor price (*stock exchange)* Mindestpreis; Niedrigstpreis

floor trade *(stock exchange)* Eigenhandel; freies Makeln

flourish blühen; florieren; gedeihen

flow Fluss; Strom; Flut; *(production)* Arbeitsablauf; Umlauf; *(to ~)* fließen

In general: sequence of events that take place consecutively.

Internet: state in which users have a positive experience from readily controlling their navigation and interaction on a web site, occurring during network navigation that is (1) characterized by a seamless sequence of responses facilitated by machine interactivity, (2) intrinsically enjoyable, (3) accompanied by a loss of self-consciousness, and (4) self-reinforcing.

flowchart Flussdiagramm; Ablaufdiagramm; Datenflussplan; Arbeitsablaufbogen

A chart used to provide a model for the flow of material, information, or people through a system. The primary purpose is to identify the activities taking place within the system and to present this information graphically.

flow diagram Flussdiagramm

flow of funds Geldstrom; Geldmittelbewegung

Economics: the way financial resources in a national economy are transferred from savings surplus units to savings deficit units through financial intermediaries.

flow of information Informationsfluss

flow of trade Handelsstrom

fluctuate schwanken; fluktuieren

fluctuating variabel; schwankend

fluctuation Schwanken; Schwankung; Fluktuieren

FOB-origin pricing fob-Preis

Geographic pricing strategy in which goods are placed free on board a carrier; the customer pays the freight from the factory to the destination.

focus group Fokusgruppe; Gruppendiskussion

A group of 8 to 12 participants, led by a moderator, who meet for an in-depth discussion of one particular topic. By skilful use of probes and other interviewing devices, the group members are encouraged to respond in depth to the moderator.

Focus groups are useful in the early stages of developing products or methods to understand the nature of business or organizational problems and for suggesting issues that should be covered in a questionnaire survey.

focused strategy fokussierte Strategie

Business strategy in which firms seek to divest themselves of all but their core activities, using the funds so raised to enhance their core skills. This strategy is a reaction to the trend towards diversification and the development of conglomerates.

follow folgen; verfolgen; *(rules)* befolgen; *(to result)* resultieren

follower Anhänger

follow-up Nachbearbeitung; Weiterverfolgung *(to ~)* weiterverfolgen

Last step in the selling process, in which the salesperson follows up after the sale to ensure the customer satisfaction and repeat business.

follow-up letter Erinnerungsschreiben; Nachfassbrief; Folgebrief

Marketing: A letter sent to a potential customer, attempting to persuade him to make a purchase; or to an existing customer, attempting to build good relations with future purchases in mind.

font Schrift; Schriftart

Style of the letters in printed material or on a web page; also called typeface. Common fonts include, Arial, Verdana and Helvetica.

food Nahrung; Nahrungsmittel; Lebensmittel; *(prepared meal)* Essen

forbid verbieten; untersagen

force Zwang; *(power)* Kraft; Stärke; *(employees)* Belegschaft; *(validity)* Gültigkeit; *(to ~)* zwingen; forcieren

forced conversion erzwungener Umtausch

Securities: situation when the conversion value of a convertible security is greater than the call price. In such a situation, the call can be used to force conversion.

forced saving Zwangssparen

force majeure (French: superior force) Höhere Gewalt

An event outside the control of either party to a contract that may excuse either party from fulfilling its contractual obligations in certain circumstances. Examples include strikes, riots, war, acts of God.

forecast Vorausberechnung; Vorhersage; Prognose; *(to ~)* vorhersagen; prognostizieren

forecast data Prognosedaten

forecaster Prognostiker

forecasting Prognoserechnung; Prognose; Vorhersage; Prognostizierung

Economics: attempts to foretell the strength of the economy, often by utilizing complex econometric models as tools to make specific predictions of future levels of inflation, interest rates, and employment.

Marketing: the art of estimating future demand by anticipating what buyers are likely to do under a given set of conditions; estimating future trends.

Securities: forecasters try to predict the direction of the stock market by relying on technical data of trading activity and fundamental statistics on the direction of the economy.

forecasting error Prognosefehler

forecasting method Prognosemethode

forecast to end of year budget Budget bis Jahresende

Attempt to see whether the business will succeed in achieving its planned objectives to year end. On the basis of the results achieved so far, the budget managers consider corrective actions and their effects.

In collaboration with the controller the quantified forecasts of cost centers, cost objects and revenue objects are assembled and consolidated to see whether the economic goals can be achieved, or after the latest estimate, how great the variance is likely to be.

foreclosure Zwangsvollstreckung

The right of a lender of money if the borrower fails to repay the money or part of it on the due date. The lender must apply to a court to be permitted to sell the property that has been held as security for the debt.

foreign Auslands-; ausländisch; auswärtig; fremd

foreign affiliate ausländische Konzerngesellschaft

foreign aid Entwicklungshilfe

foreign assignment Auslandseinsatz; Auslandsentsendung

foreign assets Auslandsaktiva; Auslandsguthaben

foreign bank Auslandsbank

foreign bond Auslandsanleihe

International bond issued by foreign borrowers in another nation's capital market and traditionally denominated in that nation's currency.

foreign branch Auslandsfiliale

foreign capital Auslandskapital

foreign competition Auslandskonkurrenz

forward contract Terminkontrakt

Arrangement calling for future delivery of an asset at an agreed-upon price.

foreign corporation auswärtige (US) Kapitalgesellschaft

In the USA, a corporation chartered under the laws of a state other than the one in which it conducts business, e.g. chartered in California, doing business in New York. A corporation from outside the US is called an *alien corporation.*

foreign country Ausland

foreign credit Auslandskredit

foreign currency Devisen; Fremdwährung

Any currency that is used outside the home market of a company. To facilitate trade between currency zones, there are exchange rates i.e. prices at which currencies (and the goods and services) can be exchanged against each other.

Currencies can be classified as either floating currencies or fixed currencies based on their exchange rate regime.

foreign currency management Devisenmanagement

foreign currency option Devisenoption

foreign currency reserves Devisenreserven

foreign currency shortage Devisenknappheit

foreign currency translation Umrechnung von Fremdwährungen

The statement of amounts denominated in one currency in terms of a second currency, by applying the exchange rate between the currencies.

foreign demand Auslandsnachfrage

foreign direct investment (Auslands-) Direktinvestition

Long-term investments by a *foreign direct investor* in an enterprise resident in an economy other than that in which the foreign direct investor is based.

foreign distributor Vertriebspartner im Ausland

foreigner Ausländer

foreign exchange Devisen

The currencies of foreign countries. Businesses require foreign exchange to purchase goods from abroad or for purposes of investment or speculation. Foreign exchange is bought and sold in foreign-exchange markets.

foreign exchange broker Devisenmakler

A broker who specializes in arranging deals in foreign currencies on the foreign-exchange markets, mostly between commercial banks and governments. Foreign-exchange brokers earn a brokerage paid on each deal.

foreign exchange dealer Devisenhändler

A person who buys and sells foreign exchange on a foreign-exchange market, usually as an employee of a commercial bank. The banks then charge fees or commissions for buying and selling foreign exchange on behalf of their customers.

foreign exchange loans Auslandsanleihen

foreign exchange market Devisenmarkt

A global market in which foreign currencies are traded. It consists primarily of foreign-exchange dealers and foreign-exchange brokers.

Currency dealing has a spot market for delivery of foreign exchange immediately and a forward-exchange market in which transactions are made for foreign currencies to be delivered at agreed dates in the future. This enables dealers and their customers who require foreign exchange in the future to hedge their purchases and sales.

foreign exchange proceeds Deviseneinnahmen

foreign exchange rate Wechselkurs; Devisenkurs

The exchange rate between two currencies specifies how much one currency is worth in terms of the other.

The spot exchange rate refers to the current exchange rate. The forward exchange rate refers to an exchange rate that is quoted and traded today but for delivery and payment on a specific future date

foreign exchange risk management Devisenkursrisikomanagement

foreign exchange swaps Devisentausch

foreign exchange trade Devisenhandel

foreign funds Devisenbestände; Auslandsgelder

foreign income ausländische Einkünfte

foreign investment Auslandsanlage; Auslandsinvestition

Investment in the domestic economy by foreign individuals or companies. Foreign investment takes the form of either direct investment in productive enterprises or investment in financial instruments, such as a portfolio of shares.

Foreign investment is often discussed controversially: while the creation of jobs and wealth is welcome, it is often argued that the country is being 'bought by foreigners'. Also, there is frequently resentment if nationals invest overseas, especially if there is domestic unemployment.

foreign investment codes Auslandsanlagecodes

foreign loan Auslandsanleihe

foreign market Auslandsmarkt; Überseemarkt

foreign order Auslandsbestellung

foreign profit Auslandsgewinn

foreign securities Auslandspapiere

foreign share Auslandsaktie

foreign shipment Auslandslieferung

foreign subsidiary ausländische Tochtergesellschaft; Auslandstochter

foreign trade Außenhandel; Außenwirtschaft

foreign trade zone Freihandelszone

An area within a country where imported goods can be stored or processed without being subject to import duty; also called *free trade zone.*

foresight Voraussicht; Vorrausschauen

forfeit Vertragsstrafe; Geldstrafe; *(forfeiture)* Verwirkung; Pfand; Buße; *(to ~)* verwirken; verfallen lassen

forfeiting Forfaitierung; Verpfändung

A method of financing foreign trade based upon the transfer of debt obligations. The forfaiter coordinates the activities of exporters, importers, and financial institutions.

forfeiture Verlust; Verwirkung

forge *(document)* fälschen; *(metal)* schmieden

forgery Fälschung; Verfälschung; Fälschen; *(law)* Herstellung falschen Beweismaterials

Preparing or altering writings or paintings with the intention of prejudicing the rights of others.

form Form; Gestalt; *(document)* Formular; Vordruck; *(to ~)* formen; bilden; *(company)* gründen

formal formal; formell; offiziell; förmlich; äußerlich

formal group formale Gruppe

Work group defined by the organization's structure, with designated work assignments, usually engaging in behavior stipulated by and directed towards organizational goals. *Example:* six members making up an airline flight crew.

formality Formalität; Förmlichkeit

formalization Formalisierung

Degree to which jobs within the organization are standardized. Employees can be expected always to handle the same input in exactly the same way, resulting in a consistent and uniform output.

formalize formalisieren; offiziell machen

formal networks formale Netzwerke

Networks, that follow the authority chain, and are limited to task-related communications. Three common types of small-group networks can be distinguished: (1) the chain rigidly follows the formal chain of command, (2) the wheel relies on the leader to act as the central conduit for all the group's communication, (3) the all-channel network permits all group members to actively communicate with each other.

format Format

formating Formatierung

formation Gestaltung; *(company)* Gründung; Errichtung

forming stage Forming

First stage in group development characterized by a great deal of uncertainty about the group's purpose, structure, and leadership.

Members are "testing the waters" to determine what types of behavior are acceptable. This stage is complete when members have begun to think of themselves as part of a group.

forming of opinion Meinungsbildung

formulate abfassen; formulieren

formulation Abfassung; Formulierung

form utility Nutzen aus Formveränderung

Changing the appeal of a product by changing its physical characteristics. For example, detergent can be produced in liquid form.

fortune Glück; *(property)* Vermögen;

Fortune 500 Liste der umsatzstärksten US-Gesellschaften

A listing prepared annually by Fortune magazine of the 500 largest US industrial corporations, ranked by sales. *Fortune* also publishes a list of nonmanufacturing firms, as well as international firms.

forward *(to ~) (to ship)* befördern; *(to send on)* nachsenden

forward buying Vorratskauf

Marketing: practice of purchasing more materials than immediately needed in order to take advantage of special discounts.

forward contract Terminabschluss

Actual purchase or sale of a specific quantity of a commodity, government security, foreign currency, or other financial instrument at a price specified now, with delivery and settlement at a specified future date.

forward dealing Terminhandel

Dealing in commodities, securities, currencies, freight, etc., for delivery at some future date at a price agreed at the time the contract is made.

This form of trading enables dealers and manufacturers to cover their future requirements by hedging their more immediate purchases.

forwarding company Spedition; Speditionsbetrieb

Business that accepts freight from other businesses or the general public and arranges for its transportation; also called *freight forwarder.*

forward cover Kurssicherung

forward currency Termindevise

forwarder Spediteur; Absender

forward exchange rate Devisenterminkurs

forwarding Beförderung; Spedition

Forwarding Agent´s Certificate of Receipt (FCR) Spediteurübernahmebescheinigung

Forwarding Agent's Certificate of Transport (FCT) Spediteurversandbescheinigung

forwarding company Speditionsunternehmen; Transportunternehmen

forward market Terminmarkt

forward pricing Preisfestsetzung für Terminkontrakte

The pricing of financial instruments for a value date in the future, which can refer to both hedging with futures or options, and forward contracting.

forward rate Terminkurs

forward trade Terminhandel

Agreement to buy or sell at rates established today for settlement in the future.

forward transaction Termingeschäft

foul bill of lading unreines Konnossement

found gründen; *(foundation)* stiften; errichten; *(metal)* gießen

foundation Fundierung; *(company)* Gründung; *(endowed institution)* Stiftung

founder *(company)* Gründer; *(endowment)* Stifter

founding year Gründungsjahr

four Ps die vier Ps

Abbreviation for the four standard marketing ingredients: *product, price, place* and *promotion.* A marketer must decide what product or service to produce, the price to charge, how products are to be distributed to the marketplace, and methods to use for promoting the product or service.

fraction Bruchteil

fractional value Teilwert

fragmented industry zersplitterte Industrie; fragmentierte Industrie

Industry characterized by many opportunities to create competitive advantages, but each advantage is small.

frames Rahmen; Frames

Internet: technique used to divide a web page into different parts such as a menu and separate content.

framework Gerüst; Rahmen

framework requirements Rahmenbedingung

framing Aufteilung in Fenster

Internet: process in which a web browser is instructed to divide itself into two or more partitions and load within a section material obtained from another web site through the execution of an automatic link.

franchise Franchise; Lizenzbetrieb; Alleinverkaufsrecht; Konzessionserteilung; *(politics)* Wahlrecht; *(to ~)* konzessionieren

A license given to a person or firm enabling them to manufacture or sell a named product or service in a particular area for a stated period.

The holder of the license (franchisee) usually pays the grantor of the license (franchisor) an initial lump sum in advance, followed by royalties on sales.

In comprehensive franchising agreements, the franchisor supplies the franchisee with a brand identity as well as finance and technical expertise. Franchises are common in the fast-food business, petrol stations, travel agents, hotels etc.

franchise agreement Konzessionsvertrag; Lizenzvertrag

franchisee Franchisenehmer; Lizenznehmer

franchising Franchising; Nutzungsrechtverleihung

A contractual relationship in which the franchisor provides a licensed privilege to the franchisee to conduct business and offers assistance in organizing, training, merchandising, marketing, and managing in return for a share of the profit.

franchisor Franchisegeber

Frankfurt Interbank Offered Rate (FIBOR) Referenzzinssatz zu dem international tätige Banken Geldmarktgeschäfte in Frankfurt abschließen

fraud Betrug; Schwindel; Schwindler;

fraudulent betrügerisch

fraudulent entry Falschbuchung

fraught with risk risikoreich

free frei; befreit; *(cost)* kostenlos; gratis; *(to ~)* befreien

free alongside ship (fas) frei Längsseite Seeschiff

free carrier frei Frachtführer

freedom Freiheit; freies (Be)Nutzungsrecht

free enterprise Unternehmerfreiheit; freies Unternehmertum

An economic system wher the individual is free to own the means of production and make management decisions independent from state control, where the allocation of productive resources is decentralised and obeys the decisions of individuals who follow their own interest.

freelance freiberuflich

freelancer Freiberufler

free market freier Markt

Market in which there is little or no control or interference by government or by any other powerful economic force or entity, such as a monopoly, cartel, or collusive oligopoly.

free of charge kostenlos; gebührenfrei

free of cost kostenlos

free on board (FOB) frei an Bord; frei Schiff

Commercial term under which the seller has the obligation to tranport the goods to a point specified in the contract. For example, "FOB, Seller's Warehouse" means that the buyer assumes all costs and risks in moving the goods from the seller's warehouse.

free on rail frei Bahnhof; frei Waggon

free on truck frei Güterwagen; frei verladen; frei Waggon

free port Freihafen; zollfreier Hafen

Port where no duties are imposed on ships that load or unload.

free trade Freihandel

free trade area Freihandelszone

The second stage of economic integration, during which a group of countries agrees to eliminate tariffs, quotas and preferences on most (if not all) goods between them.

Countries choose this kind of economic integration if their economical structures are complementary. If they are competitive, they will choose a customs union.

Unlike a customs union, members of a free trade area do not have the same policies with respect to non-members, meaning different quotas and customs.

freeware Software, die vom Urheber zur kostenlosen Nutzung zur Verfügung gestellt wird

Internet: software that is available for anyone to use, free of charge. Most freeware is still copyrighted, which means that it can't be altered.

freight Fracht; Ladung; Frachtgut; *(tonnage)* Laderaum; *(charges)* Frachtkosten

freight-absorption pricing Preisstellung mit teilweiser Übernahme der Frachtkosten

Geographic pricing strategy in which the company absorbs all or part of the actual freight charges in order to get the business.

freight car Güterwagen

freighter Frachtschiff; Frachter

freight forwarding business Spedition

freight traffic Güterverkehr

frequency Frequenz; Häufigkeit

In general: the number of times an event occurs within a specified period of time.

Advertising: number of times the average person in a target market is exposed to an advertising message during a given period.

frequency discount Mengenrabatt

Rate discount allowed an advertiser that purchases a specific schedule within a specific period of time (e.g., six ads within one year).

frequency distribution Häufigkeitsverteilung

Organization of data to show how often certain values or ranges of values occur; array of reach according to the level of frequency delivered to each group.

frequent häufig; *(to ~)* häufig aufsuchen

frequently asked questions (FAQ) häufig gestellte Fragen

Internet: list of questions and answers related to a particular issue, FAQs are intended to help users get answers to their questions without over-burdening human support staff.

fresh supply Nachschub

friendship group Freundschaftsgruppe

People brought together because they share one or more common characteristics; social alliances, which frequently extend outside the work situation, based on similar age or ethnic heritage, or the holding of similar political views.

fringe benefit Nebenleistung

Benefits provided by an employer to supplement an employee's regular salary.

front end fee Vorabgebühr

Once only charge levied on investment products, taken out of an investment when the investment is made and paid to the investment fund manager.

front office Front Office; Abteilung mit Kundenkontakt

Offices in the service industry that have direct customer contact, as opposed to the back office, where the administrative tasks are centralized.

frozen account eingefrorenes Konto; gesperrtes Konto

Bank account from which funds may not be withdrawn until a lien is satisfied and a court order is received freeing the balance.

frozen assets eingefrorene Guthaben; eingefrorene Vermögenswerte

fulfill erfüllen

fulfillment Fulfillment

Processes necessary to receive, service, and track orders sold via direct marketing.

The primary functions of fulfillment systems are (1) to respond quickly and correctly to an order by delivering the item ordered, (2) to maintain customer records, (3) to send invoices and record payments, (4) to respond to customer inquiries and complaints and resolve problems, and (5) to produce purchase and payment information on an individual customer and group basis to aid in developing marketing plans and strategies.

full voll; ganz; völlig; weit

full container load (FCL) Voll-Containerladung

full cost accounting Vollkostenrechnung

full costing Vollkostenkalkulation; Vollkostenrechnung; Vollkostenprinzip

full duplex Duplex

In computer usage, transmission of data in two directions simultaneously.

full employment Vollbeschäftigung

Rate of employment defined by government economists to take into account the percentage of unemployed who would not be employed regardless of the nation's economy.

full service bank Universalbank

full service retailer Einzelhändler mit umfassenden Service

Retailers that provide a full range of services to shoppers.

full service wholesalers Großhändler mit umfassenden Service

Wholesalers that provide a full set of services such as carrying stock, using a sales force, offering credit, making deliveries and providing management assistance.

full-time position Vollzeitstelle; Ganztagsstelle

fully diluted vollständig gelöst

function Aufgabe; Funktion; Zweck; *(social event)* gesellschaftliche Veranstaltung; *(to ~)* funktionieren; *(to act as)* fungieren

functional funktionell; fachlich; zweckmäßig

functional conflict funktionaler Konflikt

Conflict that supports the goals of the group and improves its performance.

functional discount Händlerrabatt

Price reduction offered by the seller to trade channel members that perform certain functions, such as selling, storing and record keeping.

functional intermediary funktionaler Mittelsmann; Zwischenhändler

functional organization funktionale Organisation

Structure of an organization based on functional performance; organizational departments created to fulfill organizational functions such as marketing, finance, and personnel. This type of organization has characteristics of both line and staff functions.

functional strategy funktionale Strategie

fund Kapital; Geldsumme; *(investment)* Fonds; *(stock)* Vorrat; *(to ~)* finanzieren

fundamental analysis fundamentale Aktienanalyse; Fundamentanalyse

fundamental attribution error Grundirrtum der Attribution

Tendency to underestimate the influence of external factors and overestimate the influence of internal factors when making judgments about the behavior of others.

fund assets Fondsvermögen

funded debt langfristige Verpflichtung; langfristige Verbindlichkeit

fund family Fondsfamilie

Management company that runs and/or sells shares of the fund. Fund families often offer several funds with different investment objectives.

funding Finanzierung; Refinanzierung; Bildung von Rückstellungen

fund raising Geldbeschaffung; Kapitalbeschaffung; Mittelbeschaffung

All efforts aimed at soliciting and gathering money from individuals, businesses, charitable foundations, or governmental agencies. Practiced by non-profit organizations, such as political parties in the US. Some common techniques include direct mail advertising and telemarketing.

funds Finanzmittel; Vermögen

funds from operations (FFO) Umsatzüberschuss; Mittel aus laufender Geschäftstätigkeit

Term used by real estate and other investment trusts to define the cash flow from trust operations. It is earnings with depreciation and amortization added back.

fungible fungibel; vertretbar

futile nutzlos; vergeblich

future Zukunft; zukünftig

future earnings zukünftiger Ertrag

future leaders Führungsnachwuchs

futures Termingeschäfte; Terminhandel

futures contract Terminabschluss

A contract which requires the delivery of a commodity or currency at a specified value and date in the future. The contracts themselves can be traded on the futures market.

Under a futures contract the buyer is obliged to purchase the underlying commodity and the seller to sell it. In options trading, on the other hand, the option buyer may choose whether or not to exercise the option by the exercise date.

futures market Terminmarkt

futures rate Terminsatz

futures trade Terminhandel

future value Endwert; Zukunftswert; künftiger Wert

Value of a sum of money (the present value) after investing it over one or more periods at a particular rate of interest; also called compound value.

G

GAAP

See: generally accepted accounting principles.

gain Zunahme; *(profit)* Gewinn; Profit; *(utility)* Nutzen; *(to ~) (to earn)* verdienen; erwerben; erlangen; gewinnen

gainful employment Erwerbstätigkeit

gains from trade Außenhandelsgewinne; Tauschgewinne

gain sharing Gewinnbeteiligung; Beteiligung am Produktivitätszuwachs

Incentive plan in which improvements in group productivity determine the total amount of money that is allocated. The division of productivity savings can be split between the company and employees in any number of ways, but fifty-fifty is pretty typical.

game theory Spieltheorie

Idea of business as a game, amongst them: (1) *The end game:* strategy that a company evolves for a product that seems to be on its last legs, (2) *The win-win game:* a game where both parties end up as winners, (3) *The zero sum-game:* the idea that every game has a winner and a loser. The winner's win plus the loser's loss equal zero.

gallup poll Gallup-Umfrage; Meinungsumfrage

An opinion poll for representing public opinion. Named after its inventor, the American statistician George Gallup, the poll normally uses a simple random sampling method in order to keep the level of bias to a minimum.

Gantt chart Gantt-Karte

A chart showing a planned activity as horizontal bands against a background of dates. Invented by Henry L Gantt in 1917. Used for production scheduling, it shows the various production stages and how long each stage should take.

gap Lücke; Kluft; Schlucht

gap analysis Lückenanalyse

A tabulation of all the known requirements of consumers in a particular category of products, combined with a cross-listing of all the features provided by existing products. The resultant chart shows any gaps that exist and therefore provides a pointer to any new products that could supply an unfulfilled demand.

gasoline Benzin

gasoline price hike Benzinpreiserhöhung

gatekeeper Informationsregulatoren; Personen mit Informationsfiltereigenschaft

Person in an organization's buying center who controls the flow of information to others, e.g. a secretary.

gearing Verschuldungsgrad; Fremdkapitalaufnahme; Leverage

Extent to which a firm relies on debt; also called *financial leverage.*

gender segmentation geschlechtsbezogene Segmentierung

Dividing a market into different groups based on sex/gender.

general allgemein; üblich; *(not specific)* ungefähr; unbestimmt

general agent Generalvertreter

General Agreement on Tariffs and Trade (GATT) Allgemeines Zoll- und Handelsabkommen

An international trade treaty that was in force from 1948 until 1995. Its objectives were to expand world trade and to provide a permanent forum for international trade problems. It committied signatories to lowering trade barriers and to encourage trade across national borders by the reduction of tariffs and quotas on foreign goods.

GATT was supported by 95 nations and a further 28 nations applied its rules. It was finally replaced by the World Trade Organization (WTO).

A substantial extension of free trade was achieved in eight negotiating rounds: Geneva (1947), Annecy (1948), Torquay (1950), Geneva (1956), Dillon (1960-61), Kennedy (1964-67), Tokyo (1973-79), and Uruguay (1986-94).

general average Gesamtdurchschnitt

general expenses Gemeinkosten

Costs incurred for general operations other than selling, administrative, or cost of goods sold.

generalist Generalist

Person with many abilities and interests who is able to acquire more than superficial knowledge about many different subjects.

generalized system of preferences allgemeines Präferenzsystem

general ledger Hauptbuch

Formal ledger containing all the financial statement accounts of a business. It contains offsetting debit and credit accounts. Certain accounts in the general ledger, termed *control accounts,* summarize the details booked on separate subsidiary ledgers.

Generally Accepted Accounting Principles (GAAP) Allgemein anerkannte Grundsätze der Rechnungslegung; Grundsätze ordnungsgemäßer Buchführung

A standard established by the Accounting Practices Board of the American Institute of Certified Public Accountants. These rules, conventions, and procedures define accepted accounting practices in the USA, including broad guidelines as well as detailed provisions.

general need description Beschreibung des allgemeinen Anforderungsprofils

Stage in the business buying process in which the company describes the general characteristics and quantity of a needed item.

general partner unbeschränkt haftender Gesellschafter

In a limited partnership, the general partner is responsible for managing the partnership's activities. His liability to the partnership's creditors is not limited.

general partnership Partnerschaft

Form of business organization in which all partners agree to provide the same portion of the work and cash and to share profits and losses. Each partner is liable for the debts of the partnership.

general strike Generalstreik

general tariff Einheitstarif

generate erzeugen; hervorbringen; entwickeln

generation Generation

generic generisch; gattungsmäßig; allgemein

generic product generisches Produkt

A product that carries neither a manufacturer's name nor a distributor's brand. These no-name brands offer no guarantees of quality and are produced and sold inexpensively

generic strategy generische Strategie

generous großzügig

genuine echt

geocentric staffing geozentrische Stellenpolitik

Staffing policy where the best people are sought for key jobs throughout a MNE, regardless of nationality.

geocentrism Geozentrismus

geodemographic segmentation geodemographische Segmentierung

Market segmentation strategy grouping consumers according to demographic variables, such as income and age, plus geographic variables, such as post code.

This takes two principles into account: (1) people who live in the same neighborhood, defined by a census enumeration district, are likely to share similar buying habits; (2)

neighborhoods can be categorized in terms of their populations: two or more neighborhoods with similar populations can be placed in the same category.

geographic pricing geographische Preisfestlegung

Pricing policy based on where customers are located.

geographic segmentation geographische Segmentierung

Dividing a market into different geographical units such as nations, states, regions, counties, cities, or neighbourhoods.

geographic structure geographische Struktur

gift Geschenk; Schenkung; Gabe; Begabung

gigabit

Computers: one billion bits. Used frequently to describe the bandwidth capacity of LANs and high-speed internet connections

give away verschenken; vergeben

giving away Vergabe

glass ceiling gläserne Decke

Invisible barrier that prevents qualified individuals (particularly women) from advancing beyond a certain point within their employing organization. A number of reasons have been identified to explain this phenomenon: the time factor, motherhood, and male stereotypes.

global Welt-; global; weltweit; weltumfassend

global alliance globales Bündnis

global branding globale Markenkenpolitik

global company weltweites Unternehmen

Firm that, by operating in more than one country, gains R&D, production, marketing and financial advantages in its costs and reputation that are not available to purely domestic competitors.

global demand weltweite Nachfrage

global economics Weltwirtschaft; *(study)* Weltwirtschaftslehre

global firm weltweites Unternehmen

global industry weltweiter Industriezweig

Industry in which the strategic positions of competitors in given geographic or national markets are affected by their overall global positions.

global leadership globale Führung

global learning globales Lernen

Flow of skills and product offerings from foreign subsidiary to home country and from foreign subsidiary to foreign subsidiary.

global marketing globales Marketing

Marketing that is concerned with integrating or standardizing marketing actions across different geographic markets.

global market share Weltmarktanteil

global matrix structure globale Matrixstruktur

Horizontal differentiation of a company or corporation along two dimensions: product divisions and areas.

global organization globale Organisation

Form of international organization whereby top corporate management and staff plan worldwide manufacturing or operational facilities, marketing policies, financial flows and logistical systems. The global operating unit reports directly to the chief executive, not to an international divisional head.

global top level domain names (gTLD)

Internet: part of the domain name that refers to the category of site. The gTLD is usually the rightmost part of the domain name such as *.com.*

global strategy globale Strategie

Strategy focusing on increasing profitability by reaping cost reductions from experience curve and location economies.

global web globales Web

Situation when different stages of value chain are dispersed to those locations around the globe where value added is maximized or where costs of value creation are minimized.

globalization Globalisierung

Trend since the 1990s of progressive expansion of economic activities across national borders, resulting in compex interdependencies and a huge global market.

This can take a number of forms: companies export from a few domestic production facilities, largely to enable them to reap the huge economies of scale; companies set up franchise operations in foreign markets; companies set up multinational manufacturing facilities with plants in a number of different countries.

globalization of markets Globalisierung der Märkte

A tendency to move away from an economic system in which national markets are distinct entities, isolated by barriers of distance, time, and culture, toward a system in which national markets are merging into one global market.

globalization of production Globalisierung der Produktion

Trend by individual firms to disperse parts of their productive processes to different location around the globe to take advantage of differences in cost and quality of factors of production.

goal Ziel; Zweck; *(sports)* Tor

goal congruence Zielkongruenz

goal-setting theory Zieltheorie

Theory that specific and difficult goals, with goal/feedback, lead to higher performance. The evidence strongly supports the value of goals:

1. Specific goals increase performance: specific hard goals produce a high level of output.

2. Difficult goals, when accepted, result in higher performance than easy goals.

3. Feedback leads to higher performance than does non-feedback: feedback helps to identify discrepancies between what they have done and what they want to do – feedback acts to guide behavior.

go below a limit eine Grenze unterschreiten

go down zurückgehen

going concern Going-Concern-Prinzip; Fortführungsprinzip; Grundsatz der Unternehmensfortführung

A principle of accounting that assumes businesses to be going concerns unless circumstances indicate otherwise. Particularly, it assumes that the business will continue in operation for the foreseeable future.

going-private Börsenabgang; Delisting

Situation when publicly owned shares in a firm are replaced with complete equity ownership by a private group. The shares are delisted from stock exchanges and can no longer be purchased in the open market.

going-rate pricing Marktpreisbildung; Marktpreiskalkulation

Setting price based largely on following competitor's prices rather than on company costs or demand.

gold Gold

golden handcuffs goldene Handschellen; Sonderleistung einer Firma, um Manager länger zu halten

golden handshake hohe Abfindung

golden parachute goldener Fallschirm; großzügige Abfindung

A clause in the contract of a senior manager that provides for financial and other benefits if he is sacked or decides to leave as the result of a takeover or change of ownership.

gold hoarding Goldhortung

gold holder Goldbesitzer

gold holding Goldbestand

gold par value Goldwert

Amount of a currency needed to purchase one ounce of gold.

gold producer Goldproduzent

gold reserve Goldbestand; Goldreserve

gold standard Goldstandard

A monetary system in operation until 1931, in which a country's currency unit was fixed in terms of gold and freely convertible into gold. Free import and export of gold was permitted.

gold supply Goldvorrat

good Nutzen; *(public)* Wohl; *(financially)* zahlungsfähig; solvent; reell; *(valid)* gültig; *(check)* in Ordnung

goods Waren; Güter; Artikel

goods receipt Warenempfangsschein

good till canceled bis auf Widerruf

Order to buy or sell stock that is good until one cancels it; also called "GTC". Brokerages usually set a limit of 30-60 days, at which the GTC expires if not restated.

goodwill Wohlwollen; Goodwill; Firmenwert

Intangible asset taken into account when assessing the value of an enterprise, indicating its commercial reputation and worth, and customer connection; excess of the purchase price over the sum of the book (or fair market) values of the individual assets acquired.

gopher

Internet: directory-based structure containing information in certain categories.

govern regieren; verwalten; leiten; *(to regulate)* bestimmen; *(law)* als Präzedenzfall dienen; regulieren

governing body Verwaltungsgremium; Direktorium

government Regierung; *(agency)* Behörde; *(administration)* Verwaltung

government bonds Staatsanleihen; Staatsschuldverschreibungen

government guarantee Staatsgarantie

government housing Sozialwohnung

government incentives for savers staatliche Sparförderung

government influence Staatseinfluss

government market Behördenmarkt

Governmental units – national and local – that purchase or rent goods and services for carrying out the main functions of government.

government order Behördenauftrag

government securities Staatspapiere

government subsidy Staatszuschuss

grace *(delay)* Frist; Aufschub; Zurückstellung; Zahlungsfrist

grace period Zahlungsfrist

graft Korruption; Schiebung

grade Rangstufe; Grad; *(quality)* Handelsklasse; Qualität; *(to ~)* abstufen; einteilen

graduate Absolvent; *(high school)* Abiturient; *(university)* Hochschulabsolvent; *(to ~)* einteilen; staffeln; *(from university)* Hochschule absolvieren

graduation Gradeinteilung; *(education)* Ausbildungsabschluss

grant Verleihung; *(donation)* Schenkung; *(sum)* Unterstützungssumme; Zuschuss; *(of request)* Gewährung; *(to ~)* gewähren; bewilligen; verleihen

granting of a loan Darlehensgewährung

granting of credit Kreditgewährung

grant leave beurlauben

grapevine Gerüchteküche

An informal communication network within a large organization. The grapevine has three main characteristics: (1) it is not controlled by management, (2) it is perceived by most employees as being more believable and reliable than formal communication by top management, (3) it is largely used to serve the self-interests of those people within it.

graph graphische Darstellung

graphical user interface (GUI) graphische Benutzerschnittstelle

Computers: interface that lets users interact with their computer via icons and a pointer instead of by typing in text at a command line.

graphic design Graphik-Design

graphic rating scale graphisches Stärke-Schwäche-Profil

One of the oldest and most popular evaluation method in which the evaluator rates performance factors on an incremental scale.

A set of performance factors are for example quantity and quality of work, depth of knowledge, cooperation, loyalty, attendance, honesty, and initiative.

graphics interchange format (GIF)

Internet: one of the two most common graphics formats on the web [JPEG and GIF]. GIF images are used mostly for line art, logos and similar types of graphics.

gray market grauer Markt

Any market for goods that are in short supply and sold through unofficial channels. Other than the black market it is legal

gray market imports Graumarktimporte

gratuitous unentgeltlich; gratis; kostenlos; grundlos

green card Aufenthaltsgenehmigung; grüne Versicherungskarte

greenfield development Industrie-Neuansiedlung

An industrial development on a virgin site in the country.

greenfield strategy Firmengründung auf der grünen Wiese

green chip Wachstumswert

green mailer erpresserischer Käufer eines Aktienpaketes

Similar to a blackmailer but the word "green" relating to the color of money. A shareholder, holding sufficient shares in a company to prevent his or her being bought out at the going price by a majority shareholder, is able to ask whatever price he or she requires to sell out shares.

green marketing ökologisches Marketing; umweltbewusstes Marketing

Marketing products that benefit the environment, including recyclable and biodegradable packing, better pollution controls and more energy-efficient production processes and product performance.

green-shoe provision Green-Shoe-Klausel

Contract provision that gives the underwriter the option to purchase additional shares at the offering price to cover over-allotments.

grocery store Lebensmittelladen

gross Gros; brutto; roh; dick; *(coarse)* unfein

gross domestic product (GDP) Bruttoinlandsprodukt (BIP)

The monetary value of all the goods and services produced by an economy within one year.

It is measured in three ways: (1) on the basis of expenditure, which includes the value of all goods and services bought, consumption, capital expenditure, increase in the value of stocks, government expenditure, and exports less imports; (2) on the basis of income, which includes income arising from employment, self-employment, rent, company profits (public and private), and stock appreciation; (3) on the basis of the value added by industry, which includes the value of sales less the is costs of raw materials.

gross earnings Bruttoverdienst

An accounting term which is arrived at by subtracting the cost of goods sold from the total sales.

gross fixed capital formation Bruttoanlageinvestition

Summarizes the total amount of capital invested in factories, stores, office buildings, and the like.

gross income Bruttoeinkommen

Total income before deduction for expenses and taxes.

gross margin Bruttohandelsspanne

Difference between the direct cost of products and what they are sold for.

gross national product (GNP) Bruttosozialprodukt (BSP)

The gross domestic product (GDP) with the addition of interest, profits, and dividends received from abroad by residents.

The GNP better reflects the welfare of the population, whilst the GDP better reflects the productive performance of the economy.

gross profit Rohgewinn

The difference between revenue and the cost of making a product or providing a service, before deducting overheads, payroll, taxation, and interest payments.

gross rating points (GRP) Bruttoreichweite

Advertising: the percentage of a target audience reached by an advertisement. If the advertisement appears more than once, the GRP figure represents the sum of each individual GRP.

If a TV advertisement is aired 5 times reaching 50% of the target audience, it would have 250 GRP = 5 x 50%.

gross sales Bruttoabsatz

The total invoice value of a company´s sales, before deducting customers' discounts, returns, or allowances.

group Gruppe; Klasse; *(business)* Konzern; *(to ~)* gruppieren; anordnen

Association of two or more individuals who have a shared sense of identity and who interact with each other in structured ways on the basis of a common set of expectation about each other's behavior.

group demography Gruppendemographie

Degree to which members of a group share a common demographic attribute, such as age, sex, race, educational level, or length of service in the organization, and the impact of this attribute on turnover. The group demography considers the individual's attribute in relationship to the attributes of the other group members.

group discussion Gruppendiskussion

A marketing research technique bringing six to eight respondents together for at least an hour to discuss a marketing issue under the guidance of an interviewer.

group member Gruppenangehöriger

group norms Gruppennormen

Group of Seven (G-7) Gruppe der sieben führenden Industrienationen

The seven leading industrial nations of the world: USA, Japan, Germany, France, UK, Italy, and Canada. This group holds annual meetings attended by heads of state and governement.

The original aim in 1976 was to discuss economic coordination, but the agenda has since broadened to include political issues. Since 1991 Russia attends G7 meetings, and the group is often referred to as the Group of Eight.

Group of Ten (G-10) Zehner-Gruppe

Group of Twenty-four (G-24) Vierundzwanziger-Gruppe

Group of Thirty (G-30) Dreißiger-Gruppe

Group of Seventy-seven (G-77) Siebenundsiebziger-Gruppe

group of banks Bankengruppe

group of companies Firmengruppe

group order ranking Intra-Gruppen-Ranking

Evaluation method that places employees into a particular classification such as quartiles. When used by managers to appraise employees, managers deal with all their subordinates. Therefore, if a firm had 20 employees, only four can be in the top fifth and four must be relegated to the bottom fifth.

group shift Gruppenbewegung; Verschiebung im Gruppendenken

Change in decision risk between the group's decision and the individual decision that members within the group would make; can be either toward conservatism or greater risk.

groupthink Gruppendenken

Phenomenon in which the norm for consensus overrides the realistic appraisal of alternative courses of action.

grow wachsen; zunehmen; *(to cultivate)* ziehen; anbauen

growing perpetuity wachsende ewige Rente

Constant stream of cash flows without end that is expected to rise indefinitely.

Example: cash flows to the landlord of a block of flats might be expected to rise by a certain percentage each year.

growth Wachstum; Zunahme; Vergrößerung; *(expansion)* Ausdehnung; *(development)* Entwicklung

growth forecast Wachstumsprognose

growth in earnings Verdienstzuwachs; Ertragsentwicklung

growth in sales Umsatzsteigerung

growth in the money supply Geldmengenwachstum

growth model Wachstumsmodell

growth opportunity Wachstumsmöglichkeit

growth path Wachstumspfad

growth policy Wachstumspolitik

growth prediction Wachstumsvorhersage

growth rate Wachstumsrate

growth sector Wachstumsbranche

growth-share matrix Portfolio-Matrix

Portfolio-planning method, developed by the Boston Consulting Group (BCG) in the 1960s, that evaluates a company's strategic business units or products in terms of their market growth rate and relative market share.

The results are displayed in a two-dimensional matrix, with four generic types of positions:

Cash Cows: mature businesses or products with a high market share but low growth rate. Typically, most fixed investment has already been made and a substantial cash flow is generated.

Stars: businesses or products with a high rate of growth, which are often able to generate sufficient cash to fund the necessary investment to meet increasing demand.

Question Marks: operating in a growth market, but with a low market share, most likely these business units are unable to sustain the required level of investment.

Dogs: the combination of low growth rate and low market share often typical in mature markets. Firms frequently face strategic decisions whether to support dogs further or to implement a divestment strategy.

growth stage Wachtumsphase

Stage in the product life cycle at which a product's sales begin to climb quickly.

guarantee Bürgschaft; Garantie; *(bill of exchange)* Aval *mint*; *(to ~)* bürgen; gewährleisten; garantieren; haften

Promise by another person (a guarantor) to pay the unpaid balance of a loan should the borrower fail to repay it.

guaranteed verbrieft; gewährt; garantiert; versprochen

guaranteed letter of credit avaliertes Akkreditiv

guaranteed price Garantiepreis

guarantor Bürge; Verantwortlicher

Person who makes a legally binding promise either to pay another person's debt or to perform another person's duty if that person defaults or fails to perform.

guaranty fund Bürgschaftsfonds

guest Gast

guest worker Gastarbeiter

guidance Führung; Leitung; *(counseling)* Beratung

guide *(manual)* Leitfaden; *(person)* Führer; Vorbild; *(to ~)* führen; lenken; leiten

guideline Richtlinie; Vorlage

guild Zunft; Berufsverein; Brüderschaft; Gilde

H

habit Gewohnheit; Gebrauch; Gepflogenheit

habitual gewohnheitsmässig

habitual buying behavior gewohnheitsmässiges Kaufverhalten

Consumer buying behavior in situations characterized by low consumer involvement and few significant perceived brand differences. Purchases are made out of habit, rather than a strong commitment to a brand.

hacker

Someone with a very good understanding of the functioning of computer networks, who deliberately breaks into confidential systems, sometimes with malign intentions.

half Hälftc; halb

halo effect Halo-Effekt

Drawing a general impression about an individual on the basis of a single characteristic, such as intelligence, sociability, or appearance.

The effect is most extreme when the traits to be perceived are ambiguous in behavioral terms, when the traits have moral overtones, and when the perceiver is judging traits with which he or she has had limited experience.

halt Stillstand; Rast; Halt; *(to ~)* anhalten; stocken; zögern

Hamel, Gary (* 1955)

Management thinker and consultant whose work shifted strategic thinking from positioning a company within its industry to changing the rules of that industry and creating new markets.

Important concepts developed by Hamel and his co-author Prahalad include core competencies, strategic intent and industry foresight. In their best-selling book "Competing for the Future", they argued that the sustainable health of a business could not be achieved by simply applying simple accounting rules to costs, and that managers needed to look much further into the future of the business than they had been accustomed to.

They urged managers not to take customers and markets for granted but to ask themselves what the business would look like in the medium-term future.

Biography: studied international business at the University of Michigan, where he also met C.K. Prahalad, with whom he co-authored his most important works, 1983-1993 professor of strategy at London Business School, later set up his own consultancy.

Major publications: (1994 with C.K. Prahalad) 'Competing for the future', Harvard Business Review (July/Aug), (1994 with C.K. Prahalad) Competing for the future, (1996 with C.K. Prahalad) 'Strategy as revolution', Harvard Business Review (July/Aug).

Hammer, Michael (* 1948)

Computer scientist and mathematician who became famous for his 're-engineering' concept.

Hammer defined re-engineering as 'the fundamental re-thinking and radical redesign of business processes to achieve dramatic improvements in critical measures of performance such as cost, quality, service and speed'.

Major publications: (1990) 'Reengineering work: don't automate, obliterate', Harvard Business Review (July/Aug), (1993 with J.Champy) Reengineering the corporation, (1995 with S.A. Stanton) The reengineering revolution, (1996) Beyond reengineering.

hand Hand; *(worker)* angelernter Arbeiter; Arbeitskraft; *(to ~)* aushändigen

handle Handhabe; *(grip)* Griff; Klinke; Henkel; *(to ~)* handhaben; behandeln; *(to process)* bearbeiten; erledigen

handling *(execution)* Erledigung; Handhabung; *(processing)* Bearbeitung; *(treatment)* Behandlung

handling allowance Bearbeitungspauschale

handling charges Bearbeitungsgebühr

handling objections Enwandbehandlung

Step in the selling process in which the salesperson seeks out, clarifies and overcomes customer objections to buying.

handout Prospekt; Informationsmaterial; Presseerklärung *(charity)* Almosen

Handy, Charles (* 1932)

Classical scholar and philosopher, whose studies of organizations and his ideas on the future of work and business structures decisively influenced management thinking.

Biography: studied Greek and Latin antiquity at Oxford University, worked for Shell International in Malaysia and as an economist in the city of London, spent two decisive years at MIT´s Sloan School of Management, where he was influenced by academics such as Warren Bennis, Ed Schein, and Chris Argyris, during the 1990s turned away from management to concern for the individual's struggle to find personal fulfillment in a world of uncertainty.

Major publications: (1976) Understanding organizations, (1986) Gods of management, (1984) The future of work, (1988 with J. Constable) The making of managers, (1989) The age of unreason, (1990) Inside organizations.

harbor Hafen; *(refuge)* Zufluchtsort; Versteck

hard hart; *(difficult)* schwierig; *(strenuous)* anstrengend; mühsam; *(strict)* streng

hard currency harte Währung

hardship Not; Bedrängnis; Härte; Mühsal; Not

hardware Eisenwaren; *(computer)* Hardware

harmonization Harmonisierung; Angleichung

Hawthorne effect Hawthorne-Effekt

Effect named after a famous experiment in industrial history which took place at Western Electric's factory at Hawthorne, a suburb of Chicago, in the late 1920s and early 1930s. The experiment established that workers' performance is influenced by their surroundings and by the people they are working with. It thus set the individual in a social context.

head Kopf; *(main)* Haupt; *(chief)* Chef; Leiter; *(top)* Spitze; *(to ~)* leiten; anführen; *(to direct)* lenken

head and shoulders characteristische Kurvenform

A chart formation in which a stock price reaches a peak, declines, rises above its former peak, declines and rises again but not to the second peak and then again declines.

head-hunter Personalabwerber

Professional who searches out and poaches talented employees from their employers by making them a better offer.

heading Überschrift

head manager Chefmanager

head office Hauptverwaltung

head organization Spitzenorganisation; Spitzenverband

headquarters Hauptgeschäftssitz; Hauptverwaltung; Zentrale; *(military)* Hauptquartier

health certificate Gesundheitszeugnis; Gesundheitspass; Gesundheitsattest

hearing *(deliberation)* Verhandlung; *(investigation)* Voruntersuchung; *(trial)* Verhör; *(ability)* Gehör

heavy schwer; *(large or great)* stark

Heckscher-Ohlin theory Heckscher-Ohlin-Theorie

Mathematical model of international trade, developed by Eli Heckscher and Bertil Ohlin at the Stockholm School of Economics, building on David Ricardo's theory of comparative advantage by predicting patterns of trade and production based on the factor endowments of a trading region.

The theory suggests that countries will export those goods that make intensive use of locally abundant factors of production and import goods that make intensive use of locally scarce factors of production.

hedge *(stock exchange)* Deckungsgeschäft; Absicherung; Sicherungsgeschäft; *(to ~)* Sicherungsgeschäft abschließen; absichern

Finance: an investment that is taken out specifically to reduce or cancel out the risk in another investment.

hedge fund stark spekulierender Investmentfonds

Investment fund that not only buys financial assets (stocks, bonds, currencies) but also sells them short.

hedging Kursabsicherung; Sicherungsgeschäft am Terminmarkt

The use of strategies which reduce the risk of financial loss on an investment, amongst them: "call" options, "put" options, "short" selling, or futures contracts. A hedge can help lock in existing profits. Its purpose is to reduce the potential volatility of a portfolio, by reducing the risk of loss.

height Höhe; Größe; *(summit)* Gipfel; Level; Spitze

heir Erbe; Erbin

helper Hilfsarbeiter; Gehilfe; Gehilfin

helpful hilfreich

help wanted advertisement Stellenangebot

Herzberg, Frederick (1932-2000)

Clinical psychologist whose work on human motivation divides the elements of a job into those serving animal or economic needs ('hygiene' or 'maintenance' factors) from those meeting deeper aspirations ('motivation' factors). The solution Herzberg suggested became famous as the technique called 'job enrichment'.

His book *The Motivation to Work*, published in 1959, was based on intensive questioning of 200 engineers and accountants in Pittsburg, asking them to analyze occasions when they felt exceptionally good and exceptionally bad about their work. He discovered that satisfaction and dissatisfaction with one's employment arose from quite different factors and were not simply opposing reactions to the same factors.

Biography: During the second world war his experiences as a US army volunteer decisively shaped his views. After the war he worked for the US public Health Service, when he began to work conceptually in the field of industrial psychology. After working as a consultant in industry, amongst others with AT&T, he became a professor of management at the University of Utah.

Major publications: (1959, with B. Mausner, B. Snyderman), The motivation to work, (1966) Work ant the nature of man, (1968) 'One more time: how do you motivate employees?', Harvard Business Review, (1976) Managerial choice: to be efficient and to be human.

heuristic Heuristik

Judgmental shortcuts in decision making. There are two common categories of heuristics – availability and representativeness. Each creates biases in judgment.

hierarchy of effects model Wirkungshierarchiemodell

Device that attempts to explain the impact of marketing communication. It assumes that consumers go through a series of stages when making product decisions and that communication messages are designed to assist that movement.

hierarchy of needs Bedürfnishierarchie

Abraham Maslow's hierarchy of needs is the best-known theory of motivation. He suggested that within every human being there exists a hierarchy of five levels of needs:

Physiological: includes hunger, thirst, shelter, sex, and other bodily needs

Safety: includes security and protection from physical and emotional harm

Social: includes affection, belongingness, acceptance, and friendship

Esteem: includes internal esteem factors such as self-respect, autonomy, and achievement; and external esteem factors such as status, recognition, and attention

Self-actualization: the drive to become what one is capable of becoming; includes growth, achieving one's potential, and self-fulfillment.

As each of these levels becomes substantially satisfied, the next need becomes dominant. Maslow separated the five needs into higher and lower orders. Physiological and safety needs were described as lower-order needs and social, esteem, and self-actualization needs as higher-order needs.

high Höchststand; Zustand der Hochstimmung; nach oben; hoch

high bandwidth hohe Bandbreite

high contact cultures High-Contact-Kulturen

high context cultures High-Context-Kulturen

Cultures that rely heavily on nonverbal and subtle situational cues in communication. What is *not* said may be more significant than what is said.

Examples: countries such as China, Vietnam, and Saudi Arabia. Communication implies considerably more trust by both parties and oral agreements imply strong commitments. The age, seniority, rank in the organization are highly valued and heavily influence credibility.

higher management obere Betriebsführung

higher-order needs höhere Bedürfnisse

Maslow separated the five needs of his hierarchy of needs into higher and lower orders. Higher-order needs are satisfied internally (within the person); social, esteem, and self-actualization needs.

highest level Höchststand; *(in hierarchy)* oberste Ebene

high-grade hochwertig

highly paid hoch bezahlt

high price hoher Preis

Highest (intraday) price of a stock over the past 52 weeks, adjusted for any stock splits.

high-quality hochwertig

high risk hohes Risiko

high volume business Massengeschäft

high-yield bond hochverzinsliche Anleihe

hike Anstieg; Steigen; *(walking)* Wanderung; *(to ~) (to increase)* steigern; *(to walk)* wandern

hire Einstellung; *(renting)* Miete; Arbeitslohn; *(to ~) (to employ)* einstellen; anstellen; *(to rent)* mieten

histogram Säulendiagramm; Histogramm

historic cost ursprüngliche Anschaffungskosten; Herstellungskosten; historische Kosten

historic cost principle Anschaffungskostengrundsatz

Accounting principle founded on the assumption that the currency unit used to report financial results is not losing its value due to inflation.

history Geschichte; Darstellung; *(personal)* Entwicklung; *(background)* Hintergrund

hit Treffer; Schlager; Schlag; Hieb; *(to ~)* treffen; *(to reach)* erreichen

Internet: each 'visit' on a website from a reader/user is called a *hit.* Hits form an important form of circulation estimates and are interpreted and analyzed as a marketing strategy.

hoard Vorrat; Schatz; *(to ~)* anhäufen; hamstern; horten

hold Halt; Griff; *(influence)* Einfluss; *(ship)* Laderaum; *(to ~)* halten; *(to possess)* im Besitz haben; *(capacity)* fassen; enthalten

holder *(property)* Besitzer; Inhaber

holding *(possession)* Besitz; *(inventory)* Bestand; *(share)* Beteiligung; Anteil

holding company Holdinggesellschaft; Dachgesellschaft

Corporation that owns enough voting stock in another firm to control management and operations by influencing or electing its board of directors.

holding period Halteperiode

Length of time that an individual holds a security.

holding-period return Rendite der Halteperiode

Rate of return over a given period.

home Wohnort; Heim; *(country)* Heimat; *(at home)* zu Hause; *(to go home)* nach Hause

home country Mutterland; Inland

home country national Staatsbürger seines Mutterlandes; Einheimischer

home currency Landeswährung; inländische Währung

home computer Heimcomputer

home leave Heimaturlaub

home loan financing Hausfinanzierung

homemade dividends maßgeschneiderter Dividendenstrom

Individual investor can undo corporate dividend policy by reinvesting excess dividends or selling off shares to receive a desired cash flow.

homemade leverage selbstgemachte Verschuldung

Idea that as long as individuals borrow (and lend) on the same terms as the firm, they can duplicate the effects of corporate leverage on their own. Thus, if levered firms are priced too high, rational investors will simply borrow on personal accounts to buy shares in unlevered firms.

home market Inlandsmarkt; Binnenmarkt

home office Hauptbüro; Zentrale; Büro zu Hause

homeowner Hausbesitzer

home page Homepage

Internet: index page of a web site with menu options or links to other resources on the site.

home purchase savings Bausparen

home rule Selbstverwaltung

home savings and loan association Bausparkasse

home trading Inlandsgeschäft

host Gastgeber; Veranstalter *(to ~ an event)* veranstalten

homogeneous homogen

homogeneous expectations homogene Erwartungen

Idea that all individuals have the same beliefs concerning future investments, profits, and dividends.

hop Etappe; Sprung

Communication: movement of a digital packet of information from one node to the next. In general the fewer the number of hops, the faster the packet arrives at its destination.

horizontal acquisition horizontaler Unternehmenserwerb

Merger or takeover between two companies producing similar goods or services.

horizontal differentiation horizontale Differenzierung

Horizontal differentiation occurs when products are different according to additional features that don´t affect the product itself, such as different colors.

horizontal foreign direct investment horizontale ausländische Direktinvestition

Foreign direct investment in the same industry abroad as a firm operates in at home.

horizontal marketing horizontales Marketing

Channel arrangement in which two or more companies at one level join together to follow a new marketing opportunity.

horizontal merger horizontaler Zusammenschluss

A merger of two or more firms in the same industry that are both at the same stage of production; in effect, they are competitors.

host Gastgeber

Computers: generic term that refers to any computer providing information or services to others. The term originated with large mainframe computers that acted as a "host" to a set of terminals.

Internet: refers to a webserver that functions as a host to web browsers, a file server that acts as a host to other computers on a local area network.

hostage Geisel

host country Aufnahmestaat; Gastland

host country national Staatsbürger des Gastlandes

hostile applets bösartige Applets

Internet: programs that can be used to surreptitiously access and transmit data on bald drives, including e-mail addresses, credit card records, and other account information.

hotelling Hotelkonzept

An extension of the open office concept, in which employees have no permanent work space. They are assigned space each day when they arrive and check out each day when they depart. They spend a significant percentage of their work time outside the office or in team meetings.

hour Stunde

hourly wages Stundenlohn

hours worked per week Wochenarbeitszeit

house Haus; *(firm)* Handelsfirma; *(to ~)* unterbringen; beherbergen

house air waybill eigener Luftfrachtbrief; Hausluftfrachtbrief; Spediteurluftfrachtbrief

household Haushalt

housing Unterbringung

housing allowance Mietzuschuss; Wohngeld

housing industry Wohnungswirtschaft

hub Zentrum; Nabe; *(wheel)* Nabe

human Mensch; menschlich

human capital Humankapital

The skills acquired by an individual in the course of his work experience. The concept was introduced by Gary Becker in the 1960s in order to point out that wages reflect in part a return on human capital. It can be used to explain large variations in wages for apparently similar jobs.

human development index (HDI) Index des menschlichen Entwicklungsstandes

An approach to measure human progress introduced by the United Nations Development Programme in 1990. In combining indicators of real purchasing power, education, and health, the HDI attempts to provide a more comprehensive measure of development than GNP.

humane menschenfreundlich; human

human need menschliches Mangel

human relations zwischenmenschliche Beziehungen

human relations view of conflict Human-Relations-Ansatz der Konfliktforschung

Belief that conflict is a natural and inevitable outcome in any group. The human relation view dominated conflict theory from the late 1940s through the mid-1970s.

human resource management (HRM) Personalmanagement

The management of people in an organization in order to achieve individual behavior and performance that will enhance the overall effectiveness.

HRM was traditionally called personnel management, but recent trends place greater emphasis on the morale of employees and ways of achieving consistent job satisfaction. Methods include: using more sophisticated psychological tests in selecting employees, training employees to do more than one job, and encouraging all the members of a workforce to accept responsibility.

human resource strategy Personalstrategie

human rights policy Menschenrechtspolitik

human skills soziale Kompetenzen

Ability to work with, understand, and motivate other people, both individually and in groups.

Since managers get things done through other people, they must be have good human skills to communicate, motivate, and delegate.

human want menschliches Bedürfnis

Form that a human need takes as shaped by culture and individual personality.

Humble, John (* 1925)

Management consultant who developed the concept of Management by Objectives into a practical tool for managers.

Conceived in the 1950s, Ducker's theory asked for clearly spelled out objectives for everybody in a firm. Humble developed a practical methodology by breaking down corporate aims into a series of personal objectives.

Biography: Humble was educated at the University of Cambridge and became a director of the established consultancy Urwick Orr, has been at the forefront of management development in the UK for many years, worked for the Central Training Council of the Department of Employment and as a consultant to industry.

Major publications: (1971) Management by Objectives.

hybrid marketing channels gemischte Absatzkanäle

Multi-channel distribution, as when a single firm sets up two or more marketing channels to reach one or more customer segments. A variety of direct and indirect approaches are used to deliver the firm's goods to its customers.

hygiene factors Hygienefaktoren

Characterized by psychologist Frederick Herzberg, those factors – such as company policy and administration, supervision, and salary – that, when adequate in a job, placate workers. When these factors are adequate, people will not be dissatisfied.

hype *(advertising)* Werberummel; Werbespektakel

hyperinflation Hyperinflation

Very high and self-sustaining levels of inflation levels, exceeding 50% until it has drops below that level for 12 months. Prices are rising rapidly thus reducing the purchasing power value of money.

hyperlink Hyperlink

Internet: A method of moving between one website page and another indicated to the user by text highlighted by underlining and/or a different color. Hyperlinks can also appear as graphics or as areas of differently colored.

hypermarkets Verbrauchergroßmärkte; Großeinkaufszentren

Huge stores that combine supermarket, discount and warehouse retailing; in addition to food, they carry furniture, appliances, clothing and many other products.

hypertext

Internet: simple text that, when clicked on, takes the reader to an another site or part of the same document. In most browsers, hypertext is shown underlined.

hypertext markup language (HTML)

Internet: a markup language designed for the creation of web pages with hypertext and other information to be displayed in a web browser. HTML is used to structure information and to describethe appearance and semantics of a document.

Originally defined by Tim Berners-Lee, HTML is now an international standard. Later HTML specifications are maintained by the World Wide Web Consortium (W3C).

hypothesis Hypothese; Annahme

hypothesis testing Hypothesentest; Überprüfung einer Hypothese

I

idea Idee; Begriff; Einfall

idea champion Ideenführer

Individual who takes an innovation and actively and enthusiastically promotes the idea, builds support, overcomes resistance, and ensures it is implemented.

idea generation Ideengenerierung; Ideensuche

Systematic search for new product ideas. Part of the process of new product development.

idea screening Ideenscreening

Screening new-product ideas in order to spot good ideas and drop poor ones as soon as possible.

ideal Ideal; *(model)* Vorbild; ideal; optimal; *(exemplary)* vorbildlich

identical identisch; *(copy)* gleich lautend

identifiable feststellbar; identifizierbar

identification Bestimmung; Feststellung; Identifizierung; *(identification card)* Ausweis

identification-based trust identifikationsbasiertes Vertrauen

Trust based on a mutual understanding of each other's intention and appreciation of the other's wants and desires.

Example: team members are comfortable and trusting of each other that they can anticipate each other and freely act in each other's absence.

identify ausweisen; identifizieren; *(to determine)* bestimmen

identify oneself sich ausweisen

identity Identität; Individualität; Gleichheit; Persönlichkeit

idle müßig; untätig; *(capacity)* unausgenutzt; *(capital)* tot; *(machinery)* stillstehend; stilliegend; *(to ~) (engine)* leer laufen

idleness Untätigkeit

idle shift Feierschicht

illegal unrechtmäßig; ungesetzlich; rechtswidrig; illegal; unerlaubt

illegitimate political behavior illegitimes politisches Verhalten

Extreme political behavior that violates the implied rules of the game. *Examples:* sabotage, whistle-blowing, and symbolic protests.

illustrate illustrieren; veranschaulichen

illustration Abbildung; Illustration

illustrative erklärend; erläuternd; erhellend; konkretisierend

image Bild; Image; Erscheinungsbild; *(to ~)* abbilden

imbalance Unausgeglichenheit

imitation Nachahmung; Imitation

imitation strategy Imitationsstrategie

Strategy that seeks to move into new products or new markets only after their viability has been proven by innovators. It takes the successful ideas of innovators and copies them, thus minimizing risk and maximizing profit.

immaterial unwesentlich; unerheblich; *(intangible)* immateriell; unkörperlich

immeasurable unermesslich; unmessbar

immediate sofortig; unverzüglich; dringend

immediately sofort; umgehend

immunized immunisiert; geimpft

impact Aufprall; *(force)* Wirkungskraft; Stoßkraft; *(effect)* Auswirkung; *(to ~)* einwirken auf

impair beeinträchtigen; verschlechtern; beschädigen

impartial unparteiisch; unvoreingenommen

impede behindern; vereiteln; aufhalten

impediment Behinderung; Hindernis

impetus Antrieb; Impuls; Triebkraft

impetus toward expansion Wachstumsimpuls

implement Werkzeug; Arbeitsgerät; *(instrument)* Instrument; *(to ~)* ausführen; durchführen; *(contract)* erfüllen

implementation Ausführung; Durchführung; *(contract)* Erfüllung; Implementierung

implementation date Ausführungstag

implicit models of organizational structure implizierte Modelle der Organisationsstruktur

Perceptions that people hold regarding structural variables formed by observing things around them in an unscientific fashion.

import Einfuhr; Import; *(to ~)* einführen; importieren

The act of bringing products from a foreign into a domestic market in order to sell them there.

importation Einfuhr; Import

import barrier Einfuhrschranke; Importbarriere; Importschranke

import capacity Importfähigkeit

import company Importfirma

import control Einfuhrkontrolle

import curb Importdrosselung

import demand Importbedarf

import duty Importabgabe

A tax on imported goods, either a fixed amount or a percentage of the value of the goods. Its main purpose is as barrier used to protect domestic production against foreign competition and as an important source of government revenue, especially in developing countries.

import entry form Einfuhrdokument

A form completed by a importer of goods and submitted to cstoms authorities for assessment of the import duty. When passed, the the form functions as a warrant to permit the goods to be removed from the port of entry.

importer Importeur; Importkaufmann; Importkauffrau

import goods Importware

importing Import; Einfuhr

import license Einfuhrbewilligung; Einfuhrgenehmigung

A permit allowing the importation of a stated quantity of certain goods into a country. Import licenses are needed when import restrictions are in force, such as import quotas, currency restrictions, and prohibition.

import merchandise Importgut

import of finished goods Fertigwarenimport

import organization Importorganisation

import penetration Importdurchdringung

A measure of the importance of imports in the domestic economy, usually defined as a share of total consumption.

import price Importpreis; Einfuhrpreis

import price increase Importverteuerung

import protection Einfuhrschutz

import quota Einfuhrkontingent; Einfuhrquote; Importkontingent; Importquote

A restriction imposed to reduce the quantity of certain goods allowed into a country from a particular exporting country in a stated period.

The purpose of a quota may be to conserve foreign currency if there is an unfavorable balance of payments, or to protect the home market against foreign competition. Quotas are usually enforced by means of import licenses.

import restrictions Einfuhrbeschränkungen

Restrictions imposed on goods and services imported into a country, which include tariffs, import quotas, currency restrictions and prohibition.

The reasons can be problems in the importing country's balance of payments, but restrictions may also be imposed to protect the home industry against foreign competition.

imports Einfuhren; Einfuhrware; Importartikel

import substitute Einfuhrersatz

import surcharge Importabgabe

import value Einfuhrwert

impose aufbürden; *(taxes)* auferlegen; *(charges)* erheben

imposition Belastung; Auferlegung; Erhebung; *(taking advantage)* Zumutung; Steuer; Schulden; Strafe

impression Eindruck; Wirkung; (*media*) Eindruck

Media: gross sum of all media exposures (number of people or homes) without regard to duplication.

impression management Impressionsmanagement; Kontrolle des Eindrucks

Process by which individuals attempt to control the impression others form of them.

Some of the more popular impression management techniques are: conformity, excuses, apologies, acclamation, flatter, favors, association.

improve sich bessern; verbessern; *(to refine)* veredeln

improvement Verbesserung; *(progress)* Fortschritt; *(refining)* Veredelung

imprudent unklug; unvorsichtig; unüberlegt

impulse Anstoß; Antrieb; Impuls

impulse buying Impulskauf

The purchase of a product without previous intention and without evaluation of competing brands. It is encouraged especially by prominent shelf position, and manufactures therefore try to persuade retailers to give these advantages to their products.

imputation Zurechnung; Zuschreibung

impute zurechnen; unterstellen; beschulden

imputed costs kalkulatorische Kosten

Cost elements which do not directly correspond to any type of expense found in financial accounting, either because they are accrued from financial accounting or because they involve no direct expense.

They are often opportunity costs, i.e. costs arising from missed opportunities to earn interest or income. The best-known are: imputed social security costs, imputed depreciation, imputed interest, imputed entrepreneurial salary, imputed risk costs.

inability Unvermögen; Unfähigkeit; Mittellosigkeit

inaccurate ungenau; *(false)* falsch; fehlerhaft

inadequacy Unzulänglichkeit; Unangemessenheit

inadequate unzulänglich; unangemessen

inadmissible unzulässig; unakzeptabel

inbound eingehend

inbound e-mail eingehende E-Mail

inbound telemarketing eingehendes Telemarketing

incalculable unkalkulierbar

incapable unfähig

incentive Anreiz; Ansporn

incentive pay Gratifikation; Erfolgsprämie

incentive scheme Leistungssystem; Anreizsystem

Scheme designed to increase the motivation of employees by offering them monetary or other rewards.

incidence Vorkommen; Dauer; Auftreten; *(distribution)* Verbreitung; *(frequency)* Häufigkeit

incident Zwischenfall; Ereignis

incidental gelegentlich; beiläufig

inclined *(to buy)* kaufwillig

include einschließen; einbeziehen; erfassen

inclusion Einbeziehung

inclusive einschließlich; inklusive

income Einkommen; *(receipts)* Einnahmen; *(revenue)* Einkünfte

income bond Gewinnobligationen

A bond that only pays interest if the corporation has sufficient earnings. Income bonds are commonly used during the reorganization of a failed or failing business.

income bracket Einkommensgruppe

income decrease Einkommensminderung

income-dependent einkommensabhängig

income distribution Einkommensverteilung

income group Einkommensgruppe

income segmentation Einkommenssegmentierung

Dividing the market into different income groups.

income statement Gewinn-und Verlustrechnung; Einkommensaufstellung

Financial report that summarizes a firm's performance over a specified time period; in the UK also called profit and loss account.

income tax Einkommenssteuer

A tax levied on the financial income of persons, corporations or other legal entities. Tax systems can rangie from a flat tax to a progressive tax or graduated income tax.

A tax levied on the income of companies is often called a corporate tax. Individual income taxes generally tax the total income of the individual (with some deductions permitted), while corporate income taxes often tax net income, the difference between gross receipts, expenses and additional writeoffs.

income tax allowance Steuerfreibetrag

Allowance that may be deducted from a taxpayer's gross income before calculating the liability to income tax.

incoming order Auftragseingang

incomplete unvollständig; mangelhaft; fehlerhaft

inconvertible nicht konvertierbar

inconvertibility *(bank notes)* Nichteinlösbarkeit; Nichtkonvertierbarkeit

incorporate als Aktiengesellschaft eintragen; registrieren; inkorporieren; *(to join)* vereinigen; *(to take in)* aufnehmen; *(of a town)* eingemeinden

incorporation *(registration)* Eintragung; *(forming of corporation)* Körperschaftsgründung; *(corporation)* Körperschaft; Korporation; *(of a town)* Eingemeindung

The process of forming a corporation under the laws and statutes of a specific state.

incorrect unrichtig; falsch; ungenau; unangenehm

Incoterms Incoterms

See: International Commercial Terms.

increase Anstieg; Steigerung; Erhöhung; *(increment)* Zunahme; Zuwachs; *(of capital)* Aufstockung; *(to ~)* erhöhen; steigern; *(to rise)* sich erhöhen; steigen; zunehmen

increased demand Bedarfszuwachs

increase in capital stock Kapitalerhöhung

increase in cost Verteuerung

increase in currency Geldvermehrung

increase in customers Kundenzuwachs

increase in efficiency Effizienzsteigerung

increase in imports Einfuhranstieg; Einfuhrsteigerung

increase in interest Zinsanhebung

increase in prices Kursanstieg

increase in sales Absatzsteigerung

increase in the money supply Geldmengenerhöhung; Geldmengenvermehrung

increase in turnover Umsatzanstieg

increase of capital stock Kapitalvermehrung

increase of deposits Depositenzuwachs

increment Zunahme; Zuwachs

incremental automatisch steigend; Zuwachs-; Wachstum-

incremental cash flows marginale Zahlungen

incremental costs Grenzkosten

Additional costs incurred if a company pursues a specific course of action. Similar to marginal costs, also referred to as differential costs.

incremental IRR marginaler interner Zinsfuß

IRR on the incremental investment from choosing one project rather than another, for example from choosing a larger project instead of a smaller project.

incur *(obligation)* eingehen; *(costs)* übernehmen; auf sich nehmen; erleiden

indebted verschuldet; verpflichtet

indebtedness Verschuldung; Verpflichtung; Schuldenlast

indefinite unbestimmt; unbegrenzt

indemnity Schadensersatz, Entschädigung, Abfindung

An agreement by one party to make good the losses suffered by another, usually by payment of money, repair, replacement, or reinstatement.

indemnity insurance Haftpflichtversicherung

An insurance designed to compensate the policyholder for a loss, either by the payment of money, repair, replacement, or reinstatement.

The policyholder is entitled to be put back in the same financial position as he was immediately before the event occurred, but there may be no profit resulting from it.

indenture Vertrag; Anleihevertrag

A written agreement creating or transferring an estate in land.

Bonds: written agreement between the corporate debt issuer and the lender, setting forth maturity date, interest rate and other terms.

independence Unabhängigkeit; Selbständigkeit

independent unabhängig; selbständig

independent project unabhängiges Investitionsprojekt

Project whose acceptance or rejection is independent of the acceptance or rejection of other projects.

independent variable unabhängige Variable

Presumed cause of some change in the dependent variable.

in-depth interviews (IDI) Tiefeninterviews

Semi-structured conversation with a small number of subjects.

index Index; Verzeichnis; *(statistics)* Messziffer; Kennziffer; *(file)* Kartei; *(to ~)* registrieren; *(to link to an index)* an einen Index koppeln

indexing Indexbindung; Indexierung

indicate angeben; anzeigen; *(to point out)* hinweisen; bezeugen; indizieren

indicated annual dividend angegebene jährliche Dividende

Total of the expected dividend payments over the next twelve months. It is generally the most recent cash dividend paid or declared multiplied by the dividend payment frequency, plus any recurring extra dividend.

indication Anzeichen; Angabe; *(pointing out)* Hinweis; Markierung

indication of results Ergebnisangabe

indicative bezeichnend; hinweisend

indicator Indikator; Messgröße; Anzeiger

indirect indirekt; mittelbar

indirect costs indirekte Kosten

indispensable unentbehrlich; unerlässlich

individual Einzelperson; Individuum; Einzel-; einzeln; persönlich

individual marketing individuelles Marketing

Tailoring products and marketing programs to the needs and preferences of individual customers.

individual ranking individuelles Ranking

Evaluation method that ranks employees from best to worst. The result is a clear ordering of employees, from the highest performer down to the lowest.

individual responsibility Eigenverantwortung

individualism Individualismus

Culture: orientation that places strong emphasis on individual freedom and self-expression, as opposed to obligations to groups like families or society. Individualism stressed personality, uniqueness, genius, and the fullest development of capabilities and talents.

individualism versus collectivism Individualismus und Kollektivismus

One dimension of cultural models like that of Geert Hofstede. It creates a scale with two extremes on which different cultures can located and compared.

In individualistic societies, ties between individuals are loose and individualistic behavior is valued highly. In collectivist societies, ties between individuals are tight, and the interests of groups are supposed to have precedence before those of the individual.

individualized targeting individualisiertes Targeting

induce herbeiführen; verursachen; veranlassen; *(to convince)* überreden

inducement Anreiz; Antrieb; Beeinflussung; Ansporn

inducement to buy Kaufanreiz

industrial industriell; gewerblich

industrial action Arbeitskampf

Coordinated action in an industrial dispute of employees, with or without the support of a trade union, attempting to force employers to agree to demands relating to wages, terms of employment, working conditions. etc. Common forms are: go slow, overtime ban, work-to-rule, sit-down strike or strike.

industrial goods Investitionsgüter; Industrieprodukte; Produktionsgüter

Goods bought by individuals and organizations for further processing or for use in conducting a business.

industrial marketing Industrielles Marketing

industrialism Industrialismus

industrialization Industrialisierung

industrialize industrialisieren

industrialized world industrialisierte Länder

industrial nation Industrieland; Industrienation; Industriestaat

industrial plant Industrieanlage; Industriebetrieb; Industriewerk

industrial relations Arbeitgeber-Arbeitnehmer-Beziehungen; Arbeitsbeziehungen

Area of labor relations concerned with the relationship between company management and workers, usually represented by a labor unions.

industry Industrie; Gewerbe; *(line of industry)* Branche; Industriezweig; Eifer; Bestreben

A group of businesses that share a common method of generating profits, such as the "automobile industry" or the "film industry".

It is also used to refer to an area of economic production focused on manufacturing which involves large amounts of capital investment before any profit can be realized, also called "heavy industry".

industry analysis Branchenanalyse

industry expert Industriefachmann; Industriefachfrau; Branchenkenner

industry forecast Industrieprognose

industry leader Industrieführer

industry show Industrieausstellung

industry spokesman Branchensprecher

ineffective unwirksam; wirkungslos; dienstunfähig

inefficient leistungsunfähig; unwirksam; unpraktisch

inefficient market unvollkommener Markt

Market in which prices do not reflect all available information.

inelastic demand unelastische Nachfrage

Total demand for a product that is not much affected by price changes, especially in the short run.

inept ungeeignet

inequality Ungleichheit; Uniformitätslosigkeit

inequity Ungerechtigkeit; Unfairness

inexpensive billig; preiswert

inexperienced unerfahren

infant industry junger, unterentwickelter Wirtschaftszweig

New industries in developing countries that must be temporarily protected from international competition to help them reach a position where they can compete on world markets with the firms of developed nations.

inferior untergebene Person; minderwertig; zweitklassig

inflate *(economy)* Inflation herbeiführen; *(prices)* hochtreiben; aufblähen; *(tire)* aufpumpen

inflation Inflation; Preissteigerung; Teuerung

Rise in the general level of prices, measured against some baseline of purchasing power. It may also be regarded as a decline in the purchasing power of money.

Inflation is measured by observing the change in the price of a large number of goods and services in an economy. These prices are combined to give a *price index* or *average price level*, the average price of the basket of products. The inflation rate is the rate of increase in this index.

inflation accounting inflationsbereinigte Rechnungslegung

A method of accounting that attempts to take account of the fact that a monetary unit does not have a constant value; due to the effects of inflation.

The principal methods of dealing with inflation are current cost accounting and current purchasing power accounting.

inflationary inflationär; inflationistisch; inflatorisch

inflationary factor Inflationsfaktor

inflationary pressure Inflationsdruck

inflationary tendency Inflationstendenz

inflation-escalator clause Inflationsanpassungsklausel

Clause in a contract providing for increases or decreases in price based on fluctuations in inflation which may be measured by the cost of living, production costs, and so forth.

inflation rate Inflationsrate

inflow Zugang; Zufluss; Zustrom

influence Einfluss; Einwirkung; Beeinflussung; *(to ~)* beeinflussen

influencer Beeinflusser

Marketing: Person whose views or advice carries some weight in making a final buying decision; they often help define specifications and also provide information for evaluating alternatives.

influential einflussreich

influx Zustrom

influx of funds Mittelzufluss

infomediary Info-Mediär

Intermediary business whose main source of revenue derives from capturing consumer information and developing detailed profiles of individual customers for use by third parties.

infomercial als Informationssendung getarnte Werbung

Television commercials that run as long as a typical television program designed to solicit a direct response. It is therefore a form of direct response marketing.

The ad response is delivered directly to television viewers through the television ad. In normal commercials, advertisers do not solicit a direct response from viewers, but, instead, brand their product in the market place amongst potential buyers.

inform mitteilen; informieren; benachrichtigen; *(to advise)* Auskunft geben; *(to brief)* unterrichten

informal formlos; zwanglos; informell; regelwidrig

informal group informelle Gruppe

Group that is neither formally structured nor organizationally determined; appears in response to the need for social contact.

Example: three employees from different departments who regularly eat lunch together.

informal network informales Netzwerk

informality Formlosigkeit; Zwanglosigkeit; Regelwidrigkeit

information Information; *(notification)* Benachrichtigung; Mitteilung; *(briefing)* Unterrichtung; *(knowledge)* Kenntnis; *(advice)* Auskunft

information-content effect informationsbedingte Kursentwicklung

Stock exchange: Phenomenon that the share price of a corporatioin tends to rise following the dividend signal.

information management Informationsmanagement; *(data processing)* Datenverwaltung

information overload Informationsüberlastung

Condition when information inflow exceeds an individual's processing capacity, thus creating a barrier to effective communication.

The demands of keeping up with e-mail, phone calls, faxes, meetings, and professional reading create an amount of information that is nearly impossible to process and assimilate.

information publishing Informationsveröffentlichung

Marketing: communication with the goal of disseminating persuasive information to create awareness, knowledge (cognitive step), and positive attitudes (attitude step).

information search Informationsbeschaffung

Stage of the buying process in which the consumer is tempted to search for more information; the consumer may simply have heightened attention or may go into active information search.

information technology Informationstechnologie

All activities concerned with technology and other aspects of managing and processing information, especially in large organizations.

In particular, IT deals with the use of computers and software to convert, store, protect, process, transmit, and retrieve information.

informativc lehrreich; aufschlussreich; informativ

informative advertising Informationswerbung; Aufklärungswerbung

Advertising used to inform consumers about a new product or feature and to build primary demand.

infrastructure Infrastruktur

The basic facilities, services, and installations needed for the proper functioning of an economy, such as transportation, communication, water and power supply, and institutions including schools and prisons.

Since infrastructure usually requires substantial investments and benefits the whole of a society, it is normally funded by the government using public money.

infrequent selten; nicht häufig

infringe verletzen; übertreten; *(to violate)* verstoßen; *(contract)* brechen

infringement Verstoß; Verletzung; Übergriff; Übertretung

inhabitant Einwohner

inherit erben

inheritance Erbschaft; Nachlass

initial *(letter)* Anfangsbuchstabe; Anfangs-; Erst-; anfänglich; *(to ~)* mit den Anfangsbuchstaben unterzeichnen

initial capital Anfangskapital

initial cost Anschaffungspreis

initial demand Ausgangsforderung

initial investment Erstinvestition

initial public offering (IPO) Börsengang

Securities: a company's first sale of stock to the public. The main purpose of an IPO is to raise capital for the corporation, but it also imposes heavy legal compliance and reporting requirements on the company.

IPOs generally involve one or more investment banks as underwriters. The company offering its shares, called the issuer, enters a contract with a lead underwriter to sell its shares to the public. The underwriter then approaches investors with offers to sell these shares

initial rate Einführungskurs

initial reserve Anfangsreserve

initial subscriber Erstzeichner

initiate Eingeweihter; Kenner; *(to ~)* einleiten; anbahnen; *(to introduce)* einführen; initiieren

initiating structure Aufgabenorientierung

Extent to which a leader is likely to define and structure his or her role and those of employees in the search for goal attainment. It includes behavior that attempts to organize work, work relationships, and goals.

initiation Initiierung

initiative Initiative

initiator Initiator; Urheber; Veranlasser; Anfänger; Beginner

Buying process: person who first suggests or thinks of the idea of buying a particular product or service.

injunction Vorschrift; *(judicial order)* einstweilige Verfügung

injure verletzen

injury Verletzung; *(damage)* Schaden

injustice Ungerechtigkeit; Unrecht

innovate Neuerungen einführen

innovation Neuerung; Innovation; *(innovating)* Einführung von Neuerungen

Marketing: Idea, product or technology that has been developed and marketed to customers who perceive it as novel or new. It is the result of a process of identifying, creating and delivering new products to the marketplace.

innovation strategy Innovationsstrategie

Strategy that emphasizes the introduction of major new products and services.

innovative neuerungsbereit; innovativ

innovative marketing innovatives Marketing

Principle of enlightened marketing which requires that a company seek real product and marketing improvements.

innovator Innovator; Neuerer; Erfinder

innovators Innovatoren

First 2.5% of consumers to purchase a product. They tend to be risk takers, eager to try new products (especially high-tech products), and with higher levels of education and income. They are very self-reliant, gaining information from experts and the press rather than from peers.

input *(data)* Eingabe; Input; *(materials)* Einsatzmenge

input data Eingabedaten; Inputdaten

input path Inputpfad

inquire *(letter)* anfragen; nachfragen; untersuchen; erbitten

inquiry Erkundigung; *(letter)* Anfrage; *(investigation)* Nachforschung; Ermittlung; Untersuchung

insecure unstabil; unsicher

insertion order Insertionsauftrag; Anzeigenauftrag

Advertising: printed order to run an advertisement campaign. It defines the campaign name, the web site receiving the order and the planner or buyer giving the order, the individual advertisements to be run (or who will provide them), the sizes of the advertisements, the campaign beginning and end dates, the CPM, the total cost, discounts to be applied, and reporting requirements and possible penalties or stipulations relative to the failure to deliver the impressions.

insider Eingeweihter; Mitglied; Zugehöriger

insider information Insider-Informationen; vertrauliche Informationen

Relevant information about a company that has not yet been made public. It is illegal for holders of this information to make trades based on it, however received.

insist bestehen auf; dringen auf

insistence Bestehen; Nachdruck

insolvency Insolvenz; Zahlungsunfähigkeit; Konkurs

A situation where a business entity has insufficient assets to cover the value of its liabilities, resulting in an inability to meet its financial obligations as they fall due.

insolvency proceedings Vergleichsverfahren; Konkursverfahren

insolvent Zahlungsunfähiger; insolvent; zahlungsunfähig

Person or company having insufficient assets to meet debts and liabilities.

inspect prüfen; besichtigen; untersuchen; inspizieren

inspection Prüfung; Inspektion; Untersuchung; *(on site)* Besichtigung

instability Unbeständigkeit; Instabilität

install installieren; *(office)* einsetzen; einrichten

installation Installierung; Aufstellung; Einbau *(factory)* Betriebseinrichtung; Anlage

installation cost Aufstellungskosten; Einbaukosten

installment *(payment)* Rate; *(publication)* Fortsetzung

installment credit Ratenkredit

installment payment Abzahlung

institute Institut; Anstalt; *(to~)* einrichten; einführen; *(to set in motion)* einleiten

institution Anstalt; Institut; Organ; Institution; *(order)* Einrichtung

institutional institutionell; einheitlich

institutionalization Institutionalisierung

Situation when an organization takes on a life of its own, apart from any of its members, and acquires immortality.

institutional market institutioneller Markt

Schools, hospitals, nursing homes, prisons and other institutions that provide goods and services to people in their care.

instruct anweisen; *(to teach)* unterrichten; unterweisen

instruction Anweisung; *(teaching)* Unterricht

instrument Instrument; Werkzeug; *(document)* Dokument; Urkunde; *(commercial)* Papier

instrumental behilflich; mitwirkend; dienlich

instrumental values instrumentelle Werte

Preferable modes of behavior or means of achieving one's terminal values. Examples are ambition, courage, persistence, politeness.

instruments Finanzierungsinstrumente

Financial securities, such as money market instruments or capital market instruments.

insufficient unzureichend; ungenügend

insurance Versicherung

A legal contract in which an insurer promises to pay a specified amount to the insured if a particular event occurs. The insured in exchange promises to pay an amount of money, the premium, either once or at regular intervals. The insured must also have an insurable interest.

The main branches of insurance are: accident insurance, fire insurance, holiday and travel insurance, household insurance, liability insurance, livestock and bloodstock insurance, loss-of-profit insurance, marine insurance, motor insurance, private health insurance, and property insurance.

insurance broker Versicherungsmakler

Someone who offers advice on insurance matters and arranges cover, on behalf of the client, with an insurer. His income comes from commission paid by the insurers.

insurance company Versicherungsgesellschaft; Versicherungsfirma

An organization engaged in the business of providing insurance cover to its customers in exchange for a fee, known as a premium. It also has to pay all legitimate claims that may arise from the insurance policy.

The risks covered include a very wide range, for example: accident, burial, casualty, credit life, contract performance, dental, disability, fidelity, fire, health, hospitalization, illness, life, malpractice, marine, mortgage, surety, wage protection and workers' compensation insurance.

insurance policy Versicherungspolice

A document that sets out the terms and conditions of an insurance contract, defining the benefits payable and the premium required.

insurance premium Versicherungsprämie; Versicherungsbeitrag

insure versichern

insured Versicherter

A person or company covered by an insurance policy.

insured value Versicherungswert

insurer Versicherer; Versicherungsträger

A person, company, or other organization that underwrites an insurance risk.

intangible immateriell; unfassbar; unangreifbar

intangible asset immaterielle Vermögenswerte

Any asset that can neither be seen nor touched, e.g. goodwill, patents, trademarks, and copyrights. The commercial value of intangible assets is often difficult to determine, even if it can be very substantial.

integrate eingliedern; (sich) integrieren

integrated circuit integrierter Schalkreis

The formal name for a computer chip, resulting from the integration of previously separate transistors, resistors and capacitors, all on a single chip.

integrated direct marketing integriertes Direktmarketing

Direct marketing campaigns that use multiple vehicles and multiple stages to improve response rates and profits, such as telemarketing, mailshots, and sweepstakes.

integrated logistics management integriertes Logistikmanagement

Physical distribution concept that recognizes the need for a firm to integrate its logistics system with those of its suppliers and customers. The aim is to maximize the performance of the entire distribution system.

integrated marketing communication (IMC) integrierte Marketingkommunikation

Comprehensive plan of communication that includes advertising, sales promotion, public relations, direct marketing, personal selling, and the rest of the marketing mix to provide maximum communication impact with stakeholders.

integrating mechanism integrierender Mechanismus

Mechanisms for achieving coordination between subunits within an organization.

integration Eingliederung; Integration; Zusammenschluss

integrative bargaining integrative Verhandlung

Negotiations that seek a settlement that is favourable to all parties. To succed the parties have to be open with information and candid about their concerns, and show sensitivity to the other's needs.

integrity Integrität

intellectual Intellektueller; Kopfarbeiter; intellektuell

intellectual abilities intellektuelle Fähigkeiten

Abilities required to do mental activities. Seven dimensions can be identified: number aptitude, verbal comprehension, perceptual speed, inductive reasoning, deductive reasoning, spatial visualization and memory.

intellectual property geistiges Eigentum

Products of the mind, such as books, music, computer software, designs, or technological know-how. Intellectual property can be protected by patents, copyrights, and trademarks.

intend beabsichtigen; vorhaben; wollen

intended use Verwendungszweck

intensive intensiv; konzentriert; intensiviert

intensive distribution intensiver Vertrieb

A distribution strategy aimed at using the maximum number of outlets in order to provide maximum brand exposure and consumer convenience. Examples are sweets, chewing gum, disposable razors, soft drinks.

intent Absicht; Ziel; *(resolution)* Vorsatz; *(meaning)* Bedeutung; Absicht; *(curious)* bedacht auf; gespannt

intention Absicht; *(resolution)* Vorsatz

interacting groups interagierende Gruppen

Groups in which members interact verbally and nonverbally with each other face-to-face. These groups often censor themselves and pressure individual members toward conformity of opinion.

interactionist view of conflict interaktionistischer Ansatz der Konfliktforschung

Belief that conflict is not only a positive force in a group but that it is absolutely necessary for a group to perform effectively.

interactive banner interaktiver Banner

Internet: most advanced stage of the banner. Some banners sense the position of the mouse on the web page and begin to animate faster as the user approaches. Other banners have built-in games. Still other banners have drop-down menus, check boxes, and search boxes to engage and empower the user to enter real-time information.

interactive banner advertisements interaktive Bannerwerbung

interactive marketing interaktives Marketing

Approach to marketing that uses different techniques to improve buyer-seller interaction. This includes telemarketing, direct response TV, and the Internet.

interbank transaction Interbankgeschäft

interest Interesse; *(on loan)* Zins; Zinsen; *(importance)* Bedeutung; *(to ~)* interessieren

The charge made for borrowing a sum of money. Calculated by applying an interest rate, which is expressed as a percentage of the total sum loaned for a specific period of time (usually one year). Thus, an interest rate of 10% per annum means that for every 100 € borrowed for one year, the borrower has to pay 10€ interest.

interest advantage Zinsvorteil

interest arbitrage Zins-Arbitrage

Dealings in foreign currencies between financial centers that take advantage of differentials in interest rates and between the forward and spot exchange rates.

Using these differntials, it becomes possible to make a profit by buying a foreign currency, changing it into the currency of the home market, lending it for a fixed period, and buying back the foreign currency on a forward basis.

interest arrears Zinsrückstände

interest bearing verzinslich; zinstragend

interest calculation Zinsberechnung

interest ceiling Höchstzinsen

interest charge Zinsaufschlag

interest coupon Zinsschein

interest coverage ratio Zinsdeckung

Earnings before interest and taxes divided by interest expense. Used to measure a firm's ability to par interest.

interest credit Zinsgutschrift

interest dependency Zinsabhängigkeit

interest difference Zinsdifferenz

interest differential Zinsabstand; Zinsunterschied; Zinsgefälle

interest expense Zinskosten

interest group Interessengruppe

People working together to attain a specific objective with which each is concerned.

interest income Zinseinkommen

interest level Zinsniveau

interest margin Zinsdifferenz; Zinsspanne

interest on debt Schuldzinsen; Sollzinsen

interest on deposits Bankzinsen; Habenzinsen

interest on interest Zinsen auf investierte Zinseinnahmen; Zinseszins

Interest earned on reinvestment of each interest payment on money invested.

interest on loan capital Darlehenzinsen

interest owed Zinsverpflichtung

interest payment Zinszahlung

interest policy Zinspolitik

interest rate Zinssatz; Zinsrate

Price paid for borrowing money. It can be defined as the rate of exchange of present consumption for future consumption, or the price of current cash in terms of future cash.

interest rate differential Zinssatzgefälle

interest rate increase Zinssatzerhöhung

interest rate on debt Kreditzinssatz

Firm's cost of debt capital. Also called return on the debt.

interest-rate-parity theorem Zinssatzparitäten-Theorie

Theorem that suggest that interest rate differential between two countries will be equal to the difference between the forward-exchange rate and the spot- exchange rate.

interest-rate risk Zinsrisiko

Chance that a change in the interest rate will result in a change in the value of a security.

interest rate swap Zinsswap

interest receipts Zinseinnahme

interest revenues Zinseinnahme

interest subsidy Abzugsfähigkeit der Fremdkapitalzinsen

Firm's deduction of the interest payments on its debt from its earnings before it calculates its tax bill.

interest yield Zinsertrag; Rendite

interfere sich einmischen; *(to impair)* beeinträchtigen; *(to step in)* einschreiten

interference Einmischung; *(intervention)* Eingriff; *(disturbance)* Störung

intergroup development Gruppenarbeit

Organizational development efforts to change the attitudes, stereotypes, and perceptions that groups have of each other.

interim Zwischenzeit; einstweilig; zwischenzeitlich; vorläufig

interim aid Überbrückungshilfe

interim payment Zwischenzahlung

interim ruling Übergangsregelung

interior Inneres; *(country)* Binnenland; Inland; innen-; binnen-; *(country)* binnenländisch; inländisch

intermediary Mittelsmann; Mittelsperson; Zwischenhändler; *(arbitration)* Vermittler; Schlichter; Mittelsmann

General: organization or person who helps to bring different parties such as buyers and sellers together.

Distribution: channel firms that help the company find customers or make sales to them, including wholesalers and retailers that buy and resell goods.

intermediate zwischen-; dazwischen liegend; schlichtend; *(to ~)* schlichten

intermediate goods Zwischenprodukte; Halbfabrikate

Any goods used as inputs in the production of other goods, for example partly finished goods or raw materials.

intermittent periodisch

intermittent reinforcement widerholte Verstärkung

Motivation technique that reinforces desired behavior often enough to make the behavior worth repeating, but not every time it is demonstrated.

internal innen-; intern; *(business)* innerbetrieblich; *(country)* einheimisch; inländisch

internal audit Innenrevision; interne Revision

Internal audits serve to inspect the way business is conducted, often commissioned by the board of directors.

The aims are: (1) to inspect the correctness, completeness and regularity of bookkeeping *(financial auditing),* and (2) to check the correct use of the various systems and processes, e.g. invoicing, inventory, ordering.

internal bond Inlandsanleihe

internal economic trend Binnenkonjunktur

internal efficiencies innerbetriebliches Leistungspotential

Reductions on expenses like marketing. etc. so as to effectively reduce total operations costs.

internal financing Innenfinanzierung

Financing that comes from internally generated cash flow. It is equal to: net income (after interest and taxes) plus depreciation minus dividends.

internal forward rate Terminkurs; Devisenterminkurs

Company-generated forecast of future spot rates.

internal marketing internes Marketing

Marketing by a service company to train and effectively motivate its customer-contact employees and all the supporting service people to work as a team to provide customer satisfaction.

internal rate of return (IRR) interner Zinsfuß (IZF)

Interest rate at which the net present value of a projected cash flow is zero. The IRR is a method of evaluating capital expenditure proposals.

The interest rate where the present values of cash inflows and outflows are equal, is the internal rate of return for a project under consideration. The decision to adopt a project depends on its size compared with the cost of capital.

internal records information Informationen auf Basis interner Aufzeichnungen

Information gathered from sources within the company to evaluate marketing performances and to detect marketing problems and opportunities.

internal services interne Dienstleistungen

Accounting: services that one cost center provides to another. If the services can be measured, then the internal services are calculated according to work reports. But if the exchange of services cannot be measured clearly, then the costs are apportioned according to a pre-established key.

international international

International Accounting Standards (IAS) Internationale Rechnungslegungsgrundsätze

Set of rules that serve to standardize valuation rules, presentation of results and the contents of annual reports. Their purpose is to make balance sheets, income statements and notes of annual reports comparable internationally. The main purpose of all IAS-rules is to show a true and fair view of the company.

There is no law that enforces IAS-rules in reporting, but investors, the media and banks ask more and more for presentations that are drawn up according to these rules.

The rules issued by the International Accounting Standards Committee always represent a compromise between the interpretations in different countries. This compromise is usually fixed as the minimum standard.

International Accounting Standards Committee (IASC) Internationaler Ausschuss für Rechnungslegungsgrundsätze

Organization of representatives of 106 professional accounting organizations from 79 countries that is attempting to harmonize accounting standards across countries.

International Bank for Reconstruction and Development (IBRD) „World Bank" Internationale Bank für Wiederaufbau und Entwicklung „Weltbank"

An international bank established in 1944 to help finance post-war reconstruction and to help raise standards of living in developing countries. It is owned by the governments of 151 countries. The headquarters of the Bank are in Washington.

The IBRD lends on broadly commercial terms, either for specific projects or for more general social purposes; funds are raised on the international capital markets.

International Commercial Terms (Incoterms) Internationale Regeln für die Auslegung von Handelsklauseln; Lieferbedingungen im Ausland

A series of international sales terms published by the International Chamber of Commerce that divide transaction costs and responsibilities between buyer and seller and define transportation practices.

<u>Group E - Departure:</u>

EXW: Ex Works (named place)

<u>Group F - Main Carriage Unpaid:</u>

FCA: Free Carrier (named place)

FAS: Free Alongside Ship (named loading port)

FOB: Free On Board (named loading port)

<u>Group C - Main Carriage Paid:</u>

CFR: Cost and Freight (named destination port)

CIF: Cost, Insurance and Freight (named destination port)

CPT: Carriage Paid To (named destination port)

CIP: Carriage and Insurance Paid to (named destination port)

<u>Group D - Arrival:</u>

DAF: Delivered At Frontier (named place)

DES: Delivered Ex Ship (named port)

DEQ: Delivered Ex Quay (named port)

DDU: Delivered Duty Unpaid (named destination place)

DDP: Delivered Duty Paid (named destination place).

international division internationale Abteilung

Form of international marketing organization in which the division handles all of the firm's international activities.

Marketing, manufacturing, research, planning and specialist staff are organized into operating units according to geography or product groups, or as an international subsidiary responsible for its own sales and profitability.

International Fisher Effect internationaler Fisher-Effekt

Theory that suggests that for any two countries, the spot exchange rate should change in an equal amount but in the opposite direction to the difference in nominal interest rates between countries

International Labor Organization (ILO) Internationale Arbeitsorganisation

A special agency of the United Nations, established under the Treaty of Versailles in 1919.

The aim of the ILO is to promote lasting peace through social justice. For this purpose it establishes international labor standards, runs a program of technical assistance to developing countries, and works against unemployment through its World Employment Program.

international markets Auslandsmärkte; Weltmarkt

Buyers in other countries, including consumers, producers, resellers and governments.

international marketing internationales Marketing

Marketing activities in more than one country at the same time. The main challenges are to deal with differences in culture, political, economic, social and technological conditions. If possible, companies try to standardize their approach in order to be efficient, where necessary they have to adapt to local conditions in order to still be effecive.

International Monetary Fund (IMF) Internationaler Währungsfond (IWF)

A specialized agency of the United Nations established in 1945 to promote international monetary cooperation, stabilize exchange rates, and help countries with short-term balance of payments difficulties.

The Fund is financed by subscriptions from its members, voting power is related to the amount of the contribution.

international shopping center internationals Einkaufszentrum; internationales Geschäftszentrum

Store cluster in the heart of an affluent and major international city. The international shopping center attracts shoppers from all over the country and the world.

Example: fashionable cities such as Paris, Tokyo, New York, Rome, Milan and London.

International Standards Organization (ISO) Internationale Organisation für Normung

An organization founded in 1946 to standardize measurements and other standards for industrial, commercial, and scientific purposes.

international strategy internationale Strategie

Attempts to create value by transferring core competencies to foreign markets where indigoenous competitors lack those competencies.

international trade Welthandel

The exchange of goods and services across international borders. In most countries, it represents a significant share of GDP.

International trade has existed throughout history, but with Industrialization, advanced transportation and globalization, its economic, social, and political importance has increasd in recent decades.

international unit internationale Einheit

Internet

The pyhsical network of computers acrsoss the globe, together with the infrastructure of network servers and communication links between them, which enables users to process and transport vast amounts of information.

Although often used synonymously, the Internet is not identical with the World Wide Web, which is only one application that runs on the Internet, like e-mail or FTP.

Internet service provider (ISP)

Company that provides internet access to an individual or organization on a commercial basis.

Internet Corporation for Assigned Names and Numbers (ICANN)

Organization responsible for the administration of the internet name and address system, resolving conflicts that surround the assignment and possession of domains.

internet marketing Internet-Marketing

Use of the internet and other digital technologies to achieve marketing objectives.

internet marketing metrics Internet-Marketing-Metriken

Internet Relay Chat (IRC)

Communication tool that allows a text-based 'chat' between different users who are logged on at the same time.

internet telephony Internettelefonie

Use of the internet to carry simultaneous digitized voice transmission. Also calle voice over IP (VOIP).

interpersonal skills interpersonelle Fähigkeiten

interrelation of media Medienverflechtung

interstitials Interstitials; Unterbrecherwerbung

Internet: advertisements that are usually included within a 'pop-up window'; Java-based ads that appear while the publisher's content is loading.

interval Intervall, Zeitabstand

intervene einschreiten; sich einschalten; intervenieren

intervention Einschreiten; Einmischung; Eingreifen; *(central bank)* Intervention; *(mediation)* Vermittlung

intervention price Interventionskurs

interview Gespräch; Unterredung; *(media)* Interview; Befragung; *(job)* Vorstellungsgespräch; *(to ~)* befragen; interviewen

interviewee Befragter; Interviewter

interviewer Befrager; Interviewer

in the money im Geld

Investment: Describes an option whose exercise would produce profits, for a "call" option if the strike price is less than the market price of the underlying security. A "put" option is in-the-money if the strike price is greater than the market price of the underlying security.

Example: an xyz "call" option with a 52 strike price is in-the-money when xyz trades at 52 1/8 or higher. An xyz "put" option with a 52 strike price is in-the-money when xyz is trading at 51 7/8 or lower.

intranet Intranet

Private corporate network built with internet-based protocols and software applications, in order to deliver information to a closed group of its own employees and possibly stockholders and customers.

intrapreneur Entrepreneuer in einem Unternehmen

Employee of a business who introduces and implements a significant innovation for a firm.

introduce einführen; *(to make acquainted)* bekannt machen; vorstellen; *(politics)* Gesetzesentwurf einbringen

introduction Einführung; Einleitung; *(recommendation)* Empfehlung; *(presentation)* Vorstellung

introduction stage Einführungsphase

Product life-cycle stage when the new product is first distributed and made available for purchase.

intuition Intuition; Einsicht

Feeling not necessarily supported by facts that could suggest the possible occurrence of an event in advance.

intuitive decision making intuitive Entscheidungsfindung

Unconscious process created out of distilled experience, that does not necessarily operate independently of rational analysis; rather, the two complement each other. In such a case, a person could take a decision based on his past experience and intuition.

invalid Invalide; Körperbehinderter; *(not valid)* ungültig; unwirksam; abgelaufen

invalidate ungültig machen; außer Kraft setzen

invalidity Ungültigkeit; Unwirksamkeit; Invalidität; Behinderung

invent erfinden; ausdenken

invention Erfindung

New technology or product that may or may not deliver benefits to customers.

inventiveness Erfindungsgabe

inventor Erfinder; Entwicklung

inventory Inventar; Bestand; Lagerbestand; *(inventory taking)* Inventur; Bestandsaufnahme

The quantity of goods or materials on hand, either raw materials, items available for sale, or in the process of being made ready for sale.

inventory control Bestandskontrolle

inventory cost Lagerkosten

inventory financing Lagerfinanzierung

Technique of obtaining capital for a business by borrowing money with inventory used as collateral.

inventory loan Vorratskredit

Secured short-term loan to purchase inventory.

inventory management Lagerverwaltung

inventory turnover Inventarumschlag; Lagerumschlag

Ratio of annual sales to inventory. Low turnover is an unhealthy sign, indicating excess stocks and/or poor sales.

inventory turnover ratio Umschlaghäufigkeit der Vorräte

Ratio of annual gains to average inventory that measures how quickly inventory is produced and sold.

inventory valuation Bestandsbewertung

The valuation of stocks of raw material, work in progress, and finished goods. Depending on the purpose that a inventory valuation serves (for fiscal/balance sheet valuation or business analysis), various methods can be employed. Among them are: valuing stocks at cost, the first-in-first-out method, the average cost method, the last-in-first-out method, the next-in-first-out method.

invest investieren; anlegen

investigate untersuchen; ermitteln; nachprüfen

investigation Untersuchung; Nachprüfung; Ermittlung

investigation fee Untersuchungsgebühr

investigator Prüfer; Untersucher; Untersuchungsbeamter

investment Anlage; Investition; Investierung; Investment

Capital investment: the purchase of capital goods, such as plant and machinery in a factory in order to produce goods for future consumption. The higher the level of capital investment in an economy, the faster it will grow.

Financial investment: the purchase of assets, such as securities, works of art, bank and building-society deposits, etc., with a primary view to their financial return, either as income or capital gain.

investment adviser Anlageberater

investment analyst Analyst

Someone employed by a stockbroker, bank, insurance company etc., to give advice on investments.

Investment analysits use a variety of techniques, such as technical analysis or fundamental analysis, in order to predict expected trends.

investment bank Anlagebank; Effektenbank

A bank that advises companies on mergers and acquisitions and provides finance for industrial corporations by buying shares in a company and selling them in relatively small lots to investors.

investment banker Anlagebankier; Effektenbankier

investment capital Anlagekapital

investment company Investmentgesellschaft; Anlagegesellschaft

investment cycle Investitionszyklus

investment decision Investitionsentscheidung; Anlageentscheidung

investment fund Investmentfonds

A resource managed on behalf of its clients for the purpose of maximizing the profit on invested capital. Many funds are of a specialized nature, with the portfolio representing a particular industry or country

Investment funds are listed on US and foreign exchanges. The market price may exceed the net asset value per share, in which case it is considered at a "premium." When the market price falls below the NAV/share, it is at a "discount."

investment gap Investitionslücke

investment grade bond für Investitionen empfohlene Papiere

Debt that is rated BBB and above by Standard & Poor's or Baa and above by Moody's.

investment in securities Wertpapieranlage

investment level Investitionshöhe

investment loan Investitionskredit

investment of assets Vermögensanlage

investment period Anlagedauer

investment plan Investitionsprogramm; Anlageplan

investment portfolio Wertpapierbestand; Wertpapierdepot; Effektenbestand

investment premium Investitionsprämie

investment project Investitionsvorhaben

investment proposal Investitionsantrag

investment quota Investitionsquote

investment return Kapitalertrag

investment tip Anlagetip

investment trust Investitionsgesellschaft

A company that invests the funds provided by shareholders in securities and attempts to make a profit from the income and capital gains provided by these securities.

The advantages for shareholders are: spreading the risk of investment and making use of professional managers. Investment trusts, which are not usua1ly trusts in the usual sense, bur private or public limited companies, differ from unit trusts in that in the latter the investors buy units in the fund but are not shareholders.

investor Kapitalanleger; Geldanleger; Geldgeber; Investor; Kapitalgeber; Eigenkapitalgeber

invoice Rechnung; Faktura; Quittung

Bill written by a seller of goods or services and submitted to the purchaser.

IOU ("I owe you") Schuldschein

irredeemable nicht einlösbar; nicht tilgbar

irrevocable unwiderruflich; endgültig

IS/LM curve IS/LM-Kurve

Graph that summarizes a major part of Keynesian macroeconomics.

The horizontal axis represents national income and is labelled **Y**. The vertical axis represents the interest rate **i**.

The **IS** schedule is drawn as a downward-sloping curve and equals an economy's total output and income. The initials **IS** stand for **I**nvestment/**S**aving equilibrium.

The **LM** schedule is an upward-sloping curve representing the role of finance and money. The initials **LM** stand for **L**iquidity preference/**M**oney supply equilibrium.

The graph thus represents the interface between the "real" and the "monetary" parts of the economy.

isolate isolieren; absondern

isolates isolierte Atome; Isolate

Individuals who are not connected to a social network.

isolation Isolierung; Absonderung

isolationism Isolationspolitik

isolationist Isolationspolitiker

issuance Ausgabe; *(securities)* Emission; *(document)* Ausstellung

issue *(check, document)* Ausstellung; *(book)* Ausgabe; *(debate)* Kernpunkt; *(securities)* Emission; *(to ~)* ausstellen; *(to distribute)* austilen; *(to publish)* herausgeben; *(securities)* emittieren

Securities: the number of shares or the amount of stock on offer to the public at a particular time.

issue price Ausgabekurs; Ausgabepreis

Securities: the price at which a new issue of shares is sold to the public. In public issue, the issue price is fixed by the company on the advice of its stock- brokers and bankers; in an issue by tender the issue price is fixed by the highest bidder.

issuer Aussteller, *(book)* Verleger; *(securities)* Emittent

Securities: a financial institution, usually an investment bank, that specializes in the flotation of private companies on a stock exchange.

item Gegenstand; *(accounting)* Posten; *(topic)* Punkt; *(newspaper)* Notiz

itemization Detaillierung; Aufzählung; Verzeichnung

itemized account Postenkonto

itemized billing Einzelabrechnung

itinerary Reiseroute

J

Jaques, Elliott (1917-2003)

Canadian psychologist who became famous for his work on the psychological and social factors in group behavior.

He developed a theory of measuring the value of work by the time span of 'discretion'. He pioneered the 'working-through' process. Later he developed a theory of bureaucracy in which progression up an organization was described with increasing levels of discretion.

Biography: Graduate of the University of Toronto and Johns Hopkins Medical School, served as a major in the Royal Canadian Army, founder member of the Tavistock Institute of Human Relations in London, an organization that did pioneering work on the sociology of industry and management.

Major publications: (1951) The changing culture of a factory, (1956) The measurement of responsibility, (1965), Glacier project papers, (1976) A general theory of bureaucracy, (1982) Free enterprise, fair employment, (1989) Requisite organization.

jargon Jargon

Specialized terminology or technical language that members of a group use to aid communication among themselves.

java

Programming language created by Sun Microsystems capable of operating on many different operating systems.

Java offers a number of advantages for internet developers and users and offers built-in security features that make it safer for computer users to download unfamiliar applications

JavaScript

Unrelated to Java, JavaScript is a relatively simple text-based scripting language that can be embedded in HTML documents. JavaScript lets developers add special effects to web pages.

J-curve J-Kurve

Economics: graph describing a turnaround in a trend, such as sales figures. The initial trend continues for a while, then bottoms out and turns up the right side of the J.

jeopardize gefährden

job Arbeit; *(occupation)* Beruf; Beschäftigung; Job; *(position)* Arbeitsstelle

job analysis Stellenanalyse

Analysis of a position in an organization to determine the responsibilities related to the position and the qualifications needed to fulfill its responsibilities.

job applicant Stellenbewerber; Arbeitsuchender

jobber Großhändler; Börsenhändler; Aktienhändler; Gelegenheitsarbeiter

A middleman who buys large quantities of a product from a wholesaler and sells smaller quantities to a retailer. A jobber takes title to the goods and then resells them, whilst a broker or an agent sells goods on someone else´s behalf.

job characteristics model (JCM) Modell der Arbeitsplatzmerkmale

Model developed by Hackman and Oldahm, that identifies five job characteristics (skill variety, task identity, task significance, autonomy, and feedback) and their relationship to personal and work outcomes (employee motivation, performance, and satisfaction).

job classification Stellenklassifizierung

A method designed to create a hierarchy of jobs based on such factors as skill, responsibility or experience, time and effort for the purposes of work comparison and wage comparability.

job description Stellenbeschreibung; Aufgabengebiet

A summary of the most important features of a job, describing its general nature, including duties and responsibilities, and details such as required skill, effort, responsibility and working conditions.

job design Arbeitsgestaltung; Strukturierung der Arbeitsaufgaben

job enlargement horizontale Aufgabenerweiterung; Erweiterung des Aufgabengebietes

Increasing the number and variety of tasks that an individual performs, resulting in jobs with more diversity.

job enrichment vertikale Aufgabenbereicherung; Bereicherung des Aufgabengebietes; Arbeitsbereicherung

Attempts to make jobs more rewarding and less monotonous for the individual worker, including expanding job responsibilities and giving increased control.

job involvement Arbeitsmentalität

Degree to which a person identifies himself with his job, actively participates in it, and considers his performance important to self-worth. High levels of job involvement have been found to be related to lower resignation rates.

job loss Stellenverlust

job market Arbeitsmarkt

job market condition Arbeitsmarktlage

job offer Stellenangebot

job protection Kündigungsschutz

job rotation systematischer Arbeitsplatzwechsel; systematischer Aufgabenwechsel; Stellentausch

A technique of career development where an individual is moved through a schedule of assignments designed to give him a breadth of exposure to the entire organization.

job satisfaction Arbeitszufriedenheit

Term used to describe how content an individual is with his job, expressed in a sense of joy, inner fulfillment and pride.

job security Arbeitsplatzsicherheit

Feeling of an employee of being safely established in his job. Some professions, such as the government civil service, have greater job security than others in the private sector.

job sharing Arbeitsplatzteilung; Teilzeit

Arrangement in which the responsibilities and hours of one job position are carried out by two people. Can be used as an alternative to layoffs.

job specification Qualifikationsanforderungen

Stating the minimum acceptable qualification that an employee must possess to perform a given job successfully. Job specification keeps the attention of those doing the selection on the list of qualifications necessary for an incumbent to perform a job and assists in determining whether or not candidates are qualifies.

job training Training; Einarbeitung

join sich vereinigen; sich verbinden; *(an association)* beitreten

joint account Gemeinschaftskonto

joint ownership Gemeinschaftseigentum; Miteigentum

Joint venture: a company joins investors in a foreign market to create a local business in which the company shares joint ownership and control.

joint photographic experts group (JPEG)

One of the two most common image types used on the web [GIF and JPEG], used mostly for photographic reproductions. The format allows for some degradation in image quality to enable more rapid download; also referred to as jpg.

joint stock company (US) Kapitalgesellschaft

Form of business organization in the US that combines features of a corporation and a partnership. They are recognized as corporations, but with unlimited liability for their stockholders.

joint venture Joint-Venture; Gemeinschaftsunternehmen

A commercial undertaking entered into by two or more parties. One can distinguish between equity joint ventures, when a separate company is set up, and non-equity joint ventures, when the parties just cooperate on a project basis.

The parties in a joint venture often carry on their principal businesses independently of each other. Joint ventures are becoming increasingly common as companies cooperate with each other in international markets, in order to share costs, exploit new technologies, or gain access to new markets

journal Journal; Zeitschrift; Tagebuch

Accounting: book, typically to record accounting transactions as they occur.

journal entry Journalbuchung; Grundbuchung; Tagebucheintragung

Accounting: recording of a transaction in an accounting journal, such as the general journal. The journal entry has equal debit and credit amounts, and it usually includes a one-sentence explanation of the purpose of the transaction.

journeyman Geselle

judge Richter; *(to ~)* richten; *(to evaluate)* beurteilen; urteilen

judgment Urteil; *(verdict)* Urteilsspruch; *(ability to judge)* Urteilsvermögen; *(opinion)* Ansicht

judicial gerichtlich; richterlich; kritisierend

judiciary committee Rechtsausschuss

jump Sprung; *(to ~) (price)* sprunghaft steigen

jump page Weiterleitungsseite

Internet: webpage whose primary purpose is to allow one to "jump" to another location. When a visitor clicks on a link and instead of being immediately linked to that site, they are first shown a "jump page" which reminds them that they are leaving the original site.

junior staff member Nachwuchskraft

junk bond hochverzinsliche Risikoanleihe

Bond with a credit rating of BB or lower that carries higher risk of interest or principal default. Junk bonds are often issued in leveraged buyouts and other takeovers.

junk mail Massenwerbepost; Papierkorbpost

Unsolicited mail often distributed by mass marketers. The response rate tends to be very low.

Juran, Joseph (* 1904)

Electrical engineer who believed that company-wide quality cannot be delegated. He worked contemporaneously with W. Edwards Deming on pioneering the quality revolution in post-war Japan. Juran published his Quality Control Handbook in 1951, the first manual of its kind, and was invited to Japan in 1954.

Biography: born in Romania, in 1924 he joined Western Electric, the manufacturing division of Bell Telephone System to work with Walter A. Shwehart on developing a method for controlling quality in manufacturing, in the 1950s he taught his quality philosophy in Japan, and since has acted as a consultant to many leading companies.

Major publications: (1951) Quality control handbook, (1988) Juran on planning for quality, (1989) Juran on leadership for quality: an executive handbook, (1992) Juran on quality by design.

jurisdiction Rechtsprechung; Gerichtsbezirk; *(local authority)* Zuständigkeit

Legal term that describes the ability of a court or other authority to gain control over a party through the power, right, or authority to interpret and apply laws or decisions.

Example: the U.S. Court of Appeals has exclusive jurisdiction to review decisions of the U.S. tax court and the U.S. District Courts, and the U.S. Court of Appeals of the Federal Circuit has jurisdiction over decisions from the U.S. Court of Federal Claims.

jurisprudence Rechtswissenschaft; Jurisprudenz

The science of law, including the principles, the rules, the processes, and the application; sometimes a synonym for law.

jurist Jurist

jury *(court)* Geschworenenkollegium; Geschworene; Schiedsrichter

A group of persons convened to render a verdict on a legal question, often composed of the peers of the parties or a cross section of society.

just gerecht; angemessen; *(barely)* gerade; *(only)* nur

just in time (JIT) production verwendungssynchrone Produktion; just-in-time Produktion

An approach to manufacturing that seeks to improve all performance variables, such as cost, quality, speed, dependability, and flexibility. As a result, it can reduce waste, queues and bottlenecks, the effects of poor product design, excess transport, better inventories, motion, and scrap.

Some of the key elements of JIT are: respect for the contribution that employees can make; encouragement of personal responsibility and process ownership from a multiskilled workforce; a demand- pull system in which material only flows when needed; *kanban;* standardized product design; accelerated learning-curve effects; preventive rather than reactive maintenance; level scheduling; reduction of set-up times; efficient plant layout; JIT purchasing; close liaison with suppliers; and total quality management committed to continuous improvement.

just-in-time inventory control (JIT) fertigungssynchrone Lagerkontrolle; Just-in-time Bestandskontrolle

Close cooperation between producers and suppliers in order to optimize the relationship between production and sales levels with inventory, thus reducing carrying costs.

Inventory 1evels are monitored and maintained through a computerized system ranging from the POS to the manufacturers.

justice Gerechtigkeit; *(law)* Recht; *(legal system)* Justizwesen; Gericht; *(judge)* Richter

justification Rechtfertigung; *(authorization)* Berechtigung; *(reason)* Begründung

justify rechtfertigen; *(to give reasons)* begründen

Kk

Kaizen

Japanese word made up from the two kanji-signs "kai" (to change) and "zen" (goodness), means striving after constant, systematic and gradual improvement. Kaizen is an approach that acknowledges the importance of people, since it promotes the motivation of the employees and their identification with the tasks they are performing. It does this by giving them the opportunity to share in the development of processes.

The most important element in continuous improvement is the workshop. There the participants under the guidance of a specially trained moderator, who analyses the work processes in use and work out possible improvements where weaknesses have been exposed. The participants themselves generally implement the solutions they have proposed directly after the end of the workshop.

Kanban

A Japanese method of controlling the movement of materials through a just-in-time system. Literally meaning 'visual record'.

Kanter, Rosabeth Moss (* 1943)

US sociologist who established herself as a leading authority on managing change, developing the 'post-entrepreneurial' corporation and 'empowering' human potential in organizations.

Kantar's award-winning book *Men and women of the corporation* (1977) analysed the bureaucratic factors that locked people into pre-determined roles in an industrial corporation, and how this prevented the business from fully tapping the talent within it.

Biography: born in Cleveland, Ohio, Kanter graduated from the University of Michigan, taught at Brandeis University and from 1973 at Harvard, Yale and MIT, in 1988 acted as a key economic adviser to US presidential candidate Michael Dukakis.

Major publications: (1977) Men and women of the corporation, (1983) The change masters: corporate entrepreneurs at work, (1989) When giants learn to dance, (1992) The challenge of organizational change, (1995) World class: thriving locally in the global economy, (1997)

Kaplan, Robert S (* 1940)

Co-inventor of the 'balanced business scorecard', a new kind of performance-measurement tool which allows businesses to measure their non-financial as well as financial results, covering such soft but essential areas of customer satisfaction, quality and product cycle times and effectiveness of new product development.

Biography: graduated in electrical engineering from MIT, taught at Carnegie-Mellon University, from 1984 at Harvard Business School.

Major publications: (1992 with D.P. Norton), 'The balanced scorecard: measures that drive performance', Harvard Business Review (Jan/Feb), (1993 with D.P. Norton), 'Putting the balanced scorecard to work), Harvard Business Review (Sept/Oct), (1996) The Balanced scorecard: translating strategy into action.

kbps (kilobits per second)

Measurement of data transfer rates; abbreviation for *thousands of bits per second.*

keen *(competition)* scharf; hart; eindringlich; aufgeweckt

keeping an account Kontoführung

keep ready bereithalten

Keiretsu

Japanese word which means headless combine. The name is given to a firm of corporate structure in which a number of organizations link together. Outside Japan, the word keiretsu became attached to any loose network of alliances between more than two organizations.

key Schlüssel; *(index)* Kennziffer; *(office machines)* Taste

key account Großkunde; Hauptauftraggeber

key account manager Großkundenleiter; Großkundenberater

Managers whose primary responsibility is to orchestrate the company's relationship with a major customer or prospective customer in order to achieve liaisoning and mutually beneficial exchange between the two parties.

key-area evaluation Beurteilung nach Schlüsselbereichen

Evaluation of management in eight key areas, suggested by management theorist Peter Drucker, who argued that an organization needs to have result-oriented objectives in at least eight key areas: market standing, productivity, profitability, physical and financial resources, innovation, manager performance and development, worker performance and attitudes, and public and social responsibility.

keyboard Tastatur

key buyer Hauptkäufer

key country Schlüsselland

key competitive factors zentrale Wettbewerbsfaktoren

key currency Leitwährung

key issue Hauptthema; Schlüsselfrage

Keynes, John Maynard (1883 – 1946)

An English economist, and mathematician, who became highly influential. In his book The General Theory of Employment, Interest, and Money (1936) he legitimized countercyclical political economy by providing an analytical justification for increasing government spending and decreasing taxation during hard economic times. In post-war Western economies this became an important theoretical justification for justifying state interference.

Keynesian economics keynesianische Wirtschaftstheorie

The body of economic thought originated by John Maynard Keynes. Essentially he argued that insufficient demand causes unemployment and that excessive demand results in inflation; government should therefore manipulate the level of aggregate demand by adjusting levels of government expenditure and taxation.

To avoid a depression, for example, Keynes advocated increased government spending and easy money, resulting in more investment, higher employment, and increased consumer spending.

key personnel Schlüsselpersonal

key position Schlüsselstellung

key rates Referenzsatz; Leitzinssatz

Term used for the wage rates of those occupations in the internal labor market which act as points of contact with the external market. Associated with each key rate is a job cluster; a set of associated rates for occupations of varying job content and description which are specific to the firm.

key series Hauptserie; Schlüsselserie

keywords Suchwörter; Keywords

Internet: text within an HTML file summarizing the content of the site and relevant keywords (keyword meta-tag), which are matched against the keywords typed into search engines; words listed on search engine catalogs that tell the search engines how to catalog their site so that readers can find it.

Example: if a site provides consumer information about children's safety belts, it would probably like to be listed under the following: car safety, automobile safety, infant seats, seat belts, safety equipment.

kilobit

One thousand bits; abbreviated as Kb

kit Werkzeugtasche; Werkzeugausstattung; *(unassembled components)* Zusammenbauausrüstung

kite ungedeckter Scheck; Gefälligkeitswechsel

Bill, often called "accommodation bill" drawn on a person who has received nothing in return. It is an expedient for getting credit for a short period.

knockdown Preissturz; *(machinery)* zerlegbar

know-how praktisches Wissen; Fachwissen; Knowhow

knowledgeable kenntnisreich

knowledge-based trust wissensbasiertes Vertrauen

Concept based on behavioral predictability that comes from a history of interaction. It exists when one has adequate information about someone to understand them well enough to be able to accurately predict their likely behavior. This knowledge develops over time, largely as a function of experience that builds confidence of trustworthiness and predictability.

knowledge management Wissensmanagement

Process through which organizations generate value from their intellectual and knowledge-based assets. Most often, generating value from such assets involves sharing them among employees, departments and even with other companies in an effort to devise best practices.

Kondratiev waves Kondratieff-Zyklen

Regular cycles in the modern world economy. Fifty to sixty years in length, they alternate between periods of high sectoral growth with periods of slower growth.

Kotler, Philip(* 1931)

Economist, mathematician and sociologist who became the world's leading authority on marketing. He has distilled the essence of his work in simple concepts, and argues that marketing is basically a matter of exchange in different contexts. That is 'the art of creating genuine customer value' and of 'filling needs profitably'.

Biography: born in Chicago, studied economics at the University of Chicago under Milton Friedman and at the MIT under Paul Samuelson, found his passion for marketing during a post-doctoral year at the Harvard Business School, later became professor of marketing at the Northwestern University, Illinois.

Major publications: (1967) Marketing management: analysis, planning, implementation and control, (1969 with S.J. Levy) 'Broadening the concept of marketing', (1980) Principles of marketing

Kotter, John P. (* 1947)

American academic whose work is predominantly associated with the leadership of organizations. He has made detailed studies of what differentiates leaders from managers.

He sets his research firmly in a corporate framework. For him leadership is a 'process' that sets off hundreds or thousands of 'leadership acts' within the organization. The primary function of leadership is to produce change. He defined the differences between leadership and management and the relationship between the two. Organizations need strong management and strong leadership to succeed, so that no bureaucracy develops.

Biography: graduate in electrical engineering of Massachusetts Institute of Technology, recipient of a master's degree in management from the Sloan School, Harvard, doctorate in organizational behavior, Harvard professor and since 1990 Konosuke Matsushita chair of leadership at Harvard Business School

Major publications: (1982/1990) Harvard Business Review, (1982) The General Managers, (1987) The Leadership Factor, (1990) A Force for Change, (1992) Corporate Culture and Performance, (1996) Leading Change, (1997) Matshusita Leadership

L

lab Laboratorium; Labor

label Etikett; *(brand)* Marke; *(to ~)* etikettieren; beschildern; kennzeichnen

labeling Etikettieren; Kennzeichnen

labeling laws Etikettierungsgesetz; Auszeichnungsvorschriften

Laws and regulations that prescribe the information that has to be supplied on labels, as well as safe packaging and warning labels on hazardous materials.

labor *(work)* Arbeit; *(workforce)* Arbeitskräfte

Profession: physical or mental work performed for remuneration.

Social: group or class of people who work for others performing particular jobs in organizations.

labor conflict Arbeitskonflikt

labor costs Arbeitskosten; Lohnkosten

labor court Arbeitsgericht

labor dispute Arbeitskampf

Conflict between a company´s management and its workers over the terms and conditions of employment, including: job security; working conditions, wages, job descriptions, and fringe benefits.

laborer ungelernter Arbeiter

labor force Erwerbsbevölkerung; Erwerbstätige

Economics: the number of people over 16 years of age who are gainfully employed, as calculated by statistical offices. In 2004, there were approximately 145 million men and women in the U.S. *labor force*, out of a total population of 285 million.

labor intensive arbeitsintensiv

Production process in which labor costs are more important than capital costs. *Example:* coal mining and computer programming are more labor intensive than manufacturing computer chips.

labor judge Arbeitsrichter

labor law Arbeitsrecht

labor market Arbeitsmarkt

labor organization Gewerkschaftsorganisation; Arbeiterorganisation

labor rate Lohntarif

labor relations Arbeitgeber/Arbeitnehmer-Verhältnis

labor union Gewerkschaft

An organization of employees formed to bargain with the employer in order to protect the interests of workers against that of management.

lack Mangel; Fehlen; Knappheit; *(to ~)* fehlen

lacking Mangel; fehlend; mangelnd

lading Ladung

Laffer curve Laffer-Kurve

A curve, named for U.S. economist Arthur Laffer, relating tax rates and total tax revenues. It shows that first, increases in the marginal tax rate raise total tax revenue, but eventually, a tax rate is reached beyond which total tax revenues decrease.

lag Verzögerung; Rückstand; *(to ~)* zurückbleiben

laggards Nachzügler; Bummler; Schlepper

Last 16% of buyers of new products who often adopt a product when newer products have already been introduced. They are very traditional and generally of lower socioeconomic status.

lagging indicators Spätindikatoren

Market indicators describing the general trend of an economy, either confirming or denying the trend implied by the leading indicators.

Lagging indicators are: unemployment rate, corporate expenditures, labor cost per unit, loans outstanding, bank interest rates and book value of trade inventories.

lag strategy Verzögerungsstrategie

Delaying the collection of foreign currency receivables if that currency is expected to appreciate, and delaying payables if that currency is expected to depreciate.

Laissez-faire Laissez-faire

Economic policy demanding that interference of government in business and economic affairs should be minimal. Adam Smith's *The Wealth of Nations* (1776) described laissez-faire economics in terms of an invisible hand that would provide for the maximum good for all if businessmen were free to pursue profitable opportunities as they saw them.

land Land; Ländereien; Grundbesitz; Erde; *(to ~)* landen

landholding Grundbesitz; Grund besitzend

Landing, Storage, Delivery (LSD) Löschung, Einlagerung, Auslieferung

landlord Wirt; Mietsherr; Verpächter; Hauswirt; Grundbesitzer

The owner of a house, apartment, condominium, or land which he rents or leases to another individual or business, called the tenant. The landlord retains title to the property, but the rights of the tenant, or *lessee,* are spelled out in a lease.

landowner Grundbesitzer; Grundeigentümer

landownership Grundbesitzertum

land register Grundbuch

language Sprache; *(manner of speech)* Redeweise; *(terminology)* Terminologie

language barrier Sprachenschranke

lapse Verfall; *(contract)* Erlöschen; *(manners)* Entgleisung; *(to ~)* verfallen; erlöschen

large city Großstadt

large company Großfirma

large credit Großkredit

large order Großauftrag

large plant Großanlage

large-sized großformatig

large truck Laster

last Ende; Lebensdauer; *(in a series)* letzt; *(prior)* vorig; *(to ~)* reichen; dauern

last in, first out (LIFO) LIFO-Methode; zuletzt hinein, zuerst hinaus

A method of valuing inventory which assumes that the last articles bought are the first ones to be used or sold. Items in inventory at the end of the year are treated as though they had been in the opening inventory, plus or minus acquisitions during the year. During a period of rising inventory prices, LIFO leads to lower income.

last split letzte Zuteilung

After a stock split, the number of shares distributed for each share held and the date of the distribution.

late spät; verspätet; *(deceased)* verstorben

late majority späte Mehrheit

Consumers comprising the next 34% to adopt new products, after innovators, early adopters, and early majority. These people are sceptical and generally purchase a product only after their friends already have done so. They adopt because of the desire to conform to group norms.

late-mover advantage Nachzüglervorteil

Benefits enjoyed by a company that is late to enter a new market, such as consumer familiarity with the product or knowledge gained about a market.

latent defect verdeckter Mangel

A defect which is not immediately apparent, i.e. hidden from knowledge and from sight, and normally would not be discovered. If it is discovered, the buyer may later claim misrepresentation.

lateral Neben-; seitlich

lateral partnerships laterale Partnerschaft

Competitors, not-for-profit organizations, or governments that join with the firm for some common goal but not for transactions.

lateral thinking laterales Denken

A term coined by Edward de Bono, defined as methods of thinking concerned with changing concepts and perception.

lateral transfer gleichwertiger Austausch; Konzernüberweisung

lathe Drehbank

latitude Ausdehnung; *(geog)* Breite; *(freedom of action)* Handlungsfreiheit; Spielraum

launch *(to ~)* *(boat)* zu Wasser lassen; vom Stapel lassen; *(enterprise)* gründen; *(product)* herausbringen; *(campaign)* starten.

launching Herausbringen; Starten; *(nautical)* Stapellauf; Gründen; Barkasse; Abschluss

law Gesetz; Gesetzgebung

lawful legal; rechtsgemäß; *(legitimate)* rechtmäßig; *(valid in law)* rechtsgültig; *(judicial)* rechtlich

lawmaker Gesetzgeber

law of diminishing returns Ertragsgesetz; Gesetz der abnehmenden Erträge

Economics: short form of diminishing marginal returns, the concept that each additional unit of input produces increasingly less additional output. Also known as the law of increasing opportunity cost.

law office Anwaltsfirma

law of increasing costs Gesetz der steigenden Kosten

Related to the law of diminishing returns, it states that, as the productivity of a factor of production decreases with increasing production, the cost of successive units produced must increase.

law of instrumentality Mitwirkungsrecht

law of one price (LOP) Gesetz des identischen Preises

In competitive markets free of transportation costs and barriers to trade, identical products sold in different countries must sell for the same price when their price is expressed in the same currency.

law of supply and demand Gesetz von Angebot und Nachfrage

The law in economics stating that in any free market the relationship between supply and demand determines price and the quantity produced. A change in either will lead to changes in price and/or amount produced in order to achieve equilibrium in the market.

law student Jurastudent

lawsuit Rechtsprozess; Rechtsstreit

A civil action brought before a court, in which the party commencing the action, the plaintiff, seeks a legal remedy. If the plaintiff is successful, judgment will be given in the plaintiff's favour, and a range of court orders may be issued to enforce a right, impose a penalty, award damages, impose an injunction, or to obtain a declaratory judgment to prevent future legal disputes. The conduct of a lawsuit is called litigation.

lawyer Rechtsanwalt; Jurist

A legal practitioner, certified to give legal advice to clients in legal matters. Some lawyers represent clients in courts and in other forms of dispute resolution.

In American English, the term is synonymous with licensed attorneys who practice law; attorneys who serve as judges, law clerks or legislators do not practice for the duration of their service.

In British English, the word lawyer is used loosely to refer to a broad variety of law-trained persons. It includes practitioners such as barristers, solicitors, and legal executives; and people who are involved with the law but do not practice it on behalf of individual clients, such as judges, and law clerks.

layer Schicht; Ebene; Wohltäter; *(to ~)* schichten

laying claim to Inanspruchnahme

layman Laie; Nichtfachmann

lay off entlassen

To remove someone temporarily or permanently, from employment.

layoff Entlassung

Temporary, prolonged, or final removal from employment.

lay open aufdecken; offen legen

layout *(display)* Aufriss; *(rough sketch)* Rohskizze; *(arrangement)* Anordnung; Anlage

lead *(metal)* Blei

lead *(hint)* Tip; *(to ~)* führen

lead Aufmacher; Vorspann; Spur; Haupt-; erster; führender

Marketing: New and unqualified prospect or client previously unknown to a sales person or company.

leader Leiter; Führer; *(foreman)* Vorarbeiter; Vorsitzender

A person who exhibits certain traits that are characteristic of leaders. These leadership traits include: a strong drive for responsibility and task completion, self confidence, willingness to make decisions and accept consequences of decisions, ability to influence peoples behavior and the ability to structure the social climate and systems in an organization to fit the goals at hand.

leader in the field Branchenführer

leader-member exchange theory Austauschtheorie der Führung

Theory that argues that because of time pressures, leaders establish a special relationship with a small group of their followers. These individuals make up the in-group – they are trusted, get a disproportionate amount of the leader's attention, and are more likely to receive special privileges.

Others followers fall into the out-group. They get less of the leader's time, fewer of the preferred rewards that the leader controls, and have leader-follower relations based on formal authority interactions.

leader-participation model Partizipationsmodell der Führung

Model developed by Victor Vroom and Phillip Yetton, in 1973, that gives the leadership theory that provides a set of rules to determine the form and amount of participative decision making in different situations. The model was a decision tree incorporating seven contingencies and five alternative leadership styles.

leadership Leitung; Führung

A social influence process where an individual member of a group or organization influences: the events, choices of objectives, strategies, work activities, the motivation of people, and the enlistment of support and cooperation from people inside the group.

leadership behavior Führungsverhalten

leadership competencies Führungskompetenzen

leadership characteristics Führungseigenschaften

leadership figure Führungsfigur

leadership image Führungsimage

leadership position Führungsposition

leadership quality Führungsqualität

leadership role führende Rolle

leadership stance Führungsverhalten

leading führend; maßgeblich

leading bank Konsortialführer

leading indicators Frühindikatoren

Economic statistics that offer an outlook of the future performance of an economy. Examples include the consumer price index (CPI), producer price index (PPI), retail sales, personal income, and the fed funds rate.

leading technology Spitzentechnik

leading underwriter Konsortialführer

lead market erster Einführungsmarkt

Market where products are first introduced.

lead product Spitzenprodukt

leads and lags Schwankungen im Handel

lead strategy spezielle Währungsstrategie

Finance: strategy of collecting foreign currency receivables early when a foreign currency is expected to depreciate, and paying foreign currency payables before they are due when a currency is expected to appreciate.

lead time Bearbeitungszeit; Vorlaufzeit; Beschaffungszeit

The time lag between the placement of an order and its actual receipt. Can be reduced by implementing just-in time inventory control.

leaflet Werbeprospekt; Wurfblatt; Handzettel

leak Leck; *(information)* gezielte Indiskretion; *(to ~)* durchsickern; durchsickern lassen

leakage Schwund; Leck; Loch

lean dünn; *(meager)* mager; *(profits)* dürftig; kümmerlich; *(to ~)* lehnen; *(to incline)* schief stehen; neigen; tendieren

lean production schlanke Produktion

System of flexible manufacturing technologies pioneered in the automobile industry where manufacturer's employees are organized in teams and the components are delivered to each team's work station just-in-time.

learning Lernen

Permanent changes in an individual's behavior arising from experience.

learning curve Lernkurve

learning effect Lerneffekt

learning opportunity Bildungsangebot

learning organization lernende Organisation

Organization in which people at all levels, individually and collectively, are continually increasing their capacity to produce results they really care about.

An organization that has developed the continuous capacity to adapt and change. There are five basic characteristics.(1) people put aside their old ways of thinking, (2) they learn to be open with each other, (3) they understand how their organization really works, (4) they form a plan or vision that everyone can agree upon, (5) and then work together to achieve that vision.

lease Verpachtung; *(revenue)* Miete; *(document)* Mietvertrag; *(to ~ lease to someone)* verpachten; *(to rent to so)* vermieten; *(to lease from so)* pachten; *(to rent from so)* mieten; *(car)* leasen

A contract between a lessor and a lessee for the use of an asset, either real estate, equipment, or other fixed assets, for a specified time in exchange for payment, usually in the form of rent.

An operating lease is generally a short-term cancellable arrangement, whereas a financial, or capital, lease is a long-term non-cancellable agreement.

lease financing Mietfinanzierung; Leasingfinanzierung

leasehold *(leased real estate)* Pachtgrundstück; *(leasing from someone)* Pachtung

The right to possession and use of land for a fixed period of time. The value of a leasehold depends on whether the rent is below market and on the length of the remaining lease term.

leasing Leasing

The act of hiring an asset, such as machine, to avoid the capital cost involved in owning it. The equipment remains an asset of the lessee rather than the lessor.

leasing business Leasinggeschäft

leasing charge Leasingmiete

leasing company Leasinggesellschaft

leasing rate Leasingrate

least-effort principle Prinzip des geringsten Aufwandes

Advertising: theory that consumers will tend to buy what is easily available. A consequence of this view is point-of-purchase advertising.

least preferred coworker (LPC) questionnaire LPC-Fragebogen

Questionnaire developed by Fred Fiedler as an instrument to measure whether a person is task or relationship oriented and what his basic leadership style is.

It contains 16 contrasting adjectives (such as pleasant-unpleasant, efficient-inefficient, open-guarded). It asks respondents to think of all co-workers they have ever had and to describe the one person they least enjoyed working with by rating him or her on a scale of 1 to 8 for each of the 16 sets of contrasting adjectives.

leave *(vacation)* Urlaub; *(permission)* Erlaubnis; Abwesenheitsergebnis; *(to ~)* verlassen; *(job)* ausscheiden

leave behind zurücklassen; hinterlassen; *(to outdistance)* abhängen

leave of absence Beurlaubung

Approved absence period from work without loss of seniority or other job-related perquisites. A leave of absence is often granted to employees for particular purposes, such as attending an educational program or performing a special research project.

lecture Vorlesung; Vortrag; *(to ~)* Vorlesung halten; vortragen

ledger Hauptbuch; Register

Principal book for all accounting transactions; book of accounts. Contrary to journal, in which the transactions are initially recorded.

leeway Spielraum; Bewegungsfreiheit; Abdrift

legal gesetzlich; gesetzmäßig; rechtsgemäß; juristisch; *(legitimate)* rechtmäßig; *(valid in law)* rechtskräftig; *(judicial)* rechtlich

legal conception Rechtsauffassung

legal force Rechtskraft

legal form Rechtsform

legal monopoly gesetzliches Monopol

A market situation in which a monopoly right has been granted by the government to a privately owned organization. In exchange, the company agrees to have its policies and rates regulated. *Example:* electricity and water utilities are often legal monopolies.

legal opinion Rechtsgutachten

The legal document stating the reasons for a judicial decision.

legal residence gesetzliches Domizil

legal risk Rechtsrisiko

Likelihood that a trading partner will opportunistically break a contract or expropriate intellectual property rights.

legal rule Rechtsvorschrift

legal services juristische Dienstleistungen; Anwaltsdienste

legal situation Rechtslage

legal status Rechtsstatus

legal system Rechtssystem

System of rules that regulate behavior and the processes by which the laws of a country are enforced and through which redress of grievances is obtained.

There are four major legal systems in the world today: civil law, common law, customary law, and religious law. However, each country often develops variations on each system or incorporates other features into the system

legal tender gesetzliches Zahlungsmittel

legal title Rechtsanspruch

legislation Gesetzgebung

legislative gesetzgebend

legislative proposal Gesetzesvorlage

legislative provision Rechtsvorschrift

legislator Gesetzgeber

legitimate legitim; *(lawful)* rechtlich; gesetzlich; *(according to law)* rechtmäßig; gesetzmäßig; *(genuine)* echt

legitimate power legitime Macht

Developed by French and Raven, is the power a person receives as a result of his or her position in the formal hierarchy of an organization. It includes acceptance by members of an organization of the authority of a position.

legitimate political behavior legitimes politisches Verhalten

General behavior in normal everyday politics. *Example:* bypassing the chain of command, forming coalitions, obstructing organizational policies or decisions through inaction or excessive adherence to rules, and developing contacts outside the organization through one's professional activities.

leisure Freizeit; Muße

lend leihen; verleihen; ausleihen; spenden; geben

lend Kreditgewährung

Provide money temporarily on the condition that it or its equivalent will be returned, often with an interest fee.

lender Ausleiher; Verleiher; *(creditor)* Kreditgeber

A person or a business that lends money to a borrower with the expectation of being repaid, usually with interest.

lending Ausleihung; *(granting credit)* Kreditgewährung; Darlehensgewährung

lending institution Kreditanstalt

lending law Kreditwesengesetz

lending officer Kreditsachbearbeiter

lend on beleihen

Leontief paradox Leontief-Paradoxon

Empirical finding that, in contrast to the predictions of the Heckscher-Ohlin theory, US exports are less capital intensive than US imports.

lessee Pächter; *(renter)* Mieter

A person to whom a lease is granted, i.e. the user of the asset.

lessor Verpächter; Vermieter; Leassinggeber

The person who owns an asset and grants a *lease* to another, thereby transferring to him exclusive temporary right of possession.

less than carload (LCL) weniger als Wagenladung; Stückgut

An amount of freight that is insufficient to command the lower shipping rates that apply to full carloads.

let lassen; zulassen; *(to rent)* vermieten

letter Brief; Schreiben; *(alphabet)* Buchstabe

letter of awareness Patronatserklärung; Bürgschaft

letter of comfort Patronatserklärung; Bürgschaft

A letter to a bank from the parent company of a subsidiary that is trying to borrow money from the bank. The letter gives no guarantee for the repayment of the loan but offers the bank the comfort of knowing that the parent company is aware of its intention to borrow.

letter of credit (L/C) Kreditbrief; Akkreditiv

A document issued by a bank guaranteeing the payment of a customer's drafts up to a stated amount for a specified period. It gives the buyer the financial backing of the bank and satisfies the requirements of the seller in completing the transaction; extensively used in international trade.

letter of intent Bereitschaftserklärung; Absichtserklärung

A letter expressing the intention to take (or not to take) an action, sometimes subject to certain conditions.

letter of preparedness Bereitschaftsklausel, Absichtserklärung

letter of regret Absagebrief

letter of responsibility Patronatserklärung

letter of understanding Vorvertrag

level Niveau; Höhe; *(flat)* flach; *(straight)* gerade; horizontal; auf gleichem Level

level-coupon bond Kuponanleihe

Bond with a stream of coupon payments that are the same throughout the life of the bond.

level of capacity Kapazitätsgrad; Auslastungsgrad

level of employment Beschäftigungsgrad

level of familiarity Bekanntheitsgrad

level of investment Investitionsquote

level of jurisdiction Instanz

leverage Hebelkraft; *(fig)* Einfluss; *(capital)* Verschuldung; Verschuldungsgrad

Finance: the relationship between debt and equity in a firm's capital structure. The more long-term debt there is, the greater the financial leverage.

leveraged buyout (LBO) fremdfinanzierte Übernahme

The takeover of a company with the use of borrowed money. Usually, the target company's assets serve as security for the bonds taken out by the investors, who then repay the bonds out of the cash flow of the acquired company.

leveraged company verschuldetes Unternehmen

A company with a high degree of debt in its capital structure. As a general rule, industrial companies with more than one-third of their capitalization in the form of debt are regarded highly leveraged.

leveraged equity Firmenanteil mit hohem Verschuldungsgrad

Shares in a firm that relies on financial leverage. Holders of leveraged equity face the benefits and costs of using debt.

leveraged lease durch Leihkapital finanziertes Leasing

Tax-oriented leasing arrangement that involves one or more third-party lenders.

Levitt, Theodore (1925-2006)

One of the first management thinkers to emphasize the importance of marketing. Levitt believed that the secret of success in marketing is to ask questions to develop sensitivity for customer needs. He also was one of the first to point out the effects of globalization.

Major publications: (1960) Harvard Business Review, (1962) Innovation in Marketing, (1969) The Marketing Mode, (1983) The Marketing Imagination

levy Eintreibung; *(tax)* Steuer; Steuererhebung; *(troops)* Aushebung; Einberufen; *(to ~)* erheben; eintreiben

liabilities *(bookkeeping)* Passiva; Schulden

Debts of the firm in the form of financial claims on a firm's assets.

liability Bürde; Verpflichtung; *(debt)* Verschuldung; *(debt)* Verbindlichkeit; Obligo; *(bookkeeping)* Passivposten; *(guarantee)* Haftung; Haftpflicht

Finance: anything owed by a person or company.

liability case Schadensfall

liability insurance Haftpflichtversicherung; Rückdeckungsversicherung

Insurance cover against claims arising from injuries or damage to other people or property. This is indispensable, for example, for motor vehicles, home owners, and businesses.

liability for risk Risikohaftung

liability, legal gesetzliche Haftpflicht

Liability imposed by law on individuals or corporations to pay for damage done to others.

liability, professional Berufshaftung

Liability created when a professional with certain expertise in a particular area such as a doctor or a lawyer, commits a serious mistake.

liable haftbar; haftpflichtig; verpflichtet; verantwortlich

liaison Verbindung; Zusammenarbeit; Kontakt

Key term for discussing and analyzing a sociogram; communication, contact and linking between people or groups; individuals in a social network who connect two or more clusters but are not members of any cluster.

libel Verleumdung; Anschwärzung; Schmähschrift

Defamation of an individual in a published work.

liberal aufgeschlossen; großzügig; liberal; *(generous)* freigiebig; großzügig

liberalization Liberalisierung; *(losening)* Lockerung

liberate befreien; *(capital)* flüssig machen

license Lizenz; Benutzungsrecht; *(patent)* Patentausnutzung; *(driving)* Führerschein; *(sale)* Verkaufsrecht; *(trade)* Zulassung; Konzession; Gewerbeschein; *(to ~)* genehmigen; erlauben; zulassen

Official permission to do something that is forbidden without a licence. In property law, a license is a personal privilege or permission with respect to the use of land, and is revocable at the will of the landowner.

license agreement Lizenzabkommen

license contract Lizenzvertrag

licensed lizenziert; verbrieft

licensee Lizenzinhaber; Konzessionsinhaber

Person or company to whom a license has been granted.

Law: a person who is on the property of another, despite the fact that the property is not open to the general public.

license fee Lizenzgebühr

license tax Gewerbesteuer

licensing Lizenserteilung

Method of entering a foreign market in which the company (the licensor) enters into an agreement with a licensee in the foreign market, offering the right to use a manufacturing process, trademark, patent, trade secret or other item of value for a fee or royalty. In return for giving the licensee these rights, the licensor collects a royalty fee on every unit the licensee sells.

licensor Lizenzgeber

Person or company that grants a license to someone else.

lien Zurückbehaltungsrecht; Pfandrecht

The right of one person to retain possession of goods owned by another until the possessor's claims against the owner have been satisfied.

In a general lien, the goods are held as security for all the outstanding debts of the owner, whereas in a particular lien only the claims of the possessor in respect of the goods held must be satisfied.

life cycle Lebenszyklus

Concept taken from biology to describe the movement of a firm or its product through successive stages, most often development, introduction, growth, expansion, maturity, saturation, and decline. Normally referred to as the product life cycle, but also applied as the family life cycle.

life-cycle costs Lebenszykluskosten

All the costs a system causes or will cause during its life. Konwledge of life-cyle cost is needed to take strategic decisions.

life-cycle segmentation Lebenszyklus-segmentierung

Marketing approach that recognizes the consumer's changing needs at different stages of their life.

life expectancy Lebenserwartung

Age to which an average person can be expected to live, as calculated by an actuary. Insurance companies base their projections of benefit payouts on actuarial studies of such factors as sex, heredity, and health habits and base their rates on actuarial analysis.

lifehold Nießbrauch

life insurance Lebensversicherung

life insurer Lebensversicherer; Lebensversicherungsgesellschaft

life span Lebensdauer

lifestyle Lebensstil; Lebensführung

Combination of activities, interests, opinions, and values of individuals as they affect their mode of living. It thus provides a profile of a person's whole pattern of behavior and interaction with the world.

Lifestyles are important in marketing because they influence the way in which people make purchases. They are measure by psychographics segmentation, which involves measuring primary characteristics, known as AIO dimensions (activities, interests, and opinions).

lifestyle segmentation Segmentierung nach dem Lebensstil

Segmentation of a market based on lifestyles, which are increasingly seen as good predictors of consumer behavior.

lifetime demand Lebensbedarf

lifetime employment lebenslange Anstellung

lifetime value Lebenszeitwert

Net present value of the revenue stream for any particular customer over a number of years.

LIFO method LIFO-Methode; zuletzt hinein, zuerst hinaus

lift Auftrieb; Aufzug; *(to ~)* heben; *(loan)* aufheben; beseitigen; *(to raise)* anheben

Likert, Rensis (1903-1981)

Social psychologist and researcher who set up a pioneering establishment for research into human behavior in organizations. His work had a lasting effect on organizational theory and the study of leadership. He invented the concept of 'linking plans' – individuals capable of linking each work group to the organization. In his opinion participative management was the best kind, and the most likely to produce results.

Biography: 1932 he gained a Ph.D. from Columbia University, director of research at a life insurance office in Hartford (Connecticut), 1939 director of program surveys at the Department of Agriculture in Washington, 1949-1969 Institute for Social Research an on retirement he formed his own consulting firm.

Major publications: (1961) New Patterns of Management, (1967) The Human Organization, (1976) New Ways of Managing Conflict

limit Grenze; Limit; *(barrier)* Schranke; *(amount)* Höchstbetrag; *(to ~)* begrenzen; einschränken; beschränken; limitieren

limitation Beschränkung; Einschränkung; Begrenzung

limitation of credit Kreditbeschränkung

limited company Gesellschaft mit beschränkter Haftung

A company in which the liability of the members in respect of the company's debts is limited. Form of business most common in Great Britain, where registration under the Companies Act is comparable to incorporation under state law in the United States. It is abbreviated Ltd. or PLC, public limited company.

limited liability beschränkte Haftung

The restriction of someone's potential losses to the amount invested; absence of personal liability.

Limited liability is provided to stockholders of a corporation and limited partners of a limited partnership. Those parties cannot lose more than they contribute to the corporation or partnership.

limited liability company (LLC) Gesellschaft mit beschränkter Haftung

A business structure in some states of the US that is a hybrid between a partnership and a corporation..

limited line retailer Fachhändler

limited partnership Kommanditgesellschaft

A form of partnership consisting of one or more general partners who manage the business and are liable for its debts, and one or more limited partners who invest in the business and have limited personal liability.

limited partnership interest Kommanditeinlage

limited partner Teilhaber; Kommanditist

Partner in a limited partnership whose liability is limited to the amount invested and whose role in business management is restricted.

limited price Limitkurs

limited-service retailers Einzelhändler mit beschränktem Service

Retailers that provide only a limited number of services to shoppers.

limited-service wholesalers Großhändler mit beschränktem Service

Wholesalers who offer only limited services to their suppliers and customers.

limit order Limitauftrag; limitierte Order

Stock exchange: order to buy a stock at or below a specified price or to sell a stock at or above a specified price.

line Linie; Leine; Schnur; *(text)* Zeile; *(business)* Gewerbezweig; *(product)* Warengattung; Sparte; *(assortment)* Sortiment

linear regression lineare Regression

line extension Produktlinienerweiterung

Marketing technique using a successful brand name to introduce additional items in a given product category under the same brand name, such as new flavors, forms, colors, added ingredients or package sizes.

Example: when a coffee manufacturer adds decaffeinated coffee to the same brand line of coffee products already on the market (such as regular coffee and instant coffee), a *line extension* has been made.

line function Linienfunktion

Position or activity in an organization contributing directly to the output of the organization..

line management Linenmanagement

Administration of the line functions of an organization; administration of all activities that contribute directly to an organization's output.

line of credit Kreditlinie

An commitment by a commercial bank or other financial institution to extend credit up to a certain amount for a certain time to a specified borrower.

The borrower does not have to file another application and is expected to reduce the debt after having reached the full amount of credit.

A *non-committed* line of credit is an informal agreement, a *committed* line of credit is a formal legal arrangement and usually involves a commitment fee paid by the firm to the bank.

line of export goods Exportsortiment

line of products Produktgruppe; Erzeugnisgruppe

line organization Linienorganisation

The organizational structure of activities that contribute directly to the organization's output. Every position in the organization is reporting exactly to one superior, from bottom to top. Staff organization, on the other hand, is advisory to the line function.

line supervisor Spartenchef

line total Zeilensumme

link Verbindung; Querverbindung; *(chain)* Glied; *(connection)* Anknüpfungspunkt; Verbindung; *(capital)* Kapitalverflechtung; *(to ~)* verbinden

Internet: links between two sites where one site promotes and markets the other by putting connecting links. In return, the other site also does the same. These may be a courtesy, or they may be contractually required.

Lintner's observations Lintners Beobachtung zur Dividendenpolitik

John Lintner's work (1956) suggested that dividend policy is related to a target level of dividends and the speed of adjustment of change in dividends.

liquid Flüssigkeit; *(capital)* flüssig; sofort realisierbar; liquide

liquid assets flüssige Mittel

Assets in form of cash or easily convertible into cash. In a corporation's financial statements, liquid assets are cash, marketable securities, and accounts receivable.

liquidable realisierbar

liquidate auflösen; *(business)* abrechnen; abwickeln; Geschäft auflösen; *(to balance)* saldieren; *(pay off)* tilgen

liquidation Liquidierung; Auflösung; *(debt)* Abtragung; Tilgung

The process of terminating a business including selling its assets. Liquidation occurs when a corporation ceases to be a going concern..

The shareholders surrender all of their shares in a corporation and receive, after all creditors are paid, their pro-rata share of any remaining assets and accumulated earnings and profits.

liquidation value Abwicklungswert; Liquidationswert

liquid capital flüssiges Kapital

Assets in the form of money or those easily converted into money

liquidity *(money)* Liquidität; Geldflüssigkeit

Capability of a company to punctually cover all its financial commitments with its available assets. This depends on the ability to convert assets into cash or cash equivalents without significant loss. Investments in money market funds and listed stocks are much more liquid than investments in real estate, for instance.

A distinction is made between the structural or *strategic liquidity*, which arises from the net working capital as well as from the *free credit limits*, and the *dynamic liquidity*, which is ensured by the solvency plan for short-term cash management.

liquidity assistance Liquiditätshilfe

liquidity position Liquiditätslage

liquidity problem Liquiditätsproblem

liquidity ratio Liquiditätsgrad; Liquiditätsquote

Widely-used ratio for assessing the liquidity of a company: liquid (quick) assets, i.e. the circulating capital less stock to current liabilities.

For example, a company with current assets of 25,000 € including stock of 15,000 € and liabilities of 12,000 € will have a liquid ratio of: (25,000 € - 5,000 €)/12,000 € = 0.83, i.e. 83% or 0.83:1. This may be interpreted as the company having 83 cent of liquid or current assets for every 1 € of current liabilities.

If the company should be obliged to repay the current liabilities immediately, there would be insufficient liquid assets to allow it to do so. The company may therefore be forced into selling stock at a discount to raise finance.

Although there is no rule of thumb, and there are industry differences, a liquid ratio significantly below 1:1 will give rise to concern. The liquid ratio is regarded as an acid test of its solvency and is therefore sometimes called the acid-test ratio.

liquidity squeeze Liquiditätsdruck

list Liste; Register; *(directory)* Verzeichnis; *(to ~)* notieren; aufstellen; auflisten

list broker Adressenverlag

Marketing: A company that buys and sells lists of customer addresses. Each customer address is accompanied with often detailed aggregate transaction information.

Most promotional mailings such as catalogs, coupons, promotional offers and credit offers utilize lists purchased through list brokersfirm that sells lists.

listed on the stock exchange börsennotiert

listing on the stock exchange Börsennotierung

list of precedence Rangliste

list owner Eigentümer einer Liste

Marketing: Someone who has compiled a database of names that have common characteristics and that can be used as a mailing lists used for solicitation. Mailing lists are generally sold on a price-per-name basis.

list price Listenpreis; Katalogpreis

Retailing: the price at which manufacturers recommend retailers to sell a good, which is quoted to customers before applying discounts.

list renting Mieten einer Adressliste

Marketing: the practice of renting a list of potential customers to an organization involved in direct-mail selling or to a charity raising funds. When the terms of hiring restrict the use of the list to one mail shot, it is usual for the owner of the list to carry out the mailing, so that the hirer cannot copy it for subsequent use.

LISTSERV

Program that provides automatic processing of many functions involved with mailing lists. E-mailing appropriate messages to it will automatically subscribe the e-mailer to a discussion list or unsubscribe the person. A listserv will also answer requests for indexes, FAQs, archives of the previous discussions, and other files.

literature Literatur; *(product information)* Broschüren; Prospekte

litigation Rechtsstreit; Streitsache; Prozess

livelihood Lebensunterhalt; Existenzgrundlage; Auskommen

live web site Live-Website

Internet: current site accessible to customers, as distinct from test web site.

living *(livelihood)* Lebensunterhalt; Auskommen; Leben; Existenz; *(alive)* lebend; lebendig

living conditions Lebensbedingungen; Lebensverhältnissee

living standard Lebensstandard

load Fuhre; Ladung; *(freight)* Fracht; *(burden)* Last; *(to ~)* beladen; aufladen; *(to encumber)* belasten

load fund Investmentfonds mit Gebührenabrechnung beim Verkauf

Mutual fund with shares sold at a price including a sales charge - typically 4 % to 8% of the net amount indicated.

Some "no-load" funds have distribution fees of typically 0.25%. A "true no-load" fund has neither a sales charge nor a fee. A load implies that the fund purchaser receives some investment advice or other service worthy of the charge.

loan Anleihe; Darlehen; *(to ~)* leihen; verleihen; ausleihen

A type of debt instrument in which an owner of property, called the lender, allows another party, the borrower, to use the property.

The borrower promises to return the property after a define time with a payment for its use, called interest.

loan account Kreditkonto; Darlehenskonto

loan against borrower's note Schuldscheindarlehen

loan agreement Kreditvertrag; Darlehensvertrag

loan amount Kreditsumme; Anleihebetrag

loan approval Kreditgewährung

loan association Darlehenskasse

loan bank Kreditanstalt

loan business Debitorengeschäft

loan committee Kreditausschuss

loan contract Darlehensvertrag

loan debt Darlehensschuld

loan default Kreditausfall

loan demand Kreditnachfrage

loan guarantee Anleihegarantie

loan insurance Kreditversicherung

loan on overdraft Kontokorrentkredit

loan payable Darlehensschuld

loan proceeds Anleiheerlös; *(loan program)* Darlehensprogramm

loan repayment Kreditrückzahlung

loan term Darlehenslaufzeit

loan terms Rückzahlungsbedingungen

lobby Vorhalle; Eingangshalle; *(interest group)* Interessengruppe; Machtgruppe; Interessenverband

lobbying Lobbying

Any attempt to influence decisionmakers in favor of a specific cause. Most often used in the context of legislation, as historically representatives could best be met in the lobby of a parliament.

lobbyist Interessenvertreter; Lobbyist

A person paid by another for the specific purpose of influencing legislation or the administration of rules, regulations, and policies.

local örtlich; kommunal; heimisch; *(inhabitant)* Ortsbewohner; *(trade union)* Ortsverein; *(train)* Nahzug; Vorortszug

local area network (LAN) lokales Netzwerk

Geographically limited communications network linking computers, printers and other devices. Ethernet is the most common means of creating a LAN.

local bank Hausbank

local content inländischer Wertschöpfungsanteil

Requirement that some specific fraction of a good be produced domestically.

local custom ortsüblicher Brauch; ortsübliche Sitte

local government Lokalbehörde; Gemeindeverwaltung

Administrative offices of an area smaller than a state or province. The term is used to contrast with offices at nation-state level, which are referred to as the central government, national government, or federal government.

localization Lokalisation

Attempts at adapting products, such as publications, hardware or software, for non-native environments, especially other nations and cultures.

Internetpages, for example often have to be adapted extensively. Just translating the content often alienates local users.

locality Ort; Lokalität; *(location)* Lage

local market heimischer Markt

local politician Kommunalpolitiker

locate örtlich festlegen; sich niederlassen; *(find)* finden

location Niederlassung; Standort

location economies Standortvorteile; Standorteinsparungen

Cost advantages from performing a value creation activity at the optimal location for that activity.

location-specific advantages standortspezifische Vorteile

Advantages that arise from using resource endowments or assets that are tied to a particular foreign location and that a firm finds valuable to combine with its own unique assets (such as the firm's technological, marketing, or management know-how).

lockout Aussperrung

lock out aussperren

locus of control Grad der Selbstkontrolle

Degree to which people believe they are masters of their own fate.

log file Protokolldatei

Internet: file stored on a web server that records every item downloaded by users; internet server software, a feature that records every file sent by the server along with the destination address and time sent.

log file analyzers Log-File-Analysten

*Internet: t*ools that are used to build a picture of the amount of usage of different parts of a website based on the information contained in the log file.

logistics Logistik; Versorgung; Nachschub

The management of material and information flows through an organization to its end customers.

logo Logo; Signum; Firmenzeichen; Firmenschriftzug

Unique design, symbol, or other special representation of a company name, used as a trademark.

lombard lending rate Lombardsatz

Lombard rate Lombardsatz

German term for the rate of interest charged for a loan against the security of a pledged promissory note. Particularly used by the Bundesbank, which, until 1999, maintained its Lombard rate at about 0.5 per cent above its discount rate.

London Interbank Bid Rate (LIBID) Londoner Interbankennachfragesatz

London rate at which the major banks will bid to take deposits from each other for a given maturity, normally between overnight and live years.

London Interbank Mean Rate (LIMEAN) Mittelkurs zwischen LIBOR und LIBID

Average of libid and libor.

London Interbank Offered Rate (LIBOR) Londoner Interbanken-Zinssatz

Rate that the most creditworthy banks charge one another for large loans in the London market.

London International Financial Futures Exchange (LIFFE) Londoner Internationale Finanzterminbörse

Centralized market in London where standardized currency contracts, currency options and financial futures are traded.

long position Hausseposition

Investment: a position that appreciates in value if market prices increase. An investor who owns a particular security has a long position on the security as he will benefit if the price of the security increases.

long-range plan langfristiger Plan

Plan that describes the principal factors and forces affecting the organization during the next several years, including long-term objectives, the chief marketing strategies used to attain them and the resources required.

long-run langfristig; auf lange Sicht

long-term langfristig; auf lange Sicht; lange Sicht

long-term assets langfristige Vermögenswerte

Value of property, equipment and other capital assets minus the depreciation. This is an entry in the bookkeeping records of a company, usually on a cost basis and thus does not necessarily reflect the market value of the assets.

long-term debt langfristige Schulden

An obligation having a maturity of more than one year from the date it was issued.

long-term debt/capitalization langfristige Schuld/Kapitalisierung

Indicator of financial leverage. Shows long term debt as a proportion of the capital available. Determined by dividing long term debt by the sum of long term debt, preferred stock and common stockholders' equity.

long-term liabilities langfristige Verbindlichkeiten; langfristige Verpflichtungen

Amount owed for leases, bond repayment and other items due after 1 year.

long-term orientation langfristige Orientierung

National culture attribute that emphasizes the future, thrift and persistence.

long-term use Dauernutzung

loophole Hintertürchen; Ausweg; *(law)* Gesetzeslücke; *(taxes)* Schlupfloch

An ambiguity in a law or a contract that makes it possible to circumvent the original intent without violating its letter. For instance, a tax shelter may exploit a *loophole* in the tax law.

lopsided schief; *(argument)* einseitig

lose verlieren; einbüßen; zusetzen

loser Verlierer; Verlustträger

losing verlustbringend

loss Verlust; *(disadvantage)* Nachteil; *(damage)* Schaden

loss accounting Verlustrechnung

loss area Verlustzone

loss carryback Verlustrücktrag

An accounting technique to offset the current year's net loss against net income of the previous years for tax purposes.

loss carryforward Verlustvortrag

An accounting technique to offset the current year's net operating loss against future years' net incomes for tax purposes, if a loss carryback is not possible.

loss generating verlustbringend

loss in sales Umsatzeinbuße; Umsatzverlust

loss of efficiency Effizienzverlust

loss of job Arbeitsplatzverlust

loss of pay Lohnausfall

loss of production Produktionsausfall

loss of revenue Einnahmeausfall

loss on interest Zinsverlust

lot Teil; Anteil; *(real estate)* Grundstück; *(goods)* Warenposten; Lieferposten; *(quantity)* Menge; Parzelle; Parkplatz

lottery Lotterie

Marketing: contest that requires that a purchase be made in order to qualify for a random drawing.

low *(stock market)* Tiefstand; niedrig

low-context cultures low-context-Kulturen

Cultures that rely heavily on words to convey meaning in communication. Body language or formal titles are secondary to spoken and written words.

Examples: people from Europe and North America. Enforceable contracts will tend to be in writing, precisely words, and highly legalistic and managers are expected to be explicit and precise in conveying intended meaning.

low cost producers kostengünstige Hersteller

lower senken; herabmindern

lower-cost products kostensenkende Produkte; Güter von geringen Kosten

Products introduced to compete with existing brands by offering a price advantage.

lower-order needs niedrigere Bedürfnisse

Maslow separated the five needs of his hierarchy of needs into higher and lower orders. Lower-order needs are satisfied externally (by such things as pay, union contracts, and tenure); psychological and safety needs.

lowest cost Niedrigstkosten

lowest value Niedrigstwert

low-grade bond geringwertige Anleihe

See: junk bond.

low-interest period Niedrigzinsphase

low-involvement product geringes Produktinteresse

A product that involves the consumer in little or no trouble or deliberation when making a purchase. Such products are cheap and manufacturers try to make them more interesting and appealing by means of advertising.

low price Niedrigpreis; Billigpreis

Lowest (intraday) price of a stock over a certain period of time

low-price competitor Billigkonkurrent

low-priced billig

low rate Billigtarif

loyalty Loyalität

Passively but optimistically waiting for conditions to improve, including speaking up for the organization in the face of external criticism and trusting the organization and its management to "do the right thing".

loyalty techniques Treuesysteme

Customers sign up to an incentive scheme where they receive points for repeat purchases, which can be converted into offers such as discounts, free products or cash. (Also known as online incentive schemes.)

lucrative lukrativ; *(profitable)* ertragbringend; gewinnbringend; einbringlich; einträglich

lump sum Pauschalbetrag; Pauschalsumme; Einmalzahlung

In life insurance, single payment instead of a series of installments.

luxury Luxus; Luxusartikel; Üppigkeit; *(display)* Aufwand

M

M1, M2, M3 Geldmenge M1; Geldmenge M2; Geldmenge M3

See: money supply.

Maastricht Treaty Vertrag von Maastricht

Treaty agreed to in 1991, but not ratified until January 1, 1994, that committed the 12 member states of the European Community to a closer economic and political union.

Machiavellianism Macchiavellismus

Term named after Niccoló Machiavelli, that refers to the degree to which an individual is pragmatic, maintains emotional distance, and believes that ends can justify means.

People with a high degree of Machiavellianism manipulate more and persuade less. They flourish (1) when they interact face-to-face with others rather than indirectly, (2) when the situation has a minimum number of rules and regulations, thus allowing latitude for improvisation, and (3) when emotional involvements with details distract others.

machine Maschine; Mechanismus; *(apparatus)* Apparat; *(device)* Vorrichtung; *(to ~)* maschinell bearbeiten

machine-down time Machinenstillstandszeit

The period during which a machine cannot be used, normally because of breakdown.

machine hour rate Stillstand; Maschinenstunden-Satz

machine-idle time ablaufbedingte Brachzeit

The period during which a machine is not being used, caused rather by lack of work rather than by a fault in the machine.

machine-readable maschinenlesbar

Any form of data that can be input directly into a computer.

machine life Nutzungsdauer einer Maschine

machinery Maschinenanlage; maschinelle Anlage

machine tool Werkzeugmaschine

machine works Maschinenfabrik

macroculture Gesamtkultur; Makrokultur

macroeconomic gesamtwirtschaftlich; makroökonomisch

Taking a broad view of the economy and examining general behavior

macroeconomic policy gesamtwirtschaftliche Politik

macroeconomics Makroökonomie

The study of the aggregate forces of a nation's economy as a whole, in particular total amount of goods and services produced, total income earned, the level of employment of productive resources, and the general behavior of prices.

Macroeconomic analysis can guide economic policy in its attempt to reach conflicting goals, especially economic growth, price stability, full employment and the attainment of a sustainable balance of payments.

macroeconomist Gesamtwirtschaftler; Makroökonom

macroenvironment Makroumwelt; Makrostruktur

Larger societal forces that affect the whole microenvironment - demographic, economic, natural, technological, political, and cultural forces. It consists of all stakeholders, organizations, and forces external to the organization.

made gemacht; *(manufactured)* hergestellt; angefertigt

magazine Magazin; *(periodical)* Zeitschrift

magisterial richterlich

magnate Magnat; *(industry)* Großindustrieller; einflussreiche Person

mail Post; *(items)* Postsachen; *(shipment)* Postsendung; *(to ~)* mit der Post senden; (to *post)* einstecken

mail float Scheck in der Post

Refers to the part of the collection and disbursement process where checks are trapped in the postal system.

mailing list Postversandliste; Adressenkartei

mailing list addressee *(customer)* Versandkunde; Werbeadressat

mailman Briefträger

mail order advertising Versandwerbung

Advertising by mail or periodical advertisement, leading to purchases transacted by mail.

mail-order firm Versandhaus

A company that uses a catalog to communicate with its customers and direct merchandise shipments to deliver its products. Many mail order firms market only one particular type of merchandise, for example computers or textiles.

mail-order trade Versandhandel

main Stärke; Haupt-; hauptsächlich; wichtigst-

main cashier's window Hauptkasse

main competitor Hauptkonkurrent

main computer Zentralrechner

mainframe *(computer)* Schrank; Systemzentraleinheit; Internspeicher eines Computersystems; großes oder mittelgroßes Computersystem

mainframe computer Zentralrechner; Superrechner

mainland Festland; Kontinent

main product Hauptprodukt

The product that has the greatest economic significance to a company.

main profession Hauptberuf

mainstay Hauptstütze

maintain *(equipment)* warten; instandhalten; *(office)* unterhalten; *(price)* aufrechterhalten; *(delivery, schedule)* erfüllen; *(argument)* bestehen auf; *(relationship)* aufrechterhalten

maintenance Wartung; Aufrechterhaltung; *(equipment)* Instandhaltung

Necessary activities to keep something in good working order, such as inspection, overhaul, repair, preservation and the replacement of parts.

maintenance fee Instandhaltungskosten; *(Bank)* Kontoführungsgebühr

Real estate: regular fee for operating the common elements of shared property, such as gardens or escalator of a condominium.

maintenance of assets Substanzerhaltung

Costs associated with the necessary care and management of assets. Before a profit can arise, the costs of the fixed assets installed in the business have to be covered first. This maintenance of assets is carried out by estimating depreciation.

Fixed assets become technically outdated or, because of inflation, become more expensive to replace. It follows, that for internal purposes, that depreciation is based on the replacement cost of an asset of similar value and capable of similar performance, which leads to the determination of imputed depreciation.

maintenance process Pflege; Instandhaltungsprozess

Internet: work involved with running a live web site such as updating pages and checking the performance of the site.

major Mündiger; Hauptfach; *(military)* Major; Haupt-; *(significant)* bedeutend; *(of age)* mündig

major growth area Hauptwachstumsgebiet

major industry bedeutender Industriezweig

majority Mehrheit; Stimmenmehrheit; *(legal adulthood)* Volljährigkeit

majority interest Mehrheitsbeteiligung

majority ownership Mehrheitsbesitz

majority stockholder Mehrheitsaktionär

major market bedeutender Markt; wichtiger Markt

major product Hauptprodukt; wichtiges Produkt

major supplier Hauptlieferant; wichtiger Lieferant

make *(product)* Erzeugnis; *(brand)* Fabrikat; Marke; Warenzeichen; *(to ~)* machen; *(to manufacture)* herstellen

make a bid ein Angebot machen; *(to apply)* sich bewerben

make a market einen Geldkurs angeben

Investment: Obligation of a specialist to offer to buy and sell shares. It is assumed that this makes the market liquid, because the specialist assumes the role of a buyer for investors if they wish to sell and a seller if they wish to buy.

make additional payment Geld nachschießen

make an effort sich bemühen

make more expensive verteuern

make public veröffentlichen; publizieren; herausstellen

maker Hersteller; Verfertiger; Fabrikant

Commercial law: a borrower who signs a note or endorses it before its delivery to the payee, and thereby assumes an obligation to pay the stated amount.

make up *(to catch up)* nachholen; *(cosmetics)* schminken

making delivery Leistungserfüllung

Refers to the seller' s actually turning over to the buyer the asset agreed upon in a forward contract.

male chauvinism männlicher Chauvinismus

A term first used in the 1960s by the feminist movement to describe aA variety of bahavior that derives from the belief that men are superior to women, especially discrimination against women by applying stereotyped ideas.

malfunction Nichtfunktionieren; Funktionsstörung; *(machine)* Panne; *(to ~)* nicht funktionieren; eine Panne erleiden

malicious mischief mutwillige Sachbeschädigung

Intentional vandalism, damage or destruction of somebodey else´s property.

malingerer Simultant; Scheinkranker

Sombody who pretends to be ill and intentionally reports false symptoms or subjective test responses in order to avoid a task or responsibility.

mall *(shopping)* Einkaufszentrum; Ladenstraße

A shopping area with a pedestrian character where customers park in dedicated areas and walk to the stores.

malpractice Verletzung der Berufspflicht

Any professional misconduct in the performance of one´s duties, either intentionally or through carelessness or ignorance.

Malthusian law of population Malthussches Bevölkerungsgesetz

Theory by the philosopher Thomas Malthus (1766-1834) that population increase would outpace economic growth and that, therefore, general prosperity is impossible. Malthus did not take into account the rapid increases in productivity brought on by industrialization.

mammoth Mammut; Riesen-; riesig

mammoth company Riesenunternehmen; Mammutunternehmen

manage führen; leiten; *(to administer)* verwalten; *(to operate)* bewirtschaften

Administer an organization's activities to achieve particular objectives.

manageable *(object)* handlich; *(task)* leicht zu bewältigen; machbar

managed economy Planwirtschaft

An alternative to the market economy in which government intervention plays an important role in allocating goods and resources and in determining prices.

The approach was introduced by socialist and communist parties that came to power because they sought to counterbalance the negative effects of capitalism, which relies more on market forces to direct economic activity.

managed float system System der kontrollierten Kursfreigabe; schmutziges Floaten

System under which some currencies are allowed to float freely, but the majority are either managed by government intervention or pegged to another currency.

management Vorstand; Geschäftsleitung; Geschäftsführung; Management; *(administration)* Verwaltung; *(handling)* Handhabung

Generally defined as the running of an organization, management can be seen as having two main dimensions: an organizational skill and an entrepreneurial sense. The organizational skill, involving the principles and techniques of management, can be learned; the entrepreneurial sense arguably not. This inculdes: recognizing and making use of opportunities, predicting market needs and trends, and achieving one's goals by sustained drive, skilful negotiation. and articulate advocacy.

Organizationally, on can distinguish: top management, including the chief executive of an organization, his deputy or deputies, the board of directors, and the managers in charge of the divisions or departments of the organization, and middle management, consisting largely of the managers to whom top management delegates the day-to-day running of the organization.

Furthermore, management can be broken down into the categories of line and staff management: line managers organize the production of the goods or oversee the services provided by the organization, while staff managers provide such support as personnel management, transport management, service management or legal advice.

management audit Leistungsbeurteilung von Führungskräften

A formal and comprehensive examination of the entire management system of an organization, including the performance of individual mangagers.

management by exception Management nach dem Ausnahmeprinzip; Management by Objectives

A management philosophy holding that managers should interfere in the operational activites of his employees only when the actual results differs from the expected results.

management by objectives Führung durch Zielvereinbarung

A management philosophy that seeks to judge the perfomance of employees on the basis of their success in achieving the objectives they establish through discussions with their superiors. Performance goals are jointly agreed upon by management and the employee and subsequently evaluated.

management by walking around Management durch Pflege persönlicher Kontakte

A management philosophy that seeks to establish an open-door management policy and promote effective communication between employees and managers. Employees are encouraged to express concerns, make suggestions, or obtain answers to questions.

management capacity Führungskapazität

management career Führungslaufbahn

management-held shares Anteil der Vorzugsaktien Firmenangehöriger

Percentage of shares held by persons closely related to a company, as defined by the Securities and Exchange Commission.

management committee Direktorium

management consultant Unternehmensberater; Betriebsberater; Industrieberater

Person or organization acting as professional advisors to the management of a company in order to assist them in analyzing and solving management problems. Consultants work on a fee basis, and make practical recommendations.

management contract Vorstandsvertrag

management contracting Managementvertrag

Joint venture in which the domestic firm supplies the management know-how to a foreign company that supplies the capital; the domestic firm exports management services rather than products.

management control Führungskontrolle; Unternehmenskontrolle

management cycle Managementzyklus

The established time during which a particular management operation is expected to occur.

management decision Entscheidung der Geschäftsleitung; Managemententscheidung

management fee Führungsprovision; Verwaltungsgebühr

Finance: compensation for managing an investment portfolio.

Real estate: compensation for managing someone else´s real estate, including rent collection, maintenance, and bookkeeping.

management function Managementfunktion

management information system (MIS) Managementinformationssystem; Führungsinformationssystem

A system for the collection and analysis of information for the management of such areas as control, operations, and planning.

If the information is only given in the form of predefined reports, the word Executive Information system (EIS) is adequate. EIS is only used for query and presentation purposes. A Decision Support System (DSS) is a MIS that also offers methods and algorithms for decision-taking purposes.

management network Managementnetzwerk

Network of informal contacts between individual managers.

management personnel Führungspersonal

management process Führungsprozess

management result account Managementerfolgsrechnung

Target figure for the whole operative activity of a business. It is produced by adding the *standard result* and the balance of the *variance resumé.* It is the operating result after deducting the target profit.

management science Führungslehre; Wissenschaft der Unternehmensführung

management seminar Führungsseminar

management skills Führungsfähigkeiten

management structure Führungsstruktur

management style Führungsstil

The approach adopted by managers in administering an organization, in particular in exercising authority, encouraging participation, motivating staff, delegating authority, communicating, and maintaining control.

Four basic leadership styles developed by Dr. Rensis Likert are: exploitative-authoritative, benevolent- authoritative, consultative-democratic, and participative-democratic.

management system Verwaltungssystem

management team Führungsgruppe; Verwaltungskörper

management trainees Führungsnachwuchs

manager Manager; *(administrator)* Verwalter; *(leader)* Leiter; *(supervisor)* Vorsteher

Person responsible for administering and directing the activities of an organization. The term "manager" is in principle not bound to any particular level in the hierarchy. Managers who are also members of the board of management are the executives. The organization to be managed is normally considered to be a business, but can also be a governmet unit or a basball team.

managerial führend; geschäftsleitend;

managerial accounting entscheidungsorientiertes Rechnungswesen

The branch of accounting that uses historical and estimated data in providing information to that management for its business planning decisions.

managerial area of responsibility Managementbereich

managerial grid Mangerial Grid

A behavioral leadership model developed by Robert Blake and Jane Mouton in 1964. It classifies management leadership behavior on the basis of the balance of their concern for people and tasks.

managerial problem Führungsproblem

managing leitend; geschäftsführend; verwaltend

managing director geschäftsführendes Vorstandsmitglied; Generaldirektor; Betriebsführer

managing directorship Vorstandsvorsitz

mandate Mandat; Verfügung; Auftrag; *(authority)* Vollmacht; *(to ~)* einem Mandat unterstellen

Law: a formal notice of a decision by a court of appeal to enforce a decree, judgment, or sentence.

mandatory Bevollmächtigter; obligatorisch; zwingend; zwangsläufig; verbindlich

mandatory accounting Buchführungspflicht

maneuver Manöver; *(move)* Schachzug; *(trick)* Kunstgriff; Finte; *(to ~)* manövrieren

man hour Arbeitsstunde

A time unit used in industry. It measures the work that one person produces in one hour's time and is used as a method of determining the labor content of tasks and projects.

manifest öffentliche Erklärung; Manifest; *(customs)* Zolldeklaration; *(bill of* *lading)* Ladeverzeichnis; Warenverzeichnis; offenkundig; augenscheinlich; *(to ~ a cargo)* eine Ladung anmelden

Trade: A detailed listing of the goods being transported by a carrier. One copy of the manifest has to be kept in a safe, one copy is kept on board the ship.

man in charge Hauptverantwortlicher; Chef

manipulable manipulierbar; beeinflußbar

manipulate manipulieren; beeinflussen

manipulation Manipulation; *(mech)* Handhabung; Überredungskunst

Psychology: influencing someone else, implicitly against his will.

Finance: creating a false appearance of active trading in order to influence other investors to buy or sell shares.

manipulator Manipulator; *(stocks)* Kursbeeinflusser

man-made künstlich hergestellt

manpower menschliche Arbeitskraft; *(personnel)* Personalbestand

manual Handbuch; *(rules)* Vorschriftenbuch; *(instructions)* Instruktionsbuch; *(labor)* körperlich

A small handbook generally containing information, instructions, or other related data.

manual customization manuelle Anpassung

Internet: creating systems according to explicit *a priori* instructions from the user regarding preferred content categories.

manual operation *(machine)* Handbedienung

manual skill manuelle Fertigkeit

The ability to use one's hands efficiently, also called *dexterity*.

manual training Werkunterricht

manual worker Handarbeiter

manufacture Herstellung; Verarbeitung; Fabrikation; Verfertigung; Anfertigung; Produktion; *(to ~)* herstellen; anfertigen; produzieren

The organized activity of transforming raw materials into finished goods for sale, normally in large quantities.

manufactured article Fertigprodukt

manufacturer Fabrikant; Hersteller; Erzeuger; *(producer)* Produzent; *(industrialist)* Industrieller

manufacturer's agents Vertreter der Herstellerfirma

Representative of manufacturer who usually has a franchise to sell a particular product in a clearly defined area. An agent can represent more than one seller.

manufacturer's brand Herstellermarke

Brand created and owned by the producer of a product or service.

manufacturers' sales branches and offices Verkaufsniederlassung und Büros der Herstellerfirma

Wholesaling by sellers or buyers themselves rather than through independent wholesalers.

manufacturing Fertigung; Herstellung; Produktion

manufacturing capability Fabrikationsfähigkeit; Produktionsfähigkeit

manufacturing capacity Fabrikationskapazität; Produktionskapazität; Fertigungskapazität

manufacturing company Produktionsunternehmen; Fabrikationsbetrieb; Herstellungsfirma

manufacturing costs Fertigungskosten; Herstellungskosten

All costs related directly with the manufacturing process, consisting of direct materials, direct labor, and factory overhead.

manufacturing country Erzeugerland; Herstellungsland

manufacturing facility Produktionsanlage; Herstellungsanlage

manufacturing inventory Lagerbestand im Fertigungsbereich

All the parts and materials needed for the manufacturing process that a company holds in its inventory.

manufacturing operation Produktionsvorgang

manufacturing planning and control Fertigungsplanung und -kontrolle

manufacturing plant Industrieanlage; Industriebetrieb

manufacturing process Herstellungsprozess; Fabrikationsprozess; Produktionsvorgang; Fertigungsverfahren

manufacturing program Produktionsprogramm

manufacturing schedule Fertigungsplan; Produktionsplan

map Landkarte; *(projection)* Messtischblatt; *(to ~)* kartographisch aufnehmen

margin Marge; Differenz; Spielraum; *(earnings)* Verdienstspanne; *(profit)* Gewinnspanne; *(trade)* Handelsspanne

Corporate finance: difference between the price received by a company for its products and services and the cost of producing them; also known as gross profit margin.

Banking: difference between the current market value of collateral backing a loan and the face value of the loan.

Futures: deposit an investor must put up when buying or selling a contract. If the futures price moves adversely, the investor must put up more money to meet margin requirements.

margin account Effektenkreditkonto; Einschlusskonto

Stocks: leveragable account in which stocks can be purchased for a combination of cash and a loan. The loan in the margin account is collateralized by the stock and, if the value of the stock drops sufficiently, the owner will be asked to either put in more cash, or sell a portion of the stock.

marginal knapp; kaum; am Rande; nebensächlich; gering

marginal cost Grenzkosten

Additional cost associated with producing one more unit of output. This represents the variable costs per unit of production, which are the direct costs plus the variable overheads.

As long as the total cost curve of a product is linear, the marginal costs for each manufactured piece are the same. Marginal costs and variable costs are synonymous.

marginal cost curve Grenzkostenkurve

marginal cost of capital Grenzkosten des Kapitals; marginale Kosten des Kapitals

The cost of obtaining another unit of new capital. As some sources of capital are more expensive than others, this is an important figure in discounted cash flow present value analysis.

marginal efficiency of capital Grenzleistungsfähigkeit des Kapitals

The return from incremental investments, i.e. the return earned by the last additional unit of capital; also known as marginal productivity of capital or natural interest rate.

Projects whose marginal efficiency of capital exceed the market rate of interest are profitable to undertake.

marginal product Grenzprodukt

The marginal product of a factor is the increase in output due to a unit increase in the input.

marginal propensity to consume (MPC) marginale Konsumquote

The increase in personal consumer spending that occurs with an increase in disposable income. *Example:* if 90 cents of an additional dollar of income are consumed, then MPC = 0.90.

marginal propensity to invest marginale Investitionsquote

The proportion of additional income that will be invested, rather than consumed or spent.

marginal propensity to save (MPS) marginale Sparquote

The increase in saving that results from an increase in income, i.e. the proportion of additional income that will be saved rather than consumed.

marginal revenue Grenzerlös

The extra total revenue received when selling one more unit, calculated as the change in total revenue divided by the change in quantity sold.

marginal tax rate Grenzsteuersatz

Tax rate on an additional unit of income. Due to the progressive rate structure of income taxes, an additional dollar of income could be taxed at a higher rate than all previous income.

marginal utility Grenznutzen

The additional satisfaction or benefit that a consumer derives from an additional unit of a commodity or service; also called marginal benefit.

marginal value Grenzwert

Concept used to describe the relationship between two variables. If $y = f(x)$, x is the independent variable and y is the dependent variable, i.e. the value of y will change in accordance with the change in the value of x.

If x is a discrete variable, marginal value of y will be the change in the value of y for a one unit change in the value of x. If x is a continuous variable, marginal value of y will be the ratio of two changes.

margin deposit *(securities)* Einschußzahlung

margin of profit Gewinnspanne

The income remaining from a business transaction after all expenses are paid, expressed as a ratio: returns and allowances are subtracted from gross sales to arrive at net sales; costs of goods sold are subtracted from net sales to arrive at gross profit; gross profit is divided by net sales to get the profit margin.

margin requirement Deckungserfordernis; Einschußsatz

Amount of cash an uncovered (naked) option writer is required to deposit and maintain to cover his daily position valuation and reasonably foreseeable intra- day price changes.

marital status Familienstand; Ehestand

Tax: determines the type of return filed: single, joint, married filing separately, or head of household. Different tax rates apply to the different marital statuses.

mark Kennzeichen; Zeichen; *(characteristic)* Merkmal; *(stamp)* Stempel; *(brand)* Marke; *(to ~)* markieren; auszeichnen

markdown Preisherabsetzung

Reduction in the original retail selling price, which was determined by adding a percentage factor, called a *markup,* to the cost of the merchandise. The term *markdown* does not apply unless the price is dropped below the original selling price.

market Markt; *(buyers)* Käufer; Abnehmer; *(economy)* Wirtschaftslage; *(market trend)* Konjunktur; *(to ~)* vermarkten

General: a mechanism that allows people to exchange products, normally governed by the law of supply and demand.

Customers: total of all actual and potential buyers with the necessary purchasing power to buy a product or service.

marketability Marktfähigkeit; Absatzfähigkeit; Marktgängigkeit; Gangbarkeit; *(stocks)* Börsenfähigkeit

The relative speed and ease with which an asset can be sold.

marketability study Marktfähigkeitsstudie

An analysis of the potential sales of a specific product, especially about possible prices and potential quantities to be sold.

marketable marktfähig; marktgängig; absatzfähig; *(salable)* verkäuflich; umsetzbar; realisierbar

market access Marktzugang

market action Marktgeschehen

market analysis Marktanalyse; Marktuntersuchung; Konjunkturdiagnose

Systematic investigation aimed at defining a company's current or potential markets, predict their further development, and decide how to expand the company's market share.

market area Absatzgebiet; Marktgebiet

market balance Marktgleichgewicht

market-build-tip method spezielle Marktschätzungsmethode

Method used mainly by business goods firms to estimate the market potential of a city, state or country based on determining all the potential buyers in the market and estimating their potential purchases.

market capitalization Marktkapitalisierung

Total currency value of all outstanding shares. It is a measure of corporate size and calculated by multiplying the current share price by the current number of shares outstanding.

market-centered company marktkonzentriertes Unternehmen; Firma, die sich auf Kunden und Konkurrenten konzentriert

Company that pays balanced attention to both customers and competitors in designing its marketing strategies.

market challenger Marktherausforderer

Runner-up firm in an industry that is fighting hard to increase its market share.

market clearing Markträumung

market condition Marktlage; Konjunkturlage; *(prerequisite)* Marktbedingung; *(fact)* Marktgegebenheit

market cycle Marktzyklus

market data Marktdaten

market deconstruction Marktrückbau

Removing distribution channel or other functions from the players that normally perform them.

market demand Marktnachfrage

market development Marktentwicklung; Absatzentwicklung

Strategy for company growth by identifying and developing new segments and markets for current company products.

market dominance Marktbeherrschung

market domination Marktbeherrschung

market economist Marktwirtschaftler

market economy Marktwirtschaft

Economic system that relies largely upon market forces to allocate resources and determine the prices and quantities of each good to be sold.

market equilibrium Marktgleichgewicht

Situation in a market where the quantity demanded equals the quantity supplied and the prevailing price leads producers to produce exactly the quantity demanded by consumers at that same price.

marketer Absatzfachmann; Marketer

Someone who pursues marketing activities, either as an employee of a company, or as an independent agent.

market-factor index method Methode des Marktfaktorindex

Method used mainly by consumer product firms to estimate the market potential for consumer products.

market failure Marktversagen

market follower Marktfolger

Runner-up firm in an industry that wants to hold its share without rocking the boat.

market forces Marktkräfte; *(effects)* Markteinwirkungen

The forces of supply and demand that in a free market determine the quantity available of a particular product or service and the price at which it is offered.

Normally, a rise in demand will cause both supply and price to increase. while a rise in supply will cause both a fall in price and a drop in demand.

In practice, most markets are not free. being influenced either by restrictions on supply or by government intervention that can affect demand supply or price

market forecast Marktprognose; Konjunkturprognose

market gap Marktlücke

market imperfections Marktunvollkommenheiten

market index Marktindex

A statistic which measures trends in a market, composed of weighted values of the components that make up the index. A stock market index, for example, tracks the performance of certain stocks by weighting them according to their prices and the number of outstanding shares.

marketing Marketing; Vermarktung; *(theory)* Lehre vom Warenabsatz; *(economy)* Absatzwirtschaft; *(planning)* Absatzplanung; *(sales)* Absatz; Vertrieb

Marketing is a comprehensive set of activities around the core aim of selling a company´s products or services to its customers.

There are many different, often very sophisticated, definitions of marketing. The American Marketing Association sees it as "an organizational function and a set of processes for creating, communicating and delivering value to customers and for managing customer relationships in ways that benefit the organization and its stakeholders."

The standard components of marketing are described by the four P's - product, price, place, and promotion: the selection and development of the *product,* determination of a suitable *price,* selection and design of the right distribution channels (*place*), and all aspects related to coummunicating with customers *(promotion)*.

marketing activity Absatztätigkeit

marketing area Absatzbereich; Absatzgebiet

marketing audit Vertriebsanalyse; marktpolitische Unternehmensanalyse

Comprehensive, systematic, independent and periodic examination of a company's environment, objectives, strategies and activities to determine problem areas and opportunities, and to recommend a plan of action to improve the company's marketing performance.

marketing base Absatzbasis; Vertriebsbasis

marketing boss Marketingchef; *(marketing channel)* Absatzweg; *(marketing department)* Marketingabteilung

marketing budget Marketingbudget

Section of the marketing plan that shows projected revenues, costs and profits.

marketing concept Marketingkonzept; Vertriebskonzept

Idea or strategy for marketing a product or service.

marketing control Marketingkontrolle

Process of measuring and evaluating the results of marketing strategies and plans, and taking corrective action to ensure that marketing objectives are attained.

marketing database Marketingdatenbank

Organized set of data about individual customers or prospects that can be used to generate and qualify customer leads, sell products and services, and maintain customer relationships.

marketing director Vertriebsleiter; Vertriebschef

Person in charge of all marketing activiteis within a company, including advertising, sales promotion, research, and planning.

marketing environment Marketingumfeld

All the factors external to a company that could affect its sales, including cultural traditions, technological developments, competitors' activity, government policies, and changes in distribution channels.

The marketing environment cannot be controlled by the company and requires constant monitoring.

marketing expenses Vertriebskosten

marketing expert Marketingfachmann

marketing formula Vertriebsformel; Absatzformel

marketing function absatzwirtschaftliche Funktion

marketing gimmick Absatzgag

marketing implementation Marktingdurchführung; Marketingimplementierung

Process that turns marketing strategies and plans into marketing actions in order to accomplish strategic marketing objectives.

marketing information system Marketinginformationssystem

An organized set of procedures and methods to gather, sort, analyze and evaluate accurate information for marketing decision makers.

marketing intelligence Marketing-informationen

Information about developments in the marketing environment that helps managers to prepare and adjust marketing plans.

marketing intermediary Absatzmittler; Vertriebsgesellschaft

Independent business that assist in the distribution of goods and services from producers to end-users. They include agents, wholesalers and retailers, middlemen, physical distribution firms, service agencies, and financial intermediaries.

marketing management Marketing-Management; Vertriebsleitung

All the practical activities involved in marketing a product or service, including analysis, planning, implementation and control.

marketing manager Vertriebsleiter; Marketingchef

marketing mix Marketingmix

The factors controlled by a company that influence consumer buying decisions, often called the four Ps: the product, including quality, branding, packaging, and other features; pricing, including the recommended retail price, discounts for large orders, and credit terms; promotion, including advertising and all other communication decisions, and place, including where to sell the product, which distributors and transport services to use, and desirable stock levels.

marketing myopia Marketing-Kurzsichtigkeit

A failure to take the consumers' point of view sufficiently into consideration. For example, railway companies that define their markets in terms of trains rather than transportation, fail to recognize the challenge of competition from cars, airlines, and buses.

marketing objective Marketingziel

A statement defining in measurable terms the performance an organization, business unit, or operating unit intends to achieve.

marketing plan Marketingplan

A detailed statement prepared annually outlining how a company's marketing mix will be used to achieve its market objectives.

A marketing plan normally includes consumer analysis, market analysis, competition analysis, distribution channel analysis, and detailed statements about the four Ps. It may be laid out for an individual prouct or for the entire company and all its products.

marketing policy Vertriebspolitik

marketing potential Absatzpotential; Absatzchancen

marketing process Marketingprozess

The entire process including all marketing activities, such as: analysing marketing opportunities; selecting target markets; developing the marketing mix; and managing the marketing effort.

marketing research Marktforschung; Absatzanalyse

The systematic collection and analysis of data related to a firm´s marketing activities. The aim is to generate, refine and evaluate marketing actions; to monitor marketing performance; and to improve understanding of the marketing process.

marketing services agencies Marketingdienstleistungsagenturen

Marketing research firms, advertising agencies, media firms, marketing consulting firms, and other service providers that help a company to target and promote its products to the right markets.

marketing staff Vertriebsmitarbeiter; Angestellte im Marketingbereich

marketing strategist Marketingstratege

marketing strategy Marketingstrategie; Absatzstrategie; Vertriebsstrategie

Comprehensive statement of the planned strategy for a new product that outlines the intended target market, the planned product positioning, and the sales, market share, and profit goals for the next few years.

marketing survey Absatzanalyse

marketing system Vertriebssystem

marketing test Marketingtest

market leader *(firm)* Marktführer; *(product)* Spitzenreiter

The company in an industry with the largest market share; it usually leads other firms in price changes, new product introductions, distribution coverage and promotion spending.

market letter Börsenbrief

Newsletter written by an market analyist, either provided to customers of brokerage firms, or sold independently to subscribers for a profit.

market makers Marktmacher; Primärhändler; Wertpapierhändler

Financial service companies that connect investors and borrowers, either directly or indirectly; dealers in the securities exchange who buy and sell securities for their own account to maintain an orderly market in the specific securities they manage. The basic role of the *market maker* is to maintain liquidity in the securities industry for buyers and sellers.

market mechanism Marktmechanismus

market model Marktmodell

One-factor model for returns where the index that is used for the factor is an index of the returns on the whole market.

market niche Markrtnische

Small segment of a larger market, where demand is not met by any supply.

Once a company decides to address that demand, it is working in a niche market.

market nicher Nischenfirma

Firm in an industry that serves small segments that other firms overlook or ignore.

market objective Marktziel; Absatzziel

market opportunity Absatzmöglichkeit; Absatzgelegenheit; Marktchance

market opportunity analysis Analyse der Absatzmöglichkeit

Analysis conducted by a firm upon reviewing the marketing environment, focusing on finding and selecting among market opportunities.

A traditional market opportunity analysis includes both demand and supply analysis. The demand part reviews various market segments in terms of their potential profitability, the supply analysis reviews competition in selected segments that are under consideration.

market order Marktpreisorder

Stock market: an order to buy or sell a financial instrument immediately at the best possible price.

market-oriented marktorientiert

market outlook Konjunkturaussicht

market pattern Marktgestaltung; Marktstruktur

market penetration Marktdurchdringung

Sales: the degree to which a particular product is purchased in a particular market.

Strategy: attempt to increase the sales of a product within an existing market through the use of aggressive marketing tactics, especially low price.

market-penetration pricing Preissetzung zur Marktdurchdringung

Setting a low price for a new product in order to attract large numbers of buyers and a large market share.

market performance Marktleistung

marketplace Marktplatz; Markt

market portfolio Markt-Portfolio

market position Marktposition; Marktlage; *(sales)* Absatzposition

market positioning Marktpositionierung

Arranging for a product to occupy a clear, distinctive and desirable place relative to competing products in the minds of target consumers.

The product positioning process involves the following steps: defining the market in which the product or brand will compete; identifying the attributes; collecting information about their perceptions of each product on the relevant attributes; determine each products' share of mind; determine each products' current location in the product space; determine the target market's preferred combination of attributes; examine the fit between the position of your product and the position of the ideal product; position.

market power Marktmacht

Ability of a firm to exercise control over industry prices or output.

market price Marktpreis; Verkaufspreis; Verkaufskurs; *(replacement)* Wiederbeschaffungswert

The price agreed upon by buyers and sellers, as determined by the interaction of supply and demand.

market principle Marktprinzip

market profile Marktprofil

The characteristics of a market, including the demographic description of potential buyers.

market profit Kursgewinn; Konjunkturgewinn

market rate Marktpreis; Diskontsatz; Tageskurs; Marktsatz

market rate of interest Marktzinssatz

market reach Marktbreite

market-ready marktreif

market regulation Marktregulierung; *(rule)* Marktverordnung

market report Konjunkturbericht; Geschäftsbericht

market research Marktforschung

All efforts aimed at gathering, analyzing, and interpreting information about markets, including information about consumers, competitors, distributors, and the potential effectivs of different marketing programs.

market researcher Marktforscher

market risk Marktrisiko

Systematic risk in the market. This term emphasizes the fact that systematic risk influences to some extent all assets in the market.

market scope Marktumfang

market segment Marktsegment; Marktteil; *(customers)* Kundensegment

A group of buyers or potential buyers of a product or service that have common characteristics, which can be demographic, geographic, or lifestyle-related. This group can therefore be expected to respond in a similar way to a given marketing mix strategy.

market segmentation Marktsegmentierung

Strategy of dividing a market into smaller groups of buyers with common characteristics by applying various criteria, such as demographic, geographic, social, usage, or lifestyle. Due to their common characteristics, the resulting group can be offered distinct products and marketing mixes.

For example, within the large market of detergent buyers, a certain segment might specifically look for a fresh smell in his detergent. Manufacturers can serve this segment by offering a corresponding and communicate that with a special advertising message.

market share Marktanteil

Relationship of the sales volume of a business or of a product to the volume of the relevant market in one year. In the absence of statistics for volumes, market share is often calculated on the basis of sales.

The *relative market share* compares a business's own turnover or sales volume in a given period with its biggest competitors in this market.

market size Marktgröße

market skimming Marktabschöpfung

Pricing strategy that sets a high price for a new product in order to skim maximum revenues from the segments willing to pay the high price; the company makes fewer but more profitable sales.

market spectrum Marktbreite

market strength Marktstärke

market targeting Sondierung der Kauferzielgruppe

Process of evaluating each market segment's attractiveness and selecting one or more segments to enter.

market test Markttest

Strategy of introducing a new product or services to a small sample of the entire market in order to test different marketing strategies.

market timing zeitliche Abstimmung der Marktentscheidungen

Securities: attempts to buy and sell securities with the intention of exploiting up trends and avoiding down trends in stock, bond, currency, or commodity markets.

market-to-book (M/B) ratio Marktwert-Buchwert-Verhältnis

Market price per share of an ordinary share divided by book value per share.

market upturn Marktaufschwung

market value Marktwert; Kaufwert; *(replacement)* Wiederbeschaffungswert; Handelswert; *(stocks)* Kurswert

The highest price a buyer will pay for a property and the lowest price the seller will accept.

market value added (MVA) Marktwertschöpfung

Measure to quantify the value creation of a company. MVA can only be computed for companies quoted on a stock exchange because the capitalization is needed as comparison figure.

Market Value of a company (capitalization) = number of shares x share price, where capital employed = operating assets – "free" liabilities, and MVA = Market Value - Capital employed.

market volume Marktvolumen

Total number of sales of one particular product sold by all companies in that market in one year.

marking Kennzeichnen; Markieren

markup Aufschlag; Preisaufschlag

The amount by which the cost of a product or service has been increased to arrive at the selling price. It is calculated by expressing the profit as a percentage of the cost or service.

For example, if a product cost 8 € and is sold for 12 €, the mark-up would be: 4/8 x 100 = 50%.

The margin, on the other hand, is calculated by expressing the profit as a percentage of the selling price, in this case: 4/12 x 100 = 33.3%.

mark up heraufsetzen; aufschlagen

masculinity versus femininity Maskulinität und Femininität

In masculine cultures, sex roles are sharply differentiated and traditional "masculine values" such as achievement and the effective exercise of power determine cultural ideals. In feminine cultures, sex roles are less sharply distinguished, and little differentiation is made between men and women in the same job.

Maslow, Abraham (1908-1970)

Psychologist and behavioral scientist who developed the concept 'hierarchy of needs', which has influenced many other behavioral scientists and which is widely quoted in other areas of sciences.

Biography: born in New York, trained at the University of Wisconsin, 1947-1949 worked in industry, then teacher at Brandeis University, Massachusetts, where he became a professor and head of department, later he studied Douglas McGregor's Theory X in action at a California electronics factory.

Key writing: (1970) Motivation and Personality

Maslow´s pyramid of needs Maslowsche Bedürfnispyramide

Hierarchy of five human motivational needs arranged by ascending order of importance, developed by Abraham Maslow. The five ascending needs are (1) physiological, (2) safety, (3) social, (4) esteem, and (5) self-actualization.

Maslow argued that none of these needs is absolute: as soon as one is satisfied, the fact of its satisfaction ceases to be important. Once a need is satisfied, the next level emerges as a motivator.

mass Masse; Anhäufung; *(church)* Messe; massenhaft; massig; *(to ~)* anhäufen

mass appeal Massenanreiz

mass communication Massenkommunikation

The process of communicating with many people at the same time using widely circulating media such as newspapers, magazines, television, and radio.

mass consumption Massenkonsum

mass customization Maßanfertigung in grossen Stückzahlen

Production of a wide variety of end products at a unit cost that could once be achieved only through mass production of a standardized output; preparing individually designed products and communication on large scale.

mass dismissal Massenentlassung

mass distribution Massendistribution

massive massiv; massig; *(very big)* sehr groß; *(heavy)* schwer; *(mighty)* mächtig

mass layoff Massenentlassung; Entlassungswelle

mass market Massenmarkt

mass marketing Massenmarketing

Using almost the same product, promotion and distribution for all customers.

mass media Massenmedien

Channels of communication through which messages are communicated to many people, which includes radio and television broadcast stations and networks, newspapers, magazines, and outdoor.

mass produce fabrikmäßig herstellen; in Massen produzieren

mass product Massenprodukt

mass production Massenproduktion; Massenfertigung

The process of manufacturing or processing large volumes of the same basic product, using interchangeable parts and machinery. The process is either wholly automated or a series of short, repetitive procedures.

master Meister; *(proprietor)* Eigentümer; Besitzer; *(household)* Hausherr; *(degree)* Magister; *(to ~ a skill)* meistern; *(a subject)* beherrschen; *(a problem)* bewältigen

master of business administration (MBA) Magister der Betriebswirtschaft

An academic degree awarded after one or two years of studies at a university or business school learning the common body of knowledge in business, often with a specialty such as accounting, finance, management or marketing.

master wage agreement Manteltarifvertrag

master wage agreement contract Manteltarifvertrag

mastery Meisterschaft; Beherrschung; *(rule)* Herrschaft; Macht; *(preeminence)* Vorrang; *(ascendancy)* Oberhand; *(superiority)* Überlegenheit

match Gegenstück; *(equality)* Ebenbürtiger; *(lighter)* Streichholz; *(marriage)* eheliche Verbindung; *(to ~)* passend machen; passend sein; *(to compare)* vergleichen

matching principle Kongruenzprinzip; Grundsatz der Periodenabgrenzung

Accounting concept demanding that a company should recognize expenses as it earns the revenues related to those expenses, regardless of when the company receives payment .

mate´s receipt Bordempfangsschein; Verladebescheinigung

material Material; Werkstoff; *(substance)* Substanz; Materie; *(adj)* materiell; real

material adverse clause Rückzahlungsklausel

Clause in a loan agreement or similar contract under which the loan will become repayable in the event that there should be a serious (or material) deterioration in the borrower's credit standing.

material costs Materialkosten; Sachkosten

materialist materialistisch

materiality Bilanzierungsgrundsatz der Wesentlichkeit

The extent to which an item of accounting information is material, i.e. if its omission from a financial statement could influence the decision making of its users.

Materiality is therefore not an absolute principle but dependent on the size and nature of an item and the particular circumstances.

materials and parts Materialien und Teile

Industrial products that enter the manufacturer's product completely; including raw materials and manufactured materials and parts.

materials handling Materialwirtschaft; Materiealtransport

Moving, packaging, and storing of materials in every form, ranging from raw materials to finished goods. It includes the shipping, receiving, and processing of incoming items and outgoing products, returns to suppliers, and disposal of scrap.

materials management Materialwirtschaft; Steuerung des Materialflusses

Activity that controls the transmission of physical materials through the value chain, from procurement through production and into distribution; administration of all activities concerned with the ordering, storage, and movement of materials. This includes the storage of raw materials and parts and the manning of production operation centers.

materials requirements planning Bedarfsmengenplanung; Materialbedarfsplanung

maternity Mutterschaft

maternity allowance Mutterschaftsgeld

maternity leave Mutterschaftsurlaub

maternity pay Mutterschaftsgeld

maternity protection Mutterschaftsschutz

maternity rights Mutterschaftsrechte

The rights of a woman when she is absent from work because of her pregnancy or confinement.

These rights normally inculde: pregnant employees are entitled to reasonable time off work; an employee is entitled not to be dismissed because of pregnancy or any reason connected with it; a pregnant employee is entitled to receive maternity pay, in most countries at least 26 weeks; an employee entitled to maternity leave is also entitled to return to work with her employer.

mathematical mathematisch; rechnerisch

matrix Matrize; Mater; Matrix

Mathematical term describing a rectangular array of elements (numerical data, parameters, or variables). Each element within a matrix has a unique position, defined by the row and column.

matrix management Matrixführung

matrix structure Matrixstruktur

Organizational structure that creates dual lines of authority, combining e.g. functional and product departmentalization. Employees in the matrix have two superiors – their functional department managers and their product managers.

The most obvious structural characteristic of the matrix is that it breaks the unity-of-command concept. The strength of the matrix lies in its ability to facilitate coordination when the organization has a multiplicity of complex and independent activities. It also facilitates the efficient allocation of specialists.

The major disadvantages of the matrix lie in the confusion it creates, its propensity to foster power struggles, and the stress it places on individuals.

matter Materie; Stoff; Substanz; *(thing)* Sache; *(affair)* Angelegenheit; Thema; Gegenstand

mature reif; *(instrument)* fällig; abgelaufen; zahlbar; *(to ~)* fällig werden

mature economy reife Volkswirtschaft

The state of a country's economy whose population has stabilized or is declining, and where the proportion of national income utilized for investment in new capital projects is decreasing and the proportion of national income being utilized in purchasing consumer goods is increasing.

mature industry vollentwickelte Industrie

maturity Reife; *(bond)* Fälligkeit; *(time of payment)* Verfallzeit; *(expiration date)* Ablauftermin; Termin

Legal: date when legal rights in something become due.

Marketing: stage in the product life cycle characterized by stagnating sales.

maturity date Fälligkeitsdatum

maturity-factoring Fälligkeits-Faktoring

maturity stage Reifephase

Stage in the product life cycle characterized by stagnating sales, heavy competition, alternative product options and changing buyer preferences.

maximization Maximierung

maximize maximieren; *(picture)* möglichst groß darstellen; *(to raise to highest degree)* auf ein Höchstmaß bringen

maximum Maximum; *(ceiling)* Höchstgrenze; Höchst-; Größt-; maximal

maximum amount *(money)* Höchstbetrag

maximum period of time Höchstdauer

maximum proceeds Höchstertrag; Höchstgewinn

maximum value Höchstwert

Mayo, Elton W. (1880-1949)

Pioneer of industrial sociology who identified the roots of work satisfaction as non-economic and connected them with the interest taken in a worker's performance.

Mayo achived fame with the Hawthorne Experiments. Named after Western Electric's Hawthorne Works in Chicago, the experiments ran from 1927-1932. They were conducted by a team of Harvard scientists led by May and between 75 and 100 investigators working with 20,000 Western Electric employees. It involved changes in working conditions and produced unexpected results in employee performance.

Mayo made as many as ten changes in working conditions such as shorter hours, varied rest-breaks and a number of incentives. He believed that by creating an atmosphere of spontaneous cooperation in industry could help to combat the postwar collapse in traditional values.

Biography: born in Australia, graduate of Adelaide University and a medical student in London and Edinburgh, 1911-1919 teacher of mental and moral philosophy at the University of Queensland, 1923 emigration to the US, where he worked on a three-year research project at a Pennsylvania textile mill, prior to joining Harvard University as associate professor of industrial research in 1926. He ended his career at Harvard as professor of industrial research.

Major publications: (1933) The Human Problems of an Industrial Civilisation, (1949) The social Problems of an Industrial Civilisation

McClelland's theory of needs McClellands Bedürfnistheorie

Theory developed by David McClelland, focussing on three needs: achievement, power, and affiliation.

McGregor, Douglas (1906-1964)

Social psychologist analyzing human behavior within organizations. He became famous for the formulation of 'Theory X' (authoritarian management) and 'Theory Y' (participative management) which influenced a whole generation of management theorists. McGregor believed that the way an organization is run depends on the beliefs of its manager.

Theory X assumes that most people are lazy and dislike work. They need direction and are incapable of taking responsibility. Theory Y assumes that people have a psychological need to work and want achievement and responsibility. McGregor believed that human beings were capable of far greater potential than the industrial management of his time could understand.

Biography: president of Antioch College, 1954-1964 professor of management at the Massachusetts Institute of Technology.

Major publications: (1960) The Human Side of Enterprise, (1966) Leadership and Motivation, (1967) The Professional Manager

mean Durchschnittswert; Mittelwert; *(average)* durchschnittlich; *(petty)* kleinlich; *(shabby)* schäbig; gemein; *(to ~)* meinen; *(to signify)* bedeuten

mean, arithmetic arithmetisches Mittel

The sum of n numbers divided by n, i.e. the sum of all values in the sample divided by the number of observations.

mean absolute deviation (MAD) mittlere absolute Abweichung

A measure of forecast error, e.g. when carrying out exponential smoothing of time-series data. MAD is the average forecast error, either positive or negative, calculated as the sum of the absolute value of forecast error for an periods, divided by the total number of periods evaluated.

mean deviation mittlere Abweichung

Statistics: the arithmetic mean of the deviations (positive numbers) of all the numbers in a set of numbers from their arithmetic mean.

Example: the arithmetic mean of 5, 8, 9 and 10 is 8. The deviations from this mean are 3, O, 1, and 2, giving a mean deviation of 1.5.

mean distribution of sample Durchschnittsverteilung der Probe

mean, geometric geometrisches Mittel

Value calculated by taking the *n*th root of all values in a sample multiplied together.

mean inflation rate Durchschnitts-inflationsrate

meaning *(significance)* Bedeutung; *(sense)* Sinn

meaningless *(insignificant)* bedeutungslos; *(senseless)* sinnlos; unsinnig

mean return Durchschnittsrendite

Securiies: the expected returns of a portfolio of investments.

means of promotion Werbemittel

means of subsistence Unterhaltsmittel

mean value Durchschnittswert; Mittelwert

measurability Messbarkeit

Marketing: degree to which the size, purchasing power and profits of a market segment can be measured.

measurable messbar; absehbar

measure Maß; Ausmaß; *(instrument)* Messinstrument; *(circumference)* Umfang; *(degree)* Grad; *(action)* Maßnahme; *(expedient)* Maßregel; *(to ~)* messen; bemessen

measurement Messung; *(size)* Maß

mechanic Mechaniker

mechanical mechanisch; maschinell

mechanical engineer Maschinenbauer

mechanical engineering Maschinenbau

mechanics Mechanik

mechanism Mechanismus; Triebwerk

mechanistic model mechanistisches Organisationsmodell

Organization: structure characterized by extensive departmentalization, high formalization, limited communication, and little participation in decision making.

mechanization Mechanisierung; Motorisierung

media Medien

Non-personal communication channels including television, print media (newspapers, magazines, direct mail), display media (billboards, signs, posters), and cinema.

media analysis Medienanalyse; Werbeträgeranalyse

Investigation into the relative effectiveness and the relative costs of using the various advertising media in an advertising campaign.

Marketing research first has to provide information on potential customers, such as their reading or television-watching habits.

It also has to be decided how many times the advertisers wish the potential customers to see an advertisement and how great a percentage of the marker they wish to reach. etc.

These elements all have to be considered to plan a campaign that will effectively reach its target audience at a reasonable cost.

media broker Medienmakler

Company that places advertisements for companies wishing to advertise by contacting the media owners.

media buyer Medienkäufer

An person working for an advertiser or for an advertising agency, responsible for purchasing advertising space.

media commission Medienkommission

media coverage Berichterstattung in den Medien; Medienberichterstattung

media evaluation Bewertung als Werbeträger

media event Medienereignis

media fragmentation Zersplitterung der Medien

media impact Medieneinwirkung

Qualitative value of an exposure through a given medium.

media law Mediengesetz

media magazine Medienmagazin

median Halbwert; Median; mittelwertig

The midpoint in a series of numbers; half the data values are above the median, and half are below. It is used to obtain a representation of a data set without distortion.

media option Medienoption

An advertisement or commercial in the production phase, excluding the copy and artwork.

media owners Medienbesitzer

Owners of websites (or other media such as newspapers) that accept advertisements.

media plan Mediaplan

The process of determining the exact media vehicles to be used for advertising, including the dates and times when the advertisements will appear.

media schedule Mediaeinsatzplan; Terminplanung einer Webeaktion

A schedule identifying the media to be used for an advertising program and the dates on which advertisements are to appear.

Decisions have to be made on: reach (the percentage of market expected to see the ad); frequency (how often the market would see the ad); impact (qualitative value of the ad); major media to be used (TV, radio, newspapers, etc.); media vehicles (specific media to be used, e.g. which newspaper);.media timing (the schedule of the appearance of the ads in the chosen media).

mediation Schlichtung; Vermittlung; Beschwichtigung

An approach to alternative dispute resolution using a neutral third party, the mediator.

If the mediator has power to make binding decisions, the process is known as arbitration; if the mediator can only make suggestions, it is known as conciliation.

mediation attempt Vermittlungsversuch

mediator Vermittler; Mittler

The neutral third party who facilitates a negotiated solution between two conflicting parties.

Mediation is most effective if the levels of conflict are limited. To be effective, the mediator must be perceived as neutral and non-coercive. The techniques employed by mediators include reasoning, persuasion, and suggestions for alternatives.

media vehicle Werbeträger

Specific media within each general media type, such as specific magazines, television shows or radio programs.

media weight Gesamtwerbeaufwand

A measure of the amount of media used in a campaign. It can be expressed in terms in terms of the number of commercials and advertisements, number of insertions, time parameters, and budget.

medical examination ärztliche Untersuchung

An examination by a qualified physician required of applicants for a life or health insurance to ascertain if they can be insured.

Medicare Krankenversicherung in den USA

Health insurance system in the USA that covers people who are over 65, people with a permanent illnesses, and those who have been receiving Social Security disability benefits for the past 24 months.

medium Medium; *(means)* Mittel; *(advertising)* Werbeträger

medium of exchange Tauschmittel; Zahlungsmittel

Anything accepted by people as having a certain value that can be used for exchange. The most common medium of exchange is money; but in some primitive markets other commodities, such as cattle may be used.

medium-sized enterprise mittelständischer Betrieb

medium-term mittelfristig

meet treffen; begegnen; kennen lernen; *(financial obligation)* begleichen; *(criteria)* erfüllen; *(responsibility)* erfüllen; *(demand)* decken; *(limitation)* einhalten; *(meeting)* tagen

meeting Treffen; Zusammenkunft; Zusammentreffen; *(briefing)* Besprechung; *(consultation)* Beratung; *(session)* Sitzung; *(convention)* Versammlung; Konferenz; Tagung

megabit Megabit

One million bits. Abbreviated as Mb

member Mitglied; *(family)* Angehöriger

member country Mitgliedsland

member of a banking syndicate Konsortialbank

member of the board Vorstandsmitglied

membership Mitgliedschaft; Zugehörigkeit

membership fee Mitgliedsbeitrag

membership group Zugehörigkeitsgruppe

Group to which a person belongs and that has a direct influence on a person's behavior.

membership promotion Mitgliederwerbung

membership register Mitgliedsbuch

membership roster Mitgliederliste; Mitgliedsbuch

memorandum Memorandum; Vermerk; *(note)* Notiz; Mitteilung

memorandum bill Schuldwechsel

memorandum of association Gründungsvertrag

memorandum of understanding Absichtserklärung; Vorvertrag

memory Gedächtnis; Speicher

mention Erwähnung; *(to ~)* erwähnen

mentoring Betreuung; als Mentor handeln

Long-term helping and learning relationship between an experienced person (mentor) who shares his knowledge, experience and insights with a less-experienced person who seeks to profit from this exchange. The role inculdes coaching, counseling, and sponsorship.

mercantile handeltreibend; kaufmännisch; geschäftlich; handels-

mercantile trade Warenhandel

mercantilism Merkantilismus

Economic philosophy advocating that countries should simultaneously encourage exports and discourage imports.

During the seventeenth and eighteenth century mercantilism was quite widesprad, as trading nations generated wealth and power by exporting manufactured goods in exchange for gold.

mercantile law Handelsrecht

The commercial law of a country, including those aspects that apply to banking, companies. contracts, copyrights, insolvency, insurance, patents, the sale of goods, shipping, trademarks, transport, and warehousing.

merchandise Ware; Handelsgut; Handelsware; *(to ~)* Handel treiben; handeln

Any commodity offered for sale.

merchandise account Warenkonto

merchandise appeal Kaufanreiz

merchandise balance of trade Handelsbilanz

merchandise broker Produktenmakler

An agent who brings the buyers and sellers of a merchandise together and negotiates an agreement. A merchandise broker does not take possession of the actual merchandise and is paid a commission or fee.

merchandise export Warenexport

merchandise item Wareneinheit

merchandise market Gütermarkt

merchandisers' fair Verkaufsmesse

merchandise trade Güterhandel

merchandise traffic Warenverkehr

merchandise value Warenwert

merchandising Absatzförderung; Warenhandel

Advertising: The sales efforts of retailers, wholesalers or dealers, who use such techniques as advertising, point-of-purchase displays, special sales, and in-store promotions to sell a product.

merchandising concern Handelsunternehmen

merchandising conglomerate Handelskonglomerat

Corporation that combines several different retailing forms under central ownership and that share the same distribution and management functions.

merchandising scheme Verkaufsplan

merchant Kaufmann; Kauffrau; *(dealer)* Händler; *(trader)* Handelsherr

merchant bank Handelsbank

A bank that do not offer retail banking but facitliate trade and commerce. Merchant bank also offer investment banking, counseling, mergers and acquisitions, and a variety of other services.

merchant bankers Handelsbankier

merchant banking Remboursgeschäft

merchant fleet Handelsflotte; Kauffahrtsflotte

merchant ship Handelsschiff

merchant wholesaler Großhandelsunternehmen

Independently owned business that takes title to the merchandise it handles.

Mercosur Südamerikanisches Freihandelsabkommen

Pact between Argentina, Brazil, Paraguay and Uruguay to establish a free trade area.

merge zusammenschließen: verschmelzen; fusionieren

Companies: the process of combining two companies so that only one legal entity remains.

Office: the technique of combining two or more files or lists into one.

merger Fusion; Firmenzusammenschluß; Verschmelzung; Zusammenlegung

A combination of two or more businesses on an equal footing that results in the creation of a new entity. The shareholders of the combining entities mutually share the risks and rewards of the new entity and no one party to the merger obtains control over another.

merger and acquisition (M&A) Fusion und Akquisition; Fusion und Übernahmen

merger case Fusionsfall

merit Verdienst; Vorzug; Wert; *(to ~)* *(deserve)* verdienen

meritocracy Leistungsgesellschaft

mesh Netz(-werk); *(to ~)* ineinander greifen; (to *cooperate)* zusammenarbeiten

message Nachricht; Botschaft; *(advertising)* Werbeaussage

Communication: the content of communication, encoded and sent with the intention of transfering meaning.

Advertising: The underlying theme or idea in advertisement

message source Nachrichtenquelle

Company, the brand name, the salesperson of the brand, or the actor in the ad who endorses the product.

messenger Bote; *(runner)* Läufer; *(bank)* Kassenbote

metadata Metadaten

Metadata are data that describe other data. Generally, a set of metadata describe a single set of data, called a resource.

metamorphosis Metamorphose; Umwandlung

Groups: third stage in the socialization process in which a new employee changes and adjusts to the job, work group, norms, and organization.

metal Metall

metal industry Metallindustrie

metaphor Metapher

meta search engines Meta-Suchmaschinen

Internet: meta search engines submit keywords typed by users to a range of search engines in order to increase the number of relevant pages since different search engines may have indexed different sites.

meta-tags Meta-Tags

HTML elements used to provide structured metadata about a web page. Such elements are placed as tags in the `head` section of an HTML document.

meter Meter; *(measuring device)* Messinstrument; Messapparat; *(counter)* Zähler; *(to ~)* messen; abzählen

method Methode; Verfahren; Verfahrensweise

method of computation Berechnungsmethode

method of payment Zahlungsweise

method of production Produktionsweise

metric metrisch

metrics for internet marketing Metriken für Internet-Marketing

Measures that indicate the effectiveness of internet marketing activities in meeting customer, business and marketing objectives.

metric system metrisches System

A system of measurement based on the decimal system, first formalized in France at the end of the 18th century and by the 1830s widely adopted in Europe.

metropolis Großstadt; Metropole

metropolitan großstädtisch

microchip Mikrochip

microcomputer Mikrocomputer; Kleincomputer; Mikrorechner

microculture Mikrokultur; Kleinstkultur

microeconomics Mikroökonomie

The branch of economics concerned with the economic decisions made by individuals, households, and firms.

Individuals or households are concerned with the optimal allocation of a given budget, the labor supply choice, and the effects of taxation.

The firm is largely concerned with the production process, costs, and the marketing of output, dependent on the type of competition faced.

microelectronics Mikroelektronik

microenvironment Mikroumgebung

Forces close to the company that affect its ability to serve its customers - the company, market channel firms, customer markets, competitors, and publics.

micro-function Mikrofunktion

micro-marketing Mirkomarketing

Form of target marketing in which companies tailor their marketing programs to the needs and wants of narrowly defined geographic, demographic, psychographic or behavioral segments.

micro-payments Mikrozahlungen

Digital cash systems that allow very small sums of money to be transferred, but with lower security. Such small sums do not warrant a credit card payment, because processing is too costly.

microprocessor Mikroprozessor

An integrated circuit that contains on one chip the arithmetic, logical, and control functions of the central processing unit.

microsite Mikrosite

Specialized content that is part of a web site that is not necessarily owned by the organization. If owned by the company it may be part of an extranet.

Microsoft Internet Information Server (IIS)

Web server developed by Microsoft that runs on Windows NT.

microstructure Mikrostruktur

microtechnology Mikrotechnologie

microwave Mikrowelle

middle Mitte; Mittel-; mittlere; mittelmäßig; mittelprächtig

middle class Mittelklasse; Mittelstand

middle-class zur Mittelklasse gehörend; mittelständisch

middleman Mittelsmann; *(jobber)* Zwischenhändler; *(broker)* Makler; *(intermediary)* Vermittler; *(reseller)* Wiederverkäufer

Distribution channel firms that help a company find customers or make sales to them, including wholesalers and retailers who buy and resell goods.

middle management Management auf mittlerer Führungsebene

Managers with full management responsibilities reporting to higher-level managers, e.g. departmental managers, plant managers, assistant managers, and so on.

middle of the month Monatsmitte

midsection Mittelsektion; Mittelteil

midsize mittelgroß

midyear Jahresmitte; Halbjahrespunkt

midyear result Halbjahresergebnis

migrant worker Wanderarbeiter; Gastarbeiter

Worker moving from one region or country to another to find employment. Migrant workers are used extensively for crop harvesting, mandating that they follow the harvest seasons.

militant militant; kämpferisch; aggressiv

military Militär; Militär-; militärisch

military-industrial complex militärisch-industrieller Komplex

Relationship between the military and industry. It was first described by President Eisenhower in his farewell address, where he warned of the irresponsible power of the military-industrial complex.

milking strategy kurzfristiges Profitstreben

Short-range marketing strategy planned to take the largest possible profit from an item in the shortest amount of time without regard to the item's long-range possibilities for sales.

millionaire Millionär

millions of bits per second (mbps) Millionen Bits pro Sekunde

mind mapping Mindmapping

mine Zeche; Bergwerk; Mine; *(to ~)* fördern; abbauen; *(explosives)* verminen

miner Bergarbeiter; Bergmann

mineral Mineral; mineralisch

miners Bergleute

minicomputer Minicomputer; mittelgroßer Computer

minimax principle Minimax-Prinzip

Decision criterion based on reducing to the lowest level the difference between the possible outcomes and the best possible outcome resulting from the decision. The minimax principle is used to select result(s) with the least amount of regret in case of failure.

minimize minimieren; *(to reduce)* auf ein Mindestmaß verkleinern

minimum Minimum; Mindestmaß

minimum balance requirement Mindestreserve

minimum collateral Mindestsicherung

minimum interest Mindestzins

minimum purchase Mindestabnahme; Mindestverkauf

Mutual funds: the amount required to open a new account (Minimum Initial Purchase) or to deposit into an existing account (Minimum Additional Purchase). These minima may be lowered for buyers participating in an automatic purchase plan

minimum size Mindestgröße

minimum variance portfolio Minimum-Varianz-Portfolio

Portfolio of risky assets with the lowest possible variance. By definition, this portfolio must also have the lowest possible standard deviation.

minimum wage garantierter Mindestlohn; gesetzlicher Mindestlohn

Lowest allowable hourly wage permitted by the government or a union contract for an employee performing a particular job.

minimum working hours Mindestarbeitszeit

mining Bergbaum

mining company Bergbauunternehmen

minister *(government)* Minister; *(clergy)* Pastor; *(to ~)* ministrieren; betreuen

ministerial ministeriell; verwaltungsmäßig; amtlich

minister of economic affairs Wirtschaftsminister

minister of finance Finanzminister

ministry *(government)* Ministerium; Ministeramt; Regierungsabteilung; *(area of competency)* Ressort; *(clergy)* kirchliches Amt

minor *(age)* Minderjähriger; minderjährig; (*size*) klein; jung; *(quantity)* gering; *(problem)* geringfügig.

Person under the age of maturity specified by law (18 to 21 years, depending on the state).

Certain contracts, entered into by a minor, are voidable by the minor (the other party is bound, only the minor may void them).

minority Minorität; Minderheit

minority business Betrieb ethnischer Minderheit

Small business in the US owned and operated by members of a minority, such as American Africans, officially defineds as "socially and economically disadvantaged".

The federal government is adressing their specific needs by dedicating a certain share of government contracts for minority businesses.

minority interest Minderheitsbeteiligung

The interest of individual shareholders in a company where more than 50% of the company is owned by a holding company. These shareholders will receive their full share of profits in the form of dividends although they will be unable to influence company policy as they will always be outvoted by the majority interest held by he holding company.

minority investment Minderheitsbeteiligung

minority participation Minderheitsbeteiligung

minority partner Minderheitsgesellschafter

mint Münzamt; Münzanstalt; *(brand new)* nagelneu; *(to ~)* münzen

A factory where money is produced under the authority of the government. A mint is usually responsible for the production of coins rather than paper money.

Mintzberg, Henry (* 1939)

One of the most prolific management writers, Mintzberg found that a manager's time is being fragmented by interruptions and that the manager spends as much time dealing with people outside as inside the company. Managers don't write down much of what they hear, so that the strategic data-bank of the organization isn't in the memory of its computer.

His influential work divided into three main categories: 1.) strategy-making: what managers actually do with their time 2.) how their mental processes work: the ′right brain, left brain' theories 3.) how organizations design themselves to suit their needs.

He identified ten principal managerial roles, grouped into three main areas: 1.) interpersonal 2.) informational 3.) decisional. The roles are part of an integrated whole and can not easily be separated. He concluded that most organizational structures fall into five basic categories – simple structured, machine bureaucracy, professional bureaucracy, divisionalized form and adhocracy.

Biography: born in Canada, Professor of management at McGill University (Montreal) and at International Business school at Fontainebleau in France (INSEAD), studied at the Sloan School of Management, Massachusetts Institute of Technology, international and multicultural teacher, supervising a co-operative venture by five business schools in Canada, England, Japan, France and India.

Major publications: (1973, 1980) The Nature of Managerial work, (1979) The Structuring of Organizations, (1983) Structures in Fives: Designing Effective Organizations, (1983) Power In and Around Organizations, (1989) Mintzberg on Management, (1994) The Rise and Fall of Strategic Planning, (1994) Sloan Management Review, (1996) Harvard Business Review, (1996) Harvard Business Review

minute Minute; Augenblick; Liste; *(size)* winzig

minutes Protokoll

The written records of a meeting. They are an important source of information and are normally stored for later reference.

misallocation Fehlallokation

miscalculate falsch berechnen; sich verrechnen

miscellaneous *(mixed)* gemischt; vermischt; *(different)* verschieden; verschiedenartig

misdirect fehlleiten; vergeuden; falsch leiten; *(mail)* falsch adressieren

misdirection Fehlleitung; *(mail)* falsche Adressierung; *(misinvestment)* Fehlinvestition

mislead irreführen; fehlleiten; täuschen

mismanage falsch managen; schlecht verwalten; schlecht wirtschaften

mismanagement Misswirtschaft; schlechte Verwaltung

A general term descrbing management that is careless, inefficient, and fails to achieve its goals.

misrepresentation falsche und ungenaue Angaben

A false or misleading statement made to induce a prospect to make a purchase; can be intentional or unintentional.

miss vermissen; *(omission)* versäumen; *(airplane)* verpassen; *(to miss the mark)* verfehlen

missing amount Fehlbetrag

mission statement Leitbild

Provides the ground rules for the way in which a company is managed. Mission statements are an element of corporate policy that serves to motivate all employees in the sense of understanding the corporate beliefs.

A good mission statement therefore answers the question: Who do we want to be? It is a written expression of *corporate identity*. The realization of mission statements depends largely on the will in top management to live up to these principles.

mistake Fehler; *(bad choice)* Mißgriff; *(to ~)* verwechseln

mitigate mildern; *(to moderate)* mäßigen; *(alleviate)* lindern

mitigation of damages Schadensminderung

The legal requirement that someone who has been negatively affected by the action of another must employ reasonable diligence and care to avoid aggravating the injury or increasing the damages.

mix Mischung; *(grouping)* Zusammenstellung; *(assortment)* Sortiment; *(to ~)* mischen; vermischen; *(beverage)* mixen

mixed economy Mischwirtschaft

An economic system in which both market forces and government intervention determine resource allocation and prices. Certain sectors of the economy are left to private ownership and free market mechanisms, while other sectors have significant government ownership and government planning.

mixer *(stocks)* Aktie mit hoher Rendite

mixture Mischung; *(compound)* Zusammensetzung

MM Proposition I MM-These I

Proposition of Modigliani and Miller (MM) which states that a firm cannot change the total value of its outstanding securities by changing its capital structure proportions.

MM Proposition II MM-These II

Proposition of Modigliani and Miller (MM) which states that the cost of equity is a linear function of the firm' s debt-equity ratio.

mobile mobil; *(free to move)* bewegungsfrei; *(movable)* beweglich

mobility Mobilität; Bewegungsfreiheit; *(labor force)* Freizügigkeit; *(agility)* Beweglichkeit

mobility barriers Mobilitätsbarrieren

mobility of labor Arbeitsmobilität; Arbeitskräftemobilität

The extent to which workers are willing to move from one region or country to another (geographical mobility) or to change from one occupation to another (occupational mobility).

The more highly skilled a worker, the less his occupational mobility will be, but he will often be highly geographically mobile. An unskilled worker will often be both occupationally and geographically mobile.

mobilization Mobilisierung; *(appropriation)* Bereitstellung

model Modell; *(design)* Entwurf; *(template)* Schablone; *(to ~)* modellieren

model case Beispielsfall; Musterfall

modeling Modelling; Modellbildung; Erstellen eines Modells

model of economic cycles Konjunkturmodell

modem Modem

Abbreviation for modulator-demodulator. A device that enables a computer to transmit and receive data by means of a communications link, such as a telephone line.

moderate mäßig; bescheiden; *(to ~)* moderieren; *(to mitigate)* mäßigen; *(to mediate)* vermitteln

moderation Mäßigung; *(modesty)* Bescheidenheit; *(mediation)* Vermittlung

Act of mediating between two parties, or for running discussions. There are various moderation techniques, such as brain writing, meta-planning, mind-mapping, creativity techniques, minute-taking during discussions, and chairing meetings.

moderator Moderator; *(mediator)* Vermittler; *(panel discussion)* Diskussionsleiter

modernization Modernisierung

modest bescheiden; *(moderate)* maßvoll; mäßig; *(decent)* anständig

modification Modifikation; *(change)* Änderung; Modifizierung; *(rearrangement)* Umstellung

modified rebuy modifizierter Wiederkauf

Business buying situation in which the buyer wants to modify product specifications, prices, terms or suppliers.

modify modifizieren; *(to change)* abändern

modular modular; *(building blocks)* bausteinartig

module Modul; *(building block)* Baustein; *(unit in a series)* Serieneinheit

mom-and-pop store (US) Tante-Emma-Laden

monetarism Monetarismus; Geldwirtschaft

An economic theory that emphasizes the importance of the money supply as an instrument of economic policy. Monetarists advocate a slow but steady growth in the money supply, controlled by the central bank, which would reduce inflation, encourage entrepreneurial activity, reduce unemployment and lead to economic growth.

monetarist Monetarist; Geldwirtschaftler

Economist who believes that the money supply is a key factor of economic policy. Most prominent in recent times has been Milton Friedman.

monetary Geld-; Währungs-; geldlich; finanziell; monetär

Pertaining to, or having to do with, money, money creation, money supply, and government management of money.

monetary assets Geldvermögen

monetary authority Währungsbehörde; Währungsinstanz

monetary claim Geldforderung

monetary control Kontrolle der Geldpolitik

Attempts by a government to use the central bank in order to control the money supply. This happens, for example, in the UK, whilst the European Central Bank is largely independent of government interference.

monetary fund Währungsfonds

monetary needs Währungsbedarf

monetary order Währungsordnung

monetary policy Währungspolitik; Geldmarktpolitik; Geldpolitik

Efforts by a central bank of managing money supply in order to achieve specific goals - such as constraining inflation, maintaining an exchange rate, achieving full employment or economic growth.

The tools available involve changing certain interest rates, either directly or indirectly through open market operations, setting reserve requirements, or trading in foreign exchange markets.

The basic choices are either an expansionary policy which increases the total supply of money in the economy, and a contractionary policy which decreases the total money supply. Expansionary policy is traditionally used to combat unemployment in a recession by lowering interest rates, while contractionary policy has the goal of raising interest rates to combat inflation.

monetary policy tools Werkzeug der Geldpolitik/ Währungspolitik

monetary reform Währungsreform

The revision of a country's currency by the introduction of a substantial change to the system, such a new currency. Other examples include the decimalization of the UK currency (1971), or the replacement of 12 EU currencies by the euro in 1999-2002.

monetary reserves Währungsreserven

A government's stock of foreign currency and precious metals, used to back up its currency; also called *international* reserves.

Central Bank requirements that banks keep on hand certain proportions of their deposits in cash or near-cash equivalents.

monetary system Währungssystem

The system used by a country to provide the public with money for internal use and to control the exchange of its own currency with those of foreign countries.

monetary theory Geldtheorie

monetary transaction Zahlungsverkehr

Marketing transaction in which goods or services are exchanged for money.

monetary union Währungsunion

A situation where several countries have agreed to share a single currency among them, for example, the East Caribbean Dollar. The control over monetary policy is given to a central bank independent of member governments.

A monetary union differs from an economic and monetary union, where it is not just currency but also economic policy that is pooled or co-ordinated, as in the European Union.

monetary unit Währungseinheit; Geldeinheit

The standard unit of currency in a country, related to those of other countries by a foreign exchange rate.

monetary value Geldwert

monetary variable währungspolitische Größe

monetize *(to establish the coinage standard)* den Münzfuß festsetzen; *(to establish as legal tender)* zum gesetzlichen Zahlungsmittel machen

money Geld; *(coinage)* Münze; *(legal tender)* Zahlungsmittel

A medium of exchange that also functions as a unit of account and a store of value. It enhances economic development by enabling goods to be bought and sold without the need for barter.

A problem of money has been its debasement as a store of value as a result of inflation. With the supply of money as a monopoly of the state, most governments and central banks are committed in principle to stable prices.

money and capital market Kreditmarkt

money capital Geldkapital

money debt Geldschuld

money due Geldforderung

money income Geldeinkommen

Income measured only in money. It contrasts with real income, which takes into account changes in the purchasing power of money due to inflation or deflation.

money lender Kapitalgeber; Geldgeber

money manager Geldverwalter; *(assets)* Vermögensverwalter

money management Geldverwaltung; Finanzverwaltung

money market Geldmarkt; Kreditmarkt

General term for banks and other financial institutions dealing in government securities such as bonds and treasury notes, bills of exchange, negotiable certificates of deposit, commercial paper, banker's acceptances, and others.

The money market has no central meeting place like the share market, but dealers, borrowers and lenders are connected through the telecommunications network.

money market business Geldmarkt-geschäft

money market certificate Geldmarktpapier

money market fund Geldmarktkapital; Geldmarktinvestmentfonds

Mutual fund that invests only in short term securities, such as bankers' acceptances, commercial paper, repurchase agreements and government bills.

money market interest Kapitalmarktzins

money market investment Geldmarktanlage

money market securities Geldmarktpapiere

money market transaction Geldmarktgeschäft

money receipts Geldeingang

money reserve Geldreserve

money supply Geldversorgung; *(money in circulation)* Geldmenge

The quantity of money issued by a country's monetary authorities, usually the central bank.

Economists identify several types of money supply, based on liquidity:

Ml: sum of currency, demand deposits, checking accounts, travelers' checks, etc.

M2: Ml plus savings and other highly liquid time deposits.

M3: M2 plus other very liquid instruments

If the demand for money is stable, the widely accepted quantity theory of money implies that increases in the money supply will lead directly to an increase in the price level i.e. to inflation. Since the *1970s* most western governments have attempted to reduce inflation by controlling the money supply.

money supply policy Geldmengenpolitik

money supply target Geldmengenziel

money trade Geldhandel

money transfer Geldübermittlung; Geldüberweisung

money transfers Zahlungsverkehr

monitor Abhörgerät; Abhörung; *(TV, Computer)* Bildschirm; Bildschirmgerät; *(to ~) (to supervise)* kontrollieren; *(to check)* überwachen; *(to tap)* abhören

monitor screen Bildschirm

monopolist Monopolist; Monopolbesitzer; *(sole trader)* Alleinhändler

Firm or individual entrepreneur that is the sole producer of a good and so represents the entire market supply of that good.

monopolistic monopolistisch

monopolistic competition monopolistische Konkurrenz

Monopolistically competitive markets have the following characteristics: there are many producers and many consumers; consumers have clearly defined preferences and sellers attempt to differentiate their products from those of their competitors; the goods and services are heterogeneous; there are no barriers to entry and exit.

The only difference between a monopolistically competitive market and perfect competition is the presence of heterogeneous products, and a great deal of non-price competition (based on product differentiation). This gives the company a certain amount of influence over the market; it can raise its prices without losing all the customers, owing to brand loyalty. This means that an individual firm's demand curve is downward sloping, in contrast to perfect competition, which has a perfectly elastic demand schedule.

monopolization Monopolisierung

monopolize monopolisieren; Monopol besitzen; *(exclusive control)* allein beherrschen

monopoly Monopol; *(exclusive right)* ausschließliche Berechtigung; *(company)* marktbeherrschendes Unternehmen; *(exclusive selling right)* Alleinverkaufsrecht; *(exclusive manufacturing right)* Alleinherstellungsrecht

A market situation in which there is only a single seller and many buyers. If there is a single seller and a single buyer the situation is called bilateral monopoly.

In its pure form, which is characterized by an absence of competition, a monopoly leads to high prices and a general lack of responsiveness to the needs and desires of consumers.

monopoly price Monopolpreis

The equilibrium price reached in a monopoly, which is normally higher than under competition because it maximizes the monopolist's total profit.

monopoly problem Monopolproblem

monopsony Monopson; Nachfrage-monopol

Market situation in which there is only a single buyer.

Monte Carlo method Monte Carlo Methode

A mathematical simulation method that uses random numbers to determine events. An experiment is repeated many times with different randomly generated data to allow statistical conclusions to be drawn.

monthly Monatszeitschrift; monatlich

monthly average Monatsdurchschnitt

monthly balance sheet Monatsbilanz

monthly earnings Monatsverdienst

monthly production Monatsproduktion

monthly rate Monatsrate

monthly statement of account monatlicher Kontoauszug; Monatsauszug

month's end Monatsende

moods Stimmungen; Launen

Feelings that tend to be less intense than emotions, that lack a contextual stimulus, and aren't directed at an object.

Moody's investors service Moodys Kapitalanlegerservice

Financial services company that assignes grades to debt securities, from best, high, favorable, and adequate quality, respectively. All four are investment grade or bank quality.

moonlighting Nebentätigkeit; Nebenjob; Schwarzarbeit

A colloquial term for an employee working in a second job for additional income. The term derives from the fact that many of these jobs are night jobs.

Moore's Law Moores Gesetz

Theory that suggests that the power of microprocessor technology doubles and its costs of production fall in half every 18 months.

moral appeal moralischer Reiz

An appeal in an advertisement or sales literature that is directed at the recipient's sense of what is right and proper.

morale *(workplace)* Arbeitsmoral

HRM: the attitude workers have towards the quality of their work life. For a manager, it is important to keep morale high because it motivates workers.

moral hazard subjektives Risiko; moralische Versuchung

Insurance: describes the tendency of individuals, once they are insured against a certain risk, to behave so as to make that risk more likely.

moratorium Moratorium; *(payment)* Zahlungsaufschub; *(standstill agreement)* Stillhalteabkommen

mortgage Hypothek; *(encumberment)* hypothekarische Belastung; Grundpfandrecht; *(paper)* Hypothekenbrief; *(to ~)* verpfänden; hypothekarisch belasten

A debt instrument by which the borrower (mortgagor) gives the lender (mortgagee) a lien on property as security for the repayment of a loan. The lien is removed once the obligation is fully paid.

mortgage-backed security hypothekarisch gesichertes Wertpapier

A bond in which the collateral is provided by a mortgage or portfolio of mortgages, usually insured to cover any defaults.

mortgage bank Hypothekenbank; Hypothekarinstitut

mortgage bond clearing house Pfandbriefzentrale

mortgage company Pfandbriefbank

mortgagee Geldgeber; Hypothekar

mortgage interest Hypothekenzinsen

mortgage insurance Hypothekenversicherung

Insurance that covers the lender against the losses incurred if the borrower defaults on a mortgage.

mortgage-lending institution Pfandbriefbank

mortgage loan Hypothekendarlehen; Hypothekenkredit

mortgage securities Hypothekendarlehen

Debt obligation secured by a mortgage on the real property of the borrower.

mortgagor Hypothekenschuldner; Pfandschuldner

most-favored-nation Land mit Meistbegünstigungsstatus

most-favored-nation clause Meistbegünstigungsklausel

A clause in a trade agreement between two countries stating that each will accord to the other the same treatment as regards tariffs and quotas as they extend to the most favored nation with which each trades.

motion Antrag

A proposal put before a meeting for discussion. If the motion is passed by a majority, it becomes a resolution.

motion of censure Mißbilligungsantrag

motion of no confidence Mißtrauensantrag

motivate motivieren; *(by exerting pressure)* antreiben; anregen

motivation Motivation; Beweggrund

Descriptive term for the mental processes that arouse, sustain, and direct human behavior, resulting in changes to a person´s physiological and psychological conditions.

Motivation can stem from processes within an individual (intrinsic motivation) or from the impact of factors acting on the individual from outside (extrinsic motivation); in most cases these two influences are continually interacting.

motivational research Motivationsforschung

Research conducted in order to determine the motivations behind consumer purchases, attempting to learn why people behave as they do, why they make certain purchases, and why they respond to specific types of advertising appeals. The results are used by advertisers to plan new products, to develop advertising campaigns, and to create more effective advertising.

motive Beweggrund; *(impulse)* Antrieb; Veranlassung

Need that is sufficiently pressing to direct the person to seek satisfaction of the need.

motor insurance Kfz Versicherung

A form of insurance covering loss or damage to motor vehicles and any legal liabilities for damage to other people's property.

Drivers have a legal obligation to be covered against third-party claims, but most drivers also have a comprehensive insurance, providing wide coverage of all the risks involved in owning a motor vehicle.

move *(house)* Umzug; *(strategy)* Schritt; *(to ~)* bewcgcn; *(house)* umziehen; *(proceedings)* in Vorschlag bringen; beantragen

move backwards zurückgehen

movement Bewegung; *(tendency)* Tendenz

movement of freight Güterverkehr

movement of goods Warenverkehr

mover *(proceedings)* Antragsteller; *(transport)* Fuhrunternehmer; *(household)* Möbelspediteur

moving average gleitender Mittelwert; gleitender Durchschnittswert

An average that is based on security or commodity prices over a period of time, days, months, years. It is used in charts and technical analysis, to show the trends of the price development. *Example:* a 30-day *moving average* includes prices for the past 30 days.

mp3

Popular audio file format. Files encoded in MP3 compress data at a 10:1 ratio, making it suitable for sending large, high-quality files over the internet

multibrand strategy Mehrmarkenstrategie

Strategy under which a seller develops two or more brands in the same product category.

multichannel marketing Marketing über mehrere Vertriebswege

Marketing one's products or services using two or more marketing channels, often to reach more than one marker segment. Retail chains, for example, may use the shops to distribute their products, and also use catalogue selling.

multiculturalism Multikulturalismus

Business policy emphasizing the need to be responsive to the unique conditions prevailing in different national markets.

multidimensional contribution accounting mehrdimensionale Deckungsbeitragsrechnung

Multidimensional contribution accounts are devised according to the principle that only those structure costs are deducted in steps from the CM I which are unequivocally assignable to the object in question.

As a result, a company can have clear contribution targets per sales area, profit center, distribution channel, strategic business unit, etc.

multilateral multilateral; vielseitig

multilateral agreement multilaterales Abkommen

Multilateral Agreement on Investment (MAI) multilaterals Investitionsabkommen

Agreement that would make it illegal for signatory states to discriminate against foreign investors; would have liberalized rules governing FDI between OECD states.

multilateral netting multilaterale Saldierung

Technique used to reduce the number of transactions between subsidiaries of the firm, thereby reducing the total transaction costs arising from foreign exchange dealings and transfer fees.

multilingual vielsprachig

multimedia Multimedia

Computers: digitalized information that combines different types of formats, such as text, images, animation, video and audio.

Advertising: campaign that utilizes two or more media, normally one to support the other, such as a radio commercial supporting a newspaper advertisement.

multinational multinational

multinational company (MNC) multinationales Unternehmen

A company that operates in several foreign countries and makes its major management decisions in a global context.

Multinational companies (MNC) can be divided into three broad groups:

Horizontally integrated MNCs manage production establishments in different countries producing the same or similar products.

Vertically integrated MNCs manage production establishments in certain countries to produce products that serve as input to its production establishments in other countries.

Diversified MNCs manage production establishments in different countries that are neither horizontally or vertically integrated.

multiple vielfach; mehrfach; mannigfaltig

multiple-choice question Multiple-choice Fragen

A question requiring a respondent to select an answer from a list of answers provided with the question.

multiple niching Anbieten mehrerer Nischenprodukten

Adopting a strategy of having several independent offerings that appeal to several different sub-segments of customer.

multiple rates of return mehrfache Rendite

More than one rate of return from the same project that make the net present value of the project equal to zero. This situation arises when the IRR method is used for a project in which negative cash flows follow positive ones.

multiple regression multiple Regression

Statistical technique to analyze the relation between one dependent variable and several independent variables.

multiples Multiplikator; Multipel-

multiplicity Vielfältigkeit; Vielfalt

multiplier *(quantity)* Vermehrer; *(intensification)* Verstärker; *(math)* Multiplikator

A factor applied by multiplication to estimate another value. For example, a *population multiplier* of 2 calculates that for each new job created, a city´s population will grow by two.

multiplier effect Multiplikatoreffekt

In economic theory, the spending/income multiplier effect occurs when a change in spending causes a disproportionate change in aggregate demand. It is particularly associated with Keynesian economics.

multipoint competition Mehrpunktkonkurrenz

Arises when two or more enterprises encounter each other in different regional markets, national markets, or industries.

multipoint pricing Mehrpunktpreissetzung

Occurs when a pricing strategy in one market may have an impact on a rival's pricing strategy in another market.

multipurpose Mahrzweck-; vielzweckig

multipurpose internet mail extension (MIME)

Internet e-mail protocol that allows the transmission of graphics, audio, video, binary files and other non-textual content.

Some e-mail encryption programs use a variation of this protocol, called S/MIME, to encode text messages. In addition, web servers and browsers use the mime protocol to identify new multimedia file types and to specify what kind of software is needed to decode these files

multipurpose software Multizwecksoftware; Allzwecksoftware

multisegment targeting Zielansprache mehrerer Segmente; Targeting mehrerer Segmente

multisided vielseitig

municipal kommunal; gemeindlich; *(municipally owned)* gemeindeeigen

municipal bond kommunale Schuldverschreibung; *(loan)* Kommunalanleihe; *(debt)* Kommunalobligation

A debt security issued by a state or local government body such as a county, city, town, or municipal authority. The purpose is to raise capital for expenditures like the construction of highways or other public works.

municipality; Gemeinde; Bezirk; Kommune; Stadt

municipal loan Kommunaldarlehen

Murphy's Law Murphy's Gesetz

Administrative aphorism stating that whatever can go wrong, will go wrong at the worst tıme with the worst consequences. The law originated allegedly with developmental engineer Ed Murphy in 1949, who was frustrated by a laboratory technician's error.

mushroom Pilz; *(to ~)* pilzartig aufschießen

muster Musterung; *(to ~) (to procure)* auftreiben; *(to collect)* zusammenbringen

mutual gegenseitig; wechselseitig

mutual company Gesellschaft auf Genseitigkeit

A type of corporation in the US with no capital stock. Ownership and profits are distributed among members in proportion to the amount of business they do with the company.

mutual fund Anlagefonds; Investmentfonds; *(company)* Anlagegesellschaft; Investmentgesellschaft

An investment company that raises money from shareholders and invests it professionally in stocks, bonds, options, commodities, or money market securities.

mutual insurance company Versicherungsverein auf Gegenseitigkeit

An insurance company which is owned by its policy-holders and which does not issue stock for purchase on the stock exchange.

mutually exclusive investment decisions sich gegenseitig ausschließende Investitionsentscheidungen

Investment decisions in which the acceptance of one project precludes the acceptance of other projects.

mutual savings bank Genossenschaftsbank; genossenschaftsähnliche Sparkasse

A type of bank in the US that is owned by its depositors and operates for their benefit. Most of these banks hold a large portion of their assets in home mortgage loans.

mutual stock fund Aktienfonds

Myers-Briggs type indicator (MBTI) Myers-Briggs-Typenindikator

100-question personality test that taps four characteristics and classifies people into one of 16 personality types. On the basis of the answers individuals give to the test, they are classified as extroverted or introverted (E or I), sensing or intuitive (S or N), thinking or feeling (T or F) and perceiving or judging (P or J). These classification are then combined into 16 personality types.

N

name Name; *(designation)* Bezeichnung; *(to ~)* nennen; (*to appoint)* ernennen; *(date, price)* festsetzen; bestimmen; *(to state)* angeben

name paper Solawechsel

narrowcast Netzwerk oder Programm, das für ein spezielles Publikum bestimmt ist

Electronic media term referring primarily to cable channels because they contain very focused electronic content that appeals to special-interest markets.

narrow money eng gefasste Geldmenge

An informal name for the part of the money supply that can directly perform the function of a medium of exchange, normally M0 and M1.

NASDAQ automatisiertes Kursnotierungssystem der Vereinigung der US-Wertpapierhändler

Abbreviation for: National Association of Securities Dealers Automated Quotations.

nation Nation; Volk

national Staatsbürger; Einwohner; national; staatlich

national accounts budget Nationalbudget

national advertising überregionale Werbung; landesweite Werbung

Advertising that is aimed at a nationwide market, as opposed to a regional or local market.

national bank Nationalbank

national bankruptcy Staatsbankrott

national budget Staatsbudget; Staatshaushalt

national currency Landeswährung

national debt Staatsschuld

The total amount of government borrowing still outstanding, owed to its creditors, individuals and institutions. The figure includes debt incurred at any level of government (central, federal, national, municipal, local, regional). The national debt of the United States passed the $8 trillion mark in October 2005.

national deficit Staatsdefizit

The yearly amount by which public spending exceeds revenues. All previous yearly amounts added together are the national debt.

national economy Nationalökonomie

The totality of all economic activity that takes place in one country, including that of all individuals, businesses and institutions.

national finances Staatsfinanzen

All the financial activities of government authorities in one country. More often called public finance.

national income Volkseinkommen

The total income generated by all of a country's factors of production. Some common measures are Gross National Product (GNP), Gross Domestic Product (GDP), Gross National Income (GNI), Net National Product (NNP), and Net National Income (NNI).

national income accounting volkswirtschaftliche Gesamtrechnung

Measures of national income and output to estimate the value of goods and services produced in an economy.

They use a system of national accounting and produce measures such as Gross National Product (GNP), Gross Domestic Product (GDP), Gross National Income(GNI), Net National Product (NNP).

national insolvency Staatsbankrott

nationalization Verstaatlichung; *(individual person)* Einbürgerung; Naturalisierung

The process of bringing the assets of a company into the ownership of the state.

One argument for nationalization is that if a company possesses a natural monopoly, the profits it earns should be shared by the whole population through state ownership. Another argument might be that particular industries are strategically important for the country.

Since the 1980s, Western governments have tended to reverse nationalization through privatization measures, argueing that the resulting competition increases efficiency and reduces prices.

nationalize verstaatlichen; nationalisieren

national law Bundesgesetz

national product Sozialprodukt

national wealth Volksvermögen; Nationalvermögen

nationwide überregional; landesweit

native Inländer; Einheimischer; *(aborigine)* Eingeborener, einheimisch; heimisch

natural natürlich; normal; *(customary)* üblich

natural environment natürliche Umwelt

natural gas Erdgas

natural gas pipeline Erdgasleitung

natural gas supplier Erdgaslieferant

natural gas supply Erdgasversorgung; *(delivery)* Erdgaslieferung

naturalize einbürgern; naturalisieren

natural law Naturgesetz

natural monopoly natürliches Monopol

Industry in which the most efficient producer is a monopoly. Most natural monopolies are utilities or similar entities.

natural resources Rohstoffe; Bodenschätze

All sources of wealth supplied by nature, such as coal, oil, wood, water power, and arable land.

nature Natur; Art; Beschaffenheit; Charakter

navigation Navigation; Lenkung; Schifffahrt

Internet: method of finding and moving between different information and pages on a website. It is governed by menu arrangements, site structure and the layout of individual pages.

navigation bar Navigationsleiste

Internet: using of frames to create a kind of "Table of Contents" of a site that stays available so the reader can move easily from place to place.

necessarily notwendigerweise

necessary nötig; notwendig; *(requisite)* erforderlich

necessity Notwendigkeit; Bedarf; Elend; Unumgänglichkeit

neglect Gleichgültigkeit; Nachlässigkeit; Vergessen

Dissatisfaction expressed through passively allowing conditions to worsen, including chronic absenteeism or lateness, reduced effort, and increased error rate.

need *(hardship)* Not; Bedürftigkeit; *(wish, desire)* Bedürfnis; *(requirement)* Bedarf; Notwendigkeit; *(to ~)* brauchen; bedürfen; erfordern

A need can be defined as a state of felt deprivation. The actual expression of a need is a want. Wants equipped with purchasing power constitute demand.

Needs are universal. (every human being feels hunger), wants are shaped by culture.

need category Bedürfniskategorie

need for achievement Bedürfnis nach Leistung

The drive to excel, to achieve, to succeed, and to do something better than others. High achievers differentiate themselves from others by their desire to do things better. They avoid what they perceive to be very easy or very difficult tasks.

need for affiliation Bedürfnis nach Zugehörigkeit

The desire for friendly and close interpersonal relationships. Individuals with a high affiliation motive strive for friendship, prefer cooperative situations rather than competitive ones, and desire relationships involving a high degree of mutual understanding.

need for power Bedürfnis nach Macht

The need to to have impact, to be influential, and to control others. Individuals high in power need enjoy being "in charge", strive for influence over others and prefer to be placed into competitive and status-oriented situations. They tend to be more concerned with prestige and gaining influence over others than with effective performance.

need recognition Bedarfserkennung

First stage of the buyer decision process in which the consumer recognizes a problem or need.

need satisfaction Bedürfnisbefriedigung

Act of solving a state of felt deprivation by supplying the desired want.

needs test Bedürfnisprüfung

needy bedürftig; arm

negative cash flow negativer Cashflow

A situation where income is less than expenses, i.e. the business spends more cash than it receives. Prolonged negative cash flow will eventually lead to the failure of a business.

negative covenant Negativverpflichtung

Part of the indenture or loan agreement that limits or prohibits actions that the company may take.

negative correlation negative Korrelation

An inverse relationship between two variables, i.e. as one variable becomes larger, the other becomes smaller. The correlation coefficient in a negative correlation is between 0 and –1.

negative equity Unterbilanz; negatives Eigenkapital

The difference between the value of a property and the outstanding amount borrowed against it. For example. if a property's current value is €100.000 and the borrowing against it is €110.000, it is a negative equity to the extent of £10.000. House owners who paid more for their houses than their current value are unable to sell without realizing the loss.

negative pledge Negativerklärung

A covenant in a loan agreement in which a borrower promises that no secured borrowings will be made during the time of the loan.

negative working capital negatives Betriebskapital

Financial situation when the current liabilities of a company exceed its current assets, which normally leads to bankruptcy, if not corrected. In some cases, where companies have a very high inventory turnover, this can actually become the norm. An example is Amazon.com, where products are delivered *and sold* to the customer before the company itself has to pay for them.

neglect Vernachlässigung; *(carelessness)* Nachlässigkeit; *(omission)* Versäumnis; Unterlassung; *(to ~)* vernachlässigen; versäumen; unterlassen

negligence Vernachlässigung; *(endangerment)* Fahrlässigkeit; *(carelessness)* Nachlässigkeit; Unaufmerksamkeit

Action or omission falling below the standard of care that a reasonable person would exercise in the same situation; lack of due care or failure to do what is reasonable and prudent under the circumstances.

negligent *(endangering)* fahrlässig; *(careless)* nachlässig; schlampig; unvorsichtig

negotiable verhandelbar; aushandelbar; *(bankable)* bankfähig; bankmäßig; *(endorsable)* indossierfähig; *(transferable)* begehbar; *(marketable)* handelbar; umlauffähig

A financial instrument that can be sold or transferred to another party in exchange for money or as settlement of an obligation. Negotiability is a prerequisite of secondary markets.

negotiate verhandeln; aushandeln; *(contract)* zu Stande bringen; abschließen; *(transfer)* übertragen

negotiating power Verhandlungsmacht

negotiating skill Verhandlungsgeschick

negotiation Verhandlung; *(transfer)* Übertragung

The process of communication by which parties attempt to resolve a dispute between them. The aim is to reach a mutually acceptable agreement, in a commercial context a contract.

negotiation goal Verhandlungsziel

negotiator Unterhändler; Verhandlungspartner; *(mediator)* Vermittler

neighborhood Nachbarschaft; Gegend

An area of a community with characteristics that distinguish it from other areas, which can be geographic, social, or land use. Neighborhoods often have boundaries composed of major streets, barriers, or geographic differences.

neighborhood store Nachbarschaftsladen; Laden an der Ecke

Small retail store with a limited product range, often tailored to local tastes, long opening hours, and above-average prices.

neo-charismatic theories neocharismatische Theorien

neoclassical economics neoklassische Ökonomie; neoklassische Volkswirtschaft

School thought in economic theory that reasserted the classical belief that market forces would always lead to efficient allocation of resources and full employment. It was questioned by the economic depression and challenged by the advent of Keynesian economics.

nepotism Vetternwirtschaft; Nepotismus

The practice of awarding relatives and family members preferential treatment, such as promotions, higher earnings, and other benefits.

nested ad content eingebetteter Anzeigeninhalt

Internet: refers to the situation when the person undertaking the click through is not redirected to a corporate or brand site, but is instead taken to a related page on the same site as that on which the advertisement is placed; sometimes referred to as micro-site.

net netto; per saldo

The amount remaining after all costs, charges or fees have been deducted from the total. For example, *net sales* are equal to gross sales minus discounts, returns, and allowances.

net allowance Nettozuschuss

net assets Nettovermögen; Reinvermögen

The assets of an organization less its current liabilities. The resultant figure is equal to the capital of the organization.

net asset value Reinvermögenswert; Substanzwert

The value of a share in a company calculated by dividing the amount for the net assets of the company by the number of shares in issue. The net asset value can be below the market price of a share because financial statements do not reflect the present values of all assets.

net book value Buchwert nach Abrschreibungen

The value at which an asset appears in the books of an organization (usually at the date of the last balance sheet) less any depreciation that has been applied since its purchase or its last revaluation.

net capital Nettokapital

net cash flow *(addition to liquid assets)* Nettozugang an liquiden Mitteln; Abschreibungen plus nicht ausgeschüttete Gewinne

See: after tax cash flow, cash flow.

net commodity price Nettowarenpreis

net contribution Nettobeitrag; Nettozuschuss

net cost Grundpreis; Nettopreis; *(manufacturer's cost)* Selbstkostenpreis

The costs of purchasing an asset less income received. For example, total payments for an insurance policy less premiums paid.

net current assets Nettoumlaufvermögen; Betriebskapital; Liquiditätsüberschuss

The difference between the current assets of a company and its current liabilities; another name for working capital.

net domestic product Nettoinlandsprodukt

As a measure of economic activity, the Net Domestic Product (NDP) equals the Gross Domestic Product (GDP) minus depreciation on a country's capital goods.

net earnings Reinverdienst; Nettoertrag

net export capital Nettoexportkapital

net export Außenbeitrag; Nettoexport

net gain from operations Betriebsreingewinn

net income Nettoeinkommen; Reineinkommen; *(yield)* Reinertrag

In general: the sum remaining after all expenses have been met or deducted, i.e. revenues minus depreciation, interest, taxes and other expenses; also called *net earnings* or *net profit* (net loss if the figure is negative).

Accounting: total sales minus total costs and expenses. Net income after taxes is the *bottom line.* It is out of this figure that dividends are normally paid.

net increase Nettozunahme

net interest yield Effektivzins

net investment Nettoinvestition

net loss Nettoverlust

net national product (NNP) Nettosozialprodukt

As a measure of economic activity, the Net National Product (NNP) equals the Gross National Product (GNP) minus depreciation on a country's capital goods. NNP is therefore equal to the national income, i.e. the amount of money available in the economy for expenditure on goods and services.

net operating income (NOI) Nettobetriebseinkommen

Income from business activities after operating expenses have been met, but before deducting income taxes and financing expenses (interest and principal payments).

net operating loss (NOL) Nettobetriebsverlust

Financial situation when income from business activities is lower than operating expenses.

net present value (NPV) Kapitalwert

Standard method of determining whether the expected financial performance of a proposed investment promises to be adequate.

Calculated as the present value of future cash returns, discounted at the appropriate market interest rate, minus the present value of the cost of the investment. If the NPV is positive, the required rate of return is likely to be earned and the project should be considered; if it is negative, the project should be rejected.

net present value rule Kapitalwertregel

Investment is worth making if it has a positive NPV. If an investment's NPV is negative, it should be rejected.

net price of goods Nettowarenpreis

net profit Reingewinn nach Steuern; Bilanzgewinn

The profit of a business when all incomes and expenses have been taken into account. Net profit is calculated by deducting al1 remaining expenses from the gross profit.

net pofit margin Nettoumsatzrendite

Percentage of after-tax profit as a percentage of total sales. This ratio is used in analyzing the profitability of organizations and is an indicator of the extent to which sales have been profitable.

net purchases Nettoeinkäufe

A figure for a company´s gross purchases less returns, allowances, discounts.

net quick assets Betriebskapital; Nettoumlaufvermögen

Financial ratio to calculate whether a business could meet its current liabilities with its readily convertible assets. Calculated as cash, marketable securities, and accounts receivable minus current liabilities.

net realizable value (NRV) Nettorealisationswert; realisierbarer Nettowert

The sales value of the stock of an organization less the additional costs likely to be incurred in getting the stocks into the hands of the customer.

net relevant earnings relevanter Nettoverdienst

A person's nonpensionable earned income, before deduction of personal allowances and after deduction of expenses, capital allowances and losses.

net reproduction rate Nettoreproduktionsrate

A figure to estimate population trends. Calculated by dividing the number of female children in a population by the number of female adults in the previous generation; if it exceeds unity the population is expanding.

net reserves Nettoreserve

net sales Nettoverkaufserlös; Reinumsatz

Figure representing the total sales of a business less returns and allowances, freight out, and cash discounts allowed.

net sales price Nettoverkaufspreis

net savings Nettoersparnis

net subsidy Nettosubvention; Nettozuschuß

net surplus Nettoüberschuss

net tangible assets Nettosachanlagen

The tangible assets of an organization less its current liabilities. Net tangible assets indicate the financial strength of a business in terms of being solvent.

netting Netting

The process of setting off matching sales and purchases against each other; especially of futures, options, and forward foreign exchange.

network Netzwerk; Netz; *(technical)* Netzplan; Stellennetz; *(television)* Sendernetz; *(to ~)* Verbindung mit Gleichgesinnten aufnehmen

Broadcasting: organization that provides programming and sells commercial time in programs, such as ABC television network, ESPN cable network.

Computing: a group of computers, connected by a telecommunications links, that share information and resources.

networked applications Netzwerkanwendung

Internet: Database-driven applications and methods for sharing information within an organization, such as distributed internet applications, linked corporate and legacy data, web-enabled and live applications, and object-oriented applications.

networking Netzwerk(-betrieb); vernetztes Arbeiten; Nutzung von Geschäftskontakten; Beziehungen pflegen

Broadcasting: arrangement wherein television or radio stations agree to broadcast the programs furnished by a network.

Personal relations: the use of personal and professional contacts for one´s own advancement..

net working capital Nettobetriebskapital; Nettoumlaufvermögen

network interface card (NIC) Netzwerk(-schnitt)karte

Computers: piece of hardware that fits into an expansion slot on a computer and allows it to communicate with other computer over a network.

network of contacts Kontaktnetz

net worth Nettowert; Eigenkapital

The value of an organization when its liabilities have been deducted from the value of its assets.

neutral *(gear)* Leerlauf; neutral; *(without allegiance)* parteilos; gleichgültig

neutrality Neutralität; Parteilosigkeit

newcomer Neuling; *(stranger)* Fremdling; *(marketing)* Außenseiter

New Deal New Deal

Political and economic policies aimed at combating the consequences of the great depression, that were introduced by president Franklin D. Roosevelt in the 1930s.

newfangled neumodisch; hypermodern; erneuerungssüchtig

newly industrialized country (NIC) Schwellenland

newly produced neu produziert

new product neues Produkt

new-product development Entwicklung eines neues Produktes

Development of original products, product improvement, product modification and new brands through the firm's own R&D efforts.

new product line neue Produktlinie

A product lines that is created when an existing brand name is extended to create new products in a completely different category. *Example:* the Mars brand applied to ice cream.

new-rich neureich

news Nachricht; *(news item)* Neuigkeit; *(media)* Nachrichten

news agency Nachrichtenagentur; Nachrichtenbüro; Korrespondenzbüro

newsgroup Newsgroup

Internet: communities of interest that post e-mails on electronic bulletin boards.

newsletter *(internal)* internes Rundschreiben; Rundschreiben; Informationsblatt

news magazine Nachrichtenmagazin

newspaper Zeitung; Journal; Blatt

newspaper advertisement Zeitungsannonce; Inserat; Zeitungsreklame

newsprint *(not yet printed)* Rotationspapier; *(old newspapers)* Zeitungspapier

news release Pressenotiz

A brief written statement sent to the press informing about a company's new product, product improvement, price change, or some other development of interest.

new task neue Aufgabe

Business buying situation in which the buyer purchases a product or service for the first time.

new trade theory neue Handelstheorie

Theory that suggests that observed pattern of trade in the world economy may be due in part to the ability of firms in a given market to capture first-mover advantages.

New York Stock Exchange (NYSE)

The main US stock exchange, founded by 24 merchants under a tree in 1792, moved to Wall Street in 1793; the New York Stock & Exchange Board was formally established in 1817 and renamed the New York Stock Exchange in 1983.

next-in-first-out (NIFO)

A method of stock valuation pricing units of raw material or finished goods issued from stock at the next unit price at which a consignment will be received

niche Nische; *(market)* Marktnische

Narrowly defined area of competence or of a market in which a business specializes and prospers.

niche market Nischenmarkt

Relatively small group of potential customers who share common characteristics that make them receptive to a particular product or service. They often develop from mass markets, but sometimes niche markets also develop into mass markets.

niche marketing Nischenmarketing; Marketing in Marktlücken

Targeting a small but lucrative segment of the market. The small size of the niche generally ensures efficient marketing efforts and few if any direct competitors.

nil Null; nichts

no growth Nullwachstum; statisch

Description of little or no economic growth as measured by changes in the gross domestic product.

no-interest unverzinst

noise Geräusch; Störung; Lärm; Verzerrung

no load mutual fund Anlagefonds ohne Abschlussgebühr

Open-end investment company, shares of which are sold without a sales charge nor a distribution fee.

nominal nominell; *(in name only)* nur dem Namen nach;

nominal account Erfolgskonto; Aufwands- und Ertragskonto

Income statement account (revenue and expense) that is closed out at the end of the year.

nominal amount Nominalbetrag; Nennbetrag

nominal capital Grundkapital; Nominalkapital

nominal cash flow nomineller Cashflow

Cash flow expressed in nominal terms if the actual cash amounts to be received (or paid out) are given.

nominal damages nomineller Schadensersatz

Very small sum ($1) awarded as recognition that a minor legal injury was sustained, but where no recoverable loss can be established.

nominal group technique nominale Gruppentechnik

Group decision-making method in which individual members meet face-to-face to pool their judgments in a systematic but independent fashion.

The main advantage of this technique is that it permits the group to meet formally but does not restrict independent thinking.

nominal interest Nominalzins

nominal interest rate Nominalverzinsung; Nominalzinssatz; Nominalzins

The interest rate that is actually observed in the market, in contrast to the real interest rate, which would be adjusted for inflation.

nominal rate Nominalsatz

The actual rate of return on an investment, not adjusted for the effect of inflation.

nominal value Nennwert; Nominalwert

nominal yield Nominalverzinsung; Rendite; Ertrag aus der Nominalverzinsung

The interest rate stated on the face of a bond, calculated as the percentage of interest to be paid by the issuer on the face value of the bond.

nominate nominieren; *(election)* aufstellen

nomination Vorschlag; Einsetzung

nomination of beneficiary Begünstigung

nominee Kandidat; Strohmann; Bevollmächtigter

Investment: person or firm, such as a bank official or brokerage house, which acts on behalf of a beneficial owner and into whose name securities or other properties are transferred by agreement.

non-acceptance Nichtannahme

The failure by the person on whom a bill of exchange is drawn to accept it on presentation.

nonappealableness *(sentence)* Rechtskraft

nonbank Nichtbank

noncallable unkündbar

Securities that cannot be called by the issuer prior to maturity, such as preferred stock or bonds that cannot be redeemed at the option of the issuer.

non-cash item zahlungsunwirksame Größe

Expense against revenue that does not directly affect cash flow, such as depreciation and deferred taxes.

noncompetitive nicht wettbewerbsfähig; außer Konkurrenz; nicht wettbewerbskonform; nicht wettbewerbsorientiert

noncompliance *(rule, regulation)* Nichtbefolgung

non-convertible currency nicht konvertierbare Währung

Currency is not convertible when both residents and non-residents are prohibited from converting their holdings of that currency into another currency.

noncurrent asset Anlagevermögen

An asset that is not expected to be converted into cash, sold, or exchanged in the foreseeable future, at least one year. This includes fixed assets, real estate, machinery, and other equipment.

non disclosure agreement (NDA) Stillschweigevereinbarung

Contract in which a person or business agrees to maintain the confidentiality of proprietary information or trade secrets and not disclose such information without authorization.

Example: employees, consultants, business partners and investors are often asked to sign nondisclosure agreements.

non-durable goods kurzlebige Güter; kurzlebige Konsumgüter; kurzlebige Verbrauchsgüter

Description for consumer goods that do not last long, are used up quickly, and must be replaced regularly. Examples are food, drink, newspapers, gasoline etc.

non-executive director Direktor ohne Geschäftsbereich; Aufsichtsratsmitglied

A director of a company who is not involved in the day-to-day management of the business but who is appointed to bring independent judgment to the company.

non-free-market country Land ohne freien Markt; Staatshandelsland

noninflationary inflationsfrei

non-interest-bearing zinsfrei; *(incapable of bearing interest)* unverzinslich

nonnegotiable check Verrechnungsscheck

nonobservance Nichtbefolgung

nonpayment of credit Kreditausfall

non-personal communication channel unpersönliche Kommunikationskanal

Media that carries messages without personal contact or feedback, e.g. TV, radio.

non-price competition nicht-preislicher Wettbewerb

Competition at the same price level but with the aid of advertising, sales promotion campaigns, quality, delivery time, packaging, offering free servicing and installation, or other services.

nonproductive unproduktiv; ertraglos

nonprofit gemeinnützig; nicht auf Gewinn gerichtet

nonprofit accounting Buchführung nicht gewinnorientierter Organisationen

nonprofit organization gemeinnützige Organization

A public or private entity established to provide a service efficiently and effectively to the public, but without profit objectives.

Examples include colleges, hospitals, voluntary health and welfare organizations, and charities.

non refundable nicht erstattungsfähig; nicht zurückzahlbar

Provision in a sales or other contract that forecloses the option that the money paid will be returned. For example, if a passenger does not use a ticket, the money paid for the ticket will not be returned.

nonrefundable fee nicht erstattungsfähige Gebühr

nonresident alien Ausländer ohne festen Wohnsitz

nonreturnable bottle Einwegflasche

nonstock corporation (US) nichtöffentliche Aktiengesellschaft

Corporation owned by its members under the membership charter or agreement, rather than through the issue of shares.

nonstop ununterbrochen; durchgehend; nonstop

nonstore retailing Vertrieb ohne ohne Ladengeschäft

Retailing without conventional stores, such as selling through vending machines, telemarketing, catalog sales, mail order, and others.

non-tariff trade barriers nichttarifäres, zollfremdes Handelshemmnis

Non-monetary barriers to foreign products, such as biases against a foreign company's bids or product standards that go against a foreign company's product features.

nonverbal communication nonverbale Kommunikation

nonvoting nicht stimmberechtigt; stimmrechtlos

nonvoting stock stimmrechtslose Aktie

Corporate securities whose holders have no voting powers, i.e. they may not vote on the election of directors or corporate resolutions.

norm Norm; *(rule)* Regel; *(standard)* Standard

Social rules and guidelines that prescribe appropriate behavior in particular situations.

normal normal; *(customary)* üblich; *(regular)* regelrecht

normal distribution Normalverteilung

The symmetrical bell-shaped frequency curve formed when the number of occurrences of a range of values is plotted on the vertical axis against a series of classes plotted on the horizontal axis.

The shape indicates that extreme values, large and small occur infrequently, while the more frequent occurrences are clustered around the arithmetic mean value, which in a normal distribution is also equal to the median and the mode (the value that occurs most frequently in a set of data).

normative normativ; standard; normal; nach der Regel

normative economics normative Wirtschaftswissenschaften

Approach to economics in which value judgments about the desirability of policy options are made, which are then backed up by facts and theories.

norming stage Stadium der Normierung

Third stage in group development, characterized by close relationships and cohesiveness where there is a strong sense of group identity and camaraderie. This stage is complete when the group structure solidifies and the group has assimilated a common set of expectations of what defines correct member behavior.

North American Free Trade Agreement (NAFTA) Nordamerikanische Freihandelszone

Free trade area between Canada, Mexico, and the United States formed in 1993.

The aim of NAFTA is to completely end U.S. and Mexican tariffs and quotas on imports and agricultural products mostly, with some requiring 15 years to phase out. Applies only to goods made from labor and materials originated within the countries; other imports are acceptable only if they are substantially transformed within the U.S., Mexico, or Canada.

notarial notariell; vor einem Notar

notarize noteriell beglaubigen

notarized notariell beglaubigt

notary public Notar

Public officer authorized to administer oaths, to attest to and certify certain types of documents, to take depositions, and to perform certain acts in commercial matters. The seal of a notary public authenticates a document.

not cancelable *(order)* nicht stornierbar; *(contract)* unkündbar

not considered unberücksichtigt

not dismissible *(person)* unkündbar

note *(music)* Note; *(memo)* Notiz; *(to ~)* notieren; aufschreiben; vermerken; *(to notice)* bemerken

Commerce: a negotiable record of an unsecured loan, often used in preference to bond when the principal sum is reparable in less than five years.

note payable Schuldwechsel

Written promise to pay a certain amount of money at a certain time.

note receivable ausstehender Schuldschein

A claim against a debtor, who has given a written promise to pay a certain sum of money by a certain date.

not for profit gemeinnützig

Organization in which no stockholder or trustee shares in profits or losses; usually exists to accomplish some charitable, humanitarian, or educational purpose; also called *nonprofit.*

not harmful to the environment nicht umweltschädlich

notice Aufmerksamkeit; Beachtung; *(cognizance)* Kenntnisnahme; *(advertisement)* Anzeige; *(notification)* Ankündigung; Bekanntmachung; *(warning)* Warnung; *(job termination)* Kündigung; *(to ~)* bemerken

noticeable bemerkbar; auffallend; deutlich; merklich

notice of default Anzeige der Nichterfüllung; Inverzugsetzung

A formal written notice sent to a lender that a default has occurred and legal action may be taken.

notice of deficiency Steuerbescheid

Notice sent by the tax authorities to a taxpayer, informing him about oustanding taxes.

notice of discontinuance *(contract)* Kündigung

notice of dismissal *(from a job)* Kündigung

notice of redemption *(loan)* Kündigung

notice of termination *(of a job)* Kündigung

notification Ankündigung; Bekanntmachung; Benachrichtigung; Mitteilung; Meldung

notify bekannt geben; benachrichtigen; amtlich mitteilen

notify of departure abmelden

not knowledgeable in the field sachfremd

not rated (NR) nicht bewertet; nicht klassifiziert

Investment: phrase used by rating services stating that a security or a company has not been rated, which should have neither negative nor positive implications.

nourish ernähren; nähren; pflegen

nourishment Ernährung

nouveauriche neureich

nuisance Ärgernis; störende Tätigkeit; Beninderung

Property: a legal term referring to the use of land that interferes with the use of neighboring lands.

null and void null und nichtig

A contract that is no loger enforceable, or has no longer any effect.

nullify aufheben; für nichtig erklären; zunichte machen

number Nummer; *(quantity)* Anzahl; *(digit)* Ziffer; *(to ~)* nummerieren; beziffern; *(to count)* zählen

number of applicants Bewerberzahl

number of employees Mitarbeiterzahl

number of members Mitgliederzahl

number of offers Angebotszahl

number of participants Teilnehmerzahl

number of persons employed Beschäftigungszahl

number of units Stückzahl

numerator Zähler; Zählvorrichtung; Zählwerk

numerical numerisch; zahlenmäßig

numerical data Zahlenmaterial

numerical value Zahlenwert

numerous zahlreich; viel

nursing expenses Pflegekosten

nursing insurance Pflegeversicherung

O

object Gegenstand; Sache; Ding; *(aim)* Ziel; *(purpose)* Zweck; *(taxes)* Steuerobjekt; *(to ~)* beanstanden; nicht zustimmen

objection Einspruch; Beanstandung; Einwand

objective objektiv; sachlich; Ziel

Free of personal bias and opinion, as in an *objective* evaluation.

Ultimate goal or target of an individual's or a group's efforts and strategy; striven-for future state which is precisely defined in terms of content, time scale and scope.

objective-and-task method Ziel-Aufgaben-Methode

Method of developing the promotion budget by first defining specific objectives; then determining the tasks that must be performed to achieve these objectives; and finally estimating the costs of performing these tasks. The sum of these costs is the purposed promotion budget.

objectivity Objektivität

Accounting: concept aimed at eliminating any subjective influences in the preparation of accounts.

The aim is to enabel users to compare financial statements for different companies over time.

obligate verpflichten; binden; nötigen

obligation Verpflichtung; Engagement; *(money payable)* Verbindlichkeit; Schuldverschreibung

obligation to accept Annahmepflicht

obligation to pay interest Zinsverpflichtung

obligatory obligatorisch; bindend; zwingend

oblige verpflichten; binden; *(to force)* zwingen; nötigen

obligee Gläubiger; Berechtigter

The person in whose favor an obligation is owed..

obligor Schuldner; Verpflichtender

The person who promises to another to perform some obligation.

obliterate ausstreichen; auslöschen; *(stamp)* entwerten; *(truth)* verschleiern

observance *(laws)* Einhaltung; *(directives)* Befolgung; *(observation)* Beobachtung; *(custom)* Brauch

observation Beobachtung; *(rules)* Einhaltung

observational research Forschung auf Grundlage von Beobachtungen

Gathering of primary data by observing relevant people, actions and situations.

observe beobachten; *(to observe rules)* einhalten; befolgen

observer Beobachter

obsolescence Überalterung; Veralten

The loss of value or usefulness of an object over time because of wear, changing technology or user preferences.

obsolete obsolet; überholt; veraltet

obstacle Hindernis; Hemmnis

obstruction Hemmung; *(handicap)* Behinderung; Sabotage; *(blockage)* Verstopfung

obtain erhalten; erlangen; bekommen; *(to procure)* beschaffen; auftreiben; *(yield, profit)* erzielen; erwirtschaften; *(to buy)* beziehen

obtainable erhältlich; beziehbar

obtainment *(procurement)* Beschaffung; *(goal)* Erzielung

occasion Gelegenheit

occasion segmentation Gelegenheitssegmentierung

Practice of dividing the market into groups according to occasions when buyers get the idea to buy, actually make their purchase, or use the purchased item.

occupancy level Belegungsgrad; Belegungsstufe

The number of units currently occupied in a building, city, neighborhood, or complex, expressed as a percentage of total capacity. For example, hotels need around 60% occupancy level to break even.

occupant Bewohner; *(by force)* Besetzer

occupation *(profession)* Beruf; *(employment)* Beschäftigung

The principal activity of a person, his trade, job, or business, that represents his principal means to earn a livelihood.

occupational Berufs-; beruflich

occupational category Berufsgruppe

occupational disease Berufskrankheit

A disease which is due to causes and conditions at the person´s place of employment. *Example:* black lung disease is an occupational disease associated with coal mining.

occupational group Berufsgruppe

A group of people doing the same kind of work, such as accountant or doctors.

occupational hazard Berufsrisiko

Any condition at a workkplace that can result in an accident, sickness, or the death of a worker.

Occupational Safety and Health Administration (OSHA) Arbeitsschutzorganisation in den USA

A government organization in the US which sets and enforces occupational health and safety regulations. It requires employers to inform employees of potential hazards, provide safety training and report workplace injuries.

occupy *(to keep busy)* beschäftigen; *(position)* innehaben; *(dwelling)* bewohnen; *(by force)* besetzen

occur *(to take place)* stattfinden; *(to come into existence)* entstehen; *(phenomenon)* vorkommen

occurrence *(incident)* Vorfall; *(event)* Vorkommnis; *(happening)* Ereignis; *(process)* Vorgang

odd lot krummer Auftrag; Sondermenge

odd numbers ungerade Zahlen

odd-value pricing Preisauszeichnung mit ungeraden Zahlen

The practice of setting retail prices just below even currency amounts, such as €0.99 or €5.99. It is based on the assumption that consumers will feel that they are getting a better value.

OECD (Organization for Economic Cooperation and Development) Organisation für wirtschaftliche Zusammenarbeit und Entwicklung

of age mündig

of equal rank gleichrangig

off aus; ausgeschaltet

off-balance bilanzunwirksam; bilanzneutral

off-balance sheet financing bilanzneutrale Finanzierung

Financing that is not shown as a liability on a company's balance sheet.

off-limits gesperrt; verboten

off-peak außerhalb der Spitzenzeiten

off-season außerhalb der Saison

off-the-record inoffiziell; nicht amtlich

offend beleidigen; verletzen; ärgern; *(rule)* verstoßen; sich vergehen

offer Angebot; Offerte; Vorschlag; Ware; *(to ~)* anbieten; offerieren; *(to suggest)* in Vorschlag bringen

Market: The price at which a willing seller is ready to sell. The opposite of bid, the price at which a ready buyer is ready to buy.

offer price Angebotspeis

offeree Angebotsempfänger

offerer Anbieter

office Büro; *(branch)* Zweigniederlassung; Geschäftstelle; *(function)* Funktion; *(post)* Amt; *(administration)* Verwaltungsstelle

office automation Büroautomation

office desk Büroschreibtisch

office electronics Büroelektronik

office equipment Büroeinrichtung

office equipment trade fair Büromesse

office hours Bürostunden; Geschäftszeiten

office industry Büroindustrie

office machine Büromaschine

office management Büroleitung

All activities required to organize and administer the day-to-day business in an office environment.

office of Economic Security Arbeitsamt

officer Beamter; Beamtin; *(company)* Vorstandsmitglied; Direktor; *(military)* Offizier; *(police)* Polizist; *(party)* Funktionär

Company: a person who acts in an official capacity in a company. Company officers include the directors, managers, the company secretary, and in some circumstances the company's auditors and solicitors.

office routine Bürobetrieb

office space Bürofläche; Büroraum

office technology Bürotechnik

office typewriter Büroschreibmaschine

office work Innendienst

official *(government)* Beamter; Beamtin; Sachbearbeiter; offiziell; amtlich

official act Amtshandlung

official channels Behördenweg

Official Journal *(EU)* Amtsblatt

official register Amtsblatt

official secret Amtsgeheimnis

official statement öffentliche Erklärung

officially offiziell; amtlich

officiate amtieren; fungieren

offline offline

offline promotion Offline-Werbung

offline web metric Offline-Webmetriken

Internet: offline measures are collated by marketing staff recording particular marketing outcomes such as an enquiry or a sale.

offset *(accounting)* Verrechnung; Gegenbuchung; *(printing)* Offsetdruck; *(to ~)* verrechnen; kompensieren; *(print)* drucken

Accounting: amount or position entered on the other side of a balance sheet to balance another entry.

Printing: a printing method that involves the transfer of wet ink from a printing plate onto an intermediate surface and then onto the paper.

Securities technique of liquidating a purchase of futures or options through the sale of an equal number of contracts of the same delivery month.

offset rate Tauschrate

Accounting: amount equaling or counterbalancing another amount on the opposite side of the same ledger or the ledger of another account.

offshoot Seitenzweig; Seitenlinie; Unterorganisation

offshore vor der Küste gelegen; offshore

Expression used for financial organizations situated outside the country, which implies some degree of financial secrecy in an effort to attract investment and safe taxes.

off time Ausfallzeit; Freizeit

Period of time when not in service; off time for a computer or machine is when it is not scheduled for use or needs maintenance, alterations, or repairs.

of long duration langfristig; langjährig

often oft; häufig

of the same value gleichwertig

Ohmae, Kenichi (* 1943)

Japanese business thinker. He argued that business strategy is all about, 'what distinguishes it from all other kinds of business planning, is competitive advantage.' Ohmae asserts that 'customer-based strategies are the basis of all strategy'. He identifies the 'four routes of strategic advantage' – strategy based on:

1. Company's key factor for success in its capability to increase market share and profitability

2. Exploiting any relative superiority

3. Aggressive initiatives, challenging accepted assumptions

4. 'Strategic degrees of freedom' (SDF) – development of innovations such as new markets or products

Biography: 1972 doctorate in nuclear engineering from MIT, former head of McKinsey's Tokyo office, leading international exponent of global business strategy, published about 30 books and articles on strategy,

Major publications: (1982, 1983) The Mind of the Strategist, (1985) Triad Power: The Coming Shape of Global Competition, (1990) The Borderless World, (1995) The End of the Nation State

oil-exporting Erdöl ausführend

oil facility Erdölverwertungsanlage

oil field Erdölfeld; Erdölvorkommen

old-line-factoring echtes Factoring

oligopolistic competition oligopolistischer Wettbewerb

Market situation in which there are a few sellers that are highly sensitive to each other's pricing and marketing strategies.

oligopolistic model Oligopolmodell

oligopolistic situation Oligopolsituation

oligopolistic theory Oligopoltheorie

oligopoly Oligopol

A market situation in which relatively few sellers supply many buyers. Each sellers recognizes that prices can be controlled to a certain extent and that competitors' actions will influence profits.

An oligopolistic industry is more concentrated than a competitive one but less than a monopoly. *Example:* a few large sellers of similar products, such as automobiles, dominate the market.

oligopsony Oligopson

Market situation with few large buyers and many sellers. The buyers control the purchase of a product. *Example:* in the tobacco industry there are about five major companies that purchase from numerous growers.

ombudsman Ombudsmann; Beschwerdestelle; Schiedsstelle

A neutral person or organization empowered to receive and investigate complaints about an institution, organization, or business.

omission Wegfall; *(nonperformance)* Versäumnis; Unterlassung

omit unter-; weg-; auslassen; *(dividend)* ausfallen lassen

on account gegen Kredit; Teilzahlung

Finance: denotes a purchase or sale made on open account, i.e. the seller gives the buyer the possibility to make the payment sometime after delivery, and the obligation is not documented by a note.

on balance per Saldo; unter dem Strich

on call auf Abruf

one-factor APT Ein-Faktor-Arbitrage-Pricing-Theorie

Special case of the arbitrage pricing theory that is derived from the one-factor model by using diversification and arbitrage.

It shows the expected return on any risky asset is a linear function of a single factor. The CAPM can be expressed as one-factor APF in which a single factor is the market portfolio.

one-to-one marketing Eins-zu-eins-Marketing

Unique dialog that occurs directly between a company and individual customers, defined less strictly also with groups of customers with similar needs. It involves the company listening to customer needs and responding with services to meet these needs.

one-way einfach; Einweg-

one-way street Einbahnstraße

one-year period Jahresfrist

on hand vorrätig; vorliegend

online online

Connected to a computer or connected to the Internet.

Denoting either a real-time operation that is accomplished by a dialogue between a human operator and a computer system, or a system based on such operations.

online advertising Online-Werbung

Advertisements on the internet in special sections offered by commercial online services, normally as banner ads or popups.

online auctions Online-Auktionen

Auction-style sale of merchandise via the internet.

online brand Online-Marke

online brochure Onlinebroschüre; Onlineprospekt

Small, simple website, that only displays information. This is essentially a description of a business, product, or service, with an e-mail link to allow customers to get more information.

online community Online-Gemeinschaft

Internet: users who are widely dispersed geographically but come together in cyberspace based on common interests that can range from gaming, parenting, or computing.

online computer shopping Onlineshopping

Internet: form of direct marketing conducted through interactive online computer services, which provide two-way systems that link consumers with sellers electronically.

online database Online-Datenbank

A database that is located on a computer elsewhere and that is accessed via the Internet or other channels.

online exchange Online-Austausch; Online-Tauschgeschäft

Electronic forum in which buyers and sellers meet to make transactions.

online incentive schemes Online-Treueschemata

online marketing Online-Marketing

Direct marketing conducted through interactive on-line computer services that provide two-way communication.

online observation Online-Beobachtung

Internet: monitors people's behavior by watching them in relevant situations, such as consumer chatting and e-mail posting through chat rooms, bulletin boards, or mailing lists.

online panel Online-Panel

Called single-source data systems or opt-in communities, they include a panel of people who are paid to be the subject of marketing research.

online promotion Online-Werbung

Use of various techniques on the internet to raise awareness about a site and drive traffic to it, such as links from other sites, banner advertisements or targeted e-mail messages.

online service provider (OSP) Online - Serviceprovider

Large internet service providers (ISP) who provide large amounts of premium content to their customers as part of their service.

Example: AOL, Freeserve and LineOne have a large amount of specially developed content available to their subscribers.

online shopping Online-Einkauf

online store Online-Geschäft

online web metrics Online-Web-Metriken

Internet: online measures are those that are collected automatically on the webserver, often in a server log file.

on offer im Angebot

onset Beginn; Anfang; Angriff

onshore im Küstenvorland

on speculation unverbindlich; unaufgeforderte Arbeit

Any work done for a potential client without a contract or an order. The client will only pay if he is going to use the work. Sometimes practiced by editors or by advertisers. Also called on spec.

on-the-job training (OJT) innerbetriebliche Weiterbildung

Training that is undertaken in the actual workplace while engaged in the activity.

on time pünktlich; fristgerecht

open offen; ausgesetzt sein; frei; *(to ~)* *(door)* öffnen; *(meeting)* eröffnen

open account Kontokorrent

Credit account for which the only formal instrument of credit is the invoice.

open account business Kontokorrentgeschäft

open bid offenes Angebot

An offer to perform a contract that involves quoting a price which can, however, be reduced to meet the quotes made by competitors.

open book management Managementstil der offenen Bücher

Management style where a firm's accounts are left open for their employees. It attempts to extend the feeling of responsibility, for whether a business makes money or not, to everybody in the organization.

open distribution offene Distribution

Practice of offering a product through different dealers with no restrictions regarding the number of products a dealer can sell.

open-door policy Politik der offenen Tür; Politik des freien Zugangs

Management: the policy of leaving the door open in order to encourage informal interaction with employees.

Trade: the policy of granting equal trade opportunities to all countries.

open economy offene Volkswirtschaft

An economy that permits extensive transactions with the outside world. Foreign investments, imports, and exports are easy to accomplish and play an important role.

open-end question offene Frage

Questions in a survey that allow respondents to answer in their own words.

opening Öffnung; *(meeting, branch)* Eröffnung; *(opportunity)* Gelegenheit

opening balance Eröffnungsbilanz; Anfangssaldo

opening hours Öffnungszeiten

opening inventory Anfangsbestand

opening price Anfangskurs

opening purchase Eröffnungskauf

Bonds: transaction in which the purchaser's intention is to create or increase a long position in a given series of options.

opening sale Eröffnungsverkauf

Bonds: transaction in which the seller's intention is to create or increase a short position in a given series of options.

open market freier Markt; offener Markt; Wochenmarkt

Retailing: an area where stalls are situated in a village or town and wher fresh agricultural products are sold regularly.

open-market credit Schuldscheindarlehen

open-market policy Offenmarktpolitik

openness to experience Offenheit für Erfahrung

A personality dimension characterizing someone in terms of imaginativeness, artistic sensitivity, and intellectualism.

open web offenes Web

Term normally refers to those web addresses that are available to anyone with internet access.

Example: some America Online information is available only to America Online members. Some, like the information at www.aol.com, is available on the open web - anyone with web access can visit.

operate *(a machine)* bedienen; *(an enterprise)* betreiben; führen; *(surgery)* operieren; *(to be operative)*; funktionieren; verkehren

operating *(company)* Betriebs-; *(functioning)* funktionierend

operating activities laufende Geschäftstätigkeit

Sequence of events and decisions that create the firm' s cash inflows and cash outflows before financing. These activities include buying and paying for raw materials, manufacturing and selling a product, and collecting cash.

operating capital Betriebskapital

operating cash flow Cashflow aus laufender Geschäftstätigkeit

Earnings before interest and depreciation minus taxes. It measures the cash generated from operations, not counting capital spending or working capital requirements.

operating control Betriebskontrolle

Checking on-going performance against annual plans and taking corrective action.

operating cost Betriebsunkosten

operating cycle Geschäftszyklus

Time interval between the arrival of inventory and the date when cash is collected from receivables.

operating instructions Betriebsanleitung; Betriebsvorschrift

operating lease kurzfristiger Leasingvertrag; operatives Leasing

A lease that is not a capital lease. Normally entered on a short-term basis, the lessee can acquire the use of equipment for only part of its useful life. The lessor handles all maintenance and servicing; therefore also called *service lease.*

operating leverage leistungswirtschaftliches Risiko

Degree to which a company's costs of operation are fixed as opposed to variable. A firm with high operating costs compared to a firm with a low operating leverage implies larger percentage changes in EBIT with respect to a change in the sales revenue.

operating loss Betriebsverlust

operating manual Bedienungsanweisung

operating profit Betriebsgewinn

The income before taxes; calculated as the difference between total revenues and total expenses, but exluding extraordinary transactions such as restructuring costs or goodwill amortisation. Also called net operating profit, operating income, and net operating income.

operating rate Beschäftigungsgrad

operating ratio Erfolgskennziffer; Betriebskennziffer

A financial ratio that measures a firm's operating efficiency. It is calculated by dividing operating expenses by operating revenues.

operating result Betriebsergebnis

Operating or operative result, arising from the profit and loss account, shows what the company has earned in connection with its business aims, that is to say before deduction of interest and taxes.

It is also described as EBIT (Earnings Before Interest and Taxes). The operating result is also shown in the management result account and should therefore be reconciliated with the EBIT in the profit and loss statement.

operating statement Betriebsergebnisrechnung; Ergebnisrechnung; Gewinn- und Verlustrechnung

Financial statement that shows company sales, cost of goods sold and expenses during a given period of time.

operating system Betriebssystem

Computer program that controls basic operations such as start-up routines, input and output, and memory allocation. It is also responsible for loading and executing programs.

operation *(business)* Geschäftstätigkeit; *(machine)* Bedienung; Handhabung; Arbeitsvorgang; *(enterprise)* Unternehmung; Betrieb; *(surgery)* Operation

operational area Einsatzfeld

operational capability Funktionsfähigkeit

operational headquarters Führungsstab; Zentrale; Hauptbüro

operational management Betriebsführung

operation instructions Bedienungsanleitung

operations research (OR) Systemanalyse; Unternehmensforschung

A scientific approach to industrial and commercial problems in order to arrive at the most efficient and economic method of reaching the desired objective.

The basic steps are: making a clear statement of the problem; designing a model to represent the possible solutions using different strategies; and applying the solutions obtained from the analysis of the model to the real problem.

operator *(machine)* Bedienungsperson; *(enterprise)* Unternehmer; *(telephone)* Telefonist; Arbeiter

opinion leader Meinungsführer

People within a reference group who, because of special skills, knowledge, personality or other characteristics, exert influence on others.

In certain marketing instances, it may be advantageous to direct the communications to the opinion leader alone to speed the acceptance of an advertising message.

opinion poll Meinungsumfrage

opinion research Meinungsforschung

opponent Gegner

opportunity Gelegenheit; *(possibility)* Möglichkeit; Chance

opportunity costs Opportunitätskosten

The income or benefit foregone as the result of carrying out a particular decision when resources are limited or when mutually exclusive projects are considered.

For example, the opportunity cost of building a factory on a piece of land is the income foregone by not constructing an office block on this site. Similarly, the income foregone by not constructing a factory if an office block is constructed represents the opportunity cost of an office block.

opportunity set verfügbare Anlagemöglichkeiten

Investment: Possible expected return-standard deviation pairs of all portfolios that can be constructed from. a given set of assets; also called a feasible set.

opportunity to perform Leistungsmöglichkeiten

High levels of performance are partially a function of an absence of obstacles that constrain the employee.

oppose ablehnen; Widerspruch erheben; Einspruch erheben; opponieren

opposite side Gegenseite

opposition Widerstand; Opposition

opt sich entscheiden; entschließen; optieren

opt for *(choice)* wählen ; sich entscheiden

optical character recognition (OCR) optische Zeichenerkennung

Computing: software that lets computers read printed documents input via a scanner and converts the image into a computer text file that users can edit.

optimality Optimalität

optimal capital structure optimale Kapitalstruktur

optimal planning Optimalplanung

optimal solution Optimallösung

optimization Optimierung

optimize optimieren

optimum Optimum; Bestfall; Bestwert

optimum capacity Optimalkapazität; höchstes Leistungsvermögen; Höchstaufnahmefähigkeit

opt-in wählen; votieren für

Internet: list of users who have voluntarily agreed to receive commercial e-mail about topics that might be of interest to them by simply checking a box and entering an e-mail address; also called permission marketing.

option Wahlmöglichkeit; Entscheidungsfreiheit; Alternative; *(real estate)* Vorkaufsrecht; *(stock)* Optionsrecht; Bezugsrecht; Option

Finance: a contract that gives the contract buyer the right to buy or sell on or before a future date, and the contract seller has to honour that obligation.

optional beliebig; wahlweise; freigestellt; nicht pflichtgemäß; freiwillig

optional bond Optionsanleihe; *(option price)* Optionspreis

optional-product pricing Preiskalkulation für Zusatzprodukte

Pricing of optional or accessory products along with a main product.

options market Terminmarkt; Prämienmarkt; Optionsmarkt

option to buy Vorkaufsrecht; Ankaufsoption

option trading Optionshandel; Termingeschäft

opt-out austreten; abwählen

opt-out clause Ausweichklausel; Rücktrittsklausel

order Auftrag; Bestellung; *(directive)* Bestimmung; Anweisung; Befehl; Order; *(tidiness)* Ordnung; *(to ~)* bestellen; ordern; *(to make a determination)* bestimmen; *(to direct)* anweisen; *(to put in order)* ordnen

Commerce: the stated intention to engage in a transaction, can be verbal or in writing, and commits the issuer of the order to the terms specified.

Securities: the instruction issued to a broker or dealer to buy or sell securities. There are four basic categories of orders: market order, limit order, time order, and stop order.

order backlog unerledigter Auftragsbestand; Auftragsüberhang; Auftragspolster

order bill of lading Orderfrachtbrief; Orderkonnossement

A negotiable bill of lading made out to the order of the shipper, which can be sold to anyone, not just the intended recipient of the goods. The carrier has to release the goods only when the bill of lading is given to him by the recipient.

order book Orderbuch; Bestellbuch; Auftragsbuch

order form Bestellformular; Auftragsformular

ordering activity Ordertätigkeit

orderly ordnungsmäßig; *(orders in hand)* Auftragsbestand

order to economize Sparbeschluss

order-routine specification Spezifikation der Bestellungsprozedur

Stage of the business buying process in which the buyer writes the final order with the chosen supplier, listing the technical specifications, quantity needed, expected time of delivery, return policies and warranties.

order to purchase securities Wertpapierauftrag

ordinance Verfügung; Verordnung; Anordnung; Erlass; Gesetz

ordinary interest vereinfachte Zinsberechnung

Simple interest calculation based on a 360-day year rather than a 365-day year; the latter is called exact interest.

ordinary loss negatives Ergebnis aus gewöhnlicher Geschäftstätigkeit

Any loss that is not a capital loss and that is deductible against ordinary income.

ordinary shares Stammaktien

Equity claims held by the residual owners of the firm, who are the last to receive any distribution of earnings or assets; also called common stock.

organic model organisches Modell

Organizational structure that is flat, uses cross-hierarchical and cross-functional teams, has low formalization, processes a comprehensive information network, and relies on participative decision-making.

organization Organisation; *(company)* Firma; *(association)* Verband; *(corporate legal entity)* Unternehmensform

Structure of roles and responsibilities functioning to accomplish predetermined objectives. Organizations have grown tremendously in size in the twentieth century and are found in all parts of private and public life.

organizational organisatorisch

organizational architecture Organisatorischer Ausfbau

organizational behavior Verhalten (des Einzelnen) in Organisationen

Analysis of human behavior in organizations, covering a wide array of topics such as organizational structure, group dynamics, leadership, motivation, decision making, conflict resolution, and organizational development.

organizational chart Organigramm; Geschäftsverteilungsplan; Organisationsplan

A chart that describes the administrative and functional structure of an organization, especially the interrelationships of individual positions in terms of authority and responsibility.

organizational citizenship behavior individuelles Verhalten in der Arbeitsumgebung

Discretionary behavior that is not part of an employee's formal job requirements but that nevertheless promotes the effective functioning of the organization.

Successful organizations need employees who will do more than their usual job duties and provide performance that is beyond expectations – employees who will engage in "good citizenship" behaviors such as making constructive statements about their work group and the organization and volunteering for extra job activities.

organizational commitment Einsatz des Einzelnen für und in einer Organisation

Degree to which an employee identifies with a particular organization and its goals and wishes to maintain membership in the organization. High organizational commitment means identifying with one's employing organization.

organizational culture Unternehmenskultur

The common perception held by the organization's members that provides a system of shared meaning.

There are seven primary characteristics that capture the essence of an organization's culture and give a composite picture of the organization's culture: (1) innovation and risk taking (2) attention to detail (3) outcome orientation (4) people orientation (5) team orientation (6) aggressiveness (7) stability.

organizational development Organisationsentwicklung

Collection of interventions, driven by certain ideas and values, that seek to improve organizational effectiveness and employee well-being. The organizational development paradigm values human and organizational growth, collaborative and participative processes, and a spirit of inquiry.

Techniques used in this context are sensitivity training, survey feedback, process consultation, team building, and intergroup development.

organizational planning Organisationsplanung

The process of identifying, assigning and documenting responsibilities and relationships in an organization with the aim of transforming organizational objectives into a functioning mechanism designed to achieve the objectives.

organizational structure Organizationsstruktur

The division of authority, responsibility, and duties among the members of an organization, defines how job tasks are formally divided, grouped, and coordinated.

Three common types of organizational structure are functional organization, matrix organization, and line organization.

There are six key elements that managers need to address when they design their organization's structure: specialization, departmentalization, chain of command, span of control, centralization, and decentralization, and formalization.

organization chart Stellenbesetzungsplan

organization committee Verbandsausschuss

organization cost Gründungskosten; Gründungsaufwand; organisatorische Kosten

Amounts spent to begin a business enterprise, such as legal fees, business filing fees, and franchise acquisition.

organization doctrine Organisationslehre

Organization for Economic Cooperation and Development (OECD) Organisation für wirtschaftliche Zusammenarbeit und Entwicklung

Group of the major western economic powers that promote cooperation among industrialized countries on economic and social policies.

Formed in 1961, the OECD replaced the Organization for European Economic Cooperation (OEEC). Its objectives are to assist member countries in formulating policies designed to achieve high economic growth while maintaining financial stability, contributing to world trade on a multilateral basis, and stimulating members' aid to developing countries.

Members are Australia, Austria. Belgium, Canada, Denmark, Finland, France, Germany, Greece, Hungary, Iceland, Ireland, Italy, Japan, South Korea, Luxembourg, Mexico, the Netherlands, New Zealand, Norway, .Poland, Portugal, Spain. Sweden. Switzerland, Turkey, UK, and USA Its headquarters are in Paris.

organization of the market Marktordnung

organize organisieren; gründen

organizing Organisieren

One of the management functions which includes the determination of what tasks are to be done, who is to do them, how the tasks are to be grouped, who reports to whom, and where decisions are to be made.

orient orientieren; sich zurechtfinden

orientation Orientierung; Ausrichtung; *(new employee)* Einweisung

origin Ursprung; Herkunft; Anfang

original *(document)* Urschrift; Original; Erstanfertigung; original; ursprünglich

original capitalization Erstausstattung mit Kapital

original condition Anfangszustand

original cost Anschaffungskosten; Gründungsaufwand

Accounting: the total costs associated with the acquisition of an asset.

Public utilities: the acquisition cost incurred by the entity that first devotes a property to public use.

original equipment Erstausstattung

original equipment manufacturer (OEM) Originalgerätehersteller; Original Equipment Manufacturer

A company that builds products using components from other companies and sells these products under its own name.

original-issue-discount bond Abzinsungsobligation

Bond issued with a discount from par value.

original stock Grundkapital

original store Stammladen

original subscriber *(shares)* Ersterwerber

originate ins Leben rufen; hervorbringen; *(to found)* begründen; *(to come into being)* entstehen; *(to have origin)* herstammen

originating banker Konsortialführer

originator Urheber; Erfinder; ursprünglicher Kreditgeber

Banking: the individual or organization that is initiating a money transfer instruction through the Automated Clearing House (ACH) in the US.

other current assets sonstiges Umlaufvermögen

Value of non-cash assets, including prepaid expenses and accounts receivable, due within 1 year.

other income sonstige Erträge; betriebsfremde Erträge; neutrale Erträge

Accounting: income from activities not in the normal course of business, such as interest income or profit from sale of assets; sometimes called other revenue.

other long term liabilities sonstige langfristige Verbindlichkeiten

Value of leases, future employee benefits, deferred taxes and other obligations not requiring interest payments that must be paid over a period of more than 1 year.

other receivables sonsitge Forderungen

other sources sonstige Quellen

Amount of funds generated during the period from operations by sources other than depreciation or deferred taxes. Part of free cash flow calculation.

outbound telemarketing ausgehendes Telemarketing

outcome Ergebnis; Resultat

outdoor advertising Außenwerbung, Plakatwerbung

Very large advertisements posted on road side structures, on top of buildings and on walls

outfit *(equipment)* Ausrüstung; Ausstattung; *(enterprise)* Betrieb; *(mil)* Truppenteil; *(to ~) (to equip)* ausrüsten

outflow Abgang; Abfluss

outflow of capital Kapitalabfluss

outflow of deposits Einlagenabfluss

outlaw gesetzwidrig Handelnder; Bandit; *(to ~)* ungesetzlich machen

outlay Auslage; Ausgabe; Kostenaufwand

outlet *(market)* Absatzmarkt; *(store)* Vertriebsstelle; *(high-volume customer)* Großabnehmer

outlet store Resteladen; Werksverkaufsstelle

A retail store in which a manufacturer sells his products directly to the public, in particular irregular, surplus or end-of season merchandise.

outline *(sketch)* Skizze; Umriss; *(draft)* Entwurf; *(to ~)* umreißen; skizzieren

outlook Aussicht; Vorschau; *(viewpoint)* Ansicht; Auffassung

outlook on the future Zukunftserwartung

out of außerhalb

out-of-court settlement außergerichtlicher Vergleich

out of fashion unmodern; veraltet

out-of pocket expenses Spesen

out of the money aus dem Geld

A call option is out-of-the-money if the strike price is greater than the market price of the underlying security. A put option is out-of-the-money if the strike price is less than the market price of the underlying security.

out-of-stock cost Fehlmengenkosten

out-of-town retail cluster außerstädtisches Gewerbezentrum

Cluster of stores situated out-of-town, usually in a transport node, which is very accessible by road from several regional locations. The cluster of retailers may not be organized as a unit.

outperform übertreffen; überflügeln; überragen

output *(total output)* Gesamtleistung; *(production)* Ausstoß; Produktionsleistung; *(quantity)* Produktionsmenge; *(productivity)* Leistung; Output; *(to ~) (computer)* ausgeben

output boost Leistungssteigerung; Outputsteigerung

output controls Produktivitätskontrolle

Method of control by setting goals for subordinates, expressing these goals in terms of objective criteria, and then judging performance by a subordinate's ability to meet these goals.

output data Produktionsziffern; *(data processing)* Ausgabedaten

output device Ausgabegerät

output increase Leistungssteigerung; Outputsteigerung

output path Outputpfad

outside capital Fremdkapital; Fremdmittel

outside country *(EU)* Drittland

outside director nebenamtliche Geschäftsführer; Direktor ohne Geschäftsbereich

A person elected by the shareholders to a corporation's board of directors,who is not an employee of the company. Outside directors can bring unbiased opinions and contribute experience.

outside funds Fremdmittel

outsider Außenseiter; Nichtfachmann

outsource ausgliedern

Contract internal tasks to external firms in order to accomplish one´s objectives.

outsourcing Fremdvergabe, Produktionsverlagerung; Outsourcing

The buying in of components, products or services from outside suppliers rather than by supplying them internally. Reasons for outsourcing may be lack of expertise, investment capital or capacity to do so. It may also be cheaper or quicker to outscource.

outstanding *(bill)* unbeglichen; *(sum)* ausstehend; *(issue)* offen stehend; *(excellence)* hervorragend

outstanding debt ausstehende Forderung; Geldforderung

outstrip übersteigen; überflügeln; übertreffen

outweigh überwiegen

overall total; gesamt; pauschal

overall costs Gesamtkosten

overall expenses method Gesamtkostenmethode

Accounting: technique for evaluating the cost of goods sold by dividing total expense by the number of items sold.

overall index Gesamtindex

overall loss Gesamtverlust

overall result Gesamtergebnis

overall Schutzanzug

over and above extra

over-and-short unbereinigte Verkaufsdaten

Accounting: discrepancy between recorded sales data and audited statements.

overbooked *(flight, hotel)* überbucht

Situation that arises when a business such as a hotel accepts more reservations than it can offer accommodations. The reason for this policy is that there are always people who have reserved but do not arrive and do not cancel..

overbought/oversold indicator Indikator für zu hohen Verkaufs-/Kaufwert

Securities: indicator that attempts to define when prices have moved too far and too fast in either direction and thus are vulnerable to reaction.

overcapitalization Überkapitalisierung

overcapitalize überkapitalisieren; *(corporation)* zu hohen Nennwert für das Stammkapital ansetzen

overcharge zuviel verlangen; einen zu hohen Preis verlangen

Charging a price that is too high, which is usually the result of an error and must be refunded to the customer.

overdraft Kontoüberziehung

overdraft credit Überziehungskredit; Dispositionskredit

A loan made to a customer with a bank account, in which the account is allowed to go into debit up to a specified limit (the overdraft limit). Interest is charged on the daily debit balance.

overdraw überziehen

overdue *(time)* überfällig; *(in arrears)* rückständig

overestimation Überbewertung

overextension Überschuldung

overflow *(flooding)* Überschwemmung; Überflutung; *(flood)* Flut; *(to ~)* überfließen; überlaufen

overhaul Überprüfung; Überholung; gründliche Instandsetzung; *(to ~)* überprüfen; überholen; instand setzen

overhead *(transport)* Hoch-; Luft-; oben

overhead costs Gemeinkosten; indirekte Kosten

Indirect expenses of running a business not directly associated with a particular item or service sold.

Indirect costs complement the direct costs. Whenever costs can be clearly allocated to an object (for example, cost center), it is regarded as direct costs, but if they accrue collectively for this and other objects, they are then indirect cost or overheads.

Example: wages paid to factory workers and the cost of production materials are direct costs. Electricity, insurance, and benefits paid to workers are overhead expenses.

overheat überheizen; *(economy)* sich überhitzen

overheating Überhitzung

Economy: situation of rapid expansion that can lead to a rise in inflation. Basically, too much money is chasing too few goods, which can lead to price rises.

overload überladen; *(to overburden)* überlasten; einer zu hohen Belastung aussetzen

overnight loan Tagesgeld

overpositioning Überpositionierung

Positioning error referring to too narrow a picture of the company, its product or a brand being communicated to target customers.

overprice Überpreis; *(to ~)* einen zu hohen Preis ansetzen

overproduce überproduzieren; zuviel produzieren

overproduction Überproduktion; Überschussproduktion

Economics: market situation characterized by excessive production leading to supply well beyond market demand at remunerative prices, also called glut.

override sich hinwegsetzen über; *(decision)* aufheben; *(law)* außer Kraft setzen

overrun Überschreitung; Überlauf; Überschuss; überschüssige Menge; *(to ~)* überschreiten; überlaufen

Manufacturing: production over the desired order or schedule amount, possibly due to estimating errors.

overseas Übersee; überseeisch; im Ausland

overseas buyer Auslandskunde; Kunde aus Übersee

overseas company ausländisches Unternehmen; Auslandsunternehmen

Term used in the UK for a company incorporated outside the country.

overseas market Überseemarkt

overseas operation überseeische Unternehmung; überseeische Geschäftstätigkeit

overseas trade Überseehandel; Überseegeschäft

oversell überverkaufen; in zu großer Menge verkaufen; *(stock exchange)* über den Bestand verkaufen

overstate *(to exaggerate)* übertreiben; zu hoch angeben; *(to overemphasize)* zu stark betonen; *(balance sheet)* überbewerten

oversubscribe überzeichnen

oversubscribed issue überzeichnete Emission

Investors are not able to buy all the shares they want, so underwriters must allocate the shares among investors. This occurs when a new issue is underpriced.

oversubscription privilege Überzeichnungsprivileg

Allows shareholders to purchase unsubscribed shares in a rights offering at the subscription price.

oversupply Überangebot; *(to ~)* überversorgen

overtake *(outdistance)* überholen

overtax überbesteuern; zu hoch besteuern; *(capacity)* überlasten.

over the counter (OTC) im Freiverkehr; nicht Börsen gehandelt; *(marketing)* offen; *(medication)* rezeptfrei; freiverkäuflich

Securities: a market in which transactions are conducted through telephone or computer, rather than on the floor of an exchange.

Medication: drugs that are available without a prescription.

over-the-counter market Freiverkehr; außerbörslicher Markt für Wertpapiere

Securities: network of brokers and dealers who negotiate sales of securities informally, rather than in a physical exchange location.

overtime *(working hours)* Überstunden

The time an employee worked in excess of the time agreed upon in the contract. The employees must normally be compensated for overtime work.

overtime hour Überstunde

overtrading Überspekulation; Spekulation ohne Deckung

Securities: excessive buying and selling by a broker in a discretionary account.

overvaluation Überbewertung

overvalue überbewerten; überschätzen; zu hoch ansetzen

Practice of assigning too high a value to a product.

overvalued überbewertet

overwork *(others)* überfordern; *(self)* sich überarbeiten; sich überanstrengen; *(equipment)* überlasten

owe *(money)* schulden; *(gratitude)* verdanken

owing geschuldet; offen stehend; zustehend; ausstehend

own eigen; *(to ~) (to possess)* besitzen

owned by the people volkseigen

owner Besitzer; Eigentümer; Inhaber; Eigner

owner-operator Eigenbetrieb

A person who owns his own business or the equipment used in the business and operates it at the same time.

owner's equity Eigenkapital

The amount of money in an organization that has been provided by its owners. It is calculated by subtracting total liabilities from total assets.

ownership Besitz; Eigentumsrecht

The right to possess and enjoy a thing, which is a broader concept than possession or title.

own production Eigenproduktion

own resources Eigenmittel

P

pace Schritt; Tempo

pacesetter *(company)* Schrittmacher

A leader in a market or an industry who is setting the standards which others have to follow.

pack Packen; *(bale)* Ballen; *(bundle)* Bündel; *(package)* Packung; (*US)* Päckchen; *(to ~)* verpacken

package Pack; Verpackung; Paket; Packung; *(of goods)* Warensendung; *(flat rate)* Pauschale; *(to ~)* verpacken

packaged goods abgepackte Ware

Consumer products, such as food or household products, that are packaged by manufacturers and sold through retailers.

package price Paketpreis; *(flat rate)* Pauschalpreis

packaging Packmaterial; Verpackung; Verpacken

Activities involved in designing and producing the container or wrapper for a product.

packaging concept Verpackungskonzept

Idea or thought that the packaging should convey in order to support the actual product.

packaging industry Verpackungsindustrie

packing list Packliste; Versandliste

A document which lists in detail the contents of a particular package or shipment.

packing material Packmaterial; Füllmaterial

pad Kissen; Polster; *(notepad)* Notizblock; Papierblock; *(rubber stamp)*

Stempelkissen; *(to ~)* aufpolstern; wattieren; *(expenses)* überhöhen

padding Füllmaterial; Polstermaterial; Wattierung; *(of accounting records)* Fälschen von Buchungsunterlagen

The practice of adding unnecessary material in order to increase the size or the volume of a product.

page Seite; *(to ~ for sb)* ausrufen

Internet: HTML document that may contain text, images, and other online elements, such as Java applets and multimedia files. It may be statically or dynamically generated.

page impression Seitenabrufe

A page impression occurs when a member of the audience views a web page.

page interactivity Seiteninteraktivität

Internet: ability of a user to receive either standard or tailored responses from an internet site, including search tools, forms, purchase options, and e-mail.

page request Seitenanfrage

Internet: process of a user selecting a hyperlink or typing in a uniform resource locator (URL) to retrieve information on a specific web page.

page view Seitenansicht

Internet: number of times a page was downloaded by users, often measured as a function of time ("page views per day"). The actual number of times the page was seen by users may be higher because of caching.

paid circulation verkaufte Auflage; Verkaufsauflage

A classification of subscriptions or purchases of a magazine or newspaper based on payment, in the US monitored by the Audit Bureau of Circulation (ABC).

paid-in capital eingezahltes Kapital

The capital of a corporation received from investors in exchange for a share in the ownership.

paired comparison Paarvergleich; Methode des paarweisen Vergleichs

A research technique used in marketing in which consumers are presented with pairs of competing products and asked to choose the one they prefer. The number of times each brand is selected as a preference in a large number of such tests will reveal an order of brand preference.

pallet Palette

A normed wooden frame on which certain goods are stacked in warehouses and during transport. Pallets are designed to be lifted by fork-lift trucks or pallet trucks.

paltry armselig; erbärmlich; geringfügig

pamphlet Flugblatt; Streitschrift; Pamphlet; *(brochure)* Broschüre; *(prospectus)* Prospekt

panel Tafel; Schalttafel; Verzeichnis; *(group)* Ausschuss; Gremium; *(wood)* Paneel

panic Panik; *(stock exchange)* Kurssturz

paper Papier; Dokument; Akte; *(record)* Unterlage; *(draft)* Wechsel; Wertpapier; Arbeit

paper loss Scheinverlust

paper money Banknoten; Papiergeld

Banknotes issued by the central bank as legal tender, which are accepted within the economy as reliable media of exchange.

paper profit Scheingewinn; imaginärer Gewinn

An unrealized profit on a security still held. A paper profit becomes realized only when the security is sold.

paperwork Büroarbeiten; Schreibarbeit; Dokumentation

par *(equality)* Gleichwertigkeit; *(face value)* Nennwert; Pari

The nominal- or face value of a security, not the actual value it would receive on the open market. Bills of exchange, stocks, and the like are at par when they sell for their stated value.

parade Schaustellung; Prunk; Parade Exerzieren

paradigm Beispiel; Muster; Modell; Paradigma

paragraph Absatz; Abschnitt; Paragraph

paralegal *(law)* Rechtsanwaltsgehilfe

Person employed by a law office to perform a variety of tasks associated with a law practice, but who is not member of the bar.

parallel Parallele; Vergleich; Gegenstück; parallel; *(to ~)* entsprechen

parallel port Paralleler Port

Computers: interface on a computer used for connecting printers and other devices. Most PCs have at least one parallel port along with a serial port and special ports for a mouse and keyboard.

parallel processing Paralellverarbeitung

Computing: a method of executing two or more parts of a program simultaneously rather than sequentially.

paralyze *(trade)* lahm legen; *(initiative)* lähmen; paralysieren

parameter *(statistics)* Parameter; Größe; Bestimmungsgröße

A quantifiable characteristic or feature of a statistical population. Parameters are known for certain, if the number is based on a sample, it is called an estimate.

paramount von höchstem Rang; *(decisive)* ausschlaggebend; oberst; überragend

paraphrase Umschreibung; Erklärung; Erläuterung; freie Übersetzung;*(to ~)* umschreiben

par bond Wertpapier zum Nennwert

A bond that is selling at par, i.e. the amount equal to its nominal or face value.

parcel Paket; Partie; Posten; *(land)* Grundstücksparzelle

parcel out *(to distribute)* austeilen; *(to divide up)* aufteilen; parzellieren

pare *(benefits)* beschneiden; *(expenditures)* kürzen; abschneiden; *(~ down)* gesundschrumpfen

parent company Muttergesellschaft

Company that owns a majority stake (51% or more) of another company's shares. It may have its own operations, or it may have been set up solely for the purpose of owning the operating company. Where it has no business of its own, the term holding company is often used.

parent store Stammladen

Pareto's Law Pareto-Gesetz

Theory developed by the economist Vilfredo Pareto (1848-1923), that the pattern of income distribution is constant, historically and geographically, regardless of taxation or welfare policies; also called law of the trivial many and the critical few or the 80-20 law.

Pareto´s Law can be widely extended, for example: 80% of value is locked up in 20% of inventory; 80% of car breakdowns can be fixed by 20% of the spare parts range; 80% of a company's profits will come from 20% of its product range; and 80% of system failures will be caused by 20% of possible causes.

pari passu gleichberechtigt; gleichrangig

Ranking equally. When a new issue of shares is said to rank pari passu with existing shares, the new shares carry the same dividend rights and winding-up rights as the existing shares.

parity Umrechnungskurs; Parität; Par; *(equal value)* Gleichheit

An equality between prices of commodities, currencies, or securities on separate markers.

Foreign exchange: the amount of a foreign currency equivalent to a specified sum of domestic currency at the par of exchange.

parity check Paritätskontrolle

Computers: a method of error detection that checks a unit of data for even or odd parity to determine whether a mistake has taken place in reading, writing, or transmitting information.

parity price Paritätskurs; Paritätspreis

The price for a currency, commodity or service that is pegged to another price or to some sort of index.

park Park; *(public park)* Anlage; Parkplatz; *(to ~)* parken

Parkinson's Law Parkinsonsches Gesetz

Rule by the British writer Cyril N Parkinson (1909-93) in his book *Parkinson's Law*, which includes such aphorisms as: work expands to fill the time available in which to do it, expenditure rises to meet income; and subordinates multiply at a fixed rate that is independent of the amount of work produced

According to the law, organizations become infected with a disease termed injelitis, which causes the organization to become moribund, resulting in little constructive activity and accomplishment.

parochial Gemeinde-; Pfarr-; engstirnig

part Teil; Stück; Anteil; *(spare)* Ersatzteil; Rolle; Part; Partei; Gegend; *(to ~) (company)* sich trennen; *(to divide)* teilen

partial Teil-; teilweise; parteiisch; *(to be ~ to)* eine Vorliebe haben für

partial privatization Teilprivatisierung; partielle Privatisierung

partial value Teilwert

participant Teilnehmer; Beteiligter; *(part owner)* Teilhaber

participate teilnehmen; sich beteiligen; *(to have a part)* teilhaben

participating certificate Genussschein

participation Teilnahme; *(share)* Beteiligung; *(decision-making)* Mitwirkung; Teilhaberschaft; Partizipation

participation in a fair Messebeteiligung

participative budgeting partizipative Finanzplanung

Approach to budgeting that enables key employees to provide input into the budgetary process. It is intended as a motivational tool because employes are expected to work harder for goals they have set themselves.

participative leadership partizipativer Führungsstil

Leadership style in which the manager encourages workers to participate in the decsision process. Decisions are achieved as the result of consultation and group participation. Potential advantages can be increased productivity, improved quality, and reduced costs.

participative management partizipatives Management

particular spezifisch; besonders; *(exact)* genau; *(in detail)* ausführlich; *(fastidious)* eigen

particular case Einzelfall

partition Teilung; Abteil; Aufteilen; *(in office)* Aufteilung; *(property)* Grundstücksteilung; *(to ~)* aufteilen

Computing: the creation of logical divisions on a hard disk that allows operating system-specific logical formatting.

Legal: the division into parts of property held jointly, so that each party can and control his separate estate.

partner Partner; *(shareholder)* Teilhaber; *(company)* Gesellschafter; *(partnership)* Kompagnon; *(to~)* als Partner zusammenbringen

A person who is a member in a partnership.

partnership Partnerschaft; *(registered partnership)* Personalgesellschaft; Handelsgesellschaft; Teilhaberschaft

An association of two or more people formed for the purpose of carrying on a business. Partners pool some or all of their money, abilities, and skills and divide profit or loss in predetermined proportions.

Unlike an incorporated company, a partnership does not have a legal personality of its own and therefore partners are liable for the debts of the firm. General partners are fully liable for these debts, limited partners only to the extent of their investment.

partnership agreement Gesellschaftsvertrag

partnership share Geschäftsanteil

part-time Teilzeit-; teilzeitlich; *(not regular job)* nebenberuflich

Employment involving less than the standard or customary time for an activity.

part-time employee Teilzeitarbeiter

part-time work Teilzeitarbeit

Work of less than full-time hours, which usually does not entitle to the same health insurance, retirement, and other benefits as full-time work.

party Partei; *(contract)* Vertragspartei; *(social gathering)* Party; Teilnehmer; Einladung; Trupp

par value Paritätswert; *(nominal value)* Nominalwert; Nennwert; *(parity)* Parität; Pan

Value printed on the face of a share certificate or bond and used to assess dividend, capital ownership or interest. The par value on bonds specifies the payment at maturity.

Pascale, Richard T. (* 1938)

Business consultant, who tgether with McKinsey developed the famous 'Seven-S' framework of guiding management concepts. In his description, superordinate goals held the other six parts of the framework together.

Success in organizations breeds failure unless there is a system that encourages debate, even contention and conflict, leading to a process of continued renewal.

Biography: Pascale's comparative research into US and Japanese companies, member of a faculty at Stanford University's Graduate Business School, associate fellow of Oxford University, member of a faculty at Stanford University's Graduate Business School

Major publications: (1981, 1982, 1986) The Art of Japanese Management, (1990) Managing on the Edge, (1993) Harvard Business Review, (1997) Harvard Business Review.

pass Ausweis; Passierschein; Abnahme; passieren; durchkommen; *(to ~ a law)* verabschieden; *(to approve)* genehmigen; *(to spend time)* verbringen; *(a resolution)* beschließen; in Umlauf bringen; herumgereicht werden

passage Strecke; *(throughway)* Durchgang; *(transoceanic)* Überfahrt; Übergang; Reise; *(book)* Textstelle; *(law)* Verabschiedung; *(time)* Verlauf

passenger Reisender; Passagier

passenger mile Passagiermeilen

A statistical unit of measurement in the travel industry, defined as one fare-paying passenger carried for one mile.

passenger receipts Passagierquittung

passenger terminal Passagierterminal

passenger transport Personenbeförderung

passive untätig; zinslos; passiv

passive balance Passivsaldo

passive income Einkünfte aus Kapitalvermögen

Income from business activities in which someone does not materially participate, such as income generated by rental real property or investements.

passive investor passive Anleger; passiver Investor

Person who invests money but does not manage the business or property.

passport Paß; Reisepaß; Geleitbrief

An official document issued by a state, which identifies a citizen and allows travel to foreign countries and re-entry into the home country.

password Paßwort; Losung(swort)

A string of characters that is required to log onto a computer system. It has to be kept secret, thus preventing unauthorized access.

past Vergangenheit; Imperfekt; vergangen; letzte; *(former)* ehemalig; *(prior)* früher

past due überfällig

patch Flicken; Pflaster; Korrektur

Computing: interim update to a computer program that fixes a particular problem.

patent Patent; Patenturkunde; offenkundig

The granting of an exclusive right to use and exploit an invention. A patent normally remains valid for 20 years, provided that the person to whom it has been granted (the patentee) continues to pay the appropriate fees.

patentable patentierbar

patent application Patentanmeldung

patent fee Patentgebühr

patent infringement Patentrechtsverletzung

Any violation of the rights secured by a patent, which occurs when the subject-matter is used without the owner's approval or against the terms given by him.

patent law Patentrecht

patent licensing Patentvergabe

patent monopoly Patentmonopol

A form of temporary monopoly that develops because an invetor of an innovative good or service has been granted a patent. The government itself does not grant a monompoly, but the inventor has time to collect rewards for producing successful new products.

patent of invention *(law)* Erfindungspatent

patent pending angemeldetes Patent; schwebende Patentanmeldung; Patent angemeldet

A statement issued by a Patent Office after a patent has been filed. It means that a patent search is being conducted and that the Patent Office is in the process of determining whether the invention is patentable under the law.

patent register Patentregister; Patentrolle

patent right Patentrecht

paternalism Paternalismus

A type of social structure based on male supremacy and a subordinate position of women. Applied to a business, it means an approach where management assumes ultimate responsibility for employees in such areas as benefits, job assignments, and promotions.

path-goal theory Weg-Ziel-Theorie

Theory developed by Robert House that a leader's behavior is acceptable to subordinates insofar as they view it as a source of either immediate or future satisfaction.

Effective leaders clarify the path to help their followers get from where they are to the achievement of their work goals and make the path easier by reducing roadblocks.

patron Kunde; Mäzen; *(supporter)* Förderer; *(restaurant)* Stammgast

In general: a regular customer.

patronage Protektion; *(artistic)* Gönnerschaft; Kundschaft; *(financial)* Unterstützung

The practice of supporting or favoring a person or group, which normally involves someone in a powerful position offering favors in return for support.

patronage rewards Treueprämie

Customer: rewards given for the regular use of a company's products or services; can be cash, discounts or some other form.

pattern Muster; Vorlage; *(garment)* Schnittmuster; *(habit)* Gewohnheit

pawn Pfand; Pfandsache; *(chess)* Bauer

pawnbroker Pfandleiher

A person who lends money against the security of valuable goods used as collateral.

Borrowers can reclaim their goods by repaying the loan and interest within a stated period. However, if the borrower defaults, the pawnbroker is free to sell the goods.

pawning verpfänden, pfänden

pay *(payment)* Bezahlung; *(wage)* Lohn; *(to ~)* bezahlen; *(to remunerate)* entgelten; begleichen

The act of exchanging money for goods or services received.

payable zahlbar; *(due)* fällig; rentabel

payable in advance im voraus bezahlbar

payable on delivery zahlbar bei Lieferung

payable on demand zahlbar auf Verlangen

payable to bearer zahlbar an Überbringer

A bill of exchange in which neither the payee or endorsee are named.

payables Verbindlichkeiten

Accounting: money owed by a company to trade suppliers, employees, taxes, banks or others. The term refers to current liabilities instead of all debts.

payback *(debt)* Rückzahlung; *(capital)* Kapitalrückfluss; Heimzahlen

The financial rewards of an investment, such as a machine, in relation to the original amount invested.

payback period Amortisationszeit

The length of time it takes for the net revenues of an investment to cover the initial cost of the investment.

payback period rule Amortisationsrechnung

Investment decision which states that all investment projects that have payback periods equal to or less than a particular cut-off period are accepted, and all of those that pay off in more than the particular cut-off period are rejected.

paycheck Gehaltsscheck; Lohnscheck

A check issued by a company in payment of wages or salary to an employee. It normally includes the net wages, after deductions for social security and other deductions have been made.

payday Zahltag

Day on which employees receive their paychecks.

PAYE (Pay-as-you-earn) Quellenabzugsverfahren

Method of collecting tax on wages and salaries when employer make the payments to their employees.

payee Zahlungsempfänger; Wechselinhaber

The person to whom a payment should be made, i.e. the person named on a bill of exchange, note, check or other instrument.

payer Zahler; Zahlungsleistender; Bezogener; Trassat

The person who makes a payment.

paying agent Zahlungsabwickler

Securities: the institution responsible for handling payments in a transaction, receiving funds from an issuer and paying principal and interest to bondholders and dividends to stockholders.

payload Nutzlast; Tragfähigkeit

The amount of cargo a vehicle can carry, usually expressed in weight.

payment Begleichung; Bezahlung; Zahlung; *(deposit)* Einzahlung; *(compensation)* Lohn; Entlohnung; *(additional)* Zuzahlung

payment date Zahlungstermin; Tilgungstermin; Fälligkeitsdatum

The date on which a payment has to be made, such as a debt repayment, a stock dividend or an interest payment.

payment difficulty Zahlungsproblem

payment habit Zahlungsgewohnheit

payment in advance Vorauszahlung; Vorleistung

payment instrument Zahlungsmedium; Zahlungsmittel

payment method Zahlungsart; Zahlungsmethode

The specific method of payment used by a customer, such as cash, check, money order, or credit card.

payment of dividend Dividendenzahlung

payment of interest Zinszahlung; Verzinsung

payment of wages Lohnzahlung

payment transactions Zahlungsverkehr

payoff *(reward)* Belohnung; Amortisation; *(profit)* Profit; *(yield)* Ertrag; Erfolg

pay off abzahlen; abtragen; *(to be worthwhile)* sich lohnen; (sich) auszahlen

payor Zahlender

payout Auszahlung; Geld ausgeben

payout ratio Ausschüttungsquote

Securities: the proportion of a company´s profits paid out to its owners in the form of dividends.

pay raise Lohnsteigerung; Gehaltserhöhung

payroll *(accounting)* Lohn- und Gehaltsabrechnung; Lohn- und Gehaltsliste; Gehaltsverzeichnis

All remuneration paid by a business to its employees, including wages, commissions, bonuses, overtime pay, pay for holidays, vacations and sickness. It is also used to refer to the employees of a company.

payroll account Lohnkonto

pay scale Lohnskale; Lohntabelle

peak Gipfel; Höchstpunkt; Höhepunkt; Spitze; Haupt-; Höchst-; *(to ~)* den Höchststand erreichen

peak demand Spitzenbedarf

peak year Spitzenjahr

peasant Kleinbauer; Bauer; Bäuerin; *(adv)* bäuerlich

pecking order Hackordnung

A hierarchy or a rank order between the people in an organization; derived from the behavior of chickens.

peculiar *(exclusive)* eigentümlich; *(strange)* merkwürdig; sonderbar; sondern; seltsam

pecuniary Geld-; *(monetary)* geldlich; *(financial)* finanziell; pekuniär

peg Kurs; Aufhänger; *(stock exchange)* Kursstützung; *(to ~) (price)* stützen; *(exchange rate)* ansetzen

A peg is a virtual point used for orientation. It is used to describe the practice of stabilizing the price of a security, commodity, or currency by intervening in a market.

pegged price Stützpreis; künstlich gestützter Preis

pegging Kursstützung; Preisstützung

Currencies: a form of price stabilization used to stabilize a country's currency by fixing its exchange rate with that another country

penalty Strafe; *(fine)* Geldstrafe; Strafmaß, Straf-; Handicap

A form of punishment for non-compliance or violation of the terms of a contract, such as for prepaying a loan, failing to complete a contract sale, or breaking a lease.

pen and ink Schreibzeug

pending schwebend; anhängig; noch nicht erledigt

penetrate durchdringen; *(market)* eindringen, durchsetzen; durchschauen

penetrated market eroberter Markt; durchdrungener Markt

Set of consumers who have already bought a particular product or service.

penetration Durchdringung; *(market)* Eindringen; Scharfsinn

Marketing: percentage of people (or homes) within a defined universe that are physically able to be exposed to a medium.

penetration pricing *(marketing)* Niedrigpreisstrategie

Pricing strategy that sets a low price for a new product in order to attract large numbers of buyers and a large market share. Often used to get rapid entry into a new market. After the product has been established in the market, prices can be raised again.

penny stock Aktien mit sehr niedrigen Nennbeträgen und Kursen; Kleinaktien; Pfennigaktien

A stock that sells for less than $1 a share, often issued by companies with a short or erratic history of revenues and earnings.

pension Rente; Ruhegehalt; Pension

pension adjustment Rentenanpassung

pension cut Rentenkürzung; Pensionskürzung

pensioner Rentner; Pensionär

pension fund Rentenfonds; Pensionsfonds; Rentenkasse; Pensionskasse

A fund set up by a company, union, or government, to pay the pension benefits of retired workers.

Pension funds invest the funds they hold, often billions of dollars, in the stock and bond markets in order to maximize the return for their members.

pension increase Rentenerhöhung; Rentenaufbesserung

pension payment Rentenzahlung; Pensionszahlung

pent-up demand aufgestaute Nachfrage; Nachholbedarf

people intensive personalintensiv; arbeitsintensiv

A process or industry that requires large amounts of human labor to produce goods or render services. Typical examples are hospitals, restaurants, or hotels; same as labor-intensive.

people's bank Volksbank

per pro; durch; per *(citation)* laut

per capita pro Kopf

Latin for "per head". Larger sums that are calculated per capita are divided by the number of individuals involved, such as GNP per capita.

perceive wahrnehmen; erkennen

perceived conflict wahrgenommener Konflikt

Awareness by one or more parties of the existence of conditions that create opportunities for conflict to arise.

percent Prozent; prozentig

A ratio that compares a number to 100, thus defining a given quantity as a portion of the whole.

percentage Prozentsatz; Anteil; Gehalt; Provision

percentage of sales prozentualer Umsatzanteil

percentage of sales method *(advertising)* umsatzbezogene Methode der Budgetierung

Practice of setting the promotion budget at a certain percentage of current or forecast sales or as a percentage of the sales price.

This method is popular with advertisers because of its simplicity and its ability to relate advertising expenditures directly to sales.

percentage of share Anteilsquote

percentage point Prozentpunkt

percent calculation Prozentrechnung

percentile Perzentil

A ranking scale that defines the relative position or rank of each figure. The pth percentile of a number in a list means that *p* percent of the elements in the list are less than that number.

perceptible wahrnehmbar

perception Wahrnehmung(-svermögen); Auffassung

Process by which people select, organize and interpret information to form a meaningful picture of the world. What one perceives can be substantially different from objective reality.

perceptual map Wahrnehmungslandkarte

Product positioning tool that uses multidimensional scaling of consumer's perceptions and preferences to portray the psychological distance between products and segments.

perceptual mapping Darstellung in einer Wahrnehmungslandkarte

The use of mathematical psychology to analyse the structure of a market. Consumer perceptions of different brands are plotted on a graph or map. It can be useful in determining competitors' positions and what opportunities there are in unoccupied positions.

per diem pro Tag

per diem allowance Tagegeld

A fixed daily allowance for travel, meals and/or lodging while an employee is conducting a business transaction.

perfect vollkommen; vollendet; vollenden; *(to ~)* vervollkommnen, vollständig

perfect competition vollkommener Markt; vollkommener Wettbewerb

A market situation in which there are many buyers and many sellers and no buyer or seller has the power to affect the market price of the product; also called pure competition.

Further characteristics of a perfectly competitive market are: a homogeneous product, an equal awareness of prices and volume, an absence of discrimination in buying and selling, total mobility of productive resources, and complete freedom of entry. Perfect competition exists only as a theoretical model.

perfect markets vollkommener Markt

perfection Vollkommenheit; Vollendung

perforate durchbohren; durchlöchern; perforieren; lochen

perform aus-; auf-; vorführen; leisten; erfüllen; vollziehen

performance Verrichtung; Ergebnis; Leistung; *(entertainment)* Vorstellung; *(implementation)* Durchführung; *(contract)* Erfüllung; *(presentation)* Veranstaltung

performance ambiguity mangelnde Eindeutigkeit der Leistungsbeschreibung

Occurs when the causes of good or bad performance are not clearly identifiable.

performance appraisal Leistungsbewertung; Leistungsbeurteilung

A system of measuring how well an individual employee has performed by applying objective criteria.

performance evaluation Leistungsbewertung; Leistungsbeurteilung

performance measurement Leistungsmessung; Leistungsbeurteilung

Means to determine and judge how far a manager or an employee has achieved his objective.

performance of a web site Leistungsfähigkeit einer Webseite

Internet: performance or quality of service is dependent on its availability and speed of access.

performance-related pay leistungsbezogene Bezahlung

System that relates the rewards of an individual employee to the performance of the organization that they work for. It is designed to motivate employees and to align their effort more closely with the aims of the organization.

performance review Leistungsbeurteilung; *(accounting)* Leistungsüberprüfung

Stage of the business buying process in which the buyer rates its satisfaction with suppliers, deciding whether to continue, modify or drop them.

performance shares erfolgsabhängige Aktienvergütung

Shares given to managers on the basis of performance as measured by earnings per share and similar criteria. They are therefore a control device used by shareholders to tie management to the interests of shareholders.

performing stage Leistungsstadium

Fourth stage in group development, when the group is fully functional and accepted. Group energy has moved from getting to know and understand each other to performing the task at hand. For permanent work groups, performing is the last stage in their development.

peril Gefahr; Risiko; gefährden

period Zeitraum; Periode; *(period of effectiveness)* Laufzeit; *(punctuation)* Punkt

period cost wiederkehrende Aufwendungen; Periodenkosten

periodic regelmäßig wiederkehrend; periodisch

periodical periodisch; regelmäßig erscheinend

periodical Magazin; Zeitschrift

Any publication that is issued on a regular basis, with its own distinctive title, and normally containing several articles by more than one contributor. Typical examples of periodicals are magazines and journals.

periodic inventory method Stichtags-inventurmethode; periodische Bestands-aufnahme

Accounting process used to find the cost of inventory sold or in production. Data on beginning inventory, purchases, and ending inventory are used to find the amount and cost of withdrawals from inventory.

period of adjustment Anpassungs-zeitraum; Angleichungsperiode

period of notice Kündigungsfrist

peripheral device *(computer)* Peripherie-Gerät

perishability *(goods)* Kurzlebigkeit; Leichtverderblichkeit; Vergänglichkeit

perishable leicht verderblich; *(goods)* kurzlebig

Food that will perish rapidly if not refrigerated, such as fish.

perjury Meineid schwören; Meineid leisten

The act of making a false statement willfully and knowingly while under oath. Perjury is a criminal offense.

perk Nebenleistung; Vergünstigung; (to~) sich herausputzen; sich aufmöbeln

Any form of non-wage compensation provided to employees in addition to their normal imcome.

These benefits can include insurance, retirement benefits, daycare, tuition reimbursement, sick leave, paid vacation, social security, profit sharing and others.

Executive perks include automobiles, vacations, club membership, reserved parking spaces, and use of corporate aircraft.

permanent dauernd; beständig, bleibend; permanent

permanent financing Dauerfinanzierung; langfristige festverzinsliche Hypothek

Corporate finance: method of long-term financing either through a debt instrument (bonds or long-term notes) or equity (common or preferred stock).

Real estate: a mortgage with a 15-, 20-, or 30-year term.

permanent income theory Theorie des konstanten Einkommens

Economics: theory that consumers take a long-term view of their income and do not change consumption patterns much in response to temporary income changes.

permanently unemployed person Langzeitarbeitsloser; Dauerarbeitsloser

permanent use Dauernutzung

permissible zulässig

permission Erlaubnis; Genehmigung

permission marketing Permission Marketing; Erlaubnismarketing; Marketing nach vorheriger Zustimmung

Approach when marketers ask permission before they send advertisements to prospective customers, used especially by Internet marketers, email marketers, and telephone marketers.

It is supposed to be more efficient because advertisements are not sent to people that are not interested in the product..

permit Genehmigung; Erlaubnisschein; *(permission)* Erlaubnis; *(to ~)* erlauben; genehmigen; zulassen

A document issued by a government or any other authority, that entitles the bearer to take some specific action.

perpetual ewig; dauernd; immerwährend; *(annuity)* unbefristet

perpetual inventory laufende Inventaraktualisierung

An inventory management system that keeps records up to date on all inventory items all the time. This is done by obtaining information directly from records, without resorting to a physical inventory; also called continuous inventory.

perpetuate *(to eternize)* verewigen; *(to continue indefinitely)* endlos fortsetzen

perpetuity Dauerzustand; ewige Rente

A type of annuity in which the periodic payments continue indefinitely, sometimes referred to as a perpetual annuity.

Example: fixed coupon payments on permanently invested sums of money, or scholarships paid perpetually from an endowment.

perquisite (perk) Nebenleistung; Vergünstigung; zusätzliche Leistungen des Arbeitgebers

per se an sich; für sich allein; schlechthin

persist nachdrücklich behaupten; sich hartnäckig halten; *(to persevere)* beharren; *(to last)* fortdauern

persistence *(preserving)* Beharrlichkeit; Hartnäckigkeit; *(lasting)* Nachhaltigkeit; Fortdauer

persistent *(persevering)* beharrlich; *(lasting)* nachhaltig; hartnäckig; bleibend

person Person; Individuum; Aufgabenträger; *(personal)* persönlich; privat; personell

personal account Privatkonto

personal allowances Steuerfreibetrag

The amount of income that an individual can earn before he becomes liable to income tax.

personal communication channels persönliche Kommunikationskanäle; -Kommunikationswege

Channels through which two or more people communicate directly with each other, including face-to-face, person to audience, over the telephone, or through the mail.

personal computer Personalcomputer; Kleincomputer; PC

personal controls persönliche Führung; persönliche Steuerung

personal credit Privatkredit

personal digital assistant (PDA) PDA

Any handheld device that offers a variety of computing and communication applications, ranging from calendar, address book, Internet, e-mails, video, to mobile phone, and WLAN access.

personal drawing Privatentnahme

personal effects persönliche Habe; bewegliches Eigentum

personal exemption persönlicher Freibetrag

personal income Privateinkommen

Economics: indicator that measures the total income of all households from all sources. It is defined as: national income less retained corporate profits, corporate income taxes, and social insurance contributions, plus transfer payments, interest paid to consumers, and net government interest payments. Personal income represents the amount of income actually received by households.

personal influence persönlicher Einfluß

Effect of statements made by one person on another's attitude or probability of purchase.

personalization Personalisierung

Internet: web-based personalization involves delivering customised content for the individual through web pages, e-mail or push technology.

personality Persönlichkeit

A person's distinguishing psychological characteristics that lead to relatively consistent and lasting responses to his or her own environment.

An individual's personality is a combination of lifetime experiences as well as genetic characteristics. Personality is an indelible characteristic and results in a pattern of predictable behavior.

personality-job fit theory Personality-Job-Fit Theorie

Theory by John Holland that identifies six personality types and proposes that the fit between personality type and occupational environment determines satisfaction and turnover.

The key points of this model are that (1) there do appear to be intrinsic differences in personality among individuals, (2) there are different types of jobs, and (3) people in job environments congruent with their personality types should be more satisfied and less likely to voluntarily resign than should people in congruent jobs.

Each one of the six personality types has a congruent occupational environment. The six listed personality types are: (1) realistic, (2) investigative, (3) social, (4) conventional, (5) enterprising, (6) artistic.

personality traits Persönlichkeitseigenschaften

Enduring characteristics that describe an individual's behavior.

The more consistent the characteristic and the more frequently it occurs in diverse situations, the more important that trait is in describing the individual. Popular characteristics include shyness, aggressiveness, submissiveness, laziness, ambition, loyalty, and timidity.

personalize individualisieren; individuell anpassen

personalized web page personalisierte, angepasste Webseite

Web page created with cookies that were put on the user's hard disk by the web site. Cookies help companies to personalize web pages by greeting the user by name or by listing previous purchases, thus building relationship with users.

personalized products personalisierte Produkte

personal loan Personalkredit; persönliche Anleihe; Kleinkredit

personal liability persönliche Haftung

The legal obligation of an individual to repay debts from his personal assets. Sole proprietors and general partners in a partnership are personally liable, whilst corporate stockholders can lose only their investment in the corporation.

personal property bewegliches Privateigentum

All property of an individual except real property, which includes all things movable.

personal selling *(marketing)* persönlicher Verkauf; Direktverkauf durch Vertreter

Direct personal communication between a representative of the company and a prospective customer with the intention of iinfluencing a purchase decision..

personal share Namensaktie

personal tax Vermögenssteuer

personnel Belegschaft; Personal; Mannschaft; Mitarbeiter

All the individuals who actually compose an organization's work force, i.e. the human resources of an organization.

personnel cutback Stellenabbau; Belegschaftsabbau

personnel department Personalabteilung

The department of a company responsible for hiring, training and placing employees and for setting policies for personnel management.

personnel development Mitarbeiterförderung; Personalentwicklung

personnel exchange Personalaustausch

personnel expenses Personalaufwendung; Personalkosten

personnel growth Personalzuwachs

personnel management Menschenführung; Personalleitung

personnel policy Personalpolitik

personnel turnover Personalfluktuation

person with power of attorney *(action)* Handlungsbevollmächtigter; *(representation)* Vertretungsbevollmächtigter; *(business)* Prokurist

perspective Perspektive; An-; Aussicht

persuade überreden; *(to convince)* überzeugen; (sich) einreden

persuade to buy zum Kauf überreden; umwerben

persuasion Überredung; Beeinflussung; *(conviction)* Überzeugung(skraft)

A rhetorical strategy aimed at inducing attitude changes and influencing action by appealing to reason or emotion..

In modern advertising, persuasion can be achieved through attention-getting effects, appeal to self-interest, stimulation of desire, and a call-to-action response.

persuasive überzeugend; Überredungs-

persuasive advertising auf Überzeugung zielende Werbung

Advertising used to build selective demand for a brand by persuading consumers that it offers the best quality for their money.

persuasive power Überzeugungskraft; *(advertising)* Werbekraft

pertain betreffen; gehören

pertaining to the global economy weltwirtschaftlich

pertaining to growth policy wachstumspolitisch

pertinent question relevante Frage; Sachfrage

PESTL analysis Umfeldanalyse

Analysis of the environmental influences on a firm: political, economic, social, technological, and legal.

Peter principle Peter Prinzip

Theory advanced by Lawrence J Peter that in large organizations individuals are promoted to the level of their incompetence i.e. to jobs for which they are not suited and do not display competence.

Peters, Tom (* 1942)

Management thinker who wrote, together with Robert Waterman, "In Search of Excellence". They developed the McKinsey 'Seven-S' formula to analyze an organization: structure, strategy, system, style of management, skills, staff and shared value.

Both were responsible for popularizing the study of management to a mass readership, and initiating a new direction in management thinking.

Biography: 1972 he worked in the Pentagon, where he became 'fascinated by complex organizations', 1974 joined McKinsey, Master's degree in civil engineering at Cornwall University, then serving to Vietnam, MBA at Stanford and worked again in Washington for the office of Management and Budget, founded the Tom Peters Group.

Major publications: (1982) In Search of Excellence, (1985) A Passion for Excellence, (1987, 1988) Thriving on Chaos, (1992) Liberation Management, (1994) The Tom Peters Seminar: Crazy Times Call for Crazy Organizations, (1994) The Pursuit of Wow!, (1997) Circles of Innovation

petition Antrag; *(written)* Bittschrift; Gebet; *(to ~)* beantragen; eine Eingabe machen

*Legal:*a written request to a court for an order, stating facts and circumstances relied upon as a cause for judicial action.

petitioner Bittsteller; Antragsteller

The party who filed a petition with the court.

petitioning creditor Konkursgläubiger

petroleum Erdöl; Mineralöl

petty *(character)* kleinlich; *(concern)* geringfügig; engstirnig

petty cash Portokasse; Nebenkasse

phase Stadium; *(step)* Stufe; Phase; *(to ~)* in Phasen einteilen; staffeln

phase out auslaufen lassen; abschaffen

Phillips curve Phillips-Kurve

Economics: a relationship between the inflation rate and the unemployment rate observed by A.W. Phillips in 1958: as inflation increases, unemployment decreases and vice versa.

philosophy Philosophie; *(business)* Lebens;- Weltanschauung

phone Telefon; Fernsprecher; *(to ~)* telefonieren; anrufen

phone-me Bitte um Rückruf

Internet: Call-back facility available on the web site for a company to contact a customer by phone at a later time as specified by the customer.

phone switching Umtausch von Wertpapieren über Telefon

In mutual funds, the ability to transfer shares between funds in the same family by telephone request.

photocopy Fotokopie; Ablichtung; *(to ~)* fotokopieren; ablichten

photograph Fotografie; Lichtbild-aufnahme; fotografieren

photographer Fotograf

photographic fotografisch

phrase Redewendung**;** Phrase; *(expression)* treffender Ausdruck; *(to ~)* ausdrücken

physical materiell; *(human body)* körperlich; äußerlich, physisch

physical ability physische Fähigkeiten

Ability required to do tasks demanding stamina, dexterity, strength, and similar. It includes the strength, flexibility and other related factors.

physical commodity Effektivware

Securities: the actual product that is delivered to the contract buyer at the completion of a commodity contract in either the spot market or the futures market.

physical depreciation verbrauchsbedingte Wertminderung; nutzungsbedingte Abschreibung

The depreciation of a property due to normal wear and tear. Other reasons for physical depreciation include breakage, deferred maintenance, effects of age on construction material.

physical distribution physische Distribution; Marketinglogistik

Tasks involved in planning, implementing and controlling the physical flow of materials and final goods from points of origin to points of use.

physical distribution firms Firmen in der Logistikkette

Warehouse, transportation and other firms that help a company to stock and move goods from their points of origin to their destinations.

physical examination *(of an object)* physische Durchsuchung; ärztliche Untersuchung

Medicine: the process by which a physician investigates the body of a patient for signs of disease.

physical product eigentliches Produkt

physical property *(possession)* Sacheigentum; Sachbesitz; *(characteristic)* physische Eigenschaft

physically disabled Körperbehinderter

physician Arzt

pick *(choice)* Auswahl; *(the best)* Auslese; *(to ~) (to choose)* auswählen; aussuchen

picket (Streik)Posten; Feldwache; *(fence)* Stakete

picketing Streikposten aufstellen; demonstrieren

The practice of patrolling around an employer's premises to increase the pressure in labor and political disputes.

pickup *(acceleration)* Anzugsvermögen; *(truck)* Kleinlastwagen; *(economy)* Konjunkturanstieg

pick up abholen; (to *increase)* zunehmen; (to *rally)* sich erholen

PICS

Acronym for Platform for Internet Content Selection - a standardized format for rating systems. The PICS standard lets anyone define how their rating system works.

picture Bild; Vorstellung; Verkörperung; *(to imagine)* ausmalen

picture screen *(movies)* Leinwand; *(TV)* Bildschirm

piece Teil; Figur; Rolle; Stück; *(to ~)* zusammenstücken

piecemeal stückweise

piece rate Akkordlohn; Prämienlohn; Stücklohn; Akkorrdlohnsatz; Stücklohnsatz; Stücklohntarif

A payment scheme in which an employee is paid a specific price for each unit made. The rate is therefore directly related to output and not to the required time.

Piece rate, to be attractive to workers, depends on speed of production, therefore the standard of quality and safety may suffer if adequate precautions are not taken.

piece-rate pay plan Stücklohnsystem

piece work Akkordarbeit

pie chart Kreisdiagramm; Kuchendiagramm

A circle graph used for comparing parts to the whole. The area of a circle represents the whole amount, and the areas of the sectors represent the parts.

pie model of capital structure Kreisdiagramm der Kapitalstruktur

Model of the debt-equity ratio of the firms, graphically depicted in slices of a pie that represents the value of the firm in the capital markets.

piggyback Huckepack

Transportation: carrying trailers and containers on a rail car from terminal to terminal.

piggyback exporting Huckepackexport

Method of exporting where a domestic company with no existing export channels uses the channels and the experience of some other company to enter a foreign market.

The piggyback strategy is easy, quick and reduces the risk to the company. On the other hand, it gives up control over the product and substantial share of the revenue, and misses the experience to be made in a new market.

piggy back traffic Huckepackverkehr

Pigou effect Pigou-Effekt; realer Kassenhaltungseffekt

Effect first observed by A.C. Pigou in 1943 that the stimulation of output & employment causes in increasing consumption due to a rise in real balances of wealth.

Pigou showed that a decrease in the price level increases the buying power of money that people have, and increases their consumption.

pile *(stack)* Stapel; Menge; *(heap)* Haufen; *(fabric, rug)* Noppe; *(to ~)* stapeln; anhäufen, mit Pfählen versehen

pilferage Dieberei; Mauserei; kleiner Diebstahl

pilot Pilot; *(ship)* Lotse *(experimental)* Versuchs-; Pilot; *(an airplane)* fliegen; *(to guide)* führen; *(to pilot a ship into harbor)* lotsen

pilot installation Pilotanlage

pilot plant Versuchsanlage

A small production facility built to test the large-scale feasibility of a production process, thus reducing the investment risk.

pink slip Kündigungsschreiben

The official notice sent to an employee that he has been fired from his job.

pinpoint genau lokalisieren

pin point Nadelspitze; genau bestimmter Punkt

pioneer Pionier; *(innovator)* Bahnbrecher; *(to ~)* Bahn brechen; vorangehen; bahnen; den Weg bahnen für

pioneering costs Initialkosten; Initialisierungskosten

Costs an early entrant into a market bears that later entrants avoid, such as the time and effort in learning the rules, failure due to ignorance, and the liability of being a foreigner.

pipe *(tobacco)* Pfeife; *(oil, gas)* Rohr; Röhre; *(to ~)* pumpen; mit Röhren versehen

pipeline Rohr(fern)leitung; Ölleitung

pit Grube; *(coal)* Kohlenbergwerk; *(stock exchange)* Maklerstand; *(to ~) (a fruit)* entsteinen, entkernen

pitch *(mineral)* Pech; Händlerstand; Stelle *(sales)* Warenangebot; Überredung zum Kauf; *(to ~) (to pitch goods)* Waren anbieten; feilhalten

pivot Dreh- und Angelpunkt, Drehzapfen; Angel

Pricing: level established as being significant by market's failure to penetrate or as being significant when a sudden increase in volume accompanies the move through the price level.

pivotal ausschlaggebend; entscheidend; *(vital)* lebenswichtig

Pixel Bildpunkt; Bildelement

Computers: small dots on a computer screen that are used to represent images and text. Short for 'picture element'. Used to indicate the size of banner advertisements.

place Ort; Stelle; *(employment)* Anstellung; *(to ~)* plazieren; *(to arrange)* anordnen; *(to invest)* investieren; *(a loan)* plazieren; *(to house)* unterbringen; *(in a job)* eine Stelle vermitteln

Marketing mix: all the company activities and decisions that make the product or service available to target customers.

place an advertisement inserieren

placement Unterbringung; *(employment)* Vermittlung; *(securities)* Platzierung; *(capital)*Anlage; Investierung; Stellenvermittlung

placement test Einstufungstest

A test to determine the suitability of applicants or potential employees, measuring skills, intelligence, motivation, interests, needs, and goals of the individuals.

place of business Unternehmenssitz; Betriebsstätte

plaintiff *(law)* Kläger

Person who initially brings a lawsuit. In a personal action, he seeks a remedy in a court of justice for an injury to his rights.

plan Plan; Karte; *(design)* Entwurf; *(intent)* Vorhaben; *(to ~)* planen; *(design)* entwerfen; planmäßig ordnen

plan B Plan B

An alternative plan for action if the initial plan did not achieve the desired results.

plan development Planerstellung; Planentwicklung

planned activity *(cost accounting)* Planleistung

Planned activity is the output that a cost center should achieve on average per month, expressed in output units. It can be calculated or estimated from the sales volume budget, the production program and from the operations which have to be carried out within the cost center responsible for which a budget is being set.

planned activity level *(cost accounting)* Planbeschäftigung

The planned activity level is used to calculate the planned cost rate of a cost center. In the planning process, there are two alternative possibilities for establishing the planned activity level of a cost center:

Derived: starting with the production program, the capacity demand for each manufactured product and its relevant cost center is derived from bills of material and work plans.

Expected: In businesses that manufacture directly to customer orders, it is not possible to derive the planned activity level directly from the production program. In this case the planned activity level of a cost center is estimated on the basis of past figures.

planned costs Plankosten

Planned costs are the result of cost budgeting. In every cost center the question is asked, which employees, resources, premises and other services are needed to achieve the planned output. The resulting quantities are then multiplied by the planned prices.

planned economy Planwirtschaft

An economic system in which state authorities rather than market forces determine prices, output and production.

Socialist and communist economies are to a high degree planned economies. Capitalist economies are, however, not completely market-driven, and they are therefore called mixed economies.

planned obsolescence Obsoleszenzplanung

Business strategy of causing products to become obsolete before they actually need replacement.

planned output Planziel

planner Planer

planning Bewirtschaftung; Planung;

planning Planung; Ausarbeitung; Endplanung

General: process involving the anticipation of possible future situations, the selection of desirable objectives, and the determination of relevant measures that need to be taken.

*Business:*one of the primary management functions of organizing a sequence of predetermined actions to complete future organizational objectives. Some types of planning are: operative planning, strategic planning, top-down/bottom-up planning.

planning commission Planungskommission

A planning commission normally oversees the work of a professional planning department, which prepares a comprehensive plan; also called a planning board, zoning commission, or zoning board, depending on the locality.

planning error Planungsfehler

planning framework Planungssystematik

planning model Planungsmodell

planning process Planungsprozess

planning program Planungsprogramm

planning project Planungsaufgabe; Planprojekt

planning task Planungsaufgabe

planning technique Planungstechnik

planograph Flachdruckverfahren

plant Pflanze; *(factory)* Fabrikanlage; Werk; Betrieb; Anlage; *(manufacturing)* Fertigungsanlage; *(machinery)* technische Anlage; *(to ~)* pflanzen; hinstellen; gründen; *(rumor)* ausstreuen

Accounting: the same as fixed assets, comprising land, buildings, machinery, natural resources, furniture and fixtures, and all other equipment permanently employed.

plant data collection *(cost accounting)* Betriebsdatenerfassung

plant equipment Betriebsausstattung

plant management Betriebsführung; Betriebsleitung

plant regulation Betriebsvorschrift

plastic; Kunststoff; Plastik; Kreditkarte; plastisch; aus Kunststoff

plate Teller; *(company)* Namensschild; *(car)* Nummernschild; Tafelgeschirr

platform Plattform; Rednerbühne; *(railway station)* Bahnsteig; *(oil drilling)* Bohrinsel; *(political party)* Grundsatzerklärung

Platform for Privacy Preferences (P3P)

Internet: a protocol allowing websites to declare the intended use of information they collect about users. Designed to give users more control of their personal information.

plausible einleuchtend; bestechend; plausibel; glaubhaft

plea Einrede; Einwand; Ausrede; Bitte; *(petition)* Gesuch; *(law court)* Plädoyer

plead einwenden; geltend mache; dringend bitten; *(law court)* plädieren; vorbringen; sich entschuldigen mit;

pleadings *(court)* Klageschrift; Prozessakten

Law: the formal allegations by the parties in a court case of their respective claims and defenses.

pleasing products Genussmittel

Products that give high immediate satisfaction, but may hurt consumers in the long run.

plebiscite Volksabstimmung

pledge Bürgschaft; Versprechen; *(deposit)* Pfand; *(to ~)* verpfänden; *(security)* als Sicherheit stellen; j-n verpflichten

Generally defined as a binding promise or agreement, a lien can commit personal property as security for a debt.

plenary Voll-; Plenar-; völlig; vollständig; uneingeschränkt

plentiful reichlich

plenty Fülle; Überfluss; Reichtum; *(in ~)* in Hülle und Fülle

plight Notlage; Zwangslage; Versprechen; verpfänden; versprechen; verloben

plot Stück; Komplott; Verschwörung; *(land)* Grundstück; *(scheme) (to ~)* planen; (to *chart)* einzeichnen; *(to scheme)* anzetteln; Anschlag machen auf

plowback Reinvestition; Ersatzinvestition

A ratio that measures the amount of earnings retained by a company after dividends have been paid out.

The ratio is normally higher in smaller, fast-growing companies, whilst more established firms pay out more of their profits as dividends.

plug Pflock; Priem; Stecker; Stöpsel; *(advertisement)* unbezahlte Werbebotschaft; *(to ~) (to promote)* anpreisen; (*to stop up)* verstopfen; einstöpseln; (*to close)* verstöpseln

plug and play sofort betriebsbereit

Computer: attempts to enable users to install new components into their computer system and begin using them immediately.

plug-in Zusatzprogramm; Plug-In

Internet: a program that must be downloaded to view particular content such as an animation.

plunge *(stock exchange)* Kurssturz; *(to ~) (prices)* plötzlich fallen; stürzen; eintauchen; etwas riskieren

plus Pluszeichen; *(advantage)* Vorteil; zuzüglich

plush Plüsch; *(luxurious)* luxuriös

poach wildern; *(sales territory)* ins Gehege kommen; *(employees)* abwerben;

pocket Tasche; *(to ~)* (to *keep)* behalten; *(to reap)* einheimsen; *(law)* nicht unterschreiben

point Spitze; Punkt; Stelle; Pointe; Wirkung; *(stock exchange)* Einheit; *(discussion)* Kernpunkt; *(to ~)* hinzeigen; richten

pointcast punktuelle Übertragung; Richtübertragung

Electronic media with the capability of transmitting to an audience of just one person.

point of equilibrium Gleichgewichtspunkt

point of purchase (POP) Einkaufsort; Einfkaufsstelle; Kaufort

The place at which a consumer makes a purchase. Usually a retail shop, but can also be a doorstep (in door-to-door selling), a market stall, or a mail-order house.

point-of -purchase advertising Werbung am Verkaufsort; Werbung im Einzelhandelsgeschäft

Displays and demonstrations that take place at the point of purchase or point of sale.

point-of-purchase display Werbeflächen am Verkaufsort

Device promoting consumer purchases by providing consumer information and product advice.

point of sale (POS) Verkaufspunkt/-ort

point system Punktsystem

poison pill Giftkapsel; *(takeover)* Anti-Übernahme-Strategie

A strategy employed by a company targeted for takeover to make its stock less appealing to the acquiring company, hopin to avoid the takeover.

policy politische Line; Verfahren; Politik; *(insurance)* Police; Versicherungsschein *(company)* Geschäftspolitik

policy dealer Versicherungsmakler

policy decision Grundsatzentscheidung

policy holder Versicherungsnehmer

policy maker maßgebliche Person

policy statement Grundsatzerklärung

policy trader Policenhändler

political politisch; Staats-

political behavior politisches Verhalten

Activities that are not required as part of one's formal role in the organization, but that influence, or attempt to influence, the distribution of advantages and disadvantages within the organization.

political economy Nationalökonomie; Volkswirtschft

Study of how political factors influence the functioning of an economic system.

political economist Nationalökonom

political environment politisches Umfeld

Laws, government agencies and pressure groups that influence and limit various organizations and individuals in a given society.

political risk politisches Risiko

Likelihood that political forces will cause drastic changes in a country's business environment that will adversely affect the profit and other goals of a business enterprise.

political science Politikwissenschaft

Study of the behavior of individuals and groups within a political system.

political system politisches System

A social system of politics and government, usually compared to the law system, economic system, culture, and other dimension of a society.

A political system normally includes the institutions, political organizations, interest groups (such as political parties, trade unions, lobby groups), the relationships between those institutions and the political norms and rules that govern them.

politician Politiker

politico-economic wirtschaftspolitisch

politics Politik

polluter Umweltverschmutzer

pollution Verschmutzung; Unreinheit; *(environment)* Umweltverschmutzung

In general: disposal of environmentally unfriendly and harmful waste products into air, water, and land. Also: mixing inferior product components with standard components resulting in the pollution of a product.

pollution control Überwachung der Umweltverschmutzung; *(automobile)* Abgaskontrolle

polycentrism Polyzentrismus

Generally understood as an attitude of openness towards other cultures. Actions and relationships are interpreted not only with the background of one´s own cultural experiences, but other cultures are recognized and appreciated as equivalent. The opposite is ethoncentrism.

polycentric organization polyzentrische Organisation

polycentric staffing polyzentrische Stellenverteilung

Staffing policy in a multinational company in which host-country nationals are recruited to manage subsidiaries in their own country, while parent-country nationals occupy key positions at corporate headquarters.

pool Pool; *(interest group)* Interessengemeinschaft; *(fund)* Fonds; *(between companies)* Kartell; Trust; Pool; *(to ~)* zusammenschließen; *(resources)* zusammenwerfen; ein Kartell bilden

Industry: a group of companies that cooperates to improve profits by reducing competition, normally outlawed by antitrust laws.

pooling of interests Fusion; Organschaft; Interessensvereinigung

Accounting: one method of accounting for a company merger by simply adding the balance sheets of the two companies item by item.

poor arm; *(quality)* schlecht; *(weak)* schwach; *(unfavorable)* ungünstig; *(needy)* bedürftig; mangelhaft

popular Volks-; volkstümlich; populär; beliebt; *(merchandise)* zugkräftig

popularity Beliebtheit

popularize popularisieren; populär machen; gemeinverständlich darstellen

popular price Preisschlager

population Bevölkerung; Bestand; *(statistics)* Gesamtzahl

population census Volkszählung

population density Bevölkerungsdichte

population structure Bevölkerungsaufbau

port Hafen; Backbord; *(computer)* Anschluß; Eingang

Computers: connection for sending data into or out of a PC. Also used to denote an address reserved for a particular use on an internet server

Example: most printers, for example, plug into a computer's parallel port.

portable Koffer-; tragbar; *(pension)* übertragbar

portable document format (PDF)

File format that delivers print-quality documents in downloadable form.

portal Portal; Portalseite

Internet: web site that acts as a gateway to the information on the Internet by providing search engines, directories and other services such as personalized news or free e-mail.

port bill of lading Hafenkonossement

porter Träger; Schaffner; Pförtner

Porter, Michael (* 1947)

Leading expert on competitive strategy. In his book "Competitive Strategy" he argues that a firm may possess two kinds of competitive advantage: low cost or differentiation. 'Competitive advantage is a function of either providing comparable buyer value more efficiently than competitors (low cost) and command a premium price (differentiation)'.

Firms that operate in a number of different countries can locate processes where the best advantage lies. One of Porter's favorite methods of identifying a firm's competitive position is to analyze its 'value chain' – all the activities it performs and how they interact.

Biography: graduated at Princeton in aeronautical engineering, professor at Harvard Business School.

Major publications: (1980) Competitive Strategy: Techniques for Analysing Industries and Competitors, (1985) Competitive Advantage, (1986) Competition in Global Industries, (1990) The Competitive Advantage of Nations

portfolio *(investment)* Depot; Portefeuille; Portfolio; *(case for papers)* Mappe; *(government minister)* Ressort; Geschäftsbereich

Investment: a collection of investments held by an institution or a private individual. A portfolio can contain a variety of common and preferred stocks, corporate and municipal bonds, certificates of deposit, and treasury bills. The purpose of a portfolio is to reduce risk by diversification.

portfolio analysis Portfolio-Analyse

Tool by which management identifies and evaluates the various businesses that make up the company.

portfolio concept Portfoliokonzept

In the *portfolio concept,* the business is seen as a portfolio of strategic business units. It says that differing *strategic business units* (SBU) in differing competitive positions with differing features of market attractiveness require differing strategies.

The strategic business units are represented as circles and arranged in a matrix which includes a risk-determining (external) dimension and a profit-determining (internal) dimension, from which the directions in which the strategic business units develop may be inferred. The portfolio concept has proved to be a versatile tool for strategic management.

portfolio optimization Portfoliooptimierung

portfolio management Depotverwaltung; Vermögensverwaltung

portfolio manager Vermögensverwalter; Portfolio-Manager; Wertpapierberater

Professional responsible for the securities portfolio of an individual or institutional investor.

A portfolio manager may work for a mutual fund, pension fund, profit-sharing plan, bank trust department, or insurance company, as well as for private investors.

portfolio strategy Portfolio Strategie

portfolio theory *(investment)* Portfolio-Theorie

An investment decision approach that provides a mathematical framework in which investors can minimize risk and maximize returns. Central elements of the theory are the belief that by diversifying holdings, an investor can reduce risk, and that returns are a function of expected risk.

portfolio variance Portfoliovarianz

Weighted sum of the covariances and variances of the assets in a portfolio.

portion Anteil; Portion; *(shares)* Tranche; *(to ~) (to divide)* einteilen; aufteilen

port of entry Einfuhrhafen

The port where foreign goods are examined and cleared by customs to be admitted into the receiving country.

position Position; Lage; *(employment)* Stellung; Arbeitsstelle; Stelle; Rang; *(condition)* Zustand; *(point of view)* Standpunkt; *(to ~)* platzieren; an den rechten Platz stellen

positioning Positionierung

A marketing strategy that attempts to position a company's products and services against those of its competitors in the minds of consumers.

The basic competitive strategies available are: cost leadership, i.e. the company tries to achieve lowest costs of production and distribution; and differentiation, i.e the company can persuade the consumer that certain differences, such quality, design or service, are worth paying a premium price.

position in the hierarchy Rangstelle

position of power Machtstellung; Machtposition

position power Positionsmacht

Influence derived from one's formal structural position in the organization; includes power to hire, fire discipline, promote, and give salary increases.

positive definitiv; bestimmt; überzeugt; tatsächlich; positiv; *(certain)* sicher; *(ex pressly)* ausdrücklich; *(firmly)* fest

positive confirmation *(auditing)* positive Bestätigung; vorbehaltlose Bestätigung

Accounting: a type of receivables confirmation in which the auditor of a party having financial dealings with the client requests information about the accuracy of an item.

positive correlation positive Korrelation

Statistics: a direct relationship between two variables; when one variable becomes large, the other also becomes large, and vice versa. A positive correlation is represented by correlation coefficients greater than 0.

positive covenant unbeschränktes Nutzungsrecht

Part of the indenture or loan agreement that specifies an action that the company must abide by.

positive-sum game Positivsummenspiel

Situation in which all parties in a certain situation can benefit, even if some may benefit more than others.

positive yield curve positive Zinsertragskurve

Situation in which interest rates on long-term debt securities are higher than on short-term debt securities of the same quality.

possess besitzen; sich aneignen

possession Besitz; Besitztum; Habe; Beherrschung

Legal: the situation when one has property in one's control.

possibility Möglichkeit

possible möglich; eventuell; Höchstleistung

post *(employment)* Posten; Stelle; *(mail)* Post; *(to ~) (to publish)* anschlagen; *(a letter)* aufgeben; *(accounting);* verbuchen; postieren; mit der Post schicken; ins Hauptbuch übertragen

postage Porto

postage rate Portogebühr; Porto

The price for mailing a letter or a package. The rate is set by national postal services or private carriers and depends on the size, weight, destination of the letter, and the speed of delivery.

postal Post-; postalisch

postal budget Postetat

postal charges Portokosten

postal checking account Postscheckkonto

postal consumer Postkunde

postal expert Postexperte

postal rate Porto

postal savings bank Postsparkasse

post employment benefit Pensionszahlung

poster advertising Plakatwerbung

posting Posteinlieferung; *(job)* Versetzung; *(accounting)* Verbuchung; *(law)* Aufstellen; *(commercial)* Buchungsverfahren; *(civil procedure)* öffentliche Bekanntmachung

Accounting: listing in the company's records, such as listing the detail of sales and purchases on the accounts receivable or payable records.

Civil procedure: affixing of certain required information as a substitute form of service of process.

Commercial law: procedure that a bank follows in deciding to finally pay a negotiable instrument and in recording its payment.

post-merger integration nachhaltige Integration nach Fusion / Unternehmenszusammenschluss

post office box Postfach

postpone ver-; aufschieben; zurückstellen

postponement Aufschub; Zurückstellung

postpurchase advertising Nachkaufwerbung

postpurchase behavior Verhalten nach dem Kauf

Stage of the buyer decision process in which consumers take further action after purchase based on their satisfaction or dissatisfaction.

postpurchase dissonance kognitive Dissonanz nach dem Kauf

postwar Nachkriegs-

postwar period Nachkriegszeit

potential Potential; Möglichkeit; möglich; potentiell

potential market potentieller Markt; möglicher Bedarf

Group of consumers who profess some level of interest in a product or service.

potentials for success Erfolgspotentiale

Business's strengths and at the same time critical success factors. Potentials for success are necessary but not sufficient conditions for profit and liquidity.

To find and select the right potentials for success is strategic management's main task. It is the sum of all preconditions specific to products and markets that make for success.

Critical success factors are those variables, whose characteristics contribute largely to market success, and which are essential if one wishes to be successful in competition within his industry.

pound *(weight)* Pfund; *(currency)* Pfund; Lärm; heftiger Schlag; *(to ~)* hämmern; einpferchen

poverty Armut; Dürftigkeit; Mangel

power Macht; *(authority)* Vollmacht; *(entitlement)* Berechtigung; *(authorization)* Ermächtigung; Befugnis; *(output)* Leistung; *(electricity)* Strom; *(strength)* Kraft; Rechte; Vollmacht; Potenz; *(to ~) (an engine)* antreiben

Capacity that A has to influence the behavior of B so that B acts in accordance with A's wishes. Power may exist but not be used. It is a capacity or potential. One can have power but not impose it. An important aspect of power is that it is a function of dependency.

power distance Machtdistanz

Theory of how a society deals with the fact that people are unequal in physical and intellectual capabilities.

High power distance cultures are found in countries that let inequalities grow over time into inequalities of power and wealth. Low power distance cultures are found in societies that try to play down such inequalities as much as possible.

powerful mächtig; *(strong)* stark

powerhouse Maschinenhaus

power of attorney (POA) *(law)* Bevollmächtigung; schriftliche Vollmacht; *(certificate)* Vollmachtsurkunde

A written document authorizing one person (agent) to take certain legal actions on behalf of another (principal), and to evidence this authority to third parties with whom the agent deals.

power output Leistungsabgabe

power plant Kraftwerk

power station Elektrizitätswerk

power struggle Machtkampf

power supply Stromversorgung

power tactics Machttaktiken

Ways in which individuals translate power bases into specific actions. Seven tactical dimensions or strategies can be distinguished: reason, friendliness, coalition, bargaining, assertiveness, higher authority, sanctions.

The organizational culture in which a manager works, will have a strong influence on defining which tactics are considered appropriate.

practical praktisch; brauchbar; erfahren; durchführbar

practice *(working method)* Verfahren; *(profession)* Praxis; Übung; Brauch; *(custom)* Gewohnheit; Praktik; *(to ~)* praktizieren; *(profession)* ausüben; *(pro ficiency)* üben; regelmäßig tun

practitioner; Praktiker; praktischer Arzt; Rechtsanwalt; *(expert by practice)* Fachmann

pragmatic Pragmatiker; pragmatisch

preamble Vorrede; Präambel; *(introduction)* Einleitung

preapproach Vertragsvorbereitung

Step in the selling process in which the salesperson learns as much as possible about a prospective customer before making a sales call.

prearrival stage Voreintrittsphase

Period of learning in the socialization process that occurs before a new employee joins the organization.

precarious unsicher; widerruflich; prekär

precaution Vorsicht(-smaßnahme)

precautionary vorbeugend; vorsorglich

precautionary measure Vorsorgemaßnahme

precede vorangehen; führen; vorgehen

precedence Vortritt; Vorrang; *(ranking)* Rangordnung, Vorfahrtsrecht

precedent Präzedenzfall; Beispielsfall

precept Vorschrift; Regel; Richtschnur; *(authority)* Verordnung

precious Edel-; wertvoll; kostbar; edel

precious metal Edelmetall

precise genau; präzise

precision Präzision; Genauigkeit; Fein-

preclude ausschließen; unmöglich machen

predatory räuberisch; plündernd

predatory pricing rücksichtslose Preissetzung; ruinöse Preisunterbietung

Reducing prices below fair market value as a competitive weapon to drive weaker competitors out of the market. Once these competitors are eliminated, the intent is to raise the price again to reap profits.

predecessor Vorgänger

predetermine *(planning)* vorplanen; *(cost)* vorkalkulieren

predict voraussagen; vorhersagen

predictable vorhersagbar; voraussehbar

prediction Voraussage; Vorhersage; Prognose-

An attempt to define future events based upon different estimation methods, including past patterns and projections of current data.

predisposition Neigung; Empfänglichkeit

predominance Vorherrschaft

predominant *(preponderant)* vorwiegend; *(ruling)* vorherrschend

preeminent hervorragend; unübertroffen; hervorstechen

preemptive rights Vorkaufsrechte

Finance: the right of a shareholder to purchase additional shares issued by a corporation before they are issued to new shareholders.

prefabricate vorfertigen; vorarbeiten

prefabricated vorgefertigt

A building or an element which is manufactured and assembled in a factory prior to being erected or installed on the construction site.

prefer vorziehen; bevorzugen; einreichen

preference Bevorzugung; Vorzug; Priorität; Präferenz

preference share Vorzugsaktie

preferential Vorzugs-; bevorzugt; bevorrechtet

preferential treatment Vorzugsbehandlung; Begünstigung

preferred bevorzugt

preferred dividend Vorzugsdividende

preferred stock Vorzugsaktien

Security that shows ownership in a corporation and gives the holder a claim, prior to the claim of common stockholders, on earnings and also generally on assets in the event of liquidation.

Most preferred stock pays a fixed dividend and does not usually carry voting rights. Also called prefence shares.

prejudice *(bias)* Vorurteil; *(detriment)* Beeinträchtigung; Nachteil; *(harm)* Schaden

preliminary vorläufig; einleitend;

preliminary product Vorprodukt

preliminaries Einleitung

premature vorzeitig; verfrüht; -schnell

premise Voraussetzung; Prämisse

premises Räumlichkeiten; *(business - indoor)* Geschäftsräume; *(business - outdoor)* Betriebsgrundstück ; Haus mit Grundstück

Land or a portion thereof, and the structures thereon.

premium Zuschlag; Aufschlag; *(stock exchange)* Kursaufschlag; *(insurance)* Prämie; *(at a ~)* über Pari

Stocks: price of an option contract, determined on the exchange, which the buyer of the option pays to the option writer for the rights to the option contract.

Insurance: the payment, or regular payments, that a policyholder makes to own an insurance policy. The insurance company assumes the risks of the insured (life, health, property, liability) in exchange for the premium payment, which reflects the expectation of loss or risk.

premium bond Premiumanleihe; Agioanleihe

A bond with a selling price above its face or redemption value. *Example:* if a bond with a face value of $1,000 is selling for $1,100, it is called a *premium bond.*

premium rate Prämiensatz; Tarifbeitrag; Bedarfsprämie; Überstundenzuschlag

Finance: premium fee on some stocks when borrowed for trading, as in selling short.

premium reduction Prämiensenkung

prepaid expenses *(accounting)* transitorische Posten

Amounts that are paid prior to the period they cover. Such expenses often include insurance and rent. Prepaid expenses are not tax deductible until the appropriate period. Rent paid in advance is not tax deductible even by a cash basis taxpayer.

preparation Vorbereitung; *(food)* Zubereitung; Präparat

preparatory effort Vorleistung

prepare vorbereiten; präparieren; *(food)* zubereiten

prepay vorausbezahlen

prepayment Vorausbezahlung; Vorauszahlung

Banking: a privilege in a mortgage permitting the borrower to make payments in advance of their due date without penalty, while others charge a fee.

prerequisite Voraussetzung; Vorbedingung

prerogative Vorrecht; Prärogativ

An unquestioned right or privilege reserved exclusively by a particular person or group.

prescribe *(to issue an order)* vorschreiben; *(medicine)* verordnen; verschreiben; *(law)* bestimmen; vorschreiben

prescribed clusters vorgegebene Cluster

Key term for discussing and analyzing a sociogram. These are formal groups such as departments, work teams, task forces, or committees.

prescription *(order)* Vorschrift; Verordnung; *(law)* Verjährung; *(medicine)* Rezept

Real estate: means of obtaining title to property by adverse possession by occupying it for the period determined by law.

Pharmaceuticals: product that requires a physician's authorization; the written authorization itself.

presence Gegenwart; *(attendance)* Anwesenheit; *(existence)* Vorhandensein; Äußeres

present Geschenk; *(time)* Gegenwart; gegenwärtig; *(in attendance)* anwesend; *(to ~)* präsentieren; *(a plan)* vorlegen; *(a problem)* darstellen; *(to introduce)* vorstellen

presentation Vorführung; Präsentation; *(introduction)* Einführung; *(performance)* Veranstaltung

Marketing: step in the selling process in which the salesperson tells the product "story" to the buyer, showing how the product will make or save money for the buyer.

An effective presentation is usually planned, organized, and tailored to a specific audience to help facilitate the behavior change desired by the presenter.

presentation skills Präsentatiostechniken

Professional use of free speech, appearance, interaction with audience, together with computer programs and hardware (such as beamers), in order to communicate a topic or point of view effectively to an audience.

present fairly *(auditing)* ordnungsgemäß darstellen; wirtschaftlich angemessen darstellen

An independent auditor’s unqualified opinion usually includes the phrase, “present fairly…in conformity with Generally Accepted Accounting Principles”.

The prerequisites for an unqualified opinion are sufficient disclosure, reasonable detail, and absence of bias.

present value Gegenwartswert, Tageswert; Barwert

The discounted value of a future sum or stream of cash flows, also called time value of money.

Example: at a 12% interest rate, the receipt of one dollar one year from now has a present value of $0.89286. One dollar to be received in two years has a present value of $0.79719.

present value factor Barwertfaktor

Factor used to calculate an estimate of the present value of an amount to be received in a future period.

present value method Bewertung zum Zeitwert; Zeitwertmethode; Kapitalwertmethode

The present value method, also called the discounted cash flow method, is widely used in corporate finance to evaluate a capital investment project or to measure the expected return.

Present-value calculations are facilitated by present-value tables, which are compound interest tables in reverse.

present value of annuity Rentenbarwert

The present value of an annuity is the value of a stream of expected or promised future payments that have been discounted to a single equivalent present value.

preservation Erhaltung; Bewahrung; Konservierung; Präservierung

preserve erhalten; bewahren; präservieren

preside vorsitzen; Vorsitz haben/führen; präsidieren

president Präsident; Vorsitzender; *(corporation)* Vorstandsvorsitzender

Corporation: an executive officer of a corporation, appointed by the board of directors and usually reporting directly to the board.

The president is the highest ranking officer after the chairman of the board. If he holds the title chief executive officer (CEO), the president is above the chairman.

presidential election cycle theory Präsidenschaftswahl-Konjunkturzyklustheorie

A theory stating that U.S. stock markets are weakest in the year following the election of a new president, after which the market improves again until the next presidential election.

press *(news)* Presse; *(company)* Druckerei; *(printing)* Druckerpresse; *(to ~)* pressen; *(button)* drücken; *(to urge)* drängen; *(clothes)* bügeln

press kit *(print)* Pressemappe

A collection of editorial and promotional materials about a person, product, or company. It is distributed to the media, and journalists can use these materials to research the subject and write articles about it. Press kits are a very useful tool to get media coverage, but they have to be prepared with great care.

press photographer Pressefotograf

press release Presseverlautbarung; Pressemitteilung

Document that communicates information to the press. Press releases can publicize good news such as positive earnings and new product launches, or they can help control the damage caused by bad news.

press statement Presseerklärung

pressure Druck; *fig* Drängen; *(to ~) (to exert pressure) fig* bedrängen

pressure group Interessensgruppe; Lobby

pressure of prices Preisdruck

prestige Prestige; Ansehen

prestigious angesehen

presume annehmen; *(to take for granted)* voraussetzen; *(to dare)* sich erdreisten

presumption Annahme; *(law)* Vermutung; *(impertinence)* Anmaßung

pre-tax vor Steuerabzug; brutto

pretax lump sum Vorsteuerpauschale

pretax rate of return Rendite vor Steuern

Rate of return of a particular security before deduction of taxes.

prevail *(argument)* sich durchsetzen; *(situation)* herrschen; die Oberhand gewinnen

prevent verhindern; *(to avert)* verhüten; hindern

prevention Verhinderung; *(prophylaxis)* Verhütung; Vorbeugung

preview Vorschau; Probevorführung; Vorbeurteilung; *(to ~)* vorschauen; *(to check in advance)* vorprüfen

previous vorherig; vorausgegangen; früher

previous owner Vorbesitzer

previous years value Vorjahreswert

price Preis; *(cost)* Kosten; *(stock exchange)* Kurs; Nettokurs; *(to ~) (to set a price)* mit einem Preis versehen; Preis festsetzen; *(to find out a price)* Preis feststellen

In general: amount of money charged for a product or service, or the sum of the values that consumers exchange for the benefits of having or using the product or service.

Stocks: price of a share of common stock on the date shown. Highs and lows are based on the highest and lowest intraday trading price.

price advance Preissteigerung; *(securities, currency)* Kurssteigerung

price advantage Preisvorteil; Kostenvorteil

price / book ratio betriebswirtschaftliche Kennzahl aus dem Verhältnis Marktwert/Buchwert

Compares a stock's market value to the value of total assets less total liabilities (book). Determined by dividing current price by common stockholders' equity per share (book value), adjusted for stock splits.

price change Preisänderung

price change rate Preisänderungsrate

price competition Preiskonkurrenz; Preiswettbewerb

price component Preisbestandteil; Preiskomponente

price concession Preisnachlass; Preiszugeständnis

price consciousness Preisbewusstsein

price control Preiskontrolle; Preisüberwachung

Restrictions imposed by a government on the prices of consumer products, usually on a short-term basis as a measure to control inflation.

price curb Preisdämpfung

price cut Preissenkung

price cutting Preisunterbietung

price deterioration Preisverfall

price development Preisentwicklung

price difference Preisunterschied; *(stocks)* Kursdifferenz

price differential Preisunterschied; Preisgefälle

price differentiation Preisdifferenzierung

Practice of charging different prices for the same product in different markets.

price dispersion Preisstreuung; Preisspanne

Observed spread between the highest and lowest price for a given product.

price / earnings ratio (P/E) Ertragsverhältnis

Financial ratio used to analyze the price of a security. It is calculated by dividing the price of a stock by its earnings per share. Earnings per share for the P/E ratio is determined by dividing earnings for past 12 months by the number of common shares outstanding.

If the reported earnings from the latest year are used, it is called a *trailing P/E*, if a forecast of next year's earnings is used, it is called *a forward P/E.*

price effect Preiseffekt

price-elastic preiselastisch

price elasticity of demand Preiselastizität der Nachfrage

Measure of how responsive demand for a product is to changes in price.

It shows the relationship between the total amount spent on a good in the market and the price of the good. Calculated as the percentage change in quantity divided by the percentage change in price.

If a price decrease results in larger total expenditure (and vice versa), the good is price elastic. If a price decrease results in less total expenditure (or vice versa), the good is price inelastic.

price-enhancing preistreibend

price fixing Preisabsprache

Combination or conspiracy for the purpose and with the effect of raising, lowering, or stabilizing the price of a commodity.

price fluctuation Preisschwankung; *(currency)* Kursschwankung

price increase Preiserhöhung; Preisanstieg; Preisauftrieb; *(securities)* Kursaufschlag

price increase impulse Teuerungsimpuls

price index Preisindex

A measure of the average prices of a an individual good or a basket of goods over time. Well-known price indexes are the consumer price index and the producer price index.

price inflation Preisinflation; Preissteigerungsrate

price leader *(firm)* Preisführer; *(low-priced article)* Lockvogel

A company in an industry whose pricing decisions are most followed by the rest of the industry.

price leadership Preisführerschaft

priceless unschätzbar; unbezahlbar

price level Preisniveau; Preishöhe

The average level of prices, normally measured by a price index and compared with prices of previous periods.

price list Preisliste

price margin Preisspanne; Preisraum; Handelsspanne

price mechanism Preismechanismus

price of gasoline Benzinpreis

price of gold Goldpreis

price of goods Güterpreis

price-raising preistreibend

price raising Preisheraufsetzung

price range Preisklasse; Preisraum; Preislage

price relationship Preisrelation; Preisverhältnis

price resistance Preiswiderstand

price rise Preisanstieg

price risk *(stocks)* Kursrisiko

price / sales ratio Verhältnis von Preis zu Unternehmensgewinn pro Aktie

Ratio determined by dividing a stock's current price by revenue per share (adjusted for stock splits). Revenue per share for the P/S ratio is determined by dividing revenue for past 12 months by number of shares outstanding.

price-setting preisbestimmend

price setting Preissetzung

price signal Preissignal

price spread Preisspanne

price stability Preisstabilität

price stabilization Preisstabilisierung

Intervention in a market, often by governments, in order to reduce fluctuations in price.

price structure Preisgefüge

price support Preisstützung

A legally established minimum price above the equilibrium price, designed to aid farmers or other producers of goods. If the market price drops below the supported price, the government makes up the difference.

price tag Preisschild; *(cost)* Kosten

price takers Mengenanpasser

Individuals who respond to rates and prices by acting as though they have no influence on them.

price trend Preisentwicklung; *(securities, currency)* Kursverlauf

price uncertainty Preisunsicherheit

price war Preisschlacht ; Preiskrieg

A competitive situation in a market in which two or more companies each try to increase their own market share by lowering their prices.

pricing Preiskalkulation

pricing above the market Preisfestlegung über dem gängigen Marktpreis

Pricing strategy designed to attract customers with a high price image, strong personal service, and an emphasis on quality.

pricing below the market Preisfestlegung unter dem gängigen Marktpreis

Pricing strategy designed to attract customers by underbidding the competition.

pricing method Berechnungsmethode

pricing policy Preispolitik

pricing system Preissystem

pricing theory Preistheorie

primary Haupt-; Primär-; hauptsächlich; primär; grundlegend; *(original)* ursprünglich

primary costs Primärkosten

primary data Primärdaten

Information or original data compiled, collected and studied for a specific purpose; information gathered for the first time to solve a particular problem.

It is usually more expensive and time-consuming to gather than secondary data, the data are current and they are generally more relevant to the specific problem. Primary data are also proprietary and unavailable to competitors.

primary demand Primärbedarf; Primärnachfrage

Market demand by consumers of non-capital goods; level of total demand for all brands of a given product or service.

primary distribution Primärverteilung

primary market Primärmarkt; Emissionsmarkt

Securities: The first buyer of a newly issued security buys that security in the primary market. All subsequent trading of those securities is done in the secondary market.

primary product Grundprodukt; Primärerzeugnis

primary reserve Kassenreserve

prime Spitzenqualität; vorzüglich

prime minister Ministerpräsident

prime rate Leitzins

The interest rate banks charge to their best customers. Changes in the prime rate influence changes in other rates, including mortgages and consumer credit rates.

principal Auftraggeber; Vertretender; *(capital)* Kapital; *(chief)* Leiter; *(senior partner)* Hauptteilhaber; *(proprietor)* Firmeninhaber; Haupt-; hauptsächlich

Securities: the person for whom an agent or a broker executes an order.

Mortgage: the amount of money raised by a mortgage or loan, as distinct from the interest paid on it.

principal amount Grundkapital; Kapitalsumme

Mortgage: the face value of an obligation, such as a bond or a loan, that must be repaid at maturity, as separate from the interest.

principal and interest payment (P&I) Kapital- und Zinsszahlung

A periodic payment, usually monthly, that includes the interest charges for the period plus an amount applied to amortization of the principal balance.

principal occupation Hauptberuf

principal payment Zahlung aus dem Grundkapital

principal residence Hauptwohnsitz

The home at which a taxpayer lives most of the time during the taxable year.

principal stockholder Hauptaktionär; Großaktionär

principle Grundsatz; Prinzip

A basic rule that guides or influences human conduct.

principle of diversification Diversifikationsprinzip

Investment: observation that highly diversified portfolios will have negligible unsystematic risk, i.e. unsystematic risks tend to disappear in portfolios and only systematic risks survive.

print Druck; *(edition)* Druckauflage; *(to ~)* drucken; *(publish)* verlegen; in Druckschrift schreiben

printer Drucker

printout *(computer)* Ausdruck

prior früher; vorausgehend; Vor-

priority Vorrang; Priorität; *(urgency)* Dringlichkeit

Bankruptcy: the right to be paid before other creditors out of the assets of a bankrupt company.

priority mail Expresspost

prisoner´s dilemma Gefangenen-Dilemma

A type of non-zero-sum game in game theory in which two players can cooperate or betray the other player. The only concern of each individual player is maximizing their own payoff, without any concern for the other player's payoff. In any situation, betraying is more beneficial than cooperating, all rational players will betray.

privacy Privatsphäre; Heimlichkeit; Zurückgezogenheit

State of being private, confidential or secluded; concerns that affect the personal details of individuals or companies.

privacy laws Gesetz zum Schutz des Persönlichkeitsrechts

Marketing: Laws that require advertisers to inform customers about how their data are being used and give them an opportunity to indicate they do not wish their data to be used.

private privat; persönlich; nicht öffentlich; geheim

private accountant angestellter Buchhalter

Accountant employed by an organization who records and analyzes the financial information of the company. Also called cost, managerial, industrial, corporate, or management accountant. A controller is an organization's most senior private accountant.

private attorney Sachverwalter

private bank Privatbank

private banking establishment Privatbankhaus

private brand Hausmarke; Händlermarke

Brand established by a retailer or a wholesaler rather than the manufacturer. The advantages include more freedom in setting prices, more control over product attributes, and higher margins.

private corporation Kapitalgesellschaft (US) in Privatbesitz

A corporation owned by private individuals or companies whose shares are not publicly traded on any exchange.

private enterprise Privatwirtschaft; freie Markwirtschaft

private industry Privatindustrie

private law Zivilrecht

That part of a legal system that governs relationships between private individuals, companies, or organizations. There is no interference by a public authority.

private ledger Privatkonto

private limited company (UK) Gesellschaft mit beschränkter Haftung

private limited partnership (US) Kommanditgesellschaft

A limited partnership having no more than 35 limited partners and which is therefore not registered with the Securities and Exchange Commission (SEC).

privately owned home Eigenheim

private ownership *(state of being owned)* Privathand; *(state of owning)* Privatbesitztum

private placement *(securities)* Wertpapierverkauf an Private; Privatplatzierung

Sale of a bond or other security directly to a limited number of investors.

private property Privateigentum; Privatvermögen

private sale Privatverkauf

private sector *(economy)* Privatwirtschaft; privater Wirtschaftssektor

privatization Privatisierung

The process of converting government-owned industries into private or publicly owned industries by selling company shares publicly and changing management. The opposite of nationalization.

privatize privatisieren

privilege Privileg; Vorrecht; Sonderrecht; *(advantage)* Vergünstigung; Begünstigung; privilegieren

A special right or permission to do something that is unique to one person or to a group.

prizewinning preisgekrönt

proactive zuvorkommend; proaktiv

The opposite of reactive, which involves anticipating situations and dealing with them positively, rather than reacting after a situation has already occurred and one is forced to do something.

proactive change proaktive Änderung

probability Wahrscheinlichkeit

The likelihood that an event or a particular result will occur; can be represented on a scale by a number between 0 (zero probability of the event happening, i.e. it is certain not to and 1 (certainty that it will occur).

probability sampling Stichprobenauswahl; Wahrscheinlichkeitsauswahl

Method of selecting a sample in such a way that each item or person in the population being studied has an equal likelihood of being included.

probable wahrscheinlich; mutmaßlich

probe Untersuchung; *(examination)* Prüfung; *(surgical instrument)* Sonde; *(to ~)* untersuchen; prüfen; sondieren

problem Problem; Schwierigkeit

Discrepancy between some current state of affairs and some desired state, requiring consideration of alternative courses of action.

problematic loan Problemkredit

problem recognition Problemerkennung

First stage of the business buying process in which someone in the company recognizes a problem or need that can be met by acquiring a good or a service.

problem-solving model Problemlösungsmodell

problem-solving team Problemlösungsteam

Groups of 5 to 12 employees from the same department who meet for a few hours each week to discuss ways of improving quality, efficiency, and the work environment.

In problem-solving teams, members share ideas or offer suggestions on how work processes and methods can be improved.

procedural verfahrensrechtlich; prozessual; prozeßtechnisch

procedural justice Verfahrensgerechtigkeit

Perceived fairness of the process used to determine the distribution of rewards that tends to affect an employee's organizational commitment, trust in the boss, and intention to quit.

procedural manner Verfahrensweise

procedural method Vorgehensweise; Verfahrensweg

procedural principle Verfahrensprinzip

procedural process Verfahrensgang

procedural step Verfahrensschritt

procedure Verfahren; Ablauf; Vorgang

proceed *(to continue)* weitermachen; *(to advance)* vorgehen; weitergehen; fortfahren

proceeding Vorgehen; Handlungsverlauf

proceedings Verfahren

proceeds Erlös; Ertrag; Einnahmen

The amount of money received from selling a product or a service.

process Verfahren; Vorgang; *(law)* Rechtsgang; *(to ~)* verarbeiten; weiterverarbeiten; aufbereiten; veredeln; *(paperwork)* bearbeiten

Business: a group of interrelated activities that together creates value for the customer. It normally cuts across functional departments, such as marketing, manufacturing and accounting.

process conflict Verfahrenskonflikt

Conflict over how work gets done. For process conflict to be productive, it must be kept low.

process consultation Prozessberatung

Ways of getting insights into what is going on around and within a business, often performed by outside consultants.

These might include work flow, informal relationships among unit members, and formal communication channels.

process improvement Prozessverbesserung

processing Abfertigen; Weiterverarbeitung; Aufbereitung; Veredelung; *(paperwork)* Bearbeitung

processing an order Auftragsabwicklung

processor *(computer)* Prozessor

process technician Verfahrentechniker

process value analysis Analyse der Wertschöpfungskette

Attempt at determining what the organization is more superior at delivering than its competition.

Management has to define the core processes that clearly add value to the organization's distinctive competencies. These are the processes that transform materials, capital, information, and labor into products and services that the customer values.

proclaim öffentlich bekannt geben

proclamation öffentliche Bekanntmachung; Proklamation

procure beschaffen; verschaffen; herbeiführen

procurement Beschaffung; Beschaffungswesen

The processes or functions related to buying goods and services required to carry on an enterprise, which can be materials, parts, supplies, or equipment.

Procurement normally involves needs analysis, strategic sourcing, purchasing, order management and cost and supplier performance management.

procurement of funds Mittelbeschaffung

produce Produkt; Erzeugnis; *(fruit, vegetables)* Obst und Gemüse; *(to ~)* produzieren; *(agricultural products, energy)* erzeugen; *(to manufacture)* herstellen; *(profit)* erwirtschaften

produced again neu produziert

producer Produzent; *(agricultural products)* Erzeuger; *(manufacturer)* Hersteller

producer cooperative Produzentengenossenschaft

Group of producers who set up an organization to cooperate in such areas as buying supplies and equipment and marketing their products.

producer goods Produktionsgüter; Anlagegüter; Investitionsgüter

Goods that are used as inputs in the production of other goods, such as partly finished goods, raw materials, or new machinery and equipment.

producer-price-index (PPI) *(econometrics)* Erzeugerpreisindex

An economic indicator which measures the average changes on prices received by producers for their output, sometimes called the wholesale price index. Prices are calculated before they reach the consumer.

producible produzierbar; herstellbar

producing country Herkunftsland; Förderland

product Produkt; Erzeugnis; Fabrikat; *(result)* Ergebnis

The output of a company´s production process, which can be offered to a market where it might satisfy a want or need. The product concept is comprehensive and includes physical objects, services, persons, places, organizations and ideas.

product adaptation Produktanpassung

Efforts to adapt a product to meet local conditions or wants in foreign markets.

product advertising Produktwerbung

Advertising intended to promote demand for a product or service, which normally describes features, benefits, and performance.

product-bundle pricing Preissetzung eines Produktbündels

Combining several products and offering the bundle at a reduced price.

product change Produktwechsel; Produktänderung

product choice Produktauswahl; Produktpalette

product combination Produktkombination

product concept Produktkonzept

Marketing: Idea that consumers will favor products that offer the most quality, performance and features, and that the organization should therefore devote its energy to making continuous product improvements.

product costing scheme Schema zur Stückkostenkalkulation

Method or scheme used in order to ascertain the costs of a product, which shows how the individual cost elements are to be assembled.

product costing with activity units Bezugsgrößenkalkulation

Method of calculation in which the material and manufacturing costs related to actual measured output are charged to the appropriate cost objects.

Activity unit is a cost center‘s yardstick of performance. It should be able to demonstrate the causal connection between cost center costs and cost center activity. In most cost centers the activity unit is the employee- or machine-hour.

product costs Produktkosten; Stückkosten

Costs that become part of the product, determining its physical existence. They include bill of materials, recipe and work plan.

Product costs are formulated traditionally per calculation unit – per hour, per piece, per kilogram, per order. It follows then that they are the additional costs for ‚one more unit‘. Product costs are also described as marginal costs or proportional costs.

product counterfeiting Produktfälschung

product cycle Produktzyklus; Entwicklungskurve eines Produkts

product design Produktdesign, Produktgestaltung

Process of designing a product's style and function: the challenge is to design a product that is attractive, easy, safe, and inexpensive to use and service, and simple and economical to produce and distribute.

product development Produktentwicklung

Strategy for company growth by offering modified or new products to current market segments. Developing the product concept into a physical product in order to ensure that the product idea can be turned into a workable product.

product development process Produktentwicklungsprozess

All steps required for introducing a new product or service concept and managing its development until it actually comes to market.

This includes a variety of activities to be performed normally include analyzing the market, targeting potential buyers, relating this information to the productive capacity of the company, developing a product that will fit market needs, distributing it to the marketplace, and analyzing customer feedback.

product divisions Produktsparten; Erzeugnisbereiche

Organization: an approach to structuring an organization into one divisional structure of departments by equivalent products, such as men´s ware, children´s ware, women ware.

product engineering Fertigungstechnik; Produktentwicklung

product feature Produkteigenschaft

product flow Produktfluß

Distribution the view of a channel as a system of interdependent activties and organizations that together create value as a product moves through the channel from the producer to the consumer.

product group Produktgruppe

product idea Produktidee

Idea for a possible product that the company could possibly offer to the market. If the idea is pursued, the product enters its development stage.

product image Produktimage

The way in which consumers perceive an actual or potential product.

product imitation Produktnachahmung; *(counterfeit)* Produktfälschung

product innovation Produktinnovation

product innovation charter Satzung zur Produktinnovation

New product strategy statement formalizing management's reasons or rationale behind the firm's search for innovation opportunities, the product/market and technology to focus upon and the goals and objectives to be achieved.

product invention Produkterfindung

production Produktion; Herstellung; Fertigung; *(agriculture)* Erzeugung; *(productivity)* Leistung; *(natural resources)* Gewinnung

The business activity that uses people and machinery to convert materials and parts into products. In so doing, it cerates value that can be realized when the products are sold to the customers.

production and operations management (POM) Produktions- und Verfahrensmanagement

All the activities involved in planning, coordinating, and controlling a company´s production process.

POM covers a wide area of issues, such as the location of production facilities, labor and transportation costs, and production forecasting.

production budget Produktionsbudget; Fertigungsplan

production capacity Produktionskapazität; Fertigungskapazität

production concept Produktionskonzept

A view of the market based on the belief that consumers will favor products that are available and affordable. Management should therefore concentrate on improving production and distribution efficiency.

production control Fertigungskontrolle; Fertigungsüberwachung

A variety of activites required to assure the functioning of the production process, including planning, routing, scheduling, dispatching, and inspection.

production equipment Produktionsausstattung

production facility Produktionsanlage; Fabrikationsanlage; Produktionseinrichtung

production factor Produktionsfaktor

production flow Fertigungsablauf

production forecasting Produktionsprognose

All efforts required to judge how much production is required to meet estimated sales. The decisions taken affect the overall budget and activity scheduling.

Factors to be taken into account include previous sales, the general state of the economy, consumer preferences, and competitive products.

production function Produktionsfunktion

production growth Produktionswachstum

production hall Fertigungshalle

production loss Produktionseinbuße

production manager Fertigungsleiter

production method Produktionsmethode

production network Produktionsapparat

production of gold Goldproduktion

production of goods Güterproduktion

production-oriented organization produktionsorientiertes Unternehmen

A company whose primary concern is production, as contrasted to a customer-oriented organization. Traditionally, the automobile industry has been very production-oriented.

production output Produktionsleistung; Produktionsausstoß

production planning and scheduling Produktionsplanung; Fertigungsplanung und -steuerung

All the activities required to plan the production process, which requires a comprehensive system to process large amounts of data.

The following areas have to be covered: standard quantities for materials in the bill of materials; standard times for the operations in the individual cost centers; standards for setup times and capacities of the cost centers and work places

production possibility curve Produktionsmöglichkeitenkurve

Economic: a graph that depicts the trade-off between two items to be produced by showing all possible outputs of the two goods with a fixed supply of resources that are fully employed. Practically, a production possibility curve can be useful for determining possible product mixes because it indicates the opportunity cost of increasing one item's production in terms of the units of the other forgone; also called transformation curve.

production process Herstellungsverfahren; Produktionsprozess; Fertigungsverfahren

production rate Produktionsrate

production run Produktionsschub

production schedule Produktionszeitplan

production sector Produktionssektor

production share Produktionsanteil

production side Produktionsseite

production structure Produktionsstruktur

production system Produktionssystem; Produktionsapparat

production technique Produktionsverfahren; Herstellungsverfahren

production time Produktionszeit

production unit Produktionseinheit

production volume Produktionsvolumen; Produktionsstand

production worker Produktionsarbeiter

Employee of a company directly involved in the manufacturing processes, as opposed to administrative and clerical employees; also called production line workers.

productive produktiv; *(utility)* leistungsfähig; *(capacity)* leistungsstark; *(yield)* Ertrag bringend

productivity Produktivität; *(utility)* Leistungsfähigkeit; *(capacity)* Leistungsstärke; *(yield)* Ertragsfähigkeit

A measure of the output of an organization or an economy per unit of input (labor, raw materials, capital, etc.). An organization is productive if it achieves its goals and does so by transferring inputs to outputs at the lowest cost.

Example: an increase in productivity is achieved through an increase in production per unit of labor over time.

product life cycle Produktlebenszyklus

A theoretical model describing the development of a product's sales and profitability figures over its lifetime. Normally a characteristic curve can be drawn that can be divided into five stages, each of which represents different situations and challenges for the company and its marketers.

In the development stage, the original idea is transformed into a prototype and its marketing strategy is worked out. This is followed by the introduction stage, characterized by low sales, buyers are unsure about the product and it is not stocked by all distributors. Growth stage: the product will become more widely available and sales will increase. Competitors' versions will then appear. Maturity stage: supply and demand are matched and sales stabilize, characterized by intense competition and efforts at reducing the costs of production in order to maximize returns. Sometime during the decline stage, the company will leave the market or try to relaunch the product.

product line Produktlinie

A group of products that are closely related because they function in similar manner, are sold to the same customer groups, are marketed through same types of outlets, or fall within particular price ranges.

product-line pricing Preissetzung nach Produktkategorie

Setting the price law steps between various products in a product line, based on differences in costs, competitors' prices, and how customers evaluate the different features in cur e product line.

product-line stretching Ausweitung der Produktlinie

Increasing product line by lengthening beyond its current range.

product mix Produkt-Mix; Leistungsprogramm

All the product lines and items that a particular seller offers for sale.

profession Beruf; Fach

professional Berufs-; Fach-; beruflich; berufsmäßig

professional association Fachvereinigung; Berufsverband

professional category Berufsgruppe

professional interest Fachinteresse

professional liability insurance Berufshaftpflichtversicherung

Special insurance for specialists in various professional fields, where a basic liability insurance does not offer enough protection. This is often the case in professions where individuals have above average expertise and responsibility, such as doctors or managers.

professional representation Berufsvertretung; berufsständige Vertretung

profit Profit; *(gain)* Gewinn; *(yield)* Ertrag; *(advantage)* Vorteil; Nutzen; *(to ~)* Nutzen ziehen

Accounting: the surplus of revenues generated by a company during a particular time over the expenses it incurred.

profitability Wirtschaftlichkeit; Rentabilität; Ertragskraft

General: a company's ability to generate revenues in excess of the costs incurred in producing those revenues.

Accounting: a ratio that defines the relationship between a profit figure and other business figures which have helped to bring about this profit., such as sales, total costs, total assets, or equity.

Example: return on sales measures the fraction of the profit in sales before deduction of taxes and interest (EBIT) and shows how much was earned on each monetary unit sold.

profitability index Kapitalwertrate

Method used to evaluate projects. It is the ratio of the present value of the future expected cash flows after initial investment divided by the amount of the initial investment.

profitable gewinnbringend; rentabel; wirtschaftlich; profitabel; vorteilhaft

profit accounting Gewinnrechnung

profit and loss statement Gewinn- und Verlustrechnung; Erfolgsrechnung

A financial report that summarizes a firm' s performance over a specified time period by listing revenues, costs, and expenses.

Also called profit and loss account, income statement, operating statement, statement of profit and loss or income and expense statement.

profit as shown in the balance Bilanzgewinn

profit balance Gewinnsaldo

profit center Profit Center; Ertragsbereich; Ergebniseinheit

An organizational unit that operates independently and under its own responsibility in order to make a profit.

A fully equipped profit center has its own sales and marketing organization, its own production and purchasing department, but cannot take independent investment decisions.

Example: a conglomerate with interests in hotels, food processing, and paper may consider each of these three separate profit centers.

profiteer Geschäftemacher; Profitjäger; Preistreiber

Someone in search of excessive profits, often to the detriment of others.

profit gain Gewinnzuwachs

profit growth Gewinnanstieg; Gewinnzuwachs

profit index Nutzenindex

profit margin Gewinnspanne

Indicator of profitability, determined by dividing net income by revenues for the same 12-month period.

profit maximization Gewinnmaximierung

profit objective Gewinnziel

Attempts to manage all the demands which can be made on the profit before deduction of income taxes and interest, such as: interest on borrowed capital required for business operations, distributions on equity capital, profit tax, budgeted payments to third parties, budgeted creation of new reserves, long-term provisions which cannot be regarded as cost components.

profit orientation Gewinnorientierung; Ertragsorientierung

profit oriented gewinnorientiert

profit planning Gewinnplanung

profit rate Profitrate

profit ratio Gewinnverhältnis

profit seeking Gewinnstreben

profit share Gewinnquote

profit sharing Gewinnbeteiligung; Ergebnisbeteiligung

profit sharing plan Gewinnbeteilungsplan

A type of retirement plan that allows employees a share in company profits. Annual contributions are made by the company to a profit-sharing account for each employee, which may be invested.

profit situation Ertragssituation; Ertragslage

profit squeeze Gewinndruck; Gewinnschmälerung

Situation in which a business finds it increasingly difficult to maintain the same amount or rate of profit as in the past. This may be due to various factors: reduced prices, rising production costs, financing costs, general and administrative expenses, or taxes.

profit taking Gewinnmitnahme

Stock exchange: widespread strategy of selling securities when they have risen in value in order to realized the gain an take the profit.

profit target Gewinnplanziel

profit trend Gewinntrend

pro forma pro forma; Plan-; reine Formsache; der Form halber

Accounting: a hypothetical presentation of data, such as a balance sheet or income statement, that is based on assumptions.

pro forma statements Planjahres-abschlüsse

Projected income statements, balance sheets and sources and uses statements for future years.

prognosis Voraussage; Prognose; Vorausschätzung

Forecasts based on investigations into the state of the market, the behavior of competitors, and data concerning the environment.

A prognosis is also the extrapolation of past economic trends into the future. They contribute to the database used in corporate planning.

prognosticate prognostizieren; voraussagen

program Programm; Plan; *(to ~)* Programm gestalten; *(computer)* programmieren

Computing: a set of instructions te be executed by a computer.

program financing Programmfinanzierung

programmer Programmierer

programming Programmierung

programming language Programmier-sprache

progress Fortschritt; Verlauf; fortschreiten; vorankommen

progressive fortschrittlich; fortschreitend

progressive tax progressive Steuer

A tax system in which tax rates rise as incomes rise. As a consequence, the wealthy are taxed at a higher rate than the poor or middle class.

progress payment Fortschrittszahlung; Abschlagzahlung

progress report Lagebericht; Fortschrittsbericht; Tätigkeitsbericht

prohibit verbieten; untersagen

prohibited unzulässig; verboten

prohibition Verbot; Untersagung; Prohibition

prohibitive untragbar; unerschwinglich

prohibitive tariff Schutzzoll; Sperrzoll

project Projekt; Plan; Vorhaben; *(research)* Forschungsaufgabe; *(to ~)* planen; vorausberechnen; *(an image)* projizieren

A unique venture undertaken to reach clearly defined goals.

project controlling Projektcontrolling

The planning, managing and controlling of output, costs and dead-lines of a project. The progress of the project is judged by ascertaining the stage reached (percentage of completion).

project costs Projektkosten

projected geplant; vorgeplant; *(calculated)* vorausberechnet; *(future)* zukünftig; projiziert

project execution Projektdurchführung

project financing Projektfinanzierung

project implementation Projektdurchführung

projection *(cost, time)* Vorausberechnung; *(planning)* Planung; Projektion

An estimate of future trends made by economists, corporate planners, or credit and securities analysts. For example, economists use econometric models to project gross domestic product (GDP), inflation, unemployment, and many other economic factors.

projection period Planungszeitraum

The time horizon for which a projection is valid.

project leader Projektleiter

project management Projektleitung; Projektmanagement

The overall planning and co-ordination of a project from inception to completion. Amongst many other things, it involves assigning employees to specific teams and then reassigns them back to the organization when the project is completed.

project risk Projektrisiko

projected rate vorausberechneter Kurs

Spot exchange rate forecast for the end of the budget period.

project work Projektarbeit;

proliferate sich stark vermehren; wuchern

proliferation starke Vermehrung; rasches Anwachsen

prolific fruchtbar; produktiv; reich

prolong verlängern; *(bill of exchange)* prolongieren

prominence Vorsprung; Erhebung; Prominenz; Wichtigkeit; Bedeutung

prominent prominent; bedeutend

promise Versprechen; Hoffnung; *(answer)* Zusage; *(potential)* Zukunftspotential; *(to ~)* versprechen; zusagen

promising viel versprechend; aussichtsreich; hoffnungsvoll

promissory note Schuldschein; Eigenwechsel; Solawechsel

A legally binding contract between a lender and a borrower, in which the maker agrees to pay a specific sum at a definite time.

The note contains the terms and conditions of the loan, including how and when the loan must be repaid.

promote befördern; *(to advertise)* anpreisen; werben; *(to support)* fördern

promotion *(rise in rank)* Beförderung; *(advertising)* Reklame; Werbung; *(marketing)* Verkaufsförderung; *(furtherance)* Förderung

Employment: Job advance, with higher level of pay and responsibility.

Marketing: Activities that communicate the product or service and its merits to target customers and persuade them to buy, including advertising, printing, and salesperson commissions.

Four main types of promotion exist. advertising, personal selling, publicity, and sales promotion. Each includes a variety of techniques, tools, and media.

promotional Werbe-; fördernd, verkaufsfördernd

promotional allowance *(advertising)* Verkaufsförderungsbonus

Payment or price reduction to reward dealers for participating in advertising and sales-support programs. This promotional allowance compensates the retailer for expenditures made promoting the product.

promotional gift Werbegeschenk

promotional literature Werbematerial

promotional pricing Werbepreis

Temporarily pricing products below the list price, and sometimes even below cost, to increase short-run sales; special deals in price that retailers use to encourage a first purchase, to encourage repeat business, or to close a sale.

promotional program Förderprogramm

promotion manager Werbeleiter

promotion mix *(advertising)* Verkaufsförderungsmix; Werbemix

Specific mix of advertising, personal selling, sales promotion and public relations that a company uses to pursue its marketing objectives.

prompt schnell; rasch; prompt; unverzüglich; *(punctual)* pünktlich; *(to ~) (to cause)* veranlassen; *(to suggest)* anregen; *(theater)* soufflieren

proof Beweis; *(substantiation)* Nachweis; *(means of proof)* Beweismittel; *(print)* Korrekturbogen; Probe; Abzug

proof of liquidity Liquiditätsnachweis

propaganda *(publicity)* Reklame; Propaganda; Verbreiten

propensity to consume Konsumneigung; Konsumfreudigkeit

propensity to invest Investitionsneigung; Investitionsquote

proper richtig; *(correct)* ordnungsgemäß; *(competent)* maßgebend; zuständig

property *(assets)* Vermögen; *(ownership)* Eigentum; Gut; *(land)* Grundstück;

Immobilien; Liegenschaften; *(quality)* Eigenschaft

Property describes someone's exclusive right to possess, use, and dispose of a thing, as well as the object, benefit, or prerogative that constitutes the subject matter of that right.

property management Immobilienverwaltung; Vermögensverwaltung; Grundstücksverwaltung

The management of property as a business, which includes a variety of task: collection of rents, maintenance and repair, accounting and reporting, leasing, paying taxes, provision of utilities and insurance.

property rights Eigentumsrechte

Legal rights over the use to which a resource is put and over the use made of any income that may be derived from that resource; rights to the ownership and stewardship of, and profits from, land, capital, and other goods.

property sale Grundstücksverkauf

property tax Vermögenssteuer; *(real estate)* Grundsteuer

Tax paid on privately owned property. For real estate, it is based upon the assessed value of the property. The property tax on real estate is an important source of revenue for local governments.

property value Vermögenswert

proportion Proportion; *(ratio)* Verhältnis; *(share)* Anteil

proportional Verhältnis-; verhältnismäßig

proportional costs proportionale Kosten; variable Kosten

Accounting: costs that arise because a product is manufactured or a service delivered. They are determined by the structure of the cost center or of the product (bills of material, work plans, recipes).

proportionate angemessen; entsprechend; anteilmäßig

proposal Vorschlag; *(trade)* Angebot

proposal solicitation Angeboteinholung

Stage of the business buying process in which the buyer invites qualified suppliers to submit proposals.

propose vorschlagen; Antrag stellen; beabsichtigen; *(a candidate)* aufstellen

proposition Vorschlag; Antrag; Behauptung; Lehrsatz

proprietary Eigentums-; gesetzlich geschützt; Marken-; einem Besitzer gehörig; *(patent)* patentrechtlich geschützt

proprietary product Markenprodukt

proprietor Besitzer; Inhaber; Eigentümer; Eigner; Gesellschafter

proprietor of a commercial establishment Handelsherr

proprietorship Eigentumsrecht; *(ownership)* Inhaberschaft; *(organization)* Einzelfirma; Einzelunternehmung

Organization: the simplest form of business organization, the business is owned by a single person. The individual proprietor has the right to all the profits from the business and also responsibility for all the firm's liabilities.

prorata anteilsmäßig; im richtigen Verhältnis; anteilig

Refers to proportionate allocation, i.e. dividing something, like costs, income, profits, etc. among unites or participants according to the rate in which each has contributed.

pros and cons Für und Wider; Vor- und Nachteile

The advantages and disadvantages of a particular situation or set of alternatives.

prosecution *(implementation)* Durchführung; *(law)* gerichtliche Verfolgung; Anklage; *(counsel for the plaintiff)* Anklagevertretung; Staatsanwaltschaft

prospect Aussicht; *(sales)* potentieller Kunde; Interessent; *(to ~) (mining)* schürfen

Marketing: A potential customer.

prospecting *(sales)* Kaufinteressenten finden; *(mining)* Schürfung

Marketing: Step in the selling process in which the salesperson identifies qualified potential customers.

prospective voraussichtlich; zukünftig; weitsichtig

prospectus Werbeprospekt; Emissionsprospekt

Securities: a formal written offer to sell securities which must contain all the details that an investor needs to make an informed decision.

Marketing: a piece of sales literature that provides information about a product or service, often with pictures.

prosper gedeihen; *(to flourish)* florieren; im Wohlstand leben

prosperity Wohlstand; Prospentät; Gedeihen; Hochkonjunktur

Economics: a situation of economic growth with rising profits and full employment, often accompanied by a general sense of well-being of the population.

prosperous *(wealthy)* wohlhabend; *(successful)* erfolgreich; gut gehend; blühend

protect schützen; *(to shield)* abschirmen; durch Zölle schützen

protection Schutz(-zollpolitik); Protektion

protectionism Protektionismus; Schutzzollpolitik

Trade: economic policies designed to restrict imports of goods that compete with domestic producers in order to protect domestic producers from foreign competition.

protectionist Protektionist; protektionistisch

protective Schutz-; schützend

protective covenant Schutzvereinbarung

Loan: a clause in a loan agreement that limits certain actions a company can take in order to protect the lender's interests.

protector power Schutzmacht

protector state Schutzmacht

protest Protest; *(to ~)*beteuern; protestieren

protocol Protokoll; Sitzungsordnung; Verhandlungsordnung; *(minutes)* Sitzungsbericht

Politics: formal diplomatic rules.

Computing: a set of standards that define how traffic and communications are handled by a computer or network routers.

prototype Ur-; Vorbild**;** Prototyp; Ausgangsbaumuster; erstes Modell

prototyping Entwicklung eines Prototypen

Product development: the process of building a working model (the prototype) of a product in order to test ceratin aspects, such as the design or the functionality.

protrude vorspringen; hervorragen; herausragen

prove beweisen; *(to substantiate)* nachweisen; *(to test)* prüfen; erproben; auf die Probe stellen; *(to turn out)* sich erweisen; *(to document)* belegen

provide *(to procure)* verschaffen; beschaffen; versorgen; besorgen; *(to supply)* versorgen; *(law)* bestimmen; *(regulation)* vorsehen

provident vorsorglich; haushälterisch

provider Ernährer; Versorger; *(supplier)* Lieferant

province Provinz; Gebiet; Aufgabe; *(government portfolio)* Ressort; *(competency)* Zuständigkeit

provincial Provinz-; provinziell; kleinstädtisch; Provinzbewohner; Provinzler

provision Beschaffung; *(clause)* Klausel; Verfügung; *(measure)* Maßnahme; *(planning)* Vorsorge; *(balance sheet)* Rücklage; Rückstellung; *(~ to guard against risk)* Risikovorlage; Bestimmung; Vorrat

provisional vorläufig; provisorisch

provisions *(foodstuffs)* Lebensmittel; Proviant; Mundvorrat

proviso vertragliche Bedingung; Vorbehaltsklausel

Legal: a stipulated condition that excepts something from the basic provision.

proxy Vollmacht; *(voting power)* Stimmrechtsermächtigung; *(deputyship)* Stellvertretung; in Vertretung handeln

In general: a person authorized to act or speak for another.

Business: a document given by shareholders of a corporation authorizing a specific vote on their behalf at a corporate meeting.

Internet: a server designed to offer either firewall security or provide cached content accessible through slower connections.

proxy holder Prokurist

proxy server Proxy Server

Internet: a system that stores frequently used information closer to the end user to provide faster access or to reduce the load on another server; it also serves as the gateway to the internet.

proxy server caching Proxy Server Caching

Internet: process that occurs when users access copies of websites rather than the site itself. Users accessing websites from proxy servers are not counted as new visitors.

proxy statement Stimmrechtsvollmacht; Vollmachtsformular; Vollmachtsanweisung

proxy voting power Stimmrechtsvollmacht; Proxystimmrecht

prudence Umsicht; Vorsicht; *(sagacity)* Klugheit

Displaying foresight, caution, and discretion in one's actions; not acting carelessly and recklessly.

psychographics *(advertising)* Persönlichkeitsbeschreibung; Psychographie

Techniques of measuring lifestyles and developing lifestyle classifications; it involves measuring the chief AIO dimensions (activities, interests, opinions); determining market segmentation based on consumer psychological profiles.

The two general areas include how the consumer views himself or herself in relation to the rest of the world and income characteristics.

psychographic segementation psychographische Segmentierung

Dividing a market into different groups based on social class, lifestyle, or personality characteristics.

psychological psychologisch

psychological contract psychologischer Vertrag; stillschweigende Übereinkunft

Unwritten agreement that exists between employees and their employer and sets out mutual expectations - what management expects from the employee, and vice versa.

This contract defines the behavioral expectations that go with every role:

Management is expected to treat employees justly, provide acceptable working conditions, clearly communicate what is a fair day's work, and give feedback on how well the employee is doing.

Employees are expected to respond by demonstrating a good attitude, following directions, and showing loyalty to the organization.

psychological pricing psychologische Preissetzung

Pricing approach that considers the psychology of prices and not simplify the economics; the price is used to say something about the product.

psychology Psychologie

Science that seeks to measure, explain, and sometimes change the behavior of humans.

Example: in a business environment, psychologists concern themselves with learning, perception, personality, job satisfaction, decision-making processes, and job stress.

pub Kneipe; Wirtschaft; Lokal; Pub

public Öffentlichkeit; *(audience)* Publikum; Staats-; öffentlich; staatlich

Any group that has an actual or potential interest in or impact on an organization's ability to achieve its objectives.

public accountant freier Wirtschaftsprüfer

Accountant who is not certified..

public assistance expenditure Sozialhilfeausgabe; Spezialhilfeausgabe

publication *(print)* Veröffentlichung; *(announcement)* Bekanntmachung; Publikation

public bond Staatsanleihe; Staatsschuldverschreibung

public company Aktiengesellschaft (UK)

public consumption Staatsverbrauch

public corporation Körperschaft des öffentliche Rechts; staatliche Aktiengesellschaft

A corporation formed by a government authority for specific public purposes, such as education, health, or transportation. Railroads are often public corporations.

public domain öffentlicher Bereich; öffentliche Domain

Copyright term that means a particular work is free for all to use without permission. Works in the public domain include those that were never copyrighted, those for which the copyright has expired and public documents.

public employee Angestellter des öffentlichen Dienstes

A person employed by a public authority. Public employees often enjoy certain privileges and are appointed on the basis of merit examinations.

public enterprise öffentliches Unternehmen; Staatskonzern

public expense Staatskosten

public finances öffentliche Finanzen

public fund öffentlicher Fonds; Publikumsfonds

public goods öffentliche Güter; Kollektivgüter

Goods and services that are supplied by the government because it is either not sufficiently profitable for the private sector to do so, or demanded by public security, such as police power and the military.

public interest öffentliches Interesse

Anything that is considered beneficial to the public.

public issue Emmission; Aktienemission

publicity *(advertising)* Öffentlichkeitsarbeit

Activities to promote a company or its products by planting news about it in media not paid for by the sponsor.

publicity director Werbeleiter

publicity ploy Werbemanöver; Werbetrick

publicity strategist Werbestratege

publicize bekannt machen; durch Werbung herausstellen; publizieren; öffentlich *(advertising)* Reklame machen

public key öffentlicher Schlüssel

Internet: unique identifier of a buyer or a seller that is available to other parties to enable secure e-commerce using encryption based on digital certificates.

public-key encryption Chiffrierung mit öffentlichem Schlüssel

Internet: form of internet-based encryption that includes two elements: a public key and a private key. An individual creates a public key and sends it to people with whom they exchange e-mail. Recipients then use this public key to create coded message for the sender. When someone receives a message encrypted with their public key, they use a secret private key to decode the message.

public-key infrastructure Infrastruktur zur Generierung öffentlicher Schlüssel

Internet: organizations responsible for issuing and maintaining certificates for public-key security together form the PKI.

publicly owned volkseigen; staatseigen

public offering öffentliches Zeichnungsangebot

Stock exchange: an offering of new securities to the general public at a price agreed upon by the issuer and the investment bankers.

public opinion poll öffentliche Meinungsumfrage; öffentliche Meinungsbefragung; Demoskopie

public ownership Staatseigentum; Gemeineigentum

Government: a company owned and operated by the government for the purpose of providing some good or service to citizens, such as public utilities.

public policy öffentlicher Grundsatz; öffentliche Verhaltensweise; öffentliche Ordnung

public record *(reat estate)* Grundbuch

Real estate: documents and recods that are evidence of real estate ownserhip and transactions.

public record office Staatsarchiv; Grundbuchamt

public relations (PR) Öffentlichkeitsarbeit; Meinungspflege

All activities involved in generating goodwill toward a company or a product, and building good relations with the company's various publics by obtaining favorable publicity, building up a good 'corporate image', and handling or heading off unfavorable rumors, stories, and events.

Public relations uses publicity that does not necessitate payment in a wide variety of media and is often placed as news or items of public interest. Major PR tools include press relations, product publicity, corporate communications, lobbying and counseling.

public securities Staatspapiere

public support *(opinion)* öffentliche Zustimmung; *(aid)* staatliche Unterstützung

public works öffentliche Arbeiten; *(construction)* öffentliche Bauten; öffentliche Anlagen

Facilities constructed by or for a government or public authority, such as the construction of dams, highways, schools and government buildings.

publish veröffentlichen; verlegen; allgemein bekannt geben

publisher Verleger; Herausgeber; Verlagsbuchhändler

pull *(influence)* Macht; Einfluss; *(market)* Sog; *(to ~)* ziehen; *(to tear)* reißen; *(to tug)* zerren; abziehen

pullback *(retrenchment)* Rückzug; *(curtailment)* Einschränkung

pullout *(departure)* Verlassen; *(abandonment)* Aufgabe; Ausstieg

pull strategy Pull-Strategie; Marketingstrategie zur Schaffung von Verbrauchernachfrage

Marketing strategy emphasizing mass media advertising as opposed to personal selling; promotional strategy whereby the seller concentrates marketing efforts on the end user through advertising, direct mail, flyers, and related activities.

The concept seeks to educate consumers regarding the target products so they will ask retailers to offer them to the public. Subsequently the retailers request the products from wholesalers or manufacturers.

pulsing pochen; pulsieren

Advertising: Scheduling ads unevenly, in bursts, over a certain time period.

pump priming *(economy)* Ankurbelung

Economics: various expansionary policy measures like increasing government expenditures and/or reducing taxes in order to stimulate the economy. These measures shold only be temporary, as their side-effects can be detrimental.

punched card Lochkarte

Computers: a cardbord card on which data can be recorded in the form of punched holes, depending on a a particular pattern which can be read by a computer. Punched cards were dominant in dataprocessing in the 1960s, but have since become obsolete.

punctual pünktlich

punctuality Pünktlichkeit

punctuated equilibrium model Gruppenmodell bei eingeschränktem Gleichgewicht

Temporary groups go through transitions between inertia and activity. This model is essentially limited to temporary task groups that are working under a time-constrained completion deadline.

punitive Straf-; strafend

punitive damages Entschädigung mit Strafcharakter; *(fine)* Strafschadenersatz

Legal: an award of money in favor of a victim that is intended to punish the wrongdoer and not just to compensate the victim.

purchase Kauf; Erwerb; *(to ~)* kaufen; *(to acquire)* erwerben; *(to purchase land)* ankaufen

The acquisition of something in exchange for payment, as contrasted with a gift.

purchase decision Kaufentscheidung

Stage of the buyer decision process in which the consumer actually makes the decision to buy the product.

purchase guarantee Abnahmegarantie

purchase order Auftrag; Bestellung; Kaufantrag

A document that specifies commodities ordered from a vendor, as well as their price, and the terms and conditions of that order. Once accepted by the supplier, the purchase order becomes a legally binding contract.

purchase price Kaufpreis; Anschaffungspreis

purchaser Käufer; Ankäufer; Erwerber

purchasing agent Einkäufer; Einkaufssachbearbeiter

purchasing calculation Ankaufsberechnung

purchasing commission *(percentage)* Ankaufsprovision

purchasing order Bezugsschein

purchasing power Kaufkraft

The amount of goods and services that a certain amount of money can buy. It is therefore an expression of the value of money.

The purchasing power of the euro is determined by comparing an index of consumer prices to a base year.

purchasing power parity (PPP) Kaufkraftparität

A method of comparing the relative purchasing power of different currencies, based on the law of one price, i.e. the idea that in an efficient market identical goods must have only one price. Accordingly, the long-run equilibrium exchange rate of two currencies is the rate that equalizes their purchasing power.

pure rein; *(genuine)* echt; klar

pure capitalism reiner Kapitalismus

An economic system where capitalism can reign freely, characterized especially by private ownership of resources and the functioning of prices to coordinate economic activity in free competitive markets.

pure competition vollständige Konkurrenz; vollständiger Wettbewerb

Market situation in which many buyers and many sellers meet and which has a number of characteristics: they trade in a uniform commodity, no single buyer or seller has much effect on the going market price, all information is available to everyone, and no party is large enough to have a marked effect upon the market.

In theory such a market produces the largest output at the lowest price. There are, however, no real-world markets of this nature.

pure discount bond abgezinste Anleihe

Bonds that par no coupons and only par back face value at maturity having been initially issued at a price less than face value; also called zero coupon bonds.

pure monopoly echtes Angebotsmonopol; reines Monopol

Market situation in which there is a single seller and many buyers; the seller may be a government monopoly, a private regulated monopoly or a private non-regulated monopoly.

purpose Zweck; *(intended use)* Verwendungszweck; *(intention)* Absicht

purveyor Versorger; (Lebensmittel-)Lieferant

push strategy Push-Strategie; Schubstrategie

Promotion strategy that calls for using the sales force and trade promotion to push the product through channels. The producer promotes the product to wholesalers, the wholesalers promote to retailers, and the retailers promote to consumers.

push technology Push-Technologie

Internet: delivery of web-based content to the user's desktop without the need for the user to visit a site to download information. E-mail can also be considered to be a push technology. A particular type of information is a push channel.

put Verkaufsoption; Rückprämie

put-call parity Put-Call-Parität

Value of a call equals the value of buying the share plus buying the put plus borrowing at the risk-free rate.

put option Verkaufsoption

Option contract that gives the holder the right to sell (or "put"), and places upon the writer the obligation to purchase, a specified number of shares of the underlying stock at the given strike price on or before the expiration date of the contract.

put out *(displeased)* ärgerlich; *(to ~)* herausstellen; in Auftrag geben; veröffentlichen

put provision Rückgaberecht

Gives holder of a bond the right to redeem his or her note at par on the coupon payment date.

pyramid Pyramide; pyramidenförmige Anordnung; *(stock exchange)* ständig zunehmender Börsengewinn

pyramiding Verschachteln; Verschachtelung; Mehrheitsbeteiligungen an Holdinggesellschaften

pyramid selling Schneeballverkaufssystem

A method of selling using a hierarchy of part-time workers. Usually a central instigator at the apex of the pyramid sells a franchise to regional organizers, who recruit district distributors, who each take some of the stock and, in turn, recruit door-to-door salesmen, who take smaller proportions of the stock, which they attempt to sell. In some cases the last stage consists of people who sell the goods to their friends.

Q

qualification Fähigkeit; Qualifikation; Befähigung; *(modification)* Einschränkung; Voraussetzung; *(suitability)* Eignung

qualified available market qualifizierter zugänglicher Markt

Set of consumers who have interest, income, access and qualifications for a particular product or service.

qualified opinion eingeschränkter Bestätigungsvermerk

An auditor's opinion that calls attention to limitations in the audit or exceptions the auditor has taken with the financial statements.

Typical reasons for qualified opinions are: pending lawsuits; indeterminable tax liability relating to an unusual transaction; inability to confirm a portion of the inventory.

qualified person Fachkraft

qualified prospect qualifizierter Interessent

A prospective buyer who has the necessary financial resources to make a purchase.

qualify qualifizieren; *(to entitle)* berechtigen; *(to enable)* befähigen; ausbilden; *(to be entitled)* berechtigt sein; *(modify)* einschränken; relativieren

Information-gathering process that sales people use to determine a prospect's buying potential

qualitative qualitativ

qualitative analysis qualitative Analyse

Securities: analysis that looks at qualitative factors, such as a corporation's management experience, employee morale and the status of labor relations instead of the corporation's financial data.

qualitative research *(market research)* qualitative Forschung

Market research: exploratory research used to uncover consumers' motivations, attitudes and behavior. Typical methods are focus-group interviewing, elicitation interviewing and repertory grid techniques.

quality Qualität; Güte; Wert; Beschaffenheit; *(characteristic)* Eigenschaft

The totality of features and characteristics of a product or service that together constitute its ability to satisfy customer needs.

Quality is a measure of the degree to which something meets a standard. According to the European standard ISO 8402 *quality* is the totality of features of a unit with regard to their ability to meet defined and predicted requirements.

quality assurance Qualitätssicherung

All the planned and systematic activities pursued within a quality system to assure that an entity (service, product, process, activity, organization) will fulfill the requirements for quality .

quality circles Qualitätszirkel

An imporant element of quality management in which which small groups of employees meet regularly to discuss and develop management issues and procedures.

The two main tasks of a quality circle are the identification of problems, and the suggestion of solutions.

quality comparison Qualitätsvergleich

quality competition Qualitätskonkurrenz; Qualitätswettbewerb

quality control Qualitätskontrolle; Gütekontrolle; Qualitätsüberwachung; Qualitätssteuerung; Qualitätslenkung

All the operational techniques and activities used to fulfill and verify quality requirements, such as the regular inspection of products at various points in their manufacture.

quality engineering Qualitätskontrolltechnik

All operational, managerial and engineering activities that a company employs to ensure that the product fulfills quality characteristics.

quality hierarchy Qualitätshierarchie

quality management Qualitätsmanagement; Qualitätssicherung; Qualitätswesen

The design and maintenance of quality assurance mechanisms. *See:* total quality management.

quality of life Lebensqualität

The level of enjoyment and fulfillment derived by humans from the life they live within their local economic, cultural, social, and environmental conditions.

Degree to which people value relationships, and show sensitivity and concern for the welfare of others.

quality product Qualitätsprodukt

quality standard Qualitätsnorm; Qualitätsstandard

quantitative quantitativ; mengenmäßig

quantitative analysis qualitative Bestimmung; Mengenanalyse; *(market research)* quantitative Analyse

Securities: analysis that examines mathematically measurable factors, as distinguished from such qualitative considerations as the character of management or the state of employee morale.

quantitative index Mengenindex

quantitative research *(market research)* quantitative Forschung

Market resesrch: scientific investigations in which quantitative data are used to measure different variables. Data collection normally occurs by mail or personal interview, which has to reach a sufficient volume of customers to allow statistical analysis.

quantity Menge; Quantität

quantity adjustment Mengenanpassung

quantity discount Mengenrabatt, Mengenabnahme

A reduction in the unit price offered to customers who buy large volumes; also called volume discount.

Example: if the list price of an item is €100, and the unit price drops to €75 if more than 10 are bought at a time, this represents a 25% quantity discount.

quantity of life Lebensquantität

Degree to which values such as assertiveness, the acquisition of money and material goods, and competition prevail.

quantity of supply Angebotsmenge

quantity premium Mengenzuschlag

Surcharge paid by buyers who purchase high volumes of a product.

quantity structure Mengengerüst

Manufacturing: the requirements for producing a product or a service as determined by its technical specifications. It is contained in the bill of materials.

quantity theory of money Quantitätstheorie des Geldes

The quantity theory of money centers on the equation of exchange

$$M * V = P * Q$$

Where M is the total amount of money in circulation in an economy at any one time; V is the velocity of money; P is the average price level for the economy; and Q is the total number of items purchased.

The left-hand side of the equation equals the total amount of money spent during during a specified time period, the right-hand side equals the amount of money received.

quarter Viertel; *(quarter year)* Vierteljahr; Quartal; 25-Centstück; *(to ~)* vierteilen

quarterly *(publication)* Vierteljahreszeitschrift; Quartals-; vierteljährlich; (to ~) vierteln

Corporations: usual basis on which earnings reports to shareholders are made in the US.

quarterly returns vierteljährliche Steuererklärung

quarterly review Vierteljahresprüfung

quarters *(lodging)* Quartier; Unterkunft

quartile Quartil

Statistics: a segment of a sample representing a sequential quarter, so the first quartile of a list has three quarters of the numbers in the list below it, the fourth quartile has three quarters of the numbers above it.

question Frage; Thema; Zweifel; *(to ~)* fragen; (be-)zweifeln

questionable fragwürdig; *(doubtful)* zweifelhaft

question mark Fragezeichen

Portfolio analysis: descriptive term for low-share business units in high-growth markets that require a lot of cash in order to hold their share or become stars.

questionnaire Fragebogen

A written or electronic survey instrument comprised of a series of questions, designed to measure a specific item or set of items.

questionnaire design Fragebogenplanung

queue Warteschlange

A line of customers waiting to be served.

Computing: data structure from which items are removed in the same order in which they were entered.

queuing theory Warteschlangenmodell; Warteschlangentheorie

The mathematical analysis of waiting lines attempting evaluates the ability of service facilities to handle capacity and load at different times.

quick assets flüssige Mittel und Forderungen

Accounting: a company´s cash and everything that is readily converted into cash, such as marketable securities and accounts receivable.

quick ratio Liquidität zweiten Grades

Accounting: liquidity ratio calculated by dividing cash, marketable securities, and accounts receivable by current liabilities.

By excluding inventory, this ratio focuses on the firm's more liquid assets whose values are relatively certain.

quid pro quo quid pro quo; Gegenleistung

quit *(to resign)* kündigen; *(to cease)* aufhören; *(to give up)* aufgeben; frei; los

Employees who voluntarily leave their current employment either to change jobs or to leave the labor force.

quorum Beschlußfähigkeit; beschlußfähige Mehrheit

The number of members of a group who must be present in order to officially conduct the business of that group.

quota Quote; Kontingent; Sollvorgabe; *(share in business)* Geschäftsanteil

General: a prescribed number imposed on the quantity of goods to be produced or purchased.

Trade: Import quotas are used to restrict the purchase of goods from foreign origins; export quotas are used to stabilize export earnings.

quota agreement Kontingentsvereinbarung; Quotenregelung

quota control Quotenregelung

quota limitation Kontingentierung

quota regulation Quotenregelung

quota sample *(market research)* Quotenauswahl; Quotenstichprobe

A nonprobability sample that takes into account the proportion of different categories (age, gender, etc.) within the population.

quota sampling Quotenauswahlverfahren

Sampling method in which the population is first segmented into mutually exclusive sub-groups. Then judgement is used to select the subjects or units from each segment based on a specified proportion. For example, an interviewer may be told to sample 200 females and 300 males between the age of 45 and 60.

quotation Anführung; Belegstelle; Zitat; *(price)* Preisangabe; Angebot; Offerte; *(stock exchange)* Kursnotierung; Börsennotierung

General: a statement of the price of a product, often in response to an inquiry.

Stock exchange: a price at which a market maker will trade, which usually includes the bidprice and the offer price.

quote *(price offer)* Preisangebot; *(citation)* Zitat; Anführungszeichen; *(to ~)* zitieren; in Anführungszeichen setzen; *(to state)* angeben; *(stock exchange)* notieren

quoted price Angebotspreis; angegebener Preis; angebotener Preis; *(stock exchange)* notierter Kurs

Q ratio (or Tobin's Q) Tobins Q; Marktwert-Buchwert-Verhältnis

A financial ratio measuring the market value of firm's assets divided by replacement value of firm' s assets.

R

racket Schiebung; Betrügerei; *(noise)* Krach; Spektakel; *(tennis)* Schläger

An illegal activity carried on for profit, often involving extortion or the sale of illegal substances or services.

racketeering Geschäftemacherei

radical leadership durchgreifende Führung

radio advertising Radiowerbung

Advertising over the radio, often involving an advertiser paying the cost of the program as a sponsor.

radius Radius; Umkreis; *(fig)* Wirkungskreis; Bereich

raider Räuber; Plünderer

An investor who aims to take control of a company by purchasing a controlling interest in its stock in order to install new management or to make a quick profit.

railroad Eisenbahn; Eisenbahnlinie; *(tracks)* Schienenweg; *(law)* durchjagen; -peitschen

raise *(wage)* Lohnerhöhung; *(salary)* Gehaltserhöhung; *(to ~)* erhöhen; heraufsetzen; anheben; *(to procure)* bereitstellen; lüften; züchten; abbrechen

raising efficiency Effizienzsteigerung

raising of credit Kreditaufnahme

rally *(stock excbange)* Erholung; *(price)* Preisaufschwung; *(to ~)* sich erholen

random stichprobenartig; *(coincidental)* zufällig; aufs Geratewohl; wahllos; beiläufig; ziellos

random digit dialing zufällige Nummernwahl

Telephone survey technique of calling people at random and asking specific questions.

random sample Zufallsstichprobe, Stichprobenerhebung

A statistical of a population where each member of the population has an equal chance of being selected.

random sample of consumption Verbrauchsstichprobe

random sample of income Einkommens-stichprobe

random test Stichprobe

random variable *(statistics)* stochastische Variable; Zufallsvariable

random walk Irrfahrttheorie; Zufallsbewegung

The theory that price movements in the securities markets are completely random in character, and that past prices are not a reliable indicator of future prices.

range Auswahl; Sortiment; *(limits)* Spielraum; Grenze; *(extent)* Spanne; *(scale)* Größenordnung; Umfang; *(to ~)* anordnen; *(to extend)* ausdehnen; sich erstrecken; (ein-)ordnen; umherstreifen

Statistics: the difference between the minimum value and the maximum value in a set of data.

Investment: the highest and lowest quoted prices over a period of time.

range branding strategy Strategie der sortimentsbezogenen Markenpolitik

Brand strategy whereby the firm develops separate product range names for different families of product.

range of application Anwendungsbereich

range of fluctuation Schwankungsbreite

rank Rang; Stand; *(order)* Ordnung; Reihe; Glied; Klasse; *(degree)* Grad; *(to~)* einordnen; rangieren; rechnen; zählen

rank-and-file *(of company)* Belegschaft; *(of trade union)* einfache Mitglieder

The ordinary members of an organization, excluding its officers or managers.

rank hierarchy Ranghierarchie

ranking list Rangliste

ranking system Rangsystem

rapport Übereinstimmung; *(to ~)* gut harmonieren; in Übereinstimmung sein

A relationship of mutual understanding or trust and agreement between people which leads to an environment of harmony.

rarity Seltenheit; Dünne; etwas Seltenes

ratable steuerpflichtig; (ab)schätzbar; anteilmäßig

rate Maß; Verhältnis; Höhe; Rate; *(discount)* Satz; *(wage)* Tarif; *(currency)* Kurs; *(to ~) (to place)* einstufen; *(to judge)* beurteilen; bemessen; bewerten

A special kind of ratio, involving two measurements with different units, such as miles to the gallon.

Rate Adaptive Digital Subscriber Line (RADSL) leitungsabhängiges DSL

Internet: one variation of DSL, in which the information is sent at the maximum speed the line can handle under changing conditions. This is similar to modems, which can adapt to different speeds depending on the quality of the phone line.

rate bargaining round Tarifrunde

rate base zugesicherte Mindestauflage; garantierte Auflag

The circulation of a print vehicle upon which advertising space rates are based. The rate base may or may not be guaranteed by the publication

rate card *(advertising)* Anzeigenpreisliste

*Advertising*l: a list containing pricing and descriptions of all currently available ad products and packages.

The rate card includes the space, time, mechanical requirement data, and other pertinent information.

rate ceiling Höchstgrenze; Höchsttarif

rate control Tarifkontrolle

rate dispute Tarifstreit

rated policy Versicherung zu erhöhter Prämie

Insurance: a policy issued to insure a person with a greater-than-average likelihood of loss, for which the applicant is charged a higher-than-standard premium. Examples include a person with a history of heart disease or a racing driver.

rate hike Tariferhöhung

rate making Gebührenfestsetzung; *(insurance)* Prämienfestsetzung; *(wages)* Tarifberechnung

rate of change Veränderungsrate

rate of duty Zollsatz; Zolltarif

rate of exchange Devisenkurs; Umrechnungskurs; Wechselkurs; Tauschverhältnis

See: exchange rate.

rate of growth Zuwachsrate; Wachstumsrate

rate of increase Steigerungsrate; Steigerungssatz

rate of inflation Inflationsrate

See: consumer price index; inflation rate; producer price index.

rate of interest Zinsrate; Verzinsung

See: interest rate.

rate of price increase Teuerungsrate; Preissteigerungsrate

rate of progress Fortschrittsrate

rate of return Kapitalverzinsung; Rendite; Ertrag; Rentabilität

The measure for the profitability of an investment, measured as the income obtained from an investment against its purchase price. For example: for bonds and preferred stock, current yield (dividend) divided by purchase price.

rate of return on equity Eigenkapitalrendite

Measure of the profitability of an investment, based not on total returns and total investment but on the amounts the equity owner expects to receive and has invested.

rate policy Tarifpolitik

rate regulation Tarifregelung

ratification Bestätigung; zum Inkrafttreten führende Genehmigung; Ratifizierung

The act of making something valid by formally ratifying or confirming it..

rating Schätzung; Klasse; Messung

In general: process of systematically assigning ranks to goods and services.

Credit, investment: evaluation of securities investment and credit risk by rating services such as Duff & Phelps, Fitch Investors Service, Moody's Investors Service, Standard & Poor's Corporation, and Value Line Investment Survey.

Insurance: using statistics, mortality tables, probability theory, experience, judgment, and mathematical analysis to establish the rates on which insurance premiums are based.

Advertising: percentage of a given population group consuming a medium at a particular moment. Generally used for broadcast media but can by applied to any medium. One rating point equals 1 percent of the potential viewing population.

ratio Verhältnis; Verhältniswert; Kennzahl

Algebra: the relationship between two quantities. It is expressed as the quotient of two numbers, or as two numbers separated by a colon (pronounced "to"). *Example*: the ratio of boys to girls in the class is 2:3.

ratio analysis Kennzahlenanalyse

An investigation of the financial performance of a company using a series of ratios.

There exists a wide variety of ratios. Some of the most important include: current ratio, quick ratio, activity ratio, receivable turnover, inventory turnover, return on assets, return on common stock equity, profit margin, debt ratio, equity ratio, debt to equity ratio, times interest earned, degree of financial leverage, earnings per share, price earnings ratio, book value per share.

ration Zuteilung; Ration; *(to ~)* zuteilen; mit Lebensmitteln versorgen

rational Vernunft-; vernünftig; verständig; rational

rational appeal Appel an Vernunftgründe

Message appeals that relate to the audience's self-interest and show that the product will produce the claimed benefits.

Example: appeals of product quality, economy, value, or performance.

rational decision-making model Modell der rationalen Entscheidungsfindung

Decision-making model that describes how individuals should behave in order to maximize some outcome. The six steps are:

1. Define the problem 2. Identify the decision 3. Allocate weights to the criteria 4. Develop the alternative 5. Evaluate the alternatives 6. Select the best alternative.

This model contains a number of assumption: 1. problem clarity, 2. known options, 3. clear preferences, 4. constant preferences, 5. no time or cost constraints, and 6. maximum payoff.

rationalization Rationalisierung

rationalize rationalisieren; vernunftmäßig erklären; rationalistisch handeln

rationing Zuteilung; Rationierung

Method of allocating a product when the quantity demanded exceeds the quantity available at a specific price, such as gasoline in wartime.

ratio systems Kennzahlensysteme

Mathematically or logically connected combinations of ratios, which are derived from planned values or actual data.

raw material Rohmaterial; Rohstoff; Ausgangsmaterial

Any primary or secondary material that is used to produce another product.

raw materials conglomerate Rohstoffkonzern; Rohstoffkonglomerat

raw materials production Rohstoffgewinnung

re in Sachen; bezüglich; betreffs; wegen

reach Reichweite; Strecke; Bereich; *(to ~)* reichen; ausstrecken; *(goal)* erreichen

Marketing: the degree of penetration into a target audience, either as an absolute number of individuals or as a percentage.

It measures the number of people who are likely to be exposed at least once to an ad in a given period of time. Reach counts each household only once even if they will see the ad 5 times during the campaign.

Example: if a television program has a "40% reach for women age 18-25," that means it reaches 40% of that target audience at least once during a given ad campaign.

reach an agreement übereinkommen

reach and frequency *(market penetration)* Reichweite und Häufigkeit

reactive change reaktive Änderung; rückwirkender Wandel

readiness Bereitschaft; Bereitwilligkeit; Schnelligkeit

readiness to assume risk Risikobereitschaft

readjust neu ordnen; *(company)* sanieren; neu anpassen; wieder in Ordnung bringen

readjustment Neuregelung; Umstellung

Stock corporation: The voluntary restructuring of a corporation's debt and capital structure by the stockholders themselves.

readmission Neuzulassung

readmittance Neueintrittserlaubnis

ready to negotiate verhandlungsbereit

Reaganomics Reaganomics

A set of conservative, free-market economic policies pursued by US President Ronald Reagan and his administration, 1981-1989.

real wirklich; echt; real; Grund-(Besitz)

Actual, as opposed to nominal; term in economics referring to measures such as price and income, which are corrected for inflation over time so as to permit a comparison of actual purchasing power.

RealAudio

Technology developed by Real Networks for the compression of audio multimedia.

real cash flow realer Cashflow

Cash flow is expressed in real terms if the current, or date 0, purchasing power of the cash flow is given.

real cost Realkosten

real estate Immobilien; Grundbesitz; Grundstück

Land and all physical property on, below or attached to the land; same as *realty*.

real estate fund Immobilienfonds

real estate investment trust (REIT) Immobilieninvestmentgesellschaft

An investment trust that invests in a variety of different real estate properties. Instead of investing in properties themselves, investors can buy shares in a REIT, and so reduce their risk.

real estate market Immobilienmarkt

The potential buyers and sellers of real property. This includes markets for various property types, such as housing market or the office market.

real estate sale Grundstücksverkauf

real growth reales Wachstum

realign neu ausrichten; neu aufstellen

realignment Neuausrichtung; Neuaufstellung

real income Realeinkommen; wirkliches Einkommen

The income measured in terms of the amount of goods and services it will buy, thus reflecting its purchasing power.

real interest rate realer Zinssatz

The interest rate from which the effects of inflation have been removed, calculated as the nominal interest rate minus the inflation rate.

The real interest rate shows an investor if the return on his investement is higher than the erosion in the value of the currency caused by inflation. With a bond yielding 9% and inflation of 3%, for instance, the real interest rate would be 6%.

realizability Realisierbarkeit

realizable realisierbar; ausführbar; *(convertible into capital)* kapitalisierbar; Veräußerungs-

realization *(awareness)* Erkenntnis; *(conversion into capital)* Kapitalisierung; *(conversion into fact)* Realisierung; *(goal)* Verwirklichung; Erzielung; Einsehen; Verstehen

realization of profit Gewinnerzielung

realize *(to be aware of)* erkennen; *(a goal)* realisieren; verwirklichen; *(capital)* kapitalisieren; zu Geld machen; *(profit)* erzielen; umsetzen; einsehen; verstehen

realized income Einkommenserzielung

reallocate umverteilen; neu zuteilen; neu bereitstellen

reallocation Umverteilung; Neuzuteilung; Umplatzierung

reallot repartieren; neu verteilen; wiederverteilen

real rate of return effektive Rendite

The return on an investment adjusted for inflation, which shows the return on investment expressed in actual purchasing power. For example, if an investment pays 6% annually and inflation is 2%, the real rate of return is 4% (6% - 2% = 4%).

real-space data collection Datensammlung im realen Raum

Takes place offline at points of purchase such as smart card and credit card readers and bar code scanners.

real-time chat Chat in Echtzeit

Internet: a means of having a quick written conversation with one or more people who are online at the same time. Web users type messages to each other in real time at a website.

real-time multimedia Multimedia in Echtzeit

Internet: Technology that offers opportunities such as distance learning and education, virtual reality, entertainment, and video/audio conferencing.

real-time profiling Echtzeitprofilerstellung

Internet: Occurs when special software tracks a user's movements through a Web site, then compiles and reports on the data at a moment's notice.

RealVideo

Technology developed by Real Networks for the compression of video multimedia.

real wage increase Reallohnzuwachs

real wage rate Reallohnsatz

real wages Reallohn

Economics: wages corrected for inflation over time so as to provide a measure of actual changes in purchasing power over time.

reap (ab)ernten; *(profits)* realisieren

reappoint wieder ernennen; neu bestätigen

reappointment Wiederernennung; Neueinstellung

reappraisal Neubewertung; Neuabschätzung; Neubeurteilung

reappraise neu bewerten; überprüfen; neu einschätzen

rearrangement Neuordnung; Neuregelung; Wiederherstellung; Neugestaltung

reasonable sinnvoll; *(fair)* billig

reassignment Rückübertragung; Wiederabtretung ; vernünftig; angemessen; reell

reassessment Neubewertung; Neufestsetzung; Aufwertung

Real estate: the process of updating the value estimate of property for tax purposes. Value estimates are revised regularly based on recent price changes and other data.

rebate Rabatt; Rückvergütung; Abzug; Preisnachlass; *(to ~)* Rabatt gewähren; nachlassen; abziehen

Marketing: a deduction taken from a payment after the full amount has been paid. A rebate it therefore differs from a discount which is deducted in advance of the payment.

Foreign trade: a full or partial rebate may be given on import duties paid on goods which are later re-exported.

rebound Wiederaufschwung; Reaktion; *(to ~)* zurückschnellen; *(recover)* sich erholen; neu-, wieder eingebunden

rebuild wiederaufbauen

recalculate nachrechnen; neu berechnen

recall *(product)* Rückruf; *(from a post)* Zurückberufung; *(memory)* Erinnerungsvermögen; *(loan)* Aufkündigung; *(to ~)* zurückrufen; *(from a post)* abberufen; abrufen; *(to remember)* sich erinnern; *(to give notice)* kündigen

Advertising: concept in marketing or audience research that measures a respondent´s ability to remember a particular event or experience. Recall can be aided or unaided

Product: the process when a manufacturer orders previously sold products to be returned to repair or replace defective parts.

recapitalization Neufinanzierung; Neukapitalisierung

Corporate finance: the reorganization of a company's capital structure, such as an exchange of bonds for stock, or of preferred stock for common stock.

recapiulate rekapitulieren; zusammenfassen

recapitulation Zusammenfassung; Rekapitulation

recapture *(market)* wiedererobern; zurückgewinnen; wiedererbeuten

receipt *(shipment)* Empfang; Erhalt; *(taking delivery)* Inempfangnahme; *(payment)* Quittung; Beleg; *(shipment)* Empfangsbescheinigung

A written acknowledgment that something of value has been received, often to evidence payment of an invoice. A receipt normally includes the payer's name, amount, date, and purpose of payment.

receipt book Quittungsblock; Belegheft

A book containing blank receipts and a duplicate that is retained after a receipt has been issued.

receivable (balance *sheet)* Forderung; ausstehend; offen; erhältlich

receivables *(balance sheet)* Forderungen; Debitoren; Außenstände; Kundenforderungen

See: accounts receivable, notes receivable.

receivables turnover Debitorenumschlag; Forderungsumschlag

An activity ratio measuring the ratio of credit sales to accounts receivable, based on the number of times average accounts receivable are collected in a year. If average outstanding receivables are collected in three months, the receivables turnover rate is four times per year.

receive empfangen; erhalten; vereinnahmen

receiver *(recipient)* Empfänger; Übernehmer; *(trust)* Einnehmer; *(telephone)* Hörer; *(radio)* Empfangsgerät; *(bankruptcy)* Konkursverwalter

Bankruptcy: a person, usually appointed by a court, who liquidates the assets of a bankrupt company or tries to preserve them. He takes possession of, but not title to, the assets of a business that is in a form of bankruptcy called receivership.

receivership Konkursverwaltung; Zwangsverwaltung; Amtszeit eines Konkursverwalters

The state of being under the administration of a receiver. After a bankruptcy, a court decides to remove the company in receivership from its owners, who lose their equity, and places it into the hands of a receiver. The task of the receiver is to protect the assets for the benefit of the creditors.

recession Konjunkturrückgang; Rezession; Wirtschaftsrückgang; Vertiefung; Zurücktreten

Term defined as two consecutive quarters of negative growth in the gross national product and a downturn in economic activity leading to significant reduction in employment and production, trade and investment.

recipient Empfänger; Empfangsberechtigter; empfänglich

recipient country Empfängerland

reciprocal gegenseitig; wechselseitig; beiderseits; reziprok(er Wert)

reciprocal buying wechselseitige Lieferbeziehungen

Any arrangement under which a seller of one product or service buys another product or service from one of his customers.

reciprocal effect Wechselwirkung; gegenseitige Wirkung

reciprocity Gegenseitigkeit

A relationship in which both sides agree to return the privileges granted by the other side.

reckon berechnen; kalkulieren; halten für

reckoning Abrechnung; Rechnen; Ansehen; Betrachten

The process of settling accounts by computations to achieve a total.

reclaim Rückforderung; Regenerierung; *(to ~)* zurückfordern; regenerieren; zurückgewinnen; kulturfähig machen; reklamieren

reclamation *(land)* Kultivierung; Urbarmachung; Besserung; Gewinnung; Wiedergewinnung; Rückgewinnung

reclassification Neuklassifizierung; Neueinstufung; Neueinteilung; Umstufung

reclassify neu klassifizieren; neu einstufen; umgruppieren; umstufen

recognition *(law)* Anerkennung; Erkennung

recommend *(to propose)* vorschlagen; *(testimonial)* empfehlen; *(to support)* befürworten; anvertrauen

recommendation *(proposal)* Vorschlag; *(testimonial)* Empfehlung; *(support)* Befürwortung; Vorzug

recommit neu verpflichten; sich neu binden; *(resources)* neu bereitstellen; wieder anvertrauen; neu übergeben

recompense *(service)* Entgelt; Belohnung; Vergeltung; Vergütung; *(damages)* Entschädigung; Wiedergutmachung; *(to ~)* entschädigen; vergüten; wieder-gutmachen

recompute neu errechnen; nachrechnen

reconcile versöhnen; *(accounts)* abstimmen; beilegen; in Übereinstimmung bringen

reconciliation Aus-; Versöhnung; *(dispute)* Beilegung; Ausgleich; Verbindung

The process of solving differences and bringing the parties involved back together.

reconsider neu erwägen; nachprüfen; neu bedenken; Meinung ändern; erörtern

reconsideration Neuerwägung; Nachprüfung; Meinungsänderung

reconsignment Rücksendung

reconstruct wieder aufbauen; *(enterprise)* neu gründen

reconstruction Wiederaufbau; *(business, enterprise)* Neugründung; Rekonstruktion

reconvert umwandeln; umstellen; umbauen; neu bekehren

record Aufzeichnung; Bericht; Niederlegung; *(document)* Urkunde; *(sports)* Rekord; Höchstleistung; *(gramophone)* Schallplatte; *(to ~)* aufzeichnen; niederlegen; *(to enter)* eintragen; registrieren; auf-; verzeichnen

record date *(payment of dividend)* Dividendentermin

Securities: date by which a shareholder must officially own shares in order to be entitled to a dividend.

recorder *(registrar)* Registrator; *(proceedings)* Protokollführer; *(electronics)* Aufnahmeapparat

record level Rekordstand

record profit Rekordgewinn

record result Rekordergebnis

record year Rekordjahr

recoup *(loss)* wieder einbringen; ersetzen; wiedergutmachen; entschädigen; abziehen; einbehalten

recourse *(indemnity)* Entschädigung; *(resort)* Rückgriff; *(appeal)* Rekurs; *(compensation)* Ersatzanspruch; *(legal process)* Inanspruchnahme; Zuflucht

The right of a lender to reclaim money and collateral from a borrower who has defaulted on a loan.

recover *(to get back)* wiederbekommen; -erlangen; -finden; *(debt)* einziehen; *(shipwreck)* bergen; *(health)* gesund werden; *(economy)* sich erholen; wieder ausgleichen; wiedergutmachen

recoverable *(debt)* eintreibbar; *(expenses)* erstattungsfähig

recovery *(possession)* Wiedererlangung; Zurückerlangung; *(health)* Gesundung; *(recuperation)* Erholung; *(shipwreck)* Bergung; *(money)* Eintreibung; Einziehung; Wiederherstellung

Economics: the phase in a business cycle when the economy comes out of a slump, economic activity picks up again, and the expansion phase of the cycle begins.

recovery period Abschreibungszeitraum

Depreciation: the period of time over which the cost of an asset may be written off, e.g. three years for a computer.

recreate erfrischen; sich erholen; *(to create new)* neu schaffen

recreation *(entertainment)* Freizeitvergnügen; Erfrischung; Erholung *(new creation)* Neuschaffung

recruit Neuling; Rekrut; *(labor)* neue Arbeitskraft; *(to ~)* rekrutieren; *(to enlist)* anwerben

recruiter Personalanwerber

HRM: person responsible for locating and obtaining new employees. The methods used include attending job fairs, developing advertising campaigns, and develop sources through referrals.

recruitment Rekrutierung; Anwerben

HRM: The process of seeking prospective new employees.

rectification Richtigstellung; Berichtigung; Rektifizierung

rectify richtig stellen; berichtigen; verbessern

recuperate sich erholen; gesundmachen; erlangen

recyclable wieder verwendbar; wieder verwertbar

recycle wiederaufbereiten; wiederverwerten; rückgewinnen

recycling Wiederverwertung; Rückgewinnung; Wiederverwendung; Recycling

The process by which materials are collected and used as raw materials for new products.

There are three steps in recycling: 1. Materials are source-separated and collected. 2. Materials are processed and manufactured into new products. 3. Consumers purchase the goods made with reprocessed materials

redeem einlösen; *(to buy back)* zurückkaufen; loskaufen; *(to amortize)* amortisieren; tilgen; ausgleichen

In general: buy back.

Finance: cash in, as a maturing note or bond.

redemption Einlösung; *(buying back)* Rückkauf; *(amortization)* Amortisierung; *(debt)* Tilgung; Erlösung; Ablösung; (~ sum) Ablösesumme

Debt: the process of regaining one´s possession by paying back a debt or fulfilling some other obligation.

Accounting: the acquisition by a corporation of its own stock in exchange for property.

redemption charge Tilgungsgebühr; *(investment fund)* Rücknahmespesen

Securities: commission charged by a mutual fund when redeeming shares.

redemption fee Aufschlag für vorzeitige Tilgung

Debt: a charge that has to be paid when an asset is repurchased or released from creditor claims.

redemption period Einlösungsfrist; Rückzahlungszeitraum

Debt: the period of time during which a former owner can redeem foreclosed property.

redemption price Rückkaufpreis; Rückzahlungskurs

redemption rate Rückzahlungsrate

redemption value Rückzahlungswert; Rückkaufswert

redeploy umgruppieren; umstrukturieren; *(resources)* neu einsetzen; auseinander ziehen; neu entfalten

redeployment Umgruppierung; Umstrukturierung; Neueinsatz; Neuverwendung

red goods rote Ware

Consumer goods that are consumed quickly and replaced at a fast rate. Red goods normally have a low profit margin.

rediscount Rediskont; Diskont; Abzinsung; *(to ~)* rediskontieren; diskontieren; erneut abzinsen

A way for financial institutions to generate cash by selling a security, such as a bill of exchange, which has already been discounted, i.e. sold for less than its face value.

rediscount capacity Rediskontvolumen

rediscount quota Rediskontkontingent

rediscount rate Rediskontsatz

Rate of interest charged to member banks when they borrow from the federal reserve system; also called discount rate.

rediscount volume Rediskontvolumen

redistribute neu verteilen; umverteilen

redistribution Neuverteilung; Umverteilung

red tape Bürokratismus; Papierkrieg; Amtsschimmel

A derisive term for excessive and unnecessary regulations or bureaucratic procedures.

reduce vermindern; reduzieren; *(a price)* ermäßigen; nachlassen; verbilligen; *(to shorten)* verkürzen; *(to cut)* kürzen; zurückschrauben; *(to lessen)* mindern; herabmindem; herabsetzen; senken

reduced consumption Minderkonsum

reduced expenditure Minderausgabe

reduced working hours Kurzarbeit

reduction Verminderung; Reduzierung; *(alleviation)* Ermäßigung; *(restriction)* Abbau; *(deduction)* Abzug; *(lowering)* Herabsetzung; Senkung; Verkürzung; *(diminishment)* Verringerung; *(benefits)* Kürzung

reduction of interest Zinsermäßigung

reduction of jobs Arbeitsplatzverlust; Arbeitsplatzreduzierung

reduction of the interest rate Zinssenkung

redundancies Stellenlosigkeit; freigesetzte Arbeitskraft; Entlassungen

Involuntary job losses which occur due to a reduction in manpower requirements on the part of firm.

reelection Wiederwahl

reemployment Neuanstellung; Neuengagement; Wiedereinstellung

reengineering Reengineering

Fundamental rethinking and radical redesign of business processes to achieve dramatic improvements in critical measures of performance such as cost, quality, service and speed.

reestablish *(relations)* wiederherstellen; *(business)* neu etablieren; *(value)* neu festlegen; *(reputation)* wieder erwerben; neu gründen

reestablishment Neugründung; Neueinsetzung

refer verweisen; sich beziehen; sich berufen; zurückführen auf; zuschreiben; anspielen auf

referee *(for job)* Referenz; *(law)* (Schieds-) Richter

A person to whom the court refers a pending case, including power and duty to take testimony, determine issues of fact, and report the findings.

referee in bankruptcy Konkursrichter

reference Anspielung; Bezugnahme; Hinweis; *(testimonial)* Empfehlung; Verweisung; Aktennummer

General: something that refers or points to something else, or acts as a connection or a link between two things. The objects it links may be concrete, such as books or locations, or abstract, such as data, thoughts, or memories

Employment: formal recommendation by a former employer to a potential future employer describing the person's qualifications and dependability.

reference group Bezugsgruppe

A group to which an individual belongs or wants to belong and with whose norms he is likely to conform.

reference number Bezugszahl; Aktennummer

reference price Referenzpreis; Bezugspreis

Prices that buyers carry in their minds and refer to when they look at a given product.

reference product Kontrollprodukt; Referenzprodukt

referent power Macht durch Vorbildcharakter

Referent power develops out of admiration of another and a desire to be like that person. If one admires someone to the point of modeling his behavior and attitudes after this person, this person possesses referent power over him.

referral Überweisung; Empfehlung

referral revenue Empfehlungseinnahmen

Sales from customers referred to the firm by current customers.

referrals Überweisungen; Referrals

Internet: website logs showing where visitors came from, particularly what search engines or directories. Referrals are an important way to find out what source is generating the most traffic.

refer to erwähnen; verweisen; *(mention)* sprechen von; *(person)* sich wenden an; *(relate to)* sich beziehen auf

refinance refinanzieren; umfinanzieren

refinancing Refinanzierung; Umfinanzierung; *(debt)* Umschuldung

Practice of taking out a fresh loan to repay current debts in full, when their combined repayments are no longer manageable.

It usually implies selling a new bond issue to provide funds for redemption of a maturing issue, or placing a new mortgage on a house that retires an old mortgage. Refinancing is generally used to raise cash, reduce interest rates, or both.

refine veredeln; verfeinern; *(oil)* raffinieren

refinement Veredelung; Raffination; Verfeinerung; Vervollkommnung; *(personal quality)* Bildung; Feinheit; Raffinesse

refinery Raffinerie

reflate *(loan)* neu auflegen; *(ship)* wieder flott machen; *(currency)* neu floaten.

reflation Reflation

The intentional reversal of deflation through a monetary action by a government

reflationary expansiv; stimulierend; ankurbelnd

reform Reform; *(rearrangement)* Umgestaltung; Neugestaltung; Besserung; *(reconstruction)* Umbau; *(new ordering)* Neuordnung; *(to ~)* reformieren; umgestalten; neu gestalten; umbauen; bessern

reforward nachschicken

refreezing Einfrieren

refreshment Erfrischung; Stärkung

refuel auftanken; nachtanken; *(economy)* wieder ankurbeln

refund Rückvergütung; Rückerstattung; Zurückzahlung; *(amount)* Erstattungsbetrag; *(to ~)* rückvergüten; (zurück)erstatten; zurückzahlen

The reimbursement of the purchase price of a good or service, for reasons such as faults in manufacturing or dissatisfaction with the service provided

refundable rückzahlbar; erstattungsfähig

refundable credit erstattungsfähiger Kredit

A tax credit that is not limited by the amount of an individual's tax liability.

refunding Erstattung; Refinanzierung; Umfinanzierung

Retailing: the practice of returning the sales price to a customer who is dissatisfied with a product.

Finance: a way of obtaining new funds needed to retire existing debts; same as refinancing.

refusal Ablehnung; (Ver-)Weigerung; Ablehnungsrecht; *(negative response)* ablehnende Antwort; abschlägiger Bescheid; *(payment)* Verweigerung

regime Regierung(-ssystem); Verwaltung; *(contract)* Güterrecht

regimentation Organisierung; Reglementierung

region Region; Bereich; *(area)* Gebiet; Gegend

regional regional; örtlich

regional economic integration regionale wirtschaftliche Integration

Agreements among countries in a geographic region to reduce and ultimately remove tariff and nontariff barriers to the free flow of goods, services, and factors of production between each other.

regional economic policy regionale Wirtschaftspolitik; Standortpolitik

regional office Regionalbüro

regional theory Standorttheorie

register Register; Verzeichnis; *(record)* Journal; *(account book)* Kontobuch; Schieber; *(to ~)* eintragen; registrieren; *(letter)* einschreiben lassen; *(to record)* verzeichnen; erfassen; erkennen lassen

registered check Bankscheck

A check issued and guaranteed by a bank for a customer who provides the funds for the payment of the check.

registered company eingetragene Gesellschaft

Stock exchange: a company that has issued securities and filed a registration statement with the Securities and Exchange Commission in the US, and which must therefore comply with SEC disclosure requirements.

registered mail Einschreibesendung; Einschreiben

Mail item that is registered by the post office when sent in order to assure safe delivery.

registered share Namensaktie

registrar Standesbeamter; Urkundenbeamter; Registerrichter; Registerführer

Real estate: person who is responsible for maintaining official records.

Securities: an organisation charged with maintaining a company's share register.

Internet: a company specialized in the registering of domain names with the InterNIC.

registration Registrierung; Eintragung; *(military)* Erfassung; *(hotel)* Anmeldung

Securities: process of reviewing securities to be sold on a stock exchange by the Securities and Exchange Commission. The registration statement must contain detailed financial and operational information about the company.

Internet: process whereby an individual subscribes to a site or requests further information by filling in contact details and his needs using an electronic form.

registration instruction Meldevorschrift

registration of a domain name Registrierung des Domain-Namens

Internet: process of reserving a unique web address that can be used to refer to the company web site.

registration ordinance Meldebestimmung

registration statement Antrag auf Börsenzulassung

Securities: Registratition that discloses all the pertinent information concerning the corporation that wants to make a security offering. The statement is filed with regulatory authorities.

regression Rückschritt; Regression

regression analysis Regressionsanalyse

A statistical method for determining the relationship between a dependent variable and one or more independent variables.

regressive zurückschreitend; regressiv

regroup umgruppieren; neu gruppieren

regular regelmäßig; regulär; ordnungsmäßig; Berufssoldat; Stammkunde

regular advertiser Dauerklient; Dauerkunde; Dauerkundin

regular customer Stammkunde; Stammkundin; Dauerkunde; Dauerkundin

regularity Regelmäßigkeit; *(legality)* Ordnungsmäßigheit

regularize (rechtlich) regeln; gesetzlich festlegen

regular rate Normaltarif; normale Geschwindigkeit; normale Rate

regulate regulieren; lenken; ordnen; regeln

regulated reguliert; geordnet; geregelt

regulation Regulierung; *(rule)* Vorschrift; Bestimmung; Regelung; Ausführungsverordnung

Legislation: a rule used to carry out a law, which play an important role in European legislation, as regulations are directly applicable in all member states.

regulation of accounting standards Regulierung der Bilanzierungsrichtlinien

regulation of financial markets Regulierung der Finanzmärkte

regulation of natural monopolies Bestimmungen natürlicher Monopole

regulation and pricing Regulierung und Preisbildung

regulator Ordner; *(supervision)* Aufsichtsbehörde; *(control)* Überwachungsstelle; Regulator

regulatory regulativ; regelnd; bestimmend

regulatory agency *(control)* Aufsichtsbehörde; *(competency)* zuständige Behörde

regulatory framework rechtliche Rahmenvorschriften; rechtliche Rahmenbedingungen

regulatory system Regulierungssystem

rehabilitation Rehabilitation; Eingliederung; Wiederaufbau; Wiederherstellung

rehire wieder einstellen; wieder anstellen

reimburse zurückerstatten; zurückbezahlen; *(to compensate)* entschädigen

reimbursement Zurückerstattung; Rückvergütung; *(compensation)* Entschädigung; Erstattung

Specific sum an employer awards an employee as repayment for expenditures, such as travel and entertainment expenses.

reinforce *(physically)* (ver)stärken; *(policy, argument)* unterstützen

reinforcement *(physical)* Verstärkung; *(policy, argument)* Unterstützung

reinforcement theory Verstärkungstheorie

Behavioristic approach that argues that behavior is conditioned by reinforcement, i.e. any consequence that, when immediately following a response, increases the probability that the behaviour will be repeated.

reinstate wiedereinsetzen; wieder einstellen

reinstatement Weiterversicherung; *(of employee)* Wiedereinstellung; *(law)* Wiederherstellung

Insurance: the process by which a life insurance company puts back in force a policy that had lapsed because of nonpayment of renewal premiums.

reinsurance Rückversicherung

An insurance for an insurance company, which consists of an agreement between the companies under which one accepts all or part of a risk or loss of the other.

This procedure allows an insurance company to take on clients whose coverage would be too risky for it alone.

reinsure rückversichern

reintegration Neuintegrierung; Wiedervereinigung; Neuergänzung

reintermediation Mittelrückfluss ins Banksystem

The reintroduction of an intermediary between end users (consumers) and a producer. The term applies especially to instances in which disintermediation has occurred first

reinvest wieder anlegen; reinvestieren; umdisponieren

reinvestment Reinvestition; Neuanlage; Ersatzinvestition

The use of income earned from an investment to purchase additional shares of that investment.

reinvestment rate Reinvestitionrate

reject *(defective goods)* Ausschussware; Ausgemusterter; *(to ~) (to refuse)* ablehnen; *(to repudiate)* abweisen; zurückweisen; *(to cull)* aussondern; ausscheiden

rejection Zurückweisung; *(refusal to accept)* Annahmeverweigerung; *(repudiation)* Ablehnung; *(refusal)* Absage; Ausschussartikel

related to a specific field fachbezogen

relation *(connection)* Beziehung; Zusammenhang; *(reference)* Bezug; *(ratio)* Verhältnis; Erzählen; Erzählung

relationship Beziehung; Verhältnis

relationship capital Wert der bestehenden Kundenbeziehungen

Firm's ability to build and maintain relationships with customers, suppliers, and partners: The total value of these relationships to a firm in the long term is its relationship capital.

relationship conflict Beziehungskonflikt

Focuses on interpersonal relationships.

relationship marketing Relationship Marketing; Beziehungsmarketing

Process of establishing, maintaining, enhancing, and commercializing relationships with customers and other stakeholders. It has a long-term customer orientation, involves ongoing interactive communication between a firm and selected stakeholders, and focuses on individual customers 1:1.

relative frequency relative Häufigkeit

In a series of observations, the relative frequency of occurrence of an event is the number of times the event happened over the total number of observations made.

relatively efficient markets verhältnismäßig effiziente Märkte

relative purchasing power parity (RPPP) relative Kaufkraftparität

Idea that the rate of change in the price level of commodities in one country relative to the price level in another determines the rate of change of the exchange rate between the two countries' currencies.

relative strength relative Stärke

Securities: a stock's price movement over the past year as compared to a market index (the S&fP 500).

A value below 1.0 means the stock shows relative weakness in price movement (underperformed the market); a value above 1.0 means the stock shows relative strength over the 1-year period.

relativism Relativismus

Ethics: view that the meaning and value of human beliefs and behaviors have no absolute reference, but that humans understand and evaluate beliefs and behaviors only in terms of their historical and cultural context.

relax entspannen; sich ausruhen; *(to losen)* lockern; schwächen; nachlassen

relaxation Entspannung; Erleichterung; Lockerung; Vergnügen

release Freigabe; Loslösen; Auslösen; *(press)* Veröffentlichung; *(document)* Verzichtserklärung; Übertragungsurkunde; *(resources)* Freistellung; *(to ~) (to give up a claim)* Verzicht erklären; *(to confer right to use)* freigeben; *(to publish)* veröffentlichen; *(to transfer)* übertragen; *(to unburden)* entlasten

release clause Teillöschungsbewilligung

Mortgage: a provision in a mortgage contract that gives the owner the right to pay off a portion of the principal.

relevance Belang; Sachdienlichkeit; Erheblichkeit; Bedeutung

A measure of how closely a given object (file, web page, database record, etc.) matches a user´s search for information.

Relevance has at least three dimensions: the information is available at the right time, the information enables the user to make predictions, the information has provides information about earlier expectations.

relevance ranking Ranking nach Relevanz

Internet: search engine query results are often returned in order of relevance (i.e., the most likely to be the item that the user is seeking).

relevant market relevanter Markt

relevant brand set Markenrahmen

The brand names of all articles that a consumer knows and considers when plans a purchase in a specific product category.

reliability Zuverlässigkeit; Verlässlichkeit; *(information)* Glaubwürdigkeit; *(credit risk)* Kreditwürdigkeit; Bonität

Auditing: the degree of confidence that the financial records have been prepared accurately.

Financial accounting: information that accurately presents the facts. Reliability consists of verifiability, representational faithfulness and neutrality.

reliable zuverlässig; verläßlich; *(trustworthy)* vertrauenswürdig; *(sure)* sicher; *(information)* glaubwürdig; *(credit risk)* kreditwürdig

relief *(feeling)* Erleichterung; *(burden)* Entlastung; Hilfe; Unterstützung; Abwechslung; Relief

relief action Hilfsaktion

relieve erleichtern; *(guard)* ablösen

relinquish aufgeben; *(to abandon)* verlassen; *(to cede)* überlassen; abtreten; *(to renounce)* verzichten; Verzicht leisten

relocate umsiedeln; verlagern; neu errichten; neu unterbringen

Move to another location, such as to move a business or a residence.

remain zurückbleiben; übrig bleiben

remaining restlich; übrig(geblieben)

remaining period restliche Zeit; *(contract)* Restlaufzeit

remaining time to maturity Restlaufzeit

remargin nachschießen

remark Bemerkung; Beachtung; *(to ~)* bemerken; Bemerkung machen

remedy *(legal, financial)* Rechtsmittel; Abhilfe; Mittel; *(contracts)* Rechtsbehelf; Toleranz; Remedium; *(to ~)* abhelfen

Legal: means by which a right or privilege is enforced, a violation is prevented, or a wrong is redressed.

remind erinnern; *(obligation)* mahnen

reminder Mahnung; *(letter)* Mahnbrief; Mahnschreiben

reminder advertising Erinnerungswerbung

Advertising used to keep consumers thinking about a product.

remit überweisen; weiterleiten

remittance *(payment)* Zahlung; *(by mail)* Geldsendung; *(money order)* Geldanweisung; (Geld-)Überweisung; *(electronic transfer)* Geldübermittlung

Money sent from one place or person to another, usually as payment for a product or service.

remittance order Überweisungsauftrag

remittance coupon book Überweisungsbuch

remittance slip Überweisungsträger

remnant Überbleibsel; (Über-)Rest

remodel ummodellieren; *(building)* umbauen; *(company)* umorganisieren

remove entfernen

remunerate honorieren; dotieren; *(to reimburse)*entschädigen; vergüten; *(to reward)* belohnen

remuneration Dotierung; Besoldung; *(for work)* Arbeitsentgelt; Vergütung; Honorar; Ent-; Belohnung

Monetary compensation for services rendered, can be direct, such as wages, or indirects such as fringe benefits.

remuneration for executives Lohn für Führungskräfte/ leitende Angestellte

render abgeben; *(to cede)* aufgeben; *(payment)* bezahlen; *(to give)* leisten; *(to make)* machen; übergeben; vorlegen; übersetzen; auslassen

renegotiate erneut verhandeln; neuverhandeln

Revise the terms of a contract in a legally binding fashion.

renegotiation Neuverhandlung; erneute Verhandlung

renew erneuern; *(connection)* wieder erstellen; *(to extend)* verlängern; prolongieren

renewable erneuerungsfähig; *(contract)* verlängerungsfähig; *(resources)* nachwachsend

renewal Erneuerung; Verlängerung; (Wechsel-)Prolongation

rent *(charge)* Miete; Pacht; Mietzins; *(to ~) (to rent from someone)* mieten; *(to rent* to *someone)* vermieten; verpachten

Economics: the premium that the owner of a resource receives over and above its opportunity cost.

rental Mieteinnahme; Miet-; Pachtbetrag

rental income Mietertrag; Pachtertrag

rental rate Leihgebühr; Mietspreis

Regularpayment for the use of a property.

rented apartment Mietwohnung

rent increase Mietsteigerung

reopen wiedereröffnen; wieder in Betrieb setzen; neu erschlossen *(negotiation)* wiederaufnehmen

reopening Wiedereröffnung

reorder *(new order)* Neubestellung; *(additional order)* Nachbestellung; Neuordnung; erneute Geldanweisung; *(to ~) (to order again)* neu bestellen; *(to order more)* nachbestellen

reorder point Nachbestellungspunkt; kritischer Lagerbestand

The inventory level at which new orders must be placed. The reorder point has to be set taking into consideration the time delay in receiving new inventory, the typical rate of inventory consumption, and the stock out cost.

reorganization Neugestaltung; Umorganisation; Neuordnung; *(company)* Sanierung; *(official restructuring)* Neugründung; Umstrukturierung

Bankruptcy law: financial restructuring of a company after it has filed for protection from creditors under Chapter 11 of the US bankruptcy code.

reorganization bond Gewinnobligation

reorganization measure Sanierungs-maßnahme

reorganization offer Sanierungsangebot

reorganization program Sanierungs-programm

reorganization strategy Sanierungs-strategie

reorganize umorganisieren; *(to reshape)* neu gestalten; *(company - internal reorganization)* sanieren; *(company - official restructuring)* neu gründen; umstrukturieren; umgestalten

repair Reparatur; Ausbesserung;; Wiederherstellung; baulicher Zustand; *(to ~)* reparieren; ausbessern; instand setzen; wiederherstellen; sich begeben; ausbessern; wiedergutmachen

repairs Reparaturen; Instandsetzung

The expenditure for general upkeep to maintain the property close to the original condition, without extending its useful life, as distinguished from capital improvements.

repairman Techniker; Mechaniker; *(automotive)* Autoschlosser; Handwerker

repatriate Repatriierter; Heimkehrer; Umsiedler; *(to ~)* repatriieren; in die Heimat zurückbringen

Executive or other person who returns to his home country after an extended period abroad.

repatriation Wiedereinbürgerung; Rückführung

Finance: Moving the financial assets or profits of an organization or individual from a foreign country to the home country.

repay zurückzahlen; nochmals bezahlen; vergüten; *(to retaliate)* vergelten

repayable rückzahlbar; nochmals fällig

repayment Rückzahlung; Rückvergütung; *(debt)* Tilgung; *(retaliation)* Vergeltung

repayment amount Tilgungsbetrag

repayment period Rückzahlungsfrist

repeal Widerruf; *(rescission)* Aufhebung; *(to ~)* widerrufen; *(to rescind)* aufheben

repeat business Wiederholungsgeschäft; *(additional sales)* Nachverkäufe

replace *(compensation)* wiederbeschaffen; *(to refund)* wiedererstatten; *(substitution)* ersetzen

replaceable ersetzbar; wieder beschaffbar

replacement *(substitute)* Ersatz; Ersetzung; *(compensation)* Wiederbeschaffung; *(person)* Ersatzperson; Nachfolger; Stellvertreter; *(accounting)* Anlagenerneuerung

replacement cost Ersatzkosten; Wiederbeschaffungskosten; Wiederherstellungskosten

The cost of replacing property without deduction for depreciation.

replacement cost accounting Buchführung zu Wiederbeschaffungskosten

Accounting method allowing additional depreciation on part of the difference between the original cost and current replacement cost of a depreciable asset..

replacement investment Ersatzinvestition; Reinvestition; Erhaltungsinvestition

replacement period Ersatzzeitraum

Periods for tax-free gain on the replacement of certain assets under special circumstances, such as inventory interruption, involuntary conversion, sale of principal residence.

replacement value Wiederbeschaffungswert; Erneuerungswert

Current cost of replacing the firm's assets.

report Bericht; *(oral report)* Vortrag; *(news)* Meldung; ungewisse Nachricht; Gerücht; Gutachten; *(to ~)* berichten; vortragen; melden

reportable berichtspflichtig

reporter Berichterstatter; Reporter; *(law court)* Schriftführer; Protokollführer

reporting Berichterstattung, Berichtwesen

General: Give an account or provide a detailed statement about an occurrence or situation.

Management: Reporting ensures that statements are made, written and if possible also oral, concerning about how far individual reporting units have reached their objectives, where they have come up with variances, what the most important reasons of these are, and what *corrective actions* management has taken to deal with them.

reporting currency Rechnungslegungswährung

Currency in which a company prepares its financial statements; if it has foreign subsidiaries, their statements have to be translated.

reposition neu positionieren; repositionieren

repositioned product neu positioniertes Produkt

A current product that is either targeted to different markets or promoted for new uses.

repositioning Neupositionierung; Umpositionierung

repossession Wiederinbesitznahme; Rückkaufvereinbarung

Act by which a seller takes back property for which payments have not been made according to contract.

represent erklären; klarmachen; eindringlich vorhalten; *(substitute)* vertreten; *(description)* darstellen; *(constituency)* repräsentieren

representation Vertretung; *(substituting)* Stellvertretung; Repräsentation; *(description)* Darstellung; Schilderung; *(constituency)* Vertretung

representation of interests Interessenvertretung

representative typisches Beispiel; *(person)* Stellvertreter; Repräsentant; Bevollmächtigter; Agent; *(congress)* Abgeordneter; *(sales)* Vertreter; repräsentativ; darstellend

representative democracy repräsentative Demokratie

Political system in which citizens periodically elect individuals to represent them in government.

representative heuristic Heuristik nach Analogiebildung

Assessing the likelihood of an occurrence by drawing analogies and seeing identical situations in which they don't exist.

Example: managers frequently predict the performance of a new product by relating it to a previous product's success.

representative participation (Arbeitnehmer-)Mitbestimmung

Workers participate in organizational decision making through a small group of representative employees.

The goal of representative participation is to redistribute power within an organization, putting labor on a more equal footing with the interests of management and stockholders. The two most common forms are works council and board representatives.

reprimand Verweis; schwerer Tadel; *(to ~)* streng tadeln; zurechtweisen

reprint Wiederabdruck; Wiederholungsdruck; *(new edition)* Neuauflage; Faksimile; *(to ~)* wieder abdrucken; neu drucken; nachdrucken

reproduce *(letter)* kopieren; *(to make multiple copies)* vervielfältigen; fortpflanzen; wieder hervorbringen

reproduction costs Wiederherstellungskosten

The costs that have to be incurred to make an exact duplication of a product. Whilst replacement requires the same functional utility, reproduction is an exact duplication.

repudiate zurückweisen; ablehnen

repudiation Zurückweisung; Ablehnung; Nichtanerkennung

The rejection or renunciation of a duty or obligation arising from a contract.

repurchase Rückkauf; Wiederkauf; *(to ~)* zurückkaufen; wiederkaufen

repurchase agreement Rückkaufvertrag

Short-term, often overnight, sales of government securities with an agreement to repurchase the securities at a slightly higher price.

reputable angesehen; respektiert; *(trustworthy)* vertrauenswürdig; ehr-; achtbar

reputation Leumund; Ruf; Ansehen; Ruhm; Ehre

Distinction earned in a society by meeting approved societal standards; esteem, position, character, distinction, or renown someone or something enjoys in society.

request Bitte; *(official written request)* Gesuch; *(invitation, challenge)* Aufforderung; *(procurement)* Anforderung; Nachfrage; *(to ~)* bitten; ersuchen; auffordern; anfordern

require *(to demand)* verlangen; *(to need)* benötigen; brauchen; bedürfen

required rate of return angestrebte Mindestverzinsung

requirement *(demand)* Forderung; *(quality)* erforderliche Eigenschaft; Erfordernis; *(condition)* Bedingung; *(need)* Bedürfnis; Bedarf; Voraussetzung

requisite Erfordernis; erforderlich; notwendig

requisition Anforderung; Verlangen; *(to ~) (to make a request)* anfordern; *(to seize)* erfassen; mit Beschlag belegen; requirieren

requisition slip Anforderungsschein

Production: a form sent by a company unit to the supply or materials department requesting certain materials.

reroute umleiten

rerouting Umleitung

resale Wiederverkauf; *(by default)* Selbsthilfeverkauf; *(second band)* Verkauf aus zweiter Hand; Wiederverkaufs-

reshedule *(production)* neu einteilen; *(loan)* umschulden; *(time)* neu ansetzen; neu planen

resheduling *(production)* Neueinteilung der Produktionszeit; *(loan)* Umschuldung; Neuplanung

rescind *(rule)* aufheben; *(sale)* rückgängig machen; *(agreement)* annullieren

research Forschung; Erforschung; genaue Untersuchung; *(survey result)* Erhebung; *(to ~)* forschen; erforschen; nachforschen; untersuchen

Science: the process of systematically investigating something by gathering, recording, and analyzing data.

research and development (R&D) Forschung und Entwicklung (F&E)

Marketing: the process of creating and dveloping new products and solutions from their inception until production.

research assignment Forschungsauftrag; *(project)* Forschungsaufgabe

research center Forschungszentrum

research department Forschungsabteilung

Organization: department within a company whose primary responsibility is conducting research.

research engineer Forschungsingenieur

research expenditure Forschungsaufwand

research facility Forschungsanlage

research grant Forschungsbeihilfe; -zuschuss

research institute Forschungsinstitut; Forschungsanstalt

research program Forschungsprogramm

research project Forschungsprojekt

research study Forschungsstudie; Forschungsarbeit

research team Forschungsteam

resell wiederverkaufen; weiterverkaufen

reseller Wiederverkäufer

Individuals and organizations who buy goods and services to resell them at a profit.

reseller market Wiederverkäufermarkt

reservation Vorbestellung; Reservierung; *(of company)* Vorbehalt; Vorbehaltsklausel; Zurückhalten

Booking: the written record or promise that certain services, such as accommodation, are secured in advance.

Reluctance: doubt or suspicion about something or someone.

reserve Reserve; *(capital)* Rücklage; Rückstellung; Einschränkung; Zurückhaltung; *(to ~)* reservieren;

zurückstehen; *(to book)* buchen; *(judgment)* vorbehalten; *(seat)* belegen; zurückbehalten; aufheben

Accounting: part of retained earnings used to pay for such positions as dividends, contingencies, or improvements.

Banking: cash and deposits maintained by a commercial bank to meet reserve requirements.

Economy: gold and foreign currency held by governments to pay for imports and foreign debts.

reserve adequacy Zulänglichkeit von Reserven

reserve assets Währungsreserven; Währungsguthaben; Mindestreserven

reserve currency Reservewährung

reserved reserviert; *(bebavior)* zurückhaltend; *(seat)* belegt

reserve fund Reservefonds; Reservemittel

reserve liability Nachschusspflicht

reserve position Rücklagenposition

reserve ratio Deckungssatz

reserve requirements Mindestreserveanforderungen

reserves Reservemittel

reserve system Reservesystem

reservoir Behälter; Reservoir; *(lake)* Staubecken; Speicher

reshipment Rücksendung

residence Aufenthalt(sort); Wohnsitz

resident Gebietsansässiger; Ansässiger; Einwohner; Hausgast; in einer Dienstwohnung lebend; wohnhaft; ansässig

A person who lives in a country and is liable for tax there.

resident alien Ausländer mit Aufenthaltsgenehmigung

A person who has permanent resident status but has not citizenship.

resident buyer Indentkunde

A buyer with an office in an important merchandise center.

residual Restgröße; Rest-(Betrag); restlich

residual amount Restbetrag

residual dividend approach Residualdividenden-Ansatz

Approach that suggests that a firm pay dividends if and only if acceptable investment opportunities for those funds are currently unavailable.

residual value Restwert; Veräußerungswert; Schrottwert

Depreciation: the estimated value of a capital asset at the end of its useful life.

resign resignieren; *(office)* aufgeben; anvertrauen; sich anfinden; zurücktreten; *(job)* kündigen

resignation Rücktritt(-sgesuch); Resignation; *(office)* Aufgabe; *(job)* Kündigung; Resignation

resistance Widerstand; *(material)* Resistenz

resolution Entschließung; Vorsatz; Entschlossenheit; Standfestigkeit; *(document)* Beschluß; Beschlußfassung; Resolution

General: a formal decision by a governing body, such as a corporation's board of directors.

Computing: a measure for the sharpness of a screen. High resolution implies more pixel per inch and higher quality.

resolve Resolution; Entschlossenheit; *(resolution)* Vorsatz; *(to ~)* sich entschließen; entscheiden; entschlossen sein; sich etwas vornehmen; beheben; beseitigen; überwinden

resort Ferien-; Bade-; Urlaubsort

resort to greifen nach; gebrauchen; ergreifen; sich begeben nach

resource *(means)* Mittel; *(procurement)* Bezugsquelle; *(reserves)* Vorräte;

Besitz ; Ausweg ; Zuflucht ; *(expedient)* Hilfsquelle

resource management Betriebsmittelverwaltung; Ressourcenmanagement

respect Achtung; Respekt; *(reference)* Hinsicht; Beziehung; *(to ~)* beachten; berücksichtigen

respectable ehr-; achtbar**;** respektabel; seriös; schicklich; beachtlich

respite Aufschub; Frist; Atempause; aufschieben; erleichtern

respond *(survey)* antworten; reagieren; eingehen auf

respondent Antragsgegner; Beklagter; *(survey)* Respondent

respondent authenticity Echtheit des Befragten

Internet: disadvantage of online research in which it is difficult to determine that respondents are who they say they are.

response *(answer)* Antwort; Beantwortung; Reaktion

response projection *(advertising)* Rücklaufplanung

Advertising: the total expected response to an advertisement.

responsibility Verantwortung; Verantwortlichkeit; *(competency)* Verantwortungsbereich; *(liability)* Haftung; Zuständigkeit

responsibility accounting Kostenrechnung nach Verantwortungsbereichen

Management system where the whole management accounting system is constructed on the principle of responsibility.

Since managers are also responsible for the financial results, it is important to ensure, through the creation of cost centers, cost objects and contribution accounting, that clear distinctions in the reporting are made between costs, output and revenue, as well as cost allocations applying a key or imputed figures which are directly and independently controllable during the space of one year by the person responsible.

responsibility for risk Risikohaftung

rest Rest; Restbestand; *(recuperation)* Rast; Ruhe; Pause; Reserve; *(balance sheet)* Rechnungssaldo; *(to ~)* rasten; ruhen; sich ausruhen; erfrischen; stützen; liegen; ruhen

restaurant Restaurant; Gaststätte

restitute zurückerstatten

restitution *(of price)* Rückerstattung

Law: the act of restoring something to its rightful owner.

restock aufstocken; Lager ergänzen

restore *(to give back)* zurückgeben; wiederbringen; *(to original condition)* restaurieren; instand setzen; *(rights)* wiedereinsetzen; *(to reimburse)* wiedererstatten; *(to replace)* ersetzen; heilen; stärken; zurückgeben

restrain *(to hold back)* zurückhalten; *(to restrict)* beschränken; *(to hinder)* hindern; hemmen

restraining forces hindernde Kräfte

Forces that hinder movement away from the existing equilibrium.

restraint *(reticence)* Zurückhaltung; *(restriction)* Beschränkung; *(inhibition)* Hemmung; *(obstade)* Hemmnis; *(handicap)* Behinderung; *(control)* Zügelung ; Zwang

restrict einschränken; beschränken

restricted cash Termineinlagen; Termingelder

restriction Einschränkung; Beschränkung

restrictive covenant restriktive Vereinbarung

Financing: loan provisions that place constraints on the operations of borrowers.

restructure umstrukturieren; neu gliedern

restructuring Neugliederung; Umstellung

Organization: reorganizing of a company that can change its composition and operations completely.

result Ergebnis; Erfolg; Resultat; *(to ~)* resultieren; sich ergeben; enden; hinauslaufen

result testing Erfolgskontrolle

résumé Zusammenfassung; Resümee; *(vita)* Lebenslauf

A document containing information about a person that is relevant to his potential employer, such as personal background, education, and work experiences.

A resmume can be structured chronologically or free form. The basic purpose of a resume is to market the individual to obtain an interview for employment.

resume *(activity)* wieder aufnehmen; wiedergewinnen; übernehmen; zusammenfassen; *(position)* wiedereinnehmen

retail Einzelhandel; -verkauf; direkt verkaufen; *(to ~)* im Einzelhandel verkaufen

The commercial activity of selling products and services to the general public as the ultimate consumer.

retail chain Einzelhandelskette

retail credit Einzelhandelskredit; Konsumentenkredit; Kundenkredit

Credit granted by a retailer to his customer for the payment of purchases.

retailer Kleinverkäufer; Einzelhändler

A business that purchases products in order to sell them to ultimate consumers, the general public.

retailer cooperative Einzelhandelsgenossenschaft

Contractual vertical marketing system in which retailers organize a jointly owned business to carry on joint wholesaling.

retail house Einzelhandelsgeschäft

retailing Einzelhandel; Verkauf an Endverbraucher

All activities involved in selling goods or services directly to final consumers for their personal, non-business use.

Retailing is a general concept that involves selling many different products and services to a wide variety of customers, from a store location or direct through vending machines, mail order, and many more.

retail inventory method Inventurmethoden im Einzelhandel

Inventory technique using either the physical inventory of counting merchandise on hand or the book inventory system.

retail market Einzelhandelsmarkt

Market in which products and services are sold directly to the general public as end-user customer.

retail outlet Verkaufsstelle; Ladengeschäft

Any form of store or other outlet selling merchandise and/or services directly to the general public.

retail park Einkaufszentrum

Organized cluster of retailers located either at the edge of town or out of town. The provision of car parks and other extra amenities is usually agreed and manned jointly by the retailers in the cluster.

retail rate Werbetarif; Anzeigenpreis für örtliche Einzelhändler

Advertising: media advertising rate offered to local retailers.

retail sale Einzelhandelsverkauf; Ladenverkauf

retail sales Einzelhandelsumsätze

Economy: the entirety of all goods and services sold to end-users in an economy, including automobiles, building materials, furniture, department store sales, food stores, gasoline, clothing, restaurants and drugstores.

High retail sales are an indication of economic growth and an expanding economy.

retained earnings nicht ausgeschütteter Gewinn; einbehaltene Gewinne; thesaurierte Gewinne

Accounting: the earnings of a company not paid out as dividends to its shareholders; also called undistributed profits or earned surplus.

retained earnings statement Aufstellung thesaurierter Gewinne

Accounting: summary of the retained earnings account on a company's balance sheet, listing such items as profits or losses from operations, dividends declared, and any other items charged or credited to retained earnings.

retainer *(contract)* Anwaltsbestellung; *(fee advance)* Anwaltskostenvorschuss; Gefolgsmann

retaliate vergelten; heimzahlen; Gegenmaßnahmen ergreifen

retaliation Vergeltung; Gegenmaßnahme

retard *(to delay)* verzögern; *(to slow down)* verlangsamen; *(to draw out)* hinausziehen; *(to protract)* verschleppen

retention ratio Einbehaltungsquote

Accounting: the percentage of earnings that is not paid out as dividends, calculated as retained earnings for a period divided by net income for that period.

rethink umdenken; überdenken; neu bedenken

retire zurückziehen; *(committee member)* abwählen; *(bookkeeping)* ausbuchen; *(from circulation)* aus dem Verkehr ziehen; *(debt)* tilgen; *(to go into retirement)* sich pensionieren lassen; in den Ruhestand treten; zur Ruhe setzen

retired zurückgezogen; *(pensioned)* im Ruhestand; *(committee member)* abgewählt; *(bookkeeping)* ausgebucht; *(from circulation)* aus dem Verkehr gezogen; abgelegen;

retirement Pensionierung; Ruhestand; Rückzug; *(committee member)* Abwahl; *(bookkeeping)* Ausbuchung; *(debt)* Tilgung; Rücktritt; Abgeschiedenheit

Employment: the status of a worker has reached who has left active employment permanently. His income for the remaining years of life is provided through Social Security, pensions, and savings.

retirement age Pensionsalter; Rentenalter

Employment: the age at which a worker is entitled to full retirement benefits, in most countries around the age of 65.

If the worker chooses early or deferred retirement, this will lead to a proportionate reduction or increase in benefits.

retirement benefits Altersversorgung; Pensionsbezüge

retirement income adjustment Rentenanpassung

retirement pay Pensionszahlung

retirement pension Altersruhegeld; Pension

retirement plan Alterssicherungsplan; Pensionsplan

A plan that insures that a retired person has a regular income when he is out of work. For that purpose he has to make regular payments to a fund during his working life, and the contributions are invested or appreciate over time.

retirement provision Altersvorsorge

retirement savings plan Vorsorgesparplan; Rentensparplan

retiring *(reticent)* zurückhaltend; *(unobtrusive)* unaufdringlich; *(leaving a position)* ausscheidend; Pensions-

retracement Zurückverfolgung

Price movement in the opposite direction of the previous trend.

retract zurücknehmen; einziehen

retraction Rücknahme; Einziehung

retrain umschulen; neu ausbilden

retraining Umschulung; Neuausbildung

retrenchment Einschränkung; Verminderung; Beschneidung

retrieval Wiedergewinnung; Zurückerlangung; Wiedererwerb; *(Computer)* Wiederauffindung

retrieve zurückerlangen; wieder erwerben; wieder auffinden; *(to salvage)* bergen

retroactive rückwirkend

return *(travel)* Rückkehr; Wiederkehr; *(replacement)* Rückgabe; *(report)* Meldung; Erwiderung; *(tax)* Steuererklärung; *(yield)* Ertrag; Ergebnis; *(profit)* Gewinn; *(shipment)* Rücksendung; *(to ~) (to come back)* zurückkehren; *(to give back)* zurückgeben; -tun; -bringen *(to go back)* zurückgehen; umkehren

Finance: profit earned on an investment, expressed as an annual percentage rate.

Retailing: a refund for the exchange of previously sold merchandise.

Taxes: a document giving tax authorities information about the taxpayer's tax liability.

returned zurückgesandt; retourniert; Rück-

return of capital Kapitalrückzahlung

Sum paid when a portion of an investment, such as a shareholder's investment in the stock of the company, is returned to the buyer.

return on assets Anlagenrendite; Rentabilität des eingesetzten Kapitals

A profitability ratio, calculated by dividing net income for the past 12 months by total assets. The result is shown as a percentage.

return on capital Kapitalertrag; Kapitalrendite; Kapitalrentabilität

A profitability ratio measured using net income divided by invested capital. This is equivalent to return on assets multiplied by the leverage ratio (assets/equity).

return on capital employed (ROCE) Ertrag aus investiertem Kapital; Kapitalrentabilität

A profitability ratio of those assets for which on the capital side interest is to be paid. Starting point are, like with ROI, the operating assets. From this value the "free" liabilities are deducted (mainly accounts payable). This is the capital employed..

return on equity Kapitalrendite; Eigenkapitalrendite

A profitability ratio measuring the amount, expressed as a percentage, earned on a company's common stock investment for a given period. Calculated by dividing net income for the past 12 months by common stockholders' equity (adjusted for stock splits).

return on invested capital Ertrag des investierten Kapitals; Rentabilität des investierten Kapitals

Amount, expressed as a percentage, earned on a company's total capital - its common and preferred stock equity plus its long-term funded debt calculated by dividing total capital into earnings before interest, taxes, and dividends.

return on investment (ROI) Kapitalrentabilität; Kapitalrendite

Ratio measuring the return that should come back from the investment. The ROI is the form in which the profit goal presented.

ROI = return on sales x capital turnover

The profit is related to the invested operating assets, because the management has to earn the profit with the investment, i.e. with the available assets.

return on net assets Nettorendite auf das Anlagevermögen

return on sales Gewinnspanne

Measure of net pretax profits as a percentage of net sales, indicating overall operational efficiency when compared with prior periods or with other companies in the same line of business.

returns Rückwaren; Rücksendungen; Retouren

reunification Wiedervereinigung

reusable wieder verwendbar; neu nutzbar

revaluation Neubewertung; Neubeurteilung; Zuschreibung; *(of currency)* Aufwertung

Currencies: change in the value of a country's exchange rate as a result of political decisions rather than market forces. It refers to an increase in the currency's value; devaluation refers to a decrease.

revalue *(evaluation)* neu bewerten; *(currency)* aufwerten; *(to estimate)* neu schätzen; neu beurteilen

revamp reorganisieren; flicken; neu machen; umgestalten; -bilden

Revans, Reg (1907-2003)

Management thinker who pioneered the concept of Action Learning. He developed the radical theory that managers learned better from each other in working management situations. Revans concluded that miners and managers should also learn from and with each other. He always took a holistic approach, incorporating some elements of religious belief, to the practice of management.

Action learning has been practiced all over the world and became part of many management training programs.

Biography: born in Southampton, in the 1970's he became president of the European Association of Management Training Centers.

Major publications: (1966) The Theory of Practice in Management, (1971) Developing Effective Managers, (1979) Action Learning

revenue Einnahme; Einkünfte; Betriebseinkommen; Finanzamt

The amount of money that a company actually receives from its activities, mostly from sales of products and/or services to customers.

revenue sharing Beteiligung an den Einnahmen

revenue streams Einzahlungsströme

reversal Umkehrung; Umschwung; *(counter entry)* Stornierung; *(setback)* Rückschlag; Niederlage; Rückschlag; Verlust

reverse channels Rückkanäle

Marketing: channel of distribution where products are moved from the consumer back to the producer, such as recycling and product recalls.

reverse discrimination positive Diskriminierung; Gegendiskriminierung

Discrimination against an individual or group that is traditionally in the majority. This situation can occur when an employer illegally favors the promotion of minority groups.

reverse engineering Reverse Engineering; Zerlegung von Wettbewerbsprodukten

The process of learning how a product is made by taking it apart and examining it.

reverse leverage negative Verschuldung

Situation where the interest rate on an investment is higher than the financial benefits received from it, resulting in a negative leverage.

reverse stock split Aktienzusammenlegung

Procedure whereby the number of outstanding shares is reduced, but not the value of shares of stock held by shareholders. Shareholders maintain the same percentage of equity as before the split. The aim is to boost the stock's market price and attract investors.

Example: a 1-for-3 split would result in stockholders owning 1 share for every 3 shares owned before the split.

reversing entry Stornobuchung

reversionary factor *(statistics)* Korrektur-Faktor

review Duchsicht; Überprüfung; *(survey)* Überblick; *(of film, book)* Besprechung; Kritik; Rezension; *(to ~) (play, film)* besprechen; rezensieren; *(examine)* durchsehen, überprüfen; *(general account)* einen Überblick geben über; nachprüfen

revise Revisionsbogen; umarbeiten; überarbeiten; *(examine)* überprüfen; durchsehen; revidieren

revision Überarbeitung; Überprüfung; Revision; Umarbeitung; *(examination, check)* Revidierung; *(revised edition)* Neufassung; *(revised regulation)* Neuregelung

revision of a statute Gesetzesänderung; Gesetzesüberarbeitung

revisions of existing products Überarbeitung existierende Produkte

Products that are introduced as "new and improved" and, thus, replace the old product. On the internet, firms are continually improving their brands to add value and remain competitive.

revitalize wieder beleben; neu beleben; auffrischen; revitalisieren

revival Wiederbelebung; Wiederaufleben; *(market)* Erholung; Wiedererwachen; Wiedererweckung

revive *(to revitalize)* (wieder)beleben; wiederaufleben lassen; *(to become revitalized)* wiederaufleben; *(to recuperate)* sich erholen; *(to renew)* erneuern;

revocation Widerruf; Zurücknahme

revoke widerrufen; zurücknehmen; aufheben; nicht bedienen

revolution Revolution; *(mechanics)* Umdrehung; Kreisen

Politics: a sudden and drastic change in the social or political institutions of a country; can also occur in a culture or economy.

revolving sich drehend; umlaufen; überlegen; revolvierend

revolving credit revolvierender Kredit

Banking: a line of credit extended to customers who may use it as often as desired up to a certain limit .

reward power Macht durch Belohnung

Compliance achieved based on the ability to distribute rewards that others view as valuable. These rewards can be anything that another person values. In an organizational context for example money, favorable performance appraisals, promotions, interesting work assignments, and important information.

If one can give someone something of positive value or remove something of negative value, one has reward power over that person.

reward strategy Belohnungsstrategie

reward strategies for executives Belohnungsstrategie für leitende Angestellte

rewrite umschreiben; neu fassen; redigieren; druckfertig machen

RFM analysis spezielle Datenbankanalyse

Data mining: scan of a database for three criteria: recency, frequency, and monetary value. This process allows firms to target offers to the customers who are most responsive, thus saving promotional costs and increasing sales.

rich reich; *(food)* reichhaltig; fettreich

rich media advertisements Rich-Media-Werbung

Internet: advertisements on a website that are not static, but provide animation, sound or interactivity.

Ricardo, David (1772 – 1823)

A British political economist, often credited with systematizing economics, who was one of the most influential of the classical economists. He was also a successful businessman, financier and speculator, and amassed a considerable fortune.

rig Manipulieren; Börsenmnöver; *(oil)* Bohrausrüstung; Takelung; Rüstung; Auftakelung; *(to ~)* ausrüsten; montieren; *(price)* illegal beeinflussen; manipulieren; aufrüsten

rigging *(ship)* Takelung; Aufrüstung; *(market)* Preistreiberei; *(stock exchange)* Kurstreiberei

rights issue Bezugsrechte zur Kapitalerhöhung; Bezugsrechtsemission

rights offering Möglichkeit des Bezugs von Vorzugsaktien; Bezugsrechtsangebot

Stock exchange: issuance of rights to current shareholders allowing them to purchase additional shares, usually at a discount to market price. Shareholders who do not exercise these rights are usually diluted by the offering.

right to participate Teilnahmerecht; *(decision-making)* Mitwirkungsrecht

right to recourse Regressrecht

right to social benefits Sozialanspruch

right to strike Streikrecht

right to vote Stimmrecht

right-wing totalitarianism rechtsextremer Totalitarismus

Political system in which political power is monopolized by a party, group, or individual that generally permits individual economic freedom but restricts individual political freedom, including free speech, often on the grounds that it would lead to the rise of communism.

ripe reif

rise Aufstieg; Lohnerhöhung; Anstieg; Steigerung; *(increase)* Zunahme; *(land contour)* Bodenerhebung; *(to ~)* aufgehen;auf-; ansteigen; steigen; sich erhöhen; *(to grow)* wachsen

rise in exchange rate Kursanstieg

rise in expenses Ausgabenanstieg; Ausgabensteigerung

rise in exports Exportanstieg

rise in prices Preisanstieg; *(stocks)* Kursanstieg

rise in spending Ausgabenanstieg

rising Anstieg; Erhöhung; Auferstehung; ansteigend; wachsend; *(prices)* anziehend

rising price tendency Preisauftrieb

rising sales Umsatzanstieg; Verkaufssteigerung

risk Risiko; *(endangerment)* Gefährdung; Gefahr; *(danger of loss)* Verlustgefahr; *(to ~)* riskieren; *(to dare)* wagen

The probability of harmful consequences, such as the possibility of losing or not gaining value. Risk is measurable, whilst uncertainty is not.

Among the most common types of risk are: actuarial risk, exchange risk, inflation risk, interest rate risk, inventory risk, liquidity risk, political risk, repayment (credit) risk, risk of principal, systematic risk, underwriting risk, unsystematic risk.

risk-averse risikoscheu

Investment: someone who seeks the least risk.

risk avoidance Risikovermeidung

One method of dealing with the consequences of risk, which includes not performing an activity that could carry risk.

risk class Risikoklasse

risk management Risikomanagement

All activities concerned with the identification and valuation of risks, with the definition of the risks to be run and their limitation.

risk mixture Risikomischung

risk potential Gefahrenpotential

risk premium Risikoprämie

Excess return on the risky asset that is the difference between expected return on risky assets and the return on risk-free assets.

risk spread Risikostreuung; Risikomischung

risky riskant, *(daring)* gewagt; *(dangerous)* gefährlich; bedenklic; *(high-risk)* risikoreich

ritual Ritual; Zeremoniell; Ritus; rituell

Repetitive sequences of activities that express and reinforce the key values of the organization, which goals are most important, which people are important, and which are expendable.

rival *(competitor)* Konkurrent; *(coapplicant)* Mitbewerber; Rivale; *(to ~)* rivalisieren; konkurrieren; wetteifern; gleichkommen

road to success Erfolgskurs

roaming Roaming

Using a wireless phone outside the home service area defined by the service provider. Roaming often incurs higher per-minute rates as well as daily access fees and long distance charges.

rob aus-; (be)rauben; überfallen

robot Roboter; Automat

Internet: tool, also known as a spider, that is employed by search engines to index web pages of registered sites on a regular basis.

rock Felsen; Klippe; Gestein; *(to ~) (system)* erschüttern; schaukeln

role Rolle

Set of expected behavior patterns attributed to someone occupying a given position in a social unit.

role conflict Rollenkonflikt

Situation in which an individual is confronted by divergent role expectations. It exists when an individual finds that compliance with one role requirement may make more difficult the compliance with another.

role expectations Rollenerwartungen

How others believe a person should act in a given situation, largely determined by the role defined in the context in which one is acting.

role identity Rollenidentität

Certain attitudes and actual behaviors consistent with a role. People have the ability to shift roles rapidly when they recognize that the situation and its demands clearly require major changes.

role perception Rollenwahrnehmung

Individual's view of how he or she is supposed to act in a given situation. Based on an interpretation of how one believes he is supposed to behave, he engages in certain types of behavior.

role playing Rollenspiel

Simulation exercise where the participants act out specified roles in a dramatization of an event or situation. The purpose of role playing is to achieve better understanding of a situation by experiencing a realistic simulation.

rolling stock Fuhrpark; rollendes Inventar

Any transportation vehicle that moves on wheels, including railroad cars and locomotives, tractor-trailers, and trucks.

roll over revolvieren; sich umdrehen

rope Strick; Seil; Tau (to ~) anseilen

rotate drehen; rotieren; abwechseln

rotating sich drehend; rotierend; *(work shifts)* stetig wechselnd

rotation Drehung; *(mechanics)* Umdrehung; *(regulated change)* geregelter Wechsel; Kreislauf

round Runde

round of negotiations Verhandlungsrunde

route Strecke; Kurs; Route; Marsch-(befehl); *(way, path)* Weg; *(to ~)* Route bestimmen; Strecke kennzeichnen

router Router

Telecommunications: a device that finds the best route for data packets between any two networks.

routine (gewöhnlicher) Geschäftsgang; alltägliche Arbeit Routine; *(procedure)* Prozedur; *(customary course)* üblicher Verlauf; routinemäßig; üblich; laufend

routing Streckenplanung; Wegbestimmung; Ablaufplanung

Production: technique for determining the sequence of manufacturing steps necessary to complete a product.

Telecommunications: the forwarding of data packets in packet-switched networks to the intended address.

royalty Honorar; Tantieme; *(license fee)* Lizenzgebühr; *(copyright)* Autorenanteil; Königtum; königliche Personen

Remuneration paid to the owners of technologies, patents, or trade names for the use of same; share of the product, or of the proceeds therefrom, reserved by an owner for permitting another to exploit and use his property; rental paid to the original owner of property, based on a percentage of profit or production.

Example: used for mining leases, conveyances, as well as literary works, inventions, and other intellectual productions.

R squared ***(R^2)*** R^2

A statistical measure of the degree to which two investments are related.

rubric Überschrift; Rubrik; *(heading)* Titelkopf

ruin Ruine; *(figurative)* Ruin; *(collapse)* Zusammenbruch; Zerstörung; *(to ~)* ruinieren; zugrunde richten; zerstören

ruinous vernichtend; ruinös; *(too daring)* halsbrecherisch; verfallen

rule Regel; *(directive)* Vorschrift; *(decree)* Verfügung; Herrschaft; *(guideline)* Richtlinie; *(to ~) (to regulate)* regeln; *(to decree)* verfügen; *(a market)* beherrschen; regieren

ruling *(decision)* Entscheidung; Entscheid; Beschluss; Herrschaft; Regieren; *(predominant)* vorherrschend; *(decisive)* bestimmend; regierend; beherrschend

run Lauf; Rennen; Fortgang; *(strong demand)* starke Nachfrage; *(production)* Ausstoß; *(to ~)* rennen; laufen; davon rennen; fließen; strömen; *(machine)* in Betrieb sein; *(to operate a machine)* bedienen

runaway unkontrolliert; außer Kontrolle; Ausreißer; durchgebrannt

running laufend; fließend; nacheinander; umlaufend; *(in operation)* in Betrieb

run on site Ansturm auf eine Webseite

Internet: situation where a company pays for banner advertisements to promote its services across a web site which results in high traffic.

rural ländlich; Land-

rush Eile; *(heightened activity)* Hochbetrieb; *(charge, assault)* Ansturm; Stürzen; Ansteigen; Anschwellen; *(crowding)* Andrang; *(to ~)* sich beeilen; *(to urge speed)* drängen; antreiben; stürzen; jagen

Ss

sabotage Sabotage; sabotieren; Sabotage treiben

Deliberate destruction or damage of equipment in order to interference with the productive capabilities in a factory.

sack Entlassung; Plünderung; Rausschmiss; *(to ~)* entlassen; rausschmeißen; feuern; plündern

The termination of someone's employment, leaving him free to depart, originally meaning that he picked up his sack and moved on.

safe Tresor; Safe; Schrank; sicher; heil; ungefährlich

safeguard Sicherung; *(protection)* Schutz; Geleitbrief; *(protective device)* Schutzvorrichtung; *(contract)* Sicherheitsklausel; *(to ~)* sichern; schützen; sicherstellen

safeguarding Sicherstellung; sichere Aufbewahrung

safe harbor sicherer Hafen

safekeeping Sicherstellung; sicheres Verwahren; Gewahrsam

Safe storage of valuable assets or documents, in a bank safe or deposit box.

Investment: a brokerage firm holding stock certificates and keeping track of trades.

safety margin Sicherheitsmarge

Cost accounting: Situation where the actual sales volume is higher than the break-even volume, which gives a company a safety margin before it would incur a loss.

sagacity Klugheit; Urteilsfähigkeit

sagging sinkend; nachlassend; abgeschwächt; schleppend

salable leicht verkäuflich; absatzfähig; gängig; handelbar

salaried festes Gehalt beziehend; im Gehalt stehend; besoldet

salaried employee Gehaltsempfänger

salaries and wages Personalaufwendungen; Gehälter und Löhne

salary Gehalt; Besoldung; Salär

Regular payment from the employer to the employee as compensation for the work performed. Sometimes a salary is composed of a basic wage plus performance based pay and indirect fringe benefit compensation.

salary account Gehaltskonto

salary bargaining round Gehaltsrunde

salary cut Gehaltskürzung; Lohnkürzung

salary increase Gehaltssteigerung; Gehaltserhöhung; Lohnerhöhung

salary loss Gehaltseinbuße

salary negotiation round Einkommensrunde; Gehaltsrunde

salary raise Gehaltssteigerung;

sale Verkauf; Vertrieb; Absatz; Veräußerung; *(transaction)* Geschäft; Abschluss; *(at reduced prices)* Ausverkauf; Schlussverkauf

In general: the transfer of the ownership of goods or services in exchange for money.

Marketing: a temporary price reduction for certain products.

sale of gold Goldverkauf

sale of goods Warenverkauf

sale of land Grundstücksverkauf

sales Umsatz; Absatz

The total value of goods and services sold during a specified period after making adjustments for returns, credits, and discounts.

sales agent Handelsvertreter; Geschäftsreisender

sales analyst Absatzanalytiker; Umsatzanalyst

Accounting: employee charged with tracking the company's sales by region, product, or account with the aim of making recommendations and enhancing profitability.

sale and lease-back Sale and lease back; Verkauf mit gleichzeitiger Rückvermietung an den Verkäufer

Lease arrangement whereby a firm sells its existing assets to a financial company which then leases them back to the firm. This is often done to generate cash for the firm.

sales and services Verkaufs- und Kundendienst

sales base Verkaufsbasis; Verkaufsrundlage

sales branch Verkaufsfiliale; Verkaufsniederlassung

sales budget Absatzbudget; Absatzplan

The planned amount of future sales, allocated by product, territory, or person.

sales calculation Verkaufsrechnung

sales call Vertreterbesuch; Kundenbesuch

sales charge Abschlußgebühr; Ankaufgebühren

Investment: the fee an investor has to pay when he purchases shares in a mutual fund, similar to a commission.

sales collapse Umsatzeinbruch

sales company Vertriebsgesellschaft

sales director Vertriebschef

sales district Verkaufsgebiet; Absatzgebiet

sales estimate Absatzschätzung; Umsatzschätzung

sales force Verkaufspersonal; Verkaufsmannschaft; Verkaufsstab

The employees of a business that are directly responsible for selling products or services.

sales force management Führung des Verkaufspersonals; Vertriebsleitung

Analysis, planning, implementation and control of sales force activities; designing sales force strategy; and recruiting, selecting, training, supervising and evaluating the firm's salespeople.

sales force promotion Förderung des Verkaufspersonals

Sales promotion designed to motivate the sales force and make sales force selling efforts more effective, including bonuses, contests and sales rallies.

sales forecast Umsatzprognose; Absatzprognose

Key input to the firm's financial planning process. External sales forecasts are based on historical experience, statistical analysis and consideration of various macroeconomic factors.

sales gains Umsatzzunahme; Umsatzgewinne

sales group Vertriebsgemeinschaft; Verkaufsgemeinschaft

sales incentive Verkaufsanreiz; Verkaufsprämie

Marketing: an award offered to a salesperson for exceeding some predetermined sales goal. The incentive may be in cash, or some form of prize, such as a vacation.

sales lead Interessent; Verkaufshinweis

A person who has shown some kind of interest in a product or service. The lead may have a corporation or business associated with the person. A sales lead is the starting point for all further activities in personal selling.

sales letter Werbebrief; Werbeschreiben

Letter used to introduce the selling effort of a direct-mail package. Sales letters may be individually typewritten, typeset and printed, fully computer typed, or printed as a form letter and then completed by inserting the names and addresses of prospects.

sales literature Verkaufsprospekte; Werbematerial

A variety of printed material designed to help sell a product or service.

sales loss Absatzverlust

sales management Vertriebsmanagement; Vertriebsleitung

All activities involved in planning, managing and controlling the sales function in a company.

sales manager Vertriebsmanager; Vertriebsleiter

sales office Verkaufsbüro; Vertriebsstelle

Office owned by the manufacturer located in important markets, normally without any inventory, whose primary function is to increase customer sales.

sales organization Verkaufsorganisation; Absatzorganisation; Vertriebsapparat

salesperson Verkäufer; Fachverkäufer

Employee of a company whose main task is selling a product or service to the company´s customers. Normally, this includes the following activities: prospecting, communicating, servicing, and information gathering.

sales plan Verkaufsplan; Absatzplan

sales portfolio Vertriebshandbuch

A collection of all the products or services a company offers to its customers, together with detailed information about each product, such as prices, terms, special deals, types of discounts, and available merchandising material. This handbook is an important reference tool for a salesperson.

sales proceeds Verkaufserlös

sales profit Verkaufsgewinn; Verkaufserlös

sales program Absatzprogramm; Verkaufsprogramm

sales projection Absatzplan; Absatzprognose

sales promotion Verkaufsförderung; Absatzförderung

Short-term incentives to encourage purchase or sales of a product or service; activities, materials, devices, and techniques used to supplement the advertising and marketing efforts and help coordinate the advertising with the personal selling effort.

Example: sweepstakes, special displays, coupons, promotional discounts, contests, and gift offers.

sales-promotional verkaufsfördernd; Absatzförderungs-

sales psychology Verkaufspsychologie

sales quotas Verkaufsziele; Absatzquote

Standards set by managment for salespeople, stating the amount they should sell and how sales should be divided among the company's products.

sales record Umsatzrekord

sales representative Verkaufsvertreter; Vertreter; Handelsvertreter

sales result Verkaufsergebnis; Absatzerfolg; Vertriebsergebnis

sales revenue Umsatzertrag; Verkaufserlös

sales strategy Verkaufsstrategie; strategischer Verkaufsplan; Absatzstrategie; Verkaufsmethoden

sales tax Umsatzsteuer; Verkaufssteuer

A tax imposed on the purchase of goods and services, based on the value of the item and calculated as a percentage of the retail price. Sales taxes are a major sources of revenue for most states.

sales territory Absatzgebiet; Vertriebsgebiet

sales volume Verkaufsvolumen; Absatzvolumen; Absatzmenge

salutary products gesunde Produkte

Products that have low appeal but may benefit consumers in the long run.

salvage Bergung; bergen; verwerten

slavage value Restwert; Schrottwert

sample Warenprobe; Muster; *(to ~) (to test)* probieren; nach Proben beurteilen; erproben; bemustern

Statistics: a segment of a population selected for marketing research to represent the population as a whole.

Sales promotion: a product given away for free to potential customers to enable them to experience the product.

sampling Stichprobenverfahren; Musterkollektion; Probe

Market research: a technique for choosing and studying a small group of people who are representative of a larger group. Conclusions can then be drawn from the sample and be applied to the larger group.

Sales promotion: offering a product or a small portion of it to consumers at little or no cost in order to stimulate regular usage.

sanction Unterstützung; Billigung; Beweggrund; Sanktion; Strafmaßnahme; *(approval)* Genehmigung; Billigung; *(to ~)* genehmigen; billigen; unterstützen; sanktionieren

satellite Satellit; *(communication)* Fernmeldesatellit; *(surveying)* Beobachtungssatellit

satisfaction Zufriedenheit; Befriedigung; Genugtuung; *(of a customer)* Zufriedenstellung

Psychology: the idea that individuals don't seek to maximize their benefit from a particular course of action, but rather seek something that is good enough to give them satisfaction. An understanding of this situation has important implications for marketing a product.

satisfy *(customer)* zufrieden stellen; befriedigen; erfüllen; überzeugen

satisfying zufriedenstellend; befriedigend

saturate sättigen; *(market)* durchdringen; erfüllen

saturated gesättigt; *(market)* nicht mehr aufnahmefähig

saturation Sättigung; *(market)* Marktsättigung

saturation limit Sättigungsgrenze

saturation of the Internet Sättigung des Internets

Theory that the access to the internet will reach saturation as home PC ownership reaches a limit, unless other access devices become popular.

save (er)retten; *(money)* sparen; *(for future use)* erübrigen; *(reduce requisite amount)* ersparen; außer; unbeschadet

saver Sparer

savings account Sparkonto; Sparguthaben

savings activity Spartätigkeit

Savings and Loan association (S&L) Spar- und Kreditvereinigung; Hypothekenbank

Institution in the US similar to a savings bank, except that the savings and loan association's primary purpose has been to provide loans for purchasing and building homes; also called *building and loan association.* Insurance for depositors may be provided by the Federal Deposit Insurance Company (FDIC).

savings bank Sparkasse

A bank that accepts savings deposits and invests these funds in loans primarily for commercial and residential real estate.

savings bank customer Sparkassenkunde; Sparkassenkundin

savings bank window Sparkassenschalter

savings bond Sparbrief; Sparobligation

savings book Sparbuch

savings certificate Sparbrief

savings customer Sparkunde; Sparkundin

savings deposit Spareinlage; Spargeld

savings deposits administration Spargelderverwaltung

savings funds Spareinlagenbestand

savings performanc Sparleistung; *(~ target)* Einsparungsvorgabe

savings plan Sparvertrag; Sparplan

savings premium Sparprämie

savings premium law Sparprämiengesetz

savings promotion Sparförderung

savings rate Sparquote

Economics: an important macroeconomic indicator measuring the share of their disposable income which households save. Calculate by dividing total savings by total disposable income, expressed as a percentage.

Say's law Saysches Theorem

Proposition in classical economics, that supply creates its own demand, that whatever quantity is supplied will also be demanded. It is named for the 19th-century French economist J.B.Say.

scabs Streikbrecher; Gerwerkschaftsfeinde

A person who continues to work, or who accepts employment, while the the other workers of a company are on strike.

scale Waagschale; Waage; *(graduation)* Skala; Gradeinteilung; Maßstab; Größenverhältnis; *(range)* Umfang; Größenordnung; *(to ~)* wiegen; messen; Maßstab festlegen; *(to ~ up/down)* erhöhen/senken

Economics: amount of production, as in economy or diseconomy of scale.

Labor: wage rate for specific types of employees. For example, the union *scale* for carpenters is $20.00 per hour.

Modeling: proportional relationship between the dimensions of a drawing, plan, or model and the dimensions of the physical object it represents.

scale earnings Skalenertrag

scale economies Größenvorteile; Skalenvorteile

See: economies of scale

scan Überprüfung; *(radar)* Abtastung; *(television) Bildauflö*sung; *(to ~)* überprüfen; abtasten; absuchen; prüfen; durchsehen; rastern; abtasten; abfragen; *(read)* überfliegen

scanner Radarantenne; *(computer)* Abtaster; Scanner

scanning *(checking)* Überprüfen; *(radar)* Abtasten; *(reading)* Überfliegen; überprüfend; abtastend

scarce knapp; spärlich; selten

scarcity Knappheit; Verknappung; Mangel

scarcity Knappheit; Mangel; Verknappung

A central concept of economics that exists because people's wants and needs are unlimited, while the resources to produce goods and services to meet those wants and needs are limited. Economics deals with the consquences of this situation, i.e. how scarce resources should be allocated.

scarcity value Seltenheitswert

Economics: the factor that determines an item's relative price as a function of its low supply. Whilst the price of most consumer goods is determined by manufacturing costs and competition, the price of a number of product is determined by their scarcity, such as stamps and antiques.

scenario analysis Szenarioanalyse

Analysis of the effect on a project of different scenarios, each scenario involving a confluence of factors.

scenario planning Szenariotechnik; Szenarienplanung

Structured process for organizations to think about the future. A group of executives sets out to draw a small number of scenarios about how the future may unfold and how this might affect an issue that confronts them – making choices today with an understanding of how they might turn out.

schedule Zeitplan; Aufstellung; Liste; Verzeichnis; *(table)* Tabelle; *(to ~) (to set time)* ansetzen; *(to plan)* planen; verzeichnen; vorsehen

scheduled vorgesehen; planmäßig; angesetzt

scheduler Planer; Disponent

scheduling Planen; Ansetzen; *(time)* Terminplanung; Zeitplanung; Disposition; *(procedure)* Ablaufsplanung; *(travel)* Reiseplanung

Production: taking decisions regarding the allocation of available capacity or resources (equipment, labor and space) to jobs, activities, tasks or customers over time.

Scheduling results in a time-phased plan, or schedule of activities. The schedule indicates what is to be done, when, by whom and with what equipment. Scheduling seeks to achieve several conflicting objectives: high efficiency, low inventories and good customer service.

Schein, Edgar H. (* 1928)

Social psychologist who coined the term 'the psychological contract' to express the unwritten understandings that exist within an organization, as it also includes a company's expectations about the people who work for it, such as loyalty and diligence. Another important concept by Schein is the 'career anchor'.

Schein also insisted that the key to successful leadership is managing cultural change in an organization.

Biography: he worked at MIT with Douglas McGragor of 'Theory X and Theory Y' fame.

Major publications: (1978) Career Dynamics: Matching Individual and Organizational Needs, (1980) Organizational Psychology, (1985) Organizational Culture and Leadership

schema Schema; Übersicht; Diagramm; Schema; *(printing)* Satzvorlage

scheme *(plan)* Plan; System; Harmonie; Aufeinanderabstimmung; Vorhaben; *(intrigue)* Machenschaft; Intrige; *(plot)* Komplott; *(to ~)* planen; intrigieren; Ränke schmieden

Schonberger, Richard J. (* 1937)

Schonberger is a consultant and management thinker who has played an important role in introducing just-in-time and other Japanese manufacturing techniques to the US.

He insists that world class excellence in manufacturing and services can only be achieved by regarding each function in a business as a 'customer' of the one serving it. Schonberger also believes that it does not take long to train people in industry in how to improve rapidly.

Biography: worked for eight years in US defense industries, then he took a PhD in business studies at the University of Nebraska, specializing in production management and information systems, teaching there for 13 years, he has been consultant and trainer to many leading multinational corporations.

Major publications: (1982) Japanese Manufacturing Techniques, (1986) World Class Manufacturing, (1987) World Class Manufacturing Casebook, (1990) Building a Chain of Customers, (1996) World Class Manufacturing: The Next Decade

Schumacher, E.F. (1911-1977)

Schumacher became famous for the idea 'Small is Beautiful' that came to symbolize the revolt against large and impersonal organizations during the 1970s and 1980s.

Schumacher set up the International Technology Development Group and became an adviser on economic problems to Third World countries.

Biography: born in Germany, 1950-1970 he worked for Britain's National Coal Board

Major publications: (1973) Small is Beautiful.

Schumpeter, Joseph (1883 – 1950)

American economist of Austrian origing who made substantial contributions to the history of economic thought, amongst others on business cycles and entrepreneurship.

scientific management Scientific Managment; Taylorismus

Approach to management and Industrial / Organizational Psychology initiated by Frederick Winslow Taylor in his 1911 monograph The Principles of Scientific Management

It required managers to carrying out time-and-motion studies on workers in different departments. It led to the piece-rate system in which workers were paid for their output, not for their time.

scope of business Geschäftsumfang; Geschäftsrahmen

S corporation Unternehmensform in den USA

A special type of corporation in the US with a limited number of shareholders that is treated as a partnership for tax purposes. This avoids double taxation while providing limited liability protection to shareholders.

screen resolution Bildschirmauflösung

Measurements for computer screens which specifies "dots per inch" or the amount of light rays that strike one square inch of a computer screen.

scrip Dollarnote; Berechtigungsschein; Bezugsschein

seal Siegel; Stempel; *(to ~)* (ver)siegeln, zukleben; abdichten; regeln; besiegeln

An impression on wax printed on a document in order to authenticate it.

sealed bid verschlossenes Angebot; Submissionsangebot im versiegelten Umschlag

A bid which has been submitted in a sealed envelope to prevent publication of its contents before the deadline and the submission of all bids.

sealed-bid pricing Preisbestimmung auf Basis verschlossener Angebote

Setting price based on how the firm thinks competitors will price rather than on its own costs or demand – used when a company bids for jobs.

seal of approval Gütesiegel

Seal offered by influential organizations that a product has been tested and found to meet the standards set by the organization.

search engine Suchmaschine

Internet: Web site that scans the web, searching for matches for the user' s keywords, and returns a list of websites that might have the desired information.

season Jahreszeit; Saison; Weile; *(to ~)* würzen; schmackhaft machen; altern

seasonal Saison-; jahreszeitlich bedingt; saisonbedingt; Jahreszeit bedingt

seasonal adjustment Saisonbereinigung; Ausschaltung von Saisonbewegungen

Statistical procedure of estimating seasonal effects and removing them from the original data, which allows a clearer view of non-seasonal changes in the data.

seasonal discount Nachlass außerhalb der Saison

Price reduction to buyers who buy merchandise or services out of season.

seasonal goods Saisonware

seasonality Saisonabhängigkeit; Saisonbedingtheit; Saisonbewegungen

Changes in business or economic patterns which occur predictably at given times of the year. They are the result of climate, holidays, and vacations.

seasonally adjusted saisonbereinigt

Allowances for seasonality when interpreting or projecting financial or economic data.

seasonal ticket Dauerkarte

seasonal unemployment saisonbedingte Arbeitslosigkeit

Unemployment due to changes in the climate and other seasonal conditions.

seasoned new issue Kapitalerhöhung

New issue of shares after the company's securities have previously been issued.

seclusion Abgeschiedenheit; Abgeschlossenheit; Zurückgezogenheit; Verborgenheit

secondary sekundär; *(ranking)* zweitrangig; *(not important)* nebensächlich; Zweit-; Neben-

secondary appointment Nebenamt

secondary clause Nebenbedingung

secondary data Sekundärdaten

Information that has been gathered for some other purpose but is useful for the current problem; it can be collected more quickly and less expensively than primary data.

secondary market Zweitmarkt; Sekundärmarkt

Securities: Market that provides for the purchase or sale of previously owned securities; market where securities are traded and contracts to buy and sell commodities are traded. Most trading is done in the secondary market.

Example: the New York Stock Exchange, as well as all other stock exchanges, the bond markets, etc., are secondary markets.

secondary research Sekundärforschung

Research using published or recorded data that have already been collected for some purpose other than the current study. Also called desk research.

Secondary research is normally the starting point for any research project. Only after secondary sources have been consulted, can it be determined how much primary research has to be done.

secondary reserve Sekundärreserven

second-order change Wandel zweiter Ordnung

Multidimensional, multilevel, discontinuous, and radical change involving reframing of assumptions about the organization and the world in which it operates.

seconds *(goods)* Waren zweiter Wahl; IIa-Qualität

secrecy Geheimhaltung; Heimlichkeit; Verschwiegenheit

secret Geheimnis; heimlich; geheim; verborgen

secretarial help Schreibkraft

secretarial staff Schreibpersonal

secretary Sekretär; Schreibkraft; *(government)* Minister; Botschaftssekretär; Außenminister; *(association)* Schriftführer

Secretary-General Generalsekretär

secretary of state US Aussenminister

secretary of trade US Handelsminister

secret of success Erfolgsgeheimnis

section Schnitt; Sektion; Teil; *(department)* Abteilung; Paragraph; *(to ~)* aufteilen; *(to dissect)* zerlegen

sector Sektor; Bezirk; *(segment)* Ausschnitt; *(area)* Bereich

Securities: group of stocks that belong to one industry, such as the computer sctor or the airline sector.

Economics: part of the economy describing a group of companies that have common characteristics, such as the private sector or public sector.

Computing: a division of a computer disk that represents the smalles unit of storage.

sectoral sektoral

secure sicher; verlässlich; gefahr-; sorgenfrei; gesichert; *(protected)* geschützt; *(to ~)* sichern; sicher machen; absichern; *(to obtain)* erlangen

secure/mime (S-MIME)

Internet: special version of the common mime e-mail protocol that supports encryption. All the major browsers and e-mail programs support S/MIME, allowing using users to trade encrypted e-mail even if they use different e-mail clients

secured gesichert; sichergestellt; *(protected)* geschützt

Secure Electronic Transaction (SET)

Internet: standard for transmitting credit card data securely over the internet.

SET uses a series of digital certificate exchanges to verify the identities of consumers, merchants and banks. Although most major e-commerce players endorse SET, the standard's cost and complexity have hindered its progress.

secure HTTP sicheres HTTP

secure server sicherer Server

Internet: server that uses a special code to make sensitive information difficult to read for anyone not authorized to access it.

Most companies that accept credit cards over the web do so through a secured server.

secure socket layer (SSL) SSL Verschlüsselung

Internet protocol developed by Netscape Communications for transmitting credit card numbers and other sensitive data over the internet.

Both Netscape Communicator and Microsoft Internet Explorer support SSL, which is one of the most widely used e-commerce security methods.

securities *(collateral)* Sicherheiten; *(investments)* Wertpapiere; Effekten; Sicherheiten; Bürgschaften

Securities: a financial instrument issued by a company and traded on a stock exchange, such as stock certificates, bonds, and others.

Lending: an asset to which a lender can have recourse if the borrower defaults on his loan repayments.

Securities and Exchange Commission (SEC) Börsenaufsichtsbehörde

Primary federal regulatory agency in the US of the securities industry, empowered to regulate and supervise the selling of securities, to prevent unfair practices on security exchanges and over-the-counter markets, and to maintain a fair and orderly market for the investor.

securities account Wertpapierkonto; Effektenkonto

securities business Wertpapiergeschäft; Effektengeschäft

securities exchange Wertpapierbörse; Effektenbörse

securities market Wertpapiermarkt; Wertpapierbörse

securities sector Wertpapierbereich

security *(safety)* Sicherheit; Sicherung; *(protection)* Schutz; *(loan)* Darlehenssicherheit; Sicherheitsleistung; Bürge; Bürgschaft *(investment)* Wertpapier

In general: property, money or goods pledges as an assurance that a loan will be repaid

Finance: collateral offered by a debtor to a lender to secure a loan, called *collateral security.*

Investment: instrument that signifies an ownership position in a corporation (a stock), a creditor relationship with a corporation or governmental body (a bond), or other ownership rights.

security analyst Effektenberater; Anlagefachmann; Wertpaperanalytiker

security deposit Sicherheitsleistung; Kaution; *(~ business)* Depotgeschäft

Housing: a payment required by a landlord to ensure that a tenant pays rent on time and keeps the flat in good condition. The landlord can use the security deposit to cover what the tenant owes.

security holdings Wertpapierbestand; Wertpapierportfolio; Wertpapiervermögen

security market line (SML) Wertpapierlinie

Straight line that shows the equilibrium relationship between systematic risk and expected rates of return for individual securities. According to the SML, the excess return on a risky asset is equal to the excess return on the market portfolio multiplied by the beta coefficient.

security rating Sicherheitsrating; Risikoeinschätzung

Securities: an evaluation of the credit and investment risk of securities conducted by commercial rating agencies.

security trading Wertpapierhandel

security turnover Wertpapierumsatz

seed money Gründungskapital; Startkapital

Venture capital: an initial contribution toward the financing or capital requirements of a new business.

segment *(section)* Abschnitt; Segment; *(part)* Teil; *(piece)* Stück; *(to ~)* segmentieren; (to *section)* in Segmente aufteilen

Marketing: a part of a market that combines customers with similar characteristics.

segmentation Segmentierung

Marketing: the process of dividing the market for a particular product or service into a number of different segments, each representing a group of potential customers with common characteristics.

Manufacturers can then target their marketing and advertising efforts more accurately and more profitably. In consumer markets, segmentation is usually based on demographic factors, geography, behavioral, and social factors.

segmentation basis Segmentierungsgrundlage

Markets can be segmented by applying a variety of factors: the general categories of demographics, geographic location, psychographics, benefits, and behavior, each of which has a number of variables.

segmentation strategy Segmentierungsstrategie

segmentation variables Segmentierungsvariablen

Variables used by marketers to identify and profile groups of customers.

segmented pricing Preisbestimmung auf Basis von Segmentierung

Prices adjusted by customer, location, or product.

segmented marketing segmentweises Marketing

Adapting a company's offerings so they more closely match the needs of one or more segments.

segmented pricing Preissegmentierung

Pricing that allows for differences in custom-mers, products and locations. The difference in prices are not based on differences in costs.

segment reporting Branchenberichterstattung

segregation Trennung; Segregation

segregation of duties Aufgabenteilung

Organization: company setup that insures that employees do not have responsibility for incompatible activities.

seize ergreifen; zugreifen; pfänden; beschlagnahme; begreifen

select vorzüglich; exklusiv; auserlesen; *(to ~)* aussuchen; -wählen; -lesen

selected ausgewählt; ausgesucht; exklusiv

selection *(choice)* Auswahl; *(elite)* Auslese; *(assortment)* Kollektion

selection committee Jury; Auswahlkomitee

selection process Auswahlverfahren

selective auswählend; selektiv; *(targeted)* gezielt; *(as needed)* nach Bedarf

selective attention selektive Aufmerksamkeit

Tendency of people to screen out most of the information to which they are exposed.

selective demand selektive Nachfrage

Demand for a given brand of a product or service.

selective distortion selektive Verzerrung

Tendency of people to adapt information to personal meanings.

selective distribution selektive Distribution

Marketing: Distribution strategy that uses more than one, but less than all of the intermediaries that are willing to carry the company's products.

Products are distributed only to those wholesalers or retailers who meet cerain requirements: 1.) agree to sell the product for no less than a certain price, 2.) patronize the distributor on a regular basis or for at least a certain amount annually, or 3.) meet specific requirements established by the distributor as outlined by the manufacturer.

selective perception selective Wahrnehmung

People selectively interpret what they see on the basis of their interests, background, experience, and attitudes.

selective retention selektive Erinnernerung

Tendency of people to retain only part of the information to which they are exposed, usually information that supports their attitudes or believes.

self-actualization Selbstverwirklichung

Drive to become what one is capable of becoming; includes growth, achieving one's potential, and self-fulfillment.

self-concept Selbsteinschätzung, Selbsterkenntnis

Self-image, or the complex mental pictures that people have of themselves.

self-efficacy Selbstvertrauen

Individual's belief that he or she is capable of performing a task. The higher the self-efficacy, the more confidence one has in his ability to succeed in a task. In difficult situation people with high-efficacy will try harder to master the challenge.

self-employed selbstständig erwerbstätig

A person who works for himself as a sole proprietor or as part of a partnership and who is not employed by someone else. He therefore assumes all the risks and responsibilities of the business enterprise.

self-esteem Selbstwertschätzung

Individual's degree of liking or disliking of themselves.

self-financing Selbstfinanzierung; Eigenfinanzierung

self-fulfilling prophecy selbst erfüllende Prophezeiung

A prediction that, in being made, actually causes itself to become true.

self-government Selbstverwaltung

self-interest Eigeninteresse; Eigennutz

self-mailer Self-Mailer

Direct mail piece, such as a postcard, that does not require a envelope or wrapper for mailing.

self-managed work team autonomes Arbeitsteam

Group of employees (typically 10 to 15 in number) who perform highly related or interdependent jobs and take on many of the responsibilities of their former supervisors.

Typically, this includes planning and scheduling of work, assigning tasks to members, collective control over the pace of work, making operating decisions, and taking action on problems. Fully self-managed work teams even select their own members and have the members evaluate each other's performance. As a result, supervisory positions decrease in importance and may even be eliminated.

self-management Selbstmanagement

Learning techniques that allow individuals to manage their own behavior so that less external management control is necessary.

It requires an individual to deliberately manipulate stimuli, internal processes, and responses to achieve personal behavioral outcomes. The basic processes involve observing one's own behavior, comparing the behavior with the standard, and rewarding oneself if the behavior meets the standard.

self-monitoring Selbststeuerung; Selbstkontrolle

Personality trait that measures an individual's ability to adjust his or her behavior to external, situational factors.

High self-monitors are capable of presenting striking contradictions between their public persona and their private self. Low self-monitors can't disguise themselves in that way.

self-motivation Selbstmotivation

self-perception theory Selbstwahrnehmungstheorie

Attitudes are used after the fact to make sense out of an action that has already occurred rather than as devices that precede and guide action. Attitudes are just casual verbal statements.

self-regulation Selbstregulierung

Private sector's ability to rapidly identify and resolve problems specific to its areas of competence.

self-service Selbstbedienung

self-service retailers Selbstbedienungseinzelhändler

Retailers that provide few or no services to shoppers; shoppers perform their own locate-compare-select process.

self-serving bias selbstdienliche Wahrnehmung

Tendency for individuals to attribute their own successes to internal factors while putting the blame for failures on external factors. It suggests that feedback provided to employees in performance reviews will be predictably distorted by recipients depending on whether it is positive or negative.

sell verkaufen; *(to market)* absetzen; (to *place)* anbringen; *(to dispose of)* veräußern; *(to turn over)* umsetzen

seller Verkäufer; *(supplier)* Abgeber

seller financing Händlerkredit

seller's market Verkäufermarkt; Absatzmarkt

Market situation in which there is more demand for a product than there is available supply. As a result, prices will tend to rise and the sellers are in a stron position to set the terms of sale.

seller's option Verkaufsoption

selling Verkaufen; Absetzen; Vertreiben

selling agent Handelsvertreter; Verkaufskommissionär

Someone who sells goods for others and receives a commission on successful deals.

selling concept Verkaufskonzept

Marketing: the idea that consumers will not buy enough of a company's products unless the large-scale selling and promotion efforts are undertaken.

selling organization Verkaufsorganisation; Verkaufseinrichtung

selling point Verkaufsstelle

selling power Werbekraft

selling price *(goods)* Verkaufspreis; *(securities, currency)* Verkaufskurs

selling process Verkaufsprozess

Marketing: the steps that the salesperson follows when selling, which include prospecting and qualifying, preapproach, approach, presentation and demonstration, handling objections, closing and follow-up.

selling representation Verkaufsprogramm

selling short Baissespekulation; Fixen

Securities: If an investor thinks the price of a stock is going down, he could borrow the stock from a broker and sell it. Eventually, he must buy the stock back on the open market.

Example: one borrows 1000 shares of XYZ on July 1 and sells it for $8 per share. Then, on Aug 1, he purchases 1000 shares of XYZ at $7 per share. He has made $1000 (less commissions and other fees) by selling short.

selling time Verkaufszeit

sellout Ausverkauf; Verrat

semiannual result Halbjahresergebnis

semiconductor Halbleiter

An element, such as silicon, that is intermediate in electrical conductivity between conductors and insulators. Semiconductors make it possible to miniaturize electronic components.

semiskilled angelernt

semistrong-form efficiency semi-starke Informationseffizienz

Theory that the market is efficient with respect to all publicly available information.

send senden; (ab)schicken; *(forward)* übersenden; versenden; *(remit)* überweisen; machen

sending Absenden; *(delivering)* Ausliefern; *(forwarding)* Versenden; *(transmitting)* Übersenden; Abschicken

send on nach-; voraus-; weiterschicken

Senge, Peter M. (* 1947)

A leading authority on organizational learning. His chief contribution was to identify five personal development techniques that make up a true learning organization. These were: personal mastery, mental models, shared vision, team learning and system thinking.

Senge was the first to preach that the most successful organizations of the future will be those that encourage learning at all levels. Corporate learning and knowledge are seen as the key to survival, not merely competitiveness. Senge's four 'disciplines' which are held together and informed by the fifth, 'system thinking,' are broadly defined as personal mastery, mental models, building shared vision and team learning.

Systems thinking is 'a framework for seeing interrelationships rather than linear cause-effect chains, and for seeing processes of change rather than static snapshots.'

Biography: an engineering graduate from Stanford, he has been at MIT since 1970, senior lecturer and director of the Center for Organizational Learning, chairman of the Society of Organizational Learning, works as a consultant in education, healthcare and government, has a research center at MIT

Major publications: (1990) The Fifth Discipline: The Art and Practice of the Learning Organization, (1994) The Fifth Discipline Fielbook: Strategies for Building a Learning Organization.

senior älter; dienstälter; *(rank)* ranghöher; Älterer; Dienstälterer

senior citizen Rentner

senior debenture Vorzugsobligation

seniority Rückzahlungsvorrang; längere Dienstzeit

Banking: Order of repayment. In the event of bankruptcy, senior debt must be repaid before subordinated debt receives any payment.

senior partner Hauptinhaber; Seniorpartner; Seniorchef

senior salesperson Chefverkäufer; leitender Verkäufer

seniority system auf Dienstzeit basierendes System

Organization: a system in which privileges are granted to those who have served the longest.

On this basis, it is for example determined who receives promotions and layoffs.

sense-of-mission marketing Marketing mit Mission

Principle of enlightened marketing which holds that a company should define its mission in broad social terms rather than narrow product terms.

sensitive einfühlsam; empfindlich; gefühlvoll

sensitivity Empfindlichkeit; Anfälligkeit; Gefühl

sensitivity analysis Sensitivitätsanalyse

Analysis of how sensitive outcomes are to changes in the assumptions. Used in investment decisions to determine risk and possible outcomes.

sensitivity training Sensibilitätstraining

Method in which a group of individuals exchange thoughts and feelings on a face-to-face basis. Sensitivity training gives insight into how and why others feel and helps overcome resistance to change, change employees world view and even fundamental beliefs.

separable trennbar; abtrennbar; *(divisible)* teilbar

separate einzeln; getrennt; separat; *(to ~)* separieren; trennen; *(to divide up)* aufteilen

separate assets Sondervermögen

separate estate separates Vermögen; Sondervermögen

separate voucher Einzelbeleg

separation of property Gütertrennung

separation principle Separationstheorem nach Tobin

Principle that portfolio choice can be separated into two independent tasks: 1.) determination of the optimal risky portfolio, which is a purely technical problem, and 2.) the personal choice of the best mix of the risky portfolio and the risk-free asset.

separation theorem Separationstheorem nach Fisher

Value of an investment to an individual is not dependent on consumption preferences. All investors will want to accept or reject the same investment projects by using the NPV rule, regardless of personal preference.

sequence Reihenfolge; *(data processing)* Folge; *(film)* Szenenfolge; Szene; Bildfolge

sequential product development sequentielle Produktentwicklung

New-product development approach in which one company department works individually to complete its stage of the process before passing the new product along to the next department and stage.

serial *(broadcasting)* Sendereihe; *(publication)* Serie; Veröffentlichungsreihe; Fortsetzungs-; serienmäßig; laufend

serial covariance serielle Kovarianz

Covariance between a variable and the lagged value of the variable. The same as auto covariance.

series Zahlenfolge; Serie; Reihe

Options: all option contracts of the same class that also have the same unit of trade, expiration date, and exercise price.

Stocks: shares which have common characteristics, such as rights to ownership and voting, dividends, par value, etc. In the case of many foreign shares, one series may be owned only by citizens of the country in which the stock is registered.

servant *(domestic)* Hausangestellter; Diener

serve dienen; im Dienst stehen; *(shop)* bedienen; *(summons)* zustellen; *(food)* auftragen; arbeiten; behilflich sein; bedienen; versorgen

served market bedienter Markt

Part of the qualifies available market that the company decides to pursue.

server Sever

Computer on a network that offers shared hardware or software resources to multiple users. The term may apply in a general sense to a computer that "serves" shared files or applications over a LAN, or it may apply to a computer running a specific application, such as a web server or mail server.

server log file Server Log File

server-side auf Serverseite

Internet: activities that take place on an organization's web server such as processing forms, streaming video, and accessing product databases for sending product web pages to users.

server-side data collection Datensammlung über den Server

Information about consumer surfing that is gathered and recorded on the web server.

service Dienst; Dienstleistung; Service; *(public service)* Amtstätigkeit; Stellung; *(restaurant)* Bedienung; *(delivery of a writ)* Zustellung; *(machine)* Wartung; *(military)* Wehrdienst; *(public utilities)* Versorgung; *(to ~)* warten; instand halten; *(debt)* Schuldendienst leisten

General: activity or benefit that one party can offer to another which is essential intangible and does not result in the ownership of anything.

Marketing: assistance that a manufacturer can offer a customer after he has purchased a product.

serviceable dienst-; gebrauchsfähig; nützlich; hilfreich; verwendbar

service area Servicebereich

service bureau Servicebüro

A company that specializes in providing services to other companies for a fee. Examples are list maintenance or fulfillment services. Service bureaus can normally offer services at a lower cost because they achieve considerable economies of scale.

service business Dienstleistungsgeschäft; Dienstleistungsunternehmen

A business in the service sector, i.e. not manufacturing. This includes a wide variety of activities, ranging from lawn mowing and housekeeping, restaurants and hotels, to lawyers and consultants.

service capacity Dienstleistungskapazität; Nutzungspotential

service center Reparaturwerkstätte; Dienstleistungsbetrieb; *(cost accounting)* Service Center

Cost accounting: A service center is an internal organizational unit that provides paid services to other cost centers.

A service center must attempt to adjust the services it offers according to the demand within the company and compare its prices with those companies offering equivalent services on the open market.

service characteristics Eigenschaften von Dienstleistungen

Services can be distinguished from products along a number of characteristics:

Inseparability - services are produced and consumed at the same time and cannot be separated from their providers.

Intangibility - services cannot be seen, tasted, felt, heard or smelled before they are bought.

Perishability - services cannot be stored for later sale or use.

Variability – thei quality of services may vary greatly, depending on who provides them and when, where and how.

service charge Unkostenbeitrag; Verwaltungsgebühr; Bearbeitungsgebühr; Grundgebühr

service company Dienstleistungsfirma; Dienstleistungsbetrieb; Dienstleistungsunternehmen

service department Kundendienstabteilung

Department providing services to customers, such as accepting merchandise returns and credit applications, approve checks, wrap merchantdise, etc.

service economy Dienstleistungsgesellschaft

Economy in which a high proportion of the labor force is in the service sector, producing a high share of the GDP.

service fee Bearbeitungsgebühr; Bereitstellungspreis

A fee charged for the provision of a service.

service industry Dienstleistungsbranche

service manual Wartungsanweisung; *(operation)* Bedienungsanleitung

service network Kundendienstnetz; Dienstleistungsnetz

service office *(customer service)* Kundendienstbüro

service organization Dienstleistungsorganisation

service quality Servicequalität; Bedienungsqualität

service regulation Dienstanweisung; Betriebsvorschrift

services Dienstleistungen; Dienst; Betrieb

service sector Dienstleistungsbereich; Dienstleistungssektor; Servicesektor

Sector of the economy where service businesses provide employment and contributions to the gross domestic product. The service sector employs over 80% of the American work force.

service worker Arbeiter im Dienstleistungssektor

A person who works in the service sector of an economy, which covers a wide variety of activities, from a waiter to a lawyer.

servicing Wartung; Kundendienst

In general: regular work performed on an asset, such as maintenance and routine repairs, to keep it in good working condition.

Finance: the collection of payments and management of operational procedures related to a mortgage.

servicing staff Wartungspersonal

serving Serving

Internet: Used to describe the process of displaying an advertisement on a website (ad serving) or delivering a web page to a user's web browser.

session Sitzung; Sitzungszeit; *(meeting)* Tagung; Lehrabschnitt

set Satz; Garnitur; *(adv)* fest; bestimmt; *(to ~) (a condition)* festlegen, bestimmen; *(a price)* festsetzen; bestimmen; *(a deadline)* befristen; *(to solidify)* fest werden; untergehen; stellen; setzen

setback Rückschlag; *(regression)* Rückschritt; *(stock market)* Einbruch; *(worsening)* Verschlechterung; Zurückstellung; Verzögerung; Zurückwerfen

set of contracts perspective Vertragstheorie der Unternehmung

View of company as a set of contracting relationships among individuals who have conflicting objectives, such as shareholders or managers.

set of problems Problemkomplex; Problematik

setting a date Terminfestlegung; -festsetzung

settle *(bill)* begleichen; *(claim)* zufrieden stellen; *(dispute)* beilegen; *(residence)* sich niederlassen; regeln; festlegen; erledigen; beruhigen; beständig werden

Bill: to pay an obligation.

Law: to resolve a legal dispute short of adjudication

settled *(fixed, set)* fixiert; *(agreed upon)* abgemacht; festgelegt; erledigt

settlement *(bill)* Begleichung; Regelung; Abkommen; *(account)* Zahlungsausgleich; *(claim)* Zufriedenstellung; *(dispute)* Beilegung; Einigung; Siedlung; Kolonie

Estates: distribution of an estate's assets by an executor to beneficiaries after all legal procedures have been completed.

Law: an agreement reached through negotiation.

settlement date Abrechnungsdatum; Fälligkeitstermin

Real estate: the date when a property is purchased and the deed is transferred.

Securities: the date on which payment is due for a security trade.

settlement petition Vergleichsantrag

settlement proceedings Vergleichsverfahren

settlement trustee Vergleichsverwalter

set up einrichten; aufbauen; etablieren

setup *(arrangement)* Einrichtung; *(establishment)* Etablierung; *(organization)* Organisation; Aufbau; *(trap)* Falle

setup costs Einrichtungskosten

Costs that arise when setting up a new process or a new procedure. For a manufacturing operation they can include design costs, acquisition and location of machinery, and employee hiring and training.

seven S model Sieben-S-Modell

Name of a framework developed in the late 1970s and early 1980s for analyzing organizations and looking at the various elements that make them successful.

The framework has seven aspects, each of them beginning with the letter S – strategy, structure, systems, skills, shared values, staff, and style. Companies had to pay attention to all seven of the Ss at the same time. The seven Ss were subdivided into the first three (strategy, structure, and systems), referred to as the hard Ss, and the last four, which were called the soft Ss.

severe abtrennen; scheiden; zerreißen; absondern; *(relationship)* auflösen; *(communication)* unterbrechen; abbrechen

severally *(liability)* einzeln

severance Trennung; Bruch; *(diplomatic relations)* Abbruch

severance pay Abfindung; Abfindungszahlung; Entlassungsabfindung

Payment that is made by an employer to the employee on the termination of an employment.

sexual harassment sexuelle Belästigung

Unlawful discrimination on the basis of sex, which includes unwelcome advances, requests for sexual favors, and other verbal or physical conduct of a sexual nature.

shadow economy Schattenwirtschaft

Illegal part of an economy, where the workforce, is not officially employed, normally not insured, and pays no taxes.

Estimates put the size of the shadow economy up to 10% of the real economy.

shakeout Geschäftsaufgabe der Konkurrenz; Gesundschrumpfen; Umstrukturierung

A situation in a market that makes it increasingly difficult for companies to operate profitably. As a result, many weaker companies are forced to leave the industry.

shaping behavior Verhaltensformung

Systematically reinforcing each successive step that moves an individual closer to the desired response. Reinforcement would increase as responses more closely approximated the desired behavior.

share Anteil; Geschäftsateil; *(stock)* Aktie; Kapitalanteil; Kapitalbeteiligung; *(certificate)* Investmentzertifikat; *(to ~)* teilen; teilhaben an; teilnehmen; (sich) beteiligen

Securities: a certificate evidencing ownership of a fraction of the capital of the company that issued it.

share certificate Partizipationsschein; Aktienzertifikat; Anteilsscheine

share earnings *(yield)* Aktienertrag; *(earnings)* Aktiengewinn

shareholder Aktieninhaber; Aktionär; Anteilseigner

A person who owns shares of a corporation's stock. The basic rights that derive from this share of ownership are: a claim on a share of the company's undivided assets in proportion to the number of shares held; proportionate voting power; and dividends when earned and declared.

shareholders' equity *(balance sheet)* Eigenkapital; Nettoanteil der Aktionäre

Total assets minus total liabilities of a corporation; also called stockholders' equity and net worth.

shareholders' group Aktionärskreis

shareholders' interest Aktionärsinteressen

Residual claims that shareholders have against a firm' s assets, calculated by subtracting total liabilities from total assets. It includes the claims of ordinary shareholders and preference shareholders too; also called net worth.

shareholding Aktienbeteiligung; Aktienbesitz

shareholdings Beteiligungen; Aktienbesitz; Aktienbestände

share market Aktienmarkt

A market for the trading of securities, such as company stock and associated financial instruments (including stock options, convertibles and stock index futures), operated by professional stockbrokers and stockjobbers.

share of audience Zuschaueranteil

Marketing: the percentage of homes tuned to a particular program or station.

share of authorized capital Anteil des Stammkapitals

share of business Geschäftsanteil

share of capital stock Stammkapitalanteil

share of mind Share of mind; Prozentsatz der Presonen, die eine Werbung gesehen hat

Advertising: When consumers think of a type or category of product, they have a limited list in mind (evoked set). Any product included in an evoked set has share of mind. A main task of marketers is to maximize their product's share of mind.

Relationship marketing: focusing on customer development in the long term: maintaining and enhancing. A firm using this kind of relationship marketing differentiates individual customers based on need rather than differentiating products for target groups.

share of sales Umsatzanteil

share of the market Marktanteil

share price Börsenkurs; Aktienpreis

share repurchase Aktienrückkauf

Program by which a corporation buys back its own shares in the open market.

It is usually done when shares are undervalued. Since it reduces the number of shares outstanding and thus increases earnings per share, it tends to elevate the market value of the remaining shares held by stockholders.

shares Aktien; Anteile; Beteiligungen

Securities carrying ownership rights in a company.

shares of record registrierte Aktien

shares outstanding ausgegebene Aktien

The shares of a corporation's stock that have been issued to the public and are in the hands of investors.

shareware Shareware; Vertriebsform von Software

Software that anyone can download for free and pass along to others. The creators of shareware programs usually ask users to pay a small fee it they use the product after a specified period of time

sharpen schärfen; verschärfen; *(pencil)* anspitzen; *(tools)* schleifen

shelf Fach, Auslage; Regal; Schrankwand

shelf life Lagerzeit von Beständen; Lagerfähigkeit; Haltbarkeit

The length of time that a good can be stored while still remaining useful enough to sell.

shelter Zuflucht; Schutz; *(home)* Obdach; *(tax)* steuerbegünstigte Anlage; *(to ~)* schützen; *(to bouse)* beherbergen

sheltered geschützt

sheltered shopping center überdachtes Einkaufszentrum

Large store cluster housed within a sheltered or covered building, normally having many storeys of stores and, in same countries, stretching across several blocks of buildings. The cluster consists of a broad mix of stores - general, speciality, small, large, independent and chain.

shift Verlagerung; Verschiebung; Veränderung; *(work period)* Schicht; *(automobile)* Gangschaltung; *(lever)* Schalthebel; *(to ~)* verschieben; verlagern; Standort ändern; *(capital)* umschichten; *(automobile)* schalten

Work: Time window during which an employee is assigned to work. For most professions shifts last eight hours, plus a certain time for breaks.

shift performance *(factory)* Schichtleistung

shift productivity *(factory)* Schichtleistung; Arbeitsleistung einer Schicht

ship Schiff; Raumschiff; Luftschiff; *(to ~)* verschicken; absenden; verladen; verfrachten

shipment *(by sea)* Verschiffung; *(of goods)* Warensendung; *(load)* Ladung; *(delivery)* Lieferung

shipper *(water transport)* Verschiffer; *(land transport)* Versender; *(freight forwarder)* Spediteur; *(railway)* Eisenbahnspediteur

shipping *(dispatch)* Versand; Versenden; Transport; Versand-; Schiffsbestand; Handelsflotte; Verschiffung

shipping trade Speditionsgewerbe; Seetransportgeschäft

shipping volume Transportvolumen; Ladevolumen

shirking Drückebergerei; sich vor der Verantwortung drücken

Attitude to avoid work or to do less then expected.

shoddy schäbig; wertlos; schlecht; von schlechter Qualität

shop Geschäft; Laden; Betrieb; Beruf; *(repair facility)* Werkstatt; *(to ~)* einkaufen

Manufacturing: the specific area of a business where production takes place.

shop closing law Ladenschlussgesetz

shop closing time Ladenschlusszeit

shopper Käufer; Einkäufer; *(customer)* Kunde; Kundin

shopping Ladenbesuch; *(purchasing)* Einkaufen

shopping agent Shopping Agent

Internet: Program that allow the consumer to rapidly compare prices and features within product categories. Shopping agents implicitly negotiate prices downward on behalf of the consumer by listing companies in order of best price first.

shopping cart Einkaufswagen

Internet: Program or a series of programs that let visitors to a website make selections of orders from more than one page before sending in that order.

A shopping cart on the web works just like a shopping cart in the real world - on each page, the customer can "put things into his shopping cart" but not have to actually pay for them yet. As they go from area to area of the online store, they can add more items or put items back. Finally, they get to "check-out" where they place their combined order.

shopping center Einkaufszentrum

A cluster of shops and retail stores, normally with one or more large department, discount, or food stores.

shopping goods gehobene Konsumgüter

Consumer goods that the customer, in the process of selection and purchase, characteristically compares on such bases as suitability, quality, price, and style.

shopping mall Ladenpassage; Einkaufzentrum

A building or set of buildings that contain stores and have interconnecting walkways that may be enclosed. In the United Kingdom and Australia these are called shopping centers or shopping arcades

shopping newspaper Anzeigenblatt

Newspaper for customers, usually free-of-charge, that advertises local businesses, such as stores, restaurants, and shopping centers.

shop rules Fabrikordnung; Betriebsverfassung

Basic rules of behavior in a factory.

shop steward Arbeitnehmervertreter

Worker representative elected by other union members to represent them to management.

shortage Knappheit; Verknappung; *(lack)* Mangel; *(deficiency of goods)* Fehlbestand; *(deficiency of money)* Fehlbetrag

shortage of money Geldnot

shorten verkürzen; kürzer werden

shortfall Unterschuss; *(imbalance)* Defizit; *(deficiency)* Fehlbetrag; Fehlmenge

A negative difference between the amount expected or budgeted, and the actual result.

short position kurze Position

Options: Position wherein a person's interest in a particular series of options is as a net writer (i.e., the number of contracts sold exceeds the number of contracts bought).

Stocks: Occurs when a person sells stocks he does not yet own. Shares must be borrowed, before the sale, to make "good delivery" to the buyer. Eventually, the shares must be bought to close out the transaction. Technique is used when an investor believes the stock price is going down.

short run *(short term)* kurze Sicht; *(production)* kurzer Schub

short-run kurzfristig

short-run operating activities kurzfristige Geschäftstätigkeit

Events and decisions concerning the short-term finance of a firm, such as how much inventory to order and whether to otter cash terms or credit terms to customers.

short sale Leerverkauf; spekulativer Verkauf

The sale of a security that the seller does not own but is committed to repurchasing eventually. The intention is to capitalize on an expected decline in the security's price.

short selling baissespekulation; Fixen

Occurs when an investor places a speculative bet that the value of a financial asset will decline, and profits from that decline.

short-term kurzfristig

Accounting: assets that can be converted into cash within the normal operating cycle (usually one year), or liabilities coming due in one year or less.

Investment: investment with a maturity of less than one year.

short-term debt kurzfristige Verschuldung

Obligation having a maturity of one year or less from the date it was issued.

short-term liability kurzfristige Verbindlichkeit

short-term orientation kurzfristige Orientierung

National culture attribute that emphasizes the past and present, respect for tradition, and fulfilling social obligation.

show zeigen

show a tendency tendieren

shrink schrumpfen; eingehen; zurückschrecken

shrinkage Schwund; Schrumpfung; Ladendiebstahl

shutdown Stilllegung; Schließung; *(work stoppage)* Arbeitsunterbrechung; Betriebsstörung

shut down *(factory)* stilllegen; *(to close)* schließen; sperren; zumachen

Production: a stoppage of the production process that occurs after a breakdown, shortage of orders, lack of materials, or other reasons.

shutting up shop Ladenschließung

shuttle Schiffchen; *(train)* Pendelzug; *(space travel)* Raumfähre; *(to ~)* hin- und her fahren

sick pay Krankengeld

Payment an employee receives to replace wages during the period when he is absent from work.

side-effects Nebenwirkungen

Effects of a proposed project has on other parts of the firm.

sideline Seitenlinie; *(goods)* zusätzliche Ware; Nebenprodukt; Nebenzweig; Nebenberuf; *(to ~)* beiseite schieben; *(to divert)* abzweigen; *fig* kaltstellen

sidestep Schritt zu Seite; entgehen; zur Seite treten; umgehen; *(to avoid)* vermeiden

sight draft Sichtwechsel

A draft that is payable upon presentation to the drawee, such as a bill of exchange for immediate collection.

sign Zeichen; Wink; Schild; Anzeichen; *(trace)* Spur; *(characteristic)* Merkmal; *(to ~) (document)* unterzeichnen; ein Zeichen geben; unterschreiben

signaling Meldung; Anzeige; Zeichengeben

signaling approach Signalling

Investment: theory about the determination of the optimal capital structure, stating that insiders in a firm have information that the market does not; therefore the choice of capital structure by insiders can signal information to outsiders and change the value of the firm.

signature Unterschrift; Signatur; Namenszug; Vorzeichen; Druckbogen

significance Bedeutung; Bedeutsamkeit; Wichtigkeit; *(research)* Bewertungsgrad; Stichhaltigkeit; Signifikanz

signing *(agreement)* Unterzeichnung; Unterzeichnen

silent schweigend; *(partner)* still; stumm

similar ähnlich; gleichartig

simple einfach; ehrlich; arglos; einfältig töricht

simple interest einfache Zinsen; einfache Verzinsung

Interest calculated by considering only the original principal amount.

simple linear regression einfache lineare Regression

Statistics: a regression method of modeling the conditional expected value of one variable y given the values of some other variable or variables x. It is called linear because the relation is assumed to be a linear function.

simple structure einfache Organisationsstruktur

Structure characterized by a low degree of departmentalization, wide spans of control, authority centralized in a single person, and little formalization.

simple yield einfache Rendite

Investment: a yield in its most basic form, which is basically the dividend or interest payment divided by price.

simulate vorgeben; vortäuschen; heucheln; nachmachen; simulieren

simulated fingiert; *(not genuine)* unecht; künstlich; simuliert

simulation Simulation

Statistics: imitating or estimating how events might occur in a real situation. It can involve complex mathematical modeling, role playing without the aid of technology, or combinations.

simulation models Simulationsmodelle

simultaneous product development gleichzeitige Produktentwicklung

Approach to developing new products in which various company departments work closely together, overlapping the steps in the product development process to save time and increase effectiveness.

sincere aufrichtig; echt; wahr; seriös

single einfach; *(unmarried)* ledig; *(sole)* einzig; *(individual)* einzeln; ehrlich; unentwegt

single-entry bookkeeping einfache Buchführung

Accounting: a simple bookkeeping system in which transactions are entered in only one account without the use of balancing debits and credits.

Single European Act Einheitliche Europäische Akte

An act passed in 1997 and adopted by members of the European Community, that committed member countries to establishing an economic union.

single-item production Einzelfertigung

single-loop learning Anpassungslernen; Single-loop learning

Organizational learning: in single-loop learning, individuals, groups or organizations modify their actions according to the difference between expected3 and obtained outcomes.

single-source data systems Datensystem über eine Quelle

Electronic monitoring: system that links consumers' exposure to television advertising and promotion (measured using television meters) with what they buy in stores (measured using store checkout scanners).

single stockholder Einzelaktionär

singular case Einzelfall

sink *(kitchen)* Ausguss; *(to ~)* sinken; untergehen; *(fall)* fallen; abfallen; nachgeben; sich senken; *(ship)* versenken

sinking fund Schuldentilgungsfonds; Amortisationsfond; Tilgungsfonds

Investments: a fund into which a company sets aside money over time, in order to retire its preferred stock, bonds or debentures.

sister Schwester

sister company Schwestergesellschaft

Sister companies share the same parent company or individual owner. Like a subsidiary, a sister company is a separately incorporated business.

site Stätte; Lage; Örtlichkeit; *(scene)* Schauplatz; *(plot of land)* Gelände; *(Internet)* Webseite *(building site)* Bauplatz; Baustelle; *(to ~)* errichten

Internet: short expression for a website, i.e. a collection of webpages.

site announcements Seiten-Ankündigung

Internet: Usually used to describe the dissemination of information about a new or revised web site.

site auditor Seiten-Auditor

Internet: an auditor accurately measures the usage for different sites.

site availability Seiten-Verfügbarkeit

Internet: indication of how easy it is to connect to a website as a user. In theory this figure should be 100 per cent, but for technical reasons such as failures in the server hardware or upgrades to software, sometimes users cannot access the site and the figure falls below 90 per cent.

site centric measurement seitenzentrierte Messung

Internet: Audience measurement model in which user activity is tallied at the content provider' s web site to produce audience composition statistics, page views, and other statistics.

site measurement Seiten-Messung

site re-launch Seiten-Relaunch; Wiederaufsetzen einer Seite

Internet: situation where a web site is replaced with a new version with a new look and feel.

site statistics Seiten-Statistik

Internet: collected by log file analyzers, these are used to monitor the effectiveness of a web site.

site stickiness Attraktivität einer Seite

Internet: an indication of how long a visitor stars on a site. Log file analyzers can be used to assess average visit times.

site visits Seiten-Besuche

Internet: one site visit records one customer visiting the site; not equivalent to user session.

sitemapping tools Sitemap-Werkzeuge

Internet: these tools diagram the layout of the web site, which is useful for site management, and can be used to assist users.

situation Stellung; Situation; Lage

situational leadership theory situative Führungstheorie

Management: contingency theory was developed by Paul Hersey and Ken Blanchard that focuses on follower's readiness. The emphasis on the followers in leadership effectiveness reflects that it is followers who accept or reject the leader. Regardless of what the leader does, effectiveness depends on the actions of his or her followers.

situation analysis Situationsanalyse

Marketing: review of the existing marketing plan and any other information that can be obtained about the company and its brands, as well as environmental factors, and the development of a market opportunity analysis.

six-sigma method Sechs-Sigma Methode

Production: a quality measurement and improvement program originally developed by Motorola that focuses on the control of a process to the point of ± six sigma (standard deviations) from a centerline, or put another way, 3.4 defects per million items.

size Größe; *(extent)* Umfang; Leim; *(to ~)* die Größe bestimmen; die Größe messen; sortieren

sized nach Größe geordnet

skeleton data Rahmendaten

skeleton regulation Rahmenregelung

sketch Skizze; *(drawing)* Zeichnung; *(design)* Entwurf; *(to ~)* skizzieren; zeichnen; entwerfen

sketchy umrissartig; skizzenhaft; ungenau; *(superficial)* oberflächlich; lückenhaft

skewed *(statistics)* verzerrt; verzogen; abgeschrägt

skill Geschick; Kunst; Fertigkeit; *(ability)* Können; geschickt

skill-based pay Bezahlung nach Qualifizierung

HRM: pay levels are based on how many skills employees have or how many jobs they can do. Skill-based pay encourages employees to acquire a broader range of skills; also sometimes called competency-based pay.

skill intensive wissensintensiv

Economics: an occurrence of factor intensity describing an industry or sector of the economy that relies relatively heavily on inputs of skilled labor.

skilled geschickt; *(worker)* gelernt; erfahren

skilled worker Facharbeiter; Fachkraft; ausgebildeter Arbeiter

skillful geschickt; gewandt

skills development Fähigkeitenentwicklung

skill variety Tätigkeitsvielfalt

Degree to which the job requires a variety of different activities, so the worker can use a number of different skills and talent.

skim abschöpfen; abrahmen; *(reading)* überfliegen

skimming Abschöpfungsstrategie; Hochpreisstrategie

Marketing: a pricing strategy whereby a company charges the highest possible price that buyers who most desire the product will pay. At a later point the price is reduced to offset competitive products and slowing demand.

skin Haut; *(Internet)* Erscheinungsbild einer Seite

skinned enthäutet; gehäutet; *fig* ausgeplündert; betrogen

skyrocket Signalrakete; *(to ~)* hochschnellen; hochschießen

skyrocketing Emporschnellen; Hochschießen; emporschnellend; hochschießend; sprunghaft ansteigen

slack Stillstand; *(adv)* träge; schlaff; lasch; lustlos; flau

slacken verlangsamen; lockern; *(demand)* nachlassen; *(stock market)* flau werden; sich abschwächen

slackness Abschwächung; Nachlassen; Flauheit; Flaute

slack period flaue Geschäftszeit; Flaute

slag Schlacke

slag heap Schlackenhalde

slander Verleumdung; *(to ~)* verleumden; in falschen Verdacht bringen

Law: a for of defamation, consisting of spoken words that tend to damage another's reputation.

slash Hieb; Schnitt; Schlitz; *(to ~) (price)* stark reduzieren; drastisch senken; peitschen; geißeln

slashing *(public programs)* umfangreiches Streichen; *(wages)* scharfes Senken; *(price)* starkes Herabsetzen; *(production)* starkes Einschränken

slate *(mineral)* Schiefer; *(writing tablet)* Schiefertafel; *(nomination)* Kandidatenliste; Vorschlagsliste; *(to ~) (to plan)* vorsehen; vorschlagen; verreißen

slender *(profits)* gering; dürftig; mager; *(person)* schlank; schmal; knapp

slice Scheibe; Stück; *(market)* Anteil; *(to ~)* in Scheiben schneiden; abschneiden

slide *(photography)* Diapositiv; *(stocks)* Talfahrt; Rutschbahn; *(to ~)* rutschen; gleiten; schlittern; *(to insert)* einschieben

sliding Rutschen; Gleiten; *(decline)* Absinken; *(door)* Schiebe-; *(taxes)* gestuft; gestaffelt; *(parity)* Stufen flexibel; *(scale)* gleitend

slight *(offense)* Missachtung; *(adv)* unerheblich; geringfügig; *(stature)* zierlich; schwächlich; schmächtig; schlank

slim *(slender)* schlank; dünn; *(profits)* dürftig; armselig; *(scarce)* knapp; *(poor)* armselig; *(to ~) (to reduce one's weigbt)* eine Schlankheitskur machen

slip *(paper)* Zettel; Schein; *(mistake)* Flüchtigkeitsfehler; Versehen; Schnitzer; *(garment)* Unterrock; *(to ~) (into clothes)* schlüpfen; *(on ice)* ausgleiten; ausrutschen; *(sales)* schwinden; *(prices)* abgleiten

slippage Nachgeben

Investment: the difference between estimated transaction costs and actual transaction costs.

slipping *(prices)* Abgleiten; *(sales)* Schwinden *(adv)* abgleitend; schwindend

Sloan, Alfred P. (1875-1966)

US industrialist, who virtually invented the decentralized, multi-divisional corporation of today. His only book "My Years With General Motors" has been influential on practicing managers and on the study of organizations.

At GM, Sloan fundamentally changed the entire company structure to build a new organization reducing GM's eight car companies into five operating divisions, supported by three component divisions.

Each division had its own engineering, production and sales departments but was supervised by a central corporate staff responsible for policy and finance. This was a principle which has retained its value to the present day. Sloan introduced a system of checks and balances into the divisional structure that gave engineering, manufacturing and finance equal status.

Biography: in 1900 he was the general manager of the Hyatt Roller Bearing Company, 1917, United was acquired by General Motors and Sloan, by then United's president, joined the GM board, in 1923 he became president, in 1946 chairman and from 1956-1966 honorary chairman

Major publications: (1963, 1966, 1986) My Years With General Motors.

slogan Schlagwort; Motto; *(advertising)* Werbespruch

slot Spalt; Schlitz; *(coin)* Einwurfschlitz; *(market niche)* Nische; Position; Nut; Kerbe; *(to ~)* auskerben; *(to slit)* schlitzen

slotting fees Positionsgebühr; Einstellgebühr

Payments demanded by retailers from producers before they will accept new products and find slots for them on the shelves.

slow langsam; *(dragging)* schleppend; *(retarded)* zurückgeblieben; *(sales)* flau

slowdown Nachlassen; Geschwindigkeitsverringerung; Verlangsamung; Beruhigung

Industrial dispute: a form of protest designed to bring economic pressure upon an employer without incurring the costs of a strike.

slow growth langsames Wachstum

slowing Verlangsamen; Verzögern; langsamer werdend; sich verzögernd

slow down/up verlangsamen; sich verlangsamen

sluggish *(slow-moving)* schwerfällig; träge; *(market)* stagnierend; flau

sluggishness Schwerfälligkeit; *(economy)* Flaute; Stagnation

slump Fall; *(prices)* Preisverfall; *(decline)* Baisse; *(business cycle)* Konjunkturrückgang; *(to ~)* absinken; fallen; plötzlich fallen; stürzen

Economics: a drop in economic or productive activity, but not as severe as a recession or depression.

slump in sales Absatzrückgang

small business Kleinbetrieb; mittelständiges Unternehmen

A way of classifying businesses, normally based on three sets of figures: sales, employees and profit. The precise numbers, however, differ from country to country. In the US, a business is small when it employs fewer than 100 people.

small company Kleinunternehmen

small investor Kleinanleger

small is beautiful „klein ist schön"

Management technique developed by Schumacher trying to achieve smallness within large organizations.

small loan Kleinanleihe; Kleinkredit

small office/home office (SOHO) Heimbüro

Expression used to describe the work environment of very small businesses, whith 1-10 employees, often run from the owner´s home. Equipped with faxes, modems, and personal computers, they are able to compete effectively.

small parcel Päckchen

small stockholder Kleinaktionär

small-town kleinstädtisch

small trade Handwerk

small trader Minderkaufmann

SMART metrics SMART-Metriken

An acronym stating that metrics must be specific; measurable; actionable; relevant; timely.

smartcard Chipkarte

Physical card containing a memory chip that can be inserted into a smartcard reader before items can be purchased.

Smith, Adam (1723 – 1790)

A Scottish political economist and philosopher. His book *Inquiry into the Nature and Causes of the Wealth of Nations* (1776) was one of the earliest and most influential attempts to study the historical development of industry and commerce in Europe. It helped to create the modern academic discipline of economics by providing one of the best-known intellectual rationales for free trade, capitalism and libertarianism. Key elements of his thought are still quoted today.

smokestack industry „Schornstein"-Industrien

Expression for heavy industry, such as the steel and auto industries, who used to have large smokestacks for their operations.

Smoot-Hawley Tariff US Zollgesetz

Enacted in 1930 by the US Congress, this tariff erected a wall of barriers against imports into the United States. It provoked retaliation by other countries and played an important part in initiating the Great Depression.

snail mail Schneckenpost

Traditional mail delivered offline, so called because it is slower than online mail.

snake Schlange

The European system of exchange rate setting created in April 1972 and superseded in 1979 by the European Monetary System.

sneakernet Sneakernet

Computers: process of moving files and applications manually from one computer to another without the benefit of a network.

snowball Schneeball; *(to ~) fig* exponentiell zunehmen

snowballing exponentielles Zunehmen

Economic activity that rapidly increases and builds up a strong momentum.

soar emporschnellen; rapide steigen; aufsteigen; hochfliegen

soaring Emporschnellen; schnell hochsteigend; rapide zunehmend

social gesellschaftlich; gesellig; sozial

social assistance law Sozialrecht

social benefits claim Sozialanspruch

social bonding soziale Verkettung

Stimulated social interaction between companies and customers resulting in a more personalized communication and brand loyalty.

social class soziale Klasse

Relatively permanent and ordered divisions in a society whose members share similar values, interests and behavior.

social democrat Sozialdemokrat

Person committed to achieving social ideals by democratic means.

social economy Sozialwirtschaft; Gemeinwirtschaft

social facilitation effect Gruppeneinfulss auf Leistung

Organization: theory stating that individual performance is affected by the presence of others: simple, routine tasks tend to be speeded up and made more accurate; complex work, requiring closer attention, is likely to be negatively affected.

social framework Sozialgebilde; Sozialsystem

social information processing (SIP) model soziales Informationsverarbeitungsmodell

Theory saying that employees adopt attitudes and behaviors in response to the social cues provided by others (co-workers, supervisors, friends, family members, or customers) with whom they have contact. People respond to their jobs as they perceive them rather than to the objective jobs themselves.

socialism Sozialismus

Economic and plolitical system in which government owns or controls major critical industries, but may allow collective ownership and some private ownership in agriculture, services, and less critical industries; political philosophy advocating substantial public involvement, through government ownership, in the means of production and distribution.

socialization Sozialisation

Process that adapts employees to the organization's culture. The most critical socialization stage is at the time of entry into the organization. This is when the organization seeks to mould the outsider into a good employee.

social justice soziale Gerechtigkeit; Sozialrecht

social-learning theory sozial-kognitive Lerntheorie

Theory saying that people can learn through observation and direct experience. Four processes determine the influence that a model will have on an individual. These are:

Attentional processes: people learn from a model only when they recognize and pay attention to its critical features.

Retention processes: a model's influence will depend on how well the individual remembers the model's action after the model is no longer readily available.

Motor reproduction processes: After a person has seen a new behavior by observing the model, the watching must be converted to doing.

Reinforcement processes: individuals will be motivated to exhibit the modeled behavior if positive incentives or rewards are provided.

social loafing Bummeln; Faulenzen

Tendency of individuals to expend less effort when working collectively than when working individually.

Because the results of the group cannot be attributed to any single person, the relationship between an individual's input and the group's output in clouded. So there will be a reduction in efficiency when individuals think that their contribution cannot be measured.

social mobility soziale Mobilität

Extent to which individuals can move out of the social strata into which they are born.

social network soziales Netzwerk

Specific set of linkages among a defined set of individuals.

social order Sozialordnung; Gesellschaftsordnung

social partnership Sozialpartnerschaft

social policy Sozialpolitik; Gesellschaftspolitik

social psychology Sozialpsychologie

Area within psychology that blends concepts from psychology and sociology and that focuses on the influence of people on one another.

social responsibility soziale Verantwortung

social security contribution Sozialversicherungsbeitrag

social security law *(body of laws)* Sozialrecht; *(individual law)* Sozialversicherungsgesetz

social security number Sozialversicherungsnummer

social security payment Sozialabgabe

social security system Sozialversicherungssystem

Complex system run by the state that attempts to practically fulfill society's social responsibility; in particular it tries to offer protection for weak members of the society against socially recognized needs, including poverty, old age, disability, unemployment, and others.

social security tax Sozialabgabe

social service *(concept)* Sozialfürsorge; *(benefit)* Sozialleistung; Sozialversorgung

social service contribution Sozialbeitrag

social state Sozialstaat

social system Sozialordnung

societal marketing Soziomarketing

societal marketing concept gesellschaftsfreundliches Marketingkonzept

Idea that the organization should determine the needs, wants and interests of target markets and deliver the desired satisfactions more effectively and efficiently than competitors in a way that maintains or improves the consumer's and society's well-being.

society Gesellschaft; *(club)* Verein

An extended social group having a distinctive cultural and economic organization

socket *(light bulb)* Fassung; (Augen-)Höhle; (Gelenk-)Pfanne; *(wall socket)* Steckdose

socioeconomic sozialwirtschaftlich; sozioökonomisch

sociogram Soziogramm

Diagram that graphically maps the preferred social interactions obtained from interviews or questionnaires.

sociology Soziologie

The study of the human individuals in groups and in relation to their fellow human beings.

sociometry Soziometrie

Analytical technique for studying group interactions. It seeks to find out who people like or dislike and with whom they would or would not wish to work.; also called social network mapping or organizational network analysis.

sociopolitical soziopolitisch

soft weich; matschig; sanft; *(irresolute)* nachgiebig; schwächlich; *(beverage)* alkoholfrei; *(market)* flau; *(goods)* kurzlebig

soft currency weiche Währung

A currency that is not widely accepted in exchange for other currencies; they are often fixed at unrealistic exchange rates and are not backed by gold, so that countries with hard currencies are reluctant to buy them.

soften weich machen; erweichen; *(business cycle)* abschwächen

soft selling weiche Verkaufstechnik

Technique of using low-pressure appeals in sales.

soft spot wunder Punkt; Schwachstelle

software Software; Computerprogramm

A complex set of written coded commands that tell a computer what tasks to perform.

software agents Software-Agenten

software market Softwaremarkt

sogo shosha

Japanese trading companies; a key part of the keiretsu, the large Japanese industrial groups.

sold verkauft

sole *(foot)* Sohle; *(fish)* Seezunge; *(only)* Allein-; alleinig; einzig; *(to ~)* besohlen

sole agency Alleinvertretung

*sole proprietorship** Einzelunternehmung

A business owned and operated by one person. The sole proprietor pays no corporate income tax, but has unlimited liability for business debts and obligations.

solicit *(customers)* werben; *(support)* (dringend) (er)bitten; *(to plead)* plädieren; ansprechen, belästigen

solid fest; massiv; *(dense)* dicht; *(rigid)* starr; *(strong)* stark; *(durable)* haltbar; *fig* gründlich; zuverlässig; *(financially)* kreditfähig; gediegen; ganz

solve (auf)lösen

solvency Zahlungsfähigkeit; Solvenz; Bonität

The ability to meet financial obligations on time.

solvent *(chemistry)* Lösungsmittel; *(financially)* zahlungsfähig; zahlungskräftig

sophisticated hoch entwickelt; *(on a high level)* auf hohem Niveau stehend; *(complex)* differenziert

sophistication hoch entwickelter Stand; *(technically advanced)* technisch hohes Niveau; *(complexity)* Differenziertheit

sort Sorte; *(kind)* Art; Marke; *(species)* Gattung; *(to ~)* (aus)sortieren; sichten

sound Ton; Geräusch; Schall; Klang; *(narrows)* Meeresenge; Sund; *(healthy)* gesund; *(undamaged)* unversehrt;

intakt; *(business)* solide; gut fundiert; zahlungskräftig; tüchtig; gründlich; *(to ~) (depth)* ausloten; sondieren; klingen

source Quelle; Ursprung; *(supplier)* Lieferant

source of error Fehlerquelle

source of information Informationsquelle

sources of funds Mittelherkunft

Accounting: section within the statement of changes in financial position showing the increase in funds for the accounting period.

sourcing Akquisition; Beschaffung

The process of identifying, conducting negotiations with, and forming supply agreements with vendors of goods and services.

sovereign Souverän; *(ruler)* Herrscher; *(adv)* souverän; unumschränkt; oberst; unübertrefflich

sovereign risk staatspolitisches Risiko

Risk that a government or sovereign power will default on its payment obligations, also called country risk or political risk.

sovereignty Souveränität

Politics: the exclusive right to exercise power over a geographic area or a group of people. In a nation state, sovereignty is generally vested in the people who delegate it to a government.

space Raum; Zwischenraum; *(interval)* Abstand; Entfernung; *(gap)* Lücke; *(outer space)* Weltraum; Zeitraum; *(to ~) (printing)* spationieren; sperren; in Zwischenräumen/Abständen anordnen

spacious *(roomy)* geräumig; *(extensive)* ausgedehnt

spam Spam; unerwünschte Werbe-E-Mails

Internet: slang term for unsolicited commercial e-mail. "Spamming" people with unwanted commercial e-mail solicitations is considered unethical and it is now illegal in several states.

spam filter Anti-Spam-Filter

Internet: program that has the capability of blocking unsolicited e-mails.

span (Zeit-)Spanne; Spannweite; *(bridge)* Stützweite; *(to ~)* umspannen; überspannen; umfassen

span of control Kontrollspanne; Leitungsspanne

Organization: the number of people a manager can supervise effectively.

spare *(part)* Ersatzteil; Extrastück Reserve-; übrig; *(to ~) (forbearance)* schonen; *(to do without)* erübrigen; entbehren

spate Flut; Schwall; Überschwemmung

special Sonder-; Spezial-; speziell; ungewöhnlich

special agent Sonderbevollmächtigter; Agent

A person acting for another with limited authority.

special arrangement Sonderregelung

special charge Sondergebühr

special delivery Eilzustellung; Sonderzustellung

special direct costs Sondereinzelkosten

Accounting: special direct costs of sales and production are cost items which can be unambiguously assigned to a manufacturing or customer order and so be taken into account in product costing.

Example: special tools and equipment for products, special carriage and promotion costs for a specific order or customer.

special drawing rights (SDR) Sondererziehungsrechte

A type of international money created by the International Monetary Fund and allocated to its member nations.

First issued in 1970, SDRs are designed to supplement the reserves of gold and convertible currencies, used to maintain stability in the foreign exchange market.

special fee Sondergebühr

specialist Spezialist; *(expert)* Fachmann; Sachverständiger; fachlich

In general: anyone with extensive knowledge of a small area.

specialists Fachleute

specialty goods Spezialität; Spezialerzeugnis; hochwertige Waren

Marketing: consumer goods with unique characteristics or brand identification for which a significant group of buyers is willing to make a special purchase effort.

specialty product Spezialerzeugnis

specialty store Fachgeschäft

Retail store that carries a narrow product line with a deep assortment with that line.

specialization Spezialisierung; Fachrichtung

specialize sich spezialisieren

specialized spezialisiert; fachkundig

specialized asset spezieller Anlagegenstand

Asset designed to perform a specific task, whose value is significantly reduced in its next-best use.

specialized industry spezialisierte Industrie

Industry where there are many opportunities for firms to create competitive advantages that are huge or give a high pay-off.

special levy Sondererhebung; Ergänzungsabgabe

special make Sonderanfertigung

special meeting Sondersitzung

special offer Sonderangebot

special payment Sonderzahlung

special price Sonderpreis; Vorzugspreis

special property Sondervermögen; *(characteristic)* besondere Eigenschaft

special-purpose saving Zwecksparen

special regulation Sonderregelung

special session Sondersitzung

special subsidy Sondersubvention

special tariff Sondertarif

specialty Spezialartikel; Spezialität; Besonderheit; Fachgebiet

specialty advertising Sonderwerbung

Form of advertising that uses advertising novelties as medium for the message.

Example: buttons, bumper stickers, and balloons with writing.

specialty shop Fachgeschäft

Retail store specializing in a narrow range of items for a particular clientele, such as shops specializing in, wedding gowns, lawn mowers, or bicycles.

specialty retailer Fachhändler

specific bestimmt; speziell; typisch; spezifisch; *(exact)* genau; *(express)* ausdrücklich; *(certain)* bestimmt

specific tariff Mengenzoll

Tariff levied as a fixed charge for each unit of good imported.

specification Spezifikation; Beschreibung; *(exact representation)* genaue Angabe; *(itemization)* Einzelaufstellung

Production: a written document stipulating the kind, quality, and quantity of material and labor required for a specific job.

specified spezifiziert; genau angegeben

specify spezifizieren; *(to state precisely)* genau angeben; *(to detail)* detaillieren

speculate spekulieren; gewagte Geschäfte machen; *(to think)* nachdenken; *(to ruminate)* grübeln

speculation Spekulation; *(thinking)* Nachdenken; Nachsinnen; Ansicht; Mutmaßung

The process of buying, holding, and selling any valuable thing to profit from fluctuations in its price. The objects in question can be stocks, commodities, futures, currencies, collectibles, real estate, or any other object of value.

speculative spekulativ; grüblerisch

speculative deadline Spekulationsfrist

speculative market Spekulationsmarkt

speculative period Spekulationsfrist

speculative profit Spekulationsgewinn

speculative risk Spekulationsrisiko

speculator Spekulant

speech Sprache; Sprechen; Reden; Vortrag

speed Geschwindigkeit; Tempo; Schnelligkeit; *(to ~)* zu schnell fahren; (dahin) eilen

speed of growth Wachstumstempo; Wachstumsgeschwindigkeit

spend *(money)* ausgeben; verbrauchen; verausgaben; aufwenden; *(time)* verbringen; zubringen

spending Ausgaben; *(public)* Ausgabenwirtschaft

spending behavior Ausgabenverhalten

spent *(money)* verausgabt; *(energy)* erschöpft; *(flame)* erloschen; *(Zeit)* zugebracht

spider Spinne; *(Internet)* Spider

Internet: automatic programs in search engines that search the web from site to site, page by page, and word by word. They build up a massive index or database of all the words found, where they were found, how many times they appear on each page, and so on. It is this database that is actually queried when one types in a search term.

spillover Überlauf; Nebenwirkungen

Effects of economic activity or process upon those who are not directly involved in it.

spin-off *(business)* Abstoßen eines Geschäftszweigs; *(subsidiary)* Tochtergesellschaft; *(product)* anfallendes Nebenprodukt

Organization: the process of separating a corporate unit from the parent company and establishing it as its own independent operating unit.

spiral Spirale; Aktiengeschäft; *(inflation)* Schraube; *(to ~)* spiralartig ansteigen

splash page Eingangsseite

Internet: preliminary page that precedes the normal home page of a website. Site users can either wait to be redirected to the home page or can follow a link to do this.

split Spaltung; Riss; Aufteilung; *(stocks)* Aktiensplit; *(to ~)* spalten; aufteilen; splitten

Securities: the division of the outstanding shares of a corporation into a larger number of shares.

spokesperson Sprecher; Vertreter; Wortführer; *(representative)* Vertrauensperson

Someone entrusted with speaking to the media or public on behalf of someone else or an organisation.

sponsor Förderer; Stifter; *(advertising)* Auftraggeber für Werbesendungen; *(guarantor)* Bürge; Bürgin; *(financial sponsor)* Geldgeber; *(to ~)* Patenschaft übernehmen; betreuen; tragen; veranstalten

Limited partnership: the general partner who organizes and sells the partnership.

Stock exchange: investment company that offers shares in its funds; also called the underwriter.

Advertising: the company that pays for a television or radio program by running one or more advertisements during the program.

sponsorship Sponsoring; Unterstützung; Förderung

Advertising: the act of supporting an event, activity or organisation by providing money or other resources. In return, the sponsor normally gets advertising space or part of the publicity for the event.

Internet: a long-term advertising relationship that typically involves the payment of a fixed fee to display a banner or other graphic on a website, or be included in an email newsletter.

spoofing Verschleierung; Manipulation

Internet: relies on the fact that the average person is not in a position to understand exactly how information is displayed, transferred, or stored. This lack of knowledge provides opportunities for novel deceptions, and is often used to extract sensitive information by leading a user to believe that are quest is corning from a reputable source, such as an ISP or credit card company.

spot *(locality)* Ort; Stelle; *(stain)* Fleck; *(market)* Kassa-; *(to ~) (to notice)* wahrnehmen; bemerken; erkennen; ausfindig machen; beflecken

Market of immediate delivery of a product and immediate payment.

spot check Stichprobe

Supervisory check on work performance or product quality done at random intervals. Spot checks are unannounced and can occur at any time. The purpose is to ensure a continually high performance level on the part of employees.

spot exchange rate Kassadevisenkurs

Exchange rate at which a foreign exchange dealer will convert one currency into another that particular day.

spot interest rate Spot-Zinssatz

Interest rate fixed today on a loan that is made today.

spotlight Scheinwerfer; *(theater)* Rampenlicht; Mittelpunkt des Interesses; *(to ~)* anstrahlen; *(to attract notice to)* in den Blickpunkt rücken; besonders herausstellen

spot market Kassamarkt; Spotmarkt

Exchange: a market where commodities are bought and sold for cash and immediate delivery .

spot price Kassapreis; Kassakurs; Preis bei Sofortzahlung

Current price of a commodity traded in the spot market for immediate delivery.

spot rate Kassakurs

Foreign exchange: price at which a currency can be purchased or sold and then delivered within two business days.

spot transaction Kassageschäft; Lokogeschäft

Foreign exchange: a transaction in which each party promises to pay a certain amount of currency to the other on the same day or within one or two business days.

spread *(extent)* Ausdehnung; Verbreitung; *(distribution)* Streuung; *(span)* Spanne; Spannweite; Preisdifferenz; Zinsaufschlag; *(to ~)* ausbreiten; verbreiten; ausdehnen; bedecken

General: the difference between the bid and offer prices.

Bonds: the difference between yields on securities of the same quality but different maturities.

Stocks: the difference between the bid and offer prices for a security trade on the stock exchange.

spread in interest rates Zinsspanne

spread measure Verteilungsmessung

spread sheet Kalkulationstabelle; Verteilungsbogen

A rectangular grid containing numbers arranged in rows and columns, related by formulas.

spur Sporn; *(incentive)* Ansporn; Antrieb; *(railway)* Gleis; *(to ~) (riding)* die Sporene geben; *(to urge on)* anspornen

spurt plötzliches Vorwärtsschnellen; *(water)* Hervorschießen; *(price)* plötzlicher Preisanstieg; *(to ~)* hochschnellen; vorwärtsschnellen; hervorschießen; plötzlich ansteigen

squander verschwenden; vergeuden

squandering Verschwenden; verschwenderisch

square footage Fläche; *(equiv)* Quadratmeterzahl

squatter's rights Hausbesetzerrechte

Informal expression for the right of adverse possession, i.e. the right, under certain conditions, to take ownership of property by simply living in it.

squeeze Druck; Pressen; Enge; *(tight spot)* Klemme; *(money)* finanzieller Druck; Geldverlegenheit; *(scarcity)* Knappheit; *(to ~)* drücken; unter Druck setzen; auspressen; eng packen

Finance: period of tight money, characterized by scarce funds and high interest rates, making borrowing difficult and expensive.

Pricing: a market situation in which increased costs cannot be passed on to customers in the form of higher prices.

stability Festigkeit; Stabilität; Beständigkeit; *(physical property)* dynamisches Gleichgewicht

stability analysis Stabilitätsanalyse

stability law Stabilitätsgesetz

stabilization Stabilisierung; Festigung

Currency: the buying and selling of a country's own currency to protect its exchange value; also called pegging.

stabilize festigen; stabilisieren

stable fest; beständig; gleich bleibend; *(sturdy)* stabil; haltbar; dauerhaft

stable growth beständiges/stabiles Wachstum; Dauerwachstum

staff Stab; Personal; Belegschaft; Lehrkörper; Stange; Stab; Stütze; *(to ~)* besetzen; mit Personal versorgen

General: the personnel working in an organization.

Management: supporting functions in the concepts of line and staff, such as planning, organizing, budgeting, directing, and coordinating.

staff authority Stabsauthorität

Management: the authority to advise, but not to direct, other managers, such as the legal department.

staff department Personalabteilung; Stabsabteilung

staff director Personaldirektor

staffed mit Personal versehen; personalmäßig versorgt

staff employee Stabsmitarbeiter

staffing Stellenbesetzung; Personalbesetzung

The practice of finding, evaluating, and hiring people in order to achieve the aims of the organization. It also involves maintaining working relationship with colleagues, assisting them in developing further and acquiring new skills, and setting them free them when they are no longer needed.

staffing policy Personalpolitik; Stellenbesetzungsplan

Strategy concerned with selecting employees for particular jobs.

staff manager Personalleiter

stage of development Entwicklungsstadium/stufe

stages in web site development Stufen der Webseiten-Entwicklung

Internet: Standard stages of creation of a web site are initiation, feasibility, analysis, design, development (content creation), testing and maintenance.

stagflation Stagflation

Economics: expression found by economists in the 1970s for the previously unknown combination of slow economic growth and high unemployment (stagnation) with rising prices (inflation).

stagnant stehend; stagnierend; stockend; *(market)* flau

stagnate stagnieren; stocken; abflauen; stehen

stagnation Stagnation; Stockung

Economics: period of slow economic growth (of about 1 % or less per year) or decline in real terms.

stake Stütze; *(betting)* Einsatz; *(capital)* Einschuss; *(to ~)* stützen; einsetzen; riskieren; *(to furnish with necessities)* ausrüsten; *(to advance money)* vorschießen

stakeholders Interessengruppen

Following the concept of "shareholder" the concept of "stakeholder" combines all those interest groups that have claims on the company.

Stakeholders are believed to be: employees, customers, suppliers, creditors, members, associations, the media, the general public.

stakeholder analysis Stakeholderanalyse

stakeholder communication Stakeholderkommunikation

Interaction with a stakeholder involving strategies, such as advertising, public relations, sales promotion incentives, and lead generation, that can help marketers to accomplish cognitive and attitude objectives, often at substantial cost savings over traditional methods.

stalemate Patt; Stillstand; *(to ~)* patt setzen

stalemate industry Pattindustrie

Industry that produces commodities and is characterized by a few opportunities to create competitive advantages, with each advantage being small.

stall Verkaufsstand; Marktbude; *(theater)* Sperrsitz; *(to ~) (engine)* abdrosseln; *(for time)* zögern (um Zeit zu gewinnen); hinhalten; aufhalten

stamp Stempel; *(postage)* Briefmarke; *(product)* Kennzeichen; *(to ~)* stempeln; *(coin)* prägen; pressen; stanzen; *(postage)* freimachen; frankieren

stamped abgestempelt; *(coined)* geprägt; *(postage)* frankiert

standard Standard; Standarte; Norm; *(quality)* Gütegrad; *(average)* Durchschnitt; *(coinage)* Feingehalt; *(level)* Niveau; Maßstab

standard costing Standardkostenrechnung; Plankostenrechnung; Sollkostenrechnung

Cost accounting method where all input and output units are always calculated at standardised rates. Supplies from stock are valued at the standard purchase price and outputs from cost centers at the planned cost rate.

This has the great advantage that in the comparison between budgeted and actual figures variances which have occurred in upstream systems do not appear in downstream systems. In this way the requirement of responsibility accounting is met whereby only those costs are shown that are capable of being controlled.

Standard & Poor's Corporation

US company providing a broad range of investment services, including rating securities, compiling stock indexes, and publishing a wide variety of statistical materials, and other financial information.

Standard & Poor's index

Index published by Standard & Poor's based on the average performance of 500 widely held common stocks; commonly known as the Standard & Poor's 500 (or S&P 500).

Standard & Poor's rating

Risk classification of stocks and bonds issued by Standard and Poor's Corporation.

S&P's top four grades, called investment grade AAA, AA, A, and BBB, indicate a minimal risk that a bond issue will default in its timely payment of interest and principal. Bonds or stocks rated BB or below are considered speculative.

standard deviation Normalabweichung; Standardabweichung

Statistics: a measure of the range of variation from an average of a group of measurements.

From a normal distribution, one standard deviation includes about 66% of the population; two standard deviations include about 95%.

standard error Standardfehler

standard for calculation Berechnungsmaßstab

standard format Standardformat

Standard Industrial Classification (SIC) Branchenklassifikation

Unique 4-digit code used in the US to define a unique area of business activity.

standardization Standardisierung; Normierung; Normung; Vereinheitlichung

Marketing: attempt by companies to offer the same product with the same marketing mix in all the international markets they serve. In so doing, they achieve economies of scale and reach a high level of efficiency. If this is not possible for political, economic, social or cultural reasons, the company has to adapt or localize its product.

standardize standardisieren; normieren; normen; vereinheitlichen

standardized genormt; normiert; normalisiert; standardisiert; vereinheitlicht

standardized marketing mix standardisierter Marketing Mix

International marketing strategy for using basically the same product, advertising, distribution channels and other elements of the marketing mix in all the company's international markets.

standardized normal distribution Standardnormalverteilung

Normal distribution with an expected value of 0 and a standard deviation of 1.

standardized working hours Regelarbeitszeit

standard mileage method *(equiv)* Kilometerpauschale

Taxation: method of expense deduction based on a standard mileage rate.

standard of living Lebensstandard; Lebenshaltung

Economics: a measure of the degree of prosperity in a nation, based on the quality and quantity of goods and services available to people.

standard practice übliches Verfahren; Standardverfahren

standards of performance (SOP) Performancestandards

Accounting: Yardsticks for a cost center's possible performance that belong to the structure costs. They express the productivity of performance in the administration.

They have an output too, which like that of any directly productive cost center may be planned by means of output units/activity type and rendered susceptible. SOP help to test the structure costs for their suitability. They are intended to make this part of the company's activities structure transparent. SOPs can be both quantitative (number of book entries, orders, etc.) and qualitative (fluctuation rate, customer satisfaction, etc.).

standard solution Einheitslösung

standard time Standardzeit; Normalzeit; Vorgabezeit; Akkordzeit

standard value Einheitswert; Vorgabewert

standard wage Grundgehalt; Tariflohn

HRM: normal or base salary of an employee before any overtime or premium pay is computed.

standby *(waiting)* Wartestellung; *(readiness)* Bereitschaft-; *(in reserve)* Reserve; Stellvertreter; Warte-

standby agreement Bereitstellungsvereinbarung

standby credit Reservekredit; Beistandskredit; Kreditzusage

standby fee Standby-Gebühren

Banking: fee charged by a bank to provide a standby commitment.

standby loan Bereitstellungsdarlehen

Banking: commitment by a bank to make available a sum of money at specified terms for a specified period.

standby underwriting Standby-Übernahmeverpflichtung

Agreement whereby an underwriter agrees to purchase any shares that are not purchased by the public investor.

standing Stehen; *(rank)* Rang; *(level)* Stand; *(position)* Stellung; *(importance)* Geltung; Ruf

standing order Dauerauftrag

Trade: order for repeated shipments of goods to be sent without specific reorders. Standing orders must comply with certain quantity and time limitations.

staple stock Standardprodukt

Retailing: goods that have fairly constant demand with little seasonal influence. Retailers therefore continually carry these goods in stock.

star Stern; Star

Portfolio analysis: high-growth, high-share businesses or products that often require heavy investment to finance their rapid growth.

start Start; *(departure)* Aufbruch; Beginn; *(to ~)* starten; aufbrechen; beginnen; abfahren; hochfahren

start a business ein Unternehmen gründen

starting point Ausgangspunkt

starting position Ausgangsposition

starting year Anfangsjahr

start-up Fimenneugründung; junges Unternehmen

start-up costs Gründungskosten

Costs incurred after the decision to establish a business has been made, but before it becomes operational.

start-up phase Anlaufphase

start-up problem Anlaufproblem; Anfangsproblem

state Staat; *(condition)* (Zu)Stand; Stellung; Pracht; *(position)* Lage; Status; *(government)* Staats-; *(to ~) (to state)* statuieren; *(data)* angeben; *(to remark)* ausführen; *(to present)* darlegen; feststellen

state bank Staatsbank

state combine Staatskonzern; Kombinat

stated annual interest rate Nominalzinnsatz

Interest rate expressed as a percentage per annum, by which interest payment is determined.

state-directed economy Planwirtschaft

Economy in which the state plays a proactive role in influencing the direction and magnitude of private sector investments.

stated value festgestellter Wert

state finances Staatsfinanzen

state indebtedness Staatsverschuldung

state intervention Staatsintervention; Staatsdirigismus

statement Erklärung; Feststellung; Aussage; Angabe; Darlegung; *(account rendered)* Rechenschaftsbericht; *(statement of account)* Kontoauszug; *(invoice)* Rechnung

statement of changes in financial position Bewegungsbilanz; Kapitalflussrechnung

Accounting: a financial statement which provides information as to how a company generated and spent its cash during the year.

state of the art Stand der Technik; hochmodern

state of the economy Wirtschaftslage; Wirtschaftssituation

state of the market Marktlage; Marktkonstellation

state-owned enterprise Staatsunternehmen

state planner staatlicher Planer

state subsidy Staatssubvention; Staatszuschuss

static *(radio)* Empfangsstörung; *(unchanging)* stationär; statisch

statistic statistische Angabe; *(number)* statistische Ziffer

statistical statistisch

statistical data statistische Daten

statistical demand analysis statistische Nachfrageanalyse

Set of statistical procedures used to discover the most important real factors affecting sales and their relative influence; the most commonly analyzed factors are prices, income, population and promotion.

statistical process protocol (SPC) statistisches Prozessprotokoll

statistical quality control (SQC) statistische Qualitätskontrolle

Production: technique for the control of production by statistical methods by monitoring statistically representative production samples for the purpose of determining quality.

statistical sampling statistische Stichprobenerhebung

Statistics: a method of selecting a sample by mathematical calculations and probabilities, for the purpose of making scientifically and mathematically sound inferences about the entire population.

statistician Statistiker

statistics Statistik

A branch of applied mathematics concerned with the collection and interpretation of quantitative data and the use of probability theory to estimate population parameters.

status Stellung; Zustand; Lage; Status

Society: the position achieved in a society by achievement or other means.

Status is a significant motivator, and it has major behavioral consequences when individuals perceive a disparity between what they believe their status to be and what others perceive it to be.

status symbol Statussymbol

An object or a sign that is perceived to indicate a high social status in its owner.

Example: expensive cars, homes, and boats are often seen as status symbols.

statute Gesetz; Statut

A formal, written law, issued by a legislature, that becomes law. Statutes are enacted to prescribe conduct, define crimes, create inferior government bodies, appropriate public monies, and in general promote the public welfare.

statutory satzungsmäßig; gesetzlich vorgeschrieben

statutory merger Fusion

Legal combination of two or more corporations in which only one survives as a legal entity.

steady-growth method Wachstumsgleichgewichtsmethode

Marketing: a technique to evaluate subscription sources by estimating the cost and impact on profitability of building the rate base over time via various sources.

steel mill Stahlwerk

steel worker Stahlarbeiter

steer steuern; lenken

steering Steuerung; *(car)* Lenkung

stereotyping Typisieren

Psychology: the habit of classifying people because of one unique characteristic. It is a form of prejudice that can form damaging images.

stifle ersticken; *(a rumor)* unterdrücken; *(competition)* abdrosseln

stimulate stimulieren; anregen; anreizen; *(revitalize)* beleben; *(crank up)* ankurbeln

stimulating stimulierend; anregend; auftreibend

stimulation Stimulanz; Anregung; Auftrieb; *(revitalization)* Belebung; *(cranking up)* Ankurbelung

stint Einschränkung; bestimmte Dienstperiode; Arbeitsperiode; *(to ~) (to be stingy)* knausern; kurz halten; *(to save up)* einsparen

stipend Stipendium

stipendiary Stipendiat

stipulate festsetzen; ausbedingen; vereinbaren; vorsehen

stipulated festgesetzt; ausgemacht; *(contractual)* vertragsgemäß; ausbedingen

stipulated damages Konventionalstrafe

stipulation Bedingung; Abmachung; Vereinbarung; Übereinkunft; Klausel

An agreement made between two parties in legal proceedings. It is not binding unless agreed to by the parties, and most stipulations must be in writing.

stock Stammkapital; Geschäftskapital; Aktienkapital; *(shares)* Aktien; Kapitalbeteiligung; *(inventory)* Warenlager; Vorrat; *(to ~)* lagern

Corporation: the capital raised by a corporation through the issue of shares entitling holders to an ownership interest.

Inventory: products stored in manufacturing and retailing businesses for further processing or sale.

stockable lagerungsfähig

stock allotment Bezugsschein; Aktienbezugschein

stock analyst Aktienanalyst

stockbroker Börsenmakler; Wertpapiermakler; Effektenhändler; Aktienhändler

stock broking Börsenkommissionsgeschäft; Effektengeschäft; Aktiengeschäft; Wertpapierhandel

stock dividend Gratisaktie; Berichtigungsaktie; Aktiendividende

Corporate finance: payment of a corporate dividend in the form of stock rather than cash. Stock dividends are often used to conserve cash needed to operate the business.

stocked vorrätig; auf Lager; *(carried)* geführt

stock evaluation Aktienbewertung

stock exchange Börse; Handelsplatz; Effektenbörse

An organized marketplace where brokers and dealers meet to buy and sell stocks of publicly traded companies on behalf of investors.

marketplace in which stocks, common stock equivalents, and bonds are traded by members of the exchange, acting both as agents (brokers) and as principals (dealers or traders). Such exchanges have a physical location where brokers and dealers meet to execute orders from institutional and individual investors to buy and sell securities.

stock exchange crash Börsenkrach

stock exchange order Börsenauftrag

stock exchange price list Kursblatt

stock exchange quotation Börsennotierung; Börsenkurs

stock exchange ratios Börsenkennzahlen

Attempts to apply ratio analysis to measure corporate value. Examples include CEBIT (Cash Flow Before Interest and Taxes), which is equivalent to EBITDA (Earnings before Interest, Taxes, Depreciation and Amortization).

stock exchange supervision Börsenaufsicht

stock exchange trading Börsenhandel

stockholder Aktionär; Aktieninhaber

Individual or organization with an ownership position in a corporation. Stockholders must own at least one share, and their ownership is confirmed by either a stock certificate or a record by their broker if shares are in the broker's custody; also called a shareholder or share owner.

stockholders' equity Eigenkapital; Gesellschaftskapital

Accounting: figure representing the stockholders' ownership in the company. This is also known as net worth, which is calculated as the difference between the total assets and total liabilities of a company.

stock index Börsenindex

stocking *(hose)* Strumpf; *(inventory)* Lagerung

stock investment Aktienanlage

stockjobber Börsenhändler

stockjobbing Aktiengeschäft; Spekulationsgeschäft; Effektenhandel

stockkeeping Lagerhaltung

stock keeping unit (SKU) Artikelposition; Lagerhaltungsnummer

Inventory: a unit of inventory that is carried as a separate identifiable unit.

stock market Aktienbörse; Aktienmarkt; Wertpapierbörse

Organized market, such as a stock exchange or an over the counter market, where stocks and bonds are actively traded.

stock market loss Kursverlust

stock market quotation Kurszettel

stock market report Börsenbericht; Kursblatt

stock market transaction Börsengeschäft

stock market trend Aktientendenz; Börsentendenz

stock market turnover Börsenumsatz

stock of foreign direct investment Bestand an ausländischen Direktinvestitionen

Economics: the total accumulated value of foreign-owned assets.

stock on hand Lagerbestand; Warenbestand

stock option Aktienbezugsrecht

Securities: the right to buy or sell a stock at a specified price within a stated period. Options offer an opportunity to hedge positions in other securities, to speculate in stocks with relatively little investment, and to capitalize on changes in the market value of options contracts.

stock option plan Belegschaftsaktien-system

Form of employee incentive and compensation, usually for the executives of a corporation. The employee is given an option to purchase the corporation's shares at a certain price (at or below the market price at the time the option is granted) for a specified period of years.

stockout Fehlbestand

Inventory: the situation when required material is not available for a production, sales or order.

stockpile Vorrat; Stapelbestand; *(to ~)* horten; aufstocken; stapeln

Inventory: reserve supply of raw materials or goods.

stockpiling Vorratshaltung; Lagerwirtschaft; Vorratswirtschaft; Lageraufstockung; Aufstockung; Einlagerung; *(hoarding)* Anhäufung

stock price Aktienpreis; Aktienkurs

stock price gain Kursgewinn

stock purchase warrant Optionsschein; Aktienbezugsschein

stock split Aktiensplit; Aktienaufteilung; Aktienstückelung

Increase in the number of outstanding shares while making no change in shareholders' equity.

stock subscription Kapitalbeteiligung

stocktrading Aktienhandel; Effektenhandel

stock transaction Aktientransaktion

stock transfer tax Börsenumsatzsteuer

stock turnover Lagerumschlag

Inventory: measure of the speed with which inventory moves in and out of an inventory and is an an indicator of sales volume.

stop Halt; Stopp; *(barrier)* Sperre; *(bus)* Haltestelle; *(to ~)* anhalten; *(to finish)* beenden; *(to cease)* aufhören; sperren

stopgap Lückenbüßer; Notlösung

stopgap assistance Überbrückungshilfe

stop order Limit; Stop Order

Order to sell a stock when the price falls to a specified level.

stoppage Anhalten; *(interruption)* Unterbrechung; *(funds)* Sperrung; *(work)* Einstellung; *(traffic)* Stau; Unterbrechung; Streik

storable lagerungsfähig

storage Lagerung; Aufbewahrung; Speicherung; Einlagerung; *(capacity)* Lagerraum; *(cost)* Lagerkosten

storage capacity Speicherkapazität; Lagerraum; Lagerkapazität

storage performance Speicherleistung

store Geschäft; Lager; Vorrat; *(abundance)* Fülle; *(shop)* Geschäft; *(to ~)* speichern; aufbewahren; (ein)lagern

Retailing: a commercial establishment for the retail sale of goods or services. Stores range in size from small corner shops to large modern supermarkets.

store brand Händlermarket; Eigenmarke

Marketing: a brand owned and maintained by a retailer, often used for products such as coffee, rice and canned vegetables.

storming stage Storming

Second stage in group development, characterized by intragroup conflicts. Members accept the existence of the group, but there is resistance to the constraints that the group imposes on individuality. Furthermore, there is conflict over who will control the group. When this stage is complete, there will be a relatively clear hierarchy of leadership within the group.

storyboard Storyboard

Marketing: a series of drawn panels depicting scenes, copy, and shots proposed for a television commercial. The storyboard gives the client a good idea of the agency's concept for a commercial, before extensive production charges are incurred.

storyboarding Storyboarding; Konzeptausarbeitung

stowage Staugeld; Staugebühr

The placing and securing of cargo or containers on board a vessel or an aircraft, which has to happen in a manner so as to minimize the risk to ship and cargo.

straight bill of lading Konnossement; Frachtbrief

Non-negotiable bill of lading, merely stating that the carrier is to deliver the goods to a specified person at a specified place.

straight debt reguläre Schulden

Fixed rate borrowing with no additional features such as convertibility rights or warrants.

straight-line depreciation lineare Abschreibung

A depreciation method that writes off an equal amount of the value of an asset over all periods of its estimated useful life.

straight product extension reine Produkterweiterung

Marketing: strategy of marketing a product in a foreign market without any change.

straight rebuy reiner Wiederholungskauf

Business buying situation in which the buyer routinely reorders something without any modification.

stranglehold Würgegriff; Umklammerung

strapline Werbeslogan

Slogan often used in conjunction with a brand's name, advertising and other promotions.

strapped festgeschnallt; geschlagen; unzulänglich versehen

strategic strategisch

strategic alliance strategische Allianz

Cooperative agreements between two or more firms. In general, there are two types of strategic alliance: a bilateral alliance (between two organizations), and a network alliance (between several organizations).

strategic business-planning grid strategisches Geschäftsbereichsplanungsgitter

Portfolio planning method that evaluates a company's strategic business units using indices of industry attractiveness and the company's strength in the industry.

strategic business unit (SBU) Strategische Geschäfteinheit

Unit of the company that has a separate mission and objectives and than can be planned independently from other company businesses. An SBU can be a company division, a product line within a division, or sometimes a single product or brand.

strategic commitment strategische Verpflichtung

Decision that has a long-term impact and is difficult to reverse, such as entering a foreign market on a large scale.

strategic control Strategische Kontrolle

Checking whether the company's basic strategy matches its opportunities and strengths.

strategic focus strategischer Focus

Strategic planning tool to help marketers identify ways of achieving sales and profit growth. Two routes – productivity increases and volume expansion – form the basis of analysis.

strategic group strategische Gruppe

Group of firms in an industry following the same or a similar strategy.

strategic plan Strategie; strategischer Plan

Plan that describes how a firm will adopt to take advantage of opportunities in its constantly changing environment, thereby maintaining a strategic fit between the firm's goals and capabilities and its changing market opportunities.

strategic planning strategische Planung

The process of developing and maintaining a strategic fit between a company´s goals, its potential, and its changing environment. It depends on developing a clear mission, supporting objectives, a sound business portfolio and co-ordinated functional strategies.

strategic investment decisions strategische Investitionsentscheidung

strategic tools strategische Werkzeuge

Large number of tools that have been developed for the finding, selecting and drafting of strategies for managers and others involved in the strategy development process.

It includes the analysis of the strategic base position (potential, dependencies, market position), of business units, of functional areas and of the value chain from the supplier through to the customer.

Example: value chain analysis, portfolio analysis, competition analysis, potential analysis, etc.

strategic trade policy strategische Handelspolitik

Government policy aimed at improving the competitive position of a domestic industry and/or domestic firm in the world market.

strategy Strategie

A strategy is a long term plan of action designed to achieve a particular goal.

stream Fluss; Strom; Strömung; *(influx)* Zustrom; *(to ~)* strömen; wehen

streaming audio/video Streaming

Content that is sent to the user' s computer as it is viewed versus sending an entire file before the user can view it.

streamline Stromlinienform; *(to ~)* rationalisieren; *(to modernize)* modernisieren

streamlining of services Entbürokratisierung

strength Kraft; *(character)* Stärke; *(potency)* Potenz

strengthen stärken; kräftigen; stark werden

strengthening Stärkung; *(reinforcement)* Verstärkung

stress Druck; Zwang; Spannung; Belastung; Stress; *(to ~)* hervorheben; betonen

Dynamic condition in which an individual is confronted with an opportunity, constraint, or demand related to what he or she desires and for which the outcome is perceived to be both uncertain and important. It is not necessarily bad in and on itself – it's an opportunity when it offers potential gains.

strike Streik; Arbeitsniederlegung; *(to ~)* streiken; Arbeit niederlegen; schlagen; treffen; *(balance)* abschließen

Temporary stoppage of work by a group of employees to express a grievance, enforce a demand, obtain recognition, or resolve a dispute with management.

strike against bestreiken

strike area Streikgebiet

strikebreaker Streikbrecher

Someone who works during a strike, often hired by management. Strikebreakers must cross a picket line and are resented by striking employees.

strike-free streikfrei

strike fund Streikfonds; Streikkasse

A fund that is generated during those periods when the union members are working.

strike loss Streikverlust

strike month Streikmonat

strike notice Streikankündigung

Formal notice to an employer that a union has rejected the company's latest offer and that a strike is imminent.

strike pay Streikgelder

Money paid by a union to striking members to compensate for lost income..

strike price Ausübungspreis; Basispreis; Emissionskurs; Abrechnungskurs

Options: price per share at which a call option buyer can purchase the underlying stock or a put option buyer can sell the stock.

striking Streiken; Niederlegen der Arbeit; streikend; die Arbeit niederlegend; *(noticeable)* auffallend; ins Auge fallend; eindringlich

strip mining Tagebaubetrieb

strongbox Tresor; Kassette

strong culture starke Unternehmenskultur

Cultures in which the core values are intensely held and widely shared. Strong cultures have a great impact on employee behavior and are directly related to reduced turnover.

strong-form efficiency starke Informationseffizienz

Theory that the market is efficient with respect to all available information, public or private.

structural strukturell; baulich; Bau

structural adjustment Strukturanpassung

structural bond strukturelle Schuldverschreibung; sturkturelle Anleihe

structural change Strukturwandel

structural damage Gebäudeschaden

structural effect Struktureffekt

structural inflation strukturelle Inflation; immanente Inflation

Economics: inflation that is built into an economic system, thought to be around 1 to 2% per year in industrialized states is; drastic changes in economic policy would be necessary to eliminate it.

structural plan Strukturplan

structural problem Strukturproblem

structural program Strukturprogramm

structural shift strukturelle Veränderung

structural unemployment strukturelle Arbeitslosigkeit

Economics: long-term level of unemployment that results from structural factors in the economy and exists even during periods of full employment. Those who are unemployed are in the wrong area for their job skills, are illiterate or uneducated, or are school dropouts.

structural weakness Strukturschwäche

structure Struktur; Aufbau; Gefüge; *(building)* Gebäude; Bau(werk); *(to ~)* strukturieren; aufbauen

Real estate: any constructed improvement to a property. Structures include buildings, fencing and enclosures, garages, greenhouses, kiosks, sheds and utility buildings.

structure costs Strukturkosten

Costs that create the organizational framework in purchasing, in marketing, in research into new products, in the administration, in logistics, in corporate culture, in the navigability of the business.

structuring Strukturierung

struggle Kampf; Anstrengung; *(to ~)* sich wehren; sträuben; sich anstrengen

study Studie; *(room)* Arbeitszimmer; Studium; Untersuchung; Bemühung; *(to ~)* studieren; betreiben; lernen; untersuchen; prüfen; sich befassen mit

study group Arbeitskreis; Studiengruppe; Arbeitsgruppe

style Stil; Mode; Art; *(to ~)* anreden; bezeichnen

style guide Gestaltungsrichtline

Internet: Definition of site structure, page design, typography and copy defined within a company.

subaccount Unterkonto

subassembly Teilmontage

subcategorization Untergliederung

subcommittee Unterausschuss

subcontract Nebenvertrag; Zulieferungsvertrag

subcontracting Zulieferung; Untervergabe; Auswärtsvergabe

subcontracting firm Zulieferbetrieb

subcontractor Lieferant; Unterlieferant; Subunternehmer; Zulieferer

A second and distinct company to which a primary contractor passes some portion of the work described in the contract.

subculture Subkultur

Group of people with shared value systems based on common life experiences and situateions - minicultures within an organization, typically defined by department designations and geographical separation.

subdivide aufgliedern; untergliedern; *(land)* parzellieren; unterteilen

subdivision Untergliederung; *(department)* Unterabteilung; *(ledger)* Unterspalte; *(real estate)* Parzellierung; *(housing development)* Wohnsiedlung

Real estate: piece of of land divided into lots suitable for home-building purposes.

subduct zurückziehen; wegnehmen

subject Fach; Fachgebiet; *(topic)* Thema; Gegenstand; Person

subject to charges gebührenpflichtig

subject to postage portopflichtig

subject to registration meldepflichtig

subject to report berichtspflichtig; meldepflichtig

sublease Untermiete; Untervermietung; -pachtung

A rental agreement or lease between a tenant and a new tenant (called a sublessee) who will either share the rental or take over from the first tenant.

sublet untervermieten; -verpachten

Lease from under a lease. A tenant who leases property to another has sublet.

subliminal advertising unterschwellige Werbung

The illegal practice of sending advertising messages designed to pass below the normal limits of perception. For example, the message might not be audible to the conscious mind or it might be an image transmitted briefly.

submission Unterwerfung; *(of documents)* Eingabe; Einreichung; Vorlage

submit sich unterwerfen; *(document)* einreichen; vorlegen; unterbreiten

subordinate Untergebener; untergeordnet; zweitrangig; unterstellt; niedriger als; *(to ~)* unterordnen; zurückstellen

subordinated debt nachrangige Schuld

Debt whose holders have a claim on the firm's assets only after senior debtholder's claims have been satisfied.

subordination Unterordnung

Debt: an agreement in which a creditor agrees that claims of other creditors must be fully paid before the subordinated creditor is paid.

subpart *(organization)* Unterabteilung

subscribe *(newspaper)* abonnieren; Geld zeichnen; billigen

subscriber Abonnent; Spender; Subskribent; *(newspaper)* Bezieher; *(TV, radio)* Teilnehmer

subscription *(newspaper; TV)* Abonnement; *(before availability)* Vorbestellung; *(donation)* Beitrag; *(stocks)* Option; Zeichnung; gezeichnete Summe

Business model: a contract between a subscriber and a provider of products or services for regular delivery or access.

Securities: an agreement of intent by a securities dealer to buy newly issued shares.

subscription price Bezugspreis; Zeichnungspreis

Securities: the fixed price at which a new securities issue is being offered to the public.

subsequent nachfolgend; später als

subsidiary Konzerngesellschaft; Tochtergesellschaft; *(branch)* Ableger; Filiale; *(adv)* Hilfs-; ergänzend

A company owned by a parent company; a subsidiary is a separate legal entity listed as a corporation or partnership that is required to file its own taxes and compile its own financial statements

subsidiary company Tochterunternehmen; Tochterfirma; Tochterbetrieb

A company whose voting stock is more than 50% owned by another firm.

subsidiary enterprise Tochterunternehmen

subsidiary institute Tochterinstitut

subsidization Subventionierung; Bezuschussung

subsidize subventionieren; finanziell unterstützen

subsidy Zuschuss; staatliche Unterstützung/Beihilfe; Subvention

Government financial assistance to a domestic producer; can be in the form of a payment or other favorable economic stimulus (such as remission of taxation, usually to encourage the continued existence, growth, development, and profitability of domestic companies.

subsidy funds Subventionsmittel

subsidy payment Subventionszahlung; Zuschusszahlung

subsidy reduction Subventionsabbau

subsidy requirements Zuschussbedarf; Subventionsbedarf

subsistence Existenz; Existenzminimum

The minimal economic level at which people can exist. A subsistence standard is sufficient to keep the economic unit alive and reasonably healthy, but nothing else.

subsistence rate Existenzsatz

subsistence theory of wages Mindestlohntheorie

Economics: theory that wages in the long run will tend to the minimum value needed to keep workers alive.

substandard unter der Norm; Norm unterschreitend; *(below average)* unterdurchschnittlich; *(not of full value)* nicht vollwertig; Ausschuss-

substantiality Wesentlichkeit

Degree to which a market segment is sufficiently large or profitable.

substitute Ersatz(-mann); Substitut; *(imitation)* Nachahmung; *(stand-in)* Surrogat; *(for a person)* Stellvertreter; *(to ~)* substituieren; ersetzen; vertreten; an die Stelle setzen

substitution Ersetzen; Einsetzung; Verwendung; Substitution

Banking: replacement of collateral by other collateral.

Economics: the proposition that, if one product or service can be replaced by another, their prices will reflect their substitutability.

substitution effect Substitutionseffekt

Economics: the effect of a change in price of one commodity on a consumer's consumption of other commodities.

If the price of a product falls, consumers will tend to buy it instead of others; if it rises, consumers will buy other products instead.

substitution law Substitutionsgesetz

Economics: the proposition that no good is absolutely irreplaceable, because at a certain price consumers will substitute other goods for it.

substitution slope Substitutionsfunktion

Economics: a graph illustrating relative consumption at different prices, of two or more goods out of a given income.

subtenant Untermieter

Real estate: a person who has the right to use and occupy rental property leased by a tenant from a landlord.

subtotal Zwischensumme

Mathematics: the sum of part of a group of numbers, intended to be added to others later.

subtract subtrahieren, abziehen

subtraction Subtraktion; *(deduction)* Abzug; Abziehung

suburb Vortort; Stadtrandsiedlung

A residential area located on the outskirts of a city. Suburbs usually dependent on a larger city for employment and support services.

successful erfolgreich

successful year Erfolgsjahr

succession planning Nachfolgeplanung

Methodically planned and executed process to finding a successor to the current chief executive of an organization.

successive aufeinander folgend; hintereinander

successor Nachfolger; Erbe

sue verklagen; Klage anstrengen; prozessieren; ersuchen; flehen; werben

suffice reichen; genügen; ausreichen; genug sein

sufficient genug; hinreichend; ausreichend

suffrage Stimme; Zustimmung; Stimmrecht

suggest vorschlagen; anregen; deuten; schließen lassen auf

suggested compromise Kompromissvorschlag

suggested retail price empfohlener Verkaufspreis

The price of a product the manufacturer recommends that the retailer sell it for. The suggested retail price is not mandatory.

suggestion box Mitteilungsbox; Kummerkasten

HRM: a box where employees can post anonymous or signed comments; used as a method of obtaining employee feedback.

suggestion system betriebliches Vorschlagwesen

HRM: a method of obtaining employee feedback.

suit *(man's apparel)* Anzug; *(woman's apparel)* Kostüm; *(legal action)* Rechtsstreit; Prozess; *(petition)* Gesuch; Satz; Garnitur; *(to ~) (to please)* gefallen; *(to be convenient)* passen; *(to be flattering)* gut stehen

Law: any proceeding in a court of law whereby an individual seeks a legal remedy.

suitability Eignung

suitable geeignet; verwendbar; passend

sum Summe; Betrag; Rechnung

summarize zusammenfassen

summary Zusammenfassung; *(excerpt)* Auszug; *(sketch)* Abriss; *(abstract)* Kompendium

summary budget Gesamtetat

summit talks Gipfelkonferenz; Gipfeltreffen

summons Vorladung; Aufforderung; gerichtliches Mahnverfahren

Law: a notice issued by a court to a person that an action has been commenced against him and that he is required to appear, on a named day to answer the complaint.

sum-of-the-year's-digits depreciation digitale Abschreibungsmethode

sum total Gesamtbetrag

sunk costs nichtrelevante Kosten; einmalige Kosten

Accounting: costs that have already been incurred and that cannot be recovered, such as a machine that becomes a fixed cost.

superannuate pensionieren

superannuation Pensionierung

superheated überheizt; überhitzt

superintendent Vorsteher; Aufsichtsbeamte; Aufsichtsbeamtin; Aufseher; Leiter

superior Vorgesetzter; *(adv)* überlegen; besser; ausgezeichnet; erhaben; *(excellent)* vorzüglich; *(above average)* überdurchschnittlich; *(rank)* ranghöher

supermarket Supermarkt

Retailing: a store that sells a wide variety of products that are consumed regularly. Supermarkets are normally large, low-cost, low-margin, high-volume, and self-service stores.

superstore grosser Supermarkt; Großmarkt

Retailing: a store considerably larger than a regular supermarket that offers additional services such as cleaning, film developing, photo finishing, check cashing, petrol stations and self-service car-washing facilities.

superstructure Überbau; *(railway)* Oberbau

supervise überwachen; beaufsichtigen; kontrollieren

supervising Überwachen; Beaufsichtigen; Kontrollieren; Aufsicht führend; überwachend

supervision Überwachung; Aufsichtsführung; Beaufsichtigung

supervisor Aufseher; Kontrolleur; Aufsichtsbeamte; Aufsichtsbeamtin

supervisory Überwachungs-; Aufsichts-; überwachend; Aufsicht führend

supervisory agency Aufsichtsamt

supervisory body Kontrollgremium

supervisory committee Kontrollausschuss

supplement Ergänzung; Nachtrag; *(newspaper)* Beilage; *(addition)* Zusatz; Verlegerbeilage; *(to ~)* ergänzen

supplemental ergänzend; zusätzlich

supplemental claim Nachforderung

supplementary Zusatz-; Nachtrags-; Ergänzungs-; nachträglich; *(complementary)* ergänzend

supplementary appropriation Nachtragsetat; Nachtragshaushalt

supplementary budget Nachtragsetat; Nachtragshaushalt; Ergänzungshaushalt

supplier Anbieter; Auslieferer; Lieferant; Lieferfirma; *(subcontractor)* Zulieferer

A company that supplies materials, products, or services needed by others firms.

supplier's credit Lieferantenkredit

supplier country Lieferland

supplier search Lieferantensuche

Stage of the business buying process in which the buyer tries to find the best vendors.

supplier selection Lieferantenauswahl

Stage of the business buying process in which the buyer reviews proposals and selects a supplier or suppliers.

supplies and services Hilfsstoffe und Dienstleistungen

Industrial products that do not enter the finished product at all.

supply Versorgung; Belieferung; Eindeckung; *(economics)* Angebot; *(stock)* Vorrat; Bestand; *(to ~)* versorgen; beschaffen; beliefern; verschaffen

Economics: the quantity of a product that sellers are willing to offer at a certain price at a given time and place.

supply and demand Angebot und Nachfrage

supply chain integration Integration der Lieferkette

supply chain management (SCM) Supply Chain Management, Versorgungskettenmanagement

Behind the scenes coordination of the distribution channel to deliver products effectively and efficiently to customers; also called integrated logistics.

supply contract Lieferabkommen; Liefervertrag

supplying Versorgen; *(subcontract)* Zuliefern; Eindecken a versorgend; zuliefernd; eindeckend

supply of cash Bargeldversorgung; *(cash on hand)* Bargeldvorrat

supply price Angebotspreis; Lieferpreis

Economics: the price at which a given quantity of a product is supplied; here, the supply curve is viewed from the perspective of price as a function of quantity.

supply schedule Angebotstabelle; *(delivery)* Lieferzeitplan

supply-side economics angebotsorientierte Volkswirtschaftslehre

Economics: a school of macroeconomic thougst that emphasizes the importance of tax cuts and business incentives in encouraging economic growth, championed in the late 1970s especially by Professor Arthur Laffer.

support Unterstützung; *(aid)* Hilfe; *(subsistence)* Stütze; Unterhalt; *(to ~)* unterstützen; *(idea)* bejahen; *(to give aid)* Hilfe leisten; *(financially)* unterhalten; versorgen; ernähren; tragen; stützen; unterstützen

supported unterstützt; *(stock market)* gestützt

supporting Unterstützen; Unterhalten a Hilfs-; stützend; helfend; fördernd

support payment Unterhaltszahlung

support personnel Hilfspersonal

support price Stützpreis

support program Förderprogramm

supranational übernational; supranational

surcharge Preisaufschlag; Zuschlagsgebühr; *(freight)* Frachtaufschlag; *(to ~)* überladen; überlasten

surety Sicherheit; Gewissheit; *(guarantee)* Pfand; Kaution; *(personal guarantor)* Bürge; Bürgschaftsgeber; Garant

surety bond Bürgschaft

An agreement by which one party agrees to pay the debt of another. The parties involved are the *principal,* who has primary responsibility to perform the obligation, the *surety,* who has the responsibility of performing the obligation if the principal fails to perform; and the *obligee,* to whom the right of performance is owed.

surfer Surfer

Internet: undirected information seeker who is often looking for an experience rather than information.

surge in orders Auftragsflut; Überfluss; *(balance sheet)* Überschuss

surplus Überfluss; Überangebot

General: any excess amount.

surplus accounting Gewinnrechnung

surplus allocation Rücklagendotierung

surplus capacity Kapazitätsüberschuss; freie Kapazität

surplus condition Überschusslage

surplus product Überschussprodukt

surrounding conditions Rahmenbedingungen

surtax Ergänzungsabgabe; Steuerzuschlag

surveillance Überwachung; *(supervision)* Beaufsichtigung; Kontrolle; Aufsicht

survey *(opinion research)* Umfrage; Befragung; *(inspection)* Besichtigung; Inspektion; Überblick; Vermessung; *(to ~)* befragen; prüfen; begutachten; überschauen; genau betrachten; inspizieren

survey feedback approach Survey Feedback

Use of questionnaires to identify discrepancies among member perceptions; discussion follows and remedies are suggested.

survey research Umfrageforschung

Gathering of primary data by asking people questions about their knowledge, attitudes, preferences and buying behavior.

survey year Erhebungsjahr

susceptible beeinflussbar; empfindlich; empfänglich

suspend *(to discontinue)* einstellen; *(to interrupt)* unterbrechen; *(rule)* aufheben; *(public servant)* beurlauben; außer Kraft setzen; suspendieren

suspended eingestellt; *(rule)* aufgehoben; *(public service)* vorübergehend des Dienstes enthoben; beurlaubt; suspendiert

suspension Aufschub; Einstellung; Suspendierung

HRM: a temporary prohibition to work for a certain perios, used as a disciplinary action, but less critical than a discharge or dismissal.

sustainable development nachhaltige Entwicklung

sustainable growth rate nachhaltige Wachstumsrate

Only growth rate possible with preset values for four variables: profit margin, payout ratio, debt-equity ratio and asset utilization ratio if the firm issues no new equity.

swamp Sumpf; *(to ~) (market)* überschwemmen; verschlingen; *(work)* überladen; überfordern

swap Tausch; *(deal)* Swapgeschäft; *(to ~)* aus-; (ver)tauschen; eintauschen

Foreign exchange: the simultaneous purchase and sale of the same amount of a given currency for two different dates, against the sale and purchase of another.

swap arrangement Swapabkommen; Swapvereinbarung

swap rate Swapsatz

Difference between the sale (purchase) price and the price to repurchase (resell) it in a swap.

sweatshop Ausbeutungsbetrieb

A manufacturing workplace with unacceptable working conditions, low pay, poor safety provisions, and generally inhumane treatment of employees.

sweep Schwung; Wogen; *(radar)* Reichweite; *fig* Einflusssphäre; *(to ~) (floor)* fegen; kehren; *(radar)* absuchen

sweep account Geldmarktkonto

Banking: a short-term account into which all uninvested cash balances from the non-interest bearing checking account are automatically transferred on a daily basis.

sweeping *(change)* weitreichend; extensiv; umfassend; summarisch

sweepstakes Wettspiel

Marketing: a lottery in which winners are randomly selected, often used for sales promotions.

sweeten versüßen; süßen; *(fig)* mundgerecht machen

swell anschwellen; ansteigen

swing *(extent)* Spielraum; *(margin)* Marge; *(economic shift)* Umschwung; *(to ~)* schwingen; *(back & forth)* pendeln

swinging Schwingen; Schaukeln; *(fluctuating)* Schwanken; *(back & forth)* Pendeln *(adv)* schwingend; schwankend; *(back & forth)* pendelnd

switch *(electrical)* Schalter; unechter Haarknoten; Gerte; *(to ~)* schalten; *(train)* umlenken; *(loyalty)* wechseln; *(to exchange)* auswechseln

switchboard *(factory)* Schalttafel; *(communication)* Telefonzentrale; Klappschrank

switchers Wechselkäufer

Marketing: consumers who do not display any brand loyalty, and just go for the best price.

switching *(electricity)* Schalten; *(train)* Umlenken; *(loyalty)* Wechseln; *(exchange)* Auswechseln

Investment: the practice of moving assets from one mutual fund to another.

switching costs Umstellungskosten

The costs incurred when changing suppliers, products or markets.

SWOT analysis SWOT-Analyse

Acronym for strengths, weaknesses, opportunities and threats. It summarizes the findings of the internal and external audit and draws attention to the critical organizational strength and weaknesses and the opportunities and threats facing the company..

The four features can be seen to lie along two main dimensions:

1. *Internal/external:* the internal features are the company's own strengths and weaknesses (analyzing the state of the company). The external features are the organization's opportunities and the threats to its future performance.

2. *Positive/negative:* the positive things are the strengths and opportunities; the negative ones are the threats and weaknesses.

Symmetric Digital Subscriber Line (SDSL) S-DSL

Variation of DSL, in which the information is delivered at the same speed upstream or downstream. This option is appropriate for users who want to FTP webpages or send other large files over the net.

syndicate Syndikat; Kartell; Konsortium; Korrespondenzbüro

A group of individuals or companies who join forces to undertake a venture they would be unable or unwilling to pursue alone.

syndicated lending gemeinsame Kreditwährung

syndicate transaction Konsortialgeschäft

syndication *(formation of syndicate)* Syndikatsbildung; Konsortialbildung; *(electronic media)* überregionale Ausstrahlung; *(press)* überregionale Verbreitung; Syndizierung

syndication costs Syndizierungskosten

Expenditures incurred for forming and running a syndicate.

synergy Synergie

Positive incremental gain associated with the combination of two firms through a merger or acquisition.

Example: a merger of two oil companies, one with a superior distribution network and the other with more reserves, would have *synergy* and would be expected to result in higher earnings than before.

synthetic Kunststoff; *(fiber)* Kunstfaser; synthetisch; *(artificial)* künstlich

system System; Systematik

A number of separate parts that work together for a particular purpose. For example, a computer system consists of the monitor, keyboard, the CPU unit, and any peripherals connected to it.

system analysis Systemanalyse

Analysis, usually electronically on computer, of methods involved in industrial operations so that improved systems can be devised

systematic systematisch; *(thorough)* gründlich; planmäßig

systematic risk systemimanentes Risiko

Securities: Movements in a stock portfolio's value that are attributable to macroeconomic forces affecting all firms in an economy, rather than factors specific to an individual firm (unsystematic risk) and thus cannot be eliminated by diversification. The measure of systematic risk in stocks is the beta coefficient; also known as *market* risk.

systematic risk principle Prinzip des systematischen Risikos

Principle which says that only the systematic portion of risk matters in large, well-diversified portfolios. Thus, the expected returns must be related only to systematic risks.

systematic study systematische Erforschung

Looking at relationships attempting to attribute causes and effects, and drawing conclusions based on scientific evidence. That is, on data gathered under controlled conditions and measured and interpreted in a reasonably rigorous manner.

system formation Systembildung

system integrator System-Integrator

Individual or a company that specializes in making different software and hardware systems work together. Systems integrators often specialize in particular application, such as account, enterprise resource planning or web and internet systems

system of taxation Steuersystem

systems buying Systemkauf

Buying a packaged solution to a problem and without all the separate decisions involved.

systems perspective Systemperspektive

systems theory Systemtheorie

Systems theory sees the world as a combination of interdependent systems, where each system is a whole that is more than the sum of its parts, but also itself a part of larger systems.

For example, a cell is more than just a pile of molecules and itself is a part of larger systems eg. an organ. An organ is on one level a whole in itself, but on another, it is a part of a system at the level of an individual person.

Tt

T-1

High-speed internet connection that carries data at more than 15Mbps. A faster version, called T-3, operates at speeds up to 44Mbps.

table Tisch; *(list)* Liste; Verzeichnis; *(catalog)* Tabelle; *(tablet)* Tafel; *(summary)* Übersicht; Schema; *(to ~)* *(to postpone)* vertagen; tabellieren

Calculating: systematic presentation of information with the intention of conveying a certain message.

tabloid Regenbogenpresse

A newspaper smaller than a standard size newspaper, often popular or sensational, newspaper, containing news in condensed form, with a great many photographs.

tabulate tabellarisieren; tabellarisch ordnen

tabulating Tabellarisieren; tabellarisches Ordnen

tabulation Tabellarisierung; tabellarische Darstellung

t-account T-Konto

Accounting: the use of two perpendicular lines that look like the capital letter T to represent an account, with debits on the left side and credits on the right.

tack Zwecke; Drahtstift; *(course)* Richtung; Weg; Kurs; *(to ~) (to fasten)* befestigen; heften; *(nautical)* kreuzen; lavieren

tactic taktische Maßnahme; taktischer Zug

Short-term method for resolving a particular problem.

tactical taktisch; klug; planvoll

tactics Taktik

tag Anhänger; Etikett; Anhängezettel; (Preis-)Schild; *(label)* Etikett; *(to ~)* bezeichnen; etikettieren; mit einem Anhänger versehen

tailspin *(airplane)* Trudeln; Spiralsturz; spiralartiges Fallen

take nehmen; packen; fangen; wählen

take back zurücknehmen; (to *withdraw, retract)* zurückziehen

take effect in Kraft treten

take-home pay Nettolohn

Employment: the amount of wages a worker actually receives after all deductions, such as taxes and social security, have been made.

take in *(profit)* vereinnahmen; betrügen

take into account einkalkulieren

takeoff *(airplane)* Abflug; Start

Business: the point in the development of a company, an industry, or an economy at which it becomes economically viable.

take off *(airplane)* abfliegen; starten; *(weight)* abnehmen; *(to deduct)* abziehen; *(apparel)* ausziehen; *(hat)* abnehmen

take office Amt antreten

takeover Übernahme; Machtergreifung

The acquisition of one firm by another, usually through a change in its controlling interest. A takeover may friendly or hostile in nature.

take over übernehmen

take part in decision-making mitbestimmen

taking Abnahme; Annexion; Einnahme

taking delivery Lieferung annehmen

Refers to the buyer' s actually assuming possession from the seller of the asset agreed upon in a forward contract.

tally Rechnung; Abrechnung; *(list)* Liste; *(coupon)* Kupon; Anhänger; *(to ~)* zusammenzählen; nachzählen; *(to agree)* übereinstimmen; rechnen

tallyman Ladungskontrolleur; Punkteanschreiber

A person who keeps a record of quantity or weight of goods produced, shipped or received.

tamper *(to interfere)* sich einmischen; *(to meddle)* hineinpfuschen; *(to falsify)* verfälschen; betrügerisch ändern; herumdoktern

tampering *(interference)* Einmischung; *(falsification)* Verfälschung

tangible (fixed) assets Sacheigentum; Sachanlagen; Sachanlagenvermögen; materielle Vermögenswerte

Any assets having physical existence, like real estate, gold, or machinery.

tangible expenses Sachausgaben

tangible goods materielle Güter

tangible means Sachmittel

tap *(water)* Hahn; *(telephone)* Mithöreinrichtung; reichlich vorhanden; *(to ~)* anzapfen; *(telephone)* mit-; abhören; *(natural resources)* erschließen

tape Band; *(recording)* Tonband; *(measuring)* Bandmaß; *(paper)* Papierstreifen; *(to ~)* (to *seal)* mit Klebestreifen verschließen; *(to record)* aufnehmen; auf Band sprechen

taped *(sealed)* mit Klebestreifen verschlossen; *(recorded)* aufgenommen; auf Band gesprochen

tap issue Daueremission; Staatspapiere

tapped angezapft; *(telephone)* abgehört; *(natural resources)* erschlossen

tapping Anzapfen; *(telephone)* Mithören; *(natural resources)* Erschließen

target Ziel; Soll; Zielsetzung; *(goal)* Planziel; *(to ~)* Ziel setzen; planen; vorherbestimmen

target audience Zielpublikum; Zielgruppe

Marketing: the audience at which an advertising is directed, normally defined by some characteristics, such as demography or psychographic characteristics.

target company Zielgesellschaft

Firm that has been chosen as attractive for takeover by a potential acquirer.

target complex Zielkomplex

target costing Zielkostenmanagement

Technique to support pricing decisions, which starts with deciding a target cost for a new product and works back to designing the product.

Target costing is the concept of the market-oriented target cost management which applies in the early phases of product development. With target costing products are to be developed to fulfill functional features defined by the customer, thus involving costs permitted by the customer. Costing goes hand in hand from the very beginning with product planning and settles on the price determined by market research.

target country Zielland

targeted repurchase gezielter Aktienrückkauf

Situation when a firm buys back its own shares from a potential bidder, usually at a substantial premium, to forestall a takeover attempt. It is not legal in all countries.

target firm Zielunternehmen

Firm that is the object of a takeover by another firm.

target group Zielgruppe

targeting Targeting; genaue Zielgruppenansprache

Marketing: The process of identifying the needs of specific segments, selecting one or more of these segments as a target, and developing marketing programs and ad campaigns directed towards each of them.

target market Kundenzielgruppe; Zielmarkt

Set of buyers sharing common needs or characteristics that the company decides to serve; group of persons for whom a firm creates and maintains a product mix that specifically fits the needs and preferences of that group; specified audience or demographic group that an ad, product or service is intended to reach.

target marketing Zielmarketing

Directing a company's effort towards serving one or more groups of customers sharing common needs or characteristics.

target payout ratio Zielausschüttungsquote

Firm's long-run dividend-to- earnings ratio. The firm' s policy is to attempt to pay out a certain percentage of earnings, but it pays a stated dividend and adjusts it to the target as increases in earnings occur.

target price Richtpreis; Zielpreis; Orientierungspreis

Marketing: the wholesale or retail price at which a manufacturer plans to sell his product.

tariff Tarif; Zoll, Zollgebühr

Trade: a tax levied against imported products, which raises the prices of imported goods and makes them less competitive.

tariff agreement Zollabkommen

tariff autonomy Tarifautonomie

tariff barrier Zollschranke; tarifäre Handelshemmnisse

tariff commission Tarifkommission

tariff committee Tarifausschuss

tariff control Tarifkontrolle

tariff decision Tarifentscheidung; Tarifergebnis

tariff duty Tarifzoll

tariff expert Tarifexperte; Tarifexpertin

tariff increase Tariferhöhung

tariff movement Tarifbewegung

tariff negotiation results Tarifergebnis

tariff policy Zollpolitik; Tarifpolitik

tariff preference Tarifvorzug; Zollpräferenz; Zollbegünstigung

tariff rate Gebührensatz; Zollsatz; Tarifsatz

tariff reduction *(general reduction)* Tarifsenkung; Zollsenkung; Zollabbau; *(individual reduction)* Tarifermäßigung

tariff revenue Zolleinnahmen; fiskalische Gebühr; Finanzzoll

tariff sovereignty Tarifhoheit

tariff value Zollwert; Tarifwert

tariff war Handelskrieg; Zollkrieg

International trade: a confrontation between states when one raises its tariff rates in retaliation for the other`s tariff rates or economic policies.

task Aufgabe; *(administrative)* Verwaltungsaufgabe; Arbeit

task characteristic theories Theorien über Aufgabenmerkmale

Theories that seek to identify task characteristics of jobs, how these characteristics are combined to form different jobs, and their relationship to employee motivation, satisfaction, and performance.

There are three most important task characteristics theories: requisite task attributes theory, the job characteristic model, and the social information processing model.

task conflict Aufgabenkonflikt

Conflict or lack of unanimity related to the content and goals of the work.

task force Task Force; Arbeitsgruppe; Aufgabengruppe; Arbeitsstab

Organization: a temporary organizational unit responsible for the accomplishment of a specific mission, after which it is disbanded.

task group Aufgabengruppe

Organization: a groups that represent those working together to complete a job task.

task identity Ganzheitlichkeit der Aufgabe

Degree to which the job requires completion of a whole and identifiable piece of work.

task management Aufgabenmanagment; Prozesssteuerung

Management: procedure for coordinating the procedures for the completion of a specific task.

task of reconstruction Wiederaufbauaufgabe

task significance Wichtigkeit der Aufgabe

Core dimension of the job characteristic model. Is the degree to which the job has a substantial impact on the lives or work of other people.

task structure Aufgabenstruktur; Aufgabenstrukturbild

Degree to which the job assignments are procedurized (i.e., structured or unstructured).

tax Steuer; Taxe; Last; Belastung; *(social service tax)* Abgabe; *(to ~)* besteuern; belasten; viel verlangen von

A charge against a citizen's person or property or activity for the support of government. Taxes are levied upon assets or real property, upon income, or upon the sale or purchase of goods. Examples include: ad valorem tax, excise tax, income tax, property tax, sales tax, estate tax, school tax, and use tax.

tax abatement Steuerermäßigung

A reduction of taxes or an exemption from taxes granted by a government for specific reasons. Tax abatements are often grante by governments as an incentive for a special purpose, be at families with many children or real estate or industrial development.

taxable *(subject to taxation)* steuerpflichtig; abgabenpflichtig; *(capable of being taxed)* besteuerungsfähig

taxable income steuerpflichtiges Einkommen

Individuals: the gross income from wages, investments, and other sources, reduced by deductions and certain personal exemptions.

Corporations: total income reduced by total deductions, net operating loss deduction, and special dividend deductions.

tax account Steuerkonto; *(tax advantage)* Steuervorteil

tax aid Steuerhilfe

tax assessment Steuerschätzung; *(tax burden)* Steuerbelastung; Steuerveranlagung

taxation *(imposition)* Besteuerung; *(field)* Steuerwesen

taxation guideline Steuerrichtlinie

taxation law *(body of laws)* Steuerrecht; *(individual law)* Steuergesetz

taxation laws Steuergesetzgebung

tax avoidance Steuervermeidung; Steuerumgehung

A planned strategy to pay the least amount of tax as possible by using methods permitted by law, such as the deferral of income into the following year.

tax base Steuerbemessungsgrundlage

The total value of property, income, or other taxable assets subject to taxation.

tax bonus Steuerbonus

tax bracket Steuerklasse; Steuersatz

The rate at which income at a particular level is taxed, determined by income tax rate schedules. It is expressed as a percentage to be applied to each additional income earned; also called the marginal tax bracket.

tax burden Steuerbelastung

tax computation Steuerberechnung

tax consultant Steuerberater

tax credit Steuerfreibetrag; Steuergutschrift

A specific reduction in tax liability, applied after the amount of tax liability is calculated.

tax deductible steuerabzugsfähig

An expense that can be offset against assessable income.

Depreciation, repairs, maintenance, utilities, and other ordinary and necessary expenses are tax deductible for businesses.

tax deduction Steuerabzug

A provision of the tax code that specifies an amount by which a taxpayer's tax base will be reduced in return for some behavior.

tax deficit Steuerdefizit; Steuerausfall

tax dodging Steuerumgehung; Steuerhinterziehung

tax estimate Steuerschätzung

tax evasion Steuerhinterziehung; Steuerumgehung

The deliberate failure to pay taxes, which includes any method of reducing taxes not permitted by law, such as deceit, subterfuge, camouflage, concealment, or an attempt to color or obscure events.

tax-exempt steuerfrei

tax-exempt income steuerfreies Einkommen

Income that by law is not subject to income tax, such as Social Security benefits, welfare benefits, nontaxable life insurance proceeds, nontaxable pensions, and tax-exempt interest.

tax expert Steuerfachmann; Steuerexperte

tax haven Steuerparadies; Steueroase

A country that offers with very low, or even no, income taxes, in order to attract foreign funds.

taxing authority Steuerbehörde

tax law Steuergesetz

tax liability Steuerpflicht; *(tax loss)* Steuereinbuße; *(tax moneys)* Steuergelder

taxpayer Steuerzahler; Steuerpflichtiger; Besteuerter

Any person who has to bear the liability for a tax. This can be: an individual, a corporation, a partnership, a trust or estate, a joint-stock company, an association, or a syndicate, group, pool, joint venture, or other unincorporated organization or group.

tax policy Steuerpolitik

tax progression Steuerprogression

tax rate Steuersatz; -rate

tax receipts Steuereinnahmen; Steueraufkommen

tax reduction Steuerentlastung; Steuersenkung; Steuererleichterung

tax reform Steuerreform

tax regulation Steuervorschrift

tax relief Steuerentlastung; Steuervergünstigung; Steuererleichterung; *(aid)* Steuerhilfe

tax revenue Steuereinnahme; Steueraufkommen; Steuerertrag

tax structure Steuersystem

tax treaty Steuerabkommen

Agreement between two countries specifying what items of income will be taxed by the authorities of the country where the income is earned.

Taylor, Frederick Winslow (1856-1915)

Management consultant who invented scientific management. He believed that every employee held some potential and that it was the responsibility of management to identify these possibilities and provide opportunities for improvement.

Taylor's influence can be detected in business process re-engineering. From management 's point of view, Taylorism stood for efficiency and the elimination of waste. He preached that management and workforce were independent and relied on each other to achieve the common goal of higher prosperity.

In Taylor's thinking, 'the principal object of management should be to secure the maximum prosperity for the employer, coupled with the maximum prosperity of each employee.'

Biography: worked in steel companies, chief engineer at Midvale Steel Works, then a consulting engineer in management at Bethlehem Steel Works of Pittsburgh.

Major publications: (1947) Scientific Management.

team *(sports)* Mannschaft; *(work)* Arbeitsgemeinschaft; Arbeitsgruppe; Team; (to ~ up) zusammenspannen

teambuilding Teamentwicklung

Utilizes high interaction among team members to increase trust and openness. It can be applied within groups or at the intergroup level where activities are independent.

Team building is applicable to the case of interdependency. The objective is to improve coordinative efforts of members, which will result in increasing the team's performance.

team of analysts Analystenteam

team of experts Expertenteam

team selling Teamverkauf

Using teams of people from sales, marketing, production, finance, technical support, and even upper management to service large, complex accounts.

team structure Teamstruktur

Use of teams as the central device to coordinate work activities, breaking down departmental barriers and decentralizing decision making to the level of the work teams.

This requires employees to be generalists as well as specialists, and allows lage organizations to achieve the efficiency of bureaucratic standardization, while gaining the flexibility of teams.

teamwork Gruppenarbeit; Teamarbeit; koordinierte Zusammenarbeit; Gemeinschaftsarbeit

teaser *(marketing)* Anreiz; *(advertising)* anreizende Reklame; Rätselreklame; Lockwerbung; Neckwerbung

technical Fach-; technisch; fachlich

technical analysis technische (Aktien-) Analyse

A method of evaluating future security prices and market directions based on statistical analysis of variables such as trading volume, price changes.

technical director technischer Direktor

technically inexperienced technisch unerfahren; sachfremd

technical insolvency technische Zahlungsunfähigkeit

Default on a legal obligation of the firm.

Example: technical insolvency occurs when a firm doesn't pay a bill.

technical manager technischer Leiter

technical newspapers Fachpresse

technical question technische Frage; Sachfrage

technical skills technische Kompetenzen; technische Fähigkeiten

technique (Arbeits-)Technik; technische Ausführung; *(method)* Methode; Maßnahme

technocrat Technokrat

technographics Technografie

Internet: Base of segmentation of online shoppers as identified by Forrester Research. Consumers fall into one of various groups based upon their attitude toward technology, and primary motivation to go online.

technological technisch; technologisch

technological advance technologischer Fortschritt

technological change technologische Änderung; technischer Wandel

technological environment technologische Umwelt

Forces that create new technologies, creating new product and marketing opportunities.

technological innovation technologische Neuerung

technological obsolescence technische Veralterung

The situation when a technology becomes outdated due to technological progess.

technological unemployment technologische Arbeitslosigkeit

Unemployment resulting from the introduction of a new technology, by eliminating jobs or by changing the necessary skills.

technologist Technologe; Technokrat

technology Technologie; Technik

technology strategy Technologiestrategie

technology transfer Technologietransfer

Can involve physical devices and equipment, it can be intangible, involve knowledge itself or technical know-how. It can take place in many different directions (for example from the public sector to the private sector or from rich countries to poor countries).

telecommunications Telekommunikation; *(the feld)* Fernmeldewesen; *(traffic)* Femmeldeverkehr; *(technology)* Fernmeldetechnik; Telekommunikationstechnik

The use dirrerent electromagnetic channels to transmit or receive signals for voice, data, and video communications.

telecommuting Telearbeit

Situation when employees do their work at home on a computer that is linked to their office.

teleconference Telekonferenz

Meeting conducted by telephone among people in different locations.

telegram Telegramm; Drahtnachricht; Depesche

telemarketing Telemarketing; Telefonmarketing

The use of the telephone to market goods or services directly to customers and/or to receive orders and inquiries generated by advertising.

Inbound telemarketing includes receiving orders, inquiries and complaints; outbound telemarketing is used to contact prospective customers directly.

telephone Fernsprecher; Telefon; *(to ~)* telefonieren; anrufen

telephone wire Fernsprechleitung; Telefonleitung

television advertising Fernsehwerbung

Advertising over the television with an advertiser paying the cost of the program as sponsor.

television marketing Fernsehmarketing

Direct marketing via television using direct-response advertising or home shopping channels.

television support Fernsehunterstützung

Advertising: broadcast on television to serve as a secondary part of a multimedia campaign, such as to announce a newspaper insert.

telex Fernschreiber; *(teller)* Kassierer; Kassenbeamte; Kassenbeamtin; Schalterbeamte; Schalterbeamtin

telnet Telnet

Internet-based protocol for connecting to a remote host or server. Telnet was once the main way to access other computers over the internet, and it supported a variety of text-based e-mail, file transfer, chat and information retrieval programs.

template Schablone

Internet: particular pattern applied to a website.

temporal method Zeitmethode

Translating assets valued in a foreign currency into the home currency using the exchange rate that existed when the assets were originally purchased.

temporary vorübergehend; zeitlich begrenzt; befristet

temporary arrangement Übergangsregelung

tenancy Pacht(besitz); -dauer

The right to use and occupy all or part of a property under a rental agreement.

tenant Mieter; Pächter; (to ~) bewohnen

Someone who pays rent to use land or a building that is owned by someone else.

tend dazu neigen; die Tendenz haben; beitragen zu; tendieren

ten day average daily trading volume durchschnittliches 10-tages Handelsvolumen

tendency to save Sparneigung

tender Offerte; Gebot; Angebot; Submissionsangebot; Lieferangebot; *(to ~)* anbieten; offerieren; einreichen; sich an einer Ausschreibung beteiligen

An unconditional offer by a party to a contract to perform in full an obligation to another.

tendered shares angebotene Aktien

tender offer Zeichnungsangebot; Tender Offer; Übernahmeangebot

Securities: A public offer to buy shares made to shareholders of a particular corporation. The offer is only valid if the offerer is able to obtain the total amount of stock specified in the offer.

tentative Vor-; Probe-; Versuchs-; *(preliminary)* vorläufig; *(experimentally)* versuchsweise; probeweise; vorsichtig; zögernd

tentative agreement Vorvertrag; vorläufiges Übereinkommen; *(draft)* Vertragsentwurf

tenure Besitz; Besitzen; Dauer; Amtszeit; Anstellung

Real estate: the nature of an occupant's ownership rights.

Employment: the length of time during which some position has been held.

Academia: the privilege granted to professors, allowing them academic freedom of speech and continued employment except in extraordinary circumstances.

term Frist; Zeitdauer; *(payment)* Zahlungsfrist; Termin; Gebühr; Preis; *(expression)* Ausdruck; Fachausdruck; Terminus; *(condition)* Vertragsbedingung; *(to ~)* benennen; bezeichnen

Law: period of time during which the conditions of a contract will be carried out..

term borrowing befristete Geldaufnahme

term debt befristete Schuld

term financing befristete Finanzierung

terminal Flughafengebäude; Terminal *(computer)* Endgerät; *(railway)*

Endbahnhof; Endstation; *(bus)* Endhaltestelle; *(adv)* End-; begrenzend; beendend

Computing: piece of hardware that allows commands to be sent to a computer, normally a keyboard.

terminal values terminale Werte

Refers to desirable end-states of existence; the goals that a person would like to achieve during his or her lifetime.

terminate abschließen; *(contract)* kündigen; *(to complete)* zum Abschluss bringen; beschließen; *(to finish)* beenden; auflösen

terminated abgeschlossen; *(contract)* gekündigt; *(completed)* zum Abschluss gebracht; *(finished)* beendet

termination *(completion)* Abschluss; *(dismissal)* Kündigung; *(end)* Ende; Erlöschen

terminology Terminologie; Fachsprache

term investment befristete Investition

term loan langfristiges Darlehen; Langzeitkredit

Banking: an intermediate to long-term (typically two to ten years) loan granted to a company by a commercial bank, usually to finance capital equipment or provide working capital.

term of office Amtszeit

terms Bedingungen; Vertragsbedingungen;

Contract: the conditions and arrangements specified in a contract, such as the price, conditions, and contingencies.

terms of payment Zahlungsbedingungen

Contract: the conditions and arrangements specified in a contract pertaining to the details of payment.

terms of trade reales Austauschverhältnis; Austauschrelationen; Handelsbedingungen

Trade: the ratio of prices of a country's exports to the prices of its imports, i.e. the purchasing power of a country's exports in terms of the imports it buys.

terms of sale Verkaufsbedingungen; Preisforderung; Zahlungsbedingungen

Contract: conditions on which firm proposes to sell its goods and services for cash or credit.

term structure Zinsstruktur

Relationship between interest rates and various maturities.

territorial sales force structure gebietsabhängige Verkaufspersonalstruktur

Marketing: approach to sales force organization that assigns each salesperson to an exclusive geographic territory in which he carries the company's full line.

territory Land; Gebiet; Hoheitsgebiet; Territorium; *(sales)* Vertreterbezirk; *(travel)* Reisegebiet; Bereich

tertiary reserves Reserven dritter Ordnung

tertiary sector tertiärer Sektor; Dienstleistungssektor

One of the three main industrial categories of a developed economy, the others being the secondary industry (manufacturing and primary goods production such as agriculture), and primary industry (extraction such as mining and fishing). Also called the service sector or the service industry.

test Prüfung; Aufgabe; Test; *(experiment)* Versuch; *(investigation)* Untersuchung; *(test piece)* Probe; *(to ~)* testen; erproben; *(to examine)* prüfen; *(to investigate)* untersuchen; auf die Probe stellen

test case Testfall; Musterfall

testimonial Zeugnis; Empfehlungs-schreiben; Attest

Marketing: a statement, often given by a celebrity, affirming the value of a product, event or service.

testing facility Prüfanlage; Versuchsanlage

test market Testmarkt; Versuchsmarkt

test marketing Durchführung eines Markttestes

Marketing: introduction of a new product in a restricted geographic location, which allows the manufacturer to evaluate the product performance on a small scale.

test web site Testwebseite

Internet: Parallel version of a site to use before it is made available to customers as a live website.

testing testen; überprüfen

Determination, whether a test object has the required features, ie fulfills one or several agreed, determined or expected conditions.

Testing can take place subjectively by sensory perception (visual inspection) or objectively with measuring or test devices and take place at each individual component or on a random basis.

testing phase Testphase

text Text; Textteil; *(wording)* Wortlaut; *(contents)* Inhalt

textile Web-; Textil-; Webstoff; Gewebe

textile maker Textilfabrikant

text processing Textverarbeitung

theory of competition Wettbewerbstheorie

theory of demand Nachfragetheorie

theory of economic cycles Konjunkturtheorie

theory of market trends Marktzyklustheorie

theory of production Produktionstheorie

Theory X Theorie X

Management: theory developed by Douglas McGregor representing an authoritarian supervisory approach management. He believes that managers must coerce, threaten, and closely supervise subordinates in order to motivate them.

Theory Y Theorie Y

Management: theory that given the right conditions and rewards, the average employee finds work satisfying, will exercise self-direction, seek responsibility, and is creative.

Theory Z Theorie Z

Management: theory developed by William Ouchi, describing the Japanese system of management, characterized by the worker involvement in management, high productivity, and a system of organizational and sociological rewards.

third party Dritter; Dritte

Someone other than the parties directly involved in the action or transaction; outsider with no legal interest in the matter.

third party check Verrechnungsscheck

Banking: Check negotiated through a bank. The *primary party* to a transaction is the bank on which a check is drawn. The *secondary party* is the drawer of the check against funds on deposit in the bank. The *third party* is the payee who endorses the check.

third-party logistics ausgelagerte Logistik

Situation where logistics is outsourced such that a third party manages the company's supply chain and provides value-added services such as product configuration and subassembly.

third party sale Verkauf über Dritte

Sale made by an agency acting as an intermediary between a buyer and a seller.

Third World Dritte Welt

An expression that came into use during the Cold War to distinguish the rest of the world from the two power blocs of the capitalist west (United States and Europe) and the Communist east (Soviet Union, eastern Europe and China).

It comprises the poorest nations of the world. Many depend on international aid to meet the basic needs of their population.

The term has fallen into disfavor in recent years, and is being replaced by terms such as Less-Developed Country (LDC) or developing nations.

threat Drohung; *(menace)* Bedrohung; Gefahr

threaten drohen; bedrohen

threat of dismissal Kündigungsdrohung

threat to existence Existenzbedrohung

three-component model of creativity Drei-Komponenten-Modell der Kreativität

Proposes that individual creativity requires expertise, creative-thinking skills, and intrinsic task motivation. The higher the level is of each of these three components, the higher the creativity is.

three day average daily trading volume Dreitagesdurchschnitthandelsvolumen

Stock exchange: Daily average of cumulative trading volume for the last three days.

three month average daily volume Dreimonatsdurchschnittstagesvolumen

Stock exchange: Monthly average of the cumulative trading volume during the last three months divided by 22 days.

threshold Schwelle

threshold-point ordering Lagermindestbeschaffung

Inventory: minimum ordering quantity to meet expected user demand.

thrift *(economy)* Wirtschaftlichkeit; *(thriftiness)* Sparsamkeit

thrift institution Sparkasse; Bausparkasse

A general term for savings banks and savings and loan associations.

thrifty sparsam

Person or purchase characterized as frugal or economical. A thrifty buy or product is one where the consumer gets good value for the price.

thrive gedeihen; *(to flourish)* blühen; florieren; *(to prosper)* prosperieren; Erfolg haben

thriving Gedeihen; gedeihend

through bill of lading Durchkonnossement, Durchfrachtkonnossement

A single bill of lading covering receipt of the cargo at the point of origin for delivery to the ultimate consignee, using two or more modes of transportation

throughput time Durchlaufszeit

through rate Durchgangstarif

Trade: the total cost of shipping goods from sender to receiver, when two or more carriers are used.

through transport system ungebrochener Güterverkehr; von-Haus-zu-Haus-Verkehr

Trade: mode of transportation, when no change in means of transportation between sender and receiver occurs.

throw out of power hinauswerfen; *(by force)* stürzen

thrust Stoß; Hieb;Vorstoß; *(argument)* Hauptidee; Hauptrichtung; *(to ~)* stoßen; hauen; *(fig)* vorstoßen; *(to throw)* werfen; sich voranarbeiten; drängen

tick Ticken; Abhakungszeichen; *(fig)* Pump; Kredit; (to ~) ticken; funktionieren; abhaken

Stock exchange: small upward or downward price movement in a security's trades.

ticker Ticker; Börsentelegraph

Stock exchange a computerized system that produces a running report of trading activity on the stock exchanges, also called ticker tape, showing the stock symbol, latest price, and volume of trades on the exchanges.

tick indicator Marktanzeiger

Stock exchange: Market indicator based on the number of stocks whose last trade was an uptick or a downtick. Used as an indicator of market sentiment or psychology to try to predict the market's trend.

tide over überbrücken; hinwegbringen; durchschleusen

tie Band; Schlips; *(bond)* Bindung; *(connection)* Verbindung; *(voting)* Stimmengleichheit; *(to ~)* binden; *(to connect)* verbinden

tie-in promotion Kombinationswerbung; Verbundwerbung

Marketing: special displays and gimmicks that relate to an ongoing advertising campaign. A tie-in promotion carries the same basic theme as the campaign and may be in the form of a sweepstakes offering, point-of-purchase displays, a premium giveaway, or anything else that will create immediate sales, help to introduce a product, or otherwise enhance the advertising campaign.

tie up *(ship)* vertäuen; *(to dock)* anlegen; *(to obstruct)* aufhalten; lahm legen; *(to commit)* an einen Zweck binden; *(to reserve)* einbehalten; *(a contract)* abschließen; beschränken

tight eng; gespannt; fest; dicht; undurchlässig; *(money)* knapp; *(niggardly)* knauserig; knickerig

tighten festigen; festmachen; verstärken; fester binden; *(belt)* enger schnallen; *(screw)* anziehen; *(rope)* festzurren; *(restrictions)* verschärfen

tightened gefestigt; verstärkt; *(screw)* angezogen; *(rope)* festgezurrt; *(restrictions)* verschärft

tightening Festigen; Verstärken; *(screw)* Anziehen; *(rope)* Festzurren; *(restrictions)* Verschärfen; Verschärfung

tight market enger Markt; angespannter Markt

Stock exchange: market situation characterized by active trading and narrow bid-offer price spreads. A slack market, in contrast, is characterized by inactive trading and wide spreads.

tight money knappes Geld

Economics: market situation in which credit is difficult to secure, usually as the result of central bank action to restrict the money supply.

till Kasse

time-based competition Zeit basierter Wettbewerb

Competing on the basis of speed in responding to customer demands and developing new products.

time-based management Management auf Zeitbasis

Management philosophy originating from Japan which perceives time as the critical success factor and uses it in place of costs as a yardstick for success. A more efficient handling of time as a resource should result in a fall of production costs, while at the same time improving the quality of service.

time card Stechkarte; Lohnkarte

HRM: pysical card to record actual employee hours of work.

time deposit Termineinlagen; Termingeld; Festgeld; befristete Einlage

Banking: a deposit that cannot be withdrawn immediately by the depositor, but only after due notice has been given.

time deposit rate Termingeldsatz

time deposits Termineinlagen; Termingelder

time difference Zeitunterschied

time draft Nachsichtwechsel

Banking: a draft payable at a specified date in the future, as distinguished from a sight draft, which is payable on presentation and delivery.

time estimate Zeitschätzung

time lag Zeitabstand; zeitliche Verschiebung; Zeitverzögerung

time management Zeitmanagement

Techniques aime at increase the effectiveness of a person in using the time at his disposal.

time of payment Zahlungsfrist

time series Zeitreihe

time series analysis Zeitreihenanalyse

Breaking down past sales into trends, cycle and seasonal components then recombining these components to produce a sales forecast.

Time series analysis is based on the premise that by knowing the past, the future can be forecast. It uses historical data and mathematical techniques to model the historical path of a price, demand for a good, or consumption.

timetable Zeitplan; Terminplan; Terminkalender; *(train)* Fahrplan; Kursbuch; *(airplane)* Flugplan

time utility Zeitnutzen

Marketing: enhancing a product's marketability by making it available at a convenient time.

time value Zeitwert

Options: the difference between an option's intrinsic value and the current market price, that reflects the time remaining on an option contract before expiration.

time value of money Zeitwert des Gelds

Economics: the value derived from the use of money over time as a result of investment and reinvestment, which reflects the opportunity cost of investing at a risk-free rate.

Therefore, the certainty of having a given sum of money today is worth more than the certainty of having an equal sum at a later date because money can be put to profitable use during the intervening time.

time worked in a lifetime Lebensarbeitszeit

timing Zeitwahl; Terminierung

timing of entry Wahl des Eintrittszeitpunks

International trade: Entry is early when a firm enters a foreign market before other foreign firms and late when a firm enters after other international businesses have established themselves.

tip Hinweis; Trinkgeld; Wink; Abladeplatz; Halde; Klaps; (to ~) umkippen

In general: a small payment given in appreciation for a service; also called a gratuity.

Investments: secret information about a security passed by one person to another.

title Titel; Titelseite; *(legal claim)* Rechtsanspruch; Rechtstitel; *(right)* Anrecht; Verfügungsrecht

Ownership; in property law, composite of facts that will permit one to recover or to retain possession of a thing.

title register Grundbuch

Tobin's Q Tobin's Q

Market value of assets divided by replacement value of assets. A Tobin's Q ratio greater than 1 indicates the firm has done well with its investment decisions.

toehold Ansatzpunkt; *(point of support)* Stützpunkt

token Zeichen; *(proof)* Beweis; *(coupon)* Gutschein; Bon; *(pseudo currency)* Notgeld; *(adv)* symbolisch

toll Läuten; *(fee)* Abgabe; Gebühr; Zoll; Wegegeld; Verlustziffer; *(telephone)* Fernsprechgebühr; *(bell)* läuten

Charge for the use of another's property, or for the use of public facilities such as roads, bridges and ferries.

toll-free gebührenfrei

tonnage Tonnage; *(capacity)* Tragfähigkeit; Tonnengehalt; *(volume)* Frachtraum

tool Werkzeug; Instrument; *(appliance, device)* Gerät; *(to ~)* bearbeiten

tooling Einrüstung

Production: applying the tools and support devices required for a production run.

Requirements for unique or specialized tools are scheduled through their addition to the bill of materials.

top-down budgeting hierarchische Planung

topic Gegenstand; *(theme song)* Kennmelodie; *(motif)* Motiv

top-level functionary Spitzenfunktionär

top-level talk Spitzengespräch

top management oberste Betriebsführung; oberste Leitung; Spitzenkräfte; Unternehmensspitze

top manager Spitzenmanager; Unternehmensleiter

top position Spitzenstellung

top price Höchstpreis; Spitzenpreis; Höchstkurs; Höchststand

top product Spitzenprodukt

top-ranking officeholder Spitzenfunktionär

top-ranking official Spitzenbeamter

top representative Spitzenvertreter

top-selling meistverkauft; umsatzstark

tort unerlaubte Handlung; Schaden

Civil wrong or injury that results in a legal action for damages to rectify the wrong; wrongful act that is neither a crime nor a breach of contract, but that renders the perpetrator liable to the victim for damages, such as nuisance, trespassing, or negligence.

Example: negligence is a landlord's failure to fix reported defective wiring. The law provides remedy for damages from resulting fire.

total Gesamt-; Total-; *(amount)* Gesamtbetrag; Gesamtsumme; *(to ~) (to add)* zusammenzählen; addieren; *(adv)* gänzlich; gesamt

total assets Vermögenssubstanz; Bilanzsumme; Gesamtwert der Aktiva

total asset-turnover ratio Umschlaghäufigkeit des Gesamtkapitals

Turnover divided by average total assets. Used to measure how effectively a firm is managing its assets.

total bank deposits Einlagenbestand

total borrowings Kreditvolumen

total capacity Gesamtkapazität; Gesamtleistungsvermögen

total cash flow Gesamt-Cashflow

total consumption Gesamtverbrauch

total contract amount Gesamtvertragssumme; Gesamtauftragswert

total costs Gesamtkosten

Sum of the fixed and variable costs for any given level of production.

total cost curve Gesamtkostenkurve

total customer cost gesamte Kundenkosten

Total of all the monetary, time, energy and psychic costs associated with a marketing offer.

total customer value gesamter Kundenwert

Marketing: the sum total of all the product, services, personnel and image values that a buyer receives from a marketing offer.

total demand Gesamtnachfrage

total figure Gesamtziffer

total indebtedness Gesamtverschuldung

total interest Gesamtverzinsung

total investment Gesamtanlage; Gesamtinvestition

totalitarianism Einparteiensystem; Totalitarismus

Form of government in which one person or political party exercises absolute control over all spheres of human life and opposing political parties are prohibited.

totality Gesamtheit; Vollständigkeit; Sonnenfinsternis

total loss Gesamtverlust

total market Gesamtmarkt

total market demand Gesamtmarktnachfrage

Total volume of a product or service that would be bought by a defined consumer group in a defined geographic area in a defined time period in a defined marketing environment under a defined level and mix of industry marketing effort.

total nominal amount Gesamtnennbetrag

total nominal value Gesamtnennwert

total output *(productivity)* Gesamtleistung; *(production)* Gesamtproduktion

total production Gesamtproduktion

total profit Gesamtgewinn

total quality management (TQM) Qualitätsmanagement

A comprehensive management philosophy committed to the continuous improvement of product and services with the involvement of the entire workforce.

TQM perceives quality in the broadest sense as the critical success factor and subjects it to systematic planning and control. It is top management‘s chief task to create a high level of quality awareness throughout the business through personal example and publicity. Every manager and his team is responsible for the quality of the operations in their area.

total reserves Gesamtreserven

total revenue Gesamteinkommen

The amount received from the sale of a product. It equals the price of the product multiplied by the quantity sold.

total sales Gesamtabsatz; Gesamtumsatz

total savings Gesamtersparnisse

total stock on hand Gesamtbestand; gesamter Lagerbestand

total supply *(availability)* Gesamtangebot; *(provision)* Gesamtversorgung

total value Gesamtwert

total volume Gesamtvolumen

total weight Gesamtgewicht

tourist Reisender; Tourist; Gast

tout *(racing)* Tippgeber; *(to ~) (advertising)* übermäßig anpreisen; aufdringlich Kunden werben

towage *(ship)* Schleppen; Bugsieren; *(car)* Abschleppen; *(charge)* Schleppgebühr

town-center shopping innerstädtisches Einkaufszentrum

Store cluster in the town center. Typically, smaller independent stores, variety stores, a limited number of chain stores and speciality retailers form the cluster. The stores attract mainly shoppers who work or live in or near the town.

track record Erfolgs- und Erfahrungsgeschichte

Management: the summary of a manager´s recognized accomplishments, such as the reputation for producing on a timely and economical basis.

trade Handel; *(vocation)* Gewerbe; Fach; *(business)* Gewerbebetrieb; (to ~) handeln; *(exchange)* tauschen

The voluntary exchange of goods or services. Trade may take place between two parties (bilateral trade) or more than two parties (multilateral trade), within one country (domestic trade) or more than one country (international trade).

trade acceptance Handelsakzept

Trade: a bill of exchange for a specific purchase, drawn on the buyer by the seller and bearing the buyer's acceptance. It is similar to a banker’s acceptance but more risky.

trade account Kundenkonto

trade advertising Händlerwerbung

Marketing: advertising for consumer products directed at wholesalers or retailers, designed to stimulate them to purchase the products for resale to their customers.

trade agreement Handelsabkommen

Trade: an agreement between two or more countries which encourages, regulates, or restricts elements of trade among them.

trade allowance Nachlass; Rabatt; Händlerrabatt

Marketing: a discount given to distributors or retailers as a promotional effort.

trade area Handelszone

trade association Berufsverband; Wirtschaftsverband

trade balance Handelsbilanz; Handelssaldo

trade balance deficit Handelsbilanzdefizit

trade barrier Handelsschranke

Trade: any form restriction that makes the importation of goods into a country difficult or impossible.

trade creation Handelserweiterung

Trade created due to regional economic integration; occurs when high-cost domestic producers are replaced by low-cost foreign producers in a free trade area.

trade credit Lieferantenkredit; Handelskredit

Trade: an open-account arrangement between a seller and a buyer for deferred payment. Trade credit is an important external source of working capital for a company, although such credit can be highly expensive. Trade liabilities constitute a company's accounts payable.

trade cycle phase Konjunkturphase; Phase des Wirtschaftskreislaufes

trade date Tranaktionsdatum; Schlusstag

Trade: the date on which a trade is executed. Settlement (payment) normally has to occur 1-5 business days after the trade date.

trade deficit Handelsdefizit

Economics: a negative balance of trade in which a country imports more than it exports. The difference must be made up in financial payments usually in hard currency.

trade discount Händlerrabatt; Skonto

Trade: a deduction from the list price of goods provided by a business in return for payment within a specified time frame.

trade diversion Handelsdiversifizierung

Trade diverted due to regional economic integration; occurs when low-cost foreign suppliers outside free trade area are replaced by higher-cost foreign suppliers in a free trade area.

trade exhibition Fachausstellung; Gewerbeausstellung

trade fair Handelsmesse; Gewerbemesse; Fachmesse; Verkaufsmesse

trade financing Handelsfinanzierung

trade for own account Eigenhandel

trade group Handelsgruppe

trade-in in Zahlung geben

Price reduction given for turning in an old item when buying a new one.

trade jargon Händlerjargon

trade journal Fachjournal; Handelsblatt; Fachblatt

trade magazine Handelszeitschrift; Fachzeitschrift

Publications: a magazine whose content is of interest only to persons engaged in a particular industry, occupation, or profession.

trademark Schutzmarke; Warenzeichen; Markenzeichen; (to ~) gesetzlich schützen lassen

Branding: any word, phrase, symbol, design, or combination thereof, that identifies and distinguishes one product from all others.

Trademarks can be either registered or unregistered, which involves different levels of protection.

trademark protection Markenschutz

trade name Firmenname; Handelsname; Handelsbezeichnung; Firmenbezeichnung; *(logo)* Firmenzeichen

The name under which a company conducts business, which may or may not be trademarked.

trade newspaper Handelsblatt; Verbandszeitung

trade obstruction Handelshemmnis

trade-off Kompromiss; Tausch; Austauschbeziehung

Situation where a person is forced to give up one advantage in order to gain another, such as taking a financial loss in order to gain a tax deduction that will lower total tax liability.

trade off ausgleichen; verzichten; tauschen

trade policy Handelspolitik

trade promotion Händler-Promotion

Sales promotion designed to gain reseller support and to improve reseller selling efforts, including discounts, allowances, free goods, co-operative advertising, push money, and conversations and trade shows.

trader Händler; Handeltreibender; Kaufmann;; Unternehmer; Wertpapierhändler

In general: anyone who buys and sells goods or services for profit.

Investment: a person who buys and sells securities on an exchange for his or her own account, that is, as a dealer or principal, rather than as a broker or agent.

trade rate Händlerpreis

Trade Related Intellectual Property Rights (TRIPs) Abkommen über handelsbezogene Aspekte der Rechte des geistigen Eigentums

Agreement reached in 1995, part of the World Trade Organization's (WTO) program of international treaties, which aims at protecting intellectual rights like trademarks, patents, etc. so as to provide incentives for innovation.

trade relations Handelsbeziehungen

trade representation Berufsvertretung

trade restraint Handelseinschränkung

trade restriction Handelsbeschränkung; Handelshemmnis

trade rivalry Konkurrenzkampf

trade secret Geschäftsgeheimnis; Betriebsgeheimnis

Any confidential information, such as a formula, machine, or process, that gives a business a competitive advantage.

trade service Wirtschaftsdienst

trade show Gewerbeschau; Fachausstellung

An exhibition organised for companies in a specific industry to showcase and demonstrate their new products and services. Normally not open to the general public.

tradesman Handwerker; Gewerbetreibender; Händler

trade surplus Handelsüberschuss; Handelsbilanzüberschuss

trade tax Gewerbesteuer

trade union Gewerkschaft

A group of workers organized into a voluntary association, or union, to further their mutual interests with respect to wages, hours, working conditions and other matters of interest to them.

trade union law Gewerkschaftsgesetz

trade war Handelskrieg

trading bloc Handelsblock

A group of countries that are closely associated in international trade, agreeing to give each other reduced trade tariffs and other accommodations while imposing trade barriers and restrictions on nonmember nations.

Example: the European Union, NAFTA, APEC.

trading center Geschäftszentrum

trading company Handelsgesellschaft

trading firm Handelshaus; Handelsunternehmen

trading partner Handelspartner

trading range Handelsspanne

Difference between the high and low prices traded during a period of time; with commodities, the high/low price limit established by the exchange for a specific commodity for any one day's trading.

tradition Tradition

traditional traditionell

traditional view of conflict traditioneller Ansatz der Konfliktforschung

Belief that all conflict is harmful and must be avoided. It was consistent with the attitudes that prevailed about group behavior in the 1930s and 1940s.

Conflict was seen as a dysfunctional outcome resulting from poor communication, a lack of openness and trust, and failures of managers.

traffic Verkehr; Verkehrswesen; *(commerce)* Handel; Tausch; *(Internet)* Traffic; Besucher auf einer Seite; (to ~) handeln

Internet: the number of visitors to a web page or Website, measured by hits, page accesses, etc., over a given time period.

traffic building campaign Traffic-Building-Kampagne

Internet: use of online and offline promotion techniques such as banner advertising, search engine promotion and reciprocal linking to increase the audience of a site (both new and existing customers).

trailer truck Laster mit Anhänger; Sattelzug

train Eisenbahnzug; *(to ~) (sports)* trainieren; *(job)* ausbilden; unterweisen

trained *(sports)* trainiert; *(job)* ausgebildet; vorgebildet; geschult

trainee Volontär; *(intern)* Praktikant; Lehrling; *(learner)* Azubi; Auszubildender

training *(sports)* Trainieren; *(job)* Ausbilden; Ausbildung; Vorbilden; Schulen; Schulung; Praktikum

training center Ausbildungszentrum

training school Berufsschule; Ausbildungsstätte

trait theories of leadership Eigenschaftstheorien der Führung

Theories that sought personality, social, physical, or intellectual traits that differentiate leaders from non-leaders. Six traits on which leaders tend to differ from non-leaders are ambitions and energy, to desire to lead, honesty and integrity, self-confidence, intelligence, and job relevant knowledge.

tranche Tranche; Abschnitt

transaction Abwicklung; Transaktion; Geschäftsabschluss; Durchführung; Vorgang; Geschäftsvorfall; Vorhaben

An exchange between two parties that involves at least two things of value, agreed-upon conditions, a time of agreement and a place of agreement.

A transaction can be: a sale, assignment, lease, license, loan, advance, contribution, or any other transfer of an interest, whether tangible or intangible.

transactional functions Transaktionsfunktionen

Marketing: the elements of a product or service offering that refer to tranaction-specific details, such as matching product to buyer needs, or negotiating the price.

transactional leader transaktionale Führer

Management: a leadership that emphasizes planning, organizing, coordinating, and controlling. The manager enters into a transaction with his subordinates: compliance is exchanged for reward.

transaction-based online systems Onlinesystem für Transaktionen

Internet: systems that allow organizations not only to communicate with the consumer but to sell online as well.

transaction costs Transaktionskosten

The costs incurred in making an economic exchange, such as paying a commission.

transaction exposure Transaktionsrisiko

Extent to which income from individual transactions is affected by fluctuations in foreign exchange values.

transaction for third account Kundengeschäft

transaction in securities Wertpapiergeschäft

transactions motive Transaktionsmotiv

Reason for holding cash that arises from normal disbursement and collection activities of the firm.

transactive media interactive/ transaktive Medien

Interactive channels of communication that are capable of carrying out product transactions.

transcribe übertragen; *(entry)* umbuchen; *(to remit)* überweisen; *(to, instruct)* anweisen; *(capital)* transferieren

transcript Ab-; Umschrift

Letter-perfect copy of a document, which does not seek to reproduce exact appearance of original

transcription Umschreibung; Umschrift; *(transfer)* Übertragung; *(remittance)* Überweisung; *(instruction)* Anweisung; *(capital)* Transfer; *(securities)* Umschreibung;

transferable share Inhaberaktie

transfer agent Umschreibungsstelle; Übertragungsstelle

Securities: an agent who keeps a record of each registered shareowner of a corporation by name, address, and number of shares owned.

transfer charge Übertragungsgebühr; Überweisungsgebühr

transferee *(assignee)* Zessionar; *(recipient of a remittance)* Überweisungsempfänger; *(successor)* Übernehmer; *(purchaser)* Erwerber

Transfer Control Protocol/Internet Protocol (TCP/IP)

Internet: passing of data around the internet occurs via the TCP /IP protocol. For a PC to be able receive web pages or for a server to host web pages it must be configured to support this protocol.

transfer fee Überweisungsgebühr

Bank charge for moving cash from one location to another.

transfer income Transfereinkommen

transfer in the books Umbuchung; Vortrag

transfer of funds Überweisungsverkehr

transfer order Überweisungsauftrag

transfer payment Transferzahlung; Transferleistungen

A payment made without receiving any good or service in return, such as a government payint development aid or social security.

transfer price Transferpreis; Verrechnungspreis

The price at which goods and services are transferred between subsidiary companies of a corporation.

This practice is used when each entity is managed as a profit center and must deal with the others on an arm's length basis.

transfer pricing Transferpreissetzung

transformational leaders transformative Führung

Leaders who provide individualized consideration and intellectual stimulation, and who possess charisma. The transformational leader attempts to instill in followers the ability to question not only established views but eventually those established by the leader.

transient vorübergehend

transient worker Gelegenheitsarbeiter

Employment: someone who moves from one employment to the next, whitout maintaining a permanent residence.

transit Transit; Durchfahrt; *(water)* Überfahrt; *(throughway)* Durchfuhr; *(foot passage)* Durchgang

transition Übergang; Übergangs-

transitional period Übergangsperiode; Übergangszeit

translate übersetzen; versetzen; verrücken

translation exposure Umrechnungskursanfälligkeit

Finance: the extent to which the reported consolidated results and balance sheets of a corporation are affected by fluctuations in foreign exchange values.

transnational transnational

Reaching across the borders of a single country; involving more than one country.

transnational corporation transnationale Unternehmung

Firm that seeks to simultaneously realize gains from experience curve economies, location economies, and global learning, while remaining locally responsive.

transnational financial reporting Erstellung eines transnationalen Finanzberichts

Need for a firm headquartered in one country to report its results to citizens of another country.

transnational strategy transnationale Strategie

Plan to exploit experience-based cost and location economies, transfer core competencies with the firm, and pay attention to local responsiveness.

transparency of financial statement Bilanzklarheit

transport Transport; *(to ~)* transportieren; befördern

transportable transportfähig; *(compliance with rules)* versandfähig

transportation Transport; *(means of transportation)* Verkehrsmittel

transporter Transporter; *(commercial transport)* Spedition

transport ship Frachtschiff

travel *(trip)* Reise; *(passenger traffic)* Reiseverkehr *(to ~)* reisen; als Vertreter arbeiten

travel abroad Auslandsreise; Reisen ins Ausland

travel and entertainment (T&E) expenses Spesen

Expenses paid by an employee while traveling away from home for a business.

travelers checks Reiseschecks

Issued by banks, travel agencies, American Express and Western Union for the convenience of travelers.

traveling person Geschäftsreisender; Handlungsreisender; Vertreter

treason Hochverrat; Verrat

The crime of being disloyal to one's country. A person who betrays the nation of his citizenship and in some way willfully cooperates with an enemy, is considered to be a traitor.

treasurer Finanzdirektor; Leiter der Finanzabteilung; *(club)* Schatzmeister; Kassenwart

Corporate finance: an officer of a company responsible for receiving and disbursing funds.

treasuries Schatzbriefe

Securities issued and secured by a government, with various schedules and maturities.

treasury Finanzministerium; Schatzamt; Fiskus; Schatzamt

Politics: the part of a government which manages all money and revenue operations.

treasury bill Schatzanweisung; kurzfristiger Schatzwechsel; Schuldverschreibung

Government promissory note having a maturity period of up to one year; bearing no interest, but sold at a discount to buyers. The difference is the interest income to the owner.

treasury bond Schatzanweisung

Long-term (more than five years) debt instrument issued by a government.

treasury department US Finanzministerium

Politics: the department of the U.S. government that is responsible for all money and budgetary matters.

treasury note Schatzwechsel

Politics: an intermediate-term debt obligation of the U.S. government that bears interest paid by coupon.

treat Genuss; Freihalten; *(to ~)* behandeln; *(topic)* abhandeln; ansehen als; sich befassen mit; bewirten

Treaty of Rome Römische Verträge

The treaty which established the European Economic Community (EEC) and was signed by France, West Germany, Italy, Belgium, the

Netherlands and Luxembourg on March 25, 1957.

treatment Behandlung

trend allgemeine Richtung; Trend; *(tendency)* Tendenz; *(indination)* Neigung; *(to ~)* tendieren

trend analysis Trendanalyse

Finance: analysis of a company's financial performance over time, which helps to understand overall financial performance.

trend line Trendlinie

Securities: graph used by technical analysts to chart the past performance of a security in order to predict future movements.

trespass unbefugt betreten

Unlawful entry or possession of someone else´s property.

trial and error Versuch und Irrtum; systematisches Ausprobieren

Method for obtaining knowledge by trying out alternatives. If one works, a solution is found, if not, then one tries another option.

trial balance Rohbilanz; vorläufige Bilanz

Accounting: a statement compiled at the end of an accounting period listing all the debit balances and all the credit balances throughout the ledger account system to see if they balance.

trial market Versuchsmarkt

trial offer Probe; Probeangebot

Marketing: offer to a first-time buyer to examine, use, or test a product for a limited time.

triangular arbitrage Dreiecksarbitrage

Technique of striking offsetting deals among three markets simultaneously to obtain an arbitrage profit.

tribunal Richtersitz; Tribunal; *(legal)* Gerichtshof; *(mediation)* Schiedsgericht

trickle down heruntertröpfeln; herunterrieseln

Economics: theory based on the ideas of supply side economics that economic growth can best be achieved by letting investors and businesses flourish, since their prosperity will ultimately trickle down to middle and lower-income people, who will benefit by increased economic activity.

trigger point Auslösepunkt

International trade: a price level for a particular commodity. When the price of imports falls below that trigger point, trade restrictions are implemented against that imported commodity.

trim *(ship)* Gleichgewichtslage; *(store window)* Schaufensterschmuck; Zustand; *(to ~) (to decorate)* schmücken; dekorieren; *(freight)* verstauen; *(to reduce cost)* beschneiden; kürzen; besetzen

trim back zurückschrauben

trojan horse Trojanisches Pferd

Computers: program that appears to serve a legitimate purpose but actually performs a destructive or unauthorized activity. Trojan horses differ from viruses mainly in that they do not replicate themselves.

troubleshooter Störungssucher; Fehlersucher

A person specialized in finding and solving problems.

troubleshooting Troubleshooting; Störungssuche; Fehlersuche

trough Trog; *(basin)* Mulde; *(channel)* Rinne; *(depression)* Vertiefung; *(weather)* Tief; *(fig)* Tiefpunkt

truck Transporter; Lastwagen; zweirädriger Karren;

truckload (TL) Lastwagenladung

Quantity of cargo that fills a truck.

trust Vertrauen; Treu und Glauben; *(cartel)* Konzern; Großunternehmen; Trust; *(endowment)* Stiftung; *(estate)* Treuhandvermögen; *(investment)* Kapitalanlagegesellschaft; Investmentgesellschaft; *(to ~)*

vertrauen; sich verlassen auf; Kredit einräumen

Law: an organization that is engaged as a trustee in handling trust funds for the good of another person (beneficiary).

trust agreement Treuhandvertrag; Sicherungsübereignungsvertrag

trust company Treuhandgesellschaft

Law: an arrangement used to manage real or personal property. It is established by one person (the grantor or settlor) for the benefit of another (the beneficiary). A third person (the trustee) or the grantor manages the trust.

trusted third parties (TTP) vertrauenwürdige Dritte

Companies with which an agreement has been reached to share information.

trustee Treuhänder; Bevollmächtigter Beauftragter; Verwalter; Sachverwalter

Company or person who holds legal title to property in trust for the benefit of another person.

trust transaction Treuhandgeschäft

tuition Unterricht

tuition fees Schulgeld; Studiengebühren

Academia: fees paid to an educational organization for the attendance of courses.

tumble Fall; *(crash)* Sturz; Purzelbaum; Durcheinander; *(to ~)* fallen; stürzen; zerzausen; durcheinander bringen

tune Melodie; Stimmung; Einklang; Haltung; *(to ~) (instrument)* stimmen; losheulen; *(engine)* abstimmen; *(radio)* einstellen

turn Drehung; Wendung; Kurve; *(pol change)* Wende; *(revolution)* Umdrehung; *(to ~)* drehen; umdrehen; wenden; *(to revolve)* sich umdrehen; biegen; sich ablenken lassen

turnaround Trendwende; Tendenzwende

turnkey *(building, installation)* Fertig-; komplett; *(ready for startup)* schlüsselfertig

turnkey project schlüsselfertiges Projekt; Turnkey Projekt

A project in which a company sets up an entire operating plant for a customer and hands it over when it is fully operational.

turnkey system startbereites System

turnover Umsatz; Umschlag; Fluktuation

Sales: the total sales figure of an organization in a specified time.

Inventory: the number of times an asset is replaced during the accounting period

Labor: the total number of employees divided by the number of employees replaced during a given period.

Stock markets: the volume of shares traded as a percent of total shares listed during a specified period, usually a day or a year.

turn over *(to turn upside down)* umdrehen; *(to sell)* umsetzen

turnover-dependent umsatzabhängig

turnover gain Umsatzzuwachs

turnover increase Umsatzsteigerung

twisting Täuschung

An unfair trade practice whereby an agent attempts to persuade a customer to enter into an unnecessary contract, through which the agent receives a commission.

two-part pricing zweiteiliger Tariff

Strategy for pricing services in which price is broken into a fixed fee plus a variable usage rate.

two-factor theory Zwei-Faktoren-Theorie

Theory sometimes also called motivation-hygiene theory proposed by psychologist Frederick Herzberg, agruging that an individual's relation to work is basic and that one's attitude toward work can very well determine success or failure.

Conditions surrounding the job such as quality of supervision, pay, company policies, relations with others, and job security were characterized by Herzberg as hygiene factors.

To motivate people on their jobs, Herzberg suggested emphasizing factors – so called motivation factors - associated with the work itself or to outcomes directly derived from it, such as recognition, responsibility, and opportunities for personal growth.

two-sided zweiseitig; bilateral

tycoon Industriekapitän; König

A business person who is extremely wealthy and powerful.

type Urbild; Beispiel; Typ; Grundform; *(kind)* Art; Modell; *(to ~) (typewriter)* tippen; Maschine schreiben

Type A personality Typ A Perönlichkeit

Personality type associated with aggressive involvement in a chronic, incessant struggle to achieve more and more in less and less time and, if necessary, against the opposing efforts of other things or other people.

type of cost Kostenart

type of investment Anlageform

typewriter Schreibmaschine

typify verkörpern; versinnbildlichen; typisieren; repräsentieren

Uu

ubiquitous universell

ubiquitous application universelle Anwendung

ultimate ultimativ; letzter; äußerst; endgültig

ultimate goal Endziel; höchstes Ziel

umbrella organization Dachorganisation; Spitzenverband; Spitzenorganisation

unabbreviated ungekürzt; nicht abgekürzt

unabridged ungekürzt

unacceptable unzumutbar; unannehmbar; untragbar

unaccommodating unverbindlich

unadjusted *(statistics)* nicht bereinigt; unbereinigt

unaffiliated ungebunden; *(independent)* unabhängig; selbständig

unanimous einstimmig

unauthorized unerlaubt; unbefugt; nicht bevollmächtigt; wild

unavailable *(funds)* nicht verfügbar; *(goods)* nicht erhältlich

unbalanced growth unausgeglichenes Wachstum

Economic: type of economic growth in which some sectors of an economy grow faster than others.

unbundling Entbündelung; Trennung

Utilities: the process of separating the total cost of supplies like electricity into its functional parts like production, transmission, and distribution.

unbusinesslike nicht geschäftsmäßig; unprofessionell

uncertainty Unsicherheit

uncertainty avoidance Unsicherheitsvermeidung

Culture: National culture attribute describeing the extent to which a society feels threatened by uncertain and ambiguous situations and tries to avoid them.

uncertainty factor Unsicherheitsfaktor

unchanged unverändert

uncollectable nicht einziehbar; uneinbringlich(e Forderung)

uncollected funds noch nicht gebuchte Guthaben

Banking: checks deposited in a bank account that have not yet been been collected by the depository bank.

unconsolidated subsidiary nicht konsolidierte Tochtergesellschaft

Corporation: a subsidiary of a parent company that filesindividual financial statements.

uncounted ungezählt; *(not taken into account)* ungerechnet

uncovered *(not secured)* ungedeckt; ohne Deckung; *(insurance)* unversichert

uncovered call nicht gedeckte Call-Option

Securities: a short call option position in which the writer does not own shares of underlying stock represented by his option contracts. It is much riskier for the writer than a covered call, where the writer owns the underlying stock. If the buyer of a call exercises the option to call, the writer would be forced to buy the stock at market price; also called a "naked" call.

uncovered put nicht gedeckte Put-Option

Securities: a short put option position in which the writer does not have a corresponding short stock position or has not deposited, in a cash account, cash or cash equivalents equal to the exercise value of the put. The writer has pledged to buy the stock at a certain price if the buyer of the options chooses to exercise it. The nature of uncovered options means the writer's risk is unlimited; also called "naked" put.

underbid Unterangebot; Minderangebot; *(to ~)* unterbieten

undercapitilization ungenügende Kapitalisierung

Corporate finance: a condition, caused by lack of capital, where a business does not have enough capital to carry out its normal business functions.

undercut untergraben; unterbieten; (to *work for low wages)* für niedrigeren Lohn arbeiten

undercutting Unterbieten *(price)* Preisunterbietung

underdeveloped unterentwickelt; *(backward)* rückständig; *(capable of further development)* entwicklungsfähig

underdevelopment Unterentwicklung; *(backwardness)* Rückständigkeit

underemployed nicht ausgelastet; unterbeschäftigt

A persons who is working in jobs that are below his earning capacity or level of competence.

underemployment Unterbeschäftigung; mangelnde Beschäftigung

underestimate Unterschätzung; *(cost)* zu niedriger Kostenanschlag; *(to ~)* unterschätzen

underground economy Schatten-wirtschaft

Economics: an expression used to describe that portion of the economy that goes largely undetected by taxing authorities, either because the activities are illegal or because those involved want to evade taxes.

underinsured unzureichend versichert; unterversichert

Insurance: a person who does not have sufficient insurance coverage for all necessary health care services.

to compensate in the event of loss of life or property.

underissue Minderausgabe

underlying data Basisdaten; Rahmendaten

underlying shares zugrunde liegende Anteile; *(preferred shares)* Vorranganteile

underlying stock zugrunde liegende Aktien; *(preferred stock)* Vorrangaktien

undermine unterminieren; untergraben

underpaid unterbezahlt

underpay Unterbezahlung

Employment: a situation that occurs when an employee is being paid less than his performance is worth in market or perceived terms.

underpin unterbauen; untermauern; *(fig)* unterstützen; stärken

underpositioning Unterlpositionierung

Failure to position a company, its product or brand sufficiently.

underprice unter dem Wert; unter dem angesetzter Preis; *(to ~)* Preis unter dem Wert ansetzen; unter Preis ansetzen

underpricing unterbieten

undersell *(by quantity)* zuwenig verkaufen; *(by price)* unter dem Marktpreis verkaufen; verschleudern; unterbieten

underselling Preisunterbietung; Dumping

understaffed zu schwach besetzt; unterbesetzt

understanding Vereinbarung; Verständigung; *(agreement)* Absprache; Übereinkommen

understate nicht stark genug ausdrücken; nicht genügend artikulieren; bewusst mildern; untertreiben

understated *(aesthetics)* dezent; unauffällig; absichtlich einfach

undertake unternehmen; über-; annehmen; *(to take care of)* besorgen; *(to obligate oneself)* sich verpflichten; riskieren

undertaking Unterfangen; *(enterprise)* Unternehmung; *(obligation)* Verpflichtung; *(document)* Verpflichtungserklärung; Vereinbarung; Zusage

under the counter unter dem Tisch

Transaction that is conducted secretly and unofficially, usually because there is something illegal about what is being done.

undervalue unterbewerten; *(underestimate)* unterschätzen

undervalued unterbewertet; zu niedrig bewertet

Currency: situation when a currency is traded below what is perceived to be its proper market value.

Securities: a company's stock may be undervalued when analysts believe its price is below what it merits.

underwrite Haftung übernehmen; *(insurance)* versichern; Versicherung übernehmen; *(guarantee)* garantieren

Insurance: assume a risk in exchange for a premium.

Securities: the process whereby investment bankers (underwriters) buy a new issue of securities from the issuing corporation and resell them to the public.

underwriter Versicherungsagent; Prämienfestsetzer; Assekurant; *(insurance provider)* Versicherungsgeber; Versicherer; *(securities)* Emissionsfirma; Bürge; Konsorte

Securities: financial intermediaries that buy stock or bonds from an issuer and then sell these securities to the public.

Insurance: someone trained in evaluating risks and determining what rates and coverages that will be used for them

underwriting Übernahme der Haftung; *(insurance)* Übernahme von Versicherungen; Risikoübernahme; Tätigung von Versicherungsgeschäften; *(guarantee)* Garantieren; *(securities)* Emissionsgarantie; garantierend

Securities: the process of selling securities from the issuing corporation or government entity to the public

Insurance: the process of selecting, classifying, analyzing and assuming risk according to insurability.

underwriting guarantee Abnahmegarantie

underwriting member bank Konsortialbank

underwriting syndicate business Konsortialgeschäft

underwriting transaction Emissionsgeschäft

undesirable development Fehlentwicklung

undeveloped unentwickelt; unerschlossen

undifferentiated marketing undifferenziertes Marketing

Market-coverage strategy in which a firm decides to ignore market segment differences and go after the whole market with one offer.

undifferentiated targeting undifferenziertes Zielmarktansprache

Another term for mass marketing where the firm offers one marketing mix for the entire market.

undirected information seeking ungezielte Informationssuche

undiscounted ohne Abschlag; nicht diskontiert

Sales: goods or services that are sold at their full rtail price without allowances or discounts.

undistributed profits nicht ausgeschütteter Gewinn

undue influence unzulässige Beeinflussung

Influence that disturbs the free will of a testator or donor and creates a ground for nullifying a will or a gift.

unearned income Kapitalertrag; Kapitaleinkommen; Besitzeinkommen

Accounting: income received but not yet earned, such as rent received in advance, usually classified as a current liability.

Taxation: income from sources other than wages and salaries, such as dividends, interest, and rent.

uneconomical unwirtschaftlich; unrentabel

unemployable nicht einstellbar

A person who is not acceptable for employment, due to a lack of skills, education, or experience.

unemployed arbeitslos; erwerbslos; beschäftigungslos

Economics: a person who is able and willing to work yet is unable to find a paying job is considered unemployed

unemployment Arbeitslosigkeit; Erwerbslosigkeit; Beschäftigungslosigkeit

Economics: a situation where people who are willing and able to work cannot find employment..

unemployment compensation Arbeitslosengeld; Arbeitslosenhilfe

unemployment crisis Beschäftigungskrise

unemployment figure Arbeitslosenzahl

unemployment rate Arbeitslosenquote

Economics: the number of unemployed people as a percentage of the labor force. The seasonally adjusted unemployment rate eliminates the influence of regularly recurring seasonal fluctuations which can be ascribed to weather, vacations.

unequal ungleich

unethical unethisch; unrecht.

unexpected unerwartet

unexplored ununtersucht; *(area)* unerschlossen

unfair *(unreasonable)* unbillig; unfair; unlauter

unfair competition unlauterer Wettbewerb

Any activity designed to gain an unfair advantage over competitors. This covers variety of activities: unfair, untrue, or misleading advertising; imitating a competitor's product; deception of the public; pirating a product; selling in a foreign country for less than the cost of manufacture.

unfavorable ungünstig; *(disadvantageous)* unvorteilhaft

unfavorable balance of trade negative Handelsbilanz

Trade: situation when the value of a country's imports exceeds the value of its exports.

unfeasible undurchführbar; unmöglich; unbrauchbar

unfilled *(position)* unbesetzt; *(demand)* unbefriedigt; *(order)* unerfüllt

unfinished *(task)* unvollendet; *(product)* halbfertig; *(business)* unerledigt

unforeseeable nicht vorhersehbar; unkalkulierbar

unfounded grundlos; unbegründet

unfreeze auftauen; freigeben

unfreezing Auftauen; Befreiung

Change efforts to overcome the pressures of both individual resistance and group conformity.

uniform Uniform; *(adv)* gleichmäßig; gleichartig; gleichförmig; einheitlich

uniform capitalization rules einheitliche Aktivierungsrichtlinien

Accounting: a method of valuing inventory for tax purposes that requires capitalization of direct costs, eg material and labor, and an allocable portion of indirect costs that benefit or are incurred because of production or resale activities.

uniform delivered pricing einheitliche Preisstellung frei Haus

Geographic pricing strategy in which the company charges the same price plus freight to all consumers, regardless of their location.

uniformity Gleichmäßigkeit; Gleichförmigkeit; Gleichartigkeit; Einheitlichkeit; Einförmigkeit; Eintönigkeit

uniform resource locator (URL) Internetadresse

Internet: the text address that allows users to find a particular website or webpage. The links on web pages also consist of URLs, which are embedded in the HTML code on the page. URLs comprise of a domain name followed by the file path to a particular file on that domain's web server.

unilateral einseitig

unilateral contract einseitiger Vertrag

A contract in which only one party to the contract makes any enforceable promise.

unincorporated association Verein

Organization: a group of people that form an association.

uninvested nicht angelegt; brachliegend

union Vereinigung; *(labor)* Gewerkschaft; Union; Einigkeit; Bund; Verbindung; Verband; Verein

Labor relations: Employee association designed to promote employee rights and work-related welfare.

union district Verbandsbezirk

union hall Versammlungshalle der Gewerkschaft

unionist Gewerkschaftler

union leader Gewerkschaftsführer

union personnel Gewerkschaftspersonal

union rate Gewerkschaftslohn

Employment: wage rate established by collective bargaining.

union shop Unternehmen nur mit Gewerkschaftsangehörigen

Employment: company where all the employees must be members of a union.

unique selling propositon (USP) Alleinstellungsmerkmal; einmaliges Verkaufsargument

Marketing: unique product benefit that a firm aggressively promotes in a consistent manner to its target market. The benefit usually reflects functional superiority: best quality, best services, lowest price, widest choice, best guarantee, most advanced technology.

unique users individueller Nutzer

Internet: unique individual or browser which has either accessed a site (unique visitor) or which has been served unique content and/or ads such as e-mail, newsletters, interstitials and pop-under ads.

unique visitors individueller Besucher

unissued unausgegeben; nicht ausgegeben

unissued stock nicht ausgegebenes Aktienkapital

Accounting: shares of a corporation's stock authorized in its charter but not yet issued to the public.

unit Einheit; Anteil; Stück; *(block of shares)* Aktienbündel; *(building)* Bauelement; Unternehmen; Werksabteilung

unite vereinen; verbinden

United Nations (UN) Vereinte Nationen

An international organization established in 1945, now made up of 191 states (2006).

The purposes of the United Nations are to maintain international peace and security; to develop friendly relations among nations; to cooperate in solving international economic, social, cultural and humanitarian problems and in promoting respect for human rights and fundamental freedoms.

unit labor cost Lohnstückkosten; Arbeitsstückkosten

Cost of labor needed for one unit of some good. It is calculated so that the price of the unit reflects the cost of the labor necessary to produce it.

unit of goods Wareneinheit

unit of quantity Mengeneinheit

unit of trading Kontrakteinheit; Kontraktmenge; Mindestmenge

Trade: normal number of commodities constituting the minimum unit of trading.

unit price Stückpreis; Preis je Einheit

unit profit Stückgewinn

units-of-production method Abschreibung nach Leistungseinheiten

Accounting: depreciation method where a provision for depreciation is computed at a fixed rate per unit of product, based on an estimate of the total number of units the property will produce during its service life.

unity Einigkeit

unity of command Einheit der Auftragserteilung; Einliniensystem

Organization: principle that a subordinate should have only one superior to whom he is directly responsible. As a result, there is an unbroken line of authority.

universal Welt-; Universal-; universal; allgemein(gültig); weltweit

universal bank Universalbank

universalism Universalismus; Allseitigkeit; Vielseitigkeit

Philosophy: humanist tendency to generalize about human nature as if all humans have essentially the same experience of being alive regardless of, for example, economic, gender or racial differences.

universal needs universelle Bedürfnisse

Needs that are the same all over the world, such as food, shelter and security.

Universal Product Code (UPC) UPC-Strichcode

Also called the bar code, this is scanned by retailers, wholesalers, and manufacturers for the purpose of inventory management.

universe Universum; *(statistics)* Grundgesamtheit

Statistics: a term representing all possible elements in a set..

UNIX

Computer operating system used mostly in high-end workstations and servers. A number of companies produce not completely compatible varieties of UNIX. The well-known open source Linux operating system is a variant of UNIX.

unjust ungerecht; unberechtigt

unjustifiable unvertretbar

unjustified unberechtigt; ungerechtfertigt

unlawful ungesetzlich; *(prohibited)* unerlaubt

unlimited uneingeschränkt; unbegrenzt; unbefristet

unlimited credit Blankokredit

unlimited liability uneingeschränkte Haftung

Organization: the risk incurred by a sole proprietor or a general partner, where there is no distinction between business and personal liability and the owner couled be forced to use personal assets to retire a debt.

unload *(truck)* aus-; abladen; *(ship)* löschen; *(get rid of)* abstoßen; auf den Markt werfen

unloading *(truck)* Abladen; Ausladen; *(ship)* Löschen; *(getting rid of)* Abstoßen

Finance: selling off large quantities of merchandise inventory at below-market prices, either to raise cash quickly or to depress the market in a particular product.

Investment: selling securities or commodities when prices are declining to preclude further loss.

unlock *(door)* aufschließen; *(resources)* erschließen; *(capital)* freisetzen; auflösen

unoccupied beschäftigungslos; *(not busy)* nicht beschäftigt; *(space)* unbesetzt

unpaid unbezahlt; *(bill)* unbeglichen; *(in arrears)* rückständig; frei

unpledged *(shares, collateral)* unverpfändet

unproductive unproduktiv; unergiebig

unprofitable unrentabel; nicht einträglich; ertraglos; unprofitabel

unpublished unveröffentlicht

unqualified nicht qualifiziert; unqualifiziert; *(unrestricted)* uneingeschränkt

unrealized nicht verwirklicht; nicht realisiert; *(profit)* unrealisiert; unverkauft; *(not comprehended)* unbegriffen; unerkannt

unrealized profit nicht realisierter Gewinn

Securities: a profit that is realized only when a security or commodity futures contract is actually sold.

unreliable unzuverlässig; *(business)* unsolide; unreell

unrequited transfer einseitige/unerwiderte Übertragung

unresolvable *(problem)* unlösbar; *(dispute)* unschlichtbar

unresolved ungelöst; ungeschlichtet

unrestricted unbeschränkt; uneingeschränkt

unsalable unverkäuflich; nicht verkaufbar

unsecured credit Blankokredit

unsecured debt ungedeckte Schulden

High dividend investments at a fixed rate for a fixed period, but not secured by assets of a company; hence, there is a high risk factor.

unsecured note unsichere Anleihe

High dividend investments at a fixed rate for a fixed period, but not secured by assets of a company; hence, there is a high risk factor.

unsettled unerledigt; *(uncertain)* ungewiss; unbestimmt; erschüttert; gestört; offen

unskilled *(worker)* ungelernt

A person with no formal skills, training, or education.

unskilled worker ungelernter Arbeiter

unsold unverkauft; nicht verkauft

unsought goods unbeachtete Güter

Consumer goods that the consumer either does not know about or knows about but does not normally think of buying.

unstable *(unsteady)* unbeständig; *(volatile)* volatil; instabil

unsuitable ungeeignet

unsubscribe abmelden

Internet: Option to opt out from an e-mail newsletter or discussion group.

unsystematic risk unsystematische Risiko

The risk that is unique to a company such as a strike, the outcome of unfavorable litigation, or a natural catastrophe that can be eliminated through diversification. Also known as diversifiable risk or residual risk

untapped *(natural resources)* unerschlossen; *(human resources)* ungebraucht; unverwertet; unberührt

untrained ungelernt; unausgebildet

untrustworthy nicht vertrauenswürdig; unseriös

unusable unbrauchbar; unverwertbar; *(unfit)* untauglich

unused ungebraucht; ungenutzt; frei

unwarranted *(not entitled)* unberechtigt; *(not authorized)* unbefugt; *(not justified)* ungerechtfertigt

unwillingness to compromise Kompromisslosigkeit

unwilling to take risks risikoscheu

unwilling to work arbeitsscheu

unworkable *(not realizable)* nicht ausführbar; *(unusable)* unverwendbar; nicht verwendungsfähig

up- and downturns Schwankungen

update Update; *(to~)* neu informieren; *(equipment)* modernisieren; *(inventory)* neu zusammenstellen; auf den neuesten Stand bringen

Computing: file maintenance process in an offline system that applies all necessary transactions against the old file, producing a new file reflecting all adds, deletes, and changes that have become necessary since the last update.

upfront im voraus; direkt heraus

upgrade Verbesserung; Aufstieg; *(to ~)* *(improve)* verbessern; *(in rank)* höher einstufen; *(personnel)* befördern

Advance an employee, a work process or a product in rank, earnings, price of quality.

upgraded *(improved)* verbessert; *(rank)* höher eingestuft; *(personnel)* befördert

upgrading Verbessern

Process of improving the quality or performance of something.

upholster polstern; beziehen; dekorieren

upkeep Aufrechterhaltung; *(equipment)* Instandhaltung; *(cost of maintenance)* Unterhaltungskosten; *(machine)* Wartungskosten; Wartung

Activity involved in maintaining something in good working order. Mechanical equipment needs continued maintenance to avoid a breakdown.

upload Heraufladen

Internet: the process of transferring data from the computer one is using to another computer. The opposite of download.

upsell Zusatzverkäufe machen

Sales: technique to increase the value or quantity of a sale by suggesting additional options or upgrades.

Example: a fast-food restaurant may upsell by suggesting that a customer buy a larger portion of a drink.

upside potential mögliche positive Preisentwicklung

Investment: the amount that an analyst or an investor expects a security to move upward.

upstart Emporkömmling;*(adv)* arrogant

upsurge steiler Aufstieg; Auftriebstendenz; Aufwallung

upsurge in sales Umsatzanstieg

upswing Konjunkturanstieg; Aufschwung; scharfer Preisanstieg

uptime Laufzeit

Internet: the amount of time a web site is available. The benchmark for availability is 99.99% .

Manufacturing: the time in which a machine is actually operational and a worker is occupied, the opposite of downtime.

upturn Besserung; Aufwärtsbewegung; Belebung

upward business trend Konjunkturaufschwung

upwardly mobile aufwärts mobil

A trend toward higher status in terms of income, material goods, and lifestyles.

upward mobility Aufwärtsmobilität; Aufstiegsmöglichkeit

upward movement Kursanstieg; Aufwärtsentwicklung; Aufwärtsbewegung

upward trend steigende Tendenz; Aufwärtstendenz; Aufwärtstrend

urban Stadt-; städtisch

urban center Ballungsgebiet; Ballungsraum

urban household städtischer Haushalt

urbanization Verstädterung; Urbanisierung

urbanize verstädtern

urgency Dringlichkeit; Druck

usable brauchbar; verwendbar; (be)nutzbar; betriebsfähig

usage Behandlung; (Sprach-)Gebrauch; *(custom)* Sitte; Brauch; Herkommen; *(practice)* Praxis; Usance

use *(utilization)* Gebrauch; Benutzung; *(usefulness)* Nützlichkeit; *(utility)* Nutzen; *(purpose)* Zweck; Sinn; Brauch; *(to ~)* gebrauchen; benutzen; verbrauchen

useful life Nutzungsdauer

Period of time over which a depreciable asset is expected to provide a competitive return.

usefulness Nützlichkeit

useless nutzlos; zwecklos

usenet Usenet; weltweites Informations- und Diskussionssystem

Internet service that provides thousands of discussion lists, or newsgroups, on a variety of topics. Users can read newsgroups postings or they can add their own.

Most newsgroups are completely open, although some are moderated. One can view usenet newsgroups with a special software built into browsers and e-mail programs or via one of several web-based services.

usenet newsgroup Usenet Newsgroup

Electronic bulletin board used to discuss a particular topic such as a sport, hobby or business area., traditionally accessed by special newsreader software.

use of income Einkommensverwendung

use-oriented anwendungsbezogen

user Benutzer; Anwender; Nutzer

Buying center: Members of the organization who will use the product or service; users often initiate the buying proposal and help define product specifications.

user fee Nutzungsgebühr

Charge to users of a service, often publicly owned, such as parks, swimming pools, and toll roads.

user-friendly benutzerfreundlich; anwenderfreundlich

Computer hardware or software designed to be easy for people, especially novices, to use.

user industry Anwenderindustrie; Verbraucherindustrie

user session Nutzersession; Nutzersitzung

Internet: each visit to a web site by one person.

user tax Benutzungssteuer

use to capacity Auslastung; *(to ~)* auslasten

US-GAAP (United States Generally Accepted Accounting Principles) allgemein anerkannte Grundsätze der Rechnungslegung

Accounting, valuation and presentation-principles that must be followed by all companies that are willing to quote their shares in US stock exchange markets.

According to US-GAAP, assets may not be valued higher than the historical cost at the time of the acquisition of the asset. But the value of stocks is to be calculated including the appropriate parts of structure costs for warehousing and the buying department, for manufacturing overheads as well as the appropriate parts for depreciation and interest and special direct costs of manufacturing (full cost principle).The income statement (profit and loss statement) has to be structured following the cost of sales method but there are no more detailed prescriptions.

usufruct Nießbrauch; Nutznießung

usury Wucherei; (Zins-)Wucher

The practice of charging a rate of interest greater than that permitted by law.

utilitarianism Utilitarismus

Philosophy: an ethical theory stating that all actions are to be judged in terms of their utility in promoting the greatest happiness of the greatest number.

utility Nutzen; Nützlichkeit; Versorgungsunternehmen

Economics: a measure of the happiness or satisfaction gained from a good or service.

Company: a company that performs a public service; subject to government regulation, such as water, sewerage, gas, electricity.

utilization Verwertung; Verwendung; Nutzanwendung; *(of a service)* Inanspruchnahme; *(of data)* Auswertung; Ausnutzung; Auslastung

utilization theory Nutzentheorie

utilize verwerten; verwenden; nutzen; auswerten; ausnutzen; auslasten

Vv

vacancy rate Leerstandsrate

Real estate: the percentage of housing units that are unoccupied.

vacate verlassen; aufgeben; annullieren

Real estate: to leave or move out of a premises

vacation Urlaub; Ferien; *(additional time)* Zusatzurlaub; Räumung

vacationer Urlauber

valid *(in effect)* gültig; *(legal)* rechtlich; rechtskräftig; stichhaltig

validation Bestätigung

Internet: a test for errors in HTML code which may cause a web page to be displayed incorrectly or for links to other pages that do not work.

validity Gültigkeit; Stichhaltigkeit; Geltung; *(force of law)* Rechtskraft; Validität

valuable teuer; nützlich; wertvoll

valuables Wertgegenstände; Wertsachen

valuation Einschätzung; Abschätzung; Schätzung; Bewertung; Wert; *(commercial value)* Taxierung

A value estimate or opinion, or the process of estimating value. A valuation report is usually a written document giving an opinion of a business's value as of a specified date, and is normally supported by the presentation and analysis of relevant data.

valuation of assets Bewertung des Anlagevermögens

value Wert; Betrag; Nutzen; Kaufkraft; Wirkung; *(to ~)* wertschätzen; schätzen; bewerten

Price: an attempt to measure what something is worth by expressing it as a monetary value.

Philosophy: abstract ideas about what is believed to be good, right, and desirable.

value added Werterhöhung; *(taxation)* Mehrwert; *(productivity)* Wertschöpfung

Production: the difference between the selling price of a product and the costs of externally purchased materials and services required to produce it.

value added reseller (VAR) Wiederverkäufer

Retailing: a company that modifies or improves a system in some way and then resells it. A VAR. might, for example, integrate a software application with its clients' other systems or it might buy hardware components and build complete systems

value added tax (VAT) Mehrwertsteuer

Taxation: a consumption tax levied at each step of a manufacturing process where value is added to a product, i.e. upon the difference between the purchase cost of the materials and the selling price.

value additivity (VA) principle Wertadditivitätsprinzip

In an efficient market the value of the sum of two cash flows is the sum of the values of the individual cash flows.

value analysis Wertanalyse

Approach to cost reduction in which components are studied carefully to determine if they can be redesigned, standardized or made by less costly methods of production.

value-based pricing Preissetzung auf Basis des wahrgenommenen Käufernutzens

Setting price based on buyer's perceptions of product values rather than on cost.

value chain Wertschöpfungskette

Organization: the sequence of activities performed by different units of a company working together to produce a product and satisfy market demands.

The value chain concept can also be extended to cover all activities performed on a product, from its conception until it reaches the end user, including all suppliers and retailing intermediaries.

value creation Wertschöpfung

All activities that increase the value of goods or services to consumers.

value engineering Wertanalyse

Pursues the objective of recognising and eliminating all those costs that are not necessary for the value and/or function of a product or service; also called functions cost analysis.

value judgment Werturteil

Philosophy: a judgment about the rightness or wrongness of something based on a particular set of values, which is usually a biased opinion.

value marketing wertorientiertes Marketing

Principle of enlightened marketing which holds that a company should put most of its resources into value-building marketing investments.

value measure Wertmaßstab

value of goods ordered Auftragswert

value of labor Arbeitswert

value of money Geldwert

value performance Leistungserbringung

value pricing Wert-Preiskalkulation

Pricing strategy attempting to offer just the right combination of quality and good service at a fair price.

value proposition Nutzenversprechen; Wertversprechen

Describes how an organization intends to differentiate itself to customers, especially what particular set of values it will deliver.

value setting Wertstellung

value system Wertesystem

Individual hierarchy based on a ranking of an individual's values in terms of their intensity. This system is identified by the relative importance someone assign to such values as freedom, pleasure, honesty, and equality.

value theory Werttheorie

van Lieferwagen; Transportwagen; geschlossener Güterwagen

variable Variabel; variabel

variable costs variable Kosten; Arbeitskosten

Production: those costs associated with the production of a product that change directly with the amount of production, such as direct material or direct labor needed to complete the product.

variable-interval schedule variabler Intervallplan

Psychology: a schedule of reinforcement where a response is rewarded after an unpredictable amount of time has passed. This schedule produces a slow, steady rate of response.

variable-pay program variables Entgeltsystem

System of payment where a portion of an employee's pay is based on some individual and/or organizational measure of performance.

It turns part of an organization's fixed labor costs into a variable cost, thus reducing expenses when performance declines.

variable pricing variable Preiskalkulation

Marketing: a pricing strategy that charges a different price to different customers at different times.

This strategy has been common among small businesses and for highly differentiated high value product, but it is also increasingly used on the Internet.

variable-ratio schedule variabler Quotenplan

System where reward varies relative to the behavior of the individual.

Example: salespeople on commission.

variance Abweichung; Varianz

Statistics: a measure of the statistical dispersion of a distribution, indicating how far from the expected value its values typically are.

Budgeting: the difference between the actual performance and the budgeted or projected performance.

variance analysis Varianzanalyse

Cost accounting: comparison between actual values and output on the one hand with planned figures on the other.

variances Abweichungen

Difference between planned or budgeted values and actual values.

Variances give managers the opportunity to consider possible corrective actions and to implement them. The causes of a variance from the planned or budgeted figures are ascertained by means of a *variance analysis.*

varied unterschiedlich; verschieden; mannigfaltig; abwechslungsreich

variety Vielfalt; Unterschiedlichkeit; Abwechslung

variety-seeking buying behavior Abwechslung suchendes Einkaufsverhalten

Consumer buying behavior in situations characterized by low consumer involvement, but significant perceived brand differences.

variety store Niedrigpreisgeschäft; Kleinkaufhaus

Retailing: a retail store that handles a variety of products in the low and popular price ranges, targeted for the family market. Variety stores carry items such as apparel, women's accessories, gift items, and stationery.

various verschieden(artig)

vault Gewölbe; Gruft; Stahlkammer; Höhle

vehicle currency Leitwährung

Currency that plays a central role in the foreign exchange market, such as the US dollar and the Euro.

velocity Umlaufgeschwindigkeit

Economics: the rate at which total money in circulation is spent on goods and services in a given time period. The gross domestic product is the product of total money supply and velocity.

vendor Verkäufer; *(supplier)* Lieferer; Lieferant; Verkaufsautomat

venture Wagnis; Risiko; Spekulation; *(business)* Unternehmung; *(to ~)* wagen; riskieren

Business: any initiative that entails the mobilization of resources to produce and offer a product or service, normally connected with a degree of risk.

venture capital Risikokapital; Wagniskapital

Financing: money provided by investors to support new or unusual business ventures, normally carrying an above-average degree of risk, but offering the potential for above-average future profits.

venue Platz; Ort; Örtlichkeit; Gerichtsort

Court: Place where case is tried. A change of venue may be granted with the object of securing a fairer trial.

verbal Wort-; Verbal-; wörtlich; mündlich; verbal

verbatim wörtlich

verbatims wörtliche Mitschrift

Research reports that are word-for-word duplications of interviews, without editorial comment.

verdict Gerichtsurteil; Wahrspruch; Urteil

verification Beglaubigung; *(confirmation)* Bestätigung; Beweismittel; *(scrutiny)* Überprüfung; Nachprüfung

verify beglaubigen; *(to confirm)* bestätigen; (to *scrutinize)* Richtigkeit überprüfen

version Fassung; Version

vertical senkrecht; vertikal

vertical acquisition vertikale Akquisition

Organization: acquisition in which the acquired firm and the acquiring firm are at different steps in the production process.

vertical analysis Vertikalanalyse

Financial analysis: form of analysis that presents financial statement data as a percentage of some financial statement base.

vertical differentiation vertikale Differenzierung

Marketing: form of differentiation that occurs in a market where the several goods that can be ordered according to their objective quality from the highest to the lowest.

vertical foreign direct investment vertikale ausländische Direktinvestition

Foreign direct investment in an industry abroad that provides input into a firm's domestic operations, or foreign direct investment into an industry abroad that sells the outputs of a firm's domestic operations.

vertical integration vertikale Integration; vertikale Eingliederung; vertikale Verflechtung

Merging together of two businesses that are at different levels of production, thus extending a firm's activities into adjacent stages of productions.

Example: a company controlling all steps in the production process, from the extraction of raw materials through the manufacture and sale of the final product, is fully vertically integrated.

vertical management structure vertikale Managementstruktur

Organization: analysis of the hierarchical structure and functioning of an organization in terms of the layers of management delegation of authority.

vertical marketing system (VMS) vertikales Marketingsystem

Distribution channel structure in which producers, wholesalers and retailers act as a unified system. One channel member owns the others, has contracts with them, or has so much power that they all cooperate.

vertical merger vertikale Fusion; vertikaler Zusammenschluss

Organization: a merger of two companies that are members of a vertical cannel of distribution. The aim is normally to eliminate middlemen, lower costs and increasing competitiveness.

vertical organization vertikale Organization

Organization: hierarchically structured company where all management activities are controlled by centralized management.

vertical portal vertikales Portal

Internet: Generally business-to-business site hosting content to help participants in an industry to get their work done by providing industry news, details of business techniques and product and service reviews.

vertical promotion vertikale Verkaufsförderung

Advancement or upgrading of management or supervisory responsibilities in an organization with an accompanying increase in compensation.

Example: an individual receives a vertical promotion from a department manager to the position of vice-president, including an increase in responsibilities and compensation.

Vertical Service Provider (VSP) vertikal integrierter Anwendungsdiensleister

Application Service Provider (ASP) that runs an entire business because it aggregates almost all of the value chain functions for the client business.

vertical specialization vertikale Spezialisierung

International Trade: the phenomenon that companies specialize more and more on specific products in the value chain, that are then transported to the next member of the value chain for further processin. Example: the components of a car are all produced by separate, specialized companies before they are assembled.

vested fest begründet; *(pension plan)* unentziehbar

vested interest Interessenwert

One in which there is a present fixed right of present or future enjoyment.

Example: an employee is immediately vested in his individual retirement account.

vested rights Besitzstand

veto Veto; *(objection)* Einspruch; Verbot

viability Lebensfähigkeit; Durchführbarkeit; Brauchbarkeit

viable lebensfähig; durchführbar; brauchbar; praktikabel

vicarious liability Haftung für fremdes Verschulden

Law: the responsibility of one person for the acts of another, even though that person has not done anything wrong, such as employers who are held vicariously liable for damages caused by their employees.

vice chairman stellvertretende Vorsitzender

vice president Vizepräsident

Organization: a company officer ranking immediately below a president, who may serve in the president's place under certain circumstances.

Often a vice president has responsibility over a functional department, such as the vice president of marketing or of production.

view Aussicht; Sicht; *(sketch)* Skizze; *(perspective)* Perspektive; *(opinion)* Ansicht; Vorstellung; Absicht; Plan *(to ~) (to inspect, scrutinize)* inspizieren; *(to contemplate)* betrachten

violate *(agreement)* verletzen; stören; vergewaltigen; *(contract)* brechen

violation Entweihung; Übertretung; *(agreement)* Verletzung; *(contract)* Bruch; *(law, rule)* Verstoß; Störung; Vergewaltigung

viral marketing virales Marketing

Internet: the online equivalent of word of mouth, somtimes referred to as word of mouse. It occurs when individuals forward e-mail to friends, co-workers, family, and others on their e-mail lists.

virtual eigentlich; praktisch; virtuell

virtual cash virtuelles Bargeld

virtual community virtuelle Gemeinschaft

Internet: a community on the Internet where people share common interests, using bulletin boards or websites to communicate.

virtualization Virtualisierung

Process whereby a company develops more of the characteristics of the virtual organization.

virtual mall virtuelles Einkaufshentrum

Internet: web site that brings together different electronic retailers at a single virtual location. This contrasts with a fixed location infrastructure - the traditional arrangement where retail organizations operate from retail stores situated in fixed locations such as real-world shopping malls; also known as electronic mall.

virtual merchants virtuelle Händler

Internet: retailers such as Amazon that only operate online - they have no fixed sales location infrastructure.

virtual office virtuelles Büro

virtual organization virtuelle Organization

Internet: a small, core organization that outsources major business functions. In structural terms, it is highly centralized, with little or no departmentalization.

Virtual organizations have created networks of relationships that allow them to contract out manufacturing, distribution, marketing, or any other business function. The major advantage is its flexibility, but it reduces management's control over key parts of its business.

Example: Nike, Reebok, and Dell Computers.

virtual teams virtuelle Teams

Internet: teams that use computer technology to tie together physically dispersed members in order to achieve a common goal. They allow people to collaborate on-line – using communication links such as wide area network, video conferencing, or e-mail.

They can include members from the same organization or link an organization's member with employees from other organizations The three primary factors differentiate virtual teams from face-to-face teams are (1) the essence of paraverbal and nonverbal cues, (2) limited social context, and (3) the ability to overcome time and space constraints.

virus Virus

Internet: a self-replicating computer program that infects a PC without the user's knowledge or permission. Most viruses are harmless, although some are very destructive.

visibility *(weather)* Sichtweite; *(firm, product)* Sichtbarkeit

vision Vision

Image that a business has of its goals before it sets out to reach them. This image may be as vague as a dream or as precise as a goal or a mission statement.

visionary leadership visionäre Führung

Management: the ability to create and articulate a realistic, credible, attractive vision of the future for an organization. Visionary leaders normally have the following skills: the ability to explain the vision to others; the ability to express the vision through behavior; and the ability to extend the vision to different leadership contexts.

visit Besuch

Internet: A request made for a page by a user. On any given visit, a user may request several pages as he navigates through the site. If a user makes no requests during a predetermined period of time, his next request would begin a new visit

visitor Besucher

Internet: User who visits a site; however, this does not distinguish between one-time and repeat visitors.

vogue Mode; *(popularity)* Popularität

voice Stimme; *(decision-making)* Mitsprache; Artikulierung

Actively and constructively attempting to improve conditions, including suggesting improvements, discussing problems with superiors, and some forms of union activity.

Voice over Internet protocol (VoIP)

Internet: a term used to refer to internet telephony that relies on the web to transmit phone calls, thus eliminating long-distance charges.

void leerer Raum; *(gap)* Lücke; Leere; leer; *(uninhabited)* unbewohnt; *(not valid)* nichtig; rechtsunwirksam; *(to ~)* (to *void a document)* ungültig machen

Empty; having no legal force; incapable of being ratified.

voidable aufhebbar; anfechtbar

Law: something that is capable of being later annulled.

volatile flüchtig; launisch

Prices: tending to vary often or widely. Market-related volatility in stocks is measured by the beta coefficient.

volatility Preisschwankung; Unbeständigkeit; Volatilität

Investment: Measure of risk based on standard deviation in fund performance over 3 years. Scale is 1-9; higher rating indicates higher risk.

volume Menge; Volumen; Inhalt *(book)* Band; Buch; Mappe; *(bulk)* Maß; Umfang

Stock exchange: the total number of shares, bonds, or futures traded in a market during a particular period.

volume business Mengengeschäft

volume discount Mengenrabatt

Price discount offered to customers who purchase a certain amount of volume.

volume industry Mengenindustrie

Industry characterized by few opportunities to create competitive advantages, but each advantage is huge and gives a high pay-off.

volume of business Umsatzvolumen; Geschäftsumfang

volume of money Geldmenge; Geldvolumen

volume of sales Gesamtabsatz; Verkaufsvolumen

volume of stocks traded Börsenumsatz

volume of work Arbeitsvolumen; Arbeitspensum; Arbcitsanfall

volume transaction Mengengeschäft

voluminous umfangreich

voluntary freiwillig; ehrenamtlich

voluntary bankruptcy freiwillige Insolvenz

The declaration of bankruptcy by an insolvent person or business.

voluntary export restraint (VER) freiwillige Exportbeschränkung

Quota on trade imposed from the exporting country's side, instead of the importer's; usually imposed at the request of the importing country's government.

voluntary lien freiwilliges Pfand

A lien intentionally created by a debtor, such as a mortgage.

vote Stimme; Abstimmung; Votum; Stimmrecht; *(to ~)* abstimmen; *(election)* wählen; bewilligen; vorschlagen

voting right Stimmrecht

Corporation: the right of a common stockholder to vote in person or by proxy on the affairs of a company.

voting stock Stimmrechtsaktien

Corporation: the shares in a corporation that entitle the shareholder to voting and proxy rights.

vouch haften; garantieren; urkundlich belegen

voucher Abrechnungsbeleg; Bon; Kassenzettel; Quittung; Gutschein

Law: a document which authorizes the payment of money and acknowledges a liability.

voucher check Verrechnungsscheck

Ww

wage Lohn; Werklohn; *(remuneration)* Arbeitsentgelt; *(to ~) (to undertake)* unternehmen; *(war)* führen

Employment: the payment for labor performed by an employee.

wage adjustment Lohnanpassung; Lohnausgleich

wage agreement Lohnabkommen; Tarifvertrag; Tarifabkommen; Lohnvereinbarung

wage and salary administration Lohn- und Gehaltswesen

Organization: administrative functions related to establishing and supervising wage levels and operations, normally performed in the personnel department.

wage autonomy Tarifautonomie

wage bracket Lohngruppe; Tarifgruppe

Taxation: the range income taxed at a specific rate.

wage ceiling höchster Lohn der jeweiligen Tarifgruppe

Employment: the maximum compensation within a particular wage bracket.

wage control Lohnkontrolle

Politics: limits set by government on the extent to which wages can be increased, usually in percentage terms.

wage demand Lohnforderung

wage differential Lohngefälle

wage discussion Tarifgespräch

wage floor Mindestlohn

Employment: the minimum wage set either by law or by an agreed-upon wage bracket.

wage freeze Lohnstopp

Employment: a limit, imposed by the government on wage increases.

A wage freeze may also be imposed by the management of a company in order to restrain costs.

wage incentive system Leistungslohnsystem

Employment: a method of motivating workers by paying higher wages for the higher output.

wage income tax Lohnsteuer

wage level Lohnniveau

wage negotiation Lohnverhandlung

wage negotiation talks Lohnrunde

wage paid in cash Barlohn

wage policy Lohnpolitik

wage-push inflation lohngetriebene Inflation

Economics: inflationary pressure caused if increased wages are not offset by increased productivity. As a result, costs rise which leads to higher prices.

wage rate Grundlohntarif; Tarifsatz; Lohnsatz

Employment: pay rate for a particular activity, usually on an hourly basis.

wage scale Lohntabelle

Employment: a schedule of wages paid for different jobs, determined by the type of job, its duties and responsibilities, and the general labor market.

wage stabilization Lohnstabilisierung

A collection of policies intended to bring about an end to inflationary wage increases.

wage ratio Einkommensverhältnis

Employment: a ratio measuring the relationship between different wages, such as the gender wage ratio that between men and women.

The CEO-minimum wage ratio in the US by some calculations, for example, is over 800.

wage settlement Tarifabschluss

wage structure Lohnstruktur

waiting line Warteschlange

waive verzichten; (to *exempt)* erlassen

to voluntarily forego a right

waiver Verzicht; *(declaration)* Verzichtleistung; *(document)* Verzichtleistungserklärung

Law: the voluntary relinquishment or surrender of some right or privilege.

wallet Brieftasche; Werkzeugtasche

wallflower Mauerblümchen

Stock market: Stock that has fallen out of favor with investors; tends to have a low P/E.

Wall Street

Common name for the financial district at the lower end of Manhattan in New York City, where the New York and American stock exchanges and numerous brokerage firms are headquartered.

WAN (Wide Area Network)

Communications network that covers a large geographic area; a WAN may be a public network such as the internet or it may be a closed, proprietary network run by a corporation or government agency

wanted for cash gesucht gegen bar

Statement displayed on market tickers which indicates that a bidder will pay cash for same day settlement of a block of a specified security.

WAP (wireless application protocol) drahtloses Anwendungsprotokoll

Standard that enables mobile phones to access data from the internet.

ware Ware

warehouse Lager; Lagerhaus; Warenlager; Speicher; *(distribution warehouse)* Auslieferungslager; Magazin; Depot

A commercial building for storage of goods. It can be used by manufacturers, importers, exporters, wholesalers, transport businesses, and many other businesses.

warehouse club Billiganbieter für Mitglieder

Off-price retailer that sells a limited selection of brand-name grocery items; appliances, clothing, and a hodgepodge of other goods at deep discounts to members who pay annual membership fees.

warehouse receipt Lagerempfangsschein

Commerce: a document certifying possession of a commodity in a licensed warehouse. The receipt can be used to transfer ownership of that commodity, instead of having to deliver the physical commodity.

warehousing Lagerhaltung; Lagerung

warning strike Warnstreik

warrant Ermächtigung; Berechtigung; Vollmacht; Befugnis; *(execution)* Vollziehungsbefehl; Zertifikat; Optionsschein; Durchsuchungsbefehl; *(to ~) (to vouch)* bevollmächtigen; sich verbürgen; garantieren; gewährleisten; zusichern

Commerce: an order for the payment of money or delivery of goods.

warranted garantiert; *(vouched for)* verbürgt; zugesicherte

warranty Garantie; Gewährleistung; *(against defects)* Mängelgarantie

Commerce: a promise that a product that is sold is in good condition and will perform as promised.

warranty deed Bürgschaftsurkunde; *(real estate)* Übertragungsurkunde

Real estate: a deed which conveys title to property from the seller to the buyer, whereby the seller guarantees the title to be good and unencumbered.

wash sale Scheinverkauf

Stock exchange: fictitious trading to give an appearance of activity to inactive stocks.

waste Verschwendung; Ausschuss; *(cargo)* Abgang; Verlust; *(manufacturing)* Abfall; *(scrap)* Schrott; *(rubbish)* Müll; *(to ~)* verschwenden; vergeuden; verschleudern; *(to lay waste)* verwüsten

wasted verschwendet; *(squandered)* vergeudet; *(sold at a loss)* verschleudert; *(devastated)* verwüstet

wasteful verschwenderisch

wasting Verschwenden; *(squandering)* Vergeuden; *(selling below cost)* Verschleudern; *(laying waste)* Verwüsten

wastig asset Wirtschaftsgut mit beschränkter Nutzungsdauer

Accounting: a fixed asset that has a limited useful life and is therefore subject to depreciation.

waste management Abfallwirtschaft; Entsorgung

The collection, transport, processing or disposal of waste materials, in order to reduce their effect on human health and / or the einvironment.

watch list Beobachtungsliste

Investment: a list of securities selected for special surveillance by a brokerage, exchange or regulatory organization. The companies on the watch list may for example be takeover candidates

waterfront Kai

waterway Wasserweg; Wasserstraße; *(shipping lane)* Schifffahrtsweg

wave of bankruptcies Pleitewelle

wave of dismissals Entlassungswelle

wave of price increases Teuerungswelle

waybill Frachtbrief; Luftfrachtbrief

Trade: a document for handling and accounting for a shipment of freight, normally prepared by a common carrier at the start of a shipment, listing details such as the route the goods will follow and the transportation costa. The waybill typically accompanies the shipment to its destination.

weak schwach; *(economy)* flau

weaken *(to make weak)* schwächen; abschwächen; *(to become weak)* schwach werden; *(to abate)* nachlassen

weakening *(making weaker)* Schwächung; Abschwächung; Nachlassen; *(becoming weaker)* schwächer werden; schwächend; abschwächend

weak-form efficiency schwache Informationseffizienz

Economics: a variation of the efficient market hypothesis that claims that all past prices of a stock are reflected in the current stock price.

weakness Schwäche; Schwachheit; *(economy, market)* Flaute

wealth Reichtum; Wohlhabenheit; *(assets)* Vermögen; Besitz; Fülle

wealthy vermögend; wohlhabend; *(in a good position)* gut situiert; reich *(having sufficient capital)* kapitalkräftig

wear out sich abnutzen

To exhaust or get tired through overuse or great strain or stress.

wearout Abnutzung; Verschleiß; Haltbarkeit

Advertising: the level of frequency, or a point in time, when an advertising message loses its ability to effectively communicate.

web Netz

Short term for the World Wide Web.

web addresses Webadresse

Internet: refers to particular pages on a web server, which is hosted by a company or organization. The technical name for web addresses is uniform or universal resource locators (URLs).

web browser Webbrowser

Internet: a program that allows an individual to view web pages.

webdesigner Webdesigner

Internet: the person responsible for initial design and coding of a website; also called web author, HTML author, etc..

Weber, Max (1864-1920)

German sociologist and political economist. He was the first writer on management theory to analyze the role of the leader in an organization and to examine how and why individuals respond to various forms of authority. He distinguished three types of legitimate authority: the rational, the traditional and the charismatic.

Biography: taught at the Berlin University and later became professor of economics at the universities of Freiburg, Heidelberg and Munich, in 1918 he was a member of the committee set up to draft the constitution of the Weimar Republic.

Major publications: (1930) The Protestant Ethic and the Spirit of Capitalism, (1947) The Theory of Social and Economic Organization

web form digitales Formular

Internet: a technical term for a webpage that has designated places for the user to type information. Many corporate websites sport Web forms, using them for a multitude of purposes from site registration and survey research to product purchase.

web host Webhost

Internet: a service company that operates web servers for its clients and publishes their websites.

webisode Episode auf dem Netz

Internet: episode of a TV-like program where the viewer takes a more active role. The digital product captures the user on video in the studio, performs voice-overs, and then places the user in the program.

web marketing Netzmarketing; Webmarketing

Internet: any type of internet-based promotion or marketing, including websites, targeted e-mail, internet bulletin boards, sites where customers can dial-in and download files and others.

webmaster Webmaster

Internet: the person who keeps a website running and available to its readers, like the station manager at a local television station.

web page Netzseite

Internet: a page in a web document. Unlike printed pages, a webpage may include images and other content.

web server Webserver

Internet: a computer used to store the web pages accessed by web browsers. They may also contain databases of customer or product information, which can be queried and retrieved using a browser.

website Webseite

Internet: a collection of one or more webpages, usually describing a single topic.

website content Inhalt einer Webseite

Internet: text, graphics, video, and audio that are displayed on a webpage. It can also include interactive features such as search tools, forms, purchase options, and e-mail.

website log Log einer Webseite

Internet: data about how long users spend on each page, how long they are at the site, what path they take through the site, among other things.

website measurement Website-Messung

Internet: the process whereby metrics such as page impressions are collected and evaluated to assess the effectiveness of internet marketing.

weekly average Wochendurchschnitt

weekly report Wochenbericht

weigh wiegen; abwiegen; *(consider)* abwägen; erwägen

weighing Gewichtung

weight Gewicht; Last; *(to ~)* beschweren; belasten

Advertising: number of exposures of an advertising message; number of gross rating points an advertiser wants to place in a market.

weighted average gewichteter Durchschnitt; gewichtetes Mittel

weighted average cost of capital (WACC) gewichteter Kapitalkostenansatz

Concept used to calculate an interest rate at which the total of all working capital should perform.

The assumption is that the risk to invest into a company's equity can be quantified by comparison with respective interest rates in the market. Two types of risk are distinguished:

Objective risk: risk to invest in the stock market

Subjective risk: risk to invest in shares of a given company.

This is done by calculating the *beta-factor* or simply *beta* which is used to judge the subjective risk. Beta shows how much the stock price of a given company goes up or down, when the total market changes one percentage point. Beta is thus a measure for the volatility of a title.

weighted average maturity gewogener Mittelwert der Laufzeit

Measure of the level of interest-rate risk calculated by weighting cash flows by the time to receipt and multiplying by the fraction of total present value represented by the cash flow at that time.

welfare Wohlergehen; *(social service)* Wohlfahrt; Sozialhilfe; Fürsorge

welfare committee Sozialausschuss

welfare eligibility Sozialanspruch

welfare policy Sozialpolitik

welfare state Wohlfahrtsstaat

Politics: a country in which government provides a variety of social services to its citizens, such as medical care, unemployment protection and pensions.

well-grounded fundiert; begründet; gut geschult

wellness programs Wellness-Programme

Employment: programs offered by an employer offering personal fitness and exercise programs. The aim is to improve employee productivity and reduce health care costs.

well versed sachkundig

wharfage Werftgebühr; Kainutzungsgebühr

Fee for use of piers.

what you see is what you get (WYSIWYG)

Used to describe any computer program that displays content as it will appear in its finished form. Many applications promise WYSIWYG features, but differences in output devices and screen displays make it nearly impossible to meet this goal all of the time.

wheel of retailing Entwicklungszyklus des Einzelhandels

Economics: theory that retailers go through a standard development cycle, beginning as low-margin, low-price, low-status operations but later evolving into higher-priced, higher-service operations, eventually becoming like conventional retailers.

whistle-blower Nestbeschmutzer

Organization: a person who reports unethical practices by their employer to outsiders and who are therefore perceived by management as troublemakers.

white-collar worker Angestellter

Employment: classification for employees performing nonmanual work in administrative and clerical positions.

white goods weiße Waren

Retailing: expression for all those heavy household appliances that were originally manufactured with a white enamel finish, such as refrigerators, freezers, washers and dryers, or stoves.

whole Gesamtheit; ganz; *(complete)* vollständig

wholesale Großhandel; Großverkauf; *(high volume sales)* Massenabsatz; en gros

Commerce: the commercial activity of buying and storing goods in large quantities from their manufacturers or importers, and then selling smaller quantities to retailers, who in turn sell them to the general public.

wholesale chain Großhandelskette

wholesale market Großhandelsmarkt; Großmarkt

wholesaler Engroshändler; Großhändler; Großkaufmann; Grossist

Commerce: a company engaged in buying large quantities of goods and services and selling them to other distributors and businesses rather than to the final consumer.

wholesaling Großhandel(-sgewerbe)

Commerce: all activities involved in selling goods and services to those buying for resale or business use.

wholly owned im Alleineigentum; hundertprozentiger Besitz

wholly owned subsidiary hundertprozentige Tochtergesellschaft

Subsidiary in which the firm owns 100 percent of the stock.

wide area information service (WAIS)

Internet service that has been superseded by the World Wide Web.

wide area telephone service (WATS)

Telecommunications: a special long-distance calling service offered by telecommunications companies offering reduced-rate long distance calls for commercial users.

will Wille; Wunsch; letzter Wille; *(to ~)* wünschen; mögen; wollen; testamentarisch vermachen

Law: legal document of a property-holder directing the distribution of his property after his death.

willing to take risks risikofreudig

willing to work arbeitswillig

win gewinnen; *(acquire)* erwerben; *(earn)* verdienen; erringen; erreichen; durchschlagen

windfall *(forestry)* Windbruch; Fallobst; *(lucky break)* unverhoffter Glücksfall

windfall profit unerwarteter Gewinn; Zufallsgewinn; Überraschungsgewinn

Commerce: an unexpected profit arising from causes not controlled by the recipient.

winding up Abschließen; -wickeln; Liquidation

Liquidation: the process of liquidating a corporation. The steps performed include collecting the assets, paying the expenses, satisfying creditors' claims, and distributing the net assets to shareholders.

window Fenster; Zeitfenster; *(customer service)* Schalter

Windows

Computing: operating system by Microsoft providing a graphical user interface, extended memory, and multi-tasking.

window dressing Bilanzverschleierung; Bilanzkosmetik

Accounting: deliberate manipulations in a financial statement to create a more favorable appearance than is true.

winner Gewinner; *(competition)* Sieger; *(product)* Schlager

winner's curse Fluch des Gewinners

Stock exchange: Theory that an average investor wins, i.e. gets the desired allocation of a new issue because those who knew better avoided the issue.

winning Gewinnen; *(captivating)* einnehmend; gewinnend; *(victorious)* siegreich

WinTel

Common, usually derogatory, reference to the Microsoft-Intel hegemony in the PC industry.

wire Draht; *(telegram)* Telegramm; Depesche; Drahtnachricht; *(to ~)* telegrafieren; drahten

wireless Funk-; drahtlos

Transmission technology that relies on towers to relay signals in a mode very similar to that of cell phones.

wire transfer elektronische Geldüberweisung

Electronic transfer of funds from one bank to another that eliminates the mailing and check-clearing times associated with other cash-transfer methods.

withdraw sich zurückziehen; zurücktreten; *(money)* abheben; entnehmen; *(support)* entziehen; *(statement)* zurücknehmen

withdrawal Rückzug; Zurückziehung; *(money)* Abhebung; Entnahme; *(support)* Entziehung; *(statement)* Rücknahme; Sickerverlust; Widerrufung

Banking: the removal of money from where it was kept, such as a bank account or a mutual fund.

withdrawal period *(contract)* Kündigungsfrist

withdrawal plan Entnahmeplan

withhold *(to deny)* vorenthalten; *(to keep back)* einbehalten; vorenthalten

withholding Zurückbehaltung; Vorbehaltung; *(taxes)* Abzugsverfahren; Einbehaltung

Employment: the portion of an employee's wages retained by the employer for the payment of taxes, insurance, pension plans, and other deductions.

withholding tax Quellensteuer; Absatzsteuer

Taxation: a tax on income that is levied at the source, thus diverted to the government before the recipient of the income receives it.

withholding wage tax Lohnsteuerabzug

within in; im Rahmen; *(time)* binnen; innerhalb

without amortization tilgungsfrei

without leadership führungslos

without obligation unverbindlich; ohne Obligo

without prejudice ohne Nachteil

Contract term signifying that the agreement will not injure any prior or subsequent rights

without purpose zwecklos; *(aimless)* ziellos

without ready money bargeldlos

without recourse ohne Regress

Commerce: a legal phrase indicating that the holder of a document has no recourse to the person from whom he obtained it. Used in factoring receivables to denote that the holder is not to look to the debtor personally in the event of non-payment.

with regard to hinsichtlich

woo (um)werben; zu erlangen trachten; überreden; drängen

wording of a contract Vertragstext

word of mouth Mund-zu-Mund

word-of-mouth influence Mund-zu-Mund-Propaganda; Empfehlung unter Freunden

Personal communication about a product between target buyers and neighbours, friends, family members, and associates.

word processor Textprozessor; Textverarbeitungssystem

work Arbeit; Beschäftigung; Arbeitsgang; *(to ~)* arbeiten; bearbeiten; auslasten; *(mechanism)* funktionieren

workable bearbeitungsfähig; *(capable of being carried out)* ausführbar; durchführbar; funktionsfähig

work analysis Arbeitsanalyse;

work attitude Arbeitseinstellung

work councils Betriebsräte

Groups of nominated or elected employees who must be consulted when management makes decisions involving personnel.

work enthusiasm Arbeitseifer

work environment Arbeitsumfeld; Arbeitsumgebung

worker *(blue collar)* Arbeiter; *(employee)* Arbeitnehmer; Arbeitskraft

work experience Berufserfahrung

Employment: experience gained while employed in a particular occupation.

worker interest Arbeiterinteresse

workers' council Betriebsrat

worker vote Arbeiterstimme

work force Belegschaft; Arbeitskräfte; Personalbestand

Economics: the total number of persons in an economy over the age of 16 who work for pay, as well as unemployed persons actively seeking work.

workforce diversity Vielfalt in der Belegschaft

Employment: the trend towards increasing heterogeneity in organizations with the inclusion of different groups in terms of gender, race, and ethnicity. This also includes physically challenged, gays and lesbians, and the elderly.

workgroup Arbeitsgruppe

Group that interact primarily to share information and to make decisions to help each member perform within his or her area of responsibility.

Work groups have no need or opportunity to engage in collective work that requires joint effort. So their performance is merely the summation of each group member's individual contribution. There is no positive synergy that would create an overall level of performance that is greater than the sum of the input.

working area *(factory)* Werkbereich

working atmosphere Betriebsklima

working balance Betriebsmittelguthaben

working capital Betriebskapital; Nettoumlaufkapital; Betriebsmittel

Accounting: the the excess of current assets over current liabilities of a business at any time, representing the funds invested in a company's cash, accounts receivable, inventory, and other current assets.

The size of working capital is an indicator of the liquidity and solvency of a company, particularly when related to other financial indicators.

working conditions Arbeitsbedingungen

working hours Arbeitszeit

working hours policy Arbeitszeitpolitik

working hours regulation Arbeitszeitordnung

working knowledge ausreichende Kenntnisse

working life Lebensarbeitszeit

work in progress Umflaufbestand; unfertige Erzeugnisse

Accounting: goods in the process of production that have already used an amount of raw materials, labour and other attributable costs.

workload *(burden)* Arbeitsbelastung; *(prescribed share)* Arbeitspensum; Deputat

Employment: a measure of the amount and type of work to be performed by an employee in a given time.

workload approach Ansatz zur Beurteilung der Arbeitsbelastung

Marketing: approach to setting the size of the sales force, whereby the company groups accounts into different size classes and then determines how many salespeople are needed to call on them the desired number of times.

work order Arbeitsauftrag; Betriebsauftrag

Manufacturing: a request form issued by one department asking another for the completion of specified work not normally performed.

work organization Arbeitsorganisation

work out ausarbeiten; ausrechnen

work permit Arbeitserlaubnis

Politics: a provisional status given by a government to foreigners, allowing them to work legally in the country.

workplace Arbeitsplatz; Arbeitsstätte

workplace computer Arbeitsplatz-computer

workplace convenience Arbeitsplatzkomfort

workplace risk Arbeitsplatzrisiko

work plan Arbeitsplan

Standard for the production process of a product or a service (e.g. in public administration). In the work plan the various operations are listed in the precise sequence in which they are carried out (routing information).

work process Arbeitsgang; Arbeitsvorgang

work reform Arbeitsreform

work rule Arbeitsregel; Arbeitsrichtlinie

work sampling Arbeitsproben

Work sampling tests are live simulations of a job that must be performed by applicants.

By carefully devising work samples based on job analysis data, management determines the knowledge, skills, and abilities needed for each job.

workshop *(enterprise)* Gewerbebetrieb; *(work room)* Werkstatt; *(working meeting)* Arbeitstagung; Seminar; Arbeitsgemeinschaft

work specialization Arbeitsspezialisierung

Theory that rather than an entire job being done by one individual, it is broken down into a number of steps, each step being completed by a separate individual.

In essence, individuals specialize in doing part of an activity rather than the entire activity. Managers recognize the economies it provides in certain types of jobs and the problems it creates when it's carried too far.

workstation Arbeitsplatzrechner; Großrechner

Once applied to high-powered computers used for graphics processing, scientific applications or similar uses, this term is not increasingly used to describe ordinary PCs connected to a network.

work stoppage Arbeitsniederlegung

Employment: an interruption of work by employees, usually designed to put pressure on management to improve working conditions.

work team Arbeitsteam

Team of people assigned a particular task that generates a positive synergy through coordinated effort.

Their individual efforts results in a level of performance that is greater than the sum of the individual inputs. This positive synergy will allow the organization to increase performance. The extensive use of teams creates the potential for an organization to generate greater outputs with no increase in inputs.

work unit Arbeitseinheit

world agricultural market Weltagrarmarkt

World Bank Weltbank

Officially called the International Bank for Reconstruction and Development.

Created in 1945 together with the International Monetary Fund as a result of the Bretton Woods conference.

Its purpose, after initially emphasizing the reconstruction of Europe after World War II, has been to lend funds at commercial rates and to provide technical assistance in order to facilitate economic development in its poorer member countries.

world class Weltklasse

world economy Weltwirtschaft

world export Weltexport

world finance Weltfinanz

world market Weltmarkt

world market leader Weltmarktführer

world market price Weltmarktpreis

world market share Weltmarktanteil

world ranking Weltrangliste

world trade Welthandel

World Trade Organization (WTO)

Organization that succeeded the General Agreement on Tariffs and Trade (GATT) in

1995 as a result of the successful completion of the Uruguay round of GATT negotiations.

The WTO is the legal and institutional foundation of the multilateral trading system of its member countries. It defines the principal contractual obligations for domestic trade legislation and regulations. And it is the platform on which trade relations between countries evolve through collective debate, negotiation and adjudication.

worldwide area structure weltweite Gebietsstruktur

Business organizational structure under which the world is divided into areas.

worldwide economic condition Weltkonjunktur

worldwide economic crisis Weltwirtschaftskrise

worldwide operations weltweite Geschäftstätigkeit

worldwide product division structure weltweite Produktspartenstruktur

Business organizational structure based on product divisions that have worldwide responsibility.

worldwide recession weltweite Rezession

world wide web (WWW)

Abbreviation for World Wide Web, that is an internet service that links collections of documents, or web sites, both internally and to other sites. In addition to formatted text, web pages may include graphics, audio, video and other multimedia content

worm Wurm

Internet: small, usually destructive programs that replicate themselves on a computer's memory or hard disk, often until the computer crashes or becomes unusable.

worsen sich verschlechtern

woresening Verschlechterung

worth Wert; wert

Inherent value of a commodity, good, servicc, or other economic factor. Often worth is measured in non-price terms, as in comparable worth programs designed to pay equivalent wages for work of equivalent worth, even though the market prices of the services ordinarily would differ.

writ Erlass; Befehl

Law: order issued by an authority to compel a person to do something.

write-down Wertberichtigung; Sonderabschreibung

Accounting: a reduction in an asset value on the financial statements, often following a drop in market price.

write-off *(taxation)* Abschreibung; *(bookkeeping)* Ausbuchung; Abbuchung

write off *(taxation)* abschreiben; *(bookkeeping)* ausbuchen; abbuchen; abschreiben; hinhauen

writer Aussteller

Seller of an option contract.

write to schreiben; anschreiben

writing utensil Schreibgerät

written schriftlich

written communication geschriebene Kommunikation; Schreiben

wrong falsch; *(unjust, dishonest)* unrecht; *(mistaken)* irrig

wrong decision Fehlentscheidung

Xx

X-Efficiency X-Effizienz

Situation in which a firm's total costs are not minimized because the output from given inputs is less than the maximum feasible level.

This outcome is also termed a situation of "technical inefficiency". X-Efficiency is a direct function of monopoly of market power in which competitive pressures are weakened. The term was originally applied to the manager-worker relationship but can be extended to deal with the manager-owner relationship.

XML

Advanced markup language giving better control than HTML over format for structured information on web pages.

Yy

Y2K acronym for year 2000

yankee bonds Yankee-Anleihen

Foreign bonds issued in the United States by foreign banks and corporations.

yard Yard; Hof; Platz

Enclosed area that can be used for storing materials (storage yard) or repairing equipment (repair yard).

Y-Efficiency Y-Effizienz

Effectiveness with which existing profitable market opportunities are exploited

yearbook Jahrbuch

year-end Jahresultimo

year of training Ausbildungsjahr

year-to-date (YTD) seit Jahresbeginn

Accumulation of accounts from the start of the fiscal year to the latest available period. Sales, purchases, and profits for any current week or month may be displayed year-to-date.

year under report Berichtsjahr

yellow goods Gelbe Güter

In merchandising, non-consumable household goods, such as refrigerators or ovens, that are expensive and are usually replaced only after many years of service. Generally, yellow goods have a high profit margin.

yield Ernte; Ertrag; *(result)* Ergebnis; *(interest)* Zinsertrag; Verzinsung; *(stocks)* Rendite; Nominalverzinsung; *(to ~)* erbringen; abwerfen; *(to give in)* nachgeben; aufgeben; überlassen; *(to bear interest)* Zinsen tragen

In general: the annual rate of return on an investment, expressed as a percentage.

Bonds: the coupon rate of interest divided by the purchase price, called current yield.

Lending: total money earned on a loan, that is, the annual percentage rate of interest multiplied by the term of the loan.

Stocks: percentage rate of return paid on a stock in the form of dividends.

*Taxes:*amount of revenue received by a governmental entity as a result of a tax.

Agriculture: agricultural output in terms of quantity of a crop per acre.

yield curve Ertragskurve; Zinsstrukturkurve

Graph showing the term structure of interest rates by plotting the yields of all bonds of the same quality with maturities ranging from the shortest to the longest available.

yield gap Ertragslücke

Difference between average yield on equities and a corresponding yield on long-date fixed-interest securities.

yield index Nutzenindex

yield management Yield Management

The process of maximising yield from existing resouces by allocating the right type of capacity to the right kind of customer at the right price as to maximise revenue or yield.

yield on assets Vermögensertrag

yield on interest Zinsertrag

yield on investment Anlagerendite; Anlagekapitalrendite

yield spread Renditenspanne

Investment: the difference between the quoted rates of return on two different investments as a way of comparing two financial products.

yield to call Rendite auf Kündigung

Percentage rate of a bond or note, if one were to buy and hold the security until the call date.

This yield is valid only if the security is called prior to maturity. Generally bonds are callable over several years and normally are called at a slight premium. The calculation of yield to call is based on the coupon rate, length of time to the call and the market price.

yield to maturity (YTM) Rückzahlungsrendite

Percentage rate of return paid on a bond, note or other fixed income security if one buys and holds it to its maturity date.

The calculation for YTM is based on the coupon rate, length of time to maturity and market price. It assumes that coupon interest paid over the life of the bond will be reinvested at the same rate.

yuppie erfolgsorientierte junge Großstadtmenschen

Short for young urban professional, describing young career people with relatively high incomes and education, seeking instant success and gratification.

Zz

zero-balance account (ZBA) Nullsaldenkonto

Bank account in which a zero balance is maintained by transfers of funds from a master account in an amount only large enough to cover checks presented.

zero-base budgeting (ZBB) Zero-Base Budgeting; Nullbasisbudgetierung

Budgeting: a method of budgeting that requires a justification of all expenditures. All budget lines are said to begin at a zero base and are funded according to merit.

zero coupon Nullcoupon

zero coupon bond Nullkuponanleihe; Zero Bonds

Securities: a bond that pays no interest and is initially sold at a deep discount from its face value.

zero economic growth wirtschaftliches Nullwachstum

Economics: situation when national income neither grows nor falls.

zero interest Nullzins

zero population growth (ZPG) Nullwachstum der Bevölkerung

Demographics: situation where ther is no further increase in the population of a country, which has significant. economic and business implications.

zero quota Nullquote

zero sum game Nullsummenspiel

Game theory: a situation where the sum of the amounts won and lost by all parties is zero. Whatever is gained in a zero-sum game by one participant is always achieved at the expense of the other participants.

zip code/ZIP Postleitzahl

Five-digit numerical code defined by the U.S. Postal Service to simplify and expedite mail distribution.

zip code area Postleitzahlbereich

zone Zone; *(area)* Gebiet; *(part of area)* Teilgebiet; *geo* Landstrich; Tariffgruppe; *(to ~)* in Zonen einteilen.

zone pricing regionale Differenzierung

Geographic pricing strategy in which the company sets up two or more zones. All customers within a zone pay the same total price; the more distant the zone, the higher the price.

zoning Abgrenzung regionaler Teilmärkte; Gebietsaufteilung; *(real estate)* Bebauungsplan

Real estate: the public regulation of land and building use to control the character of an area.

zero growth Nullwachstum

Situation when there is no increase or decrease on productivity levels associated with an activity. This term is usually has an economic connotation.

A

ab ex

ab Lager ex stock; ex warehouse

ab Werk ex factory

abändern to alter; to modify; *(Text)* to revise

Abandon abandonment

Abbau reduction; *(Arbeitskräfte)* dismissal; cutback; *(Bergbau)* exploitation; mining

Abbau einer Mittlerrolle disintermediation

abbauen to reduce; *(Arbeitskräfte)* to dismiss; to cut back; *(Bergbau)* to exploit; to mine

abberufen to recall; to withdraw

Abberufung recall; withdrawal

abbestellen to cancel

Abbestellung cancellation

abbilden to reproduce; to copy; (*darstellen*) to portray, to illustrate, to picture, to depict; (*nachbilden*) to model, to represent; (*zeichnen*) to draw

Abbildung illustration; figure; drawing

abbrechen to stop; *(Verbindung)* to discontinue; to sever; *(Verhandlungen)* to break off

Abbruch *(Verbindung)* discontinuance; severance; *(Verhandlungen)* breaking off; *(Arbeit)* stoppage

abbuchen *(Konto)* to charge; to debit; *(abschreiben)* to write off

Abbuchung *(Konto)* charge; debit; *(Abschreibung)* write-off

ABC Abkommen ABC agreement

ABC-Analyse ABC analysis; ABC method

abdecken to cover

Abdeckung cover

abdrosseln to stall; to stifle

Abdruck (*Produkt*) print; copy; (*erster Abdruck*) first proof; (*Vorgang*) printing, copying, proofing

abdrucken to print; to print off; to reproduce; (*wieder abdrucken*) to reprint

Abruckgenehmigung permission to reprint; copyright permission

Abfall waste; refuse; trash

Abfallarten types of waste

Abfallbehandlung waste treatment

Abfallbeseitigung waste disposal

Abfallprodukt waste product

Abfallstoff waste material

Abfallvermeidung waste avoidance

Abfallverminderung waste reduction

Abfallverwertung recycling; salvage

Abfallwirtschaft waste management

abfassen to formulate; to draft

Abfassung formulation

abfertigen to handle; to dispatch; (*Zoll*) to clear

Abfertigung handling; dispatch; check-in; (*Zoll*) clearance

abfinden to pay off; *(sich ~)* to accept

Abfindung compensation; *(Angestellter)* severance pay

Abfindung, hohe golden handshake

Abfindungszahlung payoff; severance pay; lump sum payment

Abfindungsvertrag termination agreement

Abfluss outflow

Abflauen (*Konjunktur*) slowdown; downturn

abflauen to slow down

Abgabe *(Übergabe)* delivery; *(Abschöpfung)* levy; *(Zoll)* duty; *(Gebühr)* charge; fee

Abgabefrist deadline

Abgabenordnung tax code; revenue code

Abgabepreis selling price

Abgabe von Angeboten bidding

Abgang von Anlagevermögen retirement of fixed assets

Abgaskontrolle emission control

Abgeld discount

abgeleitet derived

abgeleitete Nachfrage derived demand

Abgeordneter *(Parlament)* representative; (*UK*) member of parliament; (*Gesandter*) deputy

abgegrenzte Ertragssteuer deferred income tax

abgezinste Anleihe pure discount bond

abgezinster Geldfluss discounted cash flow

Abgleich adjustment; comparison

ableichen to adjust; to compare

abgrenzbarkeit *(Bilanz)* identifyability

Abgrenzung demarcation; *(Rechnung)* deferred earnings items; *(Bilanz)* accruals and deferrals

Abgrenzung, periodengerechte cut-off

Abgrenzung, sachliche allocation of expenses not related to the operational purpose

Abgrenzung, zeitliche allocation of expenses unrelated to accounting period

Abgrenzung von Zinsaufwand *(Bilanz)* accrued interest payable

Abgrenzung von Zinsertrag *(Bilanz)* accrued interest receivable

Abgrenzungsbogen reconciliation sheet

Abgrenzungsergebnis expense allocation statement

Abgrenzungsposten (*aktiv*) deferred charges; (*passiv*) deferred income

Abgrenzungsrechnung statement of accruals and deferrals

abgerundet in rounded figures

abgleiten to slide; to slip

abgrenzen to demarcate; *(definieren)* to define

abhaken to check; to tick

abhandeln *(Thema behandeln)* to treat; *(vom Preis)* to bargain

abhängen *(hinter sich lassen)* to leave behind

abhängen von to depend on

abhängig dependent

abhängige Unternehmen dependent companies

abhängige Variable dependent variable

Abhängigkeit dependence

abheben *(Konto)* to withdraw

Abhebung *(Konto)* withdrawal

Abholgrossist cash and carry wholesaler

Abholmarkt cash and carry

abholen to pick up; to collect

Abholung collection

abhören to monitor; to listen in; (*Schulaufgabe*) to quiz

Abhörgerät monitor; bugging device

Abitur high-school diploma

Abiturient high-school graduate

Abkommen agreement; covenant; deal

Abkommenskonto agreement account

Abkühlungszeit cooling-off period

abkürzen to abbreviate; to shorten

Abkürzung abbreviation

abladen *(Waren)* to unload; *(Abfall)* to dump

Ablader (*Fracht*) discharger

Ablage filing basket; filing system

Ablauf *(Arbeitsablauf)* procedure; course; *(Erlöschen)* expiration, expiry

Ablaufdiagramm flow chart

Ablauforganisation process organization

Ablaufplanung operations planning; scheduling

ablaufen *(fällig werden)* to expire; *(Zeit)* to elapse; to run out

Ablauforganisation operational structuring

Ablauftermin date of expiration

ablegen to lay down; *(Akten)* to file

Ableger *(Filiale)* subsidiary; branch

ablehnen to reject; to oppose; to turn down

ablehnende Antwort refusal

Ablehnung rejection; disclaimer

ableiten to derive

ablichten to photocopy

Ablichtung photocopy

abliefern to deliver

Ablieferung delivery

ablösen to detach; *(Kredit)* to redeem; *(von der Arbeit)* to relieve

abmachen to agree; *(ein Geschäft)* to settle; *(regeln)* to arrange

Abmachung agreement; *(Geschäft)* deal; *(Klausel)* stipulation; *(Regelung)* arrangement

abmahnen to warn; to serve notice

Abmahnung warning; notice

abmelden unsubscribe

abmelden, sich to notify of departure

Abnahme *(Absatz)* sale; *(Kauf)* purchase; *(Minderung)* decline; decrease; diminuition

abnehmen to take delivery; (*akzeptieren*) to pass; (*kleiner werden*) to diminish; to decrease

abnehmend diminishing

abnehmender Grenznutzen diminishing marginal utility

abnehmender Nutzen diminishing utility

Abnehmer *(Käufer)* purchaser; *(Benutzer)* user; *(Kunde)* customer

Abnehmergruppe buying group

Abnehmerland buying country

Abonnement subscription; standing order

Abonnent subscriber

abonnieren to subscribe to; to take in

Abordnung delegation

abpacken to package

abrechnen *(Rechnung, Konto)* to settle; to clear; *(abziehen)* to deduct

Abrechnung *(Rechnung, Konto)* settlement; statement; bill; (*Rechnungswesen)* account; invoicing; clearance

Abrechnungskurs settlement price

Abrechnungsperiode settlement period

Abrechnungstag settlement date; account day

Abrechnungszeitraum accounting period

Abriss summary; abstract

abrufen to recall; to call up

Abrufvertrag call-off purchase agreement

Absage *(Weigerung)* rejection; *(Auftrag, Veranstaltung)* cancellation; *(Einladung)* regret

absagen *(Auftrag, Veranstaltung)* to cancel; *(Einladung)* to decline; to regret

Absatz sales; selling; *(Verkauf)* marketing; *(Vertrieb)* distribution; *(Paragraph)* paragraph

Absatzanalyse sales analysis

Absatzbasis marketing base

Absatzbereich marketing area

Absatzbudget sales budget

Absatzchance sales potential; marketing potential

Absatzeinnahmen sales revenues

Absatzelastizität sales elasticity

Absatzentwicklung sales trend; market development

Absatzerfolg sales result

Absatzfachmann sales professional; marketer

absatzfähig salable; marketable

Absatzfähigkeit marketability

Absatzfinanzierungsinstitut factor; factoring company

Absatzförderung merchandising; sales promotion

Absatzförderung beim Handel trade promotion

Absatzformel marketing formula

Absatzforschung marketing research

Absatzgebiet sales district; sales territory; market area; marketing area

Absatzgelegenheit market opportunity

Absatzhelfer sales agent

Absatzkalkulation sales calculation

Absatzkanal sales channel

Absatzkreditpolitik sales credit policy

Absatzmarkt sales market; market; market area; *(Vertriebsstelle)* outlet

Absatzmenge sales volume

Absatzmittler marketing agent; sales representative; intermediary

Absatzmix sales mix; marketing mix

Absatzmöglichkeit market opportunity

Absatzorganisation sales organization; sales force

Absatzplan sales forecast; marketing plan

Absatzplanung sales planning

Absatzpolitik sales policy

Absatzposition market position

Absatzpotential sales potential

Absatzprognose sales forecast

Absatzrückgang decline in sales

Absatzstrategie marketing strategy; distribution strategy

Absatztätigkeit marketing function

Absatzverlust sales loss

Absatzvolumen sales volume

Absatzvorausschätzung sales forecast

Absatzweg channel of distribution; marketing channel

Absatzwegeentscheidung marketing channel decision

Absatzwirtschaft marketing

Absatzziel market objective

abschätzen to estimate

Abschätzung valuation; appraisal

abschalten to switch off; to turn off

abschicken to dispatch; to send off; *(mit der Post)* to mail; to consign; *(Geld)* to remit

abschirmen to protect

Abschlag (*Abzug*) deduction; *(Preisminderung)* discount

Abschlagsdividende interim dividend

abschlagen *(Bitte)* to deny; to refuse

abschlägiger Bescheid refusal

Abschlagszahlung payment on account; instalment payment

abschleppen to tow

Abschleppgebühr towage

abschließen *(enden)* to terminate; to end; *(Vertrag, Verhandlung)* to conclude; *(Konto)* to close

Abschluss termination; completion; (*Bilanz*) financial statement; balance sheet; *(Vertrag)* conclusion; deal

Abschlussbericht final report

Abschlussbilanz annual balance sheet

Abschlussbuchung closing entry

Abschlussdividende final dividend; year-end dividend

Abschlussgebühr acquisition fee

Abschlussprüfer auditor

Abschlussprüfung audit

Abschlusssitzung closing session

Abschlusstermin closing date

Abschlussübersicht table of balance sheet figures; work sheet

Abschnitt section; segment; paragraph; *(Zinsschein)* coupon

abschnittweise Zuteilung allotment

abschöpfen to skim; *(Abgaben)* to levy

Abschöpfung (*Preispolitik*) skimming; *(Abgabe)* levy

Abschöpfungsstrategie skimming strategy

Abschreckung deterrence

abschreiben *(Bilanz)* to depreciate; to write off; *(tilgen)* to amortize; *(kopieren)* to copy

Abschreibung (*Bilanz*) depreciation; write-off; *(Tilgung)* amortization

Abschreibung, außerplanmäßige extraordinary depreciation

Abschreibung, beschleunigte accelerated depreciation

Abschreibung, degressive declining-balance depreciation

Abschreibung, jährliche annual depreciation

Abschreibung, lineare linear depreciation; straight-line depreciation

Abschreibungen, aufgelaufene accumulated depreciation

Abschreibung auf das Anlagevermögen depreciation

Abschreibung auf Finanzanlagen write-down of financial assets

Abschreibung für Abnutzung depreciation for wear and tear

Abschreibung wegen Substanzverzehr depletion

Abschreibungsart method of depreciation

Abschreibungsbeträge capital allowances

abschreibungsfähig depreciable

Abschreibungsgrundlage depreciation base

Abschreibungsmethode depreciation method

Abschreibungsmöglichkeit write-off facility; depreciation allowance

Abschreibungsobjekt tax-saving write-off project

Abschreibungsgegenstand depreciation unit

Abschreibungsrestwert written-down value

Abschreibungssatz depreciation rate

Abschreibungssumme depreciation expense

Abschreibungsverfahren depreciation method

Abschreibung vom Wiederbeschaffungswert replacement cost depreciation

Abschrift copy

Abschrift anfertigen to copy

abschwächen to weaken; to soften

abschwächen, sich to slacken

Abschwächung weakening; slackening

absenden to send off; to dispatch; *(mit der Post)* to mail; *(Geld)* to remit

Absender sender; *(Post)* return address

Absendung dispatch; *(mit der Post)* mailing

absetzbar *(Steuern)* deductible; *(Abschreibung)* depreciable; *(Verkauf)* salable

absetzen *(verkaufen)* to sell; to dispose; *(vertreiben)* to distribute; *(abziehen)* to deduct; *(vom Amt)* to dismiss; to remove

Absetzung *(Abzug)* deduction; *(vom Amt)* removal; dismissal

Absetzung für Abnutzung (AfA) depreciation for wear and tear

Absetzung von der Einkommenssteuer income tax deduction

absichern to secure; *(Börse)* to hedge

Absicherung *(gegen Risiko)* providing security; *(Börse)* hedge

Absicherungs-Fazilität note issuance-facility (NIF)

Absicht intent; intention; *(Zweck)* purpose; *(Ziel)* aim

Absichtserklärung letter of intent

Absinken sliding

absolut absolute

absolute Abweichung absolute deviation

absolute Häufigkeit absolute frequency

absoluter Kostenvorteil absolute cost advantage

Absolvent graduate

absondern *(trennen)* to separate; to set apart; *(isolieren)* to isolate

Absonderung *(Trennung)* separation; setting apart; *(Isolierung)* isolation

absorbieren to absorb

Absorption absorption

Absprache understanding; *(geheim)* collusion

Abstand distance; *(Zeilen)* space; *(Druckrand)* margin; *(zwischen Objekten)* clearance

abstimmen to vote; *(angleichen)* to adjust; *(koordinieren)* to coordinate; *(Konten)* to reconcile

Abstimmung vote; poll; ballot; (*Koordinierung*) coordination; matching

abstoßen *(Firmenteile)* to divest; *(Effekten)* to unload; *(Lagerbestände)* to clear

abstrakt abstract

abstufen to grade

Absturz crash

abtasten to scan

Abtaster scanner

Abteilung section; division; department

Abteilungsbildung departmentalization

Abteilungsleiter division manager; head of department

Abteilungstandort division headquarters

Abteilungsstruktur divisional structure

abtragen *(Schulden)* to pay off; *(Hypothek)* to amortize

abträglich detrimental; disadvantageous

abtrennen to sever

abtreten *(aufgeben)* to relinquish; *(Besitz)* to assign; *(Rechtstitel)* to cede; *(übergeben)* to transfer; *(zurücktreten)* to resign

Abtretung *(Besitz)* assignment; *(Rechtstitel)* cession; *(Übergabe)* transfer

Abtretungsvertrag bargain and sale deed

Abtritt *(Rücktritt)* resignation

abwälzen *(Kosten)* to pass on

Abwanderung exit; migration

Abwanderung von Wissenschaftlern brain drain

abwärts downward

Abwärtsbewegung downturn

abwechseln to alternate

abwechselnd alternating

abweichen to diverge; to deviate

abweichend divergent

Abweichung divergence; deviation; variance; discrepancy

Abweichungsanalyse variance analysis

Abweichungsindikator variance indicator

abweisen to reject; to disallow

abwerben to entice; to lure away

Abwerbung enticement; headhunting

abwerten to depreciate; to devalue

Abwertung depreciation; devaluation

abwesend absent

Abwesender absentee

Abwesenheit absence

abwickeln *(erledigen)* to carry out; to handle; to operate; *(Konkurs)* to liquidate

Abwicklung clearing; *(Erledigung)* handling; settlement; *(Konkurs)* liquidation

Abwicklungswert liquidation value

abzahlen to pay off

Abzahlung instalment payment

Abzahlungsbank consumer credit bank

Abzahlungskredit consumer loan

abziehbar deductible; allowable

abziehen to deduct; *(nachlassen)* to discount; *(subtrahieren)* to substract

abzinsen to discount

Abzinsung discounting

Abzinsungssatz discount rate

Abzinsung discounting

Abzug deduction; *(Rabatt)* rebate; *(Nachlass)* reduction; allowance; *(Subtraktion)* subtraction

Abzug für Betriebsausgaben deduction from taxable income

abzüglich less, off

abzugsfähig deductible; allowable

abzugsfähiger Betrag (*Steuern*) deductible amount

Abzugsfähigkeit der Fremdkapitalzinsen interest subsidy

addieren to total; to add

Adressat receipient; addressee

Adresse address

Adressenkartei list of customers; mailing list

adressieren address

Adreßbuch directory; (*Branchen*) trade directory

Affekt affect

affektive Komponente der Einstellung affective component of an attitude

Agent representative; agent

Agentenprovision agent´s commission

Agentur agency

Agenturprovision agency commission

Agenturvertreter agency representative

Agglomeration (*retail*) agglomaration

Aggregat aggregate; aggregation

aggregiertes Angebot aggregate supply; total supply

aggregierter Bedarf aggregate demand; total demand

aggressiv militant; aggressive

aggressive Preispolitik aggressive pricing

aggressive Werbung aggressive advertising; competitive advertising

Agio premium

Agioanleihe premium bond

Agioerlös paid-in surplus

Agrar- agrarian; agricultural

Agrarmarketing agricultural marketing

Agrarsubventionen agricultural subsidies

Agrarwirtschaft agriculture

Akademiker academic; graduate

akademischer Grad degree

akklimatisieren to get used to (an environment)

Akkord piecework

Akkordarbeit to do piecework

Akkordlohn piecework pay

Akkordzuschlag piecework bonus

Akkuranz accuracy

akkreditieren to accredit

Akkreditiv letter of credit; bank credit; credit order

Akkreditiv, anweisbares assignable letter of credit

Akkreditiv, begebbares negotiable letter of credit

Akkreditiv, revolvierendes revolving letter of credit

Akkreditiv, übertragbares transferable letter of credit

Akkreditiv, unwiderrufliches irrevocable letter of credit

Akkreditiv einräumen to open a letter of credit

Akkreditiv in Anspruch nehmen to draw a letter of credit

akquirieren to acquire; to make acquisitions; to secure a deal

Akquisition acquisition

Akronym acronym

Akte file

Aktenablage filing

Aktennummer reference number

Aktenstück document

Aktentasche briefcase

Aktie share

Aktien stock

Aktienanalyse stock analysis

Aktienanalyst stock analyst

Aktienanlage stock investment

Aktienaufteilung stock split

Aktienbesitz shareholding

Aktienbewertung stock evaluation; stock rating

Aktienbezugsrecht stock option; subscription right

Aktienbezugsrechtsschein equity warrant

Aktienbörse stock market

Aktienbuch stock register

Aktiendividende stock dividend

Aktienemmissionskurs issue price of a share

Aktienertrag share earnings

Aktienfinanzierung equity financing

Aktienfonds mutual stock fund

Aktiengattung class of stocks

Aktiengesellschaft (*US*) corporation; joint-stock company; (*UK*) public limited company (plc)

Aktiengesetz corporation law

Aktiengewinn share earnings

Aktienhandel stock trading

Aktienhändler stockbroker

Aktieninhaber stockholder; shareholder

Aktienkapital share capital; capital stock; common stock

Aktienkurs stock price

Aktienmarkt stock market; equity market

Aktienrendite earnings per share; yield on stock

Aktiensplit stock split

Aktientausch stock split; exchange of stock

Aktientendenz stock market trend

Aktienumschreibung transfer of shares

Aktienzeichnung subscription of shares

Aktienzertifikat share certificate

Aktienzusammenlegung reverse split

Aktienzuteilung allocation of shares; stock allotment

Aktion action

Aktionär (*US*) stockholder; (*UK*) shareholder

Aktionärsinteressen shareholders' interest

Aktionärsklage derivative suit

Aktionärskreis shareholders' group

Aktionärsversammlung meeting of shareholders; annual general meeting (AGM)

Aktionärsvermögen shareholder value

Aktionsforschung action research

aktiv active

Aktiv-Passivmehrung positive accounting change on both sides of the balance

Aktiv-Passivminderung negative accounting change on both sides of the balance

Aktiva assets

Aktiva und Passiva assets and liabilities

Aktivierung *(Bilanz)* capitalization

Aktivierungspflicht obligation to capitalize

Aktivierungswahlrecht option to capitalize

Aktivität activity

Aktivitätskennzahl activity ratio

Aktivposten asset

Aktivsaldo credit balance

Aktivseite *(Bilanz)* assets

Aktivtausch accounting exchange on the asset side

Aktivwert asset value

Aktualisierung update

Aktualität being up-to-date

aktuell current; topical; up-to-date

Akzelerator accelerator coefficient

Akzeleratorprinzip acceleration principle

Akzept acceptance; accepted bill; bill of exchange

Akzept decken to provide for acceptance

Akzept einlösen to honor a draft

Akzeptant acceptor

Akzeptanz acceptance; acceptability

Akzeptbank acceptance bank

Akzeptfinanzierung acceptance financing

Akzeptkredit acceptance credit

akzeptabel acceptable

akzeptieren to accept; to approve; (*Wechsel*) to honor

allein alone; sole

alleinig sole; exclusive

Alleinimport sole import

Alleinverkauf exclusive sale; sales monopoly

Alleinvertretung sole agency

allgemein general; universal; common

allgemeine Personengesellschaft general partnership

Allgemeine Versicherungsbedingungen general insurance conditions

Allgemeiner indirekter Aufwand overhead expense

Allgemeines Präferenzsystem generalized system of preferences (GSP)

Allgemeines Zoll- und Handelsabkommen General Agreement on Tariffs and Trade (GATT)

allgemeingültig generally accepted

Allgemeinvollmacht general power-of-attorney

Allokation allocation

Allokationsmechanismus allocative mechanism

Allzwecksoftware multipurpose software

Almosen alms; charity

Altanlage existing installation

alteingeführt established

Altengagement existing commitment

Alternativkosten opportunity costs

Altersdiskriminierung age discrimination

Altersdiskriminierung age discrimination

Altersruhegeld retirement pension

Altersstruktur age structure

Altersversorgung retirement benefit

Altersvorsorge retirement provision

amerikanische Option american option

am Geld at the money

Amortisation repayment; pay-off; amortization; (*Anleihe*) redemption

Amortisationsdauer, dynamische discounted payback period rule

Amortisationsrechnung payback period rule

Amortisationsvergleichsrechnung payback method

Amortisationszeit payback period

amortisieren to redeem; to amortize

Amt office

amtlich official

amtliche Verlautbarung official statement

Amtsantritt taking office

Amtsblatt official register

Amtsgericht district court

Amtshandlung official act

Amtsrichter district judge *(US)*; magistrate *(UK)*

Amtssprache official language

Amtsübernahme assumption of office

Amtsweg official channels

Amtszeit term of office

analog analogous

Analogie analogy

Analyse analysis

Analysephase analysis phase

Analyse der Wertschöpfungskette process value analysis

Analysezertifikat certificate of analysis

analysieren to analyze

Analyst analyst

Analytiker analyst

analytisch analytical

analytische Kompetenzen analytical skills

anbahnen to initiate

anbieten to offer; *(als Zahlungsmittel)* to tender; *(Preis)* to quote

Anbieter supplier

Anderkonto trust account; escrow account

ändern to change; to alter; *(revidieren)* to amend

Änderung change; *(Revision)* amendment

Andrang rush

aneignen, sich to appropriate; to acquire

Aneignung appropriation; acquisition

anerkennen to acknowledge; to recognize; *(zugeben)* to admit

Anerkennung acknowledgment; recognition; *(Zugeständnis)* admission

Anfahrt drive

Anfang beginning; start; (*Einführung*) introduction

anfangen to begin; to start; to commence

anfänglich initial

Anfangs- initial

Anfangsbestand beginning inventory

Anfangsbuchstabe initial

Anfangskapital initial capital; *(AG)* capital stock

Anfangskurs (*Börse*) opening price

Anfangsphase initial stage; start-up period

Anfangsproblem start-up problem

Anfangssaldo oppening balance

Anfangszustand original condition

anfechtbar refutable; voidable; subject to appeal

anfechten to contest; to challenge

Anfechtung contestation; challenge; appeal

anfertigen to manufacture; to produce

Anfertigung manufacture; production

Anfertigungskosten manufacturing cost

anfordern to request

Anforderung demand; request; *(Anforderungsschein)* requisition

Anforderungsanalyse analysis of customer needs

Anforderungsprofil job specification; profile of qualification

Anfrage inquiry; request

anfragen to inquire

anführen to head; to lead; *(zitieren)* to quote

Angabe statement; indication; *(Einzelheiten)* data; *(Auskunft)* information

angeben to state; to name; to indicate; *(Quelle)* to cite

Angebot (*Markt*) supply; *(Vorschlag)* proposal; *(Offerte)* offer; tender; *(Kostenvoranschlag)* bid; quotation

angebotene Aktien tendered shares

Angebotsabgabe tendering; bidding; submitting an offer

Angebotsabsprache collusive tendering

Angebotsausschreibung public invitation to tender

Angebotsauswahl choice of bid

Angebotseinholung invitation to tender

Angebotsbedingungen terms of a bid; *(VWL)* supply situation

Angebotselastizität elasticity of supply

Angebotskurve supply curve

Angebotslage supply situation

Angebotsmonopol supplier's monopoly

Angebotspolitik supply-side policy

Angebotspreis bid pricen; offer price

Angebotsprüfung evaluation of bids

Angebotstabelle supply schedule

Angebotsvergleich bid comparison

angefertigt made to order

angehören to belong to

Angehörige/r relative; family member; dependant

Angelegenheit matter; concern; affair

angelernt semiskilled

angemessen just; fair; appropriate; adequate

Angemessenheit adequacy; (*Eignung)* suitability

angeschlossen affiliated

angesehen reputable; prestigious

angespannt tight

angestellt employed

Angestellter employee

angestrebte Mindestverzinsung required rate of return

angewandt applied

angewandte Forschung applied research

angewandte Psychologie applied psychology; practical psychology

angewiesen sein auf to depend on

angleichen to adjust; to align

Angleichung adjustment; alignment

angliedern to incorporate; to affiliate

angrenzen to border

Angst fear

Angstkäufe panic buying

Angstklausel qualified endorsement

anhalten to halt; to stop; *(andauern)* to last

Anhalten stoppage

anhaltend prolonged; sustained; lasting

Anhang (*Vertrag*) appendix; annex; supplement; (*Beilage*) enclosure; rider; (*Bilanz*) notes to the accounts; (*Unterstützer*) followers

anheben *(Preis, Qualität)* to raise; to lift

animierte Bannerwerbung animated banner advertisements

Ankauf acquisition

ankaufen to purchase; to acquire

Ankäufer purchaser; acquirer; buyer

Anklang appeal

Anklang finden to appeal

ankommen to arrive

Ankommen arrival

ankreuzen to check off

ankündigen to announce

Ankündigung announcement

Ankunft arrival

ankurbeln to stimulate; to boost

Anlage *(Investition)* investment; *(Einrichtung)* installation; *(Ausrüstung)* equipment; *(Betrieb)* plant; *(Brief)* enclosure; attachment

Anlagebank investment bank

Anlagebankier investment banker

Anlageberater investment adviser

Anlagebetrag investment capital

Anlagenbewertung asset valuation

Anlagedauer investment period

Anlageentscheidung investment decision

Anlagefinanzierung investment financing

Anlageform type of investment

Anlagegegenstand fixed asset

Anlagegüter capital goods; capital assets

Anlagemittel investment funds

Anlagenbau plant engineering

Anlagenbilanz balance of assets

Anlagenbuchführung asset accounting

Anlagenrechnung asset accounting

Anlagenrendite return on assets; yield on investment

Anlagetipp investment tip

Anlagenumschichtung asset redeployment

Anlagevermögen fixed assets; noncurrent assets

Anlagenverwalter asset manager

Anlagewertsteigerung capital appreciation

Anlageziel investment target; investment objective

Anlass (*Gelegenheit*) occasion; (*Grund*) reason; cause

Anlaufphase start-up phase

anlegen to invest

Anleger investor

Anleihe *(Darlehen)* loan; *(Obligation)* bond

Anleihe einer Gemeinde municipal bond

Anleihe eines Unternehmens corporate bond

Anleihegläubiger bondholder

Anleihekurs bond price

Anleihe mit variabler Verzinsung floating rate bond

Anleihevertrag loan agreement; indenture

Anleihezins coupon

Anliegen request; concern

Anmeldegebühr registration fee

anmelden to declare; to register

Anmeldeschluß cosing date; deadline

Anmeldung registration; filing; declaration

annähernd approximate

Annahme *(Lieferung)* acceptance; receipt; receiving; *(Gesetz)* passing; adoption; *(Vermutung)* assumption; presumption

Annahmepflicht obligation to accept

Annahmeverweigerung refusal of acceptance; rejection; *(Wechsel)* nonacceptance

Annahmeschluß closing date

annehmbar acceptable; admissible

Annehmbarkeit acceptability

annehmen *(Lieferung)* to accept; to receive; *(Gesetz)* to pass; to adopt; *(vermuten)* to assume; to presume

Annonce advertisment; ad; (*Kleinanzeige*) classified ad

annoncieren to advertise

Annuität annuity

Annuitätsanleihe annuity bond; perpetual bond

Annuitätsfaktor annuity factor

Annuitätsmethode annuity method

annullieren to rescind; to cancel

Annullierung cancellation

anonym anonymous

anonymer Test blind test

anordnen *(anweisen)* to order; to direct; *(platzieren)* to arrange; to place

Anordnung *(Anweisung)* order; directive; decree; *(Platzierung)* arrangement; placement; *(Graphik)* layout

anpassen to adapt; to adjust; *(angleichen)* to match; *(Kleidung)* to fit

anpassen, sich to conform; to adapt

Anpassung adjustment; adaptation; accommodation

Anpassungsanreiz adjustment incentive

Anpassungsbarrieren adoption barriers

anpassungsfähig flexible; adaptable

Anpassungsfähigkeit flexibility; adaptability

Anpassungsfortbildung updating one's skills

Anpassungsprozess process of adaptation

Anpassungszeitraum period of adjustment

anpreisen to promote; to plug

anrechenbar chargeable; (*Steuer*) allowable

anrechnen to offset; to allow; to take into account

Anrechnung (*Abzug*) allowance; deduction; (*Belastung*) charge; debit; (*Vorsteuer*) imputation

anrechnungsfähig deductible; allowable

Anrechnungsverfahren tax credit method; (*Körperschaftssteuer*) corporate tax imputation procedure

Anrecht claim; title

Anrede address

anreden to address

anregen to stimulate

anregend stimulating

Anregung stimulation

Anreiz incentive; inducement

Anruf call

anrufen to telephone; to phone; to call

Ansage announcement

ansagen to announce; to introduce; to present

Ansager announcer; presenter

ansammeln *(sammeln)* to collect; *(Vorräte)* to stockpile; to assemble; *(Kapital)* to accumulate

ansammeln, sich (*Zinsen*) to accrue; to pile up

Ansammlung accumulation; *(Zinsen)* accrual

ansässig resident

Ansässiger resident

Ansatz (*Voranschlag*) estimate; valuation; (*Budget*) appropriation; entry; (*Methode*) approach

Ansatzpunkt starting point

anschaffen to procure; to purchase; to acquire

Anschaffung purchase; acquisition

Anschaffungsdarlehen consumer loan

Anschaffungskosten costs of acquisition; historical costs

Anschaffungskostenprinzip cost method

Anschaffungsnebenkosten incidental acquisition cost

Anschaffungspreis initial cost; purchase price

Anschauungsmaterial demonstration material; visual aids

Anscheinsbeweis prima facie evidence

anschlagen (*bewerten*) to value; to assess; (*Plakat*) to post

Anschlagtafel bulletin board; board

anschließen to affiliate; *(sich ~)* to join; to associate with

Anschluss connection; link-up

Anschluss- follow-up

Anschlussfinanzierung follow-up financing

anschreiben to contact; to write to *(Kredit)* to charge up

Anschreiben covering letter

Anschrift address

Ansehen reputation; prestige

ansetzen *(abschätzen)* to estimate; to assess; *(Preis)* to quote; (*Termin*) to schedule

Ansicht point of view; outlook; *(Urteil)* judgment

Ansichtsexemplar inspection copy

Anspielung hint; allusion

Ansporn stimulus; incentive

anspornen to stimulate; to spur

Ansprache speech; address

Anspruch claim; title; demand

Anspruchsabtretung assignment of a claim

Anspruchsberechtigter beneficiary; eligible person

Anspruchsnachweis proof of claim

Anspruchsverzicht waiver of a claim

anspruchsvoll demanding

Anstalt institute; institution

ansteigen to rise; to increase

anstelle von in place of

anstellen to hire; to employ; *(ernennen)* to appoint; *(zur Arbeit heranziehen)* to enlist

Anstellung position; employment; *(Ernennung)* appointment; *(Einstellung)* engagement; hiring

Anstieg rise; hike; increase

Anstoß impulse; impetus

anstrahlen to illuminate; to spotlight

anstrengen, sich to push oneself; to make an effort

Ansturm rush; onslaught; run

Anteil share; portion; *(Prozentsatz)* percentage; *(Beteiligung)* participation; holding; *(Verhältnis)* proportion

anteilig proportionate

Anteilschein stock certificate; share certificate

Anteilseigner stockholder *(US)*; shareholder *(UK)*

anteilsmäßig pro rata

Anteilsquote percentage share

Anthropologie anthropology

Antidumpingzoll anti-dumping tariff

Anti-Dumping-Gesetz anti-dumping law

antizipative Passiva accrued expenses

antizyklisch counter-cyclical; anti-cyclical

Antrag *(Gesuch)* demand; request; application; *(Angebot)* tender; *(Parlament)* motion

Antrag auf Börsenzulassung registration statement

Antrag stellen *(Gesuch)* to apply; *(Parlament)* to file a motion

Antragsfrist application period

Antrieb *(Motivierung)* motivation; impetus; impulse; *(technisch)* propulsion

Antwort response; answer; reply

antworten to respond; to answer; to reply

anvertrauen to entrust; to commit; (*Geheimnis*) to confide

anwachsen to grow; *(Zinsen)* to accrue

Anwalt solicitor; attorney at law; lawyer

Anwaltsanderkonto solicitor's trust account

Anwaltsfirma law office; law firm

Anwaltskosten solicitor's fee; attorney's fee; legal fees

Anwaltsstand bar; legal profession

Anwärter candidate

anweisen *(überweisen)* to transfer; to remit; *(Gebrauchsanweisung)* to instruct; *(anordnen)* to direct

Anweisung order; instruction; *(Geld)* transfer; money order; *(Gebrauchsanweisung)* instruction

anwendbar applicable

Anwendbarkeit applicability

anwenden to apply; to utilize; to implement

Anwender user

Anwendung use; application; utilization

Anwendungsbereich range of application

anwendungsbezogen applied; use-oriented

anwerben to recruit

Anwerber recruiter

Anwerbung recruitment; recruiting

anwesend present

Anwesenheit presence; attendance

Anzahl number; quantity

anzahlen to pay a deposit; to make a down payment

Anzahlung deposit; down payment; advance payment

Anzahlungsgarantie advance payment guarantee

Anzeichen sign; indication

Anzeige *(Ankündigung)* notice; advice; *(Inserat)* advertisement; advert; ad; *(bei Behörde)* report; *(Zahlungsankündigung)* advice

Anzeige aufgeben to place an advertisement; to advertise

Anzeige erstatten to file charges

anzeigen *(ankündigen)* to announce; to give notice; *(inserieren)* to advertise; *(bei Behörde)* to report; *(eine Zahlung ankündigen)* to advise

Anzeigenagentur advertising agency

Anzeigenkampagne advertising campaign

Anzeigentarif advertising rate

Anzeigenteil advertising section

Anzeigentexter copywriter

Anzeigenüberschrift advertising heading

Anzeiger (*Zeitung*) gazette

anziehen to attract

anziehend attractive; appealing

Anziehungskraft attraction; appeal; pull

aperiodisch aperiodic; nonperiodical

Apparat machine; device; apparatus

Apparatur equipment; hardware

Appell appeal

appellieren to appeal

äquivalent equivalent

Äquivalenz equivalence

Äquivalenzziffer weighing figure

Ära era

Arabische Liga League of Arab States (LAS)

Arbeit work; labor; *(Tätigkeit)* activity; job; *(Stellung)* employment; occupation; *(Aufgabe)* task; assignment

arbeiten to work

arbeitendes Unternehmen going concern

Arbeiter worker; employee

Arbeitgeber employer

Arbeitgeber/Arbeitnehmer-Verhältnis labor relations

Arbeitgeberverband employers' association

Arbeitgebervertreter employer's representative

Arbeitnehmer employee

Arbeitnehmermitbestimmung worker participation

Arbeitnehmervertreter im Aufsichtsrat board representatives

Arbeit niederlegen to strike

Arbeitsablauf workflow

Arbeitsamt employment office; Labor Office

Arbeitsanalyse job analysis; work analysis

Arbeitsanfall volume of work

Arbeitsaufwand effort; energy; labor input

Arbeitsausschuss task force

Arbeitsbedingungen working conditions

Arbeitsbelastung workload

Arbeitsbescheinigung certificate of employment

Arbeitsbewertung job evaluation

Arbeitsbewilligung labor permit

Arbeitseifer work enthusiasm

Arbeitseinbindung job involvement

Arbeitseinkommen earned income

Arbeitsentgelt compensation; remuneration

Arbeitsfeld sphere of action

Arbeitsfluss work flow

Arbeitsgang operating sequence; work process

Arbeitsgebiet area of work

Arbeitsgemeinschaft team; working group; *(Schule)* study group

Arbeitsgericht labor court

Arbeitsgruppe work group; task force

Arbeitshaltung attitude to work

arbeitsintensiv labor intensive

Arbeitskampf labor dispute; industrial action

Arbeitskomfort workplace convenience

Arbeitskonflikt labor conflict

Arbeitskosten labor costs

Arbeitskraft worker; manpower

Arbeitskräfte abbauen to shed labor

Arbeitskräfte einsparen to save labor

Arbeitskräfte umgruppieren to redeploy labor

Arbeitskräfte vermitteln to place workers

Arbeitslohn pay; wage

arbeitslos unemployed

Arbeitslose unemployed person

Arbeitslosengeld unemployment compensation; unemployment benefit

Arbeitslosenhilfe unemployment aid

Arbeitslosenquote unemployment rate

Arbeitslosenunterstützung unemployment aid

Arbeitslosenzahl unemployment figure

Arbeitslosigkeit unemployment

Arbeitsmarkt labor market; job market

Arbeitsmarktlage job market situation

Arbeitsmarkttheorie labor market theory

Arbeitsmobilität labor mobility

Arbeitsniederlegung strike; work stoppage; walkout

Arbeiterorganisation labor organization

Arbeitspause break

Arbeitspensum workload

Arbeitsplan work plan; work shedule

Arbeitsplanung work sheduling; human resource planning

Arbeitsplatz job; post; position; workplace

Arbeitsplatzanalyse job analysis

Arbeitsplatzaufteilung job sharing

Arbeitsplatzbeschreibung job description

Arbeitsplatzgarantie job security; (*öffentlicher Dienst*) security of tenure

Arbeitsplatzrotation job rotation

Arbeitsplatzverlust job loss; loss of a job

Arbeitspolitik labor policy

Arbeitsproben work sampling

Arbeitsrecht labor law

Arbeitsrichter labor judge

Arbeitsrichtlinie work standard; work rule

arbeitsscheu unwilling to work

Arbeitsspezialisierung work specialization

Arbeitsstab task force

Arbeitsstätte workplace

Arbeitsstelle position; job

Arbeitstag workday; working day

Arbeitstagung workshop; business meeting

Arbeitsteam work team

Arbeitstechnik working technique

Arbeitsteilung division of labor

Arbeitsuchender job applicant

Arbeitsumfeld work environment

arbeitsunfähig disabled; (*temporär*) unable to work; unfit to work

Arbeitsunfähigkeit disability; (*temporär*) inability to work

Arbeitsunfall occupational accident; accident on the job

Arbeitsverhältnis employment; (*Vertrag*) contract of employment

Arbeitsvermittlung employment agency

Arbeitsvertrag contract of employment; labor contract

Arbeitsvorgang operation; work process

Arbeitswert value of labor

arbeitswillig willing to work

Arbeitszeit working time; working hours

Arbeitszeitgestaltung organisation of working time

Arbeitszeugnis certificate of employment; (*Empfehlung*) reference

Arbeitszufriedenheit job satisfaction

Arbitrage arbitrage; arbitration

Arbitragegeschäft arbitrage transaction; arbitrage business

Arbitragehändler arbitrager; cross trader

Arbitrage-Pricing-Theorie Arbitrage-Pricing-Theory

Arbitrageschuldverschreibung arbitrage bond

Arbitration arbitration

arglistig malicious; fraudulent

arglistige Täuschung malicious fraud

Argument argument; point; reasoning

arithmetischer Durchschnitt arithmetic mean

arm poor

Armut poverty

arrangieren to arrange

Artikel article; product; item; *(Presse)* article; story

Artikel de täglichen Bedarfs convenience goods

Artikelgruppe product line

Artikulierung tone of voice; articulation

Arzneimittel drug; medicine; (*verschreibungspflichtig*) ethical drug; (*nicht verschreibungspflichtig*) over-the-counter drug; OTC drug

ärztliche Untersuchung medical examination

ärztliches Attest medical certificate; bill of health

Aspekt aspect

Assekurant underwriter

Assessment-Center assessment center

Assistent assistant

assoziieren to associate; *(Organisation)* to enter into a partnership

Assoziierung association

Assoziierungsabkommen treaty of association

Attributionstheorie attribution theory

aufbauen to build; to construct, (*Maschine*) to assemble

Aufbau organization; set-up; structure; (*Montage*) construction; assembly

Aufbaudokumentation documentation of organizational structure

Aufbaugestaltung design of organizational structure

Aufbauorganisation organizational structure

Aufbauskizze layout

aufbereiten to prepare; to process

Aufbereitung processing

aufbewahren to store; to keep safe

Aufbewahrung storage, safekeeping

Aufbewahrungsfrist safekeeping period

Aufbewahrungsschein storage check

aufeinander folgend consecutive

auferlegen to impose

Auferlegung imposition

Auffächerung diversification

auffallend striking; noticeable

auffangen *(abmildern)* to cushion; *(Kosten)* to absorb

Auffassung outlook; opinion; perception

auffordern to request

Aufforderung request

auffrischen to revitalize

Aufgabe duty; task; job; function; *(Arbeitszuweisung)* assignment; *(Verantwortung)* responsibility; *(Amt)* office; *(Freigabe)* release; *(Preisgabe)* abandonment; pullout; *(Absendung)* dispatch

Aufgabenanalyse job analysis

Aufgabendelegation job delegation

Aufgabenerfüllung task fulfillment

Aufgabengebiet area of responsibility; job description

Aufgabengruppe task force

Aufgabenkonflikt task conflict

Aufgabenorientierung initiating structure

Aufgabenstellung assignment of tasks; job definition

Aufgabenverteilung assignment of tasks

Aufgabenwahrnehmung exercise of functions

aufgeben to assign; *(absenden)* to dispatch; to mail; *(Brief)* to post; *(Anzeige);* to insert; to place *(preisgeben)* to relinquish; to abandon; *(aufhören)* to quit; *(Amt aufgeben)* to resign

aufgelaufene Abschreibungen accumulated depreciation

aufgelaufene Dividende accumulated dividend; dividend in arrears

aufgelaufene Zinsen accrued interest

Aufgeld premium; surcharge

aufgerundet in rounded figures

aufgeschobene Rente deferred annuity

aufgeschobene Zahlung deferred payment; (*Bilanz*) deferred liability

aufgliedern to subdivide; *(Konten)* to classify; *(Kosten)* to break down

Aufgliederung; analysis; itemization; subdivision; *(Konten)* classification; *(Kosten)* breakdown

aufhalten to hold up; to retard *(zurückhalten)* to detain

aufhalten, sich to stay; to remain

aufheben (*Entscheidung*) to cancel; to rescind; to annul; *(Kontrollen)* to lift; to deregulate; to remove; *(Vollmacht)* to revoke; *(Sitzung)* to adjourn; to close; *(aufbewahren)* to keep; *(Gesetz)* to repeal

Aufhebung *(Entscheidung)* cancellation; invalidation; annulment; *(Kontrollen)* lifting; deregulation; removal; abolishment; *(Vollmacht)* revocation; *(Sitzung)* adjournment; closing *(Gesetz)* repeal

Aufhebung der Devisenkontrollen lifting of currency controls

Aufhebung eines Haftbefehls revocation of a warrant of arrest

Aufhebung eines Vertrages cancellation of a contract

Aufhebungsvertrag agreement to revoke a debt

aufhören to stop; to quit; to discontinue; to cease

aufkaufen to buy up

aufkommen to arise; *(bezahlen)* to pay for; to compensate for

aufladen to load; to charge

Auflage *(Buch)* edition; *(Zeitung)* circulation; *(Anweisung)* direction; *(Belastung)* charge

Auflagenhöhe circulation; circulation figure

auflagenschwach low-circulation

auflagenstark high-circulation

Auflagenstruktur circulation breakdown

auflaufen to accumulate; *(Zinsen)* to accrue

Auflaufen accumulation; *(Zinsen)* accrual

auflegen *(Buch)* to publish; *(Anleihe)* to float

Auflegung *(Anleihe)* flotation

auflisten to list

auflösen to dissolve; *(Firma)* to liquidate; *(Vertrag)* to cancel

Auflösung dissolution; *(Firma)* liquidation; *(Vertrag)* cancellation

Auflösung eines Kontos closing of an account

aufmachen to open; (*Zeitung*) to lead in with

Aufmacher lead story; front-page story

Aufmachung styling; design; appearance

Aufmaß measurement

Aufmaßliste list of measurement

aufmerksam attentive

Aufmerksamkeit attention

Aufmerksamkeitsspanne attention span

Aufmerksamkeitswert attention value

Aufnahme reception; *(Zulassung)* admission; acceptance; *(Herberge)* accommodation; *(Eintragung)* entry; inclusion; *(Kapital)* raising; borrowing; *(einer Tätigkeit)* assumption; *(Photo)* snapshot; *(Ton, Bild)* recording; shooting

Aufnahmeapparat recorder

Aufnahmeleiter floor manager; studio manager

Aufnahmeplan shooting shedule

Aufnahmestaat host country

aufnehmen to receive; *(zulassen)* to admit; to accept; *(beherbergen)* to accommodate; *(eintragen)* to enter; to include; *(Kapital)* to raise; to borrow; *(eine Tätigkeit)* to assume; *(Ton, Bild)* to record

Aufprall impact

Aufpreis surcharge

aufrechnen to balance; to settle

aufrechterhalten to maintain

Aufrechterhaltung upkeep; maintenance

Aufriss layout

Aufruhr disturbance

aufschieben to postpone; to defer

Aufschlag *(Preis)* additional charge; markup; *(Prämie)* premium

Aufschlagskalkulation markup pricing

aufschlüsseln to break down

Aufschlüsselung break down

aufschreiben to note; to write down

Aufschub postponement; deferral

Aufschub gewähren to allow extra time

Aufschwung upswing; boom; upturn; recovery

Aufseher supervisor; controller; superintendent

Aufsicht control; supervision

Aufsichtsamt regulatory agency

Aufsicht führend supervising; supervisory

Aufsichtsführung supervision

Aufsichtsrat board of directors; supervisory board

Aufsichtsratmitglied member of the supervisory board; board member

Aufsichtsratsmandat board of directors' seat

Aufsichtsratssitzung board of directors' meeting; supervisory board meeting

Aufsichtsratvorsitzender chairman (chairwoman, chairperson) of the board; chairman of the supervisory board

aufsteigen to rise; to advance

Aufsteiger upward climber;

aufstellen *(Bilanz)* to prepare; *(Maschine)* to assemble; to install; *(Bauten)* to erect

Aufstellung *(Bilanz)* preparation; *(Maschine)* installation; assembly; *(Liste)* list; statement

Aufstieg rise; advancement

Aufstiegsmöglichkeit opportunity for advancement; career opportunity; upward mobility

aufstocken to stockpile; *(Kapital)* to increase

Aufstockung stockpiling; *(Kapital)* increase

Auftauen unfreezing

aufteilen to split; to section; to segment; to parcel out; to divide

Aufteilung split; distribution; division

Auftrag assignment; job; charge; *(Bestellung)* order; *(Ernennung)* appointment

auftragen to charge with; *(Essen)* to serve

Auftraggeber *(Besteller)* customer; principal; client; *(Werbung)* sponsor

Auftragsabwicklung filling a contract; processing an order

Auftragsannahme order taking

Auftragsbearbeitung order processing

Auftragsbestand orders on hand

Auftragseingang incoming orders; receipt of orders

Auftragsfertigung made-to-order production; contract manufacturing

Auftragsflut surge in orders

Auftragsplanung job order planning

Auftragspolster order backlog

Auftragsüberhang order backlog

Auftragsüberwachung order control; supervision of orders

Auftragsvergabe commissioning; contract placing; *(öffentlich)* public procurement

Auftragsvolumen volume of orders; contract volume

Auftragswert value of goods ordered

Aufwand *(Ausgabe)* expenditure; expense; *(Luxus)* luxury

Aufwand, außerordentlicher non-recurring charge; extraordinary expense

Aufwand, betriebsfremder other expenses; non-operating expenditure

Aufwandsentschädigung allowance for special expenditure; fringe benefits

Aufwandskonto expense account

Aufwands- und Ertragsrechnung income statement

Aufwärtsbewegung upturn

Aufwärtsentwicklung upward movement

aufwenden to spend; to expend

aufwendig expensive

Aufwendungen expenditures; expenses

aufwerten *(Währung)* to revalue

Aufwertung *(Währung)* revaluation

aufzählen to enumerate; to list

aufzeichnen (*aufschreiben*) to note down; to write down; (*protokollieren*) to record; (*skizzieren*) to outline; to sketch; (*zeichnen*) to draw; (*Tonband, Video*) to record; to tape

Aufzeichnung note; sketch; (*Video*) record; recording

aufzinsen to compound; to accumulate

Aufzinsung compounding; accumulation

Augenwischerei eyewash

Augenzeuge eye-witness

Auktion auction

Auktionator auctioneer

Auktionsgebühr auction fee

Auktionsmarkt auction market

Ausbau *(Entwicklung)* development; *(Ausdehnung)* expansion

ausbedingen to stipulate

ausbessern to repair

Ausbesserung repair

Ausbesserungswerk repair center

ausbeuten to exploit

Ausbeutung exploitation

ausbilden to train; to educate

Ausbilder trainer

Ausbildung education; training

Ausbildungsabschluss graduation

Ausbildungsleiter training officer

ausbringen to produce

Ausbringung output; production

Ausbringungsmenge output

ausdehnen *(ausbreiten)* to spread; *(erweitern)* to expand; *(verlängern)* to extend

Ausdehnung *(Ausbreitung)* spread; *(Wachstum)* growth; *(Erweiterung)* expansion; *(Verlängerung)* extension

aus dem Geld out of the money

Ausdruck *(Wort)* phrase; expression; *(Druck)* printout

ausdrücken to phrase; to express

ausdrücklich specific; explicit; express

Auseinandersetzung dispute; argument

Auseinandersetzungsbilanz dissolution balance sheet

Ausfall *(Fehlbetrag)* deficit; *(Maschine)* breakdown

Ausfallbürgschaft indemnity bond; deficiency guaranty

ausfallen *(Veranstaltung)* to be cancelled; *(Maschine)* to break down; (*Zahlungen*) to fail; *(Ergebnis)* to turn out

Ausfallrisiko default risk

Ausfallquote failure rates

Ausfallzeit down time

Ausfuhr export; exportation

Ausfuhrabgaben export duty; export levy

Ausfuhragent export agent

Ausfuhranmeldung export notification

Ausfuhrantrag export application

Ausfuhrauftrag export order

Ausfuhrdeckung export cover

ausführbar workable; realizable; feasible

Ausführbarkeit feasibility

Ausfuhrbeschränkung export restriction

Ausfuhrbürgschaft export guarantee

Ausfuhreinnahmen export receipts

ausführen *(exportieren)* to export; *(Bestellung)* to fill; to complete; *(durchführen)* to carry out; to implement; to execute; *(erklären)* to state

Ausführer exporter

Ausfuhrerklärung export declaration

Ausfuhrerstattung export refund

Ausfuhrertrag export earnings

Ausfuhrerzeugnis export product

Ausfuhrfinanzierung export financing

Ausfuhrförderung export promotion

Ausfuhrgarantie export guarantee

Ausfuhrgenehmigung export license

Ausfuhrkontingent export quota

Ausfuhrkredit export credit

Ausfuhrland exporting country

ausführlich detailed

Ausfuhrsperre embargo

Ausfuhrsubvention export subsidy

Ausfuhrüberschuss export surplus

Ausführung *(Durchführung)* execution; implementation; *(Erklärung)* statement

Ausführung eines Auftrags execution of an order

Ausführungsanzeige confirmation of execution

Ausführungstag implementation date

Ausfuhrverbot export ban

Ausfuhrvertrag export contract

Ausfuhrvolumen export volume

Ausfuhrwert export value

Ausfuhrzoll export duty; external tariff

Ausfuhrzollstelle customs office

Ausfuhrzuwachs export growth

ausfüllen *(Formular)* to fill out; to complete

Ausfüllung *(Formular)* completion

Ausgabe *(Kosten)* expense; expenditure; *(Emission)* issue; issuance; *(Buch)* edition; *(Zeitung)* issue

Ausgabekurs issue price

Ausgabenposten expense item

Ausgabepreis issue price; offering price

Ausgabeverhalten spending behavior

Ausgabezeitpunkt date of issue

Ausgangsforderung initial demand

Ausgangsposition starting position

Ausgangspunkt starting point

Ausgangsseite starting page; exit page

ausgeben *(Geld)* to spend; to expend; *(in Umlauf bringen)* to issue; to circulate

ausgebildet trained

ausgedehnt extensive; broad

ausgegangen out of sorts

ausgehandelter Preis negotiated price

ausgegebene Aktien shares outstanding

ausgegebenes Kapital issued capital stock

ausgeglichenes Budget balanced budget

ausgehende E-Mail outbound e-mail

ausgemacht stipulated

ausgeprägt distinctive

ausgeschriebener Preis bid price

ausgesucht selected; choice

ausgewählt selected

ausgewogen balanced

ausgewogenes Portfolio balanced portfolio

Ausgleich balancing; *(Bezahlung)* payment; *(Entschädigung)* compensation; *(Konto)* settlement

ausgleichen to balance; to equalize; *(entschädigen)* to compensate; *(berichtigen)* to adjust; *(Zoll)* to countervail; *(Konto)* to settle

ausgleichend compensatory; *(Zoll)* countervailing

Ausgleichsabgabe compensatory tariff

Ausgleichsbuchung adjusting entry

Ausgleichsdividende equalizing dividend

Ausgleichsforderungen equalization claim

Ausgleichslager buffer stock

Ausgleichsposten balancing item; *(Buchhaltung)* deferred item

ausgliedern divest; break up; to outsource

Ausgliederung divestment; breakup; demerger

Ausgliederung von Betriebsfunktionen outsourcing

aushandeln to negotiate

aushändigen to deliver

Aushängeschild signboard; store sign

Auskommen livelihood

Auskunft information

Auslage *(Kosten)* expense; outlay; disbursement; *(Schaufenster)* display

Ausland foreign country

Ausländer foreigner

ausländisch foreign; external

Auslands- foreign

Auslandsanleihe foreign bond

Auslandshandelskammer chamber of foreign trade

Auslandsinvestition foreign investment; investment abroad

Auslandskunde foreign customer; overseas buyer

Auslandsschulden external debts

Auslandsüberweisung foreign currency remittance

Auslandswechsel foreign bill of exchange

Auslandswerte foreign securities

auslassen to omit

auslasten to use to capacity

Auslastung capacity utilization; operating grade

Auslastungsgrad level of capacity

auslaufen lassen to phase out

ausleihen to lend; to loan

Ausleiher lender

Auslieferer distributor; supplier

ausliefern to deliver; to supply

Auslieferung delivery

Auslieferungslager warehouse

auslöschen to obliterate

Ausmaß measure; dimension

Ausnahme exception; exclusion; (*Befreiung*) exemption

Ausnahmefall exceptional case

Ausnahmeregelung exemption

ausnutzen to utilize fully; *(ausbeuten)* to exploit

Ausnutzung utilization; *(Ausbeutung)* exploitation

Ausnutzungsgrad load factor; utilization level

ausreichen to suffice

ausreichend adequate; ample; sufficient

Ausreise outward voyage; exit

ausrufen *(Namen über Lautsprecher)* to page; to call out

ausruhen, sich to rest; to relax

ausrüsten to outfit; to equip

Ausrüster outfitter

Ausrüstung equipment; outfit

Ausrüstungsgut equipment goods

Aussage statement; (*Gericht*) evidence; testimony; *(Werbung)* message

aussagen to state; to declare; *(Zeuge)* to testify

ausschalten *(beseitigen)* to eliminate; *(Licht)* to turn off

Ausschaltung elimination

ausscheiden *(Amt)* to leave; to retire

ausschlaggebend pivotal

ausschlachten to exploit

Ausschlachtung von Unternehmen asset stripping

ausschließen to exclude; to bar

ausschließlich exclusive

Ausschließung exclusion

Ausschluss exclusion; disqualification; expulsion

ausschreiben to invite tenders; to put out to tender; (*Position*) to invite applications for

Ausschreibung tender; bid invitation; *(Stelle)* advertisement; *(Bekanntmachung)* announcement

Ausschreibung einer Emission competitive bidding

Ausschreibungsfrist deadline for tenders

Ausschreibungsunterlagen tender documents; specifications

Ausschreibungsverfahren tendering procedure; bidding process

Ausschuss panel; board; commission; committee; *(Produktion)* rejects

Ausschussware rejects; damaged goods

ausschütten *(Gewinn)* to distribute; *(Dividende)* to declare

Ausschüttung distribution; payout of dividends

Ausschüttungskennzahl payout ratio

Ausschüttungsquote payout ratio

Außendienst field service; *(Verkauf)* sales force

Außendienstleiter field service manager; sales force manager

Außenfinanzierung external financing; outside financing

Außenhandel foreign trade; external trade

Außenhandelsabteilung foreign trade department

Außenhandelsbank foreign trade bank

Außenhandelsbilanz balance of trade

Außenhandelsbürgschaft foreign trade guarantee; export guarantee

Außenhandelsdefizit trade deficit

Außenhandelsgesellschaft export trading company

Außenhandelskammer chamber of foreign trade

Außenhandelskredit foreign trade credit

Außenhandelsrisiko foreign trade risk

Außenhandelsüberschuss trade surplus

Außenpolitik foreign policy

Außenhandelsquote trade ratio

Außenhandelsstatistik foreign trade statistics

Außenseiter newcomer; outsider

Außenstelle branch; field office

Außenerbung outdoor advertising

Außenwert external value

Außenwirtschaft foreign trade

Außenwirtschaftsgesetz foreign trade law

Außenwirtschaftsrecht foreign trade legislation

Außenwirtschaftsverordnung foreign trade order

Außenzolltarif common external tariff

außergerichtlicher Vergleich out-of-court settlement

außerbörslicher Markt für Wertpapiere over-the-counter (OTC) market

außergewöhnlicher Verlust extraordinary loss

außerordentliche Aufwendungen *(Bilanz)* extraordinary expenses

außerordentliche Erträge extraordinary gain

äußerlich external

Aussenstände *(Bilanz)* accounts receivable

aussetzen to suspend; to defer; (*Maschine*) to fail

Aussetzung suspension; withholding; *(Preis)* offer

Aussetzung der Notierung suspended trading

Aussetzungsbeschluss suspension order

aussperren to lock out

Aussperrung lockout

Ausstand strike; walkout

ausstatten to equip; to outfit; *(mit Kapital)* to endow

Ausstattung equipment; outfit; *(mit Kapital)* endowment

ausstehend receivable; outstanding

ausstellen *(Scheck, Dokument)* to issue; *(Wechsel)* to draw; *(Waren)* to display; *(zur Schau stellen)* to exhibit

Aussteller *(Emittent)* issuer; *(von Waren)* exhibitor

Ausstellung *(Emission)* issuance; issue; *(Zurschaustellung)* exhibit; exhibition; *(Messe)* fair

Ausstellungsstück exhibit

Ausstoß run; output

aussuchen to select; to pick

Austausch exchange

austauschbar exchangeable

Austauschbarkeit exchangeability

Austauschbeziehung trade-off

austauschen to exchange

Austauschrelationen terms of trade

Austauschtheorie leader-member exchange (LMX) theory

Austauschverhältnis terms of trade

ausüben to practice; to exercise

Ausübender practitioner

Ausübungspreis exercise/strike price

Ausverkauf sale; sellout

Auswahl selection; choice; *(Sortiment)* assortment; range

auswählen to select; to pick; to choose

Auswahlverfahren selection process

auswärtig foreign; external

ausweichen to avoid

Ausweis pass; identification card; identification badge

ausweisen *(deportieren)* to deport; *(in Bilanz)* to report

ausweisen, sich to identify oneself

ausweiten to enlarge; to expand

Ausweitung expansion; extension

auswerten to utilize; *(Daten)* to evaluate

Auswertung utilization; *(Daten)* evaluation

auswirken, sich to have an effect; to result in

Auswirkung impact; effect; consequence

auszahlen to pay out; to disburse

Auszahlung payout; disbursement

Auszahlungsfloat disbursement float

auszeichnen *(markieren)* to mark; to distinguish

Auszeichnungssprache markup language

Auszubildender trainee; apprentice

Auszug *(Konto)* statement; extract; excerpt

Autokorrelation autocorrelation

Automat *(Verkaufsautomat)* vending machine

Automatisierung automation

autonome Arbeitsteams self-managed work teams

Autonomie autonomy

Autoresponder autoresponder

Autorität authority

Aval guaranty; surety

Avalkredit credit by way of guarantee; guaranteed credit

Avantgarde vanguard

Aversion aversion

Avis notification

avisieren to notify; to inform

Axiom axiom

Azubi (Auszubildende/r) trainee; apprentice

B

Bahn railroad; railway *(UK)*

bahnbrechend pioneering

Bahnbrecher pioneer

Bahnfracht rail freight

Bahnfrachtbrief railroad bill of lading

Bahnsteig platform

Baisse slump; drop; bear market

Baissier bear

Balanced Scorecard balanced scorecard

Ballen bale

Ballon balloon

Ballonzahlung balloon payment

Ballungsgebiet urban center; overcrowded area

Balkendiagramm bar chart

Band *(Schreibmaschine)* ribbon; *(Bandgerät)* tape; *(Verbindung)* tie; bond; *(Buch)* volume

Bandbreite spread; width; scope; (*Übertragung*) bandwidth

Bandenwerbung advertising in sports fields; perimeter advertising

Banderole package band

Bank bank

Bankaktien bank stocks

Bankaktivität banking activity

Bankakzept banker's acceptance

Bankangestellter cashier; clerk; teller

Bankanlage banking investment

Bankaufsicht bank supervision

Bankauszug statement of account; statement

Bankautomation bank automation

Bankbeamter bank officer

Bankberater bank advisor

Bankbürgschaft bank guaranty

Bankdienstleistung banking service

Bankenausschuss banking committee

Bankenkonsortium banking syndicate; bank group

Bankenkundschaft bank customers; bank clientele

Bankenliquidität bank liquidity

Bankensystem banking system

Bankentochter bank affiliate; bank subsidiary

Bankfachwissen banking expertise

bankfähig bankable; negotiable

Bankführungskraft bank executive; bank manager

Bank für Internationalen Zahlungsausgleich Bank for International Settlements (BIS)

Bankgeschäfte machen to bank

Bankgesellschaft banking corporation

Bankgewerbe banking business

Bankhaus banking house

Bankier banker

Bankkonto bank account; checking account

Bankkredit bank credit; loan

Bankkunde bank customer

Bankleistung banking service; banking performance

Bankleiter bank manager

Bankleitung bank management

Bankleitzahl bank code number; sorting code; bank identification number

bankmäßig bankable; negotiable

Bankmitarbeiter bank employee

Banknote bank note; bill

Bankplatz banking center

Bankpolitik banking policy

Bankregel banking rule

Bankrott bankruptcy; failure

bankrott gehen to go bankrupt; to fail

Bankschalter cashier´s desk; teller's window

Bankschalterbeamter cashier; clerk; teller

Bankscheck cashier's check

Bankspesen bank service charges

Banktätigkeit banking activity

Banküberziehungskredit overdraft; bank overdraft

Bankverbindung correspondent bank

Bankvermögen bank assets

Bankwesen banking

Bankzinsen interest on deposits; interest on bank bans

Bankzweigstelle bank branch

Bannerwerbung banner advertisement

bar cash

Bar-Akkreditiv clean credit

bar abzüglich Rabatt cash less discount

Barausschüttung cash distribution; cash dividend

Bardepot cash deposit

Bardividende cash dividend

Bareinnahmen cash earnings

Barerstattung cash refund

Bargeld cash

Bargeldautomat cash dispenser; automatic teller machine

Bargeldbeitrag cash contribution; cash dues

bargeldlos paid by check; without ready money; noncash

Bargeldversorgung supply of cash

Bargeschäft cash transaction

Barkredit cash credit

Barliquidität cash liquidity; cash ratio

Barlohn cash wage; money compensation

Barmittel cash

Barprämie cash bonus

Barpreis cash price

Barrabatt cash discount

Barren bar; *(Gold)* bullion

Barrendite cash yield

Barreserve money reserve; *(Bank)* minimum cash reserve

Barriere barrier

Barscheck open check; cashier's check

Barter barter

Bartergeschäft barter transaction

Barvergütung cash refund

Barverkauf cash sales

Barwert present value

Barwertfaktor present value factor

Barzahlung cash payment

Barzahlungsangebot cash offer

Barzahlungsrabatt cash discount

Barzahlungsverfahren cash-based payment system

Basis base; basis

Basisbotschaft basic message

Basisdaten basic data

Basisjahr base year

Basiskalkulation standardized cost estimate

Basisobjekt underlying asset

Basispreis base price; strike price

Basispreis einer Kaufoption call price

Basispunkt basis point

Basiswährung base currency; reference currency

Basiswert base value

Bau construction

Bauelement unit; component

bauen to construct; to build

Bauer farmer

Baufinanzierung construction financing; construction loan

Baufirma construction company

Baugelder building funds; construction loan

Baugeldkonditionen terms for construction loan

Baugenehmigung planning permission; building permit

Baugesellschaft construction company

Baugewerbe construction business; construction trade

Bauherr builder-owner; house builder

Bauindustrie construction industry; construction trade

Baumarkt do-it-yourself store (DIY)

Baumdiagramm tree diagram

Bauplatz building site

Bausparen home purchase savings

Bausparkasse home savings and loan association

Bauunternehmer developer

Bauwirtschaft construction industry

Bayes Regel Baye´s theorem

beabsichtigen to intend

Beachtung notice; attention

Beamte, **Beamtin** officer; official; civil servant

Beamtenbesoldung civil service pay

beanspruchen to claim; *(fordern)* to demand; *(belasten)* to stress

beanstanden to find fault with; *(beklagen)* to complain about; *(Widerspruch erheben)* to object

Beanstandung *(Widerspruch)* objection; *(Beklagen)* complaint

beantragen to apply for; *(erbitten)* to request

beantworten to respond; to answer

bearbeiten to process; to handle; *(Land)* to cultivate

Bearbeiter person in charge

Bearbeitung handling; processing; *(Vorbereitung)* preparation; *(Land)* cultivation

Bearbeitungsgebühr handling charge; processing fee; service fee

beaufsichtigen to supervise

Beaufsichtigung supervision; surveillance

beauftragen *(bevollmächtigen)* to authorize; to commission; *(anweisen)* to instruct; to order

Beauftragter trustee; *(Bevollmächtigter)* attorney; authorized person; commissioner; *(Vertreter)* agent

Bedarf need; demand

Bedarfsanalyse demand analysis; analysis of needs

Bedarfsartikel convenience good

Bedarfsauslösung creation of demand

Bedarfsbefriedigung satisfaction of demand

Bedarfsdeckungswirtschaft subsistence economy

Bedarfselastizität demand elasticity

Bedarfsermittlung determination of demand

bedarfsgerecht tailored to suit a market need

Bedarfsgüter staple goods; basic commodities

Bedarfsmengenplanung materials requirements planning; materials budgeting

Bedarfsplanung demand planning

Bedarfszunahme demand growth

Bedarfszuwachs increased demand

bedeuten to mean; to imply

bedeutend *(wichtig)* important; *(hervorragend)* prominent; major

bedeutsam meaningful

Bedeutung importance; significance; *(Sinn)* meaning; *(einer Person)* prominence

bedeutungslos meaningless

bedienen *(Maschinen)* to run; to operate; *(dienen)* to attend to; to serve

Bedienung *(Maschinen)* operation; *(Dienstleistung)* service; (*Verkäufer*) sales clerk

Bedienungsanleitung operating instructions; instruction sheet; service manual

Bedienungsperson operator

bedingt conditional; limited

bedingter Anspruch contingent claim

Bedingtheit conditionality

Bedingung stipulation; *(Voraussetzung)* requirement; condition

Bedingungen, allgemeine standard terms and conditions

bedrängen to pressure

Bedrängnis hardship

bedürfen to need

Bedürfnis requirement; need

Bedürfnis nach Leistung need for achievement

Bedürfnis nach Macht need for power

Bedürfnis nach Zugehörigkeit need for affiliation

Bedürfnishierarchie hierarchy of needs

Bedürfnisprüfung needs test

Bedürfnispyramide pyramid of needs

Bedürfnissegment need segment

bedürftig needy; poor

beeilen, sich to hurry; to rush

beeinflussbar susceptible; manipulable; capable of being influenced

beeinflussbare Kosten controllable costs

beeinflussen to influence; to affect; to impair

Beeinflusser influencer

Beeinflussung influence; manipulation

beeinträchtigen to impair; (*schaden)* to damage

Beeinträchtigung impairment; *(Schaden)* damage

beenden to end; to terminate; to stop; to close; (*vollenden*) to finish; to complete

Beendigung ending; termination; *(Vollendung)* completion

befähigen to qualify; to enable

befähigt fit; qualified

Befähigung qualification; competence

Befähigungsnachweis certificate of professional competence; evidence of formal qualification

befangen biased; prejudiced

Befehl order; command

befehlen to command; to order

befinden to find; to rule; to decree

befinden, sich to feel

Befinden state of health; condition

befolgen to observe; to follow; to comply with

Befolgung observance; compliance

befördern *(Karriere)* to promote; *(transportieren)* to ship; to transport; to forward; to dispatch; to carry

Beförderung *(Karriere)* promotion; advancement; *(Transport)* forwarding; shipment; transport

Beförderungsart mode of transport

Beförderungskosten transportation costs; freight charges

Beförderungsmittel means of transport

Beförderungsunternehmen carrier; transportation company

befrachten to freight; to load

Befrachter charterer; freighter; shipper

Befrachtung freightage, affreightment

befragen to interview; to question; to interrogate; *(Meinungsforschung)* to survey; to canvass

Befrager interviewer

Befragter respondent; interviewee

Befragung interview; survey; poll

Befragungsmethode interview technique

befreien to liberate; to free; to exempt

befreit free; exempt

Befreiung exemption; release; liberation

Befreiung von Abgaben exemption from duties and taxes

Befreiungsanspruch right of exemption

Befreiungsklausel exemption clause; escape clause

befriedigen to satisfy; to settle

Befriedigung satisfaction; settlement

befristen to set a time limit; to set a deadline

befristeter Vertrag fixed-term contract

Befugnis *(Vollmacht)* power; authority; authorization; *(Fähigkeit)* competence

befürworten to recommend; to advocate

Befürworter advocate; supporter

Befürwortung recommendation; endorsement

Begabung talent; gift; aptitude

Begabungstest aptitude test

begabt talented; gifted; able

begebbar negotiable

Begebung *(Wertpapiere)* flotation; issue

Begebungskosten flotation cost

begegnen to meet; to encounter

Beginn start; onset; beginning

beginnen to start; to begin; to commence

beglaubigen *(bestätigen)* to verify; *(bescheinigen)* to certify; *(bezeugen)* to attest

beglaubigte Kopie certified copy

Beglaubigung *(Bestätigung)* verification; *(Bescheinigung)* certificate

Beglaubigungsschreiben certificate; credentials

begleichen to settle

Begleichung settlement

begleiten to accompany

Begleitpapiere shipping documents

Begleitung company; (*Musik*) accompaniment

begrenzen to limit; to restrict

begrenzte Rationalität bounded rationality

Begrenzung limitation; restriction

Begriff term; concept

Begriffsmodell conceptual model

begründen *(Behauptung)* to substantiate; to justify

Begründung *(Beweisführung)* argumentation; justification

begünstigen to benefit; to favor; *(fördern)* to promote

Begünstigter beneficiary

Begünstigung favoritism; *(Gläubiger)* preferential treatment; *(Steuer)* privilege

begutachten *(Versicherung)* to survey; to appraise

Begutachtung expert opinion; appraisal

Behälter container

behandeln to treat; to deal with; *(handhaben)* to handle

Behandlung treatment; *(Handhabung)* handling

beharren to persist

beharrlich persistent

behaupten to claim; to contend; to assert

behaupten, sich to hold one's own; to assert oneself

Behauptung claim; contention; assertion

beherbergen to shelter; to accommodate

beherrschen to rule; to control; *(Markt)* to dominate; *(Fähigkeit)* to master

beherrschend dominant; controlling

Beherrschung control; *(Markt)* domination; *(Fähigkeit)* mastery

Beherrschungsvertrag control contract; contract of domination

behilflich helpful; instrumental

behindern to obstruct; to impede

Behinderung obstruction; obstacle; *(Beschränkung)* restraint; *(körperlich)* disability

Behörde government agency; authority

Behördenauftrag government order

Behördenweg official channel

behutsam cautious

beifügen *(Brief)* to enclose; to attach

Beihilfe benefit; assistance

Beilage *(Zeitung)* supplement; insert; *(Brief)* attachment; enclosure

beiläufig incidental

beilegen *(Brief)* to enclose; *(Zeitung)* to insert; *(Streit)* to settle

Beilegung settlement; reconciliation

Beirat advisory board

Beispiel example

Beispielsfall precedent; model case

Beistand assistance; helo

Beitrag contribution; *(Mitgliedsbeitrag)* dues; (*Versicherungsbeitrag)* premium

beitragen to contribute

Beitragsbemessung rating; contribution assessment

Beitragsbemessungsgrenze rating limit; income threshold

beitragsfreie Pensionskasse noncontributory pension plan

Beitragsleistender contributor

beitreten to join

bejahen to affirm; to support

Bekanntgabe (*Benachrichtigung*) notice; *(Ankündigung)* announcement; *(Aufdeckung)* disclosure

bekannt geben *(benachrichtigen)* to notify; *(ankündigen)* to announce; *(aufdecken)* to disclose

Bekanntheitsgrad degree of popularity; awareness level; level of familiarity

Bekanntheitstest awareness test

bekannt machen to introduce; *(ankündigen)* to announce

bekommen to receive; to get; to obtain

bekräftigen to affirm; to confirm

beladen to load

Belange interests; issues; concerns

belasten *(beladen)* to load; *(auferlegen)* to encumber; to burden; *(Konto belasten)* to charge; to debit

belastbar resilient; able to work under pressure; (*Hypothek*) mortgageable

Belastung handicap; *(Auferlegung);* burden; *(Konto)* charge; debit

Belastungen, außergewöhnliche extraordinary expenses

belaufen, sich to amount to

beleben to stimulate; to encourage

Belebung *(Konjunktur)* stimulation; recovery

Beleg *(Beweis)* proof; evidence; *(Buchhaltung)* voucher; *(Akte)* record; *(Urkunde)* certificate

belegen *(beweisen)* to prove; to vouch; *(Vorlesung)* to register for; *(Sitzplatz)* to reserve

belegen mit *(Steuern)* to impose

belegloser Zahlungsverkehr electronic funds transfer

Belegprinzip voucher principle

Belegschaft workforce; staff; personnel

Belegschaftsabbau personnel cutback; employee layoff

Belegschaftsfluktuation staff fluctuation; personnel mobility

Belegschaftsstärke staff level

Belegschaftsversammlung staff meeting

Belegung occupancy; booking; reservation

Belegungszeit occupied time

belehrend educational

beleihbar eligible as collateral; acceptable as collateral

beleihen to lend on; *(Grundstück)* to mortgage; to hypothecate

Beleihungsgrenze lending limit; ceiling

Beleihungswert loan value; collateral value

beliebig optional; discretionary

beliebt popular

Beliebtheit popularity

beliefern to supply

belohnen to reward; *(bezahlen)* to remunerate

Belohnung reward; *(Bezahlung)* remuneration

Belohnungssystem reward system

bemängeln to find fault with

bemerkbar noticeable

bemerken *(erkennen)* to notice; to spot; *(sagen)* to remark; to note

Bemerkung remark; comment

Bemerkung machen to comment

bemessen to rate; to assess; to measure

Bemessung rating; assessment

Bemsessungsgrundlage assessment base

Bemessungsverhältnis assessment ratio

bemühen, sich to exert oneself; to make an effort

Bemühung effort

bemustern to provide samples

Bemusterung provision of samples

benachrichtigen to notify; to inform; to advise

Benachrichtigung notification; information; communication; *(Bankanzeige)* advice

Benchmarking benchmarking

Benehmen behavior

benennen to name; to entitle

benötigen to require

Benutzer user

Benutzerfreundlichkeit user friendliness

Benutzergruppe user group

Benutzerhandbuch user´s guide; manual

Benutzungsrecht license

Benutzungssteuer user tax

Benzin gasoline

beobachten to observe; to monitor; to watch

Beobachter observer

Beobachtereffekt observer effect

beobachtete Häufigkeit observed frequency

Beobachtung observance; observation

Beobachtungsfehler observation bias

Beobachtungsgenauigkeit observation accuracy

Beobachtungsliste watch list

Beobachtungszeitraum observation period

Bequemlichkeit convenience; comfort

beraten *(Rat geben)* to counsel; to advise

beraten, sich to deliberate

beratend advisory

Berater adviser; *(für das Geschäft)* consultant; *(Recht)* counsel; counselor

Berater in der Organisationsentwicklung change agents

Berater in Verhandlungen consultant

Beratergruppe advisory group

Beratung consultation; *(Besprechung)* meeting; deliberation

Beratungs- advisory

Beratungsfirma consulting agency

Beratungsgremium advisory board

berauben to rob; to deprive

Beraubung deprivation

berechenbar calculable

berechnen *(anrechnen)* to charge; to bill; *(ausrechnen)* to calculate; to compute; *(abschätzen)* to estimate

Berechnung *(Belastung)* charge; *(Ausrechnung)* computation; calculation; *(Preisfeststellung)* pricing

Berechnungsmethode method of computation; *(Preise)* pricing method

berechtigen to qualify; to entitle

berechtigt eligible; able

Berechtigung *(Vollmacht)* power; authority; *(Rechtfertigung)* justification; *(Befähigung)* eligibility; qualification; *(Rechtsanspruch)* claim

Bereich area; sector; region

Bereichsleiter area manager, division manager

Bereicherung enrichment

bereinigen *(Statistik)* to adjust; *(Rechnung)* to settle; *(Bilanz)* to verify

bereinigt adusted

bereithalten to keep ready

Bereitschaft readiness; preparedness; *(in Bereitschaft)* on call

Bereitschaftserklärung letter of intent

Bereitschaftsklausel letter of preparedness

bereitstellen to furnish; to provide; to supply

Bereitstellung provision; supply; *(Geld)* appropriation

Bereitstellungsgebühr procurement fee; provision fee

Bereitstellungsplanung supply planning; procurement budgeting

Bergbau mining

Bergbauunternehmen mining company

bergen to retrieve; to recover

Bergleute miners

Bergungswert salvage value

Bergwerk mine

Bericht report; (*Rechenschaft*) account

Bericht, analytischer analytical review

berichten to report

Berichterstatter reporter; correspondent

Berichterstattung coverage; news coverage; reporting

berichtigen *(verbessern)* to correct; *(Buchung)* to adjust

berichtigtes Bruttoeinkommen adjusted gross income

Berichtigung correction; adjustment

Berichtigung am Jahresende *(Bilanz)* year-and-adjustment

Berichtigungsaktie stock dividend

Berichtigungsbuchung adjusted trial balance

Berichtsjahr reporting year; year under report

berichtspflichtig reportable; subject to report

Berichtswesen reporting

berücksichtigen to consider; to allow for

Berücksichtigung consideration

Beruf profession; occupation; job

beruflich professional; occupational; *(Handwerk)* vocational

Berufsabschluss training qualification

Berufsausbildung professional education; vocational training

Berufsbezeichnung job title

Berufschance career opportunity

Berufserfahrung work experience

Berufsleben working life; professional life

Berufsmöglichkeiten job opportunities

Berufsplanung career planning

Berufspraxis relevant professional experience

Berufsschule vocational school; trade school

berufstätig gainfully employed; working

Berufsverband professional association; trade association

Berufsvertretung professional representation; trade representation

Berufung *(Ernennung)* appointment; *(Rechtsmittel)* appeal; (*Mission*) vocation; calling

Berufung einlegen to appeal against a judgment

beschaffen to procure; to purchase; to buy; *(anschaffen)* to provide; to supply; *(Geld)* to raise

Beschaffenheit nature; condition

Beschaffer buyer; purchaser

Beschaffung buying; purchasing; procurement; *(Kauf)* acquisition

Beschaffungsabteilung purchasing department

Beschaffungsengpass supply bottleneck

Beschaffungskosten acquisition costs

Beschaffungsmarkt supply market; procurement market

Beschaffungsmenge order size; purchasing volume

Beschaffungsmenge, optimale optimal order size; optimal purchasing volume

Beschaffungspreis purchase price

Beschaffungsprogrammpolitik purchasing program policy

Beschaffungsprozess buying process

Beschaffungsverhalten buyer behavior

Beschaffungswesen procurement; purchasing

beschäftigen *(Angestellte)* to employ

beschäftigen, sich to occupy oneself with; to concern oneself with

beschäftigt occupied; busy

Beschäftigtenzahl number of persons employed

Beschäftigung *(Arbeit)* work; *(Beruf)* occupation; job; *(Anstellung)* employment

Beschäftigung *(Kostenrechnung)* activity level

Beschäftigungsaussichten employment prospects; employment outlook

Beschäftigungsabweichung activity level variance

Beschäftigungsgrad level of employment; *(Industrie)* operating rate

beschäftigungsintensiv labor-intensive

Beschäftigungskrise unemployment crisis

Beschäftigungslage employment situation

Beschäftigungsnachweis employment record

Beschäftigungsverhältnis employment relationship

Beschäftigungszeit period of employment

Bescheid order; verdict; ruling

bescheinigen to attest; to certify

Bescheinigung certificate; certification; written confirmation

beschichten to cover; to coat

Beschichtung cover; coating

beschildern to label

Beschlagnahme confiscation; seizure

beschlagnahmen to confiscate

beschleunigen to accelerate

Beschleunigerprinzip accelerator principle

beschleunigte Abschreibung accelerated depreciation; Accelerated Cost Recovery System

beschleunigtes Wirtschaftwachstum accelerated growth

Beschleunigung acceleration

beschließen to decide; *(Gericht)* to decree; *(Parlament)* to pass a resolution

Beschluss resolution; ruling

Beschlussfassung resolution

beschneiden to trim; to cut back

beschränken to restrain; *(einengen auf)* to restrict; to confine; to limit

beschränkte Haftung limited liability

Beschränkung restraint; *(Einengung)* restriction; limitation

beschreiben to describe

Beschreibung description

Beschwerde complaint

Beschwerdeabteilung complaints department

beschweren, sich to complain

beseitigen to eliminate; to remove; to abolish

Beseitigung removal; elimination

besetzen to occupy; *(Stelle)* to staff; to fill

besichern collateralize

besichtigen to view; *(inspizieren)* to inspect

Besichtigung inspection; *(Grundstück)* survey; *(Tourist)* sightseeing

Besitz possession; ownership; *(Eigentum)* property; *(Wertpapiere)* holding; *(Reichtum)* wealth

Besitz, ungerechtfertigter adverse possession

besitzen to possess; *(als Eigentum)* to own; *(Wertpapiere)* to hold

Besitzeinkommen unearned income

Besitzer possessor; *(Eigentümer)* owner; proprietor; *(Wohnung)* occupant; *(Wertpapiere)* holder

Besitzrecht title; right of ownership

Besitzstand vested rights

Besitzstandswahrung non-impairment of vested rights

Besitzübergang change of possession

Besoldung remuneration; salary

Besonderheit specialty; peculiarity; special feature

besorgen to provide; to supply; *(Haushalt)* to manage; *(kaufen)* to buy

Besorgnis concern; anxiety

besorgniserregend alarming

besprechen to discuss

Besprechung meeting; conference; discussion; *(Buch)* review

besser gestellt well off

bessern, sich to improve

Besserung *(Konjunktur)* upturn; improvement

Bestand (*Vorrat*) supply; holding; *(Inventar)* inventory

Bestände inventory

beständig stable; permanent

Beständigkeit stability

Bestandsaufnahme stocktaking; inventory-taking; appraisal

Bestandsarten types of inventory

Bestandsbewertung stock valuation; inventory valuation

Bestandsdaten inventory data

Bestandsgewinn inventory profit

Bestandsfehlmenge stock shortage; inventory shortage

Bestandsführung inventory management

Bestandsgröße size of stock

Bestandskonto inventory account, asset account

Bestandskontrolle inventory control

Bestandskosten carrying costs

Bestandsumschlagshäufigkeit inventory turnover rate

Bestandsveränderung change in inventory; inventory change

Bestandteil part; component; ingredient

bestätigen to verify; to confirm; to attest; *(einen Brief)* to acknowledge

bestätigter Scheck certified check

Bestätigung verification; *(Urkunde)* certificate; *(eines Briefes)* acknowledgement; authentication

Bestätigungsvermerk des Abschlußprüfers *(Bilanz)* auditor's report; auditor's opinion

beste Alternative zu einer Verhandlungslösung best alternative to a negotiated settlement (BATNA)

bestechen to bribe

bestechlich corrupt

Bestechlichkeit corruption

Bestechung corruption; bribery; graft

Bestechungsgeld bribe; bribe money; secret commission; graft; kickback

Bestellabwicklung order handling

Bestellbuch order book

Bestelleingang incoming orders; orders received

bestellen to order; (*buchen*) to reserve; *(Nachricht)* to give a message

Bestellerkredit buyer's credit

Bestellformular order form

Bestellgutschein voucher; order coupon

Bestellmenge order size; quantity ordered

Bestellmenge, optimale economic order quantity

Bestellnummer order number

Bestellpunkt order point

Bestellschein order form

Bestellung order; *(Buchung)* reservation; *(Nachricht)* message

Bestellwert order value; contract value

Bestellzettel order coupon; order slip

besteuern to tax; to assess

Besteuerung taxation; assessment

besteuerungsfähig taxable; assessable

bestimmbar determinable

bestimmen *(anordnen)* to direct; *(entscheiden)* to determine; *(ernennen)* to appoint; *(vorsehen)* to designate; to earmark; *(zuweisen)* to assign; *(identifizieren)* to identify

Bestimmungsland country of destination

bestimmt specific; definite; *(vorgesehen)* destined; *(sicher)* certain

Bestimmtheit determination

Bestimmung *(Ziel)* destination; *(Vertrag)* stipulation; clause; provision; *(Entscheidung)* determination; *(Vorschrift)* directive; *(Verordnung)* regulation

Bestimmungshafen port of destination

Bestimmungsort destination; place of destination

bestrafen punish; penalize

Bestrafung punishment; penalty

bestreiken to strike against

bestreiten to deny; to dispute; to contest; to argue; *(die Kosten)* to pay for

Bestwert optimum

Besuch attendance; visit

besuchen to attend; to visit

Besucher attendant; visitor; auditor

Besucherzahl attendance

Besuchsbericht call report

Besuchsplanung call sheduling; preapproach

Beta beta

Beta-Faktor beta coefficient

Beta-Funktion beta function

beteiligen, sich to participate; to share in

Beteiligter participant

Beteiligtsein involvement

Beteiligung participation; (*Finanzen*) investment; equity holding

Beteiligung abgeben to sell off an interest

Beteiligung haben to hold a stake

Beteiligungsfinanzierung equity financing

Beteiligungsgesellschaft investment company

Beteiligungsunternehmen holding company; joint venture; partly owned subsidiary

Beteiligungskapital equity capital

beteuern to assert; to affirm

Beteuerung assertion; affirmation

betonen to stress; to emphasize

Betonung emphasis; stress

betrachten to view

Betrachter viewer

Betrachtungswinkel viewing agle; angle

beträchtlich considerable

Betrag amount; figure; sum

Betrag abbuchen to debit an amount

Betrag bereitstellen to allocate an amount

Betrag hinterlegen to deposit an amount

Betrag überweisen to remit an amount

betragen to amount to; to add up to

betragen, sich to behave

betreffen to pertain to; to concern; to be related to

betreffend concerning; regarding

betreffs re.; referring to; concerning

betreiben (*Geschäft*) to operate; to conduct

Betreiber operator

Betreuung care; looking after

Betrieb *(Unternehmen)* business; firm; company; (*Werk*) plant; *(Fabrik)* factory; *(Vorgang)* operation;

betrieblich operational; operating; managerial

betriebliche Aufwendungen operating expenses

betriebliche Fortbildung on the job training

betriebliche Mitbestimmung codetermination

betrieblicher Ertrag operating revenue

betriebliches Umfeld external environment; business environment

betriebsam busy; active

Betriebsamkeit activity

Betriebsablaufplanung operation sequencing

Betriebsabrechnungsbogen operation sheet; cost allocation sheet; cost distribution summary

Betriebsanlage (*Fabrik*) factory; *(Werk)* plant; industrial installation

Betriebsanleitung operating instructions; (*Fabrik*) shop rules

Betriebsaufgabe closure; closing down; termination of a business

Betriebsaufwand operating costs; operating expenses

Betriebsausfall breakdown

Betriebsausgaben operating expenditure

Betriebsausrüstung plant equipment

Betriebsausstattung plant equipment

Betriebsberater management consultant

Betriebsbesichtigung plant visit; factory tour

Betriebsbuchhalter cost accountant

Betriebsbuchhaltung internal cost accounting; operational accounting

Betriebseinnahmen operating receipts; revenues

Betriebsergebnis operating income; operating result; operating profit; company earnings

betriebsfähig operational; operative

Betriebsferien plant holidays; vacation close-down

Betreibsform type of business

betriebsfremd outside

betriebsfremder Erfolg nonoperating income

Betriebsführer managing director, plant manager

Betriebsführung operational management; plant management

Betriebsgeheimnis trade secret

Betriebsgemeinkosten operating overheads

Betriebsgewinn working profit; operating income; earned surplus

Betriebsgewinnmarge trading profit margin

betriebsintern internal

Betriebskapital working capital; operating capital

Betriebsklima working atmosphere

Betriebskonto business account; trading account

Betriebskosten operating costs; operating expenses

Betriebsleiter plant manager, production manager; chief operating officer (COO)

Betriebsleitung plant management

Betriebsmittel operating resources; *(Bilanz)* working capital

betriebsnotwendiges Kapital capital employed

betriebsnotwendiges Vermögen operating assets

Betriebsprüfung external audit; outside audit of the accounts

Betriebsrat workers' council

Betriebsräte work councils

Betriebsreingewinn net gain from operations

Betriebsrente company pension

Betriebsstätte business premises; plant; manufacturing facility; place of business

Betriebsvereinbarung company agreement; labor-management contract

Betriebsverlust operating loss; trading loss

Betriebsvermögen business property

Betriebsvorschrift plant regulations; operating instructions; *(Eisenbahn)* service regulations

Betriebswirt graduate in business administration

Betriebswirtschaft business administration; business management

Betrug fraud; deceit; deception; rip-off

betrügen to defraud; to cheat; to deceive

betrügerisch fraudulent; deceitful; dishonest

betrügerisches Einverständnis collusion

beunruhigen to worry; to disturb

Beunruhigung concern; alarm

beurkunden to document; to certify

Beurkundung authentication; certification; verification

beurlauben to grant leave; *(Beamter)* to suspend

beurteilen to judge; to rate; to assess; to evaluate

Beurteilung judgement; evaluation; assessment;

Beurteilung von Angestellten employee appraisal

Beurteilung der Kreditwürdigkeit credit assessment; credit rating

Beurteilungsbogen rating sheet

Beurteilungsgespräch appraisal interview

Beurteilungsmaßstab criterion; yardstick

Beurteilungsverfahren assessment procedure

bevölkern to populate

Bevölkerung population

Bevölkerungsschicht population stratum

bevölkerungsstatistisch demographic

Bevölkerungswachstum population growth

bevollmächtigen to authorize; *(ermächtigen)* to empower

Bevollmächtigter authorized person; *(Treuhänder)* trustee; *(Vertreter)* representative; agent

Bevollmächtigung authorization; delegation of authority; *(Ermächtigung)* empowerment

bevorrechtigt preferential; preferred

bevorrechtigte Forderung preferred claim

bevorrechtigter Gläubiger preferred creditor; secured creditor

bevorzugen to prefer; *(begünstigen)* to privilege; to favor

bevorzugt preferred; preferential

bevorzugte Plazierung premium position

Bevorzugung preference; preferential treatment; positive discrimination

bewahren to preserve

Bewahrung preservation

bewährt proven; successful; well-tried

Bewährung (*Strafe*) suspended sentence

bewältigen *(eine Aufgabe)* to accomplish; *(eine Schwierigkeit)* to master; to cope with

Bewältigung *(Erledigung)* handling; *(einer Schwierigkeit)* coping with

bewandert skilled

bewegen to induce

Beweggrund motive

beweglich mobile; flexible

Beweglichkeit mobility; flexibility

Bewegungsbilanz statement of application of funds; statement of changes in financial position

Bewegungsfreiheit freedom of movement; leeway; mobility

Beweis evidence; proof; *(Zeichen)* token; *(Beweisführung)* demonstration

beweisen to prove; to demonstrate

beweiskräftig conclusive

Beweislast burden of proof

Beweismittel proof; evidence

Beweisstück document; exhibit

bewerben *(Produkt)* to advertise

bewerben, sich (*um Stelle*) to apply for; (*um Auftrag)* to tender; to bid for; *(um einen Preis)* to compete for; *(um Stimmen)* to solicit

Bewerber applicant; *(Auftrag)* bidder; *(Preis)* competitor

Bewerberauswahl shortlisting; applicant selection

Bewerberzahl number of applicants

Bewerbung application; candidature; *(Auftrag)* bid for tender

Bewerbungsformular application form

Bewerbungsfrist (*Ausschreibung*) tender period

Bewerbungsschluss deadline; closing date

Bewerbungsschreiben letter of application

Bewerbungsunterlagen application papers

Bewerbungsverfahren application procedure

bewertbar assessable; appraisable

bewerten to evaluate; to appraise; to assess

Bewertung evaluation; assessment; *(Schätzung)* appraisal; estimate

Bewertung der Aktiva valuation of assets

Bewertung der Rücklagen valuation of reserves

Bewertung des Anlagevermögens fixed-asset valuation

Bewertung des Umlaufvermögens liquid asset valuation

Bewertung des Vorratsvermögens inventory valuation

Bewertung einer Leistung performance rating

Bewertung eines Betriebs going-concern valuation

Bewertung von Forderungen valuation of claims

Bewertung von Verbindlichkeiten valuation of liabilities

Bewertung von Wertpapieren share rating

Bewertungsvorschriften (*Bilanz*) valuation rules; (*Steuer*) assessment principles

Bewertungsdurchschnitt weighted average

Bewertungsgrundsätze valuation principles

Bewertungsmodell für risikobehaftete Wertpapiere capital asset pricing model (CAPM)

Bewertungsrechte appraisal rights

Bewertungsverfahren valuation method

Bewertung zum Widerbeschaffungspreis valuation at replacement cost

bewilligen to grant; *(erlauben)* to allow; *(genehmigen)* to approve; *(Mittel im Parlament)* to appropriate

Bewilligung granting; *(Erlaubnis)* permission; *(Genehmigung)* approval; consent; *(Geldmittel im Parlament)* appropriation

bewirken to effect; to cause

bewohnen to occupy

Bewohner (*Land*) inhabitant; *(Haus)* occupant

bewußt deliberate

bezahlen to pay

Bezahlung pay; payment

Bezahlung gegen offene Rechnung payment on open account

bezeugen to attest

beziehen *(Aktien)* to subscribe; *(Geld)* to draw; *(Waren)* to obtain; to buy

beziehen auf, sich to refer to

Bezieher purchaser; buyer; *(Zeitung)* subscriber

Beziehung relation; relationship; contact

Beziehungskonflikt relationship conflict

beziehungsweise respectively

beziffern to number

Bezirk sector; district

Bezirksgericht district court

Bezirksleiter district manager

Bezogener drawee; payer

Bezug *(im Brief)* reference; *(Einkauf)* purchase; *(Gehalt)* drawing of

Bezüge earnings; income; *(Gehalt)* salary; pay

Bezugnahme reference

Bezugsberechtigter beneficiary

Bezugsgröße reference figure

Bezugsgrößenkalkulation product costing with activity units

Bezugsgruppen reference groups

Bezugsoption call option

Bezugspreis (*Abonnement*) subscription price

Bezugsquelle source of supply; resource

Bezugsrecht buying option; purchase warrant

Bezugsrecht ausüben to exercise an option

Bezugsrechtsangebot rights offer

Bezugsschein *(Aktien)* subscription warrant; stock allotment; *(Auftrag)* delivery order; *(Berechtigungsschein)* scrip; *(Materialien)* requisition slip; *(Waren)* purchasing order

Bezugsverhältnis subscription ratio

Bezugszahl reference number

Bezuschussung subsidization

bieten to bid; to offer

Bieter bidder

Bieterliste list of bidders

Bietungsgarantie tender guarantee

Bilanz balance sheet; financial statement; statement of financial condition

Bilanz ziehen to draw a balance; to balance

Bilanzabschluss financial statement

Bilanzanalyse balance sheet analysis

Bilanzaufstellung preparation of the balance sheet

Bilanzbetrug accounting fraud

Bilanzbewertung appraisal

Bilanzbuchhalter accountant

Bilanzdaten financial statement data

Bilanzgewinn balance sheet profit; net earnings; declared profit

Bilanzgliederung balance sheet layout

bilanzielle Überschuldung accounting insolvency

bilanzieren to draw up the balance sheet; to prepare a balance sheet; to report

Bilanzierung balancing of accounts; drawing up a balance sheet

Bilanzierung langfristiger Beteiligungen equity method of accounting

Bilanzierungserfordernisse accounting requirements

Bilanzierungsgrundsätze accounting principles

Bilanzierungsperiode accounting period

Bilanzierungsregeln accounting policies

Bilanzjahr financial year

Bilanzkennzahl accounting ratio

Bilanzklarheit transparency of financial statement

bilanzmäßig as shown on the balance sheet

bilanzneutrale Finanzierung off balance sheet financing

Bilanzpolitik accounting policy

Bilanzposten balance sheet item

Bilanzprüfer auditor; certified accountant; comptroller

Bilanzprüfung audit; checking of accounts

Bilanzrichtlinien accounting rules

Bilanzsaldo capital balance

Bilanzskandal accounting scandal

Bilanzstichtag financial statement date

Bilanzsumme balance sheet total

Bilanztheorie accounting theory

Bilanzvergleich comparison of balance sheets

Bilanzverlust net loss

Bilanzwert balance sheet value; book value

bilateral bilateral

Bild picture; image

bilden to form; to educate

Bildfolge sequence

Bildschirm monitor; screen; visual display unit (VDU)

Bildschirmtext Teletext

Bildung education; learning; (*Kapital*) accumulation; formation

Bildungsangebot learning opportunity

Bildungsbereich area of education

Bildungsinstitution institution of learning

Bildungswesen field of education

Bildungszentrum center of learning

Billett ticket

billig cheap; low-priced; inexpensive; *(angemessen)* reasonable

billig abstoßen to dump

Billiganbieter discounter

billigen to approve; to sanction

Billighändler discount merchant

Billigkonkurrent low-price competitor

Billigpreis low price

Billigtarif bargain rate

Billigung sanction; approval

binnen- within; (*Land*) domestic

binnen (*Frist*) within

Binnenbedarf domestic demand

Binnengrenze internal frontier

Binnenhandel domestic commerce; domestic trade

Binnenkonjunktur domestic economic activity; internal economic trend

Binnenland inland; interior

binnenländisch internal; domestic

Binnenmarkt home market; domestic market; *(Europäische Union)* unified market; single market

Binnennachfrage domestic demand

Binnenschifffahrt inland navigation

Binnenwirtschaft domestic economy

Binnenzoll internal tariff

Binominalverteilung binominal distribution

biographische Merkmale biographical characteristics

Bitte request; demand

bitten to request; to ask

Bittschrift petition

Black-Scholes-Formel zur Call-Bewertung Black-and- Scholes call-pricing equation

blanko blank; (*Kredit*) unsecured

Blankogeschäft uncovered transaction

Blankoindossament blank endorsement

Blankokredit blank credit; unsecured credit; *(unbegrenzter Kredit)* unlimited credit

Blankoquittung blank receipt

Blankoscheck blank check; counter check

Blankounterschrift blank signature

Blankovollmacht blank power of attorney

Blankowechsel blank bill

Blaupause blueprint

Blickfang eye-catcher

Blockdiagramm block diagram

bloßstellen to expose; to compromise

blühen to thrive; to flourish

Bodenreform land reform

Bodenrente ground rent

Bodenschätze natural resources

Bon voucher; cash register receipt

Bonität solvency; credit rating; credit standing

Bord-Empfangsschein mate's receipt

Bord-Konnossement bill of lading

borgen to borrow

Börse exchange; *(Wertpapiere)* stock exchange; *(Waren)* commodity exchange; *(Portemonnaie)* purse

Börsenaufsicht stock exchange supervision

Börsenauftrag stock exchange order

Börseneinführung public offering; listing on the stock exchange

börsenfähige Wertpapiere marketable securities

Börsenfähigkeit negotiability

Börsenkapitalisierung market capitalization

Börsenkennzahlen stock exchange ratios

börsengängig listed on the stock exchange

Börsengeschäft stock market transaction

Börsenhandel stock exchange trading

Börsenhändler stock trader

Börsenindex stock index

Börsenkommissionsgeschäft stock broking

Börsenkrach stock market crash

Börsenkurs stock exchange quotation; share price

Börsenmakler stockbroker; floor broker

börsennotiertes Wertpapier listed security

Börsennotierung stock quotation; stock exchange quotation

Börsenparkett trading floor

Börsenumsatz stock market turnover; volume of stocks traded

Börsenumsatzsteuer stock transfer tax

Bote messenger

Botschaft message

Botschafter ambassador

Boykott boycott

Branche industry; line of business

Branchenanalyse industry analysis

Branchenkenner industry expert

Branchenschlüssel classification of industry

Branchensprecher industry spokesman, -person, -woman

Branchenrabatt trade discount

branchenüblich customary within an industry

Brauch usage; observance

brauchbar useful; practical

Brauchbarkeit usefulness; utility

brauchen to require; to need

Break-Even-Analyse break-even analysis

brechen *(Regeln)* to violate; to break

breit broad

Breitbandtechnologie broadband technology

Brief letter

Briefkurs offer price; asked price

Briefmarke stamp

Briefpartner correspondent

Brieftasche wallet

Briefträger postman; mailman; letter carrier

Briefverkehr correspondence

Briefwechsel correspondence; exchange of letters

Broker broker; agent

Brokerhaus brokerage house

Broschüre pamphlet; brochure

Bruch breach; violation; *(Trennung)* severance; *(Waren)* breakage

Bruchteil fraction

Brücke bridge

brutto gross

Bruttoabsatz gross sales

Bruttobetriebsergebnis gross operating result

Bruttobetriebsgewinn gross trading profit

Bruttoeinkommen gross income

Bruttogewinn gross profit

Bruttogewinnspanne gross profit margin

Bruttohandelsspanne gross margin

Bruttoinlandsprodukt (BIP) gross domestic product (GDP)

Bruttoinlandsproduktion gross domestic production

Bruttoinvestitionen gross investment; gross capital formation

Bruttomarge gross margin

Bruttomenge gross quantity

Bruttosozialprodukt (BSP) gross national product (GNP)

Bruttoumsatz gross sales; raw sales

Bruttoverbuchung gross accounting procedure

Bruttoverdienstspanne gross profit; gross income margin

Bruttoverkaufspreis gross selling price

Bruttoverzinsung gross-interest return

Bruttowarenumsatz gross sales

Bruttowertschöpfung gross value added

Bruttozins gross interest

Buch book; *(Hauptbuch)* ledger

buchen *(reservieren)* to reserve; *(Konto)* to post; *(Eintragung)* to record

Buchführung accountancy; accounting; bookkeeping

Buchführung, doppelte double-entry bookkeeping

Buchführung, kameralistische governmental accounting; institutional accounting

Buchführung, ordnungsgemäße sound accounting practice

Buchführung, periodengerechte accounting on an accrual basis

Buchführungsgrundsatz accounting principle

Buchführungspflicht mandatory accounting

Buchführungsrichtlinien accounting rules; accounting principles

Buchhalter accountant

Buchhalter, geprüfter (*US*) certified public accountant; (*UK*) chartered accountant

Buchhaltung bookkeeping; accounting

Buchkredit book credit

Buchprüfer auditor; accountant

Buchprüfung auditing; checking of accounts

Buchung entry; *(Reservierung)* reservation

Buchung, debitorische debit-side entry

Buchung, durchlaufende transit entry

Buchungsposten bookkeeping entry

Buchungstag date of bookkeeping entry

Buchwert book value; asset value; depreciated cost

Buchwert pro Aktie book value per share

Budget budget

Budget aufstellen to prepare a budget

Budget ausgleichen to balance a budget

Budget einhalten to keep to the budget

Budget genehmigen to approve a budget

Budgetbeschränkung budget limitation; budget reduction

Budgetierung budgeting

Budgetkontrolle budgetary control

Budgetposten budgetary item

Budgetüberschreitung budget overrun; overspending

Budgetziel budget target

Bund union; alliance; federation

Bundes- federal

bundesstaatlich federal

Bündnis alliance

Bürde burden; liability

Bürge guarantor

bürgen to guarantee

Bürger citizen; resident (*Staatsbürger*) national

bürgerlich civil; civic; (*Klasse*) middle class

bürgerliches Recht civil law

Bürgerrechte civil rights

Bürgschaft pledge; guarantee; *(finanziell)* bond; security

Büro- clerical

Büro office

Büroangestellter office worker; white-collar worker

Büroarbeiten paperwork; clerical work

Büroautomation office automation

Bürobeschäftigter clerical worker

Bürobetrieb office routine

Bürochef chief clerk; office manager

Büroeinrichtung office equipment

Büroelektronik office electronics

Büroindustrie office industry

Bürokrat bureaucrat

Bürokratie bureaucracy

bürokratisch bureaucratic

Büroleiter chief clerk, office manager

Büromaschine office machine

Büromesse office equipment trade fair

Büroraum office space

Büroschreibmaschine office typewriter

Büroschreibtisch office desk

Bürotechnik office technology

C

Call Center call center

Carnet international customs pass; carnet

Cash-Flow cash flow

Cashflow nach Zinsen und Steuern cash flow after interest and taxes

Cashflow aus laufender Geschäftstätigkeit operating cash flow

Cash-Flow Return on Investment cash-flow return on investment (CFROI)

Cashflow-Verlauf cash flow time line

Cash-Flow, abgezinster discounted cash flow

ceteris paribus other things being equal

Chance opportunity; chance

Chancengleichheit equal opportunities

Charakter character; personality

charakteristische Wertpapierlinie characteristic line

Charge charge; batch

Chargenfertigung batch manufacturing

charakterisieren to characterize; to distinguish

Charakterisierung characterization

charakteristisch distinctive; characteristic

charismatische Führung charismatic leadership

Charterflug charter flight

chartern to charter

Chartervertrag charter agreement

Checkliste check list

Chef head; boss; chief executive

Chefetage executive suite

Chefredakteur editor-in-chief

Chefsekretärin personal assistant

Chefverkäufer senior sales manager

Chiffrierschlüssel code

Chiffrierung encryption

Chiffrierung mit öffentlichem Schlüssel *(Internet)* public-key encryption

Chipkarte smart card

C-Kurve C curve

Clearing clearing

Clearingabkommen clearing agreement

Clearingbank clearing bank

Clearingkonto clearing account

Clique clique

Cluster cluster

Clusteranalyse cluster analysis

Code code

Computerausdruck computer printout

Computerbildschirm computer screen

Computerdaten computer data

Computerfirma computer company

computergesteuert computer-controlled

Computerprogramm computer program

Computertastatur computer keyboard

Computertechnologie computer technology

Computerverfahren computer operation

conditio sine qua non absolute condition

Containerbahnhof container terminal

Containerdepot container yard

Containerladestelle container freight station

Containerumschlag container handling

Containerverkehr container traffic

Controller controller

Controlling controlling

Controlling-Kalender controlling year planner

Coupon coupon

Couponbogen coupon sheet

Couponsteuer coupon tax

Courtage brokerage; commission

Cross-Rate cross rate

Curriculum curriculum

Cyber-Intermediäre cybermediaries

D

Dachfonds fund of funds

Dachgesellschaft holding company; umbrella company

Dachmarke umbrella brand; family brand

Dachverband umbrella organisation

Damnum debt discount; (*Bank*) discount

dämpfen to damp; to slow down; to curb

dargestellte Emotionen displayed emotions

darlegen to state; to explain

Darlehen loan; credit; grant

Darlehen, bares cash loan

Darlehen, befristetes time loan

Darlehen, besichertes collateralized loan

Darlehen, kündbares callable loan

Darlehen, unverzinsliches interest-free loan

Darlehen aufnehmen to raise a loan; to take up a loan

Darlehen beantragen to apply for a loan

Darlehen geben to grant a loan; to lend

Darlehen kündigen to recall a loan

Darlehen tilgen to redeem a loan; to pay back a loan

Darlehensbestand loan portfolio

Darlehensgewährung granting of a loan; lending

Darlehenskasse loan association

Darlehenslaufzeit loan term

Darlehensprogramm loan program

Darlehensschuld loan payable; loan debt

Darlehensvertrag loan agreement; loan contract

Darlehenszinsen lending rate; interest on loan

darstellen to present; to describe

Darstellung presentation; description

Daten data

Datenaustausch data exchange

Datenbank data base

Datenbankmarketing database marketing

Datenbasis data base

Datenbestand data bank

Datenerfassung data collection

Datenmaterial data

Datenspeicherung data storage

Datenschutz data protection; privacy

Datenträger data storage medium

Datenübertragung data transmission

Datenverarbeitung data processing

Datenverwaltung information management

Datenzusammenführung data fusion

Datum date

Dauer duration

Dauerarbeitsloser chronically unemployed person; permanently unemployed person

Dauerauftrag standing order; money transfer order

Dauereinkommen continuous income

Dauerfinanzierung permanent financing

dauerhaft stable; durable

dauerhafte Güter durable goods

Dauerkunde regular customer; repeat buyer; *(Kredit)* continuous borrower; *(Werbung)* regular advertiser

dauernd permanent; perpetual; continuing

Dauernutzung permanent use; long-term use

Dauerwachstum permanent growth; stable growth

dazwischenliegend intermediate

dazwischentreten to intervene

Debitor debtor

Debitoren-Finanzierung accounts receivable financing

Debitorengeschäft loan business

Debitorenkartei accounts receivable ledger

Debitorenumschlag accounts receivable turnover; receivables turnover

Dechiffrierung decryption

Decke *(obere Grenze)* ceiling; cover

decken to cover; *(Bedarf)* to meet

Deckung cover; coverage; backing

Deckungsbeitrag contribution margin

Deckungsbeitragsrechnung contribution margin accounting; break-even analysis; direct costing

Deckungsgeschäft hedge

Deckungsgrad liquidity ratio

Deckungsguthaben compensating balance

Deckungspunktanalyse break-even analysis

deduktive Methode deductive method

defekt out of order; faulty; defective; damaged

Defekt fault; defect

defensives Verhalten defensive behavior

definieren to define

Defizit shortfall; deficit

Defizitkürzung deficit decrease

Deflation deflation

deflationistisch deflationary

Degression degression

Degressionseffekt economies of scale

degressiv declining

degressive Abschreibung declining balance depreciation

degressive Doppelraten-Abschreibung double-declining-balance depreciation

Deindustrialisierung deindustrialization

deklarieren to declare

Dekodierung decoding

Delegation delegation

delegieren to delegate

Delegierter delegate; deputy

Delkredere del credere; contingency reserves; provisions for doubtful debts

Delisting going-private transactions

Delkredereversicherung del crededere insurance

dementieren to deny; to disclaim

demographisch demographic

Demonstration demonstration

demonstrieren to demonstrate

demontieren to dismantle

Demoskopie public opinion poll

Depesche wire; telegram

Deponent depositor

Depositeninhaber depositor

Depositenkasse branch office of a bank; neighborhood bank branch

Depositenzertifikat Certificate of Deposit (CD)

Depositenzuwachs increase in deposits

Depot *(Wertpapiere)* deposit; portfolio; custodian account; *(Lager)* depot; storage

Depotaufbewahrung safekeeping

Depotbank depositary bank; custodian bank

Depotgebühr holding charge

Depotgeld fixed-date time deposit

Depotgeschäft custody business

Depotkonto custodial account

Depotverwaltung portfolio management

Depotstimmrecht proxy; proxy voting power

Depotwechsel collateral bill

Depression depression

deregulieren deregulate

Deregulierung deregulation

derzeit currently

derivativ derivative

Design design

Desinflation disinflation

Designphase design phase

Desinvestition disinvestment; negative investment

destabilisieren to destabilize

Detail detail

Detailhandel retail trade

detaillieren to specify

Detaillierung itemization

Detaillist retailer

deuten to construe; to interpret

deutlich distinct; definite

Deviationsklausel deviation clause

Devisen foreign currency; foreign exchange

Devisenabfluss outflow of foreign exchange; foreign currency drain

Devisenabkommen foreign exchange agreement

Devisenbestände foreign exchange funds; foreign exchange holdings

Devisenbestimmung exchange regulation

Devisenbewirtschaftung foreign exchange control

Devisenbilanz balance of foreign exchange payments; foreign exchange account

Devisenbonus allowance for earners of foreign currency

Devisenbörse currency market; foreign exchange market

Deviseneigenhandel foreign exchange trading for own account

Deviseneinnahmen foreign exchange proceeds

Devisengeschäft foreign exchange transaction

Devisenhandel foreign exchange dealing

Devisenhändler foreign currency trader

Devisenkassageschäft spot exchange transaction

Devisenkassakurs spot exchange rate

Devisenknappheit foreign currency shortage

Devisenkommissionsgeschäft foreign exchange transaction for customers

Devisenkontingent foreign exchange quota

Devisenkonto foreign currency account

Devisenkontrolle foreign exchange control

Devisenkurs exchange rate; foreign exchange rate

Devisenmanagement foreign currency management

Devisenmarkt currency market; foreign exchange market

Devisenmarktintervention exchange market intervention

Devisenoption foreign currency option

Devisenreserven foreign currency reserves

Devisenrisiko foreign exchange risk

Devisenschwankungen currency fluctuations

Devisentermingeschäft forward exchange transaction

Devisenterminkontrakt currency futures

Devisenterminmarkt forward exchange market

Devisentransfer currency transfer; transfer of foreign exchange

Devisenwechsel foreign exchange bill

dezentralisieren to decentralize

Dezentralisierung decentralization

Diagnose diagnosis

diagnostizieren to diagnose

Diagramm graph; chart

Dialog dialog

Dichte density

dienen to serve

Diener servant

Dienst *(Dienstleistung)* service; *(Anstellung)* employment; *(im Dienst)* on duty

Dienstanweisung service regulation; instructions

Dienstaufsicht supervision

Dienstaufsichtsbeschwerde disciplinary complaint; formal complaint

Dienstbote servant

Dienstgeheimnis official secret; industrial sercret

Dienstgrad rank

Dienstleistung service

Dienstleistungen services; invisibles

Dienstleistungsbereich service sector; tertiary sector

Dienstleistungsbetrieb service company

Dienstleistungsbilanz services account

Dienstleistungsbranche service industry

Dienstleistungsfirma service company

Dienstleistungsgebühr service charge

Dienstleistungsgeschäft service business

Dienstleistungskapazität service capacity

Dienstleistungsmarketing services marketing

Dienstleistungsnetz service network

Dienstleistungssektor service sector

Dienstleistungsunternehmen service business

Dienstleistungsverkehr trade in services

dienstlich official

Dienstplan rota; duty-roster; service shedule

Dienststelle government agency; bureau

Dienstvertrag employment contract; contract of employment

Dienstwagen company car

Dienstweg official channels; chain of command

Differenz difference; margin; spread

Differenzhandel margin trading

differenzieren to differentiate

Differenzierung differentiation

Differenzierungsstrategie differentiation strategy

Differenzinvestition fictitious investment

digitale Abschreibungsmethode sum-of-the-year's digit

digitale Marke digital brand

digitales Fernsehen digital television

digitales Bargeld digital cash

digitale Signaturen digital signatures

digitale Zertifikate digital certificates

Diktat dictation

diktieren to dictate

Diplomatie diplomacy

direkt direct

Direktabsatz direct sales

Direktanlage direct investment

Direktantwort direct response

Direktbesteuerung direct taxation

direkte Kosten direct costs

direktes Leasing direct leasing

direkte Steuern direct taxes

Direktfinanzierung direct financing

Direktinvestition direct investment; *(Ausland)* foreign direct investment

Direktive directive

Direktmarketing direct marketing

Direktor director; manager; (*AG*) officer

Direktorium governing body; management committee

Direktpost direct mail

Direktsteuer direct tax

Direktverkauf direct selling

Direktversand direct shipment

Direktversicherung direct insurance

Disagio debt discount; disagio

Diskette diskette

Diskont discount; rebate

Diskont einräumen to grant a discount

Diskonterhöhung discount rate increase

Diskontfenster discount window

diskontieren to rediscount; to discount

Diskontkredit rediscount credit

Diskontsatz discount rate; market rate

Diskontwert discounted value

Diskrepanz discrepancy

diskret discreet

Diskretion discretion; confidentiality

diskriminieren to discriminate

diskriminierend discriminatory; discriminating

Diskriminierung discrimination

Diskussion discussion

Diskussionsleiter moderator

diskutieren to discuss; to argue

Disponent procurement manager; (*Börse*) fund manager

disponibel disposable; available

disponieren *(verfügen über)* to dispose; *(Vorsorge treffen)* to arrange; to plan ahead

Dispositionskredit overdraft credit; credit line

disqualifizieren to disqualify

Disqualifizierung disqualification

Distribution distribution

Distributionskanal distribution channel

Distributionskette distribution chain

Distributionsmix distribution mix

Distributionspolitik distribution policy

distributives Bargaining distributive bargaining

Distrikt district

Diversifikation diversification; principle of diversification

Diversität workface diversity

diversifizierbares Risiko diversifiable risk

diversifizieren to diversify

diversifiziertes Unternehmen diversified company

Diversifizierung diversification

Dividende dividend

Dividendendeckung dividend payout ratio; payout ratio

Dividendendeckungsverhältnis dividend coverage

Dividendeneinnahmen dividend income

Dividendenerklärung declaration of dividends

Dividende in Form von Schuldurkunden liability dividend

dividendenlos ex dividend

Dividendenpapier dividend-paying stock; equity share

Dividendenrendite dividend yield

Dividendenschein dividend coupon

Dividendenstichtag record date; declaration date

Dividendentermin record date

Dividenden-Wachstums-Modell dividend growth model

Dividendenzahlung payment of dividend

Dividende pro Aktie dividends per share

Divisionskalkulation process costing; output costing

Dokument document; paper; *(Wertpapiere)* instrument

Dokumentation documentation

Dokumente gegen Akzept documents against acceptance

Dokumente gegen bar documents against cash

Dokumentenakkreditiv documentary letter of credit

Dokumenteneinreichung presentation of document

Dokumentengeschäft documentary business

Dokumenteninkasso collection against documents

Dokumentenwechsel documentary acceptance

dokumentieren to document

Dokumentierung documentation

dolmetschen to interpret

Dolmetscher interpreter

Domain-Name domain name

Domain-Name Registrierung domain name registration

Domain-Name System domain name system

dominante Unternehmenskultur dominant business culture

Domizil domicile; residence

Doppelausweis *(Börse)* dual presentation

Doppelbesteuerung double taxation

Doppelbesteuerungsabkommen double taxation agreement

doppeldeutig ambiguous

Doppeldeutigkeit ambiguity

Doppelgesellschaft split company; syndicate

doppelt double

Doppelverdiener dual jobholder; *(Familie)* two-income couple

Doppelwährungsanleihe dual currency bond

dotieren *(Gehalt)* to compensate; *(Stiftung)* to endow

Dotierung *(Gehalt)* compensation; *(Stiftung)* endowment

Draht wire

drahten to wire

Drahtnachricht wire; telegram

drängen to rush; to push

Drängen pressure

drangsalieren to harass; to bully

Drangsalierung harassment

drastisch senken to slash

Dreiecksarbitrage triangular arbitrage

Dreieckshandel trilateral trade

Drei-Komponenten-Modell der Kreativität three-component model of creativity

dringen auf to insist on

dringend urgent; pressing

Dringlichkeit urgency; priority

Dringlichkeitsantrag urgency motion

Dringlichkeitsgrad degree of urgency

Dringlichkeitsstufe, höchste top priority

Dritter third party

Drittland third party country; *(EU)* non-EU country

Drittlandzollsatz customs tariff for non-EU countries

drohen to threaten

Drohung threat

drosseln to curtail; to curb; to reduce

Drosselung curb; reduction

Druck pressure; squeeze; *(Buch)* print

drücken to press; *(niederdrücken)* to depress; *(zusammendrücken)* to squeeze

drucken to print

Drucker printer

Druckerei printing press

Druckschrift print; (*Brief*) printed matter

dual dual

duale Notierung dual listing

Duplikat duplicate; copy

Durchbruch breakthrough

durchdringen to penetrate; to saturate

Durchdringung penetration; saturation

Durchfahrt passage; thoroughfare; crossing; (*Grenze)* transit

Durchfrachtkonnossement through bill of lading

Durchfuhr transit

durchführbar workable; feasible

Durchführbarkeit feasibility

Durchführbarkeitsstudie feasibility study

durchführen to carry out; to execute; to implement; *(Regeln)* to enforce

Durchführung execution; implementation; *(Regeln)* enforcement

durchgehend nonstop

Durchkonnossement through bill of lading

Durchlauf run; pass

durchlaufen to pass; to run through

Durchlaufterminierung throughput scheduling

Durchlaufzeit throughput time

Durchschnitt standard; average

Durchschnitt, arithmetischer arithmetic average

Durchschnitt berechnen to average

durchschnittlich average

durchschnittlich betragen to average

durchschnittliche Buchrendite Average Accounting Return (AAR)

durchschnittliche Forderungslaufzeit average collection period

durchschnittliche Jahresrendite annualized holding-period return

durchschnittliche Kapitalkosten average cost of capital

durchschnittlicher Tagesumsatz average daily sales

Durchschnitts- average

Durchschnittsbesteuerung income averaging

Durchschnittskosten average costs

Durchschnittskostenbewertung average-cost method of valuation

Durchschnittskostenmethode weighted average cost method

Durchschnittskurs market average; stock average

Durchschnittswert average; *(Mittelwert)* mean; mean value

durchsehen to examine

durchsetzen to enforce

Durchsetzung enforcement

Durchsetzungsvermögen clout; punch

durchsickern to leak

Durchtarif trough tariff

dürftig (*Einkommen*) meager; (*Verhältnisse*) poor

Dynamik drive; dynamics

dynamisch dynamic; energetic

dynamische Amortisationsdauer discounted payback period rule

dysfunktionaler Konflikt dysfunctional conflict

E

ebenda ibidem (ibid.)

echt real; genuine; pure; *(rechtmäßig)* legitimate; *(verbürgt)* warranted; *(Urkunde)* authentic

Echtes Factoring old-line-factoring

Echtheit authenticity; genuineness

Echtzeit real time

Edelmetallbarren bullion

Effekten securities; paper securities; (*Bilanz*) investments

Effekten beleihen to advance money on securities

Effekten verpfänden to pledge securities

Effektenabrechnung stock account

Effektenanlage investment in securities

Effektenbank investment bank; trust company

Effektenbankier investment banker

Effektenberater securities advisor

Effektenbestand investment portfolio; securities holdings

Effektenbörse stock exchange; securities exchange

Effektenhandel securities trading; stock trading

Effektenhändler stockbroker; securities dealer

Effekten-Kreditkonto margin account

Effektenverwalter portfolio manager

effektiv effective; real; actual

effektive Häufigkeit effective frequency

effektiver Zins effective rate of interest

Effektivität effectiveness

Effektivklausel currency clause; real wage clause

Effektivkosten actual costs

Effektivlohn real wage; net earnings

Effektivrendite dividend yield

Effektivverzinsung effective rate of interest; market rate

Effektivzins real interest rate; effective rate of interest

Effektivzinsmethode effective interest method

Effektivzoll effective tariff

effizient efficient

effizientes Portefeuille efficient portfolio

Effizienz efficiency; performance

ehemalig past; former

Ehegatte spouse

Ehegattenfreibetrag marriage allowance

Ehegattenunterhalt matrimonial maintenance

Ehevertrag marriage contract; matrimonial agreement

ehrenamtlich honorary

Ehrenplatz place of honour

Ehrenvorsitzender honorary chairman

Ehrgeiz ambition

ehrgeizig ambitious; aspiring

Eid oath

Eid ablegen to swear an oath

eidesstattliche Erklärung affidavit

eigen own; particular; proper

Eigenbedarf own requirements; *(Handel)* domestic requirements

Eigenbehalt retention

Eigenbeteiligung own funds; equity contribution

Eigenerzeugung *(Inland)* domestic production; (*Firma*) own production

Eigenfinanzierung self financing; equity financing

Eigenhandel *(Börse)* floor trade; trade for own account

Eigenhändler market maker

Eigenheim privately owned home

Eigeninteresse self-interest

Eigenkapital *(Aktiengesellschaft)* equity; stockholders' equity; shareholders' equity; net worth; net assets; *(Bank)* capital reserves, capital resources

Eigenkapitalanteil equity ratio; own capital contribution

Eigenkapitalgeber investor; financier

Eigenkapitalsbasis equity base; net worth

Eigenkapitaldecke equity position; leverage

Eigenkapitalkosten cost of equity capital

Eigenkapitalrendite return on equity (ROE)

Eigenkapitalzuwachs aus sonstigen Quellen additional paid-in capital

Eigenkapitalzinsen equity yield rate

Eigenmittel own resources; *(Bauherr)* building capital

Eigenproduktion own production

Eigenschaft *(Merkmal)* property; quality; feature; attribute; trait; *(berufliche Kapazität)* capacity

Eigenschaftstheorien der Führung trait theories of leadership

Eigentum property; *(Besitz)* possession

Eigentümer owner; proprietor; *(Wertpapiere)* holder

Eigentümer-Unternehmer owner-manager

Eigentumsrecht proprietorship; ownership; title

Eigentumsverhältnisse ownership structure

Eigentumsvorbehalt reservation of title; reservation of proprietary rights; secret lien

Eigentumswohnung condominium; freehold apartment

Eigenverantwortung individual responsibility

Eigenvertrieb direct selling

Eigenwechsel sola bill; promissory note

Eigner proprietor; owner

Eignung qualification; *(Brauchbarkeit)* suitability

Eignungstest aptitude test; qualifying examination

Eilbeförderung special delivery

Eile hurry; rush

einbehalten to withhold

einbehaltene Gewinne retained earnings; undistributed profits

Einarbeitung job training; familiarization; orientation

Einbau installation

einbauen to install

Einbaukosten installation costs

einbehalten to withhold; to retain

einbehaltene Gewinne retained earnings

Einbehaltung withholding; retention

Einbehaltungsquote retention ratio

einberufen to convene

einbeziehen to include

Einbeziehung inclusion

einbrechen to break in; to commit burglary; *(Preis)* to cave in

einbringlich profitable; lucrative

Einbruch burglary; *(Market)* break; market break

einbürgern to naturalize

Einbürgerung naturalization

Einbuße loss

einbüßen to lose

eindecken, sich to provide; to stock up

Eindeckung supply; provision

eindringen to penetrate

Eindringen penetration

einfach simple; single; *(Fahrkarte)* one-way

einfache Verzinsung simple interest

Ein-Faktor-Arbitrage-Pricing-Theorie one-factor APT

Einfluss influence; pull; leverage; hold; clout

Einflussgröße determining factor

Einflussnahme exercise of influence; control

einflussreich influential

Einflusssphäre sphere of influence

einforderbar demandable; claimable

einfordern to call in; to demand; to claim

Einforderung calling in; demand

Einfuhr import; importation

Einfuhrabfertigung import clearance

Einfuhrabgabe import levy; import duty

Einfuhrabgaben import dues

Einfuhrabhängigkeit import dependency

Einfuhrabschöpfung import levy

Einfuhrabwehr import barriers

Einfuhrausgleichsabgabe import equalization levy

Einfuhrbeschränkung import restriction

Einfuhrbewilligung import license

Einfuhrdokument import document

einführen *(importieren)* to import; *(errichten)* to institute; *(bekannt machen)* to introduce

Einführer importer

Einfuhrerklärung bill of entry; customs declaration

Einfuhrersatz import substitute

Einfuhrfinanzierung import financing

Einfuhrgenehmigung import license

Einfuhrhändler importer; import merchant

Einfuhrkontingent import quota

Einfuhrkontrolle import control

Einfuhrkonnossement inward bill of lading

Einfuhrliste import list

Einfuhrlizenz import licence

Einfuhrmakler import broker

Einfuhrpreis import price

Einfuhrquote import quota

Einfuhrschranke import barrier

Einfuhrschutz import protection

Einfuhrsteigerung increase in imports

Einfuhrumsatzsteuer import turnover tax

Einführung introduction

Einführungskurs initial rate

Einführungsphase introduction stage; introduction phase

Einfuhrversandhändler import distributor

Einfuhrvertrag import agreement

Einfuhrware imported merchandise

Einfuhrweg import channel

Einfuhrwert import value

Einfuhrzoll import duty; customs duties on imports

Eingabe *(Bittschrift)* petition; *(Datenverarbeitung)* input

Eingabedaten input data

Eingang entrance; *(Waren)* arrival; receipt

Eingangsabfertigung inward clearance

Eingangsbenachrichtigung arrival notice

Eingangsbestätigung acknowledgment of receipt; confirmation of receipt; arrival notice

Eingangsdatum date of receipt

Eingangskorb in-tray

Eingangsseite entry page

Eingangsstempel receipt stamp

Eingangssteuersatz marginal tax rate

eingebetteter Anzeigeninhalt nested ad content

eingebrachtes Kapital contributed capital

eingehen *(ankommen)* to arrive; *(Geld)* to come in; (*Verpflichtung*) to undertake; to assume; *(Vertrag)* to enter into

eingehend detailed; incoming; inbound

eingehende E-Mail inbound e-mail

eingeräumter Kredit credit line

eingerechnet inclusive

eingeschränkt restricted; limited; qualified

eingeschränkter Bestätigungsvermerk qualified opinion

eingetragen registered; recorded; incorporated

eingetragener Aktionär stockholder of record; owner of record

eingetragener Wertpapierhändler floor trader; registered trader

Eingeweihter insider

eingezahltes Grundkapital paid-in capital

eingezahltes Kapital ohne Nachschusspflicht nonassessable capital stock

eingliedern to integrate

Eingliederung integration

Eingriff intervention; interference

einhalten *(Regeln)* to observe; to meet; *(Gesetz)* to comply with

Einhaltung *(Regeln)* observance; observation; *(Gesetz)* compliance

einheimisch domestic; native; internal

Einheimischer native; local

einheimischer Gehalt domestic content

einheimsen to pocket

Einheit *(Stück)* unit; *(Einigkeit)* unity

Einheit der Auftragserteilung unit of order

einheitlich uniform

einheitliche Richtlinien uniform rules

Einheitlichkeit uniformity

Einheitslösung standard solution

Einheitswert standard value; *(Grundstück)* assessed value

einigen, sich to reach an agreement; to come to terms

Einigkeit unity; agreement; mutual consent

Einigung settlement; *(Übereinstimmung)* agreement

einkalkulieren to take into account

einkassieren to cash; to collect; *(Wechsel)* to call in

Einkauf buying; purchase; *(Einkaufen)* shopping; *(Abteilung)* purchasing department

einkaufen to buy; to purchase; *(einkaufen gehen)* to shop

Einkäufer purchasing agent; buyer; procurement manager

Einkaufsabteilung purchasing department

Einkaufsagent buying agent

Einkaufsakkreditiv buying letter of credit

Einkaufsauftrag purchase order; indent

Einkaufsbeleg purchase voucher

Einkaufsfinanzierung purchasing finance

Einkaufsgenossenschaft purchasing association; wholesale cooperative

Einkaufsleiter chief buyer; purchasing manager

Einkaufsland country of purchase

Einkaufspreis purchase price; cost price; base price

Einkaufssachbearbeiter purchasing agent

Einkaufszentrum shopping center; shopping mall

einklagen to sue; to file a suit for

Einkommen income; earnings; revenue

Einkommen nach Abzug der Steuern income after tax

Einkommen vor Abzug der Steuern pre-tax income

Einkommen aus selbständiger Arbeit self-employment income

Einkommen aus nicht selbständiger Arbeit earned income

Einkommen aus Gewerbebetrieb industrial earnings

Einkommen aus Grundbesitz property income

einkommensabhängig income-related; income-dependent

Einkommensaktien income shares

Einkommenseinbuße loss of income

Einkommenselastizität income elasticity

Einkommensfonds income fund

Einkommensgruppe income bracket

Einkommenshöhe income level

Einkommenskonsumfunktion income-consumption function

Einkommensminderung income decrease

Einkommensrunde salary negotiation round

Einkommensteuer income tax

Einkommensteuerbemessung income tax assessment

Einkommensteuerbefreiung income tax relief

Einkommensteuererklärung income tax return

Einkommensteuererstattung income tax refund

Einkommensumverteilung income redistribution

Einkommensverteilung income distribution

Einkommensverwendung use of income

Einkünfte revenues; income

Einkünfte aus selbstständiger Arbeit self-employed income

Einkünfte aus unselbstständiger Arbeit earned income

Einkünfte vor Steuern pre-tax income

Einlage *(Bank)* deposit; *(Beilage)* insert; *(Kapital)* capital contribution

Einlagekapital capital contribution; paid-in capital

Einlagenabfluss outflow of deposits

Einlagenabzug disintermediation

Einlagenbestand total bank deposits

Einlagengeschäft deposit transaction

Einlagenversicherung deposit insurance

Einlagenzertifikat certificate of deposit

Einlagerung storage; warehousing; stockpiling

einlassen to admit; to let in

einlassen, sich auf etw. to engage in something

Einlassung (*Gericht*) testimony; defense

Einleger (*Bank*) depositor; *(Kapital)* contributor; investor

einleiten to initiate; to start; *(eröffnen)* to open; *(einführen)* to introduce; *(Gerichtsverfahren)* to institute

einleitend introductory; preliminary

Einleitung introduction; preface; preamble

Einleitung eines Konkursverfahrens institution of bankruptcy proceedings

Einleitung gerichtlicher Schritte institution of legal proceedings

einleuchtend plausible

einlösen *(tilgen)* to redeem; *(eintauschen)* to exchange; *(einen Scheck)* to cash

Einlösung *(Tilgung)* redemption; *(Scheck)* cashing; *(Eintausch)* exchange

Ein-Mann-Unternehmen sole trader business

einmalig unique; on-off; non-recurring

einmalige Gebühr nonrecurring charge

einmischen, sich to interfere

Einmischung interference; intervention

Einnahme revenue; receipts; *(Einkommen)* income

Einnahmeausfall loss of income; loss of revenue

Einnahmen-Ausgaben-Rechnung statement of revenues and expenditures; cash basis accounting

Einnahmeposten revenue item

Einnahmerückgang drop in revenue

Einnahmeseite revenue side; *(Bilanz)* income account

Einnahmeüberschuss surplus revenue; net receipts

Einnahmeüberschussrechnung net income method

Einnahmeunterdeckung negative cash flow

einordnen *(in Reihenfolge)* to rank; *(klassifizieren)* to classify; *(Akten)* to file

Einplanung planning

einreichen to submit; to file

Einreise entry

Einreisedokumente entry documents

einreisen to enter

einrichten to institute; *(ausrüsten)* to equip; *(Wohnung)* to furnish

Einrichtung *(Errichten)* setup; *(Organisation)* institution; *(Ausrüstung)* equipment; *(Möbel)* furnishing

Einrichtungsgegenstände furnitures and fixtures

Einsatz *(Verwendung)* use; deployment; *(Anzeige)* insertion; *(Wette)* stake

Einsatzbesprechung briefing

Einsatzbereitschaft stand-by duty; readiness for action

Einsatzfeld operational area

Einsatzleiter director of operations

Einsatzplanung applications planning

Einsatzzweck intended use

einschalten to switch on, to start; *(sich ~)* to intervene

Einschaltpreis für Werbespots advertising rates

Einschaltquote viewing rate; audience rate

Einschaltung intervention; *(Anzeige)* insertion

einschätzen to assess; to estimate; to value

Einschätzung assessment; estimate; valuation

einschleusen to channel

einschließen to include; to comprise

einschließlich inclusive; including

einschließlich Bezugsrechte cum rights

einschränken to restrict; to limit; *(verkleinern)* to curtail; to cut back

einschränken, sich to economize; to retrench

Einschränkung *(Beschränkung)* restriction; limitation; *(Einsparung)* economizing; retrenchment

einschreiben to register; *(als Mitglied, Student)* to enroll

Einschreiben registered mail

einschreiten to interfere; to intervene

Einschreiten intervention

Einschuss *(Differenzgeschäft)* margin; *(Kapital)* invested capital; stake

Einschussbedarf *(Differenzgeschäft)* margin requirements

Einschusszahlung margin deposit

einseitig unilateral; *(ungleichgewichtig)* lopsided

einseitige Übertragung unilateral transfer

einsenden to send in; to post

Einsendeschluss deadline; closing date

einsetzen to use; to employ *(installieren)* to install; *(gebrauchen)* to deploy

einsparen to save; to economize; *(Kosten)* to cut costs

Einsparung saving, economy

Einsparung durch Massenproduktion economies of scale

Einsparungsmöglichkeiten potential savings

Einsparungsvorgabe savings target

Einspruch objection; protest; veto

Einspruch erheben to oppose; to veto

Einstandspreis cost price

einstellbar adjustable

einstellen *(anstellen)* to hire; to engage; *(beenden)* to discontinue; to cease; *(Radio)* to tune; *(Maschinen)* to set

Einstellung *(Personal)* recruitment; hiring; employment; *(Beendung)* stoppage; cessation; *(Maschine)* set-up; adjustment; *(Haltung)* attitude; approach

Einstellungsalter hiring age

Einstellungsbedingungen conditions of employment

Einstellungsgespräch job interview; interview

Einstellungspraxis recruitment practices

Einstellungssperre recruitment stop; job freeze

Einstellungsverfahren hiring procedure

Einstellungsvertrag contract of employment

einstimmig unanimous

Einstimmigkeit unanimity

einstufen to rate; to class; to classify

einstweilig interim

einstweilige Verfügung injunction

eintauschen to exchange; to trade in; to swap

einteilen to grade; to divide; *(zur Arbeit)* to assign

Einteilung classification; division; *(zur Arbeit)* assignment

eintragen to record; to register; to enter

einträglich lucrative; rewarding

Eintragung registration; entry

Eintragungszeitraum date of record

eintreffen to arrive

Eintreffen arrival

eintreibbar recoverable; *(Schulden)* collectible

eintreiben to recover; *(Schulden)* to collect

eintreten to enter; *(Ereignis)* to occur

Eintritt entrance; entry; *(Zulassung)* admission; *(Ereignis)* occurrence

Eintrittsphase encounter stage

Eintrittspreis admission price

Einverleibung annexation

Einverständnis consent; agreement

Einwand objection

Einwand erheben to raise an objection

Einwand stattgeben to sustain an objection

Einwand zurückweisen to overrule an objection

einwandfrei correct; flawless

einwandfreie Übergabe flawless delivery

Einwegflasche nonreturnable bottle; disposable bottle

Einweggüter disposable goods

Einweihung inauguration; dedication

Einweisung *(im Betrieb)* instruction; briefing; *(Krankenhaus)* referral

einwilligen to consent; to agree

Einwilligung consent; agreement

einwirken auf to affect; to influence; to impact on

Einwirkung influence; impact

Einwohner inhabitant; resident

einzahlen to deposit

Einzahler depositor

Einzahlung payment; *(eingezahlter Betrag)* deposit

Einzelabrechnung itemized billing

Enzelanfertigung single-unit production; made to specification

Einzelauftrag individual order

Einzelbedürfnis individual need

Einzelbeleg separate voucher

Einzeldebitorenrisiko single debtor risk

Einzelfall particular case; singular case

Einzelfirma sole proprietorship

Einzelgenehmigung special permit; exclusive licence

Einzelhandel retail trade; retailing

Einzelhandelsbranche retail trade; retail industry

Einzelhandelsfirma retail firm

Einzelhandelsgeschäft retail store

Einzelhandelsgewinnspanne retail margin

Einzelhandelskaufmann retailer; shopkeeper

Einzelhandelskette retail chain

Einzelhandeslkonzession retail license

Einzelhandelspreis retail price; shop price

Einzelhandelsrabatt retail discount

Einzelhandelsspanne retail margin

Einzelhandelswerbung retail advertising

Einzelhändler retailer

Einzelheit detail

Einzelkosten unit costs; direct costs

einzeln single; sole; individual; *(getrennt)* separate

Einzelperson individual

Einzelplanung individual planning

Einzelposten single item

Einzelteil component part

Einzelüberweisung individual remittance

Einzelunternehmung sole proprietorship

Einzelwirtschaft isolated economy

einziehen to recover; *(Schulden)* to collect; *(Wohnung)* to move in

Einziehung recovery; *(Schulden)* collection

einzig only; sole

Einzug entry; entrance; (*Bank*) collection

Einzug von Schecks collection of checks

Einzugsauftrag collection order

Einzugsermächtigung direct debiting authorization

Einzugsgebühren collection charges

Einzugsverfahren direct debiting

Eisenbahngüterverkehr rail freight traffic

Eisenbahngütertarif rail freight rates; railroad rates

Eisenwaren ironware; hardware; metal goods

elastisch flexible; elastic

Elastizität flexibility; elasticity

Elektrizitätswerk utility company; power station

elektronische Geldüberweisung wire transfer

elektronische Post electronic mail (E-mail)

elektronische Mall electronic mall

elektronische Münzen electronic tokens

elektronischer Datenaustausch electronic data interchange (EDI)

elektronischer Handel electronic commerce (e-commerce)

elektronischer Wertpapierhandel automated stock trading

elektronisches Bargeld electronic cash

eliminieren to eliminate

Eliminierung elimination

Embargo embargo

Emission *(Aktien)* offering; public offering; *(Banknoten,)* issuance

Emission auflegen to float an issue

Emissionsbank underwriter

Emissionsdatum offering date

Emissionsfirma securities underwriter; investment banking house

Emissionsgarantie underwriting guarantee

Emissionsgeschäft investment banking business; *(Transaktion)* issuing transaction

Emissionskonsortium group of underwriters

Emissionskonsortionalvertrag agreement among underwriters

Emissionskurs offering price; subscription price

Emissionsmarkt primary market

Emissionsprospekt prospectus

Emissionsrendite issue yield

Emissionstag date of issue

Emissionsvertrag underwriting agreement

Emittent issuer

emittieren to issue

emotionale Arbeit emotional labor

emotionale Intelligenz emotional intelligence

emotionale Stabilität emotional stability

Emotionen emotions

Empfang *(Eingang)* receipt; reception; *(Ereignis)* reception; *(Hotel)* reception desk

Empfang bestätigen to acknowledge receipt

empfangen to receive

Empfänger receiver; recipient; *(Wechsel)* payee; *(Überweisung)* remittee; *(Brief)* addressee

Empfängerland recipient country

Empfangsbescheinigung notice of receipt

Empfangsberechtigter person authorized to take delivery

Empfangsdame receptionist

Empfangsgerät receiver

empfehlen to recommend

Empfehlung recommendation; reference; *(Einführung)* introduction

Empfehlungsschreiben letter of recommendation

empfundene Emotionen felt emotions

empfundener Konflikt felt conflict

Endabnahme final inspection

Endabnehmer end user; ultimate buyer

Endabrechnung closing statement; final account

Endauswertung final evaluation

Endbestand final inventory

Ende end; ending; finish; conclusion

Endergebnis final outcome; end result

endfällige Anleihe bullet bond

Endfälligkeitstermin expiration date

Endgerät terminal

Endgewinn bottom line

endgültig final

Endkosten final costs

Endkostenstelle final cost center

Endmontage final assembly

Endnachfrage consumer demand; aggregate demand

Endprodukt final product

Endwert accumulated value; terminal value; future value

Endziel ultimate goal

Energie energy; power; *(Person)* drive

Engagement *(Verpflichtung)* commitment; obligation; *(Theater)* employment

engagieren to engage; *(Theater)* to employ; *(Kapital)* to tie up

Engpass bottleneck

Engroshandel wholesale

Engroshändler wholesaler

Enkodierung encoding

entbündeln to unbundle

Entbündelung unbundling

Entbürokratisierung debureaucratization; streamlining of administration

entdecken to discover; to detect

Entdeckung discovery; detection; find

enteignen to dispossess; to expropriate

Enteignung expropriation; dispossession

entfallen *(nicht anwendbar)* not applicable (na)

entfallen, auf to be allotted to; to fall upon

entfernen to remove; to eliminate; *(Person)* to retire

Entfernung distance

entflechten to dissolve; to break up

Entflechtung dissolution; divestiture

entgegenkommen to accommodate

Entgegenkommen accommodation; courtesy

entgegnen to counter

Entgelt *(Bezahlung)* payment; *(Vertragsleistung)* consideration

enthalten to hold; to comprise; to contain

enthalten, sich to abstain

Enthaltung *(Stimmenabgabe)* abstention

Enthüllung disclosure; discovery

entlassen to dismiss; to fire; to remove from office; *(fristlos)* to dismiss someone without notice

Entlassung dismissal; discharge; sacking; layoff

Entlassungswelle round of dismissals; mass layoffs

entlasten to relieve; to release; *(ratifizieren)* to discharge

Entlastung relief; release; *(Ratifizierung)* discharge

entleihen to borrow

Entlohnung remuneration; payment; compensation

Entnahme *(Konto)* withdrawal

entnehmen to take out; *(verstehen)* to understand from; *(Konto)* to withdraw

entschädigen to compensate; to indemnify; *(zurückerstatten)* to reimburse

entschädigend compensatory

Entschädigung compensation; indemnification; *(Zurückerstattung)* reimbursement; recourse

Entschädigungsanspruch indemnity claim; claim for damages

Entschädigungsberechtigter indemnitee

Entschädigungsfonds indemnity fund

Entschädigungsklage action for damages

Entschädigungsleistung compensatory payment

Entschädigungssumme indemnity; award; damages

Entscheid decision; decree; ruling

entscheiden to decide; to determine; to rule

entscheiden, sich to decide; to opt

entscheidend decisive; crucial; essential

Entscheidung decision; (*Gericht*) ruling

Entscheidungsbaum decision tree

Entscheidungsbildung decision making

Entscheidungsfreiheit freedom of choice

Entscheidungsmodell decision model

Entscheidungsprozeß decision-making process

Entscheidungsrechnung decision accounting

Entscheidungsträger decision maker

entschließen, sich to decide; to resolve

Entschließung resolution

Entschluss determination; decision

entschuldigen to excuse; to apologise

Entschuldigung excuse; apology

entsorgen to dispose of

Entsorgung waste disposal; waste management

entspannen to relax; to ease

entstehen to occur; to originate; to arise

entstellen to distort

Entstellung distortion

enttäuschen to disappoint

enttäuschend disappointing

Enttäuschung disappointment

entwerfen *(Konzept)* to outline; to devise; *(Konstruktion)* to design; to sketch

entwerten to devalue

Entwertung devaluation; depreciation

entwickeln to develop; *(fördern)* to promote

entwickeln, sich to grow; to expand

Entwicklung development; *(Wachstum)* growth

Entwicklungsausschuss development committee

Entwicklungsbank development bank

Entwicklungshilfe development aid; foreign aid

Entwicklungsimpuls development impetus

Entwicklungskosten development costs

Entwicklungsland developing country; less developed country

Entwicklungslinie trend

entwicklungsorientiert development-oriented

Entwicklungsphase development phase

Entwicklungspolitik development policy

Entwicklungsprozess development process

Entwicklungsstadium stage of development

Entwicklungstendenz trend

Entwurf *(Plan)* outline; plan; *(Modell)* model; *(Konstruktion)* design; draft; sketch

Entwurfsänderung design change

Equity-Methode equity method

Erbe *(Person)* heir

Erbe inheritance

erben to inherit

Erbfolge, gesetzliche legal order of succession

erbitten to solicit; to request

Erbpacht leasehold

erbringen to yield

Erbschaft inheritance

Erbschaftsmasse estate

Erbschaftssteuer inheritance tax; death tax; estate tax

Erbschein heir's certificate; certificate of inheritance

Erdgas natural gas

Erdgasleitung natural gas pipeline

Erdgaslieferant natural gas supplier

Erdöl crude oil; petroleum

Erdölvorkommen oil field

Ereignis occurrence; incident

erfahren to experience

Erfahrung experience

Erfahrungskurve experience curve

Erfahrungswert empirical value

erfassen to cover; to include; to comprise; *(begreifen)* to comprehend; *(statistisch)* to register

Erfassung registration; inclusion *(Statistik)* coverage

erfinden to invent; to devise

Erfinder inventor

Erfindung invention

Erfindungsgabe inventiveness; ingenuity

Erfolg success; outcome; result; *(GuV)* profit or loss

erfolgreich successful

erfolgsabhängig profit-related

erfolgsabhängige Aktienvergütung performance shares

Erfolgsaussichten chances of success

Erfolgsbasis (auf) on a contingent basis

Erfolgsbeteiligung profit sharing

Erfolgsfaktor factor of success

Erfolgskennziffer operating ratio

Erfolgskonto profit and loss account

Erfolgskontrolle performance review; *(Werbung)* result testing

Erfolgskurs road to success

Erfolgspotentiale potentials for success

Erfolgsprämie incentive payment

Erfolgsrechung profit and loss statement

Erfolgsrechnung; außenwirtschaftliche balance of payments

Erfolgswirksamkeit effectiveness

Erfolgszwang pressure to succeed; drive to succeed

erforderlich requisite; necessary

erfordern to need; *(fordern)* to require

Erfordernis requirement

erforschen to explore; to research

Erforschung exploration; research

erfüllen *(eine Pflicht)* to perform; to discharge; *(einen Vertrag)* to fulfill; to implement

Erfüllung *(einer Pflicht)* performance; *(eines Vertrags)* fulfillment; implementation

Erfüllungstag settlement date

ergänzen to supplement; *(vollenden)* to complete; to amend

ergänzend supplementary; complementary

Ergänzung supplement; complement

Ergänzungsabgabe special levy; surtax

ergeben *(abwerfen)* to produce; to yield; *(betragen)* to amount to

Ergebnis result; outcome; *(Bilanz)* yield; profit or loss; *(Produkt)* product

Ergebnis ausweisen to show a result

Ergebnis erzielen to achieve a result

Ergebnis des laufenden Geschäfts operating result

Ergebnis je Aktie earnings per share (EPS)

Ergebnis nach Steuern result after tax

Ergebnis vor Zinsen und Steuern earnings before interest and tax (EBIT)

Ergebnis vor Zinsen, Steuern und Abschreibungen earnings before interest, tax and amortization (EBITA)

Ergebnis vor Zinsen, Steuern, Goodwill und Abschreibungen earnings before interest, tax, depreciation and amortization (EBITDA)

Ergebnisanalyse performance analysis

Ergebnisbeitrag contribution to operating income

Ergebnisberichtigung früherer Jahre prior period adjustment

ergebnisorientiert goal-oriented

Ergebnisrechnung profit and loss account; earnings statement

Ergebnisverwendung appropriation of net income

Erhalt receipt; preservation

erhalten *(bestehen lassen)* to preserve; to conserve; *(empfangen)* to receive; to obtain

erhältlich obtainable

Erhaltung preservation; conservation; *(Instandhaltung)* maintenance

erheblich considerable; material

Erhebung *(Umfrage)* survey; census

Erhebungsjahr census year; survey year

erhöhen to raise; to increase

erhöhen, sich to rise; to increase

Erhöhung rise; increase; step-up

erholen, sich to recover; to recuperate; *(Kurse)* to rally; *(Konjunktur)* to rebound

Erholung recovery; *(Kurse)* rally; *(Wirtschaft)* revival

erinnern to remind

erinnern, sich to remember; to recall

Erinnerung recollection; memory; *(Rechnung)* reminder

Erinnerungsanzeige reminder advertisment

Erinnerungshilfe *(Werbung)* aided recall

Erinnerungsschreiben follow-up letter

Erinnerungswerbung reminder advertising

Erkenntnis awareness; finding

Erkenntnisobjekt scientific object

Erkenntnisziel scientific aim

erklären to explain; to declare

erklärend illustrative; explanatory

Erklärung statement; explanation; declaration

Erklärungsmodell explanatory model

erkunden to explore

erkundigen, sich to inquire; to make inquiries

Erkundigung inquiry; investigation

erlangen to secure; to obtain; to attain

Erlangung attainment

Erlass ordinance; enactment

erlassen to waive; *(Schulden)* to release; *(Verordnung)* to issue

erlauben to permit; to license; to allow

Erlaubnis permit

erlaubt admissible

erläuternd illustrative

Erläuterung explanation; *(Kommentar)* annotation

Erläuterungsbericht *(Bilanz)* notes to the accounts; notes to the annual financial statements

erledigen to handle; to carry out; to execute

Erledigung handling; carrying out; execution

erleichtern to ease; to facilitate; to alleviate; *(mildern)* to mitigate

Erleichterung easing; *(Notlage)* relief; *(Strafe)* mitigation

Erlös proceeds; revenues; returns

Erlösanteil profit share

Erlösbeitrag contribution to profits

Erlöseinbruch profit slump

Erlösfunktion revenue function

Erlösmaximierung revenue maximization

Erlösminderung reduction in earnings

Erlösspanne profit margin

Erlössumme total sales revenues

erlöschen to expire; to cease; to lapse

Erlöschen expiration

ermächtigen to authorize; to empower

Ermächtigung *(Vollmacht)* power of attorney; authorization; empowerment

ermäßigen to reduce; to cut

Ermäßigung reduction; cut

Ermessen discretion; judgment

Ermessensentscheidung discretionary decision

Ermessensfreiheit discretionary powers

Ermessenskosten discretionary cost

ermitteln to investigate; *(feststellen)* to ascertain

Ermittlung ascertainment; detection; *(Berechnung)* calculation; *(Abschätzung)* appraisal; *(Untersuchung)* inquiry; investigation

Ermittlungsbeamter investigation officer

ermutigen to encourage

Ermutigung encouragement

ernähren to nourish; to feed; *(unterhalten)* to support

Ernährer provider

Ernährung food; nourishment

ernennen to appoint

Ernennung appointment

erneuerbar renewable

erneuern to renew; to revive; *(Kredit)* to revolve; to prolong

Erneuerung renovation; renewal

erneuerungsbedürftig in need of repair

erneut verpfänden to rehypothecate

Ernte harvest; yield; crop

ernten to harvest; to reap

erobern to capture; to conquer

Eroberung capture; conquest

eröffnen to open

Eröffnung *(Börse, Konto)* opening; *(Einweihung)* dedication; *(Überraschung)* disclosure

Eröffnungsbilanz opening balance

Eröffnungsbestand opening balance

Eröffnungskurs opening price

Erpressung extortion; blackmail

erproben to test; to prove

Erprobung testing; trial; test

errechnen to calculate

erreichbar *(erzielbar)* attainable; *(Ort)* accessible; *(ansprechbar)* approachable

erreichen to reach; *(erzielen)* to attain; to achieve

errichten *(gründen)* to found; to establish; *(aufbauen)* to construct; to build

Errichtung *(Gründung)* formation; *(Aufbau)* construction

Errungenschaft attainment; accomplishment; achievement

Ersatz replacement; substitute

Ersatzanspruch recourse; claim for damages

Ersatzbedarf replacement needs

Ersatzbeschaffung replacement purchase

Ersatz der Verschuldung debt displacement

Ersatzinvestition replacement investment

Ersatzkosten replacement costs

Ersatzmethode replacement method

Ersatzperson replacement

Ersatzteil spare part

erscheinen to appear; to turn up

Erscheinen appearance; emergence; *(Buch)* publication

Erscheinung appearance

Erscheinungsbild image; appearance

Erscheinungsdatum date of publication

erschließen to unlock; to tap; *(Land)* to develop

Erschließung *(Land)* development

erschöpfen to deplete; to exhaust

erschweren to hamper; to hinder; to impede

erschwinglich affordable

ersetzen to substitute; to replace; to restore; to recoup

ersparen *(sparen)* to save

Ersparnis savings; economy

Ersparnisse durch Produktionsvergrößerung economies of scale

erstatten to compensate; *(zurückgeben)* to return; to refund

Erstattung reimbursement; refund; rebate

Erstattungsanspruch claim for reimbursement

Erstattungsbescheid notice of repayment

erstattungsfähig refundable; reimbursable

Erstausstattung original equipment; *(Firma)* original capitalization

Erstinvestition initial investment

erstklassig first-rate; first-class; prime

erstklassige Aktie blue chip

erstklassiges Geldmarktpapier prime paper

erststellige Hypothek first mortgage

erstklassiges Wertpapier top-grade securities

Erstzeichner initial subscriber

ersuchen to request; to petition; to ask

Ersuchen request; application; petition

Ertrag *(Einkünfte)* earnings; receipts; revenue; *(Gewinn)* profit; gain; proceeds; *(Rendite)* yield

Ertrag pro Aktie earnings per share

ertragbringend productive; profitable

Erträge aus Beteiligungen income from investments

Erträge aus der Auflösung von Rückstellungen income from reversal of provisions for liabilities

Erträge der gewöhnlichen Geschäftstätigkeit revenues

Erträe aus anderer, als der gewöhnlichen Geschäftstätigkeit gains

ertraglos nonproductive; unprofitable

ertraglose Aktiva nonperforming assets

ertragreich profitable; productive

Ertragsausschüttung distribution of earnings

Ertragsbeteiligung profit-sharing

Ertragsfähigkeit earning capacity; earning potential; productivity

Ertragskonto revenue account

Ertragskraft earning power

Ertragslage profit situation

Ertragsmotiv profit motive

Ertragsorientierung profit orientation

Ertragsrechnung revenue account; earnings statement; profit and loss statement

Ertragsrückgang decline in earnings; diminishing returns

Ertragsschwelle break-even point

Ertragsschwelle überschreiten to achieve profitability

Ertragssteuer profit tax; tax on earnings

Ertragswert capitalized earning power; capitalized (income) value

Ertragswert-Verfahren gross rental method

Ertragszentrum revenue center; profit center

Erwägung consideration; deliberation

erwähnen to mention; to refer to

Erwähnung mention; reference

erwarten to expect; to anticipate

erwartete Rendite expected return

Erwartung expectation; anticipation

Erwartungshypothese (für Zinssätze) expectations hypothesis of interest rates

Erwartungsrechnung forecasts to the end of year

Erwartungstheorie der Wechselkurse expectation theory of foreign exchange rates

Erwartungswert expected value

erweitern to expand; to enlarge; to widen

Erweiterte Fondsfazilität Extended Fund Facility (EFF)

Erweiterung expansion; extension

Erwerb *(Kauf)* purchase; acquisition; *(Einkommen)* earnings

erwerben *(kaufen)* to purchase; to buy; to acquire; *(verdienen)* to earn; *(Fähigkeiten)* to gain

Erwerber *(Käufer)* purchaser; *(Haushalt)* provider

Erwerbsaltersgrenze age limit for gainful occupation

Erwerbsbevölkerung labor force

Erwerbseinkommen income from employment

erwerbsfähig capable of gainful employment; fit for work

Erwerbsfähigkeit ability to work; earning capacity

Erwerbskosten acquisition costs

Erwerbskurs basis price

Erwerbsmethode purchase accounting

Erwerbsoption bargain-purchase-price option

Erwerbsperson employed person

Erwerbsquote labor force participation rate

erwerbslos unemployed

Erwerbslosigkeit unemployment

Erwerbstätiger gainful person

Erwerbstätigkeit gainful employment

erwirtschaften to earn; to produce; to achieve

erzeugen to produce; to manufacture; to generate

Erzeuger producer; manufacturer; maker

Erzeugerland manufacturing country

Erzeugerpreis producer's price

Erzeugerpreisindex producer price index

Erzeugnis product; commodity

Erzeugnisgruppe product line; line of products

Erzeugnishauptstoff primary product

Erzeugnishilfsstoff secondary product

Erzeugniskapazität production capacity

Erzeugniskostenrechnung product cost accounting

Erzeugnisplanung product planning

Erzeugung production; manufacture

erziehen to educate; to train

Erziehung education; educational background

Erziehungsgeld education benefit

Erziehungsberechtigter guardian

erzielen to achieve; to obtain; *(Gewinn)* to realize

Erzielung *(Erreichen)* achievement; obtainment; *(Gewinn)* realization

erzwingen to force; to enforce

erzwungene Konversion forced conversion

erzwungener Umtausch forced conversion

etablieren, sich to establish oneself; to start a business

Etage floor

Etat budget; *(Werbeagentur)* billings; *(Kunde)* account

Etatabweichung budget variance

Etatdefizit budget deficit

Etatjahr budgetary year

Etatmanager budget manager; *(Werbung)* account manager

Etatplanung budgeting; budget planning

Etatposten budget item

Etatüberziehung budget overrun; overspending

Etatzuweisung budget appropriation

Ethik ethics

ethisch ethical

ethisches Dilemma ethical dilemma

Etikett label; tag; tally

etikettieren to label; to tag

Etikettierung labeling

Euroanleihe Eurobond

Eurodollar Eurodollar

Eurodollar-Anleihe Eurodollar bond

Eurogeldmarkt Euro-money market

Euro-Libor European London interbank offered rate

Europäische Atomgemeinschaft European Atomic Energy Community

Europäische Bank für Wiederaufbau und Entwicklung European Bank for Reconstruction and Development (EBRD)

Europäische Behörde zur Koordinierung der Forschung European Research Coordination Agency (EUREKA)

Europäische Gemeinschaft (EG) European Community (EC)

Europäische Gemeinschaft für Kohle und Stahl European Coal and Steel Community (ECSC)

Europäische Freihandelsassoziation European Free Trade Association (EFTA)

Europäische Investitionsbank (EIB) European Investment Bank

Europäische Kommission European Commission

Europäische Option European option

Europäisches Währungssystem European Monetary System (EMS)

Europäische Währungseinheit European Currency Unit (ECU)

Europäische Wirtschaftsgemeinschaft European Economic Community (EEC)

Europäische Wirtschafts- und Währungsunion Economic and Monetary Union (EMU)

Europäischer Binnenmarkt European Market

Europäischer Ausgleichs- und Garantiefonds für die Landwirtschaft European Agricultural Guidance and Guarantee Fund

Europäischer Fonds für regionale Entwicklung European Regional Development Fund

Europäischer Gerichtshof European Court of Justice

Europäischer Investitionsfond European Investment Fund

Europäischer Rat European Council

Europäischer Wirtschaftsraum European Economic Space

Europäisches Parlament European Parliament

Europäisches Währungsabkommen European Monetary Agreement (EMA)

Europäisches Währungssystem European Monetary System (EMS)

Europäisches Wiederaufbauprogramm European Recovery Program (ERP), Marshall Plan

Europäische Union European Union

Europäische Verteidigungsgemeinschaft European Defense Community

Europäische Währungseinheit European Currency Unit (ECU)

Europäische Wirtschafts- und Währungsunion European Economic and Monetary Union (EMU)

Europäische Zahlungsunion European Payment Union (EPU)

Europäische Zentralbank European Central Bank (ECB)

Europarat Council of Europe

Event-Studie event study

Eventualforderung contingent asset

Eventualverbindlichkeit contingent liability

Eventualfall contingency

eventuell possible; contingent

ewige Rente perpetuity

exakte Datumskonvention dates convention

ex-Bezugsrechte ex-rights

ex-Bezugsscheine ex-warrants

ex-Dividende ex dividend

Existenz existence; subsistence; living

Existenzbedürfnis, Beziehungsbedürfnis und Wachstumsbedürfnis–Theorie existence, relatedness, growth (ERG) – theory

Existenzgrundlage livelihood

existieren to exist

Exklusionsübernahmeangebot exclusionary tender offer

expandieren to expand

Expansion expansion

Expansionskurs expansion path

Expansionspolitik expansionary policy

Experiment experiment

experimentieren to experiment

Experte expert

Expertenbericht expert report

Expertenmacht expert power

Expertensystem expert system

Expertise expertise; expert's opinion

Explorationskosten exploration cost

Export export; exportation; export trade

Exportabteilung export department

Exportagent export agent

Exportanstieg rise in exports

Exportauftrag export order

Exportaussicht export prospects

Exportbeschränkung export restriction

Exportbestimmungen export regulations

Exportdokumente export documents

Exporteinnahmen export receipts

Exportertrag export earnings

Exporteur exporter; export firm

Exportfinanzierung export financing

Exportförderung export promotion

Exportgeschäft export house; export business; *(Handel)* export transaction

exportieren to export

Exportindustrie export industry

Exportkoeffizient export ratio

Exportkraft export strength

Exportkredit export credit

Exportland exporting country

Exportleiter export manager

Exportlizenz export license

exportorientiert export oriented

Exportsachbearbeiter export coordinator

Exportsortiment export product range

Exportsubvention export subsidy

Exportsteigerung rise in exports

Exportsubvention export subsidy

Exportüberschuss export surplus

Exportverbot ban on exports

Exportvolumen export volume

Exportwachstum export growth

Exportwirtschaft export economy

Exportzuwachs export growth

extern external

externe Finanzmittel external funds

externe Revision external audit; independent audit

extra extra; over and above

Extraausgaben sundry expenses; sundries

Extragebühr extra charge

Extrasteuer surtax

Extravergütung special allowance

Extraversicherung additional inssurance

F

Fabrik factory

Fabrikabsatz factory sales

Fabrikanlage plant

Fabrikant manufacturer

Fabrikat product; make; brand

Fabrikation manufacture; production

Fabrikationsanlage production facility

Fabrikationsbetrieb manufacturing company

Fabrikationsfähigkeit production capability

Fabrikationsfehler flaw; manufacturing defect

Fabrikationsgemeinkosten production overheads

Fabrikationskosten manufacturing costs

Fabrikationsleiter production manager

Fabrikationsmethode manufacturing process

Fabrikationsnummer serial number

Fabrikationsprozess manufacturing process

Fabrikationsrechte manufacturing rights

Fabrikationsrisiko risk of manufacture

Fabrikauslastung factory operating rate

Fabrikeinrichtung factory equipment

Fabrikgeheimnis industrial secret; trade secret

Fabrikleiter plant manager

Fabrikschließung plant closure; *(zeitweilig)* plant shutdown

fabrikmäßig herstellen to mass produce

fabrikneu brand new

Fach *(Arbeitsgebiet)* field; line; *(Geschäftszweig)* trade; profession; business; *(Unterricht)* subject; *(Schrank)* shelf; box

Facharbeiter skilled worker

Fachausbildung vocational training; technical training

Fachausdruck technical term

Fachausdrücke terminology

Fachausstellung trade exhibition; trade show

Fachblatt trade journal

Fachgebiet subject area; specialty

Fachgeschäft speciality store

Fachgroßhandel specialized wholesale trade

Fachhändler specialty retailer; limited-line retailer

Fachinteresse professional interest

Fachjournal trade journal

Fachkraft skilled worker

fachkundig expert; competent in one's field

Fachleute experts; professionals; specialists

Fachmann expert; professional; specialist

fachmännisch professional; expert

Fachmesse trade fair

Fachpresse trade press

Fachsprache terminology

Fachvereinigung professional association

Fachwissen know-how; expert knowledge

Fachzeitschrift trade magazine

fähig able; capable; competent

Fähigkeit ability; capability; qualification

Fähigkeitstest capability test

Fahrdienstleiter traffic superintendent

fahren to drive

fahrlässig negligent

Fahrlässigkeit negligence; default

Fahrplan timetable

Fahrpreis fare

Fahrt *(Reise)* trip; tour; *(Fahren)* drive; *(Überfahrt)* voyage

fairer Marktwert fair market value

Faktor factor; element; criterion

Faktoranalyse factor analysis

Faktoreinkommen factor income

Faktoreinsatz factor input

Faktorerträge factor returns

Faktorkosten factor costs

Faktorgeschäft factoring business

Faktorgrenzkosten marginal factor costs

Faktoring factoring

Faktorkombination factor combination

Faktormobilität factor mobility

Faktorpreis factor price

Faktura invoice; bill

Fakturabetrag invoiced amount

Fakturierung invoicing; billing

fakultativ optional; voluntary

Fall *(Situation)* case; circumstance; *(Sinken)* slump; decline; fall

fallen to fall; to sink; to tumble; to decline; to drop

fallende Abschreibung accelerated depreciation

fallen lassen to drop; to abandon

fällig due; *(Obligationen)* mature; *(zahlbar)* payable

Fälligkeit due date; *(Obligationen)* maturity

Fälligkeitsdatum maturity date

Fälligkeits-Faktoring maturity-factoring

Fälligkeitstabelle aging schedule

Fälligkeitstermin due date; settlement date; *(Obligationen)* date of maturity

Fälligkeitswert maturity value

fällig werden to become due; *(Obligationen)* to mature

Fallpräsentation case presentation

Fallstudie case study

falsch wrong; incorrect; *(gefälscht)* forged; falsified; *(Geld)* counterfeit; *(unecht)* fake; *(ungenau)* inaccurate

falsch berechnen to miscalculate

Falschbuchung false entry; fraudulent entry

fälschen to falsify; to fake; *(Urkunde)* to forge; *(Geld)* to counterfeit

Fälschung falsification; fake; *(Urkunde)* forgery; *(Geld)* counterfeiting

Familienabzug *(Steuer)* allowance for dependants

familienfreundlicher Betrieb family-friendly workplace

Familiengesellschaft family-owned company

Familienpolitik family policy

Familienstand marital status

Familienverhältnisse family background

Familienzuschlag family allowance

fangen to catch; to capture

Faschismus fascism

fassen *(anfassen)* to grasp; *(enthalten)* to hold; *(verstehen)* to comprehend

Fassung version; *(Lampe)* socket; *(Haltung)* composure

Fassungsvermögen capacity

Feedback feedback

fegen to sweep

Fehlallokation misallocation

Fehlbestand shortage; stockout

Fehlbetrag deficit; shortage; shortfall; missing amount

fehlen to lack; to be missing

Fehlen lack; failure; *(Person)* absence

fehlend absent; missing

Fehler mistake; error; fault; *(Material)* defect

fehlerhaft faulty; deficient

fehlerhafte Übergabe bad delivery

Fehlerhäufigkeit error rate; error frequency

Fehlerquelle source of error

Fehlerquote error rate

Fehlermeldung error message

Fehlersuche troubleshooting

Fehlfracht dead freight

Fehlinterpretation misinterpretation

Fehlinvestition bad investment; unprofitable investment

Fehlkalkulation miscalculation

Fehlkauf bad buy

Fehlkonstruktion faulty design

fehlleiten to misdirect

Fehlmenge deficiency; shortage; shortfall

Fehlmengenkosten out-of-stock costs

Fehlprognose false prognosis

Fehlschlag failure; *(Enttäuschung)* disappointment

fehlschlagen to fail

Fehlurteil miscarriage of justice; misjudgement

Fehlverhalten der Mitarbeiter employee deviance

Fehlzeiten absenteeism

Fehlzeitenquote absence rate

feilschen to haggle; to bargain

Feilschen haggling; bargaining

feindlich hostile

feindliche Übernahme hostile takeover, unfriendly takeover

Feingehalt fineness

Feld domain; field

Feldzug campaign

fern distant

Fernbleiben, unentschuldigtes absenteeism

Fernmeldewesen telecommunications; communications

Fernschreiber telex

Fernsprecher telephone

Fernsprechgebühr toll; long distance rate

Fernsprechleitung telephone wire

Fernverkehr long-distance traffic

Fertigkeit skill; capability

Fertigprodukt finished product; manufactured article

fertig stellen to finish; to complete

Fertigstellung completion; *(Produktion)* finishing

Fertigung production; manufacturing; assembly

Fertigungsablauf production flow; production sequence

Fertigungsablaufplanung production sequencing

Fertigungsanlage factory; plant

Fertigungseinzelkosten prime costs

Fertigungsgemeinkosten manufacturing overheads; indirect labor costs

Fertigungshalle production hall

Fertigungskontrolle production control; process control

Fertigungskosten manufacturing costs; production costs

Fertigungsleiter production manager

Fertigungslohn direct labor

Fertigungsplan manufacturing schedule

Fertigungsplanung production planning

Fertigungsprogramm production program; product line

Fertigungsprogrammplanung production program planning

Fertigungsprozess production process

Fertigungsprozessplanung production process planning

Fertigungsqualität manufacturing quality

Fertigungssteuerung production control

Fertigungssystem production system

Fertigungstechnik production engineering; production technology

Fertigungstiefe vertical range of manufacture

Fertigungsverfahren manufacturing process

Fertigungswirtschaft manufacturing

Fertigwaren finished goods

Fertigwarenlager finished goods inventory; stock of finished goods

fesseln to tie; to constrain; (*anziehen*) to attract; to fascinate

fest solid; firm; fixed

Festbestellung firm order

Festbewertung permanent valuation; asset valuation on a standard-value basis

feste Rente fixed annuity, guaranteed-dollar annuity

fester Wechselkurs fixed exchange rate

festes Angebot firm offer; positive offer

Festbestellung firm order

Festgeld time deposit; fixed-term deposit

Festgeldhypothek fixed mortgage

Festgeldkonto fixed deposit account

Festgeldzins fixed-period interest rate

festgesetzt stipulated; stated

festgestellter Wert stated value

festigen to stabilize

Festigkeit stability; resistance; firmness

Festigung stabilization

Festkosten overheads; fixed costs

Festland mainland

festlegen to state; *(bestimmen)* to determine; to set; *(Kapital)* to tie up

festlegen, sich to make a commitment

festnehmen to arrest; to apprehend; to detain

festschreiben *(Wertpapiere)* to lock in; to peg

festsetzbar determinable

festsetzen to stipulate; to fix; *(bestimmen)* to determine; *(Termin)* to set; to schedule; *(Normen)* to standardize

feststellbar identifiable; determinable

feststellen to determine; *(erklären)* to declare; to state; *(ermitteln)* to ascertain; to find out; to diagnose; *(Fehler)* to locate

Feststellung determination; *(Erklärung)* statement; declaration; *(Ermittlung)* finding; ascertainment; diagnosis; *(Wert)* appraisal

Festübernahme firm commitment; firm underwriting

festverzinslich fixed-interest bearing

festverzinsliches Wertpapier bond

Festzins fixed rate of interest

Festzinsanleihe fixed rate loan

Festzinsen fixed interest

Fiedlers Kontingenzmodell Fielder contingency model

Fifo-Verfahren Fifo method; first-in, first-out method

Filialbank branch bank

Filiale subsidiary; branch

Filialgeschäft chain store

Filialnetz branch network

filtern to filter

Financial-Times-Börsenindex Financial Times Stock Exchange Index (FTSE)

Finanz- finance

Finanzabgabe revenue duty; fiscal charge

Finanzabteilung finance department

Finanzaktiva financial assets

Finanzamt tax office; (US)Internal Revenue Service (IRS); (UK) Inland Revenue Office

Finanzanalyse financial analysis

Finanzanlagen financial assets; investments

Finanzanlagevermögen financial assets; long-term receivables

Finanzausgleich financial compensation; revenue sharing

Finanzauskunft status report

Finanzautonomie financial autonomy

Finanzbeamter tax inspector

Finanzbedarf financial requirements; monetary requirements

Finanzberatung financial advice

Finanzbuchhaltung financial accounting

Finanzchef chief financial officer (CFO)

Finanzcontrolling financial controlling

Finanzdienstleistungen financial services

Finanzdirektor financial director; treasurer

Finanzen finances

Finanzertrag financial yield

Finanzflussanalyse cash flow analysis

Finanzgesellschaft finance company

Finanzgericht Tax Court; Court of Claims

Finanzhilfe financial aid

finanziell financial; monetary

finanzielle Aktiva financial asset

finanzielle Lage financial condition, financial position

finanzielle Situation financial condition, financial position

finanzielles Risiko financial risk

finanzielle Vermögenswerte financial assets

finanziell unterstützen to subsidize

finanzieren to fund; to finance; to bankroll

Finanzierung financing; (*Projekt*) funding

Finanzierung aus eigener Kraft internal financing

Finanzierung durch Aktienemission equity financing; stock financing

Finanzierung durch Kredite credit financing

Finanzierung mit Lieferantenkrediten trade credit financing

Finanzierung mit Risikokapital venture capital financing

Finanzierung von Abzahlungsgeschäften hire-purchase financing

Fienanzierung von Warenforderungen accounts receivable financing

Finanzierungsanalyse financing analysis

Finanzierungsdefizit financing deficit

Finanzierungsgesellschaft finance company

Finanzierungsinstitut financing institution

Finanzierungsinstrumente instruments

Finanzierungskennzahl financing ratio

Finanzierungskosten financing costs

Finanzierungs-Leasing financial leasing; finance lease; capital lease

Finanzierungsrechnung capital finance account

Finanzierungsregel financing rule

Finanzierungssystem financial plan

Finanzierungsstrom financing flow; credit flow

Finanzierungsstruktur financing structure; capital structure

Finanzinstitut financial institution

Finanzinvestition financial investment

Finanzintermediäre financial intermediaries

Finanzkrise financial crisis

Finanzlage financial situation; financial standing

Finanzleiter treasurer; chief financial officer (CFO)

Finanzmanagement financial management; cash management

Finanzmarkt financial market

Finanzminister finance minister; (*US*) Secretary of the Treasury; (*UK*) Chancellor of the Exchequer

Finanzministerium treasury; treasury department

Finanzmittel funds; capital

Finanzmittler financial intermediary

Finanzplan budget; financial plan; financial budget

Finanzplanung budgeting

Finanzplaner chartered financial accountant

Finanzplanung financial planning; budgeting

Finanzplatz financial center

Finanzpolitik fiscal policy

Finanzpresse financial press

Finanzproblem financial problem

Finanzstärke financial strength

Finanzstrategie finance strategy

Finanzteil *(Zeitung)* financial pages

Finanzverwaltung financial management; financial administration; *(Behörde)* fiscal authority

Finanzvorstand financial director, vice-president finance

Finanzwesen finance

Finanzwirtschaft corporate finance; financial management

finanzwirtschaftliche Kennzahl financial ratio

Finanzzentrum financial center

Finanzzoll revenue tariff; customs duty

Finanzzuschuss capital grant

Finanzzuweisung allocation of funds; budget appropriation

finden to find; to locate

Finte red herring; trick

Firma firm; business; company; *(Firmierung)* business name; trade name

Firmenanwalt corporate lawyer

Firmenbetreuung corporate relations service

Firmenbezeichnung trade name

Firmenchef chief executive officer (CEO); president; director of a company

firmeneigen company-owned; in-house

Firmenfusion merger

Firmengruppe group of companies

Firmengründung company foundation; estabishment of a company

Firmenimage corporate image

Firmeninhaber owner of a company; proprietor

Firmenkredit corporate lending

Firmenkunde corporate customer; corporate client; business client

Firmenkundengeschäft corporate business

Firmenleitung corporate management

Firmenlogo company logo; corporate symbol

Firmenmantel shell company

Firmenname corporate name; trade name

Firmenorganisation corporate organization

Firmenübernahme acquisition

Firmenvermögen corporate assets

Firmenwagen company car

Firmenwert goodwill

Firmenwert-Abschreibung goodwill amortization

Firmenzeichen trade mark; brand; logo

Firmenzusammenschluss merger

firmieren to trade under a name

fiskalisch fiscal; financial

Fiskalpolitik fiscal policy

Fixkosten fixed costs

Fiskus financial administration

fixer Wechselkurs fixed exchange rate

fixierter Intervallplan fixed-interval schedule

fixierter Quotenplan fixed-ratio schedule

Fläche area

flau sluggish; soft; stagnant; weak; slow

Flaute sluggishness; slack period; slackness; weakness

flexibel flexible

flexible Fertigungssystem flexible manufacturing systems

flexibler Wechselkurs flexible exchange rate; floating currency exchange rate

flexible Zusatzleistungen flexible benefits

Flexibilität flexibility

Fließband assembly line

fließen to flow

floaten to float

florieren to prosper; to flourish

Flucht flight; escape

Fluchtkapital flight capital

Fluggesellschaft airline

Flughafen airport

Flughafengebäude airport terminal

Flugplan flight schedule

Flugzeug aircraft; airplane

Fluktuation fluctuation; *(Mitarbeiter)* employee turnover

Fluktuationsabgang attrition

fluktuationsbedingt frictional; fluctuation-induced

fluktuieren to fluctuate

flüssig fluid; *(Firma)* liquid; *(Kapital)* available; *(Stil)* fluent

flüssige Mittel liquid funds; quick assets

föderal federal

föderalistisch federal

Folge sequence; *(Wirkung)* consequence

Fonds pool; fund

Fondsvermögen fund assets; *(Kapitalanlagegesellschaft)* asset value

Förderer sponsor; patron

fordern to demand; to claim

fördern to promote; to advance; *(ermutigen)* to encourage; to boost; *(entwickeln)* to develop; *(helfen)* to aid; *(Bergbau)* to mine

fördernde Kräfte driving forces

Förderprogramm promotional program; support program

Forderung demand; request; requirement; *(Schulden)* debt; *(Anspruch)* claim; receivable

Förderung promotion; advancement; *(Ermutigung)* encouragement; *(Entwicklung)* development; *(Hilfe)* aid

Forderungen *(Bilanz)* accounts receivable; receivables; debts; debtors

Forderungen aus Lieferungen und Leistungen accounts receivable

Forderungsausfall bad debt; loss of receivables

Forderungslaufzeit days in receivables; average collection period

Forderungsumschlag receivables turnover ratio

Forfaitierung forfaiting

Form, der ~ halber pro forma

formal formal

formale Gruppe formal group

formale Netzwerke formal networks

Formalisierung formalization

Formalität formality

Formel formula

formell formal

formen to shape; to form

Formgebung design

förmlich formal; ceremonial

Förmlichkeit formality; form

formlos informal; shapeless

Formlosigkeit informality

Formular form; blank; schedule

Formular ausfüllen to fill out a form

Formularseite form

formulieren to phrase; to formulate

Formulierung phrase; formulation

forschen to research; to do research

Forschung research; analysis

Forschungsanlage research facility

Forschungsarbeit research study

Forschungsaufgabe research assignment; research project

Forschungsauftrag research assignment

Forschungsaufwand research expenditure; investment in research

Forschungsausgaben research spending

Forschungsbeihilfe research grant

Forschungsbereich area of research; field of study

Forschungsgebiet area of research; field of study

Forschungsinstitut research institute

Forschungsleiter research director

Forschungsprogramm research program

Forschungsprojekt research project

Forschungsstudie research study

Forschungszentrum research center

Forschung und Entwicklung (F&E) research and development (R&D)

Forschungs- und Entwicklungskosten research and development costs; R&D costs

Fortbestand survival; continuance

fortbilden to improve one's skills; to continue one's education

Fortbildung further training; skill enhancement

Fortbildung, außerbetriebliche off-the-job training

Fortbildung, betriebliche on-the-job training; in-house training

fortdauern to persist; to continue

fortfahren to proceed; to continue

fortführen to pursue; to continue

fortgeführter Anschaffungswert book value

fortgeschritten advanced

fortlaufend continuous

fortschreiten to progress; to advance

Fortschritt progress; advance; *(Verbesserung)* improvement

fortschrittlich progressive; forward-looking

Fortschrittsrate rate of progress

fortsetzen to continue; to sustain

Fortsetzung continuation; continuance

Fotokopie photocopy

fotokopieren to photocopy

Fracht load; freight; cargo

Frachtaufschlag freight surcharge

Frachtbrief consignment note; letter of consignment; waybill; bill of lading

Frachtbriefduplikat duplicate waybill

frachtfrei carriage paid; freight and carriage paid

Frachtführer carrier; haulage contractor

Frachtfuhrunternehmen haulage company

Frachtgebühr carriage; freight

Frachtgeld carriage; freight

Frachtgut freight; cargo

Frachtkosten freight charges

Frachtpapier shipping document; freight document; (*Konnossement*) bill of lading

Frachtraum tonnage

Frachtschiff cargo ship; freighter; transport ship

Frachtvermerk freight clause

Frachtvertrag contract of carriage; freight contract

Frachtzettel waybill; freight bill; dispatch note

Frage question; *(Problem)* problem; *(Kernpunkt)* issue

Fragebogen questionnaire

fragen to question; to ask

fragwürdig questionable; dubious

Franchisegeber franchisor

Franchisenehmer franchisee

Franchising franchising

frankieren to stamp

frankiert stamped

franko postage paid; prepaid; carriage paid

frei free; *(frei von)* exempt

freiberuflich self-employed; professional; *(Journalist)* freelance

Freibetrag personal allowance; exemption

freibleibend without obligation; subject to change without notice; not binding

freie Kapazität surplus capacity

freier Markt open market; free market

freier Wechselkurs floating exchange rate; flexible exchange rate

Freigabe release; decontrol; deregulation; clearance

freigeben to release; to float; to decontrol; to deregulate; to clear

freigiebig generous; lavish

freigegebener Wechselkurs floating exchange rate

Freihafen free port; free trade zone

Freihandel free trade

Freihandelszone free trade area; export processing zone; foreign trade zone

Freilager bonded warehouse; open-air storage

freilassen to release; to set free

Freilassung release

freimachen *(Post)* to stamp; *(Zoll)* to clear out; *(Sitz)* to vacate

freischaffend free-lance; self-employed

Freischaffender freelancer

Freispruch acquittal

Freitag, schwarzer black Friday

frei übertragbar negotiable

frei verfügbares Einkommen discretionary income

Freiverkehr *(Börse)* over the counter market

freiwillig voluntary; optional

freiwilliger Konkurs voluntary bankruptcy

Freizeit leisure; free time

Freizeit- recreational

Freizeitangebot leisure time facilities

Freizeitartikel recreation-oriented product

Freizeitbeschäftigung leisure-time pursuit

Freizeitindustrie leisure industry

Freizeitkleidung casual wear

Freizeitwert recreational value

Freizeitwirtschaft leisure industry

Freizügigkeit freedom of trade; freedom of movement; mobility

fremd *(ausländisch)* foreign; *(unbekannt)* strange; *(Kapital)* outside

Fremdenverkehr tourism

Fremdenzimmer guest room

Fremder stranger; alien; foreigner

Fremdfinanzierung borrowing; debt financing

Fremdfinanzierung, kurzfristige short-term debt financing

Fremdfinanzierung, langfristige long-term debt financing

Fremdfinanzierungsbedarf external financing requirements

fremdfinanziertes Übernahmeangebot leveraged buyout (LBO)

Fremdfinanzierungsgrad leverage; borrowing ratio

Fremdgeld borrowed money

Fremdkapital debt; outside capital; external finance

Fremdkapitalanteil capital gearing

Fremdkapitalbelastung gearing

Fremkapitalgeber outside creditor

Fremdsprache foreign language

Fremdmittel outside capital; outside funds

Fremdwährung foreign currency; foreign exchange

Fremdwährungsanleihe foreign bond

Fremdwährungskonto foreign currency account

Fremdwährungsposition foreign currency position

Fremdwährunsrisiko foreign currency exposure

freundliche Übernahme friendly takeover

Freundschaftsgruppen friendship group

Friedensstifter conciliator

Frist period of time; term; *(Aufschub)* extension; grace period; *(Ultimatum)* deadline; *(Kündigungsfrist)* notice

Fristigkeit maturity

Frist einhalten to meet the deadline

Frist setzen to set a time limit

Frist gewehren to grant additional time

fristlose Kündigung dismissal without notice

fruchtbar fruitful; prolific; *(Boden)* fertile

frühe Ausübung early exercise

Früherkennung early warning

Frühwarnung early warning

Fuhre cartload; truckload

führen to lead; to guide *(Geschäfte)* to manage; to conduct; *(Bücher)* to keep; *(Waren)* to sell; to carry; *(lenken)* to direct

führend leading; *(Funktion)* managerial

führende Rolle leadership role

Führer leader; *(Tourismus)* guide

Führer-Mitarbeiter-Beziehungen leader-member relations

Führerschein driver's license

Führung *(Geschäft)* management; leadership; direction; *(Lenkung)* guidance; *(Benehmen)* conduct

Führung durch Aufgabendelegation management by delegation

Führung durch Erfolgsmessung management by results

Führung durch Mitarbeitermotivation management by motivation

Führung durch Zielvereinbarungen management by objectives

Führung nach dem Ausnahmeprinzip management by exception

Führungsanspruch claim for leadership

Führungsansatz leadership approach

Führungsebene management level

Führungsfähigkeit leadership ability

Führungsgruppe management team

Führungsinstrument management tool

Führungskontrolle management control

Führungskraft executive; manager

Führungskraft mit Linienfunktion line executive; line manager

Führungslaufbahn management career

Führungslehre management science

führungslos without leadership

Führungsmittel managerial instruments; management tools

Führungsmodell management model

Führungsnachwuchs *(Industrie)* management trainees; *(Politik)* future leaders

Führungspersonal management personnel

Führungsposition leadership position; *(Arbeitsstelle)* executive position

Führungsprinzip leadership principle

Führungsproblem managerial problem

Führungsprozess management process

Führungsqualifikation management qualification

Führungsqualität leadership quality; management skills

Führungsschicht establishment

Führungsschwäche lack of leadership; indecisive leadership

Führungsseminar management seminar

Führungsstab executive staff; *(Militär)* operational headquarters

Führungsstil management style

Führungsstruktur management structure

Führungstätigkeit management functions

Führungsverhalten leadership stance; leadership behavior

Führungswechsel change in leadership

Führungszeugnis certificate of good conduct; (*polizeilich*) police clearance

Fuhrunternehmer carrier; haulage company; trucking company

Fülle abundance

Fund discovery; find

fundamental fundamental

Fundamentalanalyse fundamental analysis; portfolio analysis

fundiert funded; well-grounded; *(Anleihe)* consolidated; *(Firma)* sound

Fundierung foundation; *(Anleihe)* funding

Fünf-Phasen Modell der Gruppenentwicklung five-stage group-development model

fungieren to function; to act as; to serve as

Funktion office; function

funktional functional

Funktionalanalyse functional analysis

funktionaler Konflikt functional conflict

Funktionalorganisation functional organization

Funktionär official; officer

funktionieren to work; to operate; to function

Funktionsbereich area of operation

Funktionsfähigkeit operational capability

Funktionsrabatt trade discount; functional discount

funktionsübergreifende Teams cross-functional teams

Fürsorge *(staatlich)* welfare; *(Pflege)* care

Fürsprecher advocate

Fusion merger; consolidation

fusionieren to merge; to combine

Fusionsbilanz consolidated balance sheet

Fusionskontrolle merger control

Fusionsvertrag merger agreement

Fusionswelle takeover wave

G

Gabe gift; donation; *(Fähigkeit)* talent; gift

Gang an die Börse going public; initial public offering (IPO)

Ganzheitlichkeit der Leistung task identity

Ganztagsarbeit full-time employment

Garantie guarantee; security; *(des Verkäufers)* warranty

Garantieleistungen guarantee items

Garantiepreis guaranteed price

Garantieschreiben letter of guarantee

garantieren to guarantee; *(verkaufte Waren)* to warrant; *(Effekten)* to underwrite

Garantieverpflichtung indemnity bond

Garantiezeit warranty period

Gast guest; *(Fremdenheim)* boarder

Gastarbeiter guest worker

Gastgeber host

Gastland host country

Gattung kind; type; sort

Gebäude building; structure

Gebäudeschaden damage to a building; structural damages

Geber donor

Gebiet territory; zone; region; field; area

Gebietsansässiger resident

Gebietsfremder non-resident; alien

Gebietskörperschaft local authority; area municipality

Gebietsleiter area manager, regional manager

Gebietsschutz territory protection

Gebietsmonopol regional monopoly

Gebietsverlust loss of territory

Gebietsvertreter area representative; regional representative

Gebot *(Anweisung)* instruction; *(Versteigerung)* bid; offer

Gebrauch use; usage; exercise; handling; application

Gebrauchsgegenstand commodity; article of daily use

Gebrauchsgüter consumer goods; durable goods

Gebrauchsmuster sample; utility pattern

Gebrauchsmusterschutz protection of utility patents

gebrauchsunfähig unusable

Gebrauchswert value in use; trade-in value

gebraucht used; second-hand

Gebrauchtgerät second-hand machinery

Gebrauchtwarenmarkt second-hand market

Gebrechen physical handicap

gebrochener Güterverkehr combined shipment

Gebühr charge; fee; *(Zoll)* duty; *(Lizenz)* royalty; *(Telefon)* toll

gebührenfrei free of charge; *(Telefon)* toll free; (*zollfrei*) duty-free

gebührenpflichtig subject to charges; *(Post)* subject to postage; (*Zoll*) dutiable

Gedankenaustausch exchange of ideas

gedeckte Option covered option

gedeihen to thrive; to prosper; to flourish

Gedeihen prosperity

gedrückt depressed; subdued

geeignet suitable; eligible; fit

Gefahr danger; peril; *(Risiko)* risk

gefährden to jeopardize; to compromise; to endanger

Gefährdungshaftung absolute liability

Gefahrenpotential risk potential

gefährlich risky; dangerous

Gefälle slope; *(Unterschied)* differential; gap

Gefälligkeit favour; gratuitous service

Gefälligkeitspapier accommodation paper

gefälscht counterfeit; fake; falsified

Gefüge structure

Gegenbuchung counter entry; reverse entry; offset

Gegend region; area

Gegengewicht counterbalance

Gegenleistung *(Vertrag)* consideration; reward; *(Gegenwert)* equivalent; (*Erkenntlichkeit*) quid pro quo

Gegenmittel antidote; remedy; corrective

Gegensaldo counterbalance

gegenseitig reciprocal; mutual

Gegenseitigkeit reciprocity

Gegenstand object; item; matter; article

Gegenstand des Anlagevermögens fixed asset

Gegenstand des Umlaufvermögens current asset

Gegenstromverfahren mixed planning; top-down/bottom-up planning

Gegenstück counterpart

gegenüberstehen to face

Gegenvorschlag counterproposal

Gegenwart *(Anwesenheit)* presence; *(Zeit)* present

gegenwärtig present

Gegenwartswert present value

Gegenwert equivalent; counter value

Gegenwertmittel counterpart funds

Gehalt contents; *(Fassungsvermögen)* capacity

Gehalt salary; earnings; pay

Gehaltsabrechnung salary statement

Gehaltsabschluss pay settlement

Gehaltsabteilung payroll department

Gehaltsangebot salary offer

Gehaltsempfänger salaried employee

Gehaltserhöhung pay raise; salary increase

Gehaltsforderung salary demand; pay claim

Gehaltskonto payroll account; checking account

Gehaltskürzung cut in pay; cut in salary

Gehaltsrunde collective bargaining

Gehaltszuschlag salary bonus

geheim secret; *(vertraulich)* confidential

Geheimhaltung secrecy; concealment

Geheimnis secret; mystery

Gehilfe assistant; aid

gehören to belong to

gekoppelter Auftrag contingent order

Geisel hostage

gekreuzter Scheck crossed check

Gelände tract of land; area; terrain

Geld money; *(Bargeld)* cash; *(Börse)* bid; *(Kleingeld)* change

Geld abheben to withdraw money

Geld anlegen to invest money

Geld aufnehmen to raise money; to borrow money

Geld ausleihen to lend money

Geld bewilligen to grant money

Geld einfordern to demand payment

Geld einzahlen to pay in money; to deposit money

Geld herausgeben to give change

Geld nehmen *(Bestechung)* to take bribes

Geld schicken to remit money

Geld sparen to save money

Geld überweisen to remit money

Geld verdienen to make money; to earn money

Geld wechseln to change money

Geld zuweisen to appropriate money

Geldakkord money piece rate

Geldanlage money investment; cash item

Geldanleger investor

Geldanweisung remittance

Geldautomat automated teller machine (ATM)

Geldbeschaffung fund-raising; borrowing

Geldbörse purse

Geld-Brief-Spanne money spread; price spread

Geldbuße fine; penalty

Geldeingang money receipts

Geldeinheit monetary unit

Geldeinlage deposit; money paid in

Geldentwertung *(Währung)* depreciation of the currency; *(Inflation)* inflation

Geldforderung monetary claim; *(ausstehende Gelder)* money due; outstanding debt

Geldgeber financial backer; financier; investor; *(Förderer)* sponsor

Geldinstitut financial institution; finance company

Geldknappheit tight money

Geldkurs bid price; buying rate of exchange

geldlich monetary

Geldmarkt money market; financial market

Geldmarktanlage money market investment

Geldmärkte money markets

Geldmarktfonds money market fund

Geldmarktgeschäft money market business; money market transaction

Geldmarktpapiere money market securities; money market instruments

Geldmarktpolitik monetary policy

Geldmarktzertifikat certificate of deposit (CD)

Geldmenge money supply

Geldmengenerhöhung increase in the money supply

Geldmengenpolitik money supply policy

Geldmengenvermehrung increase in the money supply

Geldmengenwachstum growth in the money supply

Geldmengenziel money supply target

Geldnot shortage of money; financial straits

Geldpolitik monetary policy

Geldschöpfung creation of money

Geldsendung remittance

Geldstrafe penalty; fine

Geldsubstitut near money

Geldstück coin

Geldsumme sum of money; fund

Geldtheorie monetary theory

Geldübermittlung money transfer; remittance

Geldüberweisung remittance

Geldumlauf circulation of money

Geldverkehr money transfer; circulation of money

Geldvermehrung increase in currency

Geldvermögen monetary assets

Geldversorgung money supply

Geldverwalter financial manager; money manager

Geldvolumen volume of money

Geldwäsche money laundering

Geldwert value of money; monetary value; *(Wert in Geld)* cash value

Geldwertstabilität currency stability

Geldwesen finance; monetary system

Gelegenheit opportunity; occasion

Gelegenheitsgesellschaft joint venture

Gelegenheitskauf bargain

Gelegenheit zur Leistung opportunity to perform

gelegentlich incidental; occasional

gelten to be in force; *(Wert sein)* to be worth; *(Text)* to prevail

geltend machen *(Gesetz)* to enforce; *(Anspruch)* to assert

Geltendmachung *(Gesetz)* enforcement; *(Anspruch)* assertion

Geltung *(Ansehen)* authority; standing; *(Gültigkeit)* validity; *(Wert)* value; *(Wichtigkeit)* importance

gemäß *(angemessen)* appropriate; *(entsprechend)* in accordance with; *(zufolge)* as a result of

Gemeinde community

Gemeindeverwaltung local government

Gemeinkosten indirect costs; overhead costs; overheads; fixed costs; general expenses

Gemeinkosten, direkte direct overhead

Gemeinkostenabweichung overhead variance

Gemeinkostenansatz assessment of overheads

Gemeinkostensatz overhead rate

Gemeinkostenunterdeckung underabsorption of overheads

Gemeinkostenwertanalyse overhead-value analysis

gemeinnützig nonprofit; charitable

gemeinsam collective; common

Gemeinsamer Markt common market

Gemeinsamer Zolltarif common customs tariff *(CCT)*

gemeinsame Steuererklärung joint tax return; joint return

Gemeinschaft collective; community; alliance

gemeinschaftlich collective; joint; common

gemeinschaftliches Eigentum joint ownership

Gemeinschaftsabgabe (*EU*) Community levy

Gemeinschaftsanleihe (*EU*) Community loan

Gemeinschaftsgebiet (*EU*) Community area

Gemeinschaftsklage class action (lawsuit)

Gemeinschaftskonto joint account; omnibus account

Gemeinschaftsunternehmen joint venture

Gemeinschaftsverfahren *(EU)* Community procedure

Gemeinschaftsverordnung *(EU)* Community regulation

Gemeinschaftsvorschriften *(EU)* Community rules

Gemeinschaftszoll *(EU)* Community tariff

Gemeinschaft Unabhängiger Staaten Commonwealth of Independent States (CIS)

Gemeinschuldner bankrupt; common debtor

Gemeinwert market value

Gemeinwirtschaft social economy

gemischt mixed

gemischte Lebensversicherung endowment life insurance

genau exact; specific; precise; definite; accurate

genau angeben to specify

Genauigkeit precision; accuracy

genehmigen to approve; *(erlauben)* to permit; to authorize; *(Lizenz)* to license; *(Gesetz)* to pass; *(ratifizieren)* to ratify

Genehmigung approval; *(Erlaubnis)* permit, authorization *(Ratifizierung)* ratification

Genehmigungsantrag application for a permit; application for a license

Genehmigungsbescheid notice of approval

Genehmigungserfordernisse licensing requirements

Genehmigungsschreiben letter of approval

Genehmigungsverfahren approval procedure; licensure

Generaldirektor managing director; director general

Generalkonsul consul general

Generalkonsulat consulate general

Generalsekretär secretary general

Generalversammlung *(UN)* General Assembly

Generalvertretung general agency; sole agency

Generalvollmacht general powers; proxy power; full power of attorney

Generation generation

generisch generic

genesen to recover

genormt standardized

Genossenschaft cooperative; association

genossenschaftlich cooperative

Genossenschaftsbank cooperative bank

genug enough; sufficient

genügen to suffice; to be adequate

genügend adequate; ample

Genuss enjoyment; beneficial use

Genussmittel luxury food

Genussrecht profit participation right

Genussschein participating certificate; coupon

Gepflogenheit habit

Gerät instrument; equipment; *(Hilfsmittel)* device; *(Werkzeug)* tool; *(Haushaltsgerät)* appliance

gerecht just; equitable; fair

Gerechtigkeit justice

geregelt regulated; orderly

geregelte Wertpapierbörse organized securities exchange

Gericht court

Gericht anrufen to take legal action; to go to court

vor Gericht stehen to be on trial

gerichtlich judicial

gerichtliche Verfolgung prosecution

Gerichtsanordnung court order

Gerichtsbarkeit jurisdiction

gerichtsfähig actionable; judicable

Gerichtsgutachten opinion of the court

Gerichtshof court of justice

Gerichtsstand place of juristiction

Gerichtsurteil judgment; *(Strafprozess)* verdict

Gerichtsverfahren trial

geringfügig petty; slight; *(Betrag)* paltry

geringfügige Anleihe low-grade bond

Gerücht rumour

Gerüchteküche grapevine

Gerümpel junk

Gerüst framework; *(Bau)* scaffold

gesamt total; entire; overall; aggregate

Gesamtabsatz total sales; volume of sales

Gesamtangebot total supply; aggregate supply

Gesamtanlage total investment

Gesamtbestand total stock on hand

Gesamtbetrag total; total amount; sum total

Gesamt-Cashflow eines Unternehmens total cash flow of the firm

Gesamteinkommen entire income; total revenue

Gesamtergebnis overall result

Gesamtersparnisse total savings

gesamtes Sortiment full line

Gesamtetat total budget; summary budget

Gesamtgebiet entire territory

Gesamtgewicht total weight

Gesamtgewinn total profit; total return

Gesamtheit entirety; totality; whole

Gesamtindex overall index

Gesamtinvestition total investment

Gesamtkapazität total capacity

Gesamtkapitalausstattung capitalization, total capitalization

Gesamtkapitalrendite return on capital employed (ROCE)

Gesamtkapitalrentabilität rate of return, return on assets, ROA, return on Investment, ROI

Gesamtkosten total costs; overall costs

Gesamtkostenverfahren total cost accounting

Gesamtleistung total output

Gesamtleistungsvermögen total capacity

Gesamtmarkt total market

Gesamtnachfrage total demand

Gesamtproduktion total production; total output

Gesamtrechnung *(Volkswirtschaft)* national income accounting

Gesamtreserven total reserves

Gesamtsumme total; total amount

Gesamtumsatz total sales

Gesamtverbrauch total consumption

Gesamtvergütung compensation package

Gesamtverlust overall loss; *(Versicherung)* total loss

Gesamtverschuldung total indebtedness

Gesamtversorgung total supply

Gesamtvertragssumme total contract amount

Gesamtverzinsung total interest

Gesamtvolumen total volume

Gesamtwert total value

Gesamtziffer total figure

gesättigt saturated

Geschäft business; *(Laden)* store; shop; *(Unternehmen)* enterprise; *(Firma)* firm; *(Abschluss)* deal; *(günstiger Abschluss)* bargain

Geschäft abschließen to close a deal; to transact business

Geschäft abwickeln to carry out a transaction

Geschäft anfangen to start up a business

Geschäft aufgeben to close down; to go out of business

Geschäft betreiben to conduct business

Geschäft erweitern to expand a business

Geschäft leiten to manage a business

Geschäft liquidieren to wind up a business

Geschäft machen to make a deal

Geschäftemacherei profiteering; racketeering

geschäftlich commercial; on business

Geschäftsabschluss transaction; deal

Geschäftsanteil share of business; partnership share

Geschäftsaussichten business prospects; business outlook

Geschäftsbank commercial bank

Geschäftsbereich business line; area of operations; function

Geschäftsbericht business report; financial statement; *(Marktbericht)* market report

Geschäftsergebnis company result

Geschäftsetikette business etiquette

Geschäftsfeld business area

Geschäftsfrau businesswoman; tradeswoman; *(Händlerin)* dealer

geschäftsführend managing

geschäftsführender Gesellschafter managing partner

geschäftsführendes Vorstandsmitglied managing director

Geschäftsführer manager; managing director; chief operating officer (COO)

Geschäftsführung management; business management

Geschäftsgeheimnis trade secret

Geschäftsjahr fiscal year

Geschäftskapital (*AG*) capital stock; business capital

Geschäftskonto business account

Geschäftskosten business expenses

Geschäftskredit business loan; commercial loan

Geschäftskreditgeber commercial lender

Geschäftskunde business client

geschäftsleitend managing; *(vorübergehend)* acting

Geschäftsleitung management

Geschäftsleute businessmen; tradesmen; *(Händler)* dealers

Geschäftsmann businessman; tradesman; *(Händler)* dealer

geschäftsmäßig businesslike

Geschäftsordnung bylaws; rules and regulations

Geschäftsprozessmodellierung business modeling

Geschäftspartner business associate

Geschäftsplan business plan

Geschäftspolitik business policy

Geschäftsräume business premises

Geschäftsreise business trip

Geschäftsreisende traveling salesman, -person, -woman; sales agent

Geschäftsrisiko business risk

Geschäftsstelle agency; branch; office

Geschäftstag business day

Geschäftstätigkeit operation

Geschäftsstunden business hours

Geschäftsumfang volume of business; *(Geschäftskreis)* scope of business

geschäftsunfähig incapable of contracting; incompetent

Geschäftsusance customary business practice

Geschäftsverlauf business trend; course of business

Geschäftsvolumen business volume

Geschäftsvorfall commercial transaction; business transaction

Geschäftswelt business community

Geschäftswert goodwill

Geschäftszeit business hours

Geschäftszentrum commercial center; business center; trading center

Geschäftszweck business purpose; corporate objective

Geschäftszyklus operating cycle

Geschenk present; gift

Geschenkartikel gift; giftware

Geschenkgutschein gift voucher; coupon

Geschenksendung gift parcel

Geschick *(Fertigkeit)* skill; *(Schicksal)* fate

geschickt skilled; skillful

geschlossener Fonds closed-end investment company

Geschoss missile; projectile; *(Haus)* floor; level

geschult trained

geschützt secure; secured

Geselle journeyman

Gesellschaft (*Geschäft*) company; corporation; *(Staat)* society

Gesellschaft des bürgerlichen Rechts private partnership

Gesellschaft mit beschränkter Haftung (*US*) closed corporation; (*UK*) private limited company

Gesellschafter partner; associate; stockholder

Gesellschafteranteil partner's interest; share

Gesellschafteraufnahme admission of a partner

Gesellschafterbeschluss shareholders′ decision; corporate decision

Gesellschafterhaftung partners′ liability

Gesellschafterversammlung shareholders' general meeting

Gesellschafterverzeichnis stockholders′ register

gesellschaftlich social

gesellschaftliche Veranstaltung social function

Gesellschaftsanteil business interest; share; stock

Gesellschaftsbeiträge contributions of partners

Gesellschaftseigentum corporate property

Gesellschaftsform corporate structure; legal form

Gesellschaftsfusion corporate merger

Gesellschaftsgewinn corporate earnings

Gesellschaftskapital stockholders' equity; capitalization

Gesellschaftsorgan company organ

Gesellschaftspolitik *(Unternehmen)* company policy; *(Gesellschaft)* social policy

Gesellschaftsrecht company law; law of association

Gesellschaftssatzung articles of incorporation

Gesellschaftssteuer corporation tax

Gesellschaftsübernahme corporate takeover

Gesellschaftsvertrag *(AG)* articles of incorporation; *(Personengesellschaft)* deed of partnership

Gesellschaftsziel corporate objective

Gesetz act; law; statute

Gesetzauslegung interpretation of a law

Gesetzbuch statute; law code

Gesetz des identischen Preises law of one price (LOP)

Gesetzentwurf bill; draft

Gesetzesänderung amendment; revision of a statute

Gesetzesbegründung preamble

Gesetzesinitiative legislative initiative

Gesetzeskommentar legal commentary

Gesetzeslücke legal loophole

Gesetzesreform legislative reform

Gesetzestext wording of a law

Gesetzesumgehung evasion of the law

Gesetzesvorlage bill; legislative proposal

gesetzgebend legislative

Gesetzgeber legislator; lawmaker

Gesetzgebung legislature; legislation

gesetzmäßig legal; legitimate

gesetzwidrig illegal

gesichert secure; secured

gesichert, banküblich backed by normal banking security

gesichert, dinglich secured by property

gesichert, grundbuchlich secured by land registry charge

gesichert, hypothekarisch secured by mortgage

gesicherte Anleihe secured bond

Gesichtspunkt viewpoint; consideration; aspect

Gespräch conversation; talk; dialog; *(Einstellung)* interview

Gesprächsabwicklung handling of calls

Gesprächsaufzeichnung record of a conversation

Gesprächsführung negotiation; *(Leitung)* presiding; chairmanship

Gesprächsgegenstand topic; subject

Gesprächspartner interlocutor

Gesprächsthema subject; topic

Gestaltung design; layout; organization

Gestaltungsfreiheit freedom of scope

Gestaltungskraft creative power

Gestaltungsmerkmale constitutive criteria

Gestaltungsprinzip formal principle

Gestaltungsrichtline style guide

Gestaltungsvorgabe development target

gestaffelt graduated; graded; *(Steuer)* progressive

gestrafft tightened

gestuft sliding

gestützt supported

Gesuch request; petition

gesund well; healthy; *(solide)* sound

Gesundheit health; *(Geschäft)* soundness; *(Wirtschaft)* strength

Gesundheitsattest health certificate

Gesundheitsgefährdung health hazard

Gesundheitsmarkt health care market

gesundheitsschädlich unhealthy; harmful

Gesundheitswesen health care

Gesundheitszeugnis certificate of health; health certificate

Gesundschrumpfen slimming; shakeout

Gesundung recovery

gewagt risky; daring

Gewähr guarantee; warranty

gewähren to grant; to allow

gewährleisten to warrant; to guarantee

Gewährleistung warranty; guarantee

Gewährleistungsausschluss caveat emptor

Gewährleistungsgarantie (*Bank*) guarantee for warranty obligations

Gewährsmann *(für Informationen)* source; informant; *(Bürge)* guarantor

Gewährung granting; grant; permission; *(Zugeständnis)* concession

Gewaltenteilung division of powers

Gewerbe *(Handwerk)* trade; craft; *(Industrie)* industry; business

Gewerbe anmelden to register a trade

Gewerbe nachgehen to pursue a trade

Gewerbeabfall industrial waste

Gewerbeamt trading supervision department

Gewerbeausstellung trade exhibition

Gewerbebetrieb business; manufacturing firm; trade firm; workshop

Gewerbeerlaubnis trade concession; business licence

Gewerbeertrag operating profits; trading profits

Gewerbefreiheit economic freedom

Gewerbeimmobilie commercial property

Gewerbekapital working capital; capital employed

Gewerbemesse trade fair

Gewerbeobjekt commercial property

Gewerbeordnung trading regulations; trade law

Gewerberäume premises

Gewerbeschau trade show

Gewerbeschein trade license

Gewerbesteuer business tax; industrial tax; trade tax; license tax

Gewerbetätigkeit commercial activity

Gewerbetreibender tradesman; businessman; *(Handwerk)* craftsman

Gewerbezentrum commercial center; industrial park

Gewerbezweig branch of industry; trade

gewerbsmäßig commercial; professional; industrial

Gewerkschaft union; labor union

Gewerkschaftler unionist

gewerkschaftlich union

Gewerkschaftsbeauftragter union delegate

Gewerkschaftsbeitrag union contribution

Gewerkschaftsführer union leader

Gewerkschaftsfunktionär union official

Gewerkschaftsgesetz trade union law

Gewerkschaftssprecher union spokesman

Gewerkschaftsverband *(US)* American Federation of Labor (AFL); *(UK)* Trade Union Congress (TUC)

Gewerkschaftsvertreter union representative

gewichten to weight

gewichtete durchschnittliche Kapitalkosten weighted average cost of capital (WACC)

gewichtete durchschnittliche Laufzeit weighted average maturity

Gewichtsbescheinigung certificate of weight

Gewichtskontrolle weight control; weighing

Gewichtstoleranz weight tolcrance

Gewichtung weighting

Gewichtungsfaktor weighting coefficient

Gewinn profit; gain; *(Ertrag)* return; proceeds; earnings; *(Nutzen)* benefit

Gewinn auf Istkostenbasis current cost profit

Gewinn aus Anlageverkauf profit on asset disposal

Gewinn aus Auflösung stiller Reserven gain from writing back secret reserves

Gewinn aus Beteiligungen investment profit

Gewinn aus Buchwerterhöhungen appreciated surplus

Gewinn aus Gewerbebetrieb income from business

Gewinn aus Neubewertungen surplus from revaluation

Gewinn aus Veräußerungen sales profit

Gewinn pro Aktie earnings per share

Gewinn vor Abschreibung und Wertberichtigungen gross trading profit

Gewinn vor Steuern pre-tax profit

Gewinnabführung profit transfer

Gewinnabgabe gains tax

gewinnabhängig profit-related

Gewinnaktivierung capitalization of profits

Gewinnanstieg profit growth; rise in earnings

Gewinnanteil share of profit; *(AG)* dividend

Gewinnausfall loss of profit

Gewinnausschüttung distribution of profit; capital gains distribution; dividend distribution

Gewinnbeitrag profit contribution

Gewinnbeteiligung profit sharing; gain sharing

Gewinnbeteiligung der Arbeitnehmer employee profit sharing

Gewinnbeteiligungsplan profit sharing plan

gewinnbringend profitable; lucrative

Gewinneinbehaltung retained earnings

Gewinneinkünfte profit income

gewinnen to win; *(an Wert)* to gain

Gewinner winner

Gewinnerwartung expectation of profits

Gewinnerzielung realization of profits

Gewinnfeststellung income determination

Gewinnfunktion profit function

Gewinnmanipulation earnings manipulation

Gewinnmarge profit margin

Gewinnmaximierung profit maximization

Gewinnmitnahme profit-taking

Gewinnmultiplikator price-earnings ratio

Gewinnobligation reorganization bond, income bond

gewinnorientiert profit oriented

Gewinnorientierung profit orientation

Gewinnplanung profit planning

Gewinnplanziel profit target

Gewinnrechnung profit accounting; surplus accounting

Gewinnsaldo profit balance

Gewinnschätzung estimate of profits

Gewinnschuldverschreibung adjustment bond; profit-sharing stock

Gewinnschwelle break-even point

Gewinnschwellenanalyse break-even analysis

Gewinnspanne profit margin; gross profit margin

Gewinnstreben profit motive; profit seeking

Gewinnteilungssysteme profit-sharing plans

Gewinntrend profit trend

Gewinn- und Verlust-Konto profit and loss account

Gewinn- und Verlust-Rechnung profit and loss statement (P&L); income statement; operating statement

Gewinnung *(Bodenschätze)* extraction; production; *(Förderung)* output; *(Neuland)* reclamation

Gewinnvergleichsrechnung accounting rate of return; profit comparison method

Gewinnverhältnis profit ratio

Gewinnverteilung distribution of profits

Gewinnverwendung profit appropriation

Gewinnvortrag profit brought forward; undistributed net profit; accumulated profit

Gewinnziel profit objective

Gewinnzone profit zone

Gewinnzuschreibung allocation of profit

Gewinnzuwachs profit growth

gewiss certain; sure

Gewissen conscience

gewissenhaft conscientious; diligent

Gewissenhaftigkeit diligence; conscientiousness

Gewissheit certainty

Gewohnheit habit; usage; *(Sitte)* custom; *(Übung)* practice

Gewohnheitsrecht common law; customary right

Gewohnheitsregel convention

gewöhnlich common; ordinary; plaine

gezeichnetes Kapital subscribed capital

gezielt selective; targeted

gezielte Informationssuche directed information search

gezielter Aktienrückkauf targeted repurchase

gezogener Wechsel drawn bill of exchange

Giftkapsel poison pill

Gipfel summit; peak

Giralgeld deposit currency; bank money

Giro *(Indossament)* endorsement; *(Übertragung)* assignment; transfer

Giro, bedingtes conditional endorsement

Giro, beschränktes qualified endorsement

Giro, bestätigt confirmed endorsement

Giro, offenes blank endorsement

Giro, unbeschränktes absolute endorsement

Giro, volles direct endorsement

Giroabschnitt bank slip

Girobank clearing bank

Girokonto current account; checking account

Giroscheck clearing house check

Giroverband clearinghouse association

Giroverkehr deposit clearing system

Giro verweigern to refuse endorsement

Girozentrale clearing house

gläserne Decke glass ceiling

Glaube belief; faith

Glauben, in gutem in good faith

glaubhaft credible; plausible

Gläubiger creditor; *(Bilanz)* accounts payable

Gläubigeranspruch creditor claim

Gläubigerbank creditor bank

Gläubigerbuch creditors' ledger

Gläubigerforderung creditors' claim

Gläubigergemeinschaft body of creditors

Gläubigerland creditor country

Gläubigerposition creditor position

Gläubigerrang ranking of creditors

Gläubigerschutz creditor protection

Gläubigerstaat creditor nation

Gläubigerversammlung creditors' meeting

Gläubigerwechsel subrogation

glaubwürdig credible; reliable

Glaubwürdigkeit credibility; reliability

gleich *(identisch)* same; identical; *(gleichwertig)* equal; *(sofort)* immediately

gleichartig congenial; similar; *(einheitlich)* uniform

gleichbedeutend synonymous; equivalent

Gleichbehandlung equal treatment

Gleichbehandlung, steuerliche equal tax treatment

Gleichbehandlungsanspruch claim to equal treatment

Gleichbehandlungsgrundsatz equality principle

gleichberechtigt equal; having equal rights

Gleichberechtigung equality; equal rights; equal status

gleich bleibend stable; constant

gleichförmig uniform

Gleichförmigkeit uniformity

Gleichgewicht equilibrium; balance

Gleichgewicht, außenwirtschaftliches balance in foreign trade

Gleichgewicht, gestörtes disequilibrium; imbalance

Gleichgewicht, soziales social stability

Gleichgewichtsanalyse equilibrium analysis

Gleichgewichtsmenge equilibrium quantity

Gleichgewichtsmodell equilibrium model

Gleichgewichtspreis equilibrium price

Gleichgewichtspunkt point of equilibrium

Gleichgewichtszinssatz equilibrium rate of interest

Gleichgültigkeit neglect

Gleichheit *(Preise)* parity; *(Identität)* identity; *(Gleichberechtigung)* equality

Gleichheitstheorie equity-theory

gleichlautend identical

gleichrangig of equal rank; pari passu

Gleichschaltung coordination

gleichsetzen to equate

Gleichstellung equalization; equal treatment; equal ranking

Gleichung equation

Gleichung aufstellen to form an equation

gleichwertig equivalent; of the same value

gleichzeitig simultaneous; concurrent

Gleichzeitigkeit concurrence

gleiten to slide

gleitende Arbeitszeiten flextime

gleitender Mittelwert moving average

Gleitlohntarif sliding wage scale

Gleitzeit flexible working hours; flextime

Gleitzins variable interest rate

Gleitzoll sliding tariff

Gliederung classification; *(Text)* outline

Gliederung des Jahresabschlusses layout of the annual accounts

Gliederung in Abteilungen departmentalization

Gliederung in Geschäftsbereiche divisionalization

global global; overall; comprehensive

Globalabkommen general agreement

Globalabtretung blank assignment

Globalakkreditiv blanket letter of credit

Globalberechnung aggregate calculation

Globalbewilligung block vote

Globaldeckung comprehensive cover

globale Strategie global strategy

globales Web global web

Globalisierung globalization

Globalkredit blanket credit

Globalwertberichtigung overall adjustment

Globalzession blanket assignment

Goldabbau gold mining

Goldanleihe gold loan

Goldbarren gold bullion

Goldbasis gold basis

Goldbesitzer gold holder

Goldbestand gold holding; gold reserve

Golddeckung gold backing

goldene Handschellen golden handcuffs

goldener Fallschirm golden parachute

goldener Handschlag golden handshake

Goldfixing gold fix

Goldgehalt gold content

Goldhortung gold hoarding

Goldkrise gold crisis

Goldpreis price of gold

Goldproduktion production of gold

Goldproduzent gold producer

Goldreserve gold reserve

Goldstandard gold standard

Goldverkauf sale of gold

Goldvorrat stock of gold; gold supply

Goldwährung gold currency; gold standard

Grad degree; grade; *(Rang)* rank; *(Ausmaß)* measure

Gradeinteilung scale

Graphik chart; graph

Graphik-Design graphic design

graphische Darstellung graph; diagram

graphisches Stärke-Schwächen-Profil graphic rating scale

Gratifikation bonus; gratification

gratis free; gratuitous

Gratisaktie stock dividend

Gratisangebot free offer

Gratisbeilage free supplement

Gratisexemplar complimentary copy

Gratiszuteilung *(Aktie)* bonus distribution

Grauimporte grey market imports

grauer Markt grey market

Grauzone grey area

Gremium body; committee; panel

Grenz- marginal; border

Grenzabfertigung customs clearance

Grenzabkommen frontier agreement

Grenzausgaben marginal outlay

Grenzabgabe border tax

Grenzbelastung marginal costs

Grenzbesteuerung marginal taxation

Grenze *(Beschränkung)* limit; *(Abgrenzung)* border; *(Begrenzung)* boundary; *(Schwelle)* threshold

Grenzen constraints; limits

grenzenlose Organisation boundless organization

Grenzerlös marginal revenue

Grenzfall borderline case

Grenzkosten marginal costs; incremental costs

Grenzkostenkurve marginal cost curve

Grenzlinie border line; boundary

Grenznutzen marginal utility

Grenzplankostenkalkulation marginal cost pricing

Grenzprodukt marginal product; end product

Grenzrate der Substitution marginal rate of substitution

Grenzrate der Transformation marginal rate of transformation

Grenzsteuersatz marginal tax rate

grenzüberschreitend cross-border

grenzüberschreitende Anleihe cross-border bond

Grenzwert marginal value; critical value

Gros gross; bulk; *(Mehrheit)* majority

Groß- large-scale

Großabnahme bulk buying

Großabnehmer quantity buyer; large customer; bulk buyer

Großaktionär principal stockholder; controlling stockholder

Großanlage large-scale plant

Großanleger major investor; big investor

Großauftrag large order; *(Börse)* big-ticket order

Großbank large bank; major bank

Großbestellung bulk order; large-scale order; major contract

Größe size; dimensions; volume

Großeinkäufer bulk buyer; wholesale purchaser

Größenordnung dimension; scale; range

Größenverhältnis scale; proportions

Größenvorteil economies of scale

Großfabrikation mass production

großformatig large-sized

Großhandel wholesale

Großhandelsgewerbe wholesaling

Großhandelskette wholesale chain

Großhandelsmarkt wholesale market

Großhändler wholesaler

Großindustrie big industry

Großindustrielle business tycoon

Grossist wholesaler

Großkonzern conglomerate; big concern

Großkredit large credit

Großkunde major customer; key account

Großkundenbetreuer key account manager

Großmarkt supermarket; central market

Großstadt large city; *(Weltstadt)* metropolis

großstädtisch metropolitan; big-city

Großunternehmen big business; big enterprise

Großversuch large-scale test

großzügig liberal; generous

Grundbedürfnis basic need

Grundbesitz land; landholding; estate

Grundbesitzer landowner

Grundbesitzertum landownership

Grundbuch land register; title register

Grundbuchauszug abstract of title; certificate of title

Grunddienstbarkeit landed servitude; registered charge

Grundeigentum real estate; property; realty

Grundeigentümer landowner; real estate owner

gründen *(Gesellschaft)* to found; to form; to launch; *(einrichten)* to establish; *(erschaffen)* to create

Gründer founder

Gründerfamilie founding family

Gründergeneration founding generation

Grundform type

Grundgehalt base pay; base salary

Grundirrtum fundamental error

Grundkapital (*AG*) capital stock; equity capital; *(Bank)* fund; capital stock; *(Kapitaleinlage)* principal; *(Nominalkapital)* nominal capital

Grundkredit real estate credit; mortgage loan

Grundlage basis; foundation; base

grundlegend fundamental; basic; primary

gründlich solid; systematic

Grundlohntarif wage rate

Grundpfandrecht mortgage lien

Grundpreis base price; basic charge

Grundprodukt primary product

Grundrente economic rent

Grundsatz principle; convention

Grundsatz der Bilanzkontinuität consistency principle

Grundsatz der Einzelbewertung unit account method of valuation

Grundsatz der Gegenseitigkeit reciprocity

Grundsatz der Maßgeblichkeit der Handelsbilanz für die Steuerbilanz principle that tax accounting should be based on commercial accounting

Grundsatz der Periodenabgrenzung matching principle; accrual principle

Grundsatz der Richtigkeit und Willkürfreiheit true and fair representation

Grundsatz der sachlichen Abgrenzung matching principle

Grundsatz der steuerlichen Leistungsfähigkeit ability to pay principle

Grundsatz der Unternehmensfortführung going concern principle

Grundsatz der Vorsicht prudence concept; conservatism

Grundsatz der wirtschaftlichen Betrachtungsweise substance over form

Grundsatz von Treu und Gut Glauben principle of equity and good faith

Grundsatzentscheidung fundamental decision; policy decision

Grundsatzerklärung policy statement; *(Völkerrecht)* declaration of intention; *(Parteiprogramm)* platform

Grundsätze ordnungsgemäßer Buchführung Generally Accepted Accounting Principles (GAAP)

Grundsätze ordnungsgemäßer Prüfung Generally Accepted Auditing Standards (GAAS)

grundsätzlich basic; fundamental; *(im Prinzip)* principally; in principle

Grundsatzpapier position paper

Grundstrategie basic strategy

Grundstück lot; parcel of land; *(Grundstückseigentum)* real estate; property

Grundstücksbelastung encumbrance; land charge

Grundstückserschließung land development

Grundstücksparzelle parcel

Grundstücksverkauf sale of land; property sale; real estate sale

Gründung formation; foundation; creation, *(AG)* incorporation

Gründungsaufwand start-up costs; formation expenses

Gründungsbilanz start-up balance

Gründungsjahr founding year

Gründungskapital initial capital

Gründungsurkunde *(AG)* articles of incorporation; corporate charter

Grundvoraussetzung basic prerequisite

Grundwerte core values

Gruppe network; group

Gruppenangehöriger group member

Gruppenarbeit teamwork

Gruppendemographie group demography

Gruppendiskussion group discussion

Gruppenklage class action lawsuit

Gruppenleiter team leader

Gruppenmitglied team member

Gruppenversicherung group insurance

gruppieren to group; to classify

gültig valid; good; *(rechtsgültig)* legal; *(in Kraft)* in force; effective

Gültigkeit validity; validation; *(Rechtsgültigkeit)* legality

günstig favorable; *(vorteilhaft)* advantageous; *(vielversprechend)* promising

günstige Gelegenheit opportunity

Günstlingswirtschaft favoritism

Gut *(Besitz)* property; *(Ware)* goods; merchandise; *(Gutshof)* farm

Gutachten expert opinion; accountant's opinion; survey; report

Gutachten einholen to ask for an expertise; to obtain expert advice

Gutachten eines Schätzers appraisal report

Gutachter consultant; expert; *(Schätzer)* appraiser

Gutdünken discretion

Güte quality; *(Handelsklasse)* grade; *(Charakter)* kindness

Gütegrad standard; quality

Güter goods; commodities; merchandise

Gütergruppe category of goods

Güterhandel merchandise trade; commodities trade

Güterkonsum consumption of goods

Güterpreis price of goods

Güterproduktion production of goods

Gütertrennung separate property

Guthaben balance; credit

Gutschrift credit; credit note; credit item

Gymnasium (US) high school; (UK) grammar school

H

Haben *(Buchhaltung)* credit; assets

Habenbuchung credit entry

Habenposten credit item

Habensaldo credit balance

Habenseite credit side

Habenzins credit interest

Hafen port; harbor

Hafenkonnossement port bill of lading

Haft custody; imprisonment

haftbar liable; *(verantwortlich)* responsible

haften to be liable; *(garantieren)* to guarantee; to vouch

Haftpflicht liability

Haftpflicht, gesetzliche legal liability

haftpflichtig liable

Haftpflichtversicherung personal liability insurance; *(freie Berufe)* errors and omissions coverage

Haftpflichtversicherung für Direktoren und Führungskräfte directors´ and officers´ liability insurance

Haftungszusage acceptance of liability

Haftsumme amount guaranteed

Haftung liability; *(Verantwortung)* responsibility

Halbfabrikat intermediate goods; semi-finished goods

halbfertig semi-finished

halbfertige Erzeugnisse goods in process; semi-finnished goods

Halbjahresbericht interim report

halbjährlich semi-annual; biannual

Halbleiter semiconductor

Halbtagsarbeit part-time work

Halde waste heap; dump

Halo-Effekt halo-effect

halsabschneiderisch cutthroat

haltbar *(dauerhaft)* durable; *(fest)* solid; *(stabil)* stable

Haltbarkeit durability; life; shelf life

Haltbarkeitsdatum use-by date

Halteperiode holding period

Haltung *(Einstellung)* attitude; stance

hamstern to hoard

Handarbeiter manual worker

Handbedienung manual operation

Handbuch manual; reference book

Handel trade; commerce; *(Transaktion)* bargain; *(Geschäft)* business

handelbar marketable; tradable; *(Wertpapier)* negotiable

handeln *(Handel treiben)* to trade; to deal; *(feilschen)* to bargain; *(tun)* to act

Handels- commercial

Handelsabkommen commercial treaty; trade agreement; economic agreement

Handelsakzept trade acceptance

Handelsabteilung commercial section

Handelsbank merchant bank; commercial bank

Handelsbeschränkung trade restriction

Handelsbezeichnung trade name

Handelsbeziehung trade relations; commercial relationship

Handelsbilanz balance of trade; trade balance; (*Firma*) financial statement; commercial balance sheet

Handelsbilanzdefizit trade balance deficit

Handelsblatt trade journal

Handelsbrauch usance

Handelsdefizit trade deficit

Handelseinschränkung trade restraint

Handelsfaktura commercial invoice

Handelsfirma trading company

Handelsflotte merchant fleet

Handelsgesellschaft trading company

Handelsgesetzbuch commercial code

Handelsgruppe trade group

Handelsgut merchandise

Handelshaus commercial establishment; business enterprise; trading firm; trading house

Handelshemmnis trade barrier

Handelskammer chamber of commerce; board of trade

Handelskette chain of stores

Handelsklasse grade; quality

Handelskredit trade credit

Handelskrieg trade war

Handelsmann merchant; trader; tradesman

Handelsmakler commercial broker; agent; trade broker

Handelsmarke trade brand; private brand; private label

Handelsmesse trade fair

Handelsname trade name; business name

Handelspapier commercial paper

Handelspartner trading partner

Handelspolitik trade policy

Handelsrechnung commercial invoice

Handelsrecht commercial law

Handelsregister register of companies

Handelsschranke trade barrier

Handelsspanne margin; profit margin; mark-up

Handelsstrom flow of trade

handelsüblich customary in trade; commercially available

Handelsvertreter sales representative

Handelswert market value

Handelszeitschrift trade magazine

handeltreibend mercantile; trading

Handeltreibender trader

Handhabung handling; treatment

Händler trader; merchant; dealer

Händlerakkreditiv merchant's letter of credit

Händlerdarlehen dealer loan

Händlerjargon trade jargon

Händlernetz dealer network

Händlerorganisation dealership network

Händlernetz dealer network

Händlerpreis trade price

Händlerprovision dealer commission

Händlerrabatt trade discount

Händlerwerbung trade advertising

handlich handy; manageable

Handlung act; action; *(Laden)* business

Handlungsbevollmächtigter registered manager

Handlungskomponente einer Einstellung behavioral component of an attitude

Handlungsspielraum scope; latitude; room for maneuver

Handlungsvollmacht proxy; authority

Handlungsvollmacht, beschränkte limited authority

Handlungsvollmacht, uneingeschränkte full authority

Handwerk craft; small trade; industrial art

Handwerker craftsman; tradesman

Handzettel leaflet; flier

Hardware hardware

Härte hardness; severity; rigidity; hardship

Härtefall hardship case

Härteklausel hardship clause

harte Währung hard currency

häufig frequent; often

Häufigkeit frequency; incidence

Häufigkeitsfunktion frequency function

Häufigkeitskurve frequency curve

Häufigkeitstheorie der Wahrscheinlichkeit frequency theory of probability

Häufigkeitsverteilung frequency distribution

Häufung cluster; cumulation

Hauptabnehmer principal customer

Hauptabnehmerland principal buyer country

Hauptabrechnung general balance sheet

Hauptabsatzgebiet principal marketing area

Hauptabsatzmarkt prime market

Hauptabschlussbilanz annual balance sheet

Hauptabschlussübersicht general ledger; work sheet

Hauptabteilung central department

Hauptaktionär principal stockholder

Hauptanliegen primary concern

Hauptanteil lion's share; main part

Hauptanziehungspunkt main attraction

Hauptartikel main product; staple

Hauptberuf principal occupation; main profession; full-time job

Hauptbuch ledger; general ledger

Hauptbuchauszug ledger abstract

Hauptbuchhalter chief accountant

Hauptbüro main office; headquarters; home office

Haupteigentümer general owner

Haupteinkäufer chief buyer

Haupteinnahmequelle principal source of income

Haupteinschaltzeit prime viewing time

Hauptforderung principal; principal claim

Hauptgeschäftsführer general manager,; chief executive officer (CEO); (UK) managing director

Hauptgeschäftssitz headquarters

Hauptinhaber principal owner

Hauptkäufer key buyer

Hauptkonkurrent main competitor

Hauptkonto main account; general account

Hauptkunde main customer; *(Werbung)* key account

Hauptlieferant major supplier

Hauptmerkmal key feature

Hauptnachteil main drawback

Hauptniederlassung main office; headquarters

Hauptposition main item

Hauptproblem central issue

Hauptprodukt staple product; main product

Hauptquartier headquarters

Hauptrichtung thrust

Hauptsache main issue; essence

hauptsächlich primary; principal; main; chief

Hauptserie key series

Hauptstütze mainstay

Hauptthema key issue

Hauptumsatzträger mainstay of sales

Hauptumschlagplatz main trade center

Hauptveranlagung general assessment

Hauptverbindlichkeit principal obligation; primary liability

Hauptversammlung (HV) annual general meeting (AGM)

Hauptverwaltung head office; headquarters

Hauptwachstumsgebiet major growth area

Hauptzollamt main customs office

Hausbank principal bank; house bank

Hausbesitz home ownership

Hausbesitzer homeowner

Hausfriedensbruch trespass; unlawful entry

Haushalt household; budget

Haushalt annehmen to pass the budget

Haushalt beschneiden to prune the budget

Haushalt einhalten to keep to the budget

haushalten to economize

Haushaltsartikel household goods

Haushaltsausschuss budget committee; *(US)* Ways and Means Committee

Haushaltsbefugnis budgetary powers

Haushaltsbewilligung budget appropriation

Haushaltsdefizit budget deficit

Haushaltseinkommen household income

Haushaltsentwurf budget proposal

Haushaltsexperte budget specialist

Haushaltsgeräte household appliances; white goods

Haushaltsgleichgewicht budget equilibrium

Haushaltsjahr fiscal year

Haushaltskürzung budget cut

Haushaltslage budgetary situation

Haushaltsplan aufstellen to prepare the budget

Haushaltspolitik budgetary policy

Hauhaltsposten budget item

Haushaltsrahmen budgetary ceiling

Haushaltsrechnung budget account

Haushaltssanierung budget reorganization

Haushaltsvoranschlag budget proposal

Hausse bull market

Hausse-Position long position

Hausse-Spread bull spread

Haussier bull

Hauswirt landlord

Hebelwirkung *(Bilanz)* leverage

Heimcomputer home computer

Heimfallsrecht des Staates escheat; default of heirs

heimisch domestic; native; home; local

Heimkehrer repatriate

heimlich secret; clandestine

heißes Geld hot money

Heizkosten heating costs

Heizkostenrechnung fuel bill

hemmen to impede, to obstruct; to restrain

Hemmnis obstruction; obstacle

Hemmung restraint; inhibition; obstruction

herablassend patronizing; condescending

Herablassung condescension

herabsetzen to lower; to reduce; to decrease; *(diskreditieren)* to disparage

Herabsetzung reduction; downgrading; lowering; *(Diskreditierung)* disparagement

heraufladen upload

heraufsetzen to increase; to raise; *(Preise)* to mark up

Heraufsetzung increase; *(Preis)* mark-up

herausfordern to challenge

Herausforderer challenger; contender

Herausforderung challenge

herausgeben to issue; *(Kleingeld)* to give change; *(Buch)* to edit

Herausgeber publisher; editor

herausragend outstanding

herausstellen to point out; to highlight

herausstreichen to delete; to cross out

hergebracht customary

herkömmlich conventional; customary

Herkunft *(Handelsware)* origin; *(Abstammung)* descent

Herkunftsbescheinigung certificate of origin

Herkunftsland country of origin

Herkunftsnachweis proof of origin

herleiten to derive

Hermesbürgschaft export credit guarantee

Herrschaft rule; reign; regime

herrschen to rule; to control; to dominate

herrschend ruling; dominant

Herrscher ruler

herstellen to manufacture; to produce; to make

Hersteller manufacturer; producer; maker

Hersteller von Fremdfabrikaten other equipment manufacturer (OEM)

Herstellerhaftung manufacturers liability

Herstellerpreis manufacturer's price; factory price

Herstellerzeichen trade mark

Herstellerzeugnis manufacturer's certificate

Herstellung production; manufacture

Herstellungsanlage production facility

Herstellungsbeschränkung production restriction

Herstellungsdauer production time

Herstellungsfehler manufacturing fault; defect

Herstellungsfirma production company

Herstellungsgemeinkosten manufacturing overheads

Herstellungskosten production costs; costs of goods manufactured

Herstellungskosten der verkauften Produktion costs of goods sold

Herstellungsland country of manufacture

Herstellungsleiter production manager

Herstellungsmethode production method; production process

Herstellungsort place of manufacture

Herstellungspreis manufacturing cost

Herstellungsprozess production process

Herstellungsstufe manufacturing stage

Herstellungsverfahren manufacturing process; production technique

herunterladen download

heruntersetzen to reduce; to mark down

herunterspielen to play down; to minimize

herunterstufen to downgrade; *(Personal)* to demote

Herunterstufung demotion

hervorbringen to generate; to create

hervorheben to emphasize

Heuristik heuristic

Heuristik nach Analogiebildung representative heuristic

Heuristik nach Verfügbarkeit availability heuristic

Hierarchieabbau delayering

High-Context-Kulturen high-context cultures

Hilfe help; aid; assistance; *(Unterstützung)* support; backing

Hilfe leisten to give aid; *(unterstützen)* to support

hilfreich helpful

Hilfsaktion relief action

Hilfsarbeiter unskilled worker; helper

Hilfskraft assistant; aide

Hilfsmaßnahme emergency measure

Hilfsmittel resource; *(Notbehelf)* stopgap

Hilfspersonal support personnel

Hilfsquelle resource

Hilfsstoffe auxiliary materials; supplies

hinauslegen *(Geld)* to put out; *(Kredit)* to extend; to grant; *(Akkreditiv)* to open

hinausschieben to delay; to postpone

hinauszögern to delay; to postpone

hindern to prevent; to restrain; to hinder

hindernde Kräfte restraining forces

Hindernis hindrance; obstacle; obstruction; impediment

hinreichend sufficient

hinsichtlich with regard to; in respect to; concerning; as to

Hintergrund background; backdrop; setting

hinterlassen to leave behind; *(Testament)* to bequeath; *(Grundbesitz)* to devise

hinterlegen to deposit

Hinterleger depositor

Hinterlegungsstelle depository; custodian

Hinterlegungssumme deposit

Hinweis reference; indication

hinweisen to refer to; to indicate

hinzeigen to point

hinzufügen to add

hinzurechnen to add

historische Kosten historical costs; original costs

Hits hit

Hochachtung esteem; respect

Hochbetrieb rush; peak period

Hochkonjunktur economic boom

Hochleistung high performance

Hochleistungs- heavy-duty; high-performance

hochrechnen to project forward; to forecast; to extrapolate

Hochrechnung projection; extrapolation

hochschießen to skyrocket

hochschnellen to spurt; to skyrocket

Höchstbetrag maximum amount; *(Preisgrenze)* limit

Höchstdauer maximum period of time

Höchstertrag maximum proceeds

Höchstgrenze maximum; ceiling; upper limit

Höchstkredit line of credit

Höchstkurs maximum rate, top price

Höchstleistung record

Höchstpunkt peak

Höchstratengrenze rate ceiling

Höchststand high; highest level; *(Kurse)* top price

Höchstwert maximum value

Höchstzinsen interest ceiling

hochtreiben to inflate; to boost; to force up

hochverzinslich high-yield; high-interest

hochverzinsliche Anleihe high-yield bond

hochverzinsliche Risikoanleihe junk bonds

hochwertig high-grade; high-quality; high-class

höflich courteous; polite

Höflichkeit courtesy; politeness

Höhe height; altitude; *(Ausmaß)* extent; *(Preise)* level; *(Summe)* amount

Höhepunkt culmination; climax; peak

Höherbewertung write-up

höhere Bedürfnisse higher-order needs

höhere Gewalt force majeure

Höherstufung upgrading

Holdinggesellschaft holding company

Homepage home page

homogene Erwartungen homogenous expectations

Honorar fee; remuneration; *(Autor)* royalty

honorieren to pay; to remunerate; *(anerkennen)* to reward

Hörer *(Telefon)* receiver; *(Radio)* listener

horizontale Aufgabenerweiterung job enlargement

horizontaler Unternehmenserwerb horizontal acquisition

horizontaler Zusammenschluss horizontal merger

horten to hoard; to stockpile

Hotelkonzept hoteling

Huckepackexport piggy-back exporting

Huckepackverkehr piggy back traffic

Human-Relations-Ansatz der Konfliktforschung human relations view of conflict

Hygienefaktoren hygiene factors

hypermodern state-of-the-art; ultra-modern

Hypothek mortgage; *(mit flexibler Verzinsung)* adjustable-rate mortgage

Hypothekarinstitut mortgage bank

hypothekarisch belasten to mortgage

hypothekarische Belastung mortgage debt; encumbrance

Hypothekarkredit mortgage loan

Hypothekenablösung mortgage redemption

Hypothekenbank mortgage bank

Hypothekenbrief mortgage deed

Hypothekendarlehen mortgage loan; mortgage securities

Hypothekeninhaber mortgage creditor

Hypothekenrückzahlung mortgage capital repayment

Hypothekenschulden encumbrance; mortgage debt

Hypothekenzinsen mortgage interest

Hypothekenzusage mortgage commitment

Hypothese hypothesis

Hypothese der Zufallsbewegung Random walk hypothesis

Hypothese effizienter Märkte efficient market hypothesis (EMH)

hypothetisch hypothetical

I

ichbezogen self-centred; egocentric

Ideal ideal

Idealismus idealism

Idee idea

Ideenfindung brainstorming

Ideenführer idea champions

identifikationsbasiertes Vertrauen identification-based trust

identifizierbar identifiable

identifizieren to identify

Identifizierung identification

identisch identical

Identität identity

illegal illegal

illegitime illegitimate

illiquide illiquid

Illustration illustration

illustrieren to illustrate

Image image

im Geld in the money

Imitat imitation; copy

Imitationsstrategie imitation strategy

imitieren to imitate; to copy

immateriell intangible

immaterieller Vermögensgegenstand intangible assets

Immobilien real estate

Immobilienfonds real estate investment fund

implizierte Modelle der Organisationsstruktur implicit models of organizational structure

Import import; importation

Importabgabe import surcharge

Importbarriere import barrier

Importbedarf import demand

Importbeihilfe import subsidy

Importbestimmungen import regulations

Importbeschränkumgen import restrictions

Importdeckungsquote import cover ratio

Importdeklaration import declaration

Importdrosselung import curb

Importeinsparung import savings

Importeur importer

Importfähigkeit import capacity; importability

Importfinanzierung import financing

Importfirma import company

Importgut import merchandise

importieren to import

Importkaufmann, -frau importer

Importkontingent import quota

Importleiter import manager

Importpreis import price

Importquote import quota

Importschranke import barrier

Importverteuerung import price increase

Importware import goods

Improvisation improvisation

Impuls impulse; stimulus; imputus

Index index

Index der Großhandelspreise wholesale price index

Index der Industrieproduktion index of industrial production

Index der Verbraucherpreise consumer price index

Index-Fond index fund

indexieren to index

Indexierung indexing

Indexklausel index clause

Indexkauf buying the index

Indikation indication

Indikator indicator

indirekt indirect

indirekte Kosten indirect costs; overhead

indirekte Steuer indirect tax

Individualbedürfnis individual need

individualisieren to individualize; to personalize

Individualismus individualism

Individualität individuality

individuell anpassen to personalize; to customize

Individuum individual; person

Indizierung indexing

Indossament endorsement

Indossament aus Gefälligkeit accomondation endorsement

Indossament ohne Obligo endorsement without recourse

Indossamenthaftung endorer's liability

Indossant endorser

Indossat endorsee

indossierbar endorsable; negotiable

indossieren to endorse

indossierfähig endorsable; negotiable

industrialisieren to industrialize

Industrialisierung industrialization

Industrialismus industrialism

Industrie industry

Industrieabbau deindustrialization

Industrieanlage production plant; industrial plant; manufacturing plant

Industrieausstellung industrial show; trade show

Industriebasis industrial base

Industrieberater management consultant

Industriebereich industrial sector

Industriebetrieb manufacturing company; industrial plant

Industriebrache industrial wasteland

Industrieerzeugnisse industrial products; manufactures

Industriefachmann industry expert

Industrieförderung industrial development

Industrieführer industry leader

Industriegebiet industrial area

Industriegesellschaft industrial society

Industriekontenrahmen industrial accounting system

Industrieland industrial country; industrial nation

industriell industrial

Industrieller manufacturer; industrialist

Industrielles Marketing industrial marketing

Industriemaschinen industrial machinery

Industrienachfrage industrial demand

Industrienation industrial nation

Industrieobligation corporate bond; industrial bond

Industriepark industrial park

Industrieproduktion industrial production; industrial output

Industrieprognose industry forecast

Industrieschuldverschreibung corporate bond; industrial bond

Industriespionage industrial espionage

Industriestaat industrial nation

Industriestruktur industry structure

Industrieunternehmen industrial enterprise

Industrieverwaltung industrial management

Industriewerk factory; industrial plant

Industriezweig line of industry; branch of industry

ineinander greifen to mesh

Inempfangnahme receipt

Inflation inflation

inflationär inflationary

inflationistisch inflationary

Inflationsabbau deflation

Inflationsanpassungs-Klausel inflation-escalator clause

Inflationsauftrieb inflationary rise

Inflationsausgleich compensation for inflation

Inflationsdruck inflationary pressure

Inflationsfaktor inflationary factor

inflationsfrei non-inflationary

inflationsneutrale Rechnungslegung inflation accounting

Inflationsrate rate of inflation; inflation rate

Inflationsrisiko inflation risk

Inflationsrückgang drop in the rate of inflation

Inflationsschutz inflation hedge

inflatorisch inflationary

Infomappe briefing pack

informale Gruppe informal group

informale Netzwerke informal networks

Informatik computer science

Informatiker computer scientist

Information information; *(Nachrichten)* news; *(Kommunikation)* communication; *(Auskunft)* informationdesk

Informationsblatt newsletter

Informationsfluss flow of information; communication

Informationsflut information overloads

Informationsgehalt information content

Informationsgesellschaft information society

Informationsgespräch consultation

Informationskanal channel of information

Informationsmanagement information management

Informationsmaterial information material

Informationsnetz communication network; information network

Informationsquelle source of information

Informationsstand information desk; *(Niveau)* state of information

Informationssystem information system

Informationswert informational value

informativ informative

informell informal

informieren to inform; to brief

Infrastruktur infrastructure

Ingangsetzungskosten start-up costs

Ingenieur engineer

Inhaber *(Eigentümer)* proprietor; owner; *(Besitzer)* holder; *(Wechselinhaber)* bearer

Inhaberaktie bearer share; transferable stock; bearer stock

Inhaberobligation coupon bond

Inhaberpapier bearer note

Inhaberscheck bearer check

Inhaberschuldverschreibung bearer bond; coupon bond

Inhabersparbrief bearer savings bond

Inhalt content(s); volume

Inhalt testen testing content

Initiative initiative

initiieren to initiate

Initiierung initiation

Inkasso collection; debt collection

Inkassofloat collection float

Inkassoindossament collection endorsement; endorsement for collection

Inkassopapier collection item; collection paper

Inkassopolitik collection policy

Inkassostelle collecting agency

Inkassozession assignment of accounts receivable for collection

inklusiv inclusive; included

inkompatibel incompatible

Inkompatibilität incompatibility

inkonsequent inconsistent

Inland inland; interior; *(im Inland)* at home

Inländer *(Einheimischer)* native; *(Bürger)* citizen

inländisch interior; internal; domestic

inländische Gesellschaft domestic corporation

Inlandsanlage domestic investment

Inlandsanleihe domestic loan; internal bond

Inlandsbank domestic bank

Inlandsbestellung domestic order

Inlandsgeschäft domestic business; home trading

Inlandskapital domestic capital

Inlandsmarkt domestic market

Inlandsverbrauch domestic consumption

innehaben to occupy

Innendienst office work

Innenfinanzierung internal financing; self financing

Innenrevision internal audit

Innenrevisor internal auditor

inner- internall; interial

innerbetrieblich in-house; in-company

innerbetriebliche Leistungen internal services

innerbetrieblicher Strukturwandel re-engineering

innerer Wert intrinsic value

Innovation innovation

Innovationsstrategie innovation strategy

innovativ innovative

Input input

Inputdaten input data

Inputpfad input path

Inserat ad; advertisement

Inserent advertiser

inserieren to advertise; to place an advertisement

Insertionsauftrag space order

Insider-Geschäft insider trading

Insider-Information inside information

insolvent insolvent; bancrupt

Insolvenz insolvency; bancruptcy

Insolvenzerklärung declaration of insolvency

Insolvenzgefahr financial distress

Insolvenzkosten costs of financial distress

Insolvenzrecht bankruptcy law

Inspektion inspection

inspizieren to inspect

Instabilität instability

installieren to install

Installierung installation

instand halten to maintain

Instandhaltung upkeep; maintenance

Instandhaltungskosten maintainance costs

Instandsetzung repair; *(gründliche)* overhaul

Instanz level of jurisdiction; authority

Institut institute; institution

Institution institution

Institutionalisierung institutionalization

institutionell institutional

institutioneller Anleger institutional investor

Instrument *(Urkunde)* legal instrument; deed; *(Werkzeug)* tool

instrumentelle Werte instrumental values

Integration integration

integrieren to integrate

Integrität integrity

intensiv intensive

Intentionen intentions

interagierende Gruppen interacting groups

interaktionistischer Ansatz der Konfliktforschung interactionist view of conflict

interaktive Bannerwerbung interactive banner advertisements

Interbankgeschäft interbank transaction

Interesse interest; concern

Interessengemeinschaft *(Kartell)* trust; syndicate

Interessengruppe lobby; interest group

Interessengruppen stakeholders

Interessenkonflikt conflict of interest

Interessenkonflikt zwischen Gläubigern und Aktionären conflict between bondholders and shareholders

Interessent prospective client; potential buyer; prospect

Interessentenliste list of prospects

Interessenverband lobby; pressure group

Interessenvertreter lobbyist

Interessenvertretung lobby

interessieren to interest

interessieren, sich to be interested in

intermittierende Verstärkung intermittent reinforcement

intern internal

Interna internals

interne Ordnung internal order

international international

Internationale Bank Für Wideraufbau und Entwicklung - "Weltbank" International Bank for Reconstruction and Development - "World Bank" (IBRD)

Internationales Handelszentrum International Trade Center (ITC)

Internationalisierung internationalization

interne Mittel internal funds

interne Revision internal audit; management audit

interner Zinsfuß internal rate of return

Internet-Marketing internet marketing

Internet-Marketing-Metriken internet marketing metrics

Internet-Service-Provider internet service providers (ISPs)

interne Zinsfuß-Methode discounted cash-flow method; internal rate of return method

intervenieren to intervene

Intervention intervention

Interview interview

interviewen to interview

Interviewer interviewer

Intuition intuition

intuitive Entscheidungsfindung intuitive decision making

Inventar inventory; stock in hand

Inventarwert je Anteil net asset value per share (NAV)

Inventur stocktaking; inventory

investieren to invest

Investition investment; capital spending; *(Anlage)* capital project; capital asset

Investitionen ankurbeln to encourage investments

Investitionen kürzen to cut investments

Investitionen vornehmen to invest; to make investments

Investitionen zurückstellen to defer investments

Investitionsabbau disinvestment

Investitionsabwicklung investment management

Investitionsanalyse investment analysis

Investitionsantrag investment proposal

Investitionsausgaben capital expenditure; capital spending

Investitionsbank investment bank

Investitionsbedarf investment needs; capital expenditure requirements

Investitionsentscheidung investment decision

Investitionsentscheidungen, sich gegenseitig ausschließende mutually exclusive investment decisions

Investitionsfall cash trap

Investitionsfunktion investment function

Investitionsklima investment climate

Investitionsgüter capital goods; industrial goods; capital equipment

Investitionsgüterindistrie capital goods industry

Investitionsgütermarketing industrial marketing

Invstitionsgüternachfrage demand for capital goods

Investitionshaushalt capital budget

Investitionshöhe investment level

Investitionsklima investment climate

Investitionskontrolle investment control

Investitionskredit investment loan

Investitionslücke investment gap

Investitionsneigung propensity to invest

Investitionsplan investment plan; capital expenditure plan

Investitionsplanung investment planning; capital investment planning; capital budgeting

Investitionspolitik investment policy; capital spending policy

Investitionsprämie investment premium

Investitionsprogramm capital expenditure plan; investment plan

Investitionsquote rate of investment; investment quota

Investitionsrechnung capital expenditure budgeting

Investitionsrechnungsverfahren capital budgeting technique

Investitionsrendite return on invetsment (ROI)

Investitionssumme capital expenditure

Investitionstätigkeit investment activity; capital spending

Investitionsvolumen investment volume

Investitionsvorhaben investment project

Investitionszyklus investment cycle

Investment investment

Investmentbanker investment bankers

Investmentfonds investment fund; mutual fund

Investmentgesellschaft investment company

Investment-Philosophie investment philosophy

Investor investor

irreführen to mislead

irreführend misleading; deceptive

Irreführung deception; misdirection

irrig erroneous; false; wrong

Irrtum error; mistake

irrtümlich erroneous

Isolationspolitik isolationism

Isolationspolitiker isolationist

isolieren to isolate

Isolierung isolation; *(Haus)* insulation

Ist- actual; effective

Istbestand actual stock on hand

Istbetrag real amount; actual amount

Istdaten actual data

Ist-Gemeinkosten actual overheads

Istkosten effective costs; actual costs

Istkosten der Vergangenheit historical cost; original cost

Istkostenrechnung actual costing; current cost accounting

Istleistungen actual performance

J

Jagd hunt chase

jagen to hunt; to chase

Jahrbuch yearbook; annual book

Jahresabschluss annual financial statement; annual statement of accounts; annual balance sheet

Jahresabschluss aufstellen to draw up te annual accounts; to prepare the annual financial statements

Jahresabschluss vorlegen to present the balance sheet

Jahresabschlussanalyse financial statement analysis

Jahresabsetzungsbetrag annual rate of depreciation

Jahresanfang beginning of the year

Jahresarbeitszeit annual working hours

Jahresaufkommen annual revenue

Jahresausgleich year-end adjustment

Jahresbasis annual basis

Jahresbericht annual report

Jahresbilanz annual balance sheet

Jahresdurchschnitt annual average

Jahreseinkünfte annual income

Jahresende end of the year; year-end

Jahresergebnis annual returns; annual yield; annual output

Jahresetat annual budget

Jahresfrist one-year period

Jahresgewinn annual earnings

Jahreshauptversammlung annual general meeting (AGM)

Jahresmitte midyear

Jahresplan annual plan

Jahresproduktion annual production; annual output

Jahresschluss year-end; close of the year

Jahresstatistik annual statistics

Jahressumme annual sum; annual total amount

Jahrestagung annual convention; annual conference

Jahresüberschuss annual surplus

Jahresultimo end of the year; year-end

Jahresumsatz annual sales

Jahresverdienst annual earnings

Jahresverlauf course of the year

Jahreszeit season

jahreszeitlich seasonal

Jahrhundert century

jährlich annual

jährlicher Effektivzinssatz effective annual interest rate

Jargon jargon

Journal journal; register; magazine

Jugend youth

Jugendarbeit youth work

Jugendarbeitslosigkeit youth unemployment

Jugendgruppe youth group

Jugendkriminalität juvinile delinquency

Jugendlicher adolescent

Jungunternehmen start-up company

Junggeselle bachelor; *(Frau)* single woman

Jurist lawyer; legal practitioner; attorney

juristisch legal; judicial

Jury selection committee; *(Preisrichterausschuss)* committee of judges

justitiabel actionable; litigable

Jüstitiabilität actionability; litigability

Justitiar corporate attorney; permanent legal adviser

Justizwesen legal system

K

Kabel cable; lead; wire

Kabelanschluss cable connection

Kabelfernsehen cable television

Kabine cabin; booth

Kabotage cabotage

Kalender calendar

Kalkulation calculation

Kalkulationsfehler miscalculation

Kalkulationsgrundlage calculation basis

Kalkulationsmethode cost accounting method; pricing system

Kalkulationsschema cost accounting scheme

kalkulatorisch imputed; calculative; arithmetical

kalkulatorische Kosten imputed costs

kalkulatorischer Zinssatz imputed interest rate

kalkulatorische Zinsen imputed interest

kalkulieren to compute; to calculate; *(Kosten)* to estimate

Kammer chamber; board; *(Gericht)* court

Kampagne campaign

Kampf struggle; fight; battle

Kanal channel; *(Wasserstraße)* canal

Kandidat candidate

Kandidatenliste listof candidates

Kannibalisierung cannibalization

Kapazität capacity; *(Fachmann)* authority

Kapazitätsabbau reduction of capacity

Kapazitätsabweichung capacity variance

Kapazitätsanpassung adjustment of capacity

Kapazitätsauslastung capacity utilization

Kapazitätsgrenze capacity limit

Kapazitätsmangel capacity shortage

Kapazitätsnutzungsgrad load factor

Kapazitätsoptimum ideal capacity

Kapazitätsplanung capacity planning

Kapazitätsüberschuss surplus capacity

Kapital capital; *(Eigenkapital)* equity; net worth; *(Geldmittel)* funds; resources; *(Zinsbasis)* principal

Kapital abschöpfen to absorb capital

Kapital anlegen to invest capital

Kapital aufnehmen to raise capital

Kapital binden to ty up capital

Kapital erhöhen to increase capital

Kapital nachschiessen to inject fresh capital

Kapitalabfluss outflow of capital; capital drain

Kapitalanlage capital investment; capital asset

Kapitalanlagefonds mutual fund

Kapitalanlagegesellschaft investment trust; investment company; mutual fund

Kapitalanleger investor

Kapitalanlagevermögen capital assets

Kapitalanteil share in capital; capital interest; stock share; *(Beteiligung)* interest in a firm; *(Bilanz)* capital

Kapitalaufwand cost of capital; capital spending

Kapitalausstattung capitalization; *(Bilanz)* capital equipment

Kapitalbasis capital base; equity base

Kapitalbedarf capital requirement

Kapitalbeschaffung financing

Kapitalbeteiligung financial interest; equity participation; *(Aktienanteil)*

share; stock; *(Aktienzeichnung)* stock subscription

Kapitalbedarf capital requirements; capital needs; demand for capital

Kapitalbedarfsrechnung capital budgeting

Kapitalbereitstellung capital appropriation; provision of funds

Kapitalberichtigung capital adjustment

Kapitalbeschaffung raising of capital; fund raising; procurement of money

Kapitalbesitz capital holding

Kapitalbestand capital stock; total capital

Kapitalbeteiligung interest; stake in the equity

Kapitalbetrag amount of capital; principal amount

Kapitalbewegung movement of capital; capital flow

Kapitalbewertung capital valuation

Kapitalbewilligung appropriation of funds; allocation of funds

Kapitalbilanz balance on capital account

Kapitalbildung capital formation; creation of capital

Kapitaldecke capital base; equity base

Kapitaldeckung capital cover

Kapitaldienst debt service; interest payments

Kapitaldividende capital dividend; return on capital

Kapitaleigner capital owner; equity owner

Kapitaleinkommen unearned income; investment income

Kapitaleinlage share; contribution of capital; capital invested

Kapitaleinleger contributor of capital; investor

Kapitalerhöhung increase in capital stock; capital increase

Kapitalertrag return on capital; investment return

Kapitalexport capital export

Kapitalflucht flight of capital; capital flight; exodus of capital

Kapitalfluss cash flow; flow of funds

Kapitalflussrechnung cash flow statement; application of funds statement

Kapitalgeber investor; provider of capital

Kapitalgesellschaft incorporated company; (US) stock corporation; (UK) puplic limited company (plc)

Kapitalgesellschaft, ausländische alien corporation

Kapitalgesellschaft gründen to incorporate

Kapitalgewinn return on capital; capital gain

Kapitalgüter capital goods

Kapitalherabsetzung capital reduction; reduction of the corporate capital

Kapitalhöhe amount of capital

kapitalintensiv capital intensive

kapitalisieren to capitalize

Kapitalisierungsfaktor capitalization rate

Kapitalismus capitalism

Kapitalist capitalist

kapitalistisch capitalistic

Kapitalknappheit capital shortage

Kapitalkonsolidierung consolidation of funds; actual value method

Kapitalkonto capital account; equity account

Kapitalkosten costs of capital; capital expenditure

Kapitalkostensatz weighted average cost of capital (WACC)

kapitalkräftig financially sound; financially strong

Kapitallebensversicherung endowment insurance; cash-value life insurance; permanent insurance

Kapitalmarkt capital market; equity market; money market

Kapitalmarkteffizienz efficient market; market efficiency

Kapitalmarktemission capital market issue

Kapitalmehrheit controlling interest; *(AG)* majority stock holding

Kapitalminderung capital reduction

Kapitalmittel funds; finnancial resources

Kapitalnutzung capital utilization

Kapitalproduktivität capital productivity

Kapitalrationierung capital rationing

Kapitalrechnung capital account

Kapitalrendite return on capital employed; return on investment; return on equity

Kapitalreserve reserve capital; reserve fund

Kapitalschwund depletion

Kapitalsteuer capital tax

Kapitalstrom capital flow

Kapitalstruktur capital structure; financial structure

Kapitalüberweisung capital transfer; remittance

Kapitalumschichtung capital restructuring

Kapitalumschlag asset turnover; capital turnover

Kapitalverflechtung cross ownership

Kapitalverkehr capital movement

Kapitalverkehrsbilanz balance of capital movements

Kapitalverlust capital loss

Kapitalvermehrung increase of capital stock

Kapitalverschleiß capital consumption allowance

Kapitalverwendung capital appropriation; use of capital

Kapitalverzinsung return on capital

Kapitalwanderung capital flow; capital movement

Kapitalwert net present value (NPV)

Kapitalwertmethode net present value method

Kapitalwertrate profitability index

Kapitalwertregel net present value rule

Kapitalzusammensetzung capital structure

Kapitalzuwachs capital gain; appreciation of principal; capital growth

Kapitalzuwachs aus Schenkungen donated capital

Kapitel chapter

Karenzfrist waiting period

Karenztage unpaid day

Karriere career

Karriere machen to make one's career

Karriereaussichten prospects for personal growth

Karriereplanung career management

Karrieresprung jump in one's career

Karte card; *(Eintrittskarte)* ticket; *(Landkarte)* map; *(Visitenkarte)* business card; *(Speisekarte)* menu

Kartei card index

Katreikarte index card

Karteikasten filing box

Kartell syndicate; pool; cartel

Kartellamt antitrust agency

Kartellrecht antitrust law

Karton cardboard; *(Schachtel)* cardboard box

Kaskoversicherung comprehensive insurance policy

Kassa cash

Kassadevisenkurs spot exchange rate

Kassageschäft cash business; *(Börse)* cash transaction; *(Devisen)* spot exchange transaction

Kassakonto cash account

Kassakurs *(Aktien)* cash price; *(Devisen)* spot market rate

Kassamarkt cash market; *(Devisen)* spot market

Kassapreis cash price; *(Devisen)* spot price

Kasse pay desk; pay office; pay window; *(Registrierkasse)* cash register; *(Karten)* ticket window; *(Bank)* cashier's window; *(Theater)* box office; *(Bargeld)* cash; *(Börse)* spot cash; *(Krankenkasse)* health insurance

Kassenbestand cash on hand; cash balance; *(Bank)* real reserves

Kassenbuch cash journal

Kassenbuchführung cash accounting

Kassenführer cashier; cash manager; *(Bank)* teller

Kassenhaltung cash management

Kassenkonto cash account

Kassenlage cash position

kassieren to cash; to collect

Kassierer *(Bank)* teller; cashier

Kasten box; case

Katalog catalog

katalogisieren to catalog

Katalogpreis list price

Kategorie category

Kauf purchase; buy; *(Erwerb)* acquisition

Kaufanreiz inducement to buy; buying incentive; merchandise appeal

Kaufauftrag buy order

kaufen to purchase; to buy; *(erwerben)* to acquire

Käufer purchaser; buyer; *(im Laden)* shopper

Käuferkredit consumer credit

Käufermarkt buyers′ market

Käuferland buying country

Käuferrisiko buyers risk

Kaufhaus department store

Kaufhauskette department store chain

Kaufkraft purchasing power; buying power

kaufkräftig possessing purchasing power

kaufkraftinduzierte Rechnungslegung general price level accounting

Kaufkraftparität purchasing power parity (PPP)

Kaufkraftrisiko purchasing power risk

Kaufleute business people; merchants

Kaufmann, -frau businessman, -woman; merchant; *(Händler)* dealer; tradesman, -woman; *(kaufmännischer Angestellter)* clerk

kaufmännisch commercial

Kaufoption buying option; call option

Kaufpreis purchase price

Kaufsignal buy signal

Kaufverhalten buying behavior

Kaufvertrag contract of sale; sales contract

Kaufvertrag unter Eigentumsvorbehalt conditional sales contract

Kaufwert market value

kaufwillig inclined to buy

Kaufzurückhaltung buying resistance

Kaution surety; security deposit; bail

Kautionsversicherung fidelity bond

Kenntnis knowledge; information

Kenntnisnahme notice; information

kenntnisreich knowledgeable

Kennzahl code; reference number; *(BWL)* ratio

Kennzahlenanalyse ratio analysis

Kennzahlensysteme ratio systems

Kennzeichen sign; mark; *(Abzeichen)* badge; *(Merkmal)* feature; criterion; attribute; characteristic

kennzeichnen to mark; *(Waren)* to label; *(charakterisieren)* to characterize

Kennziffer index number

Kernkompetenzen core competencies; distinctive competencies

Kernpunkt central point; main issue

keynesianische Wirtschaftstheorie Keynesian economics

Kette chain

Kettenladen chain store

Kilometerpauschale mileage allowance

Kinderfreibetrag childrens allowance

Kindergeld family allowance

Kirchensteuer church tax

Kiste box; case; crate

Klage complaint; grievance; legal action; case; *(Gericht)* lawsuit

Klage abweisen to dismiss a claim

Klage anfechten to contest an action

Klage anstrengen to sue; to institute lagal proceedings; to file an action

Klage begründen to substantiate a claim

Klage zurückziehen to withdraw an action

Kläger claimant; plaintiff; suitor

Klang sound

Klasse class; category; *(Handelsklasse)* grade; *(Steuerklasse)* bracket; *(Wertpapiere)* denomination

Klassengesellschaft class society

Klassenlose Gesellschaft classless society

Klassenschranke class barrier

klassifizieren to classify; to rate

Klassifizierung classification; rating

klassische Konditionierung classical conditioning

Klausel clause; article

Kleinaktionär small stockholder

Kleinanleger small investor

Kleinanzeige classified advertisement

Kleinbetrieb small business

Kleincomputer personal computer

Kleine und mittlere Unternehmen small- and medium-sized enterprises (SME)

Kleingeld small coins; change

Kleinkredit small loan; consumer loan; personal loan

Kleinlastwagen pickup truck

Kleinobligation baby bond

kleinstädtisch provincial; small-town

Kleinunternehmen small company

klettern to climb

Klickrate clickthrough rate

Klickstrom click-stream

Klickverfolgung click-tracking

Klient client; patron

Klientel clientele; patronage

Klientel-Effekt clientele effect

knapp scarce; tight; *(vor Zahlen)* just under

Knappheit scarcity; shortage

Knebelungsvertrag adhesion contract

Know-how know-how

Koalition coalition

Kodex code

Kofinanzierung co-financing

kognitive Dissonanz cognitive dissonance

kognitive Fähigkeiten cognitive abilities

kognitive Komponente einer Einstellung cognitive component of an attitude

kognitive-Ressourcen-Theorie cognitive resource theory

kognitives Verhalten cognitive behavior

Kohäsion cohesiveness

Kohäsionsfond cohesion fund

Kohorte cohort

Kollegialprinzip principle of collective responsibility

Kollege colleague

Kollegin colleague

Kollektion selection; assortment; range of goods

Kollektivismus collectivism

Kolonnenführer group leader

Komfort convenience

Komitee committee

Kommanditeinlage limited partnership interest

Kommanditgesellschaft limited partnership

Kommanditist limited partner

Kommentar comment; commentary

kommentieren to comment

kommerziell commercial

kommerzieller Referenzzinssatz commercial interest reference rate

Kommission commission; committee; *(auf Kommission)* on consignment; on sale or return

Kommission einsetzen to set up a committee

Kommissionär commission mergant; factor

kommissionieren to make out a production order

Kommissionslager commission stocks

Kommissionierung consignment sale

kommunal municipal; local

Kommunalanleihe municipal bond

Kommunaldarlehen municipal loan

Kommunalobligation municipal bond; general obligation bond

Kommunalpolitiker local politician

Kommunikation communication

Kommunikationsangst communication apprehension

Kommunikationsnetzwerke communication networks

Kommunikationspolitik communication policy

Kommunikationsprozess communication process

Kommunikationsweg communication channel

Kommunismus communism

kommunistisch communist

Kompagnon partner

komparativ comparative

Kompensationsgeschäft barter deal; buy-back deal

Kompensationshandel counter trade; barter trade

Kompensationskauf counter purchase

Kompetenz competence; capacity

Komplementär general partner; partner with unlimited liability

Komplementärgüter complementary goods

komplex complex

komplexe Kapitalstruktur complex capital structure

kompliziert complex; complicated; difficult

Komplott scheme; plot; conspiracy

Komplott schmieden to plot; to conspire

Komplott vereiteln to foil a plot

Komponente component; constituant

komprimierte Arbeitswoche compressed workweek

Kompromiss compromise; agreement

Kompromiss schliessen to compromise

Kompromisslosigkeit intransigence

Kompromissvorschlag compromise proposal

Konditionen conditions; terms

Konferenz meeting; conference

Konferenz abhalten to hold a conference

Konferenz leiten to chair a conference

Konferenzablauf conference proceedings

Konferenzteilnehmer conference participant; conference delegate; conference member

Konfidenzintervall confidence interval

Konflikt conflict; clash; dispute

Konflikte bei Vertriebskanälen channel conflict

Konfliktfall conflict situation

Konfliktmanagement conflict management

Konfliktregelung conflict settlement

Konfliktverlauf conflict process

Konformität conformity

Konfrontation confrontation

konfrontieren to confront

Konglomerat conglomerate

Kongress congress

Kongresshalle congress hall; assembly chamber

Konjunktur business cycle; economic situation

Konjunkturabhänig cyclical

Konjunkturabschwung cyclical downturn

Konjunkturanstieg cyclical upturn; upward business trend

Konjunkturanzeichen economic indicator

Konjunkturaufschwung cyclical upturn; upward business trend

Konjunkturaussichten business outlook; market outlook

konjunkturbedingte Nachfrage cyclical demand

Konjunkturbelebung economic recovery; business revival

Konjunkturbericht economic report; market report

konjunkturell cyclical; economic

Konjunkturforscher economic researcher; business researcher

Konjunkturindikator economic indicator

Konjunkturinstitut business research institute; economic research institute

Konjunkturlage economic condition

Konjunkturmodell model of economic cycles

Konjunkturpolitik economic stabilization policy

Konjunkturprognose economic forecast

Konjunkturrückgang recession; slump

Konjunkturschema cyclical pattern

Konjunkturtheorie theory of economic cycles; theory of market trends

Konjunkturtief depression

Konjunkturverlauf economic trend; cyclical trend

Konjunkturzyklus business cycle; economic cycle

Konkurrent competitor; rival

Konkurrenz competition; rivalry

Konkurrenzangebot competitive offer

konkurrenzfähig competitive

konkurrenzfähige Preisfestsetzung competitive pricing

Konkurrenzfähigkeit competitiveness

Konkurrenzkampf competition; trade rivalry

Konkurrenzland competing country

konkurrieren to compete

Konkurs bankruptcy; business failure

Konkurs anmelden to file bankruptcy proceedings

Konkursantrag bankruptcy petition

Konkursantrag stellen to file a petition in bankruptcy

Konkursfall bankruptcy case

Konkurseröffnung commencement of bancruptcy proceedings

Konkursforderung claim provable in bankruptcy; claim against a bankrupt's estate

Konkursgläubiger petitioning creditor; creditor of a bankrupt's estate

Konkurskosten bankruptcy costs

Konkursmasse bankrupt estate

Konkursrichter referee in bankruptcy

Konkursverwalter receiver

Können skil; ability; competence

Konnossement bill of lading

Konnossementsgarantie bill of lading guarantee

Konnossementsteilschein delivery order

Konnossementvertrag bill of lading contract

konservativ conservative

Konsignant consignor

Konsignatar consignee

Konsignation consignment

Konsignationslager consignment stocks; custodian warehouse

konsolidieren to consolidate

konsolidierte Anleihe consolidated bond

konsolidierte Bilanz consolidated balance sheet

konsolidierte Gewinn- und Verlustrechnung consolidated income statement

konsolidierte staatliche Rentenanleihe consol

Konsolidierung consolidation

Konsortialbank member bank of a syndicate; underwriting member bank

Konsortialbildung syndication

Konsortialführer leading underwriter; originating banker; leading bank

Konsortialgeschäft syndicate transaction; business on joint account; (*Versicherung*) underwriting syndicate business

Konsortium syndicate; consortium

konstruieren to construct

konstruierter Einkommenszufluss constructive receipt

Konstruktion construction

Konsulat consulate

Konsulatsfaktura consular invoice

Konsultation consultation

Konsultationsverfahren consultation procedure

konsultieren to consult; to enquire; to seek advice

Konsum consumption

Konsumartikel consumer item; consumer goods

Konsumausgaben consumer spending

Konsumbedarf consumer needs

Konsument consumer; user

Konsumentenbefragung consumer research

Konsumentenbudget consumer budget

konsumentenfreundlich consumer-friendly

Konsumenteneinkommen consumer income

Konsumentenkredit consumer credit

Konsumentenrente consumer’s surplus

Konsumentenwunsch consumer demand

Konsumgewohnheit consumer buying habit

Konsumgüter consumer goods; consumer products

Konsumgütermarkt consumer goods market; consumer market

Konsumgütermarketing consumer goods marketing; consumer marketing

konsumieren to consume

Konsumklima consumer sentiment; buyer confidence

Konsumneigung propensity to consume

Kontakt contact

Kontaktadresse contact address

Kontaktaufnahme establishing contacts; contacting

kontaktfähig sociable

Kontenabgleichung balancing of accounts

Kontensumme account balance

Kontingent quota; *(Zuteilung)* allotment

Kontingentierung setting of quotas; rationing

Kontingentsvereinbarung quota agreement

Kontingenzvariablen contingency variables

kontinuierliche Verstärkung continuous reinforcement

Kontinuität continuity

Konto account; balance

Konto anlegen to open an account

Konto ausgleichen to balance an account

Konto belasten to charge an account

Konto blokieren to freeze an account

Konto löschen to close an account

Konto prüfen to examine an account

Konto überziehen to overdraw an account

Kontoabhebung withdrawal

Kontoabtretung assignment of an account

Kontoauflösung closing of account

Kontoauszug statement of account; account statement; *(Bank)* bank statement

Kontoführung bookkeeping; *(Abteilung)* accounting department

Kontoführungsgebühr account fee

Kontoinhaber account holder; *(Einzahler)* depositor

Kontokorrentbuch current account ledger; *(Kreditoren)* accounts payable ledger; *(Debitoren)* accounts receivable ledger

Kontokorrentkonto current account

Kontokorrentkredit overdraft; current account advance; loan on overdraft

Kontokosten bank charges

Kontonummer account number

Kontostand account balance

Kontostandabfrage request for account statement; *(Bank)* request for bank statement

Kontoüberziehung account overdraft; overdrawn account

kontrahieren to contract; to conclude an agreement

Kontrahierung contraction; contracting

Kontrahierungspolitik contracting policy

Kontrakt contract; indenture; agreement

Kontraktarbeit bargain work

Kontraktbindung contractual obligation

Kontrakterfüllung execution of a contract

Kontraktgröße contract size; trading unit; unit of trading

Kontraktmenge contract size

Kontrast contrast

Kontrollabschnitt counterfoil; slip; check

Kontrollbildschirm monitor

Kontrolle control; *(Prüfung)* examination; *(Aufsicht)* supervision; *(Überwachung)* surveillance

Kontrolleur supervisor

Kontrollgremium supervisory body; supervisory committee

kontrollieren to control; *(prüfen)* to examine; to check; to inspect; *(beaufsichtigen)* to supervise

Kontrollprodukt reference product

Konventionalstrafe penalty for non-fullfilment; fine for breach of contract

konventionell conventional

Konvergenz convergence

Konversionsquote conversion ratio

Konvertibilität (*Währung*) convertibility

konvertierbar convertible

Konvertierbarkeit convertibility

konvertieren to convert

Konzentration concentration

konzentrieren to concentrate

Konzern trust; group; concern; conglomerate

Konzernabschluss consolidated financial statement; consolidated accounts

Konzernabschlussprüfer group auditor

Konzernabschlussprüfung audit of the consolidated financial statements

Konzernbilanz consolidated balance sheet

Konzernbildung cosolidation; merger

Konzernfirma consolidated company

Konzerngesellschaft subsidiary; affiliate

Konzerngewinn consolidated profit

Konzern-Gewinn-und-Verlustrechnung consolidated profit and loss statement; consolidated income statement

Konzernlagebericht group annual report; consolidated annual report

Konzernrechnungslegung group accounting

Konzernüberweisung lateral transfer

Konzernumsatz consolidated sales

Konzernverbund affiliated group

Konzession *(Verkaufsrecht)* licence; franchise; *(Banken)* charter

Konzession beantragen to apply for a licence

Konzession haben to hold a licence

Konzession erteilen to award a licence

Konzession entziehen to withdraw a licence

konzessionieren to license; to franchise

Konzessionserteilung licensing; franchising

Konzessionsinhaber licensee; franchisee; holder of a licence

Konzessionssteuer licence tax; franchise tax

Kooperation cooperation

kooperativ cooperative

Kooperative cooperative

Koordination coordination

koordinieren to coordinate

koordinierte Zusammenarbeit teamwork

Koordinierung coordination

Koordinierungsausschuss coordinating committee

Kopie copy; dublicate; replica

kopieren to duplicate; to copy

Korb basket

körperbehindert physically handicapped

Körperschaft corporation

körperschaftlich corporate

Körperschaftsgründung incorporation

Körperschaftssteuer corporate income tax

Körperschaftssteuerbefreiung exemption from corporation tax

korrekt correct

Korrektur correction

Korrektur lesen to proofread

Korrekturbogen proof sheet

Korrelation correlation

Korrespondent correspondent

Korrespondenz correspondence

Korrespondenzbank correspondent bank

Korrespondenzbüro news agency

korrespondieren to correspond

korrupt corrupt

Korruption corruption

kostbar precious

kosten to cost; *(Essen)* to try

Kosten costs; expenses; *(Gebühren)* charges; *(Preis)* price

Kosten, abnehmende decreasing costs

Kosten, abschreibbare depreciable costs

Kosten, angefallene costs incurred

Kosten, aufgelaufene accrued costs

Kosten, durchlaufende transit costs

Kosten, entstandene incurred expenses

Kosten, fixe fixed costs; overheads

Kosten, kalkulatorische expenses for costing purposes

Kosten, laufende current costs; running expenses

Kosten, periodenbezogene expired costs

Kosten, rückläufige decreasing costs

Kosten, steigende rising costs

Kosten, variable variable costs

Kosten, verschiedene sundry expenses

Kosten abbauen to reduce costs

Kosten aufgliedern to itemize costs

Kosten aufteilen to allocate costs

Kosten berechnen to calculate costs

Kosten eindämmen to contain costs

Kosten decken to break even; to cover expenses

Kosten einsparen to reduce costs

Kosten senken to reduce costs; to cut costs

Kosten umlegen to allocate costs

Kosten zurückerstatten to refund costs

Kostenabbau cost cutting

Kostenabweichung cost variance

Kostenanstieg increase in costs

Kostenart cost type; cost category; type of costs

Kostenartenrechnung cost classification; cost-type accounting

Kostenaufwand expenditure; expense; outlay

Kostenbeschränkung cost containment

kostendeckend arbeiten to break even

Kostendeckungsbeitrag contribution profit margin

Kostendeckungspunkt break-even point

Kosteneinsparung cost cutting; cost saving

Kostenentwicklung cost trend

Kostenerhöhung cost increase

Kostenersparnis cost savings

Kostenerstattung refund; reimbursement

Kostenfunktion cost function

Kostengliederung cost structure

kostengünstig cost-efficient;low-cost

Kostenkalkulation costing; calculation of costs

Kostenkontrolle cost control

Kostenkurve cost curve

kostenlos free; free of cost; free of charge

Kostennachteil cost disadvantage

Kosten-Nutzen-Analyse cost-benefit analysis

kostenorientierte Preisbildung cost-based pricing

Kostenprogression cost rise diseconomies of scale; diseconomies

Kosten pro Tausend cost per mille (CPM)

Kosten pro zielgerichtete Tausend cost per targeted mille (CPTM)

Kostenprüfer controller

Kostenrechnung cost accounting

Kostensatz cost schedule; rate; expense ratio

Kostensenkungsstrategie cost-minimization-strategy

Kostensteigerung cost increase

Kostenstelle cost center; cost unit

Kostenstellenrechnung cost center accounting

Kostenstruktur cost structure

Kostenträger cost unit

Kostenträgerrechnung cost unit accounting; product costing

Kostenträgerstückrechnung unit-of-output costing

Kostenträgerzeitrechnung cost unit period accounting

Kostentreiber cost driver

Kostenüberschreitung cost overrun

Kostenüberwachung cost control

Kostenunterschied cost differential

Kostenvergleich comparison of costs

Kostenvergleichsrechnung comparative cost method

Kostenvoranschlag cost estimate; quotation; quote; bid

Kostenvoranschlag machen to make an estimate of the costs

Kostenvoranschlag überschreiten to exceed an estimate

Kostenvorteil price advantage; cost advantage

Kostenvorteil, absoluter absolute advantage

Kostenwirksamkeit cost-effectiveness

Kostenzuordnung cost allocation

kostspielig costly; expensive; high-priced

Kovarianz covariance

Kraft power; *(Stärke)* strength; *(Krafteinwirkung)* force; *(Energie)* energy; *(Arbeiter)* worker

Kraftfahrzeug motor vehicle; car

Kraftfahrzeug anmelden to register a motor vehicle

Kraftfhrzeughaftpflichtversicherung motor third-party liability insurance

Kraftwerk power plant

Krankenversicherung health insurance

Kreativität creativity

Kredit credit; *(Darlehen)* loan; *(mit flexibler Verzinsung)* adjustable rate loan; *(Kreditwürdigkeit)* credit rating; *(Ansehen)* reputation

Kredit abtragen to repay a credit

Kredit aufnehmen to take out a credit; to borrow

Kredit auszahlen to diburse a loan

Kredit beantragen F to apply for a loan

Kredit besichern to secure a loan

Kredit bewilligen to aprove a loan

Kredit geniessen to enjoy credit

Kredit sperren to freeze a credit

Kredit überziehen to overdra a credit

Kreditanalyse credit analysis

Kreditanstalt lending institution; credit association; loan bank

Kreditaufnahme borrowing; borrow

Kreditausfall loan default

Kreditausschuss loan committee

Kreditbeschränkung limitation of credit; credit contraction

Kreditbestand loan portfolio

Kreditbeurteilung credit rating

Kreditbrief letter of credit

Kreditexpansion credit expansion

Kreditfähigkeit borrowing power

Kreditgeber lender; loan creditor

Kreditgenossenschaft credit cooperative; credit union; cooperative savings organization

Kreditgewährung granting of credit; lending; loan approval; lend

Kreditgewerbe financial business; credit business

Kreditgrenze line of credit

Kredithilfe financial aid

Kreditinstitut financial institution; credit institution

Kreditinstrument financial instrument; credit instrument

Kreditkarte credit card; bank card

Kreditknappheit credit crunch

Kreditkonditionen credit terms

Kreditkonto loan account; credit account

Kreditlinie bank line; credit line; line of credit

Kreditmarkt financial market; money and capital markets

Kreditmultiplikator credit multiplier

Kreditnachfrage demand for credit; loan demand

Kreditnehmer borrower

Kreditor creditor

Kreditrahmen bank line; credit line; line of credit

Kreditrisiko credit risk; financial risk

Kreditrückzahlung loan repayment

Kreditsachbearbeiter lending officer

Kreditsicherungsgarantie collateral security

Kreditsumme credit amount; loan amount

Kredittilgung repayment of a loan; amortization

Kreditverbesserung credit enhancement

Kreditvereinbarungsklausel covenant

Kreditversicherung credit insurance; bad debt insurance; loan insurance

Kreditvertrag credit agreement; loan agreement

Kreditwesen lending; financing; credit system

Kreditwesengesetz banking law

kreditwürdig creditworthy; financially sound

Kreditwürdigkeit credit worthiness; credit standing; credit

Kreditwürdigkeit beurteilen to test credit standing

Kreditwürdigkeitsüberprüfung credit investigation

Kreditzinssatz interest rate on debt

Kreditzusage credit approval; loan commitment; standby-credit

Kreditzuwachs credit expansion

Kreis circle; *(Bezirk)* district; *(Landkreis)* county; *(Gruppe)* group

Kreislauf circulation; cycle

Kreuz cross

Kreuzelastizität cross elasticity

Kreuzkurs cross rate

Kreuzparität cross rate

Kreuzpreiselastizität cross price elasticity

Kriegskasse war chest

Krise crisis

Krisenmanagement crisis management

Krisenplan crisis plan; crisis strategy

Kriterium criterion

Kronjuwelen crown jewels

Kuchendiagramm pie chart

kulant accommodating; generous; fair

Kulanz fairness

Kulanzgewehrung accomodating arrangement

Kulanzregelung ex gratia payment

kultivieren to cultivate

Kultivierung cultivation

Kultur culture; civilization

kulturell cultural

kumulativ cumulative

kumulative abnormale Rendite cumulative abnormal return (CAR)

kumulative Stimmabgabe cumulative voting

kumulative Varianz cumulative variance

kumulative Vorzugsdividende cumulative preference dividend

kumulative Wahrscheinlichkeit cumulative probability

Kumulierung accumulation

Kumulierungsbereich accumulation area

kündbar callable; *(Vertrag)* terminable; subject to notice; *(Anleihe)* redeemable

Kündbarkeit terminability; redeemability

Kunde customer; client; (*Groß ~*) account; *(im Laden)* shopper; *(Verbraucher)* consumer

Kunde, anspruchsvoller demanding customer

Kunde, bevorzugter preferetial customer

Kunde, fester regular customer

Kunde, gelegentlicher occasional customer

Kunde, langjähriger standing customer

Kunde, potentieller potential customer

Kunde, unangenehmer awkward customer

Kunden abwerben to entice customers away

Kunden gezielt ansprechen to target customers

Kunden bedienen to serve customers

Kunden werben to canvass customers

Kundenbedürfnisse customer needs

Kundenberater customer service representative

Kundenberatung customer service

Kundenbesuch business call; sales call; calling on customers

Kundenbetreuer account manager; account executive

Kundendeckungsbeitragsrechnung customer contribution accounting

Kundendepot custodianship account

Kundendienst customer service

Kundendienstabteilung customer service department

Kundendienstbüro customer service office

Kundendienstleiter customer relations manager; after-sales manager

Kundendienstpolitik customer service policy

Kundenetat *(Werbung)* account

Kundenfang canvassing

Kundenforderungen *(Bilanz)* accounts receivable; receivables

Kundengeschäft transaction for third account

kundenindividuelle Massenfertigung mass customization

Kundenkarte debit card; account card

Kundenkonto trade account

Kundenkredit consumer credit; customer loan

Kundenkreditbank consumer bank

Kundenkreditgesellschaft consumer finance company

Kundenkreditgewährung consumer lending

Kundenmarketing relationship marketing

Kundennähe customer proximity

Kundenorientierung customer orientation

Kundenservice customer service

Kundenwert customer value

Kundenzufriedenheit customer satisfaction

kündigen to give notice; *(Arbeitgeber)* to dismiss; *(Arbeitnehmer)* to resign; to quit; *(Vertrag)* to cancel; to terminate

kündigen, fristgemäss to due notice

kündigen, fristlos to terminate without notice

kündigen, schriftlich to give written notice

Kündigung notice; *(Arbeitgeber)* notice of dismissal; *(Arbeitnehmer)* notice of resignation; *(Vertrag)* cancellation; notice of termination; *(Anleihe)* notice of redemption

Kündigung, außerordentliche extraordinary dismissal

Kündigung, fristlose instant dismissal

Kündigung, ordentliche statutory notice of termination

Kündigung, rechtzeitige due notice

Kündigung, ungerechtfertigte unfair dismissal

Kündigung, vorzeitige premature dismissal

Kündigungsbenachrichtigung notice of cancelation

Kündigungsfrist period of notice; *(Bank)* withdrawal period

Kündigungsgrund reason for dismissal

Kündigungsklausel (*Börse*) call provision; cancellation clause

Kündigungsmitteilung dismissal notice; *(Vertag)* notice of cancellation; *(Geld)* notice of withdrawal

Kündigungsschutz protection against dismissal; (*Miete*) security of tenure

Kundschaft customer base; clientele

Kunstfaser synthetic fiber

Kunstgriff device; trick

künstlich artificial; synthetic; manmade

Kunststoff synthetic material; plastic material; plastics

Kupon coupon; stub

Kuponanleihe level-coupon bond

Kurier courier; despatch rider; messenger

Kurs *(Aktien)* market price; price; *(Währungs-)* exchange rate; *(Termingeschäft)* forward rate; *(Notierung)* quotation; *(Unterricht)* course

Kursabschlag markdown; downtick; *(Terminhandel)* discount quotation

Kursabsicherung hedging

Kursanstieg *(Aktien)* increase in prices; upward movement

Kursaufschlag markup; *(Terminhandel)* premium

Kursblatt daily quotations; stock-market report; stock exchange price list

Kursbuch *(Eisenbahn)* schedule

Kursdiagramm chart

Kursdifferenz tail; *(Devisen)* difference in exchange rate

Kurseinbruch (*Aktien*) fall in stock prices

Kursfestsetzung quotation; fixing; price determination

Kursgewinn gain; (*Börse*) market profit; stock price gain; *(Devisengeschäft)* exchange profit

Kurs-Gewinn-Verhältnis price-earnings ratio (P/E)

Kurslimit stop price

Kursnotierung quotation

Kursschwankung *(Devisen)* exchange rate fluctuation; *(Börse)* price fluctuation

Kursschwankungsbereich trading range

Kurssicherung hedge; *(Termingeschäft)* forward guarantee

Kursspanne price range; range

Kurssturz *(Aktien)* stock market crash; plunging stock prices

Kursstützung price stabilization

Kursuntergrenze stop-out price

Kursus course

Kurswert *(Aktien)* market value

Kurszettel *(Börse)* stock market quotation

Kurve curve

Kurve effizienter Portfolios efficient set

kurz short; brief

Kurzarbeit short-time work; reduced working hours

kürzen to cut; to reduce

kurzfristig short-run; short-term

kurzfristige Anleihe short bond; short coupon

kurzfristige Geschäftstätigkeit short-run operating activities

kurzfristige Orientierung short-term orientation

kurzfristige Verbindlichkeit current liability

kurzfristige Verschuldung short-term debt

Kürzung cut; reduction; decrease; *(Buch)* abridgment; condensation

L

Labor laboratory

laden to load; to ship; (*Strom*) to charge

Laden retail shop; store

Laden eröffnen so set up a shop

Laden führen to keep shop

Laden zumachen to shut up shop

Ladenbesuch shopping

Ladenpassage shopping mall

Ladenpreis, empfohlener recommended retail price

Ladenreihe shopping mall

Ladenschluss shop closing time

Ladenschlussgesetz shop closing law

Ladenstraße shopping mall

Ladenverkauf retail sales

Laderaum storage space; cargo hold; *(Kapazität)* freight capacity

Ladeschein bill of lading; shipping note; consignment note

Ladeverzeichnis freight list; manifest

Ladung load; cargo; *(Lieferung)* shipment; *(Fracht)* freight

Lage situation; position; *(Zustand)* condition; state

Lagebericht status report; financial report

Lager *(Inventar)* inventory; stock; *(Gebäude)* warehouse; storehouse

Lager abbauen to reduce stocks

Lager auffüllen to replenish stocks

Lageraufstockung replenishing stocks

Lagerbestand stock on hand; inventory

Lagerbewertung inventory valuation

Lagerbuchhaltung inventory accounting

lagerfähig storable; stockable

Lagergeld storage charges; warehouse rent; demurrage

Lagergewinn inventory profit

Lagerhalle warehouse; storehouse

Lagerhallenkonnossement custody bill of lading

Lagerhalter warehouse keeper; stock keeper

Lagerhaltung stock-keeping; warehousing

Lagerhaus depository; warehouse; storehouse

Lagerkosten storage costs; carrying charges

lagern *(Aufbewahrung)* to store; *(Inventar)* to stock

Lagerraum storeroom

Lagerräumung clearance

Lagerschein warehouse warrant

Lagerumsatz inventory turnover

Lagerumschlag inventory turnover

Lagerung *(Aufbewahrung)* storage; *(Inventarhaltung)* stocking

Lagerverwalter stock controller

Lagerverwaltung inventory management

Lagerwirtschaft stock management; just-in-time inventory keeping

Lagerzeit von Beständen shelf life

lahm legen to paralyse; *(boykottieren)* to boycott; *(sperren)* to block

Lahmlegung stoppage; boycott; blocking

Laie layman

Land land; country

landen to land

Ländereien acreage; real estate

Länderrating country rating, country ranking

Länderrisiko country risk; sovereign risk

Landeswährung national currency

Landkarte map

Landstrich area; zone

Landwirt farmer

Landwirtschaft agriculture; farming

landwirtschaftlich agricultural; agrarian

landwirtschaftliches Erzeugnis agricultural product

langen to be sufficient

längerfristig long-term

langfristiger Kredit long-term credit

lange Sicht long term-view

langfristig long-term

langfristige Orientierung long-term orientation

langfristige Verbindlichkeit non-current liability

langjährig long-time; for many years; of long standing

langlebig long lived; *(Güter)* durable

langlebige Gebrauchsgüter durable goods

langsam slow

langsamer werden to slow down

langsames Wachstum slow growth

Langzeittrend secular trend

lassen to let; to allow

Last load; burden

lasten auf to be a burden on

Laster large truck; truck

Lastschrift debit, debit entry; debit advice

Lastwagen truck

Lauf run; *(Gewehr)* barrel

Laufbahn career

Laufbahnaussichten career prospects

Laufbahnplanung career planning

laufen to run

laufend current; running; *(routinemäßig)* routine

laufende Erträge current income

laufende Geschäftstätigkeit operating activities

laufende Rendite current yield; rate of return; running yield

laufende Transferzahlungen current transfer payments

laufendes Konto current account; demand deposit account

Läufer messenger

Laufsteg catwalk

Laufzeit duration; term

Laufzeit, durchschnittliche average maturity

laut loud; *(Zitat)* per

lavieren to manoeuvre

leasen to lease

Leasing leasing

Leasinggeber lessor

Leasinggeschäft leasing business

Leasinggesellschaft leasing company

Leasingmiete leasing charge

Leasingnehmer lessee

Leasingrate leasing rate

lebend living; alive

lebendig *(am Leben)* alive; *(lebhaft)* lively

Lebensalter age

Lebensarbeitszeit working life

Lebensbedarf *(Unterhalt)* means of subsistence; *(lebenslänglicher Bedarf)* lifetime demand

Lebensbedingungen living conditions

Lebensdauer life span; physical life

Lebenserwartung life expectancy

lebensfähig viable

Lebensfähigkeit viability

Lebensführung lifestyle

Lebenshaltung cost of living; standard of living

Lebenshaltungskosten cost of living

lebenslängliche Anstellung lifetime employment

Lebenslauf resumé; curriculum vitae; vita

Lebensmittel groceries; *(Nahrungsmittel)* foodstuffs; *(Vorrat)* provisions

Lebensmittelhändler grocer

Lebensmittelladen grocery store

Lebensqualität quality of life

Lebensquantität quantity of life

Lebensstandard standard of living

Lebensunterhalt livelihood; living

Lebensverhältnisse living conditions

Lebensversicherer life insurer

Lebensversicherung life insurance

Lebensversicherungsgesellschaft life insurance company

lebenswichtig vital; essential

Lebenszyklus life cycle

Lebenszykluskosten life cycle costs

lebhaft lively; active

leer empty; *(unbewohnt)* vacant; *(unbeschrieben)* blank

Leerlauf running idle; *(Auto)* neutral gear

leer laufen to idle

Leerverkauf short sale

legal lawful; legal

Legitimation legimitation; identification

Legitimationspapier identification paper

Legitimationsübertragung proxy statement

Legitimationsurkunde document of title

legitime Macht legitimate power

legitimes politisches Verhalten legitimate political behavior

legitimieren to legitimate; to authorize

lehnen to lean

Lehre apprenticeship; traineeship; *(Theorie)* theory

Lehrling apprentice; trainee

Lehrsatz doctrine; theorem

Lehrstelle apprenticeship position

Lehrstellenangebot apprenticeship offer

Leibrente life annuity

leicht easy; *(Gewicht)* light

Leichtigkeit ease; facility

leicht zu bewältigen easily manageable

leihen to lend; to loan; *(von jdm)* to borrow

Leihfrist lending period

Leihgebühr lending fee

Leihwagen rented car; hired car

Leihweise on loan

leisten to perform;to achieve; *(Dienst)* to render

Leistung achievement; accomplishment; *(Ausführung)* performance; *(Kapazität)* power; output; *(Nebenleistung)* benefit; *(Produktion)* production

Leistungsabgabe power output

Leistungsausfall loss of production

Leistungsaustausch *(Güter)* exchange of goods; *(Dienste)* exchange of services

Leistungsbedürfnis achievement need

Leistungsbeurteilung performance measurement

leistungsbezogenen performance-related; output related

Leistungsbilanz balance on current account; performance record

Leistungsbilanzdefizit current account deficit; deficit on current account

Leistungsbilanzsaldo balance on current account

Leistungsbilanzüberschuß current account surplus; surplus on current account

Leistungsdruck pressure to perform

Leistungseinstufung job evaluation; performance rating

Leistungsempfänger beneficiary; recipient of benefits

Leistungserfüllung making delivery

leistungsfähig *(produktiv)* productive; *(effizient)* efficient; *(gebrauchsfähig)* serviceable

Leistungsfähigkeit *(Produktivität)* productivity; *(Effizienz)* efficiency; *(Gebrauchsfähigkeit)* serviceability; *(Kapazität)* capacity

Leistungsgarantie performance guarantee

Leistungsgesellschaft meritocracy

Leistungsgrad performance level; operating ratio

Leistungsgrenze marginal productivity; upper limit

leistungsmäßig übertreffen to outperform

Leistungsprämie incentive payment; performance fee

Leistungsprinzip effiency principle; marit principle

Leistungsrechnung performance accounting

Leistungsstärke (*Kapazität*) capacity; *(Produktivität)* productivity; *(finanziell)* solvency

Leistungssteigerung performance improvement; improved performance

Leistungsstörung default; *(Recht)* frustration; impairment of performance

leistungsunfähig unproductive; inefficient

Leistungsvergleich benchmarking

Leistungsverzug failure to meet an obligation; default

Leistungsvorgabe performance standard; bogey

Leistungswille motivation

leistungswirtschaftliches Risiko operating leverage

Leistungszahlen output figures

Leistungszuzahlung insentive; bonus

Leitbild mission statement

leiten to manage; *(führen)* to head; to direct

leitend managing; executive

leitender Angestellter executive

Leiter director; manager; *(Chef)* head; chief

Leitfaden guide

Leitlinie *(Verkehr)* demarcation line

Leitung leadership; *(Führung)* guidance; direction; *(Telefon)* line

Leitungsspanne span of control

Leitungsstelle executive position

Leitwährung lead currency; key currency

Leitzins prime rate

lenken to direct; to channel; to control; *(regulieren)* to regulate; *(führen)* to head

Lenkung control; direction; *(Fahrzeug)* steering; *(Flugzeug)* navigation

lernen to learn; to study

Lernen anhand eines Durchlaufs single-loop learning

lernende Organisation learning organization

lesbar readable; legible

Leseranalyse readership analysis

Leserschaft teadership; audience

leugnen to deny

Leumund reputation; record

liberal liberal

liberalisieren to liberalize; *(freigeben)* to decontrol; to deregulate

Liberalisierung liberalization; *(Freigabe)* decontrol

Lichtbild photograph

Lieferabkommen delivery contract; supply agreement

Lieferanschrift delivery address

Lieferant *(Händler)* vendor; provider; supplier; *(Quelle)* source; purveyor; *(Auftragnehmer)* contractor

Lieferantenauswahl supplier selection

Lieferantenbeurteilung supplier evaluation

Lieferantenbuch accounts payable ledger

Lieferantenerklärung supplier's declaration

Lieferantenkredit trade credit; supplier's credit

Lieferantenpreis supplier's price

Lieferantenschulden trade creditors

Lieferantenverbindlichkeiten accounts receivable

Lieferanzeige advice of delivery

Lieferauftrag delivery order

Lieferausfall delivery failure; non-performance

lieferbar available; in stock

Lieferbarkeit availability

Lieferbedingungen terms of delivery; delivery terms; sales conditions

Lieferdatum delivery date

Lieferdienst delivery service

Lieferer supplier; deliverer; contractor

lieferfähig available; deliverable

Lieferfirma supplier; contractor; supplying company

Lieferfrist term for delivery; delivery date

Liefergarantie delivery guarantee; supply guarantee

Lieferklausel delivery clause

Lieferkonto trading account

Lieferland supplying country

Liefermenge quantity delivered

liefern to supply; to deliver; *(versenden)* to ship

Lieferort place of delivery

Lieferposten shipment; lot

Lieferschein delivery note; shipping ticket

Lieferschwierigkeiten supply dificulties

Liefersperre delivery stop; cut-off

Liefertag day of delivery

Liefertermin date of delivery

Lieferung (*Posten*) shipment; *(Auslieferung)* delivery; taking delivery

Lieferung auf Abruf delivery on call

Lieferung gegen Bar cash on delivery

Lieferung frei Bestimmungsort free delivery

Lieferung frei an Bord free on board

Lieferung frei Haus delivery free domicile

Lieferung ab Werk delivery ex works

Lieferungsangebot bid; tender

Liefervertrag supply contract; *(Auslieferung)* delivery contract

Lieferwagen delivery van

Lieferzeitplan delivery schedule

Liegenschaften real estate; realty

Liegenschaftsübertragung conveyance

Liegenschaftsverwalter estate agent

limitieren to limit

Limitkurs limited price

lindern to ease; to mitigate; to relieve

Linderung relief; mitigation

lineare Abschreibung straight-line depreciation

Linie line; *(Kredit)* limit; line

Liniendiagramm line chart

Linienflug sheduled flight

Lieneienfrachtbrief liner waybill

Lieneienfunktion line function

Linienmanager line manager

Linienorganisation line organisation

Linien-und Stabsorganisation line-and-staff organisation

Linienschiff liner

Linienschifffahrt liner trade

Liniensystem (*Organisation*) line organization

Linienverkehr regular service; liner traffic

Linienvorgestetzer line manager

Liquidation liquidation; dissolution; winding up; (*Honorar*) fee; bill

Liquidationsansprüche liquidation rights

Liquidationsantrag petition for winding up

Liquidationsbilanz liquidation balance sheet

Liqudationsgewinn winding-up profit; realization profit

Liquidationsmasse liquidation trust; total assets

Liquidationswert liquidation value; realizable value

liquide solvent; liquid; fluid

liquide Mittel, buchmäßige book cash

liquidierbar realizable; payable

Liquidierbarkeit accounting liquidity

liquidieren to liquidate; (*Firma*) to dissolve; (*Vermögen*) to sell

Liquidierung liquidation

Liquidität liquidity; solvency

Liquidität ersten Grades cash ratio; acid test ratio

Liquidität zweiten Grades quick ratio

Liquidität dritten Grades current ratio

Liquiditätsausweis proof of liquidity

Liquiditätsdruck liquidity squeeze; cash squeeze

Liquiditätsengpass cashout; liquidity squeeze; tight liquidity position

Liquiditätsfalle liquidity trap

Liquiditätsgrad degree of liquidity

Liquiditätshilfe liquidity assistance

Liquiditätskennzahl liquidity ratio

Liquiditätslage liquidity position; cash position

Liquiditätsplan cash budget

Liquiditätspolitik liquidity policy

Liquiditätsproblem liquidity problem

Liquiditätsreserve cash reserve; liquidity reserve

Liquiditätszyklus cash cycle

List ruse; ploy

Liste list; *(Tabelle)* table; *(Warenliste)* tally; catalog

Listenpreis list price

Lizenz license

Lizenzabkommen license agreement

Lizenzbetrieb licensed business

Lizenzgeber licensor; grantor of a licence

Lizenzgebühr license fee; *(Urheberlizenz)* royalty payment

Lizenzinhaber licence holder; licensee

Lizenznehmer licence holder; licensee

Lizenzvergabe licensing; granting of a license

Lizenzvertrag license contract

Lobbying lobbying

Lobbyist lobbyist

lochen to punch; to perforate

lockern to relax

Lockerung relaxation; liberalization

Logdatei log file

Log-File Analyse log file analysis

Lohn wage; pay; salary; remuneration

Lohnabkommen wage agreement

Lohnabrechnung pay slip; payroll accounting

Lohnanhebung wage increase

Lohnanspruch wage entitlement

Lohnausfall loss of pay

Lohnausgleich wage adjustment

Lohneinzelkosten direct labor

Lohn- und Gehaltsempfänger wage and salary earners

lohnen to be profitable

lohnen, sich to be worthwhile; to pay off

lohnend profitable; rewarding; worthwihle

Lohnerhöhung pay raise

Lohnforderung wage demand

Lohngefälle wage differential; wage fluctuation

Lohngruppe wage bracket

Lohnkonto payroll account

Lohnkosten labor costs; cost of labor

Lohnnebenkosten cost of fringe benefits

Lohnpolitik wage policy

Lohnquote wage share; wage ratio

Lohnrunde wage negotiation talks

Lohnsatz wage rate

Lohnsteigerung pay raise

Lohnsteuer income tax; wage withholding tax

Lohnstruktur wage structure

Lohnstückkosten unit labor costs

Lohntarif pay scale; wage rate

Lohn- und Gehälterliste payroll

Lohn- und Gehaltsabrechnung payroll accounting

Lohnverhandlung wage negotiation

Lohnzahlung payment of wages

Lokalbank local bank

Lokalbehörde local authority

Lokalisation localization

Lokalität locality

Lokoware spot commodity

Lombard collateral loan business

lombardieren to collaterate; to hypothecate; to advance money on securities

Lombardierung hypothecation

Lombardkredit collateral loan; credit against securities

Lombardsatz bank rate for collateral loans

Londoner Interbanken -Zinssatz London Interbank Offered Rate(LIBOR)

Lorokonto loro account

Los lot; batch; (*Lotterie*) lottery ticket

löschen *(Waren)* to unload; *(Schuld)* to cancel; *(Computer)* to clear; *(Tonband)* to erase; *(Feuer)* to extinguish

Löschen *(Waren)* deletion; *(Ladung)* unloading; discharge; *(Schuld)* cancellation

Löschung (*Schuld*) cancellation; (*Transport*) landing

Löschung einer Belastung registration of satisfaction

Löschung eines Eintrags cancellation of an entry

Löschung im Handelsregister deregistration

Löschung einer Hypothek extinction of a mortgage

Löschung einer Verbindlichkeit defeasance

Löschung, Einlagerung, Auslieferung landing, storage, delivery (LSD)

lose loose

lösen *(Problem)* to solve; *(Fahrkarte)* to buy

Losgröße batch size; lot size

loslösen *(Verbindung)* to dissociate; *(physisch)* to detach

Lösung solution

Lotse *(Schiff)* pilot

Loyalität loyalty

Lücke gap; *(Zwischenraum)* space; *(Leere)* void

Lückenanalyse gap analysis

lückenhaft *(zeitmäßig)* intermittent; *(Information)* sketchy

Luftfahrt aviation

Luftfahrtindustrie aviation industry

Luftfracht air freight

Luftfrachtbrief air waybill (AWB); air consignment note

Luftkorridor air corridor

Luftpost air mail

Luftrecht air law

Lufttransportgesellschaft air carrier

Luftverkehr air traffic; *(Transport)* air transportation

lukrativ lucrative; profitable

luxuriös luxurious; extravagant

Luxus luxury; extravagance; indulgence

Luxusartikel luxuries; luxury goods

M

Machiavellismus Machiavellianism

machen to make; to do; *(Obligation)* to incur; *(Zustand beeinflussen)* to render

Machenschaft ploy; scheme

Macht power; force; control *(Einfluss)* pull; clout

Machtbalance balance of power

Machtbedürfnis power need

Machtbefugnis authority to act

Machtdistanz power distance

Macht durch Belohnung reward power

Macht durch Bestrafung coercive power

Macht durch Vorbildcharakter referent power

Machtgruppe power group; *(Lobby)* lobby

mächtig mighty; *(einflussreich)* powerful

Machtkampf power struggle

Machtstellung position of power

Machttaktiken power tactics

Machtverteilung distribution of power

Magazin *(Speicher)* warehouse; *(Zeitschrift)* periodical; magazine

mager meagre; slender; lean

Magnat magnate

Mahnbrief reminder letter

mahnen *(Zahlung, Leistung)* to remind

Mahnschreiben reminder; collection letter

Mahnung reminder

Mahnverfahren collection procedure; enforcement proceedings

Makler broker; middleman; agent; (*Börse*) stockbroker

Maklergebühr brokerage charges; commission; fee

Maklergeschäft brokerage

Maklerkredit broker's loan

Maklerstand broker's pit

Makroökonomie macroeconomics

makroökonomisch macroeconomic

Management management

Managementausbildung management training

Managementberater management consultant

Managementfunktion management function

Management-Informationssystem management information system

Manager manager

Managergehalt managerial salary

Managerkrankheit stress disease

Mandant *(Recht)* client

Mandat mandate; *(Vollmacht)* authority; proxy; *(Parlament)* seat

Mangel *(Fehlen)* lack; *(Knappheit)* scarcity; shortage; *(Defekt)* fault; *(Unzulänglichkeit)* deficiency

Mängelanzeige notice of defects

Mängelbeseitigung remedy of defects

Mängelgarantie warranty against defects

Mängelliste list of defects

Mängelrüge notice of defect; letter of complaint

mangelhaft *(unzulänglich)* insufficient; inadequate; *(fehlerhaft)* faulty; defective

mangeln to lack; to fail

mangelnd lacking; wanting

mangels for want of; in absence of

Mangelware scarce commodity

Manifest manifesto

Manipulation manipulation; spoofing

Manipulator manipulator

manipulieren to manipulate

Manko *(Mangel)* deficit; shortage *(Unzulänglichkeit)* deficiency

mannigfaltig diverse; *(diversifiziert)* diversified; *(vielfach)* multiple

Mannigfaltigkeit diversity

Mannschaft team; *(Personal)* personnel

Manöver manoeuvre

manövrieren to manoeuvre

Manteltarif general wage agreement; master wage agreement

Manteltarifvertrag general wage agreement contract

Mappe *(Akten)* binder; *(Zeichnungen)* portfolio

Marge margin; spread

marginal marginal

marginale Zahlungen incremental cash flows

Margenüberschuss excess margin

Marke brand; label; trademark; make (*Post*) stamp

Markenanteil brand share

Markenartikel branded article

Markenartikelhersteller manufacturer of branded goods

Markenbetreuer brand manager

Markenbevorzugung brand preference

Markenbewusstsein brand awareness; brand preference

Markenbezeichnung brand name; brand description

Markenbild brand image

Markeneneinführung launching of a brand; brand introduction

Markeneintragung trademark registration

Markenentwicklung brand development

Markenentwicklungsindex brand development index (BDI)

Markenerzeugnis brand name product

Markenführer brand leader

Markenführerschaft brand leadership

Markenidentität brand identity

Markenimage brand image

Markenindex brand index

Markenkennzeichnung branding

Markenlieferant supplier of branded goods

Markenname brand name

Markenpiraterie brand piracy

Markenpolitik brand policy; branding

Markenpräferenz brand preference

Markenprodukt branded product; proprietary product

Markenschutz trademark protection

Markentreue brand loyalty

Markenwerbung brand advertising

Markenzeichen brand label; logo

Marketing marketing

Marketingabteilung marketing department

Marketingchef marketing manager; marketing chief

Marketingfachmann marketing expert

Marketingkontrolle marketing control

Marketingkonzept marketing concept

Marketingplan marketing plan

Marketingplanung marketing planning

Marketingstrategie marketing strategy

Marketingtest marketing test

markieren to mark; to designate

Markierung labeling; marking

Markt market; marketplace; outlet

Markt abschöpfen to skim the market

Markt aufteilen to divide up a market

Markt beeinflussen to manipulate the market

Markt beherrschen to dominate the market

Markt beleben to stimulate the market

Markt beobachten to watch a market

Markt erobern to conquer a market

Markt stützen to shore up a market

Marktabdeckung market coverage

Marktabsprache marketing agreement

Marktakzeptanz market acceptance

Marktanalyse market analysis

Marktanteil market share

Marktanteil, absolut absolute market share

Marktanteil, relativ relative market share

Marktaufschwung market upturn

Marktaustrittsschranken barriers to exit

Marktbedingungen market conditions

marktbeherrschend dominant; monopolistic

Marktbeherrschung market dominance; market domination

Marktbereinigung market adjustment; shakeout

Marktbreite *(Dimension)* market reach; market spectrum

Marktbude market stall

Marktchance market opportunity

Marktdaten market data

Marktdiversifizierung market diversification

Marktdurchdringung market penedration

Markteinführung introduction on the market; launch

Markteintritt market entry

Markteinwirkungen market forces

Marktentwicklung market development

Markterholung market recovery

Markterkundung market survey; market test

Markterschliessung market development; tapping a new market

Markterweiterung market extension

marktfähig marketable; saleable

Marktfähigkeit marketability

Marktform type of market; market form

Marktforscher market researcher

Marktforschung market research; marketing research

Marktforschungsabteilung market research department

Marktforschungsdaten market research data

Marktführer market leader

marktgängig marketable

Marktgängigkeit marketability

Marktgebiet sales territory; marketing area

Marktgegebenheiten trading conditions; market forces

Marktgerecht in line with market requirements

Marktgeschehen market action

Marktgleichgewicht market eqilibrium

Marktgröße market size

Marktindex benchmark

Marktkapitalisierung market capitalization

Marktkonstellation market conditions; state of the market

Marktkräfte market forces

Marktlage market situation; *(Zustand)* market condition

Marktleistung market performance

Marktlücke market gap; market niche

Marktmechanismus market mechanism

Marktmodell market model

Marktnachfrage market demand

marktnah close to the market

Marktnische market niche

Marktordnung market regime; organization of a market

marktorientiert market-oriented

Marktplatz market space

Markt-Portfolio market portfolio

Marktposition market position

Marktpotential market potential

Marktpreis market price; market rate; fair market value

Marktprinzip market principle

Marktprognose market forecast

Markträumung market clearing

Marktregulierung market regulation

marktreif marketable; ready for the market

Marktrisiko market risk

Marktsättigung market saturation

Marktschaffung creating a market

Marktsegment market segment

Marktsegmentierung market segmentation

Marktsegmentierungspolitik market segmentation policy

Marktstellung market position

Marktstrategie marketing strategy

Marktstruktur market structure

Marktteil market sector

Markttest market test

Marktumfang market scope; market size

Marktuntersuchung market analysis; market research

Marktverhalten market behavior

Marktvolumen market volume

Marktwert market value; current market value

Marktwert-Buchwert-Verhältnis market-to-book (M/B) ratio

Marktwirtschaft market economy

Marktwirtschaftler market economist

Marktziel market objective

Marktzinssatz market rate of interest; going rate of interest

Marktzugang market access

Maschine machine

maschinell mechanical

maschinell bearbeiten to machine

maschinelle Anlage machinery

Maschinenanlage machinery

Maschinenbau mechanical engineering

Maschinenbauer mechanical engineer

Maschineneinsatz deployment of machines

Maschinenfabrik machine works; engineering works

Maschinenhaus powerhouse

Maß *(Volumen)* volume; *(Hohlmaß)* measure; *(Messung)* measurement

maßgeblich relevant; significant

maßgefertigt custom-made

maßgeschneidert made-to-order; tailor-made

Masse mass; matter; bulk

Massenabsatz wholesale

Massenentlassung mass layoff; mass dismissal

Massenfertigung mass production

Massengeschäft high-volume business; bulk transaction

Massengut bulk commodity; bulk cargo

massenhaft en masse; in large quantity

Massenkonsum mass consumption

Massenmarketing mass marketing

Massenmarkt mass market

Massenmedien mass media

Massenprodukt mass product

Massenproduktion mass production

mäßig moderate; modest

massig bulky; massive

mäßigen to moderate; to mitigate

Mäßigung moderation

massiv massive

Maßnahme provision; measure

Maßnahmeplanung action planning

Maßregel measure

Maßstab scale

Maßstab festlegen to scale

maßvoll measured; modest

Mast mast

Mater matrix

Material material; substance; stock

Materialabgang withdrawal of material

Materialbedarf material requirements

Materialbedarfsplanung materials requirement planning

Materialbeschaffung procurement of materials

Materialbestand stock of materials; materials on hand

Materialbestandsplanung inventory planning

Materialeingang receiving materials; inventory additions

Materialeinsatz input; materials usage

Materialermüdung material fatigue

Materialfluss flow of materials

materialistisch materialistic

Materialkosten material costs; cost of supplies

Materiallager stores; stocks

Materiallagerung storage of materials

Materialprobe sample

materiell tangible

materielle Aktiva tangible assets

Materialtransport materials handling

Materialwirtschaft materials management

Materie matter

materiell physical; material

materielle Güter tangible goods

Matrixführung matrix management

Matrixorganisation matrix organization

Maut toll; road charge

maximieren to maximize

Maximierung maximization

Maximum maximum

McClellands Bedürfnistheorie McClelland's theory of needs

Mechanik mechanics

Mechaniker mechanic; *(Reparatur)* repairman, -person, -woman

mechanisch mechanical

Mechanisierung mechanization

Mechanismus mechanism

mechanistisches Modell mechanistic model

Medien media

Medienanalyse media analysis

Medienbesitzer media owner

Mediengesetz media law

Medienkäufer media buyer

Medienmakler media broker

Medienmagazin media magazine

Medienverflechtung interrelation of media

Medium medium

Meeresenge narrows; *(Sund)* sound

Mehraufwand additional expenditure; extra cost

Mehrausgabe additional expenditure

mehrdeutige Rendite multiple rates of return

mehrdimensionale Deckungsbeitragsrechnung multidimensional contribution accounting

mehren to increase in quantity

Mehrerlös *(Verkauf)* additional proceeds; *(Verdienst)* extra earnings

mehrfach multiple

Mehrheit majority

mehrheitlich by majority

Mehrheitsaktionär majority stockholder

Mehrheitsbesitz majority ownership

Mehrheitsbeteiligung majority interest; controlling interest

Mehrheitsstimmrecht majority voting; statutory voting

Mehrweg- returnable

Mehrstimmrecht cumulative voting

Mehrwert value added

Mehrwertsteuer value-added tax (VAT)

Meineid perjury

Meineid leisten to commit perjury

meinen to think; to belive; *(Bedeutung)* to mean; *(Aussage)* to state; *(Meinung sagen)* to opine

Meinung opinion; view; argument

Meinung ändern to change one's mind

Meinung durchsetzen to force one's point

Meinung einholen to optain an opinion

Meinung vertreten to advance a view

Meinungsänderung change of mind

Meinungsaustausch exchange of views

Meinungsbildung opinion making; opinion formation; forming of opinion

Meinungsforschung opinion research

Meinungspflege public relations

Meinungsumfrage opinion survey; opinion poll

Meinungsverschiedenheit *(Unterschied)* difference of opinion; *(Differenz)* disagreement

meistbegünstigtes Land most favored nation

Meistbegünstigungsklausel most favored nation clause

Meister master; foreman

meistern to master; to cope with

Meistern mastery

Meistgebot highest bid; best offer

Meldeamt registration office

Meldebestimmung registration requirements

Meldefrist registration period

melden to report; to notify; to inform; to register

Meldepflicht compulsory registration

meldepflichtig subject to registration

Meldevorschrift registration instruction

Meldung report; return

Melodie melody; tune

Memorandum memorandum

Menge *(Quantität)* quantity; amount; *(Posten)* lot; *(Aufstellung)* array; *(Masse)* bulk

Mengenabnahme bulk purchasing; quantity buying

Mengenanpasser price taker

Mengenanpassung quantity adjustment

Mengeneinheit unit of quantity

Mengengerüst quantity structure

Mengengeschäft *(Unternehmen)* volume business; *(Transaktion)* volume transaction

Mengenindex quantitative index

mengenmäßig quantitative

Mengenrabatt volume discount; quantity rebate

Mengenstandardisierung volume standardization

Mengenzuwachs volume increase

Menschenalter lifetime; generation

Menschenführung human resources management; personnel management

Menschenrechte human rights

Menschenrechtskommission Human Rights Commission

menschlich human; *(human)* humane

menschliche Arbeitskraft manpower

Mentor mentor

Merkantilismus mercantilism

Merkmal *(Zeichen)* sign; *(Markierung)* mark; *(Eigenschaft)* attribute; *(quantitativ)* key variable; characteristic

messbar measurable

Messbarkeit measurability

Messe exposition; *(Ausstellung)* exhibition; trade fair; *(Kirche)* mass

Messebeteiligung participation in a fair

Messegesellschaft exhibition corporation

Messekalender schedule of trade fairs

Messekontingent trade fair quota

Messeleitung exhibition management

messen to measure

Messeplatz exibition site

Messgröße measure; indicator

Messinstrument measure; *(Richtmaß)* gauge; *(Zähler)* meter

Messtisch plan table

Messung measurement

Metall metal

Metallindustrie metal industry

Metamorphose metamorphosis

Meta-Suchmaschinen meta search engines

Meta Tags meta-tags

Meter meter

Methode method; technique

metrisch metric

Miet- rental

Miete rent; lease; hire

Miete, kalkulatorische imputed rent

Mieteinnahme rental receipts

mieten to rent; *(pachten)* to lease; *(Flugzeug, Jacht)* to charter

Mieten renting; leasing; *(Flugzeug, Jacht)* chartering

Mieter tenant; lessee

Mietertrag rental income

Mietherr landlord

Mietsteigerung rent increase

Mietvertrag rental agreement; *(Pachtung)* lease agreement

Mietwohnung rented apartment

Mietzins rent

Mikrochip microchip

Mikrocomputer microcomputer

Mikroelektronik microelectronics

Mikrofunktion microfunction

Mikrokultur microculture

Mikroökonomie microeconomics

Mikroprozessor microprocessor

Mikrorechner microcomputer

Mikrosite micro site

Mikrostruktur microstructure

Mikrotechnik microtechnology

Mikrowelle microwave

Mikrozahlungen micropayments

mildern to mitigate; to alleviate; to soften; to ease

Militär- military

Militär military

militärisch military

Millionär millionaire

Minderausgabe *(Kosten)* reduced expenditure; *(Wertpapiere)* underissue

Minderheit minority

Minderheitsbeteiligung minority interest; minority participation

Minderheitsgesellschafter minority partner

minderjährig under age; minor

Minderjähriger minor

Minderkaufmann small trader; non-registered merchant

Minderkonsum reduced consumption

mindern to reduce; to impair

Minderung reduction; impairment

minderwertig inferior; *(Warenqualität)* cheap

Mindestarbeitszeit minimum working hours

Mindesteinzahlungsbetrag margin requirement; *(Konto)* minimum deposit

Mindestgröße minimum size

Mindestmaß *(Menge)* minimum amount; *(Größe)* minimum size

Mindestpreis minimum price; floor price

Mindestpreishöhe minimum price level; price floor

Mindestreserve minimum reserves; *(Konto)* minimum balance requirement

Mindestsicherung minimum collateral

Mindestzins minimum interest

Mine mine

Mineral mineral

mineralisch mineral

Minicomputer minicomputer

minimieren to minimize

Minimum minimum

Minimum-Varianz-Portfolio minimum variance portfolio

Minister *(US)* secretary; *(UK)* minister

Ministeramt *(US)* department; *(UK)* ministry; *(Position)* ministerial post

ministeriell ministerial

Ministerium *(US)* department; *(UK)* ministry

Ministerpräsident prime minister

Ministerrat council of ministers

ministrieren to minister

Minorität minority

Minuskorrektur markdown

Minute minute

Mischfinanzierung mixed financing

Mischkalkulation combined costing

mischen to mix

Mischform hybrid

Mischform einer Rente hybrid annuity

Mischkonzern conglomerate

Mischung mix; mixture; blend

missachten to disregard

Missachtung disregard; contempt; neglect

Missbilligung disapproval

Missbrauch abuse

missbrauchen to abuse

missbräuchlich abusive

Misserfolg failure; disappointment

Missfallen dissatisfaction; disapproval

Missgriff mistake

misslingen to fail

Missverhältnis disproportion

Misswirtschaft mismanagement

Mitarbeit cooperation

mitarbeiten to cooperate; to contribute one's services

Mitarbeiter *(Arbeitnehmer)* employee; *(Kollege)* co-worker; colleague

Mitarbeiter *(Arbeitnehmer)* employee; *(Personal)* personnel

Mitarbeiter-Aktienoption employee stock option

Mitarbeiterbefragung employee attitude survey

Mitarbeiterbeteiligung employee involvement

Mitarbeiterförderung personnel development

Mitarbeiterführung personnel management; leadership

Mitarbeiterorientierung employee-orientation

Mitarbeiterranking auf der Basis von Paarvergleichen paired comparison

Mitarbeiterzahl number of employees

Mitbegründer cofounder

mitbestimmen to codetermine; to take part in decision-making

Mitbestimmung employee participation; codetermination; representative participation

Mitbewerber *(Auftrag)* rival; *(Stellung)* coapplicant

mit Dividende cum dividend

Miteigentümer co-owner

mitentscheiden to codecide

Mitgesellschafter fellow partner

Mitglied member

Mitgliederwerbung membership campaign

Mitgliederzahl number of members

Mitglied des Aufsichtsrats member of the supervisory board

Mitglied des Verwaltungsrates member of the board of management

Mitgliedsbuch membership roster; membership register

Mitgliedschaft membership

Mitgliedsland member country

Mithöreinrichtung wire-tapping device

Mitinhaber co-owner

Mitsprache *(Entscheidungsprozeß)* voice

Mitte middle; *(Zentrum)* center

mitteilen to communicate; *(berichten) to* report; *(informieren) to* inform

Mitteilung communication; information; notification

Mittel- middle; *(Durchschnitt)* average

Mittel means; *(Ressource)* resource; *(Zahlung)* medium

Mittel, arithmetisches arithmetic mean

Mittelabfluss funds flow

mittelbar indirect

Mittelbeschaffung procurement of funds

Mittelbetrieb medium-size enterprise

Mittelbindung freezing of funds

mittelfristig medium-term; intermediate-term

mittelfristige Anleihe medium-term bond

mittelgroß mid-size

mittelgroßer Computer minicomputer

Mittelherkunft sources of funds

Mittelpunkt center

Mittelrückfluss ins Banksystem reintermediation

Mittelsektion midsection

Mittelsmann middleman; intermediary

Mittelstand middle class

mittelständisch middle class

mittelständische Unternehmen small and medium-sized businesses

Mittelteil midsection; center part

Mittelverwendung *(Zuwendung)* allocation of resources; *(Verwendung)* disposition of funds; application of funds

Mittelwert mean value; mean

mittelwertig median

Mittelzufluss influx of funds

Mittler mediator; agent

mittlere Führungskraft middle manager

Mitversicherungseffekt coinsurance effect

mitwirken *(Teilnahme)* to participate *(Zusammenarbeit)* to cooperate

mitwirkend participatory; *(bewirkend)* instrumental

Mitwirkung *(Teilnahme)* participation; *(Zusammenarbeit)* cooperation; *(Mittel)* instrumentality

Mitwirkungsrecht right to participate; law of instrumentality

mixen to mix

MM-These I MM Proposition I

MM-These II MM Proposition II

Möbelspediteur mover; moving company

mobil mobile

mobilisieren to mobilize

Mobilisierung mobilization

Mobilität mobility

Mobiltelefon cell phone; mobile phone

Mode fashion; vogue

Modell model; type

Modell der Arbeitsplatzmerkmale job characteristics model

Modell der rationalen Entscheidungsfindung rational decision-making model

modellieren to model

Moderation moderation

Moderator moderator; presenter

moderieren to moderate

modernisieren to modernize; to update

Modernisierung modernization

Modifikation modification

modifizieren to modify

Modifizierung modification

Modul module

modular modular

möglich possible; potential

möglicher Bedarf potential need; potential market

Möglichkeit *(Chance)* possibility; *(Gelegenheit)* opportunity; *(Potential)* potential

möglichst groß darstellen to maximize

möglichst klein darstellen to minimize

monatlich monthly

Monatsauszug monthly statement of account

Monatsbilanz monthly balance; monthly balance sheet

Monatsdurchschnitt monthly average

Monatsende month's end

Monatsmitte middle of the month

Monatspauschale flat monthly charge

Monatsproduktion monthly production

Monatsrate monthly rate

Monatsverdienst monthly earnings

monetär monetary

Monetarismus monetarism

Monetarist monetarist

Monopol monopoly

Monopol reines absolute monopoly

Monopol besitzen to have a monopoly

Monopolbesitzer monopolist

monopolisieren to monopolize

Monopolisierung monopolization

Monopolist monopolist

monopolistisch monopolistic

monopolistischer Markt captive market

Monopolpreis monopoly price

Monopolproblem monopoly problem

Monopson monopsony

Monotonie monotony

Montage assembly

Montagewerk assembly plant

montieren to assemble; to rig

Moratorium moratorium; standstill agreement

Motiv theme

Motivation motivation

Motivationsforschung motivation research

motivieren to motivate

Motivierung motivation

Motorisierung motorization; mechanization

Motto motto; slogan

mühsam laborious; strenuous

Mulde depression; trough

Müll waste; garbage; trash

Müllabfuhr waste disposal; garbage removal

Müllaufbereitung waste recycling

Müllhalde dump

multilateral multilateral

multilaterales Abkommen multilateral agreement

Multimillionär multimillionaire

multinational multinational

multinationale Unternehmung multinational company

Multiplikator multiplier

mundgerecht palatable

Mündel ward

mündelsichere Kapitalanlage legal investment

mündig of legal age; major

Mündigkeit majority; maturity

mündlich verbal; oral

Münzamt mint

Münze *(Geldstück)* coin; *(Münzsystem, Prägung)* coinage

Münzeneinziehung demonetization

Münzensammlung coin collection

Muße leisure

müßig idle

Muster *(Probe, Exemplar)* sample; *(Vorbild, Schablone)* pattern

Musterstück sample; prime example

mutmaßlich presumable; *(wahrscheinlich)* probable

Muttergesellschaft parent company

Myers-Briggs-Typenindikator Myers-Briggs type indicator (MBTI)

N

Nabe hub

Nachahmung imitation; *(Ersatz)* substitute

nach Bedarf according to need; *(Nachfrage)* according to demand

nachbestellen to reorder

Nachbestellung reorder

Nachdruck *(Neudruck)* reprint; *(Betonung)* emphasis; *(Beharrlichkeit)* insistence

Nachfassbrief follow-up letter

nachfolgend successive; *(anschließend)* subsequent

Nachfolgeplanung succession planning

Nachfolger successor

Nachforderung *(Nachfrage)* additional demand; *(Forderung)* supplemental claim; *(Steuer)* back charge

nachforschen *(Erkundigung)* to inquire; *(Forschung)* to research

Nachforschung inquiry

Nachfrage demand; need; market; enquiry

Nachfrage, abgeleitete derived demand

Nachfrage, anhaltende persistent demand

Nachfrage, aufgestaute pent-up demand

Nachfrage, elastische elastic demand

Nachfrage, gesamtwirtschaftliche aggregate demand

Nachfrage, fehlende lack of demand

Nachfrage, konstante steady demand

Nachfrage, schleppende sluggish demand

Nachfrage, schwankende fluctuating demand

Nachfrage, unelastische inelastic demand

Nachfrage, zusammengesetzte composite demand

Nachfrage abwürgen to choke off demand

Nachfrage ankurbeln to stimulate demand

Nachfrage befriedigen to meet demand

Nachfrage steigern to increase demand

Nachfrage übersteigen to exceed demand

Nachfrageausweitung expansion of demand

Nachfrageelastizität elasticity of demand

Nachfragefunktion demand function

Nachfragekurve demand curve

Nachfragemonopol monopsony

nachfragen to inquire; to demand

Nachfrageprognose demand forecast

Nachfragetheorie demand theory

Nachfragevorhersage demand forecast

Nachfragezuwachs demand growth

nachgeben to yield; to give in; to accommodate

Nachgebühr surcharge

nachgelagert downstream

nachgewiesene Reserven proved reserves

nachgiebig yielding; soft

nach Größe geordnet ordered by size

nachhaltig enduring; *(hartnäckig)* persistent

nachhaltige Wachstumsrate sustainable growth rate

Nachholbedarf pent-up demand; backlog demand

Nachholeffekt catch-up effect

nachholen to catch up; *(Mangel)* to make up

Nachkriegs- postwar

Nachkriegszeit postwar period

Nachlass estate; bequest; inharitance

nachlassen to weaken; to slacken; *(Rabatt)* to give a rebate

Nachlassen weakening; slowdown

nachlassend sagging

nachlässig negligent; careless

Nachlässigkeit negligence; neglect

nachlaufender volkswirtschaftlicher Indikator lagging economic indicator

nachprüfen to verify

Nachprüfbarkeit verifiability

nachprüfen to check; *(untersuchen)* to investigate

Nachprüfung check; *(Untersuchung)* investigation

nachrangige Hypothek subordinated mortgage

nachrangige Schuld subordinated debt

nachrangige Schuldverschreibung subordinated debenture

nachrechnen to recompute; to recalculate; *(prüfen)* to check

Nachricht news; message

Nachrichten news

Nachrichtenmagazin news magazine

nachrückende Führungskraft junior manager

nachschicken to send on; *(Post)* to forward

nachschießen to make additional payment; *(auf Aktien)* to pay a further call; *(Effektenlombard)* to call for additional cover

nachschüssige Rente annuity in arrears

nachschüssige Zahlungen end-of-year convention

nachsenden to forward; to redirect

Nachsendeadresse forwarding address

nachtanken to refuel

Nachteil disadvantage; *(Schaden)* detriment; loss

nachteilig disadvantageous; adverse

nachträglich after the fact; *(ergänzend)* supplementary

nachträgliche Vergütung deferred compensation

Nachtragshaushalt supplementary budget; supplementary appropriation; deficiency bill

Nachverkäufe repeat business

nachwachsend renewable

Nachweis proof; *(Beweis)* evidence

nachweisen to prove

Nachwuchskraft junior staff member; trainee

nachzählen to check; to tally

Nadelspitze pin point

nagelneu brand new; in mint condition

nahe bringen to bring dose; to approximate

nahe kommen to approach

nähern, sich to approach

Näherungswert approximation

Nahzug local train

Namensaktie registered share of stock; personal share

Namenspapier registered bond; registered security

Namensschild name plate

Namenszug signature

Nationalbank national bank

Nationalbudget national accounts budget

nationalisieren to nationalize

Nationalisierung nationalization

Nationalökonom political economist

Nationalökonomie national economy; macroeconomics

Nationalvermögen national wealth

naturalisieren to naturalize

Naturalisierung naturalization

natürlich natural

Navigation navigation

Neben- by-; auxiliary; lateral

Nebenamt *(Posten)* secondary appointment; *(Geschäftsstelle)* auxiliary office

nebenamtlich extraofficial

nebenamtlicher Geschäftsführer non-executive director

Nebenbedingung additional condition; *(Kontrakt)* secondary clause

nebenberuflich part-time

Nebenbestimmung collateral clause

Nebenkosten auxiliary costs; additional expenses

Nebenleistung *(Lohn, Gehalt)* fringe benefit; perquisite; perk

Nebenprodukt *(zusätzliches Produkt)* sideline; *(Abfall, Abfallprodukt)* by-product

nebensächlich secondary

Nebenvertrag subcontract

Nebenwert *(Börse)* secondary stock; second-tier stock

Nebenwirkungen side effects

Negativverpflichtung negative covenant

negativ negative

Negativbescheinigung clearance certificate

Negativklausel negative pledge clause

Negativkommission (*Zins*) negative interest

Negotiationskredit drawing authorization

negoziierbar negotiable

Negoziierung negotiation

Negoziierungs-Akkreditiv negotiation credit; merchant's credit

negoziieren to negotiate

neigen to lean; *(Tendenz)* to tend

Neigung *(Tendenz)* tendency; *(Trend)* trend; *(Geneigtheit)* predisposition

Nennbetrag face amount; nominal amount

nennen to call; to name

Nennwert par; par value; face value

Nennwert einer Banknote denomination

neocharismatische Theorien neocharismatic theories

Neoliberalismus neo-liberalism

Neoprotektionismus neo-protectionism

Nestbeschmutzer whistle-blower

netto net; clear; *(Preis)* after tax

Nettoanteil net worth

Nettoanteil der Aktionäre shareholders' equity

Nettoarbeitslohn net wage

Nettoaufwand net expenditure

Nettobuchwert book value; carrying value

Nettoeinkommen net income

Nettoerlös net proceeds

Nettoersparnis net savings

Nettoertrag net earnings

Nettogewinn net profit

Nettoinvestition net investment

Nettokapital net capital

Nettokapitalexport net capital export

Nettokurs *(Währung, Wertpapier)* price

Nettopreis net price

Nettorendite net yield

Nettorendite auf das Anlagevermögen net return on assets

Nettoreserve net reserves

Nettosozialprodukt net national product

Nettoüberschuss net surplus

Nettoumlaufvermögen net current assets; net working capital; working capital

Nettoumsatz net sales

Nettoumsatzrendite net profit margin

Nettoverkaufserlös net sales earnings

Nettoverkaufspreis net sales price

Nettoverlust net loss

Nettowarenpreis net commodity price; net price of goods

Nettowert net worth

Nettozunahme net increase

Nettozuschuss net allowance; *(Beitrag)* net contribution; *(Staat)* net subsidy

Netz network; net

Netzplan network

Netzplantechnik network technique; critical path method

Netzwerk network; mesh

Netzwerk; verbundenes affiliate network

Neuabschätzung reappraisal

Neuabschluss new contract; new business

Neuanlage *(Fabrik)* new plant; *(Geld)* reinvestment

neu anpassen to readjust

Neuanschaffung new acquisition; *(Kauf)* new purchase; *(Bank)* new procurement

neu ansetzen to reschedule

Neuauflage reprint; new edition

neu auflegen *(Veröffentlichung)* to reissue; *(Anleihe)* to refloat

neu aufstellen *(neu errechnen)* to recalculate

Neuaufstellung realignment; *(Errechnung)* recalculation

neu ausbilden to retrain

Neuausbildung retraining

neu ausrichten to realign

Neuausrichtung *(Unternehmensziel)* redirection; realignment

neu bedenken to rethink; to reconsider

neu beleben to revitalize

neu bereitstellen to reallocate; to recommit

neu bestätigen to reconfirm

neu bestellen to reorder

Neubestellung reorder

neu bewerten to re-evaluate; to revalue; *(Schätzungswert)* to reappraise

Neubewertung reappraisal

neu binden, sich to recommit

neu drucken to reprint

neue Arbeitskraft new employee; new recruit

Neueinsatz new deployment

neu einsetzen to redeploy

Neueinstellung new appointment

neu einstufen to reclassify

Neueinstufung *(Klassifizierung)* new classification; *(Steuer)* reassessment

neu einteilen to reapportion; *(Zeit)* to reschedule

Neueinteilung *(Anordnung)* rearrangement; *(Klassifizierung)* reclassification

Neueinteilung der Produktionszeit rescheduling

Neueintritt reentry; new entry; *(Zulassung)* readmittance

Neuemission new issue; primary offering; unseasoned new issue

Neuengagement new engagement

Neuentwicklung new development

Neuerung innovation

Neuerungen einführen to innovate

neuerungsbereit innovative

neu erwägen to reconsider

Neuerwägung reconsideration

Neuerwerbung new acquisition

neu etablieren to reestablish

neu fassen to reformulate; to rewrite

Neufassung *(Dokument)* revision; *(Gesetz)* amendment

neu festlegen to reestablish

Neufinanzierung refinancing; recapitalization

neu floaten to refloat

Neugeschäft new business; new deal

neu gestalten to redesign; to reshape

Neugestaltung reorganization; reform

neu gliedern to restructure

Neugliederung restructuring; reorganization

neu gründen to set up a company; *(wiederholt)* to reestablish

Neugründung start-up company; *(wiederholt)* reestablishment;

neu gruppieren to rearrange; to regroup

Neuigkeit news

neu informieren to update

Neukapitalisierung recapitalization

neu klassifizieren to reclassify

Neuklassifizierung reclassification

Neukredit new credit; new advance

Neuling newcomer; *(Lehrling)* apprentice; recruit

neumodisch newfangled

Neuordnung rearrangement; reform; reorganization

Neuorganisation restructuring

Neuplatzierung repositioning

neu produziert newly produced; produced again; re-produced

Neuregelung readjustment; revision; rearrangement

neureich newly rich; nouveau-riche

neu schätzen to reestimate; to revalue

neutral neutral

Neutralität neutrality

neu verhandeln to re-negotiate

Neuverhandlung renegotiation

Neuvermögen new wealth; *(Aktiva)* new assets; *(Kapital)* new funds

neu verpflichten to reobligate; to recommit

Neuverschuldung new indebtedness

neu verteilen to reallot; to reallocate; to redistribute

Neuverteilung redistribution

Neuzulassung readmission; *(Registrierung)* new registration

neu zusammenstellen to regroup; to reassemble

neu zuteilen to reallocate

Neuzuteilung reallocation

nicht abgeschriebenes Disagio unamortized bond discount

nicht abgesicherte Option uncovered option

Nichtanerkennung non-recognition; *(Schuld)* debt repudiation

nicht angelegt uninvested

nicht auf Gewinn gerichtet nonprofit

nicht ausgegeben *(Aktien)* unissued; *(Geld)* unspent

nicht ausgeschüttete Gewinne retained earnings

nicht ausschüttungsfähiger Gewinnvortrag restricted retained earnings; restricted surplus

Nichtbank nonbank

Nichtbefolgung noncompliance; nonobservance

nicht befriedigen to dissatisfy; *(enttäuschen)* to disappoint

nicht beitreibbar *(Schulden)* uncollectible

nicht bereinigt unadjusted

nicht bevorrechtigter Gläubiger general creditor

nicht börsenfähiges Wertpapier nonmarketable security

nicht eingerechnet not included; exclusive of

Nichteinhaltung default; noncompliance

Nichteinlösbarkeit inconvertibility

nicht einträglich unprofitable

nicht einziehbar uncollectible

Nichterfüllung non-fulfillment; non-performance; failure; default

nicht erhältlich unavailable

Nichtfachmann layman; amateur

Nichtfunktionieren malfunctioning

nicht geschäftsmäßig unbusinesslike

nicht gestatten to disallow

nicht gewinnbeteiligt non-participating

nicht häufig infrequent

nichtig void; null

Nichtigkeit voidness; invalidity

Nichtkonvertierbarkeit inconvertibility

nicht kumulativ non-cumulative

nicht mehr aufnahmefähig saturated

nicht originär derivative

nicht realisierter Kursgewinn unrealized gain; paper gain

nichtrelevante Kosten sunk costs

nichts nothing; nil

nicht stimmberechtigt nonvoting

nicht streuungsfähiges Risiko non-diversifiable risk

nicht übereinstimmen to disagree

Nichtübereinstimmung disagreement

nicht verfügbar unavailable

nicht verkaufbar unsalable

nicht verkauft unsold

nicht verwendungsfähig unusable

nicht verwirklicht unrealized

nicht vollwertig substandard

nicht wettbewerbsfähig not competitive

nicht zustimmen to dissent; *(Einspruch erheben)* to object

niederdrücken to depress

Niedergang downgrade; fall

niederlassen, sich to locate

Niederlassung location; establishment; *(Zweigstelle)* branch office

Niederlassungsbeschränkung restriction on the freedom of establishment

Niederlassungsfreiheit freedom of establishment

Niederlassungsleiter branch manager

Niederlegen der Arbeit work stoppage; *(Streik)* walkout

niederschreiben to record

niedrig low; depressed

niedrigere Bedürfnisse lower-order needs

niedriger einstufen to downgrade

Niedrigpreis low price

Niedrigstkosten lowest cost

Niedrigstwert lowest value

Niedrigzinsphase low interest period

Nießbrauch beneficial interest; *(Grundstück)* lifehold; usufruct

Niete rivet; *(Lotterie)* blank; *(Person)* loser

Nische niche; slot

Niveau level; standard

nochmals bezahlen to repay

noch nicht emittierte Aktien unissued capital stock

noch nicht erledigt pending

noch nicht reguliert unadjusted

noch nicht vereinbart not yet settled

nominal nominal

nominale Gruppentechnik nominal group technique

nominaler Zinssatz nominal interest rate

Nominalverzinsung nominal interest rate

Nominalwert nominal value; face value; *(Aktien)* par value

Nominalzins nominal interest rate

Nominalzinssatz stated annual interest rate

nominell nominal

nominieren to nominate

nonstop nonstop

nonverbale Kommunikation nonverbal communications

Nordamerikanisches Freihandelsabkommen North American Free Trade Agreement (NAFTA)

Norm standard; norm

normal normal; natural

Normalabweichung standard deviation

Normalkosten normal costs

Normalkostenrechnung standard costing

Normaltarif general tariff; regular rate

Normalverteilung normal distribution

normativ normative

normen to standardize

normieren to standardize

normiert standardized

Normierung standardization

Normung standardization

Nostro-Konto nostro account

Not- emergency

Not need; hardship

Notar notary

notariell notarial

Note note

Notenbank central bank

Notenbanksystem central bank system

Noteninstitut central note issuing bank

Notfall emergency; case of need

notfalls in case of need; in an emergency

Notgeld *(Bon)* token; emergency funds

notieren to note; *(Börsenkurse)* to list; to quote

notierter Kurs quoted price

Notierung quotation

nötig necessary

nötigen to obligate; to oblige; *(zwingen)* to coerce; to force

Notiz note; memorandum

Notizblock notepad

Notlage emergency

Not leidend depressed

notwendig necessary

notwendigerweise as a matter of necessity; necessarily

Notwendigkeit necessity

Novelle *(Gesetz)* amendment

null null; nil

Null zero

Nullkupon zero coupon

Nullkupon-Anleihe zero-coupon bond

Nullquote zero quota

Nullsaldenkonto zero-balance account

Nullsummenspiel zero-sum game

null und nichtig null and void

Nullzins zero interest

nummerieren to number

numerisch numerical

Nummer number; *(Bekleidung)* size

Nummernkonto numbered account

Nummernschild (*Auto*) license plate

Nummernschlüssel numerical code

nur only; just

nur dem Namen nach in name only; nominal

Nutzanwendung application; utilization

nutzbar usable; *(produktiv)* productive

nutzen to utilize; to use

nützen to be useful; to serve

Nutzen usefulness; benefit; profit; gain; good; *(Vorteil)* advantage

Nutzenindex *(Ertrag)* yield index; *(Gewinn)* profit index

Nutzenmaximierung *(Kapital)* capital maximization

Nutzentheorie utilization theory

Nutzen ziehen aus to profit from; to benefit from

nützlich useful; beneficial

nutzlos useless; futile

Nutznießer beneficiary

Nutzung utilization; *(Einkommen)* revenue; *(Ertrag)* yield

Nutzungsberechtigter beneficial owner

Nutzungsdauer useful life; *(einer Maschine)* machine life

Nutzungsdauer, betriebsgewöhnliche asset depreciation range

Nutzungsgebühr royalty

Nutzwert utility valuc

Nutzwertanalyse utility analysis; cost benefit analysis

O

Obdach shelter

oben above; *(Haus)* upstairs

Oberbau superstructure

Ober- superior; senior; upper

oberflächlich superficial; *(unvollständig)* sketchy

Obergrenze cap; upper limit

Oberhand control; upper hand

oberste Betriebsführung top management

oberste Leitung top management; top leadership

Oberverkäufer senior salesman

objektiv objective

Obligation debenture; bond

Obligationär bondholder

Obligationen-Gutschein bond anticipation note (BAN)

Obligationsdisagio bond discount

obligatorisch obligatory; mandatory; compulsory

Obligo liability; engagement; commitment

obsolet obsolete

offen open; *(Buchführung)* receivable

offenbaren to disclose

Offene Handelsgesellschaft partnership

offene Zession absolute assignment

offener Markt open market

offenes Faktoring notification factoring

offenes Zahlungsziel open account terms

Offenheit für Erfahrung openness to experience

offenkundig evident; apperent; obvious

offen legen to disclose; to lay open

Offenlegung disclosure

Offenmarktausschuss des Zentralbanksystems Federal Open Market Committee (FOMC)

Offenmarktgeschäfte open market operations

Offenmarktpolitik open market policy

offen stehend *(Rechnung)* outstanding; owing

öffentlich public

öffentlich bekannt geben to announce; *(publizieren)* to publicize; *(ankündigen)* to proclaim

öffentlich bekannt machen to publicize

öffentliche Bekanntmachung public announcement

öffentliche Arbeiten public works

öffentliche Emission public issue

öffentliche Erklärung *(Ankündigung)* public declaration; *(Erläuterung)* public explanation

öffentlicher Grundsatz public principle

öffentlicher Schlüssel public key

öffentliche Zustimmung public support

öffentliches Zeichnungsangebot public offering

Öffentlichkeit public; publicity

Öffentlichkeitsarbeit public relations; publicity

offerieren to tender; to offer

Offerte tender; quotation; offer; bid

offiziell official; formal

offiziell machen to make official; to formalize

Offizier officer

Offline-Werbung offline promotion

Offline-Webmetriken offline web metric

öffnen to open

Öffnungszeit business hours; opening hours

Offsetverfahren *(Druck)* offset printing

Offshore-Bankgeschäfte offshore banking

ohne ex; without

Ökologie ecology

ökologisch ecological

Ökonom economist

ökonometrisch econometric

Ökonomie economy

ökonomisch economic

ökonomische Aktivität economic activity

ökonomische Annahmen economic assumptions

Oligopol oligopoly

Oligopolmodell oligopolistic model

Oligopolproblem oligopoly problem

Oligopolsituation oligopolistic situation

Oligopoltheorie oligopolistic theory

Oligopson oligopsony

One-to-one Marketing one-to-one marketing

Online-Marke online brand

Online-Treueschemata online incentive schemas

Onine-Webmetriken online web metrics

Online-Werbung online promotion

operante Konditionierung operant conditioning

Operationsforschung operations research

operieren to operate

opponieren to oppose

Opportunitätskosten opportunity costs

Opposition opposition

optieren to opt

optimal optimal

Optimalität optimality

Optimallösung optimal solution

Optimalplanung optimal planning

optimieren to optimize

Optimierung optimization

Option option; *(Bezugsrecht)* subscription

Option auf Belegschaftsaktien incentive stock option

Option auf einen Index index option

Option auf Wandlung in Eigenkapital equity kicker

Optionsanleihe callable bond; usable bond; convertible bond issue

Optionsaufgabe abandonment option

Optionsausübung exercising an option

Optionshandel option trading

Optionsinhaber option holder

Optionsmarkt options market

Optionspreis option price

Optionsrecht option privilege

Optionsschein equity warrant; stock purchase warrant; warrant

Order order

Orderbuch order book

Orderladeschein warehouse warrant

ordern to order

Ordertätigkeit ordering activity

ordnen to order; *(regulieren)* to regulate; *(arrangieren)* to arrange; *(aufstellen)* to array

Ordner regulator; *(Dokumente)* file; *(Heftmappe)* binder

Ordnung order; *(Rang)* rank

Ordnungsform arrangement form; *(Klassifizierung)* classification form

ordnungsgemäß as required; proper

Ordnungsgemäßheit *(Legalität)* regularity

Ordnungskriterium classification criterion

ordnungsmäßig regular; orderly

Ordnungsrahmen regulation framework

Ordnungsstrafe fine; penalty

Organ organ; institution

Organigramm organizational chart

Organisation organization

Organisation der Erdöl exportierenden Länder Organization of Petroleum Exporting Countries (OPEC)

Organisation für europäische wirtschaftliche Zusammenarbeit Organization for European Economic Cooperation (OEEC)

Organisation für wirtschaftliche Zusammenarbeit und Entwicklung Organization for Economic Cooperation and Development (OECD)

Organisationsaufbau organizational structure

Organisationseinheit unit of organization

Organisationsentwicklung organizational development

Organisationsform organizational form

Organisationshandbuch organization manual

Organisationslehre organization doctrine; corporate doctrine

Organisationsmittel organizational means

Organisationsplan organizational chart

Organisationsstruktur organizational structure

organisches Modell organic model

organisieren to organize

organisatorisch organizational

organisatorisches Verhalten organizational behavior

Organschaft affiliation

orientieren to orient

Orientierung orientation

Orientierungsbudget draft budget

Orientierungspreis reference price

Orientierungspunkt point of reference

Original original

Ort locality; place

örtlich local

örtlich festlegen *(lokalisieren)* to localize; *(bestimmen)* to locate

Ortsbewohner local inhabitant

Ortsgebrauch local custom

Ortsverein local association

Output output

Outputpfad output path

Outputsteigerung output increase; output boost

P

Pachtabtretung assignment of lease

Pachteinnahme leasing receipts

pachten to lease

Pächter lessee; *(Grundbesitz)* tenant

Pachtgeld rent

Pachtgrundstück leased property; leasehold

Pachtsumme lease amount

Pachtung leasehold; *(Pachten)* leasing

Päckchen package; small parcel

Packen pack; *(Stapel)* pile; stack

Packliste packing list

Packmaterial packing material

Packung package; pack

Pädagogik pedagogy

pädagogisch pedagogical; educational

Paket package; parcel

Paketpreis package price

Panel (*Testgruppe*) panel

Paneleffekt panel effect

Panik panic

Panikkäufe panic buying

Panikverkäufe panic selling

Panne malfunction

Papier paper; *(Dokument)* document; instrument

Papierblock writing pad

Papierstreifen paper tape

Paragraph paragraph; *(Gesetz)* section

parallel parallel

Parallelaufträge matched orders

Parallele parallel

Parallelität parallelism

Parallelmarkt parallel market

Pari par value; parity; face value

Parität par value; parity; equality

Paritätswert par value

parken to park

Parkett floor

Parketthändler floor trader

Parkplatz car park; parking lot

Partei party

parteilos without a party; neutral

Parteilosigkeit neutrality

Partizipation participation

Partizipationsmodell leader-participation model

Partizipationsschein share certificate

partizipatives Management participative management

Partner partner; associate

Partnerbank correspondent bank

Partnerinstitut associated establishment

Partnerschaft partnership; general partnership

Partnerschaftsunternehmen partnership enterprise

parzellieren to subdivide

Parzellierung subdivision

Passagier passenger

Passagierabfertigung passenger handling

Passagieraufkommen passenger volume

Passagiereinnahmen passenger receipts; passenger revenue

Passagierraum cabin

Passagierverkehr passenger traffic

passen *(Bekleidung)* to fit; *(Arrangement)* to suit

passend machen to fit; *(angleichen)* to match; to fit

passend sein to match; to be appropriate

Passierschein pass

passiv passive; *(Bilanz)* unfavorable

Passiva liabilities

Passivposten liability item

Passivsaldo deficit

Passivseite *(Buchhaltung)* debit side

Passivüberhang *(Buchung)* debit carryover

Passung fit

Patent patent

Patentanmeldung patent application

Patentausnutzung patent license

Patentgebühr patent fee

patentierbar patentable

Patentrecht patent law

patentrechtlich geschützt proprietary; patent-protected

Patentrechtsverletzung patent infringement

Patentrolle patent registry

Patentvergabe patent licensing

pauschal overall; cross-the-board; all-inclusive; flat

Pauschalangebot all-inclusive offer; package deal

Pauschalbesteuerung flat rate taxation

Pauschalbetrag standard deduction; lump sum

Pauschale lump sum; all- inclusive price; flat rate; *(Preis)* package

Pauschalpfandrecht blanket inventory lien

Pauschalpreis flat rate; all-inclusive price

Pauschalreise package holiday; all-inclusive tour

Pauschalvergütung lump-sum payment

Pech bad luck; *(Teer)* pitch

pekuniär pecuniary

Pendel- shuttle

pendeln to swing; *(Berufsverkehr)* to commute

Pendelzug shuttle train; (*Berufsverkehr*) commuter train

Pension *(Ruhegeld)* pension; *(Gasthaus)* boarding house

Pensionär pensioner

pensionieren to retire; to pension off

Pensionierung retirement

Pensionsfonds pension fund

Pensionskasse pension plan

Pensionskürzung pension cut

Pensionszahlung *(Einkommen)* retirement pay; *(Zahlung)* pension payment; *(Leistung)* postemployment benefit

per pro *(nach)* according to

perforiert perforated

Periode period; (*Zyklus*) cycle

Periodenabgrenzung deferred items; allocation of revenues and expenses to appropriate accounting period

Periodenerfolg balance by accounting period

periodisch periodic

permanent permanent

Person person

Personal personnel; workforce; human resources; *(Stab)* staff

Personalabbau staff cuts; redundancies; cutbacks; personnel reductions

Personalabteilung personnel department

Personalabwerber head-hunter

Personalakte personnel file; personnel records

Personalanpassung personnel adjustment

Personalanwerber recruiters

Personalaufwendungen personnel expenses; salaries and wages

Personalaustausch personnel exchange; personnel turnover

Personalauswahl employee selection; personnel selection

Personalbedarf staff requirements; manpower requirements

Personalbeschaffung recruiting; recruitment

Personalbesetzung staffing

Personalbestand human resources; manpower

Personalbeurteilung employee appraisal; performance appraisal

Personalchef personnel manager

Personalcomputer personal computer

Personaldirektor personnel director

Personaleinsatz staff assignment; personnel placement

Personaleinsatzplanung personnel placement planning; deployment scheduling

Personalentlohnung remuneration; payment; compensation

Personalentwicklung personnel development; human resource development

Personalisierung personalization

Personalkosten personnel costs; labor costs; personnel expenditures

Personalleitung personnel management

personalmäßig versorgt fully staffed

Personalplanung personnel planning; human resources planning

Personalpolitik personnel policy

Personalverwaltung personnel administration

Personalwirtschaft personnel management; human resources management

Personalzuwachs personnel growth

Personengesellschaft limited company; private company; partnership; non-incorporated firm

persönlich personal; private; individual

persönlich haftender Gesellschafter general partner

persönliche Befreiung personal exemption

Persönlichkeit personality

Persönlichkeitseigenschaften personality traits

Perspektive perspective

Pfand pawn; pledge; collateral; security; deposit

Pfand auslösen to redeem a pawn

Pfandbrief bond; debenture

Pfandbriefbank mortgage lending institution; mortgage company

Pfandbriefzentrale mortgage bond clearing house

Pfandrecht lien

Pflege care; nurture; maintenance process

Pflegegeld nursing allowance; *(Vormundschaft)* guardian allowance

Pflegekosten care-giving expenses; nursing expenses

pflegen to nurse; *(Umgang)* to cultivate; *(Talent, Beziehung)* to nurture

Pflegeversicherung nursing insurance; long term care insurance

Pflicht duty

pflichtgemäß according to rule

pflichtmäßig mandatory; compulsory

Pflichtversicherung compulsory insurance

Pfund pound; *(Währung)* pound

Phase phase

Philosophie philosophy

physisch physical

physische Eigenschaft physical property

physische Fähigkeiten physical abilities

Pilot pilot

Pilotanlage pilot installation

Pilz mushroom; *(Schimmel)* fungus

pilzartig aufschießen to mushroom

Pionier pioneer

plädieren to solicit; to plead

Plädoyer plea

Plan plan; *(Schema, Intrige)* scheme; *(Programm)* program; *(Projekt)* project

planen to plan; *(Zeit)* to schedule; *(Ziel)* to target

Planen planning; *(Zeit)* scheduling

Planer planner; *(Zeit)* scheduler

Plankosten budgeted costs; target costs; standard costs

Plankostenrechnung cost accounting; standard costing

Planerstellung plan development

planmäßig according to plan; *(Zeit)* on schedule

Planung planning; *(Prognose)* projection

Planungsaufgabe planning task; planning project

Planungsfehler planning error

Planungskonzept planning concept

Planungsmodell planning model

Planungsprogramm planning program

Planungsprozess planning process

Planungssystematik planning framework

Planungstechnik planning technique

Planwirtschaft planned economy; managed economy

Planziel target; *(Produktion)* planned output

plastisch plastic

Platzkosten work center costs

Platzkostenrechnung work center costing

Platzkurs spot rate

platzieren to place; to position

Platzierung placement

pleite bankrupt; broke

Pleitefirma bankrupt company

Pleitegeier bankruptcy „vulture"; someone hoping to profit from another's bankruptcy

Pleitewelle wave of bankruptcies

plötzlich ansteigen to rise suddenly; to spurt upwards

plötzlich fallen to plunge suddenly

plündern to loot; to pillage; to ransack

Plünderung looting; pillage

Pluszeichen plus sign

Police *(Versicherung)* policy

Policenhändler policy dealer; policy trader

Politik politics; policy

Politik des freien Zugangs open-door policy

Politiker politician

Politikwissenschaft political science

politisch political

politisches Risiko political risk

politisches Verhalten political behavior

politische Wissenschaft political science

Polizist police officer

Polster bolster; cushion

Pool pool; *(Trust)* combine

Popularität popularity; vogue

Populär popular

populär machen to popularize

Portefeuille portfolio

Portemonnaie purse

Portfolio portfolio

Portfolioberater investment advisor

Portfoliobewertung porfolio evaluation

Portfolioanalyse portfolio analysis

Portfoliokonzept portfolio concept

Portfolioinvestition portfolio investment

Portfoliomanager portfolio manager

Portfoliomanagement portfolio management

Portfolio-Matrix growth share matrix

Portfoliostrategie portfolio strategy

Portfoliovarianz portfolio variance

Portfolioversicherung portfolio insurance

Porto postage; postal rate

Portokasse *(Geld)* petty cash; *(Behälter)* petty cash box

Portokosten postal charges; cost of postage

Position position; situation; *(Arbeit)* post; job

Positionierung positioning

Positionsmacht position power

Positionspapier position paper; policy document

positiv positive; beneficial ; favorable

positive Vertragsklausel positive covenant

Post *(Postsachen)* mail; *(Unternehmen)* post office

postalisch postal

Posten *(Stellung)* position; *(Buchführung)* entry; item

Postenkonto itemized account

Postetat postal budget

Postexperte, -expertin postal expert

Postfach post office box

Postgiroguthaben postal account credit balance

Postkunde postal customer

Postleitzahl postal code; zip code

Postleitzahlbereich zip code area

Postsachen mail

Postschalter post office counter

Postscheckamt postal savings bank

Postscheckguthaben postal checking account credit balance

Postscheckkonto postal checking account

Postversandliste mailing list

Postversandwerbung direct mail advertising

Potenzial potential capacity; capability

potenziell potential; prospective

potenzieller Kunde prospective customer

potenzieller Markt potential market

Präferenz preference

Präferenzabkommen most favored nation agreement

prägen to stamp; to coin

Pragmatiker pragmatist

pragmatisch pragmatic; down-to-earth

Pragmatismuns pragmatism

prägnant concise; succint

Praktik practice

Praktikant intern; trainee

Praktiker practitioner

praktisch practical

praktisches Wissen know-how

praktizieren to practice

Prämie *(Versicherung)* premium; *(Belohnung)* bonus

Prämienfestsetzer underwriter

Prämienfestsetzung rate making

Prämienmarkt options market

Prämiensenkung premium reduction

Prämisse premise

Präqualifikation pre-qualification

präparieren to prepare

präsentieren to present

Präsentierung presentation

präservieren to preserve

Präservierung preservation

Präsident president; *(Vorsitzender)* chairman

präsidieren to preside

Praxis practice; *(Brauch)* usage

Präzedenzfall precedent

präzise precise

Präzision precision

Preis price; rate; charge; cost; *(Wettbewerb)* prize; *(Belohnung)* award

Preis, administrierter administered price

Preis, angegebener quoted price

Preis, durchschnittlicher average price

Preis, empfohlener recommended price

Preis, erzielter realized price

Preis, gestützter supported price

Preis, günstiger attractive price

Preis, handelsüblicher market price; going rate

Preis, optimaler optimum price

Preis, reduzierter reduced price

Preis, schwankender flactuating price

Preis, unverbindlicher subject price

Preis, wettbewerbsfähiger competetive price

Preis absprechen to fix a price

Preis angeben to quote a price

Preis ausschreiben to offer a prize

Preis bei Sofortzahlung spot price

Preis diktieren to dictate a price

Preis erhöhen to raise a price; to mark up

Preis erzielen to realize a price

Preis festsetzen to set the price; to price

Preis manipulieren to rig a price

Preis mindern to reduce a price

Preis unter dem Wert ansetzen to price below value; to underprice

Preis vereinbaren to agree upon a price

Preis verlangen to charge a price

Preisabbau price reduction

preisabhängig dependent on price; price-related

Preisänderung price change

Preisänderungsrate price change rate

Preisangabe price quotation

Preisangebot quotation; quote; price bid

Preisanstieg price increase; price rise

Preisaufschlag surcharge; mark-up

Preisaufschwung price rally

Preisauftrieb price increase; rising price tendency

Preisausschreiben contest; competition

preisbereinigt adjusted for price

Preisbestandteil price component

preisbestimmend price-setting; *(Absprache)* price-fixing

Preisbewusstsein price consciousness

Preisbildung price formation; price fixing

Preisdämpfung price curb

Preisdifferenzierung price differentiation

Preisdruck pressure of prices; pressure on the market because of prices

Preiseffekt price effect

preiselastisch price-elastic

Preiselastizität price elasticity

Preisentwicklung price development; price trend

Preiserhöhung price increase

Preisforderung price demand; asking price

preisgarantiert price-guaranteed

Preisgefüge price structure

preisgekrönt prizewinning

Preisgleichgewicht balance of prices

Preisgleitklausel escalator clause; price adjustment clause

Preisherabsetzung markdown

Preisheraufsetzung price raising; markup

Preishöhe price level

Preisindex price index

Preisinflation price inflation

Preiskalkulation price calculation; pricing

Preisklasse price range

Preiskonkurrenz price competition

preislich with regard to price

Preisliste price list

Preismechanismus price mechanism

Preisnachlass price concession; rebate

Preisniveau price level

Preispolitik pricing policy

Preisraum price range; price margin

Preisrelation price relationship

Preisschere price gap

Preisschild price tag

Preisschlacht price war

Preisschlager best market price; popular price

Preissenkung price cut

Preissetzung price setting

Preissignal price signal

Preisstabilität price stability

Preissteigerung advance in prices; rise in prices

Preissteigerungsrate rate of price increase

Preisstrategie pricing strategy

Preissturz price slump

Preisstützung price support

Preissystem pricing system

Preistheorie pricing theory

preistreibend price-enhancing; price-raising

Preistreiberei price rigging

Preisüberhöhung price inflation

Preisüberwachung price control

Preisunsicherheit price uncertainty

Preisunterbietung underselling; price cutting

Preisuntergrenze price floor; lower price limit

Preisunterschied price difference; price differential

Preisverfall price deterioration

Preisverhältnis price relationship

Preisvorteil price advantage

preiswert reasonably priced; inexpensive

Preiswettbewerb price competition

Preiswiderstand price resistance

prekär precarious

Presse press

Presseabteilung press department

Presseagentur news agency

Presseausweis press card

Pressebericht press release; newspaper report

Presseerklärung press statement

Pressefotograf press photographer

Pressefreiheit freedom of the press

Pressegespräch press conference; conversation with the press

Presseverlautbarung press release

Prestige prestige

primär primary

Primärdaten primary data

primäre Kosten primary costs

Primärerhebung field research; primary data collection

Primärerzeugnis primary product

Primärhändler market maker; primary dealer

Primärmarkt new issue market; primary market

Primärverteilung primary distribution

Prinzip principle

Prinzip der Periodenabgrenzung accrual accounting

Priorität priority; precedence

privat private; personal

Privatbank private bank

Privatbankhaus private banking establishment

Privatbesitz private property

Privatdiskont prime rate

Privateigentum private property; personal effects

Privateinkommen personal income

Privatentnahme personal draw

private Platzierung private placement

privater Wirtschaftssektor private sector of the economy

private Unternehmung private enterprise

private Verschuldung homemade leverage

Privathand private ownership

Privatindustrie private industry

privatisieren to privatize

Privatisierung privatization

Privatkonto personal account; private ledger

Privatkredit personal credit

Privatkunde private customer

Privatplatzierung private placement

Preivatrecht civil law

Privatsphäre privacy

Privatverkauf private sale

Privatvermögen private property

Privatwirtschaft private sector

Privileg privilege

pro per; for

Probe test; *(Muster, Kostprobe)* sample

Probearbeitsverhältnis employment on probation

probeweise tentative; on a trial basis

probieren to sample; to try

Problem problem

Problematik set of problems; complex of problems

Problemkredit difficult credit; *(Anleihe)* problematic loan

Problemlösungsteam problem-solving team

Produkt product; commodity

Produkt, absatzstarkes high-volume item

Produkt, fertiges finnished product

Produkt, halbfertiges semi-finnished

Produkt einführen to launch a product

Produkt vertreiben to distribute a product

Produktakzeptanz product acceptance

Produktänderung product change

Produktangebot product offering

Produktbeschreibung product specification

Produktdifferenzierung product differentiation

Produkteigenschaft product property; product feature

Produkteinführung product launch

Produktelimination product elimination; product abandonment

Produktentwicklung product development

Produktfälschung product counterfeiting; *(Nachahmung)* product imitation; *(Piraterie)* product piracy

Produktgestaltung product design

Produktgruppe product group; line of products

Produktinnovation product innovation

Produktion production; manufacture; output

Produktion, auftragsorientierte production to specification

Produktion, computergestützte computer-aided manufacturing (CAM)

Produktion, durchlaufende continuous production

Produktion, handwerkliche manual production

Produktion, industrielle industrial production

Produktion, kostengünstige cost-efficient production

Produktion, marktorientierte market-oriented production

Produktion, schlanke lean production

Produktion ankurbeln to start up production

Produktion einstellen to stop production

Produktion erhöhen to increase production

Produktion verlagern to shift production

Produktionsanlage production facility; manufacturing facility

Produktionsanteil production share

Produktionsapparat production system; production network

Produktionsausfall loss of production

Produktionsausstattung production equipment

Produktionsausstoß production output

Produktionsbudget production budget

Produktionseinbuße production loss

Produktionseinheit production unit

Produktionsfähigkeit manufacturing capability

Produktionsfaktor production factor

Produktionsgesellschaft manufacturing company

Produktionskapazität production capacity; manufacturing capacity

Produktionsleistung production output

Produktionsmenge production volume; production output

Produktionsmethode production method

Produktionsmittel means of production; *(Investitionsgüter)* capital goods

Produktionsplan manufacturing schedule

Produktionsplanung production planning

Produktionspreis cost of production

Produktionsprogramm manufacturing program; production program

Produktionsprozess production process

Produktionsrate production rate

Produktionsschub production run

Produktionsseite production side

Produktionssektor production sector

Produktionsstand production volume

Produktionssteuerung production scheduling

Produktionsstruktur production structure

Produktionssystem production system

Produktionstheorie theory of production

Produktionsverfahren production process

Produktionsvolumen production volume

Produktionsvorgang manufacturing operation; manufacturing process

Produktionswachstum production growth

Produktionsweise method of production

Produktionszeit production time

Produktionszeitplan production schedule

Produktionsziffern production output data

Produktionszweig manufacturing sector

produktiv productive; *(Geistesarbeit)* prolific

Produktivität productivity

Produktkombination product combination

Produktkosten product costs

Produktlebenszyklus product life cycle

Produktmanager brand manager

Produktmenge product quantity

Produktmischung product mixture

Produktpalette product range; *(Auswahl)* product choice

Produktpolitik product policy

Produktplazierung product placement

Produktprüfung product testing

Produktqualität product quality

Produkttest product test

Produktverbesserung product improvement

Produzent producer; manufacturer

produzieren to produce; to manufacture

professionell professional

Profit profit; gain

profitieren to profit

Profitinteresse interest in profits

Profitrate profit rate

Pro-Forma-Rechnung pro forma invoice

Prognose prognosis; *(Vorhersage)* forecast

Prognosedaten forecast data

Prognosefehler forecasting error

Prognosemethode forecasting method

Prognostiker forecaster

prognostizieren to forecast; to predict

Programm program

Programm gestalten to program

Programmablaufplan flow chart

Programmfinanzierung program financing

programmieren to program

Programmierer programmer

Programmiersprache programming language

Programmierung programming

progressiv progressive

progressive Steuern progressive taxes

Projekt project

Projektarbeit project; porject work; *(schriftliche Arbeit)* project paper

Projektdurchführung project implementation; *(Ausführung)* project execution

Projektfinanzierung project financing

Projektion projection

Projektcontrolling project controlling

Projektgruppe task force

Projektion projection

Projektkosten project cost

Projektleiter project leader

Projektmanager project manager

Projektsteuerung project management

projizieren to project

pro Kopf per capita

Prokura power of attorney; proxy

Prokura, per per proxy

Prokura erteilen to transfer procuration

Prokurist registered manager; *(Stellvertreter)* proxy holder; *(Handlungsbevollmächtigter)* person holding power of attorney

prolongieren to extend; to prolong

Prolongation extension; prolongation

prominent prominent

Prominenz prominence

prompt prompt; expeditious; on time

Propaganda propaganda

Propaganda machen to campaign

Proportion proportion

proportionale Kosten proportional costs

proratarische Zahlung prorated payment; progress payment

Prospekt *(Broschüre)* pamphlet; *(Aktien)* prospectus

Prospekte literature

prosperieren to thrive

Prosperität prosperity

Protektion protection; *(Gönnerschaft)* patronage

Protektionismus protectionism

Protektionist protectionist

protektionistisch protectionist

Protest protest

Protokoll *(Sitzung)* minutes; record; *(Politik)* protocol

Protokoll, abfassen to write the minutes

Protokoll führen to keep the minutes

Protokollführer recorder; recording secretary

Prototyp prototype

Prototypen und Prototyping-Prozess prototypes and prototyping

Proviant provisions; supplies

Provision commission; fee; percentage; *(Makler)* brokerage

Provision berechnen to charge a commission

Provision beziehen to draw a commission

Provision gewähren to accord a commission

Provision verdienen to earn a commission

Provisionsanspruch accrued commission

Provisionseinnahme commission earnings

Provisionsertrag commission earnings

Provisionsgebühr commission rate

Provisionsgeschäft trasnaction on a commission basis

provisionspflichtig commissionable

Provisionssatz commission rate

Provisionszahlung commission payment

provisorisch provisional; temporary; makeshift

Provisorium provisional arrangement; makeshift arrangement

Prozedur procedure; routine

Prozent percent; per cent

prozentig per cent

Prozentpunkt percentage point

Prozentrechnung percentage calculation

Prozentsatz percentage

prozentual percental; percentaged; in percentage terms

prozentueller Umsatzanteil percentage share of sales

Prozess process; *(Gericht)* law suit; litigation; legal action; *(Strafverfahren)* criminal proceedings; trial

Prozess anfechten to contest an action

Prozess anstrengen to go to court; to file a lwasuit

Prozess aussetzen to suspend proceedings

Prozess einstellen to discontinue a suit

Prozess führen to litigate; to conduct a lawsuit

Prozess gewinnen to win a case

Prozess verlieren to loose a case

Prozessberatung process consultation

prozessieren to process; *(Gericht)* to sue

Prozesskostenrechnung activity-based costing (ABC)

Prozessor processor

Prozessverbesserung process improvement

Prüfanlage testing facility

prüfen to test; *(untersuchen)* to examine; *(inspizieren)* to inspect; *(sondieren)* to probe; *(begutachten)* to survey

Prüfer examiner; inspector

Prüfliste check list

Prüfung test; examination; inspection

Prüfung, externe external audit

Prüfung, interne internal audit

Prüfungsausschuss audit committee

Prüfungsbericht auditor's certificate

Prüfungsprogramm audit program

Psychologie psychology

psychologischer Kontrakt psychological contract

Publikum *(Öffentlichkeit)* public; *(Zuschauer)* audience

Publikumsfonds public fund

publizieren *(bekannt machen)* to publicize; *(veröffentlichen)* to publish

Publizität publicity; (*Unternehmensdaten*) disclosure

Publizitätspflicht disclosure obligation

pumpen to pump; *(Transport durch Rohrleitung)* to pipe

Punkt point; item

pünktlich punctual; on time

Punktsystem point system

Push-Technologie push technology

Pyramide pyramid

Q

Qualifikation *(Befähigung)* qualification; *(Berechtigung)* eligibility

Qualifikationsanforderungen job specification

qualifizieren to qualify

qualifiziert *(befähigt)* qualified; *(berechtigt)* eligible; fit

Qualität quality; grade

Qualität, beste top grade; first-rate; prime quality

Qualität, erlesene choice quality

Qualität, handelsübliche commercial quality

Qualität, mindere low-grade; infearial quality

qualitativ qualitative

Qualitätsabweichung variation in quality

Qualitätsanforderung quality standard

Qualitätsaudit quality audit

Qualitätsbewußtsein quality awareness

Qualitätserzeugnis quality product

Qualitätshandbuch quality manual

Qualitätskontrolle quality control

Qualitätsmanagement quality management

Qualitätsnorm quality standard

Qualitätsplanung quality planning

Qualitätsprodukt quality product

Qualitätsprüfung quality testing

Qualitätssicherung quality assurance

Qualitätsstandard quality standard

Qualitätssteuerung quality management

Qualitätsvergleich quality comparison

Qualitätszeugnis certificate of quality

Qualitätszertifikat certificate of quality

Qualitätszirkel quality circle

Quantität quantity

quantitativ quantitative

Quartal quarter

Quartals- quarterly

Quartier quarters

Quelle source; *(Wasser)* spring

Quellensteuer withholding tax

quittieren to acknowledge; to give a receipt

Quittung receipt; acknowledgement; voucher; *(Einzahlung)* deposit slip

Quote quota

Quotenregelung quota control; quota regulation

R

Rabatt discount; rebate; allowance

Rabatt abziehen to deduct a discount

Rabatt gewähren to grant a discount

Rabattbedingungen discount terms

Rabattgutschein discount voucher

Rabattkarte discount card

Rabattspanne margin of discount

Rabattpolitik discount policy

Radar radar

Radius radius

Raffinerie refinery

raffinieren to refine

Rahmen framework

Rampenlicht spotlight

Rand border

Rang standing; rank; echelon

rangieren range; rank

Rangordnung precedence

Rangstufe grade; class

Ranking der individuellen Leistungen individual ranking

rapide steigen to soar

rapide zunehmend soaring

Rast rest; break

rasten to rest; to take a break

Rat advice; counsel; *(Gremium)* council; board; *(Person)* councillor

Rat erteilen to advice; to give advice

Rate quota; ratio; rate; (*Zahlung*) installment

raten to advise; (*Zufall*) to guess

Ratenkauf hire purchase; instalment buying

Ratenkredit instalment credit

Ratenzahlung instalment

Rat für gegenseitige Wirtschaftshilfe Council for Mutual Economic Aid (COMECON)

Ratgeber counselor; adviser

rational rational

rationalisieren to rationalize; to streamline

Rationalisierung rationalization; improvements in productivity

Rationalität, begrenzte bounded rationality

Ratschlag counsel; advice

Räuber robber; predator

rauben to rob

räuberisch predatory

Raum space; room

Raumfähre space shuttle

Räumlichkeit premises; space

reagieren to react; to respond

Reaktion reaction; response

real real; actual

Realeinkommen real income

Realerlös real proceeds

reale Zahlungen real payments

realer Zinssatz real interest rate

Realisation realization; liquidation; sale

Realisationsgewinn liquidation gain

realisierbar realizable; feasible; viable; *(Finanzen)* convertible

Realisierbarkeit feasibility; liquidability

realisieren to implement; to put into practice; (*Finanzen*) to cash; to liquidate

realisierter Gewinn realized gain

realisierter Kursgewinn capital gain

realisierter Verlust realized loss

Realisierung realization

Realkosten real costs; actual costs

Realkredit secured credit; collateral loan; loan on securities

Reallohn real wages; actual wages

Reallohnniveau actual wage level

Reallohnsatz real wage rate

Reallohnzuwachs real wage increase

Realvermögen real assets; real wealth

Realverzinsung real yield

Realwachstum real growth

Realzins real interest rate

Rechenmaschine calculator

Rechenschaft ablegen to account; to render account

Rechenschaftsbericht account; report; statement

Rechenschaftspflicht accountability

Rechenzentrum computing center; business office

rechnen to calculate; (*rechnen mit*) to reckon

Rechner calculator

rechnerisch arithmetical; mathematical

Rechnung invoice; bill; account; tally

Rechnung, alleinige sole account

Rechnung, aussenwirtschaftliche foreign trade account

Rechnung, ausstehende accounts receivable

Rechnung, detailierte itemized account

Rechnung, fremde third-party account

Rechnung, frisierte docored account

Rechnung, gesamtwirtschaftliche national accounts

Rechnung, laufende current account; revolving account

Rechnung, offene outstanding account; unpaid invoice

Rechnung, vorläufige provisional invoice; pro-forma invoice

Rechnung abschließen to settle an account

Rechnung ausstellen to make out an invoice

Rechnung ausgleichen to balance an account; to settle an invoice

Rechnungsabgrenzung accruals and deferrals

Rechnungsabgrenzung, aktive accruals; accrued income

Rechnungsabgrenzung, passive deferrals; deferred income; accrued expense

Rechnungsabgrenzungsposten accruals and deferrals; (*Aktiva*) accrued items; prepaid expenses; (*Passiva*) deferred items

Rechnungsabschluss accounts; balancing of accounts; closing of accounts

Rechnungsführung accounting

Rechnungsgrundlage basis of calculation

Rechnungsjahr fiscal year

Rechnungskauf purchase on account

Rechnungslegungsmethode accounting method

Rechnungsperiode accounting period; fiscal period

Rechnungsprüfer auditor; controller; *(UK)* comptroller

Rechnungssaldo balance; rest

Rechnungswesen accountancy; accounting; bookkeeping

Recht law; right; justice

Recht, abtretbares transferable right

Recht, angestammtes inherent right

Recht, bestehendes valid law

Recht, bürgerliches civil law

Recht, geltendes applicable law; law of the land

Recht, herrschendes governing law

Recht, internationales international law

Recht, unabdingbares unalienable light

Recht, vertragliches contractual law

Recht abtreten to cede a right

Recht anerkennen to acknowledge a right

Recht anwenden to apply the law

Recht behalten to be right after all

Recht beschneiden to curtail a right

Recht beugen to pervert the course of justice

Recht durchsetzen to enforce the law

Recht einräumen to grant a right

Recht erwerben to aquire a right

Recht sprechen to judge; to administer justice

Recht verletzen to violate a right

Rechteck rectangle

rechtfertigen to justify; to warrant

Rechtfertigung justification; vindication

rechtlich lawful; legal; legitimate; *(gültig)* valid

rechtmäßig lawful; legitimate

Rechtsansicht legal opinion

Rechtsanspruch legal title

Rechtsanwalt lawyer; attorney

Rechtsauffassung judicial conception; legal conception

Rechtsausschuss judicial panel; judiciary committee

Rechtsberater counselor

Rechtschaffenheit integrity; honesty

Rechtsfall legal case

Rechtsform legal form

Rechtsgang legal process

Rechtsgeschäft legal transaction; legal act

Rechtsgültigkeit legal force; validity; lawfulness

Rechtsgutachten legal opinion

Rechtshilfe legal aid; judicial assistance

Rechtskraft legal force; validity; *(Urteil)* nonappealability

rechtskräftig valid; effective; final; *(~ sein)* to have legal force

Rechtslage legal status; legal situation

Rechtsprechung jurisdiction

Rechtsprozess lawsuit

Rechtssache legal case

Rechtsstaat constitutional state; free government under the law

Rechtsstreit lawsuit; litigation

Rechtstitel legal title

Rechtsvorschrift legal rule; legislative provision

rechtswidrig contrary to law; illegal

Rechtswissenschaft jurisprudence

rechtzeitig punctual; timely; on time

Recycling recycling

Redeweise mode of speaking; language; idiom

Rediskont rediscount

rediskontieren to rediscount

Rediskontkontingent rediscount quota

Rediskontvolumen rediscount volume; rediscount capacity

reduzieren to reduce; to diminish

Reduzierung reduction; diminution

Reeder ship-owner

reell realistic; fair

Referenzpreis reference price

Referenzzinssatz benchmark interest rate; reference interest rate

refinanzieren to refinance

Refinanzierung refinancing; refunding

Refinanzierungsanleihe refunding bond

Refinanzierungskredit refunding loan

Refinanzierungsrisiko refinancing risk

Reform reform

reformieren to reform

Regel rule; regulation; norm

Regelarbeitszeit normal working time; standardized working hours

Regelkreis control circuit; control loop

regellos *(Markt)* irregular; unsettled

regelmäßig regular; periodic; constant

Regelmäßigkeit regularity

regeln to regulate; to rule; to control; (*Gesetz*) to govern

regelnd regulatory

regelrecht regular; proper; correct

regenerieren to regenerate; (*Altmaterial*) to reclaim; to recycle

Regenerierung regeneration; recycling

Regie administration; management; (*Film*) direction

Regie führen to direct

regieren to govern

Regierung government; (*US*) administration

Regierungsabkommen intergovernmental agreement

Regierungsabteilung government department; *(UK)* ministry

Regierungskonferenz intergovernmental conference

Regierungsstelle department; government office

regional regional

Regisseur director

Register register; record; ledger; list

Registereintragung registration; entry in the register

Registrator registrar; recorder

registrieren to record; to register; to index; (*AG*) to incorporate

Registrierstelle registrar

registrierte Aktien shares of record

Registrierung registration

Reglementierung regimentation

Regression regression

Regressionsanalyse regression analysis

Regressionskoeffizient regression coefficient

regressiv regressive

regressive Steuer regressive tax

Regress recourse; redress; claim to damages

Regressanspruch right of recourse; claim for damages

Regresshaftung recourse liability

Regression regression

regressiv regressive

Regressklage recovery suit

Regresspflicht third-party indemnity

Regressrecht right of recourse

regulär regular; scheduled; normal

regulativ regulatory

regulierbar adjustable

regulieren to regulate; to adjust; to administer

Regulierung regulation; adjustment

Regulierungssystem regulatory system

reich rich; wealthy

reichen *(genug sein)* to suffice; to last; to reach

reichlich plentiful; abundant; ample

Reichtum wealth; riches; plenty; affluence

Reichweite range; cope; *(Werbung)* reach; coverage

reif ripe; mature

reife Branche mature industry

reifen to ripen; to age; to mature

Reihe row; series

Reihenfolge sequence

Reihenkorrelation serial correlation

rein pure; clear; *(Gewinn)* net; *(Frachtbrief)* clean

Reineinkommen net income

Reinertrag net yield

Reingewicht net weight

Reingewinn after-tax profit; bottom line; net profit; profit

Reinumsatz net sales

Reinverdienst net earnings

Reinverlust net loss

Reinvermögenswert net asset value

Reinvermögen owner's equity; net worth; net assets

reinvestieren to reinvest

Reinvestition reinvestment

Reise journey; travel; trip

Reisegebiet travel area

reisen to travel

Reisemitbringsel souvenirs

Reisepass passport

Reiseplanung travel planning; trip scheduling

Reiseverkehr tourist travel; holiday traffic

reißen to tear; to pull

reizvoll attractive

Rekapitulation recapitulation; summing up

Rekapitulieren to recapitulate; to sum up

Reklamation complaint; query; protest; objection

Reklame advertising; promotion; propaganda; publicity

Reklame machen to advertise; to publicize

Reklameartikel sales gimmick

Reklamebeilage advertising suplement

Reklamebroschüre advertising brochure

Reklamefläche billboard; advertising space

Reklamegeschenk free gift

Reklamerummel ballyhoo

Reklamesendung commercial

Reklametext advertising copy

reklamieren *(beanstanden)* to complain; *(zurückverlangen)* to reclaim; to protest

Rekord record

Rekordergebnis record result

Rekordgewinn record profit

Rekordjahr record year

Rekordstand record level

Rekrut recruit

rekrutieren to recruit

Rektaindossament restrictive endorsement

Rektaklausel restrictive clause

Rektakonnossement straight bill of lading

Rektalagerschein non-negotiable warehouse receipt

Rektapapier instrument not to order; registered share/security

Rektascheck non-negotiable cheque

Rekurs recourse

relativ relative; comparative

relative Kaufkraftparität relative purchasing power parity

relative Kosten relative costs

relative Stärke relative strength

relativer Marktanteil relative market share

Rembours reimbursement; commercial letter of credit; documentary acceptance credit

Remboursauftrag instructions to open a documentary acceptance credit

Remboursbank merchant bank; accepting bank

Remboursermächtigung reimbursement authorization

Remboursgeschäft merchant banking

Rembourskredit commercial letter of credit; documentary letter of credit

Rembourstratte documentary draft

Rembourswechsel documentary bill

Rendite return; yield; rate of return

Rendite auf durchschnittliche Laufzeit yield to average life

Rendite der Halteperiode holding-period return

Rendite einer kündbaren Anleihe yield to call

Rendite nach Steuern after-tax yield

Renditeobjekt income property

Renditespanne yield spread

Rendite vor Steuern pretax yield

rennen to run; to race

Rennen race; run

rentabel profitable; profit-making; lucrative

Rentabilität profitability; rate of return; earning power; profit ratio

Rente pension; annuity; (*Kapitalertrag*) yield; return

Rentenanleihe annuity bond

Rentenanpassung pension adjustment; retirement income adjustment

Rentenaufbesserung pension increase

Rentenbesitz bond ownership

Rentenempfänger annuitant

Rentenfonds pension fund

Rentenindex annuity index; bond index

Rentenmarkt bond market

Rentenversicherung annuity insurance

Rentenwert annuity value

rentieren, sich to give a good return; *(Betrieb)* to be profitable

Rentner pensioner

Reorganisation reorganization

reorganisieren to reorganize; to revamp

Reparatur repair

Reparaturwerkstätte repair workshop

reparieren to repair; to fix

repartieren *(Aktien)* scale down; allot; apportion

repatriieren to repatriate; to relocate; to bring home

Report report; *(Bank)* premium; *(Börse)* contango; *(Devisenmarkt)* discount forex

Reporter reporter

Repräsentant representative

Repräsentation representation

repräsentativ representative

Repräsentativstück sample

repräsentieren to represent; to typify

Reserve- reserve; spare

Reserve reserve; standby; buffer

Reservekredit standby credit

Reservelager buffer stock

Reservemittel reserve fund; reserves

Reservenzulänglichkeit reserve adequacy

Reservesystem reserve system

Reservewährung reserve currency

reservieren to reserve

reserviert reserved

Reservoir reservoir

Residualdividenden-Ansatz residual dividend approach

Resignation resignation

resignieren to resign

Resolution resolution; resolve

Resonanz resonance; *(Reaktion)* feedback; reaction

Respekt respect; esteem

respektabel respectable

respektiert reputable; respected

Respekttage *(Wechsel)* days of grace

Ressort portfolio; *(Fachgebiet)* field of study; *(Regierung)* department; *(BE)* ministry; *(Zuständigkeit)* province

Ressortchef head of department

Ressourcen resources; capabilities

Ressourcen, natürliche natural resources

Ressourcen, ökonmische economic resources

Ressourcen, strategische strategic resources

Ressourcenallokation allocation of resources

Ressourcenplanung capability planning

Rest- residual

Rest rest; remainder; *(Rückstand)* residue

restaurieren to restore

Restbuchwert book value; depreciated cost

Restbestand remainder; rest

Restbetrag residual amount

Restlaufzeit remaining period; *(Fälligkeit)* term to maturity

restlich remaining; residual

Restposten remaining stock; job lot

Restsumme balance; *(Konto)* account balance

Restwert residual value; terminal value; *(Schrott)* scrap value

Resultat result; outcome

resultieren to result

Resümee summary

retten to save; to rescue; to recover; to retrieve

revidieren *(prüfen)* to check; to examine; *(ändern)* to revise

Revidierung revision

Revision revision; examination; audit

Revision durchführen to audit

Revisionsbericht audit report

Revisor examiner; controller

revolvieren to revolve; to roll over

revolvierend revolving

revolvierende Deckung revolving cover

revolvierende Kreditlinie revolving line of credit

revolvierendes Akkreditiv revolving letter of credit

Rezept (*med)* prescription; *(Formel)* formula; *(Kochen)* recipe

Rezession recession

reziprok reciprocal

Reziprozität reciprocity

richten to judge

richten an to address to

Richter judge; justice

Richterspruch sentence; judgement

richterlich judicial; magisterial

richtig correct; true; right; correct; appropriate; proper

Richtigkeit accuracy

richtig stellen to correct; to rectify

Richtigstellung correction; adjustment; rectification

Richtlinie rule; guideline

Richtpreis target price; recommendet price

Richtschnur guideline; rule

Richtung direction; tendency; trend

Riesenunternehmen mammoth company

riesig giant; mammoth

ringen to grapple; to wrestle

Rinne trough

Risiko risk; hazard; exposure; danger; peril

Risiko, akutes imminent risk

Risiko, betribswirtschaftliches commercial risk

Risiko, deckungsfähiges coverable risk

Risiko, erhebliches substantial risk

Risiko, finanzielles financial risk

Risiko, gesundheitliches health risk

Risiko, kalkulatorisches imputed risk

Risiko, staatspolitisches sovereign risk

Risiko, technisches technical risk

Risiko, unternehmerisches business risk

Risiko abdecken to cover a risk

Risiko abwägen to calculate a risk

Risiko ausschalten to eliminate a risk

Risiko eingehen to take a risk

Risiko tragen to bear the risk

Risiko versichern to underwrite a risk

Risiko verteilen to spread the risk

Risiko-Arbitrage risk arbitrage

Risikoaversion risk aversion

Risikobereitschaft readiness to assume a risk

risikofreie Investition riskless investment

risikofreie Rendite risk-free return

risikofreudig willing to take a risk

Risikohaftung liability for risk; responsibility for risk

Risikokapital risk capital; venture capital

Risikoklasse risk class

Risikomanagement risk management

Risikomischung risk mixture; *(Fächerung)* risk spread

Risikoprämie risk premium

risikoreich risky; fraught with risk

risikoscheu risk-averse; unwilling to take a risk

Risikosumme amount at risk

Risikoversicherung risk insurance

Risikovorsorge provision to guard against risk

riskant risky

riskieren to risk; *(Kapital)* to venture; *(aufs Spiel setzen)* to stake

Rituale rituals

Rivale, **Rivalin** rival; contender

rivalisieren to rival

rivalisierend rivalling

Roboter robot

roh raw; *(unveredelt)* crude

Rohgewinn gross profit

Rohgewinnspanne gross margin

Rohmaterial raw material

Rohstoff raw material; primary product; commodity

Rohstoffabhänigkeit dependence on raw materials

Rohstoffaufbereitung processing of raw materials

Rohstoffgewinnung primary production

Rohstoffhändler commodity trader

Rohstoffknappheit scarcity of raw materials

Rohstoffkonzern raw materials conglomerate

Rohstoffmakler commodity broker

Rohstoffpreis commodity price

Rohstoffproduktion primary materials production

Rohstoffreserven reserves of raw materials

Rohstoffverbrauch consumption of raw materials

Rohstoffvorkommen raw material deposit

Rolle role; function; *(Maschine)* reel; coil

rollendes Material rolling stock

Rollenerwartungen role expectations

Rollenidentität role identity

Rollenkonflikt role conflict

Rollenwahrnehmung role perception

Römische Verträge Treaty of Rome

Rotationspapier newsprint

rotieren to rotate

rotierend rotating

Route route

Route bestimmen to route

Routine routine

Rubrik column; heading

Rückantwort reply

Rückerstattung refund

rückdatieren to date back

Rückdatierung backdating

Rückforderung reclaim

Rückführung repatriation

Rückgabe return

Rückgaberecht put provision

Rückgang decline; *(Verminderung)* decrease; *(Absinken)* drop; *(Sturz)* fall

rückgängig machen *(Vorschrift, Regel)* to rescind; *(Kontrakt)* to cancel

Rückgrat spine; backbone

Rückgriff recourse

Rückkauf buyback

Rückkaufklausel *(Börse)* call provision

Rückkaufkurs call price

Rückkaufprämie call premium

Rückkaufpreis einer Anleihe callprice of a bond

Rückkaufsklausel call provision

Rückkaufvertrag repurchase agreement

Rückkaufwert cash value; surrander value

Rückkehr return

Rückkopplung feedback

Rücklage reserve; provision

Rücklagendotierung reserve allocation

Rücklagenposition reserve position

rückläufig regressive; downward

Rücknahme retraction; redemption; *(Berufung)* withdrawal

Rücknahmepreis bid price; repurchase price

Rückruf recall

Rückrufservice callback service

Rückschlag setback; reversal; backlash

rückschleusen (*Geld*) to recycle

Rückschritt step backwards; setback

Rückseite reverse; back; (*Text*) overleaf

Rücksendung return; reconsignment; reshipment

Rücksprache consultation

Rückstand lag; *(Zahlung)* arrears; *(Summe)* arrearage; *(Aufträge)* backlog; *(Abfall)* waste

rückständig backward; behind; *(Wirtschaft)* underdeveloped; *(Rechnung)* unpaid; *(überfällig)* overdue

rückständige Dividende dividends in arrears; unpaid dividend

Rückständigkeit backwardness; state of underdevelopment

Rückstellung provision; reserve; accrual; allowance

Rückstellungen auflösen to liquidate reserves

Rückstellungen bilden to make provisions for

Rückstellungen für Abschreibungen depreciation reserves

Rückstellungen für Ausgaleichsforderungen equalization reserves

Rückstellungen für Eventualverbindlichkeiten reserves for contingencies

Rückstellungen für Ruhegeldverpflichtungen pension reserves

Rückstellungen für uneinbringliche Aussenstände bad debts provisions

Rückstellungen für unvorhergesehene Ausgaben contingency fund

Rücktritt resignation; retirement

Rücktrittsklausel escape clause; *(Börse)* market-out clause

Rückübertragung reassignment

rückvergüten to refund

Rückvergütung (*Zahlung*) repayment; *(Nachlass)* rebate; *(Erstattung)* refund; (*Börse*) surrender value; *(Entschädigung)* reimbursement

rückwärts backwards

rückwirkend retroactive; *(~ von*) backdated to

Rückwirkung retroactive effect

rückzahlbar repayable; refundable; (*Anleihe*) redeemable

rückzahlbare Vorzugsaktie callable preferred stock

Rückzahlung repayment; reimbursement; payback

Rückzahlungsfrist repayment period

Rückzahlungsklausel material adverse clause

Rückzahlungskurs redemption price

Rückzahlungsrate redemption rate

Rückzahlungsrendite yield to maturity (YTM)

Rückzahlungsvorrang seniority

Rückzahlungswert redemption value

Rückzug withdrawal; pullback

Ruf call; *(Leumund)* reputation

rügen to criticize; to censure

Ruhe rest

Ruhegehalt pension

ruhen to rest; *(Geschäft)* to be at a standstill

Ruhestand retirement

Ruin *(finanziell)* ruin

Ruine *(Bau)* ruin

ruinieren to ruin

ruinös ruinous

Rundschreiben *(Werbung)* circular; *(Neuigkeiten)* newsletter

Rutsch slide

rutschen to slide

Rutschen sliding

S

Sachanlagen fixed assets; tangible assets; plant and equipment

Sachanlagenabschreibung depreciation of fixed assets

Sachaufwand operating expenditure; material expenditure

Sachbearbeiter clerk; official in charge

Sachbesitz material assets; physical property

Sachdividende property dividend

Sache object; matter; (*Anliegen*) cause; concern

Sachgebiet subject matter

Sachgut tangible asset; physical product

Sachlage circumstances, situation

sachlich factual; objective

sachlich richtig factually correct

Sachverständiger specialist; expert; authority; *(Versicherung)* surveyor; appraiser; *(Gericht)* expert witness

Sachwertdividende property dividend

Sachwissen expertise

Safe box

Saison season

Saison- seasonal

saisonal bereinigt seasonally adjusted

saisonbedingt seasonal; seasonally

Saisonbedingtheit seasonality

saisonale Schwankung seasonal variation

saisonüblich seasonal

Saisonwaren seasonal goods

Salär salary

saldieren to balance; to liquidate

Saldierung balancing

Saldierung von Forderungen netting

Saldo balance; account balance

sammeln to collect

Sammellager consolidation warehouse

Sammelladungsspediteur consolidator

Sammellebensversicherung group life insurance

Sammelmappe binder

Sammelzollanmeldung collective customs declaration

Sammler collector

Sammlerstück collectible

Sammlung collection

sanieren to restructure; to reorganize

Sanierung restructuring; reorganization

Sanierungsbilanz capital reconstruction statement

Sanierungsmaßnahme reorganization measure

Sanierungsplan reorganization plan

Sanierungsstrategie reorganization strategy

Sanktion sanction

Satellit satellite

sättigen to saturate

Sättigung saturation

Sättigungsgrenze saturation point; absorption limit

Satz sentence; *(Garnitur)* set; *(Zinsen)* rate

Satzung articles of association; memorandum of association; *(Statuten)* bylaws; *(Aktiengesellschaft)* corporate charter; charter

Satzungsänderung amendment of the statutes

Satzungsbestimmung provisions of the articles; statutory provisions

satzungsmäßig statutory; in accordance with the articles

satzungswidrig contrary to the statutes

Satzvorlage manuscript

Säulendiagramm bar chart

Säumnisurteil default judgment

schäbig shabby; *(kleinlich)* mean

Schablone stencil; mould; pattern; *(Vorlage)* model

Schachzug move; maneuver

Schaden damage; *(Verlust)* loss; *(Nachteil)* prejudice; detriment; tort; *(Verletzung)* injury

Schadenersatz compensation

Schadensfall liability case

Schadensgutachter assessor

Schadensschätzer damage appraiser

Schadensursache cause of damage; cause of loss

Schadlosbürgschaft collateral guarantee; guarantee of collection

schädlich harmful; detrimental; *(nachteilig)* disadvantageous

schaffen to create; to set up; to establish

Schaffung creation; establishment; generation

schalten to switch; *(Getriebe)* to shift gears

Schalter *(Strom)* switch; *(Behörde)* counter; counter window

Schalterbeamte, **-beamtin** counter clerk; *(Bank)* teller

Schalthebel shift knob

Schalttafel switchboard

scharf sharp; keen

scharfes Senken sharp reduction; slashing

Schattenwirtschaft shadow economy; underground economy

Schatz treasure; hoard

Schatzamt treasury

Schatzanweisung treasury note

schätzen to estimate; to evaluate; *(taxieren)* to appraise; *(wertschätzen)* to appreciate

Schätzer appraiser; evaluator

Schatzmeister treasurer

Schatzobligation treasury bond

Schatzschuldbrief certificate of indebtedness

Schätzung *(Kalkulation)* estimate; *(Achtung)* estimation; esteem; *(Wertschätzung)* appreciation

schätzungsweise approximately

Schatzwechsel treasury bill

Schätzwert estimated value; estimated price

Schau show; *(Ausstellung)* exhibition

Schaubild diagram; chart

Schaufensterauslage store window display

Schaufensterschmuck store window decoration

schaukeln to swing; *(erschüttern)* to rock

Schauplatz scene; site

Scheck check; (*UK*) cheque

Scheck, abgerechneter cleared check

Scheck, auf den Überbringer bearer check

Scheck, avisierter advised check

Scheck, bestätigter certified check

Scheck, eingelöster cancelled check

Scheck, gefälschter forged check

Scheck, geplatzter bounced check

Scheck, offener open check

Scheck, ungedeckter bad check

Scheck, verfallener stale check

Scheck anerkennen to meet a check

Scheck ausstellen to make out a check; to draw a check

Scheck bestätigen to certify a check

Scheck einlösen to cash a check; to honour a check

Scheck einziehen to collect a check

Scheck sperren to stop payment of a check

Scheck stornieren to cancel a check

Scheck verrechnen to clear a check

Scheck ziehen auf to draw a check against

Scheckabrechnung check clearance

Scheckaussteller maker; writer drawer of a check

Scheckbegünstigter payee of a check

Scheckbetrug check fraud

Scheckbürgschaft check guaranty

Scheckdeckung check cover

Scheckeinreichung check presentation

Scheckgeld check money

Scheckheft check book

Scheckkarte check guaranty card; bank card

Scheckkonto checking account

Scheckverrechnung check clearing

Scheckvordruck check form

Scheckzahlung payment by check

Scheibe slice; *(Glas)* pane

Scheidung divorce

Schein certificate; voucher; *(Anschein)* appearance

Scheinfirma street name; bogus firm; dummy company

Scheingeschäft wash sale; paper transaction; bogus deal

Scheingewinn paper profit

Scheingewinn aus Vorratsbewertung inventory profit

Scheinverlust paper loss

Scheinwerfer searchlight; spotlight

scheitern to fail

Schema schema; *(Tabelle)* table; *(Diagramm)* diagram

schenken to make a gift; to give; *(gemeinnützige Gabe)* to donate

Schenkung gift; *(Zuschuss)* grant; *(gemeinnützige Gabe)* donation

Schenkungssteuer gift tax

Schicht layer; *(Arbeit)* shift

schichten to layer; *(stapeln)* to stack

Schichtenleistung shift performance; shift productivity

Schichtwechsel change of shift

schicken to send; to ship

Schiebe- sliding

Schiebung swindle; racket

Schiedsgericht arbitration tribunal

Schiedsgerichtsverfahren arbitration

Schiedsrichter arbitrator; *(Sport)* referee

Schiedsstelle arbitration board; ombudsman

Schiedsverfahren arbitartion procedure; arbitrage

schief lopsided; crooked

schief stehen to lean

Schienenweg railroad; *(Gleis)* track

schießen to shoot; to fire

Schiff ship; vessel; boat

Schiff, abgehendes outgoing vessel

Schiff, ausländisches foreign vessel

Schiff, im Linienverkehr liner

Schiff, auf Reede liegendes ship anchored in the roadstead

Schiff, seetüchtiges seaworthy ship

Schiff, zurückfahrendes inward-bound vessel

Schiff abwracken to break up a ship

Schiff aufbringen to arrest a ship

Schiff aufgeben to abandon a ship

Schiff ausflaggen to flag out a ship

Schiff befrachten to load a ship

Schiff chartern to charter a vessel

Schiff entladen to unload a ship

schiffbar navigable

Schifffahrtsbehörde maritime authority

Schifffahrtskonferenz conference line

Schifffahrtsweg waterway

Schiffsklasse category of ship

Schiffsladung cargo; shipment

Schiffsmakler ship broker, shipping agent

Schiffsraum shipping space; tonnage; hold

Schiffsregister register of shipping; maritime register

schikanieren to harass, to bully; to mob

Schikanierung harassment; mobbing

Schild sign; *(Anhänger)* tag

Schilderung description; representation

Schirm umbrella

Schlacke slag; waste

schlagen to beat; to hit

Schlager winner; *(Treffer)* hit; *(Lied)* hit song

Schläger *(Tennis)* racket; *(Baseball)* bat; *(Golf)* club

Schlagwort slogan

schlank slender; slim

schlecht bad; *(minderwertig)* shoddy

schlecht bezahlt badly paid

schlechte Verwaltung mismanagement

schlecht verwalten to mismanage

schlecht wirtschaften to mismanage

schleichen to creep

schleichend creeping

schleichende Inflation creeping inflation

schleichende Steuerprogression bracket creep

schleichendes Übernahmeangebot creeping tender offer

schleppen to tow

schleppend dragging; depressed; slow

Schleppgebühr towage fee

Schleuderausfuhr dumping

Schleuderpreis dumping price

schlichten to arbitrate; to mediate; to settle

Schlichter arbitrator; mediator

Schlichtung arbitration; mediation; conciliation

Schlichtungsabkommen arbitration agreement

Schlichtungsergebnis arbitration result

Schlichtungsspruch arbitration decision

Schlichtungsverfahren arbitration process

schließen to close; *(Fabrik)* to shut down; *(Ansprache)* to conclude

Schließung closure; *(Fabrik)* shutdown

Schlips necktie

Schlupfloch loophole

Schluss- final

Schluss finish; termination; *(Ende)* close; *(Fabrik)* closure

Schlussbestand ending inventory

Schlussbericht final report

Schlussbilanz closing balance sheet; final balance

Schlussbrief fixing letter

Schlusskurs closing price

Schlüssel key

Schlüsselfrage key question; key issue

Schlüsselland key country

Schlüsselmarkt key market

Schlüsselpersonal key personnel

Schlüsselserie key series

Schlüsselstellung key position

Schlüsselvariable key variable

Schlussfolgerung conclusion

Schlusstermin deadline

schmackhaft machen to make palatable

schmieden to forge

schmücken to decorate; to trim

Schmuggelware contraband

Schnäppchenjäger bargain hunter

Schneeball snowball

schnell hochsteigend soaring

Schnelligkeit speed

Schnitt cut

Schnitzer *(Fehler)* blunder; *(Holz)* carver

schonen to conserve; to preserve

schöpferisch creative

Schrank cabinet; cupboard; *(Kleider)* wardrobe

Schrank für Systemzentraleinheit mainframe cabinet

Schranke limit; *(Sperre)* bar; *(Handel)* barrier

Schraube screw; *(Inflation, Preis)* spiral

Schreibarbeit paperwork

Schreiben *(Brief)* letter; *(Benachrichtigung)* written communication; *(Aktivität)* writing

Schreibgerät writing utensil

Schreibkraft secretarial help; *(Büroangestellter)* clerk

Schreibmaschine typewriter

Schreibpersonal secretarial staff

Schreibtisch desk

Schreibtischcomputer desktop computer

Schreibzeug writing utensils

Schriftführer reporter; *(Verein)* secretary

schriftlich written; in writing

schriftlich belegen to document

Schriftsatz declaration; brief; *(Druck)* font

Schriftstück document

Schriftwechsel correspondence

Schritt step; move

Schrott scrap; *(Abfall)* waste

Schrottwert scrap value; salvage value; residual value

schrumpfen to shrink; *(sich verringern)* to diminish

Schrumpfung shrinkage; contraction

Schulabschluss school leaving certificate

Schulausbildung school education

Schuld fault; guilt; *(Verschuldung)* debt; liability; obligation

Schuld, antizipative accrued liability

Schuld, aufgelaufende accumulated debt

Schuld, fällige debt owing

Schuld, frühere previous debt

Schuld, kurzfristige short-term debt

Schuld, langfristige long-term debt

Schuld, nachrangige subordinate debt

Schuld, rückständige arrears

Schuld, uneindringliche irrevocable debt; bad debt

Schuld abarbeiten to work off a debt

Schuld absichern to collaterate a debt

Schuld anerkennen to acknowledge a debt

Schuld geben to blame

Schuldbuch debt register; debt ledger

schulden to owe; to be in debt

Schulden debts; *(Verbindlichkeiten)* liabilities; *(Buchführung)* accounts payable

Schuldendeckel debt limit

Schuldendienst debt service

Schuldendienstquote debt service ratio

Schuldendienstreduktion debt service reduction

Schuldenkonsolidierung consolidation of debts

Schuldenkrise debt crisis

Schuldenlast debt burden; *(Verschuldung)* indebtedness

Schuldenmanagement debt management

Schuldenmarkt debt market

Schuldenpolitik debt policy

Schuldenreduktion debt reduction

Schuldenrückkäufe debt buy-backs

Schuldenrisiko debt risk

Schuldensicherheit collateral; debt security

Schuldenstand debt level

Schuldentilgung discharge of debt; *(Amortisierung)* amortization

Schuldenzahlungserleichterung debt payment relief

Schuldenzahlungsverweigerung debt payment refusal; debt repudiation

Schuldforderung payment demand

Schuldner debtor

Schuldnerland debtor nation

Schuldpapier debt instrument

Schuldposten debit

Schuldsaldo debit balance

Schuldschein promissory note; *(Schuldverschreibung)* debenture; debt obligation; IOU ("I owe you")

Schuldscheindarlehen loan against borrower's note; open market credit

Schuldscheinforderung note receivable

Schuldscheinverbindlichkeit note payable

Schuldverhältnis contractual obligation

Schuldverschreibung debenture; *(Obligation)* bond

Schuldverschreibung, stark abgezinste deep-discounted bond

Schuldwechsel note payable; memorandum bill

Schuldzinsen interest on debt

Schule absolvieren to graduate from school

schulen to train

Schulung training; instruction

Schulung, berufliche vocational training; professional training

Schulung, betriebliche in-house training

Schulung, firmeninterne in-company training

Schulung, praktische on-the-job training

Schulungsleiter trainer

schürfen to scrape; *(Erze)* to prospect

Schutz- protective

Schutz *(Natur)* protection; conservation; *(Sicherung)* safeguard; *(Sicherheit)* security; *(Steuer)* shelter

Schutzanzug overall

schützen to protect; to shelter

schützend protective

Schutzgebiet protectorate

Schutzmacht protector power; protector state

Schutzmarke trademark

Schutzvorrichtung safeguard

Schutz vor vorzeitiger Kündigung call protected

Schutzvereinbarung protective covenant

Schutzzoll protective tariff

schutzzollbedürftige Industrie industry in need of tariff protection

schwach weak; *(Gesundheit)* poor

Schwäche weakness

schwache Informationseffizienz weak information efficiency

schwächen to weaken

Schwächerwerden weakening

Schwachheit weakness

Schwächung weakening

schwach werden to weaken

Schwall wave; spate

schwanken to fluctuate

Schwanken fluctuating; swinging

schwankend fluctuating; swinging

schwankend machen to destabilize

Schwankung fluctuation

Schwankung im Handel fluctuation in trade; leads and lags

Schwankungsbreite fluctuation range; degree of fluctuation

Schwarzgeld black money

Schwarzmarkt black market

schweben to hover; *(Prozess)* to be pending; to be in limbo

schwebend pending

schwebende Überweisung floating transfer

schwebendes Verfahren pending action

schweigend silent

Schwelle threshold

Schwellenland emerging market; newly industrialized country (NIC)

Schwellenpreis threshold price

schwer heavy; massive; *(schwierig)* difficult

schwer behindert severely disabled

Schwerbehinderter severely disabled person

schwerfällig sluggish; lumbering

Schwerfälligkeit sluggishness

Schwerpunkt center of gravity; focal point; emphasis

Schwester sister

Schwestergesellschaft sister company

schwierig difficult; hard

Schwierigkeit difficulty; (Problem) problem

schwinden to dwindle; to slip away

Schwinden dwindling

schwindend dwindling; slipping

schwingen to swing

Schwingen swinging

schwingend swinging

Schwund shrinkage; reduction; *(Flüssigkeit)* leakage

Schwung momentum; drive

schwungvoll spirited; bold

Seefracht maritime freight; ocean freight; sea freight

Seefrachtbrief ocean bill of lading

Seefrachtführer ocean carrier

Seehafen seaport

Seehafenspediteur shipping agent

Seekonnossement affreightment

Seetransport sea transport; marine transport; maritime transport; carriage by sea

Seetransportversicherung ocean marine insurance

segmentieren to segment

Seil rope

Seite side; *(Buch)* page; side

Seitenanfrage page request

Seiten-Ankündigung site announcements

Seitenansicht page view

Seitenbesuche site visits

Seiten-Besucher site auditors

Seitenlinie sideline; *(Zweig)* offshoot

Seiten-Messung site measurement

Seiten-Relaunch site relaunch

Seiten-Statistik site statistics

Seiten-Verfügbarkeit site availability

Seitenzweig branch; sideline; offshoot

seitlich lateral

Sekretär secretary

Sektion section

Sektor sector

sektoral sectoral

sekundär secondary

Sekundärdaten secondary data

sekundäre Kosten secondary costs

Sekundärerhebung secondary research

Sekundärmarkt aftermarket; secondary market

Sekundärreserven secondary reserves

selbständig autonomous; independent

Selbständigkeit independence

Selbstabholung collection by the customer

Selbstabholung gegen Kasse cash and carry

Selbstbedienung self service

Selbstbehalt retention; own risk

Selbstbehauptung self-assertion

Selbstbeherrschung self-control; self-command

Selbstbeteiligung own risk; retention

selbstbewusst self-confident; self-assured

Selbstbewusstsein self-confidence; self-assurance

selbstdienliche Wahrnehmung self-serving bias

Selbstfinanzierung internal financing; self-financing

Selbstkostenpreis net cost

Selbstkostenrechnung cost accounting

Selbstmanagement self-management

Selbstregierung self-government; *(Souveränität)* sovereignty; *(Autonomie)* autonomy

Selbststeuerung self-monitoring

Selbstverwaltung self-government; autonomy; home rule

Selbstverwirklichung self-actualization

Selbstwahrnehmungstheorie self-perception theory

Selbstwertschätzung self-esteem

selektiv selective

selektive Wahrnehmung selective perception

selten seldom; infrequent

Seltenheit rarity

Seminar seminar; *(Arbeitstagung)* workshop

Sendeleiter *(Radio, TV)* station director

senden to send; *(Radio)* to broadcast

Sendereihe serial program; series

Sendernetz station network

Seniorchef senior partner

senken to lower

senkrecht vertical

Senkung cut; reduction; *(Kurs)* downward movement

Sensitivitätsanalyse sensitivity analysis

Serie series; serial

serielle Kovarianz serial covariance

Serieneinheit module; series unit

seriös respectable; sincere

Server Protokolldatei server log file

Service service

Servicebereich service area

Servicequalität service quality

Servicesektor service sector

sexuelle Belästigung sexual harassment

sich selbst bewahrheitende Vorraussage self-fullfilling prophecy

sicher sure; safe; *(gesichert)* secure; *(zuverlässig)* reliable; *(gewiss)* certain; *(positiv)* positive

sichere elektronische Transaktionen secure electronic transaction (SET)

sichergestellt secured

Sicherheit security; safety; *(Versicherung)* assurance; *(Gewissheit)* certainty; *(Kredit)* collateral; surety; surety bond

Sicherheiten securities

Sicherheitsfaktor safety factor; cushion

Sicherheitsguthaben compensating balance

Sicherheitsklausel safety clause; safeguard clause

Sicherheitsleistung security; security deposit

Sicherheitsmethoden security methods

sicher machen to make sure; (*sichern*) to secure

sichern to ensure; *(schützen)* to safeguard; *(sicherstellen)* to secure; *(versichern)* to assure

sicherstellen to secure; (*schützen*) to safeguard

Sicherstellung safekeeping; safeguarding; *(Kredit)* collateral; *(Schadloshaltung)* indemnification

Sicherung safeguard; (*Kredit*) security; (*Interessen*) protection; *(Strom)* fuse

Sicherungsabtretung (*Zession*) assignment of security

Sicherungsgeschäft hedge

Sicherungsgeschäft abschließen to hedge

Sicherungsübereignungsvertrag trust agreement

Sicht-Akkreditiv sight letter of credit

sichtbar visible

Sichtbarkeit visibility

Sichteinlage demand deposit

sichten to catch sight of; *(sortieren)* to sort

Sichtpapier demand note

Sichttratte sight draft

Sichtwechsel sight draft

Sichtweite visibility range

sieben-S-Modell seven S model

Sieger victor; *(Gewinner)* winner

siegreich victorious; winning

Signatur signature

simulieren to simulate

simuliert simulated

sinken to sink; *(schwinden)* to dwindle; *(fallen)* to fall; *(abnehmen)* to decline

sinkend sinking; sagging

Sinn sense; *(Bedeutung)* meaning

sinnlos senseless; *(bedeutungslos)* meaningless

Situation situation

Situationsanalyse situation analysis

situative Führungstheorie situational leadership theory

Sitz seat; *(Kleidung)* fit

Sitzung meeting;

Sitzungsbericht minutes

Sitzungsordnung protocol

Skala scale

Skalenertrag scale earnings

Skizze sketch; *(Umriss)* outline

skizzieren to sketch; *(umreißen)* to outline

Skonto cash discount

Skonto abziehen to take a cash discount

Skonto gewähren to allow a cash discount; to grant a cash discount

SMART-Metriken SMART metrics

sofort immediately; straigth away; instantly

sofort fällige Rente immediate annuity

sofortig immediate; instant; prompt

sofort realisierbar (*Geld*) liquid

Softwareanwender software user

Softwareentwicklung software development

Sog pull

Sohle sole

Solawechsel promissory note; name paper

solide *(fundiert)* sound; respectable

Soll debit; balance due; (*Plan*) estimate; target

Sollabgrenzungsposten deferred income items; accruals

Sollangabe debit report; debit statement

Sollarbeitszeit regular working hours

Sollbuchungung debit entry

Solleindeckungszeit acquisition lead time

Soll-Ist-Vergleich variance analysis

Sollkosten budget costs; standard costs

Sollsaldo debit balance

Sollseite debit side; debit column

Soll und Haben assets and liabilities

Sollvorgabe target; quota

Sollzins interest on debit balance; interest on debt

solvent solvent; *(fundiert)* sound

Solvenz solvency; ability to pay

Sonde probe

Sonder- extra; special

Sonderabschreibung accelerated depreciation

Sonderanfertigung custom-made product; purpose-built item

Sonderangebot special offer; bargain

Sonderartikel featured article

Sonderausgabe special expense; incidental expenditure; *(Buch)* special edition

Sonderausstattung extras; special equipment

Sonderdividende extra dividend; special dividend

Sondereinzelkosten special direct costs

Sondergebühr special charge; special fee

Sonderposten *(Buchführung)* special item; *(Waren)* special lot; extraordinary item

Sonderpreis special price

Sonderrecht privilege

Sonderregelung special regulation; special arrangement

Sondersitzung special meeting; extraordinary meeting; *(Gericht)* special session

Sondersubvention special subsidy

Sondertarif (*Zoll*) special tariff; *(Versicherung)* special rate

Sondervergütung bonus

Sondervermögen separate estate; *(Aktiva)* separate assets; *(Besitz)* special property

Sonderverwahrung segregation

Sonderwirtschaftszone special economic area

Sonderzahlung special payment

Sonderziehungsrechte special drawing rights (SDR)

sondieren to probe; to sound *(untersuchen)* to explore

sonstige Verbindlichkeiten other liabilities

Sorge worry; care

sorgen *(sich ~)* to worry; *(~ für)* to care

sorgfältig careful; *(gewissenhaft)* diligent

Sorgsamkeit care; diligence

Sorte sort; *(Marke)* brand

sortieren to sort

Sortiment assortment; range of goods; choice; *(Mischung)* product mix; sales mix

Sortimentsausweitung product range extension

Sortimentsbreite range of products; product mix breadth

Sortimentslänge product mix length

Sortimentspolitik product mix policy

Sortimentstiefe product mix depth

soufflieren to prompt

souverän sovereign

sozial social; caring; (*gerecht*) socially just

Sozialabgaben social security payments; *(Steuer)* social security tax

Sozialanspruch *(Forderung)* social benefits claim; *(Berechtigung)* right to social benefits; welfare eligibility

Sozialausschuss welfare committee

Sozialbeitrag social service contribution; social security contribution

Sozialdemokrat social democrat

soziale Gerechtigkeit social justice

Sozialeinrichtung welfare institution

soziale Klasse social class

soziale Kompetenzen human skills

soziale Netzwerke social networks

sozialer Erleichterungseffekt social facilitation effect

soziales Informationsverarbeitungsmodell social information processing model

Sozialfinanzen social service finances

Sozialfürsorge social service

Sozialgebilde social framework

Sozialhilfe welfare aid; social benefits

Sozialhilfeausgaben public assistance expenditures

Sozialisierung socialization

Sozialismus socialism

sozial-kognitive Lerntheorie social-learning theory

Sozialleistung social benefit

Sozialleistung, betriebliche company benefits

Sozialleistung, gestezliche statutory benefits

Sozialordnung social system; social order

Sozialpartnerschaft social partnership

Sozialpolitik social policy; welfare policy

sozialpolitisch socio-political

Sozialprodukt national product

Sozialpsychologie social psychology

Sozialrecht *(Gerechtigkeit)* social justice; *(Gesetzgebung)* social assistance law; social security law

Sozialstaat welfare state

Sozialversicherung social security

sozialwirtschaftlich socioeconomic

Sozialwohnung welfare housing; government housing

Sozietät partnership

Soziogramm sociogram

Soziologie sociology

Spalt gap; slot

Spalte crack; *(Zeitung)* column

spalten to split; to disrupt

spaltend divisive; disruptive

Spaltung split; *(Teilung)* division; partition

Spanne span; (*Preis*) margin; mark-up; *(Ausdehnung)* spread; *(Reichweite)* range

Spar- (*US*) thrift; (*UK*) savings

Sparbanken savings and loan association (S&L)

Sparbeschluss decision to economize

Sparbetrag amount saved

Sparbrief savings bond; savings certificate

Sparbuch savings book

Spareinlage savings deposit

Spareinlagenbestand savings fund

sparen to save; to economize

Sparer saver; depositor

Sparfähigkeit ability to save

Sparförderung (*Werbung*) savings promotion; *(Anreiz)* government incentives for savers

Spargelder savings deposits; savings deposit funds

Spargelderverwaltung savings deposits administration

Sparkasse savings bank; thrift institution

Sparkassenkunde savings bank customer

Sparkassenschalter savings bank window

Sparkassenverband association of savings banks

Sparkonto savings account; deposit account

Sparkunde savings customer

Sparleistung savings performance

spärlich meager; *(dünn)* thin

Sparmaßnahme economy measure

Sparneigung propensity to save

Sparplan savings plan

Sparpotential savings capacity; savings potential

Sparprämie savings premium; *(Lebensversicherung)* initial reserve

Sparprämiengesetz savings premium law

Sparprogramm austerity program; savings program

sparsam thrifty; economical

Sparsamkeit thrift; economy

sparsam wirtschaften to economize

Sparschuldverschreibung savings bond

Spartätigkeit savings activity

Sparte division; line; *(Zweig)* branch; *(Gebiet)* field

Spartenmanager division head; division manager

Spartenorganisation divisional organization

Spartenumsatz divisional turnover; branch sales

Spar- und Kreditvereinigung savings and loan association

Sparzinssatz savings interest rate

Spediteur carrier; shipper; freight forwarder

Spediteurbescheinigung carrier's receipt

Spediteurdokumente forwarder's documents

Spediteurdurchfrachtpapier forwarding agent's certificate of transport

Spediteurdurchkonnossement forwarder's through bill of lading

Spediteurkonnossement forwarder's bill of lading

Spediteurübernahmebescheinigung Forwarding Agent's Certificate of Receipt (FCR)

Spediteurversandbescheinigung Forwarding Agent's Certificate of Transport (FCT)

Spedition forwarding; transport; *(Unternehmen)* freight forwarding business

Speditionsbetrieb forwarding company

Speditionshandel haulage industry

Speditionskaufmann forwarding merchant

Speditionsversicherung forwarding insurance

Speicher warehouse

Speicherchip memory chip

Speicherkapazität *(Lager)* storage capacity; *(Computer)* memory

Speicherleistung storage performance

speichern to store

Speicherung storage

Spekulant speculator; *(Börse)* position trader

Spekulation speculation

Spekulationsblase bubble

Spekulationsfrist *(Zeitspanne)* speculative period; *(Stichtag)* speculative deadline

Spekulationsgeschäft stock jobbing

Spekulationsgewinn speculative profit

Spekulationsmarkt speculative market

Spekulationsrisiko speculative risk

spekulativ speculative

spekulative Blase bubble

spekulieren to speculate

Spende donation; gift; *(Beitrag)* contribution

spenden to donate; *(beitragen)* to contribute; to subscribe

Spendenquittung contribution receipt

Spender donor; contributor

Sperre stop; *(Bahnhof)* barrier; bar

sperren to stop; to bar; *(Konto)* to block; to freeze

Sperrkonto blocked account

Sperrminorität blocking minority

Sperrung stoppage

Sperrzoll prohibitive tariff

Spesen expenses

Spesenfreiheit exemption from expense charges;

Spezial- special

Spezialisierung specialization

Spezialist specialist

Spezialität specialty

speziell special; *(besonders)* particular

Spezifikation specification

spezifisch specific

spezifizieren to specify

spezifiziert specified

Spiel game

Spielraum leeway; *(Marge)* margin; *(Reichweite)* range

Spieltheorie game theory

Spirale spiral

Spitze *(Führung)* head; *(Börse)* odd lot; *(Höchstwert)* peak; *(Rückversicherung)* surplus

Spitzenbeamte, **-beamtin** top-ranking official

Spitzenbedarf peak demand

Spitzenbetrag residual amount; *(Börse)* fractional amount; odd lot amount

Spitzenfunktionär top-level functionary; top-ranking office holder

Spitzengespräch top-level talk; summit talk

Spitzeninstitut top institute

Spitzenjahr peak year; *(Gewinn)* year of highest profits

Spitzenkräfte top management

Spitzenleistung excellence; first class performance; *(Produktion)* maximum capacity; peak output

Spitzenmanager top manager

Spitzenorganisation head organization

Spitzenpapiere first-rate securities

Spitzenprodukt top product; lead product

Spitzenqualität prime quality

Spitzenreiter market leader

Spitzenstellung top position

Spitzensteuersatz top income tax rate

Spitzentechnik leading technology; high technology

Spitzenverband head organization; *(Dachorganisation)* umbrella organization

Spitzenverdiener top earner

Spitzenvertreter top representative

Spitzenwert peak value; *(Aktien)* blue-chip stock

splitten to split

Sponsoring sponsorship

Sporn spur

Spotmarkt spot market

Spot-Zinssatz spot interest rate

Sprache language

Sprachenschranke language barrier

Sprecher spokesperson; spokesman; spokeswoman

Sprung jump

Spur trace; tracks; sign

Staat state; country

staatlich national; state-

staatliche Unterstützung state subsidy; public support

staatlicher Planer state planner

Staats- state

Staatsanwaltschaft prosecution

Staatsbankrott national bankruptcy; national insolvency

Staatsbudget national budget

Staatsdefizit national deficit; federal deficit

Staatsdirigismus state intervention; government control

Staatseinfluss government influence

Staatsfinanzen state finances; national finances; *(öffentliche Finanzen)* public finances

Staatsgarantie government guaranty;

Staatshandelsland state-trading nation

Staatshaushalt national budget

Staatskasse federal treasury *(US)*; exchequer *(UK)*

Staatskonzern state combine; state-owned enterprise; *(öffentliches Unternehmen)* public enterprise

Staatskosten public expense

Staatspapiere government securities; public securities

Staatsschuld national debt

Staatsschuldverschreibung public bond

Staatssekretär undersecretary of state

Staatsunternehmen state owned enterprise

Staatsverbrauch public consumption

Staatsverschuldung public debt; state indebtedness

Staatszuschuss state subsidy; government subsidy

Stab staff

stabil stable; *(stark, handfest)* sturdy

stabilisieren to stabilize

Stabilisierung stabilization

Stabilität stability

Stabilitätsanalyse stability analysis

Stabilitätsfonds balanced fund

Stabilitätsgesetz stability law

Stabliniensystem line-and-staff organization

Stabsabteilung staff department; staff division

Stabsleiter staff manager; staff director

Stabsorganisation staff organization

Stabsposition staff position

Stadium phase

Stadtgemeinde municipality

städtischer Haushalt urban household

staffeln to graduate; to stagger

Staffelung scale; graduation; grading

Staffelzinsen sliding scale interest

Stagflation stagflation

Stagnation stagnation; sluggishness

stagnieren to stagnate; to be in a stalemate

stagnierend stagnant; sluggish

Stahlarbeiter steel worker

Stahlwerk steel mill

Stammaktie common stock; common share; ordinary share

Stammgast patron

Stammkapital common stock; equity

Stammkapitalanteil *(Aktiengesellschaft)* share of capital stock *(Grundkapital)* share of authorized capital

Stammkunde regular customer

Stammladen parent store; original store

Stammvermögen capital

Stand stand; *(Rang)* rank; standing; *(Klasse)* class

Stand der Technik state of the technology

Standard standard; norm

Standardabweichung standard deviation

Standardfehler standard error

Standardformat standard format

standardisieren to standardize

standardisiert standardized

Standardisierung standardization

Standardkostenrechnung standard costing

Standardnormalverteilung standardized normal distribution

Standby-Gebühren standby fees

Standby-Übernahmeverpflichtung standby underwriting

Standort location; headquarters

Standorttheorie industrial location theory; regional theory

Standpunkt point of view; position

Stapel stack; *(Haufen)* pile

stark strong; *(fundiert)* solid; *(mächtig)* powerful

stark diskontierte Anleihe deep-discount bond

Stärke strength; power; *(Durchmesser)* diameter; *(Wind)* force

stärken to strengthen

starke Nachfrage strong demand

starkes Einschränken severe restriction

starkes Herabsetzen severe reduction

starke Unternehmenskulture strong business culture

starke Vermehrung proliferation

stark reduzieren to reduce severely; to slash

Stärkung strengthening; *(Imbiss)* refreshment

starr rigid; inflexible

starrer Wechselkurs fixed exchange rate

Start start; *(Flugzeug)* takeoff; *(Anfang)* beginning

startbereites System turnkey system

starten to start; *(Flugzeug)* to take off

Starten starting; *(Unternehmen, Kampagne)* launching

statisch static

Statistik statistics

Statistiker statistician

statistisch statistical

statistische Daten statistical data

statistische Stichprobenerhebung statistical sampling

statistische Ziffer statistical number

statistische Werkzeuge statistical tools

stattfinden to take place; to occur

Status status; *(Zustand)* state

Statussymbol status symbol

Statut rules and regulations; bylaw; *(AG)* articles of incorporation

Staubecken reservoir

steif stiff

steigen to rise; *(klettern)* to climb; *(zunehmen)* to increase

Steigen rising; *(Klettern)* climbing

steigende Tendenz upward trend

steigern to raise; to step up; *(vermehren)* to increase; *(erhöhen)* to enhance; *(eskalieren)* to escalate

Steigerung rise; step-up; *(Zunahme)* increase; *(Erhöhung)* enhancement

Steigerungsrate rate of increase

Steigerungssatz rate of increase

steiler Anstieg steep climb; upsurge

Stelle place; spot; *(Posten)* position; post; *(Stellung)* job; appointment

Stellenangebot job offer; vacancy; offer of employment; *(Inserat)* help wanted advertisement

Stellenausschreibung job advertisement; advertisement of a vacancy

Stellenbesetzung staffing

Stellenbesetzungsplan staffing plan; *(Plan)* organizational chart

Stellenbewerber job applicant

Stelleninhaber incumbent; job holder

Stellenmarkt job market; employment market

Stellenverlust job loss

Stellung *(Position)* position; job; *(Rang)* standing; rank

stellvertretend deputy; assistant

stellvertretender Vorsitzender vice chairperson; deputy chairperson

Stellvertreter deputy; substitute; *(Repräsentant)* representative

Stellvertretung representation; *(Vollmacht)* proxy

Stempel stamp; seal; mark

Stempelkissen stamp pad

stempeln to stamp

Stereotyp stereotype

stetige Verzinsung continuous compounding

Stetigkeit steadiness; continuity

Steuer tax; duty; levy; *(Auto)* steering wheel

Steuerabzug tax deduction; deduction

Steueranrechnung tax credit

Steuerausfall tax deficit

steuerbegünstigte Anlage tax-sheltered investment

steuerbegünstigtes Einkommen tax-sheltered income

Steuerbegünstigung tax shelter; shelter; depreciation tax shield

Steuerbehörde tax authority; *(UK)* internal revenue office

Steuerbelastung tax burden; *(anteilsmäßige Festsetzung)* tax assessment

Steuerbemessungsgrundlage tax base

Steuerberater tax consultant; tax counselor

Steuerberatung tax consultancy; tax counselling; tax advice

Steuerberechnung tax assessment; tax computation

Steuerbescheid tax assessment note; tax bill

Steuerbilanz tax balance sheet; tax statement

Steuerbonus tax bonus

Steuerbuchführung tax accounting

Steuereinbuße tax loss

Steuereinnahmen (*Staat*) tax revenues; *(Eingänge)* tax receipts

Steuereintreiber tax collector

Steuerentlastung tax reduction; tax relief

Steuererhebung tax collection; levy

Steuererklärung tax return

Steuererklärung abgeben to file a tax return

Steuererleichterung tax relief

Steuerfachmann tax expert

Steuerformular tax form

steuerfrei tax-exempt; tax-free

Steuerfreibetrag tax allowance; tax-exempt amount, exemption

steuerfreie Schuldverschreibung tax-exempted bond

steuerfreies Einkommen nontaxable income; tax-fee income

Steuergelder taxpayers´ money; public money

Steuergesetz tax law; *(US)* Revenue Act

Steuergesetzgebung taxation laws; internal revenue code

Steuergutschrift tax credit

Steuerhilfe tax aid; tax relief

Steuerhinterziehung tax evasion

Steuerhoheit fiscal sovereignty

Steuerjahr tax year

Steuerkonto tax account

steuerliche Doppelerfassung double taxation

steuerlicher Verlustrücktrag tax loss carryback; carry-back

steuerlicher Verlustvortrag tax loss carry-forward; carry-forward

steuern *(leiten)* to direct; *(Vehikel)* to steer

Steuernummer tax number

Steueroase tax haven

Steuerobjekt tax object

Steuerparadies tax haven

Steuerpflicht tax liability

steuerpflichtig taxable

Steuerpflichtiger taxpayer

steuerpflichtiger Gewinn taxable income

steuerpflichtiges Einkommen taxable income

Steuerpolitik tax policy

Steuerprogression tax progression

Steuerrecht taxation law

Steuerreform tax reform

Steuerrichtlinie taxation guideline

Steuersatz tax rate

Steuerschätzung tax assessment; tax estimate

Steuersenkung tax reduction

Steuerstufe marginal tax rate; tax bracket

Steuerstundung tax deferral

Steuersystem fiscal system

Steuerumgehung tax dodging; tax evasion

Steuerung steering; *(Leitung)* control

Steuervergünstigung tax concession; tax allowance

Steuervermeidung tax avoidance

Steuervorauszahlung estimated tax

Steuervorschriften tax regulations

Steuervorteil tax advantage

Steuerwesen taxation; fiscal system

Steuersystem tax structure; fiscal system; system of taxation

Steuerzahler taxpayer

Stichhaltigkeit validity; (*Argument*) soundness

Stichprobe random test; spot check

stichprobenartig at random

Stichtag deadline; call date

stiften to endow; *(spenden)* to donate; *(schenken)* to give

Stifter *(Förderer, Gönner)* sponsor; *(Gründer)* founder

Stiftung trust; *(Rechtspersönlichkeit)* foundation; *(Schenkung)* endowment

still silent; quiet

stille Beteiligung silent partnership; dormant equity holding

stille Bestätigung silent confirmation

stilllegen *(Fabrik)* to close; *(Vorgang, Maschinen)* to shut down

stille Gesellschaft silent partnership; dormant partnership

Stilllegung *(Fabrik)* closure; *(Vorgang, Maschinen)* shutdown

stille Reserve hidden reserve

stiller Gesellschafter silent partner

Stillhalteabkommen standstill agreement; moratorium

Stillstand standstill; halt; slack

stillstehend *(Maschinen)* idle

stimmberechtigt entitled to vote; with voting power

stimmberechtigte Aktie voting stock

Stimme *(Wahl)* vote; voice

stimmen *(Wahl)* to cast a vote; *(Instrument)* to tune

Stimmengleichheit tie vote

Stimmenthaltung abstention

Stimmrecht right to vote; voting rights; *(Wahlrecht)* suffrage

Stimmrechtsermächtigter proxy

Stimmrechtsermächtigung proxy

stimmrechtslos nonvoting

stimmrechtslose Aktie nonvoting stock

Stimmrechtsvollmacht proxy

Stimmung mood; spirit

Stimmzettel ballot; ballot paper

Stimulanz stimulation

stimulieren to stimulate

stimulierend stimulating; reflationary

Stock stick; *(Gebäude)* storey; level

stocken to stagnate

stockend halting; stagnant

Stockung stagnation; stoppage

Stockwerk level; floor; storey

Stoff substance; matter; *(Textilien)* fabric

Stoffrest fabric remnant

Stöpsel plug; stopper

stören to disturb

Störung disturbance

stornieren to cancel; to reverse

Stornierung reversal; cancellation

Storno cancellation ; *(Buchführung)* reversing entry; cancellation of an entry

Stornobuchung reversing entry

Stornogebühr cancellation fee

Störung disturbance; interference

Stoß push; thrust; *(Ausstoß)* batch

stoßen to push; to thrust

Stoßkraft power of thrust; *(Aufprall)* impact

Stoßpolster buffer

Straf- punitive

strafbar criminal; liable to procecution

Strafe punishment; *(Geldstrafe)* penalty; fine; *(Urteil)* sentence

strafend punitive

straffen to tighten

Straffen tightening

Straßengüterverkehr road transport; road haulage

Strategie strategy

strategisch strategic

strategische Allianz strategic alliance

strategische Planung strategic planning

strategische Werkzeuge strategic tools

strebsam striving; *(ehrgeizig)* ambitious

Strebsamkeit striving; *(Ehrgeiz)* ambition

Strecke route; *(Entfernung)* distance

Strecke kennzeichnen to route

streichen to eliminate; *(Farbe)* to paint

Streichung deletion; cancellation

Streifen strip; stripe; *(Gürtel)* belt; *(Kleber)* tape

Streik strike

Streikbrecher strikebreaker; scab

streiken to strike

Streiken striking

streikfrei strike-free

Streikgebiet strike area

Streikmonat strike month

Streikposten picket

Streikrecht right to strike

Streikverlust strike loss

Streit argument; *(streiten)* to argue; to dispute

Streitpunkt point of contention; argument

Stress stress

streuen *(Risiko)* to spread; *(Dividende)* to distribute; *(Investition, Produktion)* to diversify

Streuung *(Risiko)* spread; *(Dividende)* distribution; *(Investition, Produktion)* diversification

streuungsfähiges Risiko diversifiable risk

Streuverluste waste coverage

Strick rope

Strom electricity; power; *(Fluss)* stream; *(Fließen)* flow

Stromlinienform streamlined shape

stromlinienförmig gestalten to streamline

Stromversorgung electrical power supply

Struktur structure; pattern

Strukturanpassung structural adjustment

Struktureffekt structural effect

strukturell structural

strukturelle Veränderung structural change

Strukturfonds structural fond

strukturieren to structure

Strukturierung structuring

Strukturkosten structure costs

Strukturplan structural plan

Strukturproblem structural problem

Strukturprogramm structural program

Strukturschwäche structural weakness

Strukturwandel structural change

Stück *(Akkord)* piece; *(Einheit)* unit; *(Segment)* segment

Stückgewinn unit profit

Stückgut general cargo; mixed cargo; less-than-carload lot (LCL)

Stückgutvertrag bill of lading contract

Stückkosten unit costs; cost per unit

Stückkostenrechnung unit product costing

Stückliste parts list; bill of materials

Stücklohnsystem piece-rate pay plan

Stückpreis unit price; price per unit

stückweise piecemeal

Stückzahl number of units

Stückzinsen accrued interest

Studie study; survey

Stufe step; *(Phase)* phase

stufenflexibel sliding

stumm silent; (*Sprache*) dumb

Stunde hour; *(Unterricht)* lesson

Stundenlohn hourly wages

Stundensatz hourly rate

Sturz *(Börse)* crash; tumble

stürzen *(Börse)* to crash; to tumble; to slump; *(Kurse, Preise)* to collapse; to plunge; *(Regierung)* to overthrow

Stütze *(Unterstützung)* support; backing

stützen to support; *(Kurs, Markt)* to peg

stützend supporting

Stützpreis support price; *(Kurs)* pegged price

Stützpunkt *(Militär)* base

Stützung support; *(Börse)* pegging

Stützungsgelder backing money

Stützungskosten cost of support; *(Subvention)* cost of subsidy

Stützweite *(Bau)* support span

subjektiv subjective

subjektives Risiko (*Versicherung)* moral hazard

Subkultur subculture

Submission submission; tender

Substanz substance; *(Material)* material; *(Stoff)* matter

substanzbedingte Wertminderung depletion

Substanzerhaltung preservation of substance; maintenance of asset value

Substanzverringerung *(Vermögen)* depletion of assets

Substanzverzehr depletion

Substanzwert asset value; breakdown value; net value of tangible assets

substituierbar replaceable; substitutable

Substitut substitute; substitute product

Substitution substitution

Subtraktion subtraction

Subunternehmer subcontractor; (*Fracht*) subcarrier

Subvention subsidy

subventionieren to subsidize

Subventionierung subsidization

Subventionsabbau subsidy reduction

Subventionsbedarf subsidy requirements

Subventionsgeld subsidy funds

Subventionszahlung subsidy payment

Suchmaschine search engines

Summe sum; *(Betrag)* amount

summierbar capable of being totalled

Sumpf swamp

Supermarkt supermarket

Superrechner mainframe computer

supranational supranational

Surrogat surrogate; substitute

Swapabkommen swap agreement

Swapgeschäft swap; swap deal; swap business

Swapsatz swap rate

Swapvereinbarung swap arrangement

symbolisch symbolic; token

Syndikat syndicate

Synergie synergy

Syndikatsbildung syndication

synthetisch synthetic

systematisch systematic

systematischer Arbeitsplatzwechsel job rotation

systematische Erforschung systematic study

systematisches Risiko systematic risk

Systemanalyse systems analysis

Systemauslastung system utilization

Systembildung system formation

Systemeinheit system unit

systemimmanent inbuilt

Szenarioanalyse scenario analysis

Szenariotechnik scenario planning

T

T-Konto t-account

tabellarisch tabular; shedular

tabellarische Darstellung tabulation

tabellarischer Lebenslauf personal data sheet

tabellarisches Ordnen tabulating

tabellarisch ordnen to tabulate

tabellarisieren to tabulate

Tabellarisieren tabulating

Tabelle table; *(Plan)* schedule; *(Schaubild)* chart

Tabellierung tabulation

Tadel blame; censure

tadeln to blame; to censure

Tafel *(Schaubild)* chart; *(Tabelle)* table

Tagebaubetrieb strip mining

Tagelohn daily wage

tagen to meet; *(beraten)* to deliberate; *(Gericht)* to sit; *(Parlament)* to be in session

Tagesauszug daily statement of account

Tagesgeld *(Bankwesen)* call money; overnight loan; *(Sitzungsgeld)* per diem

Tageskurs market rate

Tagesordnung agenda; *(Gericht)* docket

Tagesordnungspunkt agenda item

Tageswert present value

Tagung meeting; congress; *(Versammlung)* convention

Takelung rigging

Takelwerk rigging

Takt *(Musik)* beat; *(Motor)* stroke; *(Feingefühl)* tact

Taktik tactics

taktisch tactical

taktische Maßnahme tactical measure

taktischer Zug tactical move

Talfahrt slide

Tante-Emma-Laden corner shop; mom and pop store

Tantieme *(Ertragsanteil)* royalty

Tarif tariff; *(Rate)* rate

Tarifabkommen collective agreement; wage agreement; labor pact

Tarifabschluss tariff agreement; labor contract

Tarifautonomie tariff autonomy; wage autonomy

Tarifberechnung rate making

Tarifbewegung tariff movement

Tarifergebnis tariff decision; tariff negotiating results

Tariferhöhung tariff increase; rate hike

Tarifermäßigung tariff reduction

Tarifexperte tariff expert

Tarifgespräch bargaining talk; wage discussion

Tarifhoheit tariff authority; tariff sovereignty

Tarifkommission *(Gewerkschaft)* collective bargaining commission; *(Zoll)* tariff commission

Tarifkontrolle tariff control; rate control

Tarifpartner bargaining agent; collective bargainer

Tarifpolitik *(Lohn)* rate policy; *(Zoll)* tariff policy

Tarifregelung *(Lohn)* rate regulation

Tarifrunde *(Lohn)* rate bargaining round

Tarifsatz *(Lohn)* wage rate; *(Zoll)* tariff rate

Tarifsenkung tariff reduction

Tarifstreit rate dispute

Tarifverhandlung collective bargaining

Tarifvertrag wage agreement

Tarifvorzug tariff preference

Tarifzoll tariff duty

Tasche bag; *(Kleidung)* pocket

Taschengeld pocket money; allowance

Tastatur keyboard

Taste key

Tastengerät keyboard; digital device

tätig employed; *(beschäftigt)* busy; *(aktiv)* active

Tätigkeit action; activity

Tätigkeitsbericht progress report

Tätigkeitsvielfalt skill variety

Tätigung von Versicherungsgeschäften insurance underwriting

Tatsache fact

tatsächlich actual

tauglich suitable; *(Zustand)* fit

Tausch exchange; swap; *(Tauschhandel)* barter; swap

Tauschbeziehung exchange relationship; barter relationship

tauschen to trade; to swap

Tauschgeschäft barter; barter trade

Tauschhandel countertrade; barter trade

Tauschhandel betreiben to engage in countertrade

Tauschmittel medium of exchange

Tauschrate exchange rate; barter rate; offset rate

Tauschrelation exchange relation; barter relation

Tauschwirtschaft barter economy; countertrade economy

Taxe tariff; tax

taxieren to appraise; *(schätzen)* to estimate

Taxierung valuation

Taxwert appraisal value

Team team

Teamarbeit teamwork

Teamentwicklung team building

Teamstruktur team structure

Technik technique

Techniker technician; *(Reparatur)* repairman, -person, -woman

technisch technical

technisch ausgefeilt technologically perfected

technische Aktienanalyse technical analysis

technische Anlage technical installation; plant

technische Analyse technical analysis

technische Ausführung technique

technische Analyse technical analysis

technische Hilfe technological assistance

technische Kompetenzen technical skills

technische Kurskorrektur technical correction

technischer Indikator technical indicator

technische Zahlungsunfähigkeit technical insolvency

technisch hohes Niveau technologically advanced level

Technokrat technocrat

Technologe, **Technologin** technologist

Technologie technology

Technologietransfer technology transfer

technologisch technological

technologische Änderung technological change

technologische Lücke technological gap

technologische Neuerung technological innovation

technologischer Fortschritt technological advance; progress

technologische Strategie technological strategy

Teil- partial

Teil part; *(Sektion)* section; *(Abschnitt)* segment; *(Anteil)* portion; *(Maschine)* spare part

Teilabschreibung writedown

teilbar divisible; *(trennbar)* separable

Teilbarkeit divisibility

Teil-Containerladung less than container load (LCL)

teilen to divide; to split; *(abgeben)* to share; *(trennen)* to part; *(abtrennen)* to partition

Teilgebiet zone; area; section

teilhaben to share; to participate

Teilhaber partner; associate; *(Teilnehmer)* participant

Teilhaberschaft partnership

Teilkosten share of total costs

Teilkostenrechnung direct costing

Teilladung less than car load (LCL)

Teillieferung partial delivery

Teilliquidation partial settlement

Teilmontage subassembly

Teilnahme participation; *(Subskription)* subscription

teilnehmen to participate; to attend

Teilnehmer participant; *(Subskribent)* subscriber

Teilnehmerzahl number of participants

Teilprivatisierung partial privatization

Teilung division

teilweise partial

Teilwert fractional value; partial value

Teilzahlung installment

Teilzahlungsverkauf installment sale

Teilzeit- part-time

Teilzeitarbeit part-time work

Telearbeit telecommuting

Telefon telephone

telefonieren to telephone; to call

Telefonvermittlungsperson telephone operator

Telefonzentrale switchboard

telegrafieren to wire

Telegramm telegram; wire

Telemarketing telemarketing

Tendenz tendency; *(Trend)* trend

Tendenzwende turnaround

tendieren to show a tendency; to tend; *(neigen)* to lean

Tensororganisation tensor organization

Termin- forward

Termin appointment; *(Endtermin)* deadline; *(Datum)* date; *(Verfallzeit)* maturity; *(Zahlung)* payment due date

Terminabschluss forward contract; futures contract

terminale Werte terminal values

Termindevisen forward currency

Termineinlage time deposit; restricted cash

Terminfestlegung setting a date

Termingelder time deposits; restricted cash

Termingeldsatz time deposit rate; fixed market rate

termingerecht in due time; *(zeitplanmäßig)* on schedule

Termingeschäft option trading; forward transaction; futures trading; futures

Terminhandel forward trade

Terminhandel mit Finanztiteln financial futures

terminieren to make an appointment

Terminierung timing; setting a deadline

Terminkalender diary; appointment schedule; appointment calendar

Terminkontrakt forward contract

Terminkontraktmarkt futures market

Terminkurs forward rate; forward exchange rate

Terminmarkt options market; forward market; futures market

Terminologie terminology; *(Sprache)* language

Terminplanung scheduling; planning

Terminpreis forward rate

Terminsatz futures rate

Termin vereinbaren to make an appointment

Territorium territory

Test test

testen to test

Testfall test case

Testgruppen focus groups

testieren to testify; to certify

testierter Abschluss audited statement

Testphase testing phase

Testwebseite test web site

teuer expensive; costly

Teuerung inflation; price increase

Teuerungsimpuls price increase impulse

Teuerungsrate rate of price increase

Teuerungswelle wave of price increases

Text text

Textil- textile

Textilfabrikant textile manufacturer

Textilwaren textiles; fabrics

Textprozessor word processor

Textstelle passage

Textverarbeiter word processor

Textverarbeitung word processing

Theke counter

Thema topic

Theorem von Bayes Baye´s theorem

theoretisch theoretical; *(spekulativ)* speculative

Theorie der kognitiven Evaluation cognitive evaluation theory

Theorien über Aufgabenmerkmale task characteristic theories

Theorie X theory X

Theorie Y theory Y

Tiefpunkt bottom; *(Wirtschaft)* trough

Tiefstand low; bottom

tilgen extinguish; *(auslöschen)* to eradicate; *(Schulden)* to delete; to retire; to redeem; to liquidate; *(Hypothek)* to amortize

Tilgung *(Anleihe)* retirement; *(Zurückzahlung)* repayment; *(Amortisierung)* redemption; *(Auflösung)* liquidation

Tilgungsanleihe callable bond; sinking fund bond

Tilgungsbetrag repayment amount; amortization amount

Tilgungsfond sinking fund

tilgungsfrei without amortization

Tilgungsfreistellung exemption from amortization

Tilgungsgebühr redemption charge

Tilgungshypothek amortization mortgage

Tilgungsrate amortization rate; sinking fund installment

Tilgungstermin payment date; redemption date

Tipp tip; lead

Tippfehler typing error

tippen to type; to typewrite

Tisch table; counter

Tischcomputer desktop computer

Tischrechner desktop calculator

Titel title

Titelkopf rubric heading

Tobins Q Tobin's Q ratio

Tochterbank subsidiary bank

Tochterbetrieb subsidiary company

Tochtergesellschaft subsidiary company; subsidiary

Tochtergesellschaft im Mehrheitsbesitz majority-owned subsidiary

Tochterinstitut subsidiary institute

Tochterunternehmen subsidiary enterprise

Todesfallversicherung whole life insurance

Ton tone; sound

Tonband audio tape

Tonnengehalt tonnage

Tor *(Sport)* goal; gate

tot dead; idle

Total- total

total total; *(gesamt)* overall; complete

traditioneller Ansatz der Konfliktforschung traditional view of conflict

tragbar portable; bearable; manageable

tragen to carry; to bear

Träger *(Bahnhof)* porter; *(Versicherung)* carrier

Tragfähigkeit tonnage capacity

trainieren to train

Trainieren training

Trampschifffahrt tramping

Tranche tranche; portion

Transaktion transaction; deal

transaktionale Führung transactional leadership

Transaktionskosten transaction costs

Transaktionsmotiv transactions motive

Transaktionswert transaction value

Transfer transfer

Transferbegünstigter transferee

Transfereinkommen transfer income

transferieren to transfer

Transfergarantie transfer guarantee

Transferpreis transfer price

Transferzahlung transfer payment

Transformation transformation

Transformationskurve tarnsformation curve

transformative Führung transformational leadership

Transit transit

Transithandel transit trade

Transithandelsgenehmigung transit trade permit

Transithandelsgeschäft merchanting transaction

Transitkonnosement transit bill of lading

Transitlager transit warehouse

transitorisch transitory

transitorische Aktiva prepaid expenses

Transport transport; *(Versand)* shipping; transportation

Transporter transporter; truck

transportfähig transportable

transportieren to transport; to convey; to remove

Transportunternehmer freight carrier

Transportvolumen shipping volume

Transportwagen van

Trassant drawer; drafter; maker

Trassat drawee; payer

trassieren to draw

Tratte draft; bill

treffen to meet; *(erzielen)* to score; *(Ziel)* to hit

Treffen meeting; gathering; rally

Treffen veranstalten to hold a meeting

Treffer hit; success

treiben to drift; *(Fahrzeug)* to drive

Treibenlassen drifting

Trend trend

Trendanalyse trend analysis

Trendbereinigung trend adjustment

Trendextrapolation extrapolating the trend line

Trendlinie trend line

Trendwende trend reversal; turnaround

trennen to part; to separate; to dissociate; *(abtrennen)* to partition

trennend disruptive

Trennung separation; severance; *(Ehescheidung)* divorce

Trennschärfe selectivity

Tresor strongbox; safe; vault

Treuesysteme loyalty techniques

Treuhandanstalt trust institution

Treuhänder trustee; fiduciary; custodian

treuhänderisch fiduciary; in trust

treuhänderisch verwaltetes Konto discretionary account; managed account

Treuhandgeschäft trust transaction

Treuhandgesellschaft trust corporation

Treuhandkonto trust account; fiduciary account; managed account

Treuhandverhältnis fiduciary relationship; trust

Treuhandverhältnis unter Lebenden inter vivos trust; living trust

Treuhandvermögen trust assets

Treuhandvertrag trust deed; indenture; trust agreement; escrow

Tribunal tribunal

Triebkraft impetus

Triebwerk engine; jet engine

Trog trough

Tropfen drop

Trudeln tailspin

Truppenteil troop outfit; troop unit

Trust combine; trust; pool

tüchtig efficient; capable; competent

Tüchtigkeit efficiency; capability; competence

Typ type; model; make

Typ A type A

Typung standardization

U

üben to practice

Überalterung *(Bevölkerung)* aging; obsolescence

Überangebot oversupply; glut

überarbeiten to overwork; *(Schriftstück)* to revise

Überarbeitung revision

Überbau superstructure

überbelasten to overburden; to overwork

überbesteuern to overtax

überbewerten to overvalue

Überbewertung overvaluation; overestimation

Überbleibsel remnant

Überblick overview; survey; *(Text)* outline

überbringen to deliver

überbrücken to bridge; to bridge a gap

Überbrückungsfinanzierung interim financing

Überbrückungshilfe stopgap assistance; interim aid

über den Bestand verkaufen to oversell

überdenken to rethink

Überdenkungsfrist cooling-off period

überdurchschnittlich above average; superior

übereinkommen to come to an understanding; to agree

Übereinkommen understanding; agreement

übereinstimmen to agree; *(Zahlung)* to tally; *(Meinung)* to concur; to conform to

Übereinstimmung agreement; *(Meinung)* concurrence; *(Konsens)* consensus; *(Einklang)* accord; accordance

Überfahrt crossing; transit

überfällig overdue; past due

überfliegen to fly over; *(Dokument)* to scan

Überfliegen flying over; *(Dokument)* scanning

Überflieger *(Karriere)* high-flyer

überfließen to overflow

überflügeln to outdistance; to outstrip

Überfluss surplus; *(Übermaß)* excess; *(Fülle)* abundance; plenty

Überflüssigkeit redundancy; *(Überfluss)* superfluity

Überflutung overflow; flooding

überfordern to overburden; *(Person)* to stress

überführen to convey; to transfer;*(Gericht)* to prove someone's guilt

Überführung transportation; *(Immobilie)* transfer; conveyance; *(Gericht)* conviction

Überfülle overabundance; *(Überfluss)* superfluity

Übergang transition; change; *(Verkehr)* crossing; *(Fußgänger)* crosswalk

Übergangsregelung temporary arrangement; interim ruling

Übergangszeit transitional period

Übergriff infringement

überheizen to overheat

überheizt superheated

überhitzen to overheat

überhitzt superheated

überhöhen to exaggerate; *(Spesen)* to pad

überholen *(reparieren)* to overhaul; *(Verkehr)* to pass; to overtake

Überholen *(Verkehr)* passing

überholt obsolete

Überholung *(Reparatur)* overhaul

Überkapazität excess capacity

überkapitalisieren to overcapitalize

Überkapitalisierung overcapitalization

Überkreuzmandat interlocking directorates

überladen excessive; ornate

überlassen to dispose of; *(aufgeben)* to relinquish; to cede

Überlassung *(Abtretung)* cession

überlasten to overload

überlaufen *(Ort)* overrun; *(überfließen)* to overflow

überleben to survive

Überlebender survivor

Überlebensrente joint and survivor annuity

überlegen superior; *(denken)* to deliberate

Überlegenheit superiority

Überliegegebühr demurrage

Übermaß excess

übermäßig excessive

übermäßig anpreisen to push; to pitch; to tout

Übernahme *(Unternehmen)* takeover; buyout; *(Verantwortung)* assumption

Übernahmeangebot *(Unternehmen)* takeover offer; tender offer

Übernahmekandidat takeover target; target company

Übernahmekonnossement received bill of lading

übernational supranational

übernehmen to take over; *(Verantwortung, Schulden)* to assume; to absorb; (*Börse*) to underwrite

Übernehmer transferee; receiver

über pari above par

Überpreis overprice

Überproduktion overproduction

überproduzieren to overproduce

überprüfen to review; *(bestätigen)* to verify; *(nachprüfen)* to check

Überprüfen checking

Überprüfung review; *(Bestätigung)* verification; *(Nachprüfung)* check

überreden to persuade; *(zum Kauf)* to make a sales pitch

Überredung persuasion; *(zum Kauf)* sales pitch

überregional supraregional; nationwide

überregionale Verbreitung syndication

überregionale Ausstrahlung *(Medien)* syndication

Überrest remnant

überschätzen to overestimate; to overvalue

überschauen to survey

überschreiten to exceed

Überschrift heading

Überschuldung excessive indebtedness; *(Unternehmen)* overextension

Überschuss surplus; *(Übermaß)* excess

Überschusslage surplus condition

Überschussprodukt surplus product

Überschussreserven excess reserves

überschwemmen to flood; to swamp

Überschwemmung flooding; *(Überlaufen)* overflow

Übersee overseas; overseas countries

Überseegeschäft overseas trade

Überseehandel overseas trade

überseeisch overseas

überseeische Unternehmung overseas operation

überseeische Geschäftstätigkeit overseas business activity

Überseemarkt overseas market; foreign market

übersenden to transmit; to send

Übersenden transmission; *(Spedition)* consignment

Übersicht general view; *(Text)* summary; synopsis

übersteigen to exceed; *(überflügeln)* to outstrip

Überstunde overtime hour

Überstunden machen to work overtime

übertragbar transferable; *(Gerät)* portable

übertragbares Akkreditiv transferable credit; assignable credit

übertragen to transfer; *(freigeben)* to release; *(zuweisen)* to assign

Übertragung transfer; *(Zuweisung)* assignment

Übertragungsbilanz net transfer payments; balance on transfer account

Übertragungsgebühr transfer charge

Übertragungsurkunde release document

übertreffen to beat; to exceed

übertreiben to exaggerate; to overstate

Übertretung violation; *(Bruch, Verstoß)* breach

überverkaufen to oversell

überversorgen oversupply

überwachen to monitor; *(beaufsichtigen)* to supervise; *(kontrollieren)* to control

Überwachen monitoring; *(Beaufsichtigen)* supervising

Überwachung control; surveillance; *(Beaufsichtigung)* supervision

Überwachung der Umweltverschmutzung environmental pollution control

Überwachungsstelle regulatory agency

Überwachungstechniker control technician; monitoring technician

überweisen to transfer; to remit

Überweisung transfer; remittance

Überweisungsauftrag transfer order; *(Zahlung)* remittance order

Überweisungsgebühr transfer charge

Überweisungsträger remittance slip

Überweisungsverkehr transfer of funds

überwiegen to outweigh; *(dominieren)* to be dominant

überzeichnen to oversubscribe

überzeichnet oversubscribed; overbooked

überzeichnete Emission oversubscribed issue

Überzeichnungsprivileg oversubscription privilege

überzeugen to convince

überzeugend convincing; persuasive

überzeugendes Argument convincing argument

Überzeugung conviction; *(Überredung)* persuasion; *(Glaube)* belief

überziehen (*Konto*) to overdraw

Überziehung (*Konto*) overdraft

Überziehungskredit overdraft facility; overdraft privilege

Überziehungszinsen interest paid on overdraft

üblich customary; *(gewöhnlich)* usual

üblicher Marktpreis fair value

üblicher Verlauf customary process

übliches Verfahren standard practice; customary procedure

übrig remaining; left over

übrig bleiben to remain; to be left over

Ultimo last trading day

umändern to alter

umarbeiten to revise; to adapt

Umarbeitung revision; adaptation

Umbau reorganization; *(Umstrukturierung)* restructuring

umbauen to remodel; *(neu organisieren)* to reorganize

umbuchen to transfer; to rebook; to reclassify; to change a reservation

Umbuchung rebooking; transfer

umdenken to rethink

umdisponieren to redispose; to rearrange; *(Investition)* to reinvest

Umdisposition redisposition; *(Investition)* reinvestment

umdrehen to turn around

Umdrehung turn; *(Rotation)* rotation; *(Motor)* revolution

Umfang volume; scale; *(Größe)* size; *(Ausmaß)* measure; *(Ausdehnung)* extent; *(Fülle)* amplitude

umfangreich voluminous; *(geräumig)* spacious; *(umfassend)* comprehensive

umfangreiche Streichungen extensive cuts

umfassen to span; to include; *(beinhalten)* to contain; *(abdecken)* to cover

umfassend comprehensive

umfassendes Qualitätsmanagement total quality management

Umfeld environment

Umfeldanalyse environmental analysis

umfinanzieren to refinance

Umfinanzierung refinancing

Umfrage survey

Umgang association

Umgebung environment

umgehen to dodge; *(vermeiden)* to avoid; to sidestep

Umgehungsmanöver dodge

umgestalten to reform; to rearrange

Umgestaltung rearrangement

umgruppieren to regroup; to rearrange; *(Klassifikation)* to reclassify; *(Einsatz)* to redeploy

Umgruppierung rearrangement; *(Einsatz)* redeployment

Umkehrung turnaround; reversal

Umkehrwechsel return bill

Umklammerung stranglehold

Umkreis radius; *(Nähe)* vicinity

Umlage contribution; *(Zuteilung)* cost allocation; apportionment

umlaufen to circulate; *(Effekten)* to float

umlaufend circulating; running; current; *(Effekten)* floating

umlaufende Aktien shares outstanding; outstanding capital stock

umlauffähig negotiable

Umlaufkapital current assets; gross working capital

Umlaufrendite current yield; net yield

Umlaufvermögen current assets; working assets

umleiten to divert

umlenken to switch

Umlenken switching

ummodellieren to remodel

Umorganisation reorganization

umorganisieren to remodel; to reorganize

Umplatzierung relocation; *(Einsatz)* redeployment

umrechnen to convert

Umrechnung conversion

Umrechnungskurs exchange rate

Umrechnung von Fremdwährungen foreign currency translation

Umrechnungsgewinn translation gain

Umrechnungsverlust translation loss

umreißen to outline

Umriss outline

Umsatz turnover; sales volume; sales

umsatzabhängig turnover dependent; dependent on sales

Umsatzanstieg increase in turnover; upsurge in sales

Umsatzanteil share of sales

Umsatzaufwendungen cost of goods sold

Umsatzeinbruch sales collapse

Umsatzeinbuße loss of sales

Umsatzentwicklung development of sales

Umsatzerlöse sales revenues

Umsatzertrag sales revenue

Umsatzkosten cost of goods sold

Umsatzkostenverfahren cost of sales accounting

Umsatz-Leverage operating leverage

Umsatzprognose sales forecast

Umsatzprovision commission on sales

Umsatzrekord sales record

Umsatzrendite profit margin

Umsatzrückgang decrease in turnover; decline in sales

Umsatzsteigerung turnover increase; rise in sales

Umsatzsteuer sales tax; turnover tax

Umsatzverlust loss in sales

Umsatzwachstum growth in sales

Umsatzzunahme sales increase

Umsatzzuwachs turnover gain

umschichten to shift; to rearrange

Umschlag turnover; *(Brief)* envelope

Umschlagkennziffer turnover ratio

Umschlagsgeschwindigkeit receivables turnover

Umschlagshäufigkeit turnover ratio; rate of inventory turnover

Umschlagshäufigkeit der Vorräte inventory turnover ratio

Umschlagshäufigkeit des Gesamtkapitals total asset-turnover ratio

Umschlagshäufigkeit des Eigenkapitals rate of equity turnover

Umschlagshäufigkeit des Warenbestandes inventory sales ratio

Umschlagskapazität handling capacity

Umschlagzeit replacement period

umschreiben to circumscribe; to paraphrase; to rewrite; *(Wechsel)* to reendorse; *(übertragen)* to transfer; *(Grundstück)* to convey

Umschreibung *(Aktien)* transfer; *(Schriftstück)* transcription; *(Grundbesitz)* conveyance

umschulden to reschedule debt payments

Umschuldung debt restructuring; debt rescheduling; *(Umwandlung)* debt conversion; *(Neufinanzierung)* refinancing

umschulen to retrain

Umschulung retraining

Umschwung turnaround; change; *(Umkehrung)* reversal

umsetzbar marketable

umsetzen to sell; *(Arbeitskräfte)* to dislocate; *(Umsatz haben)* to turn over; *(realisieren)* to realize

Umsicht circumspection; *(Vorsicht)* caution

umsiedeln to relocate

umspannen to span

Umstand circumstance; *(Tatsache)* fact; *(Faktor)* factor

umstellen to change; to convert

Umstellung change; restructuring; *(Modifizierung)* modification; (*Anpassung*) adjustment

Umstellungsprozess adjustment process

umstrukturieren to restructure; to reorganize

Umstrukturierung restructuring; reorganization

Umtausch *(Waren)* exchange; *(Währung)* conversion

Umtausch ausgeschlossen non returnable

umtauschbar convertible; exchangeable; returnable

umtauschbares Wertpapier convertible security

umtauschen *(Waren)* to exchange; *(Währung)* to convert

Umtauschgeschäft exchange offer

Umtauschrecht right to exchange; *(Börse)* exchange privilege

umverteilen to redistribute; *(neu zuteilen)* to reallocate

Umverteilung reallocation; redistribution

Umwandelbarkeit convertibility

umwandeln to convert; to change

Umwandlung conversion; transformation; reorganization

Umwandlungsbilanz reorganization balance sheet

Umwandlungswert conversion value

Umwelt- environmental; ecological

Umwelt environment; *(Ökologie)* ecology

Umweltbelastung environmental burden

umweltbewusst environmentally aware; ecology-minded

Umweltexperte, -expertin environment expert

umweltfreundlich environment friendly; not harmful to the environment

Umweltgruppe environmental group

Umweltproblem environmental problem

Umweltqualität environmental quality

Umweltschutz environmental protection

Umweltschutzauflage environmental protection amendment

Umweltschützer environmentalist; environmental activist

Umweltthema environmental topic

Umweltverschmutzer polluter

Umweltverschmutzung environmental pollution

umweltverträglich environmentally compatible

umwerben to woo; *(Reklame)* to persuade; to buy

umziehen to move

Umzug relocation; move

unabgestimmter Übernahmeversuch hostile takeover

unabhängig independent; autonomous

unabhängiges Investitionsprojekt independent project

unabhängige Variable independent variable

Unabhängigkeit independence

unabkömmlich indispensable

unanfechtbar unassailable; incontrovertible

unangemessen inappropriate

Unangemessenheit inappropriateness

unannehmbar unacceptable

unaufdringlich unobtrusive; discreet; inoconspicuous

unauffällig inconspicuous; understated

unausgebildet untrained

unausgegeben *(Aktien)* unissued; *(Geld)* unspent

unausgeglichen unbalanced; disproportionate

Unausgeglichenheit imbalance; disequilibrium

unausgenutzt underutilized; idle

unbefriedigend unsatisfactory; disappointing

unbefriedigt unsatisfied

unbefristet *(Zeit)* unlimited

unbeglichen outstanding; *(Rechnung)* unpaid

unbegrenzt unlimited; indefinite

unbegründet unfounded

unbelastet unencumbered; clear

unberechtigt unjustified

unberücksichtigt not considered

unbeschränkt unlimited

unbeschränkte Haftung unlimited liability

unbeschränkt haftender Gesellschafter general partner

unbesetzt unoccupied; vacant; *(Posten)* unfilled

unbesichert unsecured

unbesicherte Verbindlichkeit unsecured liability

unbeständig vollatile; inconsistant

Unbeständigkeit volatility; inconsistency; instability

unbestimmt indefinite

unbewohnt uninhabited; empty; void

unbezahlbar prohibitively expensive; *(unersetzlich)* priceless; *(unschätzbar)* inestimable

unbezahlt unpaid

unbillig unfair

unbrauchbar unusable

undurchführbar not feasible

uneinbringlich uncollectible

uneingeschränkt unlimited; unrestricted; plenary; *(Revision)* unqualified

uneingeschränkter Bestätigungsvermerk clean opinion; unqualified opinion

uneinig sein to disagree

unelastisch inelastic

Unelastizität inelasticity

unentbehrlich indispensable

unentgeltlich gratuitous; *(gratis)* free

unentwickelt undeveloped

unerfahren inexperienced

unerfüllt unfulfilled

unergiebig unproductive

unerheblich slight; immaterial

unerkannt unrecognized

unerlässlich indispensable; requisite

unerlaubt unauthorized; illegal; *(bürgerliches Recht)* unlawful

unerledigt unfinished

unerledigte Aufträge backlog of orders

unerledigter Auftragsbestand order backlog

unermesslich immeasurable

unerschlossen undeveloped; unexplored; *(Ressourcen)* untapped

unerwartet unexpected

unerwarteter Gewinn windfall profit

unfähig incompetent; *(außerstande)* incapable

Unfähigkeit incompetence; *(Unvermögen)* inability; *(Untauglichkeit)* disqualification

unfair unfair

Unfall accident

Unfallversicherung casualty insurance; accident insurance

Unfallversorgung casualty compensation

unfein unrefined; crude; gross

unfertig unfinished

unfertige Erzeugnisse goods in process; work in progress

unfreundliche Übernahme hostile takeover

ungebraucht unused; untapped

ungebrochener Güterverkehr through transport system

ungebunden uncommitted; unaffiliated

ungedeckt uncovered; *(Schulden)* unsecured

ungeeignet unsuitable

ungekürzt unabbreviated; *(Buchausgabe)* unabridged

ungelernt unskilled

ungelernter Arbeiter unskilled worker; laborer

ungelöst unresolved

ungenau inexact; sketchy

ungenügend insufficient; deficient

ungenutzt unutilized; unused

ungerechnet uncounted

ungerecht unjust

ungerechtfertigt unjustified

Ungerechtigkeit injustice; inequity

ungeschäftlich unbusinesslike

ungeschlichtet unresolved; *(Konflikt)* not arbitrated

ungesetzlich illegal

ungesetzlich machen to outlaw

ungesichert unsecured

ungesicherte Position *(Börse)* naked position

ungesicherter Gläubiger unsecured creditor

ungewiss uncertain; *(vieldeutig)* ambiguous

Ungewissheit uncertainty; *(Vieldeutigkeit)* ambiguity

ungewöhnlich unusual

ungezielte Informationssuche undirected information search

ungleich unequal

ungleichartig disparate

Ungleichgewicht imbalance; disequilibrium

Ungleichheit inequality; *(Ungleichartigkeit)* disparity; *(Verschiedenheit)* diversity

Unglück misfortune; *(Desaster)* disaster

Unglücksfall accident; mishap

ungültig invalid

Ungültigkeit invalidity

Ungültigkeitserklärung cancellation

ungültig machen to void; to invalidate

ungünstig unfavorable; adverse

Uniform uniform

Universalbank universal bank; full service bank

unkalkulierbar incalculable; *(unvorhersehbar)* unforeseeable

unklar unclear; *(vieldeutig)* ambiguous

unklug imprudent

Unkostengebühr service charge

unkündbar *(Personal)* not dismissible; *(Vertrag)* uncancellable; *(Börse)* noncallable

unlösbar irresolvable

unmessbar not measurable

unmittelbar direct; immediate

unmittelbare Familie immediate family

unnormal abnormal

Unordnung disorder

unparteiisch impartial; fair

unpraktisch impractical

unproduktiv unproductive; nonproductive

unrealisiert unrealized

unrecht wrong; *(Tat)* unethical

Unrecht injustice

unrechtmäßig unlawful; illegal

unreell *(unehrlich)* dishonest; *(unzuverlässig)* unreliable

unrentabel unprofitable; uneconomical

unrichtig incorrect

Unruhe restlessness; unrest; *(Störung)* disturbance

unschlichtbar irresolvable

unselbständig dependent

unseriös not respectable; untrustworthy

unsicher uncertain; precarious; *(Person)* unsure; insecure

Unsicherheit uncertainty; precariousness

Unsicherheitsfaktor uncertainty factor

Unsicherheitsvermeidung uncertainty avoidance

unsicher machen to render uncertain; to destabilize

unsolide unsound; *(unzuverlässig)* unreliable

unstabil unstable; *(unsicher)* insecure

unstetig volatile

unsystematisches Risiko unsystematic risk

untätig idle

Untätigkeit idleness

untauglich unusable; *(ungeeignet)* unsuitable

unten below; *(Treppe)* downstairs

unter under; below

Unterabteilung subdivision; subpart

Unterabschreibung underdepreciation

Unterangebot insufficient supply

Unterausschuss subcommittee

unterbauen to support; to underpin

Unterbeschäftigung underemployment

unterbesetzt understaffed

unterbewerten to undervalue; to underprice

unterbewertet undervalued

unterbezahlt underpaid

unterbieten to underbid; to undercut

unterbrechen to interrupt; *(Verhandlung)* to suspend; *(Störung)* to disrupt; *(aufhören)* to discontinue

Unterbrechung interruption; stoppage

unterbreiten to submit; *(präsentieren)* to present

unterbringen to house; *(platzieren)* to place; *(Übernachtung)* to accommodate

Unterbringung housing; *(Platzierung)* placement; *(Übernachtung)* accommodation

unter dem Marktpreis verkaufen to sell below market price

unter der Norm substandard

unter Druck setzen to pressure; to squeeze

unterdrücken to suppress; *(ersticken)* to stifle

unterdurchschnittlich below average; substandard

unterentwickelt underdeveloped

Unterentwicklung underdevelopment

Unterfangen undertaking

Untergebener subordinate

untergeordnet subordinate

untergliedern to subdivide

Untergliederung subdivision; *(Kategorie)* subcategorization

untergraben to undermine

Unterhalt livelihood; maintenance; *(Unterstützung)* support

unterhalten to support; *(Unterhalt)* to maintain; *(Unterhaltung)* to entertain

Unterhaltskosten upkeep expenses; maintenance costs

Unterhaltszahlung support payment

Unterhändler negotiator

unterkapitalisiert undercapitalized

Unterkonto subaccount

Unterkunft accommodation; living quarters

Unterlage document; paper

unterlassen to refrain from

Unterlassung omission; *(Befolgung)* failure

unterlegen inferior

Unterlieferant subcontractor

untermauern to underpin; *(unterstützen)* to support; *(verstärken)* to strengthen

Untermiete sublease; subtenancy

unterminieren to undermine

unternehmen to undertake

Unternehmen enterprise; *(Firma)* firm; *(Konzern)* concern; *(Gesellschaft)* company

Unternehmen, abhäniges controlled enterprise; dependent company

Unternehmen, angegliedertes affiliated company

Unternehmen, beteiligtes participating company

Unternehmen, einheimisches domestic enterprise

Unternehmen, gewerbliches business enterprise; commercial establishment

Unternehmen, konsolidiertes consolidated company

Unternehmen, mit hohen Liquiditätsreserven cash cow

Unternehmensberater management consultant; corporate consultant

Unternehmensbereich devision; sector

Unternehmensbericht company report

Unternehmensbewertung valuation of a company; operations audit

Unternehmensethik ethical business

Unternehmensform corporate organization; type of business ownership

Unternehmensführung business management

Unternehmensführung mit Zielvorgabe management by objectives (MBO)

Unternehmenskontrolle management control

Unternehmenskonzept corporate concept

Unternehmenskultur corporate culture; organizational culture

Unternehmensleitung company management

Unternehmensmerkmale corporate characteristics

Unternehmensplanung corporate planning

Unternehmenspolitik corporate policy

Unternehmensstrategie corporate strategy

Unternehmensstruktur corporate structure

Unternehmenszusammenschluss merger; combination

Unternehmer entrepreneur

unternehmerisch entrepreneurial

unternehmerisches Risiko entrepreneurial risk; business risk

Unternehmerlohn entrepreneurial profit

Unternehmerlohn, kalkulatorischer imputed entrepreneurial profit

Unternehmerschaft body of entrepreneurs; businesspeople

Unternehmertum entrepreneurship

Unternehmerverband entrepreneurs' association; businessmen's association

Unternehmerverhalten entrepreneurial behavior

Unternehmung (*Projekt*) undertaking; *(Wagnis)* venture; *(Betrieb)* operation; *(Unternehmen)* enterprise

Unternehmungspolitik corporate policy

unter Nennwert below par

unterordnen to subordinate

Unterorganisation subsidiary organization; *(Tochtergesellschaft)* subsidiary

unter pari below par

Unterredung interview

Unterricht instruction

unterrichten to inform; *(lehren)* to teach

Unterrichtung briefing

untersagen to prohibit; *(verbieten)* to forbid

Untersagung prohibition

unterschätzen to underestimate; to undervalue

unterscheidbar distinguishable; capable of being differentiated

unterscheiden to distinguish; *(differenzieren)* to differentiate

unterscheiden, sich to differ

unterscheidend discriminating

Unterscheidung differentiation; discrimination

Unterscheidungsvermögen ability to discriminate; discrimination

Unterschied difference

unterschiedlich different; variable; varied

unterschiedlich behandeln to discriminate

Unterschiedlichkeit difference; dissimilarity

Unterschiedsbetrag difference

Unterschiedsmerkmal differential

unterschlagen to embezzle; to defraud; to missapply

Unterschlagung embezzlement; fraud; misappropriation

unterschreiben *(Dokument)* to sign

unterschreiten to undercut; to go below

Unterschrift signature; *(Bild)* caption

Unterschuss shortfall; *(Defizit)* deficit

Unterspalte subcategory; subdivision

unterstellen to impute

unterstützen to support; to back; *(Antrag, Bewerbung)* to endorse

unterstützt supported

Unterstützung support; backing; *(Gönnertum)* patronage; *(Antrag)* endorsement; *(Hilfe)* assistance; aid

Unterstützungslinie support level

Unterstützungsdarlehen assistance loan

untersuchen to investigate; to examine; *(erforschen)* to explore; to probe; *(testen)* to test

Untersucher investigator; *(Prüfer)* examiner

Untersuchung investigation; test; *(Arzt)* examination

Untersuchungsgebühr investigation fee

unterteilen to subdivide

unterweisen to instruct

Unterweisung instruction

unterwerfen to subject; to subordinate; *(sich ~)* to submit oneself

Unterwerfung subjection; submission; *(Unterjochung)* subjugation

unterzeichnen to sign

Unterzeichner signatory

Unterzeichnung signing

untragbar unbearable; prohibitive

unübertroffen unsurpassed; preeminent

Unumgänglichkeit inevitability; *(Notwendigkeit)* necessity

unumschränkt sovereign; absolute

ununterbrochen uninterrupted; nonstop

ununtersucht uninvestigated; unexplored

unverändert unchanged

unverbindlich not binding; not obligatory; *(Umgang)* unaccommodating

unverbundene Akquisition conglomerate acquisition

unverfallbare Anwartschaften vested benefits

unvereinbar irreconcilable; disparate

unverhältnismäßig disproportionate

unverkäuflich unsalable

unverkauft unsold

unvermeidbar unavoidable

unvermeidbares Risiko nondiversifiable risk

Unvermögen inability; *(Untauglichkeit)* disqualification

unveröffentlicht unpublished

unverpackt not packaged; *(lose)* close; in bulk

unverpfändet unpledged

unversehrt undamaged; sound

Unversehrtheit soundness; integrity

unversichert uninsured; *(ungedeckt)* uncovered

unvertretbar unjustifiable; unwarranted

unverwendbar unusable; unworkable

unverwertbar unusable

unverwertet unutilized; *(Ressourcen)* untapped

unverzinslich noninterest-bearing

unverzinst not subject to interest; no-interest

unverzüglich prompt; *(sofort)* immediate

unvollendet unfinished

unvollständig incomplete

unvoreingenommen unprejudiced; *(unparteiisch)* impartial

unvorhergesehen unexpected

unvorsichtig careless; *(unklug)* imprudent

unwesentlich unessential; immaterial

unwiderruflich irrevocable

unwiderrufliches Treuhandverhältnis irrevocable trust

unwirksam ineffective; inefficient; *(ungültig)* invalid

Unwirksamkeit ineffectiveness; *(Ungültigkeit)* invalidity

unwirtschaftlich uneconomical; non-viable

Unwirtschaftlichkeit non-viability

Unzufriedenheit dissatisfaction

unzufrieden machen to dissatisfy

unzulänglich inadequate; deficient

Unzulänglichkeit inadequacy

unzulässig inadmissible; *(verboten)* prohibited

unzureichend insufficient; *(unzulänglich)* deficient

unzuverlässig unreliable

Urabstimmung plebiscite; ballot vote

Urheber originator; creator; *(Autor)* author

Urheberrecht copyright

Urkunde certificate; record; document

urkundlich festgelegt documented

Urlaub leave; *(Ferien)* vacation

Urlauber vacationer

Urlaubsort vacation resort

Ursache cause

ursächlich causal

Urschrift original

Ursprung source; origin

ursprünglich primary; original

Ursprungsland country of origin

Ursprungszeugnis certificate of origin

Urteil oppinion; *(Gericht)* sentence; verdict; judgment

urteilen to judge

Urteilsfähigkeit ability to judge

Urteilsspruch verdict; *(Urteil, Strafe)* sentence; *(gerichtliche Entscheidung)* judgment

Urteilsvermögen ability to judge

Usance usage

Utilitarismus utilitarianism

V

Valuta medium of exchange; currency

Valutaabschluss currency transaction

Valutabescheinigung estoppel certificate

Valutakonto currency account

Valutakurs exchange rate

Vallutanachweis modification note

variabel variable; *(fluktuierend)* fluctuating

variable Kosten variable costs

Variante variable

Variantenstückliste list of variants

Varianz der Wahrscheinlichkeitsverteilung variance of the probability distribution

variable Entgeltsystem variable-pay programs

variabler Intervallplan variable-interval schedule

variabler Quotenplan variable-ratio schedule

variieren to vary; *(diversifizieren)* to diversify

verabreden to agree upon

Verabredung date; *(Termin)* appointment

verabschieden to dismiss; *(Gesetz)* to pass

verabschieden, sich to take one's leave; to say goodbye

Verabschiedung *(Gesetz)* passage

veraltet superannuated; obsolete; *(Mode)* out of fashion

veränderlich changeable; adjustable; *(Kurs)* sliding

verändern to change; to alter; *(anpassen)* to adjust; *(umwandeln)* to convert

Veränderung change; *(Umänderung)* alteration

Veränderungsrate rate of change

veranlassen to cause; to bring about; *(dazu bringen)* to induce; to prompt

veranschaulichen to illustrate

Veranschaulichung illustration

Veranschlagung estimate

veranstalten to stage; *(präsentieren)* to present; *(Gastgeber)* to host; to arrange

Veranstalter organizer; *(Produzent)* producer; *(Gastgeber)* host; *(Sponsor)* sponsor

Veranstaltung performance; presentation

verantwortlich responsible; *(rechenschaftspflichtig)* accountable; *(haftpflichtig)* liable

Verantwortlichkeit responsibility; *(Rechenschaftspflicht)* accountability

Verantwortlichkeitsrechnung responsibility accounting

Verantwortung responsibility

Verantwortungsbereich area of responsibility; *(Kompetenz)* area of competence; *(Arbeitsgebiet, Ressort)* province

verarbeitbar processable; easy to handle

verarbeiten to process; to use

Verarbeitung processing; *(Fertigung)* manufacture

verausgaben *(ausgeben)* to spend; *(erschöpfen)* to exhaust

verausgabt spent; *(physisch)* exhausted

veräußern to dispose of; to divest; *(verkaufen)* to sell

Veräußerung divestiture; sale

Veräußerungswert residual value; salvage value

verbal verbal

Verband organization; confederation; *(Handel)* trade association

Verbandsarbeit association work

Verbandsbezirk association district; *(Gewerkschaft)* union district

Verbandssatzung articles of association

Verbandsvertreter association representative

Verbandszeitung trade newspaper

verbergen to hide

verbessern to improve; *(höher einstufen)* to upgrade; *(intensivieren)* to enhance

verbessernd corrective

verbessert improved; revised; *(erhöht)* upgraded

Verbesserung improvement; enhancement; *(Schrift)* correction

verbieten to forbid; *(untersagen)* to prohibit

verbilligen to cheapen; *(Preis reduzieren)* to reduce in price

Verbilligung price reduction

verbinden to link; *(zusammentun)* to join; *(Unternehmen)* to associate; *(Telefon)* to connect

verbindlich obligatory; *(Umgang)* obliging

Verbindlichkeit debt; obligation; *(Passiva)* liability; *(Verpflichtung)* commitment

Verbindlichkeiten *(Buchführung)* accounts payable

Verbindlichkeiten aus Aktzeptkrediten acceptance liabilities

Verbindlichkeiten aus der Ausstellung eigener Wechsel notes payable

Verbindlichkeiten gegenüber Banken bank debts

Verbindlichkeiten gegenüber Kunden ammounts owed to depositors

Verbindlichkeiten abdecken to meet liabilities

Verbindlichkeiten begleichen to discharge liabilities

Verbindlichkeiten nachkommen to meet obligations

Verbindlichkeit mit kurzer Restlaufzeit maturing liability

Verbindung connection; contact; *(Gesellschaft)* association; *(Kombination)* combination; *(Information)* communication

Verbindungsglieder liaisons

Verbleib whereabouts

Verbleibsnachweis proof of whereabouts

Verbot prohibition; prescription; ban

Verbrauch consumption; usage

verbrauchen to consume; *(aufbrauchen)* to use up

Verbraucher *(Konsument)* consumer; *(Benutzer)* user

Verbraucherbelastung consumer burden

Verbrauchergroßmarkt hypermarket

Verbrauchermarkt consumer market; convenience store

Verbrauchernachfrage consumer demand

Verbraucherpreis consumer price

Verbraucherpreisindex consumer price index

Verbraucherschutz consumer protection

Verbraucherumfrage consumer survey

Verbraucherverband consumer association

Verbraucherverhalten consumer behavior

verbrauchsabhängig usage-bound

Verbrauchsland country of consumption

Verbrauchsmaterial consumables

Verbrauchssteuer consumption tax; excise tax

Verbrauchs- und Aufwandssteuer excise tax

Verbrauchsstichprobe random sample of consumption

Verbrauchsstruktur consumption pattern

verbreiten to spread; *(streuen)* to disperse; to disseminate

Verbreitung spread; *(Vorkommen)* incidence; *(Information)* dissemination

verbrieft certified; chartered; *(lizenziert)* licensed; *(zugesichert)* guaranteed

verbriefte Bankeinlagen certificate of deposit

verbringen *(Zeit)* to spend

verbuchen to post; *(eintragen)* to enter

verbünden to ally

verbundene Netzwerke affiliate networks

Verbündeter ally

Verbundverkauf cross-selling

Verbundvorteile economies of scope

verbürgen to warrant

verbürgt warranted

verdanken to owe

verdeckt hidden; covered

verderblich perishable

verdienen *(Geld, Respekt)* to earn; *(berechtigt sein)* to merit; *(gewinnen)* to gain

Verdiener earner

Verdienst *(Einkommen)* earnings; *(Leistung)* merit; credit

Verdienstspanne margin of earnings

Verdienstzuwachs growth in earnings; *(Gewinn)* profit increase

verdoppeln to double

verdrängen to displace; to squaze out; to replace; to eliminate

Verdrängungswettbewerb crowding out; cutthroat competition

Veredeler *(Fabrikation)* processor

veredeln *(verarbeiten)* to process; *(verfeinern)* to refine; *(verbessern)* to improve; *(fertig stellen)* to finish

Veredelung refinement; *(Verbesserung)* improvement

Verein association; *(Gesellschaft)* society; *(Klub)* club; *(Gewerkschaft)* union

vereinbar compatible

vereinbaren to arrange; *(ausbedingen)* to stipulate; to agree

Vereinbarung arrangement; *(Ausbedingung)* stipulation; *(Übereinkommen)* agreement

vereinen to unite; *(Ziele)* to combine

vereinheitlichen to standardize

vereinheitlicht standardized

Vereinheitlichung standardization

vereinigen to unite; *(zusammenlegen)* to join; *(konsolidieren)* to consolidate

vereinigt united; consolidated

Vereinigung union; coalition

vereinnahmen to take in; (*empfangen)* to receive

Vereinte Nationen United Nations (UN)

vereiteln *(verhindern)* to prevent; *(besiegen)* to defeat

verewigen to perpetuate

Verfahren procedure; *(Gericht)* proceedings; *(Prozess)* process; practice; method

Verfahren einstellen to dismiss an action

Verfahrensgang procedural process

Verfahrensgerechtigkeit procedural justice

Verfahrenskonflikte process conflict

Verfahrensprinzip procedural principle

Verfahrensrecht procedural law

verfahrensrechtlich procedural

Verfahrenstechniker process technician

Verfahrensweg procedural path

Verfahrensweise procedural method

Verfall *(Wertpapier)* lapse; *(Zusammenbruch)* collapse; *(Verderben)* ruination

verfallen *(überfällig werden)* to lapse; *(Gebäude)* to go to ruin

verfallenen Option lapsed option

verfallen lassen to forfeit; *(Gebäude)* to allow to go to ruin

Verfallsdatum expiration date

Verfallszeit maturity

verfälschen *(Waren)* to adulterate; *(Urkunde)* to falsify

Verfälschung adulteration; tampering

Verfahren operation; practice; procedure; method

Verfahrens- procedural

Verfahrensablauf procedure

Verfahrensdauer duration of proceedings

Verfahrensfehler procedural error

Verfahrensnummer processing number

Verfahrensrecht procedural law

Verfassung *(Zustand)* condition; *(Gesetz)* constitution

verfassungsmäßig constitutional

verfechten to maintain; to advocate; to contend

Verfechter advocate; champion

verfehlen to miss

verfeinern to refine

Verfeinerung refinement

Verfertiger manufacturer; maker

Verfertigung manufacture

Verflechtung *(Abhängigkeit)* interdependence; *(Verstrickung)* entanglement; *(Vernetzung)* meshing

verflochten interwoven; *(gegenseitig abhängig)* interdependent

verflüssigen to liquidate

Verflüssigung liquidation

verfolgen to pursue; to persecute; *(Plan, Absicht)* to follow

verfrachten to fraight, to consign; to ship

Verfrachter consigner; shipper; carrier

verfrüht premature

verfügbar available

verfügbare Anlagemöglichkeiten opportunity set

verfügbarer Vermögenswert available asset

verfügbares Einkommen disposable income

Verfügbarkeit availability

Verfügbarkeitsklausel disposition clause

verfügen to dispose; to direct; *(Gericht)* to rule

Verfügung rule; provision; *(Verordnung)* ordinance; *(Anordnung)* disposition; directive

Verfügungsgewalt power of disposal; control

Verfügungsrecht title

Vergabe giving away; *(Auftrag)* placing; *(Stipendium)* awarding

Vergangenheit past

vergeben to give away; *(Auftrag)* to place; *(Kontrakt)* to award

vergeblich in vain

vergelten to retaliate; to repay

Vergeltung retaliation; repayment

Vergeltungszoll retaliatory tariff

vergeuden to squander; *(verschwenden)* to waste; *(zerstreuen)* to dissipate

Vergleich comparison; *(Schlichtung)* compromise; arrangement

vergleichbar comparable

Vergleichbarkeit comparability

vergleichen to compare

vergleichend comparative

Vergleichsanmeldung settlement declaration

Vergleichsantrag settlement petition

Vergleichsbilanz comparative balance sheet

Vergleichseffekt contrast effect

Vergleichsjahr basis year

Vergleichsverfahren settlement proceedings; *(Bankrott)* insolvency proceedings

Vergleichsverwalter settlement trustee

vergleichsweise comparatively; by way of comparison

vergrößern to enlarge; *(vermehren)* to augment

Vergrößerung enlargement; *(Wachstum)* growth; *(Zunahme)* augmentation

Vergünstigung privilege; *(Vorteil)* benefit

vergüten to remunerate; *(kompensieren)* to recompense

Vergütung remuneration; *(Entgelt)* recompense; *(Entschädigung)* compensation; allowance

verhaften to arrest

Verhalten conduct; behavior

verhalten, sich to conduct oneself; to behave; to act

Verhaltensänderung behavior modification

Verhaltensformung shaping behavior

Verhaltensgitter managerial grid

Verhaltensmodifikation behavior modification

Verhaltensnorm behavioral norm

Verhaltenssteuerung behavior control

Verhaltenstheorien der Führung behavioral theory of leadership

verhaltensverankerte Beurteilungs-skalen behaviorally anchored rating scales

Verhaltensweise behavioral pattern

Verhältnis relation; *(Proportion)* proportion; *(Beziehung)* relationship

verhältnismäßig relative; *(Proportion)* proportional; proportionate

Verhältniswert ratio

verhandelbar negotiable

verhandeln to negotiate; *(aushandeln)* to bargain

Verhandlung negotiation; *(Anhörung)* hearing; *(Strafrecht)* trial

verhandlungsbereit ready to negotiate

verhandlungsfähig negotiable

Verhandlungsgeschick negotiating skill

Verhandlungsmacht negotiating power

Verhandlungsordnung protocol

Verhandlungspartner negotiator

Verhandlungsrunde round of negotiations; *(Löhne)* bargaining round

Verhandlungsstärke bargaining strength

Verhandlungsziel negotiation goal

verheerend ruinous; desastrous

verheimlichen to keep something secret; *(verstecken)* to hide; to conceal

verhindern to prevent

Verhinderung prevention

verhören to interrogate; to question

Verhör interrogation; questioning

verhüten to prevent

Verhütung prevention

Verkauf sale

Verkauf aus zweiter Hand resale

verkaufen to sell

Verkaufen selling

Verkäufer seller; *(Händler)* vendor; *(Handelsvertreter)* sales representative; salesman; salesperson; saleswoman

Verkäufermarkt sellers' market

verkäuflich for sale; *(verkaufsfähig)* salable; marketable

Verkauf mit gleichzeitiger Rückmiete leaseback

Verkaufsagentur dealership

Verkaufsauftrag sell order

Verkaufsbasis sales base

Verkaufsbedingungen terms of sale

Verkaufsberechnung sales calculation

Verkaufsbüro sales office

Verkaufs-Deckungsgeschäft short hedge

Verkaufsergebnis sales result

Verkaufserlös rvevenues; sale proceeds

Verkaufsfiliale sales branch

verkaufsfördernd sales-promotional

Verkaufsförderung sales promotion

Verkaufsgebiet sales district

Verkaufsgemeinschaft sales association

Verkaufsgewinn sales profit

Verkaufshinweis sales lead

Verkaufskurs *(Effekten)* selling price; market price

Verkaufsleitung sales management

Verkaufsmannschaft sales team; sales force

Verkaufsmesse trade fair; merchandisers' fair

Verkaufsniederlassung sales branch

Verkaufsoption seller's option; *(Börse)* put; put option

Verkaufsorganisation sales organization; *(Außendienst)* field sales force

Verkaufsort point of sale

Verkaufspersonal sales force

Verkaufsplan sales plan; merchandising scheme

Verkaufspreis selling price; market price

Verkaufsprogramm sales program

Verkaufspsychologie sales psychology

Verkaufsrecht license to sell

Verkaufssignal sell signal

Verkaufsstand sales stall

Verkaufsstelle retail outlet

Verkaufssteuer sales tax

Verkaufsstrategie sales strategy

Verkaufstipp sales lead

Verkaufs- und Kundendienst sales and customer service

Verkaufsvolumen sales volume

Verkaufszeit selling time; *(Geschäftszeit)* business hours

verkauft sold

Verkehr traffic; *(Umgang)* association; *(geschäftlich)* dealings

verkehren *(Handel)* to trade; *(Umgang)* to associate

verkehrsfähig negotiable

Verkehrsfähigkeit marketability

Verkehrswesen transportation; *(Beförderung)* transport

verklagen to sue; to take to court

Verknappung scarcity; shortage; stringency

verkürzen to shorten; *(Text)* to abbreviate; *(Rechte)* to curtail; *(vermindern)* to reduce

Verkürzung shortening; *(Text)* abbreviation; *(Lohn)* reduction; *(Rechte)* curtailment

verladen to load; to ship

Verladen loading; *(Spedition)* shipping

Verlader *(Spediteur)* shipper

Verladung loading; *(Spedition)* shipping

verlagern to relocate; to shift

Verlagerung shift; dislocation; *(neu lagern)* relocation

verlangen to require; to demand

verlängern to prolong; to extend; *(Kontrakt)* to renew

Verlängerung prolongation; extension; *(Kontrakt)* renewal

verlängerungsfähig renewable

verlangsamen to slow down; to retard; to decelerate

Verlangsamung slowdown; deceleration

verlassen to leave; to abandon

Verlassen leaving; abandonment; pullout

verlässlich reliable; dependable

Verlässlichkeit reliability; dependability

Verlauf progress; course; *(Zeit)* passing

verlaufen *(Vorgang)* to progress; *(Zeit)* to pass

verlegen to misplace; *(Buch)* to publish; *(Zustand)* embarrassed

Verlegenheit dilemma; embarrassment

Verleger publisher

verleihen to lend; to loan; *(Titel)* to confer

Verleiher lender; *(Kredit)* credit grantor; *(Pfand)* pawnbroker

Verleihung grant; *(Titel)* conferment

verletzen to hurt; to injure; *(Vorschrift, Regel)* to violate

Verletzung injury; *(Vorschrift)* violation; infringement; *(Bruch)* breach

Verleumdung libel; slander

verlieren to lose; *(verwirken)* to forfeit

Verlierer loser

verloren gehen to become lost; *(verschwinden)* to disappear

verlosen to draw; to raffle

Verlosung drawing

Verlust loss; *(Schaden)* damage; *(Defizit)* deficit

Verlustabzug deductible loss

Verlustausgleich loss adjustment; offsetting losses

verlustbringend loss-generating; losing

Verlustgefahr risk of loss

Verlustrechnung loss accounting

Verlustrücktrag carryback; carryover

Verlustträger loss-maker

Verlust vor Steuern pretax loss

Verlustvortrag (*Buchführung*) debit carryover; loss brought forward; loss carryforward

Verlustzone loss area

vermarkten to market

Vermarktung marketing

vermehren to increase; to augment

Vermehrung increase; augmentation

vermeidbar avoidable

vermeidbares Risiko diversifiable risk

vermeiden to avoid; *(umgehen)* to sidestep; to dodge

vermeidlich avoidable

Vermerk notation

vermerken to note; *(bestätigen)* to endorse

vermieten to rent; *(verpachten)* to lease; to let

Vermieter lessor; *(Mietsherr)* landlord

vermindern to decrease; *(reduzieren)* to reduce

verminderter Wert reduced value; discounted value

Verminderung decrease; reduction; diminution; *(Ausgaben)* retrenchment

vermischen to mix

vermischt mixed; *(verschiedenartig)* miscellaneous

vermissen to miss

vermitteln to mediate

Vermittler mediator; intermediary; *(Unterhändler)* negotiator; *(Moderator)* moderator

Vermittlung *(Verhandlung)* mediation; *(Stelle)* placement; intercession

Vermittlungsgeschäft brokerage

Vermittlungsprovision comission

Vermittlungsverfahren conciliation proceedings

Vermittlungsversuch mediation attempt

Vermögen wealth; fortune; *(Aktiva)* assets; *(Besitz)* property; *(Macht)* power

vermögend wealthy

Vermögensangabe declaration of assets

Vermögensanlage investment of assets

Vermögensbildung formation of wealth

Vermögensertrag yield on assets

Vermögenserwerb acquisition of assets

Vermögensgegenstand asset

Vermögensmasse estate

vermögensrechtlich proprietary

Vermögenssteuer property tax; personal tax

Vermögensübertragung asset transfer; capital transfer

Vermögensverhältnisse financial circumstances

Vermögensverwalter portfolio manager; money manager

Vermögenswert financial worth; property value; asset

vermögenswirksam asset-creating

Vermögenszuwachs capital growth; capital appreciation

Vermutung presumption; *(Annahme)* assumption

vernachlässigen to neglect

veröffentlichen *(Presse)* to publish; *(Information)* to release

Veröffentlichung publication

verordnen *(Arzt)* to prescribe; *(Erlass)* to decree

Verordnung ordinance; decree; *(Klausel)* provision

verpachten to lease; to let

Verpächter lessor; *(Pachtherr)* landlord

Verpachtung lease

verpacken to package; *(einpacken)* to pack; *(Karton)* to box

Verpackungsindustrie packaging industry

verpassen to miss

verpfänden to pledge; to mortgage; to hypothecate

Verpfändung pawning; *(Grundbesitz)* hypothecation

Verpfändungsvereinbarung hypothecation agreement

Verpflegung food; board; provisions

verpflichten to obligate; *(vertraglich)* to bind; *(zu Dank)* to oblige; *(anstellen)* to engage

verpflichten, sich to undertake

verpflichtet obligated; *(haftbar)* liable; *(verschuldet)* indebted

Verpflichtung commitment; *(zu einer Leistung)* obligation; *(gesetzlich)* liability; covenant; *(Schulden)* indebtedness

Verpflichtungserklärung undertaking

Verquickung involvement

verrechnen to offset; to set off; *(abrechnen)* to clear; *(ausgleichen)* to balance

verrechnen, sich to miscalculate

Verrechnung offset; *(Abrechnung)* clearance; clearing

Verrechnungseinheit clearing unit

Verrechnungskonto claering account; settlement account

Verrechnungskonto in Drittwährung offset account

Verrechnungspreis transfer price

Verrechnungssaldo clearing balance; *(Scheckverkehr)* clearinghouse balance

Verrechnungsscheck nonnegotiable check; voucher check

Verrechnungsverkehr clearing system

verrichten to perform

Verrichtung *(Aufgabe)* performance

verringern to decrease; to downsize; *(reduzieren)* to reduce; *(erschöpfen)* to deplete

Verringerung reduction; decrease; cutback

versagen to fail; to flop; *(Maschine)* to break down

versammeln to assemble

versammeln, sich to congregate; *(Kongress, Konferenz)* to convene

Versammlung assembly; *(Sitzung)* meeting

Versand shipping; dispatch; transportation

Versand gegen Nachnahme collect on delivery (c.o.d.)

versandfähig transportable

Versandhandel mail order trade; direct mail selling

Versandhaus catalog firm; mail-order firm

Versandpapiere shipping documents; dispatch papers

Versandschein consignment note; certificate of shipment

Versandtermin shipping date; date of dispatch

versäumen *(Pflicht)* to neglect; *(Termin)* to miss

Versäumnis neglect; omission

Verschachtelung interlocking; *(Verkaufspyramide)* pyramiding

verschaffen *(beschaffen)* to procure; *(versorgen)* to provide; *(liefern)* to supply

verschärfen to tighten

Verschärfen tightening

verschärft tightened

Verschärfung *(Gesetz)* strengthening; *(Beschränkung)* tightening

verschenken to give away

verschicken to ship; to dispatch; to mail; to send out

verschieben to shift; to dislocate

Verschiebung shift; dislocation; *(Termin)* change

verschieden different; *(ungleichartig)* diverse

verschiedenartig various; diverse; *(verschieden)* different

Verschiedenartigkeit diverseness

Verschiedenheit disparity; diversity

Verschiffer shipper

Verschiffung shipping; shipment

verschlechtern to worsen; (*beeinträchtigen)* to impair

Verschlechterung worsening; deterioration; *(Rückschlag)* setback; *(Verfall)* decline

verschleiern to obscure; *(verbergen)* to conceal

Verschleierung concealment; disguise; cover-up

Verschleiss wear and tear

verschleissen to wear out

verschleudern *(Ressourcen)* to squander; to waste; *(verkaufen)* to undersell; to dump

Verschleudern squandering; *(Verschwenden)* wasting

verschleudert (*Ressource*) squandered; *(verschwendet)* wasted

verschlimmern to aggravate

verschlimmern, sich to worsen

Verschluss closure; *(Aufbewahrung)* safekeeping

Verschlüsselung encryption

Verschmelzung merger

Verschmutzung pollution

verschreiben to prescribe

verschulden to cause; to be responsible for; *(Geld)* to incur debts

Verschulden fault; blame

verschuldet indebted; *(Unternehmen)* leveraged

Verschuldung indebtedness; *(Verbindlichkeit)* liability; *(Schuld)* debt

Verschuldungsfähigkeit debt capacity

Verschuldungsgrad debt ratio

Verschuldungsgrenze debt ceiling

Verschuldungskrise debt crisis

verschwenden to waste; *(vergeuden)* to squander

Verschwenden wasting

verschwenderisch wasteful

verschwendet wasted; *(vergeudet)* squandered

Verschwendung waste; squandering

verschwinden to vanish; to disappear

Versehen error; *(Fehler)* mistake

versenden to send

Versenden sending; *(Verladung)* shipping

Versender shipper

versenken to sink

Versicherer insurer; *(Agent)* insurance underwriter; *(Lieferer)* insurance provider; *(Träger)* insurance carrier

versichern to insure; to underwrite; *(beteuern)* to assure

Versicherung insurance; underwriting; *(Zusicherung)* assurance; guarantee; promise

Versicherungsagent insurance agent; underwriter

Versicherungsbeitrag insurance contribution; insurance premium

Versicherungsfirma insurance company

Versicherungsnehmer insured person; policyholder

Versicherungspolice insurance policy

Versicherungsschaden insured loss

Versicherungsschein policy; certificate of insurance; insurance policy

Versicherungsschutz insurance coverage

Versicherungsträger insurance carrier; insurer

Versicherungswert *(Nominalwert)* face value of policy; *(Barwert)* cash value

versöhnen to reconcile

versorgen to provide for; *(liefern)* to supply

versorgend supplying

Versorgung supply; *(Dienstleistung)* service

Versorgungsunternehmen utility; public utility

verspätet late

versprechen to promise

Versprechen promise

verstaatlichen to nationalize

Verstaatlichung nationalization

verstädtern to urbanize

Verstädterung urbanization

Verständigung understanding; *(Übereinkommen)* accommodation

verstärken to reinforce; to strengthen; *(intensivieren)* to intensify

Verstärker *(Radio)* amplifier; *(Linse)* magnifier

verstärkt reinforced; strengthened; *(vermehrt)* increased; *(Radio)* amplified; *(intensiviert)* intensified

Verstärkung reinforcement; strengthening; *(Nachschub)* reinforcements

Verstärkungstheorie reinforcement theory

verstecken to hide

versteigern to auction

Versteigerung auction; public sale

versteuern to pay taxes on

verstorben deceased

Verstoß violation; *(Verletzung)* infringement; *(Bruch)* breach; contravention

Versuch attempt; *(Test)* test; *(Experiment)* experiment

versuchen to try; to attempt

Versuchsanlage pilot plant

Versuchsmarkt test market; trial market

Versuchsreihe experimental series

versuchsweise experimentally; tentatively

versüßen to sweeten

vertagen to defer; to postpone; *(Komitee)* to table; *(Gerichtsverhandlung)* to continue

Vertagung postponement; *(Gericht)* continuance; deferment

verteidigen to defend

Verteidigung defense

verteilen *(austeilen, ausstreuen)* to distribute

Verteilernetz distribution network

verteilt angelegt diversely invested

Verteilung distribution

Verteilungsbogen spread sheet

Verteilungsfunktion distribution function

Verteilungsgerechtigkeit equity

Verteilungssystem distribution system

verteuern to incrrease the price; to make more expensive

Verteuerung price increase; rise in price

Vertiefung *(Boden)* depression; *(Einschnitt)* indentation

vertikal vertical

vertikale Akquisition vertical acquisition

vertikale Aufgabenbereicherung job enrichment

vertikale Diversifikation vertical diversification

vertikale Fusion vertical merger

vertikale Integration vertical integration

vertikales Portal vertical portal

Vertrag treaty; *(Kontrakt)* contract; *(Abkommen)* agreement

Vertrag abschließen to close a contract; to contract

verträglich compatible; agreeable

vertraglich contractual

vertragliche Beschränkungen restrictive covenants

Verträglichkeit agreeableness

vertraglich verpflichten to bind by contract; to obligate

vertraglich verpflichten, sich to contract; to undertake

Vertragsabschluß conclusion of an agreement

Vertragsbedingung terms of contract

Vertragsbruch breach of contract

Vertragsentwurf tentative agreement; draft contract

Vertragserfüllung fulfillment; execution of the contract

Vertragserfüllungsgarantie *(Bank)* performance bond, contract bond

vertragsgemäß according to contract

Vertragsklausel contract clause

Vertragspartei contract party

Vertragsstrafe forfeit; penalty

Vertragssumme contract amount

Vertragstext wording of a contract

Vertragsverletzung contract violation; default on contract

Vertragswidrigkeit infringement of contract

vertrauen to trust; to have confidence

Vertrauen trust; confidence

Vertrauensmann *(Repräsentant)* representative; *(Sprecher)* spokesman

Vertrauenswerbung public relations

vertrauenswürdig trustworthy; *(zuverlässig)* reliable; *(angesehen)* reputable

vertrauenswürdiger Dritter trusted third party (TTP)

vertraulich confidential

Vertraulichkeit confidentiality

vertreiben to distribute; to market; *(Konkurrenz)* to drive away

vertretbar defensible; justifiable; *(Argument)* tenable

vertreten to represent; to replace

Vertreter replacement person; *(Repräsentant)* representative; *(Agent)* agent

Vertreterbesuch sales call

Vertreterbezirk sales territory

Vertretung representation; *(Agentur)* agency

Vertrieb marketing; *(Verkauf)* sales; *(Verteilung)* distribution

Vertriebsagentur distributorship

Vertriebsanalyse marketing analysis

Vertriebsbasis marketing base

Vertriebschef sales director; marketing director

Vertriebsformel marketing formula

Vertriebsgebiet sales territory

Vertriebsgemeinschaft sales group

Vertriebsgesellschaft sales company

Vertriebskosten marketing costs

Vertriebsleiter marketing manager

Vertriebsleitung marketing management

Vertriebsnetz distribution network

Vertriebspolitik marketing policy

Vertriebsprovision distribution allowance

Vertriebsstab marketing staff

Vertriebsstelle sales office; outlet

Vertriebsstrategie distribution strategy

Vertriebssystem marketing system; distribution system

Vertriebsweg distribution channel

veruntreuen to embezzle, to missappropriate

Veruntreuung embezzlement; misappropriation

verursachen to cause; *(hervorbringen)* to induce

verurteilen to censure; *(Gericht)* to sentence

vervielfältigen to duplicate; *(kopieren)* to copy

vervollkommnen to perfect

Vervollkommnung perfecting; *(Veredelung)* refining

verwahren to store; to keep

Verwahrer custodian; safekeeper, depository

Verwahrung safekeeping; depositing; *(Obhut)* custody

Verwahrungsort repository

verwalten to administer; *(managen)* to manage; *(leiten)* to govern

verwaltend administrative

Verwalter administrator; *(Manager)* manager

Verwaltung administration; management

Verwaltungs- administrative

Verwaltungsaufgabe administrative task

Verwaltungsaufwand administrative expense

Verwaltungsausgabe administrative expense

Verwaltungsfähigkeiten administrative skills

Verwaltungsgebühr administration fee; *(Unkostengebühr)* service charge

Verwaltungskörper management

verwaltungsmäßig administrative

Verwaltungsrecht administrative law

Verwaltungsstelle administrative office; *(Behörde)* administrative agency

Verwaltungssystem administrative system

verwässern to dilute; to water down

Verwässerung dilution

verwechseln to confuse; *(verkennen)* to mistake; *(durcheinander bringen)* to mix up

verweigern *(Erlaubnis)* to deny; *(Leistung)* to refuse

Verweigerung refusal

Verweis censure; *(Tadel)* reprimand

verweisen to censure

verweisende Seite referring site

verwendbar usable; serviceable; *(zweckmäßig)* appropriate; *(anwendbar)* applicable; *(geeignet)* suitable

verwenden to utilize; to use

Verwendung use; utilization

Verwendungsmöglichkeit use; application

Verwendungszweck purpose; application; intended use

verwerten to use; to utilize; *(Altmaterial)* to recycle

Verwertung exploitation; *(Gebrauch)* utilization; application

Verwertung von Vermögenswerten liquidation

verwickeln to involve; *(verstricken)* to entangle

verwirken to forfeit

verwirklichen to realize

Verwirklichung realization

verwirkt forfeited

Verwirrung confusion; *(Unordnung)* disorder

verwüsten to lay waste; to devastate

Verwüstung devastation

verwüstet devastated; ravaged

Verzehr *(Essen)* consumption

verzeichnen to register; to document; to chronicle

Verzeichnis *(Tabelle)* table; *(Liste)* list; *(Register)* index; catalog

verzerren to distort; *(Daten)* to skew

verzerrt distorted; *(Daten)* skewed

Verzicht renunciation; *(legaler Verzicht)* waiver

Verzicht erklären to renounce; *(freigeben)* to release

Verzicht leisten to waive; *(aufgeben)* to relinquish

Verzichtleistung *(Dokument)* waiver

Verzichtserklärung waiver declaration; release declaration

Verzichtsurkunde release document

verzinsen to charge interest

verzinslich interest-bearing

Verzinsung *(Ertrag)* interest yield; *(Zinssatz)* interest rate; *(Zinszahlung)* interest payment

verzögern to retard; *(aufschieben)* to delay

Verzögern delaying; *(Verlangsamen)* slowing

Verzögerung delay; *(Zurückbleiben)* lag

Verzug *(Zahlung)* default; *(Verzögerung)* delay

Verzugszinsen defaulted interest

Verzweigtheit complexity

Veto veto

Vetorecht veto right

vielfach multiple

Vielfältigkeit multiplicity

vielseitig all-round; versatile; *(multilateral)* multilateral

vielsprachig multilingual

viel versprechend promising

Vielzahl multitude

Vielzweck- multipurpose

Viertel quarter; *(Bezirk)* district

Vierteljahr quarter

Vierteljahresprüfung quarterly review

Vierteljahreszeitschrift quarterly magazine

vierteljährlich quarterly

Virtualisierung virtualization

virtuell virtual

virtuelle Einkaufsstarsse virtual mall

virtuelle Gemeinschaft virtual community

virtuelle Händler virtual merchants

virtuelle Organisation virtual organization

virtuelles Bargeld virtual cash

virtuelles Unternehmen virtual enterprise

virtuelles Team virtual team

visionäre Führung visionary leadership

Vizepräsident vice president

volatil volatile

Volatilität volatility

Volksbank people's bank; credit union

volkseigen owned by the people; publicly owned

Volkseinkommen national income; aggregate income

Volksvermögen national wealth

Volksvertretung representation of the people

Volkswirtschaft national economy

Volkswirtschaft, geschlossene closed economy

volkswirtschaftliche Fundamentalwerte business fundamentals

volkswirtschaftliche Gesamtrechnung national product; macroeconomic accounting

volkswirtschaftliche Frühindikatoren leading economic indicators

volkswirtschaftliches Wachstum economic growth

Volkswirtschaftslehre economics; macroeconomics

Volkszählung census; population census

voll full; *(ganz)* entire

Vollarbeitsplatz full-time position

Vollbeschäftigung full employment

Voll-Containerladung full container load (FCL)

vollbringen to accomplish

vollendet accomplished; perfect; *(fertig)* completed

Vollendung perfection; *(Abschluss)* completion

vollentwickelte Industrie mature industry

Vollindossament full indorsement; endorsement in full; full-term endorsement; unqualified endorsement

Volljährigkeit majority

Vollkasko *(Versicherung)* comprehensive coverage

Vollkaufmann general merchant; registered trader

vollkommen perfect; accomplished; complete

vollkommene Kapitalmärkte perfectly competitive financial markets

Vollkommenheit perfection

Vollkosten full costs

Vollkostenbasis absorbed cost basis

Vollkostenrechnung full cost pricing; absorption costing

Vollmacht power; authority *(Stimmrecht)* proxy; *(Handlungsvollmacht)* power of attorney; *(Mandat)* mandate

Vollmachtsanweisung proxy statement

Vollmachtserklärung letter of authority

Vollmachtsstimmrecht proxy voting power

Vollmitglied regular member

vollständig whole; complete

vollständiges Sortiment complete assortment; full line

vollständige Verwässerung fully diluted

vollstrecken to enforce; *(Urteil)* to execute

Vollstreckung enforcement; *(Urteil)* execution

vollziehen to execute; *(ausführen)* to carry out; to perform

Vollziehung execution; *(Erfüllung)* fulfillment

Vollziehungsbefehl warrant

Volontär intern; trainee

Volumen volume

vorangehen to precede; *(Neuerung)* to pioneer

vorankommen *(Karriere)* to get ahead; *(Fortschritt)* to progress

Voranschlag estimate; *(Berechnung)* calculation

Vorarbeiter foreman; lead worker

vorausberechnen to precalculate; *(Voranschlag)* to project cost

vorausberechnet precalculated; *(Voranschlag)* projected

Vorausberechnung projection

vorausbezahlen to prepay; to pay in advance

Vorausbezahlung prepayment

Voraussage prediction; forecast

voraussagen to predict; to forecast

Vorausschätzung advance estimate; *(Prognose)* prognosis

voraussehbar predictable

voraussetzen to assume; *(Qualifikation)* to require

Voraussetzung premise; prerequisite; *(Annahme)* assumption

Voraussicht foresight

voraussichtlich probable; *(erwartet)* expected

vorauszahlen to advance money; *(im Voraus bezahlen)* to pay in advance; to prepay

Vorauszahlung advance payment

Vorbedingung prerequisite; *(Voraussetzung)* requirement

Vorbehalt reservation; proviso

vorbehalten to reserve

Vorbehaltszahlung conditional payment

vorbereiten to prepare

Vorbereitung preparation

Vorbesitzer previous owner

vorbestellen to order in advance; to reserve; to subscribe

vorbestellt subscribed

Vorbestellung advance booking; reservation; subscription

Vorbild example; *(Ideal)* ideal

Vorbilden training

vorbildlich exemplary

Vorderseite front; *(Gebäude)* face

Vordruck *(Formular)* form; blank

Voreintrittsphase prearrival stage

vorenthalten to withhold; to deprive of

Vorfall occurrence

Vorfälligkeitsklausel acceleration clause

vorfertigen to prefabricate

vorführen *(zeigen)* to show; *(demonstrieren)* to demonstrate

Vorführung *(präsentieren)* presentation; *(demonstrieren)* demonstration

Vorgabe standard; parameter; target

Vorgabezeit standard time; time allowance

Vorgang occurrence; process; *(Angelegenheit)* transaction; *(Verfahren)* procedure

Vorgänger predecessor

vorgeben to pretend; *(simulieren)* to simulate

vorgebildet skilled; trained

vorgegebene Cluster prescribed clusters

vorgehen *(vorausgehen)* to precede; *(Maßnahme ergreifen)* to proceed

Vorgehen approach; *(Methode)* method

Vorgehensweise procedural method

vorgelagert upstream

vorgeplant projected; planned in advance

Vorgeschichte *(Hintergrund)* background; *(Geschichte)* history

vorgesehen scheduled; destined

Vorgesetzter superior; senior; boss

vorhaben to intend

Vorhaben scheme; project; plan

vorhanden existing; existent; *(zur Verfügung)* available; in stock

Vorhandensein existence; *(Verfügbarkeit)* availability

vorherbestimmen to predetermine; *(zum Ziel setzen)* to target

vorherig previous

Vorherrschaft predominance

vorherrschend ruling; predominant

vorhersagbar predictable

Vorhersage prediction; forecast

vorhersagen to predict; to forecast

Vorjahreswert previous year's value

Vorjahreszeitraum previous year; period

vorkalkulieren to calculate in advance

Vorkaufsrecht option; option to buy; preemptive right

Vorkehrung arrangement

Vorkehrungen treffen to make arrangements

vorkommen to occur

Vorkommen incidence; occurrence; *(Bergbau)* deposit

Vorkommnis occurrence

Vorlage *(Unterbreitung)* submission; *(Beispiel)* example; *(Muster)* sample; *(Schablone)* stencil

vorläufig preliminary; tentative; *(provisorisch)* provisional; *(einstweilig)* interim

vorlegen to submit; to present

Vorleistung preparatory effort; *(Zahlung)* payment in advance

Vorlesung lecture

vorliegend present; *(Dokument)* on hand

Vorortszug suburban train; local train

Vorprodukt preliminary product

vorprüfen to pretest; to preview

Vorrang precedence; priority

Vorrangaktien underlying stock

Vorranganteile underlying shares

vorrangig preferential; prior-ranking

vorrangige Verbindlichkeit senior debt

Vorrat store; supply; *(Geld)* fund; *(Anhäufung)* hoard

Vorräte inventory

vorrätig on hand; *(Inventar)* in stock

Vorratshaltung stockpiling

Vorratskredit inventory loan

Vorratslager buffer stock

Vorratsvermögen inventories; stock-in-trade

Vorratswirtschaft stockpiling; inventory management

Vorrecht prerogative; privilege

Vorrichtung device; apparatus; machine

Vorru[illegible] early retirement

Vorsa[illegible]on; *(Beschlussfassung)* reso[illegible]*cht)* intent

Vorsch[illegible]w; *(Aussichten)* outlook

vorschauen to preview

vorschießen *(Geld)* to advance

Vorschlag suggestion; *(schriftlich)* proposal; proposition; *(Angebot)* offer; *(Empfehlung)* recommendation

vorschlagen to suggest; to propose; *(empfehlen)* to recommend

Vorschlagsentwurf draft proposal

Vorschlagsliste recommended list

Vorschlagswesen company suggestion plan

vorschreiben to stipulate; to dictate; *(verordnen)* to prescribe

Vorschrift regulation; directive; *(Regel)* rule; *(Erfordernis)* requirement; *(Verordnung)* precept; prescription

Vorschriftenbuch manual of rules

Vorschuss advance; advance payment; *(Lohn)* wage advance

Vorschussakkreditiv red clause credit

vorschüssige Rente annuity due; annuity in advance

Vorsicht caution; prodence; circumspection

vorsichtig careful; cautious

Vorsichtsmaßnahme precautionary measure

Vorsitz haben to preside; to chair

vorsitzen to preside; to chair

Vorsitzende/r chairwoman; chairman; chairperson

Vorsorge provision; precaution; (*Sparen*) thrift

Vorsorgemaßnahme precautionary measure

Vorsorgesparplan retirement savings plan

vorsorglich precautionary; provident

vorspringen to jump ahead

Vorstand board of management; corporate management

Vorstandschef chief executive officer (CEO)

Vorstandskollege fellow board member

Vorstandsmitglied member of the executive board; corporate officer

Vorstandssekretär executive secretary

Vorstandssitzung board meeting

Vorstandssprecher/in spokesman, spokeswoman, spokesperson of the board

Vorstandsvertrag management contract

Vorstandsvorsitz managing directorship

Vorstandsvorsitzende/r president; chief executive; chairperson of the board

Vorsteher principal; headman; master

vorstellen to present; *(bekannt machen)* to introduce; *(sich ~)* to introduce oneself

Vorstellung *(Bekanntmachung)* introduction; (*Theater*) performancc; *(Idee)* idea; conception; notion

Vorstellungsgespräch job interview; interview

Vorsteuer pretax

Vorsteuerabzug input tax reduction; pre-tax allowance

Vorsteuerpauschale pretax lump sum

Vorsteuergewinn pre-tax profit

Vorstoß thrust; *(Vorrücken, Fortschritt)* advance

vorstoßen to forge ahead; *(vorrücken)* to advance

Vorteil advantage; benefit; *(Gewinn)* profit

vorteilhaft advantageous; beneficial

Vortrag speech; talk; *(Bericht)* report; *(Buchführung)* balance carried forward; *(Umbuchung)* transfer in the books; *(Vorlesung)* lecture

Vortritt precedence

Voruntersuchung preliminary hearing

Vorurteil prejudice

Vorverkauf advance booking; pre-selling

Vorverkaufsrecht preemptive right

vorwärts forward; ahead

vorwärts bringen to advance

vorwärts kommen to advance

Vorwegnahme presumption; *(Voraussehen)* anticipation

vorwegnehmen *(vorgreifen)* to anticipate

vorwiegend predominant; prevailing; prevalent

vorzeitig premature

vorzeitige Ausübung premature exercise

vorziehen to prefer

Vorzug *(Vorteil)* advantage; *(Präferenz)* preference; *(Verdienst)* merit

vorzüglich select; *(erstklassig)* prime; *(überlegen)* superior

Vorzugsaktie preference stock; preferred stock; preferred share

Vorzugsaktie mit variabler Dividende adjustable-rate preferred stock

Vorzugsbehandlung preferential treatment

Vorzugsdividende preferred dividend

Vorzugsobligation senior debenture

W

Waage scales

Waagschale scale

wachsen to grow; to rise

wachsend growing; *(steigend)* rising

wachsende ewige Rente growing perpetuity

Wachstum growth

Wachstumsaktie growth stock

Wachstumsbedingung condition necessary for growth

Wachstumsbranche growth sector

Wachstumsfonds growth fund

Wachstumsimpuls growth impulse

Wachstumskraft growth strength

Wachstumsmodell growth model

Wachstumsmöglichkeit growth opportunity

Wachstumspfad direction of growth; growth path

Wachtumsphase growth stage

Wachstumspolitik growth policy

wachstumspolitisch pertaining to growth policy

Wachstumsproblem growth problem

Wachstumsprognose growth prognosis; growth forecast

Wachstumsprozess growth process

Wachstumsrate growth rate

Wachstumstempo speed of growth

Wachstumstheorie growth theory

Wachstumsvorhersage growth prediction

wagen to dare; *(Kapital)* to venture; *(riskieren)* to risk

Waggonladung carload

Wagnis risk; *(Kapital)* venture

Wagnis, kalkulatorisches imputed risk

Wagniskapital venture capital

Wagniskapitalfonds venture-capital fund

Wahl choice; *(Stimmenabgabe)* election; *(Abstimmung)* vote

Wählbarkeit eligibility; for election

wählen to choose; *(Politik)* to elect; *(sich entscheiden)* to opt for; *(Stimme abgeben)* to vote

Wählerschaft constituency

wahllos indiscriminate; at random

Wahlmöglichkeit option

wahlweise optional

Wahlzettel ballot paper

wahrgenommener Konflikt perceived conflict

wahrnehmbar perceptible; noticeable

wahrnehmen to notice; to discern; *(empfinden)* to perceive; *(ausfindig machen)* to spot

Wahrnehmung perception

wahrscheinlich probable; likely

Wahrscheinlichkeit probability; likelihood

Wahrscheinlichkeitsverteilung probability distribution

Währung currency

Währung, abgewertete devalued currency

Währung, fremde foreign currency

Währung, harte hard currency

Währung, konvertierbare convertible currency

Währung, regulierte managed currency

Währung abwerten to devalue a currency

Währung aufwerten to revalue a currency

Währung stützen to support a currency

Währungsausgleich currency adjustment

Währungsbedarf currency requirement; monetary requirement

Währungsbehörde monetary authority

Währungsebene currency level

Währungseinheit monetary unit

Währungsfonds currency fund; monetary fund

Währungsgewinn currency profit

Währungsguthaben reserve monetary assets

Währungsinstanz monetary authority

Währungsklausel currency clause

Währungskontrollen exchange controls

Währungskorb basket of currencies; basket

Währungskurs currency rate; *(Wechselkurs)* exchange rate

Währungsordnung monetary order

Währungspolitik monetary policy

währungspolitische Größe monetary variable

Währungsreserven currency reserves

Währungsrisiko foreign exchange risk

Währungsstabilität currency stability

Währungssystem currency system

Währungsumrechnung currency translation

Währungsumtausch currency exchange

Wandel change; alteration

Wandelanleihe convertible loan; convertible bond

Wandel erster Ordnung first-order change

Wandel zweiter Ordnung second-order change

wandeln *(ändern)* to change; *(verändern)* to alter

Wandelprämie conversion premium

Wandelschuldverschreibung convertible bond

Wandelverhältnis conversion ratio

wandern to wander; to hike

Wandlungskurs conversion price

Wandlungsprämie conversion premium

Wandlungspreis conversion price

Wandlungsrecht conversion privilege

Wandlungsverhältnis conversion ratio

Ware commodity; *(Erzeugnis)* product; *(Handelsware)* merchandise; *(Güter)* goods; *(Börse)* offering

Waren, abgepackte packaged goods

Waren, bestellte goods on order

Waren, empfindliche sensitive goods

Waren, gemischte mixed goods

Waren, knappe scarce goods

Waren, lebenswichtige essential goods

Waren, leicht verderbliche perishable goods

Waren, zollpflichtige bonded goods

Waren abnehmen to take delivery of goods

Waren absetzen to sell goods

Waren anbieten to offer goods

Waren bestellen to order goods

Waren führen to stock goods; to handle goods

Waren verzollen to clear goods

Warenangebot range of goods

Warenangebotsmischung marketing mix

Wareneinheit unit of goods; merchandise item

Warenexport merchandise export

Warengattung line of goods

Warenhandel merchandising; mercantile trade

Warenhaus department store

Warenkonto goods account; merchandise account

Warenkorb basket of available commodities; basket of goods

Warenkredit commercial credit

Warenliste stock list; tally

Warenpolitik product policy

Warenposten lot

Warenpreis commodity price

Warenprobe sample; pattern

Warenqualität product quality

Warenschuld commercial debt

Warensendung shipment; consignment

Warenterminbörse commodity futures exchange

Warentermingeschäfte commodities futures

Warenterminhandel commodity futures trade

Warenterminoption commodity option

Warentest product test

Warenverkauf sale of goods; commodity sale

Warenverkehr movement of goods; merchandise traffic

Warenverkehrsbescheinigung movement certificate

Warenversand consignment of goods; commercial shipment

Warenverzeichnis *(Ladung)* manifest

Warenwechsel commercial paper

Warenwert merchandise value

Warenzeichen trademark; *(Marke)* brand; *(Symbol)* logo

warnen to warn; to caution

warnend cautionary

Warngerät monitor

Warnstreik warning strike

Warnung warning; *(Bekanntgabe)* notice

warten to wait; *(Wartung)* to service; to maintain

Wärter attendant

Warteschlange waiting line; queue

Wartestellung standby position

Wartung service; maintenance

Wartungskosten maintanance cost; cost of upkeep

Wartungspersonal maintenance staff; servicing staff

Wasserstraße waterway

Webadresse web addresses; universal resources locator

Webbrowser web browsers

Webseite web site

Webseiten-Messung web site measurement

Webserver web servers

Webstoff textile

Web-TV WebTV

Wechsel draft; bill of exchange; paper

Wechselbank acceptance bank; exchange bank

Wechselbürgschaft draft guarantee

Wechselgeld change

Wechselkredit draft credit

Wechselkurs exchange rate; foreign exchange rate

Wechselkurs, flexibler floating currency exchange rate

Wechselkursänderung exchange rate change

Wechselkursanstieg exchange rate increase

wechselkursbedingt dependent on the exchange rate

Wechselkursgewinn exchange rate profit

Wechselkursmechanismus exchange rate mechanism (ERM)

Wechselkursmodell exchange rate model

wechseln to switch; *(umtauschen)* to exchange; *(Kleidung)* to change

Wechselportefeuille bills in hand; bill holdings

wechselseitig reciprocal; mutual

Wechselwirkung reciprocal effect

Weg way; *(Pfad)* path; *(Bahn)* track; *(Route)* route; *(Dienstweg)* channel

Wegbestimmung routing

Wegfall *(Aufhören)* cessation; *(Auslassung)* omission

wegwerfbar disposable

Wegwerfgüter disposable goods

Weg-Ziel-Theorie path-goal theory

Wehrdienst military service

weich soft

weich machen to soften

Weigerung refusal

Weisung directive; instruction; order

Weisungsbefugnis right of command; discretionary power; managerial authority

Weisungsgruppe command group

weit wide; broad; far

weit entfernt distant; far removed; *(idiomatisch)* far from it

weiterbilden to educate oneself

Weiterbildung further education; continuing education

Weieterentwicklung further development

Weiterführung continuation

Weitergeben to pass on

weitermachen to continue; to proceed

weiterverarbeiten to process; to finish

Weiterverarbeitung processing; finishing

weiterverkaufen to resell

weitreichend far-reaching; sweeping

Wellness-Programme wellness programs

Welt- global

Weltagrarmarkt world agricultural market

Weltbank World Bank; International Bank of Reconstruction and Development

Weltbanktochter World Bank subsidiary; World Bank affiliate

Weltexport world export; global export

Weltfinanz global finance

Welthandel world trade; international trade

Welthandelsorganisation World Trade Organization (WTO)

Weltklasse world class

Weltkonjunktur global economic condition

Weltkonzern global corporation

Weltmarkt global market; international market

Weltmarktanteil global market share

Weltmarktführer global market leader

Weltmarktpreis world market price

Weltorganisation für geistiges Eigentum World Intellectual Property Organization (WIPO)

Weltrangliste global ranking; worldwide ranking

Weltraum outer space

Weltwährungsfonds International Monetary Fund (IMF)

weltweit global

weltweite Geschäftstätigkeit worldwide operations

weltweite Nachfrage global demand

weltweite Rezession worldwide recession

Weltwirtschaft world economy

weltwirtschaftlich pertaining to a global economy

Weltwirtschaftskrise global economic crisis

Weltwirtschaftslehre global economics

Wende turn; *(Wirtschaft, Markt)* turnaround

wenden to turn around

wenden, sich to turn

Wendung turn; twist

Werbe- advertising; promotional

Werbeadressat mailing list addressee

Werbeagentur advertising agency

Werbeaufwendung advertising expenditure

Werbeaussage advertising message

Werbebetreuer advertising consultant; advertising account executive

Werbebild advertisement picture

Werbebotschaft advertising message; advertising slogan

Werbebrief sales letter

Werbebudget advertising budget

Werbechef advertising director

Werbedrehbuch advertising script; commercial script

Werbeeffekt advertising effect; advertising impact

Werbeeinfall advertising idea

Werbeetat advertising budget

Werbeerfolg advertising effectiveness

Werbefeldzug advertising campaign

Werbefernsehen television advertising

Werbefotograf commercial photographer

Werbefunk promotional broadcasting

Werbegeschenk promotional gift

Werbegestaltung advertising design

Werbeidee advertising idea

Werbekampagne advertising campaign

Werbekosten advertising expenses

Werbekraft persuasive power; advertising appeal; selling power

Werbekreis advertising circle

Werbekrieg advertising war

Werbekunde advertiser; client

Werbeleiter advertising manager; promotion manager; *(Publizität)* publicity director

Werbemasche advertising gimmick

Werbemaßnahme advertising tactic; publicity ploy

Werbemittel advertising material; promotional literature; *(Träger)* advertising medium; *(Händler)* dealer aids; *(Vertreter)* sales kit

Werbemotto advertising slogan

werben to advertise; *(Kundschaft)* to solicit; to advertise

Werbenetzwerke advertising networks

Werbeplattform advertising rostrum

Werbeprospekt advertising brochure; *(Reklamezettel)* handbill; *(Faltblatt)* leaflet; *(Gesellschaftsgründung)* prospectus

Werber advertiser

Werbeschlacht advertising battle

Werbesendung commercial broadcast; *(Werbespot)* advertising spot; commercial

Werbeslogan advertising slogan

Werbespruch advertising slogan; *(Reim)* jingle

Werbestratege, **-strategin** advertising strategist; publicity strategist

Werbetext advertising copy

Werbeträger advertising medium; advertising vehicle

werbewirksam effective in advertising

Werbung promotion; *(Publizität)* publicity; *(Anzeige)* advertisement

Werbungskosten advertising costs; *(Steuer)* income-related expenses; *(Freibetrag)* professional allowance

Werdegang career; background

werfen to throw; *(vorwärts werfen)* to thrust

Werk plant; factory; *(Anlage)* facility; *(Schöpfung)* creation; work

Werkbereich working area

Werkhalle factory work floor; factory work room

Werklohn wage; compensation

Werkschließung factory closing

Werkstatt factory; workshop

Werkstoff material; raw material

Werktag business day; working day

werktätig working

Werkunterricht manual training

Werkzeug tool; *(Gerät)* implement; *(Instrument)* instrument

Werkzeugausstattung tool kit

Werkzeugmaschine machine tool

Werkzeugtasche tool kit

Wert value; *(Qualität)* quality; *(Verdienst)* merit; *(Grundkapital)* equity

Wertanalyse value analysis

Wertberichtigung value adjustment

Werte values; *(Statistik)* data; *(Effekten)* securities

Werterhöhung rise in value; *(Mehrwert)* added value

Wertesystem value system

Wertgerüst value structure

wertlos without value; worthless; *(minderwertig)* shoddy

wertmäßig according to value

Wertmaßstab value measure

Wertminderung deterioration; *(Steuererklärung)* depreciation

Wertpapier security; commercial paper; *(Schuldverschreibung)* bond

Wertpapier; erstklassiges blue chip

Wertpapieranlage investment in securities

Wertpapierauftrag order to purchase securities

Wertpapierberater investment adviser

Wertpapierbereich securities sector

Wertpapierbestand portfolio; securities holdings; *(Bilanz)* investment portfolio

Wertpapierbörse stock market; securities exchange

Wertpapierdepot investment portfolio

Wertpapiere securities

Wertpapiereinstufung rating

Wertpapierfonds investment fund

Wertpapiergeschäft securities business; transaction in securities

Wertpapierhandel securities trading

Wertpapierhändler trader

Wertpapierkonto securities account

Wertpapierlinie security market line (SML)

Wertpapiermakler stockbroker

Wertpapiermarkt securities market

Wertpapierumsatz securities sales

Wertpapierverkauf *(an Private)* private placement

Wertpapiervermögen security holdings

Wertschätzung *(persönlich)* esteem; appreciation; *(Abschätzung)* appraisal

Wertschöpfung creation of value; *(Werterhöhung)* net value added

Wertschöpfungskette value chain

Wertsteigerung appreciation; rise in value

Wertstellung value date; availability date

Werttheorie value theory

Wertverhältnis value ratio

wertvoll valuable; *(kostbar)* precious

Wertzoll ad valorem duty

Wertzuwachs appreciation; rise in value; accretion

Wesen essence; *(Charakter)* character; *(Rechtspersönlichkeit)* entity

wesentlich substantial; material; essential; integral

Westeuropäische Union West European Union (WEU)

Wettbewerb competition; contest; rivalry

Wettbewerb, freier free competition

Wettbewerb, harter fierce competition; stiff competition

Wettbewerb, lauterer fair trade

Wettbewerb, ruinöser cutthroat competition

Wettewerb, unlauterer unfair competition

Wettbewerb ausschalten to eliminate competition

Wettbewerb behindern to prefent competition

Wettbewerb fördern to promote competition

Wettbewerb verzerren to distort competition

Wettbewerber competitor; rival

Wettbewerbsargument argument supporting competition

Wettbewerbsdynamik competitive dynamics

wettbewerbsfähig competitive; capable of competing

Wettbewerbsfähigkeit competitiveness

Wettbewerbsnachteil competitive disadvantage

Wettbewerbsposition competitive position

Wettbewerbsstrategie competitive strategy

Wettbewerbstheorie theory of competition

Wettbewerbsvorteil competitive advantage

Wette bet; *(Einsatz)* wager

wetteifern to compete; *(rivalisieren)* to rival

wetten to bet; to gamble; to wager

Wettkampf contest; *(Wettbewerb)* competition

Wichtigkeit importance; significance; *(Prominenz)* prominence

Wichtigkeit der Aufgabe task significance

Widerruf *(Güter)* recall; *(Gesetze)* repeal; *(Rechte)* revocation; *(Ungültigkeitserklärung)* rescission

widerrufen to revoke; *(Gesetz)* to repeal; *(für ungültig erklären)* to rescind

Widerspruch objection; protest; contradiction

Widerspruch erheben to lodge a protest; to object; to contradict; *(opponieren)* to oppose

Widerstand resistance; opposition

Widerstandslinie resistance level

Wiederabdruck reprint

wieder abdrucken to reprint

wieder ankurbeln to restart; *(Wirtschaft)* to refuel

Wiederanlagesatz reinvestment rate

wieder anlegen to reinvest

wieder anstellen to rehire

Wiederaufbau reconstruction; rehabilitation

wiederaufbauen to reconstruct; to rebuild

wiederaufbereiten to recycle

Wiederaufbereitung recycling

wieder auffinden to retrieve

Wiederauffindung retrieval

wiederaufleben to revive

Wiederaufleben revival; *(Neubelebung)* revitalization

Wiederaufnahme resumption; renewal

wiederaufnehmen to resume; *(Verhandlung)* to reopen

Wiederaufschwung rebound; *(Erholung, Gesundung)* recovery

Wiederaufstieg comeback

wieder beleben to revitalize

Wiederbelebung revitalization; *(Wiederaufleben)* revival

wiederbeschaffen to replace

Wiederbeschaffung replacement

Wiederbeschaffungskosten replacement costs

Wiederbeschaffungswert replacement value; *(Marktwert)* market value

wiederbringen to restore

wieder einbringen to recoup

Wiedereinbürgerung repatriation

wiedereinsetzen to restore; to reinstate

wiedereinstellen to rehire; *(wiedereinsetzen)* to reinstate

Wiedererlangung recovery

wieder ernennen to reappoint

Wiederernennung reappointment

wiedererobern to recapture

wiedereröffnen to reopen

Wiedereröffnung reopening

wiedererstatten to repay; *(ersetzen)* to replace; *(zurückerstatten)* to restore

Wiedererwerb reacquisition; retrieval

wiedererwerben to retrieve; to reacquire

wieder flott machen *(Schiff)* to refloat; to restart

wiedergutmachen to recompense

Wiedergutmachung compensation; *(Kriegsschuld)* reparation

wiederherstellen *(Ordnung)* to restore; *(erneuern)* to renew; *(reparieren)* to repair; *(neu etablieren)* to reestablish

Wiederherstellung restoration; *(Reparatur)* repair

Wiederholungsdruck reprint

Wiederholungsgeschäft repeat business

wieder in Betrieb setzen to reopen

Wiederkauf repurchase

Wiedervereinigung reunification; *(Neuintegration)* reintegration

Wiederverkauf resale

wiederverkaufen to resell

Wiederverkäufer reseller; *(Zwischenhändler)* middleman; *(Verteiler)* distributor

Wiederverkaufs- resale

wieder verwendbar reusable; recyclable

wieder vorlegen to resubmit

Wiederwahl reelection

wiegen to weigh

Wille will; *(Entschlossenheit)* determination

Willenserklärung statement of purpose; statement of intention

willkürlich arbitrary

Windhund-Verfahren first come-first served principle

winzig tiny; minute

wirkliches Einkommen (*Realeinkommen)* real income

wirksam effective

Wirksamkeit effectiveness

Wirkungskraft effective force; impact

Wirkungskreis *(Effekt)* area of effectiveness; *(Kompetenz)* radius of operation

Wirt landlord

Wirtschaft economy; economic system; *(Gastwirtschaft)* restaurant; *(Kneipe)* pub

wirtschaften to keep house; to manage

wirtschaftlich economic; *(sparsam)* economical; *(effizient)* efficient; *(ertragbringend)* profitable

wirtschaftliche Grundlage economic basis

wirtschaftliche Nutzungsdauer economic life

Wirtschaftlichkeit profitability; *(Sparsamkeit)* thrift; *(Effizienz)* efficiency

Wirtschaftlichkeitsrechnung profitability accounting; economic appraisal

Wirtschaftsablauf economic process; *(Zyklus)* business cycle

Wirtschaftsaufschwung economic boom

Wirtschaftsberater economic advisor

Wirtschaftsbereich economic domain

Wirtschaftsbotschaft economic signal

Wirtschaftsbüro economic bureau

Wirtschaftsdialog economic dialogue

Wirtschaftsdienst economic service; trade service

Wirtschaftseinheit economic entity; *(Betrieb)* self-contained unit

Wirtschaftsentwicklung economic development

Wirtschaftsexperte, **-expertin** economic expert

Wirtschaftsfachmann economic specialist; *(Theoretiker)* economist

Wirtschaftsflaute economic stagnation

Wirtschaftsforscher economic researcher

Wirtschaftsforschung economic research

Wirtschaftsgeschehen economic process

Wirtschaftsgut asset

Wirtschaftsindikator economic indicator

Wirtschaftsjahr fiscal year

Wirtschaftskonferenz economic conference

Wirtschaftskrise economic crisis

Wirtschaftskurs economic trend; course of the economy

Wirtschaftslage economic position; economic condition

Wirtschaftsleben economic life; business

Wirtschaftsleistung economic performance; *(Produktivität)* productivity

Wirtschaftsmagazin business magazine

Wirtschaftsminister secretary of commerce

Wirtschaftsmodell economic model

Wirtschaftsordnung economic order; economic system

Wirtschaftsplan economic plan

Wirtschaftspolitik economic policy

wirtschaftspolitisch pertaining to economic policy

Wirtschaftsprophet economic prophet

Wirtschaftsprüfer financial auditor; accountant; Certified Public Accountant (CPA)

Wirtschaftsprüfung audit

Wirtschaftsrat council of economic advisors

Wirtschaftsrecht commercial law; business law

Wirtschaftsrückgang economic recession

Wirtschaftssanktionen economic sanctions

Wirtschaftssituation state of the economy

Wirtschaftssprecher economic spokesperson

Wirtschaftsstatistik economic statistics

Wirtschaftsstruktur economic structure

Wirtschaftssystem economic system

Wirtschaftsteil *(Zeitung)* business section

Wirtschaftstheorie economic theory

Wirtschafts- und Währungsunion economic and monetary union

Wirtschaftsunion economic union

Wirtschaftsverlauf course of the economy

Wirtschaftswachstum economic growth

Wirtschaftswissenschaftler economist

Wirtschaftswunder economic miracle

Wirtschaftszeitung economic journal; *(Fachzeitschrift)* trade paper; *(Geschäftsjournal)* business journal

Wirtschaftszone economic zone

Wirtschaftszweig branch of the economy; *(Sektor)* economic sector

wissenbasiertes Vertrauen knowledge-based trust

Witwe widow

Witwenrente widow's pension

Wochenarbeitszeit hours worked per week

Wochenbericht weekly report

Wochendurchschnitt weekly average

Wohlergehen wellbeing; *(Prosperität)* prosperity

wohlerworben honestly acquired; vested

Wohlfahrt welfare; social services

Wohlfahrtseinrichtung welfare facility; charitable institution

Wohlfahrtsstaat welfare state

wohlhabend wealthy; prosperous; affluent

Wohlstand prosperity; wealth

wohlüberlegt well thought out; deliberate

Wohnort place of residence; home

Wohnsiedlung residential subdivision; residential development

Wohnung apartment

Wohnungswirtschaft housing industry

Wortführer spokesman

Wortlaut text

Wortverdrehung distortion; *(falsches Zitat)* misquotation

Wucher usury; extortion

Wucherei usury

Wuchergesetz usury law

wuchern *(Wucherei)* to engage in usury; *(Wachstum)* to grow unchecked; to proliferate

Wunsch wish; desire

wünschenswert desirable

Würgegriff stranglehold; chokehold

Y

Yankee-Anleihen Yankee bonds

Z

Zahl *(Nummer, Anzahl)* number; *(Ziffer, Preis)* figure

zahlbar payable; *(Wertpapier)* mature

zählen to count; *(nummerieren)* to number; *(rechnen mit)* to reckon

Zahlenfolge series of numbers

zahlenmäßig numerical

Zahlenmaterial numerical data; figures

Zahlenreihe column of numbers

Zahlenwert numerical value

Zahler payer

Zähler meter; counter; *(Bruch)* numerator

zahlreich numerous

Zahlstelle paying agent

Zahltag *(Lohn)* payday

Zählung count; *(Volkszählung)* census

Zahlung payment; *(aus dem Kapital)* principal payment

Zahlung bei Lieferung cash on delivery (COD); delivery versus payment (DVP)

Zahlung leisten to remit

Zahlungsanweisung money order; draft

Zahlungsaufforderung demand note

Zahlungsaufschub payment deferral; moratorium; *(Verlängerung)* extension

Zahlungsausgleich clearance; settlement; *(international)* exchange equilibrium

Zahlungsbedingungen terms of payment

Zahlungsbilanz balance of payments

Zahlungsbilanzkrise balance of payments crisis

Zahlungsbilanzlage balance of payments Position

Zahlungseinstellung stoppage of payment; *(Versäumnis)* default; *(Nichteinhaltung)* failure

Zahlungsempfänger payee

zahlungsfähig solvent; financially sound

Zahlungsfähigkeit ability to pay

Zahlungsfrist term; time of payment; *(gewährter Aufschub)* extension of time; *(Wechsel)* grace period

Zahlungsgarantie payment guarantee

Zahlungsgewohnheit payment habit

zahlungskräftig solvent; sound

Zahlungsmedium payment instrument

Zahlungsmittel medium of exchange; *(Geld)* money; currency

Zahlungsort place of payment

Zahlungsproblem payment difficulty

Zahlungstermin payment date

zahlungsunfähig insolvent; illiquid

Zahlungsunfähiger insolvent person

zahlungsunwirksame Größe non-cash item

Zahlungsverkehr money transfers; payment transactions

Zahlungsverzug default

Zahlungsweise method of payment

Zahlungsziel credit period; term of payment

Zählvorrichtung counter

Zählwerk counting device

Zeche *(Bergwerk)* mine

Zedent assigner; granter

Zeichen sign; *(Merkmal)* mark; *(Beweis)* token; *(Anzeichen)* indication

zeichnen to draw; to sketch; *(unterschreiben)* to sign; *(Aktien)* to subscribe

Zeichnung drawing; *(Skizze)* sketch

Zeichnungsangebot tender offer

Zeichnungsfirst subscription period

Zeichnungskurs offering price; subscription price

zeigen to show; *(zur Schau stellen)* to display

Zeile line

Zeilensumme line total

zeitabhängig dependent on time

Zeitabstand time interval

Zeitalter age; *(Ära)* era

Zeitdauer time period

Zeitgenosse; **-genossin** contemporary

zeitgenössisch contemporary

Zeithorizont time horizon; horizon

zeitliche Verschiebung time lag

Zeitplan timetable; schedule

Zeitraum period

Zeitreihe time series

Zeitrente annuity

Zeitschätzung time estimate

Zeitschrift periodical; *(Magazin)* magazine

Zeitung newspaper

Zeitungspapier newsprint

Zeitungsreklame newspaper advertisement

Zeitunterschied time difference

Zeitverlust time loss; *(Verspätung)* delay

Zeitwahl timing

Zeitwert present value (PV)

Zeitwert des Geldes time value of money

Zensur censorship; *(Note)* grade; mark

Zentral- central

zentral central

Zentralbank central bank; *(US)* Federal Reserve Bank

Zentralbankchef chairperson of the central bank; *(US)* chairperson of the Federal Reserve Bank

Zentralbankgeld central bank money

Zentralbankrat governing board of the central bank

Zentralbanksystem Federal Reserve System

Zentrale headquarters; home office

Zentralinstitution central institution

Zentralisation centralization

zentralisieren to centralize

Zentralisierung centralization

Zentralrechner mainframe computer; main computer

Zentralstelle center

Zentralverband central association

Zentrum hub; center

zerlegbar reducible; knockdown

zerlegen to disassemble; to section

Zerrbild distorted picture; distortion

zerren to wrench; to pull; to tug

Zerrüttung disorganization; *(Zerfall)* disintegration

Zerschlagung (*Kartell)* breakup

zerstören to destroy

zerstörerisch destructive

Zerstörung destruction

zerstreuen to disperse; to scatter; *(Bedenken)* to dispel; to dissipate; *(belustigen)* to divert

Zertifikat certificate; warrant

Zertifizierungsbehörde certification authority (CA)

Zession assignment

Zessionar transferee

Zettel slip of paper

Zeugenaussage witness account; *(beglaubigt)* deposition

Zeugnis certificate; *(Diplom)* diploma; *(Empfehlung)* reference; testimonial

ziehen to pull; to draw

Ziehung drawing

Ziehungsrecht drawing right

Ziel target; aim; goal; objective; *(Zweck)* object; *(Absicht)* intent; *(Ort)* destination

Zielausschüttungsquote target payout ratio

zielbewusst systematic

zielen to aim; *(Ziel setzen)* to target

Zielfunktion end function

Zielgesellschaft target company; takeover target

Zielgruppe target group

Zielhafen port of destination

Zielkomplex target complex

Zielkonflikt goal conflict; conflict of aims

Zielland target country

Zielpreis target price

Zielpublikum target audience

Ziel setzen to set a goal; to target

Zielsetzung target; goal; aim

Zieltheorie goal-setting theory

Zielunternehmen target firm

Zielvorgabe target setting

Zielvorstellung objective

Ziffer digit; *(Nummer)* number; *(Zahl, Preis)* figure

Zins interest

Zinsabhängigkeit interest dependency

Zinsabstand interest differential

Zinsabzug discount

zinsähnlich interest-like

Zinsanhebung increase in interest

Zinsanteil interest share; *(prozentual)* interest percentage

Zinsaufschlag interest increase

Zinsberechnung interest calculation

Zinsbestandteil interest percentage

zinsbewusst interest-conscious

Zinsdeckung interest coverage ratio

Zinsdifferenz interest difference; *(Marge)* interest margin

Zinseinkommen interest income

Zinseinnahme interest revenues; interest receipts

zinsempfindlich interest-sensitive

Zinsen interest

Zinsen abwerfen to earn interest; *(tragen)* to yield interest

Zinsendienst debt service

Zinsentwicklung interest rate development; interest rate trend

Zinserhöhung interest increase

Zinsermäßigung interest rebate; interest reduction

Zinsertrag yield; yield on interest

Zinsertragskurve yield curve

Zinseszins compound interest

zinsfrei interest free; no-interest; non-interest-bearing

Zinsgefälle interest rate differential; difference in interest

Zinsgutschrift interest credit

Zinskosten interest expense; *(Anleihe)* cost of money; interest expense

Zinskurve interest curve

zinsloses Darlehen flat loan

Zinsnachteil interest disadvantage

Zinsniveau interest level

Zinsoption interest rate option

Zinssatzparitäten-Theorie interest-rate-parity theorem

Zinspolitik interest policy

Zinsrate interest rate

Zinsrisiko interest rate risk

Zinsrechnung computation of interest

Zinsrückgang decrease in the interest rate

Zinsrückstände interest arrears

Zinsrutsch downward slide of interest rates

Zinssatz interest rate

Zinssatzparitäten-Theorie interest-rate-parity theorem

Zinsschein coupon; interest coupon

Zinssenkung interest rate reduction; cut in interest rates

Zinssicherung interest hedge

Zinssicherungsinstrument interest rate hedging instrument

Zinsspanne spread in interest rates; interest margin

Zinsstruktur interest rate structure

Zinssubvention interest subsidy

Zinsswap interest rate swap

zinstragend interest-bearing

Zinsterminkontrakt interest rate future

Zinsüberschuss interest surplus

Zinsunterschied difference in interest rates; interest differential

zinsvariable Anleihe floater

Zinsverlust loss on interest

Zinsverpflichtung obligation to pay interest; *(Zinssumme)* interest owed

Zinsvorteil interest advantage

Zinszahlung interest payment

zirka circa; approximately

Zitat quotation; quote

zitieren to quote

zögern to hesitate; to delay; *(um Zeit zu gewinnen)* to stall for time

Zögern hesitation; reluctance

Zoll *(Handel)* tariff; *(Gebühr)* duty; *(Behörde)* customs; *(Maß)* inch

Zollabbau tariff reduction

Zollabfertigung customs clearance

Zollabkommen tariff agreement

Zolllager bonded warehouse

Zolllagerverfahren customs warehouse proceedure

zollamtlich abfertigen to clear through customs

Zollanmeldung customs declaration

Zollbefreiung exsemption from customs

Zollbegünstigung tariff preference

Zollbehörde customs authority

Zollbescheid notice os assessment

Zolldeklaration customs declaration; *(Exportlieferung)* manifest

Zolleinfuhrschein bill of entry

Zollerklärung customs declaration

Zollfaktura customs invoice

Zollfahndung customs investigation

Zollforderung duty charge; duty claim

Zollformular customs form

Zollfrei duty free

Zollfreibetrag duty free allowance

Zollfreizone duty free area

Zollgarantie customs guarantee

Zollgebiet customs territory

Zollgebühr duty

Zollpräferenz tariff preference

Zollrückvergütung drawback

Zollsatz tariff rate; rate of duty

Zollschranke tariff barrier

Zollsenkung tariff reduction

Zollspedition customs expediting firm; customs forwarding firm

Zollstelle customs office; customs house

Zolltarif customs tariff; rate of duty

Zollunion customs union

Zollverwaltung *(Behörde)* customs authority; *(Personal)* customs officials

Zollwert tariff value

Zone zone

Zubehör accessories ; attachments; equipment ; material

zuerkennen to award; *(zusprechen)* to adjudge; *(zuteilen)* to apportion

Zuerkennung award; *(Zuteilung)* apportionment

zufällig accidental; by chance

Zufallsfaktor coincidence factor

Zuflucht shelter

Zufluss inflow

zufrieden content; *(zufrieden gestellt)* satisfied

Zugabe extra benefit

Zugang access

zugänglich accessible

Zugangsschutzsystem *(Internet)* firewall

zugeben to admit

Zugehörigkeit belonging; *(Mitgliedschaft)* membership

Zugehörigkeitsbedürfnis need for affiliation

zugelassen admitted; accredited

Zügelung restraint

Zugeständnis concession; admission

zugestehen to concede

zugkräftig popular; attractive

zugreifen to seize; to help oneself

Zugriff *(Datenverarbeitung)* access

zugrunde liegend *(Anteile, Aktien)* underlying

zugrunde richten to ruin

zugunsten in favor of

Zuhörerschaft listeners; *(Publikum)* audience

Zukunft future

zukünftig future

zukünftiger Ertrag future earnings

Zukunftserwartung future expectation; *(Aussichten)* future outlook

Zukunftsmarkt future market

zulassen *(erlauben)* to allow; to permit; *(aufnehmen)* to admit; *(Konzession)* to license

zulässig permissible; *(Gericht)* admissible; *(zu erlauben)* allowable

Zulassung admittance; *(Lizenz)* license; *(Aufnahme)* admittance

Zulassungsvorschriften *(Börse)* listing requirements

Zulieferant subcontractor

Zulieferbetrieb subcontracting firm; *(Tochterunternehmen)* manufacturing subsidiary; *(Fabrik)* feeder plant

Zulieferer supplier; subcontractor

Zuliefern supplying

Zulieferung subcontracted supply

Zulieferungsvertrag subcontract

zum Abschluss bringen to bring to a dose; *(fertig machen)* to finish; *(beendigen)* to terminate

zum Abschluss gebracht finalized; *(fertig)* completed

zum gesetzlichen Zahlungsmittel machen to monetize

Zunahme increase; gain; *(Erhöhung)* rise; *(Wachstum)* growth

zunehmen to increase; *(wachsen)* to grow; *(Umsatz)* to pick up

Zunft *(Handwerk)* guild

zurechnen to add; to impute; to attribute

Zurechnung addition; imputation; attribution

Zurschaustellung display; exhebition

Zurückbehaltung withholding; *(Reserve)* reserve

Zurückbehaltungsrecht retention of goods; lien

Zurückberufung recall

zurückbleiben *(dableiben)* to stay behind; *(nicht Schritt halten)* to fall behind; to lag behind

zurückdatieren to backdate

zurückerlangen to recover; *(wiedergewinnen)* to regain

Zurückerlangung recovery

zurückerstatten to refund; *(entschädigen)* to reimburse

Zurückerstattung refund; *(Entschädigung)* reimbursement

zurückfordern to reclaim

zurückführen *(Idee)* to attribute; *(umsiedeln)* to resettle

zurückgeben to give back; to restore; to return

zurückgeblieben *(Entwicklung)* backward; slow

zurückgehen to return; *(abnehmen)* to decrease; *(Aufträge)* to go down; *(Einnahmen)* to fall ott; *(Konjunktur)* to move backwards; *(Preise)* to decline; *(Qualität)* to deteriorate

zurückgesandt returned

zurückgestellt *(Mittel)* reserved

zurückgewinnen to recapture

zurückgezogen withdrawn; secluded; retired

zurückhalten to hold back; *(hemmen)* to restrain; *(aufhalten)* to detain

zurückhaltend reserved; retiring

Zurückhaltung restraint

zurückkaufen to buy back, to repurchase; *(einlösen)* to redeem

zurückkehren to return

Zurücknahme *(Ware)* return; *(Rechte, Privilegien)* revocation

zurücknehmen to take back; *(Behauptung)* retract; *(Rechte, Privilegien)* to revoke

zurückrufen to recall; *(telefonieren)* to call back

zurückschnellen to rebound

zurückschrauben to trim back; *(reduzieren)* to reduce

zurückstellen to subordinate; *(Mittel)* to reserve; *(Termin)* to postpone

Zurückstellung subordination; *(Mittel)* reserves; *(Termin)* postponement

zurücktreten (*Kandidatur*) to withdraw; *(Position)* to step down; *(Amt)* to resign

zurückweisen *(Behauptung)* to repudiate; *(Vorschlag)* to reject; *(Argument)* to dismiss

Zurückweisung (*Behauptung*) repudiation; *(Vorschlag)* rejection; *(Argument)* dismissal

zurückzahlen to repay; *(Entschädigung)* to reimburse; *(Rückerstattung)* to refund

Zurückzahlung refund; *(Entschädigung)* reimbursement

zurückziehen to recall; *(Einspruch)* to subduct; *(Forderung)* to take back

zurückziehen, sich to withdraw; *(Ruhestand)* to retire

Zurückziehung withdrawal; *(Ruhestand)* retirement; *(von Anlagekapital)* disinvesting

Zusage *(Zusicherung)* assurance; *(Versprechen)* promise

zusagen to agree; to answer in the affirmative; *(versprechen)* to promise; *(Einladung)* to accept

Zusammenarbeit cooperation; collaboration

zusammenarbeiten to cooperate; to collaborate

Zusammenbauausrüstung assembly kit

zusammenbrechen to collapse

Zusammenbruch collapse; ruin; *(Maschine)* breakdown

zusammenfassen to sum up; to summarize

Zusammenfassung summary; recapitulation

zusammengefasst summarized

zusammengesetzt *(Mechanik)* assembled; composite; *(vermischt)* compound

Zusammenhang context; relation

Zusammenkunft gathering; *(Treffen)* meeting

zusammenlegen to combine; *(konsolidieren)* to consolidate

Zusammenlegung consolidation; combination; *(Unternehmen)* merger; amalgamation; *(Verwaltung)* centralization

zusammenpassend compatible

zusammenrechnen to add up

Zusammenrechnung addition

zusammenschließen to pool; *(vereinigen)* to combine; *(verschmelzen)* to fuse; *(fusionieren)* to merge

zusammenschließen, sich *(verschmelzen)* to fuse; to amalgamate; *(sich vereinigen)* to unite

Zusammenschluss merger; *(Integration)* integration; *(Kombination)* combination

zusammenschrumpfen to shrink; *(dahinschwinden)* to dwindle

zusammensetzen to put together; *(Montage)* to assemble

Zusammensetzung mixture; *(Chemie)* compound

Zusammenstellung compilation; *(Mischung)* mix

zusammenstoßen to collide; *(Kulturen)* to clash

zusammenstückeln to piece together

zusammentreffen to meet; *(Termine, Ziele)* to coincide

Zusammentreffen meeting

zusammenwerfen to pool

zusammenzählen to total; (*nachzählen)* to tally

Zusammenziehung contraction

Zusatz supplement; *(Hinzufügung)* addition; *(Teil)* amendment

Zusatzgerät auxiliary unit; *(Zubehör)* attachment; *(Stecker)* adapter

Zusatzleistung additional contribution; *(Produktion)* additional output

zusätzlich additional; supplemental; extra

zusätzlich eingezahltes Kapital additional paid-in capital; paid-in surplus

zusätzlicher Anreiz sweetener

zusätzliches Nettoumlaufvermögen additions to net working capital

Zusatzurlaub additional vacation time

Zusatzverzinsung additional interest

Zuschlag premium; extra amount

Zuschlaggebühr surcharge

zuschreiben to attribute

Zuschreibung attribution; *(Widmung)* dedication; *(Bilanz)* write-up

Zuschuss allowance; *(Subvention)* subsidy; *(Stipendium)* grant

Zuschussbedarf subsidy requirement

Zuschusszahlung subsidy payment

zusetzen *(einbüßen)* to lose; *(belästigen)* to pester

Zusicherung assurance

Zustand condition; state; *(Lage)* position

zu Stande bringen to achieve; to accomplish

zuständig in charge; competent

zuständige Behörde competent agency

Zuständigkeit jurisdiction; competence

zustellen to send; *(ausliefern)* to deliver

Zustellung *(Auslieferung)* delivery

zustimmen to agree; *(bestätigen)* to endorse; *(einwilligen)* to consent; *(genehmigen)* to approve

Zustimmung agreement; *(Bestätigung)* endorsement; *(Einwilligung)* consent; *(Genehmigung)* approval

Zustrom influx

zutage treten to come to light; to become evident; *(auftauchen)* to emerge

zuteilen to apportion; to allocate; to ration; *(verteilen)* to distribute; to allot

Zuteilung allocation; apportionment; *(Aufgabe)* assignment; *(Wertpapiere)* allotment; *(Ration)* ration

zutreffend applicable; *(passend)* fitting

zuverlässig reliable; dependable; trustworthy

Zuverlässigkeit reliability; dependability; trustworthiness

zuversichtlich confident

zuviel produzieren to overproduce

Zuwachs increment of growth; accrual

Zuwachsrate incremental growth rate

zu Wege bringen to accomplish

zuweisen *(Aufgabe)* to assign; *(Mittel)* to apportion; to allocate

Zuweisung *(Aufgabe)* assignment; *(Mittel)* allocation

zuwenden *(Mittel)* to allocate; *(Geld)* to channel

Zuwendungsempfänger donee

Zuzahlung additional payment; *(Effekten)* assessment

zuzüglich plus; additionally

Zwang coercion; compulsion

zwanglos informal; casual; relax

Zwangsanleihe forced loan; compulsory loan

Zwangslage plight; tight spot

zwangsläufig inevitable; unavoidable

Zwangsräumung eviction

Zwangssparen forced saving

Zwangsvollstreckung distraint; foreclosure; lawenforcement

Zwangsvollstreckungsbefehl warrent of attachement; foreclosure decree

Zweck purpose; object; *(Ziel)* goal; aim

zweckdienlich expedient; convenient

zweckgebunden *(Mittel)* committed; earmarked

zwecklos useless; without purpose; *(ziellos)* aimless

zweckmäßig functional

Zweckmäßigkeit utility; convenience

zwecks for the purpose of

Zwecksetzung goal setting; goal establishment

Zwecksparen special purpose saving

zweideutig ambiguous; *(Witz)* suggestive

Zweideutigkeit ambiguity; double entendre; *(Witz)* suggestiveness

Zwei-Faktoren-Theorie two-factor theory

zweifelhaft doubtful; *(fragwürdig)* questionable

Zweiggesellschaft affiliate

Zweigniederlassung branch office

Zweigstelle branch

zweiseitig bilateral

Zweitausfertigung duplicate; copy

zweitklassig second-rate; inferior

Zweitmarkt secondary market

zweitrangig second-rank; subordinate

zwingen to coerce; to force; to compel; to oblige; to constrain

zwingend obligatory; *(pflichtmäßig)* mandatory; *(zwangsmäßig)* compulsory; *(Grund)* compelling

Zwischenbericht interim report

Zwischendividende interim dividend

Zwischenfall unforeseen occurrence; incident

Zwischenfinanzierung interim financing

Zwischenhändler middleman; intermediary

Zwischenkredit bridge loan

Zwischenprodukt intermediate product

Zwischenraum interval; *(Lücke)* gap

Zwischenschein scrip

Zwischensumme subtotal

Zwischenverkauf vorbehalten subject to prior sale

Zwischenzahlung interim payment

Zwischenzeit interim time

zyklisch cyclical

Zyklus cycle

A

A2A Administration to Administration
A2B Administration to Business
A2C Administration to Customer
AAA American Arbitration Association; American Automobile Association; Triple A
AA Always Afloat; After Arrival; Advertising Association
AAD Annual Aggregate Deductible
AADFI Association of African Development Finance Institutions
AAEI American Association of Exporters and Importers
AAIB Arab-African International Bank
AAII American Association of Individual Investors
AAP Affirmative Action Program
AAR Against All Risks; Average Accounting Return
AATPO Association of African Trade Promotion Organizations
ABA American Bankers Association
ABB Activity-Based Budgeting
ABC Activity-Based Costing; Audit Bureau of Circulation; American Business Center
ABCA Association des Banques Centrales Africaines
ABDNT Abandonment
ABEDA Arab Bank for Economic Development in Africa
ABI American Business Initiative; Automated Broker Interface; Association of British Insurers
ABO Accumulated Benefit Obligation
ABS Asset Backed Securities; American Bureau of Shipping; Able-Bodied Seaman; Automated Bond System
ABT About
ABTA Association of British Travel Agents
A/C Account Current
A/CDS Antidumping/Countervailing Duty System
ACA Associate of the Institute of Chartered Accountants
ACAB Association of Central African Banks
AC Account
ACA Air Cargo Agent
ACAB Association of Central African Banks
ACAS Advisory, Conciliation and Arbitration Service
ACAT Automated Customer Account Transfer
ACC Administration Committee on Coordination; United Nations Administrative Committee on Co-ordination; Arab Cooperation Council; Acceptance; Accepted
ACCJ American Chamber of Commerce in Japan
ACCT Agence de Cooperation Culturlle et Technique; Agency for Cultural and Technical Cooperation, Account
ACDA Arms Control and Disarmament Agency
ACE Active Corps of Executives
ACEP Advisory Committee on Export Policy
ACES Advance Computerized Execution System
ACH Automated Clearing House
ACI Advertising Council, Inc.
ACII Associate of Chartered Insurance Institute
ACMA Associate of the Chartered Institute of Management Accountants
ACORN A Classification of Residential Neighborhoods
ACP African, Caribbean, and Pacific Developing Countries; Anchors and Chains Proved
ACPC Association of Coffee-Producing Countries
ACRS Accelerated Cost Recovery System
ACS Automated Commercial System
ACT Advance Corporation Tax; Association of Corporate Treasurers; Amazonian Cooperation Treaty
ACTPN Advisory Committee on Trade Policy and Negotiations
ACU Asian Clearing Union; Asian Currency Units

ACV Air Cushion Vehicle
AD Antidumping
ADA Americans with Disabilities Act
ADB Asian Development Bank; African Development Bank; Adjusted Debit Balance
ADC Andean Development Corporation; Anti-Dumping Clause
ADD Antidumping Duty
ADEA Age Discrimination in Employment Act of 1967
ADF African Development Foundation; African Development Fund; Asian Development Fund
ADFAED Abu Dhabi Fund for Arab Economic Development
ADO Antidumping Duty Order
ADP Automated Data Processing; Antidumping Petition
ADR American Depositary Receipt; Asset Depreciation Range; Acquisition-Development-Retention
ADRs Advance Determination Rulings; American Depository Receipts
ADS Agent Distributor Service; American Depository Share
ADSL Asymmetric Digital Subscriber Line
ADST Approved Deferred Share Trust
AD VAL Ad Valorem
AEA American Economics Association
AECA Arms Export Control Act
AEF Africa Enterprise Fund
AEN Administrative Exception Note
AERP Automated Export Reporting Program
AEX Amsterdam Exchange
AF Advanced freight
AFAA As Far As Applicable
AFAIK As Far as I Know
AFC African Groundnut Council
AFDB African Development Bank
AFDF African Development Fund
AFESD Arab Fund for Economic and Social Development
AFF Air Freight Forwarder
AFG Affiliated Foreign Group
AFKN Armed Forces Korea Network
AFL-CIO American Federation of Labor-Congress of Industrial Organizations
AFM Amman Financial Market
AFREXIMBANK African Export-Import Bank
AG Australia Group
AGI Adjusted Gross Income
AGM Annual General Meeting
AGRICOLA Agricultural OnLine Access
AGRIS Agriculture Information System
AGT Agent; Against; Agreement
AGV Automated Guided Vehicle
AGWI Atlantic, Gulf, West Indies Limits
AFIC Asian Finance and Investment Corporation
AFM Amman Financial Market
AFTA Asean Free Trade Area
AH After Hatch
AHF American Hull Form (insurance policy)
AI Artificial Intelligence
AIAFD Association of African Development Finance Institutions
AIB Arab International Bank
AIBD Association of International Bond Dealers
AICPA American Institute of Certified Public Accountants
AID Agency for International Development
AIES Automated Information Exchange System
AIG Airbus Industries Group
AIM Alternative Investment Market
AIMR Association for Investment Management and Research
AIMS Agriculture Information and Marketing Services
AIMU American Institute of Marine Underwriters
AIOEC Association of Iron Ore Exporting Countries
AIRMIC Association of Insurance and Risk Managers in Industry and Commerce
AIST Agency for Industrial Science Technology
AIT American Institute in Taiwan
AITS Automated Information Transfer System
AKA Also Known As
ALADI Asociación Latinoamericana de Integración
ALGOL Algorithmic Language

ALIDE Associación Latinoamericana de Institutiones Financieras
ALJ Administrative Law Judge
AMA American Management Association
AMB Ambassador
AMCHAM American Chamber of Commerce
AMEX American Stock Exchange
AMF Arab Monetary Fund; Accord Multi Fibre
AMI Alternative Mortgage Instrument
AML Adjustable Mortgage Loan; Absolute Maximum Loss
AMPS Auction Market Preferred Stock
AMPTC Arab Maritime Petroleum Transport Company
AMS Agricultural Marketing Service; Automated Manifest Systems; Arab Monetary Fund
AMSC African Management Services Company
AMSCO African Management Services Company
AMT Alternative Minimum Tax
AMU Arab Maghreb Union
AMVER Automated Mutual-Assistance Vessel Rescue
AMVI Amex Market Value Index
AMW Average Monthly Wage
ANF Arrival Notification Form
ANOVA Analysis of Variances
ANRPC Association of Natural Rubber Producing Countries
ANS Ansvarlig Selskap
ANSI American National Standards Institute
A/O Account Of
AOVOY Any One Voyage
AOA Activity-On-Arrow
AOB Any One Bottom
AOE Any One Event
AOL Any One Loss; America Online
AOLOC Any One Location
AON All or None Order; Activity-On-Node
AOO Any One Occurrence
AOR Any One Risk
AOS Automated Order System
AOSIS Alliance of Small Island States
AOV Any One Vessel
AP Additional Premium
APAC Auto Parts Advisory Committee
APACS Association for Payment Clearing Services
APB Accounting Principles Board
APC Advance Postcard
APDF Africa Project Development Facility
APEC Asian Pacific Economic Cooperation
APEX Advance-Purchase Excursion
API American Petroleum Institute
APICORP Arab Petroleum Investment Corporation
APL As Per List; A Programming Language
APO Administrative Protective Order; Army Post Office; Asian Productivity Organization
APP Appendix
APPD Approved
APR Annual Percentage Rate; Auction Preferred Stock
APSC Arab Petroleum Services Company
APT Arbitrage Pricing Theory; Automated Pit Trading
APV Adjusted Present Value
APY Annual Percentage Yield
AR Administrative Review; All Risks; Against All Risks
ARBS Arbitrageurs
ARF Andean Reserve Fund
ARITT Arrangement Regarding International Trade in Textiles
ARM Adjustable-Rate Mortgage
ARO Average Rate Option
ARP Adjustable-Rate Preferred Stock; Auction Rate Preferred Stock
ARR Average Rate of Return; Accounting Rate of Return
ARRTL Arranged Total Loss
ARS African Regional Organization for Standardization
ARSO African Regional Organization for Standardization
A/S After Sight; Account Sales; Alongside (chartering)
ASA Advertising Standards Authority
ASAP As Soon As Possible
ASB Accounting Standards Board
ASBC Asset Backed Securities Corporation

ASCII American Standard Code for Information Interchange
ASDF Asian Development Fund
ASE Athens Stock Exchange; American Stock Exchange
ASEA Association of South-East Asia
ASEAN Association of Southeast Asian Nations
ASO Administrative Service Only
ASP Application Service Provider; Active Server Page; American Selling Price
AST Automated Screen Trading
ASX Australian Stock Exchange
A/T American Terms (grain trade)
ATCA Agreement on Trade in Civil Aircraft
ATFP Arab Trade Financing Program
ATI American Traders Index; Andean Trade Initiative
ATL Actual Total Loss; Atlantic
ATLAS Automated Trade Locator Assistance Network
ATM Automated Teller Machine; At the Moment
ATMIC Agricultural Trade and Marketing Information Center
ATO African Timber Organization
ATO Agricultural Trade Offices
ATP Advanced Technology Products; Arbıtrage Trading Program; Air Trade Provision
ATPA Andean Trade Preference Act
ATPI Andean Trade Preference Initiative
ATST At the Same Time
ATWT Atomic Weight
AUP Acceptable Use Policy
AUX Auxiliary Vessel
A/V Average; Ad Valorem (according to value)
AVC Additional Voluntary Contribution
AVDISBTS Average Disbursements
AVE Ad Valorem Equivalent
AVMS Administered Vertical Marketing System
AWB Airway Bill

B

B2A Business To Administration
B2B Business To Business
B2C Business To Consumer
BAA Buy American Act; British Airports Authority
BAC Bank Advisory Committee
BACS Bankers Automated Clearing System
BACAT Barge Aboard Catamaran
BADEA Banque Arabe pour le Développement Economique en Afrique
BAETC Bank Affiliate Export Trading Company
BAGGAGE General License-BAGGAGE
BAL Balance
BAN Bank Anticipation Note; Bond Anticipation Note
BANCOMEXT Banco Nacional de Comercio Exterior
BAR Barrel
BARs Buy American Restrictions
BAS Caribbean/Central America Business Advisory Service
BASIC Beginner's All-Purpose Symbolic Instruction Code
BB Bill Book; Below Bridges
BBA Bachelor of Business Administration, British Bankers´ Association
BBB Better Business Bureau
BBS Bulletin Board System
BBCL Both to Blame Collision Clause
BBLs Barrels
BC Blind Copy; Bristol Channel; Basel Convention
BCA Bilateral Clearing Agreement
BCAP British Code of Advertising Practice
BCAS Bank of Central African States
BCC Blind Carbon Copy
BCEAO Banque Centrale des Etats de l'Afrique de l'Ouest
BCG Boston Consulting Group
BCH Bristol Channel
BCIE Banco Centroamericano de Integraciön Econömico

BCIU Business Council for International Understanding
BC-NET Business Cooperation Network
BCS Border Cargo Selectivity
BD Bank Draft, Bar Draft (grain trade); Bound, Bond
BDEAC Banque de Développement des Etats de l'Afrique Centrale
BDEGL Banque de Développement des Etats du Grand Lac
BDI Both Dates Inclusive
BDMA British Direct Marketing Association
BDL Bundle
BDS Boards (timber)
BDS Broker's Daily Statement
BDV Budget Day Value
BE Bill of Exchange, Bill of Entry
BEA Bureau of Export Administration
BEAC Banque des Etats de l'Afrique Centrale
BEACON Boston Exchange Automated Communication Order-Routing Network
BEARS Bonds Enabling Annual Retirement Savings
BECAO Banque Centrale des Etats de l'Afrique de l'Ouest
BECC Border Environment Cooperation Commission
BEET Business Executive Enforcement Team
BELFOX Belgian Futures and Options Exchange
BENELUX Belgium, Netherlands, and Luxembourg Economic Union
BERI Business Environment Risk Index
BEU Benelux Economic Union
BEXA British Exporters Association
BFC Business Facilitation Center
BFCE Banque Francaise du Commerce Extérieur
BFO Business Facilitation Office
BFOQ Bona Fide Occupational Qualification
BFP Bona Fide Purchaser
BG Bondage Goods; Bag
BGC Bank Giro Credit
BH Bill of Health; Bordeaux to Hamburg
BHC Bank Holding Company; British High Command; British High Commission
BHP Brake Hore-Power
BIA Best Information Available
BIC Business Income Coverage, Bank Identifier Code; Bank Investment Contract
BID Banco Interamericano de Desarrollo
BIE Bureau of International Expositions
BIF Bank Insurance Fund
BIFFEX Baltic International Freight Futures Exchange
BIIBA British Insurance & Investment Brokers' Association
BIM British Institute of Management
BIMBO Buy-In Management Buy-Out
BIMCO Baltic and International Maritime Conference
BIO Business Information Office
BIOTAC Biotechnology Technical Advisory Committee
BIS Bank for International Settlements
BISNIS Business Information Service for the Newly Independent States
BIT Bilateral Investment Treaty; Binary Digit
BIL Bill of Lading
BK Back; Backwardation; Book
BKGE Breakage; Brokerage
BLADEX Banco Latinoamericano de Exportaciones
BLEU Belgium-Luxembourg Economic Union
BLL Blue Lantern
BLS Bales; Barrels
BM Board Measure (timber)
BMIR Below-Market Interest Rate
BO Buyer's Option; Branch Office; Brought Over
BOAD Banque OuestAfricaine de Developpement
BOGOF Buy One Get One Free
BOM Bill of Materials
BOQ Bill of Quantitites
BOP Business Owners Policy; Balance of Payments
BOS Bill of Sight; Bill of Sale
BOT Balance of Trade; Board of Trade
BOTB British Overseas Trade Board
BOVESPA Bolsa de Valores de Sao Paulo

BOY Beginning of Year
BP Bills Payable; Between Perpendiculars
BPB Bank Post Bill
BPI Business Proprietary Information
BPR Business Process Re-engineering
BPPCF Business and Personal Property Coverage Form
BR Bills Receivable; Builders' Risks; Bordeaux or Rouen (grain trade)
BRAD British Rates and Data
BRC Broker Regulatory Committee (Lloyds's); Brokers Registration Council
BRI Builders' Risks Insurance
BRITE Basic Research in Industrial Technologies in Europe
BRL Barrel
BROU Banco de la Republica Oriental del Uruguay
BS Boiler Survey; Balance Sheet; Bags; Bales; Bill of Sale; Bill of Store
BSA Bilateral Steel Agreement
BSAs Bilateral Steel Agreements
BSE Bombay Stock Exchange; Brussels Stock Exchange
BSI British Standards Institution
BSFF Buffer Stock Financing Facilities
BSP Business Sponsored; Between Show Promotion
BST British Summer Time
BT Berth Terms
BTG British Technology Group
BTN Brussels Tariff Nomenclature
B2B Business to (2) Business
B2C Business to (2) Customer
B&TCL Blocking & Trapping Clause
BTHU British Thermal Unit
BTN Brussels Tariff Nomenclature
BTU Bow Thrust Unit(s)
BTW By the Way
BU Bushels
BV Bureau Veritas
BVRJ Bolsa de Valores de Rio de Janeiro
BXA Bureau of Export Administration

C

C2A Customer to Administration
C2B Customer to Business
C2C Customer to Customer
C&D Collected and Delivered
C&F Cost and Freight
C&I Cost and Insurance
C&M Care and Maintenance
C&/or J China and/or Japan
C/D Carried Down
C/F Carried Forward
CA Chartered Accountant; Consumers Association
CAATS Computer-Assisted Audit Techniques
CABEE Consortia of American Businesses in Eastern Europe
CABEI Central American Bank for Economic Integration
CABNIS Consortia of American Businesses in the Newly Independent States
CAC Codex Alimentanus Commission
CACEU Central African Customs and Economic Union
CACM Central American Common Market
CACTLVO Compromised &/or Arranged &/or Constructive Total Loss of Vessel Only
CAD Cash Against Documents; Computer-Assisted Design; Computer Aided Design
CADICAM Computer Aided Design/Computer Aided Manufacturing
CAE Computer-Assisted Education; Computer-Assisted Engineering
CAEU Council of Economic Arab Unity
CAF Corporación Andina de Fomentó
CAFR Comprehensive Annual Financial Report
CAFTA Central American Free Trade Association
CAI Computer-Assisted Instruction

CAM Certified Administrative Manager; Computer Aided Manufacturing
CAMA Continental Advertising and Marketing Association
CAMPS Cumulative Auction Market Preferred Stocks
CANC Cancelled
CANCL Cancelling
CAP Common Agricultural Policy; Capacity; Country Action Plan
CAPAR Computer Assisted Panel Research
CAPI Computer Assisted Personal Interview; Common Application Interface
CAPM Capital Asset Pricing Model
CAPS Convertible Adjustable Preferred Stock
CAPX Capital Expenditures
CAR Compound Annual Return; Computer-Assisted Retrieval; Commercial Activity Report; Cumulative Abnormal Return
CARs Certificates of Automobile Receivables
CARD Certificates of Amortized Revolving Debt
CARICOM Caribbean Community; Caribbean Common Market
CARIFTA Caribbean Free Trade Association
CASDB Central African States Development Bank
CASE Council of American States in Europe
CASI Computer Aided Self Interview
CAT Computer-Assisted Trading; Computer-Assisted Transcription; Conventional Arms Transfer; Charges Access and Terms
CATI Computer Aided Telephone Interviewing
CATS Certificate of Accrual on Treasury Securities
CATV Community Antenna Television (cable TV)
CB&H Continent Between Bordeaux and Hamburg
CBA Capital Builder Account
CBD Central Business District; Cash Before Delivery; Commerce Business Daily
CBERA Caribbean Basin Economic Recovery Act
CBI Caribbean Basin Initiative; Confederation of British Industry
CBM Conventional Buoy Mooring
CBO Collateralized Bond Obligation
CBOE Chicago Board Options Exchange
CBT Computer-Based Trading; Computer-Based Training; Chicago Board of Trade
CBW Chemical and Biological Weapons
CC Carbon Copy; Current Cost; Civil Commotions Cancellation Clause; Continuation Clause
CCA Current Cost Accounting ; Chambre de Cooperation de l'Afrique de l'Ouest
CCAO Chambre de Cooperation de l'Afrique de l'Ouest
CCC Canadian Commercial Corporation; Commodity Credit Corporation; Customs Cooperation Council
CCCE Caisse Centrale de Coope'ration Economique
CCCN Customs Cooperation Council Nomendature
CCD Conseil de Coope'ration Douanie're
CCF CoCom Cooperation Forum
CCFF Compensatory and Contingency Financing Facility
CCH Commerce Clearing House
CCI Chambre de Commerce International
CCIR Comite Consultatif International des Radiocommunications
CCISG Convention Contracts of International Sale of Goods
CCITT Consultative Committee for International Telephone and Telegraph; Comite' Consultatif International Te'le'graphique et Telephonique
CCL Commerce Control List
CCNAA Coordination Council for North American Affairs
CCY Convertible Currency
CD Certificate of Deposit; Commercial Dock; Consular Declaration; Clean Draft; Creative Director; Confidential Document
CDB Caribbean Development Bank

CDC Commonwealth Development Corporation
CDFC Commonwealth Development Finance Company
CDI Capital Development Initiative
CDN Canadian Dealing Network
CD-ROM Compact Disk Read Only Memory
CCSA Collective Company Signing Agreement
CD Country Damage
CDB Caribbean Development Bank
CDC Commonwealth Development Corporation
CDI Capital Development Initiative
CDSC Contingent Deferred Sales Charge
CDT Center for Defense Trade
CDV Current Domestic Value
CE Committee of Experts; Communautes Europe'enes; Conformite Europe'ene; Council of Europe
CEA Council of Economic Advisers; Chinese Economic Area
CEAO Communaute Economique de l'Aftique de l'Ouest
CEAU Council of Economic Arab Unity
CEBS Certified Employee Benefit Specialists
CEC Commodities Exchange Center
CECA Communaute Europeenne du Charbon et de l'Acier
CEE Commission Economique pour l'Europe
CEEAC Communaute Economique des Etats de l'Afrique Centrale
CEEB Customs Electronic Bulletin Board
CED Committee for Economic Development
CEEB Customs Electronic Bulletin Board
CEFTA Central Europe Free Trade Association
CEG Canadian Exchange Group
CEN Comite Europeen de Normalisation
CENELEC European Committee for Electrotechnical Standardization
CEO Chief Executive Officer
CEPAL Comision Económica para America Latina y el Caribe
CEPGL Communaute Economique des Pays des Grands Lacs
CEPT Conference Europeénne des Administrations des Postes et Telecommunications
CERN Centre Europeén de Recherche Nucleaire
CES Comprehensive Export Schedule
CET Common External Tarrif
CETA Comprehensive Employment and Training Act of 1975
CF Cubic Feet; Carried Forward; Clean Float
CFA Chartered Financial Analyst; Communaute Financiere Africaine
CFAT Cash flow After Taxes
CFC Chartered Financial Consultant; Common Fund for Commodities; Controlled Foreign Corporation
CFCE Centre Francais du Commerce Exterieur
CFI Cost, Freight and Insurance
CFIS Center for Foreign Investor Services
CFIUS Committee on Foreign Investment in the United States
CFO Chief Financial Officer; Channel for Orders; Coast for Orders; Calling for Orders
CFP Certified Financial Planner
CFR Code of Federal Regulations; Cost and Freight
CFS Container Freight Station; Country Focused Seminar
CFTA Canadian Free Trade Agreement
CFTC Commodities Futures Trading Commission
CFY Cash Flow Yield
CG Consul General; Consulate Generale; Cairns Group
CGA Cargo's Proportion of General Average
CGIAR Consultative Group on International Agricultural Research
CGL Comprehensive General Liability (insurance)
CGSA Carriage of Goods by Sea Act
CGT Capital Gains Tax
CH&H Continent between Havre and Hamburg
CHAPS Clearing House Automated Payments System
CHB Customhouse Broker

CHESS Clearing House Electronic Subregister System
CHG Charge d'Affaires
CHGWC Change in Working Capital
CHIPS Clearing House Interbank Payment System
CHX Chicago Stock Exchange
CI Consular Invoice; Certificate of Insurance
CIA Cash in Advance
CIAT Centro Internacional de Agricultura Tropical
CICA Confederation Internationale du Credit Agricole
CIDA Canadian International Development Agency
CIE Captain's Imperfect Entry (Customs)
CIF Cost, Insurance, and Freight; Corporate Income Fund
CIF&E Cost, Insurance, Freight and Exchange
CIFCI Cost, Insurance, Freight, Commission and Interest
CIFLT Cost, Insurance, and Freight London Terms
CII Chartered Insurance Institute
CILSS Comite' Permanent Intere'tats de Lutte contre la Secheresse
CIM Computer-Integrated Manufacturing
CIMMYT Centro Internacional de Mejoramiento de Maiz y Trigo
CIMS Commercial Information Management System
CIPs Commodity Import Programs
CIR Center for International Research
CIRR Commercial Interest Reference Rates
CIS Commonwealth of Independent States; Compuserve
CISG Convention on Contracts for the International Sale of Goods
CIT Court of International Trade
CITA Committee for the Implementation of Textile Agreements
CITES Convention on International Trade in Endangered Species
CIV Customs Import Value
CIX Commercial Internet Exchange
CJ Commodity Jurisdiction
CK Cask
CKD Completely Knocked Down
CL Craft Loss
CLC Commercial Letter of Credit
CLD Cleared
CLDP Commercial Law Development Program
CLU Chartered Life Underwriter
CMA Common Monetary Agreement
CMBS Commercial Mortgage Backed Securities
CME Chicago Mercantile Exchange
CMEA Council for Mutual Economic Assistance
CML Capital Market Line
CMO Collateralized Mortgage Obligation; Common Market Organization
CMP Country Marketing Plan
CMPL Completed
CMSA Consolidated Metropolitan Statistical Area
CN Consignment Note; Cover Note; Credit Note; Combined Nomenclature
CNAR Compound Net Annual Rate
CNS Continuous Net Settlement
CNUSA Commercial News USA
CO Certificate of Origin; Cash Order; Case Oil
COAP Cottonseed Oil Assistance Program
COB Cargo on Board
COBOL Common Business-Oriented Language
COCOM Coordinating Committee on Multilateral Export Controls; Coordinating Committee for Multilateral Strategic Export Controls
COBRA Consolidated Omnibus Budget Reconciliation Act
COCA Confederation Internationale du Credit Agricole
COCOM Coordinating Committee on Multilateral Export Controls
COD Cash on Delivery
CODEX Codex Alimentanus Commission
COD Cash on Delivery; Cancellation of Debt
CODA Cash or Deferred Arrangement
COE Council of Europe; Conseil de l'Europe
COFACE Compagnie Francaise d'Assurance pour le Commerce Exterieur
COFC Container on Flat Car

COGS Cost of Goods Sold-Labor
COLA Cost-of-Living Adjustment
COLTS Continuous On-Line Trading System
COM Costs of Manufacture; Chief of Mission; Computer Output Microfilm; Commission
COMECON Council for Mutual Economic Assistance
COMEX Commodity Exchange Inc.
COMSAT Communications Satellite Corporation
CONSGT Consignment
CONT Continent of Europe
CONTAH Continent, Antwerp-Hamburg Range
CONTBH Continent, Bordeaux-Hamburg Range
CONTHH Continent, Havre-Hamburg Range
CONUS Contiguous United States
CONV Conveyance
COO Chief Operation Officer
COP Cost of Production
COPAL Cocoa Producers Alliance
COPANT Comision Panamericana de Normas Tecnicas
COR Club of Rome
CORECT Committee on Renewable Energy, Commerce, and Trade
COST European cooperation on Scientific and Technical Research
CP Charter Party; Custom of Port; Control Panel; Copy Protected
CPA Certified Public Accountant; Claims Payable Abroad; Closest Point of Approach; Critical Path Analysis
CPCM Comite' Permanent Consultatif du Maghreb
CPCU Chartered Property and Casualty Underwriter
CPD Charterers' Pay Dues
CPE Centrally Planned Economy; Cost Per Enquiry
CPI Consumer Price Index
CP/M Control Program for Microcomputer
CPM Cost Per Mille
CPNT Comision Panaamericana de Normas Tecnicas
CPO Cost Per Order
CPP Current Purchasing Power; Controllable Pitch Propellers
CPS Characters per Second; Certified Professional Secretary
CPSC Consumer Product Safety Commission
CPT Carriage Paid To
CPTM Cost Per Targeted Mille
CSCE Conference on Security and Cooperation in Europe
CPU Central Processing Unit
CR Credit; Creditor; Current Rate; Company's Risk; Carrier's Risk
CRM Customer Relationship Management
CRO Cancelling Returns Only
CRP Capacity Requirements Plan
CS Collections System
CSCE Conference on Security and Cooperation in Europe
CSD Closed Shelter Deck
CSE Cincinnati Stock Exchange
CSI Commissioners Standard Industrial Mortality Table
CSIS Center for Strategic and International Studies
CSO Commissioners Standard Ordinary Mortality Table
CSP Common Standard Level of Effective Protection
CSS Customized Sales Survey
CST Central Standard Time
CSTAC Computer Systems Technical Advisory Committee
CS&CE Coffee, Sugar & Cocoa Exchange
CT Countertrade; Corporation Tax
CTA Cumulative Translation Adjustment
CTD Committee on Trade and Development
CTF Certified Trade Fair
CTIS Center for Trade and Investment Services
CTL Constructive Total Loss
CTLO Constructive Total Loss Only
CTMs Certified Trade Missions
CTP Composite Theoretical Performance
CTs Crates
CTT Capital Transfer Tax
CULS Convertible Unsecured Loan Stock
CUM Cumulative
CUSIP Committee on Uniform Securities Identification Procedures

CV Corporate Venture; Constructed Value; Chief Value
CVC Customs Valuation Code
CVD Countervailing Duty
CVMS Contractual Vertical Marketing System
CVS Corporate Venturing Scheme
CW Commercial Weight; Cash With Order
CWC Chemical Weapons Convention
CWO Cash With Order
CXT Common External Tariff
CY Container Yard

D

D District Office; Draught; Delivery; Delivered
D/A Documents Against Acceptance
D/P Documents Against Presentation
DA Development Assistance; Discharged Afloat
DAA Documents Against Acceptance
DAC Development Assistance Committee
DACON Data on Consulting Firms
DAE Dynamic Asian Economies
DAF Delivered at Frontier
DANIDA Danish International Development Assistance
DASH Dual Access Storage Handling
D&B Dun and Bradstreet
DB Data Base; Day Book; Defined Benefit
DBA Doing Business As
DBB Deals, Battens and Boards
DBGLS Development Bank of the Great Lakes States
DBK Drawback
DBM Disk By Mail
DBMS Database Management System
DBP Development Bank of the Philippines
DC Delivery Clause
DCF Discounted Cash Flow
DCI Direct Computer Interviewing
DCM Deputy Chief of Mission
DCS Defense Conversion Subcommittee
DD Double Deck; Date Draft; Damage Done; Days after Date; Days' Date; Demand Draft; Delivered at Docks; Diversionary Dumping
DDB Double-Declining-Balance
DDC Damage Done in Collision
DDE Direct Data Entry
DDM Discounted Dividend Model; Dividend Discount Model
DDO Despatch Discharging Only
DEC District Export Council
DECs District Export Councils
DED Deductible
DEFAC Deferred Account
DEIP Dairy Export Incentive Program
DEP Department of Export Promotion

DET Detained
DEZs Development Economic Zones
DF Dead Freight; Direction Finder; Designated Federal Officer
DFA Development Fund for Africa
DFOR Deductions for Adjusted Gross Income
DFP Duty-Free Port
DFROM Deductions Form Adjusted Gross Income
DFT Draft
DIDA Danish International Development Assistance
DISC Domestic International Sales Corporation
DIF Data Interchange Format
DIS Discount
DISBT Disbursements
DISC Domestic International Sale Cooperation
DISH Data Interchange in Shipping
DISPL Displacement
DJI Dow Jones Index
DJIA Dow Jones Industrial Average
DK Don't Know; Deck
DL Distribution License
DLO Dispatch Loading Only
DM Decimeter; Definitional Mission
DMA Direct Marketing Association
DMOU Defense Memoranda of Understanding
DMA Direct Marketing Association
DMP District Marketing Plan
DMU Decision Making Unit
DMSB Direct Mail Sales Bureau
DMSSB Direct Mail Services Standard Board
DN Debit Note
DNI Do Not Increase; Digital Networked Individuals
DNRO Do Not Reduce Order
DNS Domain Name Server
DO District Office; Delivery Order
DOA Documents on Acceptance
DOC Driver Other Car Insurance
DOS Disk Operating System; Department of State
DOT Designated Order Turnaround System; Department of Transport
DP Direct Port; Documents against Payment; Draft Proposal; Data Processing
DPA Defense Production Act
DPAS Defense Priorities and Allocation System
DPR Daily Pro Rata
DR Debit; Deposit Receipt; Dock Receipt
D-RAM Dynamic Random Access Memory
DRC Damaged Received in Collision
DREE Direction des Relations Economiques Exteneures
DRP Dividend Reinvestment Plan
DRTV Direct Response Television
D/S Days After Sighting; Delivered Sound (grain trade)
DSB Dispute Settlement Body
DSR Debt Service Ratio
DSS Decision Support System
DST Daylight Saving Time
DST Double-Stacked Container Train
DTAG Defense Trade Advisory Group
DTBA Days to be Agreed, Date to be Advised
DTC Defense Trade Controls; Depository Trust Company; Depository Transfer Check
DTI Department of Trade and Industry
DTP Desktop Publishing; Defense Trade Policy
DTR Defense Trade Regulations
DTSA Defense Technology Security Administrations
DTWG Defense Trade Working Group
DUS Dollar Unit Sampling
DV Dual Valuation
DVC Delivery Verification Certificate
DW Deadweight; Dock Warrant
DWAT Deadweight All Told
DWC Deadweight Capacity
DWT Deadweight Tonnage

E

E&OE Errors and Omissions Excepted
EA Escrow Account
EAA Export Administration Act
EAC Export Assistance Center; East African Community; Equivalent Annual Cost
EADB East African Development Bank
EAEC East Asian Economic Caucus; European Atomic Energy Community
EAFEI European Australian and Far East Index
EAI Enterprise for the Americas Initiative
EAITC External Affairs and International Trade Canada
EAON Except As Otherwise Noted
EAP Employee Assistance Program
EAR Exported Administration Regulations
EARB Exported Administration Review Board
EASD European Association of Securities Dealers
EASDAQ European Association of Securities Dealers Automated Quotation
EB Eastbound
EBB Economic Bulletin Board
EBIAT Earnings Before Interest after Taxes
EBIT Earnings Before Interest and Taxes
EBITD Earnings Before Interest, Taxes and Depreciation
EBITDA Earnings Before Interest, Taxes, Depreciation, and Amortization
EBRD European Bank for Reconstruction and Development
EBT Earnings Before Taxes
EC European Communities
ECA Economic Commission for Africa; Export Credit Agency
ECASS Export Control Automated Support System
ECB European Central Bank
ECCAS Economic Community of Central African States
ECCB East Caribbean Central Bank
ECCN Export Control Classification Number; Export Commodity Classification Number
ECCNs Export Control Commodity Numbers
ECCP East Coast Coal Port
ECD Exporter Counseling Division
ECDG Export Credit Guarantee Department
ECE Economic Commission for Europe; Export Credit Establishment
ECGB East Coast of Great Britain
ECGD Export Credit Guarantee Department
ECGLC Economic Community of the Great Lakes Countries
ECI East Coast of Ireland
ECJ European Court of Justice
ECL Export Control List
ECLA Economic Commission for Latin America
ECLAC Economic Commission for Latin America and the Caribbean
ECLS Export Contact List Service
ECM Enterprise Content Management; Emerging Company Marketplace
ECME Economic Commission for the Middle East
ECNR European Center for Nuclear Research
ECO Economic Cooperation Organization
E-CON Electronic Computer Originated Mail
ECOSOC Economic and Social Council
ECOWAS Economic Community of West African States
ECP Euro-Commercial Paper
ECRT European Community of Research and Technology
ECS European Committee for Standardization
ECSC European Coal and Steel Community
ECU European Currency Unit
ECUK East Coast of United Kingdom
ECV Each Cargo Voyage
EDB Exporter Data Base
EDC Export Development Corporation; Electronic Data Capture
EDF European Development Bank
EDI Electronic Data Interchange

EDIFACT Electronic Data Interchange for Administration, Commerce, and Transportation
EDO Export Development Office
EDP Electronic Data Processing
EDSP Exchange Delivery Settlement Price
EE Errors Excepted
EEA European Economic Area; Each and Every Accident
EEBIC Eastern Europe Business Information Center
EEC European Economic Communities
EEL Each and Every Loss
EEO Each and Every Occurrence
EEOC Equal Employment Opportunity
EEP Export Enhancement Program
EEPROM Electronically Erasable Programmable Read-Only Memory
EEZ Exclusive Economic Zone
EFF Extended Fund Facility
EFT Electronic Funds Transfer
EFTA European Free Trade Association
EFTPOS Electronic Funds Transfer at Point of Sale
EGM Extraordinary General Meeting
EI Each Incident
EIB European Investment Bank
EIS Enterprise Investment Scheme; Environmental Impact Statement; Executive Information Service
EIS Export Information System
EITC Earned Income Tax Credit
EL Employer's Liability
ELAIN Electronic License Application and Information Network
ELAN Export Legal Assistance Network
ELP Export Limitation Period
ELVIS Export License Voice Information System
EM Effective Margin; Export Merchant
EMA European Monetary Agreement
EMC Export Management Company
EMCF European Monetary Cooperation Fund
EMFI Emerging Markets Free Index
EMH Efficient Market Hypothesis.
EMI European Monetary Institute
EMPL Estimated Maximum Probable Loss
EMS Export Management System; European Monetary System; Electronic Mail Survey
EMU European Monetary Union
EMV Expected Monetary Value
EN European Norm
EO Evidence of Origin
EOE European Options Exchange
EOHP Excepted Otherwise Herein Provided
EOM End of Month
EONIA Euro Overnight Indexed Average Rate
EOP European Patent Office
EOQ Economic Order Quantity
EOTC European Organization for Testing and Certification
EOY End of Year
EP European Parliament; Export Promotion
EPA Environmental Protecting Agency
EPC Economic Policy Council; European Patent Convention
EPCI Enhanced Proliferation Control Initiative
EPI Earned Premium Income
EPIRB Emergency Position Indicator Radio Beacon
EPO European Patent Office
EPOS Electronic Point of Sale
EPP Executive Pension Plan
EPROM Erasable Programmable Read-Only Memory
EPS Earnings Per Share; Export Promotion Services
EPZ Export Processing Zone
EQ Export Quotas
EQA European Quality Award
ERA Equal Rights Amendment; Export Restraint Agreement
ERDF European Regional Development Fund
ERISA Employee Retirement Income Security Act
ERLC Export Revolving Line of Credit
ERM European Exchange Rate Mechanism; Exchange Rate Mechanism
ERNIE Electronic Random Number Indicating Equipment
ERO Electronic Return Originator
ERP European Recovery Program

ERS Economic Research Service
ERTA Economic Recovery Tax Act of 1981
ERV Each Round Voyage
ESA European Space Agency
ESAF Enhanced Structural Adjustment Facility
ESCAP Economic and Social Commission for Asia and the Pacific
ESCB European System of Central Banks
ESCWA Economic and Social Commission for Western Asia
ESD Echo-Sounding Device
ESF Economic Stabilization Fund; Economic Support Fund
ESOP Employee Stock Ownership Plan
ESOT Employee Share Ownership Trust
ESP Exporter's Sale Price; Emotional Selling Proposition
ESPRIT European Strategy Program for Research in Information Technologies
ESQ Esquire
EST Eastern Standard Time; Estimated
ETA European Technical Approval; Estimated Time of Arrival
ETAC Electronics Technical Advisory Committee
ETC Export Trading Company
ETF ElectronicTransfer of Funds
ETM Escrowed to Maturity
ETSI European Telecommunications Standards Institute
ETUC European Trade Union Confederation
EU European Union
EUCLID European Cooperation for the Long Term in Defense
EURAM European Research in Advanced Materials
EURATOM European Atomic Energy Community
EUREKA European Research Coordination Agency
EUREX European Derivatives Exchange
EURIBOR European Interbank Offered Rate
EURL Entreprise Unipersonnelle Responsabilite Limitee
EUROMTN Euro-Medium Term Note
EUROSTAT Statistical Office of the European Community
EUROTRA European Research and Development Program for a Machine Translation System of Advanced Design
EV Expected Value
EX Excluding; Examined; Exchange; Executed
EXCEL Export Credit Enhanced Leverage
EXIMBANK Export/Import Bank of the United States
EXPAT Expatriate
EXW Ex Works

F

F&AP Fire and Allied Perils
FA Free Astray; Foreign Affiliate; Framework Agreement
FAA Federal Aviation Administration; Free of All Averages
FAAS Foreign Affairs Administrative Support
FAC Fast as you Can; Facultative
FAC/OBLIG Facultative/Obligatory
FAD Fonds Africain de Development
FAIR Fair Access to Insurance Requirements
FAK Freight All Kinds
FAO Food and Agricultural Organization
FAQ Fair Average Quality; Free Alongside Quay; Frequently Asked Question
FAS Foreign Agricultural Service; Free Alongside Ship; Financial Accounting Statement; Firsts and Second
FASB Financial Accounting Standards Board
FAVR Fixed and Variable Rate Allowance
FAX Facsimile
FAZ Foreign Access Zone
FBIS Foreign Broadcast Information Service
FBL Foul Bill of Lading
FBO Foreign Branch Office
FBP Foreign Buyer Program
FBSEA Foreign Bank Supervision Enhancement Act
FC&S Free of Capture and Seizure
FCA Free Carrier; Freight Carriage
FCAR Free of Claim for Accident Reported
FCC Federal Communications Commission
FCIA Foreign Credit Insurance Association
FCII Fellow of the Chartered Insurance Institute
FCL Full Container Load
FCM Futures Commission Merchant
FCO Foreign and Commonwealth Office
FCPA Foreign Corrupt Practices Act
FC&S Free Of Capture and Seizure
FCS Foreign Commercial Service
FCSC Foreign Claims Settlement Commission
FCV Full contract value; Full Completed Value
F&D Freight and Demurrage
FD Free Discharge; Food for Development; Free Delivery; Free Dispatch; Free Docks
FDA Food and Drug Administration
FDI Foreign Direct Investment
FDIC Federal Deposit Insurance Corporation
FDIUS Foreign Direct Investment in the United States
FDO For Declaration Purposes Only
FECA Foreign Exchange Control Act
FECDAP Foreign Exchange and Currency Deposit Brokers Association
FED Federal Reserve System
FEDMA Federation of European Direct Marketing Associations
FEMA Foreign Extraterritorial Measure Act of 1984
FEMIDE Federacion Mundial de Instituciones Financieras de Desarollo
FEOID Foreign Exchange Operations and Investment Department
FETs Foreign Economic Trends
FETC Foreign Economic and Trade Commission
FEU Forty-foot Equivalent Unit
FF Freight Forwarder
FFA Free From Average; Free From Alongside, Free Foreign Agency
FFEU Forty-Foot Equivalent Unit
FFF Foreign Freight Forwarder
FFO Funds From Operations; Fixed and Floating Objects
FFP Food For Progress
FGA Foreign General Average
FGIS Federal Grain Inspection Service
FH Fore Hatch
FHA Federal Housing Administration
FHFB Federal Housing Finance Board
FHLMC Federal Home Loan Mortgage Corporation
FI Free In; Foreign Investment

FIA Full Interest Admitted; Fellow of the Institute of Actuaries
FIAS Foreign Investment Advisory Service
FIATA Federation Internationale des Associations de Transitaires
FIB Free Into Bunkers; Free Into Barge
FIBOR Frankfurt Interbank Offered Rate
FICA Federal Insurance Contributions Act
FICO Financing Corporation
FICS Fellow of the Institute of Chartered Shipbrokers
FIDIC Federation Internationale des Ingenieurs-Conseils
FIFO First In, First Out
FII Foreign Investment Insurance
FIL Foreign Insurance Legislation
FIMBRA Financial Intermediaries, Managers and Brokers Regulatory Association
FIO Free In and Out
FIONIA Frankfurt Overnight Indexed Average Rate
FIOS Free In and Out Stowed
FIOST Free In and Out Stowed and/or Trimmed
FIOT Free In and Out Trimmed
FIRA Foreign Investment Review Agency
FIRPTA Foreign Investment in Real Property Tax Act of 1980
FIRREA Financial Institutions Reform, Recovery and Enforcement Act
FIT Foreign Independent Tour; Free of Income Tax
FIW Free in Wagon
FLAIR Food-Linked Agro-Industrial Research
FLASH Feeder-LASH
FLE Fire, Lightning and Explosion
FLSA Fair Labor Standards Act
FMAN February, May, August, and November
FMC Federal Maritime Commission
FMCG Fast-Moving Consumer Goods
FMD Foreign Market Development Program
FMEA Failure Mode and Effect Analysis
FMHA Farmer's Home Administration
FMIFD Federacion Mundial de Instituciones Financieras de Desarollo
FMLA Family and Medical Leave Act
FMRR Financial Management Rate of Return
FMS Foreign Military Sales
FMs Fathoms (timber)
FMV Foreign Market Value
FMS Flexible Manufacturing System
FNMA Federal National Mortgage Association
FO Free Out; For Orders; Firm Offer; Full Out Terms (grain trade)
FOA Foreign-Owned Affiliate
FOB Free on Board
FOC Flag of convenience, Free of Commission; Free of Charge; Free of Claims; Father of Chapel
FOD Free of Damage
FOFT Federal Office for Foreign Trade
FOGS Functioning of the GATT System
FOK Fill or Kill Order
FOIA Freedom of Information Act
FOK Fill-or-Kill Order
FOM Flag, Ownership and Management
FOMC Federal Open Market Committee
FOMEX Fondo para ei Fomentö de las Exportaciones de Productos
FONASBA Federation of National Association of Shipbrokers and Agents
FONPLATA Fondo Financiero Para ei Desarrollo de la Cuenca del Plata
FOOTSIE Financial Times Stock Exchange 100 Share Index
FOQ Free on Quay
FOR Free on Rail
FORDTIS Foreign Disclosure and Technical Information System
FOR/FOT Free on Rail/Free on Truck
FOREX Foreign Exchange
FORIFOT Free on Rail/Free on Truck
FORT Full Out Rye Terms
FORTRAN Formula Translation
FOS Free on Steamer
FOSFA Federation of Oils, Seeds & Fats Associations
FOT Free on Truck
FOW Free on Wagon; First Open Water
FGLs Fourth-Generations Languages
FOW First Open Water
FP Food for Peace; Foreign Person; Free Port; Fully Paid; Floating (or open) Policy
FPA Free of Particular Average

FPAAC Free of Particular Average American Conditions
FPAEC Free of Particular Average English Conditions
FPC Federal Power Commission; Foreign Policy Control
FPFS Fines, Penalties, and Forfeitures System
FPG Foreign Parent Group
FPIL Full Premium if Lost
FPM Flexible-Payment Mortgage
FPO Fleet Post Office
FPT Forepeak Tank
F/R Freight Release
FRA Forward Rate Agreement
FRAC Frequency, Recency, Amount, Category
FRB Federal Reserve Board
FR&CC Free of Riot and Civil Commotion
FRC Free of Reported Casualty; Financial Reporting Council
FRCD Floating-Rate Certificate of Deposit
FREIT Finite-Life Real Estate Investment Trust
FRN Floating-Rate Note
FRO Fire Risk Only
FROF Fire Risk on Freight
FRRP Financial Reporting Review Panel
FRS Federal Reserve System
FRT Freight
FS Foreign Service
FSA Freedom Support Act; Foreign Sales Agent
FSBR Financial Statement and Budget Report
FSC Foreign Sales Corporation
FSI Foreign Service Institute
FSL Full Signed Line (insurance)
FSLIC Federal Savings and Loan Insurance Corporation
FSM Foreign Military Sales
FSN Foreign Service National
FSO Foreign Service Officer; Fund for Special Operations
FSR&CC Free of Strikes, Riots and Civil Commotions
FS Feasibility Study
FSU Former Soviet Union
FT Financial Times; Full Terms; Feet
FTA Free-Trade Agreement; Free-Trade Area; Freight Transport Association and Agents
FTC Federal Trade Commission
FTD Foreign Trade Division
FTH Fathom
FTI Foreign Traders Index
FTO Foreign Trade Organization
FTP File Transfer Protocol
FTRR&I For Their Respective Rights and Interests
FTS Federal Telecommunication System
FTSR Foreign Trade Statistical Reporting
FTZE Foreign Trade Zone Entry
FTZs Foreign Trade Zones
FTZSZ Foreign Trade Zone-Subzone
FUTA Federal Unemployment Tax Act
FVC Fishing Vessel Clauses
FWD Fresh Water Damage; Forward
FWL Full Written Line (insurance)
FWPCA Federal Water Pollution Control Act (USA)
FWR FIATA Warehouse Receipt
FWT&GD Fair Wear, Tear and Gradual Deterioration
FX Foreign Exchange
FY Fiscal Year
FYI For Your Information
FZ Franc Zone

G

G-5 Group of Five
G-7 Group of Seven
G-10 Group of Ten
G-11 Group of Eleven
G-15 Group of Fifteen
G-24 Group of Twenty-Four
G-77 Group of Seventy-Seven
GA General Average
GAAP Generally Accepted Accounting Principles
GAAS Generally Accepted Accounting Principles
GAB General Arrangements to Borrow
GACON General Average Contribution
GADEP General Average Deposit
GADV Gross Arrived Damaged Value
GAFTA Grain & Feed Trade Association
GAO General Accounting Office
GAB General Arrangements to Borrow
GASV Gross Arrived Sound Value
GATC German Agency for Technical Cooperation
GATS General License-Aircraft on Temporary Sojourn
GATT General Agreement on Tariffs and Trade
GAW Guaranteed Annual Wage
GC Grandfather Clause
GCC Gulf Cooperation Council
GCCI Global Contract Comprehensive Insurance
GCG General License-Shipments to Agencies of Cooperating Governments
G-COCOM General License-COCOM
GCT General License
G-DEST General License-Destination
GDP Gross Domestic Product
GDS General Depreciation System
GE General Exception
GEF Global Environmental Facility
GEM Growing-Equity Mortgage; Global Export Manager
GE General Exception
GEF Global Environmental Facility
GEM Global Export Manager
GEMSU German Economic Monetary and Social Union
GF Government Form (chartering)
GFA Good Fair Average
GFCIDC German Financing Company for Investments in Developing Countries
GFW General License-Free World
GIC Guaranteed Income Contact; Guaranteed Investment Contract
GIE Groupement d'Int~et Economique
GIF Graphic Interchange File
GIFT General License
GIGO Garbage In, Garbage Out
GIM Gross Income Multiplier
GKS Gold Key Service
GL General License
GLOG General License
GLR General License Return (Replacement)
GLS General License-Safeguard
GLSS General License-Ship Store
GLV General License-Shipments of Limited Value
GMB Good Merchantable Brand
GMC Guaranteed Mortgage Certificate
GMI Gray Market Imports
GMQ Good Merchantable Quality
GMT Greenwich Mean Time
GNEPI Gross Net Earned Premium Income
G-NGO General License
GNMA Government National Mortgage Association
G-NNR General License-Nonnaval Reserve
GNP Gross National Product
GOB Going-out-of-Business Sale; Good Ordinary Brand
GOP Gross Original Premium
GPM Graduated-Payment Mortgage
GPO Government Printing Office
GPP&P Government Procurement Policies and Practices
GPR Guaranteed Premium Reduction Insurance
GQ Global Quota
GR Grain; Gross
GRAT Grantor-Retained Annuity Trust
GRIT Grantor-Retained Interest Trust
GRM Gross Rent Multiplier
GRT Gross Register Tons; Gross ton

GRU Grantor-Retained Unitrust
GRW Gross Weight
GS Good Safety
GSM General Sales Manager; Good Sound Merchantable
GSE Government-Sponsored Enterprise
GSP Generalized System of Preferences
GSS General Statistical Service
GT General Tariff
GTC Good-Till-Canceled Order
GTDA General License-Technical Data Publicly Available
GTDR General License-Technical Data Restricted by Written Assurance
GTDU General License-Technical Data Restricted Without Written Assurance
G-TEMP General License-Temporary Export
GTF-US General License
GTMO Good-This-Month Order
GUAR Guaranteed
GUI Graphical User Interface
GULP Group Universal Life Policy
GYC Gyro Compass

H

H Hour
HA Hectares; Helsinki Accord; Horn of Africa
HAD Havre, Antwerp or Dunkirk Harbor
HBR Harbour
HC High Commission; Hard Currency; Held Covered (insurance); Hold Cleaning
HCFA Health Care Financing Administration
HETC Horizontal Export Trading Company
HEX Helsinki Exchange
HH Havre to Hamburg
HHD Hogshead
HIBOR Hong Kong Interbank Offered Rate
HIP Human Information Processing
HIPC Heavily Indebted Poor Countries Trust Fund
HK Hook Damage
HKFE Hong Kong Futures Exchange
HLT Highly Leveraged Transaction
H&M Hull and Machinery
HMHC Her Majesty's High Commission
HMO Health Maintenance Organization
HMP Home Market Price
HMSO Her Majesty´s Stationary Office
H&O Hook and Oil Damage
HOW Homeowner Warranty Plan
HP Hire Purchase; Hours Purposes; Horsepower
HPN Horse-Power Nominal
HRM Human -esource Management
HS Harmonized System; Harmonized Commodity Description and Coding System
HSC Harmonized System Committee
HSSC Heating, Sweating and Spontaneous Combustion
HT Half-time
HTML Hypertext Markup Language
HTS Harmonized Tariff Schedule
HTTP Hypertext Transfer Protocol
HTWG High Technology Working Group

HUD Housing and Urban Development (Department of)
HWD Heavy Weather Damage
HWM High Water Mark
HWOST High Water Ordinary Spring Tides

I

IA Internet Access; Information Acceleartion
IAs International Agreements; Internal arrangements
IACAC Inter-American Commercial Arbitration Commission
IACC International Anticounterfeiting Coalition
IACO Inter-African Coffee Organization
IADB Inter-American Development Bank
IAEA International Atomic Energy Agency
IAED International Association of Exchange Dealers
IAEL International Atomic Energy List
IAF International Accreditation Forum
IAIGC Inter-Arab Investment Guarantee Corporation
IAND/ORO In and/or Overdeck
IAP Internet Access Provider
IAPH International Association of Ports and Harbours
IARCs International Agricultural Research Centers
IAS International Accounting Standards
IASC International Accounting Standards Committee
IA-ECOSOC Inter-American Economic and Social Council
IATA International Air Transport Association
IAU International Accounting Unit
IB Invoice Book; In Bond; Issuing Bank
IBA International Banking Act
IBC International Banking Center; Institute Builders' Clauses
IBEC International Bank for Economic Cooperation
IBEL Interest-Bearing Eligible Liabilities
IBES Institutional Brokers Estimate System
IBEX Iberian Exchange
IBF International Banking Facility
IBL Inland Bill of Lading

IBLCB International Bidding Local Competitive Bidding
IBMBR Inter Bank Market Bid Rate
IBNR Incurred But Not Reported
IBOR Interbank Offered Rate
IBOS International Business Opportunities Service
IBPGR International Board for Plant Genetic Resources
IBRD International Bank for Reconstruction and Development
IBRS International Business Reply Service
IBS In-Bond System
IC Import Certificate; Information Coefficient; Ice Clause; Imports for Consumption; Inspection Certification; Insurance Certificate; Integrated Carriers; Intermediate Consignee; Integrated Circuit; Inland Carrier
ICA International Cocoa Agreement; International Coffee Agreement; International Commodity Agreement
ICAC International Confederation of Agricultural Credit
ICADLF International Cooperation Administration and Development Loan Fund
ICAO International Civil Aviation Organization
ICARDA International Center for Agricultural Research in Dry Areas
ICB International Competitive Bidding
ICBL International Competitive Bidding Limited
IC&C Invoice Coast and Charges
ICC Interstate Commerce Commission; International Chamber of Commerce; Institute Classification Clauses; Institute Cargo Clauses
ICD Inland Clearance Depot
ICE Istituto Nazionale per il Commercio Estero
ICEP Instituto do Com~rcio de Portugal
ICES International Council for the Exploration of the Sea
ICFTU International Confederation of Free Trade Unions
ICGEB International Center for Genetic Engineering and Biotechnology
ICGP Intermediate Credit Guarantee Program
ICHCA International Cargo Handling Coordination Association
ICJ International Court of Justice
ICMS Imposto Dobre Circulacäo de Mercadorias y Servicos
ICO International Cocoa Organization; International Coffee Organization; International Congress Office; Islamic Conference Organization
ICON Indexed Currency Option Note
ICP Industry Consultations Program
ICRAF International Centre for Research in Forestry
ICRISAT International Crops Research Institute for the Semi-Arid Tropics
ICS Investment Climate Statement; Institute of Chartered Shipbrokers; International Chamber of Shipping
ICSs Investment Climate Statements
ICSA Institute of Chartered Secretaries and Administrators
ICS&HCP International Convention on the Simplification and Harmonization of Customs Procedures
ICSHT International Center for Science and High Technology
ICSID International Centre for the Settlement for Investment Disputes
ICSU International Council of Scientific Unions
ICTF Intermodal Container Transfer Facility
IDA International Development Association
IDB Industrial Development Bond; Inter-American Development Bank; International Data Base; Islamic Development Bank
IDC Industrial Development Certificate; Intangible Drilling and Development Costs
IDEM Italian Derivatives Market
IDIN International Development Information Network
IDF Industrial Development Fund
IDR International Depository Receipt
IDRC International Development Research Center
IE Infrequent Exporter; Indirect Exporting
IEA International Energy Agency

IEC International Electrotechnical Commission
IEEPA International Emergency Economic Powers Act
IENT Institut Europeen des Normes des Telecommunication
IEP International Economic Policy
IEPG Independent European Program Group
IESC International Executive Service Corps
IF In Full
IFA Independent Financial Adviser
IFAC Industry Functional Advisory Committee
IFAD International Fund for Agricultural Development
IFC International Finance Corporation; Institute Freight Clauses
IFCE International Federation of Consulting Engineers
IFF Institute of Freight Forwarders
IFE International Fisher Effect
IFPS Integrated Financial Planning System
IFRB International Frequency Registration Board
IFS In-Flight Survey
IFU Industrialization Fund for Developing Countries
IFVC Institute Fishing Vessel Clauses
IGADD Inter-Governmental Authority on Drought and Development
IGC Interagency Group on Countertrade
IHP Indicated Horse-Power
II International Investment; Infant Industry
IIB International Investment Bank
IIC Inter-American Investment Corporation; International Import Certificate
IIL International Industrial List; Insurance Institute of London
IIMI International Irrigation Management Institute
IIPA International Intellectual Property Alliance
IIT Instruments of International Traffic
IITA International Institute of Tropical Agriculture
IIUPL International Institute for the Unification of Private Law
IL Industrial List; Import License
ILA International Longshoremen's Association
ILC Irrevocable Letter of Credit
ILCA International Livestock Center for Africa
ILO International Labor Organization
ILRAD International Laboratory for Research on Animal Diseases
ILU Institute of London Underwriters
ILZSG International Lead and Zinc Study Group
IM Institute of Management
IMA Institute of Management Accountants
IMF International Monetary Fund
IMI International Market Insight
IMIF International Maritime Industry Forum
IML International Munitions List
IMM International Monetary Market
IMO International Maritime Organization
IMR International Market Research
IMRO Investment Management Regulatory Organization
IMTA International Meat Trade Association
INCE Insurance
INCEWTIEs Insurance warranties
INCOTERMS International Commercial Terms
INDIS Industrial Information System
INIBAP International Network for the Improvement of Banana and Plantain
INMARSAT International Maritime Satellite Organization
INPI Instituto Nacional de Propriedade Industrial
INR Initial Negotiating Right
INSTINET Institutional Networks Corporation
INT Interest
INTELSAT International Telecommunications Satellite Organization
INTIB Industrial and Technological Information Bank
I/O Input/Output; In and/or Overdeck
IO Interest Only
IOC Immediate or Cancelled Order
IOGA Industry-Organized, Government-Approved Mission

IOM International Organization for Migration; Index and Option Market
IOS International Organization for Standardization
IOSCO International Organization for Securities Commissions
IOU I Owe You
IP Internet Protocol
IPA Institute of Practitioners in Advertising
IPAC Industry Policy Advisory Committee
IPE International Petroleum Exchange
IPF Intaken Piled Fathom
IPL Investment Product Line
IPM Institute of Personnel Management
IPO Initial Public Offering
IPRC Institute Port Risks Clauses
IPR Intellectual Property Right; Institute of Public Relations
IPS Investment Promotion Services
IQA Import Quota Auctioning
IR Import Restrictions; Inland Revenue; Import Rate
IRA Individual Retirement Account
IRB Industrial Revenue Bond
IRC International Research Council; Internet Relay Chat
IRCC International Radio Consultative Committee
IRO In Respect of
IRR Internal Rate of Return
IRRI International Rice Research Institute
IRS Internal Revenue Service; Interest Rate Swaps; Indian Register of Shipping
IRSG International Rubber Study Group
IRU International Road Transport Union
IS Import Substitution; Import Surcharge; Installment Shipments
ISA Individual Savings Account; Industry Subsector Analysis; International Sugar Agreement
ISAC Industry Sector Advisory Committee
ISBA Incorporated Society of British Advisers
ISDA International Swaps and Derivatives Association; International Swap Dealers Association
ISDB Islamic Development Bank
ISDN Integrated Services Digital Network
ISE Italian Stock Exchange
ISF International Shipping Federation
ISIS Intermarket Surveillance Information System
ISLP Investment Sector Loan Program
ISMA International Security Market Association
ISNAR International Service for National Agricultural Research
ISO Insurance Service Office; Incentive Stock Option; International Standards Organization; Independent Service Organization
ISONET International Standards Organization Information Network
ISP Internet Services Provider; Institute of Sales Promotion
ISRO International Securities Regulatory Organization
ISSA International Social Security Association
IT Information Technology; Income Tax; Indirect Tax
ITA International Tin Agreement
ITAR International Traffic in Arms Regulations
ITC International Trade Center; International Trade Commission; Institute Time Clauses
ITDCs International Trade Development Centers
ITE Immediate Transportation Entry
I&TO International and Territorial Operations
ITO International Trade Organization
ITS Intermarket Trading System; International Telecommunications Services
ITT Instruments of International Traffic
ITTCC International Telegraph and Telephone Consultative Committee
ITU International Telecommunication Union
IV Inherent Vice; Invoice Value; Increased Value
IVANS International Value-Added Network Services
IVC Institute Voyage Clauses (Hulls)
IVL Individually Validated License
IWC International Whaling Commission

IWTO International Wool Textile Organization
IYC Institute Yacht Clauses

J

J/A Joint Account
JAJO January, April, July, and October
JASDAQ Japanese Association of Securities Dealers Automated Quotation System
JCC Joint Cargo Committee
JCIT Joint Committee for Investment and Trade
JCP Japan Corporate Program
JCRA Joint Common Risks Agreement
JDB Japan Development Bank
JEC Joint Economic Committee of Congress
JEIC Japan Export Information Center
JESSI Joint European Submicron Silicon
JETRO Japan External Trade Organization
JETRRO Japan Exports Trade Recovery Organization
JEXIM Export/Import Bank of Japan
JHC Joint Hull Committee
JHF Joint Hull Formula
JHIU Japanese Hull Insurers' Union
JHU Joint Hull Understandings
JICA Japan International Cooperation Agency
JINCAR Joint Industry Committee for National Readership
JICRAR Joint Industry Committee for Radio Audience Research
JIS Japanese Industrial Standards
JIT Just-in-Time
JODA Japan's Official Development Assistance
JOP Joint Venture Program
JOV Joint Venture
JPRS Joint Publication Research Service
JSE Johannesburg Stock Exchange
JSF Japan Special Fund
JTPA Job Training Partnership Act
J&WO Jettison and Washing Overboard

K

KBO Kangera Basin Organization
KC Kyoto Convention
KCAB Korean Commercial Arbitration Board
KCBT Kansas City Board of Trade
KD Knocked Down
KDC Knocked Down Condition
KDD Kokusai Denshin Denwa
KFAED Kuwait Fund for Arab Economic Development
KFTA Korea Foreign Trade Association
KG Kilogram
KHZ Kilohertz
KIPO Korean Industrial Property Office
KISS Keep it Short and Simple
KL Kiloliter
KLCE Kuala Lumpur Commodities Exchange
KLOFFE Kuala Lumpur Options and Financial Futures Exchange
KLSE Kuala Lumpur Stock Exchange
KM Kilometer
KOBACO Korea Broadcasting Advertising Company
KOTRA Korea Trade Promotion Corporation

L

L/A Letter of Authority; Landing Account; Lloyd's Agent
L&R Lake and Rail Transport
LA Limited Appointment; Louvre Accord
LAADFI Latin American Association of Development Financing Institutions
LAC Labor Advisory Committee
LAEB Latin American Export Bank
LAES Latin American Economic System
LAFTA Latin American Free Trade Association
LAIA Latin American Integration Association
LAN Local Area Network
LANBY Large Automatic Navigation Buoy
LAS League of Arab States
LASH Lighter Aboard Ship
LAT Linseed Association Terms
LATF Lloyd's American Trust Fund
LAUTRO Life Assurance and Unit Trust Regulatory
L&B Leakage and Breakage
LBO Leveraged Buyout
L/C Letter of Credit
LC London Clause (chartering), Label Clause; Lome Convention
LCs Lusophone Countries
LCB Local Competitive Bidding; Limited Competitive Biddings
LCE London Commodity Exchange
LCBC Lake Chad Basin Commission
LCH London Clearing House; Legal Charges
LCD Liquid Crystal Display
LCE London Commodity Exchange
LCL Less Than Carload; Less Than Container Load; Less Developed Country
LCM Lower of Cost or Market
LCP Life-Cycle Processing
LCTA London Corn Trade
L&D Loss and Damage
LDC Less-Developed Country
LDCs Least Developed Countries

LDD Loss During Discharge
LDF Long-Dated Forward
LDEF Latent Defect
LDG Loading
LDG&DLY Landing and Delivery
LDL Loss During Loading
LDS Loads
LDT Light Displacement Tons
LEAPS Long-Term Anticipation Securities
LEXIS Legal Exchange Information Service
LHAR London, Hull, Antwerp or Rotterdam
LIAB Liability
LIB Limited International Bidding
LIBC Lloyd's Insurance Brokers' Committee
LIBID London Interbank Bid Rate
LIBOR London Interbank Offered Rate
LIC Life Insurers Conference
LIFFE London International Financial Futures and Options Exchange
LIFO Last In, First Out
LIM London Insurance Market
LIMDSM London Insurance Market Data Standards Manual
LIMEAN London Interbank Mean Rate
LIMNET London Insurance Market Network
LIMRA Life Insurance Marketing and Research Association
LIMTCG London Insurance Market Technical Co-ordination Group
LIP Life Insurance Policy
LISBOR Lisbon Interbank Offered Rate
LLB Limited Liability Company
LL&COs Lloyd's and Companies
LLC Limited Liability Company
LLDCs Least Developed Countries
LLT London Land Terms
LMC Lloyd's machinery certificate
LMCC Lloyd's Machinery Certificate, Continuous survey
LME London Metal Exchange
LMFE London Meat Futures Exchange
LNG Liquified Natural Gas Carrier
LNYD Liability Not Yet Determined
LOA Length Overall
LOC Letter of Credit
LO/LO Lift On/Lift Off
LOMA Life Office Management Association
LOP Law of One Price
LP Linear Programming; Laisser Passer
LPFA London Potatoes Futures Association
LPG Liquified Petroleum Gas Carrier
LPSO Lloyd's Policy Signing Office
LR Lombard Rate
LRMC Lloyd's Refrigerating Machinery Certificate
LRS Lloyd's Register of Shipping; Line Release System
LS Lump Sum; Liquidation System
LSCLS Livestock Clauses
LSE Lisbon Stock Exchange; London Stock Exchange
LSHWLIAB Longshoremen's and Harbor Workers' Liability
LST Local Standard Time
LTA Long Term Agreement
LTC Long-Term Care
LTD Limited (Liability)
LTFV Less Than Fair Value
LTGE Lighterage
LTL Less Than Truckload
LTOM London Traded Options Market
LTR Lighter
LTV Loan-to-Value Ratio; Light-Vessel
L/U Laid Up; Letter of Undertaking; Leading Underwriter
LUA Lloyd's Underwriters' Association
LUAA Lloyd's Underwriting Agents Association
LUAMC Leading Underwriter Agreement for Marine Cargo
LUAMH Leading Underwriter Agreement for Marine Hull
LUCRO Lloyd's Underwriters' Claims and Recoveries Office
LUF Lifting Unit Frame
LUPAC Life Underwriter Political Action Committee
LUTC Life Underwriting Training Council
LUTIRO Life and Unit Trust Intermediaries Regulatory Organization
LUXIBOR Luxembourg Interbank Offered Rate
LW Low Water

LWOST Low Water, Ordinary Spring Tides
LYON Liquid Yield Option Note
LZF La Zone Franc

M

M&A Mergers and Acquistions
MA Memorandum of Association; Market Access; Multilateral Agreement
MACRS Modified Accelerated Cost Recovery System
MAD Mean Absolute Deviation
MAGI Modified Adjusted Gross Income
MALD Malicious Damage
MAP Military Assistance Program; Merchant Account Provider
MATAC Materials Technical Advisory Committee
MAVIS Marine Audio-Visual Instruction Systems
MB Megabyte
MBA Master of Business Administration
MBD Machinery breakdown
MBNQA Malcom Baldrige National Quality Award
MBO Management by Objectives; Management Buy-out
MBS Mortgage-Backed Securities
MBSCC Mortgage-Backed Securities Clearing Corporation
MBWA Management by Walking Around
M/C Metalling Clause (marine insurance); Machinery Certificate; Multinational Corporation
MC Minister Counsellor; Machinery Certificate; Mixed Cargo; Mixed Credit; Mobile Crane
MCA Management Consultants Association
MCCA Mercado Comün Centroamericano
MCI Marine Cargo Insurance
MCT Mainstream Corporation Tax
MCTL Militarily Critical Technologies List
M/D Malicious Damage; Memorandum of Deposit
M&DP Minimum and Deposit Premium
MD Managing Director ; Market Disruption
MDA Multiple Discriminant Analysis

MD&A Management Discussion and Analysis
MDBs Multilateral Development Banks
MDS Multi-dimensional Scaling
MDSE Merchandise
MEs Matchmaker Events
MEA Ministry for Economic Affairs
MERCOSUR Mercado Común del Cono Sur
MFA Multifiber Arrangement
MFER&T Ministry of Foreign Economic Relations and Trade
MFL Maximum Foreseeable Loss
MFN Most Favored Nation Treatment
MGIC Mortgage Guarantee Insurance Company
MH Main Hatch
MHS Manufactured Housing Securities
MHW Ministry of Health and Welfare
MHWS Mean High Water Spring
MHZ Megahertz
M&IE Meals and Incidental Expense
MIA Marine Insurance Act
MICEX Moscow Interbank Currency Exchange
MICR Magnetic Ink Character Recognition
MIF Multilateral Investment Fund; Mercato Italiano Futures
MIGA Multilateral Investment Guarantee Agency
MIME Multipurpose Internet Mail Extensions
MINBL Minimum Bill of Landing
MINDEP Minimum and Deposit Premium
MIP Marine Insurance Policy; Monthly Investment Plan; Maximum Investment Plan
MIPRO Manufactured Imports Promotion Organization
MIPS Monthly Income Preferred Security
MIRAS Mortgage Interest Relief at Source
MIS Management Information System ; Marketing Information System
MIT Market-if-Touched
MITI Ministry of International Trade and Industry
MJSD March, June, September, and December
MKR Matchmaker Program
MLP Master Limited Partnership
MLR Maximum Lending Rate
MLS Multiple Listing Service
MLWS Mean Low Water Springs
MM Made Merchantable; Merchant Marine
MMA Merchandise Marks Act
MMC Monopolies and Mergers Commission
MMDA Money Market Demand Account; Money Market Deposit Account
MNC Multinational Cooperation
MNE Multinational Enterprise
MNSC Managed Network Steering Committee
MO Modus Operandi; Marks of Origin
MOA Memorandum of Agreement
MOC Market-on-Close
MOCP Market-Oriented Cooperation Plan
MOFERT Ministry of Foreign Economic Relations and Trade
MOH Medical Officer of Health
MOL Ministry of Labor
MONEP Marche des Options Negociables de Paris
MORI Market and Opinion Research International
MORT Mortality
MOS Monthly Operational Summary
MOSS Market-Oriented, Sector-Selective
MOTO Mail Order / Telephone Order
MOU Memorandum of Understanding
MP Missing Package
MPA Major Projects Agreement
MPC Marginal Propensity to Consume; Market Performance Committee
MPETAC Materials Processing Equipment Technical Advisory Committee
MPL Maximum Probable Loss
MPP Market Promotion Program
MPS Marginal Propensity to Save; Master Production Shedule
MPT Modern Portfolio Theory; Ministry of Posts and Telecommunications
MR Mate's Receipt
MRA Mutual Recognition Agreement
MRP Manufacturer´s Recommended Price; Material Requirements Planning
MRS Market Research Society
MRU Mano River Union

M/S Months after Sight
MS Motor Ship; Machinery Survey
MSA Multilateral Steel Agreement; Metropolitan Statistical Area
MSAC Most Seriously Affected Countries
MSCI Morgan Stanley Capital International
MSIE Microsoft Internet Explorer
MS-DOS Microsoft Disk Operating System
MSP Matched Sale-Purchase Agreement
MST Mountain Standard Time; Multistate Tax Commission; Measurement
MT Mean Time; Maastricht Treaty
MTAG Missile Technology Analysis Group
MTCR Missile Technology Control Regime
MTEC Missile Technology Export Control Group
MTFA Medium-term Financial Assistance
MTL Mean Tidal Level
MTM Methods-Time Measurement
MTN Multilateral Trade Negotiations; Medium-term Note
MTO Multilateral Trade Organization; Multimodal Transport Operator
MTOPS Million Theoretical Operations Per Second
MU Memoranda of Understanding
MUD Municipal Utility District
M&W Marine and War Risks

N

N/A No Advice; No Account; Not Applicable
NA Information not Available; Net Absolutely
NAA National Apartment Association; Not Always Afloat
NAARS National Automated Accounting Research System
N/C New Charter; New Crop
NAC National Advisory Council on International Monetary and Financial Policies
NACE North American Commission on the Environment
NAD North American Development Bank
N/F No Funds
NAFIN Nacional Financiera
NAFO North Atlantic Fisheries Organization
NAFTA North American Free Trade Agreement
NAHB National Association of Homebuilders
NAIC National Association of Insurance Commissioners
NAL National Agricultural Library
NAM Nonaligned Movement
NAR National Association of Realtors
NASD National Association of Securities Dealers
NASDA National Association of State Development Agencies
NASDAQS National Association of Securities Dealers Automatic Quotation System
NASDA National Association of State Departments of Agriculture; National Association of State Development Agencies
NASDAQ National Association of Securities Dealers Automated Quotations
NADIM National Association of Securities Dealers and Investment Managers

NAM Non-Aligned Movement
NATO North Atlantic Treaty Organization
NAV Net Asset Value
NBA Net Book Agreement; Niger Basin Authority
NBP National Bank of Poland
NBV Net Book Value
NC Nordic Council
NCAR No Claim for Accident Reported
NCI New Community Instrument
NCV No Commercial Value
NCT National Chamber of Trade
NDAA National Defense Authorization Act
NDER National Defense Executive Reserve
NDP Net Domestic Product
NDW Net Dead Weight
NE Not Exceeding
NEA Nuclear Energy Agency
NEBS New Exporters to Border States
NEDC National Economic Development Council
NEO Nonequity Option
NEP Not Elsewhere Provided; New Economic Program
NES Not Elsewhere Specified
NFA National Futures Association
NFF No Fault Found
NFI Net Foreign Investment
NG Negotiating Group
NGO Non-Governmental Organization
NHO Not Held Order
NHP Nominal Horse-Power
NIA Nearest International Airport
NIB Nordic Investment Bank
NIBOR New York Interbank Offered Rate
NIC National Intelligence Council; Net Interest Cost; Newly Industrializing Countries
NICs Newly Industrializing Countries
NIE Newly Industrialized Economy
NIEs Newly Industrializing Economies
NIF Note Issuance Facility
NIFO Next In First Out
NIPA National Income and Product Accounts
NIS Newly Independent States
NIT Negative Income Tax
NKK Nippon Kaiji Kyokai
NKORL No Known or Reported Loss
NL No Liability
NLA Net Leasable Area
NLQ Near Letter Quality
NLRB National Labor Relations Board
NLV National Language Version
N/M No Mark
NMA (Lloyd's) Underwriters Non-Marine Association
NME Non-Market Economy
NMS National Market System; Normal Market Size
N/N Not North of
NN Netscape Navigator
NNP Net National Product
NNPA Nuclear Nonproliferation Act
NNPT Nuclear Non-Proliferation Treaty
N/O No Orders (banking)
NOBS Notes Over Bonds Spread
NOC Notice of Cancellation
NOE Not Otherwise Enuemrated
NOHP Not Otherwise Herein Provided
NOI Net Operating Income
NOIBN Not Otherwise Indicated by Number; Not Otherwise Indexed by Name
NOL Net Operating Loss
NOND Non Delivery
NOP Not Otherwise Provided
NORAD Norwegian Agency for Development Cooperation
NOS Not Otherwise Specified
NOW Negotiable Order of Withdrawal
NP Net Proceeds
NPD New Product Development
NPIS New Product Information Service
NPT Nuclear Nonproliferation Treaty
NPV Net Present Value
NPVGO Net Present Value of Growth Opportunities
NR Not Rated; No Risk; Net Register
NRAD No Risk After Discharge
NRBP Natural Resource Based Products
NRC Nuclear Regulatory Commission
NRP National Revolutionary Party (Mexico)
NRPB Natural Resource Based Products
NRT Net Registered Tonnage
NRV Net Realizable Value
NS Not Sufficient; Netscape
NSB National Savings Bank
NSC National Security Council

NSCC National Securities Clearing Corporation
NSD National Security Directive
NSDDs National Security Decision Directives
NSE National Stock Exchange
NSF Not Sufficient Funds
NSG Nuclear Suppliers Group
NSO National Security Override
NSPF Not Specifically Provided For
NTBs Non-Tariff Barriers
NTDB National Trade Data Bank
NTE National Trade Estimates Report; New-To-Export
NTF Nigeria Trust Fund
NTM New-To-Market
NTMs Non-Tariff Measures
NTPA National Tourism Policy Act
NTT Nippon Telegraph and Telephone Corporation
NV Norske Veritas
NVOC Non-Vessel Owning Carrier
NVOCC Non-Vessel Operating Common Carrier
NVOMTO Non-Vessel-Operating Multimodal Transport Operator
NVQ National Vocational Qualification
NYMEX New York Mercantile Exchange
NYCE New York Cotton Exchange
NYFE New York Futures Exchange
NYMEX New York Mercantile Exchanges
NYSE New York Stock Exchange

O

O&M Organization and Methods
O&R Ocean and Rail
O/A On Account of
OA Over All; Open Account
OAG Official Airline Guide
OAL Overall Length
OAPEC Organization of Arab Petroleum Exporting Countries
OAR Overall Rate of Return
OAS Organization of American States; Option Adjusted Spread
OASI Old-Age and Survivors Insurance
OATUU Organization of African Trade Union Unity
OAU Organization of African Unity
O/B On Board; On or before
OBC Offshore Banking Center
OBL Ocean Bill of Lading
OBO Oil/Bulk/Ore Carrier
OBR Overseas Business Report
OBSF Off Balance Sheet Finance
OBU Offshore Banking Unit
O/C Overcharge, Open Cover
OC Operating Committee
OCAS Organiztion of Central American States
OCB/L Ocean Bill of Landing
OCC Options Clearing Corporation; Occurrence
OCIMF Oil Companies International Marine Forum
OCONUS Outside Contiguous United States
OCR Ordinary Capital Resources; Optical Character Recognition
O/D Overdeck
ODA Official Development Assistance; Overseas Development Administration
ODS Operating Differential Subsidy
OE Operation Exodus
OEA Organizacition de los Estados Americanos
OEB Office Europeen de Brevets
OECD Organization for Economic Cooperation and Development

OECF Overseas Economic Cooperation Fund
OECS Organization of Eastern Caribbean States
OEEC Organization for European Economic Cooperation
OEIC Open-ended Investment Company
OEL Office of Export Licensing
OEM Original Equipment Manufacturer
OER Operating Expense Ratio
OETCA Office of Export Trading Company Affairs
OFAC Office of Foreign Assets Control
OFD Ocean Freight Differential
OFF Ocean Freight Forwarder
OFT Office of Fair Trading
OFTEL Office of Telecommunications
OGPI Original Gross Premium Income (reinsurance)
OH Off Hook
OIC Organization of the Islamic Conference
OICD Office of International Cooperation and Development
OID Original Issue Discount; Original Issue Discount Debt
OILSR Office of Interstate Land Sales Registration
OIP Open Insurance Policy
OJT On-the-Job Training
OLR Off-line Reader
OM Offshore Manufacturing
OMA Orderly Marketing Agreement
OMB Office of Management and Budget
OMC Office of Munitions Control
OMCAS Outstanding Marine Claims Advisory Settlements
OMPI Organisation Mondiale de la Propne'te Intellectuelle
OMV Open-market Value
O/N Order Notify
ONMS Open Network Management System
ONPI Original Net Premium Income (reinsurance)
ONR Original Net Rate
O/O Order of
OP Open (or floating) Policy
OPEC Organization of the Petroleum Exporting Countries
OPIC Overseas Private Investment Corporation
OPT Optimized Production Technology
O/R Overriding Commission
OR Operating Research; Owner's Risk; Original Rate; Official Receiver
ORAN Organisation Regionale Africaine de Normalisation
ORE Other Real Estate
OREO Other Real Estate Owned
O/S On Sample; Out of Stock; On Sale or Return
OS&D Over, Short, and Damage
OSD Open Shelter Deck
OSHA Occupational Safety and Health Act
OSP Online Service Provider
O/T On truck
OT On Truck or Railway
OTB Open-To-Buy
OTC Over The Counter; Good-Till-Cancelled
OTE On Target Earnings
OTM Old-To-Market
OTS Office of Thrift Supervision
OVs Orientation Visits

P

P Package
P2P Peer to Peer
PA Particular Average; Power of Attorney; Private Account; Personal Accident; Plaza Accord; Purchasing Agent; Personal Assistant
PAC Political Action Committee; Planned Amortization Class; Preauthorized Checks; Pacific Coast Ports
PACBOND Planned Amortization Class Bond
PACE Price, Assortment, Convenience, Entertainment
PAD Preauthorized Electronic Debits
PAL Passive Activity Loss
PAN Premium Advice Note
PAP Personal Automobile Policy
PASC Pan American Standards Commission
PATS Partly Assisted Trading System
PAU Pan American Union
PAYE Pay As You Earn
PB Permanent Bunkers
PBAS Polish Business Advisory Service
PBEC Pacific Basin Economic Council
PBFDF Plata Basin Financial Development Fund
PBEC Pacific Basin Economic Council
PBGC Pension Benefit Guarantee Cooperative
PBO Projected Benefit Obligation
PBOT Philadelphia Board of Trade
PBX Private Branch Exchange
PC Personal Computer; Participation Certificates; Price Current; Petty Cash; Percent; Particular Charges; Profit Commission; Paris Club; Paris Convention
PC-DOS Personal Computer Disk Operating System
PCP Permissible Capital Payment
PCT Patent Cooperation Treaty
PD Per Diem; Public Domain; Port Dues; Passed; Paid; Prior Deposit
PDA Personal Digital Assistant
PDE Prepared Data Entry
PDO Property Damage Only
PDR Price Dividend Ratio
P/E Price/Earnings
PEC President's Export Council
PECC Pacific Economic Cooperation Council
PECSEA President's Export Council, Subcommittee on Export Administration
P-E or P/E Price-Earning Ration
PEFC Private Export Funding Corporation
PEFCO Private Export Funding Corporation
PEGRATIO Prospective Earnings Growth Ratio
PEP Personal Equity Plan
PERC Preferred Equity Redemption Stock
PERLS Principal Exchange-Rated-Linked Securities
PERT Program Evaluation and Review Technique
PEST Political, Economic, Social, Technological
PESTL Political, Economic, Social, Technological, Legal
PET Potentially Exempt Tax
PF Programmable Function Key
PFI Pro Forma Invoice
PFO Portfolio
PFP Policy Framework Paper
PG Persona Grata
PGs Product Groups
PHARE Poland and Hungary Action for Reconstructing the Economy
PHC Personal Holding Company
PHI Private Health Insurance; Permanent Health Insurance
PHLX Philadelphia Stock Exchange
P&I Principle and Interest Payment; Protection and Indemnity
PI Profitability Index; Personal Injury
PIA Primary Insurance Amount; Peril Insured Against; Personal Investment Authority
PIANC Permanent International Association of Navigation Congresses
PIBOR Paris Interbank Offer Rate
PICDCS Permanent Interstate Committee for Drought Control in the Sahel
PIBS Permanent Interest Bearing Share

PIC Product Innovation Charter
PICS Platform for Internet Content Selection
PIG Passive Income Generator
PIK Payment In Kind
PIL Premium Income Limit
PILF Piferage
PIM Personal Information Manager
PIMS Profit Impact of Market Strategies
PIN Personal Identification Number
PINC Property Income Certificate
PIP Post-Initiated Promotion
PIRG Public Interest Research Group
PITI Principle, Interest, Taxes, and Insurance Payment
P&L Profit and Loss; Profit and Loss Statement
PL Public Liability; Partial Loss
PLA Port of London Authority
PLC Public Limited Company; Pre-License Check; Project Loan Certificate
PM Premium; Preventative Maintenance
PMI Private Mortgage Insurance
PML Probable Maximum Loss
PMTS Predetermined Motion-time Standards
PMSA Primary Metropolitan Statistical Area
PMV Private Market Value
PN Project Notes; Promissory Note
PNG Persona Non Grata
PO Principal Officer; Principal Only; Protective Order
POA Power of Attorney
POC Port of Call
POD Paid on Delivery; Port of Distress
POM Production and Operations Management
POP Point of Purchase
POS Point of Sale
PP Purchase Price; Picked Ports; Per Procurationem (on behalf of); Primary Product
PPA Protocol of Provisional Application
PPD Prepaid
PPI Producer Price Index; Policy Proof of Interest
PPP Penultimate Profit Prospect; Purchasing Power Parity
PPT Prompt Loading
PR Public Relations; Port Risks; Prorata; Pacific Rim; Performance Requirements; Premiums reducing; Premium Reserve
PRO Public Relations Officer
PRP Profit Related Pay
PRT Petroleum Revenue Tax
PS Postscript; Public Sale; Port Shipping; Principal Supplier; Protest System; Petrograd Standard (timber trade)
PSA Public-Service Announcement; Public Securities Administration
PSBR Public Sector Borrowing Requirement
PSR Profit Sharing Ratio
PSSG Price by Sales over Sales Growth
PST Pacific Standard Time
PSV Post-Shipment Verification
PT Premium Transfer; Private Terms
PTA Preferential Trade Area; Preferential Trade Area for Eastern and Southern Africa States
P2P Path to Profitability
PUD Planned Unit Development
PV Present Value
PVBP Price Value of a Basis Point
PVOs Private Voluntary Organizations
PW Packed Weight
PWG Policy Working Group
PYB Proceeding Year Basis

Q

QFD Quality Function Development
QLF Quality Loss Function
QLTY Quality
QM Quadrilateral Meetings
QN Quotation
Q&QS Quotas and Quota System
QRSs Quantitative Restrictions
Q-TIP Qualified Terminable Interest Trust
QWL Quality of Work Life
QRs Quantitative Restrictions
QS Quota Share

R

R&CC Riots and Civil Commotions
R&D Research and Development
R&O Rail and Ocean
R&R Rest and Recreation
RA Refer to Acceptor
RACE Research in Advanced Communications in Europe
RADAR Radio Detection and Ranging
RADO&TSI Revocation of Antidumping Duty Order & Termination of Suspended Investigation
RAFT Revolving Acceptance Facility by Tender
RAM Read-Access Memory; Reverse Annuity Mortgage
RAN Revenue Anticipation Note
RAP Regulatory Accounting Procedures
RAT Rapeseed Association Terms
RBPs Restrictive Business Practices
RC&L Rail, Canal, and Lake
RC Red Clause
RCC&S Roils, Civil Commotions and Strikes
RCH Recognized Clearing House
RCLC Restricted Commercial Letter of Credit
RCS Regular Catalog Show
RD Running days; Refer to Drawer
RDA Romanian Development Agency
RDPMU Reciprocal Defense Procurement Memoranda of Understanding
RDS Roads
REDs Refunding Escrow Deposits
REF Refrigerating Machinery
REFCORP Resolution Funding Corporation
REFG Refrigerating, Refrigeration
REIT Real Estate Investment Trust
REMIC Real Estate Mortgage Investment Conduit
REO Real Estate Owned
RESPA Real Estate Settlement Procedures Act
RFP Request for Proposals
RI Registro Italiano
RIC Regulated Investment Company

RICO Racketeer Influenced and Corrupt Organization
RIE Recognized Investment Exchange
RLC Revocable Letter of Credit
RN Rotation Number
RNLI Royal National Life-boat Institution
R/O Request/Offer
RO/RO Roll-On/Roll-Off
ROA Return on Assets; Reinsurance Offices Association
ROB Remaining on Board
ROCE Return on Capital Employed
ROD Rust, Oxidation and Discoloration
ROE Return on Equity
ROG Receipt of Goods
ROI Return on Investment
ROL Reduction-Option Loan
ROM Read-Only Memory
ROR Release on Recognizance
RORO Roll On Roll Off
RP Return Premium; Return of Post for Orders; Reverse Preferences
RPA Repurchase Agreement
RPB Recognized Professional Body
RPFB Russian Project Finance Bank
RPI Retail Price Index
RPM Resale Price Maintenance
RPPP Relative Purchasing Power Parity
RPTAC Regulations and Procedures Technical Advisory Committee
RUIE Russian Union of Industrialists and Entrepreneurs
RR Registered Representative; Residual Restrictions
RR&I Respective Rights and Interests
RRM Renegotiated-Rate Mortgage
RRP Recommended Retail Price
RRSP Registered Retirement Savings Plan
RS Revised Statutes; Recommended Standard; Request to Send
RS&CC Riots, Strikes and Civil Commotions
RT Rye Terms; Register Tonnage; Reserve Tranche
RTA Rubber Trade Association
RTC Resolution Trust Corporation
RUF Revolving Underwriting Facility
RWA Returned Without Action
RWG Regulatory Working Group

S

S&A Signing and Accounting (procedure)
S&D Special and Differential Treatment
S&FA Shipping and Forwarding Agent
S&H/EXCT Sundays and Holidays Excepted in Lay Days
S&L Savings and Loan Association; Sue & Labor
S&P Standard & Poor´s Corporation
S/A Subject to Acceptance (insurance); Subject to Approval
SA Sociedad Anonima; Sociedad Anönima; Socie'te' Anonyme; Salvage Association; Supply Access; Switch Arrangements
SA de CV Sociedad Anönima
SAARC South Asian Association for Regional Cooperation
SABIT Special American Business Internship Training Program
SACU Southern African Customs Union
S&DT Special and Differential Treatment
SADC Southern African Development Community
SAEF Stock Exchange Automatic Execution Facility
SAF Structural Adjustment Facility
SAFEX South African Futures Exchange
SAFTA South Asia Free Trade Area
SAIF Savings Association Insurance Fund
SALM Single Anchor Leg Mooring
SAM Shared-Appreciation Mortgage
SANR Subject to Approval no Risk
SAPTA South Asia Preferential Trade Agreement
SARL Socie'te'ä Responsabilite' Limite'e
SARSEP Salary Reduction SEP
SAS Statement of Auditing Standards; Société par Actions Simplifiée
SASO Saudi Arabian Standards Organization
SAYE Save As You Earn
SB Short Bill
SBA Small Business Administration
SBIC Small Business Investment Company

SBM Single Buoy Mooring
SBU Strategic Business Unit
SBS Survey Before Shipment
SC Salvage Charges; Soft Currency; Southern Cone; Summit Conference
SCA Settlement of Claims Abroad
SCE Securities Commodities Exchange
SC&S Strapped, Corded, and Sealed
SCLP Simplified Commercial Lines Portfolio (insurance policy)
SCM Southern Common Market
SCO Senior Commercial Officer
SCOR Scientific Commission on Oceanic Research
SCORE Service Corps of Retired Executives
SCP Single Currency Peg
SCS Société en Commandite Simple
S/D Sight/Draft
SD Sea Damage; Short Delivery; Scope Determinations; Sailed
SDA Single Administrative Document
SDD Store Door Delivery
SDDE Simultaneous Direct Data Entry
SDFS Same-Day Funds Settlement
SDHF Standard Dutch Hull Form
SDN Specially Designated National
SDR Special Drawing Right
SDR Special Drawing Right
SEA Single European Act
SEAQ Stock Exchange Automated Quotation System
SEATO Southeast Asia Treaty Organization
SEB Swiss Electronic Bourse
SEC Securities and Exchange Commission
SECA Self-Employment Contributions Act
SECOFI Secretaria de Comercio y Fomento Industrial
SED Shipper's Export Declaration
SEED Support for East European Democracy
SEHK Stock Exchange of Hong Kong
SELA Sistema Economico Latinoamericano
SEM Shared-Equity Mortgage; Seminar Mission
SEP Simplified Employee Pension; Subject to Endorsement on the Policy
SEPD State Export Program Database
SERPS State Earnings Related Pension Scheme
SES Stock Exchange of Singapore
SET Secure Electronic Transaction; Securities Exchange of Thailand
SF Survey Fee; Solo Fair (overseas procured)
SFA Securities and Futures Authority
SFAS Statement of Financial Accounting Standards
SFE Sydney Futures Exchange
SFO Serious Frau Office; Solo Fair
SFSC Shared Foreign Sales Corporation
SFW Solo Fair (Washington procured)
SG South Group
SG&A Selling, General, and Administrative Expenses
SGA Selling, General and Administrative (Expenses)
S&HEX Sundays and Holidays Excepted
S&HINC Sundays and Holidays Included
SHP Shaft Horse-Power
SI Short Interest; Sum Insured; International System of Units (System International); Summary Investigation; Suspension of Investigation
SIA Securities Industry Association
SIAC Security Industry Automated Corporation
SIB Securities and Investment Board
SIBOR Singapore Interbank Offered Rate
SIC Standard Industrial Classification
SICA Securities Industry Committee on Arbitration
SICE Sistema de Informaciön al Comercio Exterior
SID Security Identification Number; System Identification
SIDA Swedish International Development Authority
SIFIDA Société Internationale Financière pour les Investissements, et le Développement en Afrique
SII Structural Impediments Initiative
SIJORI Singapore-Johor-Riau Growth Triangle
SIMEX Singapore International Monetary Exchange
SIMIS Single Internal Market Information Service

SIPC Securities Investor Protection Corporation
S/IOGA State/Industry-Organized, Government-Approved
SIOGAM State Industry Organized Government Approved Mission
SITC Standard International Tariff Classification
SITPRO Simplification of Industrial Trade Procedures Board
SK Sack
SKD Semi Knocked Down
SL Salvage Loss; Sue and Labor; Soft Loan; Suspension of Liquidation; Specification Limits
S/LC Sue and Labor Clause
SL/CH Sue and Labor Charges
SL&C Shipper's Load and Count
SLC Strategic Level of Controls
SL&T Shipper's Load and Tally
SLD Sold Last Sale; Sailed
SLIP Specialized Lines of Industry Practice
SLMA Student Loan Marketing Association
SLOB Separate Lines of Business
SMART Software for Market Analysis and Restrictions on Trade
SMBS Stripped Mortgage Backed Securities
SMIPC Small and Medium Industry Promotion Corporation
SML Security Market Line
SMP Special Multiplier Policy; Security Market Plane; Statutory Maternity Pay
SMSA Standard Metropolitan Statistical Area
SN Shipping Note; Swap Network
SNC Societä in Nome Collettivo; Societe en Nom Collectif
SNEC Subgroup on Nuclear Export Coordination
SO Ship's Options; Shipping Order; Seiler's Option
SOAP Sunflower Seed Oil Assistance Program
SOEC Statistical Office of the European Communities
SOES Small Order Execution System
SOFFEX Swiss Options and Financial Futures Exchange
SOGAIIOGA State/Industry Organized, Government Approved Mission
SOHO Small Office/Home Office
SOL Ship Owner's Liability
SOP Standard Operating Procedure
SOS Service of Suit
SP Supra Protest; Separation Procedure (signing and accounting)
SPA Società Per Azioni; Special Priorities Assistance
SPBEC South Pacific Bureau for Economic Cooperation
SPC Statistical Process Control
SPCT South Pacific Trade Commission
SPD Shipped; Steamer Pays Dues
SPDA Single-Premium Deferred Annuity
SPDR Standard & Poor's Depositary Receipt
SPEC South Pacific Bureau for Economic Cooperation
SPF South Pacific Forum
SPL Set Priority Level; System Programming Language
SPM Single Point Mooring
SPOT Single Property Ownership Trust
SQC Statistical Quality Control
SR&CC Strikes, Riots, and Civil Commotions
SR Sales Representative
SRF Supplementary Reserve Facility
SRL Società a Responsabilite' Limitata; Ship repairers' liability
SRO Self-Regulatory Organization
SS Shipside; Short Supply; Substantial Suppliers
SSA Sub-Saharan Africa
SSAP Statement of Standard Accounting Practice
SS&C Same Sea and Country or Coast
SSC Simultaneous Settlements Clause
SSL Secure Socket Layer
SSM Soft Systems Methodology
SSN Standard Shipping Notice
SSP Statutory Sick Pay
ST Short Ton
STA Semiconductor Trade Arrangement
STAC Sensors Technical Advisory Committee
STABEX System for the Stabilization of Export Earnings

STAGS Sterling Transferable Accruing Government Securities
STD Standard (timber trade)
STDs Standards
STELA System for Tracking Export License Applications
STE State Trading Enterprise
STG Sterling
STK Stock
STL Stevedores' Liability
STM State Trade Mission
STR Steamer
STS Station to Station
STR Steamer
SV Sailing Vessel
SW Shipper's Weights
SWD Seawater Damage
SWEDECORP Swedish International Enterprise Development Corporation
SWG Standard Wire Gauge
SWIFT Society for Worldwide Interbank Financial Telecommunications
SYD Sum-of-the-Years' Digits
SYN Syndicate
SYSMIN System of Stabilization of Export Earnings from Mining Products

T

T&CC Technical and Clauses Committee
T&E Travel and Entertainment
T&G Tongued and Grooved (timber trade)
T&S Touch and Stay
TA Trade Assistant; Tariff Anomaly
TAA Trade Adjustment Assistance; Tactical Asset Allocation
TAAC Trade Adjustment Assistance Centers
TAB Tax Anticipation Bill
TAC Technical Advisory Committee; Targeted Amortization Class; Tied Aid Credit
TACBOND Targeted Amortization Class Bond
TACIS Technical Assistance for the Central Independent States
TALISMAN Transfer Accounting Lodgment for Investors and Stock Management
TAN Tax Anticipation Note
TAO Taxpayer Assistance Order
TAPO Trade Assistance and Planning Office
TAR Throughput Accounting Ratio
TARIC Integrated Tariff of the European Community
TASF Technical Assistance Special Fund
TB Trial Balance; To be Advised; To be Agreed
TBA To Be Announced
TBL Through Bill of Lading
TBs Tariff Bindings
TBT Technical Barrier to Trade
TC Till Countermanded
TCE Tax Consulting for the Elderly
TCI Third-Country Initiative; Time Charterer's Interest
TCMD Third-Country Meat Directive
TCMP Taxpayer Compliance Measurement Program
TCN Third-Country National
TCPA Target Closest Point of Approach
TD Treasury Decision
TDA Trade and Development Agency

TDF Transborder Data Flow
TDO Table of Denial Orders
TDR Transfer Development Rights
TDS Technical Data Sheets
TDW Tonnage Deadweight
TE Trade Expenses; Tariff Escalation
TEA Targeted Export Assistance Program
TEE Trans-Europe Express
TEFRA Tax Equity and Fiscal Responsibility Act of 1982
TETAC Telecommunications Equipment Technical Advisory Committee
TEU Twenty-foot Equivalent Unit
TF Tropical Freshwater; Trade Fair (Overseas-Recruited)
TFC Trade Fair Certification
TFW Trade Fair (Washington-Recruited)
TGB Tongued, Grooved and Beaded
TGI Target Group Index
TH Tonnes per Hour
TIAS Treaties and Other International Acts Series
TIB Temporary Importation under Bond; Trimmed in Bunkers
TIC Trade Information Center
TIEA Tax Information Exchange Agreement
TIFTs Trade and Investment Facilitation Talks
TIGR Treasury Investment Growth Receipts
TIMS Textiles Information Management System
TIN Taxpayer Identification Number
TIPS Technological Information Pilot System
TIR Transport International Routier
TIV Total Insured Value
TL Truckload; Total Loss; Tied Loan
TLF Transferable Loan Facility
TLO Total Loss Only
TLVO Total Loss of Vessel Only
TO Transfer Order
TQM Total Quality Management
TM Trade Mission
TNC Trade Negotiations Committee; Transnational Corporation
TOCOM Tokyo Commodity Exchange
TOP Trade Opportunities Program
TOPIC Teletext Output Price Information Computer
TOR Terms of Reference; Time on Risk
TOT Terms of Trade
TOVALOP Tanker Owners' Voluntary Agreement Concerning Liability for Oil Pollution
TPC Trade Policy Committee
TPCC Trade Promotion Coordinating Committee
TPI Tons per Inch
TPIS Trade Policy Information System
TPL Third Party Liability
TPM Total Productive Management; Trigger Price Mechanism
TPND Theft, Pilferage and Non-Delivery
TPRG Trade Policy Review Group
TPRM Trade Policy Review Mechanism
TPSC Trade Policy Staff Committee
TQ Tale Quale (as found); Tariff Quota
TQM Total Quality Management
TRANSTAC Transportation and Related Equipment Technical Advisory Committee
TRIMs Trade-Related Investment Measures
TRIPs Trade-Related Aspects of Intellectual Property Rights
TRO Temporary Restraining Order
TS Trade Specialist; Transhipment; Tariff Schedule; Tariff Surcharges
TSB Textile Surveillance Body
TSE Tokyo Stock Exchange; Toronto Stock Exchange
TSI Total Sum Insured
TSUS Tariff Schedules of the United States
TSUSA Tariff Schedules of the United States Annotated
TT Telegraphic Transfer; Technology Transfer
TTF Timber Trade Federation
TTM Time To Market
TUC Trade Union Congress
TV Television; Terminal Value; Threshold Value
TVR Television Rating
TW Tare Weight
TWEA Trading With the Enemy Act
TWG Technical Working Group
TWMC Transport, Wages, Maintenance and Care

U

UA Underwriting Account
UAE United Arab Emirates
UBECs Union of Banana Exporting Countries
UBI Unrelated Business Income
UBIT Unrelated Business Income tax
UBO Ultimate Beneficial Owner
UC Under Cdsonstruction
UCB Unless Caused by
UCC Uniform Commercial Code
UCP Uniform Customs and Practices
UCS Unified Claims System
UD Underdeck
UDEAC Union Douanie're et Economique de l'Afrique Centrale
UDITPA Uniform Division of Income for Tax Purposes Act
UGMA Uniform Gifts to Minors Act
UIT Union Internationale des Telecommunications
UK/C United Kingdom or Continent
UK/CBH United Kingdom or Continent (Bordeaux-Hamburg range)
UK/CGH United Kingdom or Continent (Gibraltar-Hamburg range)
UK/CHH United Kingdom or Continent (Havre-Hamburg range)
UKFO United Kingdom for Orders
UKHAD United Kingdom, Havre, Antwerp or Dunkirk
ULCC Ultra Large Crude Carrier
ULS Unsecured Loan Stock
UMA Union du Maghreb Arabe
UMLER Universal Machine Language Equipment Register
UMOA Union Monetaire Ouest-Africaine
UMR Usual Marketing Requirements
UN United Nations
UNCDF United Nations Capital Development Fund
UNCED United Nations Conference on Environment and Development
UNCHS United Nations Commission on Human Settlements
UNCITRAL United Nations Commission on International Trade Law
UNCJIN United Nations Criminal Justice Information Network
UNCLOS U.N. Conference on the Law of the Sea
UNCST United Nations Conference on Science and Technology
UNCTAD United Nations Conference on Trade and Development
UNDP United Nations Development Program
UNDRO United Nations Disaster Relief Organization
UN/ECE United Nations Economic Commission for Europe
UNEP United Nations Environment Program
UNESCO United Nations Educational, Scientific, and Cultural Organization
UNFPA United Nations Fund for Population Activities
UNGA United Nations General Assembly
UNHCR United Nations High Commissioner for Refugees
UNICEF United Nations Children's Fund
UNIDO United Nations Industrial Development Organization
UNIDROIT International Institute for the Unification of Private Law
UNITAR United Nations Institute for Training and Research
UNL Ultimate Net Loss
UNRISD United Nations Research Institute for Social Development
UNRWA United Nations Relief and Works Agency
UNU United Nations University
U/O Use and Occupancy
UP Under Proof
UPC Universal Product Code
UPEB Union de Países Exportadores de Banano
UPS United Parcel Service
UR Under repair
URAR Uniform Residential Appraisal Report
URL Universal Resource Location; Uniform Resource Locator
US&FCS U.S. and Foreign Commercial Service

USA U.S. Affiliate
USAEDC U.S. Agricultural Export Development Council
US-AEP U.S.-Asia Environmental Program
USC U.S. Code
USCIB U.S. Council for International Business
USDA U.S. Department of Agriculture
USDIA U.S. Direct Investment Abroad
USEC U.S. Mission to the European Community
USIA U.S. Information Agency
USIT Unit Share Investment Trust
USITC U.S. International Trade Commission
USML U.S. Munitions List
USNH United States, North of Cape Hatteras
USP Unique Selling Proposition; U.S. Price
USPAP Uniform Standards of Professional Appraisal Practice
USPIRG U.S. Public Interest Research Group
USSA United States Salvage Association
USTR U.S. Trade Representative
USTTA U.S. Travel and Tourism Administration
USUN U.S. Mission to the United Nations
UT Unlimited Transhipment
UTA Unit Trust Association
UTC Universal Time Coordinated
UTMA Uniform Transfers to Minors Act
UTP Unfair Trade Practice

V

VA Veterans Administration
VAC Value Added Counseling
VAD Value Added Dealer
VAL Value
VAR Value-at-Risk
VAT Value-Added Tax
VC Valuation Clause
VCPO Value for Customs Purposes Only
VCT Venture Capital Trust
VD Value Date; Valued
VER Voluntary Export Restriction
VETC Vertical Export Trading Company
VITA Volunteer Income Tax Association
VL Variable Levy
VLCC Very Large Crude Carrier
VMS Vertical Marketing System
VOA Voice of America
VOMTO Vessel-Operating Multimodal Transport Operator
VOP Value as in Original Policy
VP Vice-President
VR Virtual Reality
VRA Voluntary Restraint Agreement
VRDB Variable-Rated Demand Bond
VRM Variable-Rate Mortgage
VRN Variable-Rate Note
VSE Vancouver Stock Exchange
VTS Vessel Traffic Systems
VW Visa Waiver

W

WA With Average
WACC Weighted Average Cost of Capital
WACH West African Clearinghouse
WADB West African Development Bank
WAEC West African Economic Community
WAMU West African Monetary Union
WAN Wide Area Network
WAP Wireless Application Protocol
WAOB World Agricultural Outlook Board
WARC World Administrative Radio Conference
WARDA West Africa Rice Development Association
WARN Worker Adjustment and Retraining Notification Act
WARO Weighted Average Rate Option
WATS Wide Area Telephone Service
WB Water Ballast; Warehouse Book; Way Bill; World Bank
WB/EI West Britain/East Ireland
WBS Without Benefit of Salvage
WC West Coast
WCB Will Call Back
WCL World Confederation of Labor
WCSA West Coast of South America
WD Warranted
WDA Writing Down Allowance
WDF Wireless Direction Finder
WDG Wording
WDV Written-Down Value
WEBS World Equity Benchmark Series
WECM Warranted Existing Class Maintained
WEU Western European Union
WF Wharf
WFC World Food Council
WFDFI World Federation of Development Financing Institutions
WFP World Food Program
WFTU World Federation of Trade Unions
WG Weight Guaranteed
WHO World Health Organization
WI When Issued
WIFI Wireless Fidelity
WIMAX Worldwide Interoperability for Microwave Access
WIP Work in Progress
WIPO World Intellectual Property Organization
W/M Weight and /or Measurement
WMO World Meteorological Organization
WNA Winter North Atlantic
WOB Washed Overboard
WP Without Prejudice; Weather Permitting; Word Processor
WPA With Particular Average
WPP Waterproof Paper Packing
WR Warehouse Receipts; Without Reserve
WRO War Risk Only
WRTD Without Reference to Date
WS Workstation
WT Weight
WTBA Wording to be Agreed
WTD Warranted
WTDR World Traders Data Report
WTM World Tourism Market
WTO World Tourism Organization; World Trade Organization
WTY Warranty
WW Warehouse Warrant
WWD Weather Working Days
WWW World Wide Web; World Weather Watch
WYSIWYG What You See is What You Get

X

XC Xerox Copy; Ex Coupon
XD Ex Dividend
XIN Ex Interest
XR Ex-Rights
XSL Excess Loss Reinsurance
XSPT Excess Point
XW Ex-Warrants

Y

YAR York/Antwerp Rules
YT Yacht
YTD Year-to-Date
YTM Yield to Maturity

Z

ZBA Zero Balance Account
ZBB Zero-Base Budgeting
ZC Zangger Committee
ZEP Zone d'Exchanges Pre'ferentiels pour les Etats de l'Afrique de l'est et de l'Afrique Australe
ZF Zone Franc
ZPG Zero Population Growth
ZF LaZoneFranc